# Dependable Computing

## About IEEE Computer Society

IEEE Computer Society is the world's leading computing membership organization and the trusted information and career-development source for a global workforce of technology leaders including: professors, researchers, software engineers, IT professionals, employers, and students. The unmatched source for technology information, inspiration, and collaboration, the IEEE Computer Society is the source that computing professionals trust to provide high-quality, stage-of-the-art information on an on-demand basis. The Computer Society provides a wide range of forums for top minds to come together, including technical conferences, publication, and a comprehensive digital library, unique training webinars, professional training, and the Tech Leader Training Partner Program to help organizations increase their staff's technical knowledge and expertise, as well as the personalized information tool my Computer. To find out more about the community for technology leaders, visit http://www.computer.org.

## IEEE/Wiley Partnership

The IEEE Computer Society and Wiley partnership allows the CS Press authored book program to produce a number of exciting new titles in areas of computer science, computing, and networking with a special focus on software engineering. IEEE Computer Society members receive a 35% discount on Wiley titles by using their member discount code. Please contact IEEE Press for details.

To submit questions about the program or send proposals, please contact Mary Hatcher, Editor, Wiley-IEEE Press: Email: mhatcher@wiley.com, John Wiley & Sons, Inc., 111 River Street, Hoboken, NJ 07030-5774.

# Dependable Computing

## Design and Assessment

### Ravishankar K. Iyer
*Department of Electrical and Computer Engineering and*
*Coordinated Science Laboratory*
*University of Illinois at Urbana-Champaign*
*Urbana, Illinois, USA*

### Zbigniew T. Kalbarczyk
*Department of Electrical and Computer Engineering and*
*Coordinated Science Laboratory*
*University of Illinois at Urbana-Champaign*
*Urbana, Illinois, USA*

### Nithin M. Nakka
*Cisco Networking Engineering group*
*Cisco Systems, Inc.*
*San Jose, California, USA*

IEEE
**computer society**

**IEEE**Press

WILEY

Published by John Wiley & Sons, Inc., Hoboken, New Jersey.
Published simultaneously in Canada.

For general information on our other products and services or for technical support, please contact our Customer Care Department within the United States at (800) 762-2974, outside the United States at (317) 572-3993 or fax (317) 572-4002.

Wiley also publishes its books in a variety of electronic formats. Some content that appears in print may not be available in electronic formats. For more information about Wiley products, visit our web site at www.wiley.com.

*Library of Congress Cataloging-in-Publication Data for:*

Hardback ISBN: 9781118709443

Cover Design: Wiley
Cover Image: © Yuichiro Chino/Getty Images

Set in 9.5/12.5pt STIXTwoText by Straive, Pondicherry, India

SKY10072364_041124

*This book is dedicated to my wife Pamela for her unwavering support and encouragement in my academic pursuits, from my PhD to the present day.*
*– For Ravishankar K. Iyer*

*This book is dedicated to my wife, whose unfailing support kept me moving forward to the completion of this work.*
*– For Zbigniew T. Kalbarczyk*

*This book is dedicated to my parents, whose sacrifices have shaped what I am.*
*– For Nithin M. Nakka*

# Contents

About the Authors *xxiii*
Preface *xxv*
Acknowledgments *xxvii*
About the Companion Website *xxix*

## About the Authors

**Professor Ravishankar K. Iyer** is George and Ann Fisher Distinguished Professor of Engineering at the University of Illinois Urbana-Champaign. He holds joint appointments in the Departments of Electrical and Computer Engineering (ECE) and Computer Science, the Coordinated Science Laboratory (CSL), the National Center for Supercomputing Applications (NCSA), the Carle Illinois College of Medicine, and the Carl R. Woese Institute for Genomic Biology. He is also a faculty Research Affiliate at the Mayo Clinic. Professor Iyer was the founding Chief Scientist of the Information Trust Institute at UIUC – a campus-wide research center addressing security, reliability, and safety issues in critical infrastructures. He leads the DEPEND Group at CSL/ECE at Illinois, with a multidisciplinary focus on systems and software that combine deep measurement-driven analytics and machine learning with applications in two important domains: (i) management and control of large infrastructures including autonomous systems that span resilience, safety, and security and performance and (ii) health and personalized medicine that spans computational genomics and health analytics focused on neurological disorders, pharmacogenomics, and predicting cancer metastases. His group has developed a rich AI analytics framework that has been deployed on real-world applications in collaboration with industry, health providers, and government agencies including the National Science Foundation, the National Institutes of Health, the Department of Energy, the Defense Advanced Research Projects Agency, and the Department of Defense.

Professor Iyer is a Fellow of the American Association for the Advancement of Science (AAAS), the Institute of Electrical and Electronics Engineers (IEEE), and the Association for Computing Machinery (ACM). He has received several awards, including the Jean-Claude Laprie Award, IEEE Emanuel R. Piore Award, and the 2011 Outstanding Contributions Award by the Association of Computing Machinery. Professor Iyer is also the recipient of the degree of Doctor Honoris Causa from Toulouse Sabatier University in France.

**Dr. Zbigniew T. Kalbarczyk** is Research Professor at the Department of Electrical and Computer Engineering and the Coordinated Science Laboratory of the UIUC. Dr. Kalbarczyk's research interests are in the design and validation of reliable and secure computing systems. His current work explores: (i) emerging computing technologies, such as resource virtualization to provide redundancy and assure system resiliency to accidental errors and malicious attacks; (ii) machine learning-based methods for early detection of security attacks, including defense against smart malware; (ii) analysis of data on failures and security attacks in large computing systems to characterize system resiliency and guide development of methods for rapid diagnosis and runtime detection of problems; and (iv) development of techniques for automated validation and benchmarking of dependable and secure computing systems using formal (e.g., model checking) and experimental methods (e.g., fault/attack injection). Dr. Kalbarczyk led the design and commercialization of (i) ARMOR high-availability software middleware to support resilient distributed applications and (ii) NFTAPE software framework to support fault injection-based resiliency assessment. He served as a program chair of Dependable Computing and Communication Symposium (DCCS), a track of the International Conference on Dependable Systems and Networks (DSN) 2007, and Program Co-Chair of Computer Performance and Dependability Symposium, a track of the DSN 2002. He was Associate Editor of IEEE Transactions on Dependable and Secure Computing. He has published over 230 technical papers and is regularly invited to give tutorials and lectures on issues related to the design and assessment of complex computing systems. He is a member of the IEEE, the IEEE Computer Society, and IFIP Working Group 10.4 on Dependable Computing and Fault Tolerance.

**Dr. Nithin M. Nakka** received his BTech (hons.) degree from the Indian Institute of Technology, Kharagpur and his MS and PhD degrees at the University of Illinois at UIUC. Currently, he is Technical Leader at Cisco Systems. While at Cisco, he has worked on most layers of the networking software stack, from network data-plane hardware, control plane at Layer-2 and Layer-3, network controllers, up to and including network fabric monitoring. This along with doing what he enjoys – sharing his expertise through mentoring many incoming employees. He has been leading the development of solutions for network day-2 operations to monitor fabrics and analyze, understand, troubleshoot network issues, and possibly predict impending network failures. His innovative approximation heuristics in Algorithms for Memory Array Redundancy Analysis during his work at Nextest Systems Corporation brought the company to world-class excellence in this niche computational problem domain, generally known to be NP-complete. He also worked for Motorola's mobile devices group, on pioneering efforts in Bluetooth stereo audio transmission (A2DP) and Bluetooth security. His areas of research interest include systems reliability, network telemetry, and hardware implemented fault tolerance. Dr. Nakka has previously held positions as a research faculty in UIUC, and Northwestern University in Evanston, Illinois, and contributed to the area of dependability in high-performance computing systems.

# Preface

Dependability of systems has transitioned over the years from a feature to a necessity for end users, and from an add-on to a core design principle for those who are designing and implementing computing or computer-based systems. The need for dependability has grown not just in its breadth in terms of the areas where it is applicable but also in depth. Given any one of the many systems where dependability techniques are applied, their relevance is seen in every layer of the system stack. The aim of this book is to help readers navigate through the evolution of dependability, from taxonomy, mathematical concepts, and fundamental theory to design, implementation, validation, deployment, measurement, and monitoring. Finally, the book brings its audience right up to the modernity of the field by looking at critical societal applications such as autonomous vehicles, large-scale clouds, and engineering solutions for healthcare, illustrating the emerging challenges faced in making artificial intelligence (AI) and its applications dependable and trustworthy.

Sections of the book are intensely pedantic and technical. However, with the support of practical case studies and use cases from both academia and real-world deployments, we have attempted to guide our audience through their journey in fathoming the developments in this ever-growing field. For a beginner, a systematic study from the beginning will help in building strong foundations, but we encourage all readers to whet their appetite with any of the case studies that spark their interest. For seasoned designers and academicians in the area, we attempt to provide a near-current reference for dependability research and development.

The prerequisites for the content of this book are a basic understanding of statistical concepts, computer systems and organization, and, preferably, a course on distributed systems. Above all, a keen interest in delving into this exciting field to unravel and possibly discover new techniques will maintain a reader's enthusiasm, as it has done ours over the past years. Certainly, well-written texts are already available in this area. However, the authors felt that we lacked a single compendium spanning the myriad areas in which dependability has been applied, providing theoretical concepts and applied knowledge with content that would excite a beginner yet rigor that would satisfy an expert. That feeling led us to embark on the long journey of bringing forth this book.

Chapters 1 and 2 describe dependability taxonomy and briefly compare and contrast classical techniques with their modern counterparts or extensions. Chapters 3–7 help the readers walk up the system stack, from the hardware logic via operating systems up to software applications, with respect to how those layers are hardened for dependability. Chapters 8–12 expand into the domain of distributed systems to explore the techniques and applications therein. Those chapters also delve a great deal into a measurement-based understanding of the systems being studied, an aspect that the authors feel honored to have had the opportunity to significantly contribute. Chapter 13 focuses on the most recent and upcoming trends that are shaping developments in dependability. Finally, looking into the future, Chapter 14 delves deeper into the novel challenges that are being faced in making AI systems dependable and trustworthy.

In summary, with the support of practical case studies and use cases from both academia and real-world deployments, we guide our audience through a journey of developments, including the impact of AI and machine learning on this ever-growing field.

# Acknowledgments

In writing this book, we were inspired by Professor Dan Siewiorek's groundbreaking research and the unmatched book *The Theory and Practice of Reliable System Design* by Siewiorek and Swarz, now in its third edition, as well as the foundational work of Professors Ed McCluskey and Al Avižienis, which continues to impact the field today.

We are indebted to many of our current and former students, postdoctoral associates, and academic and industry colleagues whose research contributed in important ways to material in this book, including Karthik Pattabiraman, Lelio DiMartino, Bob Horst, Saurabh Bagchi, Homa Alemzadeh, Long Wang, Tim Tsai, Saurabh Jha, Phuong Cao, Keywhan Chung, Shengkun Cui, and Archit Patke. Some of our colleagues have also adopted a draft version of this book in teaching dependability courses to graduate and senior students in their respective institutions, which has bolstered our confidence in the usefulness of this content. The administrative and technical proofreading staff members, including, Carol Bosley, Heidi Leerkamp, Jenny Applequist, and Kathleen Atchley, have contributed immensely to this effort by their critical linguistic polish of this technical content and also by their logistical work in keeping the authors and publishers in synchrony to accomplish this massive task. We are grateful to all of them as well as many others who shared their insights.

Special thanks to our colleagues at the University of Illinois Urbana-Champaign who provided a rich, supportive environment that allowed us to pursue this project.

The research presented in this book was supported by numerous funding agencies and industry partners, including NSF, NIH, NASA, DoD, DARPA, DOE, IBM, Sandia National Lab, Nvidia, the Mayo Clinic, Infosys, and Xilinx.

Apart from the immense technical support we have received, we are very grateful to our families, who have been ever so patient in supporting us. They have transformed their "Are we there yet?" to "Looks like we are getting close" to keep our enthusiasm alive on an emotional front while we gave all we could to tame

this mammoth. In spite of all the support that we have received both profession-
ally and personally, added to our over 100 years of combined experience in this
area, we feel that our attempts to gather all that we could in this ever-expanding
and interesting field may have fallen short in some application domains, not given
enough justice to some, or even at times made unintentional errors in compre-
hending and explaining the content. A significant portion of our time was spent
in making sure that we kept the content current and relevant for our audience.
However, as the field is growing at the rate that it is, we had to reconcile ourselves
to the hope that we may offer more in a future edition! We invite readers to send
us their feedback on the content or any errors that may have escaped our scruti-
nous efforts to maintain relevance and correctness.

## About the Companion Website

This book is accompanied by a companion website:

**www.wiley.com/go/iyer/dependablecomputing1**

The website includes PDF's of slides describing material in the book; problem sets and select solutions by chapters; as well as in-class and semester long projects students can undertake.

# 1
# Dependability Concepts and Taxonomy

## 1.1 Introduction

Every single failure in any computing device is a potential cause for concern. Reliable computing and fault tolerance, or, to use a more current term, *dependable computing*, is a longstanding area of research and practical implementation. This broad area of study started in the mid-fifties with John von Neumann's construction of reliable systems from unreliable systems or components. Over the years, significant advancements and deployments have been made in commercial telecommunications, defense, and business applications that address a wide range of potential failures. Today, an explosion in the complexity of systems, applications, and operating systems has resulted in ever-expanding failure sources. That, combined with explosive growth in computing as an enterprise in all areas of human endeavor, has brought forth new challenges and opportunities in designing dependable systems. Further, early detection, rapid concurrent/online diagnosis, and efficient and complete recovery are key to the design of systems that continue to operate in the event of errors. They must be complemented by ongoing analysis and monitoring of failures, supported by strong statistical models. In dependability, an understanding of real failures is critical in the design, implementation, deployment, and validation of reliability techniques. Design and validation must go hand in hand in developing new systems. While dependability techniques protect systems against known faults, their greatest efficacy comes from their ability to safeguard against unanticipated failures due to accidental errors or malicious attacks.

This chapter sets the theme of the book by first placing classic work on dependability techniques in perspective and relating their importance for current computing systems. That assessment is followed by a description of the complexity of systems built using present-day hardware designs, architectures, and software

*Dependable Computing: Design and Assessment*, First Edition. Ravishankar K. Iyer, Zbigniew T. Kalbarczyk, and Nithin M. Nakka.
© 2024 The IEEE Computer Society. Published 2024 by John Wiley & Sons, Inc.
Companion website: www.wiley.com/go/iyer/dependablecomputing1

technologies that pose compelling challenges in providing continuous availability against a vast array of potential failures. Examples are provided of the developmental (or changing) trends in these areas that motivate the need for a newer perspective on dependability. The purpose of this chapter is to bring forth the recent challenges and opportunities in the reliability domain. (Possible solutions and techniques for fault tolerance and security will be explained as the book unfolds in the remaining chapters.) The discussion concludes with an introduction of dependability concepts, definitions, a taxonomy of failures, and a sample set of measurements from real systems in preparation for the next chapter's description of basic techniques.

The entire book follows the theme set by this chapter in introducing fundamentals of techniques with examples of prior deployment of the techniques in systems currently in use, with the goal of educating the reader on the applicability of these techniques, and any modifications or adaptations they need for use in modern and upcoming systems.

## 1.2 Placing Classical Dependability Techniques in Perspective

The earliest diagnostic techniques were developed for testing and failure recovery in the ILLIAC machine at the University of Illinois [1, 2] in the 1950s. When ILLIAC I (1950) and ILLIAC II (1961) were built at Illinois, fault diagnosis consisted of a battery of programs that exercised different sections of the machine. Typically, the test programs compared answers computed in two different ways, or stressed what was suspected to be a vulnerable part. In the ILLIAC II, the arithmetic and control units were designed to operate asynchronously, using a double handshake for each control signal and its acknowledgment. That protocol simplified the fault diagnosis, as it was used as an automatic fault detection mechanism. Most faults caused the control to wait for the next step in the asynchronous handshake protocol; that next step was identified using indicator lights for the flip-flops.

Spaceborne computing systems were one of the earliest avenues for dependability design. Early work on dependability in space-mission systems was performed on the JPL-STAR (Jet Propulsion Laboratory Self-Testing and Repair) computer (1971) [3] and on Voyager [4], leading to work on the Boeing 777 [5]. Although the craft carrying the JPL-STAR computer never went into space, its development resulted in the design and implementation of a range of techniques that are considered standard today. The Voyager computer (launched in 1977) used block redundancy (a form of a standby redundancy whereby redundancy is provided at the subsystem level, e.g., at the altitude control subsystem, rather than internally in each subsystem) for fault tolerance. Heartbeat-based hardware- and software-implemented techniques were used for error detection. For example, an error would be detected in the hardware if a command for the primary (in the dual-redundant configuration) arrived before the current command had been completely processed, and in software error detection, an error would be detected when the output unit in the primary remained unavailable for more than 14 seconds. Further developments in dependability in aviation were used in the design of the Boeing 777 fly-by-wire system, which used triple modular redundancy for all hardware resources, including the computing system, airplane electrical power, hydraulic power, and communication path.

The basic techniques established for hardware redundancy and software-based fault and failure management, exceptions, and their handling in software, and the use of error codes in memory systems, transmission, and disk systems have been the mainstay of practical and commercial systems such as the AT&T No. 5 ESS [6], IBM S/360, and IBM S/370 [7]. These systems included a combination of hardware and software techniques and diagnostics that significantly advanced the theory and practice of dependable computing. The methods have since been augmented with computational algorithms and protocols to achieve consistency and reliable operation in distributed systems [8].

While parity, ECC (error correcting codes) and redundant array of independent disks have been widely used for commodity systems, the use of massive redundancy in hardware and software has led to high overheads in performance costs, hardware components, and software development costs. For example, the IBM MVS operating system devotes 50% of its software code base to fault management [9], while the IBM G5 processor dedicates 35% of its processor silicon area to fault detection and tolerance hardware [10]. In addition to those overheads, the validation of such systems has become increasingly complex and difficult. Thus, the use of the techniques discussed above to build "one-size-fits-all" architectures has become reserved for high-end, high-cost systems such as those used in military, telecommunication, and financial applications. Until recently, those application domains depended on traditional techniques in which redundancy in the hardware, combined with hooks into the operating system, together supported some level of software redundancy. On the other hand, until recently, failures in commodity environments did not have such a big cost impact and hence were either not addressed or at best marginally addressed.

With the explosion of computing devices, and in particular a variety of mobile/handheld devices in a wide variety of applications, computing has become a social enterprise. Massive computing data centers are distributed geographically, logically, and physically, servicing networked entities from telecom to Internet service providers to banks (i.e., high-dependability domains). On the one hand, the likes of Amazon and Google have increasingly adopted and invested in high-performance computing systems. On the other hand, ubiquitous computing, present in everyday appliances such as washing machines and microwaves, vehicles such as automobiles and airplanes, and applications such as e-commerce and health monitoring, has dramatically changed the impact of computing system failures on the world's social and economic machinery. With computing now a common enterprise, such outages can no longer be ignored or brushed aside with a marginal or cursory solution. Dependability requirements for these systems are nearly as high as those for the legacy systems that extensively used redundancy throughout the system. However, the cost margin for high availability is typically small, precluding the use of traditional techniques for commodity systems. New, low-cost techniques that are tailored to the specific needs of the application are required for the emerging domains. On the other end of the spectrum from embedded, ubiquitous computing are new large-scale, high-performance computing systems (i.e., supercomputers) for which dependability (or the ability to compute through failures) is paramount for providing sustained performance at scale. Such systems pose another important challenge with respect to dependability. The domain-specific requirements of the varied systems discussed thus far, failures during recovery in any system significantly change the dependability dynamics of the system [6, 11]. However, this aspect has not been adequately considered in either the design or the assessment of computing systems.

## 1.3 Taxonomy of Dependable Computing

In this section, we introduce dependability concepts and definitions as preparation for the descriptions of dependability techniques that follow in the rest of the book.

Avižienis and Laprie [12] described a taxonomy for dependable systems and certain dependability measures. A subsequent publication by Avižienis et al. [13] described a taxonomy that also included secure computing, as well as methodologies for evaluating the availability of a system with greater rigor. It introduced dependability as a global concept that subsumes attributes such as reliability, availability, safety, integrity, and maintainability. The consideration of security brings in concerns for confidentiality, in addition to availability and integrity. Although there have been attempts at quantification, e.g., [14], a consensus has not yet emerged on how to measure dependability and security.

Figure 1.1 shows a refined dependability and security tree as described by Avižienis et al. [13].

Since this book is primarily focused on dependability design and assessment, this section will present a taxonomy related to dependability that draws on the work mentioned above. We direct the reader to the referenced papers for more in-depth understanding.

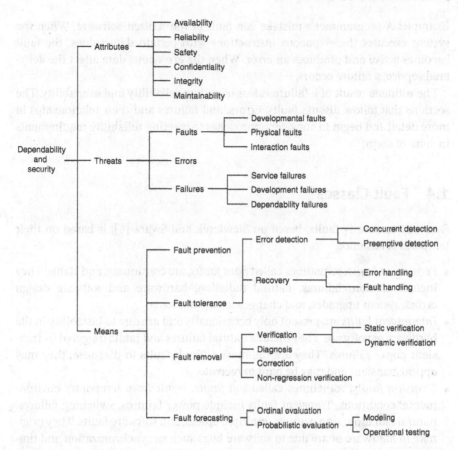

**Figure 1.1** A refined dependability and security tree. *Source*: Avižienis et al. [13]. © IEEE.

## 1.3.1 Faults, Errors, and Failures

Within a computing system, it is useful to distinguish among faults, errors, and failures as follows:

- A *failure* is a deviation of the delivered service from compliance with the specification, i.e., a failure is a departure from the service required of a system and is a property of the external behavior of a system.
- An *error* is part of the system state that has been damaged by the fault and, if uncorrected, can lead to a failure. Here, fault tolerance is based on detection of latent errors before they become active, followed by replacement of the erroneous part of the state with an error-free state.
- A *fault* is the adjudged or hypothesized cause of an error.

Example: A programmer's mistake is a fault in the written software. When the system executes the erroneous instructions with certain data values, the fault becomes active and produces an error. When the erroneous data affect the delivered service, a failure occurs.

The ultimate result of a failure is loss of system reliability and availability. The sections that follow discuss faults, errors, and failures and their relationships in more detail and begin to consider approaches to meeting reliability requirements in spite of them.

## 1.4 Fault Classes

One way to classify faults, based on Siewiorek and Swarz [6], is based on their temporal persistence:

- *Permanent faults*, sometimes called *hard faults*, are continuous and stable. They include random failures, natural radiation, hardware and software design errors, system upgrades, and changes to requirements.
- *Intermittent faults* are present only occasionally and are due to instability in the hardware or software. They include natural failures and faults triggered by transient power failures. They are the most difficult faults to diagnose; they may appear transient and may be hard to recreate.
- *Transient faults*, sometimes called *soft faults*, result from temporary environmental conditions. Transient faults include power failures, switching failures, natural radiation, single upsets, multiple upsets, and software faults. They originate in hardware or are due to software bugs such as synchronization and timing errors. Ninety percent of field errors are due to transient faults [15].

Faults may also be classified by their origin, again following [6]:

- *Physical faults* stem from physical phenomena internal to the system, such as shorts, or from external changes, such as vibration.
- *Human-made faults* include design and procedural faults as well as human-machine interaction faults that occur during maintenance or operation.

## 1.5 The Fault Cycle and Dependability Measures

Four important metrics measure system dependability: reliability, maintainability, availability, and safety. They are defined in terms of the concepts of *mean time to failure* (MTTF) or *mean time to error* (MTTE), *mean time between failures* (MTBF), *mean time to catastrophic failure* (MTTCF), *fault latency, error latency,*

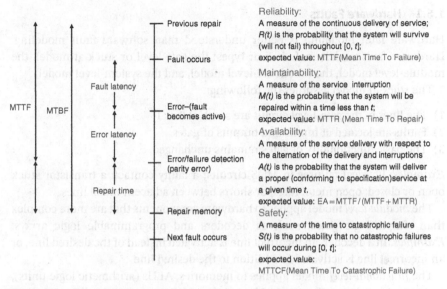

**Figure 1.2** Dependability measures in relation to the fault cycle.

*and repair time*; all are understood with reference to the fault cycle, as shown in Figure 1.2.

Note that increased error latency increases the likelihood that multiple errors will occur, placing a greater burden on recovery mechanisms. It also increases the likelihood of error propagation, which is why error containment boundaries are important.

Figure 1.2 also defines basic dependability metrics: (i) *reliability* (a measure of the continuous delivery of services), (ii) *maintainability* (a measure of the service interruption), (iii) *availability* (a measure of service delivery with respect to the alternation of the delivery and interruptions), and (iv) *safety* (a measure of the time to catastrophic failure).

Note that in theory, high availability can be achieved with a low MTTF, as long as the MTTR is very low. In practice, however, those two quantities are closely related: they tend to increase together. In other words, it is very unlikely that a system that crashes frequently will offer a very fast and robust recovery service.

# 1.6 Fault and Error Classification

This section provides a brief, somewhat generic discussion of broad classes of faults/errors. The purpose is not to be comprehensive, but to articulate major differences between hardware and software faults/errors.

### 1.6.1 Hardware Faults

Hardware fault modeling is better understood than software fault modeling. Hardware fault models include four types: the gate level or stuck-at model, the module-level model, the functional-level model, and the system-level model.

The *stuck-at* model assumes the following:

1) The lines in the gate-level circuit are stuck at 0 or 1.
2) Faults are located at inputs and outputs of gates.
3) The basic functionality of gates remains unchanged.

*Examples:* Physical failures in MOS circuits; a faulty contact; a transistor stuck open or closed; open metal lines; or shorts between adjacent metal lines.

The *module-level* model applies to hardware components that are more complex than simple logic gates, such as decoders and programmable logic arrays. *Examples:* In a decoder, an incorrect line is activated instead of the desired line, or an incorrect line is activated in addition to the desired line.

The *functional-level* model applies to memories, ALUs (arithmetic logic units), and network switches. *Examples:* Memory in which one or more cells are stuck at 0 or 1, one or more cells fail to undergo 0–1 or 1–0 transition, two or more cells are coupled, a 1–0 transition in one cell changes contents in another cell, more than one cell is accessed during a READ or WRITE, or a wrong cell is accessed during a READ or WRITE.

The *system-level* model applies to higher-level system components, e.g., several CPUs, or a memory, network, or disk subsystem. *Example:* In a parallel processor topology, a processor or a communication link between processors is faulty.

### 1.6.2 Software Faults and Errors

Software faults are often referred to as software *bugs*. Computer pioneer Grace Hopper described how that term was coined after a malfunction in an early electromechanical computer was caused by a "moth trapped between points at Relay #70, Panel Γ, of the Mark II Aiken Relay Calculator while it was being tested at Harvard University, 9 September 1945. . . .. The operators affixed the moth to the computer log, with the entry: First actual case of bug being found [. . .]". They thus coined the term *bug* and joked that they had "debugged" the machine – thus also introducing the term *debugging* now used to describe removal of software faults from a computer program [16].

Most software bugs are mistakes made by people during the design or coding of a program, and a few are caused by compilers that produce incorrect code. Software bugs have been classified as permanent and transient; Gray [17], for example, classified software faults into "Bohrbugs" and "Heisenbugs." *Bohrbugs,* whose name was inspired by the Bohr model of the atom, are permanent design faults. By nature they are very nearly deterministic. During testing and debugging (i.e., the early deployment phase), Bohrbugs can be easily identified and weeded out. On the other hand, *Heisenbugs* (whose name was inspired by the Heisenberg uncertainty principle in physics) are intermittent and, as such, belong to the class of temporary internal faults. Heisenbugs are, in essence, permanent faults with activation conditions that occur rarely and are not easy to reproduce. Such faults give rise to transient failures, and if the software is restarted, the failures will not necessarily recur. Heisenbugs are likely to circumvent testing, as the bug-catcher may perturb the situation enough to make the Heisenbug disappear [17].

The majority of studies on failure data have shown that a significant proportion of software failures are transient [15, 17] and are caused by phenomena such as timing, overloads, and exception errors. Studies of failure data from Tandem's fault-tolerant computer system reported that 70% of its failures were transient, triggered by faults such as race conditions and timing problems [11].

### 1.6.2.1 The GUARDIAN90 Operating System

Lee and Iyer [11] presented an analysis of software failure data on the Tandem GUARDIAN90 operating system. The analysis examined a collection of memory dumps of field reports on software failures, and resulted in the classification scheme presented in Table 1.1. A total of six classes of software errors were distinguished.

### 1.6.2.2 IBM-MVS (zOS) and IBM Database Management Systems

Table 1.2 presents a classification of error types obtained from failure reports from the IBM-MVS operating systems [18] and two large IBM database management systems, DB2 and IMS [19]. A total of 12 classes of faults were distinguished in these studies. It was observed that the overall error-type distributions for the three

**Table 1.1** Error classes for Tandem GUARDIAN90.

| Incorrect computation | Arithmetic overflow or use of incorrect arithmetic function |
| --- | --- |
| Data fault | Use of an incorrect constant or variable |
| Data definition fault | Fault in declaring data or in defining data structure |
| Missing operation | Omission of a few lines of source code |
| Side effect of code update | Not all dependencies between software modules were considered when software was being updated |
| Unexpected situation | Routines to handle rare but legitimate operational scenarios not provided |

**Table 1.2** Error classes for IBM-MVS and IBM database management systems.

| | |
|---|---|
| Allocation management | Module uses a memory region after deallocating it. |
| Copying overrun | Program copies data past end of buffer. |
| Pointer management | Variable containing address of data was corrupted. |
| Wrong algorithm | Program works but uses wrong algorithm. |
| Uninitialized variable | Variable used before it is initialized. |
| Undefined state | System goes into state designers did not anticipate. |
| Data error | Program produces or reads wrong data. |
| Statement logic | Statements executed in the wrong order or are omitted. |
| Interface error | Module's interface is defined or used incorrectly. |
| Memory leak | Program does not deallocate memory it has allocated. |
| Synchronization | Error occurs in locking or synchronizing code. |

products (IBM-MVS, DB2, and IMS) differ significantly. However, some aspects of the error type distributions are invariant, for instance, the dominating error type, *undefined state*.

An important contribution to the classification and understanding of software faults/errors was the development of Orthogonal Defect Classification (ODC) [20]. ODC was proposed by R. Chillarege at IBM T.J. Watson to bring measurement into the software development process. By measuring and analyzing software defects, ODC provides methods for understanding and controlling the design and test process.

ODC's roots go back to the early stages of software-implemented fault injection (SWIFI). The concept of *ODC Trigger* reflects the need to understand the error mechanisms for fault injection by studying real field failures [18]. A *defect*, defined as a necessary change to software that must be made for the software to be usable [21], is the target of the final repair actions that follow the discovery of a fault. Since defects can exist through the entire development process and field life of a product, they are an excellent source of information that can be used to understand and characterize all stages of the software development process.

ODC requires that each defect be categorized/characterized by a prescribed attribute value set. A rigorous empirical process is employed to determine the attribute values that describe the defect and produce a specific measurement of the development process [22]. For example, *Defect Type* and *Trigger* are two key ODC attributes. The *Defect Type* captures the meaning of the fix, expressed in a value set that describes design or programming terms and maps to the development process via a set of associations and probabilities. The defect type attributes were initially established empirically [20]. The *Trigger* maps into the test process and expresses conditions that lead to the surfacing of a defect.

The classes of software faults identified using ODC were used as a basis for emulation of software faults using fault injection. Based on the observation that a large percentage of faults can be characterized in a precise way, a set of emulation operators was established to mimic software faults. A software fault injection technique (G-SWFIT) based on emulation operators derived from field study was proposed [23].

## 1.7 Mean Time Between Failures

We also know that mean time between failures (MTBF) can vary greatly between systems designed for fault tolerance and other systems. For example, consider the data in Table 1.3.

The Los Alamos National Laboratory collected and published data regarding the failure and usage of 22 of their supercomputing clusters [24]. The root causes of the failures were classified into the following categories: (i) Facilities, (ii) Hardware, (iii) Human Error, (iv) Network, (v) Undetermined, and (vi) Software. The data were previously analyzed by Schroeder and Gibson [25] from CMU to study the statistics of the data in terms of the root causes of the failures, mean time between failures, and the mean time to repair.

Table 1.3 provides the details of the systems. In the "Production Time" column, the range of times specifies the node installation-to-decommissioning times. A value of "N/A" indicates that the nodes were installed before the observation period began. For those machines, the beginning of the observation period (January 1996) was used as the starting date for calculating the production time. For some machines, multiple ranges of production times were provided because the systems were upgraded during the observation period; each production time range corresponds to a set of nodes within the system. For the sake of simplicity, for all such machines, we consider the production time to be the longest range among the specified ranges.

The failure data for a single system include the following fields:

*System*: The number of the system under study (as specified by the Los Alamos National Laboratory).

*Machine type*: The type of the system (smp, cluster, numa).

*Number of nodes*: The number of nodes in the system.

*Number of processors per node*: Notably, some systems are heterogeneous in that they contain nodes with different numbers of processors per node.

*Number of processors total*: Total number of processors in the system = $\sum_{i}^{k} n_i \times p_i$,

where, for a system, $k$ is the number of node types in the system, $n_i$ is the number of nodes of type $i$, and $p_i$ is the number of processors in a node of type $i$.

Table 1.3  MTTF, MTTR, and availability data for various real-world systems.

| System | | | | | | MTTF (h) | MTTR (h) | Availability |
|---|---|---|---|---|---|---|---|---|
| Tandem GUARDIAN98 | | | | | | 98 | N/A | N/A |
| Tandem NonStop UNIX | | | | | | 480 to 2040 | N/A | N/A |
| Network of 69 SunOS Workstations | | | | | | 96.44 | 0.72 | 99.25% |
| LAN of NT machines (using system logs from 68 mail servers) | | | | | | 284 | 1.97 | 99.31% |
| Blue Waters Petascale system | | | | | | 154.04 | 5.16 | 96.76% |
| Amazon EC2 | | | | | | 99.95 | 0.05 | 99.95% |

| Type | Cat | System | # of procs | # of nodes | # of procs/node | Network topology | Production time | MTTF (h) | MTTR (h) | Availability |
|---|---|---|---|---|---|---|---|---|---|---|
| A | Smp | 7 | 8 | 1 | 8 | N/A | N/A–12/99 | 34 315.6 | 4.43 | 99.987% |
| B | Smp | 24 | 32 | 1 | 32 | N/A | N/A–12/03 | 69 377.7 | 6.26 | 99.991% |
| C | Smp | 22 | 4 | 1 | 4 | N/A | N/A–04/03 | 63 522.3 | 5.73 | 99.991% |
| D | Cluster | 8 | 328 | 164 | 2 | GB Ethernet Tree | 04/01–11/05 | 34 300.8 | 34.30 | 99.90% |
| E | Cluster | 21 | 512 | 128 | 4 | Dual Rail Fat Tree | 09/01–01/02 | 2925.6 | 2.40 | 99.918% |
| F | Cluster | 14 | 256 | 128 | 2 | Single Rail Fat Tree | 09/03–11/05 | 19 629.5 | 98.52 | 99.500% |
| G | Cluster | 2 | 6152 | 49 | 128/80$^a$ | Multi Rail Fat Tree | 01/97–11/05 | 77 438.0 | 2.37 | 99.997% |
| H | Numa | 15 | 256 | 1 | 256 | N/A | 11/04–11/05 | 9477.7 | 2.31 | 99.976% |

[a]Depending on the function of the processor, if it is used for front-end graphics it has 80 procs per node. If it is used for back-end computing/graphics, it has 128 procs per node.

*Production time*: The time between the installation and decommission of the system. If the system was in production at the end of the observation period, we consider that to be the end time.

*Mean time between failures (MTBF) (in hours, h)*: The average time between failures of the system, calculated as the ratio of the production time and the number of failures.

*Mean time to repair (MTTR) (in hours, h)*: The average time for which the system was unavailable due to repair.

*Availability*: Calculated as $\left(\dfrac{(MTBF - MTTR)}{MTBF}\right)$.

## 1.8 User-perceived System Dependability

Some studies on failure data analysis have attempted to measure dependability as it is perceived by customers/users. From the user's perspective, dependability characterizes the ability of a machine or system to provide service, not just to survive.

In 2000, Chandra and Chen [26] evaluated the hypothesis that generic recovery techniques such as process pairs can survive most application faults without using application-specific information. They examined three large, open-source applications examined. Information from the bug reports and source code were used to classify faults related to the faults' dependence on the operating environment. A quite large percentage of the faults (72–87%) were found to be independent of the operating environment, and recovery from the failures caused by these faults required the use of application-specific knowledge. Of the remaining faults, half depended on a condition in the operating environment that was likely to persist on retry, and the failures caused by these faults were also likely to require application-specific recovery. Only 5–14% of the faults were triggered by transient conditions (e.g., timing and synchronization) that inherently self-correct during recovery. Results from this study showed that classical application-generic recovery techniques (e.g., process pairs) would be insufficient to enable applications to recover from the majority of failures caused by application faults.

For example, a study [27] of a LAN of Windows NT-based mail servers indicates that while the measured availability of the system was 99%, the user-perceived availability was only 92%, i.e., the system was often alive but unable to provide a required service. A later analysis [28] reports similar figures on system availability of a Windows NT cluster consisting of two thousand workstations and servers. The need to account for the user's perception of system dependability is also stressed in an analysis of Windows 2000 dependability [29].

## 1.9 Technology Trends and Failure Behavior

As technology matures, the user set changes, the degree of product sophistication increases, and new sources of failures become prominent. It is important to understand these trends to determine the techniques that would be most effective in preventing, detecting, and recovering from the new sources of errors. One of the main trends driving the design of modern dependable systems has been the change in failure rates as well as the change in the dominant sources of failures. By and large, we can conclude that hardware failure rates are currently down, while the relative contribution of software in failures is up.

Through the years, transient faults have typically been associated with the corruption of stored data values. The phenomenon was reported in adverse operating conditions as early as 1954, first in areas close to nuclear bomb test sites and later in space applications [30, 31]. Since 1978, dense memory circuits (both DRAM and SRAM) have been known to be at risk from soft errors caused by alpha particles from both IC packaging and cosmic rays. Following a transient failure, a hardware device can recover its full capability. Nonetheless, such a failure can be catastrophic for the correct execution of a program; a corrupted intermediate value, if not handled, can corrupt all subsequent computations.

Continuously decreasing feature sizes and supply voltages of devices will lessen capacitive node charge and noise margin. Inevitably, even flip-flop circuits will become susceptible to soft errors [32]. The high clock rate of modern processors makes the problem worse by increasing the probability of a new failure mechanism whereby a momentarily corrupted combinational signal is latched by a flip-flop. Continual pushing of the processor performance envelope will soon place users and developers in an unfamiliar realm where logically correct implementations alone cannot guarantee correct program execution with acceptable confidence. Explicit error detection and correction techniques have long been incorporated into the architectures provided by vendors of high-availability platforms. The basic techniques involve space redundancy (achieved by carrying out the same computation on multiple independent pieces of hardware at the same time and corroborating the redundant results to expose errors), information redundancy (e.g., parity and ECC), and time redundancy (whereby redundant computation is obtained by repeating the same operations multiple times on the same hardware).

Memory arrays can be ECC-protected relatively efficiently because the cost of the coding logic can be amortized over the array. Application of ECC to individual registers in a processor may require a significant amount of overhead and increases the critical path delay. Typically, information redundancy is reserved for memory, caches, and perhaps register files, whereas space- and time-redundant techniques are employed elsewhere in the processor. A shortcoming of time redundancy is that persistent hardware faults may introduce identical errors to all redundant results, making errors indiscernible. A complementary shortcoming of space redundancy is that a transient failure may affect the space-redundant hardware identically, again making errors indiscernible.

Table 1.4 summarizes the changes over the last four decades in terms of the technology, error/fault sources, number of users, and their level of sophistication/ training [33]. One consequence of the dropping hardware failure rate is that other failure modes have become more prominent. Increasing software complexity has gradually contributed to a larger proportion of system outages. Throughout the 1980s, as fault tolerance methods were being developed for hardware and the incidence rate of hardware failures was dropping, software failures became more prominent. At the same time, the focus on software reliability methods was marginal. In the high-end server business, most of the development budgets were focused on new functionality, as that was a growth segment into the 1990s. The PC segment was at its inception, and functionality was the focus there as well. As a consequence, software failures – a class of problems whose damaging effects could be as significant as hardware outages that took down entire systems – became more evident.

An important development in providing runtime mechanisms for handling software failures was the inception of design diversity. The seminal academic work materialized as the N-Version Programming [34], Recovery Blocks [35], and N-Self-Checking [36] approaches. Extensive experimental studies (e.g., [37]) were conducted to assess the effectiveness of the proposed solutions. Examples of industrial use span embedded control systems, in particular in the avionics and railway domains; e.g., [38, 39].

The following sections briefly discuss the issues that have emerged at the hardware and platform levels. We then turn to a discussion of cloud computing as an example of a computing paradigm that encompasses new technological trends while still being impacted by the aforementioned challenges.

## 1.10 Issues at the Hardware Level

- If standard redundancy techniques were to be applied as is, they would scale costs by a factor of the degree of integration of the processing elements.
  - For instance, consider this quick back-of-the-envelope calculation. For the $200 million Blue Waters supercomputer deployed at the University of

**Table 1.4** Fault sources, levels of integration, users, and user sophistication over the past decades.

| Topics / Decade | 1970s | 1980s | 1990s | 2000s |
|---|---|---|---|---|
| Typical systems | Mainframes | Workstations | Personal computers | Mobile devices (e.g. cellphones, PDAs) |
| Fault/error sources | Hardware | Hardware, network | Hardware, network, software, human errors | Hardware, software, wired/wireless networks, environment (e.g. frequent connectivity loss, malicious faults) |
| Integration/complexity | Close systems, highly custom designs where both hardware and OS are fully controlled by vendor | Mostly close systems, network connectivity, standard interfaces exposed to users | Open systems, wide access to network, COTS operating systems, third-party hardware and software | Open systems, proprietary and COTS operating systems, highly integrated PC-like systems |
| People/users | Tens of thousands | Millions | Tens of millions | Hundreds of millions |
| Level of user sophistication/training | BS in engineering; 5000 hours | Basic knowledge in computing; 500 hours | Basic computing; 50–100 hours | Training at the time of a purchase of a device; couple of hours |

Source: Siewiorek et al. [33]. © IEEE.

Illinois [40], requiring a hardware overhead of 35% would incur approximately $70 million in costs ($200M × 0.35), a sizeable amount.

- Process variations are an additional factor that has grown more important over time because of the decreasing feature size and increasing complexity that are resulting from greater and greater levels of integration.
- With decreasing feature sizes, issues such as negative bias temperature instability (NBTI) [41] have arisen as key reliability concerns at the device level.
  - The bug in Intel's Cougar Point SATA (Serial Advanced Technology Attachment) port on the 6-Series Chipset is an example of the impact of failures on device-level integration [42]. Cougar Point (Intel's 6-Series Chipsets, H67/P67) has two sets of SATA ports: four that support 3-Gbps operation, and two that support 6-Gbps operation. Each set of ports requires its own PLL (phase-locked loop) source. On 31 January 2011, Intel announced that it had identified a bug in the 6-Series Chipset, specifically in its SATA controller [43]. Intel stated that "in some cases, the Serial-ATA (SATA) ports within the chipsets may degrade over time, potentially impacting the performance or functionality of SATA-linked devices such as hard disk drives and DVD drives." Intel began shipping the corrected version of the chipset in late February of 2011. The recall reduced Intel's revenue by around $300 million, and it cost around $700 million to completely repair and replace affected systems.

## 1.11 Issues at the Platform Level

The use of virtual machine-based systems has drastically transformed the system view by introducing the hypervisor in between the operating system and the hardware. The relationship between the hypervisor/virtual machine monitor (VMM) and a guest operating system is analogous to the former relationship between the operating system and the application processes running atop it. The hypervisor introduces a new set of interactions (with both the operating system and applications) and consequent system failure modes.

The non-uniform, dynamic geographic distribution of nodes (in the current cloud computing environment) violates the assumptions of traditional distributed systems regarding communication overheads, resulting in a need to adapt these systems for efficiency in spite of the additional performance-deterring factors. Legacy techniques such as synchronous and asynchronous checkpointing already incur significant overhead and cannot be applied naïvely in the new scenario without investigation. Added to that are the high and nondeterministic costs that result from the dynamic nature of distributed systems.

## 1.12 What is Unique About this Book?

While this book reflects the experience and expertise of the authors in design and validation of dependable systems, it also introduces a holistic view of dependability and discusses techniques and approaches for achieving dependability from the system perspective.

System or application failures can originate in faults/errors at different levels of the system hierarchy (hardware, operating system, communication layer, middleware, or application). Therefore, a system (hardware and software) perspective is needed to properly handle design issues in dependable computing. Figure 1.3 depicts a basic system hierarchy and poses relevant questions that a system designer or developer must answer before building a dependable computing system.

At each system level – applications, middleware, communications, operating system, hardware, and network – we can ask ourselves what reliable dependability-supporting mechanisms are provided and what mechanisms can be added. In answering those questions, we must consider how hardware and software techniques can be combined; specifically, how fast error detection in hardware and high-efficiency detection and recovery in software can be coordinated, bearing in mind that fault-tolerance mechanisms in both hardware and software must themselves be self-checking and fault tolerant. We must also consider how to assess whether the dependability achieved is sufficient to meet system requirements. State-of-the-art techniques available to us at each of the four levels (and discussed in this book) are shown in Figure 1.4.

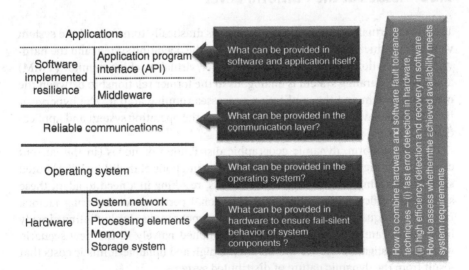

**Figure 1.3** Dependability requirements at various system levels.

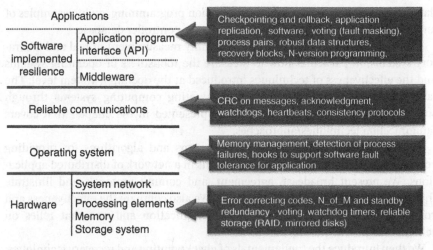

**Figure 1.4** Techniques available at each system level.

## 1.13 Overview of the Book

The intended audience of this book ranges from students who wish to learn the fundamentals of dependable computing, to dependability researchers and engineers and software and hardware developers. The goal of this book is to present the fundamentals of designing computer systems for dependability. We will begin by introducing key terms and concepts and go on to illustrate and explain a wide range of design and implementation techniques. Because the design of dependable systems is as much an art as a science, our approach will be to provide, through real-life examples, a repertoire of ideas and techniques that you, the designer, can draw upon and adapt according to your constraints and requirements. We will discuss issues and techniques from both hardware and software viewpoints in the context of selected dependable systems, including distributed systems and networks.

To interest readers in the potential applications of dependability, in Chapter 5, we start with a set of illustrative case studies of systems that have paved the way for modern dependability and still remain relevant. At the same time, we present a spectrum of computing paradigms in which dependability has applications. We are going to present a system-level perspective that encompasses both hardware and software. To do so, we will first introduce hardware redundancy techniques. We will then present a variety of error-detecting and -correcting codes as well as noncoding detection techniques. Fault-tolerance techniques employed at the processor level in academic research and commercial systems will be presented. We will describe software fault tolerance techniques, including process pairs, robust data structures, recovery blocks, and N-version programming, giving examples of an online transactional processing system and a controller database.

An entire chapter is devoted to dependability measurement of real and laboratory systems, in particular how to measure the robustness of operating systems and the effectiveness of techniques introduced at the operating system level. The fault models and primitives used in evaluating computing systems through software-implemented fault injection are presented in the chapter that covers fault injection techniques/approaches.

Network-specific issues include mechanisms and algorithms for providing consistent data and reliable communications in a network of distributed applications. We present broadcast, agreement, and commit protocols and illustrate them in the context of a reliable platform. We also compare the effectiveness and costs of a reliable design that relies on replication and one that relies on self-checking.

We then introduce the fundamentals of checkpointing and recovery techniques, followed by a discussion of the additional considerations involved in checkpointing large-scale systems. Checkpointing and rollback recovery are illustrated using three examples: a commercial, distributed database system (a "macro" example); checkpointing of multi-threaded processes (a "micro" example); and an operating system that supports checkpointing and recovery.

Validation is a key step, often overlooked or inadequately executed, in the design of any dependable system. Early validation of a system using modeling has been dealt with in detail by many others, e.g., Trivedi [44] and Sahner and Trivedi [45] (SHARPE), Clark et al. [46] (Möbius), and Ciardo and Miner [47] (SMART). In this book, we will address validation through field measurements and fault injections. Fault injection is an effective and common method for validating a dependability technique. Fault injection techniques can be implemented at various levels in a system, either in hardware or in software.

The book concludes with a chapter on understanding the dependability challenges of modern-day systems and paradigms: virtualization and cloud systems in software and system architecture, multicore processors in hardware, and stream processing in applications. We look into the dependability techniques applied in those areas in light of the techniques discussed in all the previous chapters.

# References

1 Iyer, R.K., Sanders, W.H., Patel, J.H. et al. (2004). The evolution of dependable computing at the University of Illinois. *Building the Information Society: IFIP 18th World Computer Congress Topical Sessions* (ed. R. Jacquart), Toulouse, France (22–27 August 2004), 135–164. Boston, MA, USA: Kluwer Academic Publishers.

**2** Abraham, J.A., Metze, G., Iyer, R.K. et al. (1987). The evolution of fault tolerant computing at the University of Illinois. In: *The Evolution of Fault Tolerant Computing. Dependable Computing and Fault-Tolerant Systems*, vol. 1 (eds. A. Avižienis, H. Kopetz and J.C. Laprie), 271–288. Vienna, Austria: Springer-Verlag.

**3** Avižienis, A., Gilley, G.C., Mathur, F.P. et al. (1971). The STAR (self-testing and repairing) computer: an investigation of the theory and practice of fault-tolerant computer design. *IEEE Transactions on Computers* C-20 (11): 1312–1321.

**4** Jones, C.P. (1979). Automatic fault protection in the Voyager spacecraft. AIAA Paper No. 79-1919, Jet Propulsion Laboratory, California Institute of Technology, Pasadena, CA.

**5** Yeh, Y.C. (1996). Triple–triple redundant 777 primary flight computer. *Proceedings of the IEEE Aerospace Applications Conference*, vol. 1, Aspen, CO, USA (10 February 1996), 293–307. IEEE.

**6** Siewiorek, D.P. and Swarz, R.S. (1998). *Reliable Computer Systems: Design and Evaluation*, 3e. Natick, MA, USA: A K Peters/CRC Press.

**7** Carter, W.C., Montgomery, H.C., Preiss, R.J. et al. (1964). Design of serviceability features for the IBM system/360. *IBM Journal of Research and Development* 8 (2): 115–126.

**8** Garg, V.K. (2002). *Elements of Distributed Computing*. Wiley.

**9** Iyer, R.K. and Velardi, P. (1985). Hardware-related software errors: measurement and analysis. *IEEE Transactions on Software Engineering* SE-11 (2): 223–231.

**10** Spainhower, L. and Gregg, T.A. (1999). IBM S/390 Parallel Enterprise Server G5 fault tolerance: a historical perspective. *IBM Journal of Research and Development* 43 (5): 863–874.

**11** Lee, I. and Iyer, R. (1993). Faults, symptoms, and software fault tolerance in the Tandem GUARDIAN90 operating system. *Proceedings of the 23rd International Symposium on Fault-Tolerant Computing*, Toulouse, France (22–24 June 1993), 20–29. IEEE.

**12** Avizienis, A. and Laprie, J.C. (1986). Dependable computing: from concepts to design diversity. *Proceedings of the IEEE* 74 (5): 629–638.

**13** Avizienis, A., Laprie, J.C., Randell, B. et al. (2004). Basic concepts and taxonomy of dependable and secure computing. *IEEE Transactions on Dependable and Secure Computing* 1 (1): 11–33.

**14** Sharma, V.S. and Trivedi, K.S. (2007). Quantifying software performance, reliability and security: an architecture-based approach. *Journal of Systems and Software* 80 (4): 493–509.

**15** Gray, J. (1990). A census of Tandem system availability between 1985 and 1990. *IEEE Transactions on Reliability* 39 (4): 409–418. http://bnrg.eecs.berkeley. edu/~randy/Courses/CS294.F07/10.1.pdf (accessed 22 October 2020).

**16** Naval History and Heritage Command (2020). NH 96566-KN: the first "computer bug." https://www.history.navy.mil/content/history/nhhc/our-collections/

photography/numerical-list-of-images/nhhc-series/nh-series/NH-96000/
NH-96566-KN.html (accessed 25 May 2020).

**17** Gray, J. (1985). Why Do Computers Stop and What Can Be Done About It?
Technical Report 85.7. Tandem Computers.

**18** Sullivan, M. and Chillarege, R. (1991). Software defects and their impact on
system availability: a study of field failures in operating systems. *Digest of Papers,
the 21st International Symposium on Fault-Tolerant Computing*, Montreal,
Quebec, Canada (25–27 June 1991), 2–9. IEEE.

**19** Sullivan, M. and Chillarege, R. (1992). A comparison of software defects in
database management systems and operating systems. *Digest of Papers, the 22nd
International Symposium on Fault-Tolerant Computing*, Boston, MA, USA
(8–10 July 1992), 475–484. IEEE.

**20** Chillarege, R., Bhandari, I.S., Chaar, J.K. et al. (1992). Orthogonal defect
classification: a concept for in-process measurements. *IEEE Transactions on
Software Engineering* 18 (11): 943–956.

**21** Chillarege, R. (1994). ODC for process management, analysis, and control.
*Proceedings of 4th International Conference on Software Quality*, McLean, VA,
USA (3–5 October 1994).

**22** Chillarege, R., Kao, W.-L., and Condit, R.G. (1991). Defect type and its impact on
the growth curve. *Proceedings of the 13th International Conference on Software
Engineering*, Austin, TX, USA (13–16 May 1991), 246–255. IEEE.

**23** Durães, J. and Madeira, H. (2006). Emulation of software faults: a field data study
and a practical approach. *IEEE Transactions on Software Engineering* 32 (11):
849–867.

**24** Nakka, N. and Choudhary, A. (2010). Failure data-driven selective node-level
duplication to improve MTTF in high performance computing systems. In: *High
Performance Computing Systems and Applications. HPCS 2009. Lecture Notes in
Computer Science*, vol. 5976 (eds. D.J.K. Mewhort, N.M. Cann, G.W. Slater, et al.),
304–322. Berlin, Heidelberg: Springer.

**25** Schroeder, B. and Gibson, G.A. (2006). A large-scale study of failures in high-
performance computing systems. *Proceedings of the International Conference on
Dependable Systems and Networks*, Philadelphia, PA, USA (25–28 June
2006). IEEE.

**26** Chandra, S. and Chen, P.M. (2000). Whither generic recovery from application
faults? A fault study using open-source software. *Proceedings of the International
Conference on Dependable Systems and Networks*, New York, NY, USA
(25–28 June 2000). IEEE.

**27** Kalyanakrishnam, M., Kalbarczyk, Z., and Iyer, R. (1999). Failure data analysis
of a LAN of Windows NT based computers. *Proceedings of the 18th IEEE
Symposium on Reliable Distributed Systems*, Lausanne, Switzerland (22 October
1999). IEEE

28 Kalyanakrishnan, M., Iyer, R.K., and Patel, J.U. (1999). Reliability of Internet hosts: a case study from the end user's perspective. *Computer Networks* 31 (1–2): 47–57.

29 Murphy, B. and Levidow, B. (2000). Windows 2000 Dependability. Microsoft Research Technical Report MSR-TR-2000-56.

30 Ziegler, J.F., Curtis, H.W., Muhlfeld, H.P. et al. (1996). IBM's experiments in soft fails in computers. *IBM Journal of Research and Development* 40 (1): 3–18.

31 Normand, E. (1996). Single event upset at ground level. *IEEE Transactions on Nuclear Science* 43 (6): 2742–2750.

32 Faccio, F., Kloukinas, K., Marchioro, A. et al. (1999). Single event effects in static and dynamic registers in a 0.25 $\mu$m CMOS technology. *IEEE Transactions on Nuclear Science* 46 (6): 1434–1439.

33 Siewiorek, D.P., Chillarege, R., and Kalbarczyk, Z.T. (2004). Reflections on industry trends and experimental research in dependability. *IEEE Transactions on Dependable and Secure Computing* 1 (2): 109–127.

34 Avižienis, A. (1985). The *N*-version approach to fault tolerant software. *IEEE Transactions on Software Engineering* SE-11 (12): 1491–1501.

35 Anderson, T., Barrett, P.A., Halliwell, D.N. et al. (1985). Software fault tolerance: an evaluation. *IEEE Transactions on Software Engineering* SE-11 (12): 1502–1510.

36 Laprie, J.-C., Arlat, J., Beounes, C. et al. (1990). Definition and analysis of hardware- and software-fault-tolerant architectures. *Computer* 23 (7): 39–51.

37 Brilliant, S.S., Knight, J.C., and Leveson, N.G. (1990). Analysis of faults in an *N*-version software experiment. *IEEE Transactions on Software Engineering* 16 (2): 238–247.

38 Kantz, H. and Koza, C. (1995). The ELEKTRA railway signalling system: Field experience with an actively replicated system with diversity. *Digest of Papers, 25th International Symposium on Fault-Tolerant Computing*, Pasadena, CA, USA (27–30 June 1995), 453–458. IEEE.

39 Traverse, P. (1991). Dependability of digital computers on board airplanes. *Proceedings of the 1st International Working Conference on Dependable Computing for Critical Applications*, Santa Barbara, CA, USA (August 1989), 133–152 (ed. A. Avižienis and J. Laprie), *Dependable Computing and Fault-Tolerant Systems*, vol. 4. Vienna: Springer.

40 About Blue Waters (2020). National Center for Supercomputing Applications, University of Illinois at Urbana-Champaign. http://www.ncsa.illinois.edu/ BlueWaters/ (accessed 31 July 2020).

41 Schroder, D.K. and Babcock, J.A. (2003). Negative bias temperature instability: road to cross in deep submicron silicon semiconductor manufacturing. *Journal of Applied Physics* 94 (1): 1–18.

42 Shimpi, A.L. (2011). The source of Intel's Cougar Point SATA bug. *AnandTech* (31 January). http://www.anandtech.com/show/4143/the-source-of-intels-cougar-point-sata-bug (accessed 31 July 2020).

**43** Intel Newsroom. (2011). Intel identifies chipset design error, implementing solution. https://newsroom.intel.com/news-releases/intel-identifies-chipset-design-error-implementing-solution/#gs.09015p (accessed 31 January).

**44** Trivedi, K.S. (2002). *Probability and Statistics with Reliability, Queuing and Computer Science Applications*, 2e. Chichester, UK: Wiley.

**45** Sahner, R.A. and Trivedi, K.S. (1987). Reliability modeling using SHARPE. *IEEE Transactions on Reliability* R-36 (2): 186–193.

**46** Clark, G., Courtney, T., Daly, D. et al. (2001). The Möbius modeling tool. *Proceedings of the 9th International Workshop on Petri Nets and Performance Models*, Aachen, Germany (11–14 September 2001), pp. 241–250. IEEE.

**47** Ciardo, G. and Miner, A.S. (1996). SMART: simulation and Markovian analyzer for reliability and timing. *Proceedings of the IEEE International Computer Performance and Dependability Symposium*, Urbana-Champaign, IL, USA (4–6 September 1996), 60. IEEE.

# 2

# Classical Dependability Techniques and Modern Computing Systems: Where and How Do They Meet?

## 2.1 Illustrative Case Studies of Design for Dependability

In this chapter, we attempt to engage the interest of the reader by beginning with a brief discussion of examples of real systems to illustrate the deployment of traditional techniques in legacy systems. The examples show how fault tolerance needs to be considered as part of the design requirements, starting in the initial stages of a system development cycle. The first example, IBM System/360 [1, 2] (which ran on the proprietary IBM MVS operating system) introduced many dependability techniques and was a commercial success. The design of the system presents an instructive example of the use of fault tolerance techniques in a traditional architecture. The second example, the Tandem Integrity system [3, 4] was the first commercial, loosely synchronized, TMR (Triple Modular Redundancy), fault-tolerant system that ran the UNIX operating system, which made it possible to support many standard applications on a high-availability platform. The Integrity system succeeded in bringing together many methods that were part of sophisticated fault-tolerant systems to establish something that approximated a commodity environment. The third example is Blue Waters, a petaflop HPC system capable of delivering approximately 13.1 petaflops (at peak) for a range of real-world scientific and engineering applications.

### 2.1.1 IBM System S/360

During the early planning for the IBM System/360 [2], the goal was to significantly improve serviceability performance over that of existing systems. Based on that general goal, the following serviceability objectives for the System/360 were

*Dependable Computing: Design and Assessment*, First Edition. Ravishankar K. Iyer, Zbigniew T. Kalbarczyk, and Nithin M. Nakka.

established: (i) to reduce the (a) maximum, (b) median, and (c) mean durations of unanticipated downtime and (ii) to develop a set of standard servicing programs and procedures.

The ability to reduce the duration of unanticipated downtime depends on whether another unit can perform the task performed by the failed unit. If the failing unit has an alternate unit, then execution is continued on the alternate after decoupling of the failed unit. If there is no alternative unit, the solution is to reduce the time required to repair the unit.

Since intermittent failures are difficult to reproduce, they must be detected immediately upon occurrence, and the system state at the time of the error must be recorded. The IBM S/360 has checking circuits distributed throughout the system to detect errors as close in time and space as possible to their occurrence.

Recording of the system state at the time of error is straightforward for the CPU and some particular I/O units. It is done by halting the CPU or the I/O unit and recording the state of their control and data path storage elements, and then resuming the execution. However, for some I/O units, the operation in the device cannot be stopped instantaneously because of, e.g., the inertia of mechanical motion. If the state stored in the control unit for such an I/O device is partial, then the remaining part of the device state must be read from the unit. The IBM System/360 had an extensive automatic fault-location system that was introduced to reduce the duration of service calls. It is described below.

*Fault Locating Tests.* The IBM S/360 provided a set of tests whose sequence and order of correct and incorrect responses could help in pinpointing a failing circuit element. For hard or permanent failures, the failed portion of the circuit had to be isolated. However, for transient failures, it might suffice to repeat the affected computation on the same hardware. Faulty circuit isolation could be implemented efficiently for I/O devices and storage arrays, but not for the CPU. In the case of transient errors in the CPU, the S/360 provided the instruction retry mechanism to repeat the execution of a CPU instruction.

A program called the *diagnostic monitor* provided a set of functions common to many of the maintenance routines. The diagnostic monitor had the following capabilities: (i) self-loading, (ii) initializing of the system, (iii) handling of interruptions, (iv) decoding of messages that originated externally, (v) recognition of priority interruptions, (vi) loading of unit diagnostics, (vii) control of the sequence in which the units were treated, and (viii) running of option control.

### 2.1.2 The Tandem Integrity System

The design objectives for the Integrity system [3, 4] were that the system should include the following capabilities:

- Run UNIX (System V) applications in a fault-tolerant environment with minimal modification to the application software,
- Continue to operate despite hardware and software faults, without loss of performance or data integrity, and
- Provide a high degree of fault tolerance and data integrity for applications that require very high system dependability, specifically that
  - No single hardware failure should corrupt data stored or manipulated in the system, and
  - System outages due to the operating system should be minimal.

*System Architecture.* The system architecture of Tandem Integrity is shown in Figure 2.1. The three CPUs were loosely synchronized; they synchronized (voted) whenever there was a write to global memory.

*Design Decisions and Discussion.* The design decisions on the system were reflected in the system's hardware and software. From the hardware perspective, the design included the following features:

- Triple redundancy of processors and buses; specifically, there were three identical CPUs and three independent buses.
- Two self-checking voters, which voted on processor output for each I/O operation.
- Duplicate global memory protected by parity.

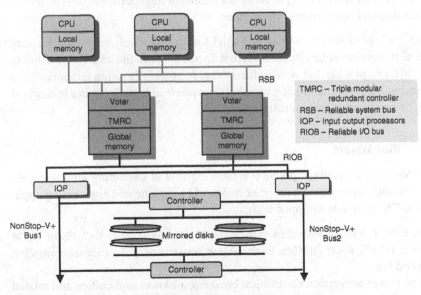

**Figure 2.1** Architecture of the Tandem Integrity system.

- Primary backup TMR controller.
- Acknowledgment after each memory operation.
- DMA (direct memory access) transfer with an automatic checksum calculated for data integrity.
- Duplicate heartbeat timer.
- Duplicate I/O controllers.
- Mirrored disks.
- Power supplies with battery backup.

From the software perspective, the design included the following features:

- Subscription-based services: An entity in the OS that required notification of an event could subscribe to occurrences of that event (including component failures).
- Consistency checks to detect errors.
- Assertions: Forward recovery routines were used to determine the validity and consistency of various data structures (with the goal of avoiding panics).
- Three recovery states: Recovery on fault detection, execution under probation, and panic on error.
- Nonvolatile memory checksumming by software.
- Memory scrubbers implemented in the OS to detect and correct latent errors in memory.
- Power-on Self -Test (POST) to verify the health of the board.
- Disabling and reintegration of modules.

It may be argued that a TMR design might be prohibitively expensive for very large-scale systems or for applications that do not demand the levels of availability that TMR can provide, but would either degrade gracefully (often temporarily) in the presence of faults or fail in a way that does not lead to major losses in terms of time, revenue, safety, or user satisfaction.

### 2.1.3 Blue Waters

Blue Waters is a sustained petaflop system capable of delivering approximately 13.1 petaflops (at peak) for a range of real-world scientific and engineering applications. The system is equipped with:

- 276 Cray liquid-cooled cabinets hosting 26 496 nodes and 1.47 PB of RAM across 197 032 RAM DIMMs. Each cabinet consists of an L1 cabinet controller, several fan
- trays, power conversion electronics, breakers, a blower and chiller, and related piping. Each cabinet is organized in three chassis, and each chassis hosts eight blades.

- 22 640 compute nodes (based on AMD Opteron processors) with a total of 724 480 cores.
- 3072 GPU hybrid nodes equipped with NVIDIA K20X GPU accelerators and AMD Opteron processors.
- 784 service nodes with a total of 5824 available cores.
- The high-speed Cray Gemini network, to provide node connectivity.
- The online storage system, consisting of 198 Cray Sonexion 1600 storage units equipped with 20 196 disks, and 396 SSDs (used to store file system metadata) that provide access to 26 petabytes (36 raw) of usable storage over a Lustre distributed file system.
- 300 petabytes (380 raw) of usable near-line tape storage.

*Compute Node Hardware.* Compute nodes are hosted in 5660 Cray XE6 blades (see Figure 2.2a), with four nodes per blade. System memory is protected with x8 Chipkill [5], code that uses eighteen 8-bit symbols to make a 144-bit ECC word made up of 128 data bits and 16 check bits for each memory word. The x8 code is a single-symbol correcting code, i.e., it detects and corrects up to 8-bit errors. L3, L2, and L1 data caches are protected with ECC, while all the others (tag caches, TLBs, and L2 and L1 instruction caches) are protected with parity.

*GPU Node Hardware.* GPU nodes are hosted in 768 Cray XK7 blades (see Figure 2.2b), with four nodes per blade. The DDR5 RAM memory used in XK7 blades is protected with ECC.

*Service Node Hardware.* Service nodes are hosted on 166 Cray XIO blades and 30 XE6 blades, with 4 nodes per blade. A service node can be configured as (i) a boot node to orchestrate system-wide reboots; (ii) a system database node to collect event logs; (iii) a MOM node for scheduling jobs; (iv) a network node to bridge external networks through Infiniband QDR IB cards; or (v) an Lnet (Lustre file system network) node to handle metadata (via Lustre metadata servers, or MDSes, to keep track of the location of the files in the storage servers) and file I/O data (via Lustre Object Storage Servers, or OSSes, to store the data stripes across the storage modules) for file system servers and clients.

*Network.* Blue Waters' high-speed network consists of a Cray Gemini System Interconnect. The topology is a three-dimensional (3D) $23 \times 24 \times 24$ reentrant torus: each node has six possible links toward other nodes, i.e., right, left, up, down, in, and out.

*Hardware Supervisor System (HSS) and System Resiliency Features.* Every node in the system is checked and managed by the HSS. Core components of the HSS system are (i) the HSS network; (ii) blade (L0, see Figure 2.2) and cabinet (L1) controllers in charge of monitoring the nodes, replying to heartbeat signal requests, and collecting data on temperature, voltage, power, network performance counters, and runtime software exceptions; and (iii) the HSS manager in

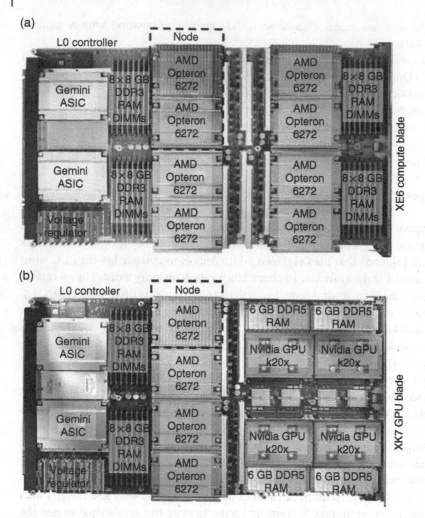

**Figure 2.2** Blue Waters blades: (a) compute (Cray XE6), (b) GPU (Cray XK7).

charge of collecting node health data and executing the management software. Upon detection of a failure, e.g., a missing heartbeat, the HSS manager triggers failure mitigation operations. They include (i) warm swap of a compute/GPU blade to allow the system operator to remove and repair system blades without disrupting the workload; (ii) service node and Lustre node failover mechanisms, e.g., replacement of IO nodes with warm-standby replicas; and (iii) link degradation and route reconfiguration to enable routing around failed nodes in the topology. The procedure in the communication path route consists of (i) waiting 10 seconds to aggregate failures; (ii) determining which blade(s) is/are alive; (iii) quiescing the Gemini network traffic; (iv) asserting a new route in the Gemini chips; and (v) cleaning up and resuming Gemini. The total time to execute that procedure is around 30–60 seconds. In the case of Gemini link failures, applications running on the affected blades are either killed or, in the case of a warm swap-out, allowed to complete. In the case of inactivity or miscommunication of one of the agents, the HSS manager switches the node state to "suspect" or "down." The job currently running on the node, if not failed, is allowed to complete.

*System Software.* Compute and GPU nodes execute the lightweight kernel Compute Node Linux (CNL) developed by Cray. The operating system is reduced to a bare minimum to minimize the overhead on the nodes and includes only essential components.

*File System Features.* All blades are diskless and use the shared parallel file system for IO operations. Blue Waters hosts the largest Lustre installation to date. It consists of a parallel file system used to manage data stored in Cray Sonexion 1600 [6] storage modules. Each Lustre service node and Sonexion module is configured as an active-passive pair connected to a shared storage device. In that configuration, the passive replica node becomes active when the HSS detects a failure of a Lustre node; the shared storage device is then mounted in a read-only mode to avoid data inconsistency until the failed node has been replaced with the standby replica.

With the background of the aforementioned systems that demonstrate classical dependability, we are in a position to explore in the upcoming sections more recent and upcoming computing paradigms and domains. Dependability is of paramount importance in all these systems, yet the techniques and their applicability need to be adapted to the specific computing system at hand.

## 2.2  Cloud Computing: A Rapidly Expanding Computing Paradigm

With the development of new computing paradigms and the pervasive use of embedded devices in many aspects of our daily life, the social and enterprise computing landscape has taken a new direction, posing varied and formerly unknown challenges in providing user satisfaction. Those trends have forced system developers to reconsider dependability more as a user-perceived level of service provided by the system despite failures and less as a technical specification of the product [7]. Multiple technologies, such as multicore processor architectures, virtual machines that host multiple operating systems on a single platform, and high integration of hundreds of thousands of processing elements via a high-speed network, have emerged as enabling technologies for cloud computing.

> Cloud Computing refers to both the applications delivered as services over the Internet and the hardware and systems software in the datacenters that provide those services. The services themselves have long been referred to as Software as a Service (SaaS). The datacenter hardware and software are what we will call a Cloud. When a Cloud is made available in a pay-as-you-go manner to the general public, we call it a Public Cloud; the service being sold is Utility Computing. We use the term Private Cloud to refer to internal datacenters of a business or other organization, not made available to the general public. [8]

With the participation of many large enterprises as cloud service providers, such as IBM, Microsoft, Google, and Amazon, cloud computing has been adopted by an increasing number of people with dynamic computing requirements. For customers, the cloud is viewed as a potential solution to replace costly in-house server farms and self-managed data centers. Paying for computing resources on an as-needed basis, which mitigates the risk of over-provisioning or under-provisioning in IT management, is the feature that differentiates cloud computing from traditional IT infrastructures. Those advantages promise the stable growth of cloud computing.

Multicore processors and network-based processor integration are used to build cloud computing infrastructure, whereas virtual machines form the basis for cloud computing platforms. In relation to those component technologies, we discuss the challenges that have emerged for system dependability in the face of the introduction of new technologies, with cloud computing as an example. The issues mentioned in Section 1.10 of the previous chapter are related to multicore processor technologies, whereas those detailed in Section 1.11 have a direct impact on virtual machine-based systems.

## 2.2.1 Layered Architecture of Cloud Computing

Figure 2.3 shows the layered architecture of cloud computing. The cloud architecture is generally defined by four distinct layers: (i) the system level, (ii) core middleware, (iii) user-level middleware, and (iv) the user level, from physical hardware to end user applications. The bottommost level (*system level* in Figure 2.3) of the stack is formed by physical resources, such as spare desktop machines, clusters, and data centers; on top of it, the virtual infrastructure is deployed. Infrastructures

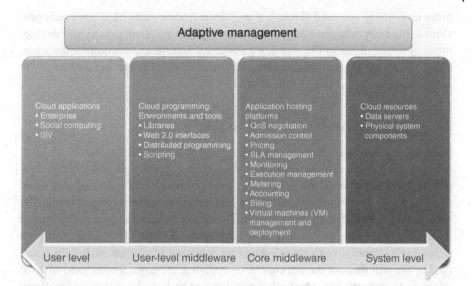

Figure 2.3 Cloud computing's layered architecture.

that support large-scale cloud deployments are more like data centers that host hundreds to thousands of machines. However, small-scale, in-house clouds offer a much more heterogeneous scenario in which the idle CPU cycles of spare desktop machines are used to leverage the compute workload. That lowest level provides the "horsepower" of the cloud.

The *core middleware level's* objective is to manage the physical infrastructure, providing an appropriate runtime environment for applications and maximizing the use of the physical resources. To provide advanced services (e.g., application isolation, quality of service, and sandboxing), the core middleware relies on virtualization technologies. Among the various solutions for virtualization, programming language-level virtualization and hardware-level virtualization are the most popular. Hardware-level virtualization ensures complete isolation of applications and a fine partitioning of the physical resources (such as memory and CPU) via virtual machines. Programming-level virtualization provides sandboxing and managed execution for applications developed with specific technologies or programming languages. In addition, the core middleware provides a set of services (e.g., negotiation of the quality of service, admission control, execution management, monitoring, accounting, or billing) that assist service providers in their delivery of professional and commercial services to end users.

The core middleware, together with the physical infrastructure, represents the platform on top of which applications are deployed in the cloud. It is very rare to have direct access to this layer; the services delivered by the core middleware are more commonly accessed through a user-level middleware. That approach provides for the environments and tools that simplify the development and deployment of applications in the cloud, e.g., Web 2.0 interfaces, command-line tools, libraries, and programming languages. The user-level middleware constitutes the access point of applications to the cloud.

## 2.2.2 Reliability Issues in Cloud Computing

In the design of cloud computing systems, the general trend in the commercial sector is to assume graceful degradation of the system. For example, most cloud computing infrastructure offerings promise a proportionate reduction in quality of service in the event of failures. However, failures do occur in ways that violate the assumption of graceful degradation (see examples that follow), potentially forcing both providers and consumers to incur huge losses. In light of the impact of such failures, it is imperative to provide low-cost solutions to prevent such failure scenarios. We will discuss the drawbacks of applying the basic techniques, without adapting them to the new computing paradigm, at both the hardware and platform levels. Solutions that are aware of the application characteristics and are adapted to specific dependability requirements are needed for the emerging applications.

However, the need to provide a higher level of reliability and availability is one of the biggest challenges [8] that must be addressed in order for cloud computing to attract more customers. Customers who have migrated their services to a cloud must not encounter problems such as the 22-hour outage of Microsoft Azure that once occurred (on 13 March 2009) as a result of a malfunction in the hypervisor, Amazon's S3 outage that occurred (on 20 July 2008) because of a single bit error in the gossip message, the outage of Google AppEngine that occurred (on 17 June 2008) because of a programming error, or the system failure in the Microsoft Sidekick service (on 2 October 2009) that resulted in data loss [9].

*The Azure Failure.* On Friday, 13 March 2009, during a routine operating system upgrade, the deployment service within Windows Azure began to slow down because of networking issues, causing a large number of servers to time out and fail. Any application that was running only a single instance went down when its server went down. While very few applications running multiple instances went down, some were degraded because one instance was down. The ability to perform management tasks via the web portal appeared to be unavailable for many applications because the Fabric Controller was backed up with work during the serialized recovery process.

To prevent such occurrences in the future as well as to safeguard its ability to handle possible malfunctions quickly and gracefully, Microsoft addressed the network issues by refining and tuning its recovery algorithm. To ensure uninterrupted availability during upgrades, application owners are advised to deploy their applications with multiple instances of each role. The second instance of an application will not be counted against quota limits, allowing customers to run two instances of each application role.

*Amazon S3 Failure.* The eight-hour outage of Amazon services on 20 July 2008 was caused by a single bit error in messages communicated (using a gossip protocol) between the servers. In their postmortem analysis, system engineers at Amazon determined that "there were a handful of messages. . . that had a single bit corrupted such that the message was still intelligible, but the system state information was incorrect. We use MD5 checksums throughout the system, for example, to prevent, detect, and recover from corruption that can occur during receipt, storage, and retrieval of customers' objects. However, we didn't have the same protection in place to detect whether this particular internal state information had been corrupted. As a result, when the corruption occurred, we didn't detect it and it spread throughout the system. . .." [10].

*The Amazon EC2 Outage.* The EC2 faced a major outage on 21 April 2011 that lasted for more than 36 hours. The outage had a serious impact on many popular websites, including Reddit, Quora, FourSquare, Hootsuite, parts of *The New York Times*, ProPublica, and about 70 other sites. To compensate costumers, Amazon promised to keep customers' sites up and running 99.95% of the year or reduce customers' monthly bills by 10%. The Amazon EC2's availability design is based on the concept of "availability zones," of which there are five, geographically distributed across the globe; each contains multiple data centers. The system had been designed so as to isolate faults within an availability zone, but from an initial failure analysis, Amazon surmised that "a *networking event* caused a domino effect across other availability zones in that region, in which many of its storage volumes created new backups of themselves. That filled up Amazon's available storage capacity and prevented some sites from accessing their data. Amazon didn't say what that *networking event* was." [11].

Indeed, similar failure patterns were observed in an error-injection-based experimental analysis [12] of the Ensemble Group Communication System (GCS), a robust communication layer for distributed dependable applications [13]. The study shows that about 5–6% of application failures are due to an error that escapes the GCS error-containment mechanism and manifests as silent data corruption. While GCS was formally specified and verified, it constituted only about 5% of the entire code base, i.e., the remaining 95% consisted of unverified third-party runtime environment. It is important to note that although the observed silent data corruption errors are rare, such errors constitute an impediment to achieving high dependability, because recovery from failures can involve significant downtime in system operation.

While those examples show how an accidental error can negatively impact system reliability and availability, memory corruption due to accidental or intermittent errors can also lead to security compromises. In [5], the authors of this book modeled and experimentally evaluated the error-caused security violations of two Linux kernel firewalls (IPChains and Netfilter). The results indicate that under a realistic error rate of 0.1 error/day, during a one-year period in a networked system (e.g., a large university campus) protected by 20 firewalls, two machines (on average) will experience security violations. The error injection experiments showed that about 2% of errors injected into the firewall code segment cause security vulnerabilities. That indicates that hardware error-caused security vulnerabilities are a non-negligible source of security threats to a highly secure system.

We are not reporting the above anecdotes as indictments of specific systems, which are often well-engineered products. Rather, we want to point out that observed data corruptions, application failures, and data integrity violations often result from subtle runtime faults (accidental or malicious) that expose (i) implementation deficiencies and (ii) unverified assumptions made during the design of systems, applications, and protocols. For example, designers of many group communication systems have assumed that the crash/omission failure semantic will hold, but it may not always do so in real-world systems. Similarly, the gossip protocol (from the Amazon case), although well-fortified against errors during data transmission, could not survive when the data were corrupted before they were sent over the network. Furthermore, even in presumably well-protected systems (e.g., credit card databases), the defenses can be bypassed if foreign code can be implanted into the system/application. In the next section, we will look at several examples of systems to provide insights on the dependability and security challenges of designing them. Except for the embedded medical electronics applications, they are all suitable for execution on the cloud computing platform.

In summary, the challenges and opportunities that arise from the emerging cloud computing paradigm are as follows.

- As feature sizes are shrinking, combinational circuits are becoming increasingly susceptible to errors, and the ever-increasing clock frequencies of processors increase the likelihood that an upset in the combinational logic will be latched by a flip-flop.
- Increasing levels of integration at the device level and complexity in hardware increase the costs of validation and introduce nondeterminism in intermediate states of application execution.
- Higher levels of device-level integration make it prohibitively expensive to apply redundancy in a traditional all-or-none approach.
- Increasing integration at the node level to produce large computing clusters again prohibits the straightforward application of replication techniques at the system level.

- Multicore systems provide inherent redundancy and opportunities to customize idle cores to enhance fault tolerance and security.
- Diversified design can make it easier to deal with software faults in redundant architectures (and thereby reduce the risk of common mode failures).
- Virtualization introduces an additional layer between the low-level hardware layer and the high-level application layer, and thereby introduces additional failure modes at the interface of the hypervisor with the hardware and the operating system.
- In providing transparent service to customers, cloud computing systems must abstract underlying, geographically disparate execution platforms. That calls for reevaluation of the applicability and efficacy of traditional algorithms for distributed systems, as those algorithms may assume deterministic and bounded communication times.

## 2.3 New Application Domains

Above and beyond all the trends and developments in system design and implementation are factors related to application development. While the influence of computing systems has spread to literally every possible field, they are also being entrusted with greater and greater responsibilities within specific fields. Examples of overarching sensitive applications include smart and secure power grids, financial applications that affect critical market transactions, and high-performance scientific computing. We envision an emerging landscape that presents compelling new research, business, and societal challenges – driven by the multidisciplinary nature of societal problems – that are at the nexus of food, health, and energy.

The next major innovations in computer science and engineering are likely to come from "intelligent" deployment of human-centric systems that must interact optimally with other manmade and natural systems, with a focus on seamless availability of dynamic decision-making capabilities. The driver will be our need to measure, model, communicate, and manage our vast natural and social enterprise, based on the recognition that our physical world is complex and requires a level of dynamic adaptation and automation that is unprecedented. Innovation and creative new approaches will be essential for handling the envisioned problems of scale and complexity.

Different applications have evolved to require different levels of reliability. We classify applications into three broad categories based on their requirements: (i) *the application does not tolerate any failure within the mission time* (e.g., a space mission system, an airplane navigation system, or a medical monitoring system in an operating room or intensive care unit); (ii) *the application allows the user to restart without leading to a catastrophic safety failure* (e.g., a remote car ignition system with acknowledgment that allows a restart even in the case of a failure, even though the cause of the failure may still need to be addressed); and (iii) *erroneous instances of the results affect the output of the application temporarily, but it remains within the limits of safety and user acceptance* (e.g., stream processing applications that operate on the incoming input stream of data to provide recommendations for purchase or in rating certain services).

New emerging systems and applications have spawned a level of complexity such that traditional fault tolerance cannot form the backbone of providing truly dependable systems. If one assumes (for example) that only a single fault will occur in a system, that faults are independent, or that hardware and software interactions are low, those assumptions are foiled in the new setting. Thus, a new set of fault models and failures have evolved, and they must be carefully dealt with, either through intelligent improvement of traditional techniques or by introduction of new techniques for error detection and recovery. The factors mentioned above have also increased the need to consider issues related to validation of systems and of the fault-tolerance techniques themselves.

In that context, it is surely important to understand the basics, which is why we have dedicated a sizeable portion of this book to detailing the theory and implementation of some fault-tolerance techniques that have been deployed in both existing and decommissioned systems. New techniques that are suitable for the current computing paradigms, environment, and applications may need to build upon older theories (e.g., with respect to redundancy and coding), but with modifications that accommodate the nuances of the current situation. The techniques must be application-specific in order to be low-cost and viable.

The following sections provide examples of emerging new systems and provide insights on the dependability and security challenges that they impose.

## 2.3.1 Smart Power Grid Application

In recent years, the electric power grid has undergone major organizational and structural changes in order to improve interoperability and ensure high reliability, security, and efficiency of operation. The smart power grid vision has become one of the drivers of transformative change in energy production and usage. While smart power grids ask for consumers' active participation and promise cost efficiency, they also bring new challenges in terms of ensuring reliable and secure operation in the presence of accidental failures and malicious attacks. In the past, the power grid had very little computing hardware infrastructure, but that has been changing rapidly as computing infrastructure support has become increasingly integrated with power distribution networks that can span an entire country (or even multiple countries). That integration means that failures could have potentially devastating effects, even crippling the function of large regions or a nation as a whole. Thus, the changes require grids to have greater reliability and much more security. The opportunity is there to introduce techniques at the node, substation, control center, and corporate networking levels.

One application that demonstrates such needs involves provision of continuous monitoring and control of loads in the households of customers. Figure 2.4 illustrates the envisaged application scenario. The loads in the household include refrigerators, air conditioning/heating devices, entertainment, and battery recharging of electric cars.

A unified hub provides an entry/exit point for remote control and monitoring. A public network is used to enable communication channels between households and the Control and Monitoring Facility (CMF). The CMF is responsible for collecting measurements from the remote customer sites and communicating actions/commands to be enforced at the neighborhood or individual household levels. The specific actions initiated by the CMF are based on analysis of data coming from individual households and additional information (e.g., energy demand and pricing) from energy providers. We envisage three modes of operation for the CMF: (i) passive mode (i.e., non-intrusive monitoring of loads at the household level); (ii) active user participation mode (i.e., monitoring with user involvement

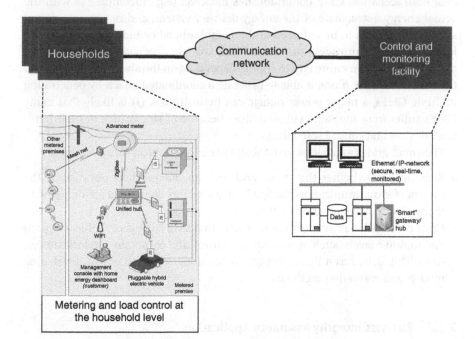

**Figure 2.4** A typical scenario in smart power grids.

in applying actions/commands); and (iii) autonomous mode (i.e., automated monitoring and execution of actions/commands).

The example settings discussed above (see Figure 2.4) provide the basis for autonomous (or semiautonomous, with active end-user involvement) measurement and control of loads at the customer site. However, these settings also make the system vulnerable to accidental failures and malicious attacks. As an example, consider two scenarios that involve malicious or accidentally induced failures. In the two scenarios, we assume that in the case of a malicious attack, the attacker will try to cause damage while hiding the trail of the malicious activity.

*Scenario 1*: An attacker exploits an application vulnerability (e.g., a buffer overflow) and takes control of the CMF. A maliciously crafted command from the CMF can be sent to a customer site to alter/overwrite data collected on the end user site, and that corrupts the aggregated information later sent to the CMF(s) by the end user.

*Scenario 2*: An attacker mimics the normal protocol (e.g., using valid commands) to obtain data from the end user and then sends a valid but malicious command to force invalid actions to be taken (e.g., unexpected switch-off of the loads on the customer site). The same effect could result from an accidental failure in the mechanism that regulates the power supply to the loads on the customer site.

In both scenarios, CMF communicates incorrect (e.g., incompatible with the actual energy usage, state of the energy delivery system, and/or energy pricing) actions/commands to be enforced at the neighborhood or individual household level. As a result, intruders can cause blackouts (e.g., because of massive shutdown of loads) in an entire city or region, depending on the area served by a given CMF. Furthermore, if one is able to generate a coordinated attack by penetrating multiple CMFs, a major power outage can be instigated. (It is likely that many CMFs suffer from the same vulnerabilities because of similarities in their hardware devices and control software.)

The smart grid is analogous to the world's telecommunication systems.

- Regardless of whether the smart grid uses an independent network or the Internet for communication, the levels of availability demanded are on par with those of telecommunication systems.
- Error propagation is a concern in networks that span large geographical regions and multiple levels, such as substation, control, and corporate network subsystems. This issue has a direct impact on the underlying science of developing models and evaluation methods.

### 2.3.2 Business Integrity Assurance Application

Business systems have been prevalent for a long time and consist of a variety of applications that provide varied business services, such as marketing and payroll.

Those applications execute on IT infrastructure, most of which has been assembled from commodity off-the-shelf hardware and software components. They rely on continuous availability of the underlying computing infrastructure. Since enterprises are interested in IT infrastructure that is optimized for overall business value, it is essential to address the provision of dependability in the presence of accidental errors and malicious attacks. That requires (i) understanding of how the various business processes are mapped to the underlying IT resources and (ii) quantification of the business impact of accidental errors and violation of the security properties (i.e., integrity and availability) that are supported by the IT system components underlying the business processes.

The major question for such systems is not simply to find out (either experimentally or analytically) the availability of the system, but to understand whether the system can deliver the service required by the business and, if not, to determine the cost impact on the business of an outage, regardless of its rarity.

Loss of availability due to accidental or malicious failures can be costly or even catastrophic for an enterprise. As an example, consider two scenarios involving high-impact malicious attacks: (i) a *user/admin credential compromise,* in which stolen user credentials provide attackers with what are essentially insider privileges and (ii) *network sniffing,* through which the attacker, once inside an enterprise network, can install a network sniffer to gather passwords for services such as instant messengers, and then penetrate further into the enterprise. Those example attacks can cause significant disruption to the availability of the IT infrastructure (e.g., a credential compromise attack can require all users to change their passwords, which may result in many hours of system downtime) and impose a high recovery cost on the company.

To understand the impact of the example attack scenarios, consider a business application that consists of two components: *order management* and *customer support,* as depicted in Figure 2.5.

The order management process supports web-based retail transactions and includes a credit card verification service and a shipping service. The customer support process is limited to phone-based communication with customers and includes answering of general product questions and creation/updating of customer account information. The order management process is the most critical, and the integrity and availability of all the entities associated with the process are vital to the company's reputation and income; disruptions to the process have direct revenue impact. The customer support process is important from a reputation standpoint. Since sensitive customer information is accessed and manipulated during the process, the integrity of this information is of concern. The company can incur significant costs from the theft of data, such as credit card information. In achieving high-availability services, it is essential to analyze such things in order to understand and assess the impact of failures on the business. An example of a corporate breach was the 2011 external intrusion into the Sony

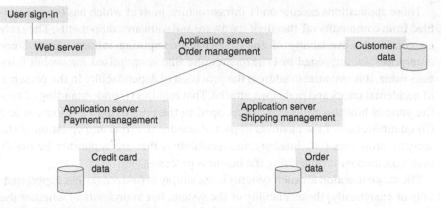

**Figure 2.5** IT infrastructure of an example business application.

PlayStation Network website. "Sony has confirmed that user data – names, email addresses, home addresses, passwords, and possibly even credit card information – have been compromised in the "illegal and unauthorized intrusion" that occurred between 17 April and 19 April [2011] and has resulted in the worldwide PSN outage. . .. By Sony's count, 70 million users subscribe to the cloud-based PSN" [14].

### 2.3.3 Medical Devices and Systems

Computing devices are now being massively deployed in medical monitoring and diagnostic systems and function as recommender systems to physicians. They are certainly life-critical applications, if the physician has to place any amount of faith in them. Medical electronics is a domain in which the impact of failures is severe and intolerable.

The development of new technologies has dramatically increased the number of audio and/or visual alarms available in intensive care units (ICUs) to alert medical physicians on either changes in a patient's condition or equipment malfunction [15]. The alarms are expected to monitor vital physiological conditions and to increase patient safety by allowing early detection of any abnormality. Alarms on clinical devices are intended to call the attention of caregivers to conditions of patients or devices that deviate from a predetermined "normal" status [16].

Some instances of false alarms are inevitable. However, frequent false alarms are a nuisance for patients and caregivers [17]. Often, the alarms are distracting and interfere with physicians' ability to perform other critical tasks effectively. Alarms also contribute to desensitization of nurses to the devices, such that alarms for real events are less likely to catch the attention of medical staff [16] or lead to sleep deprivation [6] and continuous stress [18] for both nurses and patients.

As devices become more sophisticated, complexity increases. Caregivers are charged with effectively managing numerous bedside devices, and each device has an alarm. Furthermore, nurses must deal with a high frequency of false alarms (e.g., a tachycardia alarm triggered by the effect of a patient's movement on an electrocardiogram) and nuisance alarms that do not indicate a clinically important condition (e.g., a "high pressure" ventilator alarm caused by a patient's cough). All those challenges are placing increasing requirements on the training and operations of nursing staff.

Some studies have demonstrated that even experienced nurses are able to recognize only 38% of vital alarms [19]; similar results have also been reported for operating rooms and ICUs [20]. In Tsien and Fackler's study [21], 86% of 2942 alarms were found to be false positives, and an additional 6% were classified as clinically irrelevant true alarms. Only 8% of all alarms tracked were determined to be true alarms with clinical significance. Similar results regarding the frequency and reliability of alarms in the monitoring of cardiac postoperative patients were reported by Koshi et al. [22]. Of 1307 occasions when an alarm was activated during the study period, only 139 (10.6%) were significant.

In medical electronics, application safety is a major concern.

- Particularly when there is a human in the loop, the system needs to be standardized and carefully designed to prevent any inconvenience to the patient under observation.
- These systems are stateful, and novel checkpointing techniques are needed for this low-power domain.
- The reliability and high-availability infrastructure must have a small footprint in terms of hardware and software.
- The low-power and low-area overhead requirements make formal verification and modeling important in terms of validation.
- Real-time constraints further complicate the development of high-availability techniques.

A recent study [23] of safety-critical computer failures in medical devices indicates that such equipment is often subject to a non-negligible number of failures with potentially catastrophic impact on patients. Specifically, the analysis found that:

- Although software failures remain the major cause (~64%) of recalls of computer-based medical devices, hardware, battery, and I/O are also significant contributors to failures that can lead to potentially life-critical hazards.
- In many cases, the design process of recalled devices had not included identification and handling of safety issues, or the safety mechanisms weren't designed or implemented correctly.

Those issues emphasize the importance of designs with well-defined safety requirements and implementations that employ robust error-detection techniques and rigorously validated fail-safe mechanisms.

The next section discusses an example application that aims at providing real-time, accurate monitoring of the health of the subject (in this case, a soldier in combat) in the field and the requirements for reliably monitoring health as well as communicating the observations reliably and in time for the necessary curative actions to be taken. The section also proposes a solution based on embedding of monitoring devices in a modified battlefield helmet.

### 2.3.3.1 Monitoring of Soldiers for Blast Impact in a Battlefield Scenario

Transient blast events can result in blast injury; such injuries can involve cognitive and communication impairments related to TBI (traumatic brain injury), swallowing impairments, aphasia, motor speech impairment, medical conditions that require tracheostomy and ventilation, and hearing loss. When blast events occur on the battlefield, the levels of blast injury (LBI) are unknown to first responders and emergency and surgical medical field hospital personnel. It is critical for soldier survival and treatment that first responders and medical teams have timely information on the level of blast exposure to the brain as well as data regarding the physiological functioning of cortical systems. The recording of blast events and physiological responses using smart nanotechnology embedded into helmet-supporting structures can provide such vital information. The use of a combination of sensor inputs designed to monitor brain function, both pre- and post-blast exposure, could provide important insights into the prediction of recovery from battlefield blast exposure and TBI.

One possible solution would be to develop a modified battlefield helmet integrated with (i) smart nanotechnology sensors to measure and record, in real time, blast pressure and acceleration, oxygen saturation, EEG, blood flow, and other vital signals from the human subject (e.g., a soldier), and (ii) small-footprint, low-power-consumption, and ARM-based processing to enable rapid processing of collected data in order to determine the extent of blast-induced injury [24, 25].

The sensors can be embedded within helmet straps, nap pad, while the processing unit in headband to create a compact, lightweight, highly robust solution, as shown in Figure 2.6. Along with the transceivers and processor that comprise its hardware, the processing unit employs individual software modules responsible for sensor data management, data feedback through sensory (audio/visual/tactile) output, and self-monitoring. Levels of blast injury algorithms (LBIAs) can be developed to characterize (or quantify) TBI based on physiological data on pre- and post-blast exposure. It has to be ensured that the sensor data are clinically relevant and trustworthy despite potential temporary misbehavior or permanent damage of some of the sensors.

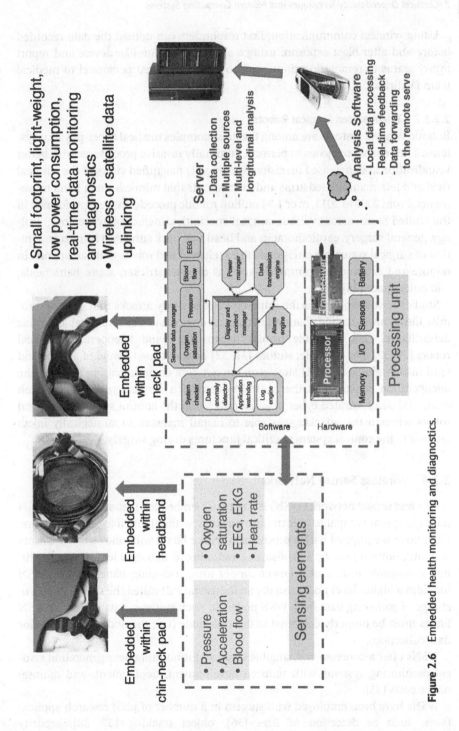

**Figure 2.6** Embedded health monitoring and diagnostics.

- Small footprint, light-weight, low power consumption, real-time data monitoring and diagnostics
- Wireless or satellite data uplinking

**Analysis Software**
- Local data processing
- Real-time feedback
- Data forwarding to the remote serve

**Server**
- Data collection
- Multiple sources
- Multi-level and longitudinal analysis

Embedded within neck pad

Embedded within headband

Embedded within chin-neck pad

**Sensing elements**
- Pressure
- Acceleration
- Blood flow
- Oxygen saturation
- EEG, EKG
- Heart rate

**Software**

Sensor data manager
- Oxygen saturation
- Pressure
- Blood flow
- EEG

Power manager

Data transmission engine

Display and control manager

Alarm engine

System checker

Data anomaly detector

Application watchdog

Log engine

**Hardware**

Transceiver

Processor

Memory | I/O | Sensors | Battery

**Processing unit**

Using wireless communication, first responders can upload the data recorded before and after blast exposure using a small cell-phone-like device and report injury status to remote locations prior to moving injured personnel to medical team facilities.

### 2.3.3.2 Teleoperated Surgical Robots

Robotic surgical systems are among the most complex medical cyber-physical systems. They enable surgeons to perform minimally invasive procedures with better visualization and increased precision by using 3D magnified views of the surgical field and tele-manipulated arms and instruments that mimic human hand movements. From 2007 to 2013, over 1.74 million robotic procedures were performed in the United States across various surgical specialties, including gynecology, urology, general surgery, cardiothoracic, and head and neck surgery. The next generation of surgical systems is envisioned to be teleoperated robots that can operate in remote and extreme environments, such as disaster-stricken areas, battlefields, and outer space [26].

Studies have emphasized the importance of security attacks that can compromise the communication channels in medical devices such as implantable cardiac defibrillators [27], wearable insulin pumps [28], and teleoperated surgical robots [29–32]. For example, studies [31, 32] demonstrated denial of service and man-in-the-middle (MITM) attacks on the network communication between the teleoperation console and the control system of a surgical robot. Alemzadeh et al. [33] demonstrated cyber-physical attacks on the control system of surgical robots wherein the attacker was able to install malware to strategically inject faults into the control system at critical junctures during surgery.

### 2.3.4 Wireless Sensor Networks

A wireless sensor network (WSN) is a network-embedded system composed of $N$ nodes [34] that is capable of forming a network without any fixed infrastructure. Each node is equipped with a processor, a sensor board with one or more sensors (c.g., humidity sensor or thermistor), a radio board that enables wireless multi-hop communication, and a power supply unit, including batteries. The WSN includes a higher level node (usually an industrial PC) called the *sink*, which is in charge of gathering data from WSN nodes. In such systems, data sensed by WSN nodes must be properly delivered to the sink node (i.e., the node responsible for data collection).

WSNs offer a concrete and tangible solution for building next-generation critical monitoring systems with reduced development, deployment, and maintenance costs [35].

WSNs have been employed with success in a number of pilot research applications, such as detection of fires [36], object tracking [37, 38], security monitoring [39], supply chain monitoring [40], and stability monitoring of buildings [41], railroad tunnels [42], and dams [43]. Industrial entities in the field of wired sensing and monitoring infrastructures are drawn to WSNs because of some of their interesting features, along with the possibility of reducing deployment and management costs. However, while the technology for WSNs is relatively mature, real, large-scale industrial applications are lacking. That shortcoming is due in part to a number of unsolved problems that afflict WSNs, including their somewhat low dependability.

WSN are highly unstable, highly susceptible to accidental errors (in software and hardware components), and easy targets of security attacks. Importantly, these problems stem from the very nature of wireless networks; i.e., node mobility; deployment in harsh environments; need for low-cost solutions; limited availability of communication, computation, and energy resources; and broadcast communication.

Nodes' behavior is directly impacted by sensor faults and network reconfiguration events, and vice versa. The workload is influenced by the number of packets sent over the multi-hop network. The path followed by packets depends on the routing algorithm, topology, and wireless propagation. The energy profile is affected by the workload, number of forwarded packets, and battery technology. All of those factors have an impact on failure behavior; e.g., a node can fail because of battery exhaustion. A node can also fail independently because of faults in the sensing hardware. In turn, a failure of a node may induce a partition of the network into two or more subsets, causing unavailability (e.g., isolation) of a large set of nodes that can no longer deliver data to the sink. That high degree of interdependence and high dynamicity complicate assessment and design such that canonical techniques are inadequate. While analytical models are acceptable ways to measure nonfunctional properties, such as performance and dependability, via simulation, their widespread use in this field is limited by the complexity and dynamicity of WSN. That complexity leads to unaffordable modeling costs. The definition of analytical models for WSNs is a challenging task due to highly variable networking conditions and operating behavior that make it difficult to reuse models or adapt them to different scenarios. In addition, models raise the concern of how to obtain realistic values for their parameters – parameters that may change during the lifetime of the WSN. Hence, the values of some model parameters, such as packet loss rate and energy consumption, could depend on initial assumptions that may or may not hold true during the evolution of the WSN.

## 2.3.5 Mobile Phones

The cell phone network is made up of millions of low-cost cell phone gadgets that interface with the stationary cell phone networking infrastructure. Each new generation of mobile and embedded devices, such as smartphones and PDAs (personal digital assistants), supports a full range of applications, from web browsing to entertainment software to gaming. Challenges are presented by the characteristics of today's marketplace, where the time-to-sell demands force manufacturers to deliver products with new features within a very short time window (e.g., six months), often sacrificing the testing efforts for these products. That environment has resulted in increasing susceptibility of handheld devices to accidental errors and malicious attacks. An example is the first reported mobile phone virus, Cabir, which in 2007 affected smartphones that had the Symbian OS.

Reliability is becoming even more important as new critical applications are being developed for mobile phones. Such critical applications include, but are not limited to, ones for robot control [44, 45], traffic control [46] and telemedicine [47]. In such settings, a phone failure that affects an application could result in a significant loss or hazard, e.g., causing a robot to perform uncontrolled actions.

Following the above sampling of the wide spectrum of systems, paradigms, and domains where dependability is employed, we can now delve deeper into each layer, beginning with the hardware redundancy techniques in the following chapter.

### 2.3.6 Artificial Intelligence (AI) Systems

The emergence of AI systems and their ubiquitous adoption in automating tasks that involve humans in critical application domains (e.g., autonomous vehicles (AVs), medical assistants/devices, manufacturing, agriculture, and smart buildings) means that it is of paramount importance that we be able to place trust in these technologies.

In a broad sense, a trustworthy AI system must be dependable[1] (i.e., ensure safety, resilience, robustness, and security of its own and its operational environment) and reasonable (i.e., provide the reasoning behind produced decisions/actions). Indeed, the absence of these features not only makes people reluctant to deploy technology in the field despite successful demonstrations but also leaves systems vulnerable to security hacks and crashes that ultimately impact human safety and wellbeing. Artificial Intelligence (AI) changes the landscape, where computers can now infer relationships, discover patterns, react, and adapt to changes while keeping its original strengths in speed, scale, and scope. In the new era of smart systems, AI has successfully demonstrated the possibility of accelerating and automating processes that were a job of human actors until now

---

1 While trustworthiness and dependability might have distinct definitions, in a system engineering's perspective, we use the terms interchangeably.

(e.g., driving, diagnosis, or navigating). The success of AI is changing the paradigm in system design.

In conventional systems, humans in the decision loop monitor, reason, and validate the decision (if not made by the human him/herself) and the feedback that follows. In contrast, in AI systems (once in the production system), the decision is inferred by AI models and actuators execute action, often, without human validation although human-AI systems interactions are becoming increasingly common. Such a change in paradigm, where a human is no longer the core in the decision-loop, asserts a need to assure trustworthiness of AI systems and the actions that follows. Further, the proximity to and direct interaction with humans (and our surrounding environment) and the probabilistic nature of the underlying algorithm raises concerns on the trustworthiness of such systems.

For instance, AVs use Machine Language (ML) methods to derive real-time driving decisions. With the benefits of enabling autonomous control and management, or rapid response to anomalous events in a system/application behavior, these technologies bring new challenges in terms of the robustness, resilience, and safety. ML algorithms, in particular the ones used in AVs, are known to be brittle in rare driving scenarios, perturbations (both accidental and malicious) introduced in the AVs and their environment. Further, uncertainty in the environment and the decision process, software/hardware run-time errors, design bugs, and malicious attacks, can contribute to the erratic behavior of AVs. Erratic decisions may lead to safety hazards, such as accidents, which often lead to loss of human life or property damage. In March 2018, an automated test vehicle fatally injured a pedestrian crossing the road where there was no crosswalk while pushing a bicycle by her side. The automated driving system (ADS) failed to classify the victim as a pedestrian or predict her path. The ADS determined the likeliness of a collision only after the situation exceeded the response specifications of the braking system. The vehicle operator was responsible for monitoring the ADS and for responding to emergency situations (i.e., resume control from the ADS), but the vehicle operator was glancing away from the road and redirected her gaze ahead only about a second before impact [48].

System trustworthiness, also known as dependability and security, is a well-studied concept in computing systems. For instance, Avizienis et al. describe a trustworthy system in the context of availability, reliability, safety, confidentiality, integrity, and maintainability. Accordingly, variations of measures and methods have been developed to assess the trustworthiness of critical systems (e.g., space programs, high-speed trains, large-scale computing infrastructure) or detect, prevent, and tolerate incidents that corrupt the operation of such systems [49–54]. However, the aforementioned resilience and safety challenges cannot be solved by conventional methods (which are broadly used in aircrafts, satellites, and power grids).

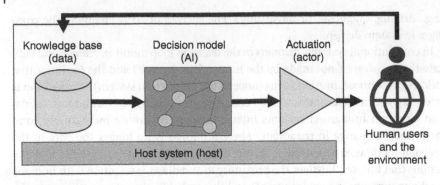

**Figure 2.7** Generic representation of an AI system/application.

As depicted in Figure 2.7, an AI system can be abstracted into three core components; the knowledge base (data) to infer the intelligence, the learning algorithm (AI) that derives/infers a representative model from the data, and an actuation module (actor) that executes the action and interacts with the surrounding environment and the human users.[2] The challenges in ensuring trustworthiness in mission- and life-critical AI systems originates from uncertainties in each key layer of an AI system:

1) **Uncertainty in the inputs.** The challenge is to identify and handle the uncertainty in the input caused by (i) the measurement errors, and (ii) adversarial perturbations. For example, recent research report that an AV may fail to recognize the stop sign or estimate target object trajectories due to corrupted inputs from the sensors due to a fault or an adversarial attack. Further, ML systems, in general, were shown to be vulnerable to noisy inputs. For instance, an AI-driven eye screening system that demonstrated a promising detection rate during its development struggled with significant rejection rates, when deployed in practice. Post-deployment investigation showed that numerous factors such as the expertise of the staff, procedures taken, or the environmental settings (e.g., darkness) affected the quality of the input.

2) **Uncertainty in ML models.** The challenge is to identify and handle the uncertainty in decision models derived by AI, which are caused by (i) lack of comprehensive training data and inability of ML model to handle rare inputs, (ii) underfitting/overfitting of ML model parameters (e.g., neural network weights and Kalman Filter parameters), (iii) implementation and integration of ensemble of ML models (e.g., uncertainty propagating and snowballing

---

2 Not all AI systems are feedback systems. While Figure 2.7 depicts a closed-loop AI system, there are open-loop and non-loop systems.

from object detectors to vehicle actuation commands). Resolving the uncertainties in the model outputs does not lend itself to conventional methods.

3) **Uncertainty in the system operation.** The challenge is in handling the uncertainty in the behavior of the underlying system components, executing the ML models and vehicle kinematics, caused by a wide range of failure modes across system components. Examples include faults in mechanical components such as engine and brakes, performance anomalies, bugs and faults in software and hardware components. Although most of such challenges can be handled using traditional resiliency techniques, some failures may escape the fault containment domains impacting the inference of the ML models.

For AI-driven methods to become an integral part of decision making, current methods of decision and control algorithms need to be augmented so as to incorporate the uncertainties inherent in AI models. In particular, we need formal verification, experimental methods, and better models that build upon current methods. For instance, verification, validation, and testing methods provides means of assessing the dependability of systems. However, unlike conventional systems whose logic is static, that of AI systems are rather dynamically derived and inferred by the data used for training. Further, the inference of the logic derived by AI is not easily interpretable, making the system difficult to assess and validate. Addressing this challenge will require developing innovative model-driven fuzzing, falsification, and fault injection techniques to understand system behavior across a wide range of inputs and faults. Further, while assessing the AI system's response to unknown corner cases has become a critical task, often one can derive the consequence and impact of a decision only through interaction with the surrounding environment. Hence, it is imperative to develop a comprehensive testbed that enables testing the full AI system stack (i.e., both hardware and software). Further, by augmenting the testbed with advanced assessment and validation techniques, we can strategically generate rare corner case inputs and systems states for a thorough stress test and eventually minimize unexpected behavior on rare input or events.

Critical applications increasingly consider adopting AI into their core decision loop. AVs, one of the most complicated AI systems, is undoubtedly the most active industry domain in conducting AI research. Further, its increased use in healthcare, from interpreting images to a new generation of surgical robots and assisting physicians in complex decision making, is rapidly becoming a reality. Despite the advances in state-of-the-art AI research, the issues of reliability, security, and robustness of such systems have not been adequately addressed so far. If such AI systems are to become widely accepted and deployed, the issues of dependability must be thoroughly researched.

## 2.4 Insights

Foundational work in dependability included concepts such as redundancy and coding. The extensive use of these techniques is evident from thecase studies presented in Section 2.1 of this chapter. The IBM System S/360 tries to minimize the impact on performance due to reliability by implementing duplicated instruction execution units. However, in spite of such heavy use of spatial redundancy it still incurs about a 35% overhead in program execution due to the instruction result comparison and retry logic. Reliability is surely very desirable but it has to be understood that it comes at some cost.

The techniques used in the IBM System S/360, Tandem Integrity systems remain relevant with appropriate modifications for current and future systems. The example of the Blue waters system illustrates this by building upon and extending these core dependability features.

The need for reliability has only grown over the years as digital computing spread its influence on domains that were previously deemed beyond its scope. However, as we have seen in the descriptions of all the emerging computing domains the applicability of fundamental techniques needs to be evaluated with the domain knowledge in perspective.

## References

1 Siewiorek, D.P. and Swarz, R.S. (1998). *Reliable Computer Systems: Design and Evaluation*, 3e. A K Peters.

2 Carter, W.C., Montgomery, H.C., Preiss, R.J. et al. (1964). Design of serviceability features for the IBM System/360. *IBM Journal of Research and Development* 8 (2): 115–126.

3 Jewett, D. (1991). Integrity S2: a fault-tolerant Unix platform. *Digest of Papers, the 21st International Symposium on Fault-Tolerant Computing*, Montreal, Quebec, Canada (25–27 June 1991), 512–519. IEEE.

4 Horst, R., Jewett, D., and Lenoski, D. (1993). The risk of data corruption in microprocessor-based systems. *Proceedings of the 23rd International Symposium on Fault-Tolerant Computing*, Toulouse, France (22–24 June 1993), 576–585. IEEE.

5 Chen, S., Xu, J., Iyer, R.K. et al. (2002). Evaluating the security threat of firewall data corruption caused by instruction transient errors. *Proceedings of the International Conference on Dependable Systems and Networks*, Washington, DC, USA (23–26 June 2002). IEEE.

6 Aaron, J.N., Carlisle, C.C., Carskadon, M.A. et al. (1996). Environmental noise as a cause of sleep disruption in an intermediate respiratory care unit. *Sleep* 19 (9): 707–710.

**7** Siewiorek, D.P., Chillarege, R., and Kalbarczyk, Z.T. (2004). Reflections on industry trends and experimental research in dependability. *IEEE Transactions on Dependable and Secure Computing* 1 (2): 109–127.

**8** Armbrust, M., Fox, A., Griffith, R. et al. (2009). Above the Clouds: A Berkeley View of Cloud Computing. Technical Report No. UCB/EECS-2009-28, Electrical Engineering and Computer Sciences, University of California at Berkeley. https://www2.eecs.berkeley.edu/Pubs/TechRpts/2009/EECS-2009-28.pdf (accessed 8 August 2020).

**9** Ionescu, D. (2009). Microsoft red-faced after massive data Sidekick data loss. *PCWorld* (12 October). http://www.pcworld.com/article/173470/microsoft_redfaced_after_massive_sidekick_data_loss.html (accessed 3 August 2020).

**10** Amazon S3 Team. (2008). Amazon S3 availability event: 20 July 2008. *Amazon Web Services.* http://status.aws.amazon.com/s3-20080720.html (accessed 3 August 2020).

**11** Goldman, D. (2011). Why Amazon's cloud Titanic went down. *CNN Money* (22 April). https://money.cnn.com/2011/04/22/technology/amazon_ec2_cloud_outage/ (accessed 3 August 2020).

**12** Hayden, M. (1997). *The Ensemble system. Ph.D. thesis.* Cornell University.

**13** Basile, C., Wang, L., Kalbarczyk, Z. et al. (2003). Group communication protocols under errors. *Proceedings of the 22nd International Symposium on Reliable Distributed Systems,* Florence, Italy (6–8 October 2003), 35–44. IEEE.

**14** Smith, C. (2011). Sony admits PlayStation Network hacker stole user data. *The Huffington Post* (26 April). https://www.huffpost.com/entry/playstation-network-hacker-stole-user-data_n_854106 (accessed 3 August 2020).

**15** Chambrin, M.C., Ravaux, P., Calvelo-Aros, D. et al. (1999). Multicentric study of monitoring alarms in the adult intensive care unit (ICU): A descriptive analysis. *Intensive Care Medicine* 25 (12): 1360–1366.

**16** Korniewicz, D.M., Clark, T., and David, Y. (2008). A national online survey of the effectiveness of clinical alarms. *American Journal of Critical Care* 17 (1): 36–41.

**17** Mondor, T.A. and Finley, G.A. (2003). The perceived urgency of auditory warning alarms used in the hospital operating room is inappropriate. *Canadian Journal of Anesthesia* 50 (3): 221–228.

**18** Kam, P.C.A., Kam, A.C., and Thompson, J.F. (1994). Noise pollution in the anaesthetic and intensive care environment. *Anaesthesia* 49 (11): 982–986.

**19** Cropp, A.J., Woods, L.A., Raney, D. et al. (1994). Name that tone, the proliferation of alarms in the intensive care unit. *Chest* 105 (4): 1217–1220.

**20** Momtahan, K., Hetu, R., and Tansley, B. (1993). Audibility and identification of auditory alarms in the operating room and intensive care unit. *Ergonomics* 36 (10): 1159–1176.

**21** Tsien, C.L. and Fackler, J.C. (1997). Poor prognosis for existing monitors in the intensive care unit. *Critical Care Medicine* 25 (4): 614–619.

**22** Koshi, E.M.J., Mäkivirta, A., Sukuvaara, T. et al. (1990). Frequency and reliability of alarms in the monitoring of cardiac postoperative patients. *Journal of Clinical Monitoring and Computing* 7 (2): 129–133.

**23** Alemzadeh, H., Iyer, R.K., Kalbarczyk, Z. et al. (2013). Analysis of safety-critical computer failures in medical devices. *IEEE Security & Privacy* 11 (4): 14–26.

**24** Cheriyan, A.M., Jarvi, A., Kalbarczyk, Z., et al. (2009). Pervasive real-time biomedical monitoring system. *Proceedings of the 2009 International Conference on Biomedical and Pharmaceutical Engineering*, Singapore (2–4 December 2009). IEEE.

**25** Cheriyan, A.M., Jarvi, A.O., Kalbarczyk, Z., et al. (2009). Pervasive embedded systems for detection of traumatic brain injury. *Proceedings of the 2009 IEEE International Conference on Multimedia and Expo*, New York, NY, USA (18 June–3 July 2009), 1704–1707. IEEE.

**26** Rosen, J. and Hannaford, B. (2006). Doc at a distance. *IEEE Spectrum* 43 (10): 34–39.

**27** Halperin, D., Heydt-Benjamin, T.S., Ransford, B. et al. (2008). Pacemakers and implantable cardiac defibrillators: Software radio attacks and zero-power defenses. *Proceedings of the 2008 IEEE Symposium on Security and Privacy*, Oakland, CA, USA (18–22 May 2008), 129–142. IEEE.

**28** Li, C., Raghunathan, A., and Jha, N.K. (2011). Hijacking an insulin pump: security attacks and defenses for a diabetes therapy system. *Proceedings of the 2011 IEEE 13th International Conference on e-Health Networking, Applications and Services*, Columbia, MO, USA (13–15 June 2011), 150–156. IEEE.

**29** Tozal, M.E., Wang, Y., Al-Shaer, E. et al. (2011). On secure and resilient telesurgery communications over unreliable networks. *Proceedings of the 2011 IEEE Conference on Computer Communications Workshops*, Shanghai, China (10–15 April 2011), 714–719. IEEE.

**30** Lee, G.S. and Thuraisingham, B. (2012). Cyberphysical systems security applied to telesurgical robotics. *Computer Standards & Interfaces* 34 (1): 225–229.

**31** Bonaci, T., Yan, J., Herron, J., et al. (2015). Experimental analysis of denial-of-service attacks on teleoperated robotic systems. *Proceedings of the ACM/IEEE Sixth International Conference on Cyber-Physical Systems* (14–16 April 2015), 11–20. New York, NY, USA: ACM.

**32** Bonaci, T., Herron, J., Yusuf, T. et al. (2015). To make a robot secure: An experimental analysis of cyber security threats against teleoperated surgical robots. arXiv:1504.04339.

**33** Alemzadeh, H., Chen, D., Li, X. et al. (2016). Targeted attacks on teleoperated surgical robots: dynamic model-based detection and mitigation. *Proceedings of the 2016 46th Annual IEEE/IFIP International Conference on Dependable Systems and Networks*, Toulouse, France (28 June–1 July 2016), 395–406. IEEE.

**34** Di Martino, C., Cinque, M., and Cotroneo, D. (2012). Automated generation of performance and dependability models for the assessment of wireless sensor networks. *IEEE Transactions on Computers* 61 (6): 870–884.

**35** Levis, P. and Culler, D. (2004). The firecracker protocol. *Proceedings of the 11th ACM SIGOPS European Workshop*, Leuven, Belgium (19–22 September 2004). ACM.

**36** Chih-Yu, L., Wen-Chih, P., and Yu-Chee, T. (2006). Efficient in-network moving object tracking in wireless sensor networks. *IEEE Transactions on Mobile Computing* 5 (8): 1044–1056.

**37** Oh, S., Sastry, S., and Schenato, L. (2005). A hierarchical multiple-target tracking algorithm for sensor networks. *Proceedings of the 2005 IEEE International Conference on Robotics and Automation*, Barcelona, Spain (April 2005), 2197–2202. IEEE.

**38** He, T., Krishnamurthy, S., Luo, L. et al. (2006). VigilNet: an integrated sensor network system for energy-efficient surveillance. *ACM Transactions on Sensor Networks* 2 (1): 1–38.

**39** Evers, L. and Havinga, P. (2007). Supply chain management automation using wireless sensor networks. *Proceedings of the 2007 IEEE International Conference on Mobile Adhoc and Sensor Systems*, Pisa, Italy (8–11 October 2007). IEEE.

**40** Ceriotti, M., Mottola, L., Picco, G.P., et al. (2009). Monitoring heritage buildings with wireless sensor networks: the Torre Aquila deployment. *Proceedings of the 2009 International Conference on Information Processing in Sensor Networks*, San Francisco, CA, USA (13–16 April 2009), 277–288. IEEE Computer Society.

**41** Xu, N., Rangwala, S., Chintalapudi, K.K. et al. (2004). A wireless sensor network for structural monitoring. *Proceedings of the 2nd International Conference on Embedded Networked Sensor Systems*, Baltimore, MD, USA (3–5 November 2004), 13–24. New York, NY, USA: ACM.

**42** Cinque, M., Di Martino, C., and Testa, A. (2009). iCAAS: Interoperable and configurable architecture for accessing sensor networks. *Proceedings of the 3rd International Workshop on Adaptive and Dependable Mobile Ubiquitous Systems*, London, UK (13–17 July 2009), 19–23. New York, NY, USA: ACM.

**43** Astarita, V. and Florian, M. (2001). The use of mobile phones in traffic management and control. *Proceedings of the 2001 IEEE Intelligent Transportation Systems Conference*, Oakland, CA, USA (25–29 August 2001), 10–15. IEEE.

**44** Aziz, A.A. and Besar, R. (2003). Application of mobile phone in medical image transmission. *Proceedings of the 4th National Conference on Telecommunication Technology*, Shah Alam, Malaysia (14–15 January 2003), 80–83. IEEE.

**45** Sekman, A., Koku, A.B., and Zein-Sabatto, S. (2003). Human robot interaction via cellular phones. *Proceedings of the 2003 IEEE International Conference on Systems, Man and Cybernetics*, vol. 4, Washington, DC, USA (8 October 2003), 3937–3942. IEEE.

**46** Kubik, T. and Sugisaka, M. (2001). Use of a cellular phone in mobile robot voice control. *Proceedings of the 40th SICE Annual Conference*, Nagoya, Japan (27 July 2001), 106–111. IEEE.

**47** Chillarege, R., Bhandari, I.S., Chaar, J.K. et al. (1992). Orthogonal defect classification: a concept for in-process measurements. *IEEE Transactions on Software Engineering* 18 (11): 943–956.

**48** National Transportation Safety Board (2019). Accident Report: Collision Between Vehicle Controlled by Developmental Automated Driving System and Pedestrian, Tempe, Arizona, 18 March 2018. Technical Report. https://www.ntsb.gov/investigations/AccidentReports/Reports/HAR1903.pdf.

**49** Alur, R. (2011). Formal verification of hybrid systems. *Proceedings of the Ninth ACM International Conference on Embedded Software (EMSOFT)*, Taipei, Taiwan (9–14 October 2011), 273–278. IEEE.

**50** Henzinger, T.A., Kopke, P.W., Puri, A., and Varaiya, P. (1998). What's decidable about hybrid automata? *Journal of Computer and System Sciences* 57 (1): 94–124.

**51** Kalra, N. and Paddock, S.M. (2016). Driving to safety: how many miles of driving would it take to demonstrateautonomous vehicle reliability? *Transportation Research Part A: Policy and Practice* 94: 182–193.

**52** Koymans, R. (1990). Specifying real-time properties with metric temporal logic. *Real-time Systems* 2 (4): 255–299.

**53** Mitra, S., Wang, Y., Lynch, N., and Feron, E. (2003). Safety verification of model helicopter controller using hybrid input/output automata. In: *International Workshop on Hybrid Systems: Computation and Control*, 343–358. Springer.

**54** Abbas, H., Fainekos, G., Sankaranarayanan, S. et al. (2013). Probabilistic temporal logic falsification of cyber-physical systems. *ACM Transactions on Embedded Computing Systems (TECS)* 12 (2): 1–30.

# 3

# Hardware Error Detection and Recovery Through Hardware-Implemented Techniques

## 3.1 Introduction

A *reliable* computer system is one that provides its normal level of service even in the presence of hardware and software faults [1, 2]. There are two philosophies on how to achieve reliability: *fault avoidance,* wherein techniques prevent the occurrence of faults; and *fault tolerance,* wherein techniques allow the system to continue to execute despite the occurrence of faults. This discussion focuses on methods for achieving fault tolerance.

Fault tolerance can be achieved using either of two basic approaches: *error masking,* in which the system avoids the effect of an error through some form of redundancy; and *error detection and recovery,* in which the system notices the presence of an error, locates and isolates the error, reconfigures in a spare system, and restarts the system [3].

This chapter and the next three chapters (Chapters 3–6) will discuss example experiences of applying error detection techniques to actual systems. We first introduce and characterize a variety of hardware- and software-based error detection techniques, illustrating them in real-world systems and applications. Quantitative evaluation (in terms of error coverage and performance overhead) will also be provided for many of the techniques presented. The techniques discussed here can be implemented in hardware and/or in software, and they can be applied to uniprocessor, multiprocessor, distributed, or networked systems.

This chapter discusses hardware-implemented techniques that are primarily focused on detecting errors in the underlying hardware platform (logic or memory). Although not specifically targeted toward faults in the software layer, these techniques may be able to provide detection for them as well. Such corollary advantages of these techniques will be brought forth where applicable.

*Dependable Computing: Design and Assessment,* First Edition. Ravishankar K. Iyer,
Zbigniew T. Kalbarczyk, and Nithin M. Nakka.
© 2024 The IEEE Computer Society. Published 2024 by John Wiley & Sons, Inc.
Companion website: www.wiley.com/go/iyer/dependablecomputing1

## 3.2 Redundancy Techniques

In this section, we discuss three basic forms of redundancy: *passive*, *active*, and *hybrid*.

*Passive hardware redundancy* relies on majority voting mechanisms to mask the occurrence of faults. It does not employ fault detection or system reconfiguration. The most common form of passive redundancy is called *triple modular redundancy* (TMR). TMR triplicates the hardware necessary to perform the required operations and uses a voter to determine the output of the system. It is assumed that the triplicated hardware module failures are both independent and identically distributed. In this approach, the primary difficulty is the voter. If the voter fails, the entire system fails. A theoretical approach to avoiding that problem is to use three voters and provide three independent outputs.

One can interconnect several stages of TMR by connecting the outputs of the voters of one TMR stage via the inputs of modules of the next TMR stage. The voting can be performed by either a hardware voter (which performs the voting quickly but requires extra hardware logic) or a software voter (which performs the voting on processors that are also executing normal computations but is generally slower). However, in the end, you still need a single, nonredundant voter or computer that will remain a single point of failure. The argument in support of such a design is that the final voter has very simple logic and hence can be made highly reliable. The implementation of the TMR is nontrivial and requires some care, as discussed in the Tandem example in Chapter 1 and in [4].

A generalization of the TMR approach is *N-modular redundancy* (NMR), which uses *N* copies of a module instead of three. For example, the NASA Space Shuttle onboard computer system consists of five *general-purpose computers* (GPCs) that control the avionic subsystems. Four GPCs run the same software and support flight-critical functions (e.g. guidance and navigation). The outputs of the four computers are voted on to ensure highly reliable control [5]. The fifth GPC is responsible for non-flight-critical avionic functions. The system can operate in two modes: *quad/triplex* and *duplex*. In quad/triplex mode, each computer is used to perform the computation and check the correctness of the operations performed by the remaining computers. That process is achieved by means of bit-by-bit comparison of critical data and an I/O transactions timeout test [5]. The results from each computer are then put through a hardware voter that outputs a success (or failure) signal if the outputs of all the computers agree or at most one computer disagrees.

Upon a first failure, the exclusion logic excludes the failed computer and switches to triplex mode. On a second failure, the system switches to duplex mode. In duplex mode, comparison of the outputs of the two working computers can detect disagreement. A combination of a built-in test and a watchdog timer is then used to identify the failed computer. Using 4-modular redundancy (and gradual degradation from quad to triplex and duplex operation modes), the Space Shuttle's onboard computer system achieves a very high level of error detection coverage, higher than what can be provided using self-testing techniques (e.g. duplex mode) alone. Preflight testing of the architecture demonstrated high efficiency in detecting malfunctioning GPCs and preventing catastrophic failures during the flight [6].

In 1989, Tandem Computers launched the Integrity S2 hardware architecture, which was based on a TMR [7]; the voter design and synchronization are discussed in Section 3.2.3. Integrity S2 used three CPU modules operating as one TMR logical processor. The three CPUs executed the same instructions, and then compared and voted on the output. The main difference between Integrity S2 and traditional TMR architectures is that Integrity S2 used three independently clocked CPUs. Hence, while they executed the same instruction stream, they did not necessarily execute the same instruction at the same time. The CPUs were synchronized whenever interrupts were presented to them. Two self-checking voter modules connected to and monitored the CPU modules. Voting occurred when the global memory had to be accessed or an interrupt needed to be processed.

*Active hardware redundancy* can be *static* or *dynamic*. Static redundancy attempts to achieve fault tolerance by fault detection, fault location, and fault recovery. The most common form of fault detection is duplication and comparison, with which two identical pieces of hardware perform the same computations in parallel and compare the results.

A second form of active redundancy is *standby sparing*, also referred to as *dynamic redundancy*, illustrated in Figure 3.1. It consists of one active module with one or several backup (spare) modules. It relies on failure detection and system reconfiguration actions (hence *dynamic* redundancy). The action of switching to a backup module is called *failover*. The advantage of standby sparing is that in a system that contains $n$ identical modules, such as $n$ identical multiprocessors, fault tolerance can be provided with $k < n$ spare modules. The assumption here is

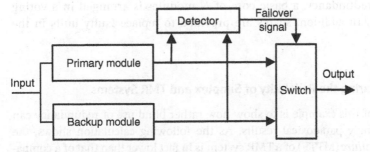

**Figure 3.1** Standby redundancy.

that the active modules will eventually manifest silent failures, detectable value failures, or signaled failures. Consequently, various fault detection schemes are used to determine when a module has become faulty, and fault location is used to determine exactly which module is faulty. The reconfiguration operation in standby sparing can be viewed conceptually as a switch whose output is selected from one of the modules that provide inputs to the switch.

Standby sparing can bring a system back into full operation after occurrence of a fault, but it requires a momentary disruption in performance while reconfiguration is being performed. Depending on the technique used to activate the spare module, standby sparing can be classified as *hot, warm,* or *cold. Hot* standby sparing techniques force the spare to operate synchronously with the online modules and be prepared to take over at any time. While the spare module does not perform any useful work during regular operations, it ages at the same rate and consumes as much power as the active module. *Warm* standby techniques rely on the use of checkpoints of the status of the active module. The backup module is powered and will load the most recent checkpoint upon a failover. During regular functioning of the active module, the standby module can perform useful work. However, the technique requires twice the power of a single active module and presents a high failure rate because two modules are operating. In addition, warm standby techniques require more time to replace the failed module with a standby, because of the use of the checkpoint. *Cold* standby sparing uses checkpoints and unpowered spares that must be powered up and initialized before the module is brought into active service. It presents an overall lower failure rate than warm or hot standby techniques and lower power consumption. However, it needs a longer period to boot up and initialize the spare module from the checkpoint.

*Hybrid hardware redundancy* combines the attractive features of both the active and passive approaches [8]. Fault masking is used to prevent the system from producing erroneous results, and fault detection, location, and recovery are used to reconfigure the system in the event of a fault. The most common form of hybrid redundancy is that of $N$-modular redundancy with spares. In that approach to redundancy, a basic core of $N$ modules is arranged in a voting configuration. In addition, spares are provided to replace faulty units in the NMR core.

### 3.2.1 Comparing the Reliability of Simplex and TMR Systems

The purpose of this example is to show how rather blind use of redundancy can lead to seemingly paradoxical results. As the following calculation shows, the *mean time to failure* (MTTF) of a TMR system is in fact lower than that of a comparable simplex (nonredundant) system. A system with triple-modular redundancy

(TMR) includes three components, two of which are required for the system to function properly. Assuming that the reliability of a single component is given by[1]

$$R_{simplex} = e^{-\lambda t} \tag{3.1}$$

where $\lambda$ is the failure rate of the simplex component, the MTTF for a simplex system is:

$$MTTF_{simplex} = \int e^{-\lambda t} = \frac{1}{\lambda}$$

The reliability of a TMR system can be expressed as:

$$R_{TMR} = e^{-3\lambda t} + \binom{3}{2} e^{-2\lambda t}\left(1 - e^{-\lambda t}\right) = 3e^{-2\lambda t} - 2e^{-3\lambda t}$$

and consequently:

$$MTTF_{TMR} = \frac{3}{2\lambda} - \frac{2}{3\lambda} = \frac{5}{6\lambda}$$

$$MTTF_{simplex} > MTTF_{TMR}$$

Figure 3.2 shows the reliability of TMR and simplex systems as functions of $\lambda t$. Note that

$$R_{TMR}(t) \geq R(t) \quad 0 \leq t \leq t_0$$

$$R_{TMR}(t) \leq R(t) \quad t_0 \leq t < \infty$$

$$\text{where } t_0 = \frac{\ln 2}{\lambda} \approx \frac{0.7}{\lambda}$$

TMR improves reliability for short missions ($t \leq t_0$). For long missions ($t > t_0$), TMR actually degrades reliability. The explanation of that phenomenon is rather simple. Until the first failure, the system operates in a TMR configuration, and $R_{TMR} > R_{simplex}$. After the first failure, the two remaining components "compete" to fail, resulting in a lower reliability than would be seen for a plain simplex with the same failure rate.

### 3.2.2 M-out-of-N Systems

In $M$-out-of-$N$ systems, the critical factor is mission time rather than MTTF. The reliability of $M$-out-of-$N$ systems is very high in the beginning, when the spare

---

1 Details on probability theory and the analytical formulas used throughout this book can be found in [9].

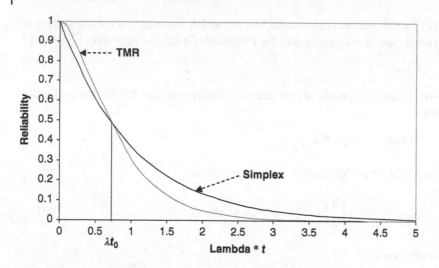

**Figure 3.2** Comparative reliability of TMR and simplex systems.

components tolerate failures. But reliability falls sharply as time goes on, system redundancy is exhausted, and more hardware is subject to failure. *M*-out-of-*N* systems are useful in contexts, such as aircraft control, in which very high reliability is needed for a short period of time. *M*-out-of-*N* systems are also used in fault-tolerant multiprocessors (FTMP) [10] and software-implemented fault tolerance (SIFT) [11].

For the general *M* and *N*, *M* modules out of *N* need to function for the system to be operational. The reliability of such a system is given in the following expression:

$$R_{MN} = \sum_{i=0}^{N-M} \binom{N}{i} R_m^{N-i}\left(1-R_m\right)^i$$

where $R_m$ is the reliability of a single module.

**Example** Computer systems used onboard spacecraft must guarantee long-term uninterrupted operation (often for years) despite permanent failures induced by radiation present in space and by random events. Standby redundancy for both processors and memory is usually a technique of choice. The below example addresses the design of memory units with redundancy and the evaluation of their reliability. To improve reliability, each *k*-bit memory word is expanded by *s* spare cells, so each row contains $k+s$ memory cells. There are *n* rows in the memory system. Assume that each memory chip contains *n* rows, and each row contains only one cell. The entire memory system then contains $k+s$ chips. Each chip has a failure rate of $\lambda$ and obeys the exponential failure law.

To compute the reliability of the complete memory system using column sparing, the expression must account for fault coverage. Suppose that $k = 16$,

$\lambda = 9.15 \times 10^{-6}$ failures occur per hour, and fault coverage is $C = 0.97$. Designers might consider determining the number of spares that will maximize the reliability of the memory at the end of a 10-year space mission, and comparing the obtained reliability to that of the memory system at the end of 10 years if there are zero spares.

### Solution

We have a memory system with $k$ main and $s$ spare memory chips. The chips fail at the same rate: $\lambda = 9.15 \times 10^{-6}$ per hour. The error coverage factor is $C = 0.97$. We wish to know the reliability of the system at the end of 10 years. There are $\binom{k+s}{i}$ ways for $i$ chips to fail. The probability that $i$ specific chips will fail and the remaining $((k+s) - i)$ will not is $R_1(t)^{k+s-i}(1 - R_1(t))^i$, and the probability that $i$ failures will be detected and covered is $C^i$. Consequently, the reliability is the sum of the probabilities that $0, 1, \ldots, s$ chips will fail and can be expressed as follows:

$$R(t) = \sum_{i=0}^{s} \binom{k+s}{i} R_1(t)^{k+s-i} (1 - R_1(t))^i C^i$$

$R_1(t)$ is the probability that a particular memory chip will not fail by time $t$, and it is given by $R_1(t) = e^{-\lambda t}$.

Solving the equation above, we find that for $s = 29$ (when $k = 16$ and $t = 10$ years), the reliability has optimal value. For $s = 0$, $R(t) = 2.7 \times 10^{-6}$, and for $s = 29$, $R(t) = 0.44$. Clearly, the 29 spares provide a significant improvement in reliability.

The problem becomes more complicated if the spare chips have a lower failure rate than the $k$ primary chips do.

To compute the probability that $n$ chips will fail, we need to compute the probability that $a$ main chips will fail and $b$ spare chips will fail for all combinations of $a$ and $b$ such that $a + b = n$. That can be done as shown below:

$$R(t) = \sum_{i=0, j>0, j\geq i-k}^{s} \sum^{i} \binom{k}{i-j}\binom{s}{j} R_{\lambda_1}(t)^{k-i+j} R_{\lambda_2}(t)^{s-j} (1 - R_{\lambda_1}(t))^{i-j} (1 - R_{\lambda_2}(t))^j C^i \quad (3.2)$$

where $R_{\lambda_1}(t) = e^{-\lambda t}$ is the reliability of the main chips, and $R_{\lambda_2}(t) = e^{-\lambda st}$ is the reliability of the spare chips.

### 3.2.3 The Effect of a Voter

The previous expression (Eq. 3.1 in Section 3.2.1) for reliability of a TMR system assumes a voter that is 100% reliable. If we assume voter reliability of $R_v$, we have:

$$R_{\text{TMRV}} = R_V \left( R_m^3 + \binom{3}{2} R_m^2 (1 - R_m) \right)$$

In general, a voter can be implemented in either the hardware or the software. Design and implementation of a robust voting mechanism is often considered a relatively simple task. In reality, the set of functions that a voter (or voting mechanism) can support depends on the system and the application. The functions might include

- Guaranteeing a majority vote on the input data
- Providing the ability to detect its own errors (i.e. the voter should be self-checking)
- Determining the faulty application replica (node)
- Handling voting in loosely synchronized (or loosely coupled) systems
- Handling voting in tightly synchronized (or tightly coupled) systems

A very instructive example of an actual voter implementation is the hardware voting mechanism used in Tandem's TMR architecture to guarantee that the three processing units synchronously serve external interrupts arriving to the system [12, 13].

The three processors in TMR systems were configured to operate together as a single logical processor. For them to do so, their instruction streams had to be identical. The synchronization mechanisms were designed so that if the code stream of any processor diverged from the code stream of the other processors, then a failure was indicated. The TMR architecture was a loosely synchronized system that required synchronization of inputs to the voter. It may also be difficult in such systems to determine voter timeout, because of differences in the relative speeds of the machines and variations in network communication delays. Tightly synchronized systems, on the other hand, generally do not require external synchronization of inputs to the voter.

Interrupt synchronization presents one of most difficult challenges in maintaining a single logical processor view. All interrupts are required to be synchronous to virtual time, which is referred to as the *cycle count*. The cycle count can be thought of as a representation of the virtual time, just as seconds are a representation of the real time. The reference point for virtual time is a specific software event or instruction. The code stream after the reference point must be identical for the three processors.

External exceptions (interrupts) are not inherently synchronous to virtual time. All interrupts that are generated by the I/O devices must be synchronized to virtual time (i.e. made synchronous with the individual processor's instruction stream) before they are presented to the processor. If an external interrupt is presented directly to the processor (i.e. without synchronization to virtual time), then the three processors could start to process the interrupt at different instructions, and this could lead to an unacceptable, inconsistent state of the system.

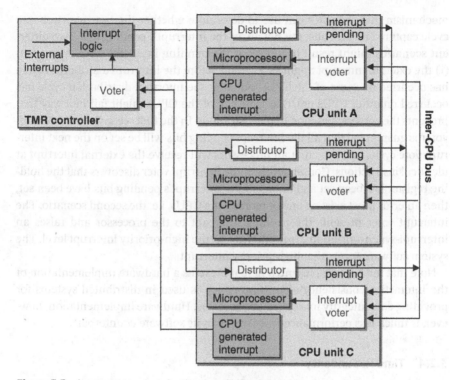

**Figure 3.3** Interrupt synchronization in a TMR system.

An interrupt is synchronized to virtual time through means of a distributed vote on the interrupt followed by presentation of the interrupt to the processor on a predetermined cycle count (virtual time). Figure 3.3 gives a block diagram of the interrupt synchronization logic. An external interrupt is delivered to the distributor present on each processing board (i.e. CPU unit). The distributor broadcasts the delivered interrupt to the other two CPUs via the inter-CPU bus. As a result, there are three pending interrupts, one from each CPU. The interrupt voter (also present on each processing board) captures the pending interrupts and performs a vote to verify that all the CPUs did receive the external interrupt request. On a predetermined cycle count, the interrupt voter presents the interrupt to the microprocessor. Thus, all the microprocessors will receive the interrupt on the same cycle count, so the interrupt will be synchronized to virtual time.

The interrupt voter uses a dedicated register (a holding register, not shown in Figure 3.3) to save state information on whether all CPUs have captured and distributed an external interrupt. In an error-free scenario, as described above, that state information is unneeded, i.e. external interrupts can be synchronized to virtual time without the use of a holding register. The holding register provides a mechanism that the voter can use to determine whether the last interrupt vote cycle captured at least one, but not all, of the interrupt's pending bits. Two different scenarios might result in not all of the pending interrupt's bits' being set: (i) the external interrupt might be asserted before the interrupt distribution cycle has occurred on some of the CPUs, but after the interrupt distribution cycle has occurred on other CPUs or (ii) at least one of the CPUs might fail in a way that prevents the correct operation of the distributor. In the first scenario, the interrupt voter is guaranteed that all the interrupt pending bits will be set on the next interrupt vote cycle, and thus that all processors will receive the external interrupt at identical instructions. Consequently, if the interrupt voter discovers that the holding register has been set and not all of the interrupt's pending bits have been set, then an error must exist on one or more of the CPUs, i.e. the second scenario. The interrupt voter presents the pending interrupt to the processor and raises an interrupt-synchronization-error interrupt on the high-priority interrupt level. The system software serves that high-priority interrupt.

Note that the scheme presented here represents a hardware implementation of the interactive consistency algorithm, which is used in distributed systems for providing data integrity for replicated processes. Hardware implementation, however, is much less performance-intensive than its software counterpart.

### 3.2.4 Time Redundancy

The fundamental concept of time redundancy can best be defined as the repetition of computations, two or more times, followed by a comparison of the results to conclude whether a discrepancy exists. Should an error be detected, computations can be performed once more to determine whether the disagreement remains or if it has disappeared. While such approaches are reliable in detecting errors that result from transient faults, they cannot protect against errors due to permanent faults.

Another form of time redundancy for handling permanent faults modifies how computations are performed the second time. One approach applies alternating logic for self-dual combinational circuits [14], performing a function on some set of inputs in one time instant and then performing the equivalent function on the complemented input in a subsequent time instant. The output should be the complement of the original function value of the original input. Should the second value of the function not be the complement, an error is detected.

A method of error detection called *recomputing with shifted operands* (RESO) was proposed and analyzed for *arithmetic and logic units* (ALUs) [15]. It represented the first time a unified method was used for both arithmetic and logic units. RESO was different from the previous work on self-checking logic;

it assumed a far more general fault model, which was suitable for the emerging VLSI circuits. A variable amount of fault coverage was provided depending on the number of shifts used for the recomputed step, e.g. if $k$ shifts were used in an adder, then any $(k - 1)$ consecutive failed cells would be covered, although the cells might fail in any arbitrary way. RESO was then applied to more complex circuits of multiply and divide arrays [16] and further extended to arbitrary one-dimensional iterative logic arrays [17].

## 3.3 Watchdog Timers

*Watchdog timers* have been used since the early days of digital systems as an inexpensive method of error detection. A timer is implemented separately from the process that it monitors. The process being watched must reset the timer before the timer expires; otherwise, the watched process is assumed to be faulty.

Traditionally, watchdog timers have been used to detect control flow errors that result in the timer's not being reset [18]. When the timer expires, the system is reset. Alternatively, instead of a system reset, an interrupt can be triggered to initiate a recovery from the error. Watchdog timers can also be used in much the same way that timeouts are used to monitor the behavior of a single subsystem [19]. Timeouts differ from watchdog timers in that they provide a finer check of control flow.

Watchdog timers can be implemented either in hardware, where the timer is generally an external one that can be reset with a signal, or in software. Software implementations often run on the same processor as the process being monitored, but the timer is maintained as a separate process [20].

A novel implementation that achieves the watchdog timer effect without using a timer is the technique of extended-precision, checksum-based, control-flow checking [21]. Extended-precision checksums are taken off a branch-free block of instructions as the sum total of the instructions or some transformation of the instructions. Before each block, the checksum value is sent to a buffer. As the instructions execute, they are subtracted from the buffer. When the block ends, or a branch occurs, a zero check signal is sent. If the buffer becomes zero or negative before the signal is set, a control flow error has occurred. If the buffer is positive when the signal is set, that also means that an error has occurred.

### 3.3.1 Example Applications of Watchdog Timers

*Bell System Telephone Switches.* An example of a system that employed watchdog processors to detect errors was the telephone-stored program switching system developed by the Bell System [22]. External watchdog timers monitored proper program operation by triggering recovery when timers were not periodically reset. That allowed early detection of problems caused by software errors (before the error propagated and caused severe damage to the system) and consequently made recovery easier. It should be noted that in spite of watchdog-based error detection, software techniques such as audit were the main line of defense against errors in this system.

*Mars Sojourner.* NASA's 1997 Mars Pathfinder mission with the Sojourner rover demonstrated a watchdog timer's ability to detect errors [23]. The computer system that controlled the Sojourner rover used a real-time, preemptive, multi-threaded operating system. Tasks were scheduled based on priorities that reflected their relative urgency. Because of a design flaw, a condition known as *priority inversion* could occur. Priority inversion occurred when a mutex or critical section held by a lower-priority thread delayed the running of a higher priority thread when both were competing for the same resource. To illustrate priority inversion, consider the following example execution scenario: (i) a low-priority thread $L$ obtains a mutually exclusive lock to access shared data $D$; (ii) a high-priority thread $H$, which needs $D$, is started and put in the wait set for the resource $D$; and (iii) a medium-priority task $M$, which does not need $D$, is started after $H$. As a result, $L$ is preempted by $M$, and $H$ is blocked after $L$ because $L$ cannot relinquish $D$.

Through use of a watchdog timer, the above scenario was detected, and the system was restarted. However, full restart caused loss of data, and the repetitive resets seriously limited the correct work of the Mars rover's system. The problem was eventually diagnosed, and the software was patched to reestablish proper behavior.

In that system, the recovery method applied when the watchdog signaled a timeout was a traditional system reset, a drastic but robust measure representing good engineering practice. The availability of the system was much more important than the loss of data due to the system reset.

### 3.3.2 Limitations of Watchdog Timers

Watchdog timers are not ideal for detecting errors in digital systems, for four reasons:

1) While the error detection is not limited to any particular fault model, watchdog timers only detect errors of a very specific type. The assumption is that any error will manifest itself as a control flow error that will prevent the system from continuing to reset the timer (i.e. timing and silent failures). If a control flow error occurs but the program resets the timer in time, the error will go undetected.

2) Timer resets must be placed with care to be effective. They cannot be placed inside interrupt routines or loops (to avoid the possibility of an infinite

loop), but they must occur often enough that the timer cannot expire during a normal operation.

3) Only processes with relatively deterministic runtimes can be checked, since the error detection is based entirely on the time between timer resets. If the set time is shorter than the longest possible runtime of the checked process, it can expire even though there is no error. On the other hand, if the time is set too long, then even if a control flow error occurs, the process may have enough time to get back to the point at which the timer is reset, and the error will not be detected.

4) A watchdog timer provides only an indication of possible process failure; a partially failed process may still be able to reset the timer. Coverage is limited, as neither the data nor the results are checked. When used to reset the system, a watchdog timer can improve availability (because the mean time to recovery is shortened) but not reliability (because failures are just as likely to occur). When the availability of a digital system is more important than the loss of data under some conditions, the use of a watchdog timer to reset the system on the detection of an error is an appropriate choice.

## 3.4  Information Redundancy

*Information redundancy* is the addition of redundant information to data to allow fault detection, fault masking, and fault tolerance. An example of information redundancy is a *single error correction-double error detection* (SEC-DED) code. A code's error detection and correction properties are based on its ability to partition a set of $2^n$ words, each $n$-bit wide, into a code space of $2^m$ words and a non-code space of $(2^n - 2^m)$ words. Each code is constructed such that no combination of fewer than a certain number of bit errors can transform one codeword into another valid codeword. Decoding circuits detect errors by identifying any word outside the code space. Error-correcting codes for any given number of bit errors require more redundancy in the codeword than error-detecting codes do for the same number of bit errors. Error-correcting codes also uniquely associate a non-code space word with the original codeword transformed by the errors.

### 3.4.1  A Brief History of Coding Theory

Claude Shannon founded the field of *information theory* with his landmark 1948 paper "A Mathematical Theory of Communication" [24, 25] Since then, research in information theory has given rise to a plethora of encoding and decoding pairs for error control in communication systems, digital computers, storage systems, and so on.

In a broad sense, coding schemes can be categorized into two classes: *block codes* and *convolutional codes*. Block codes were the primary area of coding theory research in the 1950s. *Hamming codes* were the first known linear binary block codes. They could detect and correct single errors and detect double errors, depending on the number of check bits introduced. The different classes of *parity-check codes* are discussed in Section 3.4.4.

In 1961, Meggitt [26] proposed a decoder structure that is generally applicable to all *cyclic codes*. However, it was not practical for an implementation. The approach was improved by Rudolph and Mitchell [27] and Kasami [28]. Melas and Gorog [29], Fire [30], and Abramson [31] proposed systematic cyclic codes for burst error correction. Cyclic codes are discussed in Section 3.4.5.

*BCH codes* were invented in 1959 by Hocquenghem [32], and independently in 1960 by Bose and Ray-Chaudhuri [33]. BCH codes have been an important set of codes for multiple-error correction. Their advantage is that they can be decoded using an algebraic decoding mechanism implemented as a simple decoder. They can detect multiple-burst errors in a transmitted word and have a wide variety of parameters for the block and code rates. Peterson [34] devised the first decoding algorithm for BCH codes. It was later improved by Berlekamp [35], Massey [36], Chien [37], Forney [38], and Lin and Costello [39]. Reed and Solomon proposed a subset of BCH codes, called *Reed-Solomon codes*, which have become popular in disk storage and communication systems [40]. Reed-Solomon codes are discussed in Section 3.4.9.

The discovery of *convolutional codes* by Elias in 1955 [41] was a major leap forward in coding theory. The lack of practical decoding algorithms, however, hindered their popular use until the 1960s, when several decoding algorithms were presented and implemented. Wozencraft and Reiffen [42] presented the sequential decoding algorithm for decoding convolutional codes in 1961. In 1963, a newer version of the sequential decoding algorithm, called the *Fano algorithm*, was proposed by Fano [43]. The Z-J stack algorithm, another version of the sequential decoding algorithm, was proposed by Zigangirov [44] and Jelinek [45] independently in 1966 and 1969, respectively. In 1967, Viterbi proposed the Viterbi algorithm as the maximum-likelihood decoding algorithm [46]. Those decoding algorithms are all in the category of *probabilistic decoding*. An algebraic decoding algorithm for convolutional codes, called *threshold decoding*, was proposed by Massey in 1963 [47]. It is less powerful than the Viterbi algorithm but is easier to implement.

*Low-density parity check (LDPC) codes* were first developed in 1963 by Robert Gallager as part of his PhD dissertation at the Massachusetts Institute of Technology (MIT) [48]. They were forgotten for a long time because, at the time of their development, they were impractical to implement.

*Tornado codes* were developed by Michael Luby et al. in 1997 and are known to have very fast encoding and decoding algorithms [49]. Software-based implementations of tornado codes are about 100 times faster on small lengths and about 10000 times faster on larger lengths than software-based Reed-Solomon erasure codes, while having only slightly greater overhead. Tornado codes work on the principle of reconstructing lost blocks of data using XOR-based parity. Checksums are used to detect and discard corrupted blocks, while XOR-based parity is used to iteratively reconstruct lost blocks of input data.

Forney proposed *concatenated coding schemes* [50], first introduced as a method for achieving large coding gains by combining two or more relatively simple building block or *component codes*. *Turbo codes* were developed in 1993 by Berrou et al. [51]. They are based on the concepts of concatenated coding and iterative decoding. To minimize error propagation from one encoding scheme to another, the output data from one encoder are interleaved (or permuted) before passing to the next encoder, and, conversely, the output of a decoder is de-interleaved before passing to the next decoder. Turbo codes are being widely used in deep-space satellite communications and other applications. Turbo codes rely on soft-decision decoding, wherein one decoder passes probabilistic soft decisions to another; after a few iterations, that process is expected to lead to reliable decisions.

### 3.4.2 Outline of the Description of Coding Techniques

Broadly, coding schemes can be classified as block codes or convolutional codes. In a block code scheme, the codeword for a data block depends only on the current block of data, whereas for convolutional codes, it depends on the current and a fixed number of previous blocks of data. Different classes of block codes are discussed in Sections 3.4.4–3.4.9. Convolutional codes are introduced briefly in Section 3.4.10.1.

In a linear block code, the modulo-2 sum of any two codewords is also a codeword. One class of linear block codes that use parity, and examples of such techniques, are discussed in Section 3.4.4. In cyclic coding schemes, which are a subclass of linear block codes, a circular shift of any codeword also belongs to the code. Cyclic codes are discussed in Section 3.4.5. Arithmetic codes to check the correct operation of functional units are described in Sections 3.4.7 and 3.4.8. Reed-Solomon codes, used extensively in disk storage systems and communication systems, are discussed in Section 3.4.9. A category of coding techniques called *two-level interleaved encoding techniques* has proven to be effective in practical disk storage systems [52]; the approach is described with a real example in Section 3.4.11. The above coding schemes bring parity-check codes and cyclic codes together into a single coding scheme, which is employed at different levels.

### 3.4.3 Fault Detection Through Encoding

The basic idea behind an error-detecting scheme is to add redundant information to the data being transmitted or stored to determine whether errors have been introduced. The amount of check information involved is the respect in which error-detecting and error-correcting codes diverge. Error-detecting codes use only enough redundant information to allow the receiver to determine that an error has occurred, but not to locate it. Error-correcting codes, on the other hand, add enough redundancy to allow the receiver or reader to deduce what the original clock or data must have been.

At the logic level, codes provide a means of masking or detecting errors. Formally, the code is a subset $S$ of the universe $U$ of possible vectors. A noncode-word is a vector in the set $U$-$S$. Those relations are shown in Figure 3.4. In the figure, $X_1$ is a codeword <10010011>, which, due to a multiple bit error, becomes noncodeword $X_3$ = <10011100>, which is *detectable*. The codeword $X_2$ becomes another codeword $X_4$, which is *not detectable*.

The ability of a code to detect and correct errors is determined by the minimum separation, or *Hamming distance,* between the words of a *code space,* which is the minimum number of bit positions by which two words from the code can differ. The Hamming distance of a code is the minimum Hamming distance between the two members of all pairs of codewords. For example, for two codewords $x = (1011)$ and $y = (0110)$, the Hamming distance is $d(x, y) = 3$.

Using the notion of Hamming distance, it can be shown that, to detect all error patterns of a Hamming distance $\leq d$, the code distance must be $\geq d + 1$; for example, a code with a distance of 2 can detect patterns with a distance of 1 (i.e. single-bit errors). To correct all error patterns with a Hamming distance of $\leq c$, the code distance must be $\geq 2c + 1$. To detect all patterns with a Hamming distance of $d$ and to correct all patterns with a Hamming distance of $c$, the code distance must be $\geq 2c + d + 1$. (Note that $d$ corresponds to the number of additional bit errors that can be detected beyond the correction capability of the code.) For example, code with a distance of 3 can detect and correct all single-bit errors (i.e. $c = 1$ and $d = 0$). A code with a distance of 4 can detect all triple-bit errors ($c = 0$ and $d = 3$) or can detect all double-bit errors and correct all single-bit errors ($c = 1$ and $d = 1$).

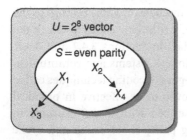

**Figure 3.4** Logic of error masking/detecting code.

### 3.4.4 Parity

One of the simplest error-detecting codes is the parity code, with which, given an $n$-bit word, one attaches an extra bit to convert it to an even or odd parity word. A simple decoding circuit using a set of XOR gates will detect any single-bit error in the parity-coded word. The single-bit parity code has a minimum Hamming distance of 2. Parity codes have been used for many years in computers to check errors in busses, memory, and registers.

Table 3.1 compares parity codes for memory. In a computer system, memory can be organized to distribute a single memory word across different memory units, also called *banks*. A bank is a physical memory module or a chip. It is assumed that memory is constructed from individual chips, where each chip contains several bits of data. Parity can be applied to a memory word across memory banks or to the data within a memory bank. Five strategies for calculating parity

**Table 3.1** Comparison of parity codes.

| Parity code | Advantages | Disadvantages |
| --- | --- | --- |
| Bit-per-word: one parity bit per data word | Detects all single-bit errors | Certain errors undetected, e.g. a word, including parity bit becomes all 1s, due to a failure of a bus or a set of data buffers |
| Bit-per-byte: each data portion (e.g. a byte) is protected by a separate parity bit; the parity of one group should be even and the parity of the other group should be odd | Detects all-1s and all-0s conditions | Ineffective for multiple errors, e.g. the whole-chip failure |
| Bit-per-multiple chips: one bit from each chip is associated with a single parity bit | Detects failure of entire chip | Cannot locate failure of complete chip |
| Bit-per-chip: each parity bit is associated with one chip of the memory | Detects single-bit errors and identifies chip with erroneous bit | Susceptible to whole-chip failure, i.e. a single-chip error can result in multiple bits to be corrupted and this may go undetected |
| Interlaced: similar to the bit-per-multiple chips; must ensure that no two adjacent bits are from the same parity group | Detects errors in adjacent bits | Parity groups are not based on physical organization of the memory |

are considered: (i) bit-per-word parity, (ii) bit-per-byte, (iii) bit-per-multiple-chips, (iv) bit-per-chip, and (v) interlaced parity.

In high-speed memories, single-bit error-correcting and double-bit error-detecting (SEC-DED) codes are the most commonly used. The data, before being written to the memory, are passed to a parity generator. The generated parity bit(s) are then stored in the memory together with the data. On a read operation, the data bits are passed into the parity checker, which regenerates the parity bit(s) and compares them with the parity bit(s) that were stored in the memory when the original data were written to the memory. The following description provides more details on Hamming codes.

In Hamming single-error correction code, $c$ parity bits are added to a $k$-bit data word, forming a codeword of $k+c$ bits. The following expression can be used to determine the number of check (parity) bits needed to protect $k$ bits of information: $2^c \geq c+k+1$.

Consider a data word of four information bits ($d_3$, $d_2$, $d_1$, $d_0$). According to the above expression, three parity bits ($p_3$, $p_2$, $p_1$) are needed to protect the four bits of data. To illustrate how the parity (check) bits are generated and checked, assume that the bits in the codeword are numbered from 1 to $k+c$. Positions numbered as a power of two are reserved for the parity bits. The grouping of bits for parity generation and checking is based on a list of the binary numbers from 0 to ($2^k - 1$), as illustrated in Figure 3.5.

The first group is formed by the data bits in the positions corresponding to the 1-bits in the least significant bit of the binary count sequence (i.e. bits 1, 3, 5, and 7). The second group is formed by the data bits in the positions corresponding to the 1-bits in the second significant bit of the binary count sequence (i.e. bits 2, 3, 6, and 7), and so on. Note that each group of bits starts with the number that is a power of 2. Those numbers are also the position numbers (in codewords) for the

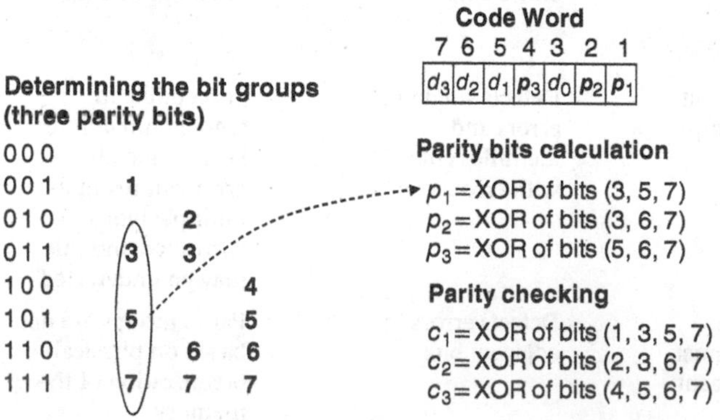

**Code Word**

| 7 | 6 | 5 | 4 | 3 | 2 | 1 |
|---|---|---|---|---|---|---|
| $d_3$ | $d_2$ | $d_1$ | $p_3$ | $d_0$ | $p_2$ | $p_1$ |

**Determining the bit groups
(three parity bits)**

```
0 0 0
0 0 1     1
0 1 0         2
0 1 1     3   3
1 0 0             4
1 0 1     5       5
1 1 0         6   6
1 1 1     7   7   7
```

**Parity bits calculation**

$p_1 =$ XOR of bits (3, 5, 7)
$p_2 =$ XOR of bits (3, 6, 7)
$p_3 =$ XOR of bits (5, 6, 7)

**Parity checking**

$c_1 =$ XOR of bits (1, 3, 5, 7)
$c_2 =$ XOR of bits (2, 3, 6, 7)
$c_3 =$ XOR of bits (4, 5, 6, 7)

**Figure 3.5** Determining parity/check bits for Hamming code.

parity bits. The individual parity bits are calculated by XOR operations on the data bits specified by a given group. For parity checking, the XOR operations also include the parity bit itself. As a result, the original data are encoded via generation of a set of parity bits $(p_3 p_2 p_1)$. To check correctness, the encoding process is repeated, and a set of check bits $(c_3 c_2 c_1)$ is generated. The binary word represented by the check bits $c_3 c_2 c_1$ forms a *syndrome*, which points directly to the position of the erroneous bit.

The Hamming code discussed above can only detect and correct single-bit errors. Through the addition of an extra parity bit, the Hamming code can be used to correct single-bit errors and to detect double errors. In the example of a data word consisting of four information bits, the additional parity bit, $p_0$, can be calculated as parity (XOR) over the first seven bits of the codeword. For parity checking, the additional check bit, $c_0$, is calculated over all eight bits of the codeword. Figure 3.6 illustrates the four kinds of single-error correction (SEC) and double-error detection (DED) Hamming code. In general, one can extend any code that has an odd Hamming distance by adding a parity bit to form a code with a Hamming distance that is greater by one, and thus even.

### 3.4.5 Cyclic Redundancy Checks

*Cyclic redundancy checks* (CRCs) are used to detect errors in communication channels, tapes, and disks. Cyclic codes are parity check codes with the additional property that the cyclic shift of a codeword is also a codeword. The wide use of CRCs is due mainly to the following three factors. (i) CRC calculators are simple to implement; the needed hardware includes linear feedback shift registers and XOR gates. In particular, CRCs have the advantage that the data can be streamed through the CRC calculator in both directions (send and receive) and, when all the data have passed, depending on the direction, the CRC check bits or error detection syndromes are generated. (ii) CRC has the ability to detect single-bit errors, multiple adjacent bit errors affecting fewer than $(n - k)$ bits (for an $(n, k)$ code), all odd-bit

| $c_3$ | $c_2$ | $c_1$ | $c_0$ | |
|-------|-------|-------|-------|---|
| 0 | 0 | 0 | 0 | No errors |
| $x_3$ | $x_2$ | $x_1$ | 1 | Single error (in a position $x_3 x_2 x_1$) is detected and can be corrected |
| $y_3$ | $y_2$ | $y_1$ | 0 | Double error is detected but cannot be corrected |
| 0 | 0 | 0 | 1 | Error in parity bit $p_0$ |

**Figure 3.6** Error detection and correction using SEC-DED code.

errors (with proper choice of the generator polynomial), and burst transient errors (which are typical of communication applications). (iii) CRC codes and implementations are independent of message length, with the caveat that if we place a limit on the message length, CRC can detect any two-bit error.

The basic idea in cyclic codes is to append a checksum to the end of the data frame in such a way that the polynomial represented by the resulting frame is divisible by the generator polynomial $G(x)$ upon which the sender and receiver have agreed. When the receiver gets the checksummed frame, it divides it by $G(x)$; if the remainder is not zero, there has been a transmission error. Hence, the best generator polynomials are those less likely to divide evenly into a frame that contains errors. CRCs are distinguished by the generator polynomials they use. Using the above relation between the codewords of the cyclic code, it can be concluded that if a polynomial g(x) of degree $n - k$ divides $(x^n - 1)$, then g(x) generates a cyclic code and can be used as a generator polynomial.

We present a proof that there is a unique monic[2] polynomial, $g(x) = x^{r-1} + g_{r-2} x^{r-2} + \ldots + g_1 x + g_0$ of *minimum degree* in a cyclic code in which $g_0 \neq 0$. g(x) is the generator polynomial for the cyclic code.

*Proof.* By contradiction.

A) To prove g(x) is unique.

Let us suppose that g(x) is not unique. Then, there exists another monic polynomial $g'(x) = x^{r-1} + g'_{r-2} x^{r-2} + \ldots + g'_1 x + g'_0$ of the same degree, $(r - 1)$. Since g(x) and $g'(x)$ belong to the cyclic code, $g'(x) - g(x)$ must also belong to the cyclic code. Therefore, $g''(x) = g'(x) - g(x) = (g'_{r-2} - g_{r-2}) x^{r-2} + (g'_{r-3} - g_{r-3}) x^{r-3} + \ldots + (g'_1 - g_1) x + (g'_0 - g_0)$ is also a code polynomial. Since the degree of $g''(x) < (r-1)$, this contradicts the initial assumption that g(x) is the polynomial of *minimum degree* in the code. Therefore, $g''(x) = 0$, which means $g'(x) = g(x)$.

B) To prove $g_0 \neq 0$.

Let us suppose that $g_0 = 0$. Then, $g(x) = x(x^{r-2} + g_{r-2} x^{r-3} + \ldots + g_1)$. Then the $(n-1)$th cyclic shift of g(x) gives another code polynomial $x^{n-1} g(x) \bmod(x^n - 1)$. That is nothing but $x^n(x^{r-2} + g_{r-2} x^{r-3} + \ldots + g_1) \bmod(x^n - 1)$. Therefore, $g'''(x) = x^{r-2} + g_{r-2} x^{r-3} + \ldots + g_1$ is also a code polynomial. Since the degree of $g'''(x)$ is less than the degree of g(x), this contradicts the initial assumption that g(x) is the polynomial of *minimum degree* in the code. Therefore, $g_0 \neq 0$.

---

2 A polynomial $x^n + c_{n-1} x^{n-1} + c_{n-2} x^{n-2} + \ldots + c_1 x + c_0$, where the coefficient of the highest-order term is 1.

Consider a generator polynomial $g(x) = x^3 + x + 1$ and the message 10011010 or $d(x) = x^7 + x^4 + x^3 + x$. Then the codeword

$$\begin{aligned}
c(x) &= g(x)d(x) \\
&= \left(x^7 + x^4 + x^3 + x\right)\left(x^3 + x + 1\right) \\
&= x^{10} + x^8 + x^6 + x^5 + x^4 + x^3 + x^2 + x.
\end{aligned}$$

Hence, the codeword is 10101111110.

The multiplication of the polynomials modulo-2 is shown below:

$$
\begin{array}{r}
10011010 \quad x^7 + x^4 + x^3 + x \\
\times \quad 1011 \quad x^3 + x + 1 \\
\hline
10011010 \\
100110100 \\
0000000000 \\
10011010000 \\
\hline
10101111110 \quad x^{10} + x^8 + x^6 + x^5 + x^4 + x^3 + x^2 + x
\end{array}
$$

*A Practical Use of CRC in Communication Protocols.* CRC is widely used in network communication protocols, including the well-known Ethernet protocol. Consider a host *A* on an Ethernet network that wishes to send 10 000 bytes to another host *B* on the same Ethernet network. The Ethernet protocol specification allows each frame to have 1500 bytes of data. Therefore, the application data (in this case, 10 000 bytes) are broken into chunks of at most 1500 bytes.[3] In our example, there would be seven frames, of which the first six contain 1500 bytes each, while the seventh contains the last 1000 bytes of the application data. The format of each frame is shown in Figure 3.7 below. The CRC field (with shading) is calculated on the body field that contains the data payload for that frame. The receiving end checks the CRC and rejects the frame upon detecting an error.

*Circuit to Generate Cyclic Code.* Cyclic codes require less hardware than parity check codes do. Parity check codes require complex encoding and decoding circuitry involving arrays of EX-OR gates, AND gates, and so on. Cyclic codes require

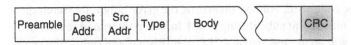

| Preamble | Dest Addr | Src Addr | Type | Body | | CRC |
|----------|-----------|----------|------|------|--|-----|

**Figure 3.7** Ethernet frame format.

---

3 Note that the Ethernet specification also requires a minimum data payload length of 46 bytes, even if it means that the data have to be padded with additional zeros.

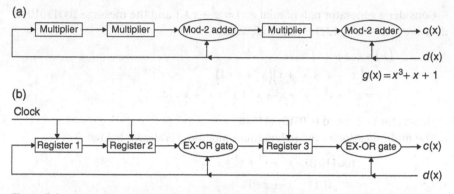

**Figure 3.8** Example representations of circuits to generate cyclic code. (a) The circuit representation using multipliers and modulo-2 adders. (b) The circuit representation using storage elements (registers) and EX-OR gates. *Source:* Adapted from Johnson et al. [8].

linear feedback shift registers (LFSRs) that involve a simple combination of registers and EX-OR gates. The circuit for generating the cyclic code for the generating polynomial $g(x) = x^3 + x + 1$ is shown in the examples (a) and (b) in Figure 3.8.

In Figure 3.8a the blocks labelled (multipliers) represent multipliers and the blocks labelled (modulo-2 adders) represent modulo-2 adders. One could represent the same circuit in another way (see Figure 3.8b) by replacing the multipliers with storage elements (registers) and the modulo-2 adders with EX-OR gates.

The initial state of the registers (*Reg1*, *Reg2*, *Reg3*) is 0. The bits of the data word are shifted inward, going from the least significant bit to the most significant bit. When the LFSR is clocked $m + k$ times, where $m$ is the degree of $d(x)$ and $k$ is the degree of $g(x)$, the bits are shifted out at $c(x)$ from the codeword. (The least significant bit is shifted out first.)

The property of cyclic code is often expressed as $(n, k)$, where $n$ is the total length of each cyclic codeword and $k$ is the length of the redundancy code. The characteristics of a cyclic code depend on $n$ and $k$, and on the code's generating polynomial. All generating polynomials have a common factor $(X + 1)$ that enables the resultant cyclic code to detect all odd-bit errors. The error polynomial, $E(X)$, is the symmetric difference between the received message codeword and the correct message codeword. For odd-bit errors, the error polynomial contains an odd number of terms, and substituting $X = 1$ in this polynomial results in a sum of 1. An error will go undetected by a CRC algorithm if and only if the error polynomial is divisible by the CRC polynomial. Since $(X + 1) = 0$ for $X = 1$ and $(X + 1)$ is a factor of the generator polynomial, the generator polynomial also evaluates to 0 for this value of $X$. Therefore, since $E(X)$ is not divisible by $G(X)$, the odd-bit error is detected.

IBM SDLC (Synchronous Data Link Control) is a transmission protocol that employs CRC-16, which has 16 bits of redundancy code with a $G(X) = X^{16} + X^{15} + X^2 + 1$ generating polynomial. Large transmission systems, such as Ethernet and Token Ring, use a 32-bit CRC for data protection. Other CRCs widely used in link-level protocols include CRC-8, CRC-10, and CRC-12. The authors of [53] discuss their corresponding generator polynomials.

One of the problems with cyclic code is that we cannot directly specify the error bit position during the decoding process. If the nonzero remainder does not contain enough data to determine the error bit position, the receiver cannot correct the error and has to request that the sender retransmit. That process requires a large buffer for both the sender and receiver in order (i) to store all the transmitted data to be retransmitted and (ii) to reconstruct the correct receiving order [54]. The retransmission procedure is time-consuming, but if the error rate is not too high, it is efficient. One approach to realizing error correction is to use lookup tables [55]. Lookup tables contain all possible patterns of nonzero remainders and the position of the corrupt bit in the received data. They can be implemented quickly but require a huge amount of data storage. In some applications, the use of a lookup table is impractical because of its cost and overhead.

### 3.4.6 Checksums

*Checksums* are commonly used in communication applications. The idea is to add up all the words to be transmitted and then transmit the sum (called the *checksum*) along with the data. At the receiving end, the checksum is recalculated, and the result is compared with the original. If any of the data, including the checksum, were corrupted during transmission, the comparison results in a mismatch. The method will not protect against errors that cause data words to arrive out of order. Checksum codes differ in the way the checksum is generated.

Performing the modulo-2 addition of the words to be transmitted and ignoring any overflow generates the *single-precision checksum*. Its weakness is that errors that cause the original and recalculated checksums to differ only in the ignored bit position are not detected, as illustrated in Figure 3.9. A most significant data line stuck at 1 is an example of an error that exposes this flaw.

In the *Honeywell checksum*, adjacent data words are concatenated prior to computation of the checksum; thus, $K$ $n$-bit words are grouped into $K/2$ $2n$-bit words. That structure can detect a bit error that affects all words in the same bit position because it makes the two checksums differ in two locations. Nevertheless, overflow can still cause loss of carry-bit information.

Checksums have the advantage that, like CRC, they allow variable-length messages and can be calculated on streaming data. Checksums are used in the TCP/IP protocol, specifically because the more costly CRC checks are performed at the

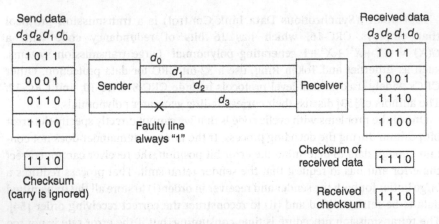

**Figure 3.9** Error scenario not detected by single-precision checksum. An error caused by a most significant data line stuck at 1 goes undetected. *Source:* Adapted from Johnson et al. [8].

lower levels. Thus, a basic sanity check, such as a checksum on the header info, provides sufficient error detection capability. The key disadvantage of checksums is their limited capability to diagnose the cause of a problem. An observed problem can be due to (i) an error in a checksum calculation, (ii) a transmission error or (iii) a corruption of the original data (before the checksum computation). In using a checksum, one cannot tell which of those occurred.

### 3.4.7 Arithmetic Codes

*Arithmetic codes* detect errors in arithmetic units like adders and multipliers. Arithmetic codes are useful in checking arithmetic operations, where parity codes would not be preserved under addition and subtraction. *Separate* arithmetic codes separate check symbols from data symbols. *Nonseparate* arithmetic codes combine check and data symbols. Some types of arithmetic codes are *AN* codes, *residue* codes, and *bi-residue* codes.

#### 3.4.7.1 AN Codes

In AN arithmetic codes, data $X$ are multiplied by check base $A$ to form $A.X$. Addition of codewords is performed modulo $M$, where $A$ divides $M$. That yields $A(X +_m Y) = AX +_m AY$. Dividing the result by $A$ checks the operation's correctness. If the result is zero, there is no error; otherwise, there is an error. For more information about coding in reliable computer systems, the reader is referred to [56, 57].

#### 3.4.7.2 Berger Codes

Berger codes are separate codes that detect all unidirectional errors. For a given binary data word, $(a_n a_{n-1} \ldots a_1)$, the number of zeros in the word are appended to the word as check bits. Thus, each Berger code uses $\lfloor \log_2(n+1) \rfloor$ check bits for a data word with $n$ (binary) symbols. For example, for the 16-symbol data word 1010010110100111, the number of zeros is 7. Therefore, the check bits 0111 are appended to the data word and transmitted. Let $NZ_d$ and $V_c$ be the number of zeros in the data part and the value of the check bits. In an error-free scenario, $NZ_d = V_c$. If that relationship is not satisfied in the received word, then an error is detected. Table 3.2 presents the different scenarios of unidirectional errors, their effect on $NZ_d$ and $V_c$, and how Berger codes can detect these unidirectional errors.

### 3.4.8 Residue-Inverse Residue Codes

Residue codes are separate arithmetic codes of the form $(X, R)$, where $X$ is the data word and $R$ is the residue of $X$ for divisor $A$. $A$ is called the *check base*. In short:

$$R = N \bmod A$$

The codeword for the inverse residue code is $(X, (A - R))$.

Because of an interesting property of residue codes, described below, they can be used to check whether an arithmetic operation has executed correctly. Let $X_1$ and $X_2$ be two positive integers and $R_1$ and $R_2$ be their respective residues for divisor $A$. Then:

$$\left(N_1 \pm N_2\right) \bmod A = \left(R_1 \pm R_2\right) \bmod A$$

$$\left(N_1 \times N_2\right) \bmod A = \left(R_1 \times R_2\right) \bmod A$$

Therefore, arithmetic addition, subtraction, and multiplication can be checked using the above properties. In other words, these equations mean that the residue

**Table 3.2** Berger code's capabilities in detecting unidirectional errors.

| Error type in | | Effect on | | Relationship between $NZ_d$ | |
|---|---|---|---|---|---|
| Data | Check | $NZ_d$ | $V_c$ | and $V_c$ | Error detected |
| $0 \to 1$ | None | ↓ | None | $NZ_d < V_c$ | Yes |
| $1 \to 0$ | None | ↑ | None | $NZ_d > V_c$ | Yes |
| None | $0 \to 1$ | None | ↑ | $NZ_d < V_c$ | Yes |
| None | $1 \to 0$ | None | ↓ | $NZ_d > V_c$ | Yes |
| $0 \to 1$ | $0 \to 1$ | ↓ | ↑ | $NZ_d < V_c$ | Yes |
| $1 \to 0$ | $1 \to 0$ | ↑ | ↓ | $NZ_d > V_c$ | Yes |

of the result of an operation on two positive integers is equal to the residue (modulo $A$) of the result of the same operation on the residues of the two integers.

### 3.4.9 Reed-Solomon Codes

*Reed-Solomon codes* are block-based error-correcting codes that have been applied widely in digital communications and storage. The Reed-Solomon encoder takes a block of digital data and appends extra redundant or check bits. Thus, it is a separated or systematic code. The decoder processes each block and, if there are errors, attempts to correct the errors and recover the original data. The number and type of errors that can be corrected depend on the specific characteristics of the Reed-Solomon code.

A Reed-Solomon code is denoted by RS($n$, $k$) with $s$-bit symbols, where $k$ is the number of data symbols of $s$ bits each, and $n$ is the number of symbols in the final codeword after the check symbols are appended. Thus, there are $n - k$ check symbols of $s$ bits each. In terms of communication latency, Reed-Solomon codes have the important advantage that as long as any $k$ symbols of the $n$-symbol codeword are received, it is possible to reproduce the $k$ symbols of the original data word. A Reed-Solomon decoder can correct errors in up to $t$ symbols in a codeword, where $2t = n - k$. Figure 3.10 shows the layout of a Reed-Solomon codeword.

As an example, RS(255,223) with 8-bit symbols is a commonly used Reed-Solomon code. In this case, each codeword contains 255 codeword bytes, of which 223 bytes are data and 32 bytes are check bytes. For this example code:

$$n = 255, k = 223, s = 8$$

$$2t = 32, t = 16$$

The decoder can automatically correct any 16-symbol errors in the codeword: i.e. errors in up to 16 bytes anywhere in the codeword.

For a given symbol size $s$, the maximum codeword length ($n$) for a Reed-Solomon code is given by $n = 2^s - 1$. For example, the maximum length of a code with 8-bit symbols ($s = 8$) is 255 bytes.

Reed-Solomon codes are particularly well suited to correcting burst errors, in which a series of bits in a codeword are received in error. That is a common, realistic error model in communication systems. A symbol error occurs when one or

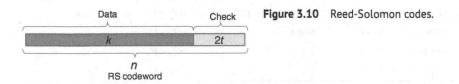

**Figure 3.10** Reed-Solomon codes.

all of the bits of a symbol are corrupted. For example, the RS(255, 223) code can correct 16-bit errors or $16 \times 8$ bit errors occurring in 16 symbols.

An *erasure* is a special class of error in which the location of the symbol that is in error is known (usually because data were lost in transmission or a disk block is unreadable). Reed-Solomon codes can detect both errors and erasures. It can readily be seen that the same coding technique can detect at least as many (or more) erasures than the number of errors that it can detect, since in the case of erasures, some additional information about the error occurrence is available to the decoder. An RS($n$, $k$) code can detect up to $2t$ erasures. Upon decoding of a codeword, one of the following three possibilities can occur:

1) If $2s + r < 2t$ ($s$ errors, $r$ erasures), then the original codeword can always be recovered.
2) The decoder discovers that it cannot recover the original codeword and indicates this fact.
3) The decoder mis-decodes and recovers an incorrect codeword without any indication.

The probability of each of those possibilities depends on the particular Reed-Solomon code and on the number and distribution of errors and erasures.

The computation of Reed-Solomon codes is based on a mathematical concept known as *Galois fields* or *finite fields*. The codeword is generated using a special polynomial referred to as the *generator polynomial*. The generator polynomial is related to all the codewords in that each codeword is exactly divisible by that polynomial. The general form of an RS generator polynomial is

$$g(x) = \left(x - \alpha^i\right)\left(x - \alpha^{i+1}\right)\ldots\left(x - \alpha^{i+2t}\right)$$

The codeword is generated by:

$c(x) = g(x). i(x)$, where $c(x)$ is a valid codeword, $g(x)$ is the generator polynomial, $i(x)$ is the block of information being encoded, and $\alpha$ is called the *primitive element* of the field. The Reed-Solomon encoder and decoder can be implemented either in software or in special-purpose hardware.

### 3.4.10 Communication Codes and Protocols

The medium for data exchange in networked systems – ranging from local and smaller distributed computing systems to the geographically widespread and gargantuan Internet – is subject to more frequent errors than the part of the system that performs the computation. Yet data integrity must be maintained during communication in spite of the errors. As we have discussed, the mechanisms for encoding a data packet before transmitting it over the error-prone channel and decoding it after receiving it can aid in achieving reliable communication in spite of the errors in the communication channel.

The block codes, cyclic codes, and convolutional codes discussed above were developed toward that end and are an area of continuing research. Those coding techniques enable detection of a class of errors and the successful correction of a subset of them. Protocols for requesting retransmission of erroneous data have also been developed at higher layers in the communication stack.

Examples of block codes are parity, checksum, and Hamming codes. Cyclic codes include CRC techniques, Reed-Solomon codes, and BCH codes. Multiple mechanisms for decoding, such as sequential decoding, maximum-likelihood decoding, and the Stack algorithm have been proposed for convolutional codes. In the previous sections, we looked at block codes and cyclic codes in some detail. This section describes convolutional codes and Automated Repeat reQuest (ARQ) protocols, which are now widely used in communication systems.

### 3.4.10.1 Convolutional Codes

Research on block codes, discussed briefly in Section 3.4.4, constitutes most of the studies related to coding schemes. For an $(n, k)$ block code, $n - k$ check symbols are added for every block of $k$ symbols to detect and correct a certain class of errors (single- or multiple-bit errors, or single- or multiple-burst errors). The $n - k$ check symbols depend entirely on the $k$ symbols of the information being transmitted. Thus, block codes can be said to be memoryless. In other words, for block codes, the check symbols for the current block of information do not depend on any previous blocks of information. An encoder for block codes can be implemented using a combinational circuit with $k$ inputs and $n$ outputs.

Convolutional codes, on the other hand, introduce the concept of memory into the coding functions. The codeword to be transmitted at any time $t$ depends on the information encoded during a fixed number of previous time slots. For an $(n, k, m)$ convolutional code (also referred to as an $(n, k)$ convolutional code of memory order $m$), at each time instant, $k$ information symbols are provided as input to the encoder. The encoder outputs the codeword with $n$ symbols. The $n$ symbols depend on the information symbols produced during the $m$ previous time instances aside from the current time instance. In short, the $n$ output symbols at any time depend on $m \times k$ additional information symbols. The encoder for a convolutional code can be constructed by using a sequential circuit with $m$ memory symbols and having $k$ inputs and $n$ outputs.

Convolutional codes are seen to require a lower complexity decoder than block codes do, with lower values of both $k$ and $n$. In spite of the lower values of $k$ and $n$, the probability of an error in decoding can be reduced by choosing an appropriate value of $m$. Of course, the additional reliability is achieved at the cost of increased complexity of the decoder and a consequent degradation in decoding performance. However, it has been seen that convolutional codes can meet the specified performance requirements for many practical applications.

Elias proposed the concept of convolutional codes for the first time in 1955 as an alternative to block codes. Many decoding techniques were proposed during the 1960s that made the use of convolutional codes practical in many applications [41]. As seen in the previous sections, the decoding of block codes is primarily algebraic, meaning that there is a fixed (combinational circuit) algorithm that translates received codewords into corresponding data symbols or detects and corrects any errors in the received codewords. On the other hand, convolutional codes have mostly been decoded using probabilistic decoding.

### 3.4.10.2 Communication Protocols for Reliable Transmission

Many coding techniques have been discussed so far, for both error detection and error correction. These techniques, when used in a communication system, can detect and correct errors in the messages exchanged between two nodes, the sender and the receiver. Where the errors can be successfully corrected by the coding scheme, the receiver accepts the corrected frame. However, not all the bit and burst errors that occur in a practical communication medium can be corrected by the coding scheme. When the error can be detected but not corrected, the message (or packet or frame) that was received must be discarded, and a mechanism to retrieve the discarded messages must be in place.

To enable retrieval or retransmission of corrupted or lost messages, each message is identified with a sequence number. The successful receipt of a message is indicated by an acknowledgment of the message. Acknowledgments are used along with timeouts to request and provide retransmission of messages. The protocols for retransmission could be classified as either *stop-and-wait* or *continuous*.

*Stop-and-wait ARQ Protocol.* In this protocol, the sender sends a message and starts a timer, setting a fixed time to wait until it receives an acknowledgment from the receiver of the receipt of the message. If the acknowledgment is received, the sender sends the next message. If the timer expires before the acknowledgment is received, the sender assumes that the receiver has not received the message and retransmits it. A 1-bit sequence number would suffice for this category of ARQ protocols. The sequence number is necessary to distinguish between a duplicate receipt of a message and receipt of a lost message. For example, consider this scenario:

1) The sender $A$ sends a message with sequence number 0.
2) The receiver $B$ receives the message and acknowledges receiving the message along with its sequence number.
3) If the acknowledgment is lost in transit, $A$ would time out waiting for the acknowledgment and retransmit the message with sequence number 0.

4) Upon receiving the second message with sequence number 0, *B* discards the message, understanding it to be a duplicate transmission.
5) However, if sequence numbers are not being used, then *B* accepts the second copy of the message as the subsequent message and adds it to the application data stream. This is undesirable.

*Continuous ARQ Protocol.* In a continuous-transmission ARQ protocol, the sender does not wait for an acknowledgment from the receiver for every message that it sends. Rather, it continues transmitting messages while storing the unacknowledged messages in a buffer. A reasonably large sequence number is used to avoid repetitions due to wraparound of the number. The receiver also is not bound to acknowledge every message separately. When the receiver acknowledges the receipt of a message with a certain sequence number, it acknowledges every message with a sequence number below that number. The acknowledged messages are cleared from the buffer, and the window of unacknowledged messages is shifted to start from the first unacknowledged message. This is called a *sliding window* ARQ protocol.

Within a sliding window ARQ protocol, there can be two flavors of repeat requests: (i) *go-back-n*, wherein, upon receiving a request from the receiver for retransmission of a message with a particular sequence number, the sender sends all unacknowledged messages up to and including the requested message, and (ii) *selective repeat*, wherein the receiver requests the retransmission of a message with a specific sequence number, indicating that it has received all the previous messages correctly. The selective repeat algorithm is more efficient than the go-back-n protocol if frequent errors are detected by the receiver or if the transmission time from the sender to the receiver is high, as those situations require a higher upper bound on the sequence number. As intuition would suggest, the servicing of retransmission requests on the sender side and the detection of duplicates on the receiver side in the go-back-*n* protocol are simpler than those in the selective repeat protocol.

### 3.4.11 Two-Level Integrated Interleaved Codes

Cyclic redundancy codes and Reed-Solomon codes are effective in detecting a single burst of errors but are ineffective in the event of multiple bursts of errors. Patel from IBM proposed a coding architecture that uses a two-level coding scheme to enable correction of multiple bursts of errors in each record in a typical disk storage application [52].

The coding technique used in the first level is designed to provide reliability guarantees that may suffice for most applications in their routine disk accesses. The second-level coding, being more expensive, is called upon only if the first-level coding fails to correct an error pattern. In particular, because of manufacturing defects, it is possible that one out of many devices could be *weaker*, i.e. have a higher defect density than a normal disk. In such a scenario, the normal devices could use the low-cost, first-level coding technique, while the weaker device could also use the second-level coding scheme, provided performance requirements are met.

In the case of Reed-Solomon and CRC techniques, coding is performed at the granularity of a *block*. A block consists of data bytes and check bytes. The basic two-level architecture extends that idea of blocks and consists of subblocks within a block. The first-level coding scheme is applied at the granularity of a subblock. Multiple subblocks constitute a block, and the second-level code is calculated on the block. Figure 3.11 shows the data format for one particular implementation of the level scheme in the IBM 3380 J and 3380 K file systems. As shown in the figure, a subblock is made up of two interleaved codewords, each with 48 data bytes ($B_{49}$ to $B_2$) and 3 check bytes ($B_1$, $B_0$, and $C_3$). In addition, for error detection at the second level, one check byte ($C_0$) is added for each set of interleaved code-words in the subblocks of each block. The check bytes $B_1$, $B_0$, and $C_3$ are calculated using an extended Reed-Solomon code. The check byte $C_0$ at the second level is a modulo-2 sum of all the bytes in the subblocks, except the $C_3$ bytes, within a block. In this text, we omit the details of the specific coding schemes used at the first and second levels. We refer readers to [52] for detailed descriptions of the coding functions and the hardware implementation of the encoding and decoding functions.

In the case of many errors, which the codes at both levels may not be able to handle, it is possible that corrections made to the data word will transform it into a valid but incorrect codeword. To guard against any such mistaken corrections,

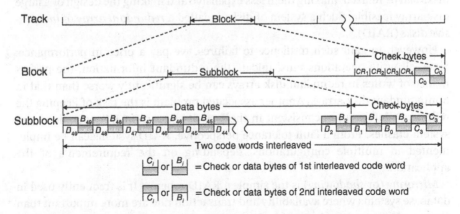

**Figure 3.11** IBM two-level interleaved coding scheme [52]. *Source:* Courtesy of International Business Machines Corporation, © (1989) International Business Machines Corporation.

four more bytes, $CR_{1-4}$, are appended at the end of each block to implement a data integrity check on the data bytes.

## 3.4.12 RAID: Redundant Array of Inexpensive Disks

To bridge the gap between the speeds of microprocessors and secondary storage systems, disk arrays that organize multiple, independent disks into a large, high-performance logical disk have been proposed [58]. Disk arrays stripe data across multiple disks so that they can be accessed in parallel. That enables higher data transfer rates on large data accesses and higher I/O rates on small data accesses [59, 60]. Such a distribution of data also provides a uniform balance of the load across all the disks. From the standpoint of temperature-induced failures, which is important because it eliminates hot spots that otherwise saturate a small number of disks while the majority of disks sit idle.

As we have learned from comparing the TMR system to a simplex system, as the number of components in a system increases, the probability that one of them will fail increases. Large disk arrays, therefore, are highly vulnerable to disk failures. The probability of the failure of a disk array with five disks is five times higher than that of a single-disk array. If a single disk has an MTTF of 200000 hours (approximately 23 years), the disk array with 100 disks has an MTTF of only 2000 hours, or approximately three months. One trivial solution is to employ redundancy in the form of error-correcting codes to tolerate disk failures whenever they occur. That allows a redundant disk array to avoid losing data for much longer than is possible on an unprotected single disk. Also, since the array of disks provides tolerance to failures, the fault tolerance requirements for the individual disks can be relaxed, making them less expensive and making the design of a large disk array feasible. Such a system of disks is called a *redundant array of inexpensive disks* (RAID).

However, to gain such resilience to failures, we pay a price in performance. Since all write operations must update the redundant information, the performance of writes in redundant disk arrays can be significantly worse than that in nonredundant disk arrays. Another associated problem is the task of keeping the redundant information consistent in the face of concurrent I/O operations and system crashes. From a fault tolerance perspective, RAID systems can be implemented in multiple configurations, depending on the requirements of the application.

*Mirroring* (or *shadowing*) is the simplest RAID scheme. It is frequently used in database systems where availability and transaction rate are more important than storage efficiency. It is depicted in Figure 3.12. All the data are duplicated, and a complete backup is available if a disk fails. Disks are grouped into mirror pairs, where one copy of each data block is stored on each disk in the pair. The scheme

**Figure 3.12** Mirroring RAID.

| Disk 0 | Disk 1 | Disk 2 | Disk 3 | Disk 4 | Disk 5 |
|--------|--------|--------|--------|--------|--------|
| D0 | D0 | D1 | D1 | D2 | D2 |
| D3 | D3 | D4 | D4 | D5 | D5 |
| D6 | D6 | D7 | D7 | D8 | D8 |
| D9 | D9 | D10 | D10 | D11 | D11 |

provides high availability, but the cost is a high storage overhead. The number of redundancy disks is equal to the number of data disks. The arrangement can tolerate up to $N/2$ disk failures, where $N$ is the total number of disks (redundancy + data).

Another possible scheme, called the *Hamming-coded RAID array*, is shown in Figure 3.13. With it, data are striped in bits or bytes. $N$ data disks and $G$ redundancy disks store a Hamming error-correcting code computed over the data stored in each stripe. Since $G \sim \log(N+G)$, the storage efficiency $\left(\dfrac{N}{N+G}\right)$ increases with $N$. A single redundancy disk is sufficient to detect a single disk failure, but more disks are required to identify which one has failed and to perform error correction. A disadvantage of the scheme is that only one request can be serviced at a time because each request, be it a read or a write, accesses all the disks. The bit-interleaved parity scheme also stripes data by bits or bytes. Errors are detected using parity computed over the bytes stored in multiple disks. An example illustrating that scheme is shown in Figure 3.14. Here, $dx$ is a bit or a byte, and $px - y$ is the parity computed over $dx$ to $dy$. One parity disk is needed. The configuration suffers from the drawback that only one request at a time can be serviced.

**Figure 3.13** Hamming-coded RAID.

| Disk 0 | Disk 1 | Disk 2 | Disk 3 | Disk 4 | Disk 5 |
|--------|--------|--------|--------|--------|--------|
| d0 | d1 | d2 | d3 | h0–3 | |
| d4 | d5 | d6 | d7 | h4–7 | |
| d8 | d9 | d10 | d11 | h8–11 | |
| d12 | d13 | d14 | d15 | h12–15 | |

**Figure 3.14** Bit-interleaved parity.

| Disk 0 | Disk 1 | Disk 2 | Disk 3 | Disk 4 | Disk 5 |
|--------|--------|--------|--------|--------|--------|
| d0 | d1 | d2 | d3 | d4 | p0–4 |
| d5 | d6 | d7 | d8 | d9 | p5–9 |
| d10 | d11 | d12 | d13 | d14 | p10–14 |
| d15 | d16 | d17 | d18 | d19 | p15–19 |

| Disk 0 | Disk 1 | Disk 2 | Disk 3 | Disk 4 | Disk 5 |
|--------|--------|--------|--------|--------|--------|
| D0 | D1 | D2 | D3 | P0–3 | Q0–3 |
| D6 | D7 | P4–7 | Q4–7 | D4 | D5 |
| P8–11 | Q8–11 | D8 | D9 | D10 | D11 |
| D12 | D13 | D14 | D15 | P12–15 | Q12–15 |
| D18 | D19 | P16–19 | Q16–19 | D16 | D17 |

**Figure 3.15** $P + Q$ redundancy.

$P + Q$ redundancy employs multiple redundancy schemes, including parity ($P$) and Reed-Solomon codes ($Q$), to detect and correct errors. It can tolerate up to two disk failures and requires two redundancy disks, one for parity and the other for the Reed-Solomon code. Figure 3.15 shows the implementation of that scheme, where again $Px - y$ and $Qx - y$ are the parity and Reed-Solomon codes over $Dx$ to $Dy$.

### 3.4.12.1 A Commercial RAID-Based Storage System

This section describes a hierarchical simulation approach for the dependability analysis and evaluation of a highly available, commercial, cache-based RAID storage system [61]. The architecture is complex and includes several layers of overlapping error detection and recovery mechanisms. The storage architecture shown in Figure 3.16 is designed to support a large amount of disk storage and provide high performance and high availability. The storage system supports a RAID architecture composed of a set of disk drives storing data, parity, and Reed-Solomon coding information, which is striped across the disks [58]. The architecture tolerates the failure of up to two disks. If a disk fails, the data from the failed disk are reconstructed on the fly using the valid disks. The reconstructed data are stored on a hot spare disk without interrupting service.

Data transfer between the hosts and the disks is supervised by the array controller, which is composed of a set of control units. The control units process user requests received from the channels and direct the requests to the cache subsystem. Data received from the hosts are assembled into tracks in the cache. The number of tracks corresponding to a single request is application-dependent. Data transfers between the channels and the disks are performed by the cache subsystem via reliable, high-speed control and data busses. The cache subsystem consists of (i) a cache controller organized into cache controller interfaces to the channels and the disks, plus cache controller interfaces (made of redundant components to ensure a high level of availability) to the cache memory and (ii) cache volatile and nonvolatile memory. Communication between the cache controller interfaces and the cache memory is provided by redundant, multidirectional busses (denoted by "Bus 1" and "Bus 2" in Table 3.3). The cache volatile memory is

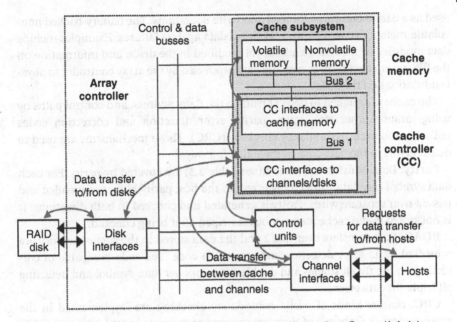

**Figure 3.16** Array controller architecture, interfaces, and data flow. *Source:* Kaâniche et al. [61]. © IEEE.

**Table 3.3** Error detection efficiency with respect to location and number of errors.

| Error location | Error detection mechanism | | | |
| --- | --- | --- | --- | --- |
| | FE-CRC | Parity | EDAC | PS-CRC |
| Transfer: channel to cache | X | | | |
| CCI to channels/disks | X | | | |
| Bus 1 | X | X | | |
| CCI to cache memory | X | | | |
| Bus 2 | X | | X | |
| Cache memory | X | | X | |
| Transfer: cache to disk | X | | | X |
| Disks | | | | X |
| Error detection condition | <4 ds with errors | Odd no. of errors per ds | <4-bit errors per ds | <4 ds with errors |

CCI, cache controller interface; ds, data symbol

used as a data staging area for read and write operations. The battery-backed non-volatile memory is used to protect critical data against failures. Examples include data modified in the cache and not yet modified in the disks, and information on the file system necessary to map the data processed by the array controller to physical locations on the disks.

The cache is designed to detect errors in the data, address, and control paths by using, among other techniques, parity, error detection and correction codes (EDAC), and cyclic redundancy checking (CRC). Those mechanisms are used to detect errors in the data path in the following ways.

**Parity.** Data transfers over Bus 1 (see Table 3.3) are covered by parity. For each data symbol (i.e. data word) transferred on the bus, parity bits are appended and passed over separate wires. Parity is generated and checked in both directions. It is not stored in the cache memory but is striped after being checked.

**EDAC.** Data transfers over Bus 2 and the data stored in the cache memory are protected by an error detection and correction code. The code is capable of correcting on the fly all single- and double-bit errors per data symbol and detecting all triple-bit data errors.

**CRC.** Several kinds of cyclic redundancy checking are implemented in the array controller. Only two of them are checked or generated within the cache subsystem: the frontend CRC (FE-CRC) and the physical sector CRC (PS-CRC). FE-CRC is appended by the channel interfaces to the data sent to the cache during a write request. It is checked by the cache controller. If the FE-CRC is valid, it is stored with the data in the cache memory. Otherwise, the operation is interrupted, and a CRC error is recorded. FE-CRC is checked again when a read request is received from the channels. Therefore, extra detection is provided to support recovery from errors that may have occurred while the data were in the cache or in the disks and escaped the error detection mechanisms implemented in the cache subsystem and disk array. PS-CRC is appended by the cache controller to each data block to be stored in a disk sector. The PS-CRC is stored with the data until a read from disk operation occurs. At that time, it is checked and striped before the data are stored in the cache. The same algorithm is implemented to compute FE-CRC and PS-CRC. The algorithm guarantees detection of three or fewer erroneous data symbols in a data record.

Table 3.3 summarizes the error detection conditions for each mechanism presented above, taking into account the component in which the errors occur and the number of uncorrected errors that occur between the computation of the code and the time when it is checked. An "X" means that errors affecting the corresponding component can be detected by the mechanism indicated in the column. It is noteworthy that the number of check bits and the size of the data symbol ($ds$) mentioned in the error detection condition are different for parity, EDAC, and CRC.

## 3.5 Capability and Consistency Checking

### 3.5.1 Capability Checking

*Capability checking* limits access to objects (e.g. memory segments or I/O devices) to those users (processors or processes) that have the proper authorization. Examples include checking of address validity by virtual address management (MMU), checking of permission versus activity (if the permission is not valid, an error trap is executed, usually in hardware), and password checking (usually executed in software). Capability checking can be implemented (i) as a hardware mechanism, e.g. the hardware-supported error traps mentioned above or (ii) as a part of the operating system, e.g. by a firewall. For example, the firewall in Linux is an integral part of the operating system and enables automated checking of an incoming packet's attributes against a predefined set of rules. If any of the specified rules is violated, the packet is rejected, and access to the system is denied.

### 3.5.2 Consistency Checking

*Consistency checking* determines whether the state of various objects in the system or of results from computations is reasonable based on their intended usage and purpose according to the system design and specification. Examples of consistency checking include *range checking*, *address checking*, and *opcode checking*. Address checking verifies that the address to be accessed exists, and opcode checking verifies the validity of an opcode of the instruction to be executed. Address and opcode checking are commonly used in most computer systems. For example, executing instructions without verifying the validity of their opcodes could lead to performance of a random sequence of operations. That could have unpredictable consequences for system integrity, including a total system crash or corruption of other components (subsystems) of the overall environment due to error propagation. Underflow and overflow checking are other examples of typical range checking in computer systems.

## 3.6 Insights

This chapter presented multiple hardware and combined hardware and software approaches for enhancing the reliability of systems. On a node level, one can use watchdog monitors that plug into a computer system as a Peripheral Component Interconnect card. The watchdog periodically polls the operating system kernel to check if the operating system is continuing to schedule processes and can be configured to reboot the system if the watchdog does not receive heartbeats within a certain prespecified period. However, if the system crashes, the driver for the watchdog card will also be unavailable. To overcome that problem, two server systems, one backing up the other, have been used to design a failover mechanism with heartbeats as the method of detecting a failure of the primary server. When the primary fails, the secondary server assumes the role of the primary. To provide a failover capability to the server that is transparent to the client, we need the backup server to respond to requests to the same IP address as the primary server, and that requires IP migration. It is achieved by having the backup server take over the IP address of the primary server by means of Address Resolution Protocol spoofing. As a result, all communications between the client and the server are redirected to the backup server. In the emerging computing paradigms, such as utility and cloud computing, heartbeats can be relatively easy to deploy through the central management routines that control the allocation, configuration, and deallocation of resources for users. Surely, with the addition of heartbeat mechanisms themselves, system availability can be raised above 2 nines, but commercial-, mission-, and life-critical systems would require further fault tolerance through redundancy.

Hardware redundancy using duplication or triplication enables high fault detection coverage; however, it significantly increases costs. Use of duplication may require support of checkpointing and rollback. The state of the system that needs to be included in the checkpoint must be decided upon, and the components of the system that are stateless and stateful must be identified to arrive at the state to be checkpointed. The next question to be decided on regarding checkpointing is the period of checkpointing. It depends on the expected failure rate of the system and should be slightly larger than the failure rate, to avoid corruption of the checkpointed state itself by a failure. However, the period cannot be arbitrarily small, as checkpointing itself introduces unnecessary overhead for the application. When TMR is used in the system, it is possible to tolerate any failure in a single replica.

In both duplication and TMR, the frequency with which results are compared needs to be established. It would be ideal to synchronize replicas by checking their results after every clock cycle. However, a lock-step architecture would require control over the CPU design, which may be impractical. The nondeterminism within a processor chip (particularly that due to cache inconsistencies) and don't-care nodes cause the signals read at the external pins of the chip to be different, even though the execution, and hence the final application result, is correct. The ability to synchronize the multiple processors at every clock cycle would require a complex and expensive *phase locked loop* design for timing skew reduction among the clocks of the replicas.

An example of the lock-step processor architecture is the IBM G6 processor, in which the results of the dual instruction and execution units are compared at the completion of every instruction. The instruction unit (*I-unit*) gets the instruction as an input from the cache, decodes the instruction, and forwards the output to the execution unit. The execution unit (*E-unit*) takes the decoded instruction from its corresponding I-unit to perform fixed-point and floating-point operations. However, to achieve the lock-step behavior, designers restricted the CPU to a single-issue processor. In performance-critical logic areas, the error checking may not be completed in the same cycle and could be detected a few cycles later. That requires mechanisms to control error propagation and avoid contamination of recovery information.

Another complication is the design of the exclusion logic that isolates the faulty component, switches control to a working standby, and seamlessly integrates a failed component after it has been repaired. More expensive techniques are widely used in highly critical systems, such as TMR in the Boeing 777 and duplication in telecommunication systems, spaceborne systems, computing systems, and railway safety-based switching systems.

Hardware redundancy can be used in a cloud computing environment to provide the customer with reliability in addition to other quality-of-service guarantees.

TMR can be directly applied if multiple computing nodes/cores that might otherwise be underutilized are available. While data are replicated over multiple geographical locations (e.g. in the Amazon Cloud), the synchronization is controlled by distributed protocols.

Information redundancy is employed in the memory hierarchy starting from the register file, cache, and on-chip and off-chip memories and going up to the current storage systems for persistent data. Single-error-correction/double-error-detection (SEC/DED) codes are commonplace in most system memories of today. It has to be noted that use of error-correcting codes does not protect against any errors in the execution engine of the processor. Rather, an incorrect result produced by the execution units in the processor, when sent to memory, can be used to calculate the "correct" error correction code (for that incorrect result) and be stored in memory. In such a case, the error goes undetected and can propagate to other parts of the application execution and the system. Information redundancy and hardware redundancy are key in supporting various generations of RAID, as discussed in Section 3.4.12.

An important observation made in independent experiments is that only a small percentage of lower level faults translate to application-level errors. Measurements conducted on an avionic process and reported in [62] show that 87% of gate-level faults and 98% of component-level faults were masked and never manifested at the application level. Independent experiments discussed in [63–67] showed that almost 75–85% of low-level errors do not surface as errors in the final outcome of an application to become observable by the user. SEC codes in the main memory end up detecting and correcting many such errors that are benign to the application. DED also detects many such low-level errors, invoking the recovery method of choice (e.g. checkpoint and rollback or instruction retry) and incurring additional overhead, which may not be needed for application correctness. (The percentage of such benign errors depends on the nature of the application.) The situation calls for *application-aware checking*, an approach to the design of detection and recovery methods that focuses on the point of view of the application (the final point of an error's impact) rather than on the origin of errors.

In most cloud computing and virtualized environments, heartbeats can be easily and effectively deployed by using the hypervisor layer to monitor not only the application and a specific user's activity but also the underlying operating system. At the application level, understanding the semantics of the application can help in developing capability and consistency checks that can be executed in parallel with the application and thus reduce the impact on performance.

## References

1 Avizienis, A. and Laprie, J.C. (1986). Dependable computing: from concepts to design diversity. *Proceedings of the IEEE* 74 (5): 629–638.

2 Laprie, J.C. (ed.) (1992). *Dependability: Basic Concepts and Terminology, Dependable Computing and Fault-Tolerant Systems*, vol. 5. Vienna: Spinger-Verlag.

3 Rennels, D.A. (1984). Fault tolerant computing: concepts and examples. *IEEE Transactions on Computers* C-33 (12): 1116–1129.

4 Avižienis, A., Gilley, G.C., Mathur, F.P. et al. (1971). The STAR (self-testing and repairing) computer: an investigation of the theory and practice of fault-tolerant computer design. *IEEE Transactions on Computers* C-20 (11): 1312–1321.

5 Sklaroff, J.R. (1976). Redundancy management technique for Space Shuttle computers. *IBM Journal of Research and Development* 20 (1): 20–28.

6 Approach and Landing Test Team, National Aeronautics and Space Administration. (1977). *Space Shuttle Orbiter Approach and Landing Test Evaluation Report: Captive-Active Flight Test Summary*. National Aeronautics and Space Administration, Lyndon B. Johnson Space Center, Technical report JSC-13045 (NASA-TM-75011). https://ntrs.nasa.gov/archive/nasa/casi.ntrs.nasa.gov/19780002256.pdf (accessed 4 August 2020). (See section 6.6.)

7 Norwood, P. (1991). Overview of the NonStop-UX operating system for the Integrity S2. *Tandem Systems Review* 7 (1): 10–23. http://www.hpl.hp.com/hpjournal/tandem/vol7num1apr91.pdf (accessed June 2021).

8 Johnson, B.W. (1989). *Design and Analysis of Fault-Tolerant Digital Systems*. Boston, MA, USA: Addison-Wesley.

9 Trivedi, K.S. (2002). *Probability and Statistics with Reliability, Queuing, and Computer Science Applications*, 2e. New York, NY, USA: Wiley.

**10** Lala, J.H. (1983). Fault detection, isolation and reconfiguration in FTMP: methods and experimental results. *Proceedings of the 5th AIAA/IEEE Digital Avionics Systems Conference*, Seattle, WA, USA (31 October–3 November 1983), 21.3.1–21.3.9. IEEE.

**11** Wensley, J.H. (1972). SIFT: Software Implemented Fault Tolerance. *Proceedings of the AFIPS Fall Joint Computer Conference* (5–7 December 1972), Part I, 243–253. Association for Computing Machinery (ACM).

**12** Cutts, R.W., Jr., Norwood, P.C., Debacker, K.C. et al. (1991). Fault-tolerant computer with three independently clocked processors asynchronously executing identical code that are synchronized upon each voted access to two memory modules. US Patent 5,193,175, filed 6 March 1991 and issued 9 March 1993.

**13** Jewett, D. (1991). Integrity S2: a fault-tolerant Unix platform. *Digest of Papers, the 21st International Symposium on Fault-Tolerant Computing*, Montreal, Quebec, Canada (25–27 June 1991), 512–519. IEEE.

**14** Reynolds, D.A. and Metze, G. (1978). Fault detection capabilities of alternating logic. *IEEE Transactions on Computers* C-27 (12): 1093–1098.

**15** Patel, J.H. and Fung, L.Y. (1982). Concurrent error detection in ALU's by recomputing with shifted operands. *IEEE Transactions on Computers* C-31 (7): 589–595.

**16** Patel, J.H. and Fung, L.Y. (1983). Concurrent error detection in multiply and divide arrays. *IEEE Transactions on Computers* C-32 (4): 417–422.

**17** Cheng, W. and Patel, J. (1984). Concurrent error detection in iterative logic arrays. *Digest of Papers, the 14th International Symposium on Fault-Tolerant Computing*, Kissimmee, FL, USA (20–22 June 1984), 10–15. IEEE.

**18** Prasad, V.B. (1989). Fault tolerant digital systems. *IEEE Potentials* 8 (1): 17–21.

**19** Orenstein, S.M., Crowther, W.R., Kraley, M.F. et al. (1975). Pluribus: a reliable multiprocessor. *Proceedings of the AFIPS National Computer Conference and Exposition* (May 1975), 551–559. New York, NY, USA: ACM.

**20** Siewiorek, D.P. and Swarz, R.S. (1998). *Reliable Computer Systems: Design and Evaluation*, 3e. A K Peters.

**21** Saxena, N.R. and McCluskey, E.J. (1990). Control-flow checking using watchdog assists and extended-precision checksums. *IEEE Transactions on Computers* 39 (4): 554–559.

**22** Connet, J.R., Pasternak, E.J., and Wagner, B.D. (1972). Software defenses in real-time control systems. *Digest of Papers, 2nd International Symposium on Fault-Tolerant Computing*, Newton, Massachusetts, USA (June 1972), 94–99.

**23** Jones, M. (1997). What really happened on Mars Rover Pathfinder. *The RISKS Digest: Forum on Risks to the Public in Computers and Related Systems* 19 (49) http://catless.ncl.ac.uk/Risks/19/49#subj1.1 (accessed 3 August 2020).

**24** Shannon, C.E. (1948). A mathematical theory of communication. *The Bell System Technical Journal*, July 1948 27 (3): 379–423. https://doi.org/10.1002/j.1538-7305.1948.tb01338.x.

**25** Shannon, C.E. (1948). A mathematical theory of communication. *The Bell System Technical Journal*, October 1948 27 (4): 623–656. https://doi.org/10.1002/j.1538-7305.1948.tb00917.x.

**26** Meggitt, J.E. (1961). Error-correcting codes and their implementation for data transmission systems. *IRE Transactions on Information Theory* 7 (4): 234–244.

**27** Rudolph, L.D. and Mitchell, M.E. (1964). Implementation of decoders for cyclic codes. *IEEE Transactions on Information Theory* 10 (3): 259–260.

**28** Kasami, T. (1964). A decoding procedure for multiple-error-correcting cyclic codes. *IEEE Transactions on Information Theory* 10 (2): 134–138.

**29** Melas, C.M. and Gorog, E. (1963). A note on extending certain codes to correct error bursts in longer messages. *IBM Journal of Research and Development* 7 (2): 151–152.

**30** Fire, P. (1959). *A Class of Multiple-Error-Correcting Binary Codes for Non-Independent Errors*. Stanford Electronics Laboratories, Technical Report No. 55.

**31** Abramson, N.M. (1959). A class of systematic codes for non-independent errors. *IRE Transactions on Information Theory* 5 (4): 150–157.

**32** Hocquenghem, A. (1959). Codes correcteurs d'erreurs. *Chiffres* 2: 147–156.

**33** Bose, R.C. and Ray-Chaudhuri, D.K. (1960). On a class of error correcting binary group codes. *Information and Control* 3 (1): 68–79.

**34** Peterson, W.W. (1960). Encoding and error-correction procedures for the Bose-Chaudhuri codes. *IRE Transactions on Information Theory* 6 (4): 459–470.

**35** Berlekamp, E.R. (1965). On decoding binary Bose-Chaudhuri-Hocquenghem codes. *IEEE Transactions on Information Theory* IT-11 (4): 577–579.

**36** Massey, J.L. (1969). Shift-register synthesis and BCH decoding. *IEEE Transactions on Information Theory* IT-15 (1): 122–127.

**37** Chien, R.T. (1964). Cyclic decoding procedures for Bose-Chaudhuri-Hocquenghem codes. *IEEE Transactions on Information Theory* 10 (4): 357–363.

**38** Forney, G.D. Jr. (1965). On decoding BCH codes. *IEEE Transactions on Information Theory* IT-11 (4): 549–557.

**39** Lin, S. and Costello, D.J. Jr. (1983). *Error Control Coding*. Englewood Cliffs, NJ, USA: Prentice-Hall.

**40** Reed, I.S. and Solomon, G. (1960). Polynomial codes over certain finite fields. *Journal of the Society for Industrial and Applied Mathematics* 8 (2): 300–304.

**41** Elias, P. (1955). Coding for noisy channels. *IRE Convention Record* 3 (4): 37–46.

**42** Wozencraft, J.M. and Reiffen, B. (1961). *Sequential Decoding*. Cambridge, MA: MIT Press.

**43** Fano, R.M. (1963). A heuristic discussion of probabilistic decoding. *IEEE Transactions on Information Theory* 9 (2): 64–74.

**44** Zigangirov, K.S. (1966). Some sequential decoding procedures. *Problemy Peredachi Informatsii* 2 (4): 13–25.

**45** Jelinek, F. (1969). Fast sequential decoding algorithm using a stack. *IBM Journal of Research and Development* 13 (6): 675–685.

**46** Viterbi, A.J. (1967). Error bounds for convolutional codes and an asymptotically optimal decoding algorithm. *IEEE Transactions on Information Theory* IT-13 (2): 260–269.

**47** Massey, J.L. (1963). *Threshold Decoding*. Cambridge, MA, USA: MIT Press.

**48** Gallager, R.G. (1963). *Low-Density Parity-Check Codes*. MIT Press.

**49** Luby, M.G., Mitzenmacher, M., Shokrollahi, M.A. et al. (1997). Practical loss-resilient codes. *Proceedings of the 29th Annual ACM Symposium on Theory of Computing*, El Paso, TX, USA (4–6 May 1997), 150–159. New York, NY, USA: ACM.

**50** Forney, G.D. Jr. (1966). *Concatenated Codes*. Cambridge, MA, USA: MIT Press.

**51** Berrou, C., Glavieux, A., and Thitimajshima, P. (1993). Near Shannon limit error-correcting coding and decoding: Turbo-codes. *Proceedings of the IEEE International Conference on Communications*, Geneva, Switzerland (23–26 May 1993), 1064–1070. IEEE.

**52** Patel, A.M. (1989). Two-level coding for error control in magnetic disk storage products. *IBM Journal of Research and Development* 33 (4): 470–484.

**53** Peterson, L.L. and Davie, B.S. (1996). *Computer Networks: A Systems Approach*. Morgan Kaufmann.

**54** Benelli, G., Favalli, L., and Filigheddu, G. (1995). Error recovery for ATM transmissions over wireless channels. *Electronics Letters* 31 (16): 1325–1326.

**55** Maniatopoulos, A., Antonakopoulos, T., and Makios, V. (1995). Single-bit error-correction circuit for ATM interfaces. *Electronics Letters* 31 (8): 617–618.

**56** Rao, T.R.N. and Fujiwara, E. (1989). *Error Control Coding for Computer Systems*. Prentice Hall.

**57** Blahut, R.E. (1983). *Theory and Practice of Error Control Codes* (corrected ed.). Addison-Wesley.

**58** Chen, P.M., Lee, E.K., Gibson, G.A. et al. (1994). RAID: high-performance, reliable secondary storage. *ACM Computing Surveys* 26 (2): 145–185.

**59** Salem, K. and Garcia-Molina, H. (1986). Disk striping. *Proceedings of the 1986 IEEE 2nd International Conference on Data Engineering*, Los Angeles, CA, USA (5–7 February 1986), 336–342. IEEE.

**60** Livny, M., Khoshafian, S., and Boral, H. (1987). Multi-disk management algorithms. *Proceedings of the 1987 ACM SIGMETRICS Conference on Measurement and Modeling of Computer Systems*, Banff, Alberta, Canada (11–14 May 1987), 69–77. New York, NY, USA: ACM.

**61** Kaâniche, M., Romano, L., Kalbarczyk, Z. et al. (1998). A hierarchical approach for dependability analysis of a commercial cache-based RAID storage architecture. *Proceedings of the 28th Annual International Symposium on Fault-Tolerant Computing*, Munich, Germany (23–25 June 1998). IEEE.

**62** McGough, J.G. and Swern, F.L. (1983). Measurement of Fault Latency in a Digital Avionic Mini Processor Part II. NASA Contractor report 3651.

**63** Ries, G.L., Choi, G.S., and Iyer, R.K. (1994). Device-level transient fault modeling. *Proceedings of the IEEE 24th International Symposium on Fault-Tolerant Computing*, Austin, TX, USA (15–17 June 1994), 86–94. IEEE.

**64** Cha, H., Rudnick, E.M., Patel, J.H. et al. (1996). A gate-level simulation environment for alpha-particle-induced transient faults. *IEEE Transactions on Computers* 45 (11): 1248–1256.

**65** Wang, N.J., Quek, J., Rafacz, T.M. et al. (2004). Characterizing the effects of transient faults on a high-performance processor pipeline. *Proceedings of the International Conference on Dependable Systems and Networks*, Florence, Italy (28 June–1 July 2004). IEEE.

**66** Saggese, G.P., Vetteth, A., Kalbarczyk, Z., et al. (2005). Microprocessor sensitivity to failures: control vs. execution and combinational vs. sequential logic. *Proceedings of the 2005 International Conference on Dependable Systems and Networks*, Yokohama, Japan (28 June–1 July 2005).

**67** Li, M.-L., Ramachandran, P., Sahoo, S.K. et al. (2008). Understanding the propagation of hard errors to software and implications for resilient system design. *Proceedings of the 13th International Conference on Architectural Support for Programming Languages and Operating Systems*, Seattle, WA, USA (1–5 March 2008), 265–276. New York, NY, USA: ACM.

# 4
# Processor Level Error Detection and Recovery

## 4.1 Introduction

Traditionally, transient faults have been linked to the corruption of stored data values. As early as 1954, the phenomenon has been reported in adverse operating conditions, e.g., near nuclear bomb test sites and in space applications [1, 2]. Beginning in 1978, dense memory circuits (both DRAM and SRAM) have been known to be at risk to soft errors caused by alpha particles from IC (integrated circuit) packaging [3] and cosmic rays [4]. A hardware device can generally recover its full capability after a transient failure. Nonetheless, such failures can be catastrophic for the proper execution of a program, as a corrupted intermediate value, if not dealt with, can corrupt subsequent computations. Through the years, means to guard against soft errors in memory devices have evolved to include physical techniques in cell and gate design [5] and in packaging materials [6], in addition to error correction codes (ECC). These techniques are now routinely used, even in commodity PC memories. Even so, except in extremely critical applications, protection against transient failures has been given very little commercial attention other than for the memory subsystem. While soft-error rates vary significantly depending on device types and operating conditions, current estimates typically are in the range of one failure per one million hours [7].

Continuously decreasing feature sizes and supply voltage of devices reduce capacitive node charge and noise margin, making even flip-flop circuits inevitably susceptible to soft errors [8]. The high clock rate of modern processors further exacerbates the problem by increasing the probability of a new failure mechanism wherein a momentarily corrupted combinational signal is latched by a flip-flop. Constant pushing of the processor performance envelope will shortly place us in an unfamiliar realm in which logically correct implementations alone cannot ensure correct program execution with sufficient confidence.

*Dependable Computing: Design and Assessment*, First Edition. Ravishankar K. Iyer, Zbigniew T. Kalbarczyk, and Nithin M. Nakka.
© 2024 The IEEE Computer Society. Published 2024 by John Wiley & Sons, Inc.
Companion website: www.wiley.com/go/iyer/dependablecomputing1

Even at the present day, there are no commercial ICs guaranteed to operate "perfectly." When additional confidence in reliability is required, vendors of high-availability platforms have as a matter of course incorporated explicit error detection and correction techniques into their architectures.

The high cost of fault tolerance, combined with the low probability of errors in today's technologies, has meant that fault-tolerant processor designs are seen as justified only in specialty systems and high-end mainframes/servers meant for mission-critical applications. IBM's G5 [9] and Compaq's NonStop Himalaya [10] are examples of commercial fault-tolerant systems. The IBM G5 uses two fully duplicated lock-step pipelines. When the pipelines disagree in an instruction's result, the processor reverts to millicode to execute extensive hardware checks, and, on transient errors, it can restore the program state from a special hardware checkpoint module. The entire process can take up to several thousand processor cycles. Although these processors provide outstanding fault tolerance, they are high-end specialty items whose design trade-offs are considerably different from those of commodity microprocessors. The Compaq NonStop Himalaya system encompasses two stock Alpha processors running the same program in lockstep; faults are detected through comparison of the outputs of the processors at the external pins on every clock cycle. If the two processors disagree, they are immediately halted to prevent errors from corrupting the memory and storage subsystems. While Compaq is able to leverage its commodity workstation processors in the NonStop Himalaya systems, it is not able to provide hardware support for seamless recovery following a transient failure.

Duplication clearly has more than 100% hardware overhead for both the execution and the comparison hardware. It is believed that duplication incurs no additional performance penalty except from the comparison of results, which may be done by introducing an additional stage in the pipeline. Duplication covers faults only in those parts of the system that have been duplicated, and duplicating an entire processor system is cost-prohibitive. As described above, it is affordable only for specialty systems. Vijaykumar et al. [11] have proposed duplicate execution and recovery in simultaneous multithreaded processors through use of redundant hardware. That is an extension of earlier work done by Reinhardt and Mukherjee [12] to provide transient fault detection through duplicate execution of an application as communicating threads. They have shown, using software simulation, that the overhead for fault detection due to duplication is 21 and 27% for integer and floating point (FP) programs, respectively. If recovery is added, the additional overhead incurred is 1 and 7% for integer and FP programs, respectively. An important point is that those results were obtained using software simulation. The duplication techniques introduce additional data structures not only to support duplication but also to optimize it. The actual hardware implementation of such structures would reveal a higher hardware overhead, accessing these structures that are on the critical path of the pipeline takes a finite amount of time and would increase the length of the clock cycle for the processor. Duplication suffers not only from the overhead due to the synchronization of the duplicate threads but also from an inherent performance overhead due to the additional hardware introduced. Another disadvantage of duplication at the processor level is that the application is not given the choice of selectively duplicating its execution.

Over the years, three main types of measures to protect against soft errors at the hardware platform level have evolved: device-level, logic- or circuit-level, and architectural techniques.

- *Device-level techniques* include forward body bias; forward-biasing of the MOSFET body-source junction increases the junction capacitance, decreases the junction depletion charge collection volume, and creates a stronger feedback loop within the transistor to hold the state. The following factors decrease the probability that a particle strike can flip the output of a device: (i) transistor sizing (because increasing the transistor aspect ratio increases output capacitance and hardens the transistor against charge injected by cosmic radiation), (ii) conservative design practices (e.g., using high-reliability components and excluding radiation-sensitive circuit styles such as dynamic-logic styles), and (iii) incorporating a sufficient functional margin in circuit designs to account for anticipated shifts in circuit characteristics.
- *Logic- or circuit-level techniques* can be classified as those that avoid and those that detect and, possibly, recover from errors. Combinational circuit and flip-flop hardening are the common techniques for increasing immunity against soft errors. They can be achieved by placing resistors in latches to slow down the regeneration (feedback) path for single-event transients to flip a circuit, adding an explicit capacitor on the feedback/keeper node to increase the cell-level power, using two specifically designed latch sections that store the same data, and providing specific state-restoring feedback to recover corrupted data from the uncorrupted section. Logic-level error detection and recovery are achieved in combinational circuits through the use of a redundant circuit or a self-checking circuit, such as an output parity generation circuit, to validate the output of the combinational circuit. It is achieved in flip-flop elements by using redundant latches or by reusing scan flip-flops to hold redundant copies of flip-flop data.
- *Architectural techniques* include use of duplicate functional units or independent hardware to mimic and verify pipeline execution, or replication of application execution through multiple communicating threads.

This chapter discusses time, space, and information redundancy techniques that are applied for error detection (and recovery) at the processor architecture level.

The description focuses on the fault tolerance methods and techniques employed in industry and in experimental research.

## 4.2 Logic-level Techniques

In this section, we discuss some previous work on logic-level single-event upset (SEU) avoidance, detection, and recovery. The following subsections describe techniques for radiation hardening of latches and combinational circuits, selective node engineering, and hardening of memory.

The Razor flip-flop [13] has been proposed for detecting and recovering from SEUs caused primarily by dynamic voltage scaling (DVS) of a chip. Scan-based designs use inherent redundancy of latches. Through use of a Muller C-element in BISER (built-in soft-error resilience) to exploit redundancy, errors in the latch are detected and tolerated [14]. Elakkumanan et al. [15] propose a slightly modified approach to detecting and recovering from errors in the combinational logic feeding the scan-based flip-flop.

### 4.2.1 Radiation Hardening

A *radiation-hardened* device is designed to meet its functional and parametric specifications under worst-case operating conditions. For SEU avoidance, radiation hardening of latches and combinational circuits was used in the SA3300 [16] single-chip 16/32 microprocessor. It contained a full 32-bit arithmetic logic unit (ALU) and 32-bit data registers, with an external interface through a 16-bit data bus.

All latches were SEU-hardened. SEU hardening can be done in either of two ways: (i) by making the transistors large enough to provide SEU immunity while maintaining the setup time or (ii) by adding an SEU resistor to slow down the regeneration (feedback) path for single-event transients. The latches on high-capacitance buses and input latches on the external data bus were designed using the former approach. All the remaining latches in the processor were hardened using the latter approach. There was a minimal or no penalty for resistors themselves, as they were incorporated into the usual interconnections within the latch. The transistors on the data bus had to be made more than twice the size of those using resistors. The small number and locality of the data bus transistors helped keep the overhead in die size to a minimum.

The latch hardening using resistors is shown in Figure 4.1. Though the registers slow down the regeneration path, they do not affect data propagation times to latch outputs. However, the added resistors do affect performance. In the D-latch (Figure 4.1a), the resistor increases setup time and minimum clock pulse width. In the RS-latch (Figure 4.1b), the minimum pulse widths for set and reset signals are increased because of the addition of the SEU resistors.

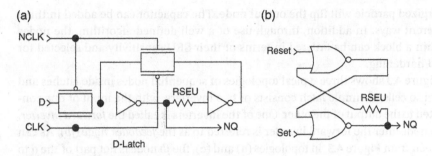

**Figure 4.1** SEU-hardened latches. (a) D-latch, (b) RS-latch. *Source:* Hass et al. [16]. © IEEE.

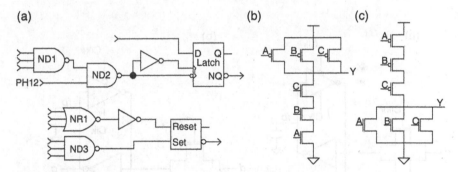

**Figure 4.2** SEU effects in logic: three-input NAND and NOR gates. (a) Combinational circuits. (b) CMOS three-input NAND gate. (c) CMOS three-input NOR gate. *Source:* Hass et al. [16]. © IEEE.

The transistor widths of specific transistors in selected gates were increased appropriately to nullify the effect of a spurious pulse on combinational circuits. For example, three-input NAND gates (ND1 and ND3 in Figure 4.2a) have poor drive for logic zero. A cosmic particle that strikes one of the turned-off p-channel transistors (see the transistor diagram in Figure 4.2b) in one of those gates will cause a spurious high-level pulse at the gate output. This pulse may be wide enough to cause the latch to change to an erroneous state. Similarly, the three-input NOR gate (NR1 in Figure 4.2a) has poor drive for logic ones, and a hit to a turned-off n-channel transistor (see transistor diagram in Figure 4.2c) will cause a logic zero pulse that may reset the latch.

### 4.2.2 Selective Node-Level Engineering

Karnik et al. [17] presented a new method for selectively hardening sequential/domino cells inside large circuit blocks against single-event upsets (SEUs). Another approach they took [17] adds an explicit capacitor to the feedback/keeper node to increase the cell-level power, thus reducing the chance that an energized particle will flip the output node. The capacitor can be added in three different ways. In addition, through use of a well-defined algorithm, the nodes within a block can be ordered in terms of their SEU sensitivity and selected for SEU hardening.

Figure 4.3 shows three typical topologies of sequential nodes inside latches and domino cells. A simple latch consists of two inverters, with the input of one connected to the output of the other. One of the inverters is called the *forward inverter*. The node after the forward inverter is referred to as the *feedback node (fb)*. As can be seen from Figure 4.3, in topologies (a) and (c), the *fb* node is not part of the *d* to *q* path; hence, it is called *path-exclusive* cell. A capacitor is added on the feedback

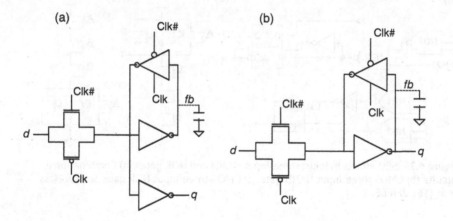

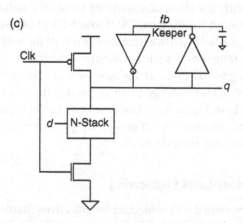

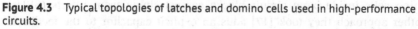

**Figure 4.3** Typical topologies of latches and domino cells used in high-performance circuits.

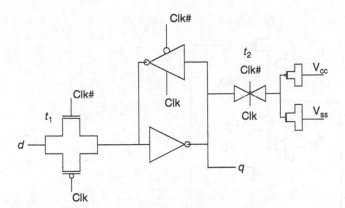

**Figure 4.4** Switched capacitor technique.

node, as shown by the dotted connection. It introduces performance and power overheads.

Figure 4.4 shows the second method of adding the cell-level capacitance for SEU resistance. The explicit capacitor is constructed by the P-MOS, N-MOS pair, with the drain and source connected to $V_{cc}$ and $V_{ss}$, respectively. While the latch is being written, the explicit capacitor is automatically disconnected (through the transmission gate $t_2$; when the clock is at "0," $t_1$ is ON and $t_2$ is OFF). However, the transmission gate adds a series resistance to the capacitor. Widening of the transistors in $t_2$ decreases the series resistance and improves the SER, but there is a cost in terms of area and power. Another stack-node technique for introducing the explicit capacitance is presented in Figure 4.5. The feedback driver circuit (with four stacked transistors) contains two transistors that are clocked. The capacitors are split and switched through these clocked transistors. The capacitors provide the desired SEU protection by having a high value for one logic state and a low value for the opposite logic state on the *fb* node.

It is clear that a performance penalty is paid in return for SER tolerance. However, by selectively hardening only the latches/dominos belonging to non-critical paths, it is possible to reduce the performance penalty. Selective node engineering is performed as follows. First, timing analysis is done on the block, and the latches are ranked according to their max and min delay criticality. The criterion for ordering the latches is to choose the least maxDelay-critical latch that improves minDelay violations. When that latch is hardened, it causes a delay change. That may change the order of the max and minDelay criticality; therefore, timing analysis needs to be performed iteratively to choose the next candidate latch for SEU protection. The SER improvement has been shown to increase by a factor of 3 at the cell level, a factor of 1.8 at the block level, and by 1.3 times at the

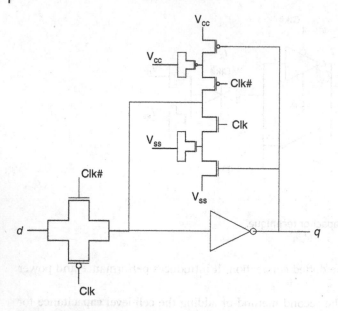

**Figure 4.5** Stack node capacitor technique.

chip level, without any performance or area penalty. The estimate of the additional power expended was <3%.

## 4.2.3 SEU Hardening for Memory Cells

One method of providing SEU immunity to storage cells is by duplicating the latches and providing feedback. However, that method is impractical for high-density circuit architectures because of multiple factors, including (i) high area overhead, (ii) high power dissipation, and (iii) critical transistor sizing. Calin et al. [18] present a novel storage cell design called Dual Interlocked Storage Cell (DICE) that achieves upset immunity while avoiding those drawbacks. They hardened memory cells by using a novel idea called *dual node feedback control*, wherein two nodes in a memory circuit maintain redundant data. Should one of the nodes be corrupted by an SEU, the uncorrupted node will provide a feedback path for restoring the data on the corrupted node. That approach was extended by Hazucha et al. [19] to harden path-exclusive latches. DICE does not put any constraints on transistor sizes and thus is immune to the total dose of the ratioed designs. It has a lower area overhead than other logic design-hardening techniques for both CMOS and static RAM cells and sequential logic elements (latches, flip-flops, registers, and so on).

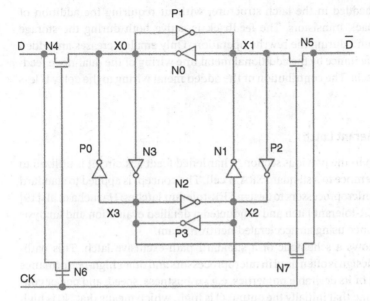

**Figure 4.6**   DICE memory cell's principle of operation. *Source:* Calin et al. [18]. © IEEE.

Figure 4.6 illustrates the principle of operation of the upset-immune storage cell. It uses a novel four-node redundant structure and employs two conventional cross-coupled (horizontal) inverter latch structures, N0–P1 and N2–P3, connected by bidirectional feedback (vertical) inverters N1–P2 and N3–P0. The four nodes X0. . .X3 store the data as two pairs of complementary values (i.e., 1010 or 0101), which are simultaneously accessed using transmission gates for a write or read operation. According to the principle of *dual node feedback control*, the logic state of each of the four nodes of the cell (X0. . .X3) is controlled by two adjacent nodes located on the opposite diagonal. In an actual implementation, the inverters shown in Figure 4.6 can be implemented using N- or P-MOS transistors. N0 to N3 are implemented using N-MOS transistors, while P0 to P3 are implemented using P-MOS transistors. If a transient pulse flips the value at a node, it would affect only one of the adjacent nodes (clockwise, if it is a negative pulse, i.e., a negative pulse on $X_i$ will affect $X_{i+1}$; and anticlockwise, if it is a positive pulse). However, the other adjacent node and the node directly opposite to the affected node on the diagonal are unaffected. Because of the state-restoring feedback from those unaffected nodes, the affected nodes will be restored to the original correct value after the transient pulse has expired.

Regardless of the electrical charge collected at the perturbed node, the cell recovers its initial state. Electrical simulations show that the recovery process is tremendously fast (much less than 1 ns). The reason is that the restoring feedback function is embedded in the latch structure, without requiring the addition of oversized feedback transistors. The feedback is active both during the storage cell's idle state and during the rewrite operation. Only small increases are added to cell node capacitance by the additional metal line wiring of the dual-node feedback interconnects. The contribution of the added metal wiring to the delay is less than 3%.

### 4.2.4 SEU-tolerant Latch

As we have seen in the previous section, a hardened feedback circuit is utilized to provide SER tolerance to a standard SRAM cell. The concept is applied to standard latches used in microprocessors to design SER-tolerant latches. Hazucha et al. [19] designed the SER-tolerant latch and conducted a detailed evaluation and analysis of its SER tolerance using an accelerated neutron beam.

Figure 4.7 shows a schematic of a standard path-exclusive latch. This path-exclusive latch design is often used in microprocessors and other high-performance circuits because of its desirable properties, e.g., robustness, speed, and power consumption. Assume that initially the output $Q$ is high, which means that N0 is high and N1 is low. If an SEU occurs at the nodes of transistors T1 and T7 connected to N0, the node is discharged to low. In turn, that switches transistor T4 to ON, and the output stabilizes to a flipped low state. One can improve the reliability by adding capacitance to the most sensitive node, but there would be a performance cost due to the increased setup time of the latch.

Figure 4.8 shows a schematic of the SER-tolerant latch. The standard clocked keeper has been replaced with a redundant clocked keeper much like the SER-tolerant SRAM cell. The transmission gate T0, T1 has been divided with the intent

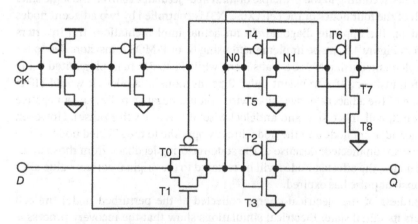

**Figure 4.7** Standard path-exclusive latch.

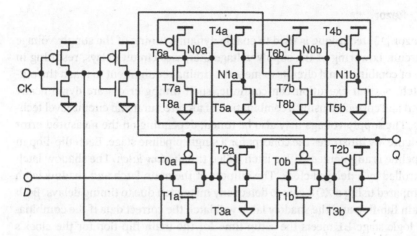

**Figure 4.8** SER-tolerant path-exclusive latch.

to drive two storage nodes N0a, N0b. The output buffer T2, T3 has been divided to balance the capacitive load on the storage nodes. The divided buffer also decreases the amplitude of spurious glitches at output $Q$ that could occur during cell recovery.

#### 4.2.4.1 Recovery from a Particle Strike

The SER-tolerant latch employs four nodes, N0a, N1a, N0b, and N1b, to store bit values $L$ or $II$ as logic values $LHLH$ or $HLHL$, respectively. Consider a scenario in which an SEU at *N0a* changes its state from high to low. That leads the latch into a temporary state $LLHL$. The gate of transistor T4a goes to $L$, switching it to ON. It next tries to pull N1a high. However, the transistor T5a is also ON because the N0b is $H$. The voltages at N0b and N1b are dynamically preserved and as a result maintain their original state. For that reason, the pull-down transistor T5a eventually discharges node N1a to $L$, and the pull-up transistor T6a restores the value of N0a to $H$. Given sufficient time, the latch recovers to the original state, $HLHL$. Notice that a glitch appears at output $Q$.

So that the SER benefit of the SER-tolerant latch as compared to the standard latch could be assessed, both latches were fabricated on the same chip, and SER measurements were performed on them. The test chips were irradiated with neutrons since atmospheric neutrons are the dominant cause of induced SEUs in latches. No workload was executing on the chip during the exposure. Without affecting performance, the SER-tolerant latch offered 10 times better SEU tolerance than the standard latch. Also, power and area overhead at the chip level can be held to a minimum if the technique is applied selectively to critical sequential elements.

### 4.2.5 Razor

The Razor [13] technique is used to enable dynamic tuning of the supply voltage of a circuit. Lowering of the supply voltage increases circuit delays, resulting in failure of combinational circuits to meet the timing requirement to reach the output latch. So that execution can continue, such timing errors are dynamically detected and corrected using a combination of architectural and circuit-level techniques. The supply voltage may also be tuned, depending on the measured error rate. Figure 4.9 illustrates the concept for a single pipeline stage. Each flip-flop in the pipeline is augmented with a latch called the *shadow latch*. The shadow latch is controlled by a delayed clock. The outputs of the main latch and shadow latch are compared using a XOR gate to detect any mismatch due to timing delays. Both the main flip-flop and the shadow latch will latch the correct data if the combinational logic stage L1 meets the setup time for the main flip-flop for the clock's rising edge. However, the main flip-flop will latch an incorrect value if the combinational logic L1 does not complete its computation in time, and the shadow latch will latch the late-arriving correct value. In such a situation, the output of the XOR comparator will be high, triggering the recovery mechanism. The correct value is restored from the shadow latch into the main flip-flop and is then available to stage L2.

#### 4.2.5.1 Pipeline Error Recovery
It must be ensured that, even in the presence of errors that are detected by Razor, the architectural state (registers and memory) is not corrupted. Three approaches for implementing pipeline error recovery were proposed in [13]. The first is based on clock gating, while the other two use pipelining to perform recovery.

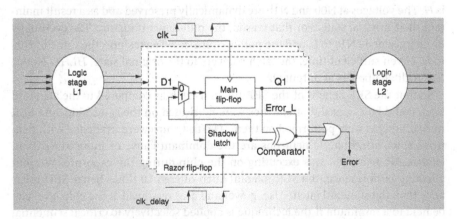

**Figure 4.9** Pipeline stage augmented with Razor latches and control lines.

*Clock Gating:* In this approach, when an error is detected, the global clock is gated for one cycle to stall the pipeline. During that cycle, each pipeline stage recomputes its result, using the input from the shadow latch. It does so to replace the erroneous values that were read from the main flip-flop in the previous cycle. Since all stages participate in the recovery from the shadow latch input, multiple errors in different stages of the pipeline in a cycle can be tolerated through introduction of a pipeline stall of a single cycle.

*Counterflow Pipelining:* Counterflow pipelining is a technique for recovering without having to gate a clock, because clock gating may be prohibitively expensive in a high-frequency digital circuit. In this method, a bubble is introduced in the pipeline to nullify the computations based on the erroneous main flip-flop. In the next cycle, the computation is performed on the inputs from the shadow latch of that stage, which are assumed to be correct. The bubble signal is propagated forward to subsequent stages to clear an empty slot in the pipeline. After that, it is necessary to invalidate all instructions that were partially executed in the pipeline prior to the affected stage. For that purpose, a *flush train* is propagated backward in the pipeline, nullifying all previous instructions in the pipeline. When the flush train signal reaches the beginning of the pipeline, the execution is resumed from the instruction following the errant instruction.

*Micro-rollback:* Micro-rollback keeps a first-in first-out queue of length $N$ to log the pipeline registers for the past $N$ cycles [14]. When the pipeline needs to be stalled, the backing storage reinjects the old value for the stage register into the pipeline, thus simulating a stall. The stall signal must be propagated to all stages. Since there are $N$ entries in the backup store, the technique allows $N$ cycles for the stall signal to propagate to the other stages in the pipeline.

### 4.2.5.2 Discussion

There are drawbacks to be aware of in implementing and using a shadow-latch-based design such as Razor [13]. Some of them are listed below.

*Increased Susceptibility to Soft Errors.* Shadow latches, as used in Razor, protect only against timing errors that occur because of DVS. But the scaling down of supply voltages reduces the charge collected on the output nodes, thus making them increasingly susceptible to soft errors.

*No Protection Against Soft Errors.* The technique does not protect against any errors in the combinational circuit that feeds both the main and shadow latches. The protection is confined to the limited region of errors in the main and shadow latches of the processor pipeline. That leaves unprotected a significant portion of the processor, which has been made more susceptible to soft errors due to DVS.

*Power Overhead Estimation.* It has been shown that the energy overhead due solely to the shadow latches is less than 1% for an Alpha processor. The error detection circuit and the metastability detectors that are included for every shadow latch need to be included in the power estimations.

Most importantly, a delayed clock is to be distributed all along the chip to clock the shadow latch. The delayed clock can also be generated locally at the site of the flip-flop to reduce the power incurred in driving two clock signals. However, in both scenarios, the power consumption needs to be taken into account.

*Nonzero Probability of Metastability.* There is also an additional complexity in trying to reduce the probability of error in detecting a metastability in the latches due to a decrease in the supply voltage. *Metastability* is an abnormal situation in which the output of the latch does not resolve to a definite high or low voltage.

### 4.2.6 Built-in Soft-Error Resilience Using Scan Flip-Flop Reuse

A typical microprocessor scan flip-flop design has two distinct components: a system flip-flop and a scan portion. The scan flip-flops in a microprocessor are all connected in one or more shift registers to enable observation of the values at the system flip-flops at a particular cycle. In BISER [20], the scan flip-flop design is reused to reduce the impact of soft errors that affect latches. A schematic of the technique is shown in Figure 4.10. In normal system operation mode, the scan clocks SCA, SCB, UPDATE, and TEST are reset to low, while the CAPTURE signal is set to high. That transforms the scan portion of the flip-flop into a master-slave flip-flop that now operates as a shadow of the system flip-flop.

In BISER, the outputs of the system flip-flop and the scan flip-flop are inputs to a C-element. The truth table for the C-element is shown in Figure 4.10. When O1

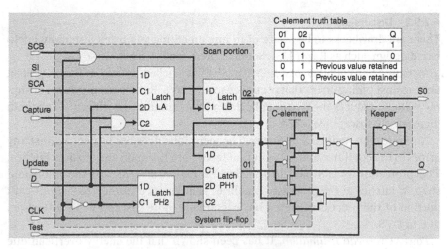

**Figure 4.10** SER-tolerant scan flip-flop using C-element.

and O2 hold the same value, the C-element passes the inverse of this value to the output Q. When the clock signal CLK is 0, the logic value at input D is passed into latches LA and PH2. Latches PH1 and LB are not driven by an active input (i.e., their clock signals are 0) and hence are susceptible to soft errors. If a soft error occurs in PH1 or LB, the logic value on O1 will not agree with O2. In that case, the C-element does not forward the erroneous value to the output. Rather, with the help of the keeper latch, it maintains the previous value at the output Q, which is assumed to be correct. When the CLK returns to 1, the erroneous value in PH1 or LB will be overwritten by the correct subsequent values from PH2 or LA, respectively. A similar situation occurs when latches PH2 and LA become susceptible to errors when CLK = 1. The C-element ensures that errors that occur in those latches during the vulnerable period do not propagate to the output Q.

### 4.2.7 Discussion

Some key limitations of the BISER technique are the following.

1) The scan flip-flop is used as a redundant latch for the main latch. It is assumed that the scan latch is alongside the main latch on the die.
2) The C-element used at the output of the latch to tolerate faults in any of the redundant flip-flop discharges, and therefore an associated keeper circuit, is added, introducing an additional source of error susceptibility.
3) The protection is limited only to errors in the latches that have scan functionality. The combinational circuitry and the rest of the latches are not protected.

## 4.3 Error Protection in the Processors

A variety of time and space redundancy techniques can be applied to a processor/microprocessor design [21]. To illustrate error detection and recovery mechanisms in processors, we discuss examples of techniques employed in Intel, AMD, and IBM processor architectures.

### 4.3.1 Reliability Features of Intel P6 Processor Family

With the increasing awareness of the occurrence of transient errors and the shift toward use of commercial off-the-shelf processors even for critical applications, the P6 family of Intel processors (Pentium Pro, Pentium II, Celeron, and Pentium III) include high-end features supporting reliability that are available to the mass market [21]. All processor registers in the P6 microarchitecture are parity-checked. The 64-bit data path between the CPU core and the level-2 cache is protected by

ECC. Through machine-check interrupts, the P6 improves support for check-pointing; however, it requires that the operating system be written to take advantage of such features.

Other support for enhanced data integrity and reliability includes (i) an enhanced machine check architecture (MCA); (ii) ECC on the L2 data cache and parity on the L2 cache tags; (iii) parity on the L1 cache and TLB (translation lookaside buffer); (iv) built-in self-test; and (v) FRC (functional redundancy checking).

#### 4.3.1.1 Machine Check Architecture (MCA)

The MCA is an internal architecture subsystem that detects and captures errors occurring within a microprocessor's logic. MCA covers five major subsystems within the processor: external bus logic, back-side bus logic, the data cache unit, the data translation lookaside buffer, and the instruction fetch unit.

#### 4.3.1.2 Functional Redundancy Checking (FRC)

FRC increases the integrity of critical applications by comparing the outputs of the two members of a processor pair and alerting the system if it detects any differences between the two outputs. The P6 supports full FRC to compare the outputs of multiple processors and checks for discrepancies. In an FRC pair, one processor acts as a master, and the other acts as a checker. The two chips are lashed together to constantly verify each other's results. The checker signals the system if it detects any differences between the processors' outputs.

### 4.3.2 Reliability Features in Itanium

Itanium (introduced in 2001) represents a family of 64-bit Intel microprocessors targeting enterprise servers and high-performance computing systems [22]. The Itanium architecture provides several reliability features, some of which are detailed in the following subsections, to support rapid detection and containment of runtime errors at the hardware level [23].

#### 4.3.2.1 Protection of On-Chip Memory Arrays

The instruction TLB1, data TLB1, and data TLB2 are protected by parity. When an error is detected, a hardware bus reset is performed because the memory transaction may already have been sent to the memory subsystem. The tag and data arrays of the L1I instruction cache are protected by parity. A local MCA is raised on error detection and results in an entire cache invalidation recovery action. The L1D (data cache) tag and data arrays are also protected by parity. L1D, however, has one parity bit per byte to avoid a read-modify-write operation for stores of size less than one word. In addition, there is redundant error detection in the L1D cache, such that a local MCA is raised whenever there is an error in any of the four ways in a set. Bit interleaving of single cache lines converts multiple-bit errors into single-bit errors in multiple cache lines.

The L2 cache data array is protected by SEC-DED (72, 8) error-correcting code, i.e., every 64 bits of data are protected by 8 bits of ECC. That has the disadvantage that all lower granularity stores require a read-modify-write operation. The L2 cache tag array is protected by parity and redundant error detection as in the L1D data cache. If a cache line is in the clean or shared state when an error is detected, a local MCA is generated so that the cache can be invalidated. However, if the cache line is in the modified state, a global MCA is raised to terminate all processes that might be affected.

The L3 cache tag is protected by 3 parity bits, and the data are protected by 8 ECC bits per 64 bits. The errors are corrected by the hardware without the intervention of the Processor Abstraction Layer (PAL). Single-bit errors in a cache line are corrected on the fly while being sent to the processor or while being written back to the system memory (or other processors). The state of the L3 cache lines is represented using 4 bits instead of 2 to provide redundancy and reliability.

*Processor buses.* The processor backside, system address, and command buses are protected using 8-bit ECC per 64 bits, which can detect 4-bit block errors as well. A single-bit error on the data bus would be corrected on the fly, whereas a double-bit error would trigger a data-poisoning event.

### 4.3.2.2 Error Containment

Error containment in the Itanium prevents the processor from allowing the effect of a fault to propagate to and beyond the system bus. A hierarchical error containment strategy is used.

At the *instruction level*, instructions with single-bit errors in the L1I instruction cache are detected and never executed. Any single-bit errors in instructions (or data) in the L2 and L3 caches are corrected on the fly. At the *process level*, detected errors in the L1 and L2 caches that cannot be corrected raise an MCA before the data are consumed. For double-bit errors in the L2 caches that are detected by ECC but cannot be corrected, a data-poisoning mechanism (described in "Counterflow Pipelining") is used.

At the *cluster level*, a global MCA sets off a restoration action by the system, e.g., turning off memory traffic to the I/O regions and then shutting down the affected node or cluster. A global MCA can be raised by an error in the tag bits of a dirty cache line. All MCA events in Itanium are in one of two categories, depending on the hardware reporting mechanism used. The two categories are

1) CPU errors: Errors that either occur within components of the CPU, such as the caches, or are detected on the CPU front side bus (FSB) during an external transaction.

2) Platform errors: Errors that are delivered to the CPU through external pins responsible for reporting MCA events.

The vast majority of MCA events correspond to hardware errors; however, not every single hardware error is reported as an MCA event. For instance, a failure in a memory device in the system memory would be reported as an MCA event, yet a component failure due to a hard disk drive would most likely not be reported to the operating system as an MCA event.

### 4.3.2.3 Data Poisoning

To prevent errors detected in memory from bringing down the entire system, the Itanium processor employs a data-poisoning mechanism. Erroneous data from the memory are marked as bad (poisoned) in the processor cache, and all processes that use the poisoned data are terminated, allowing the rest of the processes to continue executing. The rules for handling a poisoned cache line within a processor are as follows:

1) A load or fetch from a poisoned cache line signals a local MCA.
2) A store to a poisoned cache line is ignored. The line in the cache remains unchanged and poisoned.
3) A snoop or eviction causes the processor to write back the cache line with the double-bit ECC error to the system bus and signals a corrected machine check interrupt.

### 4.3.2.4 Error Promotion

On the Itanium processor, less severe errors may be promoted to more severe ones via a configuration model-specific register manipulated via a defined PAL interface. The following promotion options are implemented:

- A hardware-correctable error may be promoted to take a local MCA.
- A local MCA (including a promoted one from a hardware-correctable error) may be promoted to signal a global MCA.
- A global MCA (including a promoted one from a local MCA) may be promoted to take a hardware bus reset.

### 4.3.2.5 Watchdog Timer

The processor implements a 64-bit watchdog timer, whose size roughly corresponds to a time interval of eight seconds. The timer measures the time elapsed between two instructions that are retired and is reset on every instruction retirement. On timeout, the processor initiates a hardware bus reset, breaking a potential system hang condition in which the system is not executing.

#### 4.3.2.6 Error Detection and Correction Logging

The processor provides an extensive error information logging capability. Each error log is implemented as a model-specific register, which can be accessed via an internal processor bus by the processor abstraction layer error handler during the error-handling process. The Itanium provides important error information early to the system maintenance staff to improve system availability. Early notification enables corrective action before a correctable error becomes uncorrectable. As an example, if the processor is experiencing an unusually high number of correctable errors, it may be prudent to preemptively replace the processor – or the entire processor board, if the number of errors exceeds an empirical threshold.

### 4.3.3 POWER7

POWER7 [24], was the first multicore processor from IBM. It inherited almost all the reliability features of its predecessor, the POWER6, and built upon them. From a reliability perspective, POWER7 faces challenges, but also derives benefits, from its multicore architecture. An example of the challenges is the need to provide additional protection for the processor fabric bus. The benefits stem mainly from additional spare resources (both processing and array) that are available on-chip for proactive and reactive repair strategies.

Continuing the POWER microprocessors tradition, the POWER7 provides processor-wide error checkers and fault isolation registers (FIRs) that capture the state of the processor on the first error. The mechanism is called First Failure Data Capture, and the data are logged for further offline analysis by engineering support staff.

For the memory arrays, POWER7 attempts to provide a self-healing architecture. The L1 instruction and data caches have parity checking with fetch retry from higher layers of memory. The L2 and L3 caches implement DED/SEC (double-error detection and single-error correction) codes to detect failed lines. For recovery, errors correctable by ECC are corrected on a read. Cache lines with persistent correctable errors are predictively deallocated. In POWER7+, the larger L3 cache (80 MB, whereas POWER7 has 32 MB) warrants and allows for spare cache lines that dynamically replace deleted cache lines.

The memory bus on the POWER7 provides cyclic redundancy code (CRC) checking for all data transfers. The processor-to-processor bus provides spare lines that can dynamically replace a failed bus line. POWER7, owing to its Power-On Reset Engine, is the first processor for which such a replacement of a faulty bus line does not require a system reboot. A system reboot was a requirement in all prior processors that attempted to provide spare bus lines, since the initialization values for the processors using the bus had to be changed. (In other words, the processors needed to be informed about which wires to use.)

Within a processor core, the POWER7 provides instruction retry for failed instructions. The cores themselves are viewed as logical entities, not physically tied to a particular partition. Rather, they are provided with a fluid capability of drifting between partitions depending on the performance and reliability requirements. That enables predictive processor deallocation to be seamless, such that any partition that is executing on a core that is being proactively deallocated can be migrated to another (or a set of) working cores.

### 4.3.4 NonStop Himalaya Systems

All components of a NonStop Himalaya system [10], including processors, I/O adapters, storage devices, communications lines, and the system area network (SAN) itself, which connects all the components together (see Figure 4.11), are duplicated. The system thus avoids having any single point of failure that, when failed, could crash a user application.

All the components are designed to be self-checking and "fail-fast." A component is said to be *fail-fast* if it either works correctly or (if an error is detected by the in-built detection mechanisms or by external monitoring) removes itself from the system. That isolates the fault to the failing component, preventing it from propagating to the rest of the system.

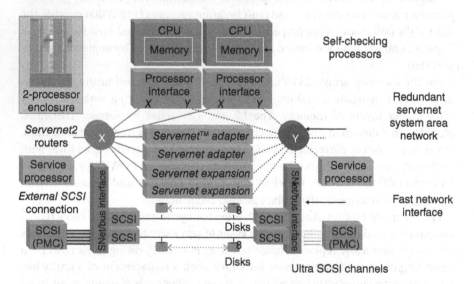

**Figure 4.11** NonStop system architecture. *Source:* Modified from Hewlett Packard Enterprise [10].

In addition to the fully duplicated hardware subsystem, the operating system, NonStop Kernel, is also designed to enhance reliability. Along with the usual operating system features, the NonStop Kernel employs *Process Pairs*, a novel approach for handling permanent and transient hardware and software errors. The primary process performs the actual work of the pair and communicates state changes to the backup process, which is executing on another processor, via inter-processor messages. To ensure data integrity and enable recovery, duplicate file images (a primary and a backup) are created. *Primary* periodically sends checkpoint information to *Backup*. *Backup* reads checkpoint messages and updates its data, file status, and program counter. The checkpoint information is inserted in the corresponding memory locations of the *Backup* and, hence, enables fast recovery (in the case of a *Primary* failure) such that processing can be resumed without requiring disk accesses. The *Backup* takes over if the system reports that *Primary* is down, i.e., *Primary* fails to respond to an "I am alive" message. All file activities by *Primary* are performed on both the primary and backup file copies. *Primary* periodically asks the OS if a *Backup* exists. If there is no *Backup*, the *Primary* can request the creation of a copy of both the process and file structure.

The system area network (SAN) that connects all the hardware components in the NonStop system is ServerNet. The SAN is used for both inter-processor communications and input/output (I/O). The SAN connects all processors to each other as well as to all I/O adapters. As shown in Figure 4.11, the SAN fabric is itself duplicated to prevent a system failure in the event of a single failure in one of the network fabrics. Corrupted packets are detected using a CRC checksum. If packets are lost, they are retransmitted. An attempt is made to retransmit the lost packet on the same network fabric. If that fails, then the fabric is assumed to have failed, and retransmission is attempted on the other fabric.

Data stored on permanent storage are protected using end-to-end checksums and mirrored volumes. The checksums can be used for error detection, and the mirrored volumes can be used for recovering from a single error. All writes to disk are passed on to both the volumes. An optimization for reads is to allow a read from the most proximal copy. If a read from one copy fails, the read can be reissued to be served by the other copy. In a scenario in which an entire physical disk volume fails, it is possible to plug out the failed disk and swap in a new disk. The data from the mirrored disk volume are copied to the new disk to restore the original duplicated disk configuration.

To ensure the integrity of individual blocks of data on the disk, end-to-end checksums are used. The processor calculates the checksum of a block and writes it to the disk along with the data. This checksum is verified on a read to that block.

## 4.4 Academic Research on Hardware-level Error Protection

This section describes selected work (mainly academic research) on handling transient faults through spatial and/or time redundancy at the processor hardware level.

The inherent hardware redundancy in simultaneous multithreading (SMT) [25] and the chip multiprocessor (CMP) architectures make the two approaches ideal bases for space- and time-redundant fault-tolerant designs. However, in normal operation, these multithreaded/multiprocessor architectures are throughput-optimized and depend on the existence of multiple threads for maximum performance. In the AR-SMT architecture, fault tolerance is achieved by executing two copies of the same program [26]. The two copies, known as the A-thread and the R-thread, proceed with a slight lag between them. Mechanisms are introduced to verify the correctness of the outcome of the two threads on an instruction-by-instruction basis. While the AR-SMT architecture provides a means for detecting errors, recovery strategies are not included. Later work developed similar concepts in the context of CMPs [27, 28].

The SMT-based fault-tolerant design is further enhanced by checking only instructions whose side effects are visible beyond the boundaries of the processor core, permitting looser coupling between the redundant threads [12]. That mechanism is termed *Simultaneously and Redundantly Threaded (SRT) processors*. No recovery scheme has been suggested to complement this coarse-grained detection scheme.

Another, quite different, fault-tolerant processor architecture has been proposed in the DIVA (Dynamic Instruction Verification Architecture) design [29, 30]. DIVA comprises an aggressive out-of-order superscalar processor and, on the same die, a simple in-order checker processor. The checker processor verifies the output of the complex out-of-order processor and triggers a recovery action when an inconsistency is found. In addition to providing transient fault tolerance, the checker processor can also correct errors due to design mistakes in the aggressive front-end processor, assuming that the simple DIVA checker processor is free of errors. DIVA offers an interesting solution for combatting processor design complexity, but the static nature of its hardware redundancy prevents it from regaining additional performance when reliability is not warranted. The following sections discuss in more detail the merits and demerits of some of the techniques mentioned above. So that they can be contrasted with the hardware-implemented techniques. Table 4.1 summarizes some of the architectural techniques for reliability described in the following sections.

**Table 4.1** Summary of some of the architectural techniques for reliability.

| | Technique | Features and description | Merits | Disadvantages |
|---|---|---|---|---|
| Space redundancy | Dynamic Instruction Verification Architecture (DIVA) [29, 30] | A simple in order checker processor checks a complex out-of-order core processor. | ⋏ Checker uses intermediate results from the core processor.<br>⋏ The simple checker can be formally verified. | ⋗ Design of checker for a superscalar core is non trivial.<br>⋗ Errors causing omission of prediction stream entries are not covered. |
| Time redundancy in hardware | Using multithreaded processors: SRTR [11], SRT [12], AR-SMT [26], Saxena [31]. | The process is duplicated into two communicating threads executing at a phase lag. | ⋏ Utilizes spare hardware in multithreaded processors.<br>⋏ Leading thread provides intermediate results to trailing thread. | ⋗ Introduces data structures, accessing which increases cycle time.<br>⋗ Error detection limited to sphere of replication – includes only execute stage.<br>⋗ Application cannot choose reliability through duplication. |

*(Continued)*

**Table 4.1** (Continued)

| Technique | Features and description | Merits | Disadvantages |
|---|---|---|---|
| Time + redundancy in software | Instructions are duplicated in software at compile time. Hardware executes the two copies of the instruction and the results are compared. Data are also diversified while maintaining a mapping between original and duplicated data. | ⋏ No additional hardware required. ⋏ Can be used easily with COTS components. ⋏ Idle hardware in super scalar processors can be put to use. ⋏ Technique targeted at energy efficiency. | ≻ High-performance penalty. ≻ High-power penalty. ≻ Selective insertion hard. ≻ High error-detection latency. |
| Space + time redundancy | Instructions are replicated when dispatched to reservation station and results in re-order buffer compared before commit. | ⋏ Dispatch mechanism is modified to support replication. ⋏ Recovery is achieved using the mechanism that recovers from a branch misprediction. | ≻ Effective dispatch and commit bandwidths reduced by a factor of $R$, redundancy. ≻ Effective utilization of re-order buffer (ROB) and register rename table decreased by a factor of $R$. ≻ Does not provide selective replication. |

Using diverse data and duplicated instruction [32], duplicated instructions in superscalar processors [33], and selective procedure call duplication [34].

Dual use of superscalar datapath [35]

| Reuse of existing performance enhancing checkpointing hardware | ReStore: symptom-based soft error detection in microprocessors [36] | Symptoms – such as exceptions, control-flow misspeculations, and cache or translation look-aside buffer misses – that hint at the presence of soft errors trigger restoration of a previous checkpoint. | ✓ Incurs little overhead over traditional soft error detection techniques.<br>✓ Reuses existing checkpointing hardware. | ➤ Sacrifices some error detection as all errors do not lead to the symptoms being monitored.<br>➤ Can incur unnecessary performance overhead due to rollback on false alarms. |
| Concurrent checking in pipeline | Signature monitor for concurrent detection of data-access errors [37] | Data structures are appended with a signature which is read at runtime and compared against a reference signature in the processor pipeline. | ✓ Performance overhead due to signature access is masked due to spatial locality.<br>✓ Runtime signature computed in parallel with instruction execution.<br>✓ Exception conditions are handled. | ➤ Custom augmentation of the pipeline to provide specific protection (against data-access faults) to the application.<br>➤ Does not cover errors in data or computation unit within pipeline. |

Source: Modified from Iyer et al. [38].

### 4.4.1 SRTR: Transient Fault Recovery Using Simultaneous Multithreading

Simultaneously and redundantly threaded processors with recovery (SRTR) is an enhancement of the SRT technique that provides transient fault detection [11]. It uses the concept of a *sphere of replication*, which is the logical extent of redundant execution. An SRT processor provides transient fault coverage by running identical copies of the same program as two independent threads, one called the *leading thread* and the other the *trailing thread*. The leading thread executes ahead of the trailing thread and maintains a minimum slack. SRT allows the leading thread to commit before the trailing thread completes the instruction execution and before the comparison of the result is done. If there is an error, the trailing thread triggers detection. In SRTR, to ensure that the effects of a faulty instruction can be undone, no instruction in the leading thread can commit before checking has occurred. Three SRT techniques are useful in supporting recovery in SRTR:

- Use of a *load value queue (LVQ)* to hold values loaded by the leading thread and to enable the trailing thread to load data from LVQ instead of repeating the load from the cache. That ensures that the two threads load exactly the same values. (Note that replication of the cached loads may lead to inconsistency because memory locations may be modified between the accesses by the leading and trailing threads.)
- Exploitation of the slack (of about 256 instructions) by which the leading thread is running ahead of the trailing thread to hide the leading thread's memory latencies and branch mispredictions from the trailing thread. The branch outcomes are forwarded from the leading thread to the trailing thread.
- Ability to limit the checking to stores and uncached loads by taking advantage of the fact that a fault propagates through computations and eventually reaches a store.

SRTR makes use of the time between the completion and commit of the leading instruction to allow for slack between the two threads, thus preventing the leading thread from stalling for a long time. To exploit complete to commit time of instructions, the slack between the leading thread and trailing thread should be short. However, it should not be *too* short, or the trailing thread will stall for lack of branch outcomes and loads. To make the slack shorter, the leading thread provides branch predictions instead of branch outcomes. Therefore, slack is determined by the complete to commit times of the instructions and the memory access latency (for forwarding of load values). Either the leading thread or the trailing thread can complete execution first. The first thread to complete its execution places its results in the temporary buffer data structures (e.g., LVQ), and the thread that completes later compares its results against those in the buffer. In the following discussion, the leading thread is assumed to complete first, even though the arguments hold even when the trailing thread is the one to complete first.

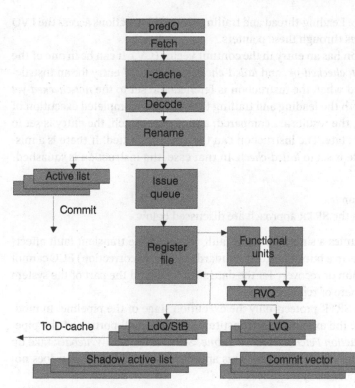

**Figure 4.12**   Processor pipeline with extensions for SRTR.

The data structures used by SRTR are depicted in Figure 4.12 and briefly described below.

- Each thread's active instructions are kept in the thread's *active list* (AL) in the predicted order. Leading-thread and trailing-thread instructions occupy the same positions in their respective ALs.
- To avoid increasing the pressure on the register file for checking, SRTR uses a *register value queue* (RVQ). The ALU, floating point unit (FPU), and branch instruction from the leading thread place their results in the RVQ and set the Full/Empty bit for that entry.
- As in SRT, SRTR uses the *load value queue (LVQ)* to store the load values and addresses of the leading thread. An address generated by the trailing thread is compared to the leading thread's result address, and the trailing thread uses the value in the LVQ.
- A *store buffer (StB)* is used, as in SRT, by the leading thread to place committed store values and addresses. The trailing thread checks its store values and addresses against StB entries.
- A *shadow active list (SAL)* is employed to keep LVQ and RVQ lengths small. LVQ and RVQ entries are allocated only when needed, and pointers to the entries are

kept in the SAL. Leading-thread and trailing-thread instructions access the LVQ and RVQ entries through these pointers.

- Each instruction has an entry in the commit vector (CV). It can be in one of the *not-checked-yet*, *checked-ok*, and *failed-check* states. A CV entry for an instruction is allocated when the instruction is fetched and set to the *not-checked-yet* state. When both the leading and trailing threads have completed execution of an instruction, the results are compared, and if they match, the entry is set to the *checked-ok* state. The instruction can then be committed. If there is a mismatch, the state is set to *failed-check*. In that case, the instruction is squashed.

### 4.4.1.1 Discussion

Some issues with the SRTR approach are discussed below.

- The SRTR assumes a single-transient-fault model. If the transient fault affects multiple bits, as in a burst of errors, standard (single-bit correction) ECC cannot support detection or recovery for the data structures and the part of the system outside the sphere of replication.
- Duplication in SRTR protects only the execution stage of the pipeline. In modern processors, the execute stage constitutes only a small portion of the pipeline. The *Instruction Fetch*, *Decode*, *Rename*, *Scheduling*, and *Writeback* take up many more stages in the pipeline. This approach to duplication thus does not cover a major portion of the processor.
- SRTR can detect but cannot recover from an error in a register after the register has been written back and the instruction that produced the value has been committed. The reason is that the leading and trailing threads use separate register files.
- The complexity of the dependence chain queue (DCQ), the data structure used to extract register-level (true) dependencies and maintain the chain structure, has not been clearly addressed.
- The assessment of the approach has focused mainly on performance and not on evaluation of the error coverage, which is an important metric from the fault tolerance perspective.

### 4.4.2 DIVA: A Reliable Substrate for Deep Submicron Microarchitecture Design

DIVA is a fault-tolerant processor architecture that comprises an aggressive out-of-order superscalar processor and, on the same die, a simple in-order checker processor [29, 30]. The checker processor verifies the output of the complex out-of-order processor and triggers a recovery action when an inconsistency is found.

The core processor executes the program and creates the prediction stream that contains all the executed instructions with their input values and any memory addresses referenced. The instructions in the prediction stream are delivered in program order to the checker processor before retirement. The checker processor verifies the core processor by re-executing all the program computations. The prediction stream sent to the checker processor helps to simplify the design of the checker because it eliminates all the processing hazards like branch mispredictions, cache misses, and data dependencies. Thus, the checker processor is a simple in-order processor pipeline that executes the computations for the instruction in each stage at the same time, i.e., it executes the fetch, decode, execute, and memory stage computations for the instruction at the same time because of the availability of the inputs for all stages in the same cycle.

The checker processor has its own register file and a small, dedicated L0 cache, which is loaded with whatever data the core pipeline touches. It taps off the output of the L1 cache (which is accessed by the core). Store queues are also added to both the core and the checker in order to increase performance.

If there is no error in any of the stages, then the instruction is retired and the state is copied to the architectural state. But if there is an error in any of the stages, then the checker fixes the errant value in the prediction stream, flushes the entire core pipeline, enters the execute state by reconfiguring itself to do single-serial-instruction processing, executes the faulty instruction and commits the values if there are no errors, and restarts the core pipeline at the instruction following the errant instruction. If there are any errors in the re-execution, the checker is assumed to have failed. Figures 4.13 and 4.14 show the generation of the prediction stream by the core processor and the checker that is using the prediction stream to check an instruction without undergoing any control or data hazards.

### 4.4.2.1 Discussion

The main assumptions, the features, and the deficiencies of the DIVA technique are discussed below.

- The DIVA approach's assumption that speculative execution is fault-tolerant is not necessarily true. The speculative mechanism of the processor contains the branch target buffer (BTB) and the mechanism that checks whether a prediction is correct, and when the speculative mechanism is in error, that changes the control flow of the program.
- If the core pipeline is wide, then a single checker cannot match the retirement bandwidth of the core pipeline. Thus, multiple checker pipelines are required.
- The checker has a dedicated register file. Some outstanding issues with the use of a dedicated register file for the checker need to be addressed. (i) How does the checker update the register file? (ii) What relation does the checker register file

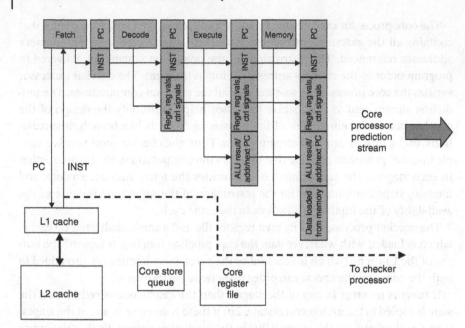

**Figure 4.13** Generation of prediction stream by the core processor.

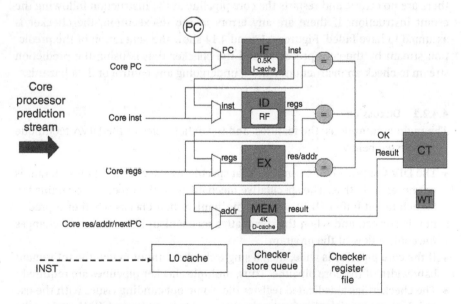

**Figure 4.14** Checker processor performs the check on the predication stream. *Source:* Based on Austin [29].

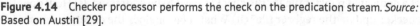

have to the core register file (RF)? (iii) How does the register file state get committed to the architectural state?

If the checker does not use its own program counter, there are two scenarios in which it cannot detect errors:

1) *There is an error in the program counter of the core pipeline.* Since the core and the checker fetch the instruction from the same location, the error is masked.

2) *An error causes an entry in the prediction stream corresponding to an instruction to be overwritten by an entry of another instruction.* The checker cannot detect this omission error because the checker uses the program counter (PC) provided in the prediction stream to check the instruction results.

If the checker uses its own program counter, then for a *single-wide checker* pipeline, it is easy to maintain the PC. When a wider checker pipeline is used, however, it is a nontrivial task to determine which checker pipeline would check which instruction. In other words, it is nontrivial to maintain the PC for each individual checker pipeline. Data dependencies and control dependencies are introduced in the execution of the instructions by the checker, and the checker would have to ensure that instructions are committed in program order.

### 4.4.3 Microprocessor-based Introspection (MBI)

Microprocessor-based introspection (MBI) [39] is a time-redundancy-based, transient fault detection technique that schedules the redundant execution of a program during idle cycles, particularly when a long-latency cache miss is being serviced. MBI operates in either of the following two modes. (i) In the *performance mode*, instructions are processed for the first time. It is only during this mode that the architectural state (i.e., architectural registers and memory) is updated. (ii) In the *introspection mode*, to provide redundant execution and therefore fault tolerance, instructions are processed again. Instruction results that are produced during performance mode are then verified in the introspection mode.

A block diagram of MBI incorporated in a processor microarchitecture is shown in Figure 4.15. For the performance mode, instructions are performed as in a normal pipelined processor, and the results of each committed instruction are then stored in a structure known as the *backlog buffer*. Upon encountering a long-latency cache miss while in the performance mode, the processor enters the introspection mode. After the cache miss is serviced, the processor reverts back to the performance mode. In the introspection mode, the instructions that were retired in the performance mode (and the results stored in the backlog buffer) are executed again in program order. A comparison is completed of the results of the re-execution against the results stored in the backlog buffer. If the comparison shows

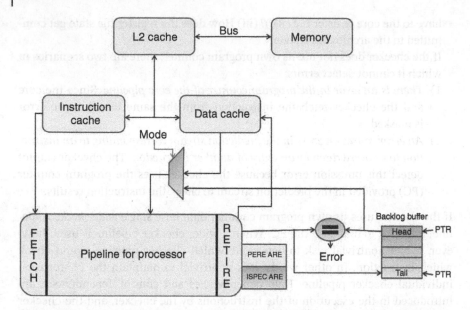

**Figure 4.15** Microarchitecture support for the backlog buffer. *Source:* Based on Qureshi et al. [39].

a match, then the entry in the backlog buffer for that instruction is removed, under the assumption that the instruction was executed error-free. However, if the two results do not match, it signals an error condition.

It is important to note that the backlog buffer is continuously filled in the performance mode and that it is emptied only in the introspection mode. However, if the processor does not enter the introspection mode because of a lack of long-latency cache misses, the backlog buffer will be full. At that juncture it is not possible for any more instructions to be retired in the performance mode, since their results cannot be stored in the backlog buffer. In that circumstance, the processor has no choice but to enter the introspection mode. When the backlog buffer again becomes empty, the processor returns to the performance mode.

The MBI architecture has some similarities to the DIVA architecture, in that just as the main pipeline passes the results for each instruction to the checker core through a prediction stream, the instructions in the performance mode write their results to the backlog buffer for use in the introspection mode. Therefore, as in the case of the prediction stream, the operation of writing to the backlog buffer is susceptible to omission and overwriting errors. If there is an error in the PC during the performance mode, it will lead to a control-flow error, which cannot be detected in the introspection mode. The reason is that the performance mode provides the control-flow information for the introspection mode.

Other errors in the instruction wake-up logic while the processor is in either the performance or introspection mode cannot be detected by the above mechanism. There has to be an independent heartbeat mechanism to detect such errors.

Errors in the memory interface logic that cause data errors propagate from the performance mode to the introspection mode, because instructions in the introspection mode do not access the D-cache but use the results stored in the backlog buffer by the corresponding instructions in the performance mode.

### 4.4.4 Phoenix: Detection and Recovery from Permanent Process Design Bugs

Phoenix is a tool for analyzing and repairing design defects in modern microprocessors [37]. It has been used to analyze processors made by various manufacturers, such as AMD, Intel, IBM, and Motorola, for design defects. Most of the errors discovered were found in the periphery of the core and in the cache hierarchy.

Depending on the criticality of the structures in which it occurs, a design defect is categorized as either Critical or Noncritical (as shown in Figure 4.16). Noncritical structures include performance counters, error-reporting registers, and hardware for breakpoint support. Those structures support and enhance the operation of the processor, but their correctness is not essential for the correct execution of the application on the main processor core. Firmware defects are also classified as Noncritical, as they can be corrected with patches.

A further classification of Critical defects is based on the complexity of the event (or set of events) that led to the activation of the defects. If a defect is activated by a relatively simple combination of concurrent signals, then it is classified as a Concurrent defect. Other Critical defects that depend on more complex event

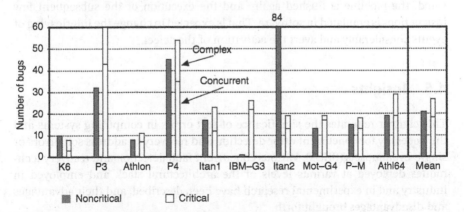

**Figure 4.16** Classification of design defects in each processor.

combinations, such as the processor's being in a specific internal state during which a specific sequence of events needs to occur, are categorized as Complex defects.

The impacts of activating a critical defect range from corruption of caches or memory to processor hangs, I/O failures, incorrect computations, and accessing of invalid data locations, among others. Some critical defects may have unpredictable consequences, ranging from application errors to processor shutdown. Most events that lead to unpredictable results can be traced to defects in the temperature or power manager. The specific solutions for those defects may have to be incorporated in the hardware, firmware, operating system, or compiler. Not surprisingly, it is possible that the identified defect may not have a solution that can be applied in the field. On average, it has been observed that about 60% of critical defects can be avoided through patches applied to the system in the field.

As mentioned before, Phoenix aims to detect and patch the design defects in a processor in the field. The Phoenix hardware, co-located with a buggy processor, is programmed to monitor the relevant control signals involved in the activation of one or more defects, and to raise an alert when the specific combination of control signals that leads to a specific defect is reached. The Phoenix hardware can be reprogrammed if a new defect is detected and a patch is released by the vendor to be applied to the chip in the field.

The specific action taken when Phoenix raises an alert depends on the type of defect that was activated. As an initial measure, the pipeline is flushed before control is transferred to the specific recovery handler. The goal in recovery is to avoid the reoccurrence of the specific combination of events that led to the defect, while attempting to re-execute all uncommitted instructions. It is expected that when the instruction execution begins again, refilling the pipeline, the exact same combination of events would not occur again. However, if the defect is again activated, the pipeline is flushed again, and the execution of the subsequent few instructions is emulated in software. That is expected to change the interleaving of events considerably and avert the activation of the defect.

## 4.5 Insights

This chapter reiterates the significance of soft errors in computing systems and the necessity for concurrent error detection and recovery to address soft errors or single-event upsets (SEUs). Various concurrent fault detection and recovery techniques deployed at various levels of the architectural stack and employed in industry and in experimental research have been described, and their advantages and disadvantages brought forth.

Radiation-hardening techniques are used at the device level to improve tolerance of single-event upsets. Apart from the additional hardware overhead, the performance impact due to slower devices affects applications, even when there is no single-event upset. As we have seen, the majority of upsets at the device level are benign to applications. Therefore, unless there is a high incidence of single-event upsets, the overhead due to radiation hardening is not justified. For that reason, radiation-hardened devices have been used primarily on space missions or missions with extreme climatic conditions, such as polar or mountaineering expeditions. Single-event upsets due to cosmic rays are significantly more frequent in such conditions, and applications can benefit greatly from fault tolerance techniques.

One of the important issues addressed in this chapter is the common belief that duplication can provide 100% coverage, incurring only a hardware overhead and little or no performance overhead. In studies that performed software simulations and through the synthesis of a processor with a triplicated ALU, it has been shown that duplication also incurs significant performance overhead.

An effective (though costly) approach to processor-level duplication has been implemented in the IBM G5/G6 processors. The IBM G series processors are high-end processors used in high-availability servers. In addition to processor-level techniques, the IBM MVS operating system provides high availability through high-level techniques, e.g., job restart. Compare that to a commodity processor such as the Intel P6 processor family or the Itanium processor. Because of prohibitive performance or hardware costs, the fault-tolerance techniques in commodity processors are restricted to protecting the different levels of on-chip cache arrays with error-control coding. One can also provide higher-level protection, such as memory with ECC. Protection at higher layers can be provided by operating systems that offer exception handling, such as Linux.

Design decisions need to be carefully evaluated to ensure that designs use less resources than the G5/G6 processor does, yet provide higher availability than current commodity processors. New architectures should be evaluated in terms of their cost and resiliency to faults. Typically, architectures are proposed and simulated but not evaluated via fault injection. Comparison with the best commercial techniques that are already in use is seldom completed. Even when fault injection is done, it is only to show that the particular fault detection technique protects against a particular fault model. The fault injection experiments should be comprehensive and should evaluate the technique's effectiveness against a broad set of faults. The real value of an error detection technique is in how much of the fault space it covers, rather than whether it covers a particular fault model. A related question that could be answered is, "How much of the fault space is covered by the fault model against which the technique is being evaluated?"

The approach employed by IBM G5/G6 has a high cost and a high payoff. The flip side of the coin is that many faults that are detected and recovered from are benign. The question that arises is, "What kind of design should one have so that one does not try to detect and recover from faults that are benign?" The lower the layer in the architectural stack at which the fault detection technique is deployed, the higher the number of benign faults detected. The actual effect of a fault is known in terms of the impact on application outcome [40–44].

The remainder of this chapter provides a brief critique of some of the error detection/recovery techniques discussed earlier in this chapter.

The Razor technique uses shadow latches to guard against timing errors. An important practical concern in using shadow latches that are triggered by a delayed clock is the generation and distribution of the delayed clock signal, which require significant silicon area as well as power overhead.

Functional redundancy checking (FRC), as in the P6 family of Intel processors, checks the outputs of a processor pair, one acting as a master and the other as a slave. The processors in a multiprocessor design can be configured to act as masters or slaves. However, the FRC mode was eliminated by Intel in April 1998. That may have indicated that there was inherent difficulty in running two superscalar processors in lock-step in order to compare their outputs for integrity checking.

In academic research, SRTR were proposed to provide time-redundant duplicate execution for fault detection and recovery. The sphere of replication defined in the work is critical to the efficacy of the technique. The technique assumes protection mechanisms, such as error correcting codes (ECC), to ensure integrity outside the sphere of replication. Incorrect results, when presented to an ECC mechanism, would generate the "correct" code, and hence the errors would be masked. Further, ECC is not scalable (in terms of performance and hardware overheads) for protection from errors in increasing number of bits. It is to be noted that the number of hardware structures required in order to support time-redundant duplication and recovery is significant.

DIVA brings forward interesting questions. From the viewpoint of a computer architect, it may be acceptable to claim that speculative execution is fault-tolerant. However, from the standpoint of reliability, for which one would scrutinize all points of failure (including the checkers themselves), the mechanism that checks whether the prediction is correct should not be overlooked. Errors in that mechanism could cause otherwise correct programs to execute incorrectly, thus introducing additional failure modes in the system. If the main processor is superscalar, it is not clear how the checker processor would be able to match the retirement bandwidth of the processor. It is possible that the problem will not be solvable even through the use of multiple checker pipelines to handle cases in which more than one instruction is retired in a single cycle. It is nontrivial to maintain the correspondence of the program counter for the multiple checker pipelines to ensure proper commitment of instructions in program order.

Time-redundant duplication of an application is justified on the grounds that modern processors are heavily underutilized. Hence, processor idle cycles can be utilized to execute the redundant stream of instructions and thus achieve very small overheads. However, experiments that evaluated the SRTR technique and the MBI technique showed that time-redundant execution incurs, on average, 30% overhead.

# References

1 Ziegler, J.F., Curtis, H.W., Muhlfeld, H.P. et al. (1996). IBM experiments in soft fails in computer electronics. *IBM Journal of Research and Development* 40 (1): 3–18.

2 Normand, E. (1996). Single event upset at ground level. *IEEE Transactions on Nuclear Science* 43 (6): 2742–2750.

3 May, T.C. and Woods, M.H. (1978). A new physical mechanism for soft errors in dynamic memories. *Proceedings of the 16th International Reliability Physics Symposium*, San Diego, CA, USA (18–20 April 1978), 33–40. IEEE.

4 Ziegler, J.F. and Landford, W.A. (1979). Effect of cosmic rays on computer memories. *Science* 206 (4420): 776–788.

5 Anghel, L., Nicolaidis, M., and Alzaher-Noufal, I. (2000). Self-checking circuits versus realistic faults in very deep submicron. *Proceedings of the 18th IEEE VLSI Test Symposium*, Montreal, Quebec, Canada (30 April–4 May 2000). IEEE

6 Hasnain, Z. and Ditali, A. (1992). Building-in reliability: soft errors: a case study. *Proceedings of the 30th Annual Reliability Physics Symposium*, San Diego, CA, USA (31 March–2 April 1992), 276–280. IEEE.

7 Tezzaron Semiconductor. (2004). Soft errors in electronic memory: a white paper, https://tezzaron.com/media/soft_errors_1_1_secure.pdf (accessed 4 August 2020).

8 Faccio, F., Kloukinas, K., Marchioro, A. et al. (1999). Single event effects in static and dynamic registers in a 0.25 μm CMOS technology. *IEEE Transactions on Nuclear Science* 46 (6): 1434–1439.

9 Slegel, T.J., Averill, R.M., Check, M.A. et al. (1999). IBM's S/390 G5 microprocessor design. *IEEE Micro* 19 (2): 12–23.

10 Hewlett Packard Enterprise (2018). HPE NonStop OS: provide the availability and scalability advantage to your business at a low TCO. Technical white paper 4AA0-6149ENW, rev.3. https://h20195.www2.hpe.com/v2/getpdf. aspx/4aa0-6149enw.pdf.html (accessed 4 August 2020).

11 Vijaykumar, T.N., Pomeranz, I., and Cheng, K. (2002). Transient-fault recovery using simultaneous multithreading. *Proceedings of the 29th Annual International Symposium on Computer Architecture*, Anchorage, AK, USA (25–29 May 2002). IEEE.

**12** Reinhardt, S.K. and Mukherjee, S.S. (2000). Transient fault detection via simultaneous multithreading. *Proceedings of the 27th International Symposium on Computer Architecture*, Vancouver, BC, Canada (12–14 June 2000), 25–36. IEEE.

**13** Ernst, D., Kim, N.S., Das, S. et al. (2003). Razor: a low-power pipeline based on circuit-level timing speculation. *Proceedings of the 36th Annual IEEE/ACM International Symposium on Microarchitecture*, San Diego, CA, USA (3–5 December 2003), 7–18. IEEE.

**14** Tamir, Y., Tremblay, M., and Rennels, D.A. (1988). The implementation and application of micro rollback in fault-tolerant VLSI systems. *Digest of Papers, the 18th International Symposium on Fault-Tolerant Computing*, Tokyo, Japan (27–30 June 1988), 234–239. IEEE.

**15** Elakkumanan, P., Prasad, K., and Sridhar, R. (2006). Time redundancy based scan flip-flop reuse to reduce SER of combinational logic. *Proceedings of the 7th International Symposium on Quality Electronic Design*, San Jose, CA, USA (27–29 March 2006). IEEE.

**16** Hass, K.J., Treece, R.K., and Giddings, A.E. (1989). A radiation-hardened 16/32-bit microprocessor. *IEEE Transactions on Nuclear Science* 36 (6): 2252–2257.

**17** Karnik, T., Vangal, S., Veeramachaneni, V., et al. (2002). Selective node engineering for chip-level soft error rate improvement. *Digest of Technical Papers, 2002 Symposium on VLSI Circuits*, Honolulu, HI, USA (13–15 June 2002), 204–205.

**18** Calin, T., Nicolaidis, M., and Velazco, R. (1996). Upset hardened memory design for submicron CMOS technology. *IEEE Transactions on Nuclear Science* 43 (6): 2874–2878.

**19** Hazucha, P., Karnik, T., Walstra, S. et al. (2004). Measurements and analysis of SER-tolerant latch in a 90-nm dual-*VT* CMOS process. *IEEE Journal of Solid-State Circuits* 39 (9): 1536–1543.

**20** Mitra, S., Seifert, N., Zhang, M. et al. (2005). Robust system design with built-in soft-error resilience. *Computer* 38 (2): 43–52.

**21** Mendelson, A. and Suri, N. (2000). Designing high-performance and reliable superscalar architectures: the out of order reliable superscalar (O3RS) approach. *Proceedings of the International Conference on Dependable Systems and Networks*, New York, NY, USA (25–28 June 2000). IEEE.

**22** Intel Corporation (2020). Intel 64 and IA-32 architectures software developer's manual, vol. 3A. System programming guide, part 1. https://www.intel.com/content/dam/www/public/us/en/documents/manuals/64-ia-32-architectures-software-developer-vol-3a-part-1-manual.pdf (accessed 27 October 2020)

**23** Quach, N. (2000). High availability and reliability in the Itanium processor. *IEEE Micro* 20 (5): 61–69.

**24** Henderson, D., Mitchell, J., and Ahrens, G. (2012). *POWER7 System RAS: Key Aspects of Power Systems Reliability, Availability, and Serviceability*. IBM Systems and Technology Group.

**25** Tullsen, D.M., Eggers, S.J., and Levy, H.M. (1995). Simultaneous multithreading: Maximizing on-chip parallelism. *Proceedings of the 22nd Annual International Symposium on Computer Architecture*, Santa Margherita Ligure, Italy (22–24 June 1995), 392–403. IEEE.

**26** Rotenberg, E. (1999). AR-SMT: a microarchitectural approach to fault tolerance in microprocessors. *Digest of Papers, the 29th Annual International Symposium on Fault-Tolerant Computing*, Madison, WI, USA (15–18 June 1999). IEEE.

**27** Purser, Z., Sundaramoorthy, K., and Rotenberg, E. (2000). A study of slipstream processors. *Proceedings of the 33rd Annual IEEE/ACM International Symposium on Microarchitecture*, Monterey, CA, USA (10–13 December 2000), 269–280. IEEE.

**28** Sundaramoorthy, K., Purser, Z., and Rotenberg, E. (2000). Slipstream processors: Improving both performance and fault tolerance. *ACM SIGOPS Operating Systems Review* 34 (5): 257–268.

**29** Austin, T.M. (1999). DIVA: A reliable substrate for deep submicron microarchitecture design. *Proceedings of the 32nd Annual ACM/IEEE International Symposium on Microarchitecture*, Haifa, Israel (16–18 November 1999). IEEE.

**30** Weaver, C. and Austin, T. (2001). A fault tolerant approach to microprocessor design. *Proceedings of the International Conference on Dependable Systems and Networks*, Goteborg, Sweden (1–4 July 2001), 411–420.

**31** Saxena, N.R., Gomez, S.F., Huang, W.J. et al. (2000). Dependable computing and online testing in adaptive and configurable systems. *IEEE Design & Test of Computers* 17 (1): 29–41.

**32** Oh, N., Mitra, S., and McCluskey, E.J. (2002). ED4I: error detection by diverse data and duplicated instructions. *IEEE Transactions on Computers* 51 (2): 180–199.

**33** Oh, N., Shirvani, P.P., and McCluskey, E.J. (2002). Error detection by duplicated instructions in super-scalar processors. *IEEE Transactions on Reliability* 51 (1): 63–75.

**34** Oh, N. and McCluskey, E.J. (2002). Error detection by selective procedure call duplication for low energy consumption. *IEEE Transactions on Reliability* 51 (4): 392–402.

**35** Rotenberg, E., Q. Jacobson, Sazeides, Y., and Smith, J. (1997). Trace processors. *Proceedings of 30th Annual International Symposium on Microarchitecture*, Research Triangle Park, NC, USA (3 December 1997), 138–148.

**36** Wang, N. and Patel, S. (2006). ReStore: symptom-based soft error detection in microprocessors. *IEEE Transactions on Dependable and Secure Computing* 3 (3): 188–201.

**37** Sarangi, S.R., Tiwari, A., and Torrellas, J. (2006). Phoenix: detecting and recovering from permanent processor design bugs with programmable hardware. *Proceedings of the 2006 39th Annual IEEE/ACM International Symposium on Microarchitecture*, Orlando, FL, USA (9–13 December 2006), 26–37. IEEE.

**38** Iyer, R.K., Nakka, N.M., Kalbarczyk, Z.T. et al. (2005). Recent advances and new avenues in hardware-level reliability support. *IEEE Micro* 25 (6): 18–29.

**39** Qureshi, M.K., Mutlu, O., and Patt, Y.N. (2005). Microarchitecture-based introspection: a technique for transient-fault tolerance in microprocessors. *Proceedings of the 2005 International Conference on Dependable Systems and Networks*, Yokohama, Japan (28 June–1 July 2005), 434–443. IEEE.

**40** Ries, G.L., Choi, G.S., and Iyer, R.K. (1994). Device-level transient fault modeling. *Proceedings of the IEEE 24th International Symposium on Fault-Tolerant Computing*, Austin, TX, USA (15–17 June 1994), 86–94. IEEE.

**41** Cha, H., Rudnick, E.M., Patel, J.H. et al. (1996). A gate-level simulation environment for alpha-particle-induced transient faults. *IEEE Transactions on Computers* 45 (11): 1248–1256.

**42** Wang, N.J., Quek, J., Rafacz, T.M. et al. (2004). Characterizing the effects of transient faults on a high-performance processor pipeline. *Proceedings of the International Conference on Dependable Systems and Networks*, Florence, Italy (28 June–1 July 2004). IEEE.

**43** Saggese, G.P., Vetteth, A., Kalbarczyk, Z. et al. (2005). Microprocessor sensitivity to failures: Control vs. execution and combinational vs. sequential logic. *Proceedings of the 2005 International Conference on Dependable Systems and Networks*, Yokohama, Japan (28 June–1 July 2005), 760–769. IEEE.

**44** Li, M.-L., Ramachandran, P., Sahoo, S.K. et al. (2008). Understanding the propagation of hard errors to software and implications for resilient system design. *Proceedings of the 13th International Conference on Architectural Support for Programming Languages and Operating Systems*, Seattle, WA, USA (1–5 March 2008), 265–276. New York, NY, USA: ACM.

# 5

# Hardware Error Detection Through Software-Implemented Techniques

## 5.1  Introduction

Even if multiple layers of hardware reliability are being used, fault manifestations may escape one, or more, or all, of the applied techniques. In that scenario, a software-level technique can provide an additional layer of error detection and recovery for such fault modes.

In addition to detecting errors that escape the hardware techniques, software techniques can also be geared toward detection of software bugs and application errors, which are not directly visible to the hardware. This chapter aims at describing techniques implemented in software that are geared toward detection of errors in hardware that evade hardware-level detection and surface up to the operating system or application layer.

Techniques implemented in software benefit from the flexibility available in developing and installing software, compared to the costs of fabricating and deploying hardware. Software-level techniques can also benefit from detailed knowledge of the application in question, which is irrelevant to most general-purpose hardware, which will have been designed to support a wide range of applications. At the same time, software-level techniques have the drawback that they more heavily impact performance, relative to similar techniques implemented in hardware. We analyze that trade-off in discussing techniques such as duplication, control-flow checking, and heartbeats. A symbiotic scenario could occur if application characteristics can be made available to hardware, while enabling programmability at the hardware layer to tailor the hardware to the reliability needs of the application. Processor-level selective replication is an example of such a hardware-implemented, application-aware technique.

## 5.2 Duplication-based Software Detection Techniques

In building reliable systems, hardware redundancy is not always the most practical and economical solution. As an alternative, redundancy in the form of duplication can be applied at the software level. Duplication in software can be introduced at the source-code level, at the instruction level, or at the intermediate-code level.

A software-based approach to duplication has several advantages over hardware approaches. The most attractive feature of software techniques is that they do not necessitate any changes in the hardware. In addition, it is well-known that even the most optimized hardware scheduler may leave slacks in scheduling instructions, and this slack time can be utilized by the compiler to minimize the performance impact due to the duplication. Also, software-based duplication gives programmers the flexibility to vary the error detection and handling mechanism within the program. As an example, the programmer could choose to selectively check only critical code sections in a program, or to handle detected errors in a special manner so as to provide the best experience to the user.

However, software duplication has some disadvantages compared to hardware approaches. The main ones are memory overhead due to the redundant source code added, and the performance overhead due to execution of redundant code and comparison of the results from the redundant execution. Another drawback of software-based redundancy techniques is the reduction in the effective instruction bandwidth available to the processor, i.e., the effective rate of the number of instructions fetched and available for the processor to execute. The reason is that for every replicated instruction, all the replicas of the instruction need to be fetched from memory. The situation is getting worse as the gap between the speeds offered by the CPU execution and the memory access mechanisms is widening.

One approach to reducing the memory access overhead is to refrain from duplicating loads and stores. If loads are not duplicated, the result of the load needs to be copied to a duplicate register. However, that has the disadvantage that errors in the loads/stores will not be detected. Another approach is to selectively duplicate portions of the application that are reliability-critical. To reduce the performance overhead due to the checking, the checking can be delayed until a variable is stored. To illustrate that approach, consider the code segment in Figure 5.1, described in [1]:

```
ld r12 = [GLOBAL]
add r11 = r12,r13
st m[r11] = r12
```

**Figure 5.1** Original code segment. *Source:* Reis et al. [[1]]. © IEEE.

When we duplicate the code (at the instruction level), we obtain the following code:

In the duplicated code, instructions 1 and 6 replicate the load and store. The checking is done before the store instruction to prevent writing of incorrect values to memory. Instructions 3, 4, and 5 compare and check the operands of the store. However, it is not sufficient to check the replicas only before the store instructions, because an incorrect branch may cause (i) the execution of stores to be skipped, (ii) incorrect stores to be executed, or (iii) incorrect operands to be provided to the store instruction. Therefore, the comparison and checking must also be performed at branch instructions, further increasing the performance overhead.

In a distributed system, in which multiple processes communicate with each other through shared memory, it is possible that the two replicas of a load instruction will return different values. That can happen when a context switch occurs after one of the loads has been executed in the duplicated process and the process that starts executing has modified the value that was loaded by the previous process. In such a case, there would be a mismatch between the values, and it would result in flagging of an error even though there was no error. Ironically, the error was an artifact of the duplication mechanism whose purpose is to reduce errors.

As mentioned before, one of the optimizations that can be applied to the code in Figure 5.2 is avoidance of the duplication of memory access instructions, loads, and stores, as shown in Figure 5.3. That would eliminate the scenario described above. However, it would also eliminate the ability to perform detection at the load instruction. The memory access due to the load is not duplicated; rather, the result of the load, written to **r12**, is copied from **r12** to the redundant register **r22** via instruction 1. The store to memory is also not duplicated.

**Figure 5.2** Duplicated code segment [1]. © IEEE.

```
   ld r12 = [GLOBAL]
1: ld r22 = [GLOBAL + offset]
   add r11 = r12,r13
2: add r21 = r22,r23
3: cmp.neq.unc p1,p0 = r11,r21
4: cmp.neq.or p1,p0 = r12,r22
5: (p1) br faultDetected
   st m[r11] = r12
6: st m[r21+offset] = r22
```

**Figure 5.3** Duplicated code with performance optimizations.

```
   ld r12=[GLOBAL]
1: add r22 = r12,0
   add r11 = r12,r13
2: add r21 = r22,r23
3: cmp.neq.unc p1,p0 = r11,r21
4: cmp.neq.or p1,p0 = r12,r22
5: (p1) br faultDetected
   st m[r11] = r12
```

Another approach to preventing the introduction of new error scenarios while duplicating loads is to use the compiler to prevent the replicas of a load instruction from being split across instructions. The compiler can use its knowledge of which instruction may lead to such mismatches and enforce the scheduling only for this class of instructions.

## 5.2.1 Examples of Software-based Duplication Techniques

In the technique called Error Detection by Duplicated Instructions (EDDI) [2], the compiler duplicates instructions at compile time to detect errors at application runtime. Different registers and variables are used for the new instructions. In contrast to hardware redundancy, EDDI does not require hardware modifications to provide the error detection capability. Duplicated instructions in EDDI do not affect the results of the program, but detect errors in the system during runtime. In a superscalar architecture, idle resources are available, as it may not be possible to find enough independent instructions in every cycle from the window of instructions fetched and waiting to be executed to keep all the functional units busy. To lessen the performance overhead of duplication, those idle resources can be used as much as possible to schedule the duplicate instructions.

The original instruction in the source code is referred to as the *master instruction (MI)*. The duplicated instruction introduced into the code is called a *shadow instruction (SI)*. The CPU registers and memory are partitioned into two groups for the sets of master and shadow instructions. The registers and memory for the MI and SI are compared using a comparison instruction (CI) to detect any mismatches due to errors. When an error is detected, an error handler can be invoked to take the appropriate recovery action.

The results of every MI and its corresponding SI could be checked with a CI immediately after their execution; however, this would lead to prohibitive performance overhead. Instead, an optimization can be applied that delays the comparison until the point at which the register values are to be stored in memory, or before control is switched to resolve an unconditional or conditional branch instruction. It is assumed that the intermediate computation results would eventually propagate to a store instruction that writes the values to architectural state. As discussed before, branch instructions are also checked because they could cause a store instruction to be skipped or an incorrect store to be executed.

Consider the code segment in Figure 5.4.

After EDDI is applied to this code segment, instructions are scheduled so as to issue as many instructions as possible that are independent, and to avoid using the same functional unit. That achieves the conflicting goals of minimizing performance impact and avoiding common mode failures. The scheduled instructions that would be used for the runtime scheduling optimization are shown in Figure 5.5. (In the figure, the MIs, SIs, and CIs are indicated in the code segment.)

**Figure 5.4** Original code segment.

$I_1$: add r1 = r2,r3

$I_2$: sub r4 = r1,r7

$I_3$: and r5 = r1,r2

$I_4$: mul r6 = r4,r5

$I_5$: st m[r5] = r6

| **Figure 5.5** EDDI code segment after performance optimizations. | | | |
|---|---|---|---|
| | $I_1$: | add r1 = r2,r3 | MI |
| | $I_2$: | sub r4 = r1,r7 | MI |
| | $I_1'$: | **add r11 = r12,r13** | **SI** |
| | $I_3$: | and r5 = r1,r2 | MI |
| | $I_2'$: | **sub r14 = r11,r17** | **SI** |
| | $I_4$: | mul r6 = r4,r5 | MI |
| | $I_3'$: | **and r15 = r11,r12** | **SI** |
| | $I_4'$: | **mul r16 = r14,r15** | **SI** |
| | $I_{c1}'$: | **cmp.neq.unc p1,p0 = r5,r15** | **CI** |
| | $I_{c2}'$: | **cmp.neq.or p1,p0 = r6,r16** | **CI** |
| | $I_{c3}'$: | **(p1) br faultDetected** | **CI** |
| | $I_5$: | st m[r5] = r6 | MI |
| | $I_5'$: | **st m[r15] = r16** | **SI** |

A "basic block" is a branch-free sequence of instructions, i.e., control cannot be transferred to (from) a basic block except to (from) the first (last) instruction. Similarly, a *storeless basic block* (SBB) is defined as a special case of a basic block in which there is no store instruction except for the last instruction. The last instruction of an SBB could be a store or a branch instruction. An attempt is made to schedule the duplicated SIs within an SBB, as much as possible, on the idle resources. A CI is placed before the last instruction of an SBB if it is one of the following:

1) An indirect branch instruction that uses a register to compute its target address.
2) A conditional branch instruction that uses a register to determine its direction.
3) A store instruction that stores a register to memory.

### 5.2.1.1 Duplication at the Level of Source Code

Software-based duplication can also be carried out at the source-code level. An example of that approach is RECCO [3], a source-code-level tool that uses code reordering and variable duplication to detect data errors occurring in the system memory or in the registers. RECCO extracts reliability-critical variables from the source code by calculating the reliability weight of a variable by using the *lifetime* and *functional dependency* heuristics. In a code reordering phase, it tries to reduce the reliability weight of the code. Finally, it performs variable duplication at the source-code level. The main disadvantage of source-code-level duplication is that the redundant code may be optimized away by the compiler, thus removing the duplicated code. Further, many code segments that are added by the compiler (e.g., stack manipulation code) would not be duplicated in this approach.

### 5.2.1.2 ED$^4$I

Error Detection by Data Diversity and Duplicated Instructions (ED$^4$I) [4] is a technique that detects temporary as well as permanent errors. ED$^4$I executes two "different" programs with identical functionality but with different data sets, and compares outputs.

The "different" programs with diverse data are generated as follows. A given program is transformed automatically to a new program wherein all variables and constants are multiplied by a diversity factor of $k$. Outputs of the transformed program are checked to ascertain whether the outputs are $k$ times greater than the results of the original program. The value of the factor $k$ establishes the hardware fault detection capability of the technique. The factor $k$ should fulfill two goals. The main one is to guarantee data integrity, namely, the probability that the two programs do not produce identical erroneous outputs. The ancillary goal is to ensure that error detection is possible by maximizing the likelihood that the two programs will produce different outputs for the same hardware fault. The factor $k$, however, should not trigger an overflow in the functional units.

One disadvantage of ED$^4$I is its high overhead (estimated at around 90%) due to the execution of two programs on the processor. Another is that programs have to be recompiled using ED$^4$I, so the source code must be available. Also, there is overhead, although a one-time overhead, in determining the optimal value of $k$ for the application and generating the transformed program.

## 5.3 Control-Flow Checking

Control-flow errors can cause a divergence from the sequence of program counter values seen during the error-free execution of the application. These errors can lead to data corruption, process crashes, or fail-silence violations.[1] Control-flow errors have been shown to account for between 33% [6] and 77% [7] of all errors.

---

1 A fail-silent application process either works correctly or stops functioning (i.e., becomes silent) if an internal failure occurs [5]. A violation of this premise is termed a *fail-silence* violation. In distributed applications, fail-silence violations can have potentially catastrophic effects by causing fault propagation.

The authors of [8] show that about one-third of the activated errors in the application code of a non-data-intensive application lead to control-flow errors.

### 5.3.1 The State of the Art

Broadly speaking, state-of-the-art techniques detect between 15 and 30% of injected errors; the remaining errors are detected by the system detection techniques, such as raising of an operating system signal. Furthermore, the unstated assumption in providing error detection is that system detection (i.e., process crash) is an acceptable way of detecting an error. From a recovery point of view, it is questionable whether a process crash is an acceptable form of detection. Data from real systems have shown that while many crashes are benign, severe system failures often result from latent errors that cause undetected error propagation, which results in crashes or hangs and severe recovery problems [9–13]. Further, application recovery time is higher when recovery involves spawning of a new process (after a crash) rather than creation of a new thread (in the case of multi-threaded processes).

This section provides (i) a brief survey of the approaches to hardware- and software-based control-flow checking; (ii) discussion of ECCA (enhanced control checking with assertions) [14] and PECOS (preemptive control signature) [8], two representative examples of software-implemented techniques for control-flow error detection; and (iii) a summary of results from the fault-injection-based evaluation of ECCA and PECOS. ECCA is an example of *nonpreemptive* control-flow checking; the correctness of a control flow is checked after the execution flow has changed (e.g., a branch or jump instruction has been executed). PECOS facilitates preemptive control-flow checking, as it verifies the correctness of the control flow of a program before any change in the execution flow occurs.

#### 5.3.1.1 Hardware Schemes

The field of control-flow checking has evolved over the years. The earliest paper, by Yau and Chen [15], outlines a general control-flow checking scheme that uses the program specification language PDL. Mahmood and McCluskey [16] present a survey of the various techniques in hardware for detecting control-flow errors. Many schemes for checking control flow in hardware have been proposed [17–22].

A summary of some of those techniques is presented in Table 5.1. The basic scheme is to divide the application program into *blocks*. Each block has a single entry and a single exit point. A *golden signature* (or *reference signature*) is associated with the block. It represents an encoding of the correct execution sequence of the instructions in the block. At runtime, the watchdog processor calculates the selected signature. The watchdog validates the application program at the end of a block by comparing the block's runtime signature with its golden signature.

**Table 5.1** Survey of representative control-flow error detection techniques.

| Technique | Outline of scheme | Workload, coverage, resources | Comments |
|---|---|---|---|
| Signatured instruction stream (SIS) [23] | The signature is embedded in the application instruction stream at the assembly code level. An optimization called *branch address hashing* reduces memory overhead by eliminating reference signatures at branch points. | Quicksort, string search, matrix transpose on MC-68000<br>*Coverage:* 36%<br>*Hardware:* Watchdog processor with cyclic code signature generator<br>*Software:* Modified assembler and loader | Needs runtime support to rehash branch addresses before target address calculation. |
| Path signature analysis (PSA) [19] | Signatures are computed for paths, i.e., sequences of branch-free intervals (or nodes). Program graph is decomposed into path sets, with all paths in a path set starting and ending at the same node. All paths in a path set have the same signature. | Fifty unspecified programs from data manipulation to I/O control routines on MC-68000<br>*Coverage:* Not available<br>*Hardware:* Watchdog processor<br>*Software:* Modified assembler | Requires complicated parser for finding path sets. Error detection latency can be significant, since detection is done at the end of the path. |
| On-line signature learning and checking (OSLC) [24] | Application is decomposed into sections, each having a number of branch-free intervals. On receiving Exit-From-Block signal from the signature generator, the checker checks the runtime signature against signatures of all blocks in the same section. | Pseudo-random number generator, string search, bit manipulation, quick sort, prime number generator on Z-80<br>*Coverage:* 86.3%<br>*Hardware:* Watchdog processor<br>*Software:* Exhaustive tester | Requires exhaustive path activation to generate golden signatures. Synchronization required between the application processor, signature generator, and the checker. |

| | | | |
|---|---|---|---|
| Time–time-address signature checking [25] | Program is decomposed into branch-free blocks (BFB).<br><br>The watchdog starts a timer on getting notification of beginning of BFB. If notification of end of BFB is not received before timeout expires, an error is detected.<br><br>At block exit, watchdog checks that exit is made at (start address + size). | Linked list manipulation, matrix manipulation, quicksort on MC6809E (8-bit CPU)<br><br>*Coverage:* 23.9% (heavy ion radiation), 48.6% (power system disturbance)<br><br>*Hardware:* Timer, watchdog processor<br><br>*Software:* Software to decompose application into BFB and embed signature instructions | Difficult to determine time bounds for the watchdog.<br><br>Sending frequent signals to the external watchdog may result in performance degradation. |
| Concurrent process monitoring with no reference signatures [21] | A known signature function is applied to the instruction stream at compilation time.<br><br>When the accumulated signature forms an $m$-out-of-$n$ code or a branch point is reached, the instruction is tagged.<br><br>At runtime, a watchdog verifies that, at a tagged instruction, an $m$-out-of-$n$ code has been accumulated.<br><br>No reference signatures are required. | Possibly no implementation exists<br><br>*Coverage:* Not Available<br><br>*Hardware:* Watchdog processor<br><br>*Software:* Software to indicate checkpoints where code word needs to be checked and tag memory | One extra word per branch is required to force the accumulated signature to become an $m$-out-of-$n$ code.<br><br>Better at detecting control bit errors, than control flow errors. |
| Block signature self checking (BSSC) [26] | The program is divided into basic blocks, and each block is assigned a signature (the address of the first instruction in the basic block).<br><br>A call instruction at the end of the block fetches the signature from the variable and compares it to an embedded signature following it. A mismatch signals an error. | Linked list manipulation, quicksort, matrix manipulation on MC6809<br><br>*Coverage:* 15–22%<br><br>*Hardware:* None<br><br>*Software:* Software to identify blocks, assign calls and signatures | The assertions introduce control flow instructions of their own.<br><br>The technique assumes absolute addresses for the start of the basic block. This will preclude using it for relocatable code. |

*(Continued)*

**Table 5.1** (Continued)

| Technique | Outline of scheme | Workload, coverage, resources | Comments |
|---|---|---|---|
| Enhanced control-flow checking with assertions (ECCA) [14] | The entry and the exit points of the branch-free intervals in a high-level language are fortified through assertions inserted in the instruction stream. In case of a control flow error, the BID (Branch Free Interval Identifier) computation will cause a divide-by-zero error. | Two SPEC Int92 benchmarks<br>*Coverage:* 18.4–37.5% (022.li), 27.8–73.0% (espresso)<br>*Hardware:* None<br>*Software:* C-language lexer, filter and parser, signature generator | A parser for high-level code can be complex because of larger variations in code structure in the high-level language. |
| Preemptive control signature (PECOS) [8] | An assertion is embedded at the assembly level before each control flow instruction. Determination of the runtime target address and its comparison against the valid addresses is done before the jump to the target address, i.e., preemptively. In case of an error, the assertion block raises a divide-by-zero exception. | Dynamic Host Configuration Protocol (DHCP)<br>*Coverage:* 87.5% (control flow instructions)<br>*Hardware:* None<br>*Software:* Parser, which embeds assertions into the application assembly code. | The parser for embedding the assertions blocks must take into account specifics of the instruction set of a given processor. |

| Technique | Description | Benchmark / Coverage / Hardware / Software | Results |
|---|---|---|---|
| Abstract control signatures (ACS) [27] | The approach is based on the insight that control flow that exhibits simple but repeated properties of correctness is almost always entirely correct. ACS achieves abstraction by checking simpler properties (e.g., path length) and promoting control flow signature checking from individual basic blocks to group of blocks. | SPECINT2000 benchmark suite. *Coverage:* 96.6% (the percentage of faults out of total injected faults that do not result in Silent Data Corruptions). *Hardware:* None. *Software:* Parser, which takes LLVM Intermediate Representation of the code to embed signature computations and checks. | ACS reduces the number of SDCs while incurring only 11% performance overhead. |
| Control flow checking by software signatures (CFCSS) [28] | The program is divided into basic blocks. All basic blocks are assigned different arbitrary numbers (signatures), which are embedded into the program. During program execution, a run-time signature is stored in one of the general-purpose registers and compared with the stored signature of the node whenever control is transferred to a new node | Benchmark programs: LZW (compression), FFT (Fast Fourier Transform), matrix multiplication, quick sort, insert sort, Hanoi, Shuffle. (R4400 MIPS processor). *Coverage:* 96.9% (only 3.1% of branching faults produced undetected incorrect outputs). *Hardware:* None. *Software:* Signatures are embedded into assembly source code, and the resulting assembly code is compiled. | A high-performance overhead from 16.2 (for FFT) to 69.2% (for Insert Sort). |

Among the hardware schemes, two broad classes of techniques have been defined that access the precomputed signature in different ways. *Embedded signature monitoring* (ESM) embeds the signature in the application program itself [20, 22], while *autonomous signature monitoring* (ASM) stores the signature in memory dedicated to the watchdog processor [17]. Upadhyaya and Ramamurthy [21] explore an approach in which no reference signatures need to be stored, and the runtime signature is any $M$-out-of-$N$ codeword.

Use of hardware schemes in distributed environments suffers from several limitations:

1) Hardware schemes are quite suitable for embedded processors running single programs, but they do not scale well to complex modern processors. If multiple processes (or threads) execute on the main processor, then the memory access pattern observed by the external watchdog will not correspond to the signature of any single process, and hence errors will be flagged by mistake. The cause is the different possible interleavings among the multiple processes being executed.

2) The underlying assumption is that in the presence of errors, runtime memory accesses observed by the watchdog will differ from the reference signature. Consequently, an error after an instruction has been fetched from memory, e.g., while it is residing in the cache of the main processor, will not be caught even if it causes application misbehavior. For current processors with increasingly large cache sizes, such errors are no longer negligible, and a watchdog would have to be embedded in the processor itself, which in turn would present new challenges.

3) Hardware watchdog schemes require transmission on the system bus to communicate information to the external watchdog (e.g., the OSLC signature generator communicates the runtime signature to the checker). Transmission errors on the bus (address or data) during those transmission cycles would potentially reduce the coverage of the signature techniques.

### 5.3.1.2 Software Schemes

The software techniques partition the application into blocks, either in the assembly language or in the high-level language and insert appropriate instrumentation at the beginning and/or end of the blocks. The checking code is inserted in the instruction stream, eliminating the need for a hardware watchdog processor. Representative software-based control-flow monitoring schemes include Block Signature Self Checking (BSSC) [26], Control Checking with Assertions (CCA) [29], ECCA [14], and PECOS [8].

Table 5.1 presents a survey of representative hardware and software techniques for control-flow error detection. The first five techniques require additional hardware, while the last two are software-based approaches. The table mentions the results of evaluations of the available techniques. For the results, an attempt has been made to remove the cases in which the detection was done by something other than the technique under consideration; e.g., system detection, which crashes the application process, has been removed from the error detection coverage number.

Recent research also indicates certain inefficiencies of CFC techniques that do not seem to justify incurring performance overheads (when implemented in software) and power/silicon area overheads (when implemented in hardware) [30]. This will depend on the fault model that is being targeted.

The remainder of this section describes example experimental evaluations of software-implemented control-flow checking techniques ECCA and PECOS to substantial applications.

## 5.3.2 Enhanced Control-Flow Checking with Assertions (ECCA)

### 5.3.2.1 Insertion of ECCA Assertions

*Enhanced control-flow checking using assertions* (ECCA) is a means of detecting control-flow errors at both the high code level (i.e., a high-level language such as C) and the intermediate code level (i.e., the *register transfer language*) of applications. In applying ECCA, the following steps are used: (i) *branch-free intervals* (BFIs) in a given high- or intermediate-level program are identified, and the entry and exit points of these intervals are determined; (ii) consecutive BFIs are grouped into blocks whose sizes are determined based on overhead-coverage trade-off analysis; and (iii) assertions are inserted in the blocks for use in the run-time detection of control-flow errors. In the discussion presented here, we focus on the implementation of ECCA at the high-level language, in this case C.

### 5.3.2.2 SET and TEST Assertions in ECCA

As indicated earlier, in ECCA the program in the high-level language is divided into blocks. Each block consists of consecutive branch-free intervals (BFIs) and is protected with two assertions, neither of which contains a branch. If each block contains only one BFI, that arrangement provides maximum coverage but incurs maximum overhead. After a unique prime number ID larger than 2, called the *block identifier* (BID), is assigned to each block, the two assertions are added. The *first assertion* (called *SET*), a simple assignment executed upon entry to the block, is of the following form:

$$id \leftarrow \frac{BID}{\left(id \bmod BID\right) \cdot \left(id \bmod 2\right)},$$

where the elements in the assignment are as follows: (i) id is a global integer variable updated during execution time upon entry into and exit from the block and (ii) BID is a unique prime number larger than 2 generated for the block during the preprocessing phase. (BID is hard-coded into the program.) The assignment will result in a divide-by-zero error if either $\overline{\text{id} \bmod \text{BID}} = 0$ or id mod 2 = 0. In other words, the SET assertion makes it possible to detect the following types of errors: (i) a branch from the middle of a block (i.e., BFI) to another block, (ii) a branch to the middle of a BFI, and (iii) a branch to an illegal block.

The *second assertion* (called TEST), also an assignment, is executed immediately before the block is left. It is of the following form:

$$id \leftarrow \text{NEXT} + \overline{(id - \text{BID})},$$

where NEXT is an integer generated in the preprocessing phase and equal to the product of blocks' BIDs, which can be accessed from the current block, i.e., NEXT $= \prod \text{BID}_{\text{Permissible}}$. Observe that the result of $\overline{(id - \text{BID})}$ is either 0 or 1. The TEST assertion ensures that, at the exit from a block, the value assigned to the id of the block is such that if an error occurs, a subsequent execution of the SET assertion (in the following block of the execution flow) will generate a divide-by-zero exception and thus detect the error.

To automate the process of embedding the assertions in the application code, a dedicated ECCA preprocessor places assertions at the boundaries of the program blocks. The preprocessor consists of three major components: a pseudo control-flow C-parser, a lexical analyzer, and a translation unit located between the parser and the lexical analyzer to filter out segments of code that do not change the program's control flow. The following code is an example of high-level code that needs to be preprocessed using ECCA [14]. For simplicity, a block contains only one BFI.

```
...
/* Beginning of original code */
foo=1;

if foo
{boo=10}

else
{hoo=20}
foo=0;
/* End of original code */
```

Preprocessing modifies the code, inserting assertions as follows:

```
...
/* Beginning of preprocessed code */
/* <BID> is 3 */
foo=1;
id=35+!!(id-3);
/*Note: 35 is the result of multiplying permissible
blocks' BIDs, i.e., 5*7 */

if foo
{
/* <BID> is 5 */
id=5/(((!(id%5))*(id%2));
boo=10;
id=11+!!(id-5);
}

else
{
/* <BID> is 7 */
id=7/(((!(id%7))*(id%2));
hoo=20;
id=11+!!(id-7);
}
/* <BID> is 11 */
id=11(((!(id%11))*(id%2));
```

### 5.3.2.3 ECCA Error Detection

A *control-flow error* is an error that incorrectly transfers control from one block to another. It can be analytically demonstrated [14] that the ECCA approach can detect all single control-flow faults that cross block boundaries. Such faults include branches (i) from the middle of a block to another block, (ii) from a block to the middle of another block, and (iii) from a block to an illegal block. Data-value errors are not covered by the ECCA method, e.g., illegal branches that do not cross a block boundary and incorrect decisions on conditional branches.

Although ECCA is designed to detect all single control-flow errors, it can also detect most multiple control-flow errors. The only situation that will cause a multiple control-flow error to go undetected by ECCA is one in which the first block and the last block in the sequence are the same.

To go beyond terminating the system upon detection of a control-flow error, i.e., to determine the cause of the error or to recover from it, requires mechanisms beyond those described thus far. Specifically, it is necessary to determine whether a divide-by-zero exception was caused in the original code or the inserted code. There are two ways to do so: via an *if–then* statement or via an *exception handler*.

*If–then.* An if–then statement can be used to transfer control to a control-flow error-handling routine. The obvious drawback of this approach is that it introduces an additional branch in the assertion and thus reduces coverage. This type of assertion at the beginning of a block would be as follows:

```
/*Beginning of block*/
if !((!(id%<BID>))*(id%2))
        ...go to handling routine...
else
{
        id=<BID>; ...body of block...
```

Exception handling makes it possible to separate the error case from the normal case, thus increasing performance. To install an exception handler, one can use a global routine *catchfpe()* (found in *signal.h* of the system library).

```
/*Beginning of program*/
#include <signal.h>
...
#define SIGFPE 8
...
void catchfpe() {
        if id is prime, then data divide by zero
        else control flow error divide by zero we then
                go to handling routine
}
```

### 5.3.2.4 Experimental Evaluation of ECCA

FERRARI [31], a software-based, fault/error-injection tool, has been used to evaluate ECCA [29]. FERRARI can inject transient errors that last for only one instruction cycle and permanent errors that may persist throughout the entire execution of the application. The platform for evaluation was a SUN SPARC workstation. A target application was instrumented with ECCA, and its behavior when injected with errors was studied.

The error models were carefully chosen to represent a wide range of transient hardware errors and some software bugs.[2] The chosen errors and bugs are listed in

---

2 For example, a pointer overflow error may be modeled by a hardware bit flip in the data line when the operand of a load instruction is being fetched.

**Table 5.2** Transient error models.

| Error model | Description |
|---|---|
| ADDIF | Address line error resulting in execution of a different instruction taken from the instruction stream |
| DATAIF | Data line error when an opcode is fetched |
| DATAOF | Data line error when an operand is fetched |
| ADDIF2 | Address line error resulting in execution of two different instructions taken from the instruction stream |
| ADDOF | Address line error when an operand is fetched |
| ADDOS | Address line error when an operand is stored |
| DATAOS | Data line error when an operand is stored |
| CndCR | Errors in condition code flags |

*Source:* Alkhalifa et al. [14]. © IEEE.

Table 5.2. For each experiment, errors belonging to a single category were injected one at a time. Transient hardware errors/failures served as the error model for the experiments[3] for two specific reasons: (i) previous studies indicated that more than 90% of the physical failures in computers are transient [32, 33], and (ii) failures that span many cycles are easily detected, even by relatively simple error detection mechanisms [7, 34].

Errors were injected into the registers as well as into the code segment of the application. For error injections into the registers, the specific register to be corrupted was selected randomly. For the code segment injection, the application code that was injected also included the libraries. The target location where the error was to be injected was chosen randomly. For each run, the bit position(s) that needed to be flipped were also chosen randomly. When the program execution reached the target address, the program was stopped, and a software trap was activated. At that point, the error was injected via modification of the internal state of the processor with respect to the requested error model. The program was then allowed to proceed.

The number of runs for each experiment was chosen to obtain the same system behavior (±0.5%) even after the number of runs was increased. The system behavior is defined by the percentages of detected and undetected errors and the contribution of each of the embedded error detection mechanisms. In each experiment conducted, a selected application was first run without having any errors injected into the system. The output of that initial run, called the *reference*, was written to

---

3 Permanent failures are usually covered by dedicated hardware detection mechanisms, including periodic sampling to check the status of hardware components.

**Table 5.3** Error detection coverage for *espresso* without ECCA.

| Error Models | System detection | Timeouts | User detection | Undetected | Overall coverage |
|---|---|---|---|---|---|
| | Detection coverage without ECCA | | | | |
| AddIF | 76.4% | 1.9% | 12.6% | 9.1% | 90.9% |
| AddIF2 | 90.1% | 0.7% | 5.4% | 3.8% | 96.2% |
| AddOF | 91.6% | 0.9% | 4.7% | 2.8% | 97.2% |
| AddOS | 88.8% | 0.8% | 7.3% | 3.0% | 97.0% |
| DataIF | 86.9% | 1.0% | 8.0% | 4.1% | 95.9% |
| DataOF | 77.8% | 1.8% | 12.2% | 8.2% | 91.8% |
| DataOS | 80.4% | 3.7% | 10.6% | 5.3% | 94.7% |
| CndCR | 26.7% | 0.0% | 53.3% | 20% | 80.0% |

*Source:* Alkhalifa et al. [14]. © IEEE.

a file for future comparisons. A fault or error was then injected into the system while the application was running. If no error detection mechanism was triggered, the output of that run was compared with the reference. A difference indicated that an undetected error had resulted in incorrect output, indicating a lack of coverage of the ECCA error detection/recovery mechanism.

The following three test programs were used to demonstrate the capabilities of ECCA: (i) Test1 had all the C language branch constructs; (ii) Test2 was SPEC Benchmark Release 1 008.*espresso*, an integer benchmark; and (iii) Test3 was SPEC Benchmark Release 1 022.*li*, a CPU-intensive integer benchmark. Tables 5.3 and 5.4 present fault injection results for the *espresso* application.

The experimental results show that ECCA is capable of detecting data line, address line, control line, and register errors with high coverage. The memory and performance overhead can also be reduced by selectively inserting the assertions. The architectural portability of ECCA allows its implementation in heterogeneous distributed systems.

### 5.3.3 Preemptive Control Signature (PECOS)

PECOS monitors the runtime control path taken by an application and compares it with the set of expected control paths to validate the application's behavior. The scheme can handle situations in which the control paths are either statically or dynamically (i.e., at runtime) determined. Figure 5.6 depicts the basic PECOS instrumentation and the resulting change to the application code structure. The application is decomposed into blocks, and a group of PECOS instructions called

**Table 5.4** Error detection coverage for *espresso* with ECCA.

| Error models | System detection | Timeouts | User detection | ECCA | Undetected | Overall coverage |
|---|---|---|---|---|---|---|
| | | | **Detection Coverage with ECCA** | | | |
| AddIF | 32.8% | 0.5% | 10.6% | 55.0% | 1.1% | 98.9% |
| AddIF2 | 65.0% | 0.8% | 2.5% | 30.8% | 0.8% | 99.2% |
| AddOF | 69.4% | 0.9% | 1.3% | 27.8% | 0.6% | 99.4% |
| AddOS | 61.3% | 0.3% | 3.4% | 34.3% | 0.6% | 99.4% |
| DataIF | 47.0% | 0.0% | 3.8% | 48.1% | 1.1% | 98.9% |
| DataOF | 35.1% | 0.9% | 5.1% | 56.4% | 2.5% | 97.5% |
| DataOS | 17.3% | 1.1% | 7.1% | 73.0% | 1.5% | 98.5% |
| CndCR | 25.0% | 0.0% | 0.0% | 75.0% | 0.0% | 100.0% |

*Source:* Alkhalifa et al. [14]. © IEEE.

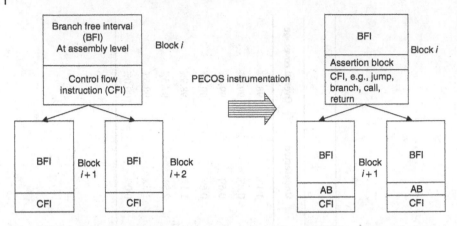

**Figure 5.6** Change in the code structure due to insertion of PECOS assertion blocks.

*assertion blocks* (ABs) are embedded in the instruction stream of the application to be monitored. Normally, each block is a basic block in the traditional compiler sense of a branch-free interval (i.e., the decomposition of the code is performed at the assembly-code level), and each basic block is terminated by a *control-flow instruction* (CFI), which is used as a trigger for PECOS. As shown in Figure 5.6, the PECOS ABs are inserted at trigger points. The AB contains (i) the set of valid target addresses (or address offsets) the application may jump to, which are determined either at compile time or at runtime and (ii) code to determine the runtime target address. The determination of the runtime target address and its comparison against the valid addresses is done *before* the jump to the target address is made. If an error occurs, the AB raises a divide-by-zero exception, which is handled by the PECOS signal handler. The signal handler checks whether the problem was caused by a control-flow error[4], and, if it was, takes a recovery action, e.g., terminates the malfunctioning thread of execution.

Experiments with random error injection into the text segment of an application process have shown that with a nonpreemptive scheme, a significant number of cases lead to a process crash before detection by the technique. For example, experiments using a SPECInt benchmark application instrumented with ECCA showed that 29–70% of random errors resulted in system detections (i.e., process crashes). A crash of the entire application process incurs a higher recovery overhead [8].

---

4 The PECOS signal handler examines the PC (program counter) from which the signal was raised, and, if it corresponds to a PECOS AB, concludes that a control-flow error raised the signal.

Recall that PECOS is a preemptive technique, i.e., it determines the runtime target address and compares that against the valid addresses *before* the jump to the target address is made. As a result, with PECOS (unlike other techniques), execution of instructions from an invalid target location is unlikely.

At compile time, the PECOS tool instruments the application assembly code with ABs placed at the end of each block. Note that the assertion block itself does not introduce additional CFIs. The task of the assertion block can be broken down into two subtasks:

- Determine the runtime target address of the CFI (referred to as $X_{out}$ in the following discussion).
- Compare the runtime target address with the valid target addresses determined by a compile-time analysis. In general, the number of valid target addresses can be one (jump), two (branch), or many (calls or returns). For two valid target addresses, $X_1$ and $X_2$, the resulting control decision implemented by the assertion block is shown below. The comparison is designed so that an impending illegal control flow will cause a divide-by-zero exception in the calculation of the variable ID, indicating an error.

1) Determine the runtime target address $\left[ = X_{out} \right]$
2) Extract the list of valid target addresses $\left[ = \left\{ X_1, X_2 \right\} \right]$
3) Calculate ID: $X_{out} \times 1/P$,

$$\text{where,} \quad P = ! \left[ \left( X_{out} - X_1 \right) \times \left( X_{out} - X_2 \right) \right]$$

### 5.3.3.1 PECOS Error Detection

In the following example, PECOS is applied to protect a conditional branch statement. The target address of the CFI is static, i.e., it is a constant embedded in the instruction stream. We will discuss how an error in the CFI or in the assertion block instruction is captured.

Figure 5.7(i) shows a basic block (for the SPARC architecture) terminated with the conditional branch instruction. Figure 5.7(ii) shows the same block with the assertion block inserted into the object code by the PECOS tool. Instructions 1–3 load the runtime instruction, which has the branch opcode and the runtime target address combined, into register $l7$.[5] In that computation, SPARC uses program-counter-relative offsets for addressing. Instructions 4–5 load the valid

---

5 The assertion uses local registers $l5$, $l6$, and $l7$, which were not used by the applications in our study.

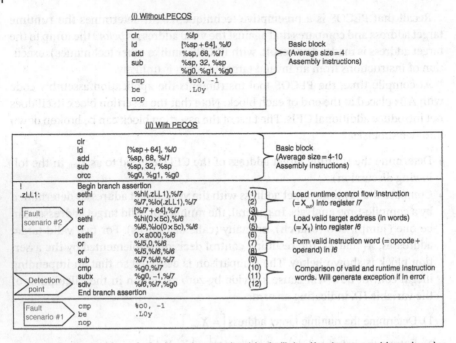

**Figure 5.7** Assembly code for branch assertion block. (i) Application assembly code prior to PECOS instrumentation. (ii) Application assembly code instrumented with PECOS AB.

target offset[6] in bytes into register *l6*. The offsets are determined by the usual compile-time creation and analysis of the application's control-flow graph. Instructions 6–8 form the valid instruction by combining the valid offset with the opcode, and then load it into register *l6*. Instructions 9–12 compare the valid instruction word (in *l6*) with the runtime instruction word (in *l7*) and raise a divide-by-zero floating-point exception if there is a mismatch.

Now consider an error case. In the fault/error scenario in Figure 5.7(i), an error in the memory word storing the conditional branch instruction causes a corruption of the correct memory word (hex value: 0x02800017) to an incorrect value (hex value: 0xffffffff). In the absence of a preemptive control-flow error detection scheme like PECOS, execution would have reached the incorrect memory word, and the operating system would have generated the illegal instruction signal, which, in the absence of a signal handler, would have caused the application process to crash. Now consider the assembly code segment with the PECOS

---

6 In this case, there is only one valid target offset. In the general case, one can load multiple valid offsets and compare the runtime offset against each of them.

assertion block in place. At the end of instruction 3, the incorrect memory word 0xffffffff is loaded into register *l7*. The correct memory word is loaded into register *l6*, and a subsequent comparison between the two register values causes a floating-point exception signal to be raised. By examining the PC, the PECOS signal handler will determine that the signal was raised because of a control-flow error.

By design, the exception is raised before the CFI is executed; therefore, the error cannot propagate, and the PECOS signal handler can take appropriate recovery action, e.g., shut down the offending thread. Similarly, any error that hits the PECOS assertion block, e.g., changing of the operand of *sethi* in instruction 4 from, e.g., 0x5c to 0xfd (the fault/error scenario shown in Figure 5.7(ii)), will also be detected by the comparison and division in instruction 12.

### 5.3.3.2 Experimental Evaluation of PECOS

In this section, we describe the evaluation of PECOS applied to a substantial real-world application: the *Dynamic Host Configuration Protocol* (DHCP) application. Error injection campaigns were conducted in the baseline (uninstrumented) DHCP first and then into DHCP instrumented with PECOS. The goal was to evaluate relative improvements in the dependability metrics, including percentages of system detection, hangs, and fail-silence violations. NFTAPE, a software-implemented fault injection tool, was used to conduct the error injection campaigns [35].

### 5.3.3.2.1 *Target Application*

*DHCP.* The Dynamic Host Configuration Protocol (DHCP [23]) application is widely used in mobile and wireless environments to provide configuration information to hosts on an IP network. DHCP supports dynamic allocation of IP addresses in which the server allocates an IP address to the client for a limited amount of time (termed the *lease time*), after which the server can reclaim the address.

The protocol operates in two phases. In Phase 1, the client broadcasts a DHCPDISCOVER message on its local physical subnet. One or more servers on the network respond to the client request by sending a DHCPOFFER message, which contains a tentative offer of an IP address and configuration parameters. In Phase 2, the client collects the DHCPOFFER responses from all the servers that have responded and chooses one server to interact with via a DHCPREQUEST broadcast message. On receiving the DHCPREQUEST message, the chosen server commits the binding of the IP address of the client to a lease database in stable storage and responds with a DHCPACK message. If the selected server is unable to satisfy the DHCPREQUEST message, then the server responds with a DHCPNAK message. When the client's lease is close to expiration, it tries to renew the lease by resending the DHCPREQUEST message.

**Table 5.5**   Cumulative results from directed injection to control-flow instructions.

| Category | Without PECOS | With PECOS | Improvement Factor {(measured value w/o PECOS)/(measured value with PECOS)} |
|---|---|---|---|
| Error not activated | 1380 | 1446 | n/a |
| Error activated but | | | |
| Not manifested | 426 (38.0%) | 46 (4.3%) | n/a |
| PECOS detection | n/a | 922 (87.5%) | n/a |
| System detection | 612 (54.6%) | 75 (7.1%) | 7.7 |
| Application hang | 18 (1.6%) | 5 (0.5%) | 3.2 |
| Program aborted | 24 (2.2%) | 5 (0.5%) | 4.4 |
| Fail-silence violation | 40 (3.6%) | 1 (0.1%) | 36.0 |
| Total | 2500 | 2500 | n/a |

Table 5.5 presents the results of the injections directed into control-flow instructions. Each row in the table gives a sum of the number of cases from all error injection campaigns. The fourth column gives the improvement due to the PECOS instrumentation. Reductions in system detections, hangs, program aborts, and fail-silence violations are considered improvements.

The results in Table 5.5 characterize the effectiveness of PECOS in detecting errors when an error directly affects a CFI (i.e., effectiveness in detecting the errors that PECOS was designed to protect against). The major improvements gained by instrumenting the DHCP server with PECOS are as follows: (i) PECOS detects more than 87% of all activated errors; (ii) fail-silence coverage is improved by about a factor of 36; (iii) system detection is reduced by a factor of 7.7; and (iv) application hang cases are reduced by about 3.2 times.

In a second experiment, faults were injected randomly in any instruction in the instruction stream (control-flow or not). Table 5.6 shows the results for this fault injection experiment. Some of the important observations in these results are that PECOS greatly reduces the changes of an application hang by pre-emptively detecting the error. Other failure symtoms such as fail-silence violations and program abort also are reduced. It is interesting to note that about 30% of the faults

**Table 5.6** Cumulative results from injection to random instructions from the instruction stream.

| Category | Without PECOS | With PECOS | Improvement factor {(measured value w/o PECOS)/(measured value with PECOS)} |
|---|---|---|---|
| Error not activated | 2486 | 2476 | n/a |
| Error activated but | | | |
| Not manifested | 770 (50.9%) | 513 (33.7%) | n/a |
| PECOS detection | n/a | 480 (31.5%) | n/a |
| System detection | 610 (40.3%) | 483 (31.7%) | 1.3 |
| Application hang | 22 (1.4%) | 2 (0.1%) | 14.0 |
| Program aborted | 40 (2.6%) | 24 (1.6%) | 1.6 |
| Fail-silence violation | 72 (4.8%) | 22 (1.4%) | 3.4 |
| Total | 4000 | 4000 | n/a |

that were activated did not manifest in any manner that impacts the functionality of the application.

### 5.3.3.2.2 *Performance Measurements*

Performance measurements for the DHCP application with and without PECOS instrumentation were performed from the server side as well as the client side. The server-side measurement gave the time between the server's receiving of a request from the client and its sending out of a response. The time on the client side includes that time plus the time spent in the network. The performance measurements are presented in Table 5.7. The measurements for the two main phases of the protocol are given separately.

Note that PECOS allows selective instrumentation of the application. Performance measurements are made once with the entire DHCP server instrumented, and once with only the core protocol engine instrumented. Server overhead is the percentage overhead seen at the server, and the client overhead is that seen from the client side, including the network overhead. The entire DHCP server consists of 30 source files (written in C) and includes all the support functions, such as receiving of a packet from the network, used by the core protocol

**Table 5.7** Performance measurements for DHCP instrumented with PECOS.

| Phase 1 DHCPDISCOVER → DHCPOFFER | | Phase 2 DHCP REQUEST → DHCPACK/DHCPNAK | |
|---|---|---|---|
| Server overhead | Client overhead | Server overhead | Client overhead |
| Exhaustive instrumentation of DHCP server | | | |
| 25.03% | 15.34% | 29.91% | 25.17% |
| Selective instrumentation of DHCP server (only the core protocol engine) | | | |
| 5.20% | 10.92% | 13.80% | 18.07% |

engine. In terms of lines of source code, the DHCP core protocol engine constitutes 11% of the entire DHCP server code. In terms of the size of the object code, the DHCP core protocol engine is 7.2%. However, the proportion of time spent in the core protocol engine is much greater than the relative code size of the protocol engine.[7] The results show an overhead in the range of 5–10%, depending on the fraction of the target software instrumented.

## 5.4 Heartbeats

A *heartbeat* is a common approach to detecting process and node failures in a distributed (networked) computing environment. There are two basic ways in which information about component failures is propagated in the system: the *push model* and the *pull model*. A combination of the two can also be used [36].

In the push model, the monitored objects are active and periodically send heartbeat ("I am alive") messages to report their aliveness to the monitoring entity. If the monitoring entity does not receive a heartbeat from a monitored object within specific time bounds, it declares the monitored object to have failed, and appropriate recovery action is initiated. This method is efficient, since only one-way messages are sent in the system.

In the pull model, the monitored objects are passive. Periodically, the monitors send aliveness requests to monitored objects. A reply by a monitored object means it is alive. This model may not be as efficient as the push model, since two-way messages are involved. On the other hand, it is easier for the application developer to use the pull model. If the monitored objects are passive, they do not need to have any knowledge of time factors, e.g., they do not have to know the frequency with which the monitor expects to receive messages.

---

7 However, there is no easy way to determine the proportion of time spent in one particular file.

The push and pull models have their pros and cons and are essentially complementary. A choice of which to use depends on the nature of the application. A *dual protocol*, which is a combination of the two models, has also been proposed. It consists of two distinct phases. During the first phase, all the monitored objects are assumed to use the push model and hence to send heartbeat messages. After some delay, the monitors switch to the second phase, in which they assume that all monitored objects that did not send a heartbeat during the first phase use the pull model. In the second phase, the monitors send an aliveness request to each monitored object and expect an aliveness message (similar to that used the push model) in return. If the monitored object does not send this message within some specific time bound, the monitor declares a failure.

### 5.4.1 Timeout Mechanism

In general, *timeouts* are of two kinds:

- *Static* (or *fixed-value+*) timeouts are used in the vast majority of existing approaches. For example, in the Microsoft DCOM Architecture [37], a pinging mechanism is used in which clients send "I am alive" messages to objects on the server. If a client does not send an "I am alive" message for a prespecified number of successive timeouts of fixed duration, then the server declares the client to have crashed, and all the resources allocated to that client during the execution are revoked.

- *Dynamic* or *adaptive* timeouts are employed by heartbeat protocols that try to adapt dynamically to variability in the behavior of the application, system, and network. Chen et al. [38] propose an adaptive timeout algorithm that uses a linear combination of the previous $n$ arrival times of the heartbeat that is added to a constant safety margin to estimate the arrival time for the next heartbeat. If the next heartbeat does not arrive within that time, the process is declared to have failed. Bertier et al. [39] propose a slight modification of that algorithm that replaces the constant safety margin with a dynamically estimated round-trip time (RTT) for the heartbeat, calculated based on Jacobson's algorithm. Their approach has a lower detection time than Chen et al.'s but a greater number of false alarms. Basile et al. [40] propose an adaptive timeout heartbeat mechanism that uses Jacobson's algorithm to calculate the roundtrip time and retransmission timeout for their pull-based heartbeat protocol. The RTT is estimated as a linear combination of a fixed number of previous samples of the RTT. To calculate the retransmission timeout, the estimated RTT is multiplied by the mean deviation of the RTT, which serves to handle the case in which the variance of the RTT goes up. Adaptive timeouts are further discussed in the next section.

Aguilera et al. [41, 42] propose a class of heartbeat failure detectors used to provide quiescent reliable communication in the presence of process crashes. A protocol is said to be *quiescent* if eventually no process sends or receives messages. In Aguilera et al.'s approach, each process sends "I am alive" messages to its neighbor. Every process maintains a heartbeat counter for each of its neighbors and increments it upon receiving an "I am alive" message. The application compares the previous and current values of the heartbeat counter to decide whether the process has crashed.

### 5.4.2 Limitations of Traditional Heartbeats

Two major problems are associated with the traditional heartbeat scheme:

1) The timeout period is prenegotiated by the two parties or sometimes even hard-coded by the programmer. The predefined timeout value cannot adapt to changes in network traffic or to load variability on individual nodes. In cases of high network traffic, high load on the nodes, or a slow node, the timeout value can be too short and cause the monitoring node to declare a healthy node faulty. Such a false alarm is undesirable in a distributed environment, especially for critical applications, such as those used in commercial banking and in database systems.

2) The monitored node is assumed to be healthy if it can respond to a heartbeat message. That approach is usually acceptable for a single-threaded application. However, in a multithreaded application, an independent thread of execution is usually responsible for replying to the heartbeat message. The healthy operation of that thread does not necessarily imply the healthy operation of the entire multithreaded application. Other threads inside the process may be in a deadlock that keeps the entire process from making progress. Alternatively, other threads could be operating in a corrupted state that keeps the process from providing proper service.

### 5.4.3 Designing Adaptive, Smart Heartbeats

A heartbeat algorithm is called *adaptive* if the timeout value used by the monitor is not fixed but rather periodically negotiated between the two parties so that they can adapt to changes in the network traffic or node load. A heartbeat algorithm is called *smart* if the entity being monitored invokes a set of predefined checks to verify the robustness of the entire process and only then responds to the monitoring process. To illustrate the concept of adaptive and smart heartbeats, we consider two independent, multithreaded processes: the *heartbeat monitor* and the *heartbeat replier* [40].

The *heartbeat monitor* is the monitoring entity that is responsible for periodically sending heartbeat request messages to the target node. The *heartbeat replier* is the monitored entity that responds to the heartbeat request messages sent by the monitor. The *adaptive* scheme uses Jacobson's algorithm [43], which allows for adjusting the timeout value according to measured network performance in terms of RTT in message transmission. The heartbeat algorithm uses a null test message inside the process to test the healthy operation of all the threads within the process. In the following sections, we present implementations of these two schemes (i.e., adaptive and smart heartbeats).

The heartbeat protocol is depicted in Figure 5.8. Periodically, the heartbeat monitor sends a heartbeat message to the heartbeat replier, clears the counter *ack_missed,* and starts the timer. The duration of the timer is dictated by the current value of the timeout variable associated with the heartbeat replier.

On the other side, the heartbeat replier responds with a heartbeat acknowledgment message. If a heartbeat acknowledgment message is received by the heartbeat monitor before the time expires, the monitor assumes that the remote process is alive; otherwise, the counter *ack_missed* is increased. If the counter has not reached its maximum value, a further heartbeat message can be sent from the heartbeat monitor to the heartbeat replier; otherwise, the remote process is assumed to be faulty.

The values of the timeout and the heartbeat period are crucial for the protocol. In general, the heartbeat period can be fixed as a multiple of the current value of the timeout. It is, however, desirable to have a timeout value that adapts to the current response time of the remote process. The response time, as seen by the heartbeat monitor, is a function of the current load on the remote machine and the time required to transfer the heartbeat message and he heartbeat acknowledgment, i.e., the response time is a function of the RTT.

**Figure 5.8**  Protocol for adaptive heartbeat.

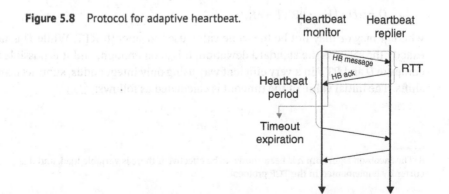

To calculate the RTT, it is sufficient to include in the heartbeat message a timestamp whose value is the sending time. This timestamp will be sent back to the monitor by the replier. Therefore, when the monitor receives a heartbeat acknowledgment, it can calculate the instantaneous RTT as the difference between the current time and that timestamp. However, it turns out that such a solution still does not perform well in the case of a variable workload. The main problem is the variability of the instantaneous RTT value, which can present substantial oscillations. A more accurate and smoother estimation of the RTT is required.

An approach to the problem is found in [43].[8] For each heartbeat replier, the heartbeat monitor maintains a variable RTT, which is the best current estimate of the RTT to the destination in question. When a heartbeat message is sent, a timer is started. If the heartbeat acknowledgment gets back before the timer expires, the monitor measures how long it took for the acknowledgment to arrive; let $M$ be this value. The monitor then updates RTT according to this formula:

$$RTT_{(i)} = \alpha RTT_{(i-1)} + (1 - \alpha) M,$$

where $\alpha$ is a smoothing factor that determines how much weight is given to the old value. Typically, $\alpha$ is set to 7/8.

Even given a good value of RTT, choosing a suitable timeout value is nontrivial. One choice would be to use $\beta$RTT, but the trick is how to choose $\beta$. Moreover, experience has shown that a constant value for $\beta$ is inflexible because it fails when the variance of the RTT goes up. Tanenbaum [43] proposes to make $\beta$ proportional to the standard deviation of the acknowledgment arrival time probability density function. That way, a large variance means a large $\beta$ and vice versa. In particular, he suggests using the mean deviation as a cheap estimator of the standard deviation. His algorithm requires that another smoothed variable, $D$, the deviation, be kept track of. Whenever a heartbeat acknowledgment comes in, the difference between the expected and observed values, $|RTT - M|$, is computed. A smoothed value of that difference is maintained in $D$ by the formula:

$$D = \alpha D + (1 - \alpha) |RTT - M|,$$

where $\alpha$ may or may not be the same value used to smooth RTT. While $D$ is not exactly the same as the standard deviation, it is good enough, and it is possible to compute $D$ and RTT in a very efficient way using only integer adds, subtracts, and shifts. The initial value of the timeout is calculated as follows:

---

8 The Jacobson algorithm has been shown to be effective if there is variable load, and it is currently implemented in the TCP protocol.

$$\text{RTT} = \frac{7}{8}\text{RTT} + \frac{1}{8}M; \quad D = \frac{3}{4}D + \frac{1}{4}|\text{RTT} - M|$$

Using those two quantities, we can calculate the timeout value as Timeout = RTT + 4 · D. Moreover, if the timer expires before the heartbeat monitor has received the heartbeat acknowledgment, the value of the timeout is doubled.

### 5.4.4 Evaluation of Smart Heartbeats

The *smart* heartbeat scheme is implemented inside the *heartbeat replier* process. Upon receiving a heartbeat request message from the *heartbeat monitor*, the replier thread initiates a round of surrogate messages (*MSG_HB_NULL_TEST*) to all threads inside the process. To process a message, a given thread first acquires a lock to the local data structure. It then increments a counter inside the message and releases the lock to the element data structure. If the process operates properly, i.e., there is not a deadlock, the counter inside the null message will eventually reach the total number of threads currently active inside the process. The last thread in the chain that sees this condition satisfied sends a *MSG_HB_NULL_TEST_REPLY* back to the heartbeat replier. Upon receiving *MSG_HB_NULL_TEST_REPLY*, the replier element assumes that the entire process is in a healthy, deadlock-free state and then sends a heartbeat acknowledgment back to the monitor. If, however, there are threads inside the process in a deadlock state, the null test message is blocked, and the replier does not send a heartbeat acknowledgment back to the monitor. The monitor eventually times out and declares the failure of the monitored process.

#### 5.4.4.1 Experimental Methodology

To test the effectiveness of the proposed heartbeat scheme in adapting to oscillations in network load, we used an artificial sinusoidal load generator. The load generator generated identical processes such that the number of processes satisfied a discrete sinusoidal function. To make the load due to other processes negligible, we ensured that the generated artificial load was relatively large. The desired function is of the form:

$$d(t) = M\sin(\omega t\pi) + \frac{3}{2}M,$$

where $M$ and $\omega$ are given parameters. To compute the number of processes, a discrete approximation of the above function is used:

$$n(t_{k+1}) = \begin{cases} n(t_k)+1 & \text{If } d(t_k)-n(t_k) > 0.5 \\ n(t_k) & \text{If } |d(t_k)-n(t_k)| \le 0.5 \\ n(t_k)-1 & \text{Otherwise} \end{cases}$$

The time axis is divided into small intervals $t_k$, and for each interval, a number $n(t_k)$ of processes to be generated is calculated. (Note that to ensure the accuracy of the above approximation, the time slot must be sufficiently small.)

The size of the kernel ready queue is used to measure the load. To test our algorithm, we artificially generated deadlock situations inside a monitored process.

### 5.4.4.2 Experimental Results

Figure 5.9 shows the results from running the adaptive heartbeat scheme together with the load generator and measurement program. The curve in the lower part of the chart is the measured load. It is a normalized value in terms of the number of processes in the kernel ready queue. The curve in the upper part of the chart shows how the estimated timeout value adapted to the changing load. The timeout value is out of phase with the load of the node, but it eventually adapts to the changes in the generated load. The observed latency is due to (i) the convergence time required by the timeout estimation algorithm, (ii) communication delay between the two nodes, and (iii) the generated load's frequent oscillations, to which the algorithm cannot adapt quickly enough. (An actual environment usually will not have such rapid load changes.)

Figure 5.10 shows the effectiveness of the smart heartbeat algorithm. The *x*-axis is time, and the *y*-axis is the timeout value estimated by the algorithm. At around time 420 000 ms, a deadlock situation is created, and the heartbeat monitor process begins to miss heartbeat reply messages from the heartbeat replier. Each time

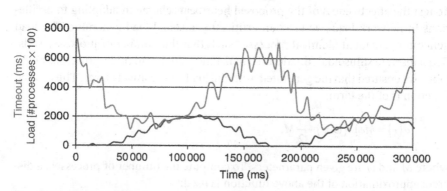

**Figure 5.9** Adaptive heartbeat with load generator.

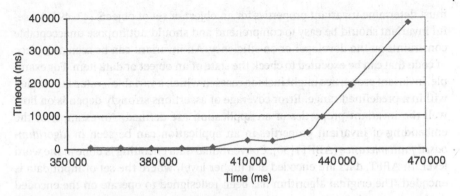

**Figure 5.10** Effectiveness of smart heartbeat.

the monitor misses an acknowledgment, it doubles its timeout value until it has given up on too many timeouts and declares that the process has failed.

## 5.5 Assertions

*Assertions* are highly valued and useful automated techniques with a distinguished history in the annals of software engineering and programming language design. They are available for detecting faults and then providing information about the locations of the faults, even faults that are traversed during execution but do not lead to failures. Assertions were initially developed as a way of stating expected or desired program properties as a necessary step in constructing formal, deductive proofs of program correctness. Over time, assertions have found many other applications in software engineering, although largely in later stages of development and primarily in the development and execution of source code. Assertions are a critical element of *model checking*, an actively studied approach to program verification, in which the state space resulting from a program's execution is checked against logical assertions expressing temporal safety and aliveness properties (e.g., SPIN [44]). Embedded in the type systems of numerous programming languages that support strong typing of data and objects (e.g., Java [45]), assertions are commonly used in an informal fashion by developers to better describe module interfaces to other developers. Here, however, we focus on the application of assertions that has the greatest impact on development practice: their use for automated runtime fault detection in which formal assertion checks are instrumented into a program for execution along with the program's application logic [46].

An assertion represents a logical expression that implements a check on the objects in a program and is evaluated at runtime. To enable an assertion, the user must determine invariant properties for an object or set of objects [47–49]. A useful invariant should be easy to comprehend and should not impose unacceptable constraints on the developer or on efficiency. An invariant can be seen as a piece of code that can be executed to check the state of an object or data item. For example, invariant properties might include cases in which a variable's value is bounded within a predefined range. Error coverage of assertions strongly depends on how well the invariant properties of an application are defined. An example of the embedding of invariant properties in an application can be seen in *algorithm-based fault tolerance* (ABFT) [50]. Conventional data encoding is done at the word level. In ABFT, data are encoded at a higher level, where the set of input data is encoded. The original algorithm has been redesigned to operate on the encoded data and to produce encoded output data. That redundancy enables recovery of the correct data, or at least recognition of the error. This technique has been applied to perform computations such as matrix operations, fast Fourier transforms, sorting, and filtering [51].

## 5.6 Insights

Duplicated execution is the mainstay of aircraft systems that have been in commission for many decades. They employ full duplication for mission-critical applications. In emerging systems such as the autonomous vehicles, duplicated execution is used extensively. It is important to note that, theoretically, the reliability of a system with a duplicated stream execution engine is lower than a system executing a single stream due essentially to the increase in the number of components that can fail now. This is accounted for by falling back to an independent backup system in case of a mismatch of the two primary stream execution engines.

Early control flow checking techniques limited themselves to checking the validity of the path taken by the program after the jump instruction has been executed, e.g., ECCA. This was further enhanced by pre-emptively checking the control flow even before the jump is executed as is done in PECOS. This greatly reduces the possibility of a unintended process crash, which can have other undesirable consequences and may also not lend itself to a graceful recovery mechanism for the application. An interesting insight provided by the PECOS experiments is that about 34% of all faults injected randomly in the instruction stream and that were activated (erroneous instruction was executed) did not manifest in any user perceivable change in the functionality of the application. This shows the possibility of benign errors in the system. PECOS was able to detect 31% of the activated errors, while another 32% were detected by the system through process crash.

Important aspect of most control flow checking techniques is that they are unable to detect valid but incorrect control flow and focus primarily on invalid control flow errors. Overall, they should be considered as complementary techniques that support other mainstream methods, such as assertions, coding, and duplication.

Heartbeats are heavily used in large-scale enterprise systems and super computers. One application is to detect if remote nodes in the system have failed. Though adaptive heartbeats have been around, their adoption has been slow. This can be attributed to the fact that the tuning of the heartbeats depends not only on the nature of the system but also on the environment in which it is operating which is highly deployment specific.

Assertions still hold currency in the applications such as artificial intelligence. Most software programs and their associated unit and integration test frameworks heavily utilize assertions to validate updates for any collaterals that they may pose.

# References

1 Reis, G.A., Chang, J., Vachharajani, N. et al. (2005). SWIFT: software implemented fault tolerance. *Proceedings of the International Symposium on Code Generation and Optimization*, New York, NY, USA (20–23 March 2005). IEEE.

2 Oh, N., Shirvani, P.P., and McCluskey, E.J. (2002). Error detection by duplicated instructions in super-scalar processors. *IEEE Transactions on Reliability* 51 (1): 63–75.

3 Benso, A., Chiusano, S., Prinetto, P. et al. (2000). A C/C++ source-to-source compiler for dependable applications. *Proceedings of the International Conference on Dependable Systems and Networks*, New York, NY, USA (25–28 June 2000). IEEE.

4 Oh, N., Mitra, S., and McCluskey, E.J. (2002). ED$^4$I: error detection by diverse data and duplicated instructions. *IEEE Transactions on Computers* 51 (2): 180–199.

5 Brasileiro, F.V., Ezhilchelvan, P.D., Shrivastava, S.K. et al. (1996). Implementing fail-silent nodes for distributed systems. *IEEE Transactions on Computers* 45 (11): 1226–1238.

6 Ohlsson, J., Rimen, M., and Gunneflo, U. (1992). A study of the effects of transient fault injection into a 32-bit RISC with built-in watchdog. *Digest of Papers, the 22nd International Symposium on Fault-Tolerant Computing*, Boston, MA, USA (8–10 July 1992), 316–325. IEEE.

7 Schuette, M.A. and Shen, J.P. (1987). Processor control flow monitoring using signatured instruction streams. *IEEE Transactions on Computers* C-36 (3): 264–276.

8 Bagchi, S., Srinivasan, B., Whisnant, K. et al. (2000). Hierarchical error detection in a software implemented fault tolerance (SIFT) environment. *IEEE Transactions on Knowledge and Data Engineering* 12 (2): 203–224.

**9** Chandra, S. and Chen, P.M. (1998). How fail-stop are faulty programs? *Digest of Papers, the 28th Annual International Symposium on Fault-Tolerant Computing*, Munich, Germany (23–25 June 1998), 240–249. IEEE.

**10** Iyer, R.K., Rossetti, D.J., and Hsueh, M.C. (1986). Measurement and modeling of computer reliability as affected by system activity. *ACM Transactions on Computer Systems* 4 (3): 214–237.

**11** Iyer, R.K. and Rossetti, D.J. (1986). A measurement-based model for workload dependence of CPU errors. *IEEE Transactions on Computers* C-35 (6): 511–519.

**12** Thakur, A. (1997). Measurement and analysis of failures in computer systems. Master thesis. University of Illinois at Urbana-Champaign.

**13** Tsao, M.M. and Siewiorek, P. (1983). Trend analysis on system error files. *Digest of Papers, the 13th International Symposium on Fault-Tolerant Computing*, Milano, Italy (28–30 June 1983), 116–119.

**14** Alkhalifa, Z., Nair, V.S.S., Krishnamurthy, N. et al. (1999). Design and evaluation of system-level checks for on-line control flow error detection. *IEEE Transactions on Parallel and Distributed Systems* 10 (6): 627–641.

**15** Yau, S.S. and Chen, F.-C. (1980). An approach to concurrent control flow checking. *IEEE Transactions on Software Engineering* SE-6 (2): 126–137.

**16** Mahmood, A. and McCluskey, E.J. (1988). Concurrent error detection using watchdog processors: a survey. *IEEE Transactions on Computers* 37 (2): 160–174.

**17** Michel, T., Leveugle, R., and Saucier, G. (1991). A new approach to control flow checking without program modification. *Digest of Papers, the 21st International Symposium on Fault-Tolerant Computing*, Montreal, Quebec, Canada (25–27 June 1991), 334–341. IEEE.

**18** Miremadi, G. and Torin, J. (1995). Evaluating processor behavior and three error detection mechanisms using physical fault injection. *IEEE Transactions on Computers* 44 (3): 441–454.

**19** Namjoo, M. (1982). Techniques for concurrent testing of VLSI processor operation. *Digest 1982 International Test Conference*, Philadelphia, PA, USA (November 1982), 461–468.

**20** Schuette, M.A., Shen, J.P., Siewiorek, D.P. et al. (1986). Experimental evaluation of two concurrent error detection schemes. *Digest of Papers, the 16th International Symposium on Fault-Tolerant Computing* Vienna, Austria (1–4 July 1986), 138–143.

**21** Upadhyaya, S. and Ramamurthy, B. (1994). Concurrent process monitoring with no reference signatures. *IEEE Transactions on Computers* 43 (4): 475–480.

**22** Wilken, K. and Shen, J.P. (1990). Continuous signature monitoring: Low-cost concurrent detection of processor control errors. *IEEE Transactions on Computer-Aided Design of Integrated Circuits and Systems* 9 (6): 629–641.

**23** Droms, R. (1997). Dynamic host configuration protocol. Request for comments RFC-2131, RFC Editor, March 1997. https://www.rfc-editor.org/info/rfc2131 (accessed June 2021).

**24** Madeira, H. and Silva, J.G. (1991). On-line signature learning and checking. *Proceeding of the 2nd IFIP Working Conf. on Dependable Computing for Critical Applications (DCCA-2)* (February 1991), 170–177. IEEE.

**25** G. Miremadi, J. Ohlsson, M. Rimen, J. Karlsson. (1995). Use of time and address signatures for control flow checking. *Proceeding of the 5th IFIP Working Conf. on Dependable Computing for Critical Applications (DCCA-5)* (1995), 113–124. IEEE.

**26** Miremadi, G., Karlsson, J., Gunneflo, U., et al. (1992). Two software techniques for on-line error detection. *Digest of Papers, the 22nd International Symposium on Fault-Tolerant Computing*, Boston, MA, USA (8–10 July 1992), 328–335. IEEE.

**27** Khudia, D.S. and Mahlke, S. (2013). Low cost control flow protection using abstract control signatures. In: *Proceedings of the 14th ACM SIGPLAN/SIGBED Conference on Languages, compilers and tools for embedded systems (LCTES'13)*. New York, NY, USA: ACM. 3–12. https://doi.org/10.1145/2491899.2465568.

**28** Oh, N., Shirvani, P.P., and McCluskey, E.J. (2002). Control-flow Checking by Software Signatures. *IEEE Transactions on Reliability* 51 (1): 111–122.

**29** Kanawati, G.A., Nair, V.S.S., Krishnamurthy, N. et al. (1996). Evaluation of integrated system-level checks for on-line error detection. *Proceedings of the IEEE International Computer Performance and Dependability Symposium*, Urbana-Champaign, IL, USA (4–6 September 1996), 292–301. IEEE.

**30** Rhisheekesan, A., Jeyapaul, R., and Shrivastava, A. (2019). Control flow checking or not? (For soft errors). *ACM Transactions on Embedded Computing Systems* 18 (1): 1–25. https://doi.org/10.1145/3301311.

**31** Kanawati, G.A., Kanawati, N.A., and Abraham, J.A. (1995). FERRARI: a flexible software-based fault and error injection system. *IEEE Transactions on Computers* 44 (2): 248–260.

**32** Lala, P.K. (1985). *Fault Tolerant and Fault Testable Hardware Design*. New York, NY, USA: Prentice Hall International.

**33** Siewiorek, D.P. and Swarz, R.S. (1998). *Reliable Computer Systems: Design and Evaluation*, 3e. Natick, MA, USA: A K Peters.

**34** Madeira, H. and Silva, J.G. (1994). Experimental evaluation of the fail-silent behavior in computers without error masking. *Proceedings of the IEEE 24th International Symposium on Fault-Tolerant Computing*, Austin, TX, USA (15–17 June 1994), 350–359. IEEE.

**35** Stott, D.T., Floering, B., Burke, D. et al. (2000). NFTAPE: a framework for assessing dependability in distributed systems with lightweight fault injectors. *Proceedings of the IEEE International Computer Performance and Dependability Symposium*, Chicago, IL, USA (27–29 March 2000), 91–100. IEEE.

**36** Felber, P., Defago, X., Guerraoui, R., et al. (1999). Failure detectors as first class objects. *Proceedings of the International Symposium on Distributed Objects and Applications*, Edinburgh, Scotland, UK (5–6 September 1999), 132–141. IEEE.

**37** Eddon, G. and Eddon, H. (1998). Understanding the DCOM wire protocol by analyzing network data packets. *Microsoft Systems Journal* https://web.archive.

org/web/20040712062651/http://www.microsoft.com/msj/0398/dcom.aspx (accessed June 2021).

**38** Chen, W., Toueg, S., and Aguilera, M.K. (2000). On the quality of service of failure detectors. *Proceedings of the International Conference on Dependable Systems and Networks*, New York NY, USA (25–28 June 2000). IEEE.

**39** Bertier, M., Marin, O., and Sens, P. (2002). Implementation and performance evaluation of an adaptable failure detector. *Proceedings of the International Conference on Dependable Systems and Networks*, Washington, DC, USA (23–26 June 2002). IEEE.

**40** Basile, C., Wu, Y., and Xu, J. (2000). Adaptive and Smart Heartbeat. Final project for ECE 442 class, Fall 2000 (instructor R.K. Iyer), University of Illinois at Urbana-Champaign.

**41** Aguilera, M.K., Chen, W., and Toueg, S. (1997). Heartbeat: A Timeout-Free Failure Detector for Quiescent Reliable Communication. Computer Science Tech. Rep. 97-1631, Dept. of Computer Science, Cornell University. https://ecommons. cornell.edu/handle/1813/7286.

**42** Aguilera, M.K., Chen, W., and Toueg, S. (1999). Using the heartbeat failure detector for quiescent reliable communication and consensus in partitionable networks. *Theoretical Computer Science* 220 (1): 3–30.

**43** Tanenbaum, A.S. (1996). *Computer Networks*, 3e. Prentice Hall.

**44** Holzmann, G.J. (1997). The model checker SPIN. *IEEE Transactions on Software Engineering* 23 (5): 279–294.

**45** Gosling, J., Joy, B., and Steele, G. (1996). *The JavaTM Language Specification*. Reading, MA, USA: Addison-Wesley.

**46** Clarke, L.A. and Rosenblum, D.S. (2006). A historical perspective on runtime assertion checking in software development. *ACM SIGSOFT Software Engineering Notes* 31 (3): 25–37.

**47** Leveson, N.G. and Harvey, P.R. (1983). Analyzing software safety. *IEEE Transactions on Software Engineering* SE-9 (5): 569–579.

**48** Mahmood, A., McCluskey, E.J., and Lu, D.J. (1983) Concurrent fault detection using a watchdog processor and assertions. *Proceedings of the 13th IEEE International Test Conference* (October 1983), Philadelphia, PA, USA, 622–628. IEEE Computer Society.

**49** Saib, S.H. (1977). Executable assertions: an aid to reliable software. *Conference Record, 1977 11th Asilomar Conference on Circuits, Systems, and Computers*, Pacific Grove, CA, USA (7–9 November 1977), 277–281. IEEE.

**50** Huang, K.-H. and Abraham, J.A. (1984). Algorithm-based fault tolerance for matrix operations. *IEEE Transactions on Computers* C-33 (6): 518–528.

**51** Abraham, J.A., Banerjee, P., Chen, C.-Y. et al. (1987). Fault tolerance techniques for systolic arrays. *Computer* 20 (7): 65–75.

# 6

# Software Error Detection and Recovery Through Software Analysis

## 6.1 Introduction

From the initial days of ILLIAC I – the first von Neumann architecture to be built using the stored program concept – software has evolved to become a very large and failure-prone component of computer systems. Failures of software systems can occur because of runtime errors (e.g. hardware transients) or bugs introduced at any phase in their lifecycles (development, deployment, or maintenance). Those errors should be detected and recovered from with minimum impact on system/application availability. To achieve that goal, software can be fortified with a fault/error detection mechanism at any of the phases in its lifecycle. During the development stage, software specifications can be implemented by independent groups of programmers to provide what is commonly called *N-version programming*. Alternatively, a recovery-blocks scheme can be used to enable redundant execution and rapid recovery. During the implementation phase, formal proof techniques can be utilized to prove the correctness of the software from both functional and nonfunctional standpoints. Compile-time techniques – which might be implemented as additional passes in a compiler – include static invariant detection, duplication, diversification of code at the source, or application-specific assertions and can be used to provide the required resiliency. Runtime checking techniques, such as array bounds checking, memory leak protection, or runtime verification using assertions, can detect runtime errors in the system.

This chapter presents a spectrum of software techniques for (i) uncovering of software bugs through static or dynamic program analysis and (ii) runtime detection of hardware/software errors. The techniques are divided into several broad groups as shown in Table 6.1. The static techniques listed in the table are geared toward detection of errors at compile time, while the dynamic analysis techniques

*Dependable Computing: Design and Assessment*, First Edition. Ravishankar K. Iyer, Zbigniew T. Kalbarczyk, and Nithin M. Nakka.
© 2024 The IEEE Computer Society. Published 2024 by John Wiley & Sons, Inc.
Companion website: www.wiley.com/go/iyer/dependablecomputing1

**Table 6.1** Classification of software-based detection techniques.

| Class | Example | Comments |
|---|---|---|
| Static analysis techniques | Data flow analysis: Prefix [1], ESP [2], LCLINT [3] | Checks the program based on a well-understood fault model, usually specified based on common programming bugs (e.g. NULL pointer dereferences). The techniques attempt to locate errors across all feasible paths in the program (i.e. program paths that correspond to actual executions of the program). Determining feasible paths is known to be an impossible problem in the general case. Therefore, these techniques make approximations that result in discovery of errors that will never occur in a real execution, leading to wasteful detections |
| Static analysis techniques | Inferring specifications from code: [4, 5] | Learns program patterns from source-code analysis and considers violations of these patterns to be program bugs. Patterns are learned from localized code samples and extended to the whole code base. The techniques are useful for finding common programming errors such as copy-and-paste errors. It is unclear whether they can be used to detect more subtle errors that occur in well-tested code, such as timing and memory errors, as such errors may not be easily localized to code sections. Further, these techniques suffer from a high rate of false positives, i.e. many errors are not real bugs |
| Dynamic analysis techniques | Application-specific (critical data or variables): [6] | Extracts application characteristics that are critical from a reliability perspective (e.g. critical variables that, if corrupted, lead to program failure), formulates an assertion that captures the identified system property, and enforces the assertion at runtime |
| Dynamic analysis techniques | DAIKON: [7] | Derives code invariants such as the constancy of variables, linear relationships among sets of program variables, and inequalities involving two or more program variables. DAIKON's primary purpose is to present the invariants found to programmers. The invariants are derived based on the execution of the application with a representative set of inputs. Note that certain inputs that are not present in that set may result in violation of the invariants even if there is no error in the program |

| | | |
|---|---|---|
| Duplication techniques | DIDUCE: [8] | Uses the invariants learned during an early stage of the program execution to detect errors in the subsequent part of the execution. It is unclear how the invariants learned during the early stages represent the entire application's execution. That may lead to false detections |
| | Rule-based: [9–11] | Derives error detectors based on rule-based templates, wherein the choice of templates and the parameters are either manually specified or automatically derived. The problem with rule-based detectors is that they are specific to an application domain (e.g. specific embedded applications), and it is difficult to make them work for general-purpose applications. Further, the rules learned may not be representative of all inputs to the application and may be violated even when there is no error in the application |
| | Duplication at source, instruction, or intermediate levels: [12, 13] (EDDI), [14] (SWIFT) | Replicates the entire program, which can result in high performance overheads (90–100%). An important issue in all low-level replication techniques is that they result in the detection of many errors that have no impact on the application (i.e. benign errors). This constitutes wasteful detection (and subsequent recovery) from the application's viewpoint. Further, duplication-based techniques offer limited protection from software faults and permanent hardware faults because both the original program and the replica can incur common-mode faults |
| | Runtime verification: JavaMac [15], Java PathExplorer [16] | Checks whether the program violates a programmer-specified safety property by constructing a model of the program and checking the model based on the actual program execution. The checking is done at specific program points that depend on the model. However, if there is a general error in the program, there is no guarantee that the program will reach the check before crashing. Since the papers describing these techniques only consider errors that are directly detectable (by the checking technique), the coverage for a random hardware or software error is not clear |

(Continued)

**Table 6.1** (Continued)

| Class | Example | Comments |
|---|---|---|
| Runtime checking techniques | Memory safety checking: [17–19] | Checks every program store that is performed through a pointer (at runtime) to ensure that the write is within the allowed bounds of the pointer. The techniques are effective in detecting common problems due to buffer overflows and dangling pointer errors. It is unclear whether they are effective in detecting random errors that arise because of incorrect computation, unless such an error causes a pointer to write outside its allowed bounds. The techniques also require checking of every memory write, which can result in prohibitive performance overheads (5×–6×). |
| | Race condition detection: [20, 21] | Checks for race conditions in a multithreaded program. A race condition occurs when a shared variable is accessed without explicit and appropriate synchronization. The techniques check for races in lock-based programs by dynamically monitoring lock acquisitions and releases. However, these approaches involve instrumenting and dynamically monitoring memory writes to shared variables in programs, which can result in prohibitive performance overheads (6×–60×). Moreover, conventional race-detection techniques may find races that have no impact on the program's output (i.e. benign races), resulting in wasteful detections |
| Diverse programming | N-version programming: [22, 23]. | In N-version programming, the specifications for a software system are implemented by multiple independent sets of programmers to arrive at multiple versions of the program. The results of these diverse versions of the software are compared to check for correctness. |
| | Recovery blocks: [24–26] | In recovery blocks, several reliability-critical sections (or the entire program) are identified within the program. If a failure is detected through use of an acceptance test executed at the section/program, control is transferred to an alternative implementation of that section/program, such that the state is rolled back to what it was before the beginning of the execution of this section/program and the alternative implementation is executed |

are geared towards providing feedback to the programmer for bug finding. Both types are *fault-avoidance* techniques (i.e. in which the fault is removed before the program is operational) [27]. Despite the existence of these techniques and rigorous program testing, subtle but important errors, such as timing errors, may persist in a program [28, 29]. Software replication can detect many such errors; however, it not only incurs significant performance overheads but also results in the detection of a large number of benign errors that have no impact on the application [30], and thereby result in wasteful recovery. Thus, there is a compelling need for a technique that takes advantage of application characteristics and detects arbitrary errors at runtime without incurring the overheads of replication.

## 6.2 Diverse Programming

Duplication is an effective way to deal with transient hardware faults. However, duplication-based techniques offer limited protection from software faults and permanent hardware faults because the original program and the duplicated program can suffer from common mode errors. To deal with common mode errors, *diverse execution techniques* that execute two different versions of the same program and compare the results can be used. We study three such methods in this section.

### 6.2.1 N-Version Programming

*N-version programming* (NVP) (first introduced in 1978 by Chen and Avižienis [22, 31]) is a design diversity technique in which independent individuals or groups, who cannot communicate with each other, implement different versions of the same program. It promotes the use of different algorithms and different implementations on the assumption that different people will approach solutions to the same problem in different ways. The specification of the program is provided in a formal specification language that states the functional requirements as unambiguously as possible, while providing the programmers with a wide choice in terms of the implementation. The versions are executed simultaneously, and the results of their executions are compared. The assumption is that the versions produced by the independent teams will suffer from different kinds of errors, and hence that an error in any one version of the software will be detected and possibly masked through use of the results from the other versions.

Thus, in the ideal case:

$$\text{Prob}\big(\text{failure of the N-version system}\big) = \Big[\text{Prob}\big(\text{failure of one version}\big)\Big]^N$$

However, Knight and Leveson [23] showed that in practice, even independently produced versions of software are likely to exhibit similar failures. The reason is that people tend to make the same mistakes, e.g. treat boundary conditions incorrectly, when implementing algorithmic solutions for more difficult parts of an overall problem. Further, NVP requires a significant investment in terms of programmer time and resources, which, in turn, means that NVP is typically applied only to mission-critical systems.

$ED^4I$ is a diverse execution technique that attempts to overcome the problems of NVP by introducing diversity in an automated way [32]. The original program is transformed into a different program in which each data operand is multiplied by a constant value $k$. Since the transformed program operates on a different set of data operands from the original program, it is able to mask hardware errors in processor functional units and memory. However, the technique cannot detect errors that result from incorrect computation in both the original and transformed programs.

The main difference between space-redundant hardware systems and fault-tolerant software units is that the simple replication of one design that is effective against random physical faults in hardware is not sufficient for software fault tolerance. Each copy of a piece of software contains the same faults as the original software; therefore, each version of the software in the N-version system needs to be developed separately and independently of the other versions. That is the concept of software *design diversity*.

A set of $N \geq 2$ diverse simplex units by themselves cannot provide fault tolerance. Figure 6.1 shows the *N-version software* (NVS) model of a fault-tolerant software unit. Each diverse unit is called a *version*. The NVS uses a generic *decision algorithm* (or *voter*) that looks for a *consensus* of two or more outputs among $N$ member versions. When there are only two versions in the NVS, the systems can

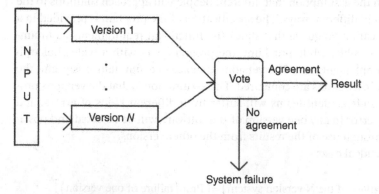

**Figure 6.1** The N-version software model.

detect disagreements between the versions, but cannot determine a consensus. A possible action on a disagreement is to safely shut down the system. NVP is the process by which the NVS versions are produced [22].

### 6.2.1.1 Applications of N-Version Programming

Because of its cost (e.g. in additional system resources and software development), practical use of NVP is usually limited to safety-critical applications, such as flight control systems for aircraft. In such applications, the probability of a critical failure must be less than $10^{-10}$ per flight hour.

To illustrate the use of N-version programming, we present two examples of fault-tolerant flight control systems deployed by Boeing and Airbus in their commercial aircraft to cope with design faults (in hardware and/or software) [33]. Two different forms of software redundancy are employed:

- N-version programming (e.g. Boeing 777).
- N-self-checking programming (e.g. Airbus A320 or A330).

NVP was discussed in the preceding section; here, we briefly introduce *N-self-checking programming (NSCP)*, a variation of N-version programming. In N-self-checking programming, a self-checking component is considered to have resulted either (i) from the association with each variant (labeled "version *i*" in Figure 6.2) of an acceptance test (labeled "AT") on the output results of the variant or (ii) from the association of two variants together with a comparison algorithm (labeled "compare"). Graphical representations of the two types of self-checking components are presented in Figure 6.2.

*Airbus Approach to Design Diversity*. The Airbus architecture employs multiple self-checking flight computers [34]. Two computers, a *primary* and a *backup*, are used. Each computer has two channels: *control* (e.g. to govern a control surface) and *monitoring* (to ensure correct operation of the control channel); see Figure 6.3. The two computers are designed and fabricated by different manufacturers to eliminate common manufacturing faults. To achieve further protection, one computer is based on a 68010 microprocessor and the other on an 80186 microprocessor. That

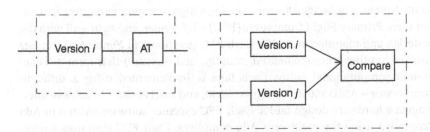

**Figure 6.2** N-self-checking programming.

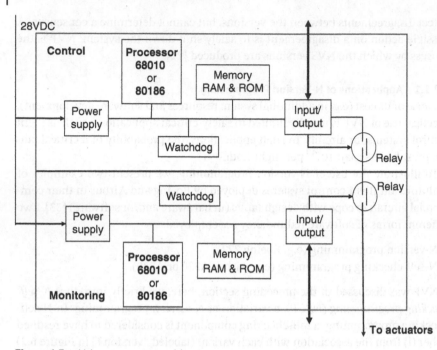

**Figure 6.3**  Airbus computer architecture.

architecture results in four different entities and, hence, four independently developed software packages designed and implemented to common specifications.

Each channel consists of a processor, memory, I/O interfaces, power supply, and a specific software package. At runtime, when the results produced by the two channels (in the same computer) differ, the channel that detects the discrepancy (i.e. failure) cuts the connection to the actuators, and the control is transferred to the backup computer. The detection is based on a comparison of the commands issued by the control and monitoring channels. Different teams will have developed the software for each channel (in the two computers), using different programming languages.

*Boeing Approach to Design Diversity.* Boeing's flight computer architecture consists of three Primary Flight Computers (PFC) – *left, center,* and *right* – all with the same design and manufacturer [35]. Each PFC (as shown in Figure 6.4) consists of three computing lanes (*command, standby,* and *monitor*) that form a triple-redundant computational entity. Each lane is implemented using a different microprocessor – AMD 29050, Motorola 68040, and Intel 80486 – to achieve tolerance against hardware design faults. Each PFC executes software written in Ada and compiled using three different Ada compilers. Each PFC lane uses a dedicated ARINC 629 terminal to connect to the data bus.

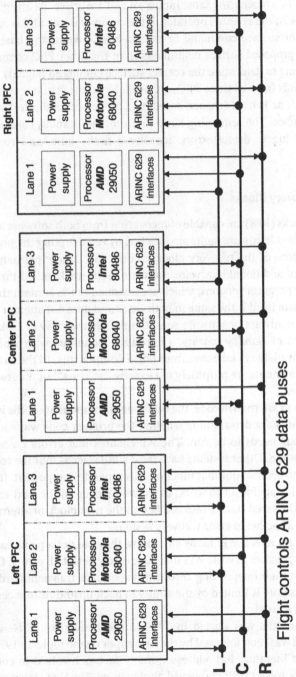

**PFC – primary flight control**

| Left PFC | | | | Center PFC | | | | Right PFC | | |
|---|---|---|---|---|---|---|---|---|---|---|
| Lane 1 | Lane 2 | Lane 3 | | Lane 1 | Lane 2 | Lane 3 | | Lane 1 | Lane 2 | Lane 3 |
| Power supply | Power supply | Power supply | | Power supply | Power supply | Power supply | | Power supply | Power supply | Power supply |
| Processor AMD 29050 | Processor Motorola 68040 | Processor Intel 80486 | | Processor AMD 29050 | Processor Motorola 68040 | Processor Intel 80486 | | Processor AMD 29050 | Processor Motorola 68040 | Processor Intel 80486 |
| ARINC 629 interfaces | ARINC 629 interfaces | ARINC 629 interfaces | | ARINC 629 interfaces | ARINC 629 interfaces | ARINC 629 interfaces | | ARINC 629 interfaces | ARINC 629 interfaces | ARINC 629 interfaces |

L
C
R

**Flight controls ARINC 629 data buses**

**Figure 6.4** Boeing computer architecture.

All three PFCs receive the same inputs and all are active. At any given moment, only one lane in the channel operates in the command role and is responsible for generating the surface command to its data bus. A command lane in each PFC receives the proposed surface commands from the other PFC channels and uses majority voting to determine the correct surface command (signal). Selected surface commands from all three PFCs are available to the actuator control electronics, and only one is used (chosen based on a predetermined priority schedule) to drive the surface. The remaining lanes (monitor and standby) are used for cross-lane monitoring to detect errors, identify a faulty lane, and reconfigure the controller.

## 6.2.2 Recovery Blocks

Recovery blocks (RBs) are capable of recovering from both software and hardware faults. Transient hardware faults are handled by reattempting the processing, and some extensions of the recovery block scheme can handle permanent faults by making use of additional hardware. Software faults are handled through the use of secondary program versions, which are assumed not to contain the same fault. The mechanism itself is the same in both cases and does not attempt to determine whether the hardware or software was at fault. Another way of looking at RBs is in the context of *standby sparing*, a hardware technique with which duplicate hardware is available to take over from failed components. In the case of RBs, the software components are purposely not exactly the same, but otherwise serve the same function.

In addition to alternative code, the other main component of RBs is the AT. The AT is responsible for determining whether the primary code was successful, or if secondary code needs to be run. The AT ensures that errors do not propagate within the system. Other systems have used similar ideas, but the recovery block was the first to abstract out that function as a separate component. It is necessary to save system state for AT to work, as we will explain in the next section. When the AT fails, the saved state is restored before the next block of alternative code is run, forming a backward error-recovery system.

While RBs are effective in many situations, they are not a panacea. In practice, it may not be possible to write ATs that adequately detect all errors. Complex ATs may also have their own coding defects or experience transient hardware errors. Also, recoverability is limited by the ability to back up and restore certain devices (such as hard drives).

Research on RBs was started in 1971 at the University of Newcastle upon Tyne [24] and was soon followed by the first paper on the topic, in 1974 [26]. Since that time, the literature has addressed many factors involved in combining the recovery block model with real-world applications. The first step was support for distributed applications, i.e. handling of cooperating processes with reasonable performance. Real-time constraints have also led to extensions in another direction, such that multiple RBs are run concurrently as a form of forward error recovery. So long as one block succeeds, the result can be returned without any further delays. That method for forward recovery has also been combined with the distributed recovery block model, for use with multiple sets of computer nodes that are running a distributed application protected by RBs. We consider some of the extensions to the recovery block scheme in the rest of this section.

### 6.2.2.1 Sequential Recovery Block Scheme

In [26], Horning et al. describe the initial recovery block scheme, in which the focus was on sequential programs running independently on one machine. They describe the reasoning behind the recovery block design by noting that recovery after error detection is a difficult problem. Checking for errors after every instruction would add high overhead and determining the correct recovery step for each possible error would be very time consuming and error prone. Instead, RBs look at a set of instructions as a whole, examining the output at the end of the set.

RBs can also be nested, allowing processes to be subdivided into increasingly smaller parts. If one recovery block cannot recover from a fault, it will signal a fault to its enclosing block, which will then attempt recovery steps by failing its own AT. Thus, recovery is highly structured, composed of discrete parts that potentially can be well tested.

To define RBs more formally, a block is composed of three parts. The *primary try block* is the preferred block of code to complete a given task. A recovery block then has any number of *alternate try blocks* coded with secondary ways of completing the task. To minimize coincident errors, alternate try blocks should be as independent as possible from the primary try block. (If they aren't, an input that causes an error in the primary could cause an error in the alternate.) There is no requirement that the alternate try blocks implement the same function as the primary. In many applications, there may be slightly different actions that are acceptable. Last, the *AT* determines whether the executed block was successful. Figure 6.5 illustrates how the components fit together.

The ordering of alternate try blocks should be set based on how well they perform actions. Another measure could be the efficiency, with the primary block being highly optimized but not always successful and backed up by an alternate block that is slow and highly accurate. Alternate try blocks might also be previous versions of the primary.

### 6.2.2.2 Designing an Acceptance Test

There are a wide variety of possible approaches to ATs [36]. ATs should be as strict as possible, but if alternate blocks are performing different calculations

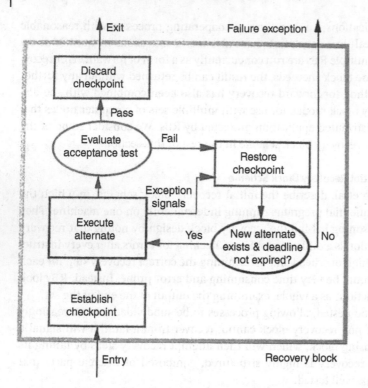

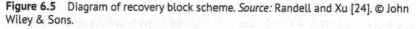

**Figure 6.5** Diagram of recovery block scheme. *Source:* Randell and Xu [24]. © John Wiley & Sons.

from the primary block, the AT will necessarily need to be more lenient. Empirical evidence shows that the fault coverage of ATs is frequently below 90%, with a significant amount of false alarms [37]. A study described in [38] shows the extent of the problem; of 24 students attempting to write self-checks for code, only 11 managed to write tests that actually detected a fault! If it is desirable, the values that cause an AT failure can also be logged for further analysis and to help revise the test [25].

The starting values of variables are available for the AT to access, and that greatly enhances the possible tests. For example, some scientific quantities (velocity and temperature) are expected to be fairly stable, and the difference between the starting and ending values can be checked [39]. It may also be possible for the AT to determine whether modified values are subsequently accessed in the block, and thus detect errors of omission if such a value is not subsequently accessed [25]. ATs, however, do not have access to the local values of a block; those values go out of scope prior to the start of the AT [26]. The AT should not have any side effects, since it may be run multiple times within the recovery block [40].

In general, the AT is a sanity check: is the block's output satisfactory for processing by the rest of the program, or does error recovery need to occur? The AT can also be an integrity check, verifying the integrity of data values and data structures. At a basic level, a data value can be constrained to be within a certain range, or more complex tests can be performed. Functional tests are another sphere of ATs, ensuring the reasonableness of the output given the input and the block's function. For example, an AT for a sorting algorithm would ensure that the algorithm's output has the same number of values as the unsorted data set (that was provided as the input to the algorithm), and that the sorted data output was successfully sorted. Secondary blocks, in this case, could be less efficient, but more reliable sorting algorithms.

When an AT fails, the system must be restored to its state at the beginning of the recovery block. Similar behavior ensues if the AT is not reached within a certain time limit, indicating that a hang has occurred. One option for restoring state is checkpointing, but in general it is too inefficient. Instead, various mechanisms have been proposed for determining when a nonlocal variable is being changed within the recovery block for the first time, and then recording its previous value for use in the AT and in case rollback is necessary. In that manner, the "recovery cache" stores only modified values, and not the entire state. Hardware support can be used to make this more efficient.

### 6.2.2.3 Distributed Applications: Recovery Block Conversations

Sequential RBs work very well, but their applicability toward many real-world applications is limited. Randell [25] thus introduced the concept of a recovery block conversation, allowing cooperating processes to use the recovery block (RB) scheme efficiently. The main issue with distributed applications is handling of the rollback upon an AT failure. For a distributed application, if one process rolls back, other processes that use that process's output, or send it input, must often roll back as well. Without proper structuring there could be a domino effect, such that all processes ultimately roll back to the initial starting point.

For the domino effect to occur, the processes must have both uncoordinated RBs, and dependencies such that a failure of one causes the others to roll back. Since preventing the latter would change the nature of the program, the conversation scheme prevents the former. Conversations coordinate the saving of state, such that failures will at worst cause a rollback to the start of the conversation. Conversations are entered asynchronously; the coordination is in saving state before entering. The members of a conversation must be known at the start, and once the conversation has formed, communication with other processes must be prohibited. Conversations, like normal RBs, can be nested. Intersecting conversations, however, would violate the prohibition against communication across conversation boundaries and are not allowed. Figure 6.6 illustrates the proper

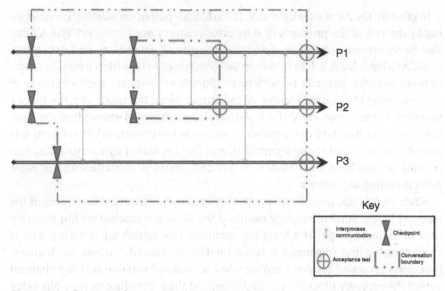

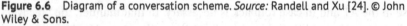

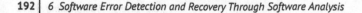

**Figure 6.6** Diagram of a conversation scheme. *Source:* Randell and Xu [24]. © John Wiley & Sons.

structure of a conversation. A conversation can be considered a recovery block, with multiple RBs nested inside (one for each node).

At the end of a conversation, each node will run its respective AT. All nodes must pass their ATs before the conversation is considered finalized. The set of ATs forms the *test line*, and for the conversational recovery block can be referred to as a *conversation* AT [41]. If one or more tests fail, all nodes roll back to the start of the conversation (the *recovery line*) and continue processing with their alternate blocks. In some situations, it might make sense for the successful nodes to continue with their primary blocks, but one must be careful that the node failure was not due to bad input from a succeeding node. When all nodes are running their primary blocks, that is known as the *primary interacting session* (PIS); when alternate blocks are being used, it is an *alternate interacting session* (AIS) [42]. To increase performance, an interrupt mechanism should be implemented to abort other processes when the first one fails its AT, minimizing the amount of unnecessary work performed [43].

One performance bottleneck is that processes must wait at the AT stage until all other processes have finished. That delay adds significant overhead [41]. One solution is *look-ahead execution* [42], with which processes will go past the end of the conversation, though keeping their recovery points from the start of the conversation in case rollback is needed. The downside is that rollback becomes more involved, but the benefits outweigh the costs, as we will discuss shortly.

It may be possible for a nested conversation to finish, including all its AT, while its processes are still waiting for the enclosing conversation to finish. If that happens, the nested conversation is considered unfinished, since it may need to be rolled back if the enclosing conversation enters recovery. Implementations may choose to limit how far ahead processes can get, and should prevent the occurrence of output that cannot be undone.

Kim and Yang present performance models for lookahead execution [42] and explore some implementation details concerning conversations in [43], e.g. use of a "recovery cache" to support lookahead execution. Romanovsky [44] explores use of a group communication (GC) service as an underlying implementation to take advantage of membership atomicity and failure atomicity in supporting RBs.

### 6.2.2.4 Advanced Recovery Block Models and Real-Time Systems
The recovery block schemes described up to this point involve fault-tolerant systems that are capable of handling many real-world applications but are not suitable for real-time systems. With many alternate blocks, the RB may process for quite some time before either issuing a result or declaring failure. That latency has been solved by using multiple computers to run the primary and alternate try blocks concurrently, and having the succeeding node supply the answer to the system. That newer approach also converts the recovery block scheme from a backward error recovery model to a forward error recovery model. That is, when a primary try block fails, an alternate try block has already calculated a correct value.

The technique just described is called the *distributed recovery block* (DRB) scheme [45]. For simplicity, the literature commonly describes DRB models in terms of a primary try block and a single alternate, and we will do so here. In a DRB model, each computer runs just one try block at a time. In [45], the first computer (the primary computer) runs just the primary try block. The second computer (the shadow computer) is responsible for the alternate. However, both computers have try blocks and will switch roles as needed. It is possible to extend the models by including additional try blocks as further shadows of the nodes.

After each computer has run its try block, it will pass the output through the AT. If the primary succeeds, it will notify the shadow, and the primary node will send the output. If the message is lost, the backup may also send its output (as if the primary had crashed), and thus the output might need to be tagged so that the duplication can be detected [42]. That situation could also cause both computers to believe they are the primary, a situation that would need to be detected and resolved. If the primary fails, it switches roles with the shadow, and the shadow sends the output of its AT. Failure is detected either if the primary signals that it failed the AT, or if the backup's watchdog timer indicates that the primary failed to respond. When switching roles, the failed node will roll back and execute its new try block in an attempt to synchronize its state with the new primary.

It should be clear that the two try blocks should have the same output (a stricter requirement than found in non-concurrent RBs) or else the two computers could have divergent states even when both pass their ATs. Such divergence is actually allowed in [45], but in some systems will be undesirable. In a non-concurrent recovery block scheme, the alternate block will be used only when the primary fails. But in the DRB scheme, the shadow node will always use the alternate block. If the alternate block results in less desirable output, and then there is a role switch, the node running the primary block will have its state determined by many iterations of the substandard alternate block. The impact will depend upon the application.

An extension of the DRB scheme for process control applications is known as the *Extended Distributed Recovery Block* (EDRB) [46]. The EDRB scheme can be thought of as a system of multiple DRBs controlled by a supervisor node. Combination of the conversation and DRB models results in the distributed real-time conversation (DRC) scheme [47]. The DRC scheme is designed to provide fault tolerance for cooperating processes (which themselves might be DRBs) that cannot tolerate the delays associated with backward error recovery.

## 6.3 Static Analysis Techniques

Many techniques have been proposed for finding bugs in programs based on static analysis of the application code [1–3]. These techniques validate the program based on a well-understood fault model, which has usually been specified based on common programming bugs (e.g. NULL pointer dereferences). The techniques attempt to locate errors across feasible paths in the program, i.e. program paths that correspond to actual executions of the program. Static determination of all feasible paths is known to be an impossible problem in the general case. Therefore, the techniques either overapproximate the set of feasible paths, leading to wasteful detections, or do not explore all feasible paths in the program, leading to missed detections.

To illustrate the problems faced by static analysis techniques, consider, for example, the code fragment in Figure 6.7. In the code, the pointer *str* is initialized to NULL, and the pointer *src* is initialized to a constant string. The length of the string *src* is computed in a *while* loop. If the computed length is greater than zero, a new buffer of that length is allocated on the heap, and its address is stored in the pointer *str*. Finally, the string pointed to by the pointer *src* is copied into the buffer pointed to by the pointer *str*.

**Figure 6.7** Example code fragment to illustrate feasible path problem faced by static analysis techniques.

```
int size = 0;
char* str = NULL;
char* src = "A String";
while (src[size]! = '\0')
    ++ size;
if (size > 0) {
    str = malloc(size + 1);
}
strcpy(str,src size );
```

Consider a static analysis technique that checks for NULL pointer dereferences. In the program shown in Figure 6.7, the tool needs to resolve whether the value of *str* is NULL before the *strcpy* statement is executed. For *str* to be NULL, the *then* branch of the *if* statement should not be executed, and that, in turn, means that the predicate in the *if* statement, namely (*size* > 0), should be false. The value of *size* is initialized to zero outside the *while* loop and incremented inside the loop. The technique needs to statically evaluate the *while* loop in order to conclude that the value of *size* cannot be zero after execution of the loop and before the *if* predicate.[1] In the interest of scalability, many static analysis tools would not perform such an evaluation. In fact, the evaluation of the loop may not even terminate in the general case (although in this example, it would terminate, because the string is a constant string). Therefore, the technique would report a potential NULL pointer dereference of *str* in the call to *strcpy*. The problem is that the control path in which the *then* part of the *if* statement is not executed does not correspond to a real execution of the program. However, the static analysis technique does not have enough resolution to determine whether the *then* part of the *if* statement is or is not executed, and consequently it overapproximates the set of feasible paths in the program, resulting in wasteful detections.

In the general case, it is impossible for a static analysis technique to resolve all feasible paths in a program. In practice, different static analysis techniques provide varying degrees of approximations for handling the feasible path problem. We consider the following three examples of static analysis techniques:

- **LCLINT** performs dataflow analysis to find common programming errors in C programs [1]. The analysis is coarse-grained and approximates branch predicates to be both true and false, effectively considering all paths to be feasible. LCLINT may produce many spurious warnings and requires programmer annotations to suppress such warnings.

---

1 In this example, evaluation of a single iteration of the loop is enough to support the conclusion that *size* cannot be zero. However, in the general case, it may be necessary to evaluate the entire loop.

- **ESP** also uses dataflow analysis to determine whether a program satisfies a given temporal property [2]. However, the dataflow analysis is path-sensitive and takes into account specific execution paths in the program. To perform exact verification, any branch in the program that affects the property being verified must be modeled. The main approximation made by ESP is that it is sufficient to model the branches along which the property being verified differs on the two sides of the branch. ESP can correctly identify feasible paths when two branches are controlled by the same predicate, or when one branch predicate implies another. However, for more complex branch predicates, ESP relies on programmer-supplied annotations to resolve feasible paths in the program.
- **Prefix** performs symbolic simulation of the program, rather than dataflow analysis [3]. The Prefix tool follows each path through a function and keeps track of the exact state of the program along that path. To keep the simulation tractable, only a fixed number of paths (typically 50) are explored in each function. Hence, Prefix may miss errors that occur on the unexplored paths. The main assumption made by Prefix is that the incremental benefit of finding more defects as the number of paths increases is small. It is unclear whether the assumption holds for operational defects that may manifest along infrequently executed paths in the program, or along paths that occur deep in the program space. We discuss the ESP technique in more detail below, to explain how it addresses the feasible path problem.

### 6.3.1 ESP: Path-Sensitive Program Verification in Polynomial Time

Consider the code snippet (extracted from the gcc compiler's source code) shown in Figure 6.8a (based on [2]). Suppose we want to check the temporal property that "a file must be opened before it can be closed and can be written to only when it is open." We want to avoid opening an already opened file and closing an already closed file. This property can be expressed using the state machine shown in Figure 6.8b, in which the *Error* state corresponds to the disallowed transitions.

Assume that a file can be opened only through an fopen() call and closed only through the fclose() call. The C language does not offer a mechanism for expressing such invariants; hence, we need to map program operations to states in the state machine. Assume that the fopen() call is mapped to the Open operation and the fclose() call is mapped to the Close operation in the state machine.

In the code shown in Figure 6.8a, there are four feasible paths, which correspond to the following combinations of the *dump* and $p$ variables: (i) dump $= 0$, $p = 0$; (ii) dump $= 1$, $p = 0$; (iii) dump $= 0$, $p = 1$; and (iv) dump $= 1, p = 1$. The file is opened and closed on paths 1 and 4 and neither opened nor closed in paths 2 and 3. Hence, for all feasible paths in the code, the property in Figure 6.8b is

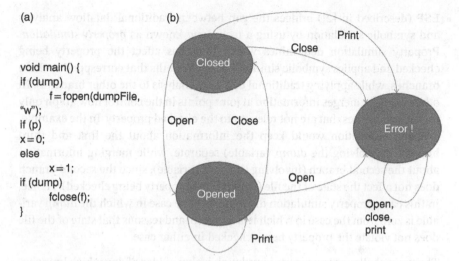

(a)

```
void main() {
if (dump)
    f = fopen(dumpFile,
"w");
if (p)
x = 0;
else
    x = 1;
if (dump)
    fclose(f);
}
```

(b)

**Figure 6.8** Code sample and property FSM.

obeyed, and the paths capture the correlation between the *dump* variable and the file state.

Next, we discuss how different analysis approaches would reason about the above program.

- **Traditional dataflow analysis** (of the kind described in [1]). Since dataflow analysis merges the values of the variables at merge points in the control flow graph, the information about the state of the dump variable will be lost at the statement following the first branch. Similarly, the state of the file can be either *Opened* or *Closed*. When the subsequent branch involving *dump* is taken, the file is closed, and a transition from the *Closed* state to the *Closed* state is taken and an error is declared. The error is a false positive, as it does not occur on a feasible path in a real execution. Rather, it is introduced because of the approximations made by the dataflow analysis.
- **Symbolic simulation approach** (of the kind described in [1]). A symbolic simulation approach would systematically explore all feasible paths in the program by exhaustively considering every possible branch condition and its negation. Such an approach will be effective at finding that a property is not violated along any feasible path, but it needs to explore all four feasible paths before arriving at this conclusion. The result may be exponential complexity; hence, symbolic simulation approaches explore only a fixed number of paths. The most that a symbolic simulation approach can say is that a property was not violated along the explored paths.

- **ESP** (described in [2]) bridges the gap between traditional dataflow analysis and symbolic simulation by using a technique known as *property simulation*. Property simulation determines which branches affect the property being checked and applies symbolic simulation for the paths that correspond to these branches, while applying traditional dataflow analysis to the other branches. In other words, it merges information at joint points in the control flow graph only for those branches that are not relevant to the checked property. In the example, property simulation would keep the information about the first and third branches (involving the *dump* variable) separate, while merging information about the second branch (involving the *path* variable), since the second branch does not affect the state of the file (which is the property being checked). Hence, in this case, property simulation distinguishes the case in which the *dump* variable is zero from the case in which it is nonzero, and reasons that state of the file does not violate the property being checked in either case.

The main challenge in property simulation is that of identifying which branches are relevant to the property being checked. While in the example it is simple to make that determination, generally speaking, branch predicates may be arbitrarily complex, and it may be difficult for property simulation to decide ahead of time which branches are relevant to the property being checked. An example for which property simulation does not work is shown in Figure 6.9 (which is also from [2]). In this example, different variables control the branches leading to *fopen* and *fclose*. Although the variables have the same value, property simulation will incorrectly assume that the first branch does not affect the state of the file and will merge the program state after analyzing the first branch. As a result, it will not be able to uncover the correlation between the *dump* and *flag* variables, and hence will reason that there is a feasible path in which flag = 0 and dump = 1. That path will cause the file to be closed without being opened, which is a violation of the property. Hence, property simulation will incorrectly declare an error for the program in Figure 6.9. That shows that property simulation can also result in false positives (wasteful detections) when branch predicates are correlated in complex ways.

```
if (dump)
flag = 1;
else
flag = 0;

if (flag)
f = fopen(dumpFile,"w");

if (dump)
fclose(f);
```

**Figure 6.9** Example showing the limitation of property simulation.

## 6.3.2 PR-Miner: Automatically Extracting Implicit Programming Rules and Detecting Violations in Large Software Code

Apart from the specific logical flow of a program, programmers tend to implicitly follow some programming rules. One example of such a rule is the invocation of the pair of functions lock and unlock: if there is a call to lock, then a call to unlock should follow later in the program. Other implicit rules have likewise been observed in large software code bases. However, such rules are rarely documented or written down in comments. For example, in PostgreSQL, a widely used, open-source database server, a call to ReleaseSysCache must follow a call to SearchSysCache. That implicit rule in the program is depicted in Figure 6.10. The rule exists because the function SearchSysCache returns a cached copy of a specified tuple. After the function that called SearchSysCache finishes using the tuple, it must make a call to ReleaseSysCache to release the tuple so that the cached copy can be replaced by other data. There are 209 occurrences of that rule in PostgreSQL, and a violation of it would cause the buffer cache in PostgreSQL to leak memory.

Programming rules can be more complex than the example shown above. A rule may involve more than two elements. Elements can be of various types: a function, a variable, or a data type. For example, Figure 6.11 shows an example of

**Figure 6.10** A function-pair rule in PostgreSQL. *Source:* Li and Zhou [4]. © ACM, Inc.

```
postgresql-8.0.1/src/backend/catalog/dependency.c:
1733 getRelationDescription (StringInfo buffer, Oid relid)
1734 {
1735   HeapTuple relTup;
.....
1740   relTup = SearchSysCache (...);
.....
1796   ReleaseSysCache (relTup);
1797 }
```

**Figure 6.11** A complex programming rule in PostgreSQL. *Source:* Li and Zhou [4]. © ACM, Inc.

```
postgresql-8.0.1/src/backend/commands/tablecmds.c:
5686 AlterTableCreateToastTable(Oid relOid, bool silent)
5687 {
.....
5692   Relation class_rel;
.....
5853   class_rel = heap_openr (...);
.....
5863   simple_heap_update (class_rel, ...);
.....
5866   CatalogUpdateIndexes(class_rel, ...);
.....
5870   heap_close (class_rel, ...);
.....
5891 }
```

a more complex programming rule, derived from PostgreSQL. It involves one variable and four function calls. The rule formally specifies the correct sequence of events to be followed in replacing a tuple. Specifically, the rule requires that before the tuple is replaced via the function simple_heap_update, the function heap_openr must be called to open the relation. The index remains consistent by calling the function CatalogUpdateIndexes. Further, after simple_heap_update returns, a call to heap_close must be made to close the relation.

Some complex rules show correlations among variables, and these variables may need to be accessed together or be modified consistently. For example, according to the rule shown in Figure 6.12, in Linux, the two variables ic.command and ic.driver should be accessed together. This rule has 98 occurrences in the source code of Linux.

A correct software implementation requires the use of such programming rules. Unfortunately, the rules are implicit and usually not documented, as doing so would be too tedious. In addition, maintaining such rules across multiple versions of the same software poses a problem, as some rules may change in subsequent versions. On top of that, when software scales, the number of rules also scales, possibly nonlinearly. For those reasons, it is quite easy for programmers to violate rules unwittingly, especially if they are unaware of the rules. Therefore, it is highly desirable to derive the programming rules automatically, directly from the source code.

The rules thus derived can be used as a specification that can be a reference for programmers. They also make it easier to detect their violations and thus achieve more robust software. The detection of a violation is based on the hypothesis that a programming rule is obeyed in most cases and is violated in only a small percentage of cases.

PR-Miner (Programming Rule Miner) is a method that automatically derives *general* programming rules from programs that are written in C/C++, a widely used programming language [4]. The methodology also detects violations of the rules with minimal effort from programmers by using *data mining*, a technique for extracting patterns from large amounts of data. Figure 6.13 shows the

```
linux-2.6.1 1/drivers/isdn/hisax/config.c:
771 void 11_stop(struck IsdnCardState *cs)
772 {
773     isdn_ctrl ic;
775     ic.command = ISDN_STAT_STOP;
776     ic.driver = cs->myid;
777     cs->iif.statcallb(&ic);
779 }
```

**Figure 6.12** A programming rule for variable correlation in Linux. *Source:* Li and Zhou [4]. © ACM, Inc.

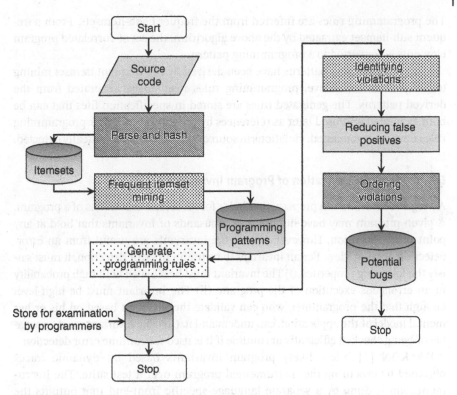

**Figure 6.13** Flowchart of PR-Miner. *Source:* Modified from Li and Zhou [4].

flowchart of PR-Miner. In extracting rules automatically, PR-Miner attempts to derive associations among elements of different types by searching for elements that appear together frequently in the source code. After identifying those elements, with a relatively high level of confidence, PR-Miner can formulate the correlation between elements as a programming rule.

PR-Miner follows the following initial steps, as depicted in Figure 6.13, to convert the problem of finding correlations between program elements to a frequent itemset (a set of numbers) mining problem, a common data mining approach.

1) Each program element is encoded as hash code.
2) The definition of a function is mapped into an itemset and is written into the itemset database as a row.

Through that procedure, the entire program is converted into a database containing many itemsets. With a frequent itemset mining algorithm like *FPclose*, the database is mined to provide the frequent sub-itemsets that occur many times.

The programming rules are inferred from the frequent sub-itemsets. From a frequent sub-itemset extracted by the above algorithm, the set of correlated program elements is converted to a programming pattern.

After programming patterns have been derived by the frequent itemset mining technique detailed above, programming rules need to be generated from the derived patterns. The generated rules are stored in specification files that can be both examined and used later as references by programmers. After programming rules have been generated, violations in source code can be automatically detected.

### 6.3.3 Dynamic Derivation of Program Invariants

A *program invariant* is a property that holds for all correct executions of a program. A given program may have hundreds of thousands of invariants that hold at any point in its execution. However, not all the invariants are useful from an error-detection point of view. For an invariant to be useful in error detection, it must satisfy the following properties. (i) The invariant must be violated with high probability in an erroneous execution of the program. (ii) The invariant must be high-level enough that the programmer, who can validate the invariant based on his or her mental model of the application, can understand it. (iii) The invariant must be capable of being checked efficiently at runtime if it is used for runtime error detection.

**DAIKON** [7] infers likely program invariants based on dynamic traces obtained by executing the instrumented program over a test suite. The instrumentation is done by a separate language-specific front-end that outputs the values of specific program variables at certain program points to a trace. The instrumented program is executed over multiple test cases, and the resulting traces are gathered. An offline analysis procedure then runs through the traces and searches for specific invariant patterns in them. The patterns include constancy of a variable, a linear relationship among sets of program variables, and membership in a set or a value that is bounded in a range. To ensure that the invariants are characteristic of the program, DAIKON computes the probability that the invariant will hold by accident (or chance). Only if that probability is less than a certain threshold does DAIKON consider the invariant for inclusion in the set of derived invariants. DAIKON presents the invariants to the programmer in increasing order of the probability that the invariant will hold by chance, so that the programmer can focus on the invariants that are highly likely to be characteristic of the program.

Since the invariants inferred by DAIKON are based on dynamic traces over a test suite, it is important for the test suite to be representative of the operational settings of the application. Otherwise, there is a danger that the derived invariants will be characteristic of the test suite rather than the application. That could result in violation of invariants in production settings if the invariants differ significantly from those in the test suite, even if no error is present in the application (i.e. false positives).

**DIDUCE** [8] is a dynamic invariant detection approach that uses invariants learned during an early phase of the program's execution (i.e. a training phase) to detect errors in subsequent phases of the execution. Since the invariants are learned during the application's execution, DIDUCE does not require a representative test suite. The main assumption made by DIDUCE is that invariants learned during the training phase well represent the entire application's execution. It is unclear whether that assumption holds in practice, especially for applications that exhibit phased behavior.[2] Further, when DIDUCE detects an invariant violation, it does not stop the program, but saves the program state for reporting back to the user, so that spurious invariant violations do not stop program execution.[3] That approach is useful from the point of view of debugging operational failures, but not from the point of view of providing online error detection for applications. Finally, DIDUCE does not take error propagation into account when checking for invariant violations, and hence it is possible that the application state may already have been corrupted when an invariant violation is detected (at which point, it may be too late).

### 6.3.3.1 DAIKON

DAIKON derives invariants at entries and exits of procedures in the program. The assumption is that invariants represented as function preconditions and postconditions are especially useful to the programmer in finding bugs in the application. That limits the use of the generated invariants as assertions for error detection, since the program may crash before it reaches the assertions inserted by DAIKON, or the error may not propagate to the location at which the assertion was placed.

DAIKON can also be used to infer data structure invariants and to repair data structures at runtime [48]. The idea is to infer constraints about commonly used data structures in the program and monitor the data structure with respect to these constraints at runtime. If a constraint violation is detected, the data structure is "repaired" to satisfy the constraint. The repaired data structure may or may not be the same as the original data structure, and hence the program may produce incorrect output after the repair (although it continues without crashing). In general, however, continuing to execute the program after an error has been detected can lead to harmful consequences. Further, the technique described in [48] only considers errors in the program data structure being monitored. It is intriguing to analyze how the technique can be extended to detect general faults in the application's data. To detect general faults, the fault must propagate to the

---

2 Application behavior varies in phases during program execution.
3 The DIDUCE paper does not present the percentage of spurious invariants found by the tool.

data structure's fields and violate one or more of the derived invariants for the data structure. Our experience indicates that it is more likely that an application will crash because of a general error in its data, than that an error will propagate to specific locations in the program's data, unless error propagation was taken into consideration when the locations (within the code) were chosen.

To illustrate DAIKON's operation, consider a Java program for implementing a stack. The interface of the stack class is shown in Figure 6.14.

When DAIKON was run on the program containing the stack class with a sample test suite, it came up with the invariants shown in Figure 6.15 [7]. The invariants were observed at the entries and exits of method calls. The invariants are

```
void push(Object x) // Insert x
void pop() // Remove most recently inserted item
Object top() // Return most recently inserted item
Object topAndPop() // Remove and return most recently inserted item
boolean isEmpty() // Return true if empty; else false
boolean isFull() // Return true if full; else false
void makeEmpty() // Remove all items
```

**Figure 6.14**  Interface definition for a stack class.

```
Object-level invariants (valid on entry and exit of every method):
  • this.theArray != null
  • this.theArray.getClass() == java.lang.Object[].class
  • this.topOfStack >= -1
  • this.topOfStack <= this.theArray.length - 1
  • this.theArray[0..this.topOfStack] elements != null
  • this.theArray[this.topOfStack+1..] elements == null

Precondition for the StackAr constructor:
  • capacity >= 0

Postconditions for the StackAr constructor:
  • orig(capacity) == this.theArray.length
  • this.topOfStack == -1
  • this.theArray[] elements == null

Postconditions for the isFull method:
  • this.theArray == orig(this.theArray)
  • this.theArray[] == orig(this.theArray[])
  • this.topOfStack == orig(this.topOfStack)
  • (return == false) <==> (this.topOfStack < this.theArray.length - 1)
  • (return == true) <==> (this.topOfStack == this.theArray.length - 1)
```

**Figure 6.15**  Invariants derived by DAIKON for the stack program. *Source:* Modified from Ernst et al. [7].

classified based on the name of the method call at which they were observed and whether they are preconditions (which hold at method entry) or postconditions (which hold at method exits). The common invariants that are observed at the entries and exit of all method calls are also grouped together as object-level invariants for the stack.

All of the object-level invariants derived by DAIKON are examined below, and their use as error detectors is considered.

1) **this.theArray!=null and this.theArray.getClass()==java.lang.Object[].class**

   These two invariants ensure that the array pointer is not null and that it is in fact of the right type. This prevents accidental corruption of the array object and incorrect calling of the method with an object of a type that is different from the default class.

2) **-1 <= this.topOfStack <= this.theArrayLength – 1**

   This invariant ensures that the top of the stack is within the range of the array bounds. Checking of this invariant can prevent array out-of-bound exceptions. Moreover, it ensures that the array is big enough to hold the stack.

3) **theArray[0..this.topOfStack] elements != null && theArray[this.topOfStack+1..] elements == null**

   This invariant ensures that the stack is fully occupied from its start to the topmost eleme and unoccupied beyond the topmost element. That prevents errors that result in skipping of a stack location for storing an object.

Thus, the invariants are useful from the point of view of establishing a consistent global view of the stack data structure and can catch errors that violate this view. However, they do not capture structural or temporal relationships among the stack parameters, and hence are not effective in catching errors that result in subtle violations of the stack semantics. For example, consider an omission error in the *push* method that results in the object's not being pushed on the stack. The error would not be detected by any of the above invariants, as they do not capture the correlation between the state of the array *theArray* and the *top* variable. Further, there is no invariant that states that only the objects that have been added by the *push* method and have not yet been removed by the *pop* method may belong to the array. Such an invariant is necessary to ensure that objects do not accidentally get corrupted in the array. Finally, the invariants do not say anything about the state of the stack inside a method call, and it is possible for a method either to crash or to hang without violating the above invariants. As a result, it is unclear how effective DAIKON's assertions are as runtime error detectors.

The detectors derived by DAIKON can be used by a programmer in conjunction with static inspection of the application code to find errors. For example, assume that there is an error in a program that allowed *top* to be incremented beyond the bounds of the stack array. Such an error might be caused by the (buggy)

```
void push(Object obj)
{
    if (this.topOfStack < this.theArrayLength)
    {
        this.theArray[this.topOfStack + 1] = obj;
    }
    this.topOfStack = this.topOfStack + 1;
}
```

**Figure 6.16** Buggy implementation of the push function.

implementation of the *push* function, as shown in Figure 6.16. The bug causes *top* to be incremented even if the array is full, causing the value of *top* to be out of sync with the actual contents of the array. Note, however, that no exception is thrown in the program, as the object is not added to the array outside its bounds.

Assume that the programmer runs DAIKON with a test suite that covers the case in which the array becomes full. If that happens, DAIKON will observe that the value of *topOfStack* has gone outside the range of the array's allowed size and also that not all objects in the array from *topOfStack* have been allocated. Hence, DAIKON will not report the second invariant and will report a different invariant in place of the third invariant. An astute programmer may notice the omission and reason that DAIKON did not report the second invariant because the invariant no longer held. However, to have such a realization, a programmer would need to understand DAIKON's internal operations, and not all programmers would be inclined to notice the omission. Such an error might be easier to observe if the programmer already had a correct implementation of the stack that obeyed the invariant and is trying to validate his or her implementation against the correct one. On the other hand, the programmer may be trying to refactor or modify the code and has a copy of the derived invariants from prior to the modifications. Thus, while DAIKON is effective as a code understanding or refactoring test tool, its utility as a bug detection tool remains unclear.

### 6.3.4 Statically Derived Application-Specific Detectors

This section presents a methodology for deriving application-specific error detectors based on compiler-based static analysis. The derived detectors detect data errors in the application. A *data error* is defined as a divergence in the data values used in a program from those found in an error-free run of the program for the same input. Data errors can result from (i) incorrect computation (which would not be caught by generic techniques such as ECC in memory) and (ii) software defects (bugs).

Note that the detectors introduced in this section are runtime detectors, as they detect errors when the program is being executed. Thus, they do not suffer from the problems of finding feasible paths, unlike the approaches in Section 6.3.1, which operated entirely at compile time. Further, they can detect runtime errors and are not limited to design errors that manifest at compile time.

### 6.3.4.1 Terms and Definitions

The **backward program slice** of a variable at a program location is the set of all program statements/instructions that can affect the value of the variable at that program location [49].

A **critical variable** is a program variable that exhibits high sensitivity to random data errors in the application. Placing checks on critical variables achieves high detection coverage for data errors.

A **checking expression** is an optimized sequence of instructions that recompute the critical variable. It is computed from the backward slice of the critical variable for a specific acyclic control path in the program.

A **detector** is the set of all checking expressions for a critical variable, one for each acyclic, intraprocedural control path in the program.

### 6.3.4.2 Steps in Detector Derivation

The main steps in error detector derivation are as follows:

1) *Identification of critical variables.* The critical variables are identified based on an analysis of the dynamic execution of the program. The application is executed with representative inputs to obtain its dynamic execution profile, which is used to choose critical variables for detector placement. *Critical variables* are variables with the highest dynamic fanouts in the program, as errors in these variables are likely to propagate to many locations in the program and cause program failure. An approach for identifying critical variables was presented in [10], where it was shown (experimentally) to provide 85% coverage with approximately 10 critical variables in the entire program.[4] However, in the analysis in [50], critical variables are chosen on a per-function basis in the program; i.e. each function/procedure in the program is considered separately to identify critical variables. That approach was taken so that the analysis could scale to large programs.

2) *Computation of backward slice of critical variables.* A backward traversal of the static dependence graph of the program is performed starting from the instruction that computes the value of the critical variable going back to the beginning of the function. The slice is specialized for each acyclic control path that reaches the computation of the critical variable from the top of the function. The slicing algorithm used is a static slicing technique that considers all possible dependencies between instructions in the program regardless of program inputs. Hence, the slice will be a superset of the dependencies

---

4 Ideal detectors are considered that can detect any deviation from the correct value.

encountered during an execution of the program and will encompass all valid inputs.

3) **Check derivation, check insertion, and instrumentation.**
   - *Check derivation:* To form the checking expression, the specialized backward slice for each control path is optimized to consider only the instructions on the corresponding path.
   - *Check insertion:* The checking expression is inserted in the program immediately after the computation of the critical variable.
   - *Instrumentation:* The program is instrumented to track control paths followed at runtime in order to choose the checking expression for each control path.

4) **Runtime checking in hardware and software.** The control path followed is tracked (by the inserted instrumentation) at runtime. The path-specific inserted checks are executed at appropriate points in the execution, depending on the control path followed at runtime. The checks recompute the value of the critical variable for the runtime control path. The recomputed value is compared with the original value computed by the main program. If there is a mismatch, the original program is stopped, and recovery is initiated.

### 6.3.4.3 Example of Derived Detectors

We will illustrate the derived detectors by using a simplified example of an *if-then-else* statement, shown in Figure 6.17. In the figure, the original code is shown on the left, and the checking code added is shown on the right. Assume that the detector placement analysis procedure has identified $f$ as one of the critical variables that need to be checked before their use in the following basic block. For brevity, only the instructions in the backward slice of variable $f$ are shown in Figure 6.17.

In Figure 6.17, there are two paths in the program slice of $f$, corresponding to the two branches. The instructions on each path can be optimized to yield a checking expression that checks the value of $f$ along that path. In the case of the first path ($path = 1$), the expression reduces to $(2 * c - e)$, which is assigned to the temporary variable $f2$. Similarly, the expression for the second path ($path = 2$), which corresponds to the *else* branch statement, reduces to $(a + e)$ and is also assigned to $f2$. Instrumentation is added to keep track of paths at runtime. At runtime, when control reaches the inserted check, the appropriate checking expression for $f$ is chosen based on the value of the *path* variable, and the value of $f2$ is compared with the value of $f$ computed by the program. If there is a mismatch, an error is declared, and the program is stopped. Note that an error that affects the branch expression ($a == 0$) can also be detected by the inserted check.

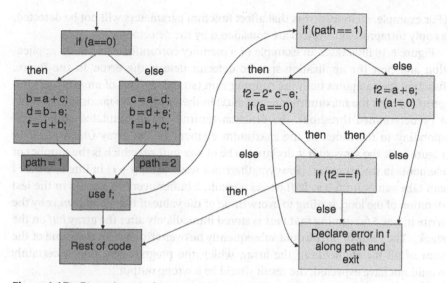

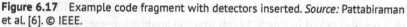

**Figure 6.17** Example code fragment with detectors inserted. *Source:* Pattabiraman et al. [6]. © IEEE.

#### 6.3.4.4 Software Errors Covered

Since the application-specific error detectors (as discussed above) enforce the compiler-extracted source-code semantics of programs at runtime, such detectors can uncover any software error that violates the source program's semantics at runtime. Such errors include software errors caused by pointer corruptions in programs (memory corruption errors) as well as those caused by missing or incorrect synchronization in concurrent programs (timing errors).

##### 6.3.4.4.1 Memory Corruption Errors

Languages such as C and C++ allow pointers to write anywhere in memory (to the stack and heap). Memory corruption errors are caused when pointers in the code write outside their intended objects[5] (according to C language semantics), thereby corrupting other objects in memory. However, static analysis performed by compilers typically assumes that objects are infinitely far apart in memory and that a pointer can write only within its intended object. As a result, the backward slice of critical variables extracted by the compiler includes only those dependences that arise through explicit assignment of values to objects via pointers to the object. Therefore, application-specific error detectors capture all memory errors that corrupt one or more variables in the backward slice of critical variables, as long as the shared state between the check and the main program is not corrupted.

---

5 The term *object* refers to both program variables and memory objects.

(For example, memory errors that affect function parameters will not be detected, as only intraprocedural slices are considered by the detectors.)

Figure 6.18 illustrates an example of a memory corruption error in an application and how the application-specific detector detects the error. In the figure, function *foo* computes both the running sum (stored in *sum)* of an array of integers (*buf)* and the maximum integer (*max*) in the array. If the maximum exceeds a predetermined threshold, the function returns the accumulated sum corresponding to the index of the maximum element in the array (*maxIndex*). In Figure 6.18, the array *sum* is declared to be of size *bufLen*, which is the number of elements in the array *buf*. However, there is a write to *buf*[$i+1$] in line 5, where $i$ can take values from 0 to *bufLen*. As a result, a buffer overflow occurs in the last iteration of the loop, leading to overwriting of the value of the variable *max* by the write in line 5 (assuming that *max* is stored immediately after the array *buf* on the stack). The value of *max* would subsequently be overwritten with the value of the sum of all the elements in the array, which the programmer almost certainly would not have expected; the result would be a wrong output.

In the above example, assume that the variable *max* has been identified as critical and is being checked in line 9. Recall that the application-specific error detectors will detect a memory corruption error *if and only if* the error causes corruption of the critical variable (as it does in this example). If that happens, the checking expression for *max* will depend on whether the branch corresponding to the *if* statement in line 6 is taken. If the branch is not taken, the value of *max* is the value of *max* from the previous iteration of the loop. If the branch is taken, then the value of *max* is computed to be the value *buf*[$i$]. These are the only possible values for the *max* variable, and both values are represented in the detector. The memory corruption error in line 5 will overwrite the variable *max* with the value

```
int foo(int buf[]) {
1:      int sum[bufLen];
2:      int max = 0; int maxIndex = 0;
3:      sum[0] = 0;
4:      for (int i = 0; i< bufLen; ++i) {
5:          sum[i + 1] = sum[i] + buf[i];
6:          if (max < buf[i]) {
7:              max = buf[i];
8:              maxIndex = i;
9:          }
10:     }
11:     if (max > threshold)      return
sum[maxIndex];
12:     return sum[bufLen];
}
```

**Figure 6.18** Example of a memory corruption error. *Source:* Pattabiraman et al. [6]. © IEEE.

*sum*[*bufLen*], thereby causing a mismatch in the detector's value. Hence, the error will be detected.

Note that the detector does not isolate the line of code or the variable at which the memory error occurs. Therefore, it can detect any memory corruption error that affects the value of the critical variable, independent of where the error occurs. As a result, we do not need to instrument all unsafe writes to memory, as is done by conventional memory-safety techniques [17–19].

#### 6.3.4.4.2 *Race Conditions and Synchronization Errors*

Race conditions occur in concurrent programs because of a lack of synchronized accesses to shared variables. When they are extracting dependencies in programs, static analysis techniques typically do not take into account asynchronous modifications of variables. As a result, the backward slice only includes modifications to the shared variables made under proper synchronization. Hence, race conditions that result in unsynchronized writes to shared variables will be detected provided the write(s) are to the variables in the backward slice of critical variables that are not shared between the main program and the checking expressions. However, race conditions that result in unsynchronized reads may not be detected unless the result read by the read propagates to the backward slice of the critical variable. Note that the technique would not detect benign races (i.e. race conditions in which the final value of the variable is not affected by the order of the writes), as it checks the value of the variable being written to rather than whether the write is synchronized.

Figure 6.19 shows a hypothetical example of a race condition in a program. Function *foo* adds a constant value to each element of an array *a* that is passed to function *foo* as a formal parameter. *Foo* is also passed an array *a_lock*, which maintains fine-grained locks for each element of *A*. Before operating on an element of the array, the thread acquires the appropriate lock from the array *a_lock*, thus ensuring that another thread cannot modify the contents of array *a*[*i*], provided that the other thread tries to acquire the lock before modifying *a*[*i*].

**Figure 6.19** Example for race condition detection. *Source:* Pattabiraman et al. [6]. © IEEE.

```
1: void foo(int* a, mutex* alock, int n, int c) {
2:     int i = 0;
3:     int sum = 0;
4:     for (i = 0; i<n; i++) {
5:         acquire_mutex( alock[i] );
6:         old_a = a[i];
7:         a[i] = a[i] + c;
8:         check( a[i] == old_a + c )
9:         release_mutex( alock[i] );
10:    }
}
```

Therefore, the locks by themselves do not protect the contents of $a[i]$ unless all threads adhere to the locking discipline. The property of adherence to the locking discipline is hard to verify using static analysis alone because (i) the thread modifying the contents of array $a$ could be in a different module from the one being analyzed, and the source code of the other module might not be available at compile time and (ii) precise pointer analysis is required to find the specific element of $a$ being written to in the array. Such precise analysis is often unscalable, and static analysis techniques perform approximations that result in missed detections.

However, such a detector would detect illegal modifications to the array $a$ even by threads that do not follow the locking discipline. Assume that the variable $a[i]$ in line 7 has been determined to be a critical variable. The detector should be placed to check on $a[i]$ to recompute it in line 8. Now assume that the variable $a[i]$ was modified by an errant thread that does not follow the locking discipline. That would cause the value of $a[i]$ computed in line 7 to be different from what it should have been in a correct execution (namely its previous value added to the constant $c$). Therefore, the error is detected by the recomputation check in line 8.

The following points about the example should be noted. (i) The source code of the errant thread is not needed to derive the check and hence can be in a different module. (ii) The check will fail only if the actual computed value is different from what it should have been in a correct execution (which is its previous value added to the constant $c$) and is therefore immune to benign races that have no manifestation in the computation of the critical variable. (iii) Finally, in the example, it is enough to analyze the code of the function *foo* to derive the check for detecting the race condition.[6]

### 6.3.4.5 Hardware Errors Covered

Hardware transient errors that result in corruption of architectural state are considered in the fault model. Examples of hardware errors covered include the following:

- **Instruction fetch and decode errors:** Either the wrong instruction is fetched, (OR) a correct instruction is decoded incorrectly, resulting in data value corruption.
- **Execute and memory unit errors:** An ALU instruction is executed incorrectly inside a functional unit, (OR) the wrong memory address is computed for a load/store instruction, resulting in data value corruption.
- **Cache/memory/register file errors:** A value in the cache, memory, or register file experiences a soft error that causes it to be incorrectly interpreted in the program (assuming that ECC is not used).

---

6 This may not hold if modification is done prior to the function call, in which case we need an inter-procedural analysis.

#### 6.3.4.6 Performance and Coverage Measurements

The derivation of detectors based on static analysis of the code has been implemented as a custom compiler pass in the LLVM compiler. We conducted a set of measurements to evaluate the performance and the detection coverage. We measured the performance by timing the execution of the program that had been compiled with the custom compiler pass, and we measured the coverage through fault injection experiments conducted using software-based fault injection.

##### 6.3.4.6.1 *Performance Measurement*

All experiments were carried out on a single-core Pentium 4 machine with 1 GB RAM and 2.0 GHz clock speed, running the Linux operating system. The following performance overheads of each individual component were measured:

*Modification overhead, i.e. performance overhead due to the extra code introduced by the VRP for instrumentation and checking.* This code may cause cache misses and branch mispredictions and incur performance overhead.

*Checking overhead, i.e. the performance overhead of executing the instructions in each check to recompute the critical variable and compare the recomputed value with the original value.* This also includes the cost of branching to the check, choosing the checking expression to be executed, and branching back to the program's code.

We did not consider the overhead of path tracking while measuring performance overheads because a specialized hardware module was used to do the path tracking in parallel with the execution of the main program. The path-tracking module could execute asynchronously and needed to be synchronized with the main processor only when the check was performed.

We emulated the path-tracking module and measured the performance overheads of the application with both path tracking and checking enabled. The application overhead with only path tracking enabled was measured and subtracted from the earlier result to obtain the checking overheads. To obtain the code modification overheads, we executed the application with both path tracking and checking disabled and measured the increase in execution time relative to the unmodified application.

##### 6.3.4.6.2 *Coverage Measurements*

*Fault Injection.* To measure coverage, we injected faults into the data of the application protected with the derived detectors. A custom compiler pass was implemented to insert calls into a special *faultInject* function after the computation of each program variable in the original program. The variable to be injected was passed as an argument to the *faultInject* function. The uses of the program variable in the original program were substituted with the return value produced by the *faultInject* function.

At runtime, the call to the *faultInject* function corrupted the value of a single program variable by flipping a single bit in its value. The value into which the fault was injected was chosen at random from the entire set of dynamic values used in an error-free execution of the program (that are visible at the compiler's intermediate code level). To ensure controllability, only a single fault was injected in each execution of the application.

Only the values in the original function prior to instrumentation were considered for fault injection. No faults were injected into the detectors themselves because we assumed that no more than one fault could occur during the application's execution. Injecting faults into detectors will at worst lead to false detections, i.e. detection of an error when none exists. However, we did inject errors into states shared between the detectors and the program in order to emulate common-mode errors.

*Error Detection.* After a fault is injected, the following program outcomes are possible: (i) the program may terminate with a hardware exception (crash); (ii) the program may continue and produce correct output (success); (iii) the program may continue and produce incorrect output (fail-silent violation); or (iv) the program may time out (hang). The injected fault may also cause one of the inserted detectors to detect the error and flag a violation.

In the experiments, when a violation was flagged, we allowed the program to continue (although in reality it would be stopped) so that the final outcome of the program under the error could be observed. The coverage of the detector is classified based on the final outcome of the program. For example, a detector is considered to have detected a crash if, upon encountering an error, it flags a violation, and subsequently the program crashes. Hence, when a detector detects a crash, it is preempting the crash of the program.

*Error Propagation.* The goal of our experiments was to measure the effectiveness of the detectors in detecting errors that propagate before causing the program to crash. For errors that do not propagate before the crash, the crash itself may be considered the detection mechanism. (For example, the state can be recovered from a clean checkpoint.) In the experiments, error propagation was tracked by observing whether an instruction that used the erroneous variable's value was executed after the fault had been injected. If the original value into which the error was injected was overwritten, the propagation of the error was no longer tracked. The error propagation was tracked through use of instrumentation inserted into the program through a new LLVM pass. The instrumentation was inserted just before the definitions of variables that are dependent on the fault-injected value.

### 6.3.4.6.3 Benchmarks

Table 6.2 lists the programs we used to evaluate the performance and coverage of detectors derived based on static analysis of the code. The first nine programs in

**Table 6.2** Benchmark programs and characteristics.

| Benchmark | Lines of C | Description of program |
|---|---|---|
| IntMM | 159 | Matrix multiplication of integers |
| RealMM | 161 | Matrix multiplication of floating-point numbers |
| Oscar | 270 | Computes fast Fourier transform |
| Bubblesort | 171 | Sorts a list of numbers using bubblesort |
| Quicksort | 174 | Sorts a list of numbers using quicksort |
| Treesort | 187 | Sorts a list of numbers using treesort |
| Perm | 169 | Computes all permutations of a string |
| Queens | 188 | Solves the N-queens problem |
| Towers | 218 | Solves the towers of Hanoi problem |
| Health | 409 | Discrete-event simulation (using linked lists) |
| Em3d | 639 | Electromagnetic wave propagation (linked lists) |
| Mst | 389 | Computes minimum spanning tree (graphs) |
| Barnes-Hut | 1427 | Solves N-body force computation problem (octrees) |
| Tsp | 572 | Solves traveling salesman problem (binary trees) |

*Source:* Pattabiraman et al. [6]. © IEEE.

the table are from the Stanford benchmark suite [51], and the next five are from the Olden benchmark suite [52]. The Stanford set consists of small programs that perform a multitude of common tasks, while the Olden set consists of pointer-intensive programs.

### 6.3.4.6.4 *Results*
Below we report on the performance and coverage for the case in which five critical variables were chosen in each function.
1) *Performance Overheads.* The performance overhead of the derived detectors relative to the normal (not instrumented) program's execution is shown in Figure 6.20. Both the checking overhead and the code modification overheads are represented. The results can be summarized as follows:
   - The average checking overhead introduced by the detectors was 25%, while the average code modification overhead was 8%. Therefore, the total performance overhead introduced by the detectors was 33%.
   - The worst-case overheads were incurred in the case of the *tsp* application, which had a total overhead of nearly 80%. *tsp* has high overhead because it is a compute-intensive program that involves tight loops. Checks within loops introduce extra branch instructions and increase the execution time.

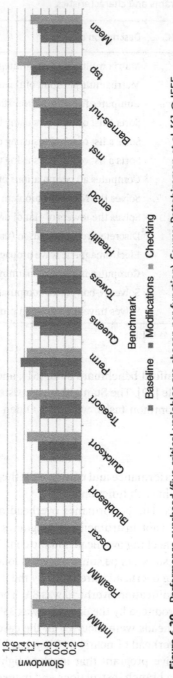

**Figure 6.20** Performance overhead (five critical variables are chosen per function). *Source*: Pattabiraman et al. [6]. © IEEE.

**Table 6.3** Coverage with five critical variables per function.

| Apps | Prop. crashes (%) | FSV (%) | Hang (%) | Success (%) |
|---|---|---|---|---|
| IntMM | 100 (97) | 100 | | 9 |
| RealMM | 100 (98) | | | 0 |
| Oscar | 57 (34) | 7 | 60 | 0.5 |
| Bubblesort | 100 (73) | 100 | 0 | 5 |
| Quicksort | 90 (57) | 44 | 100 | 4 |
| Treesort | 75 (68) | 50 | | 3 |
| Perm | 100 (55) | 16 | | 0.9 |
| Queens | 79 (61) | 20 | | 3 |
| Towers | 79 (78) | 39 | 100 | 2 |
| Health | 39 (39) | 0 | 0 | 0 |
| Em3d | 79 (79) | | | 1 |
| Mst | 83 (53) | 79 | 0 | 5 |
| Barnes-Hut | 49 (39) | | 23 | |
| Tsp | 64 (64) | | 0 | 0 |
| Average | 77 (64) | 41 | 35 | 2.5 |

*Source:* Pattabiraman et al. [6]. © IEEE.

2) *Detection Coverage.* For each application, 1000 faults were injected, one in each execution of the application. The error-detection coverages (when five critical variables were chosen in each function) for different classes of failure are reported in Table 6.3. A blank entry in the table indicates that no faults of the type were manifested for the application. For example, no hangs were manifested for the *IntMM* application in the fault injection experiments. The second column of the table shows the number of errors that propagated and led to crashes of the application. The numbers within parentheses in the second column indicate the percentage of propagated, crash-causing errors that were detected before propagation.

## 6.4 Error Detection Based on Dynamic Program Analysis

In the previous section, we discussed techniques for deriving detectors for an application based on static analysis of the program. Static analysis techniques do not depend on the inputs of the program, and hence the detectors are applicable to all possible inputs of the program. Unfortunately, that approach opens up the possibility that the detectors will be too broad, limiting their error detection coverage. In contrast to the detectors derived by static analysis techniques, those derived by dynamic analysis depend on the inputs used to execute the program, which means they are much tighter and provide higher coverage.

The technique for deriving detectors based on dynamic analysis has four steps, as follows:

1) The *analysis* phase identifies the program locations and variables for detector placement, based on the dynamic dependence graph (DDG) of the program. The DDG of the program is specific to the input of the application. Detectors are derived for a representative set of inputs and applied against inputs in the field. It is possible to choose the detector variables and locations without performing fault injections. (In the following discussion, we choose the locations for detector placement based on the *Fanouts* heuristic [53].) The program code is then instrumented to record the values of the chosen variables at the locations selected for detector placement.

2) The *design* phase uses the dynamic traces of recorded values over multiple executions of the application in order to choose the "best" detector that matches the observed values for the variable, based on a set of predetermined generic detector classes (Section 6.4.2). The best detector is the one that maximizes detection coverage with the lowest cost, as defined in terms of a probability model. After the best detector has been chosen, it can be either integrated into application code as software assertions or implemented in hardware. In this chapter we consider a hardware implementation of the derived detectors in order to minimize the detection latency and performance overheads.

3) The *synthesis* phase converts the generated assertions to a hardware description language (HDL) representation that is synthesized in hardware. It also inserts special instructions in the application code to invoke and configure the hardware detectors.

4) Finally, during the *checking* phase, the custom hardware detectors are deployed in the system to provide low-overhead, concurrent runtime error detection for the application. When a detector detects a deviation from the application's behavior learned during the design phase, it flags an error and halts the program.

Note that the analysis and design phases are related to the derivation of the detectors, while the synthesis and checking phases are related to the implementation and deployment of the derived detectors, respectively.

## 6.4.1 Fault Model

The fault model covers *errors* in the data values used in the program's execution, including faults in (i) the instruction stream (if the faults would result in execution of the wrong opcode or in reading or writing of the wrong registers by the instruction), (ii) the functional units of the processor (if the faults would result in incorrect computations), (iii) the instruction fetch and decode units (if the faults would result in fetching or decoding of incorrect instructions), or (iv) the memory and data bus (if the faults would cause fetching or writing of the wrong values in memory and/or processor register file). Note that these errors would not be detected by techniques such as ECC (error correcting codes) in memory, as they originate in the computation.

It is important to understand that not all the faults mentioned above will necessarily result in data value errors; if they don't, they would not be detected by the proposed technique. However, studies have shown that 60–70% of errors in the processor result in data value corruption [50, 54].

The fault model also represents certain types of *software errors* that result in data-value corruptions, such as (i) synchronization errors or race conditions that result in corruptions of data values due to incorrect sequencing of operations; (ii) memory corruption errors, e.g. buffer overflows and dangling pointer references that can cause overwriting of arbitrary data values in memory; and (iii) use of uninitialized or incorrectly initialized values, as these could result in the use of unpredictable values, depending on the platform and environment. These software errors often escape conventional testing and debugging techniques and manifest themselves in the field [28].

## 6.4.2 Derivation: Analysis and Design

An *error detector* is an assertion based on the value of a single variable[7] of a program at a specific location in its code. A detector for a variable is placed immediately *after* the instruction that writes to the variable. Since a detector is placed in the code, it is invoked each time the detector's location is reached.

Consider the sample code fragment in Figure 6.21. Assume that the detector placement methodology has identified variable $k$ as the critical variable to be checked within the loop. Although this example illustrates a simple loop, the

**Figure 6.21** Example code fragment.

```
void foo() {
    int k = 0;
    for (; k<N; k++) {
    ....
    }
}
```

---

7  In this chapter, a *variable* is any register, cache, or memory location.

technique is general and does not depend on the structure of the source program (or even require the program's source code). Nevertheless, the source-level representation of the code is shown for clarity.

In the example code, variable $k$ is initialized at the beginning of the loop and incremented by 1 within the loop. Within the loop, the value of $k$ is dependent on its value in the previous iteration. Hence, the rule for $k$ can be written as "either the current value of $k$ is zero, or it is greater than the previous value of $k$ by 1." The current value of the detector variable $k$ is denoted by $k_i$ and the previous value by $k_{i-1}$. Thus, the above detector can be expressed as $(k_i - k_{i-1} == 1)$ or $(k_i == 0)$.

As seen from the above example, one can construct a detector for a target variable by observing the dynamic evolution of the variable over time. The detector consists of (i) a rule describing the allowed values of the variable at the selected location in the program, and (ii) an exception condition to cover correct values that do not fall into the rule. If the detector rule fails, then the exception condition is checked, and if it too fails, the detector flags an error. Detector rules can belong to any one of six generic classes and are parameterized for the variable checked. The rule classes, shown in Table 6.4, were chosen based on observations about the behavior of program variables and are similar to those in Hiller [9].

**Table 6.4** Generic rule classes.

| Class name | Generic rule ($a_i, a_{i-1}$) | Description |
| --- | --- | --- |
| Constant | $(a_i == c)$ | The value of the variable in the current invocation of the detector is a constant given by parameter $c$ |
| Alternate | $((a_i == x \land a_{i-1} == y))$ $\lor (a_i == y \land a_{i-1} == x)$ | The value of the variable in the current and previous invocations of the detector alternates between parameters $x$ and $y$ |
| Constant-difference | $(a_i - a_{i-1} == c)$ | The value of the variable in the current invocation of the detector differs from its value in the previous invocation by a constant $c$ |
| Bounded-difference | $(min <= a_i - a_{i-1}$ $<= max)$ | The difference between the values of the variable in the previous and current invocations of the detector lies between *min* and *max* |
| Multi-value | $a_i \in \{x, y, \ldots\}$ | The value of the variable in the current invocation of the detector is one of the set of values $x, y, \ldots$ |
| Bounded-range | $(min <= a_i <= max)$ | The value of the variable in the current invocation of the detector lies between the parameters *min* and *max* |

*Source:* Pattabiraman et al. [11]. © IEEE.

The exception condition involves equality constraints on the current and previous values of the variable, as well as logical combinations (*and*, *or*) of two of these constraints. The equality constraints take the following forms: (i) $a_i == d$, where $d$ is a constant parameter; (ii) $a_{i-1} == d$, where $d$ is a constant parameter; and (iii) $a_i == a_{i-1}$. However, not all combinations of the above three clauses are logically consistent. For example, the exception condition ($a_i == 1$ and $a_i == 2$) is logically inconsistent, as $a_i$ cannot take two different values at the same time. Of the 27 possible combinations of the clauses, only 8 are logically consistent. Hence, there are a total of 48 rule class, exception pairs that can be used to construct a detector for a particular location.

For the example (discussed at the beginning of this section) involving the loop index variable $k$, the rule class is *Constant-Difference* of 1, and the exception condition is ($k_i == 0$).

### 6.4.2.1  Dynamic Derivation of Detectors

This section describes the overall methodology for automatically deriving the detectors based on the dynamic trace of values produced during the application's execution. By *automatic derivation*, we mean the determination of the rule and the exception condition for each of the variables targeted for error detection. The basic steps in the algorithm are as follows:

1) The program is instrumented to record the runtime evolution of the values of the detector variables at their respective locations and executed over multiple inputs. This obtains dynamic traces of the checked values.
2) The dynamic traces of the values obtained are analyzed to support the choice of a set of detectors that matches the observed values.
3) A probabilistic model is applied to the set of chosen detectors to find the best detector for a given location. The best detector is characterized in terms of its tightness and execution cost.
4) The program points at which detectors are placed (both variables and locations) are chosen based on the DDG of the program, as shown in [53].

### 6.4.2.2  Detector Tightness and Execution Cost

A qualitative notion of the *tightness* of a detector was first introduced in [55]. Here, *tightness* is defined as the conditional probability that the detector will detect an error, given that there is an error in the value of the variable that it checks. Note that tightness is not the same as coverage, as the *coverage* of a detector is the probability that it will detect an error given that there is an error in *any* value used in the program. Hence, coverage depends not only on the tightness but also on the probability that an error will propagate to the detector's variable.

**Table 6.5** Probability values for computing tightness.

| Symbol | Explanation |
| --- | --- |
| $P(R\|R)$ | Probability that an error in a value that originally satisfied the rule (in a correct execution) will also cause the incorrect value to satisfy the rule |
| $P(R\|X)$ | Probability that an error in a value that originally satisfied the exception condition (in a correct execution) will cause the incorrect value to satisfy the rule |
| $P(X\|R)$ | Probability that an error in a value that originally satisfied the rule (in a correct execution) will cause the incorrect value to satisfy the exception condition |
| $P(X\|X)$ | Probability that an error in a value that originally satisfied the exception condition (in a correct execution) will cause the incorrect value to satisfy the exception condition |

*Source:* Pattabiraman et al. [11]. © IEEE.

To characterize the tightness of a detector, we need to consider both the rule and the exception condition, as the error will not be detected if either passes. The tightness also depends on the parameters of the detector and the probability distribution of the observed stream of data values in a fault-free execution of the program. For an incorrect value to go undetected by a detector, either the rule or the exception condition, or both, must evaluate to true. That can happen in four mutually exclusive ways, listed in Table 6.5.

The tightness of a detector is defined as $(1 - P(I))$, where $P(I)$ is the probability that an incorrect value will pass undetected through the detector. It can be expressed using the terms in Table 6.5 as follows:

$$P(I) = P(R)\Big[P(R|R) + P(X|R)\Big] + P(X)\Big[P(R|X) + P(X|X)\Big]$$ (6.1)

where $P(R)$ is the probability that the value belongs to the rule, and $P(X)$ is the probability that the value belongs to the exception condition; both are derived from the observed value stream on a per-application basis.

The computation of tightness can be automated, since there are only a limited number of rule-exception pairs.[8] The probabilities can be precomputed as a function of the detector's parameters as well as the frequency of elements in the observed data stream for each rule-exception pair. We do not list all the probabilities, but instead illustrate them with an example.

---

8 There are 6 types of rule classes and 8 types of exception conditions, leading to a total of 48 rule-exception pairs.

**Table 6.6** Probability values for computing tightness of detector "Bounded-Range (5, 100) except $(a_i==0)$".

| Symbol | Value | Explanation |
| --- | --- | --- |
| $P(R|R)$ | $(95/N)$ | Each rule value can turn into any of the other 95 rule values with equal probability |
| $P(R|X)$ | $(96/N)$ | An exception value can turn into one of the 96 rule values with equal probability |
| $P(X|R)$ | $(1/N)$ | A rule value can incorrectly satisfy the exception condition if it turns into 0 |
| $P(X|X)$ | 0 | An exception value cannot change into another exception value, as only one value is permitted by the exception condition. (In this example, the value is 0) |

*Source:* Pattabiraman et al. [11]. © IEEE.

*Example of Tightness Calculation.* Consider a detector in which the rule expression belongs to the class *Bounded-Range* with parameters $min = 5$ and $max = 100$ and the exception condition is of the form $(a_i == 0)$. We make the following assumptions about errors in the program: (i) the distribution of errors in the detector variable is uniform across the range of all possible values the variable can take for its type (say, $N$); (ii) an error in the *current* value of the variable is not affected by an error in the previous value of the variable; and (iii) errors in one detector location are independent of errors in another detector location.

Those are optimistic assumptions, so the estimation of tightness is an upper bound on the actual value of the detector's tightness (and therefore its coverage). Relaxing the assumptions may yield higher accuracy but will require prior knowledge of the application's semantics and error behavior in the application, and that cannot be obtained through dynamic analysis. Table 6.6 shows the precomputed probability values for the detector in terms of $N$ and the detector's parameters.

By substituting symbolic expressions in Eq. (6.1) with probability values given in Table 6.6, we get:

$$P(I) = P(R)\left[95/N + 1/N\right] + P(X)\left[96/N + 0\right] = (96/N)\left[P(R) + P(X)\right] = 96/N$$

The above derivation uses the fact that $P(R) + P(X) = 1$, since the value must satisfy either the rule or the exception in an error-free execution, and since the two events are mutually exclusive.

Consider a new detector in which the rule belongs to the *Constant* class (with parameter 5). Let us assume that the exception condition is the same as for the old detector. For the new detector,

$$P(R|R) = 0, P(R|X) = 1/N,$$
$$P(X|X) = 0 \text{ and } P(X|R) = 1/N$$

Substitution of the above values in Eq. (6.1) yields the following expression for P(I):

$$P(I) = P(R)\left[0 + 1/N\right] + P(X)\left[1/N + 0\right] = (1/N)\left[P(R) + P(X)\right] = 1/N$$

Note that the probability of missing an error in the first detector is 96 times the probability of missing an error in the second detector. The tightness of the first detector is correspondingly much lower than the tightness of the second detector (which matches our intuition).

The above model is used only to compare the relative tightness of detectors, and not to compute actual probability values, which may be very small. The range of values for the detector variable represented by the symbol N gets eliminated in the comparison among detectors for the same variable/location and does not influence the choice of the detector.

*Execution Cost.* The execution cost of a detector is the amortized computation cost of executing the detector over multiple values observed at the detector point. The execution cost of a detector is calculated as the number of basic arithmetic and comparison operations that are executed in a single invocation of the detector, averaged over the entire lifetime of the program's execution. An operation usually corresponds to a single arithmetic or logical operator. Note that the computation of the execution cost assumes an error-free execution of the program.

For example, the detector considered above has two comparison operations for the rule and one comparison operation for the exception. Assume that the rule is satisfied 80% of the time, implying that the exception condition is satisfied the remaining 20% of the time, i.e. 80% of the data points in the trace satisfy the rule while 20% satisfy the exception condition. Therefore, the total execution cost for the detector is (2 * 0.8 + 3 * 0.2 =) 2.2 operations.[9]

### 6.4.2.3 Detector Derivation Algorithm

For each location identified by the detector placement analysis in [53], the detector derivation algorithm first chooses the rule class that corresponds to the detector location and then forms the associated exception condition. The algorithm attempts to maximize the *tightness* to *execution cost* ratio for the detector. The evolution of a program variable over time is called the *stream of values* for that variable. The steps in the algorithm are as follows.

9 When a detector is invoked, the rule is checked; only if that check fails is the exception condition checked for the value.

1) To derive the rule, all of the rule classes in Table 6.4 are tried in sequence against the observed value stream to find which of the rule classes satisfy the observed value stream. The parameters of the rule are learned based on appropriate samples (for each rule class) from the observed stream. For the same location, it is possible to generate multiple rules that are considered candidates for exception derivation in the next step.
2) For each rule derived in step 1, the associated exception condition is derived. Each of the values in the stream that does not satisfy the rule is used as a seed for generating exception conditions for that rule (through exhaustive search among the exception conditions). If it is not possible to derive an exception condition for the observed value as per the conditions in Section 6.4.2, the current rule is discarded, and the next rule is tried from the set of rules derived in step 2.
3) For each rule-exception pair generated, the tightness and execution cost of the detector are calculated. The detector with the maximum tightness-to-execution cost ratio is chosen as the final detector for that location and is exported to a text file for synthesis to hardware.

The time complexity of the above algorithm is directly dependent on the number of values observed at each detector location (say $m$), the number of detector locations considered in the application (say $n$), and the number of streams or inputs on which the algorithm is trained (say $k$). The time also depends on the number of rules and exception classes, both of which are constants. Therefore, the overall time complexity of the algorithm is given by $O(m * n * k)$.

### 6.4.3 Experimental Evaluation

This section describes the experimental infrastructure and application workload we used to evaluate the coverage and overheads of the derived detectors. We used fault injection on the application executed in a processor simulator to evaluate the coverage of the derived detectors, and we used an implementation on FPGA hardware to evaluate their performance and area overheads.

#### 6.4.3.1 Application Programs

The system was evaluated with six of the seven programs in the Siemens suite [56] of programs. Each of the programs consists of a few hundred lines of C code and has been extensively used in software testing and verification. The benchmarks are listed in Table 6.7.

#### 6.4.3.2 Infrastructure

We performed the tracing of the application's execution and the fault injections using a functional simulator in the *SimpleScalar* family of processor simulators [57]. The simulator allows one to perform fine-grained tracing of an

**Table 6.7** Benchmarks and their descriptions.

| Benchmark | Description |
|---|---|
| Replace | Searches a text file for a regular expression and replaces the expression with a string |
| Schedule, Schedule2 | A priority scheduler for multiple job tasks |
| Print_tokens, Print_tokens2 | Breaks the input stream into a series of lexical tokens according to prespecified rules |
| Tot_info | Offers a series of data analysis functions |

*Source:* Pattabiraman et al. [11]. © IEEE.

application without modifying the application's code and provides a virtual sandbox in which to execute the application and study its behavior under faults.

We modified the simulator to track dependencies among data values in both registers and memory by shadowing each register/location with four extra bytes (invisible to the application), which stored a unique tag for that location. For each instruction executed by the application, the simulator printed (to the trace file) the tag of the instruction's operands and the tag of the resulting value. The trace file was analyzed offline by specialized scripts to construct the DDG and compute the metrics for placing detectors in the code as described in [53].

We used fault injection to assess the effectiveness of the detectors. Fault locations were specified randomly from the dynamic set of tags produced in the program. The tags were tracked by the simulator, but the executed instructions were not written to the trace file. When the tag value of the current instruction equaled the value of a specified fault location, a fault was injected by flipping of a single bit in the value produced by the current instruction.

Once a fault had been injected, the execution sequence was monitored to see whether a detector location had been reached. If it had, the value at the detector location was written to a file for offline comparison with the derived detectors for the application. The above process continued until the application ended. Note that we injected only a single fault into each execution of the application, because a transient fault is likely to occur at most once during an application's execution.

Since the simulator did not model the operating system or other aspects of a real system, such as virtual memory management, we had to modify it to represent real-world counterparts more accurately. We used the mapping in Table 6.8 to translate the errors detected by the simulator to their corresponding real-world consequences. We calibrated the simulator by injecting faults into the real system and comparing the results to those from the simulated system [53].

**Table 6.8** Types of errors detected by simulator and their consequences.

| Type of error | Consequence | Simulator detection mechanism |
|---|---|---|
| Invalid memory access | Crash (SIGSEGV) | Consistency checks on address range |
| Memory alignment error | Crash (SIGBUS) | Check on memory address alignment |
| Divide-by-zero | Crash (SIGFPE) | Check before divide operation |
| Integer overflow | Crash (SIGFPE) | Check after every integer operation |
| Illegal instruction | Crash (SIGILL) | Check instruction validity before decoding |
| System call error | Crash (SIGSYS) | None, as simulator executes system calls on behalf of application |
| Infinite loops | Program hang (live-lock) | Program executes double the number of instructions as in the golden run |
| Indefinite wait | Program hang (deadlock) | Program execution takes five times longer than the golden run |
| Incorrect output | Fail-silent violation | Compare outputs at the end of the run |

*Source:* Pattabiraman et al. [11]. © IEEE.

#### 6.4.3.3 Experimental Procedure

The experiment was divided into four parts, as follows.

1) **Placement of detectors and instrumentation of code.** We obtained the dynamic instruction trace of the program from the simulator and constructed the DDG from the trace. The detector placement points (both variables and locations) were chosen based on the technique described in [53]. For each application, up to 100 detector points were chosen by the analysis; that corresponds to less than 5% of the static instructions in the assembly code of the benchmark programs (excluding libraries).

2) **Deriving the detectors based on the training set.** The simulator recorded the values of the selected variables at the detector locations for representative inputs. The dynamic values obtained were used to derive the detectors based on the algorithm in Section 6.4.2.3. The training set consisted of 200 inputs, which were randomly sampled from a test suite consisting of 1000 inputs for each program. The test suites are available as part of the Siemens benchmark suite [56].

3) **Fault injections and coverage estimation.** We performed the fault injection experiments by flipping single bits in data values chosen at random from the set of all data values produced during the program's execution. After each fault

was injected, we recorded the data values at the detector locations and classified the outcome of the simulated program as a crash, hang, fail-silent violation, or success (benign). The values recorded at the detector locations were then checked offline by the derived detectors to assess their coverage. The coverage of a detector is expressed in terms of the type of program outcome it detects, i.e. a detector is said to *detect* a program crash if the program would have crashed had the detector not detected the error. If the detector does not detect an error at all, its coverage is counted as zero for all four outcome categories.

4) **Computation of false positives.** The application code instrumented with the derived detectors was executed for all 1000 inputs, including the 200 inputs that were used for training. No faults were injected in those runs. If any one of the derived detectors detected an error, then that input was considered to be a false positive, as an alarm was raised even though no error had been injected. (The assumption was that there were no residual errors in the test suite used for training, so any detection during the training phase was a false positive.)

For the fault injection experiments, we executed each application over 10 inputs chosen at random from those used in the training phase. For each input, 1000 locations were chosen at random from the data values produced by the application. Each fault injection run consisted of a single bit-flip in one of the 1000 locations. Five runs were performed for each application-input combination; that corresponds to about 50 000 fault injection runs per application.

## 6.4.4 Results

The following are the results of the experimental evaluation discussed in Section 6.4.3.

### 6.4.4.1 Detection Coverage of Derived Detectors

We used fault injections to evaluate the coverage of the detectors derived using the algorithm in Section 6.4.2.1. Figures 6.22–6.24 respectively show the coverage for crashes, fail-silent violations (FSV), and hangs obtained for the target applications (expressed as percentages) as a function of the number of detectors placed in each application, which ranged from 1 to 100. The following trends may be observed in the figures. The coverage for each type of failure increases as the number of detectors increases, but less than linearly, as there is an overlap among the errors detected by the detectors. Further, the individual error coverage of the derived detectors depends on the type of failure (crash, FSV, or hang) detected and the application. In general, crashes exhibit the highest coverage, followed by FSVs and hangs.

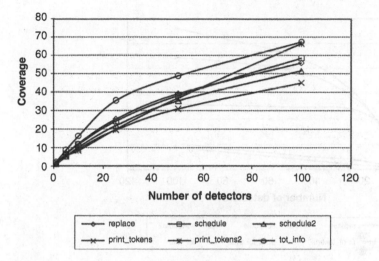

**Figure 6.22** Crash coverage of derived detectors. *Source:* Pattabiraman et al. [11]. © IEEE.

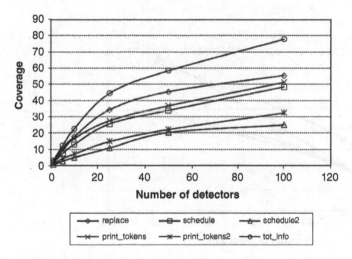

**Figure 6.23** FSV coverage of derived detectors [11].

Figure 6.25 shows the percentages of total manifested errors (crash, hang, and FSV) that were detected by the derived detectors. Those percentages were obtained by considering the detection coverage for the individual failure categories (in Figures 6.22–6.24) along with the fraction of observed errors that resulted in each failure category (not shown in the figures). The coverage obtained for each type of failure is summarized in Table 6.9 for a scenario in which 100 detectors were placed in each application. The derived detectors were able to detect 50–75% of

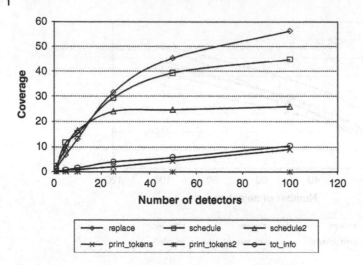

**Figure 6.24** Hang coverage of derived detectors [11].

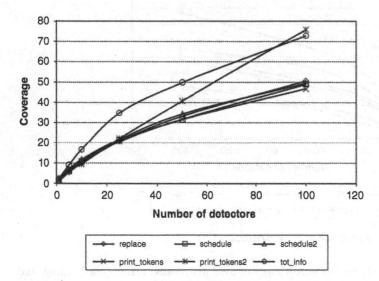

**Figure 6.25** Total error coverage for derived detectors [11].

the errors that manifested in the application, because the majority of errors that manifest in an application are crashes (70–75%) and the rest are fail-silent violations (20–30%) and hangs (0–5%); hence, the coverage for the total manifested errors is dominated by crashes.

**Table 6.9** Range of detection coverage for 100 detectors.

| Type of failure | Minimum coverage | Maximum coverage |
|---|---|---|
| Program crash | 45% (print_tokens) | 65% (tot_info) |
| Fail-silent violation (FSV) | 25% (schedule2) | 75% (tot_info) |
| Program hang | 0% (print_tokens2) | 55% (replace) |
| Program failure | 50% (replace, schedule2, print_tokens, tot_info) | 75% (schedule, print_tokens2) |

*Source:* Pattabiraman et al. [11]. © IEEE.

The results for coverage correspond to errors that occur in any data value used within the program, not just errors that occur in the data values checked by the detector. For example, if even a single bit-flip occurs in a single instance of any data value used in the program, and the error results in a program crash, hang, or fail-silent violation, then one of the 100 detectors placed in the program will detect the error 50–75% of the time. As mentioned in Section 6.4.3.1, 100 detectors correspond to less than 5% of program locations in the static assembly code of the program.

### 6.4.4.2 False Positives

False positives occur when a detector flags an error even though there is no error in the application. A false positive for an input can occur when the values at the detector points for the input do not obey either the detector's rule or the exception condition learned from the training inputs. That can occur if the training set is not comprehensive enough, i.e. it does not cover all the values that might be exhibited by a variable checked by a detector.

The training set for learning the detectors consisted of 200 inputs, and the false positives were computed across 1000 inputs for each application. No faults were injected in these runs. Therefore, any alarm raised by the detectors for any of the 1000 inputs was a false positive. If even a single detector detected an error for a particular input, then the entire input was treated as a false positive.

Figure 6.26 presents the percentage of false positives for each of the target applications as a function of the number of detectors placed in the program. Across all applications, the false positives were no more than 2.5% when 100 detectors were placed in the program. For the *replace, schedule2, print_tokens,* and *print_tokens2* applications, the false positives were observed in less than 1% of the inputs, while for the *schedule* and *tot_info* applications, the false positives were observed in around 2% of the inputs. While the number of false positives increased as the

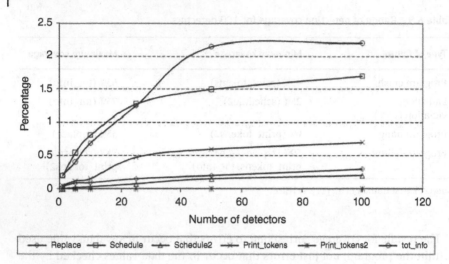

number of detectors increased, it reached a plateau as the number of detectors increased beyond 50. The reason is that a false-positive input is likely to trigger multiple detectors once the number of detectors has passed a certain critical threshold (which is around 50 in the benchmark programs). However, no such plateau was reached for the coverage results in Figure 6.25, even for up to 100 detectors.

*Effect of False Positives.* When a detector raises an alarm, one needs to determine whether an error was really present or whether the alarm was a false positive. If the error was caused by a transient fault (as the technique assumes), then it is likely to be wiped out when the program is re-executed. If, on the other hand, the detection was a false positive and hence a characteristic of the input given to the program, the detector will raise an alarm again during re-execution. If that happens, the alarm can be ignored, and the program can be allowed to continue. Thus, the impact of a false positive is essentially a loss in performance due to re-execution overhead. Since the percentage of false positives is less than 2.5%, the overhead of re-execution is small. It is possible to reduce the overhead further by using checkpointing and restarting schemes [58].

Note that rollback recovery or re-execution may not always be possible in certain systems. For example, in real-time systems, re-execution can lead to missed deadlines, and in distributed systems, it may trigger systemwide rollback. In such systems, false positives may have an impact that goes beyond loss of performance – for example, violations of the system's specifications.

## 6.5 Processor-Level Selective Replication

System-level replication has been widely used to detect and possibly tolerate transient errors in both commercial systems and research prototypes. Processor-level replication is one such technique [59]. The two basic approaches for processor-level replication are hardware redundancy and time redundancy. (i) Hardware redundancy [60] is achieved by carrying out the same computation on multiple, independent pieces of hardware at the same time and comparing the redundant results. (ii) Time redundancy [60, 61] is achieved by executing the same operation multiple times on the same or idle hardware. In both types of redundancy, all instructions of the application are replicated and checked for correct execution. However, the application cannot choose to use redundancy for a specific code section and run in a normal, unreplicated mode for the rest of the code. In other words, it is a "one size fits all" approach.

An alternative approach is hardware-based, selective replication to replicate only critical portions of the application rather than the entire application, thus reducing performance overhead [30]. The application chooses the portions that need to be replicated and the degree of redundancy. It does so using an extension of a technique described in [53] for identifying strategic locations for placement of detectors. Critical variables and, hence, critical code sections that need to be replicated are derived from that analysis. The application is then instrumented with special CHECK instructions, which are an extension to the instruction set architecture (ISA), to invoke reconfiguration of the underlying hardware and provide the specified level of replication to the critical code sections.

Another advantage of selectively replicating an application is the reduction in detection of processor-level errors that do not affect the final outcome of the application (i.e. benign errors). Fault-injection-based experiments by Wang et al. [62] and Saggese et al. [63] showed that 80–85% of errors did not manifest as errors in the application outcome. Full replication at the hardware level aims to detect all errors in the processor, even those that are benign. That leads to false alarms, which are considered undesirable from a safety perspective. Selective replication, on the other hand, aims to detect only the errors that result in application failure.

One must address the following two questions to provide selective replication:

1) Which sections of the code need to be replicated?
2) How can we modify the fetch, renaming, and commit mechanism to handle a specified level of redundancy for portions of the code?

Processor-level replication was implemented earlier [61, 64]. However, it is a nontrivial task to extend it to support selective replication of portions of the application, as doing so requires a reconfiguration of the fetch, rename, and commit mechanisms in the processor. In addition, to let the application select the portions to replicate, the hardware needs to expose an API that can be used to trigger the reconfiguration of the replication mechanism. We detail the mechanism of selective replication in a superscalar processor and present a possible implementation. The results show that selective replication detects about 87% of the instruction errors and 97% of the data errors detected by full duplication. Further, it incurs only 59% of the performance overhead of full duplication. Moreover, the detection of errors benign to the application outcome is reduced by only about 18% compared to full duplication.

### 6.5.1 Application Analysis

In this section, we show how the properties of an application are leveraged by selective replication in order to identify what to replicate in the application. The analysis consists of three main steps, which are carried out at compile time prior to deployment of the application. The first two steps are carried out by an offline analysis based on the DDG of the application, which represents the dependencies among instructions in a real execution of the application. The third step is carried out using an enhancement made to the compiler, using the information obtained from the first two steps. The three steps are explained in more detail as follows.

1) ***Identification of critical variables.*** In [53], the authors show that it is feasible to identify critical variables in an application, which, when in error, are highly likely to cause application/system failures (crashes and fail-silent violations). Selective replication leverages the results of [53] to replicate only those portions of the application that compute the critical variables. To identify the critical variables, one can use an approach similar to the one described in [53]. The criticality of variables to error-free execution of a program has been evaluated using metrics like lifetime and fanout. An analysis presented in [53] demonstrated that ideal detectors placed at locations with high fanout give higher coverage, where an *ideal* detector is one that can detect any data error that propagates to the location at which it is placed. That analysis was done on the program's DDG. For multiple inputs, faults were injected into the program variables that were being evaluated for criticality (with high fanout, lifetime, and so forth). For each input, the effect of each fault was traced, using the DDG for that input, to locations of the program where the program might crash. If the error led the program to a potential crash location, a detector at the critical point was said to have detected an impending program crash.

*Observation:* if the computations of the critical variables are replicated, it will substantially enhance application dependability and, at the same time, incur only a small performance penalty compared to that of full replication.

2) **Extraction of the critical code sections.** Any part of the application that affects the value of a critical variable is a critical code section (consisting of critical instructions). A critical code section includes:

- Instructions that define critical variables.
- Instructions that produce a result that is subsequently consumed by critical instructions (i.e. a backward program slice of a critical instruction [65]).

A reverse depth-first search algorithm on the DDG can be used for automated identification/extraction of instructions that directly or indirectly affect the values of critical variables. The algorithm extracts the backward slice of the instruction that defines a critical variable [65]. Backward slicing using static analysis techniques is known to be imprecise [49]. If the DDG is used, the precision of backward slicing can be improved [66]. That is important from the point of view of selective replication, as imprecise slicing algorithms can increase the number of instructions that need to be replicated.

3) **Insertion of CHECK instructions.** The compiler places a special CHECK instruction before and after each duplicated instruction to notify the hardware of the change in the level of replication. Note that the critical instructions can also be consecutive to each other. In such a case, for each block of contiguous critical instructions, one CHECK instruction is placed before and one is placed after the block of instructions to notify the replication module that it is entering into and exiting from replication mode. That reduces the overhead of switching between replication modes as well as the number of CHECK instructions inserted.

### 6.5.2 Overview of Selective Replication

This section describes the selective replication technique in detail. Instructions are fetched as in a normal pipeline. The dispatch mechanism, which allocates reorder buffer (ROB) entries to the currently fetched instructions, broadly operates in two modes: the *unreplicated* mode and the *replicated* mode. In the unreplicated mode, a single copy of each instruction is dispatched, renamed, and allocated to the ROB. In the replicated mode, $r$ copies of each instruction are dispatched, where $r$ is the degree of replication. If any instruction, $i$, in the replicated code consumes a value produced by a preceding unreplicated instruction, $j$, then all copies of $i$ receive their input from $j$. If a replicated instruction $i_1$ is dependent on another replicated instruction $i_2$, then the copy of $i_1$ in every replica is dependent on the copy of $i_2$ in the same replica. The register operands of the instructions are renamed accordingly.

After instruction execution is complete, the result is stored in the ROB itself. When an instruction at the head of the ROB is ready to commit, all copies of the instruction are checked to see if they are ready to commit. If all copies are ready to commit, then their results (stored in their corresponding ROB entries) are compared. If all of them match, the instruction is committed. If there is even a single mismatch, an appropriate recovery action is taken, such as retrying of the instruction execution.

### 6.5.3 Mechanism of Replication

In this section, we describe the implementation of selective replication in a superscalar out-of-order processor. Implementation of selective replication in a superscalar processor involves modifying the instruction fetch and dispatch, register renaming, and commit mechanisms of the processor.

The block diagram in Figure 6.27 shows a processor pipeline (top) with the modifications required for selective replication (bottom).

Before we describe the mechanism of execution in the replicated mode, it will be helpful to describe some key hardware data structures that are used in the execution.

The register alias table (RAT) is used in dynamic scheduling in the rename state of the pipeline. It contains as many entries as the number of architectural registers. The $i$th entry in the RAT contains information on the source of the most recent value of register $i$. If the most recent instruction-producing register $i$ has been committed to the architectural state, the $i$th entry in the RAT contains a special sentinel value indicating that the value of a register is ready and available in the architectural register file. If the most recent instruction-producing register $i$ is still executing and is in the ROB, the entry in the RAT contains the index of the ROB entry that contains the instruction. Thus, the RAT holds information on the RAW (read-after-write) dependencies among instructions.

The load/store queue (LSQ) contains entries for all the memory access instructions (loads and stores) that are currently in flight. The LSQ can be used to optimize loads by forwarding the data from the immediately preceding store, if both

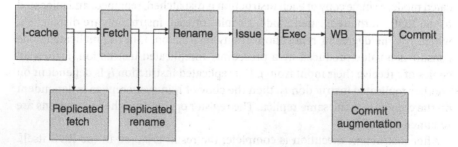

**Figure 6.27** Modifications to pipeline for selective replication. *Source:* Nakka et al. [30]. © IEEE.

generate the same effective address and are writing the same number of bytes. The replicated fetch mechanism shown in Figure 6.27 provides multiple copies of a fetched instruction to the dispatcher.

*Replicated Rename.* The mechanism for renaming multiple copies of an instruction, based on the replica index, is shown in Figure 6.28. If a replicated instruction $d$ reads from register $x$, the RAT entry for $x$ is looked up. If the value of $x$ is available in the architectural register file, then all copies of $d$ get the value for a source operand from the architectural register file. Otherwise, the value of $x$ is the result of an in-flight instruction, $p$, that is written to the ROB entry $k$. If $p$ is an unreplicated instruction (as indicated by the REPL bit in entry $k$), for all replicas $d_1, d_2, \ldots, d_r$, the source operand register is renamed to read from entry $k$. If $p$ is a replicated instruction, the register operand $x$ of $d_i$ is renamed to read the output from instruction $p_i$, where $i = 1, 2, 3, \ldots, r$.

*Instructions Issued to Functional Units.* With the above renaming mechanism, the issue of instructions to functional units can be done without any modification to the already existing scheduling mechanism.

*Execution and Storing of the Result.* The instructions in the unreplicated mode are always executed in a normal out-of-order fashion. The instructions in the replicated mode also execute in an out-of-order fashion. Although that complicates the mechanism for detecting the completion of all copies of the instruction, it

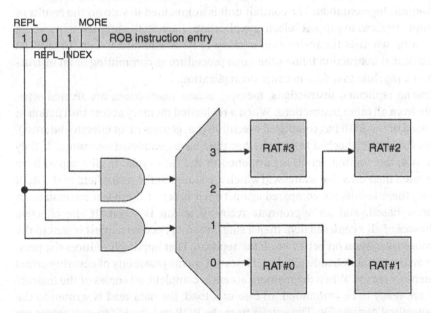

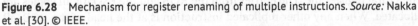

**Figure 6.28** Mechanism for register renaming of multiple instructions. *Source:* Nakka et al. [30]. © IEEE.

provides the benefits of superscalar out-of-order execution by exploiting the instruction-level parallelism and increasing the utilization of the multiple functional units available for instruction execution.

The ROB need not be empty before it switches from the unreplicated mode to the replicated mode because the information in the RAT is maintained across the two modes. In other words, if one of the replicated instructions reads from a register that was produced by the previous unreplicated instruction (which was not committed and still holds an entry in the ROB), then all copies of the replicated instruction read from the result of the same unreplicated instruction. For dependencies among instructions within the replica, a replicated instruction that is dependent on another replicated instruction gets its input from the producing instruction in the same replica.

For switching from the replicated mode to the unreplicated mode, however, the constraint is that the ROB must be empty before the switch is maintained. The reason is that an unreplicated instruction $i$ that is dependent on an instruction $j$ in the preceding replicated code is effectively dependent on all the copies of $j$. Before $i$ is issued, all copies of $j$ must have completed execution, and their results must have been matched so that results can be forwarded to instruction $i$.

After an instruction has completed execution in the functional unit, the result is stored in the ROB entry corresponding to that instruction. For memory access instructions, the result of the address generation is stored in the ROB entry.

*Commit Augmentation.* The commit unit is augmented to vote on the results of multiple replicas to support selective replication. Each ROB entry contains a field indicating whether the instruction is ready to be committed. Committing of an unreplicated instruction follows the same procedure as committing of an instruction in a pipeline that does not support replication.

Among replicated instructions, memory access instructions are treated separately from all other instructions. When a replicated memory access instruction at the head of the ROB has completed execution (i.e. generated an effective address), all its copies are checked to see whether they have completed execution. If they have not, the commit action is postponed to the next cycle. If all $r$ copies have generated their effective addresses (which are stored in the result field of the ROB entry), these results are compared against each other. If there is a mismatch, an error is raised, and an appropriate recovery action is taken. If the effective addresses of all $r$ copies match, then a single memory access request is sent to the memory subsystem on behalf of all the replicas. That approach reduces the pressure on the memory bandwidth but misses out on the possibility of covering errors in memory access. When the memory access is complete, all copies of the instruction are ready to be committed. In case of a load, the data read is written to the architectural register file. The entries from the ROB and the LSQ for all copies are deallocated. When any other replicated instruction is at the head of the ROB, all its copies are checked to see whether they are ready to be committed. If all $r$ copies are ready to be committed, the result fields in their ROB entries are compared to verify the computation. If all $r$ fields match, the instruction is committed, and the result is committed to the architectural register file.

## 6.6 Runtime Checking for Residual Software Bugs

The sooner errors are detected in the cycle of software development and deployment, the better. However, inadequate information can cause some errors to escape detection by compile-time techniques. Runtime checks can be used to detect some of those escaped errors. Examples of errors that can be detected at runtime include invalid pointer accesses, array bound violations, invalid control-flow accesses, use of uninitialized variables, and dynamic race conditions. Runtime checking, however, incurs a high cost by increasing the execution time of the application. The high cost limits the use of runtime checks to the program development phase, when most of the program errors are being detected and corrected.

Runtime checking could result in a performance overhead of up to 1000% for a program [67]. Such delays are unacceptable to most users. Notably, after deployment of a well-tested program in the field, most runs have no errors, so programs are assumed to be correct once the testing phase in their development is over and the runtime checks have been disabled. However, an error in a heavily used program could be catastrophic if it causes the program to crash, or, worse, if the program does not crash but continues to execute and generates an incorrect result. Program crash errors that happen in the field may not be easy to reproduce in the development lab. In addition, debugging of long-running programs can be prohibitively time consuming. According to a study by Miller et al. [68], it is not very rare to have undiscovered errors in heavily used programs. As computers are being more widely used in security-critical applications in commerce, transportation, communication, and government, there is a stronger case for enabling runtime checks in programs. That introduces the challenge of needing to reduce the overheads either by making the checks more efficient or by selectively targeting a specific class of errors. We consider two such error classes in the next section.

### 6.6.1 Race Condition Checking in Multithreaded Programs

Multithreading is a programming technique that has commonly been used in many important real-world applications, such as web servers. Because of the complex interactions of threads, an error in implementing the synchronization between the threads can lead to a timing-sensitive error that is activated only in a specific state of the threads and not in the rest of the system. Such errors are very expensive, as they are difficult to reproduce and hence to analyze and fix. In fact, in most well-tested programs, the bugs that remain are usually the difficult-to-track timing errors [28]. A *data race* is a situation in which the value of a shared location depends on the timing or sequence of events that access and modify the location. Since programs are expected to be deterministic, such data races need to be eliminated. Doing so requires explicit enforcement of the ordering of events that can access or modify the shared data, e.g. through the use of locks for synchronization.

In a lock-based program, all the interactions of threads through shared memory need to be synchronized to avoid a data race. A *locking discipline* is a policy that enforces the ordering of the events that try to modify and access a shared location, thus ensuring the absence of data races.

*Eraser* [20] dynamically detects data races in multithreaded programs that use lock-based synchronization. Eraser detects data races by checking whether all accesses to shared memory follow a consistent locking discipline. All threads that need to access a shared memory location must acquire a mutual exclusion lock for that location. Only a thread that has the lock associated with a memory location can access that memory location. After the thread has completed its operations on the data, it must release the lock so that other threads can access the data. Eraser ensures that each access to the shared data is preceded by an attempt to acquire a mutual exclusion lock for the data. However, the determination of which locks protect which data is made based on dynamic analysis, which may result in false positives.

## 6.6.2 Array Bounds Checking

Languages such as C/C++ are not memory-safe, in the sense that it is possible for a pointer to write anywhere in memory. (Java, on the other hand, is memory-safe.) In C/C++ programs, it is therefore necessary to carry the bounds information of a pointer with it to check the bounds of an access by using that pointer. One way to do so is to enhance the representation of the pointer to include its storage region's base address and limit, which are used to check whether the particular index is legal. Since the representation of the pointer has changed, changes at the C compiler are required. (For C++, one can make such changes through use of a separate class and operator overloading [69].) This simple approach, however, has the drawback that the modified pointer representation is not compatible with code that has not been compiled with bounds checking enabled.

The authors of [17] avoid the compatibility problem by representing pointers as simple addresses, as in C programs. A table containing all known storage objects is maintained, and the entry for an object contains the base, extent, and any additional information for error reporting. A pointer is mapped to the entry of an object into which it points. When the program performs any pointer arithmetic, the result is checked to see whether the pointer still points to the object to which it initially referred. During program execution, the creation and deletion of objects are tracked, and an ordered list of objects is maintained. Unfortunately, the conversion of pointers to arithmetic is frequent and time consuming and hence introduces high-performance overhead.

The overhead of checking the pointers can be reduced through use of appropriate structures like splay trees, tries, and skip lists. However, even if a specialized structure is used as a splay tree, overheads are about 400–500%. Those high overheads can be attributed to the size of a single monolithic splay tree. If the global splay tree is partitioned into many small trees in a way that ensures that the tree to search is known at compile time, the overhead can be reduced. That can be done using a compile-time transformation called *Automatic Pool Allocation* [70]. Other optimizations to reduce the overhead include (i) omitting single-element arrays from the splay tree, (ii) exploiting temporal locality of accesses by using small lookup caches, and (iii) using loop-invariant code motion, among others [71].

### 6.6.3 Runtime Verification

Despite tremendous growth in computing facilities, complete verification of real-life systems remains a computationally intractable problem. The main reason is the ever-growing size and complexity of software, which have far outpaced the improvements in verification techniques or computational power. Another reason is that verification is performed on a "suitable" abstraction of a system and not on the system itself. However, the final implementation of the system contains many more elements (such as the runtime execution libraries) than the abstraction that has been verified, and errors can occur in this additional portion of the application. As a result, during system operation, it is hard to guarantee that the current execution of the system is correct.

One approach to bridging the gap between the implementation and the design is to continuously verify an operational system with respect to a formal requirement specification. At first glance, that approach might not seem very beneficial because the user may not be very interested in just detecting errors. For example, if the detection mechanism simply reports that the system has crashed, that is not very useful. However, runtime monitoring can help users not only detect errors but also correct them. First, without comprehensive runtime monitoring and checking, it is very hard to detect subtle errors. Second, errors may not cause an immediately observable consequence such as a program crash or hang, but could be latent and surface later in the program execution as incorrect results. Those results can sometimes be catastrophic, as they appear valid but can result in drastically different outcomes. For example, an aircraft collision avoidance system that incorrectly directs an aircraft to "go up" instead of "go down" could cause a crash. It should be noted that the result to "go up" is also one of the valid outputs of the system, yet catastrophically incorrect in this case. Runtime monitoring and checking can find such errors quickly and help users take recovery actions before critical failures happen.

An example runtime verification system is Java PathExplorer [72], which monitors Java programs by analyzing particular execution traces. The general idea is that state events are extracted from an executing program via appropriate instrumentation into the target program and then analyzed via a remote observer process. The observer performs two kinds of verification, namely logic-based monitoring and error-pattern analysis. Logic-based monitoring checks formal requirement specifications against the executing program. Error-pattern analysis takes an execution trace of the program for a specific input and extracts relevant events from the trace. Various error-detection algorithms are applied to the event trace to identify errors, such as unhealthy locking disciplines, that may lead to data races and/or deadlocks. However, since the analysis is dependent on the specific input used, it suffers from false positives and offers relatively low coverage in detecting errors in the program.

## 6.7 Data Audit

In the telecommunications industry, the term *data audit* typically refers to a broad range of custom and ad hoc application-level techniques for detecting and recovering from errors in a switching environment. Data-specific techniques deeply embedded in the application are generally believed to provide significant improvement in availability, although few or no actual assessments of these techniques are available.

Application-layer, self-checking maintenance software has been successfully deployed to achieve high availability in systems such as the AT&T 5ESS® switch [73]. The techniques employed include in-line defensive checks, data audits, process activity and resource checks, and modular, hierarchical error recovery.

A related approach to data audit is the use of *robust data structures* to detect and correct errors in stored data structures that contain carefully deployed redundancy. Taylor, Black, and Morgan [74–77] present examples of robust storage structures and their practical implementation.

Commercial off-the-shelf database systems (e.g. Oracle [78]) include utilities for performing consistency checks of database integrity. For example, in relational databases, the core database engine supports a set of rules for identifying relations/dependencies between tables or records in the database. The rules can be used to detect structural and semantic errors in the database by performing referential integrity checking or structural checking. However, the lack of a fault-tolerant infrastructure that ties the database error detection and recovery elements together is a major limitation in the existing systems, especially when continuous availability and integrity of the database are required.

The below discussion provides examples of actual data audit techniques applied in a database used to support a call-processing application. In addition to error detection techniques, the description outlines possible means for error recovery.

### 6.7.1 Static and Dynamic Data Check

*Detection and Recovery.* The audit function detects corruption in static data by computing a golden (reference) checksum of all static data at startup and comparing it to a periodically computed checksum (e.g. 32-bit cyclic redundancy code). The standard recovery technique used for static data corruption is to reload the affected portion from permanent storage.

To make an audit of dynamic data possible in the target database, the range of allowable values for database fields is stored in the database system catalog. That information allows the audit program to do a range check on the dynamic fields in the database. If the audit detects an error, the field is reset to its default value, which is also specified in the system catalog. In addition, if the table where the error occurred is dynamic, the record is freed as a preemptive measure to stop error propagation.

### 6.7.2 Structural Check

The structure of the database in the controller system is established by header fields that precede the data portion of every record of each table. The header fields contain record identifiers and indexes of logically adjacent records.

*Detection.* The structural audit element calculates the offset of each record header from the beginning of the database based on record sizes stored in system tables. (All record sizes are fixed and known.) The database structure (in particular, the alignment of each record and table within the database) is checked by comparing all header fields at computed offsets with expected values.

*Recovery.* A single error in a record identifier is correctable because the correct record ID can be inferred from the offset within the database. However, multiple consecutive corruptions in header fields are considered a strong indication that tables or records within the database may be misaligned, and the entire database is then reloaded from the disk to recover from the structural damage.

### 6.7.3 Semantic Referential Integrity Check

*Detection.* Referential integrity checking traces logical relationships among records in different tables to verify the consistency of the logical loops formed by the record. That allows us to detect invalid data that are impossible to find when records are examined independently of each other. Corruption of key attributes in a database leads to lost records, e.g. records that participate in semantic relationships disappear without being properly updated. We refer to that phenomenon as *resource leak*. Commercial databases provide some support for referential integrity checking. However, since no timestamps or process IDs for the last access of a record are maintained, automatic recovery actions cannot be taken. Also, recovery actions require specific knowledge of the application, and such support is not offered in generic database packages.

As an example, consider the data structure established when a voice connection is serviced. A thread must be spawned to manage the connection; the process needs to allocate hardware resources and record information related to the call (e.g. the IDs of the parties involved) in the connection table. Thus, a new record needs to be written into each of the following three tables:

- *Process Table (Process ID, Name, Connection ID, Status, . . .),*
- *Connection Table (Connection ID, Channel ID, Caller ID, . . .),*
- *Resource Table (Channel ID, Process ID, Status . . .)*

The three new records form a semantic loop: the process record refers to the connection record via the Connection ID attribute, the connection record refers to the resource record via the Channel ID field, and the resource table closes the loop by pointing back to the process record via the Process ID. Thus, the audit program can follow these dependency loops for each active record in each of the three tables to detect violations of semantic constraints.

*Recovery.* The recovery actions include freeing of "zombie" records and preemptive termination of the clients that use these records. Preemptive process termination is desirable because it keeps system resources available even though an active connection may be dropped. The termination is made possible through modification of the database API to maintain, along with each database record, the ID of the client process that last accessed the record. The redundant data structure (added without modifying the original database) also includes the time of last access and counters that maintain database access frequencies.

### 6.7.4 Optimization Using Runtime Statistics

The audit techniques presented in the previous section use rules determined offline to perform data checks. While those static rules allow the audit process to detect many errors, they do not take actual runtime system behavior into account and therefore are not adaptive. Below, we present two audit optimization strategies that use statistics collected during system operation: (i) *prioritized audit triggering* and (ii) *selective monitoring of attributes*. A detailed assessment of these audit strategies can be found in [12].

*Prioritized Audit Triggering.* A prioritized audit is based on the assumption that database objects have different levels of importance and that their levels of importance vary during system operation. We use the following criteria to determine the importance of database objects:

1) *The access frequency of database tables.* The tables containing data that are more frequently updated are more liable to be corrupted by software misbehavior and are more likely to cause error propagation to processes that use the data. Hence, the tables with higher access frequencies are checked more often.
2) *The nature of the database object.* This criterion takes into account the criticality of database objects. For example, the database system catalog is a crucial component because it is referenced on every database access and consequently should be checked more often.
3) *The number of errors detected in each table.* This criterion is based on the assumption of temporal locality of data errors, i.e. an area where more errors occurred in the recent past is likely to contain more errors in the near future. The audit process can make better use of system resources by focusing on the trouble spots and thereby achieve higher error-detection coverage and lower detection latency.

To support prioritized audits, information on access frequency and error history is collected at runtime by the modified database read/write API. In addition, the audit process maintains an error log that contains the number of errors detected in the last audit cycle for each table. Those pieces of information are combined to derive a weighted measure of importance that is used to rank the database tables and to direct the audit to critical sections of the database.

*Selective Monitoring of Attributes.* The selective monitoring of certain table attributes (fields) is motivated by the lack of good static audit rules in some cases. For example, although the database catalog provides the facility to record the lower and upper bounds of each table attribute, not all ranges are specified, because of the difficulty of characterizing certain attributes whose values cannot be predicted with relative certainty. If the values of such attributes are monitored at runtime, adaptive rules can be generated for use by the audit process to detect data errors. To derive the set of correct values of an attribute in the database, the audit program periodically examines the values of that attribute in all active records of the relevant table. An average number of occurrences is computed across all attribute values. A threshold value for the number of occurrences is then calculated using a certain fraction of the average. Any value that has appeared less frequently than the threshold is marked as suspect, and further actions, such as semantic audit, are triggered to make a final decision.

## 6.8 Application of Data Audit Techniques

This section discusses data audit techniques and exemplifies their use. The example use is in protecting the structure and semantics of the database employed by the call-processing environment in a digital mobile telephone network controller [79].

### 6.8.1 Target System Software and Database Architecture

The target system is a small-scale digital wireless telephone network controller that integrates many functions (including call switching, packet routing, and mobility management) in standard wireless telephone network components. The three key components of the application software running on the controller are the *call processor* (which sets and terminates clients' calls), the *database* (which supports information about system resources), and the *support environment*.

Call processing is the key component that provides customer-visible functionality. This process dynamically creates a call-processing thread to handle activities associated with a voice/data connection. Specifically, the thread is responsible for subscriber authentication, hardware resource allocation/deallocation, mobility management, and support of basic and supplementary telephony features. The failure of call processing alone could render the entire system unavailable from a user's point of view. Since call processing requires database access, we refer to the call processing component as a database or call-processing *client*. The database subsystem contains data (including static system configuration data and runtime data that indicate resource usage and process activities) necessary to support the call-processing client.

To satisfy the real-time constraints, the entire database is loaded from disk into memory at startup time and resides completely in memory during system operation. The memory region that contains the database is contiguous and is shared among all processes that require database access. To remove the possibility of a memory leak and to ensure continuous system operation, the space for all tables in the database is preallocated, and no dynamic memory allocation is used in the database.

Although the entire space is statically allocated, some tables are dynamic in nature, while others are static. *Static data* in tables usually refers to the system configuration (e.g. the number of CPUs in the system), which stays constant during operation. In contrast, *dynamic data* are often updated, e.g. on every incoming

**Table 6.10** Examples of database API functions.

| | |
|---|---|
| DBinit | Initialize client connection to the database |
| DBclose | Close client connection to the database |
| DBread_rec | Read a record (row) in a table |
| DBread_fld | Read a field in a table record |
| DBwrite_rec | Write a record (row) in a table |
| DBwrite_fld | Write a field in a table record |
| DBmove | Move a record to another logical group |

call. Note that each table usually contains a mixture of static and dynamic data. The database subsystem exports an API that is used by other processes to access the database. Some API functions, along with brief explanations, are shown in Table 6.10.

*Errors in the Database.* The database is subject to corruption from a number of sources: human operator error, software bugs or faults, and hardware faults. The effects of these errors appear in several ways. The most serious consequence occurs if errors are introduced in the system catalog (i.e. metadata), which contains information used by the database API to access records and consists of several database tables that are referenced on each database operation. Errors in the system catalog can cause all database operations to fail, thus bringing down the whole controller.

Resource leakage is another possible effect of a data error. If any data indicating resource status are corrupted, the particular resource in question could falsely appear to the rest of the controller to be busy, leading to a reduction in system capacity. If such errors are allowed to accumulate, system availability is reduced. Other errors may have a local effect only. For example, a damaged call record related to a particular connection will likely bring down that connection prematurely but not affect other active connections.

### 6.8.2 Audit Subsystem Architecture

The overall design of the database audit process and its interaction with other system components is shown in Figure 6.29. The right half of the figure shows the database, a client process, and the database API (*DB API*) that is used by client processes to access the database. An interprocess communication channel (the *IPC message queue*) is added between the database API and the audit process to transmit events from client activities. The audit process consists of a dedicated thread (the *main thread*), which acts as the interface to other components. The function of the main thread is to translate information from external entities

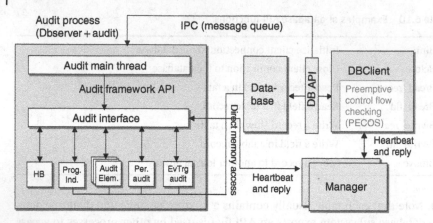

**Figure 6.29** Target system with embedded audit and control flow checking. *Source:* Bagchi et al. [79]. © IEEE.

(e.g. the database client) into audit messages via the *audit framework API*. Such an audit framework provides audit functionality and consists of a top-layer shell (the *audit interface*) and the individual elements that implement specific audit-triggering, error-detection, and recovery techniques.

To reduce contention with database clients, the audit elements access the database directly instead of through the database API. Bypassing of the locking and access-control mechanisms managed by the API reduces performance penalty, but it means that the audit process must detect database access conflicts between clients and ensure the validity of audit results.

The manager performs administrative tasks such as starting, stopping, monitoring, and recovering the audit process; it is also responsible for overseeing the overall state of the environment. The manager starts the audit process and monitors it by means of heartbeats, as shown in Figure 6.29. If the audit process fails, the manager restarts it on the same or another node.

The audit framework provides high modularity and transparency, allowing for easy extensibility of the audit subsystem. New error detection and recovery techniques can be implemented, encapsulated in new elements, and added to the system. A new element to be incorporated into the system must define and communicate to the audit main thread the set of messages that the element is capable of processing. Different audit elements can be quite independent of each other, allowing for easy customization of the audit subsystem.

Other elements include the heartbeat (*HB*), the progress indicator (*Prog. Ind.*), and the audit element (*Audit Elem.*), which encapsulates a set of error detection and recovery techniques. In addition, the periodic audit (*Per. audit*) and the event-triggered audit (*EvTrig audit*) support, respectively, periodic and event-triggered invocations of different audit techniques provided by the audit element.

### 6.8.2.1 The Heartbeat Element

Periodically, the manager process sends a heartbeat message to the heartbeat element in the audit process, and the database client waits for a reply. If the entire audit process has crashed or hung, or if there is a scheduling anomaly on the controller system that prevents the audit process from running, the manager times out and restarts the audit process.

### 6.8.2.2 The Progress Indicator Element

The progress indicator element is used to detect deadlock in the controller database and thus ensure uninterrupted system operation. If a client process terminates prematurely without fully committing its transaction, the locks left behind by this process would prevent other client processes from accessing the database or portions of it.

*Detection.* A standard POSIX IPC message queue is added between the database API and the audit process. The database API is modified to send a message to the audit process whenever any API function is called. The message contains the client process ID information and the database location being accessed. If the audit process receives no message for an extended period of time, the progress indicator element will time out and trigger recovery.

*Recovery.* The progress indicator element, via the manager, can terminate a client process that has been holding a lock for longer than a predetermined threshold duration; this termination releases the lock. While the threshold for a client to hold a lock is typically small (e.g. 100 milliseconds), the progress indicator timeout value is much larger (e.g. 100 seconds) in order to reduce runtime overhead.

### 6.8.2.3 Audit Elements

Specific audit techniques are implemented as separate audit elements in the audit process. The invocation of the audit elements can be done either by a *periodic trigger* or by an *event trigger*. The periodic trigger is based on a fixed time period. The event trigger is provided by some specific database operations, e.g. a database write operation. The periodic audit element uses as its basis the periodic heartbeat query discussed earlier as the trigger to perform the following audits: static data integrity check, dynamic data range check, structural audit, and referential integrity audit. The auditing has fine enough granularity that if an intervening update happens after an audit process has read a record, the results are not invalidated. However, in a referential audit, if there is an intervening update to a record being accessed by the audit element while the audit is in progress, the result of the audit run will be invalidated. Note also that the active audit thread shares processor time with the client accessing the database. That introduces a small overhead in the processing of the client request.

### 6.8.3 Evaluating the Audit Subsystem

To assess the performance overhead and effectiveness of different audit techniques, we conducted the following two experiments.

1) *Audit effectiveness with emulated call-processing client.* This experiment used an emulated call-processing client as the workload and measured the effectiveness of the audits in preventing database errors from corrupting the client.
2) *Overhead in database API.* This experiment measured the performance overhead introduced into the database API functions that were modified to communicate with the audit process and to maintain the support data structure.

To demonstrate the usefulness of the audit process in protecting database clients from errors in the database, we used a simple call-processing client. The client provides the basic call-processing service of setting up and tearing down a call without additional features such as call waiting or paging. The program uses multiple threads to handle incoming calls concurrently. The steps followed in each call-processing thread include authentication, resource allocation, and other phases in a typical call setup, as shown in Figure 6.30.

Table 6.11 shows a breakdown of the results of running the call-processing client program with database audit at a fixed error rate of one error every 20 seconds. The error rate used mimics a burst of transient errors affecting the database. The results show that structural audit and static data audit are both very effective in detecting and removing errors and that both achieve 100% coverage. Dynamic data audit, on the other hand, has lower coverage and can detect and remove a total of 79% (45 + 34%) of all errors in dynamic fields through range check and referential integrity check. Fourteen percent of errors escape because the application process uses the erroneous data before the audit can detect them. More frequent invocation of audit is needed to reduce the number of errors that escape because of timing. Four percent of the errors escaped detection because of the lack of enforceable rules in dynamic data audit. Suitable constraints need to be added to the database to improve audit coverage in this category.

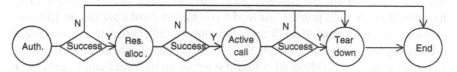

**Figure 6.30** Call-processing phases emulated in the client program. *Source:* Bagchi et al. [79]. © IEEE.

**Table 6.11** Breakdown of inserted and detected errors.

| Error types | Structural | | Static data | | Dynamic data | | | | |
| --- | --- | --- | --- | --- | --- | --- | --- | --- | --- |
| | | | | | Detected | | Escaped | | |
| | Detected | Escaped | Detected | Escaped | By range check | By semantic check | Due to timing | Due to lack of rule | No effect |
| Number of errors | 194 | 0 | 623 | 0 | 975 | 751 | 313 | 89 | 55 |
| Percentage | 100 | 0 | 1000 | 0 | 45 | 34 | 14 | 4 | 3 |

*Source:* Bagchi et al. [79]. IEEE.

## 6.9 Insights

Software-based error detection techniques fall broadly into three categories: (i) static analysis, (ii) dynamic analysis, and (iii) runtime checking. *Static analysis techniques* attempt to verify properties of the program at compile time, before the program is executed. The main problem with them is that of determining feasible paths, i.e. program paths that can be executed. Existing static analysis techniques overapproximate the list of feasible paths, leading to many spurious errors. Techniques such as ESP [2] attempt to reduce the spurious errors by tracking branches that lead to different outcomes for the property studied, but they are not foolproof. Another class of static analysis techniques, such as PR-Miner [4], attempt to find violations of implicit programming rules and flag these violations as errors. While those techniques are useful for finding known kinds of errors, they may not be as effective for unknown kinds of runtime errors.

*Dynamic analysis techniques* attempt to formulate invariants based on program execution traces and use these invariants for error detection. Unlike static analysis techniques, they do not suffer from the feasible paths problem because they are based on the actual runtime information. However, these techniques are limited to inferring invariants on the program paths that are executed, which means that the invariants may not hold on other paths. Such invariants are known as the *false positives*. One can reduce false positives by considering a large number of test cases during the inference process, in the hope that the test cases will cover a large number of paths. Another issue with using the invariants derived by dynamic analysis as error detectors is that the program may crash or suffer an assertion failure even before the error has reached the detector, thus rendering the detector ineffective at detecting the error.

In the case of runtime checking, error checks are executed at runtime, and hence do not suffer from the feasible paths problem found with detectors based on static analysis. Further, the properties to be checked are prespecified, thus avoiding the false-positive problem found with dynamic analysis. Because of its potentially prohibitive overheads, however, runtime checking is often done only for selected properties such as race condition detection or memory corruption errors, for which the property is known a priori. Such approaches employ compile time and runtime optimizations to reduce the overhead of the checking. Alternatively, the property can be specified using formal temporal logic and checked at the relevant code locations. That has the advantage that the programmer can choose what to check at runtime; however, it may incur high performance overheads.

We also looked at how static and dynamic analysis techniques can be used to derive error detectors for runtime checking. The static analysis technique extracts the backward slices of critical variables from the program's source code and converts them into checking expressions, which are used to recompute the value of the critical variable. Any discrepancy between the recomputed value and the original value indicates an error. The dynamic analysis technique observes the program's execution over multiple runs (inputs), and formulates detectors based on the observed values. The detectors are derived from a collection of rule templates, and an algorithm is applied to find the best detector that matches an observed stream of values as tightly as possible. Both the static and dynamic detector derivation approaches yield high fault coverage with low-performance overheads.

Software-based duplication is an alternative to hardware-based duplication, as it allows the programmer to control the granularity and sphere of duplication. Software duplication techniques often incur high overheads due to the redundant instructions inserted, both for the replica and for the comparisons. Between those two sources, the overhead from comparisons is often the dominant one, and hence attempts have been made to reduce it. For example, comparisons are done only after branches and store instructions, to prevent erroneous values from influencing the control flow and from being written to memory.

NVP is a technique in which multiple teams are used to design and implement a software program, given its detailed functional specifications. To prevent common-mode failures, teams are not allowed to communicate with each other. The versions developed by the teams are run in parallel and their results compared for every input; a mismatch indicates an error. The assumption is that the different software versions produced by the teams will fail in different ways for the same input, and hence that errors can be detected. However, studies have shown that that is often not the case, as what is difficult for one programmer is likely to be difficult for another, so that the teams make the same kinds of errors in implementing software versions. Therefore, errors are not masked. That limitation, coupled with the high cost of deploying NVP in practice, has limited its practical adoption.

RBs are an alternative to NVP as an approach for masking both oftware and hardware errors. With RBs (unlike NVP, in which multiple versions are run in parallel), only one version is run, and its output is fed to an AT, which determines whether the output is acceptable. If it is not, the state of the program is rolled back to the beginning, and another version of the program is tried. Again, the assumption is that the AT and the software do not have correlated errors. The AT is thus a crucial element of the RB approach, although it can be challenging to design a robust AT in practice.

## References

1 Bush, W.R., Pincus, J.D., and Sielaff, D.J. (2000). A static analyzer for finding dynamic programming errors. *Software Practice and Experience* 30 (7): 775–802.

2 Das, M., Lerner, S., and Seigle, M. (2002). ESP: path-sensitive program verification in polynomial time. *Proceedings of the ACM SIGPLAN 2002 Conference on Programming Language Design and Implementation*, Berlin, Germany (17–19 June 2002), 57–68. New York, NY, USA: Association for Computing Machinery.

3 Evans, D., Guttag, J., Horning, J. et al. (1994). LCLint: a tool for using specifications to check code. *Proceedings of the 2nd ACM SIGSOFT Symposium on Foundations of Software Engineering*, New Orleans, LA, USA (6–9 December 1994), 87–96. New York, NY, USA: Association for Computing Machinery.

4 Li, Z. and Zhou, Y. (2005). PR-Miner: automatically extracting implicit programming rules and detecting violations in large software code. *Proceedings of the 10th European Software Engineering Conference Held Jointly with the 13th ACM SIGSOFT International Symposium on Foundations of Software Engineering*, Lisbon, Portugal (5–9 September 2005), 306–315. New York, NY, USA: Association for Computing Machinery.

5 Engler, D., Chen, D.Y., Hallem, S. et al. (2001). Bugs as deviant behavior: a general approach to inferring errors in systems code. *Proceedings of the 18th ACM Symposium on Operating Systems Principles*, Banff, Alberta, Canada (21–24 October 2001), 57–72. New York, NY, USA: Association for Computing Machinery.

6 Pattabiraman, K., Kalbarczyk, Z.T., and Iyer, R.K. (2011). Automated derivation of application-aware error detectors using static analysis: the Trusted Illiac approach. *IEEE Transactions on Dependable and Secure Computing* 8 (1): 44–57.

7 Ernst, M.D., Cockrell, J., Griswold, W.G. et al. (2001). Dynamically discovering likely program invariants to support program evolution. *IEEE Transactions on Software Engineering* 27 (2): 1–25.

8 Hangal, S. and Lam, M.S. (2002). Tracking down software bugs using automatic anomaly detection. *Proceedings of the 24th International Conference on Software Engineering*, Orlando, FL, USA (19–25 May 2002), 291–301. New York, NY, USA: Association for Computing Machinery.

9 Hiller, M. (2000). Executable assertions for detecting data errors in embedded control systems. *Proceedings of the International Conference on Dependable Systems and Networks*, New York, NY, USA (25–28 June 2000). IEEE.

10 Pattabiraman, K., Saggese, G.P., Chen, D. et al. (2006). Dynamic derivation of application-specific error detectors and their implementation in hardware. *Proceedings of the 6th European Dependable Computing Conference*, Coimbra, Portugal (18–20 October 2006). IEEE.

11 Pattabiraman, K., Saggese, G.P., Chen, D. et al. (2011). Automated derivation of application-specific error detectors using dynamic analysis. *IEEE Transactions on Dependable and Secure Computing* 8 (5): 640–655.

12 Oh, N., Shirvani, P.P., and McCluskey, E.J. (2002). Error detection by duplicated instructions in super-scalar processors. *IEEE Transactions on Reliability* 51 (1): 63–75.

**13** Benso, A., Chiusano, S., Prinetto, P. et al. (2000). A C/C++ source-to-source compiler for dependable applications. *Proceedings of the International Conference on Dependable Systems and Networks*, New York, NY, USA (25–28 June 2000). IEEE.

**14** Reis, G.A., Chang, J., Vachharajani, N. et al. (2005). SWIFT: software implemented fault tolerance. *Proceedings of the International Symposium on Code Generation and Optimization*, New York, NY, USA (20–23 March 2005). IEEE.

**15** Kim, M., Viswanathan, M., Kannan, S. et al. (2004). Java-MaC: a run-time assurance approach for Java programs. *Formal Methods in System Design* 24 (2): 129–155.

**16** Havelund, K. and Rosu, G. (2004). An overview of the runtime verification tool Java PathExplorer. *Formal Methods in System Design* 24 (2): 189–215.

**17** Jones, R.W.M. and Kelly, P.H.J. (1997). Backwards-compatible bounds checking for arrays and pointers in C programs. *Proceedings of the 3rd International Workshop on Automated Debugging*, Linköping, Sweden (26–27 May 1997), 13–26. Linköping, Sweden: Linköping University.

**18** Dhurjati, D., Kowshik, S., and Adve, V. (2006). SAFECode: enforcing alias analysis for weakly typed languages. *Proceedings of the 27th ACM SIGPLAN Conference on Programming Language Design and Implementation*, Ottawa, Ontario, Canada (10–16 June 2006), 144–157. New York, NY, USA: Association for Computing Machinery.

**19** Ruwase, O. and Lam, M.S. (2004). A practical dynamic buffer overflow detector. *Proceedings of the 11th Annual Network and Distributed System Security Symposium*, San Diego, California, USA (2004), 159–169.

**20** Savage, S., Burrows, M., Nelson, G. et al. (1997). Eraser: a dynamic data race detector for multithreaded programs. *ACM Transactions on Computer Systems* 15 (4): 391–411.

**21** Engler, D. and Ashcraft, K. (2003). RacerX: effective, static detection of race conditions and deadlocks. *ACM SIGOPS Operating Systems Review* 37 (5): 237–252.

**22** Avizienis, A. (1995). Chapter 2 – The methodology of N-version programming. In: *Software Fault Tolerance* (ed. M.R. Lyu), 23–46. Wiley.

**23** Knight, J.C. and Leveson, N.G. (1986). An experimental evaluation of the assumption of independence in multiversion programming. *IEEE Transactions on Software Engineering* 12 (1): 96–109.

**24** Randell, B. and Xu, J. (1995). The evolution of the recovery block concept. In: *Software Fault Tolerance* (ed. M. Lyu), 1–22. Wiley.

**25** Randell, B. (1975). System structure for software fault tolerance. *IEEE Transactions on Software Engineering* SE-1 (2): 220–232.

**26** Horning, J.J., Lauer, H.C., Melliar-Smith, P.M. et al. (1974). A program structure for error detection and recovery. *Proceedings of the International Symposium on*

*Operating Systems*, Rocquencourt, France (23–25 April 1974), 171–187. *Lecture Notes in Computer Science*, vol. 16. Berlin and Heidelberg, Germany: Springer-Verlag.

**27** Avizienis, A., Laprie, J.C., Randell, B. et al. (2004). Basic concepts and taxonomy of dependable and secure computing. *IEEE Transactions on Dependable and Secure Computing* 1 (1): 11–33.

**28** Gray, J. (1986). Why do computers stop and what can be done about it. *Symposium on Reliability in Distributed Software and Database Systems*, Los Angeles, CA, USA (13 January 1986), 3–12.

**29** Sullivan, M. and Chillarege, R. (1991). Software defects and their impact on system availability: a study of field failures in operating systems. *Digest of Papers, the 21st Symposium on Fault-Tolerant Computing*, Montreal, Quebec, Canada (25–27 June 1991), 2–9. IEEE.

**30** Nakka, N., Pattabiraman, K., and Iyer, R. (2007). Processor-level selective replication. *Proceedings of the 37th Annual IEEE/IFIP International Conference on Dependable Systems and Networks*, Edinburgh, Scotland, UK (25–28 June 2007), 544–553. IEEE.

**31** Chen, L. and Avizienis, A. (1995). N-version programming: a fault-tolerance approach to reliability of software operation. *Twenty-Fifth International Symposium on Fault-Tolerant Computing, Highlights from Twenty-Five Years*, Pasadena, California, USA (27–30 June 1995), 113–119. (Reprinted from FTCS-8 1978, pp. 3–9).

**32** Oh, N.S., Mitra, S., and McCluskey, E.J. (2002). ED$^4$I: error detection by diverse data and duplicated instructions. *IEEE Transactions on Computers* 51 (2): 180–199.

**33** Sghairi, M., de Bonneval, A., Crouzet, Y. et al. (2007). Challenges in building fault-tolerant flight control system for a civil aircraft. *IAENG International Journal of Computer Science* 35 (4) http://www.iaeng.org/IJCS/issues_v35/issue_4/IJCS_35_4_07.pdf.

**34** Brière, D. and Traverse, P. (1993). AIRBUS A320/A330/A340 electrical flight controls a family of fault-tolerant systems. *Proceedings of the 23rd International Symposium on Fault-Tolerant Computing*, Toulouse, France (22–24 June 1993), 616–623. IEEE.

**35** Yeh, Y.C. (1996). Triple-triple redundant 777 primary flight computer. *Proceedings of the 1996 IEEE Aerospace Applications Conference*, vol. 1, Aspen, CO, USA (3–9 February 1996), 293–307. IEEE.

**36** Yau, S.S. and Cheung, R.C. (1975). Design of self-checking software. *Proceedings of the International Conference on Reliable Software* (April 1975), 450–455. New York, NY, USA: Association for Computing Machinery.

**37** Vaidya, N.H., Singh, A.D., and Krishna, C.M. (1993). Trade-offs in developing fault tolerant software. *IEEE Computers and Digital Techniques* 140 (6): 320–326.

**38** Leveson, N.G., Cha, S.S., Knight, J.C. et al. (1990). The use of self checks and voting in software error detection: an empirical study. *IEEE Transactions on Software Engineering* 16 (4): 432–443.

**39** Hecht, H. (1976). Fault-tolerant software for real-time applications. *ACM Computing Surveys* 8 (4): 391–407.

**40** Anderson, T. and Kerr, R. (1976). Recovery blocks in action: a system supporting high reliability. *Proceedings of the 2nd International Conference on Software Engineering*, San Francisco, CA, USA (October 1976), 447–457. Washington, DC, USA: IEEE Computer Society Press.

**41** Kim, K.H. and Yang, S.M. (1986). An analysis of the execution overhead inherent in the conversation scheme. *Proceedings of the Symposium on Reliability in Distributed Software and Database Systems*, Los Angeles, CA, USA (13 January 1986) 159–168.

**42** Kim, K.H. and Yang, S.M. (1988). An analysis of the performance impacts of lookahead execution in the conversation scheme. *Proceedings of the 7th Symposium on Reliable Distributed Systems*, Columbus, OH, USA (10–12 October 1988), 71–81. IEEE.

**43** Yang, S.M. and Kim, K.H. (1992). Implementation of the conversation scheme in message-based distributed computer systems. *IEEE Transactions on Parallel and Distributed Systems* 3 (5): 555–572.

**44** Romanovsky, A.B. (1997). Conversational group service. *ACM SIGOPS Operating Systems Review* 31 (1): 54–63.

**45** Kim, K.H. and Welch, H.O. (1989). Distributed execution of recovery blocks: an approach for uniform treatment of hardware and software faults in real-time applications. *IEEE Transactions on Computers* 38 (5): 626–636.

**46** Hecht, M., Agron, J., and Hochhauser, S. (1989). A distributed fault tolerant architecture for nuclear reactor control and safety functions. *Proceedings of the Real-Time Systems Symposium*, Santa Monica, CA, USA (5–7 December 1989), 214–221. IEEE.

**47** Kim, K.H.(K.) and Bacellar, L. (1997). Time-bounded cooperative recovery with the distributed real-time conversation scheme. *Proceedings of the 3rd International Workshop on Object-Oriented Real-Time Dependable Systems*, Newport Beach, CA, USA (5–7 February 1997), 32–39. IEEE.

**48** Demsky, B., Ernst, M.D., Guo, P.J. et al. (2006). Inference and enforcement of data structure consistency specifications. *Proceedings of the 2006 International Symposium on Software Testing and Analysis*, Portland, Maine, USA (17–20 July 2006), 233–244. New York, NY, USA: Association for Computing Machinery.

**49** Tip, F. (1995). A survey of program slicing techniques. *Journal of Programming Languages* 3 (3): 121–189.

**50** Mehdizadeh, N., Shokrolah-Shirazi, M., and Miremadi, S.G. (2008). Analyzing fault effects in the 32-bit OpenRISC 1200 microprocessor. *Proceedings of the 2008*

*3rd International Conference on Availability, Reliability and Security*, Barcelona, Spain (4–7 March 2008), 648–652. IEEE.

**51** Weicker, R.P. (1990). An overview of common benchmarks. *Computer* 23 (12): 65–75.

**52** Carlisle, M.C. and Rogers, A. (1995). Software caching and computation migration in Olden. *Proceedings of the 5th ACM SIGPLAN Symposium on Principles and Practice of Parallel Programming*, Santa Barbara, CA, USA (19–21 July 1995), 29–38. New York, NY, USA: Association for Computing Machinery.

**53** Pattabiraman, K., Kalbarczyk, Z., and Iyer, R.K. (2005). Application-based metrics for strategic placement of detectors. *Proceedings of the 11th Pacific Rim International Symposium on Dependable Computing*, Hunan, China (12–14 December 2005), 95–102. IEEE.

**54** Ohlsson, J., Rimen, M., and Gunneflo, U. (1992). A study of the effects of transient fault injection into a 32-bit RISC with built-in watchdog. *Digest of Papers, the 22nd International Symposium on Fault-Tolerant Computing*, Boston, MA, USA (8–10 July 1992), 316–325. IEEE.

**55** Voas, J. (1997). Software testability measurement for intelligent assertion placement. *Software Quality Control* 6: 327–336.

**56** Hutchins, M., Foster, H., Goradia, T. et al. (1994). Experiments on the effectiveness of dataflow- and control-flow-based test adequacy criteria. *Proceedings of the 16th International Conference on Software Engineering*, Sorrento, Italy (16–21 May 1994), 191–200. IEEE.

**57** Austin, T., Larson, E., and Ernst, D. (2002). SimpleScalar: an infrastructure for computer system modeling. *Computer* 35 (2): 59–67.

**58** Wang, N.J. and Patel, S.J. (2006). ReStore: symptom-based soft error detection in microprocessors. *IEEE Transactions on Dependable and Secure Computing* 3 (3): 188–201.

**59** Iyer, R.K., Nakka, N., Kalbarczyk, Z.T. et al. (2005). Recent advances and new avenues in hardware-level reliability support. *IEEE MICRO* 25 (6): 18–29.

**60** Weaver, C. and Austin, T. (2001). A fault tolerant approach to microprocessor design. *Proceedings of the 2001 International Conference on Dependable Systems and Networks*, Göteborg, Sweden (1–4 July 2001), 411–420. IEEE.

**61** Ray, J., Hoe, J.C., and Falsafi, B. (2001). Dual use of superscalar datapath for transient-fault detection and recovery. *Proceedings of the 34th Annual ACM/IEEE International Symposium on Microarchitecture*, Austin, TX, USA (1–5 December 2001), 214–224. Washington, DC, USA: IEEE Computer Society.

**62** Wang, N.J., Quek, J., Rafacz, T.M. et al. (2004). Characterizing the effects of transient faults on a high-performance processor pipeline. *Proceedings of the International Conference on Dependable Systems and Networks*, Florence, Italy (28 June–1 July 2004), 61–70. IEEE.

**63** Saggese, G.P., Vetteth, A., Kalbarcyzk, Z. et al. (2005). Microprocessor sensitivity to failures: control vs. execution and combinational vs. sequential logic. *Proceedings of the International Conference on Dependable Systems and Networks*, Yokohama, Japan (28 June–1 July 2005), 760–769. IEEE.

**64** Vijaykumar, T.N., Pomeranz, I., and Cheng, K. (2002). Transient-fault recovery using simultaneous multithreading. *Proceedings of the 29th Annual International Symposium on Computer Architecture*, Anchorage, AK, USA (25–29 May 2002), 87–98. IEEE.

**65** Weiser, M. (1981). Program slicing. *Proceedings of the 5th International Conference on Software Engineering*, San Diego, CA, USA (9–12 March 1981), 439–449. IEEE Computer Society.

**66** Agrawal, H. and Horgan, J.R. (1990). Dynamic program slicing. *Proceedings of the ACM SIGPLAN 1990 Conference on Programming Language Design and Implementation*, White Plains, NY, USA (20–22 June 1990), 246–256. New York, NY, USA: Association for Computing Machinery.

**67** Steffen, J.L. (1992). Adding run-time checking to the portable C compiler. *Software – Practice and Experience* 22 (4): 825–834.

**68** Miller, B.P., Lars, F., and So, B. (1990). An empirical study of the reliability of Unix utilities. *Communications of the ACM* 33 (12): 32–44.

**69** Meyers, S. (1996). *More Effective C++: 35 New Ways to Improve Your Programs and Designs*. Boston, MA, USA: Addison-Wesley.

**70** Lattner, C. and Adve, V. (2005). Automatic pool allocation: improving performance by controlling data structure layout in the heap. *Proceedings of the 2005 ACM SIGPLAN Conference on Programming Language Design and Implementation*, Chicago, IL, USA (12–15 June 2005), 129–142. New York, NY, USA: Association for Computing Machinery.

**71** Dhurjati, D. and Adve, V. (2006). Backwards-compatible array bounds checking for C with very low overhead. *Proceedings of the 28th International Conference on Software Engineering*, Shanghai, China (20–28 May 2006), 162–171. New York, NY, USA: Association for Computing Machinery.

**72** Havelund, K. and Roşu, G. (2001). Java PathExplorer: a runtime verification tool. *Proceedings of the 6th International Symposium on Artificial Intelligence, Robotics and Automation in Space*, Montreal, Canada (2001).

**73** Haugk, G., Lax, F.M., Royer, R.D. et al. (1985). The 5ESS switching system: maintenance capabilities. *AT&T Technical Journal* 6 (6): 1385–1416.

**74** Black, J.P., Taylor, D.J., and Morgan, D.E. (1980). An introduction to robust data structures. *Digest of Papers, the 10th International Symposium on Fault-Tolerant Computing*, Kyoto, Japan (1980).

**75** Taylor, D.J., Morgan, D.E., and Black, J.P. (1980). Redundancy in data structures: improving software fault tolerance. *IEEE Transactions on Software Engineering* 6 (6): 585–594.

**76** Taylor, D.J., Morgan, D.E., and Black, J.P. (1980). Redundancy in data structures: some theoretical results. *IEEE Transactions on Software Engineering* 6 (6): 595–602.

**77** Taylor, D.J. and Black, J.P. (1985). Guidelines for storage structure error correction. *Digest of Papers, the 15th Annual International Symposium on Fault-Tolerant Computing*, Ann Arbor, MI, USA (19–21 June 1985).

**78** Oracle (2015). Checking for consistency in data. *Oracle® FLEXCUBE Universal Banking Interest and Charges User Guide*. https://docs.oracle.com/cd/E64763_01/html/Int_Chargs/IC10_Check.htm (accessed June 2020).

**79** Bagchi, S., Liu, Y., Whisnant, K. et al. (2001). A framework for database audit and control flow checking for a wireless telephone network controller. *Proceedings of the 2001 International Conference on Dependable Systems and Networks*, Göteborg, Sweden (1–4 July 2001), 225–234. IEEE.

# 7
# Measurement-based Analysis of System Software: Operating System Failure Behavior

## 7.1  Introduction

The dependability of a computing system, and consequently of the services it provides to the end-user, depends largely on the failure resilience of the underlying operating system. Understanding a system's sensitivity to errors and identifying its error propagation patterns and single points of failure are of primary importance in selecting a computing platform and assessing trade-offs involving cost, reliability, and performance.

The dependability of a system can be experimentally evaluated at different phases of its lifecycle. In the design phase, computer-aided design (CAD) environments are used to evaluate the design via simulation, including simulated fault injection. The feedback from simulation can be instrumental in the cost-effective redesign of the system. Simulation, however, requires accurate input parameters and validation of output results. Although the parameter estimates can be obtained from past measurements, doing so is often complicated by design and technology changes.

In the prototype phase, the system runs under controlled workload conditions. In this stage, controlled physical fault injection is used to evaluate the system behavior under faults, including the detection coverage and the recovery capability of various fault tolerance mechanisms. Fault injection on the real system can provide information about the failure process from fault occurrence to system recovery, including error latency, propagation, detection, and recovery (which may involve reconfiguration). Physical faults can be injected at the hardware level (in which case they would be logic or electrical faults) or at the software level (in which case they would be code or data corruption faults). Heavy-ion radiation techniques can also be used to inject faults and stress a system. A

*Dependable Computing: Design and Assessment*, First Edition. Ravishankar K. Iyer,
Zbigniew T. Kalbarczyk, and Nithin M. Nakka.
© 2024 The IEEE Computer Society. Published 2024 by John Wiley & Sons, Inc.
Companion website: www.wiley.com/go/iyer/dependablecomputing1

detailed treatment of the instrumentation involved in fault injection experiments, using real examples and including several fault injection environments, is given by Pradhan [1].

In the operational phase, a direct measurement-based approach can be used to measure systems in the field under real workloads. The collected data contain a large amount of information about naturally occurring errors/failures. Analysis of the data can provide an understanding of actual error/failure characteristics and insight into analytical models.

All three approaches – simulated fault injection, physical fault injection, and measurement-based analysis – should be considered complementary for accurate dependability analysis.

This section focuses on the operational phase of the system software. It is aimed at determining the major reasons for system software failures and what methods are or can be used to handle errors and prevent error propagation. Examples of actual operational systems are used to illustrate different approaches and to introduce measurement and analysis methods for failure characterization of systems and assessment of error-handling mechanisms. The selected examples range from the highly robust custom designs of the IBM-MVS and Tandem (now HP) GUARDIAN operating systems to COTS operating systems, such as Linux.

The operational phase of mature software is very different from the development phase. In the operational phase, a typical state of affairs involves frequent changes and updates installed either by system managers or vendors. Often, without notification to the installation management, the vendor can install a change (patch) to fix a fault found at some other installation. In a sense, the system being measured represents an aggregate of all such systems being maintained by the vendor. In addition, system software reliability in the operational phase is attributed to workload effects, hardware problems, and environmental factors. Thus, software reliability in the operational phase cannot be characterized by simply applying analytical models proposed for the design or development phase.

In the following sections, we will provide a review of dependability, error detection, and recovery features in commercial systems. We will then review several other previous and contemporary dependability evaluation and protection mechanisms employed in operating systems.

## 7.2  MVS (Multiple Virtual Storage)

Multiple generations of the MVS operating system have provided a robust computing platform for many applications that require high dependability and data integrity. MVS was the most commonly used operating system on System/370 and System/390 IBM mainframe computers. First released in 1974, MVS evolved from MVS/XA (eXtended Architecture) and MVS/ESA (Enterprise Systems Architecture) through OS/390 (where UNIX System Services were added for the first time) to the current generation of z/OS (when 64-bit support was added on the zSeries models). All the generations were fundamentally based on the same operating system, and, by design, programs written for MVS can still run on z/OS without modification. MVS originally supported 24-bit addressing; as the underlying hardware progressed, it came to support 31-bit (XA and ESA) and now (as z/OS) 64-bit addressing.

Based on the same solid foundation, the z/OS continues the tradition of providing a highly robust computing platform and offers uninterruptable operation to applications despite failures due to both permanent and transient errors. Following technological advances in the underlying hardware (e.g. hardware duplication in G5 and G6 microprocessor technology [2, 3]), there has been further enhancement and development of new RAS (reliability, availability, and serviceability) mechanisms and strategies for z/OS. For example, the first failure data capture (FFDC) technique was designed to capture data and identify problems that occur during operation without impacting system availability. While FFDC has been a core component of MVS since 1974, in z/OS, FFDC has been further enhanced to allow a rapid copy of a failed task (including the associated data and system control blocks) to another location in memory, where the task either continues to execute or can be restarted by associated recovery routines. More information on the z/OS architecture can be found in [4].

### 7.2.1 MVS Error Detection and Recovery Processing

Time-stamped, low-level error, and recovery data from MVS, collected during normal operation of a system, formed the basis for developing a model that provides a quantification of the system error characteristics and gives insight into the interactions among the various software error and recovery processes that occur during normal system operation. Before presenting the method for deriving the software reliability model, we introduce the error detection and recovery mechanisms provided in the MVS operating system.

### 7.2.2 MVS Error Detection

Automatic error detection in MVS is achieved through both hardware and software facilities.

- The hardware detects conditions (denoted by HWDSWERR) such as memory violations, program errors (e.g. arithmetic exceptions or invalid operation codes), addressing errors, and password checking on critical system resources.
- The software provides detection of more complex error conditions (denoted by SWDSWERR). The data management and supervisor routines ensure that valid data are processed, and nonconflicting requests are made. Examples are the

incorrect specification of a parameter in a control structure or in a system macro or a supervisor call issued by an unauthorized program. The installation can improve the system error detection capability by means of a software facility called the resource access control facility (RACF). The RACF is used to build detailed "profiles" of system software modules. The profiles are defined in order to inspect the correct usage of system resources.

The user can also employ other software facilities to detect the occurrences of selected events. Appendages are routines that enable the user to get control during different phases of an I/O operation. Serviceability-level indication processing (SLIP) also aids in error detection and diagnosis. The SLIP command gives the user access to traps that cause program interruptions when particular events are intercepted. Further, the user can define his or her own detection mechanisms by means of the set program interruption element (SPIE) macro. It detects programmer-defined exceptions, such as using an incorrect address or attempting to execute privileged instructions.

- The operator may detect some evident error conditions (denoted by OPERDERR) and decide to cancel or restart the job. For example, the operator can detect loop conditions or endless wait states.

### 7.2.3 Recovery Processing

Recovery in MVS is designed as a means by which the system can prevent total loss. Whenever a program is abnormally interrupted because of the detection of an error, the Supervisor gets control. If the problem is such that further processing could degrade the system or destroy data, the Supervisor gives control to the *Recovery Termination Manager (RTM)*. If a recovery routine is available for the problem program, the RTM gives control to it before deciding to terminate the program.

The purpose of a recovery routine is to free the resources kept by the failing program (if any), to locate the error, and to request either a continuation of the termination process or a retry. Recovery routines are generally provided to cover critical MVS functions.

More than one recovery routine can be specified for the same program; if the latest recovery routine asks for termination of the program, the RTM can give control to another recovery routine (if another has been provided). That process is called *percolation*. The percolation process ends if either routine issues a valid retry request or no more routines are available. In the latter case, the program and its related subtasks are terminated. The termination of a program might imply the termination of the job step. If a valid retry is requested, a retry routine restores a valid status by using the information supplied by the recovery routine(s) and gives control to the program. For a retry to be valid, the system should verify that there is no risk of error recurrence and that the retry address is properly specified.

An error may have four possible effects: (i) RETRY: The system successfully recovers and returns control to the problem program, (ii) TASK TERMINATION: The program and its related subtasks are terminated, but the system is not affected, (iii) JOB TERMINATION: The job in control at the time of the error is aborted, and (iv) SYSTEM DAMAGE: The job or task in control at the time of the error was critical for system continuation. Thus, a job/task termination results in system failure.

Figure 7.1 illustrates the steps in the recovery process.

A variety of system recovery procedures are included in MVS to support attempts to recover from different classes of hardware errors. For I/O, CPU, and main storage errors, *instruction retry* is used. If instruction retry is not possible, the main storage is refreshed via loading a new copy of the affected module into the main storage. It may be possible to identify the specific program creating a problem and terminate it using the *selective termination* routine. I/O recovery is achieved via I/O retry or by choosing another channel path or control unit. MVS has a hierarchy of error recovery procedures, ranging from functional recovery that retries the interrupted operation and system recovery that terminates the affected task, to system-supported restart and system repair.

### 7.2.3.1 Hardware Error Recovery

Hardware recovery is done for the processor via the Machine Check Handler (MCH) and Alternate CPU Recovery (ACR), and for the I/O device via the Missing Interrupt Handler (MIH), the Dynamic Device Reconfiguration (DDR), and Hot I/O recovery (HIR). The Channel Subsystem is repaired using Alternate Path Recovery and the Subchannel Logout Handler.

Machine checks originate in the processor, I/O subsystem, or storage. Depending on the source and the severity of the machine check, the MCH transfers control to the RTM, the I/O Supervisor (IOS), or the Real Storage Manager (RSM). Machine

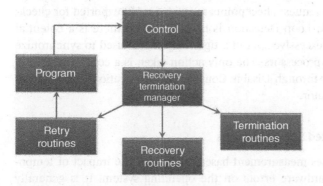

**Figure 7.1** Software handling of software errors on MVS (adapted from [5]).

checks are classified into three types. (i) *Soft* machine checks can be corrected by hardware, but they degrade performance. (ii) With *hard* machine checks, the RTM takes control and invokes the appropriate recovery routine, and the job is retried or terminated. (iii) A *terminating* machine check is an unrecoverable failure. On a uniprocessor, the system is placed in a disabled wait state, and it waits for the re-initial program load (IPL) to be initiated. On a multiprocessor, the processor is placed in a check stop state, and control is passed to the ACR to enable recovery using another processor.

ACR removes the failing processor by marking its related control areas in the operating system as inactive. The resources held by the failed processor are released with the help of the RTM. The ACR then initiates the recovery routines for the failed task. The service processor is instructed to remove the failed processor from the configuration.

If an interrupt is expected to arrive and does not do so within a specified time interval, the MIH is invoked. MIH tries to determine the cause and possibly correct it. The most common recovery action is to clear the current I/O operation and restart. However, on an I/O device hardware error, the DDR can recover by moving a demountable volume from one device to another or by substituting one unit record device for another.

### 7.2.3.2 MVS Software Error Recovery

The *RTM* function of the MVS/XA performs both software error recovery and recovery from errors propagated to the software from the hardware. *Recovery routines* are provided to isolate the error and recover from it, if possible. They also log error information to facilitate the servicing of the system by personnel. *Resource managers* are invoked by the RTM to clean up after a recovery routine has been executed. To break out of an endless loop or a wait state, a *Restart Function* (RF) is used. After the RF is initiated, the RTM is started to attempt software recovery. MVS provides a checkpointing/restart facility through the Job Control Language (JCL). Applications can request checkpoints through an API exported for checkpointing. Excessive Spin Loop Detection is triggered when there is a potential error indication due to excessive spin in a tight loop that is used to synchronize events among multiple processors. The only action taken is a conservative one: warning of the operator through Disable Console Communication. The recovery action is left to the operator.

### 7.2.4 Hardware-related Software Errors

This subsection discusses measurement-based analysis of the impact of temporary and permanent hardware errors on the operating system. It is generally believed that the operating system is seldom able to diagnose a software error related to a hardware error or failure. To determine the extent and nature of the problem, we built a data set of software errors considered to be hardware-related. Three different types of software incidents are designated as software errors in MVS and hence in this study. They range in severity from minor data-related inconsistencies to major software failures: (i) abnormal job or task terminations (ABEND), (ii) invalid supervisor calls, and (iii) program checks.

From that data set, we extracted a subset consisting of software errors that occurred in proximity to hardware errors (e.g. disk and channel errors). Thus, the software errors considered in this study range from minor problems, like a data inconsistency in the presence of hardware transients, to a software design deficiency in the presence of major hardware malfunctions. We define those errors as hardware-related software errors, denoted by *HW/SW*. Since errors occur quite infrequently (on the order of 2–3 a day), matching hardware and software errors is not a random event and represents a specific pattern. The relationship, however, may be either cause-effect (i.e. the hardware error caused the software error) or symptomatic (i.e. both the hardware error and the software error are symptoms of another, yet unidentified, problem). HW/SW errors are further subdivided as follows:

1) Software errors found to be related to temporary hardware errors (denoted by *HW/SW-Temp*).
2) Software failures found to be related to permanent hardware failures (denoted by *HW/SW-Perm*).

Our analysis differentiates between the terms *error* and *failure*. A *failure* is an error that causes the termination of the system (i.e. a system failure). Thus, an error, in general, may or may not result in a system failure.

Our analysis procedure demonstrates a methodology for measuring the interaction between hardware and software as it relates to system reliability. The analysis showed that the operating system could seldom tell that a software error may be hardware-related. Importantly, nearly 35% of all software failures are found to be hardware-related. We evaluated the impact of HW/SW errors on the system by measuring the effectiveness of system recovery in containing the propagation of such errors. We found that the system recovery management was significantly less effective in handling hardware-related software errors than software errors in general.

### 7.2.4.1 Processing of Error Data

The automatic detection of a software error in MVS can be accomplished through either hardware or software facilities. Data on the type of detection (hardware or software) and recovery are logged by the system into a data set called *SYS1. LOGREC*. A detailed description of error detection and recovery processing in MVS can be found in [6–9].

The LOGREC data include CPU, channel, and device errors. For initial analysis, we selected the software error records on the two IBM 308ls. Each error record contains a number of bits describing the type of error, its severity, and the result of hardware and software attempts to recover from the problem. The general software error status indicators are *TYPE* (of detection), *EVENT* (that caused the detection), and *ERRCODE* (i.e. a code or symptom of the error). The SYS1. LOGREC data set was decoded and compacted so as to cluster (i.e. coalesce) error records believed to reflect repeated occurrences of the same problem. The number of observations in a cluster and the timespan of the cluster were also added to the record. The creation of the database is discussed in detail in [5].

For this study, we generated two additional data sets, denoted by *HW/SW-Temp* and *HW/SW-Perm*, that contained information on hardware/software interaction. Those error categories were briefly defined in the previous section.

We created the HW/SW-Perm data set by matching software errors with a log of hardware failures manually maintained at the Center for Information Technology (CIT) at Stanford University, i.e. the HW/SW-Perm data set contained pairs of hardware and software errors/failures that both occurred within a short period of time (within a minute or so of each other). The matched records were then inspected to confirm that the resulting data (on nearly 70 failures) did indeed correspond to hardware-related software failures.

We obtained the HW/SW-Temp data set through a similar matching of software errors with temporary channel and disk errors. The data on channel errors came from the Channel Check (CCH) records and Missing Interruption Handling (MIH) records. The data on disk errors came from the system Out-Board Records (OBR). Again, we carefully inspected the merged data set to confirm that the errors corresponded reasonably well to hardware-related software errors (see [10, 11] for a detailed description of these records). Table 7.1 summarizes the error data. A detailed examination of the data (both HW/SW-Perm and HW/SW-Temp) indicates that the system is seldom able to correctly diagnose a hardware-related software error.

**Table 7.1** Summary of the data (period of study: March 1982–May 1983) [5].

| Data set | Source | Frequency |
| --- | --- | --- |
| All SW errors | SW records | 1547 |
| All permanent HW failures | UNILOG | 264 |
| All temporary HW errors | CCH, OBR, MIH | 4461 |
| SW errors related to temporary HW errors | SW records/CCH, OBR, MIH | 108 |
| SW errors related to permanent HW failures | SW records/UNILOG | 69 |

### 7.2.4.2 Analysis of Error Detection

This section investigates the detection of software errors in MVS. In particular, the following points are considered:

1) The relationship between the type of software error and the type of detection (i.e. hardware or software).
2) The impact of hardware or software detection on system recovery.
3) The detection of software errors found to be hardware-related (i.e. of HW/ SW errors).

### 7.2.4.3 Error Classification and Detection

As is commonly done in analyses of this type, we grouped the ERRCODE provided by the system into classes of similar errors. We chose the error classes to reflect commonly encountered problems. It was important to ensure that each error category contained a statistically significant number of errors. We defined seven classes of errors as follows.

1) A *control* error indicates the invalid use of control statements and invalid supervisor calls.
2) An *I/O and Data Management* error indicates that a problem occurred during I/O management or during the creation and processing of data sets.
3) A *Storage Management* error indicates an error in the storage allocation/deallocation process or virtual memory mapping.
4) A *Storage Exception* indicates that nonexistent or inaccessible memory locations have been addressed.
5) A *Programming Exception* is a program error other than a storage exception.
6) A *Timing* error indicates a system- or operator-detected endless loop, endless wait-state, or violation of system- or user-defined time limits.
7) A *Lost Record* error indicates that the error-recording process itself was affected by an error.

Table 7.2 gives the percentage distribution of the errors found during the analyzed period. On average, the two major error categories are storage exceptions (26%) and storage management (27%). Recall that a major feature of the MVS operating system is the multiple virtual storage organization. Storage management is a high-volume activity and is critical to the proper operation of the system. One might therefore expect its contribution to errors to be significant.

Significant differences exist between the error distributions of the two detection mechanisms. It can be seen that all exception errors are hardware-detected, and storage management errors are software-detected. Software is more than twice as likely as hardware to detect control and I/O errors. An analysis of the hardware-detected control and I/O errors showed that the errors were, in fact, forced

**Table 7.2** Distribution of error categories.

| Error type | Hardware detected Freq. | % | Software detected Freq. | % | All[a] % |
|---|---|---|---|---|---|
| Storage management | 11 | 1.9 | 395 | 44.2 | 27.7 |
| Storage exceptions | 382 | 67.0 | 0 | 0.0 | 26.1 |
| Timing | 0 | 0.0 | 310 | 34.6 | 21.2 |
| I/O and data management | 45 | 7.9 | 116 | 13.0 | 11.0 |
| Programming exceptions | 114 | 19.9 | 0 | 0.0 | 7.8 |
| Control | 18 | 3.2 | 50 | 5.6 | 4.6 |
| Unclassified | 1 | 0.1 | 23 | 2.6 | 1.6 |
| Total | 571 | 100.0 | 894 | 100.0 | 100.0 |

[a] Does not include lost records and operator-detected errors [5].

program checks and were detected as a result of specific software traps. Note from Table 7.2 that storage-related problems dominate both hardware- and software-detected errors.

### 7.2.4.4 Error Detection and Recovery

In MVS, recovery is aimed at containing the propagation of an error and thereby preventing a system failure. The system can recover from an error via a retry or by aborting the job or task (i.e. a module of the job) in progress [8, 9]. If the job or task is critical for system continuation, abortion will most likely result in system failure (SYSDAMAG). The data show that a hardware-detected error is more likely than a software-detected error to result in a system failure (~30 vs. ~18%) and less likely than a software-detected error to be retried successfully (24 vs. 36%).

Table 7.3 relates the provision of recovery routines to the detection mechanisms. Recovery routines are specified in MVS for major system functions [6]. We found that recovery routines are specified for almost twice as many software-detected errors as hardware-detected errors. The table shows that software-detected errors are handled better (i.e. a higher chance of a recovery than hardware-detected errors). We found that the availability of a recovery routine significantly improves the recovery probability of software-detected errors. An important reason for the better performance for software-detected errors is that software detects most (or all) management problems. Since storage management is an important function of MVS, it is more carefully designed and better protected by recovery routines.

**Table 7.3**  Effect of recovery routines [5].

| Detection | Recovery routine provided (%) | Failures (recovery routine provided) (%) | Failures (recovery routine not provided) (%) |
|---|---|---|---|
| Hardware | 43.5 | 27.6 | 31.6 |
| Software | 84.8 | 13.3 | 42.1 |
| All | 66.1 | 16.8 | 34.8 |

### 7.2.4.5  Detection of HW/SW Software Errors

Recall that the error data set (HW/SW) used in this study contains information on software errors and failures related to both temporary and permanent hardware problems. Further data analysis led to an interesting observation that the lost records (LOSTRECS) are a significant proportion of hardware-related software errors. Thus, software error data collection itself is affected by the occurrence of HW/SW errors. Further investigation revealed that the job names of the hardware records associated with software errors tagged "LOSTRECS" generally indicated a system-critical job. In addition, lost records commonly appear in large clusters (indicating the persistency of a problem and the inability of the system to limit error propagation) and usually result in system termination. Such a pattern is frequently a symptom of an HW/SW problem.

## 7.2.5  Analysis of Hardware-related Software Errors

In this section, we analyze temporary and permanent hardware-related software errors. Significant features of hardware-related software errors are determined, and their effect on recovery management is examined. Overall, the data analysis shows that the key features of hardware-related software problems are that they are very likely (i) to affect the system error detection/collection mechanisms, (ii) to have large error-handling times, and (iii) to involve many jobs.

### 7.2.5.1  Recovery from HW/SW Errors

First, we evaluate the effectiveness of system recovery management in containing the propagation of HW/SW errors and thereby preventing system failures. Recall that in handling a software error, the system can recover by issuing a retry or by aborting the current job or task (again, a module of the job) in progress. If that job is critical for system continuation, a system failure (SYSDAMAG) will result.

Table 7.4 evaluates the effectiveness of recovery routines in handling HW/SW errors. If we compare data in Table 7.4 to the data on all SW errors, we find that recovery routines are less likely to be specified for HW/SW errors than for SW errors in general (56 vs. 66%). The percentage of failures (i.e. failure probability)

**Table 7.4**  Specification of recovery routines for HW/SW errors [5].

| Error type | Recovery routine provided (%) | Failures (recovery routine provided) (%) | Failures (recovery routine not provided) (%) |
| --- | --- | --- | --- |
| HW/SW-Temp | 62.9 | 20.6 | 84.2 |
| HW/SW-Perm | 46.4 | 100.0 | 100.0 |
| All HW/SW | 56.5 | 46.0 | 92.0 |

for HW/SW errors is close to three times for SW errors in general (46 vs. 16% when recovery routines are provided, and 92 vs. 34% when recovery routines are not provided).

Table 7.4 also shows that software errors related to permanent hardware failures have a significantly lower probability of having recovery routines provided than do software errors related to temporary hardware errors (46 vs. 63%). Furthermore, the recovery routines are singularly ineffective in handling permanent hardware problems (100% failure). If we compare Tables 7.3 and 7.4, we can see that recovery routines are not nearly as effective in handling HW/SW-Temp errors. Although recovery routines are specified for almost the same proportion of HW/SW-Temp errors as for all SW errors, a higher percentage of HW/SW-Temp errors result in failure.

Detailed analysis of the data indicates that MIH (missing interruption handling) causes the highest number of job and task terminations. These are most closely related to timing errors since MIH errors are due to interrupts that are not completed in a specified time. Timing errors are most commonly due to the detection of a wait state or an endless loop. More than 40% of the channel-related software errors result in a lost record. In most of those cases, it was observed that both the hardware and the software problem had large clusters associated with them. The disk and channel errors most commonly manifest as storage problems or exceptions, which could imply that the real problem was not in the channel but, perhaps, in main storage, so that both the channel error and the software record resulted.

Significantly, 23% of HW/SW temporary errors result in system failure. Taking this and HW/SW permanent failures into account, we found that about 27% of all software failures are hardware-related. In addition, most of the lost records in our data also resulted in system termination. Thus, the true percentage of software failures (in our data) that are hardware-related is nearly 35%.

In summary, the analysis shows that the failure probability for HW/SW errors is close to three times that for SW errors in general, indicating poor recovery management of HW/SW errors. In many instances, the system could have been designed to continue in a degraded mode. That is an important observation because it points to a particularly weak aspect of the systems in general. At the very least, the software should be capable of recognizing a hardware failure and taking the offending component offline or putting the system in a wait state.

One reason for the low fault tolerance for HW/SW errors may be inadequate communication between the hardware and software regarding the occurrence of errors. It can be argued that a better provision of recovery routines specifically geared toward the hardware–software interaction could considerably alleviate the problem. If a hardware error could be diagnosed and tagged as a potential software error, it is possible that better recovery methods could be designed. That would be especially true if a system were geared to recognize certain patterns in errors (e.g. those observed here) and classify them as potential software problems.

### 7.2.6 Summary of MVS Analysis

To study the error recovery processes in the MVS system, we used real error data to develop a semi-Markov model for quantifying system error characteristics and the interaction between different types of errors. For example, we described a detailed model and analysis of multiple errors, which constitute about 17% of all software errors and result in considerable overhead. Other systems can be similarly analyzed and modeled so that a wide range of realistic models of software reliability in an operational environment can be established.

We also demonstrated how the failure data (from minor data-related inconsistencies to major software failures) can be used for analyzing the interaction between hardware and software as it relates to system reliability. The methodology introduced enables quantification of the impact of HW/SW errors on the system. Although data-specific conclusions are derived in the context of MVS systems, the approach can easily be modified to suit other systems with automatic recovery features. Since MVS (and its newest generation, z/OS) is a widely used operating system, the estimated measures have inherent value to system designers. Analysis of data finds a strong correlation between poor resolution on software errors and the occurrence of a corresponding hardware error, i.e. the system cannot tell that a software error may be hardware-related. HW/SW errors are often catastrophic. Nearly 35% of all software failures were determined to be hardware-related. The system recovery management is significantly less effective in containing the propagation of that class of errors than software errors in general. The system failure probability for HW/SW errors is nearly three times that for all software errors.

## 7.3 Experimental Analysis of OS Dependability

While the preceding sections discuss means of using failure data (system-generated error logs or human-written error reports) to characterize operation, the following sections discuss experimental use of fault/error injection methods to characterize operating system dependability. The focus is on technology, methods, and scientifically sound procedures for evaluating dependability metrics, e.g. reliability and error coverage, of operating systems. The broader objective is to create a dependability benchmark for operating systems.

Several approaches have been proposed for evaluating the robustness of operating systems, for example 10 [12, 13]. Those studies address robustness at the user-visible interfaces and constitute an important component in operating system benchmarking. We believe that a critical aspect of system dependability assessment is the ability to quantify the impact of a broad range of faults that can occur in the processor, the memory, the I/O, and the network interfaces of the underlying hardware and the corresponding system and application software. For example, fault severity (as measured by the extent of the damage caused by the fault in the system) and associated performance loss due to recovery are two metrics that characterize a system's response to faults and its ability to survive catastrophic events [14, 15]. Sound fault/error injection methods and tools are essential for either direct or indirect quantification of those metrics. While there are many outstanding issues in terms of how, where, and when faults/errors should be injected so that operating systems can be measured and compared, we believe (and substantiate the claim in this chapter) that fault/error injection should be an integral part of any benchmarking procedure.

Ultimately, a quest for a comprehensive benchmark requires us (i) to evaluate different approaches in assessing system dependability, (ii) to analyze their pros and cons, and (iii) to use the resulting knowledge to define the sound procedures, methods, and tools required to enable experimental OS benchmarking. For dependability benchmarking, unlike performance benchmarking, it is doubtful that a benchmark based entirely on the external characteristics of a system would be satisfying and acceptable. We envisage that a combination of a "black box" approach and a "white box" approach will emerge.

### 7.3.1 What to Measure and Why?

Several measures (or metrics) have been identified as useful in quantifying operating system dependability. They include the following:

- *Detection and recovery coverage (for a given set of faults):* How useful the redundancy is that has been introduced into the system.
- *Recovery time (for each recovery mechanism or strategy):* The contribution of each recovery mechanism to system downtime.
- *Fault/error latency (the amount of time from a fault/error's occurrence to activation of the fault/error):* The danger of having multiple faults/errors in the system.
- *Error detection latency (the amount of time from an error's occurrence to its detection):* The window of system vulnerability (during which the error is active and the system's behavior is unpredictable).

This section presents the use of software-implemented fault injection in conducting experimental studies and deriving quantitative dependability measures. In doing so, we stress a broad range of system components, including operating system code, data and stack sections, and processor registers. The systematic approach enables the following:

- *Assessment of fault severity and the efficiency of detection and recovery mechanisms* (present in the system) under variable workloads (real or synthetic applications). The resulting figures quantify the recovery mechanism's coverage and the system's ability to recover.
- *Measurements of the detection latency*, which are of particular importance in characterizing the probability that errors will (i) propagate between system components and (ii) escape beyond the containment boundaries defined by a computing node, e.g. in the form of fail-silence violations or silent data corruption. For example, our study (discussed in this chapter) of the Linux kernel's sensitivity to errors on Pentium- and PowerPC-based platforms shows a nonnegligible percentage of cases in which the crash latency (defined as the time between an error's activation and the resulting system failure) exceeds hundreds of millions of CPU cycles. In other words, the processor can execute millions of instructions in the presence of an active error before it finally crashes. During that time, errors can propagate, causing the system to produce bad data or make incorrect decisions.
- *Insight into how architectural characteristics of the target processors impact the error sensitivity of the operating system*, which is crucial in selecting a hardware platform.

In addition, by exercising (with faults) critical execution paths within code, one can pinpoint the error-sensitive system components/locations, which may become dependability bottlenecks. That information, in turn, provides feedback to the developers on potential ways to integrate enhancements.

To illustrate the approach, in Section 7.6, we discuss our experiences and lessons we learned from assessing the error sensitivity of the Linux kernel executing on PowerPC G4 and Pentium 4 processors. The goal was to provide a methodology and environment to enable (i) comparisons of the Linux kernel's varying behaviors under a broad range of errors on two target processors; and (ii) understanding of how the architectural characteristics of the target processors impact the error sensitivity of the operating system.

## 7.4 Behavior of the Linux Operating System in the Presence of Errors

This section presents an example of experimental (fault-injection-based) evaluation of the Linux operating system's sensitivity to errors [16].

## 7.4.1 Methodology

The objective was to develop a sound approach for experimental assessment (benchmarking) of operating systems. The components of the approach include:

1) *Methods* to stress the system, i.e. to generate runtime errors
2) *Procedures* to specify a set of measurements in terms of error types, error frequency, and workloads
3) *Metrics* to quantify dependability attributes of the operating system
4) *Tools* to set up and carry out experiments, collect and analyze the measurement data, and calculate the dependability metrics.

Software-implemented error injection was employed to experimentally assess the error sensitivity of the Linux kernel executing on the PowerPC G4 and Pentium 4 processors. Single-bit errors were injected into kernel stacks, kernel code sections, kernel data structures, and CPU system registers while benchmark programs were being run. NFTAPE [17], a software framework for conducting fault/error injection experiments, was used to conduct the tests.

## 7.4.2 Error Injection Environment

We developed a driver-based Linux kernel error injector to enable error injection campaigns. The injection driver (a kernel module), attached to the kernel, exploits the CPU's debugging and performance-monitoring features (i) to inject errors automatically; (ii) to monitor error activation, error propagation, and crash latency; and (iii) to log the data reliably to remote persistent storage (*crash data storage*).

The error injection environment, shown in Figure 7.2, consists of (i) kernel-embedded components (injectors, crash handlers, and a data deposit module) for the P4 and G4 architectures; (ii) a user-level NFTAPE control host, which prepares the target addresses/registers (to be injected), starts the workload using benchmark (UnixBench [18]), and logs injection data for analysis; (iii) a hardware monitor (watchdog card) to detect system hangs/crashes to provide an auto-reboot if needed; and (iv) a remote crash data collector that resides on the control host computer to receive crash data by UDP connections. That last capability is an important extension to the existing NFTAPE framework; it allows reliable collection of the crash data even if the underlying file system (on the target node) is not accessible. The instrumentation for collecting data on error latency (cycles-to-crash) is also added.

### 7.4.2.1 Approach

An automated error injection process, illustrated in Figure 7.3, includes the following three major steps:

*STEP 1: Generate injection targets.* The *target address/register generator* provides error injection targets for the following: (i) for *code injection*, an

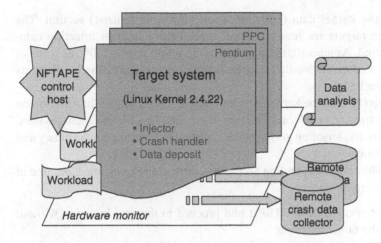

**Figure 7.2** Error injection environment [16] / with permission of IEEE.

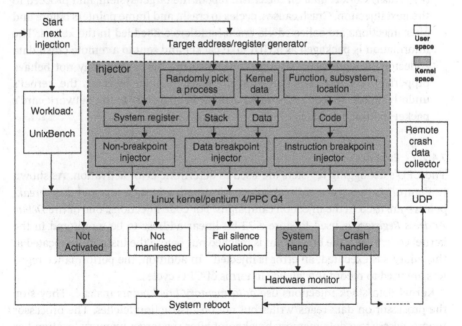

**Figure 7.3** Automated process of injecting errors [16] / with permission of IEEE.

instruction breakpoint location based on selected kernel functions, kernel subsystems, and kernel code address ranges; (ii) for *stack injection*, the bit patterns to inject at randomly chosen (at runtime) kernel processes; (iii) for *system register injection*, system registers to inject; and (iv) for *data injection*, random locations in the kernel data (both initialized and uninitialized) section. The error injection targets are generated and stored before an error injection campaign is initiated. As a result, the activation rate might not be 100%, as some of the pre-generated errors would never be injected if corresponding breakpoints were never reached.

STEP 2: *Inject errors*. The kernel injector obtains pre-generated information on the injection target and performs the error injections. This process includes starting the benchmark, enabling performance registers to measure crash latency and injection of errors.

STEP 3: *Collect data*. Depending on the outcome of the error injection, one of the following actions is taken:

1) *Error Not Activated*. Go to STEP 1 and proceed to the next injection without rebooting the target machine.
2) *Error Activated*. (a) *(Not Manifested, Fail Silence Violation, System Hang)* Log the results, reboot the target system, and proceed to the next injection; (b) *(Crash)* Collect data on the crash, reboot the target system, and proceed to the next injection. Crash causes, cycles to crash, and frame pointers before and after injections are collected via crash handlers embedded in the kernel. The information is packaged as a UDP-like packet and sent to a remote crash data collector through a UDP connection. Since the file system may not behave properly when the kernel crashes, the crash handler bypasses the kernel's underlying file system and supplies the packets directly to the network card's packet-sending function.

### 7.4.2.2 Error Activation

The CPU's debugging registers are used to determine error activation. As shown in Figure 7.3, two types of breakpoints – *instruction breakpoints* and *data breakpoints* – are used in the injection campaigns. For code injections, one of the *Debug Address Registers* is used to store a 32-bit linear address to be monitored in the kernel code. When the breakpoint is reached but before the instruction located at this address is executed, an error is injected.[1] In addition, the performance registers are used to record the latency in terms of CPU cycles.

Kernel data/stack injections use *data memory breakpoints* instead. They stop the processor on data reads/writes but not on instruction fetches. The processor reports access to a data memory breakpoint after the target memory location has been accessed (i.e. data read/write). Note that an *instruction breakpoint* is reported before the target instruction is executed. Consequently, our injector inserts an

---

1 While this discussion is in the context of the Pentium 4 processor, the PowerPC G4 injection scheme is similar.

**Table 7.5** Experiment setup summary [16] / with permission of IEEE.

| | Hardware | | System software | | |
|---|---|---|---|---|---|
| Processor | CPU clock (GHz) | Memory (MB) | Distribution | Linux Kernel | Compiler |
| Intel Pentium 4 | 1.5 | 256 | RedHat 9.0 | 2.4.22 | GCC 3.2.2 |
| Motorola MPC 7455 | 1.0 | 256 | YellowDog 3.0 | 2.4.22 | |

error before a data memory breakpoint is set. If the breakpoint is not reached, the original value at the location is restored, and the error is marked as *not activated*. If the data memory breakpoint is triggered, one of the following actions is taken: (i) a *data write access*, in which the injected error is overwritten by the write operation and, thus, needs to be re-injected and is marked as *activated* or (ii) a *data read access*, in which the injected error is not overwritten and is marked as *activated*.

*Target System Configuration.* Table 7.5 summarizes the experimental setup. To speed up the experiments, three P4 and two G4 machines were used in the injection campaigns. Watchdog cards driven by Linux drivers were embedded in those machines to enable automated system reboot after hangs.

### 7.4.2.3 Error Model

The error model assumed in this study is not contingent upon the error origin, i.e. an error could have occurred anywhere in the system – the disk, network, bus, memory, or CPU. Single-bit errors were injected into the instructions of the target kernel functions, the stack of the corresponding kernel process, the kernel data structures, and the corresponding CPU's system registers. Previous research on microprocessors [19] has shown that most (90–99%) device-level transients can be modeled as logic-level, single-bit errors. Data on operational errors also show that many errors in the field are single-bit errors [20].

While in a well-designed system, multiple mechanisms for protecting against errors may be available (e.g. parity, ECC,[2] or memory scrubbing), errors still exist. Errors could, for example, be timing issues due to hardware/software problems, due to a noise source such as undershoot or overshoot, or due to noise on the address bus that results in writing/reading of the wrong data to/from the memory. In the latter case, the data may be unaltered due to the address bus noise, but the wrong location is accessed. Our error injection experiments employed memory

---

2 As indicated by manufacturers, logic failure rates may erode the efficacy of ECC in designs. Hardened logic libraries or schemes to mask logic sensitivity (such as spatial and/or temporal redundancy on critical paths) may be needed to account for the deficiency.

errors and system register errors to emulate the diverse origins and impacts of actual errors. Four attributes characterize each error injected:

*Trigger (When?).* An error is injected when (i) a target datum is read/written for stack/data injection, (ii) a target instruction in a given kernel function is reached, or (iii) a system register is used. The kernel activity is invoked by the execution of a user-level workload program (i.e. the benchmark programs).

*Location (Where?).* (i) This can be a randomly selected kernel stack location, a location within the initiated/uninitiated kernel data, or a system register. (ii) For kernel code injection, the location is pre-selected based on the profiling of kernel functions; i.e. the kernel functions most frequently used by the workload are selected for injections.

*Type (What?).* (i) This is a single-bit error per data word in the case of stack, data, and system register injections. (ii) For kernel code injections, it is a single-bit error per instruction.

*Duration (How Long?).* A bit is flipped in the target to emulate the impact of a transient event that results in the corruption of data, code, or CPU registers. (i) For data, stack, and system register injections, the duration of an error may be as short as the time it takes the corrupted data item to be overwritten because of normal system activities. (ii) For code injections, an error may persist throughout the execution time of the benchmark.

### 7.4.2.4 Outcome Categories

Outcomes from error injection experiments are classified according to the categories given in Table 7.6. In addition, the crash category is further divided into

**Table 7.6** Outcome categories [16] / with permission of IEEE.

| Outcome category | Description |
| --- | --- |
| Activated | The corrupted instruction/data is executed/used |
| Not manifested | The corrupted instruction/data is executed/used, but it does not cause a visible abnormal impact on the system |
| Fail silence violation | Either operating system or application erroneously detects the presence of an error or allows incorrect data/response to propagate out. Benchmark programs are instrumented to detect errors |
| Crash | Operating system stops working, e.g. bad trap or system panic. Crash handlers embedded into the operating system are enhanced to dump failure data (processor and memory state). Off-line analysis of this data allows determining causes for most of the observed crashes |
| Hang | System resources are exhausted, resulting in a nonoperational system, e.g. deadlock. |

subcategories; Tables 7.7 and 7.8 provide crash subcategories for the Pentium (P4) and PPC (G4) processors, respectively.

*Latency (cycles-to-crash)* is defined as the number of CPU cycles between an error activation and the resulting crash. (Note that for system register injections, crash latency represents the time between error injection and the observed crash.) Typically, latency includes three stages, as shown in Figure 7.4.

**Table 7.7** Crash cause categories: Pentium (P4) [16] / with permission of IEEE.

| Crash category (P4) | Description |
| --- | --- |
| NULL pointer | Unable to handle kernel NULL pointer de-reference |
| Bad paging | A page fault: the kernel tries to access some other bad page except NULL pointer |
| Invalid instruction | An illegal instruction that is not defined in the instruction set is executed |
| General protection fault | Exceeding segment limit, writing to a read-only code or data segment, loading a selector with a system descriptor, reading an execution-only code segment |
| Kernel panic | Operating system detects an error |
| Invalid TSS (task state segment) | The selector, code segment, or stack segment is outside the limit, or stack is not writeable |
| Divide error | Math error |
| Bounds trap | Bounds checking error |

**Table 7.8** Crash cause categories: PPC (G4) [16] / with permission of IEEE.

| Crash category (G4) | Description |
| --- | --- |
| Bad area | A page fault: the kernel tries to access a bad page, including NULL pointer or bad memory access |
| Illegal instruction | An invalid instruction that is not defined in the instruction set is executed |
| Stack overflow | Stack pointer of a kernel process is out of range |
| Machine check | An error is detected on the processor-local bus, including instruction machine-check errors and data machine-check errors |
| Alignment | Load/store or other specific instructions' operands are not word-aligned |
| Panic | Operating system detects an error |
| Bus error | Protection fault |
| Bad trap | Unknown exception |

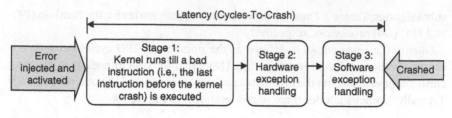

**Figure 7.4** Definition of *cycles-to-crash* [16] / with permission of IEEE.

*Stage 1.* A target location is reached, an error is injected, and a performance register is started to measure the time until the potential crash; the kernel keeps running until a bad instruction is executed, e.g. a NULL pointer is referenced. That may take from zero (i.e. if there is an immediate crash after execution/accessing the injected instruction/data) to millions of CPU cycles.

*Stage 2.* The CPU's hardware exception handling takes over to determine the exception vector, evaluate correctness, and save and load necessary data; this may consume more than 1000 CPU cycles.

*Stage 3.* The hardware transfers control to the software exception handler, which typically executes about 150–200 instructions.

### 7.4.3 Overview of Experimental Results

Tables 7.9 and 7.10 summarize the results of all injection campaigns conducted on the P4 and G4 platforms.[3] They reflect over 115 000 error injections. The major conclusions to be drawn from the tables can be summarized as follows:

- While the error activation rates are generally similar for both processors, the manifestation rates for the Pentium 4 are about twice as high.
- For stack errors, there is a significant difference between the two processors in the manifestation rates (56% for P4 vs. 21% for G4). A similar trend is observed in the case of errors in the kernel data (66% for the P4 vs. 21% for the G4). The observed difference between the two platforms can be explained by the disparity in the ways they use memory. The G4 processor always operates on 32-bit-wide data items, while the P4 allows 8-, 16-, and 32-bit data transfers. As a result, it is possible for many stack and data errors on the G4 platform to corrupt unused data bits in a target data item.

---

3 Percentage figures in the third columns of the two tables were calculated with respect to all injected errors; all other percentages are given with respect to activated errors.

**Table 7.9** Statistics on error activation and failure distribution on P4 processor [16] / with permission of IEEE.

| Intel Pentium 4 campaign | Injected | Error activated | Activated | | | |
|---|---|---|---|---|---|---|
| | | | Not manifested | Fail silence violation | Known crash | Hang/ unknown crash |
| Stack | 10143 | 2973 (29.3%) | 1305 (43.9%) | 0 (0%) | 1136 (38.2%) | 532 (17.9%) |
| System registers | 3866 | N/A | 3459 (89.5%) | 0 (0%) | 305 (7.9%) | 102 (2.6%) |
| Data | 46000 | 226 (0.5%) | 77 (34.1%) | 0 (0%) | 96 (42.5%) | 53 (23.4%) |
| Code | 1790 | 982 (54.9%) | 308 (31.4%) | 13 (1.3%) | 455 (46.3%) | 206 (21.0%) |
| Total | 61799 | | | | | |

**Table 7.10** Statistics on error activation and failure distribution on G4 processor [16] / with permission of IEEE.

| Motorola PPC G4 campaign | Injected | Error activated | Activated | | | |
|---|---|---|---|---|---|---|
| | | | Not manifested | Fail silence violation | Known crash | Hang/unknown crash |
| Stack | 3017 | 1203 (39.9%) | 949 (78.9%) | 0 (0%) | 172 (14.3%) | 84 (7.0%) |
| System register | 3967 | N/A | 3774 (95.1%) | 0 (0%) | 69 (1.7%) | 124 (3.1%) |
| Data | 46000 | 704 (1.5%) | 551 (78.3%) | 7 (1.0%) | 55 (7.8%) | 91 (12.9%) |
| Code | 2188 | 1415 (64.7%) | 580 (41.0%) | 33 (2.3%) | 576 (40.7%) | 226 (16.0%) |
| Total | 55172 | | | | | |

- For register errors, the trend in manifestation rates is similar to the above, although the manifestation rates for both platforms are lower (5% for G4 and over 11% for P4).[4]
- While the percentages of FSVs (fail-silence violations) are small for code segment injection (1.3% for P4 and 2.3% for G4), they have significant error

---

4 Register injections target the system registers, e.g. the flag register, stack registers, and memory management registers. While we cannot determine the exact percentage of activated errors, the way the system is using those registers results in a high probability that errors will be activated.

propagation potential and hence are a cause for concern. Observe that the P4 data injection does not cause any FSVs, while on the G4, 1% of activated data errors manifest as FSVs.

### 7.4.4 Crash Cause Analysis

Figures 7.5 and 7.6 show the distribution of the causes of known crashes (i.e. those for which crash dump information was logged). The crash cause distributions for the two platforms have some similarities:

- About 67% of crashes on the G4 (i.e. *Bad Area* crashes) and 71% of crashes on the P4 (i.e. the sum of the *Bad Paging* and *NULL Pointer* crashes) are due to invalid memory accesses; illegal instructions contribute to 16% of crashes on both platforms.
- As will be discussed in Section 6.4.1, the P4 does not explicitly report stack overflow (a category that is not present in the pie chart in Figure 7.5). On the P4, such stack errors propagate, and most of them manifest as *Bad Paging* or *General Protection Fault*. The impact of the propagation is discussed in a later section in connection with an analysis of error latency.
- On both platforms, about 0.1% of crashes were due to a system *Panic* (i.e. the OS detected an internal error).

#### 7.4.4.1 Stack Injection

In this section, we analyze the manifested stack errors. Stack injections on the G4 primarily result in *Stack Overflow* (41.9%) and *Bad Area* (53.5%), while *Bad Paging* (45%) and *Null Pointer* (31%) dominate P4 results (see Figure 7.7).

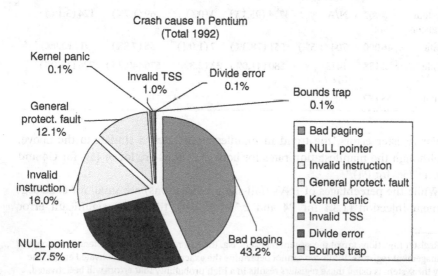

**Figure 7.5** Overall distribution of crash causes (*Known Crash* category) on P4 [16] / with permission of IEEE.

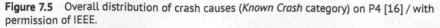

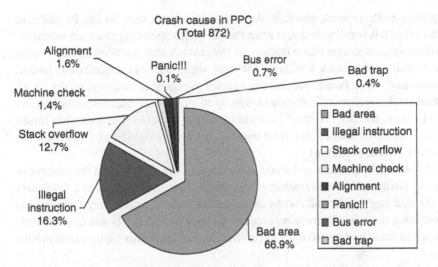

**Figure 7.6** Overall distribution of crash causes (*Known Crash* category) on G4 [16] / with permission of IEEE.

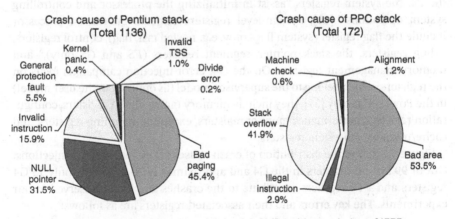

**Figure 7.7** Crash causes for kernel stack injection [16] / with permission of IEEE.

*Stack Overflow* is caused by the corruption of frame pointers stored on the stack. As a result, the kernel attempts to access memory beyond the currently allocated space for the stack, causing an exception to be generated. While the *Stack Overflow* category constitutes a significant percentage of crashes (41.9%) on the G4 processor, it does not appear to occur on the P4 platform. One could look for the explanation in the relative sizes of the runtime stacks used by the two processors. While the average size of the runtime kernel stack on the G4 is twice that of the P4 stack, the average number of function frame pointers concurrently kept on each of the two stacks is very much the same (5–7 frames).

But the main reason why stack overflows are not being reported on the P4 is that the Linux kernel on the P4 platform does not provide an exception to explicitly indicate stack overflow. An analysis of crash data on the P4 platform shows that it is possible to detect error patterns corresponding to a stack overflow. This analysis indicates that a fraction of the crashes that manifest as *Bad Paging* are actually due to stack overflow. Moreover, some crashes categorized as *Invalid Opcode* and *NULL Pointer* are also due to stack overflow. In addition, on the P4, an actual stack overflow will often lead directly to a *General Protection* exception. As will be seen, the fact that the P4 does not indicate stack overflows also has implications for error latency (the time between an error injection and the resulting crash or system detection).

The above observations and analysis also explain the difference in the number of crashes attributed to *invalid memory access* for the two processors: 53 and 76% (sums of the *Bad Paging* and *Null Pointer* cases) for G4 and P4, respectively. Our analysis shows that some invalid memory accesses on the P4 are actually due to stack overflows and could be detected if the P4 (or the OS) could explicitly capture such events.

### 7.4.4.2 System Register Injection

Register error-injection campaigns on both processors target system registers. In the P4, the system registers "assist in initializing the processor and controlling system operations" [11]. System-level registers targeted on the P4 processor include the flag register (system flags only, e.g. nested task flag), control registers, debug registers, the stack pointer, segment registers (*FS* and *GS* only),[5] and memory-management registers. On the G4, error-injection campaigns focus on the registers, which belong to the supervisor model (as opposed to the user model) in the PowerPC family [21]; they include memory management registers, configuration registers, performance monitor registers, exception-handling registers, and cache/memory subsystem registers.

Figure 7.8 shows the distribution of crash causes for system register injections. Out of 99 system registers in the G4 and approximately 20 in the P4, only 15 G4 registers and 7 P4 registers contribute to the crashes and hangs observed in our experiments. The key errors and their associated registers are as follows:

- *General Protection* errors observed on the P4 platform are due to corruption of the control register *CR0,* and the segment registers *FS* and *GS*. *CR0* contains system control flags that control the operating modes and states of the processors. (11 bits are used as flags, while the rest are reserved.) In an error scenario, a single-bit error disables protected-mode operation and causes a general protection exception – injections to the P4 stack pointer (*ESP*) cause either *NULL Pointer* or *Bad Paging* errors.

---

5 These two segment registers are stored for each context switch as part of TSS (task state segment).

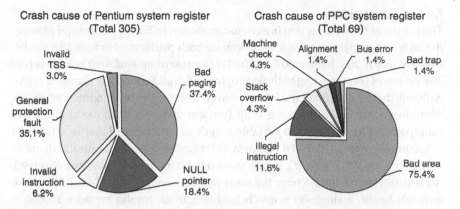

**Figure 7.8** Crash causes for system register injection [16] / with permission of IEEE.

- Few crashes on the P4 are due to *Invalid TSS (Task-State Segment)*. All such events are caused by corruption of the *NT* (nested task) bit in the *EFLAGS Register*. The *NT* bit controls the chaining of interrupted and called tasks. Changing the state of that flag results in an attempt to return to an invalid task after an interrupt.

- On both platforms, injections into the system registers can cause crashes due to *Invalid Instructions*: 6 and 12% on the P4 and G4, respectively. On the P4 platform, invalid instructions occur because of injections into the kernel process instruction pointer (*EIP*), which may force the processor to access memory corresponding to a random place in an instruction binary.

- On the G4, most crashes due to *Invalid Instructions* are caused by errors in the register *SPR274*, which is one of several registers dedicated to general operating system use and used by the stack switch during exceptions. Corrupting the contents of this register can force the operating system to try executing from a random memory location that does not contain a valid instruction and generate an *Invalid Instruction* exception. A small percentage of *Invalid Instructions* are due to errors in the register *SPR1008*, which is used to control the state of several functions within the CPU, e.g. enabling of the instruction cache or branch target instruction cache. In an error scenario (from our experiments), a single-bit error enables the branch target instruction cache when the content of the cache is invalid. As a result, the system crashes because of an invalid instruction exception.

- A small percentage of crashes on the G4 are due to the raising of a *Machine Check* exception. These crashes are caused by corruption of the *Machine State Register* (*MSR*), which defines the state of the processor. In particular, the two bits responsible for enabling/disabling the instruction address translation (*IR*) and data address translation (*DR*) are error-sensitive.

### 7.4.4.3 Code Injection

The results of the code section injections are shown in Figure 7.9. *Invalid Memory Access* is a characteristic of code injections on both platforms. However, for the P4, they are nearly 20% higher: 50% on the G4 (representing *Bad Area* errors) versus 70% on the P4 (representing both *Bad Paging* and *Null Pointers*). A plausible explanation is that a bit error on the P4 can convert a single instruction into a sequence of multiple instructions that are valid (but are incorrect from the application's standpoint). The cause is the variable length of instruction binaries on the P4 (CISC architecture). On the P4 platform, this error may lead to an invalid memory access (often a *NULL Pointer*); hence, more invalid memory accesses are observed. All instructions on the G4 have the same length (owing to the 32-bit RISC architecture); hence, a single-bit error (in addition to an invalid memory access) is more likely to result in an invalid instruction.

*Stack Overflows* resulting from code errors are a small fraction of (about 5%) on the G4; compare this with the results of stack injections that result in stack overflow (41.9%). The reason is probably that the G4 has a large number of general-purpose registers (GPRs). However, very few of them (often *GPR1* and *GPR31*) are used to operate on the stack (e.g. to keep the stack pointer). Crashes due to stack overflow would require altering a register name used by a given instruction to operate on the stack. Given the number of GPRs, the likelihood of stack overflow is low.

The *Illegal Instruction* exceptions detected on the two platforms are also quite different: 24% on the P4 versus 41% on the G4. The difference is partly due to the inability of the P4 to diagnose many instruction-level faults because of variable-length instructions (as explained earlier).

The preceding sections highlight the role of the hardware in detecting errors. Data injections discussed next highlight the operating system's detection capabilities since the impact of errors in data must be detected at the operating system level.

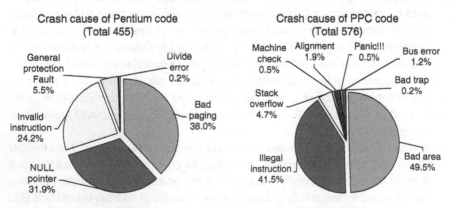

**Figure 7.9** Crash causes for code injection [16] / with permission of IEEE.

#### 7.4.4.4 Data Injection

Recall that only a small percentage of kernel data errors are activated. On both processors, the majority of manifested data errors (see Figure 7.10) result in invalid memory accesses: 89% (representing *Bad Area* errors) and 80% (representing *Bad Paging* and *Null Pointers* errors) for the G4 and P4, respectively. There is also a significant percentage of *Invalid/Illegal Instruction* cases: 9 and 18% for the G4 and P4, respectively.

The key reason that twice as many invalid instruction cases are observed on the P4 platform is that the Linux kernel (for both the P4 and G4 architectures) raises the *Invalid Instruction* exception to handle a variety of error cases, some of which have nothing to do with invalid instructions.

#### 7.4.4.5 Summary

Several more generic conclusions can be drawn based on the analysis of crash data:

- The variable-length instruction format on the P4 leads to poorer diagnosability because a bit error can alter a single instruction into a sequence of multiple valid (but incorrect in the context of the application semantic) instructions. The error may subsequently lead to an invalid memory access and cause, e.g. a *NULL Pointer* exception, making it difficult to locate the actual reason for the crash. All instructions on the G4 have the same length (32 bits); hence, a single-bit error is more likely to result in an invalid instruction.
- Though less compact, fixed 32-bit data and stack access make the G4 platform less sensitive to errors. The sparseness of the data can mask errors. For example, the larger presence of unused bits in data items means that the alteration of any unused bit is inconsequential, even if the corrupted data instruction is used. The more optimized access patterns on P4 increase the chances that accessing a corrupted memory location will lead to problems.

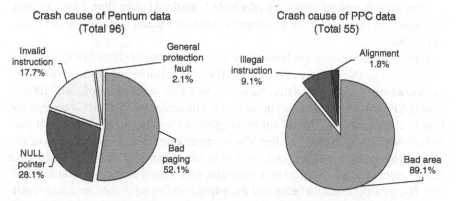

**Figure 7.10** Crash causes for kernel data injection [16] / with permission of IEEE.

- The data from stack overflows and the lazy detection of instruction corruptions indicate that the P4 kernel (and possibly the hardware strategy) reduces the performance overhead that runtime error checks might incur but increases the risk of error propagation and the potential for serious damage to the system. In contrast, the G4 kernel is more likely to perform checking closer to an error's origin. While the G4 approach may have a performance cost, it provides early detection and reduces the chance that errors will propagate.

### 7.4.5 Crash Latency (*Cycles-to-Crash*) Analysis

To explore further differences/similarities of Linux behavior on the two platforms, this section discusses crash latency. Figure 7.11 depicts the crash latency for all the error injection campaigns we conducted and details crash latency distributions. The major findings can be summarized as follows:

- The majority (80%) of stack errors on the G4 platform are short-lived (less than 3000 cycles). On the P4 platform, the majority (80%) of stack errors result in longer crash latencies (3 000–100 000 cycles). The primary reason for the disparity is the ways the two platforms handle exceptions. For example, the kernel on the G4 platform provides quick detection of stack overflow errors, while the kernel on the P4 architecture converts stack overflow events into other types of exceptions (e.g. *Bad Paging*), resulting in inherently slower detection.
- Errors impacting the kernel code show an opposite trend in crash latency (compared to stack errors). Here, 45% of the errors on the P4 platform are short-lived (less than 3 000 cycles), while about 50% of the errors on the G4 have a latency between 10 000 and 100 000 cycles. The dissimilarity is due to the differences in the numbers of general-purpose registers provided by the two processors (32 on the G4 and 8 on the P4).

Most system register errors are relatively long-lived (more than 10 000 cycles). The reason is that most of them are not visible to users and typically are not modified often.

*Stack Injection.* The crash latency for stack injections is given in Figure 7.11a. About 80% of the crashes observed on the G4 platform are within 3 000 CPU cycles, whereas about 80% of the crashes on the P4 are in the range of 3 000–100 000 cycles. The crash cause analysis in Section 6.4 indicates that 40% of G4 crashes are due to stack overflow. The G4 kernel employs a checking wrapper before it executes a specific exception handler. The wrapper examines the correctness of the current stack pointer. If the stack pointer is out of kernel stack range (8 KB), the kernel raises a *Stack Overflow* exception and forces itself to stop as soon as possible. The wrapper executes before the exception handler is invoked, and, as a result, the detection of the corrupted stack pointers is relatively fast. The kernel

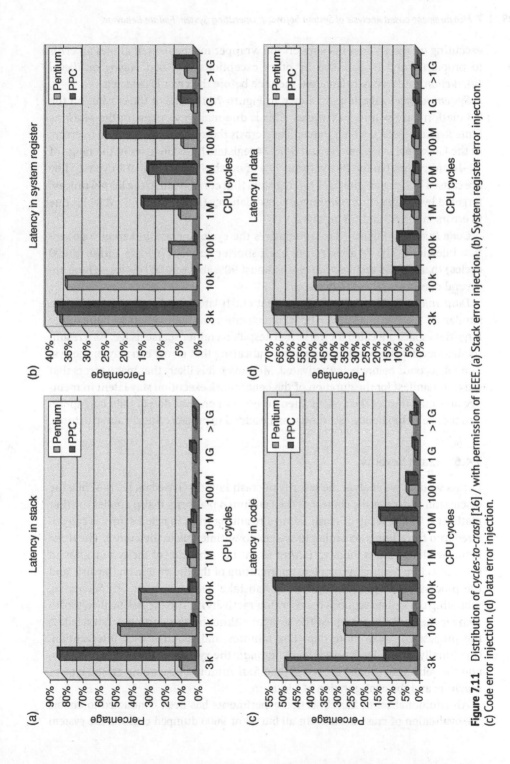

**Figure 7.11** Distribution of *cycles-to-crash* [16] / with permission of IEEE. (a) Stack error injection. (b) System register error injection. (c) Code error injection. (d) Data error injection.

executing on the P4 does not support the wrapper mechanism. It allows an error to propagate and be captured by other exceptions, e.g. *Bad Paging* or *Illegal Instruction*, and that may lengthen the time before the error is detected.

*System Register Injection.* As shown in Figure 7.11b, 35% of the crashes on the G4 platform are within 3000 cycles. This is due mainly to errors in the *Machine State Register* (*MSR*), which immediately crash the system. Crashes due to errors in the G4 kernel stack pointer and *SPR274* registers have latencies in the range of 10–100 M cycles. On the P4 platform, 70% of crashes are within 10 K cycles. They are caused by errors in the *ESP*, *EIP* registers that correspond to the kernel process targeted by the injection. The longest crash latency (larger than 1 G cycles) is due to errors in the *FS* and *GS* registers.

*Code Injection.* Figure 7.11c summarizes the cycle-to-crash in kernel code section injections. The P4 architecture has a shorter latency (70% are within 10 000 cycles) than the G4 architecture (with almost 90% above 10 000 cycles). There are several reasons for the difference.

*Data Injection.* Figure 7.11d shows that crash latencies due to data errors are similar on the two platforms. The error activation is small (about 1%) due to the large data space allocated for the kernel despite its rather sparse usage. As a result, the latency distribution has a long tail, indicating that errors can stay in the system for seconds before being activated. Moreover, it is likely that many errors that did not manifest for the duration of the benchmark execution stay latent in memory and may impact the system later. To prevent crashes due to data corruption and reduce error latency, assertions can be added to protect critical data structures.

### 7.4.6 Crash Severity

In this section, we analyze the severity of crash failures (based on [22]). While the discussion addresses the context of the Pentium 4 platform, it also applies to other platforms. The severity of crash failures resulting from injected errors is categorized into three levels according to system downtime due to the failure. The three identified levels are as follows. (i) *Most severe*, i.e. rebooting of the system after an error-injection requires a complete reformatting of the file system on the disk, and the process of bringing the system up can take nearly an hour. (ii) *Severe*, i.e. rebooting the system requires the user (interactively) to run the *fsck* facility/tool to recover the partially corrupted file system; although reformatting is not needed, the process can take more than five minutes and requires user intervention. (iii) Finally, at the least severe level, *normal*, the system automatically reboots, and the rebooting usually takes less than four minutes, depending on the type of machine and the configuration of Linux.

An additional set of fault injection experiments has been conducted to enable the evaluation of crash severity. In all but 34 of 9600 dumped crashes, the system rebooted automatically. There were 25 cases in the severe category and 9 cases that required reformatting of the file system. Table 7.11 reports on those nine cases, four of which were repeatable and could be traced using *kdb* (the kernel debugger).

We note that (i) most of the severe crashes happened under a fault injection campaign in which a fault was injected to reverse the condition of a branch instruction, and (ii) although severe damage to the system usually results in a crash, we observed one case in which the system did not crash after an injected error but could not reboot. The availability impact of the most severe crashes is clearly of concern. While a "valid but incorrect branch" error is rare, it is, in our experience, plausible. For example, to achieve 5 nines of availability (5 minutes of downtime per year), one can afford only one such failure in 12 years, no more than one *severe crash* in 2 years, and no more than one *crash* per year.

### 7.4.6.1 Lessons Learned

The lessons learned extend beyond the particular study just described and provide valuable insight into the future development and deployment of dependability benchmarks. The experimental observations can be grouped into two categories:

**Table 7.11** Summary of most severe crashes [22] / with permission of IEEE.

| No. | Repeatability | Injected subsystem: function name | Possible causes for repeatable most severe crash |
|-----|---------------|-----------------------------------|--------------------------------------------------|
| 1 | Yes | fs: open_nami() | Error results in truncating the file size to 0. No crash is observed, but on reboot, *init* reports: *error while loading shared libraries: /lib/i686/ libc.so.6 file too short* |
| 2 | No | mm: do_wp_page() | |
| 3 | No | fs: link_path_walk() | |
| 4 | No | fs: link_path_walk() | |
| 5 | No | fs: sys_read() | |
| 6 | No | fs:get_hash_table() | |
| 7 | Yes | mm: do_wp_page() | Error makes the kernel reuse the page (inside the swap area), which is in use. |
| 8 | Yes | fs: generic_commit_write() | Error reduces the *inode* size (*inode->isize*) |
| 9 | Yes | mm: do_generic_file_read() | Undetected error of an incomplete read of the file (data or executable) to the cache page |

(i) What is the unique value in employing fault/error injection to benchmark a computing system, and (ii) What is expected from benchmarking tools?

### 7.4.6.2 Value in Employing Fault Injection

*Characterization of Crash Severity.* It is commonly assumed that crashes are benign and that systems have mechanisms to ensure that when a program encounters an error (that ultimately leads to a crash), the application will crash instantaneously. While many crashes are benign, severe system failures often result from latent errors that cause undetected error propagation that results in file corruption (e.g. corruption of the OS image on the disk), remote process failures, or checkpoint corruption.

*Measurement of Detection Latency and Validation of Crash-failure Semantic.* Assumption of crash failure semantic for a program or a system behavior is not good if one cannot provide efficient mechanisms for rapid error detection to ensure that the assumption holds in practice. Measurement of detection latency must be an integral component of the benchmarking procedure. For example, we demonstrated that crash latency can be as large as hundreds of millions or billions of cycles.

*Characterization of Recovery Latency.* Measurement of recovery time is crucial to assessing system downtime and hence to quantifying availability. Benchmarking must enable validation of system behavior when multiple detection mechanisms have been triggered because of the same or a propagated error.

### 7.4.6.3 Toolset and Benchmark Procedures

*Complexity.* Benchmarking of fault tolerance requires complex procedures and tools. (The process is far more complex than the one for performance benchmarking.) It is often more time-consuming to deploy the toolset than to conduct the measurements.

*Multiple Platforms (Hardware, Operating System).* The use of multiple tools to conduct the measurement studies creates the risk that the benchmark will measure the effectiveness of the tools rather than the dependability of the target system. Portability across computing platforms is key to the wide acceptance of a benchmarking toolset.

*Multiple-fault Models.* There is a need to support multiple-fault models and provide well-defined interfaces to enable extensions for new fault models. Evaluation of complex systems benefits from injection of a wide variety of faults, such as communication faults, bit-flip faults to memory and registers, and high-level faults specific to an application. The more diverse the fault set, the more one can learn about the target system.

### 7.4.7 Summary

This section describes a fault/error-injection-based approach to the experimental assessment of operating system dependability. The methodology has been applied to characterize and compare the error sensitivity of the Linux kernel executing on PowerPC G4 and Pentium 4 processors. Findings from that case study indicate that the proposed approach can provide a solid basis for (i) comparing different platforms and (ii) providing feedback to system designers to help them remove dependability bottlenecks and integrate potential enhancements to improve the robustness of their systems. Major findings from the comparison of how the Linux kernel runs on two different hardware platforms are outlined below:

- While the activation[6] of errors is generally similar for both processors, the manifestation percentages for the Pentium 4 are about twice as high.
- For stack errors, there is a significant difference between the two processors in manifestation percentages (56% for P4 vs 21% for G4). A similar trend is observed in kernel data errors, where 66% (for P4) and 21% (for G4) of injected errors manifest as crashes.
- The variable-length instruction format of the P4 makes it possible for a bit error to alter a single instruction into a sequence of multiple valid (but incorrect from the application semantic point of view) instructions. On the one hand, that leads to poorer diagnosability; execution of an incorrect instruction sequence may crash the system and generate an exception, which does not isolate the cause of the problem and obstructs diagnosis. On the other hand, the same feature has the potential to reduce crash latency: executing an incorrect instruction sequence is likely to make the system fail fast.
- Less compact, fixed 32-bit data and stack access make the G4 platform less sensitive to errors. The sparseness of the data can mask errors, e.g. a larger presence of unused bits in data items means that altering any unused bit is inconsequential, even if the corrupted data are used. The more optimized access patterns on the P4 increase the chances that accessing a corrupted memory location will lead to problems.

## 7.5 Evaluation of Process Pairs in Tandem GUARDIAN

An approach for achieving high-availability computing systems, called *process pairs*, was proposed by Tandem. The proposed architecture was intended to handle permanent and transient hardware and software errors in loosely coupled redundant architectures with message-passing process communication, which is typical for a transactional system. The approach makes two important assumptions about the system: (i) hardware and software modules are designed to fail fast, i.e. to detect errors rapidly and subsequently terminate processing,

---

6 We cannot identify error activations while we are injecting errors into system registers, as we do not have the ability to monitor kernel access to these registers.

and (ii) errors can be corrected by re-executing the same software copy in the changed environment.

### 7.5.1 Data Integrity

Data integrity is preserved through the mechanisms of I/O "process pairs"; one I/O process is designated the primary, and the other is designated the backup. All file modification messages are executed by the primary I/O process. The primary sends a message with checkpoint information to the backup so that it can take over if the primary's processor or access path to the I/O device fails. Files can also be duplicated on physically distinct devices controlled by an I/O process pair on physically distinct processors. All file modification messages are delivered to both I/O processes. Thus, in the event of physical failure or isolation of the primary, the backup file is up to date and available.

### 7.5.2 User Applications

User applications can also take advantage of the process pairs approach (see Figure 7.12). The application executes as a *Primary* process, which starts a *Backup* in another processor. To ensure data integrity and enable recovery, duplicate file images (primary and backup) are created. *Primary* periodically sends checkpoint information to *Backup*. *Backup* reads checkpoint messages

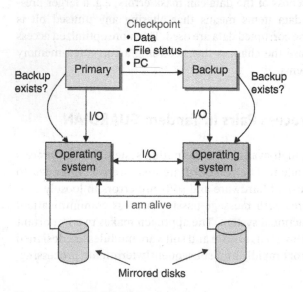

**Figure 7.12** Shadow processor in Tandem.

and updates its data, file status, and program counter. The checkpoint information is inserted in the corresponding memory locations of the *Backup* and hence (in the case of a *Primary* failure) makes it possible to recover without the need for disk accesses before resuming the processing. The *Backup* takes over if the system reports that the *Primary* is down, which would happen if the *Primary* fails to respond to an "I am alive" message. All file activities by *Primary* are performed on both the primary and backup file copies. *Primary* periodically asks the OS if a *Backup* exists. If there is no *Backup*, the *Primary* can request the creation of a copy of both the process and file structure. More information on the operating system and the programming of NonStop applications can be found in [23].

This section evaluates the software fault tolerance of process pairs in the Tandem GUARDIAN system. Two types of analyses were performed. First, we used human-generated software failure reports to investigate the level of software fault tolerance achieved using process pairs and the detailed reasons for software fault tolerance. Next, we conducted Markov reward analysis using online processor halt logs to evaluate the impact of software failures on system performance and the effectiveness of the built-in single-failure tolerance of the Tandem system against software failures.

### 7.5.3 Software Fault Tolerance of Process Pairs

It has been observed that process pairs allow the Tandem system to tolerate certain software faults [24, 25]; that is, in many processor halts caused by software faults, the backup of a failed primary can continue the execution. This observation is rather counterintuitive because the primary and backup run the same copy of the software. The phenomenon was explained by the existence of subtle faults, often referred to as *transient software faults*, which are not exercised again on a restart of the failed software. Field software faults were not identified during the testing phase, and many of them could be transient. Since the technique (i.e. the process pairs) is not explicitly intended for tolerating software faults, the study of field data is essential for understanding the phenomenon and measuring the effectiveness of the technique for tolerating software faults.

This section uses human-generated field software failure reports to investigate the user-perceived ability of the Tandem system to tolerate faults in its system software. Two conditions must be mentioned. First, only the faults in the system software that cause processor failures are considered. Thus, we are not looking at the entire set of software faults. Second, only the software fault tolerance achieved specifically by the user of process pairs is considered. The description in this section is based on [26].

The evaluation is important because, although process pairs are specific to Tandem systems, they are an implementation of the idea of checkpointing and restart, which is a general approach. This evaluation is also important because there are no efficient techniques for achieving software fault tolerance in large, continually evolving software systems. Attempts have been made to make use of the transient nature of some software faults for tolerating these faults in user applications that use checkpointing and restart [27, 28].

### 7.5.3.1 Measure of Software Fault Tolerance

The Tandem Product Report (TPR) database is a component of the Tandem Product Reporting System (PRS). TPR was used to report all problems, questions, and requests for enhancements by users or Tandem employees concerning any Tandem product. 179 TPRs were generated because of software faults during the measured period. Since each TPR reports just one problem, sometimes two TPRs are generated as a result of a multiple-processor halt. There were five such cases, meaning that the true total of software failures during the measured period was 174. Table 7.12 shows the severities of the 174 software failures. A single-processor halt implies that the built-in single-failure tolerance of the system masked the software fault that caused the halt. All multiple-processor halts were grouped because, in the Tandem system, a double-processor halt may cause additional processor halts because of the system architecture. That is, if the system loses a set of disks as a result of a double-processor halt and the set of disks contains files required by other processors, additional halts can occur in the other processors.

In this evaluation, the term *software fault tolerance* (*SFT*) refers to the system's ability to tolerate software faults. Quantitatively, it is defined as

$$SFT = \frac{\text{number of software failures in which a single processor is halted}}{\text{total number of software failures}}$$

**Table 7.12** Severity of software failures [29] / with permission of IEEE.

| Severity | # Failures |
| --- | --- |
| Single-processor halt | 138 |
| Multiple-processor halt | 31 |
| During system cold load | 1 |
| Unable to classify | 4 |
| All | 174 |

SFT represents the user-perceived ability of the system to tolerate faults in its system software through the use of process pairs.

Table 7.12 shows that process pairs provide a significant level of software fault tolerance in distributed transaction-processing environments. The measure of software fault tolerance is estimated to be 82% (138 out of 169). That measure is based on reported software failures. The issue of underreporting was discussed in [24]. The consensus among experienced Tandem engineers was that about 80% of software failures were not reported as TPRs and that most of them were single-processor halts. If that assessment is true, then the software fault tolerance may be as high as 96%.

### 7.5.3.2  Outages Due to Software

Our evaluation first focused on the multiple-processor halts. We investigated the first two processor halts for each multiple-processor halt to determine whether the second halt occurred on the processor executing the backup of the failed primary process. In those cases, we also investigated whether the two processors halted because of the same software fault. Table 7.13 shows that in 86% (24 out of 28, excluding "Unable to classify" cases) of the multiple-processor halts, the backup of the failed primary process was unable to continue the execution. In 81% (17 out of 21, excluding "Unable to classify" cases) of those halts, the backup failed because of the same fault that caused the failure of the primary. In the remaining 19% of the halts, the processor executing the backup of the failed

**Table 7.13**  Reasons for multiple-processor halts [29] / with permission of IEEE.

| Reasons for multiple-processor halts | # Failures |
| --- | --- |
| The second halt occurs on the processor executing the backup of the failed primary | 24 |
| –The second halt occurs due to the same fault that halted the primary | (17) |
| –The second halt occurs due to another fault during job takeover | (4) |
| –Unable to classify | (3) |
| The second halt is not related to process pairs | 4 |
| –The system hangs | (1) |
| –Faulty parallel software executes | (1) |
| –There is a random coincidence of two independent faults | (1) |
| –A single processor halt occurs, but system coldload is necessary for recovery | (1) |
| Unable to classify | 3 |
| All | 31 |

primary halted because of another fault during the job takeover. The level of software fault tolerance achieved with process pairs is high but not perfect. A single fault in the system software can manifest itself as a multiple-processor halt, which the system is not designed to tolerate. About half of the multiple-processor halts resulted in system cold loads. The data showed that, in most situations, the system lost a set of disks that contained files required by other processors as a result of the first two processor halts, and other processors also halted. That result shows the major failure mode of the system because of software.

### 7.5.3.3 Characterization of Software Fault Tolerance

The information in Table 7.12 poses the question of why the Tandem system loses only one processor in 82% of software failures and, as a result, tolerates the software faults that cause these failures. We identified the reasons for successful software fault tolerance in all single-processor halts and classified them into several groups. Table 7.14 shows that in 29% of single-processor halts, the fault that caused a failure of a primary process was not exercised again when the backup re-executed the same task after a takeover. Such situations occur because some software faults are exposed in a specific memory state (e.g. running out of buffer), on the occurrence of a single event or a sequence of asynchronous events during a vulnerable time window (timing), by race conditions or concurrent operations among multiple processes, or on the occurrence of a hardware error.

**Table 7.14** Reasons for software fault tolerance [29] / with permission of IEEE.

| Reasons for software fault tolerance | Fraction (%) |
| --- | --- |
| The backup re-executes the failed task after takeover, but the fault that caused a failure of the primary is not exercised by the backup | 29 |
| –Memory state | (4) |
| –Timing | (7) |
| –Race or concurrency | (6) |
| –Hardware error | (4) |
| –Others | (7) |
| The backup, after takeover, does not automatically re-execute the failed task | 20 |
| It is the effect of error latency | 5 |
| A fault stops a processor running a backup | 16 |
| The cause of a problem is unidentified | 19 |
| Unable to classify | 12 |

Figure 7.13 shows a real example of a fault that is exercised in a specific memory state. The primary of an I/O process pair, represented by "SIOP(P)" in the figure, requested a buffer to serve a user request. Because of high activity in the processor executing the primary, the buffer was not available. However, the buffer management routine returned a "successful" flag because of a software fault instead of an "unsuccessful" flag. The primary used the returned, uninitialized buffer pointer, and a halt occurred in the processor running the primary because of an illegal address reference by a privileged process. Clearly, such a situation was not tested during the development phase. Since a memory dump is taken only from a halted processor in a production system, a memory dump of the processor running the backup is not available. Our best guess is that the backup process served the request again after takeover but did not have a problem because a buffer was available on the processor running the backup.

Table 7.14 also shows that in 20% of single-processor halts, the backup of a failed primary process does not serve the failed request after a successful takeover. The reason is that some faults are exposed while serving requests that are important but are not automatically resubmitted to the backup upon a failure of the primary. Figure 7.14 illustrates an example of such situations. In the figure, process "PK" is an execution of a tool to check and change a processor configuration, such as the number of active processes and I/O lines. Process PK does not run as a process pair because if the processor being monitored or reconfigured halts while executing PK, there is no need to monitor or reconfigure the halted

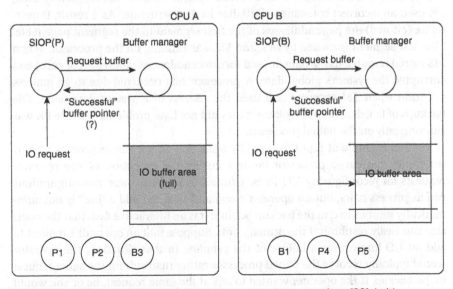

**Figure 7.13** Differences between the primary and backup executions [29] / with permission of IEEE.

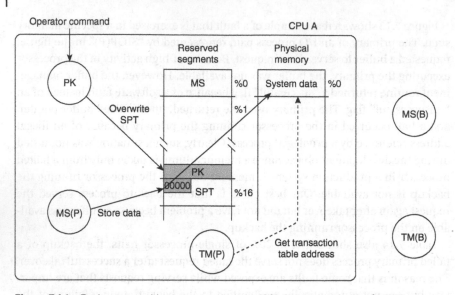

**Figure 7.14** Faults exposed by non-process pairs [29] / with permission of IEEE.

processor any longer. Process MS collects resource usage data, and process TM is in charge of concurrency control and failure recovery. Both MS and TM run as process pairs.

When the operator ran PK with a certain option, which is not frequently used, PK used an incorrect constant to initialize its data structure. As a result, it overwrote (cleared) the page addresses of the first segment in the segment page table. The first segment is owned by MS, and MS was running on the processor. When MS stored resource usage data, it used incorrect addresses (addresses of zero) and corrupted the system's global data. A processor halt occurred due to an address violation when TM accessed and used the address of a system data table. The backups of failed primaries took over; they did not have problems because PK was running only on the halted processor.

Another example of faults exposed by tasks that do not run as process pairs is the faults that cause processor failures during the execution of the operator requests for reconfiguring I/O lines. Utilities to perform these reconfigurations run as process pairs, but an operator command such as "add a line" is not automatically resubmitted to the backup because it is an interactive task that the operator can easily resubmit if the primary fails. Suppose that an operator's request to add an I/O line causes a failure of the primary. In that situation, the operator would typically recover the halted processor rather than submit the same request to the backup. If the operator wanted to repeat the same request, he or she would normally repeat it on the primary after the halted processor had been reloaded. If the operator submitted the request to the backup instantly upon a failure of the primary, one of two situations can be expected: the backup would also halt, or the backup would serve the request without any problem for the reasons discussed in Table 7.14.

In the above examples, the task (i.e. process PK or a command to add an I/O line) does not survive the failure. But process pairs allow the other applications on the halted processor to continue to run. That approach is not, strictly speaking, software fault tolerance but a side benefit of using process pairs. If these failures are excluded, the estimated measure of software fault tolerance is reduced to 78%.

Table 7.14 also shows that 19% (31 out of 169) of single-processor halts are failures of backup processes. That indicates that the software fault tolerance does not come without cost; the added complexity due to the implementation of process pairs introduces additional software faults into the system software. The estimated measure of software fault tolerance (77%) is adjusted again to 72% when those failures are excluded. All unidentified failures were single-processor halts, which is understandable because single-processor faults are caused by subtle faults that are very difficult to observe and diagnose. The reason that an unidentified problem caused a single-processor halt is unknown. Based on their symptoms, we speculate that a significant number of unidentified problems were single-processor halts because of the effect of error latency.

### 7.5.4 Discussion

The results in this section have several implications. First, subtle faults exist in all software, but software fault tolerance is not achieved if the backup execution is a replication of the original execution (i.e. the same sequence of events in the same processor state). The results show that the source of software fault tolerance lies in differences between the original and backup executions in the processing environment (i.e. the processor state and the sequence of events). The loose coupling between processors in the measured system causes those differences. This result confirms that there is another dimension to achieving software fault tolerance in distributed environments. The actual level of software fault tolerance achieved by the user of process pairs will depend on the degree of difference between the original and backup executions in the processing environment. Each processor in a Tandem system has an independent processing environment; therefore, the system naturally provides such differences. (The advantages of using checkpointing, as compared with lock-step operation, in tolerating software faults are discussed in [25].) It's likely that another reason why we observed a high level of software fault tolerance is that the operating system we were measuring is a mature software system whose faults are mostly subtle.

Second, the results indicate that process pairs can also allow the system to tolerate nontransient software faults because software failures can occur while the system is executing important tasks that are not automatically resubmitted to the backup on a failure of the primary. If that happens, the failed task does not survive, but process pairs allow the other applications on the failed processor to survive.

Third, short error latency with error confinement within a transaction is desirable [30]. In actual designs, such a strict error confinement might be rather difficult to achieve. In Tandem systems, the unit of error confinement is a processor, not a transaction [25]. Errors generated during the execution of a transaction may be detected during the execution of another transaction. Interestingly, long error latency and error propagation across transactions sometimes help the system tolerate software faults. This result should not be interpreted to suggest that long error latency or error propagation across transactions is a desirable characteristic but instead as a side effect of the system having subtle software faults. Long error latency and error propagation across transactions can make both online recovery and offline diagnosis difficult.

Finally, an interesting question is, if process pairs are good, are process triples better? Our results show that process triples may not necessarily be better because the faults that cause double-processor halts with process pairs may cause triple-processor halts with process triples.

### 7.5.5  First Occurrences Versus Recurrences

Table 7.15 uses the 174 software failures to compare the severity of the three types of software failures. There were two special cases ("Others" in the table): a multiple-processor halt that occurred because of a parallel execution of faulty code (a system cold load was not required) and a software failure that occurred in the middle of a system cold load. With only a single observation in each case, the significance of these situations is unclear, and they were not considered in the subsequent analysis.

Table 7.15 indicates that a recurrence is slightly less likely to cause a double-processor halt than is a first occurrence. We used the binomial test to test that observation because binomial tests can construct a confidence interval without requiring any assumption about the underlying distribution [31]. Each failure was treated as a random trial, and the probability of a double-processor halt was 0.23 (9 out of 39, following the statistics for the first occurrence). By calculating the probability that there will be 19 or fewer double-processor halts out of 103 trials, we tested the hypothesis that the probability that a recurrence will cause a double-processor halt is equal to the probability that a first occurrence will cause a double-processor halt. The $p$-value was 0.16; that is the hypothesis was rejected at the 20%

**Table 7.15** Severity of software failures by failure type [29] / with permission of IEEE.

| Failure type | # Failure instances | # Double CPU halts | # System cold loads | Severity unclear | # Others |
| --- | --- | --- | --- | --- | --- |
| First occurrence | 41 | 9 | 6 | 1 | 1 |
| Recurrence | 107 | 19 | 12 | 3 | 1 |
| Unidentified | 26 | 0 | 0 | 0 | 0 |

significance level. Although the trend was not strong, a recurrence is less likely than a first occurrence to cause a double-processor halt. The reason is probably that a fault that is likely to cause a double-processor halt (a possible outage in Tandem systems) gets attention, and a fix is likely to have been propagated and installed promptly. The fault is thus less likely to recur over the long run. Table 7.15 also indicates that a recurrence is less likely than a first occurrence to cause a system cold load. The *p*-value was 0.18 in this case.

Two of the six system cold loads due to first occurrences were single-processor halt situations (Table 7.13). Those two failures captured the secondary failure mode of the system because of software that causes the system to be cold-loaded to recover from a severe single-processor halt.

### 7.5.6 Impact of Software Failures on Performance

One key measure in evaluating gracefully degraded systems is the impact of failures on system performance or service capacity. Performability models [32] and reward models [33] have been widely used to evaluate performance-related dependability measures. To evaluate the loss of service incurred by software failures and the effectiveness of the Tandem system's built-in single-failure tolerance of software failures, we performed a Markov reward analysis [34, 35]. The processor halt log collected from a 16-processor in-house Tandem Cyclone system was used. The measurement period was 23 months.

We built a continuous-time Markov model using the processor halt log. Figure 7.15 shows the model structure. In the figure, $S_i$ represents the system state in which there are $i$ failed processors because of software faults, and $n$ represents the total number of processors in the system. In the model, transition rates between states were estimated using two reward functions defined in the analysis. The first function (NSFT) assumes no fault tolerance. In it, each processor halt causes degradation, and the loss of service is proportional to the total number of processors halted. The second function (SFT) reflects the fault tolerance of the Tandem system. In it, the first processor halt causes no degradation. For additional processor

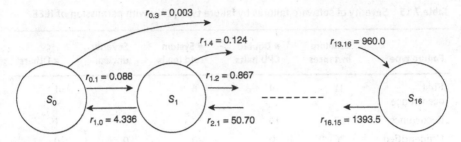

**Figure 7.15** Measurement-based Markov model.

halts, the loss of service is proportional to the number of processors halted. The difference between the two functions allows us to evaluate the improvement in service achieved by providing the built-in single-failure tolerance.

$$r_{ij} = \frac{\text{total number of transitions from } S_i \text{ to } S_j}{\text{cumulative time the system was in } S_i}$$

NSFT (No Single-Failure Tolerance):

$$r_i = 1 - \frac{i}{n} \quad \text{if } 0 \le i \le n$$

SFT (single-failure tolerance):

$$r_i = \begin{cases} 1 & \text{if } i = 0 \\ 1 - \dfrac{i-1}{n} & \text{if } 0 < i < n \\ 0 & \text{if } i = n \end{cases}$$

Given the Markov reward model described above, the expected steady-state reward rate, $Y$, can be estimated as described in [33].

$$Y = \sum_i p_i r_i,$$

where $p_i$ is the steady-state probability that the system is in state $i$. The steady-state reward rate represents the relative amount of useful service the system can provide per unit of time in the long run; it is a measure of service-capacity-oriented software availability. The steady-state *reward-loss rate* (or simply *reward loss*), $1 - Y$, represents the relative amount of useful service lost per unit of time because

**Table 7.16** Estimated loss of service.

| Measure | | Software | Non-software | All |
|---------|-----|----------|--------------|-----|
| NSFT | $1 - Y$ | 0.00062 | 0.00205 | 0.00267 |
| | Percent | 23.2 | 76.8 | 100 |
| SFT | $1 - Y$ | 0.00007 | 0.00016 | 0.00023 |
| | Percent | 30.4 | 69.6 | 100 |
| Improvement | | 89% | 92% | 91% |

of software failures. If we consider a specific group of failures in the analysis, the reward loss quantifies the service loss incurred by this group of failures.

The results of analysis are given in Table 7.16. The table shows the estimated reward losses incurred by software and non-software failures with SFT and NSFT. The bottom row of the table shows the improvement in service time (i.e. decrease in reward loss) achieved by providing fault tolerance. The single-failure tolerance of the measured system reduces the service loss incurred by software failures by 89%, which clearly demonstrates the effectiveness of the single-failure tolerance of the measured system against software faults and corroborates the results obtained in the previous section. The table also shows that the single-failure tolerance reduces the service loss incurred by non-software failures by 92%. That clearly demonstrates the effectiveness of the implemented fault tolerance mechanisms against non-software failures, as well as software failures. Software problems accounted for 30% of the service loss in the measured system (with SFT). Although the system was working in a high-stress environment, the overall reward loss was small ($10^{-4}$ with SFT). That reflects the high availability of the measured system.

A census of Tandem system availability [24] has shown that after the reliability of its hardware and maintenance was significantly improved, software emerged as the major source (62%) of outages in the Tandem system. However, it would be inappropriate to compare our number (30%) directly with Gray's (i.e. 62%) because Gray's is an aggregate of many systems, and ours is a measurement of a single system. Besides, the sources of the data and analysis procedures are different. The analysis performed in this section is based on automatically generated event logs. Some non-software problems requiring the replacement of faulty hardware can result in long recovery times and, therefore, great reward loss. Also, because of the experimental nature of the measured system, non-software problems caused by operational or environmental faults may have been exaggerated. An operational or environmental fault can potentially affect all processors in the system.

### 7.5.7 Summary

This section evaluated the software fault tolerance of process pairs in the Tandem GUARDIAN system by using human-generated software failure reports and online processor halt logs automatically generated by the operating system. The results of an evaluation using software failure reports showed that hardware fault tolerance is essential to achieve software fault tolerance: process pairs in Tandem systems tolerate about 70% of reported field faults in the system software that cause processor failures. That result shows that in a distributed transaction-processing environment, a significant level of software fault tolerance can be achieved by using checkpointing and restart, a technique for tolerating hardware faults. The loose coupling between processors, which results in a backup execution that is different (in terms of the processor state and the sequence of events) from the original execution, is a major reason for the measured software fault tolerance.

The results indicate that the actual level of software fault tolerance achieved by using checkpointing and restart depends (i) on the degree of difference between the processing environments of the original execution and the restart, and (ii) on the proportion of subtle faults in software. While process pairs may not provide perfect software fault tolerance, it is not as prohibitively expensive to implement them as it would be to develop and maintain multiple versions of large software programs.

The results of Markov reward analysis using processor halt logs showed that the single-failure tolerance of the measured system reduces the service loss incurred by software failures by 89%. That result corroborates the results obtained using software failure reports. The results also show that single-failure tolerance reduces the service loss incurred by non-software failures by 92% and that software failures account for 30% of the service loss in the measured system (with SFT).

## 7.6 Benchmarking Multiple Operating Systems: A Case Study Using Linux on Pentium, Solaris on SPARC, and AIX on POWER

This section presents an approach to conducting experimental studies for the characterization and comparison of error behavior in various computing systems. We apply the proposed approach to characterize and compare the error behavior of three commercial systems (Linux 2.6 on Pentium 4, Solaris 10 on UltraSPARC IIIi, and AIX 5.3 on POWER5) under hardware transient faults. We obtained the data by conducting extensive fault injection into kernel code, kernel stack, and system registers with the NFTAPE framework while running the Apache Web

Server as a workload. The error behavior comparison shows that the Linux system has the highest average crash latency, the Solaris system has the highest hang rate, and the AIX system has the lowest error sensitivity and the smallest number of crashes in the more severe categories. The descriptions in this section are based on material presented in [36].

### 7.6.1 Introduction of Case Study

One of the difficulties in establishing a dependability benchmark is defining and collecting a set of measures through a well-defined and easily repeatable procedure that can be used to compare the error behaviors of diverse computing systems, i.e. different combinations of operating systems (OS) and underlying hardware. In addressing this challenge, this section presents an approach to conducting experimental studies for characterizing and comparing the error behavior of different computing systems and describes a demonstration of its use on three commercial systems. The proposed approach defines (i) methods for stressing the system, i.e. for injecting runtime errors; (ii) procedures for obtaining measurements; (iii) metrics for quantifying the dependability attributes of the system; and (iv) tools for setting up and carrying out the experiments, collecting and analyzing the measurement data, and calculating the dependability metrics. In particular, this case study made the following contributions:

- An error behavior comparison of three computing systems, each with a different OS and hardware. This addresses some of the challenges in establishing a benchmark, such as the development of an easy portable toolset and the collection of comparable data on various systems. Previous dependability studies involving the comparison of multiple systems were all in the area of robustness testing with respect to faults induced by applications to the OS through system-call API injection [12, 37]. Past studies on the impact of transient faults focused mostly on a single OS and a single hardware platform [13, 38], except [16], which compared the error behavior of Linux on a Pentium and a PowerPC. In this section, we compare three operating systems on three different hardware platforms.
- Introduction of a set of common generalized crash cause categories (i.e. underlying reasons for kernel crashes) and mapping of the crash cause categories specific to each target system onto the common categories. This enables us to compare the crash cause data collected from the three systems.
- Establishment and demonstration of an evaluation procedure (based on the NFTAPE framework [17]). This provides a common injection environment for conducting fault injection experiments on all three systems and quantifying the dependability metrics: error sensitivity, failure severity, and error detection latency.

In this section, *Software-Implemented Fault Injection* is employed to experimentally assess and compare the error behavior of three computing systems: (i) SUSE Linux 9 on the Intel Pentium 4 processor; (ii) Solaris 10 on the Sun UltraSPARC IIIi processor; and (iii) AIX 5.3 on the IBM POWER5 processor. We refer to these three combinations of a particular OS and underlying hardware as the *Linux system*, the *Solaris system*, and the *AIX system*, respectively. We deployed the same fault injection procedure using the NFTAPE framework on all three platforms. Single-bit faults were injected to emulate hardware-transient faults that affected the OS code segment, the OS-level stack segment, and system registers within the microprocessor. (We define *system registers* as registers that are accessible only by the privileged kernel, e.g. the machine state register.) The Apache Web Server was used as a common workload on the target platforms to create sufficient kernel activity for activating the injected faults. We considered transient faults because earlier studies showed that soft errors had emerged as key challenges in designing reliable computing systems (e.g. [39, 40]).

The NFTAPE framework logs injection and crash data, which we used to obtain the following measures: *error sensitivity*, characterized by error manifestation rates; *failure severity*, characterized by distribution of injection outcomes between failures of different levels of severity, including crashes, hangs, and application detect/fail-silence violations (AD/FSV); and *error detection latency*, defined as the time between a fault's activation (i.e. when the corrupted instruction/data is executed/accessed) and error detection by the kernel (e.g. kernel-raised exceptions). The error behavior comparison shows that the Linux system has the highest average crash latency (~50k–500k instructions), the Solaris system has the highest hang rate (~3–7 times more likely), and the AIX system has the lowest error sensitivity and the smallest number of crashes in the more severe categories.

## 7.6.2 Experimental Setup

We deployed NFTAPE, a software-implemented fault injection framework, on all three systems to conduct injection experiments and collect data.

### 7.6.2.1 Fault Model

The fault model considered in this study uses device-level transient faults that can originate anywhere in the system: in the processor, memory, bus, network, or disk. The assumption is that faults, regardless of their origin, eventually manifest in the memory or system registers. Rimén et al. [19] have shown that most device-level transient faults (98–99%) can be emulated with software-implemented fault injection that uses bit-flips. In our study, single-bit faults were injected into the code segment of kernel functions, the process kernel stack area, and system registers. Although multiple-bit injection is also supported by NFTAPE, we only considered transient faults that resulted from a single bit-flip in this study.

#### 7.6.2.2 Target Systems

Table 7.17 outlines the hardware and software configuration of each target system. The current implementation of NFTAPE does not fully support multiprocessor or multicore architectures; thus, we configured each system to run on a single processor.

#### 7.6.2.3 Experimental Environment

Figure 7.16 summarizes an instance of the experimental setup that we used in conducting automated fault injection experiments for each computing system. Each setup consisted of two machines: (i) a *target machine*, one of the three systems under study, and (ii) a *control host machine*, a dedicated machine that ran the NFTAPE Control Host software. Two primary components of the NFTAPE framework, *Control Host* and *Process Manager* resided on the control host machine and the target machine, respectively. The Control Host monitored and orchestrated the injection experiment by communicating with the Process Manager through the network. The Process Manager executed commands on the target machine on

**Table 7.17** Target systems [36] / with permission of IEEE.

| | Hardware | | System software | | |
|---|---|---|---|---|---|
| **Processor** | **CPU (GHz)** | **Memory (MB)** | **Distribution** | **Kernel** | **Compiler** |
| Pentium 4 | 3.00 | 1024 | SUSE 9 | 2.6.5–7.97 | gcc-3.3.3 |
| UltraSPARC IIIi | 1.36 | 2048 | Solaris 10 | 5.10 | gcc-3.4.3 |
| POWER 5 | 1.65 | 2048 | AIX 5.3 | TL 05 | XL C V8 |

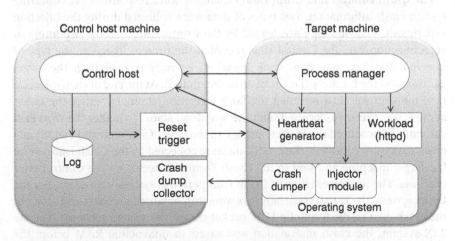

**Figure 7.16** Experimental setup [36] / with permission of IEEE.

behalf of the Control Host, invoking the necessary software processes to conduct and control the fault injection campaigns.

The *Workload* process helped (i) to identify comparable kernel functions from the three target systems and (ii) to generate sufficient kernel activity to activate an injected fault. Because of the size of the kernel, it would be impractical to target every kernel function for fault injection when evaluating the code segment of kernel functions. Depending on the workload, different kernel functions are activated with different frequencies. By profiling each OS kernel with the same workload, we obtain the relative execution frequency of kernel functions for each system. (We used the utility tools OProfile, tprof, and er_kernel to profile Linux, AIX, and Solaris, respectively.) Since the three operating systems are POSIX-compliant, the workload invoked similar kernel services on all three systems, and the profiling results identified the kernel functions that implement these services. Targeting of those functions enabled us to compare the error behaviors of the three systems.

The *Injector Module* enabled fault injection into different parts of the host OS. It was implemented as a kernel module and, as such, had the privilege to access kernel memory and system registers. The implementation of this module was OS- and platform-dependent.

A *Heartbeat Generator* was instantiated on the target machine to indicate liveness to the Control Host to enable detection of a target system crash or hang. When a crash happened, the target system rebooted itself by default. When there was a system hang, the Control Host detected it through the absence of heartbeat messages or progress indications from the process manager for a predetermined timeout period. When a hang was detected, the Control Host triggered a reset sequence to reboot the target machine.

The *Crash Dumper* and *Crash Dump Collector* were responsible for collecting system crash information. Two types of data were collected during the injection experiment. The first type was logged by the Control Host. At the beginning of each injection run, the Control Host recorded the time of injection, the type of injection (i.e. text injection, stack injection, or register injection), the target address, and the bit-mask (i.e. the bit to be corrupted). At the end of each injection run, the Control Host recorded the fault activation status (whether the target address was executed/accessed) and the workload status (whether the workload still ran and produced the correct output). In the case of a kernel crash, additional crash data were collected. The crash data were collected by the Crash Dumper on the target machine and sent to the Crash Dump Collector on the Control Host machine. The implementation of Crash Dumpers was system-dependent. For the Linux system, the kernel crash handlers were implemented to collect and send out the crash data in the form of a UDP packet before the system rebooted. For the AIX system, the crash information was saved to nonvolatile RAM before the system rebooted. After the reboot, the stored data were retrieved and sent to the Crash Dump Collector. The Solaris system worked much like the AIX system, except that instead of saving to nonvolatile RAM, Solaris saved the crash information to a dump device (i.e. a dedicated swap memory).

### 7.6.3 Evaluation Procedure

The procedure for characterizing the error behavior of the target systems involved the following steps: (i) the generation of injection targets, (ii) the execution of fault injection campaigns, and (iii) the collection and analysis of data. Each step is described in detail below. The Apache Web Server was selected as the common workload to create system activity sufficient to activate the injected faults.

#### 7.6.3.1 Generation of Injection Targets

*Kernel Text Injection:* To compare the target systems fairly, we conducted the fault injection experiments on sets of kernel functions from each system that provided similar services. We identified the kernel functions by profiling each kernel while running the selected workload (the Apache Web Server). The most frequently used kernel functions in each system were selected as the injection targets. Because of the way injection targets were selected, the results obtained from the experiments are representative of the systems' behavior under the selected workload.

*Kernel Stack Injection:* Since stack was dynamically allocated, it would not have been possible to generate a list of injection targets beforehand. Instead, we located the kernel stack region of the workload process at runtime and selected a random address in that region as the target.

*System Register Injection:* Because all the system registers for each system were known from the design specifications, we generated a random list of system registers as targets.

#### 7.6.3.2 Execution of Fault Injection Campaigns

We used the NFTAPE framework to inject single-bit faults into the kernel text, kernel stack, and system registers in an automated fashion. We use the term *injection campaign* for a set of injection runs. An *injection run* is the injection of a single fault when the workload is being executed. Each injection run consisted of three steps: (i) invoking the injector, (ii) starting the workload, and (iii) verifying the result.

When the injector was invoked (in the case of kernel text and kernel stack injections), a breakpoint was set at the target address. The processor debug registers were used to enable the setting of the breakpoint and the triggering of the fault injection when the program arrived at the breakpoint. After the breakpoint was set, the workload was started. The program was allotted a 30-second observation window, started when the injector was invoked, within which to reach the breakpoint.[7] When the breakpoint was reached, a fault was injected at the target address (for text and stack injections), and the injection run was marked as *activated* since the corrupted instruction/data would be immediately used. If the target address was not reached within the observation window, the injection run was marked as *not activated*. For each activated fault, regardless of whether the error caused a system failure, we rebooted the machine before the next run to ensure the independence of each run. No breakpoint mechanism was available for triggering the injections to system registers, so the register content was corrupted immediately upon the injector invocation.

### 7.6.3.3 Collection and Analysis of Data

Each fault injection run with an activated fault fell into one of the following outcome categories: *not manifested, crash, hang,* or *application detection/fail-silence violation*. If the fault injection outcome was a crash, then the information on *crash latency* and *crash cause* was also collected. Definitions of the terms are given below:

- *Not Manifested (NMF)*: The injected fault does not cause any observable effect on the OS or the workload within the observation window. In this case, the error can be (1) *benign*, meaning the error never manifests (e.g. the corrupted bit is not used in the instruction set architecture), or (2) *latent*, meaning it can manifest sometime later if we wait long enough.
- *Crash*: The kernel raises an exception and reboots itself (e.g. the operating system detects an illegal instruction and panics).
- *Hang*: The system becomes totally or partially unresponsive (e.g. a deadlock or an infinite loop).
- *Application Detection/Fail-Silence Violation (AD/FSV)*: Two cases are possible: either (i) the kernel detects the error and returns an error code, or (ii) the kernel does not detect the error, but the error affects the application, causing an incorrect output to be produced or an invalid action to be taken. We classify case 1 as an *application detection* since this error is visible and detected by the application. We classify case 2 as a *fail-silence violation (FSV)* or *silent data corruption* since incorrect information propagates from the kernel to the user and affects the process-produced output. The two cases are put into a single outcome category because we cannot always distinguish them. FSVs are detected by running a verifier to check the workload output. However, the coverage of this detection

---

7 We conducted a set of experiments to establish the length of the observation window. The measurements indicated that most injected faults activate within ~10–15 seconds of the injection. Increasing the observation time beyond 30 seconds does not increase the manifestation rate.

mechanism is limited because the FSV may affect only the outputs of processes other than the workload.

- *Crash Latency*: Crash latency is measured in terms of the number of instructions executed between the time a fault is activated and the time the error is detected by the system. A performance counter is used to count the instructions.
- *Crash Cause*: The crash cause indicates why the kernel crashed, e.g. an illegal instruction or stack overflow. Unfortunately, each system reports crash causes at different granularity levels and using different categories. To enable comparison of the target systems, we analyzed the existing crash cause categories and introduced a set of common generalized crash cause categories that apply across the three systems. Table 7.18 gives the definitions of the new categories, and Table 7.19 shows the mapping from the crash categories observed in the experiments to the new crash cause categories. There were situations in which crash information was not collected, for example when the kernel crashed in such a way that it did not generate a crash dump, or the crash dumper was unable to collect crash information. We categorize these crashes as *unknown* in Table 7.18.

### 7.6.4 Results

Over 27 000 injections were attempted. Table 7.20 summarizes the results of the injection experiments conducted on all three systems and shows (i) the number of injections attempted, (ii) the fault activation rate as a percentage of attempted injections, and (iii) the distribution of activated errors across the defined outcome

**Table 7.18** New crash cause categories [36] / with permission of IEEE.

| Crash cause categories | Definition |
| --- | --- |
| Illegal instruction | The CPU attempts to execute an instruction with invalid opcode or operand |
| Instr. access exception | Any exception that occurs during an instruction memory access |
| Data access exception | Any exception that occurs during a data memory access. |
| Assertion | Any crash due to a failed assertion embedded in the kernel |
| Others | Other categories including architecture or OS-specific exceptions |
| Unknown | Crash cases with no crash information |

**Table 7.19** Crash cause mapping [36] / with permission of IEEE.

| Crash cause categories | Linux system | Solaris system | AIX system |
|---|---|---|---|
| Illegal instr. | Invalid opcode | Illegal instr. fault | Invalid operation |
| Instr. access exception | | Instr. access exception<br>Instr. access MMU miss | Instr. storage |
| Data accessexception | General protection<br>Seg. not present<br>Stack segment | Data access exception<br>Data access MMU miss<br>Data access protection<br>Bad kernel MMU trap<br>NULL pointer<br>Alignment error<br>Bad stack overflow | Data storage |
| Assertion | Invalid operand | Assertion | Illegal trap instruction |
| Others | Int3, overflow<br>Co-proc. seg. overrun<br>Divide error | Bad unknown trap<br>Bad reg windowtrap | Unknown interrupt |

**Table 7.20** Injection outcome summary [36] / with permission of IEEE.

| Type | System | Injection attempt | Fault activated | Activated | | | | |
|---|---|---|---|---|---|---|---|---|
| | | | | Crash | Hang | AD/FSV | C/H | NMF |
| Text | Linux | 3792 | 46% | 61% | 5% | 1% | 0% | 32% |
| | Solaris | 6710 | 13% | 49% | 14% | 0% | 0% | 37% |
| | AIX | 3545 | 44% | 56% | 2% | 0% | 0% | 41% |
| Stack | Linux | 2530 | 48% | 26% | 0% | 0% | 2% | 72% |
| | Solaris | 3026 | 29% | 22% | 4% | 0% | 6% | 69% |
| | AIX | 3588 | 22% | 13% | 1% | 0% | 0% | 86% |
| Reg | Linux | 1221 | N/A | 25% | 0% | 0% | 0% | N/A |
| | Solaris | 1650 | N/A | 6% | 1% | 0% | 0% | N/A |
| | AIX | 1004 | N/A | 13% | 0% | 0% | 0% | N/A |

categories (crash, hang, AD/FSV, C/H, and NMF). The C/H (crash or hang) outcome category corresponds to the cases in which an error caused either a system crash or hang but based on the data logged from the experiments, we were unable to determine which.

Detailed data on the crash latency and the distribution of crash causes are shown in Figures 7.17–7.19 for text injections and Figures 7.20–7.22 for stack injections. In those figures, the x-axis represents the crash latency in terms of the number of executed instructions. The y-axis gives the crash cause categories. The z-axis is the percentage of crashes that fall into each *crash cause + crash latency*

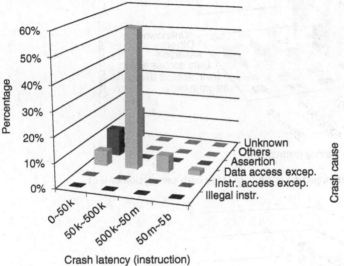

**Figure 7.17** Linux text injection crash data [36] / with permission of IEEE.

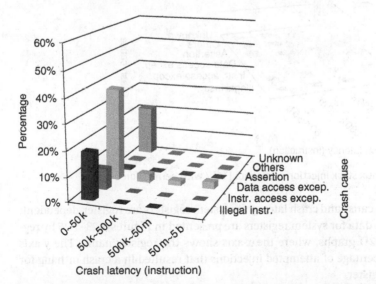

**Figure 7.18** Solaris text injection crash data [36] / with permission of IEEE.

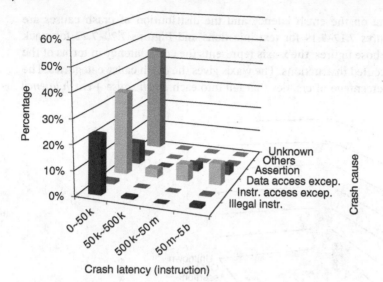

**Figure 7.19** AIX text injection crash data [36] / with permission of IEEE.

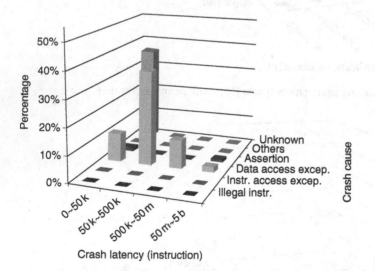

**Figure 7.20** Linux stack injection crash data [36] / with permission of IEEE.

pair. The crash cause and crash latency for system registers are register-dependent; thus, the crash data for system registers are presented in Figures 7.23–7.25 by register name as 2D graphs, where the *x*-axis shows the register name. The y-axis shows the percentage of attempted injections that resulted in a crash or hang for a particular register.

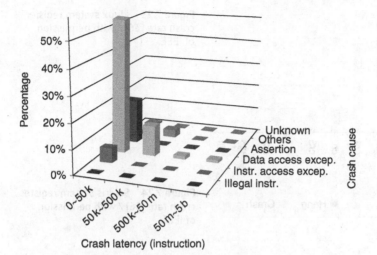

**Figure 7.21** Solaris stack injection crash data [36] / with permission of IEEE.

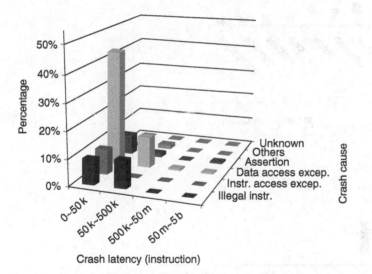

**Figure 7.22** AIX stack injection crash data [36] / with permission of IEEE.

*Fault Activation Rate.* As shown in Table 7.20, the fault activation rate for Solaris is much lower than for the other two systems. To obtain enough data points (i.e. activated errors), we attempted twice as many injections for the Solaris system. Because we injected into every instruction of the selected kernel functions, the low activation rate meant that a lower percentage of injected functions was actually executed in each execution run. By inspecting the kernel functions of each

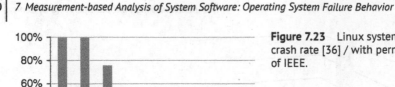

**Figure 7.23** Linux system register crash rate [36] / with permission of IEEE.

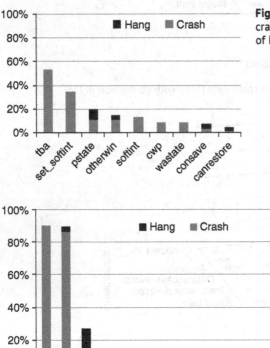

**Figure 7.24** Solaris system register crash rate [36] / with permission of IEEE.

**Figure 7.25** AIX system register crash rate [36] / with permission of IEEE.

injected function, we found that the selected Solaris kernel functions generally had more lines of code (300–1000 assembly instructions) and hence that those functions would be more likely to have some execution paths that were never executed while our workload was running. Linux kernel functions are relatively small (20–200 assembly instructions) and hence have a smaller number of potential execution paths and a higher fault activation rate.

*System Hangs.* The Solaris system had the highest hang rate among the three systems (see Table 7.20). System hangs are usually due to an infinite loop in the kernel or the infinite waiting of a kernel thread on an event that never occurs (i.e. deadlock).

### 7.6.4.1 Comparison of Target Platforms' Error Behavior

Here, we use the data obtained from the experiments to characterize error sensitivity, failure severity, and error detection latency.

*Error Sensitivity.* Error sensitivity is the probability that an activated fault in a system will lead to system/application failure. Assuming that the observation window is long enough that all latent errors manifest within the window period, the error manifestation rate characterizes error sensitivity and is computed as follows:

$$\text{Error manifestation rate} = 1 - \text{not manifested rate } (\text{NMF}).$$

All three systems have similar error sensitivities, with AIX being the least sensitive. In the AIX system, between 59 and 68% of the activated faults caused failures in text injection, and 14–28% of the activated faults caused failures in stack injection. Consequently, with respect to error sensitivity, the AIX system might be preferred over the other two systems when one is running the Apache Web Server workload.

*Failure Severity:* Failure severity is characterized by the distribution of the fault injection outcomes among the outcome categories (crash, hang, and AD/FSV). We consider:

1) *AD* and *crash* to be *less severe* because, in both cases, the kernel detects the error. In the former case, the kernel can recover or continue in a degraded mode. In the latter case, the kernel is unable to recover and panics to prevent error propagation.

2) *FSV* and *hang* to be *more severe* because in both cases, the kernel does not detect the error, and therefore it is more likely that the error will propagate. While a hang can be detected with an additional detection mechanism (e.g. an external heartbeat), the detection latency can be significant. FSV is the most severe error type and usually causes the application to produce incorrect data or take invalid actions. Detection of an FSV is difficult and relies solely on application-level mechanisms. Table 7.20 shows that the Solaris system has a much higher hang rate than the other two systems. The hang rates for the Solaris system are 14, 4, and 1% for text, stack, and register injections, respectively, whereas the Linux and AIX systems have hang rates of less than 5, 1,

and 1% for text, stack, and register injections, respectively. Table 7.20 also shows that only a few cases of AD/FSV were observed in our text injection experiments (1% for the Linux system and less than 1% for the AIX and Solaris systems). Since detecting and recovering from a hang or FSV is usually time-consuming and can result in more significant system downtime, the platform with the lower level of hangs or FSVs should be preferred. Consequently, our results indicate that AIX is the preferred computing platform overall when running the particular workload.

*Error Detection Latency.* Error detection latency indicates how fast errors are detected, and the longer the crash latency, the higher the error propagation probability. It is shown in Figures 7.17–7.22 that for the majority of crashes in the Linux system, the crash latency is between 50k and 500k instructions, whereas the figures for the AIX and Solaris systems are between 0 and 50k instructions. That is consistent with the results from a previous study [16], which shows that Linux on a PowerPC processor has a shorter crash latency than Linux on a Pentium processor. The explanation given is that a single bit-flip in a CISC architecture (such as Pentium) can change a valid instruction into multiple valid but logically incorrect instructions, allowing the program to continue until the error manifests as a different failure. Between the Solaris and AIX systems, AIX has more crash cases in the higher latency range. However, hangs and FSVs can be considered as having a relatively long detection latency that depends on the specific detection mechanism (e.g. watchdog or heartbeat) employed in the system. In that case, all other things being equal, the Solaris system would have the worst error detection latency (followed by the Linux and AIX systems) because it has the highest hang rate. Therefore, AIX is also the preferred computing platform – in terms of detection latency – for the particular workload used in this study.

### 7.6.4.2 Feedback for Reliability Enhancements
In this section, an in-depth analysis of the fault injection data is used to provide feedback to designers and developers and potentially lead to enhancement of systems' reliability.

- Injections into the system registers indicate that each of the three processors (the Pentium 4, UltraSPARC IIIi, and POWER5) has two to three critical registers that are very sensitive to errors: IDTR, GDTR, and CR4 in the Pentium 4; TBA and SET_SOFTINT in the UltraSPARC IIIi; and SPRG1, IAR, and MSR in the POWER5. Protecting those registers could improve the reliability of a corresponding system. One way to do so would be to duplicate them. Because there are very few critical registers per processor, the overhead would be small.

- The majority of the crashes that are detected via assertions in the Solaris system are related to the use of mutex locks. That may imply that Solaris's synchronization mechanisms have high error sensitivity. In addition, the Solaris system has the highest hang rate for text injections among the three target systems: 14%, compared to 5% for Linux and 2% for AIX. More comprehensive assertion checks for synchronization variables or improved synchronization mechanisms are needed to reduce system hang.
- The registers introduced to manage the register window in the SPARC architecture are particularly error-sensitive and contribute to more than 50% of the hang cases for the Solaris system. This result indicates that the use of the register window can create unexpected reliability problems, although it may improve performance.

### 7.6.5 Detailed Discussion and Analysis

In this section, OS- and hardware-specific knowledge is applied to explain the obtained data. The discussion is divided into three subsections, which address text injection (Figures 7.17–7.19), stack injection (Figures 7.20–7.22), and register injection (Figures 7.23–7.25).

#### 7.6.5.1 Text Injection Analysis

*Illegal Instructions.* Both the Solaris and AIX systems have a significant number of crashes that manifest as illegal instructions – 19 and 26%, respectively – whereas the Linux system has less than 1%. The Linux system's low percentage is due to the variable-length instruction format on the Pentium processor, making it possible for a bit error to alter a single instruction into a sequence of multiple valid (but incorrect) instructions. Execution of an incorrect instruction sequence may crash the system because of a cause other than an invalid instruction.

*Data Access Exceptions.* In all three systems, the majority of crashes manifest as data access exceptions: 72, 49, and 53% for the Linux, Solaris, and AIX systems, respectively. That result is to be expected because memory access instructions make up a significant portion of most programs.

*Assertions.* The AIX and Linux systems both have a significant number of crashes that are caught by the assertions embedded in the kernel: 12 and 18%, respectively. In the Solaris system, on the other hand, only 1% of crashes are detected via kernel assertions. The high hang rate and low assertion-based detection rate in the Solaris system indicate the need for (i) the development of more precise assertions embedded in the kernel to detect possible hangs and (ii) the identification of locations in the kernel code for the strategic placement of existing or newly developed assertions to enhance detection coverage (see [41, 42] for studies on the strategic placement of detectors).

### 7.6.5.2 Stack Injection Analysis

The outcomes of stack injections are intrinsically related to the data placed on the stack. While similar information is stored on the stacks in all three of our systems, each uses the stack in a slightly different way, causing the faults to manifest in distinct ways. The SPARC processor, unlike the x86 and POWER architectures, manages the call stack via register windows. That is an architectural modification that was added to avoid the need for memory reads/writes every time a function was called. Each register window contains 32 general-purpose registers and shares 8 registers with each of the two adjacent windows. When going up or down, procedure calls, function arguments, return values, and return addresses are passed through the shared part of the register window, thus reducing memory traffic. However, when the register windows are all full or all empty, the register contents must be copied to or from the stack.

*Illegal Instructions.* In the AIX system, about 20% of crashes manifest as illegal instructions. The percentage is much lower for the other two platforms (both of which have 0%). Illegal instruction exceptions are due to errors in the return address stored on the stack, which cause the processor to access a memory location with an invalid instruction. In the Solaris system, the return address is stored in the register window (as explained above), and therefore we do not observe crashes due to illegal instructions. In the Linux system, the variable-length instruction format on the Pentium processor (as explained in the previous section) significantly reduces the chance of Linux system crashes due to illegal instructions.

*Data Access Exceptions.* Most of the crashes for the three systems manifested as data access exceptions, i.e. 61, 70, and 57%, for the Linux, Solaris, and AIX systems, respectively. In the Solaris system, data access exceptions fell mainly into three categories: alignment errors, null pointers, and data access MMU (memory management unit) misses. The Linux and AIX systems allow unaligned memory access to data, which is one reason why they have smaller percentages of data access exceptions than the Solaris system does.

*Assertions.* The AIX system and the Solaris system both have significant numbers of crashes that are detected by assertions (11% for AIX and 18% for Solaris). In the Solaris system, the majority of assertions are related to mutex checks. When a thread accesses a mutex lock, it does so via a function that takes a reference to a global mutex data structure as an argument. The reference is then stored in a local variable placed on the stack (when a register window spill happens). If the reference is corrupted, the wrong mutex data structure is accessed, resulting in a mismatch between the current thread and the thread owner stored in the mutex data structure. Some of the hang cases for Solaris are caused by corruptions of synchronization data that are not caught by assertions. No assertion details are available for the Linux and AIX systems.

### 7.6.5.3 Register Injection Analysis

*Linux System.* Figure 7.23 shows the crash rate due to errors in Pentium processor system registers. Among the system registers, IDTR (the interrupt descriptor table register), GDTR (the global descriptor table register), and CR4 (control register 4) have the highest crash rates (100, 100, and 76, respectively).

IDTR holds the address that points to the interrupt descriptor table, whereas GDTR holds the address that points to the global descriptor table (which stores the memory segment descriptors). Both tables are frequently referenced for memory access, so these registers are very sensitive to errors. Note that injections into LDTR (the local descriptor table register) have no observable effect on the system because LDTR is not used by Linux.

CR0–CR4 are the control registers. They control the general behavior of the processor and hence have a higher sensitivity to errors. For example, CR3 holds the page-table base address that enables the processor to translate virtual addresses to physical addresses.

*Solaris System.* Figure 7.24 summarizes the crash and hang rate of the SPARC processor system registers. Registers that support process contexts are responsible for the register window management. For example, CWP maintains the current window pointer, and any error in the least significant three bits causes the current program to use an incorrect register window. CANSAVE holds the number of clean windows still available. When CANSAVE reaches zero, a spill-window trap is invoked to push each register window to its corresponding procedure's stack. When CANRESTORE reaches zero, a fill-window trap is invoked to fill the register windows if they were previously spilled. Corruption of CANRESTORE results in bad register window traps, and corruption of CANSAVE results in bad stack overflows. Note that corrupting the least significant bits of CANSAVE, CANRESTORE, and OTHERWIN may cause the system to hang.

Software-interrupt registers are used to schedule software interrupts and hence are very sensitive to errors. For example, bits 1–15 of the SOFTINT register specify the interrupt level. Errors injected into these bits cause the interrupt to trap with an incorrect trap number.

Another highly error-sensitive register is the PSTATE, which holds the current state of the processor (e.g. interrupt enable or privilege mode). Our experimental data show that corruption of certain bits of this register (e.g. PSTATE.PRIV) results in a system hang.

*AIX System.* Figure 7.25 summarizes the crash distribution for the system registers in the POWER5 processor. Our injection results show that the three registers most sensitive to errors are SPRG1, IAR, and MSR. SPRG1 is a general special-purpose register used to hold the address of the current context save area. Corruption of this register generally results in a crash, which half the time will manifest as an assertion, and the other half of the time will lead to a *memory access exception*. The IAR (Instruction Address Register) is commonly known as the *program counter*. Corrupting it will result in an incorrect execution flow and subsequent system crash. MSR (the Machine State Register) holds the state of the processor. Corruption on certain reserved bits of MSR resulted in system crash.

### 7.6.6 Conclusions

This section presented an approach for using fault injection to conduct experimental studies that characterize and compare the error behaviors of different computing systems. Unlike the approaches used in previous studies, this approach was demonstrated on three diverse systems. We obtained the proposed metrics – error sensitivity, failure severity, and error detection latency – by conducting extensive fault injections into kernel code, kernel stack, and system registers while running the Apache Web Server as a workload. Our error behavior comparison shows that the Linux system has the highest average crash latency, the Solaris system has the highest hang rate, and the AIX system has the lowest error sensitivity and the smallest number of crashes in the more severe categories.

## 7.7 Dependability Overview of the Cisco Nexus Operating System

In the previous section, we presented detailed descriptions of the reliability features in the MVS and Linux operating systems. This section presents a brief overview of the dependability design of Cisco Nexus, a commercial operating system used in network switching and routing systems [43]. The Cisco Nexus operating system, or NX-OS for short, has the following features for avoiding or reducing the likelihood of a traffic disruption if there is a hardware or software failure:

- *Redundancy:* Compute, environment, and power system module redundancy provide physical redundancy, while redundancy in the system software architecture provides software-level redundancy.
- *Isolation of planes and processes:* There is clear isolation between the control plane (i.e. the software/hardware that sets up the network topology based on the user's configuration) and the data plane (i.e. the software/hardware that is responsible for forwarding the data in the network). That isolation prevents a failure in one plane or process from propagating to the other plane.
- *Restartability:* The software architecture has been designed from the ground up to be high availability aware. Thus, most system functions and services can be restarted independently after a failure, as they are isolated from other services that continue to run. Updates to system state, including messages in transit

between services, are written to persistent storage. That allows system services to perform stateful restarts that are transparent to other services.

- *Supervisor stateful switchover:* There are two physical supervisor modules: one configured to be the active one and another acting as a standby. To provide seamless and stateful switchover in the event of an unrecoverable supervisor module failure, all updates to state and configuration are synchronized between the two supervisor modules.

- *Nondisruptive upgrades:* The active/standby supervisor module configuration, along with data forwarding line-card soft reset features, allows the user to upgrade device software while the switch continues to forward traffic. In-Service Software Upgrade (ISSU), as the name suggests, allows software upgrades while the switch is servicing network traffic, thus reducing or eliminating the downtime caused by software upgrades.

Figure 7.26 depicts the hierarchical reliability provided at various levels of the network in the Cisco Nexus family of switching systems. The switch layer directly connected to the server is called the access layer. Since there is a single link from the host to the access switch, the switch could be made robust through use of duplicate supervisor modules, which allow for stateful switchover (failover) in the event of a control plane failure. Redundant power supplies, fan trays, and fabric modules provide additional levels of reliability. The connection to the access layer is fortified via multiple physical links bundled in what is called a *port-channel*. It is a logical link consisting of one or more physical links, with abilities for load

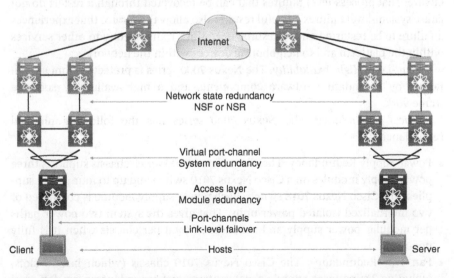

**Figure 7.26** Hierarchical reliability in Cisco Nexus switches for production-scale networks.

balancing and failover. It covers failures in the data plane by providing redundant data paths for traffic.

The next layer above access is called the aggregation layer. In this layer, multiple access switches are connected to an aggregation switch. The reliability mechanism for both link and system-level failure is called the *virtual port-channel* (*vPC*). In this, two switches acting as peers (one primary and the other secondary) maintain state consistency while sharing the traffic load. If there is a link or system failure, traffic instantly hashes toward the remaining peer, and the failure is thus tolerated. Those features, along with service-level high availability, are described in further detail below.

*Service-Level High Availability.* A modularized architecture that compartmentalizes components enables fault isolation, redundancy, and resource efficiency in the Cisco NX-OS. The Cisco NX-OS software is composed of processes known as *services*, each of which performs a function or set of functions for a subsystem or feature set. To align to the goal of having a modular software architecture, each service and service instance runs as an independent, protected process. That enables a highly fault-tolerant software infrastructure and fault isolation between services. A failure in a service instance will not affect any other services running at that time. Further, each instance of a service runs as an independent process, which means that two instances of a routing protocol can run as separate processes.

*Process Restartability.* Each process/service in the Cisco NX-OS runs in a protected memory space independently of other processes and the kernel. That provides fault containment and enables rapid restarts. Stateful process restartability ensures that process-level failures that can be recovered through a restart do not cause system-level failures. Stateful restarts also allow the service that experiences a failure to be restarted and to resume operations transparently to other services within the platform and to neighboring devices within the network.

*System-Level High Availability.* The Nexus 7000 series is protected from system failure by redundant hardware components and a high-availability software framework.

*Physical Redundancy.* The Nexus 7000 series has the following physical redundancies:

- Power Supply Redundancy: The Cisco Nexus 7000 series chassis supports three power supply modules on a Cisco Nexus 7010 switch and up to four power supplies on a Cisco Nexus 7018 switch. Each power supply module is composed of two internalized isolated power units. That gives the system two power paths per modular power supply and six paths in total per chassis when it is fully populated.
- Fan Tray Redundancy: The Cisco Nexus 7010 chassis (which has 10 slots, including 2 supervisor module slots) contains two redundant system fan trays

for I/O module cooling and two redundant fan trays for switch fabric module cooling. One fan tray from each pair is sufficient to provide system cooling. There is no time limit for replacing a failed Cisco Nexus 7010 fan tray, but to ensure the proper airflow, the failed fan tray must be left in place. The Cisco Nexus 7018 chassis (which has 18 slots, including 2 supervisor module slots) contains two fan trays, each of which is required to cool the modules in the chassis. The upper fan tray cools slots 1–9 and the fabric modules. The lower fan tray cools slots 10–18. Each of the fan trays is hot swappable. However, a failed fan tray must be replaced within three minutes of removal, or else the switch will shut down.

- Fabric Redundancy: Switching fabric availability is provided through redundant switch fabric modules. A single Cisco Nexus 7000 series chassis can be configured with one to five switch fabric cards for capacity and redundancy. I/O modules installed in the system automatically connect to and use all functionally installed switch fabric modules. Failure of a switch fabric module triggers an automatic reallocation and balancing of traffic across the remaining active switch fabric modules. Conversely, when an additional fabric module is inserted and brought online, traffic is redistributed across all installed fabric modules, and redundancy is restored.

- Supervisor Module Redundancy: The Cisco Nexus 7000 series chassis supports dual supervisor modules in which only one of the supervisor modules is active at any given time, while the other acts as a standby backup. That provides redundancy for the control and management plane. Updates to state and configuration are synchronized between the two supervisor modules to provide a seamless and stateful switchover if the active supervisor module undergoes an unrecoverable failure.

*In-service Software Upgrade (ISSU).* As noted earlier, the Cisco NX-OS allows one to perform an in-service software upgrade, also termed a *non-disruptive upgrade.* It is facilitated by the modular software architecture of the Cisco NX-OS. The supervisors and switching modules perform complete image upgrades with little or no impact on other modules. The data-forwarding plane is not impacted during the entire upgrade procedure.

*Virtual Device Context (VDC).* On the Nexus 7000 series of switches, the Cisco NX-OS allows multiple logical/virtual instances of a device to operate simultaneously on the same physical switch. Such a logical operating environment is known as a *virtual device context* or *VDC*. VDCs provide logically separate device environments that can be independently configured and managed. That provides fault isolation along with security and administrative benefits. In the event of a human error or failure conditions on one VDC, the configuration and state are isolated within a given virtual device, allowing the remaining VDCs on the same physical switch to continue operation transparent to the failure. While virtual device contexts are not primarily a high-availability feature, the operationally independent fault domains contribute to availability and prevent the service disruptions that are associated with device configuration.

*Network-Level High Availability.* In the event of a failure, network convergence is optimized by tools and functions that make both failover and fallback transparent and fast.

## 7.8  Evaluating Operating Systems: Related Studies

This section provides a brief summary of related studies on experimental evaluation of operating systems.

*User-level Testing by Executing API/System Calls with Erroneous Arguments.* Ballista [12] project provides a comprehensive assessment of 15 POSIX-compliant operating systems and libraries, as well as the Microsoft Win32 API. Ballista bombards a software module with combinations of exceptional and acceptable input values. The responses of the system are classified according to the first three categories of the C.R.A.S.H severity scale [44]: (i) catastrophic failures (OS corruption or machine crash), (ii) restart failures (a task hang), and (iii) abort failures (abnormal termination of a task).

Fuzz [45] project tests system calls for responses to randomized input streams. The study addresses the reliability of a large collection of UNIX utility programs and X-Window applications, servers, and network services. Injection of erroneous inputs to system calls has been used to evaluate the robustness of Windows 2000, NT4, and XP [37] and to compare Windows with Linux [46].

*OS Robustness with Respect to Faults in Device Drivers.* The impacts of faults in three different drivers for Windows CE .NET were tested by the authors of [47]. The study addressed operating system robustness by using three different error models for corruption of function call parameters and verified the effectiveness of each model. The robustness of the device driver architectures in Windows XP, 2003 Server, and the prerelease Vista is studied in [48]. The results were obtained by corrupting the device driver interface parameter values, and the evaluation was done by verifying the percentages of hang, crash, and file system corruptions. A study reported in [49] introduced a technique based on mutation at the machine-code level to emulate software faults and used this technique to evaluate the impact of software faults in device drivers for Windows XP, 2000, and NT. Work described in [50] injected common programming errors into device drivers to verify a fail-resilient OS design that can recover from dead drivers.

*Error Injection into Both Kernel and User Space.* Several studies have directly injected faults into the kernel space and monitored and quantified the responses.

FIAT [51], an early fault injection and monitoring environment, experiments on SunOS 4.1.2 to study fault/error propagation in the UNIX kernel. FINE [38] injects hardware-induced software errors and software faults into UNIX and traces the execution flow and key variables of the kernel.

Xception [52] uses the advanced debugging and performance-monitoring features that exist in most modern processors to inject faults and monitor the activation of the faults and their impact on target system behavior. Xception targets PowerPC and Pentium processors and operating systems ranging from Windows NT to proprietary, real-time kernels (e.g. SMX), and parallel operating systems (e.g. Parix). A more recent study Xception was used to evaluate the impact of transient faults in LynxOS on the PowerPC processor [13]. The measurements included data integrity, error propagation, application termination, and correctness of application results.

MAFALDA 10 analyzes the behavior of Chorus and LynxOS microkernels in the presence of faults. It applies both input parameter corruption and fault injection on the internal address space of the executive (both code and data segments). In [53], the authors describe how User Mode Linux (equivalent of a virtual machine that represents a kernel) was executed on top of the real Linux kernel to perform Linux kernel fault injection via the *ptrace* interface. In [16], the impact in the code segment of the Linux kernel is characterized.

The authors of [54] employed SWIFI to guide the design and implementation of the Rio File Cache system on top of the FreeBSD operating system. The use of fault injection for hardening kernel device drivers is presented in [55], which describes how a state machine was constructed to track the state of hardware and to support the injection of faults at a specific runtime state.

*Other Methods for Evaluating an Operating System.* Researchers have evaluated operating systems by studying the source code, collecting memory dumps, and inspecting the error logs. For example, in [56] a study of Linux and OpenBSD kernel errors found by automatic, static compiler analysis at the source-code level is presented. In [26], authors discussed the collection of memory dump analyses of field software failures in the Tandem GUARDIAN90 operating system to identify the effects of software faults. In [57], the authors examined Windows NT cluster reboot logs to measure dependability. The authors of [58] used 250 randomly sampled reports to study MVS operating system failures.

## 7.9 Insights

The focus in this chapter has been on reliability in operating systems (OS). We have discussed operational data on Linux, the IBM MVS operating system (now z/OS), and the GUARDIAN operating system, which employ different ways of providing error detection and recovery. The MVS operating system provides recovery functions for major if not all functions and is supported by the RTM. If, in the event of a failure, further processing might degrade the system or destroy data, control is handed to the RTM, which in turn picks the appropriate recovery routine if it is available. If an appropriate recovery routine is not available, RTM can terminate the program/application.

The MVS operating system has a hierarchical recovery structure that terminates in the RTM (see Figure 7.1). In contrast, the GUARDIAN operating system employs process pairs as the primary technique for fault detection, leading to a flatter recovery structure. A significant percentage of the code in MVS is dedicated to fault management, such as assertions and exception handling. We believe that it is about 40–60%. Similarly, a sizeable portion of GUARDIAN's code base relates to fault detection and recovery. In such a case, it is important to test the fault management code thoroughly for robustness.

The GUARDIAN operating system is founded on the principle that every component should be duplicated and that any component that can't be duplicated should be self-checking. The process pairs mechanism ensures recovery. In the Linux operating system, recovery is dependent on the exception-handling mechanism. Because Linux is a commodity system that recovery mechanism is not very extensive, and the high availability is not very high.

In High-Availability Linux (HA-Linux), the heartbeat mechanism is used as a daemon that provides cluster infrastructure (communication and membership) services to its clients. That allows clients to know about the health of peer processes on other machines and easily exchange messages with them. To be useful to users, the heartbeat daemon needs to be combined with a cluster resource manager (CRM), which has the task of starting and stopping the services (e.g. IP addresses and web servers) that the cluster will make highly available.

There is significant value in doing error propagation analysis. Such analysis gives insights on containing the effects of errors within components and optimal distribution of resources in building a high-availability system.

## References

1 Pradhan, D.K. (1996). *Fault-tolerant Computer Systems Design*. Prentice Hall.
2 Mueller, M., Alves, L.C., Fischer, W. et al. (1999). RAS strategy for IBM S/390 G5 and G6. *IBM Journal of Research and Development* 43 (5/6): 875–888.
3 Slegel, T., Averill, R.I., Check, M. et al. (1999). IBM's S/390 G5 microprocessor design. *IEEE Micro* 19 (2): 12–23.
4 IBM (2005). *z/Architecture, Principles of Operation*. Order Number: SA22-7832-04. IBM Corporation.

5 Iyer, R. and Velardi, P. (1985). *Hardware-related software errors: measurement and analysis. IEEE Transactions on Software Engineering* SE-11 (2): 223–231.

6 Auslander, M.A., Larkin, D.C., and Scherr, A.L. (1981). *The evolution of the MVS operating system. IBM Journal of Research Development* 25: 471–482.

7 IBM (1979). *OS/VS2 MVS, System Programming Library: SYS1.LOGREC Error Recording*. IBM Corporation.

8 IBM (1980). *OS/VS2 MVS, Overview*. IBM Corporation.

9 IBM (1980). *OS/VS2 MVS, System Programming Library: Supervisor*. IBM Corporation.

10 Butner, S.E. and Iyer, R.K. (1980). A statistical study of reliability and system load at SLAC. *Proceedings of 10th International Symposium on Fault-Tolerant Computing, FTCS-10*, Kyoto, Japan (October 1980).

11 IA-32 Intel Architecture Software Developer's Manual (2003). System Programming Guide, vol. 3.

12 Koopman, P. and DeVale, J. (2000). The exception handling effectiveness of POSIX operating systems. *IEEE Transactions on Software Engineering* 26 (9): 837–848.

13 Madeira, H., Some, R., Moreira, F., Costa, D., and Rennels, D. (2002). Experimental evaluation of a COTS system for space applications. *Proceedings of the International Conference on Dependable Systems and Networks*, Bethesda, MD, USA (23–26 June 2002), 325–330.

14 Tsai, T., Hsueh, M.-C., Zhao, H. et al. (Nov 1999). Stress-based and path-based fault injection. *IEEE Transactions on Computers* 48 (11): 1183–1201.

15 Tsai, T., Iyer, R., and Jewitt, D. (1996). An approach towards benchmarking of fault-tolerant commercial systems. *Proceedings of Annual Symposium on Fault Tolerant Computing*, Sendai, Japan (25–27 June 1996), 314–323.

16 Gu, W., Kalbarczyk, Z., and Iyer, R.K. (2004). Error sensitivity of the Linux kernel executing on PowerPC G4 and Pentium 4 processors. *Proceedings of International Conference on Dependable Systems and Networks (DSN)*, Florence, Italy (28 June–1 July 2004), 887–896.

17 Stott, D.T., Floering, B., Burke, D., Kalbarczpk, Z., and Iyer, R.K. (2000). NFTAPE: a framework for assessing dependability in distributed systems with lightweight fault injectors. *Proceedings of the IEEE International Computer Performance and Dependability Symposium* (27–30 March 2000), 91–100.

18 UnixBench (2021). https://github.com/kdlucas/byte-unixbench (accessed 21 July 2023).

19 Rimén, M., Ohlsson, J., and Torin, J. (1994). On microprocessor error behavior modeling. *Proceedings of FTCS'94* (15–17 June 1994), 76–85.

20 Iyer, R., Rossetti, D., and Hsueh, M.-C. (Aug 1986). *Measurement and modeling of computer reliability as affected by system activity. ACM Transactions on Computer Systems* 4 (3): 214–237.

**21** Freescale Semiconductor, Inc. (2017). Motorola MPC7450 RISC Microprocessor Family User's Manual https://www.nxp.com/docs/en/reference-manual/MPC7450UM.pdf (accessed 21 July 2023).

**22** Gu, W., Kalbarczyk, Z., Iyer, R.K., and Yang, Z. (2003). Characterization of Linux kernel behavior under errors. *Proceedings of the International Conference on Dependable Systems and Networks*, San Francisco, CA, USA (22–25 June 2003), 459–468.

**23** Bartlett, J.F. (1978). A 'nonstop' operating system. *Proceedings Hawaii International Conference System Sciences* (January 1978), 103–119.

**24** Gray, J. (1990). A census of Tandem system availability between 1985 and 1990. *IEEE Transactions on Reliability* 39 (4): 409–418.

**25** Gray, J. (1985). *Why Do Computers Stop and What Can We Do About It?* Cupertino, CA, USA: Tandem Computers, Inc.

**26** Lee, I. and Iyer, R.K. (1993). Faults, symptoms, and software fault tolerance in Tandem GUARDIAN90 operating system. *Proceedings 23rd International Symposium on Fault-Tolerant Computing (FTCS-23)*, Toulouse, France (22–24 June 1993).

**27** Huang, Y. and Kintala, C. (1993). Software implemented fault tolerance: technologies and experience. *Proceedings 23rd International Symposium on Fault-Tolerant Computing (FTCS-23)*, Toulouse, France (22–24 June 1993).

**28** Wang, Y.M., Huang, Y., and Fuchs, W.K. (1993). Progressive retry for software error recovery in distributed systems. *Proceedings 23rd International Symposium on Fault-Tolerant Computing (FTCS-23)*, Toulouse, France (22–24 June 1993).

**29** Lee, I. and Iyer, R.K. (1995). Software dependability in the Tandem GUARDIAN system. *IEEE Transactions on Software Engineering* 21 (5): 455–467.

**30** Cristian, F. (1982). Exception handling and software fault tolerance. *IEEE Transactions on Computers* C-31 (6): 531–540.

**31** Hogg, R.V. and Tanis, E.A. (ed.) (1988). *Probability and Statistical Inference*, 3e. New York, NY: Macmillan Publishing Co., Inc.

**32** Lala, J.H. and Alger, L.S. (1988). Hardware and software fault tolerance: a unified architectural approach. *Proceedings 18th International Symposium on Fault-Tolerant Computing (FTCS-18)* (27–30 June 1988), Tokyo, Japan.

**33** Trivedi, K.S., Muppala, J.K., Woolet, S.P., and Haverkort, B.R. (1992). *Composite performance and dependability analysis. Performance Evaluation* 14: 197–215.

**34** Lee, I. and Iyer, R.K. (1992). Analysis of software halts in the Tandem GUARDIAN operating system. *Proceedings 3rd International Symposium on Software Reliability Engineering*, Research Triangle Park, North Carolina (7–10 October 1992).

**35** Lee, I., Tang, D., Iyer, R.K., and Hsueh, M.-C. (1993). *Measurement-based evaluation of operating system fault tolerance. IEEE Transactions on Reliability* 42 (2): 238–249.

**36** Chen, D., Jacques-Silva, G., Kalbarczyk, Z., Iyer, R.K., and Mealey, B. (2008). Error behavior comparison of multiple computing systems: a case study using Linux on Pentium, Solaris on SPARC, and AIX on POWER. *14th IEEE Pacific Rim International Symposium on Dependable Computing, 2008. PRDC '08* (15–17 December 2008), 339–346.

**37** Kalakech, A., Kanoun, K., Crouzet, Y., and Arlat, J. (2004). Benchmarking the dependability of Windows NT4, 2000 and XP. *Proceedings of DSN'04* (28 June–1 July 2004), 681–686.

**38** Kao, W.-I., Iyer, R., and Tang, D. (1993). FINE: a fault injection and monitoring environment for tracing the UNIX system behavior under faults. *IEEE Transactions on Software Engineering* 19 (11): 1105–1118.

**39** Mukherjee, S.S., Emer, J., and Reinhardt, S.K. (2005). The soft error problem: an architectural perspective. *Proceedings of HPCA'05* (12–16 February 2005), 243–247.

**40** Mitra, S., Zhang, M., Mak, T.M. et al. (2005). *Logic soft errors: a major barrier to robust platform design. Proceedings of the IEEE International Test Conference* (8–10 November 2005)

**41** Hiller, M., Jhumka, A., and Suri, N. (2002). On the placement of software mechanism for detection of data errors. *Proceedings DSN-02* (23–26 June 2002).

**42** Pattabiraman, K., Kalbarczyk, Z., and Iyer, R.K. (2005). Application-based metrics for strategic placement of detectors. *Proceedings of PRDC'05* (12–14 December 2005), 75–82.

**43** Cisco Systems, Inc. (2022). Cisco Nexus 7000 Series NX-OS High Availability and Redundancy Guide. https://www.cisco.com/ (accessed 11 August 2023)

**44** Kropp, N.P., Koopman, P.J., and Siewiorek, D.P. (1998). Automated robustness testing of off-the-shelf software components. *Proceedings of the 10th International Symposium on Fault-Tolerant Computing* (23–25 June 1998), Munich, Germany.

**45** Miller, B., Koski, D., Lee, C.P. et al. (1995). *Fuzz Revisited: A Re-examination of the Reliability of UNIX Utilities and Services*. Madison: University of Wisconsin.

**46** Jarboui, T., Arlat, J., Crouzet, Y., Kanoun, K., and Marteau, T. (2002). Analysis of the effects of real and injected software faults: Linux as a case study. *Proceedings of PRDC'02* (16–18 December 2002), 51–58.

**47** Johansson, A., Suri, N., and Murphy, B. (2007). *On the selection of error model(s) for OS robustness evaluation. Proceedings of DSN'07* (25–28 June 2007), 502–511.

**48** Mendonça, M. and Neves, N. (2007). Robustness testing of the windows DDK. *Proceedings of DSN'07* (25–28 June 2007), 554–564.

**49** Duraes, J. and Madeira, H. (2003). Multidimensional characterization of the impact of faulty drivers on the operating systems behavior. *IEICE Transactions on Information and Systems* E86-D (12): 2563–2570.

**50** Herder, J.N., Bos, H., Gras, B., Homburg, P., and Tanenbaum, A.S. (2007). Failure resilience for device drivers. *Proceedings of DSN'07* (25–28 June 2007), 41–50.

**51** Barton, J., Czeck, E., Segall, Z., and Siewiorek, D. (1990). Fault injection experiments using FIAT. *IEEE Transactions on Computers* 39(4).

**52** Carreira, J.H., Madeira, H., and Silva, J. (1998). Xception: a technique for the evaluation of dependability in modern computers. *IEEE Transactions on Software Engineering* 24 (2): 125–136.

**53** Belli, F. and Jedrzejowicz, P. (1991). Comparative analysis of concurrent fault tolerance techniques for real-time applications. *Proceedings International Symposium on Software Reliability Engineering* (17–18 May 1991).

**54** Ng, W. and Chen, P.M. (1999). The systematic improvement of fault tolerance in the Rio File Cache. *Proceedings FTCS-29* (15–18 June 1999).

**55** Edwards, D. and Matassa, L. (2002). An approach to injecting faults into hardened software. *Proceedings of Ottawa Linux Symposium* (26–29 June 2002).

**56** Chou, A., Yang, J., Chelf, B., Hallem, S., and Engler, D. (2001). An empirical study of operating systems errors. *Proceedings 18th ACM Symposium on Operating Systems Principles* (21–24 October 2001).

**57** Xu, J., Kalbarczyk, Z., and Iyer, R.K. (1999). Networked windows NT system field failure data analysis. *Proceedings Pacific Rim International Symposium on Dependable Computing* (16–17 December 1999).

**58** Sullivan, M. and Chillarege, R. (1991). Software defects and their impact on system availability – a study of field failures in operating systems. in *Proceedings FTCS-21* (25–27 June 1991).

# 8

# Reliable Networked and Distributed Systems

## 8.1   Introduction

In a distributed or networked system, many interconnected computers can cooperate to achieve a common goal. Usually, the cooperating computers maintain some shared state. Two broad classes of distributed/networked systems are defined based on the manner in which state (or information) is shared: (i) systems based on tightly coupled processors with shared memory, and (ii) systems based on loosely coupled processors with distributed memory.

In tightly coupled systems, all computers (or processors) have equal access to a shared memory used for inter-computer (or inter-processor) communication. The difficulty with that approach is that the interconnection between the processors and the shared storage becomes a performance bottleneck as the number of processors grows. Therefore, many commercial solutions using shared memory have a limited number of processors.

In loosely coupled systems, each computer/processor has a local physical memory (usually in addition to global memory), and processors cannot access one another's memory. To cooperate, processors exchange messages over an interconnection network (so that such systems are often characterized as *message-passing*). Although message passing adds extra overhead, the advantage of distributed memory systems is their scalability. This type of system can scale to thousands of processors without the performance or cost bottlenecks of shared memory systems.

The design of fault tolerance support for distributed computers is conditioned on the specific characteristics of the system at hand. For example, in a distributed memory system, a faulty processor can impact other processors only if an error (that was caused by the processor's misbehavior) propagates across the network. Consequently, it is relatively easy to define and build error containment

*Dependable Computing: Design and Assessment*, First Edition. Ravishankar K. Iyer, Zbigniew T. Kalbarczyk, and Nithin M. Nakka.

boundaries. In contrast, in the shared memory model of multiprocessing, a processor may be able to corrupt a computation undetectably at any time through disruption of the shared store. On the other hand, fault management in the distributed setting can be quite complex, particularly when errors can escape (imperfect) containment boundaries.

The general challenges in building dependable distributed systems can be broken down into a set of questions that must be answered in the design process. Examples include the following:

- How can we guarantee reliable communication, i.e. message delivery?
- How can we ensure that all entities participating in computation have a consistent view of the overall system?
- How can we synchronize the actions of dispersed processors and processes?
- How can we contain errors or achieve fail-silent behavior of components to prevent error propagation?
- How can we adapt the system architecture to changes in the availability requirements of an application?

Answering those questions requires efficient techniques for supporting consistent data and coherent behavior of system components despite failures. In the following sections, we first provide some introductory material on system/failure modeling; then, we present general problems (briefly introduced below) whose solutions, in the form of algorithms or protocols, constitute the following building blocks for solving application-specific problems:

- *Agreement*, to ensure that all participants are consistent on common information (e.g. an action to take).
- *Broadcast/group communication*, to ensure reliable message delivery to all participants in the system.
- *Software-based replication*, to tolerate failures in the system by means of space redundancy.
- *Atomic commit*, to ensure the atomic behavior of participants in transactional systems (e.g. distributed databases).

While a substantial part of this chapter focuses on the theory of reliable distributed systems and this topic has been of significant research interest, the future applications are in public and commercial large-scale multi-cloud systems. Many vendors like Google, Microsoft, IBM, AWS, etc., are developing solutions in this space conforming to the specifications delineated by CXL (Compute Express Link) consortium – an open industry standards group establishing technical specifications that facilitate breakthrough performance for these emerging applications. Of particular interest is the rapidly growing deployment of memory- and storage-disaggregation, and going forward compute- and accelerator-disaggregation. This combination offers the opportunity to execute large data projects and provide rapid response to failures and performance bottlenecks and continuous adaptivity. This novel paradigm of distributed computing has the possibility of significantly changing the computing infrastructure landscape. There is a distinct trend toward developing resilient systems and architectures that are reliable, consistent, and provide rapid recovery. The upcoming sections (8.2–8.9) describe the theory and techniques of prior and current research in reliable distributed systems, followed by challenges and opportunities in the new architectures and systems space in Section 8.10.

## 8.2   System Model

We model a *network system* as a collection of computing elements (processes) located at the nodes of a directed network graph $G = (V,E)$. Each process $p \in V$ has a set of states (possibly infinite) and exchanges messages with an adjacent process $q$ through a communication channel (link), which is associated with the edges $(p,q) \in E$ for incoming messages, or the edge $(q,p) \in E$, for outgoing messages.

The *synchronous* model assumes known upper bounds on (i) the execution speed of processes and (ii) the communication delay of links. The synchronous model does not exactly adhere to what happens in most distributed systems, in which messages may be delayed for an arbitrary amount of time, e.g. because of congestion. Nevertheless, this model is useful for isolating general problems and typically constitutes a useful intermediate step toward understanding solutions for relatively realistic models. In addition, it is sometimes possible for a real distributed system to "simulate" a synchronous system in logical time, with the help of adequate synchronization algorithms.

In the *asynchronous* model, separate processes take steps at arbitrary relative speeds, and the communication delay of the link is unbounded. An advantage of this model is that it does not assume any timing constraints. So, algorithms designed for it are guaranteed to run correctly in networks with arbitrary timing guarantees. However, the asynchronous model is often too weak to solve important problems of distributed computing (e.g. consensus). Intuitively, that weakness originates in the impossibility of distinguishing a failed process that has stopped executing (i.e. a process that has experienced a *crash failure*) from a correct process that is executing infinitely slowly. One way to overcome this weakness of the asynchronous model is by attaching to each process an *unreliable failure detector* [1], a component that provides the process with a list of processors that are "suspected" to have failed. To generate that list, the failure detector uses, for example, heartbeats and timeouts, and therefore can make mistakes (e.g. when links drop or delay messages). However, the failure detector must eventually stop making mistakes, i.e. it must eventually provide a list that accurately describes the system. Therefore, actual asynchronous algorithms are required to solve the targeted problem only if the unreliable failure detectors eventually behave like perfect failure detectors ($P$). Formally, an eventually perfect failure detector ($\diamond P$) is required to satisfy the following two properties:

- *Strong completeness*: For every correct process $p$, if a process $q$ remains unreachable from $p$, then eventually $p$ will always suspect $q$.
- *Eventual strong accuracy*: For every correct process $p$, if a process $q$ remains reachable from $p$, then eventually $p$ will no longer suspect $q$.

Theoretically, the deterministic implementation of the required failure detector is impossible in asynchronous systems. However, if they are satisfied, the properties of strong completeness and eventually strong accuracy reflect the stability condition of the distributed system (including both the network and processes) that is necessary for a considered problem to be solvable.

It is assumed that known upper bounds exist for the execution speed of the processes and the communication delay of the links; these bounds are respected most of the time, and violations constitute process/link *timing failures*. In addition, each process has access to a local physical clock, which is assumed to give a value that is monotonically increasing. The resulting model is so-called *timed-asynchronous*.

The timed-asynchronous model is the most realistic since real systems are not arbitrarily asynchronous, although they may manifest periods of instability due to, for example, link/process failures or high load. Therefore, actual asynchronous algorithms are required to solve the targeted problem only if the system eventually stops exhibiting timing failures.

It is assumed that each process can generate random values. That ability is used by a class of algorithms called *randomized algorithms*, which can solve problems such as consensus with a probability that asymptotically tends to 1. It is, however, important to note that solving a problem deterministically and solving a problem with probability 1 are not equivalent.

## 8.3 Failure Models

Computer systems are designed to execute/run user applications. Regardless of the specific system configuration, users judge systems based on the quality of the delivered service, characterized in terms of reliability, availability, security, and performance. One must understand application failure models in order to build efficient error-handling mechanisms. A network system can exhibit various types of failures, including *process failures* and *link failures*, as illustrated above. (See Figure 8.1 for an example classification of process failure models.)

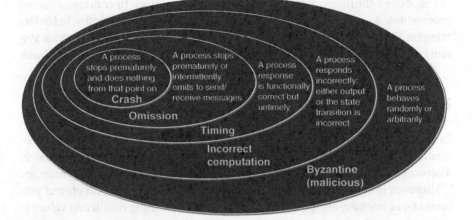

**Figure 8.1** Process failure models. *Source:* Data based on Mullender [2]/Association for Computing Machinery (ACM).

A faulty process can exhibit a *crash failure* if it stops executing and, before the failure, it does not perform incorrect state transitions. A process may fail to send or receive a message required by the protocol or algorithm it is executing and, hence, exhibit an *omission failure*. A *timing failure* occurs if a process violates a timing constraint (note that this does not apply to the asynchronous model). If a process generates an incorrect output, whether to the console, to the file system, or to another process in the form of a message, an *incorrect computation* failure is said to have occurred. A faulty process can also exhibit an *arbitrary failure* (i.e. *Byzantine failure*), which imposes no constraints on the process's behavior. The process may, for instance, send a message or perform state transitions without following its intended specifications. As a result, the faulty process could send a spurious message, send an inaccurate message, or not respond to a received message correctly. Arbitrary faults[1] are very broad in nature, and all conceivable faults can be treated as such. In practice, one often considers only a case of Byzantine failures called *authenticated* Byzantine failures. A process exhibiting such failures can behave arbitrarily; however, it is assumed that processes have access to some authentication mechanism (e.g. digital signatures) that makes it possible to detect the forgery of valid messages by Byzantine processes. Much like processes, links can also be subject to crashes, omissions, timing, and Byzantine failures. For instance, a crashed link is one that drops every message; a Byzantine link can duplicate messages, corrupt the message contents, or generate spurious messages. Communication failures can also cause network partitions.

---

1 Also referred to as *malicious faults*, in the security context.

The above definitions characterize faulty processes/links. In contrast, a *correct* process/link is a process/link that never expresses any of the faulty behaviors mentioned above. Note that correct/incorrect are predicates over the whole system execution: a process/link that crashes at time *t* is already incorrect before time *t*.

## 8.4 Agreement Protocols

In a dependable distributed system, the individual processes that compose a distributed application are often required to reach mutual agreement on a common value. In a networked environment, that agreement is achieved through exchange of messages.

However, in the presence of failures, faulty processes can prevent correct processes from reaching an agreement (for example, by sending conflicting values to other processes). Therefore, it is necessary for processes to exchange their values and relay values received from other processes multiple times. Thus, they can isolate the effects of faulty processes.

We now address the following three major classes of agreement problems (based on [3]).

1) *The Byzantine agreement problem*: One of the processes proposes a single value that needs to be agreed upon and broadcasts the value to all other processes; all nonfaulty processes must agree on that value. Formally, the properties to satisfy are:
   - *Agreement*: All nonfaulty processes agree on the same value.
   - *Validity*: If the source process is nonfaulty, then the common value agreed on by the nonfaulty processes must be the initial value from the source. If the source is faulty, then the nonfaulty processes must agree on a common value.
2) *The consensus problem*: Every process has its own initial value, which is broadcast to all other processes, and all nonfaulty processes must agree on a single, common value that was proposed by one of the processes. Formally, the properties to satisfy are:
   - *Agreement*: All nonfaulty processes agree on the same value.
   - *Validity*: If all nonfaulty processes start with the same initial value $v$, then all nonfaulty processes can agree only upon $v$. If the initial values of the nonfaulty processes are different, then all nonfaulty processes can agree on any common value.
3) *The interactive consistency problem*: Every process has its own initial value, which it broadcasts to all other processes, and all nonfaulty processes must agree on a set of common values that were proposed by the processes. Formally, the properties to satisfy are:
   - *Agreement*: All nonfaulty processes agree on the same value vector $(v_1, v_2, ..., v_n)$, where $n$ is the number of processes in the system.

- *Validity*: If the $i$th process is nonfaulty and its initial value is $v_i$, then the $i$th value to be agreed on by all nonfaulty processes is $v_i$. If the $i$th process is faulty, then all nonfaulty processes can agree on any common value for $v_i$.

Note that in the above definitions, we do not constrain the behavior of faulty processes. Indeed, in the case of arbitrary failures, it is not possible to do so. If we restrict ourselves to crash failures only, then it is possible (and useful) to formulate a *uniform* version of the above problems, which requires faulty processes (i.e. processes that eventually crash) that fail only after deciding to agree on the same value on which the nonfaulty processes have agreed.

### 8.4.1 Byzantine Agreement Problem: Solution

In this section, we describe a solution to the Byzantine agreement problem for a synchronous network system in which links do not fail and at most $f$ of the $n$ processes can fail arbitrarily. In addition, we assume that processes run in lockstep: in each step/round, a process receives messages (that were sent to it in the previous step), performs computation, and sends messages to neighbor processes, which will receive the messages at the next step.

It can be shown that in a fully connected network:

1) It is impossible to reach an agreement if the number of faulty processes $f$ exceeds $\frac{n-1}{3}$. For example, with three processes, the Byzantine agreement problem cannot be solved even in the event of a single failure [4].
2) Any solution requires at least $f + 1$ rounds of message exchange [5].
3) If authenticated messages are used, the above bound is relaxed, and agreement can be reached for any number of faulty processes.

Here we illustrate two situations in which three processes $p_0$, $p_1$, and $p_2$, one of which is faulty, are unable to reach agreement (on a binary value) because of the faulty process. Assume that $p_0$ proposes the initial value.

In Figure 8.2, $p_2$ is the faulty process. Suppose that $p_0$ broadcasts 1 to both $p_1$ and $p_2$ while $p_2$ acts maliciously by sending 0 to $p_1$, which must agree on 1 if the Byzantine problem is to be solved. However, since $p_1$ receives two conflicting values, it cannot decide on 1, the correct value.

In Figure 8.3, $p_0$ is the faulty process. Suppose that $p_0$ broadcasts 1 to $p_1$ and 0 to $p_2$. In consequence, $p_2$ communicates 0 to $p_1$, which thus

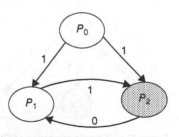

**Figure 8.2** $P_0$ is correct. *Source:* Data based on Singhal and Shivaratri [3]/Association for Computing Machinery (ACM).

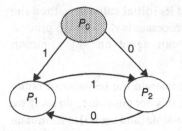

**Figure 8.3** $P_0$ is faulty. *Source:* Data based on Singhal and Shivaratri [3]/Association for Computing Machinery (ACM).

receives two conflicting values. Hence, no agreement is possible.

### 8.4.1.1 Oral Message Algorithm, *OM(f)*

The Oral Message algorithm [3], *OM(f)* for short, is a recursive algorithm that solves (deterministically) the Byzantine agreement for $3f + 1$ or more processes in the presence of at most $f$ faulty processes [6]. The algorithm has message complexity $O(n^f)$, and is recursively defined as follows:

1) Algorithm *OM(0)*
   a) The source process sends its value to every process.
   b) Each process decides on the value received from the source. (If it does not receive any value, then it decides on a default value of 0.)
2) Algorithm *OM(k)*, $k > 0$
   a) The source process sends its value to every process.
   b) For each $i$, let $v_i$ be the value that process $i$ receives from the source. Process $i$ acts as a new source and initiates *Algorithm OM(k − 1)*, wherein it sends the value $v_i$ to each of the $n − 2$ other processes.
   c) For each $i$ and each $j$ ($\neq i$), let $vj$ be the value that process $i$ received from $j$ in step (2) using *Algorithm OM(k − 1)*. (If no value is received, then a default value of 0 is used.) Process $i$ uses the *majority* value among $(v_1, v_2, \ldots, v_{n-1})$.

Consider a system with four processes $p_0, p_1, p_2$, and $p_3$. Assume that $p_0$ proposes the initial value and that $p_2$ is faulty. To initiate the agreement, $p_0$ executes $OM(1)$, wherein it sends 1 to all processes (see Figure 8.4).

At step 2 of the $OM(1)$ algorithm, $p_1$, $p_2$, and $p_3$ execute the algorithm $OM(0)$. Since $p_1$ and $p_3$ are nonfaulty, the former sends 1 to $\{p_2, p_3\}$, and the latter sends 1 to $\{p_1, p_2\}$. $P_2$ is faulty and sends 1 to $p_1$ and 0 to $p_3$ (see Figure 8.5). After receiving all messages, $p_1$, $p_2$, and $p_3$ execute step 3 of $OM(1)$ to decide on the majority value, as follows:

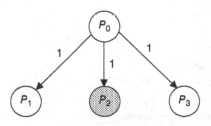

**Figure 8.4** Sample execution of *OM(1)*, Step 1. $P_2$ is faulty. *Source:* Data based on Singhal and Shivaratri [3]/Association for Computing Machinery (ACM).

1) $p_1$ received $\{1, 1, 1\}$ and decides on 1;
2) $p_2$ received $\{1, 1, 1\}$ and decides on 1;
3) $p_3$ received $\{1, 1, 0\}$ and decides on 1.

Both conditions of the Byzantine agreement are satisfied.

Consider now the case in which $p_0$ is the faulty process and, hence, sends conflicting values (see Figure 8.6). Under step 1 of $OM(0)$, $p_1$, $p_2$, and $p_3$ each send the received values to the other two processes. Eventually $p_1$, $p_2$, and $p_3$ execute step 3 to decide on the majority value:

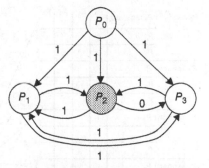

1) $p_1$ received $\{1, 0, 1\}$ and decides on 1;
2) $p_2$ received $\{0, 1, 1\}$ and decides on 1;
3) $p_3$ received $\{1, 1, 0\}$ and decides on 1.

Both conditions of the Byzantine agreement are satisfied.

**Figure 8.5** Sample execution of $OM(1)$, Step 2. $P_2$ is faulty. *Source:* Data based on Singhal and Shivaratri [3]/ Association for Computing Machinery (ACM).

### 8.4.2 Interactive Consistency Obtained by Running the Byzantine Agreement Protocol

In this section, we illustrate an example in which interactive consistency is achieved by solving multiple Byzantine agreement problems, one for each process in the system.

Consider a system with four processes $p_0$, $p_1$, $p_2$, and $p_3$, which have the following initial values: $v_0 = 1$, $v_1 = 1$, $v_2 = 1$, and $v_3 = 1$. In addition, assume that at most, one process can fail and that, in particular, $p_0$ is faulty. The interactive consistency problem is solved by having each process

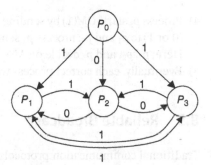

**Figure 8.6** Sample execution of $OM(1)$. $P_0$ is faulty. *Source:* Data based on Singhal and Shivaratri [3]/ Association for Computing Machinery (ACM).

initiate an $OM(1)$ protocol, as explained in the following steps (see Figure 8.7):

1) Process $p_0$ (faulty) starts $OM(1)$ by sending 0 to $p_1$ and $p_2$, and 1 to $p_3$. Process $p_1$, after receiving 0 from $p_0$, runs $OM(0)$ by sending 0 to $p_2$ and $p_3$; similarly, $p_2$ sends 0 to $p_1$ and $p_3$, and $p_3$ sends 1 to $p_1$ and $p_2$. Here, $p_1$, $p_2$, and $p_3$ decide on 0.
2) Process $p_1$ starts $OM(1)$ by sending 1 to $p_0$, $p_2$, and $p_3$. Process $p_0$ sends any value (0 or 1) to $p_2$ and $p_3$; process $p_2$, after receiving 1 from $p_1$, sends 1 to $p_0$ and $p_3$; and $p_3$ sends 1 to $p_0$ and $p_2$. Here, $p_1$, $p_2$, and $p_3$ decide on 1.
3) Process $p_2$ starts $OM(1)$ by sending 1 to $p_0$, $p_1$, and $p_3$. Process $p_0$ sends any value (0 or 1) to $p_1$ and $p_3$; process $p_1$ sends 1 to $p_0$ and $p_3$; and $p_3$ sends 1 to $p_0$ and $p_1$. Here, $p_1$, $p_2$, and $p_3$ decide on 1.

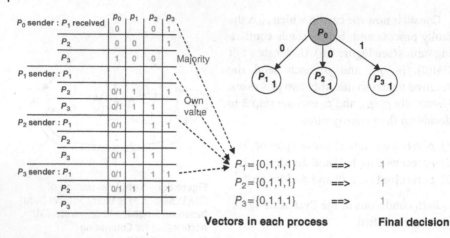

**Figure 8.7** Interactive consistency example.

4) Process $p_3$ starts $OM(1)$ by sending 1 to $p_0, p_1$, and $p_2$. Process $p_0$ sends any value (0 or 1) to $p_1$ and $p_2$; process $p_1$ sends 1 to $p_0$ and $p_2$; and $p_2$ sends 1 to $p_0$ and $p_1$. Here, $p_1, p_2$, and $p_3$ decide on 1.
5) Eventually, each correct process will have obtained the vector (0,1,1,1).

## 8.5 Reliable Broadcast

Traditional communication protocols like TCP support point-to-point communication among processes. Such protocols were designed for applications involving communication between no more than two processes at a time, like the common client-server applications. Many applications today in the distributed systems field do not adhere to that model and require multipoint-to-multipoint communication among processes in a group. A failure during such communication can lead to inconsistency and can compromise the integrity of the distributed system (e.g. if only a subset of the processes delivers a broadcast message). To cope with process/ link failures, reliable broadcast/multicast protocols offer stronger semantics than best-effort communication primitives such as IP multicast.

To make it easier to understand the implementation issues for group communication services (GCSs) (the topic of the next section), we initially assume the presence of a unique, static group that contains the entire set of processes. In addition, we suppose that the links do not fail and that the network does not partition. As a result, we eliminate the need for a group membership service since group memberships can be statically encoded in each process. Therefore, in this section, we use the term *broadcast* (reserving the term *multicast* for the next section) since in our scenario, a process sending a message addresses the entire set of processes (the singleton group).

In summary, the following assumptions are made in the following presentation on reliable broadcast:

- The system consists of a set of processors/nodes that are interconnected by a network and communicate by exchanging messages.
- Processes' execution speed and links' communication delay have known upper bounds, i.e. the system is synchronous. As a result, process failures can be detected by timeouts.
- Failures in processes are limited to either crashes or omissions.
- Communication is reliable, i.e. we do not consider link failures. In particular, we assume that the network is not partitioned.

Reliable broadcast algorithms employ low-level communication primitives, such as message sends and receives provided, for example, by the TCP/IP communication stack. The broadcast and delivery of a message primitive exposed to and invoked by the application usually require execution of multiple instructions and potentially multiple sends and/or receives that use low-level communication primitives. Figure 8.8 depicts the layering of communication primitives used by applications and broadcast algorithms.

In the following, we introduce and characterize the semantics of communication primitives employed in implementing reliable broadcast algorithms/protocols. Examples include *reliable broadcast*, *FIFO broadcast*, *causal broadcast*, and *atomic broadcast* and are discussed according to the level of guarantees on message delivery they provide.

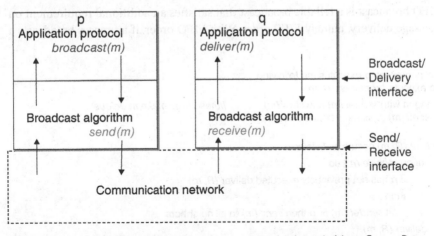

**Figure 8.8** Layering of application/broadcast communication primitives. *Source:* Data taken from Mullender [2]/Association for Computing Machinery (ACM).

### 8.5.1 Reliable Broadcast

We begin our discussion by introducing the semantics of reliable broadcast. Among the examples of broadcast algorithms/protocols considered in this section, reliable broadcast provides the weakest guarantees on message delivery. However, the other broadcast algorithms extend the basic semantics of reliable broadcast to provide stronger guarantees on message delivery. The following definitions of the key properties guaranteed by reliable broadcast were adapted from [2]:

- *Validity*: If a correct process broadcasts a message *m*, then all correct processes eventually deliver *m*, i.e. all correct processes agree on the set of messages they deliver.
- *Agreement*: If a correct process delivers a message *m*, then all correct processes eventually deliver *m*, i.e. all messages broadcast by correct processes are delivered.
- *Integrity*: For any message *m*, every correct process delivers *m* at most once and only if *m* was previously broadcast by a sender, i.e. no spurious messages are ever delivered.

Figure 8.9 gives the pseudo-code of a reliable broadcast algorithm by message diffusion (adapted from [2]).

While the introduced semantics does not impose restrictions on the order of message delivery, it guarantees that if a process fails during a broadcast, then the message is delivered either by all correct processes or by none. To impose an order on message delivery, an algorithm/protocol with enhanced semantics is required.

### 8.5.2 FIFO (First-In-First-Out) Broadcast

FIFO broadcast is a reliable broadcast that satisfies an additional requirement on message delivery, namely *FIFO order*. With FIFO order, if a process broadcasts a

---

```
Every process p executes the following:
To execute broadcast (R, m)
    tag m with sender(m) and seq#(m)        //these tags make m unique
    send (m) to all neighbors including p

deliver (R, m) occurs as follows:
    upon receive (m) do
        if p has not previously executed deliver (R, m)
        then
            if sender (m) != p then send (m) to all neighbors
        deliver (R, m)
```

**Figure 8.9** Reliable broadcast by message diffusion. *Source:* Mullender [2].

Every process *p* executes the following:
Initialization:
*msgBag* := Ø                   //set of messages that *p* received
                                //but has not yet FIFO-delivered
*next[q]* := 1 for all *q*  //sequence number of next message from *q*
                                //that *p* will FIFO-deliver


To execute *broadcast(F, m)*
    *broadcast(R, m)*

*deliver(F, m)* occurs as follows:
    upon *deliver(R, m)* do
        *q* := *sender(m)*
        *msgBag* := *msgBag* ∪ *{m}*
        while ( ∃*m'* ∈ *masgBag*: *sender(m')* = *q* and *seq#(m')* = *next[q]* do
            *deliver(F, m')*
            *next[q]* := *next[q]* +1
            *msgBag* := *msgBag* − *{m'}*

**Figure 8.10** FIFO broadcast using reliable broadcast. *Source:* Mullender [2].

message *m* before it broadcasts a message *m'*, then no correct process delivers *m'* unless it has previously delivered *m*, i.e. messages sent by the same sender are delivered in the order in which they were broadcast. Figure 8.10 gives the pseudo-code of a FIFO broadcast that uses the reliable broadcast algorithm discussed in the previous section (adapted from [2]).

## 8.5.3 Causal Broadcast

The FIFO order requirement is not sufficient if a message *m* depends on messages that the sender of *m* delivered before broadcasting *m*. For example, consider a network news application with which users distribute their articles using FIFO broadcast, as follows:

- *User 1* broadcasts an article.
- *User 2* delivers that article and broadcasts a response that can be properly handled only by a user who has the original article.
- *User 3* delivers *user 2*'s response before delivering the original article from *user 1* and consequently misinterprets the response.

Causal broadcast prevents that problem by introducing the notion of a message that depends on another message and by ensuring that a message is not delivered until all the messages on which it depends have been delivered. Causal broadcast is reliable broadcast that satisfies an additional requirement on message delivery,

Every process *p* executes the following:
Initialization:
*prevDlvrs* :=⊥          /* sequence of messages that p causal-delivered
                                        since its previous causal-broadcast */

To execute *broadcast(C, m)*:
    *broadcast(F, <prevDlvrs ‖ m>)*
    *prevDlvrs* :=⊥

*deliver(C, m)* occurs as follows:
    upon *deliver(F, <m₁, m₂, ..., mᵢ>)* for some *l* do
        for *i* := 1...1 do
            if *p* has not previously executed *deliver(C, mᵢ)*
            then
                    *deliver(C, mᵢ)*
                    *prevDlvrs* := *prevDlvrs ‖ mᵢ*

**Figure 8.11** Causal broadcast using FIFO broadcast. *Source:* Mullender [2].

namely *causal order*, which means that if the broadcast of message *m* causally precedes the broadcast of message *m'*, then no correct process delivers *m'* unless it has already delivered *m*. Figure 8.11 gives the pseudo-code of a causal broadcast that uses the FIFO broadcast algorithm introduced in the previous section (adapted from [2]).

### 8.5.4 Total Order Broadcast

Causal broadcast does not impose an order on messages that are not causally related (adapted from [2]). To illustrate, consider the following scenario:

- A replicated database has two copies of a bank account *client_acnt* resident at two different sites. Initially, *client_acnt* has a balance of $1000.
- A user deposits $150, triggering a broadcast of *msg₁*={add $150 to *client_acnt*} to the two copies of *client_acnt*.
- At the same time, at the other site, the bank initiates a broadcast of *msg₂*={add 8% interest to *client_acnt*}.
- Since the two broadcasts are not causally related, causal broadcast allows the two copies of *client_acnt* to deliver these updates in different order, creating an inconsistency in the database.

Total order broadcast, also referred to as *atomic broadcast*, prevents such problems by providing strong message ordering. Atomic broadcast is reliable broadcast that satisfies an additional requirement on message delivery, namely *total order*. Total order means that if correct processes *r* and *s* both deliver messages *m* and *m'*, then $r$ delivers $m$ before $m'$ if and only if $s$ delivers $m$ before $m'$, i.e. messages sent concurrently are delivered in identical order to the selected destinations.

## 8.6 Reliable Group Communication

A GCS provides for multipoint-to-multipoint communication between processes by organizing processes into groups. A *group* is a set of processes that are members of the group and is typically associated with a logical name. (In mobile computing, a group may also be associated with a geographic zone.) The two main services of a group communication system are (i) the *group membership* and (ii) the *reliable multicast* services. The task of a membership service is to maintain the currently active and connected processes in a group. (Processes may voluntarily leave the group or fail.) The output of the membership service is called a *view*. The task of the reliable multicast service is to deliver messages to the current view members. Processes can communicate with other group members by sending a message to the group name; the reliable multicast service delivers the message to all group members. (The description in this section is based on [7].)

### 8.6.1 Specification of Group Communication Service

Consider a system in which a set $P$ of processes communicates via message passing. The underlying communication network provides unreliable message delivery. The system is *asynchronous*, i.e. we do not make assumptions about the links' communication delay (e.g. a message may be delayed for an infinite amount of time) or on the processor execution speed (a correct processor may execute infinitely slowly). Processors may fail by *crashing* and may later *recover*, and messages may be lost or reordered; in addition, the network may partition into disjoint components, and partitions may merge back. Byzantine failures are not considered.

Figure 8.12 shows, at a process $p$, the various actions that can be performed as part of the interaction between the GCS and (1) the application and (2) the environment.

1) The application multicasts a message $m$ to the group by performing an action *mcast(p,m)*.
2) The GCS delivers $m$ to the application by performing an action *deliver(p,m)*.
3) The GCS notifies the application of a new membership view $V$ by performing an action *view_chng(p,V)*, where $V$ is a pair *<id,members>* that includes the view *id* and the set of processes in the view.
4) The events *crash(p)* and *recover(p)* are the crashing and recovery of process $p$, respectively.

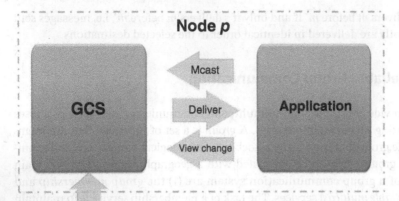

**Figure 8.12** Group communication system.

In the following, the notation "$e_1$ before $e_2$" indicates that an event $e_1$ occurs before an event $e_2$.

### 8.6.1.1 Specification of Group Membership Service

A group membership protocol manages the formation and maintenance of a set of processes called a *group*. For example, a group may be a set of processes that are cooperating on a common task (e.g. the primary and backup servers of a database), a set of processes that share a common interest (e.g. clients that subscribe to a particular newsgroup), or the set of all processes in the system that are currently deemed to be operational. In general, a process may leave a group because it has failed, because it voluntarily asks to leave, or because it is forcibly expelled by other members of the group. Similarly, a process may join a group (e.g. it may have been selected to act as a replicate for the other processes in the group). A group membership protocol must manage such dynamic changes in a coherent way; each process has a local view of the current membership of the group, and processes in the group need to agree on these local views despite failures.

For the case of group membership services that aim to maintain a single agreed-upon view of the current membership of a group, it has been shown that group membership is not solvable deterministically in asynchronous systems, in which communication is reliable and, at most, one process may crash. These are called *primary-component group membership services* and are intended for systems with no network partitions, or for systems with strong consistency requirements, which allow the group membership to change in at most one network partition, the *primary component*.

To allow for network partitions and to relax the strong consistency requirement, so-called *partitionable group membership services* have also been proposed. They allow multiple views of a group to coexist, i.e. different views of the membership of the group may evolve concurrently and independently of each other. In particular, there may be several disjoint subsets of processes such that processes in each subset agree that they are the current members of the group. Such group membership services allow group splitting (e.g. when the network partitions) and group merging (e.g. when communication between partitions is restored).

However, such partitionable group membership services run into another problem: their specification must be strong enough to rule out useless group membership protocols (in particular, protocols that can capriciously split groups into several concurrent views of the same group or capriciously install new views that exclude correct and nonsuspected processors), yet it should be weak enough to remain solvable. Several group membership specifications have been proposed over the years.

We now illustrate the properties that typical group membership services are required to satisfy. We distinguish between safety properties and liveness properties. Informally, a *safety* property requires that something "bad" must never happen; a *liveness* property requires that something "good" must eventually happen. It can be shown that every system property can be written as the conjunction of a safety property and a liveness property.

*Safety properties.* The typical safety properties of a group membership service are reported below:

- *Self-inclusion*: If a process $p$ installs a view $V$, then $p$ is a member of $V$:

  $view\_change(p,V) \Rightarrow p \in V.members.$

  This property requires that a process always be a member of its own view.
- *Local monotonicity*: If a process $p$ installs view $V$ after installing view $V'$, then the identifier of $V$ is greater than that of $V'$:

  $view\_change(p,V') \ before \ view\_change(p,V) \Rightarrow V'$
  $.id < V.id$

  This property requires that view identifiers of the view that each process installs are monotonically increasing, which has two important consequences: it guarantees (i) that a process will not install the same view more than once, and (ii) that if two processes both install the same two views, they will install the views in the same order.
- *Initial view event*: Every pair of *mcast* and deliver event occurs within some view:

  $e = mcast(p,m) \lor e = deliver(p,m) \Rightarrow viewof(e) \neq \bot$

  GCSes require that events must occur in the context of views. However, that cannot be the case for events that occur before the first view, i.e. events that do not occur in any view. To cope with the situation, GCSes typically install an initial view at startup time and upon recovery from a crash.

- *Primary component membership*: There is a one-to-one function $f$ from the set of views installed in the system to the natural numbers, such that $f$ satisfies the following property. For every view $V$ with $f(V) > 1$, there exists a view $V'$ such that $f(V) = f(V') + 1$, and a member $p$ of $V$ that installs $V$ in $V'$. (i.e. $V$ is the successor of $V'$ at process $p$.)

This property implies that for every pair of consecutive views, there is a process that survives from the first view to the second. Such a surviving process may convey information about message exchange in the first view to the members of the second.

*Liveness property.* Before defining the liveness property for a group membership service, we define *stable component* to mean a set of processes that are eventually alive and connected to each other, and to which all the channels from all other processes (that are not in the stable component) are down. Note that because of partitioning, at a given time, a network can consist of more than one stable component.

Ideally, one would like a (partitionable) membership service to be precise, i.e. to deliver a view that correctly reflects the network situation to all the live processes. The definition is formalized below:

*Precise membership*: A membership service is *precise* if, for every stable component $S$, there exists a view $V$ with the member set $S$ such that $V$ is the last view of every process $p$ in $S$.

Unfortunately, it is impossible to implement such a precise membership service in purely asynchronous environments that are prone to failures. To circumvent that impossibility, we assume that the GCS uses an external *unreliable failure detector* [1] and require that the liveness properties of the GCS hold only in executions in which the unreliable failure detector behaves as an eventually perfect failure detector ($\diamond P$), i.e. it eventually stops making mistakes.

### 8.6.1.2 Specification of Reliable Multicast Service
GCSes typically provide various types of multicast services, with different QoS and delivery ordering guarantees. As for the group membership service, we distinguish between safety properties and liveness properties.

#### Safety Properties
- *Delivery integrity*: For every deliver event, there is a preceding *mcast* event of the same message:

```
deliver(p,m) ⇒ ∃ q : mcast(q,m) ∧ mcast(q,m) before
deliver(p,m).
```

This property is trivially implemented by all GCSes.

- *No duplication*: Two different *deliver* events with the same content cannot occur at the same process:

$$e_1 = deliver(p,m) \ \wedge \ e_2 = deliver(p,m) \ \Rightarrow \ e_1 = e_2.$$

Most GCSes eliminate duplication. However, when a GCS is configured to provide the same QoS as the underlying communication layer (e.g. UDP), duplication is not eliminated.

- *Sending view delivery*: If a process $p$ receives message $m$ in view $V$, and some process $q$ sends $m$ in view $V'$, then $V = V'$.

In GCSes, send and receive events occur in the context of views to guarantee that messages will be delivered in the contexts of the views in which they were sent. Sending View Delivery can be exploited by applications to minimize the amount of context information sent with each message. For example, there are cases in which applications are only interested in processing messages that arrive in the view in which they were sent. That is usually the case with state transfer messages, sent to synchronize processes of different groups when a new view is installed because of group merging. When Sending View Delivery is used, such applications do not need to tag each state transfer message with the view in which it was sent, so that messages sent before the last view change can easily be discarded.

It has been shown that to satisfy Sending View Delivery, it is necessary for processes to block sending of messages for a certain period of time before a new view is installed. To notify the application that it needs to stop sending messages, the GCS sends a *block* request to the application. The application responds with a *flush* message, which follows all the messages sent by the application in the old view. The application then refrains from sending messages until the new view is delivered.

To avoid blocking the application, some GCSes weaken the Sending View Delivery property and require only that a message be delivered in the same view at every process that delivers it. That approach is defined as follows:

- *Same view delivery*: If processes $p$ and $q$ both receive message $m$, they receive $m$ in the same view.
- *Virtual synchrony*: If processes $p$ and $q$ install the same new view $V$ in the same previous view $V'$, then any message received by $p$ in $V'$ is also received by $q$ in $V'$. Virtual synchrony is very useful for applications that implement data replication using the state-machine approach. Such applications change their state upon receiving application messages. To keep the replicas in a consistent state, application messages are disseminated using totally ordered multicast. Whenever the network partitions, a disconnected replica may diverge and reach different states. When previously disconnected replicas reconnect, they perform

a *state transfer*, i.e. they exchange special state messages in order to reach a common state. A GCS that supports virtual synchrony allows processes to avoid state transfer among processes that "continue together" from one view to another.

- *Safe messages*: Distributed applications often require "all or nothing" semantics, i.e. either all the processes deliver a message or none of them does. Unfortunately, "all or nothing" semantics is impossible to achieve in distributed systems in which messages may be lost. An approximation of the "all or nothing" semantics is the notion of *safe* messages. A safe message $m$ is delivered to an application at process $p$ only when $p$'s GCS knows that the message is *stable*, i.e. all members of the current view have received this message from the network. In this case, each member of the current view will deliver the message unless it crashes, even if the network partitions.

An alternative approach is to decouple notification of a message's stability from its delivery. Thus, instead of deferring delivery until a message becomes stable, messages are delivered as they are received from the network, without additional delay. That delivery approach is augmented with later delivery of safe indications from the GCS to the application. An advantage of this method is that it changes the semantics of safe indications to refer to application-level rather than network-level stability: a message is stable when all members of the current view have delivered the message to the application (and not just received it from the network).

*Ordering and reliability*. Group communication systems typically provide various multicast services with a variety of ordering and reliability guarantees. The ordering properties restrict the order in which messages are delivered to the application, and the reliability properties extend the ordering properties by prohibiting gaps in the order within views. Here we describe the most common service types: *FIFO*, *causal*, and *totally ordered* (sometimes called *atomic* or *agreed*) multicast.

- *FIFO multicast*: This service type guarantees that messages from the same sender arrive in the order in which they were sent and that there are no gaps in the FIFO order within views. It is formally defined through the following properties:
  - *FIFO delivery*: If a process $p$ sends two messages, then the messages are received in the order in which they were sent at every process that receives both.
  - *Reliable FIFO*: If process $p$ sends message $m$ before message $m'$ in the same view $V$, then any process $q$ that receives $m'$ receives $m$ before $m'$.
- *Causal multicast*: This service type extends the FIFO order by requiring that a response $m'$ to a message $m$ always be delivered after the delivery of $m$. Causal multicast guarantees that messages from the same sender arrive in causal order,

and that there are no causal gaps within each view. It is formally defined through the following properties:

- *Causal delivery*: If two messages *m* and *m'* are sent so that *m* causally precedes *m'*, then every process that receives both messages receives *m* before *m'*.
- *Reliable causal*: If a message *m* causally precedes a message *m'*, and both are sent in the same view, then any process *q* that receives *m'* receives *m* before *m'*.

• *Totally ordered multicast*: In contrast with causal broadcast, totally ordered multicast also imposes order on messages that are not causally related. That is captured by the following property:

- *Strong total order*: If processes *p* and *q* both deliver messages *m* and *m'*, then *p* delivers *m* before *m'* if and only if *q* delivers *m* before *m'*, i.e. messages sent concurrently are delivered in the same order to their destinations.

The discussion above focuses on ordering semantics within a single multicast group, but GCSes generally allow processes to join multiple groups. When multicast groups overlap, one must determine the ordering semantics of messages that are sent in different groups.

*Atomic multicast* requires that messages be delivered in a total order by all the destination processes, including those that are at the intersection of the groups. For instance, if two distinct messages are sent to two different overlapping process groups, then all the processes, including those at the intersection of the two groups, should deliver the two messages in the same order.

It has been shown that unless additional assumptions (such as reliable failure detection or reliable groups) are imposed on the system model, solving atomic multicast requires sending of messages to additional processes that are not members of the group to which the message is addressed. For example, in Ensemble, the application can configure the protocol stack to use atomic multicast: messages are first sent to a daemon, where they are totally ordered, and then they are multiplexed by the daemon to the different groups.

### 8.6.2 Example Implementations of Group Communication Systems

In this section, we cite some of the most well-known systems that have been proposed.

The *Isis* toolkit [8] was probably the first group communication system. It provides the programmer with an API to manage process groups, multicast messages to groups, synchronize between processes, and manage replicated data. The notion of virtual synchrony is also introduced through Isis, in which all replicas in a group see the same view changes in the same order. *Horus* [9] extended Isis by providing a more flexible protocol stack through which group communication occurs. The protocol stack is configurable through layering of microprotocols to provide various combinations of services. Examples of microprotocols include low-level access to IP and UDP, a negative acknowledgment (ACK) multicast protocol, a consensus protocol to realize virtual synchrony, a flow-control layer, and a layer to guarantee total-order message delivery. Configurations are limited to a set of permissible combinations of microprotocols stacked in a valid order. The design gives the application programmer the flexibility to change the protocol stack at runtime. The enhanced version of Horus is called *Ensemble* [10].

*Totem* [11] provides totally ordered multicast over local area networks, utilizing hardware broadcasts where available. Totem introduces the notion of extended virtual synchrony, by means of which it can recover from network partitions. *Transis* [12] has goals similar to Totem's, with the addition of safe multicasting (which requires that all processes in a group receive a message before the message can be delivered).

The *SecureRing* [13] group communication protocols provide reliable ordered message delivery and group membership services despite Byzantine faults. The approach adopted by SecureRing to protect against Byzantine faults is to optimize the performance for normal (fault-free) operation and to pay a performance penalty when a Byzantine fault is detected, which is expected to happen rarely. In SecureRing, a group member embeds digests (i.e. hashed values of digital signatures) for the messages it has multicast into a signed token that it multicasts to reduce the performance penalty.

*Rampart* [14] is a toolkit for the development of survivable services, i.e. distributed services that can tolerate arbitrary corruption of a server component by an attacker. Even if an attacker penetrates some servers, the provided service as viewed by clients will continue to be correct. At the core of Rampart are protocols such as synchronous group membership, reliable multicast (Byzantine agreement), and atomic multicast. Using these protocols, Rampart supports the development of high-integrity services via the technique of state machine replication [15].

## 8.7 Replication

Replication is a typical example of the use of space redundancy to achieve fault tolerance. In hardware, the two basic techniques for replication are *fault-masking* and *standby spares*. The software counterparts of those techniques are typically referred to as *active* and *passive replication*. Replication uses multiple instances of the same component (e.g. a logical circuit in hardware or a user application in software) so that independent failures can be assumed. With active replication (as with fault-masking), multiple instances of a component simultaneously perform the same work. Each component is presented with the same set of inputs and produces, in the absence of faults, the same outputs. Usually, an extra component (i.e. a voter) is used for majority voting on outputs from replicas to produce a single response from the replicated system and to mask potential errors/failures. The resulting system is indistinguishable from a single, nonfaulty component. With passive replication (as with standby spares), the computation is done by only one component (i.e. the primary). One or more additional instances of the component (i.e. backups) are ready to switch over when a fault is detected in the primary.

Although hardware-based and software-based replication schemes share the same principles, their actual implementations must cope with different issues stemming from the specifics of the hardware and software. In hardware, information can be broadcast to multiple components (simply by increasing the number of wires in the system), without incurring significant performance loss.

Moreover, it is relatively easy to guarantee that inputs will arrive at replicated components in the same order. In software-based replication, reliable broadcasting and consistency of information constitute major difficulties to overcome in the implementation of replicated systems. Those issues have been deeply investigated and resulted in many flavors of group communication protocols. Because the protocols execute in a network (whose speed is orders of magnitude less than the speed of processors), the performance overhead incurred is a major factor in determining the performance of the overall replicated system.

Another fundamental issue is the potential nondeterminism in the execution of different instances of a replicated component. To ensure the correct behavior of the replicated system, the algorithms implemented by replicas must be deterministic in nature, i.e. they should produce the same output if provided with identical initial states and if identical sets of inputs arrive in the same order.

One might think that for simple logic circuitry (e.g. combinatorial circuits), behavior can be assumed to be deterministic. However, as the complexity of a circuit reaches that of a microprocessor, additional synchronization among replicas may be required to prevent different replicas' behaviors from diverging from each other. For instance, in a TMR system, such as the Integrity S2 from Tandem, to guarantee that the three processors execute the same instruction streams, the processors were constantly synchronized (i) on global memory accesses, (ii) on hardware interrupts, and (iii) periodically (every 4096 run cycles).

In software, the nondeterminism issue is harder to deal with because the system is intrinsically heterogeneous. The first work on software-based replication tried to emulate in software what was done in hardware, e.g. replicas were synchronized at the hardware interrupt level. Although that strategy was reasonably efficient in hardware (because synchronization signals can easily be propagated in parallel to all processors with additional wires and logic), in software it caused a large performance overhead (because synchronization information is transferred over a network). Another approach was to require the programmer to implement replicas to avoid the use of possible causes of nondeterminism (e.g. local timers, local random numbers, and multithreading). Several studies dealt with multithreading by using a nonpreemptive deterministic scheduler (NPDS) that guarantees the same scheduling on all replicas. However, because the scheduler is nonpreemptive, it strongly limits concurrency; on uniprocessor machines, I/O and CPU usage cannot be overlapped, and on multiprocessor machines, only one processor can be used by the replica threads. In consequence, a replicated server cannot scale well as the number of concurrent client requests increases.

In the rest of this chapter, work that we consider to be among the most significant on hardware-based or software-based replication is briefly presented, with the intent of highlighting strengths and weaknesses. Leveraging our experience, we will also identify issues that still require investigation.

## 8.7.1 Replication in Hardware

*The Self-Test and Repair (STAR)* experimental computer developed by the Jet Propulsion Laboratory (JPL) can be considered a milestone in fault-tolerant system design. The STAR was a prototype for a real-time satellite-control computer intended for a 10-year mission to the outer planets of the solar system. It employed a mixture of error-detection coding, online monitoring, standby redundancy, replication with voting, component redundancy, and repetition in order to attain hardware-controlled self-repair and protection against faults. A transient fault was corrected by re-execution of a segment of the current program; a permanent fault was eliminated by replacement of the faulty functional unit with one of the spares. The resulting hardware was a full-custom fault-tolerant computer system. The "hard-core" monitor of the STAR system was the test and repair processor (TARP), which monitored the operation of the STAR computer in two ways: (i) by checking the validity of the error code of every word sent over the data busses, and (ii) by checking the status messages from the functional units. Three fully powered copies of TARP were operated together with $n$ standby spares. The outputs of the TARPs were decided by a 2-out-of-$(n + 3)$ threshold vote. To recover the system when one powered TARP disagreed with the other two, an attempt was made to set the internal state of the disagreeing unit to match the other two units. If the attempt failed the disagreeing unit was unpowered, and one of the standby units received power, set its internal state to match the other two units, and joined the powered triplet. The computer was then restarted, a rollback was performed, and standard operation mode continued. Because the TARP was triplicated, design effort was concentrated on minimizing its complexity [16].

*The Electronic Switching Systems (ESSes)* were developed by Bell Laboratories to provide commercial telephone services. These systems handle the routing of telephone calls through central offices, so have a severe availability goal: only three minutes of downtime per year. The ESS systems take advantage of the natural redundancy present in the telephone network and in the data conveyed. (Telephone users will redial if they get a wrong number or are disconnected.) However, there is a user aggravation level that must be avoided; users will redial only if they aren't forced to redial too frequently. To meet the availability requirements, redundant components and a self-checking duplicated processor are used. When a hardware failure occurs in any of the subunits, the system is reconfigured in a working configuration around the defective unit. The system will go down only if two faults occur simultaneously [17].

*Integrity S2* [18] was a fault-tolerant, UNIX-based computing system developed by Tandem Computers, Inc., for use as a high-availability computing platform for commercial transactional processing. Fault tolerance was completely transparent to user applications and was achieved by means of massive redundancy intended to mask faults. One objective of the architects was to use CPUs, I/O devices, and an operating system that were commercially available. The system was a RISC-based, triple modular redundant (TMR) processing core, with duplexed global memory and an I/O subsystem. The operating system was derived from an MIPS port of System V Release 3. Scrubbers, implemented in the operating system, were used to detect, and if possible correct, latent errors in memory.

*Synchronization and voting.* Two time domains are defined: (i) physical time, which is the ordinal time, and (ii) virtual time, which is measured by the execution of instructions on a given CPU. Each CPU module measures the local virtual time by means of a counter (i.e. a cycle counter), which is incremented only when the pipeline of the CPU advances (i.e. an instruction has been executed).

The three identical CPUs are loosely synchronized, as each one uses a local clock and a local memory (for caching the most frequently used data). To execute the same instruction stream, CPUs are synchronized (i) on global memory references, (ii) periodically, and (iii) on external interrupts, as explained below:

- *Global memory references*: The global memory system consists of two identical self-checking memory modules that store duplicates of the same data. The two global memories both perform all write requests received from the CPUs or the I/O busses, so that both are kept up to date, but only one memory module (the primary) presents read data in response to read requests. Data written to global memory have associated parity bits, and parity is checked when data are retrieved by each memory module. Global memory references by the three CPUs are made by three independent busses connected to three separated ports of the two memory modules. All global memory references are voted on. As a memory request arrives from one of the CPUs, the memory operation is started, but it is not complete until the last CPU request has been received and voted good. Hence, global memory references synchronize CPUs in physical time.

- *External interrupts*: CPU-generated interrupts are sent from CPUs to the two global memory modules, where the interrupts are voted on. The two votes from the two memory modules are OR-ed and presented to the CPUs as external interrupts. External interrupts (i.e. voted, CPU-generated interrupts and I/O interrupts) are synchronized in virtual time via a distributed vote on the interrupts followed by a presentation of each interrupt to the CPUs on a predetermined cycle count. Each CPU contains a distributor that captures the external interrupt on a predetermined cycle count $C'$ and distributes it to the other two CPUs. In each CPU, a voter circuit captures the distributed interrupts (i.e. pending interrupts) and votes on them. The voter presents the majority vote to the interrupt pin of its respective microprocessor on a predetermined cycle count $C''$. Because all microprocessors receive the interrupt on the same cycle count $C''$, the interrupt will be synchronized in virtual time. Note that the algorithm described is the counterpart of the agreement protocol [19] employed in software-based replication.
- *Periodic synchronization*: Each CPU has a modulo-4096 counter whose overflow signal is used to generate a coprocessor-busy (*CP-busy*) signal to stall the microprocessor. A logic circuit present in each CPU receives the stall signals from all CPUs. Once all three CPUs have stalled, that circuit releases the CP-busy signal, and processors will come out of the stall in synchrony again.

*Error recovery and reintegration.* Global memory is duplicated, and backup memory is kept continuously synchronized with the content of the primary memory. In fact, all memory operations from the three CPUs are performed on both memories. When there is a read request, only the primary memory loads the read value on the memory busses; however, both memories return information on the status lines of the busses. Using that information, CPUs can determine whether there was any error in the primary memory. After a memory operation has been issued by the CPUs, if the primary memory returns a data error on the status lines of the memory busses, but the backup memory does not return any error (i.e. the operation executed successfully on the backup memory), then the CPUs will generate an interrupt. The interrupt will eventually cause the backup memory to take over from the failed primary memory. The system is thus reconfigured with the new primary memory (i.e. the previous backup memory) and can continue operating with the single global memory. The fault condition is signaled to the operator, which can replace the board containing the faulty memory. Eventually, reintegration can take place, as explained next.

The system is able to reintegrate a new memory board without a shutdown by using a two-step process. (i) First, all data are read from the good memory and written to both memory modules (location by location). That activity is interleaved with normal operation, except that write requests from I/O busses are suspended. (ii) Then, the system proceeds as in step 1, except that now write requests from I/O busses are not suspended. At the end of the process, the two memory modules contain identical data, and either of them can be designated as the primary.

When a CPU is found to be faulty (e.g. by the voter embedded in the global memory modules, which checks whether all CPUs make identical memory requests), the other two CPUs continue to operate. The bad CPU board is isolated and can be replaced without system shutdown. When the new CPU board is inserted into the system and completes its power-on self-testing routines, it signals this to the other CPUs. All CPUs then execute a revive routine as follows. (i) The two good CPUs copy their states to global memory. (ii) All three CPUs execute a "soft reset" whereby the CPUs reset and start executing from their initialization routines (which are contained in the ROM present on each CPU board). (iii) Eventually, all the CPUs will come up at the same point in their instruction stream and will be synchronized. (iv) The saved state is copied back into all three CPUs, and the task that was previously executed is continued.

### 8.7.2 Replication in Software

In this subsection, we discuss examples of software replication at different levels of the system software stack.

#### 8.7.2.1 Replication at the Level of the Operating System

The TARGON/32 system uses a process-pair scheme to ensure that an arbitrary process can survive any single hardware failure. The system consists of a local area network of 2–16 machines connected via a dual bus. Each machine is a shared-memory, three-processor machine. One of the processors executes the kernel code to handle incoming and outgoing messages and the creation, maintenance, and recovery of backup processes. The remaining two processors execute UNIX-style processes and most of the system-call-related kernel code. The UNIX operating system was rewritten to provide backup creation, checkpointing, and recovery transparently to user processes. Since only processes survive a crash, critical operating system functions were moved out of the kernel into recoverable server processes. The backup and recovery schemes used require atomic three-way message delivery,[2] which is implemented by the bus hardware and low-level software driver protocols. To force deterministic execution of UNIX processes, all asynchronous events (e.g. UNIX signals) are transformed into synchronous

---

2 Messages between backed-up processes are sent to three destinations: the target process and both the sender's and the receiver's backups.

messages delivered to the destination process and its backup. Moreover, the system ensures that a system call will return the same value to a recovered backup as it did to the primary. After a crash, a machine can be repaired and reinstalled in the system. Once the machine has been rebooted, processes that were running create new copies of themselves. Benchmarks running on a fault-tolerant, two-machine system show a 60% performance improvement relative to a standard single-processor UNIX machine [20].

### 8.7.2.2 Replication at the Level Between the Hardware and the Operating System

When replication is implemented in hardware, a design cost is incurred for each new realization of the architecture. Support of replication via hardware is expensive (in terms of time and hardware resources) and consequently may have a negative impact on the cost/performance ratio. Adding replication to an existing operating system has proven to be difficult, since mature operating systems are complex.

The hypervisor system provides primary/backup replication transparently to the operating system and user applications. To force the backup machine to execute the same instruction stream as the primary machine, the hypervisor system takes advantage of the hardware instruction counter available in the HP PA-RISC architecture. A virtual machine layer, inserted beneath the operating system, uses the hardware instruction counter to count the instructions executed between two hardware interrupts. That information is collected on the primary machine for a specific period called an *epoch*. The information collected during each epoch is sent over the network to the backup machine. The backup uses instruction counts to mimic the effects of hardware interrupts that occurred at the primary. Moreover, to enforce determinism on nondeterministic instructions (e.g. instructions for reading the time-of-day clock, loading the interval timer, and performing I/O), the instructions are simulated by the hypervisor. Thus, the execution of the backup will be identical to that of the primary machine, but there will be a lag between the execution of the primary and the execution of the backup. A prototype implementation was tested with both a CPU-intensive workload and an I/O-intensive workload. For epochs that were not too long (i.e. under 8K instructions), workloads involving I/O experienced approximately 70% of the performance overhead. The CPU-intensive workload required much longer epochs (e.g. 32K instructions) before the performance overhead decreased to 84% [21].

### 8.7.2.3 Replication at the Level Between the Operating System and the User Application

The Transparent Fault Tolerance (TFT) software system provides transparent fault tolerance via primary/backup replication at the operating system call interface. TFT coordinates replicas by interposing a supervisor agent between the application and the operating system. On UNIXWARE systems, it does so by replacing the C runtime library with calls to the supervisor. On Windows NT, the Win32 DLLs were replaced. To enforce deterministic computation, nondeterministic system calls (e.g. *gettimeofday*, *read*, and *write*) are emulated,[3] while exceptions (e.g. asynchronous signals and nonblocking I/O completion notifications) are delivered at the same points in the instruction streams through use of a software emulation of an instruction-counter register, much as the hypervisor system does.

### 8.7.2.4 Replication at the User-Level

SIFT (Software Implemented Fault Tolerance) was one of the earliest attempts to provide fault tolerance substantially through software rather than hardware. With SIFT, a program executes independently on a number of redundant modules, each consisting of a processor and memory. The processor places its output in memory, and the consuming task performs majority voting on values from all processors before using the data. A process in SIFT consists of several iterations, and voting is done at the beginning of each iteration. Hence, the processing modules need only be loosely synchronized at iteration boundaries, not tightly synchronized at the instruction or interrupt level [22].

The Delta-4 project aimed to provide fault tolerance by means of an atomic multicast protocol and specialized network attachment controllers (NACs) capable of running the complete communication stack. The controllers produced by Delta-4 have enhanced self-checking mechanisms to enforce fail-silent execution of replicas. The system provides user applications with (i) passive replication, in which backup replicas are regularly updated by means of checkpoints of the primary replica; (ii) semi-active replication, in which only the *leader* replica provides output messages, while the *follower* replicas update their state either by direct processing of input messages or by means of "notifications" from the leader replica; and (iii) active replication, in which all replicas process all input messages concurrently so that their internal states are synchronized. Replica determinism is required for active replication. To handle nondeterministic execution in semi-active process replication, applications need to be modified to adhere to the polling event model. Interrupts are queued until the application program executes a polling routine, in which all replicas synchronize and agree on which interrupts were received and the order in which they are to be processed [23].

In the software approaches discussed to this point, the entity to replicate is a process; e.g. in the client/server paradigm, fault tolerance is achieved through replication of the server process. More recent work, following the object-oriented

---

3 The primary performs the operation, and the backup simulates the operation by returning the same transformation in state as the primary.

paradigm, has focused on object replication. Replication at the granularity of an object offers greater flexibility than server replication does in configuration management of the number of replicas and their assignment to different hosts. Replicated objects can invoke the methods of other replicated objects independently of the physical location of those objects. A common trend in object replication work has been to integrate fault tolerance via replication in CORBA applications, which is discussed next.

### 8.7.2.5 CORBA

An early approach to fault-tolerant CORBA was to integrate replication mechanisms in the ORB itself, providing a fault-tolerant ORB (e.g. *Isis* [8] and *Maestro* [24] follow that approach). Since replication is integrated with the ORB, this approach can be made efficient. On the other hand, the resulting ORB is nonstandard and typically does not support portions of the CORBA standard.

Another approach has been to provide fault tolerance through CORBA services above the ORB (e.g. *OGS* [25] follows that approach). The main drawback is that replication is made explicit to the programmer through use of the provided fault tolerance services, so existing CORBA applications need to be modified. Furthermore, since fault tolerance is implemented at a high level in the communication stack, performance inefficiency can become an issue.

Yet another approach has been to intercept messages from the ORB and send them via a group communication protocol to ensure reliable delivery. The advantage of this approach is that it is independent of the underlying ORB and is application-transparent. Eternal [26] implements the interception as a collection of library interposers, with each interposer overriding a specific subset of the standard library. In particular, it diverts the CORBA application's TCP/IP-based IIOP communication to the Totem [11] group communication protocol through a socket library interposer.[4]

Eternal supports different replication styles (active, cold passive, warm passive, and hot passive) of both the client and the server objects. *AQuA* [27] uses a proxy approach to intercept CORBA message invocations, redirect them to AQuA gateways that are on top of the ORB, and forward the messages into a group communication system without going through the ORB.

### 8.7.3 The Problem of Nondeterminism

Replication requires replica determinism to ensure that no undesirable or unforeseen side effects cause the state of replicas to be inconsistent. Unfortunately, many practical applications use nondeterministic mechanisms, such as local timers,

---

4 To tolerate arbitrary faults, Eternal exploits the SecureRing protocol [13].

processor-specific functions, and multithreading. Among those, multithreading is the most crucial, because without it, the overall performance and scalability of an application can be significantly compromised. In uniprocessor machines, multi-threading allows for overlapping of I/O with CPU usage; in multiprocessor machines, different threads can be scheduled to run simultaneously on different CPUs, possibly allowing significant speed-up relative to a sequential implementation of the same application.

The traditional solution to nondeterminism in replica execution has been to force replicas to serve hardware interrupts at the same point in the instruction stream. In hardware-based replication, the Integrity S2 system used dedicated hardware to count the run cycles of a RISC processor. In software-based replication, the idea was to use a hardware instruction counter available in many processors or a software emulation of the counter. When interrupt synchronization is implemented entirely in hardware, it can be made efficient; however, when interrupts are synchronized in software, the overhead becomes substantial because the extra communication needed is done over a network. Software-based replication approaches that allow nondeterminism in replica behavior, such as TARGON/32, the hypervisor system, and TFT, provided only primary/backup replication. Because those approaches synchronized replicas at the interrupt level, using active replication would significantly degrade performance. Moreover, voting would require additional synchronization and hence introduce extra overhead.

The Eternal system addresses the use of multithreading for replicated CORBA applications in a way that is transparent both to the application and to the ORB. To achieve that goal, Eternal employs a NPDS and allows the execution of only one logical thread at a time. Concurrency is thereby strongly limited. In uniprocessor systems, it is not possible to overlap I/O with CPU usage. In multiprocessor systems, a process that contains replicated objects cannot take advantage of multiple CPUs and executes sequentially on only one CPU (i.e. only one thread can be scheduled at a time) [26].

Transactional Drago employs a deterministic, nonpreemptive scheduler to enforce deterministic behavior of multithreaded replicas. The algorithm targets transactional applications and allows the concurrent execution of several transactions. Since the algorithm is nonpreemptive, threads cannot be interrupted, e.g. because of high-priority traffic. The scheduler cannot exploit all the concurrency obtained by overlapping the I/O and computation, since it allows the execution of only one thread at a time. Scheduling of another thread can be done only when the running thread reaches a scheduling point. Scheduling points are service requests, selective receptions, lock requests, server calls, and end of execution. Similarly, the scheduler cannot take advantage of the presence of multiple CPUs on multiprocessor machines, since to enforce determinism, it supports only one running thread. Unlike Eternal, Transactional Drago allows the execution of more than one logical thread at a time; however, like Eternal, it can schedule only one physical thread at a time (even though multiple CPUs are available). Transactional Drago therefore suffers from limitations similar to Eternal [28].

### 8.7.4 Paxos and Read-Write Quorums: A Practical Approach to Achieving Eventual Consistency

In a distributed memory system, various hardware, system, and software components can fail, leading to unavailability of data. One possible approach to dealing with such failures is to create multiple replicas or copies of the memory location. A key challenge in doing so is to create a coherent view of replicated data, but that can be achieved by using consistency protocols. In this section, we will explore two protocols that offer different kinds of consistency guarantees for replicated data in distributed systems: Paxos [29] and read-write quorums [30].

#### 8.7.4.1 Paxos

At its core, Paxos is a distributed consensus algorithm used to enable multiple processes to agree upon a single value. In general, consensus algorithms, including Paxos, can be used to maintain consistency between reads and writes to shared memory/storage locations. Paxos has been widely adopted in commercial systems such as ZooKeeper [31], Hadoop [32], Kafka [33], and Ceph [34].

*Fault models.* Paxos offers a consistent data view under the following fault models:

- *Network delay*: Paxos assumes that messages are eventually delivered within a bounded delay (which might not be known ahead of time).
- *Network/storage failures*: If there are $N$ replicas of the storage location, Paxos assumes that at most $N/2$ replicas (and network messages originating in them) can end up in a crash failure. If the number of crash faults is greater than $N/2$, Paxos may not terminate. Moreover, consistency is not guaranteed under silent data corruption and malicious or Byzantine behavior.
- *Request serialization*: Paxos assumes that read-write requests can be performed concurrently.

*Algorithm summary.* Paxos assigns each replica one or both of two roles: proposer and/or acceptor. Note that each replica may have multiple roles at the same time. The Paxos algorithm proceeds in two phases, as follows. In phase I, a proposer selects a proposal number $n$ and sends a "prepare" request to a majority of the acceptors, asking them not to reply to or accept any other proposal with a lower number. If an acceptor receives a *prepare-request* for proposal $n$, and has not responded to a *prepare-request* with a higher number, it will make a promise to accept values from that request in the future. In phase II, if a proposer receives affirmation from a majority of its *prepare-requests*, it sends an *accept-request* with a proposed value. If an acceptor receives an *accept-request* for proposal *n*, and has not responded to a *prepare-request* with a higher number, it accepts the proposal.

### 8.7.5 Read-Write Quorums

Read-write (R/W) quorums are consistency protocols used in distributed databases. They handle read and write requests differently. Read-write quorums are said to provide "weak tunable consistency" because they have a weaker fault model than Paxos, which requires parameter setup. R/W quorums have been adopted by Netflix, Amazon's DynamoDB [35] and Facebook's Cassandra [36].

*Fault models.* Read-write quorums offer a consistent view under the following fault models:

- *Network delay*: Read-write quorums assume the same network delay model as Paxos, i.e. messages are eventually delivered within a bounded delay (that might not be known ahead of time).
- *Network/storage failures*: Read-write quorums assume that replicas may be inaccessible due to failures in underlying storage devices or network paths. The number of tolerable failures depends on the level of replication.
- *Request serialization*: Read-write quorums assume that requests are received serially. Concurrent requests can lead to inconsistent scenarios; hence, the read-write quorums approach is a weakly consistent algorithm.

*Algorithm.* Quorum values for read ($R$) and write ($W$) replicas are chosen prior to algorithm execution. For consistency, the condition is that $R + W > N + F$, where $F$ is the number of crash faults that need to be handled and $N$ is the number of replicas. Each read or write request is sent to all $N$ replicas, and when $R$ or $W$ replicas respond back (depending on the type of request), the request completes. Quorums ensure consistency because at least one replica contains the latest value of the memory location.

In summary, both Paxos and read-write quorums offer consistency for replicated data but have different fault models. The primary differences are in the number of crash faults that can be tolerated and in request serialization. If requests are serial (such as memory addresses protected by locking primitives), R/W quorums offer better fault tolerance. However, when requests are concurrent, consistency breaks, and stronger protocols such as Paxos are required. In the distributed memory context, concurrent requests may occur in order to acquire and release locks.

## 8.8 Replication of Multithreaded Applications

In software-based active replication, to ensure the correct behavior of the replicated system, the algorithms implemented by the replicas must be deterministic, i.e. they should produce the same outputs when provided with identical initial states and if they have identical sets of inputs arriving in the same order. Software-based replication is typically quite expensive in terms of performance overhead [27, 37, 38]; that is a major reason for its limited acceptance in real-world applications. Multithreading can help improve performance by exploiting concurrency in thread execution; however, since the thread/process scheduling performed by operating systems such as UNIX is asynchronous with replica execution, multi-threaded replicas can exhibit *nondeterministic* behavior.

Solutions for replicating multithreaded applications/objects are based on a NPDS, which achieves determinism in replica state updates by enforcing the same interleaving of threads on all replicas. In eternal, determinism is achieved through sequential processing of application threads (each of which serves a client request); it is effectively a single-threaded solution [26]. In Transactional Drago, the executions of multiple logical threads are interleaved. If the running thread starts an I/O operation, the thread is suspended while waiting for I/O to complete, while another thread may be scheduled [28].[5] Nonpreemptive deterministic schedules, although they provide consistent replica behavior, cannot exploit concurrency in thread execution, since only one physical thread is scheduled at a given time. This results in poor scalability and performance of the replicated system.

In contrast, strong replica consistency can be enforced without requiring interleaving of the same thread on all replicas, thus preserving concurrency. It can be achieved by intercepting mutex lock/unlock operations performed by application threads upon accessing the shared data. To that end, we discuss two algorithmic solutions for enabling low-overhead multithreaded replication [39]:

- The loose synchronization algorithm (LSA), wherein one replica (leader) decides on the mutex acquisition order and propagates it to other replicas (followers), which enforce the leader-dictated order on the execution of their threads (only on a per-mutex basis) [13].
- The Preemptive Deterministic Scheduling (PDS) algorithm, with no leader/follower structure and no inter-replica communication. Replica consistency is achieved by breaking a replica execution into a sequence of rounds. The mechanism is such that when a new round fires, all threads' mutex requests

---

5 To guarantee determinism, there are situations in which the algorithm waits for the I/O to complete (while keeping the CPU idle), although another thread can be scheduled.

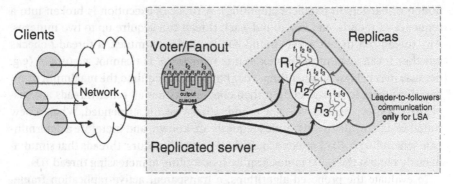

**Figure 8.13** Active replication architecture. *Source:* Basile et al. [39]/IEEE.

are known, and thus mutex acquisitions can be deterministically scheduled for the round [14].

The algorithms presented in this section are discussed in the context of the active replication architecture depicted in Figure 8.13, where a single voter/fanout component accepts requests from the clients, dispatches client requests to the multithreaded replicas (via a FIFO-ordered reliable multicast), collects (unicast) replica outputs and votes on them (on a per-replica thread basis), and delivers the majority outputs to the clients. Voting on a per-thread basis is necessary because, to preserve concurrency in replica thread execution, we cannot guarantee ordering of replica outputs. Note that the proposed algorithms are applicable to other replication schemes that use duplicated voter/fanout or embedded voter within each client. The considered replication mechanism employs an underlying group communication layer (e.g. [10, 14]), which provides virtual synchrony through group membership and FIFO-ordered reliable multicast services.

In NPDSs, an *LSA* ensures the deterministic behavior of replicas while preserving concurrency [39]. The algorithm enforces a compatible sequence of state updates in all replicas without requiring the same thread to interleave. It does so by intercepting mutex lock/unlock operations performed by application threads upon accessing the shared data. Interception of mutex lock/unlock operations was first suggested in [40] for message logging-based recovery. In the LSA algorithm, one replica (the leader) decides on the mutex acquisition order and propagates it to other replicas (followers), which enforce the leader-dictated order on the execution of their threads. While the method preserves a large degree of concurrency, the presence of inter-replica communication can affect overall system dependability.

To overcome that limitation, a *PDS* algorithm, with no leader/follower structure and no inter-replica communication, has been proposed. In PDS, the key mechanism for ensuring determinism is the concept of *rounds* (which is similar to the notion of barriers in parallel computing). A replica's execution is broken into a sequence of rounds, and in a round, each thread can acquire up to two mutexes. Any thread can trigger a new round. On requesting a mutex, a thread $t$ checks whether it can acquire the mutex $m$ it is requesting. If $t$ cannot acquire $m$ (e.g. because $m$ is held by another thread or $t$ has already acquired the maximum number of mutexes for that round), it then checks whether all other threads are suspended. If they are, $t$ starts a new round; otherwise, $t$ is suspended. When a new round is started, all threads' mutex requests are known, and therefore a deterministic scheduling (DS) of mutex acquisitions naturally occurs: threads that simultaneously request the same mutex acquire it according to increasing thread IDs.

To evaluate the proposed algorithms, a transparent active replication framework was developed. The framework consists of (i) an implementation of the LSA and PDS algorithms; (ii) a *virtual socket layer*, which provides transparent replication; and (iii) an adaptive *voter/fanout* component, which detects errors (crashes, hangs, and value errors), excludes faulty replicas, and reliably multicasts client requests to the replicas. The framework has been used to replicate the multithreaded version of the Apache web server, a substantial real-world application. Results show a performance degradation of about 23% for an Apache web server triplicated with the LSA algorithm, relative to a noninstrumented, TCP-based version of the same server.

While most algorithms for providing fault tolerance services are formally proved for correctness, the use of fault/error injection is essential for sound assessment of a proposed algorithm's dependability. Employing fault/error-injection allows us to study the failure behavior of an overall system (including the algorithm) under realistic scenarios, which cannot be achieved using formal methods alone.

A performance evaluation showed that PDS and LSA outperform NPDS. The reason is that PDS and LSA can schedule multiple threads to execute at the same time. PDS provides lower throughput than LSA; however, it provides additional benefits in terms of system dependability and hence can be considered to offer a trade-off between performance and dependability.

A fault/error-injection-based evaluation of dependability showed that because LSA relies on an inter-replica communication channel for efficient scheduling of mutex acquisitions, the algorithm is relatively sensitive to the underlying communication layer's fail silence violations. That leads to a larger number of catastrophic failures (i.e. cases in which the entire replicated system fails) for LSA than for PDS. (NPDS dependability characteristics are similar to those of PDS because neither uses inter-replica communication.) Therefore, if minimizing of downtime is crucial (as it is for highly available systems), PDS is a more appropriate choice than LSA; if performance concerns have priority over minimizing of downtime, then LSA can be preferred to PDS.

### 8.8.1   System Model: Definitions and Assumptions

A system consists of a set of identical multithreaded processes (i.e. replicas) running on different nodes. Each replica consists of a set of threads $T$ and a set of mutexes $M$ used to protect partitions of shared data. ($T$ and $M$ can be infinite.) It is assumed that the same thread/mutex IDs are associated with corresponding threads/mutexes of different replicas; this can be enforced by using a hierarchical thread/mutex naming scheme. We define three atomic actions: (i) *request(m,t)*, which corresponds to thread $t$'s request for a mutex $m$; (ii) *acquire(m,t)*, which corresponds to thread $t$'s acquisition of mutex $m$; and (iii) *release(m,t)*, which corresponds to thread $t$'s release of a mutex $m$. Two mutex acquisitions are said to be *conflicting* if they are made by different threads on the same mutex. In general, the order in which conflicting mutex acquisitions are made may affect the result of a computation.

The *history of a replica* is the sequence of mutex acquisitions by its threads at a given time. Since threads within a replica $r$ execute on the same node, the order of the mutex acquisitions in the history is determined by the time (based on the node's local clock) when the threads make the acquisitions. Enforcing the same history on all replicas (under the assumption of determinism, as defined later) makes all replicas behave in the same way. This, however, is a stronger requirement than necessary since only the causal dependencies between mutex acquisitions need to be preserved.

The notion of *causal precedence* between two mutex acquisitions in a multithreaded process is analogous to the notion of causal precedence between two events in a distributed system [41]. As concurrent events in distributed systems are not causally related, concurrent mutex acquisitions in a multithreaded process are those acquisitions whose actual order of execution does not affect the result of the computation. To preserve concurrency, we allow replicas to schedule concurrent mutex acquisitions independently. Based on the notion of causal precedence, the following definition introduces the causal set of a mutex acquisition, which represents all mutex acquisitions upon which a given mutex acquisition is causally dependent.

A **deterministic scheduling algorithm** must assume that threads behave deterministically between two consecutive mutex acquisitions. The assumption is somewhat similar to the piecewise deterministic assumption made by proponents of message-logging checkpointing [42]. While determinism is traditionally expressed in terms of state, the causal set is used as an abstraction to represent a thread's view of the replica's state at the moment of a given mutex acquisition.

A multithreaded **application with piecewise deterministic threads is defined to be correct** if: (i) Each application thread releases only mutexes it owns; (ii) If an application thread executes infinitely often, then the thread (a) eventually releases each mutex it acquires and (b) requests mutexes infinitely often;

and (iii) The mutex dependency graph is acyclic. The correctness of a DS algorithm is defined with respect to a correct application as the conjunction of an internal correctness property, which defines the behavior of the algorithm only with respect to one replica, and an external correctness property, which defines the behavior of the algorithm with respect to other replicas.

### 8.8.2 Specification of the LSA Algorithm

In the following, it is assumed that replica nodes are interconnected by means of a network. One replica is designated the leader; the others are followers. A FIFO-order reliable multicast and group membership services are available for leader-to-followers communication; the network does not partition.

Replica nodes are interconnected by means of a synchronous network that does not partition. FIFO-ordered reliable multicast and group membership services are available for inter-replica communication. (In practice, if it is ensured that LSA communication and voter-replica communication occur in different multicast groups, these services can be provided by the same group communication layer used by the replication infrastructure.) One replica is designated as the leader; the others are followers. (The selection can be done by means of a deterministic rule, e.g. pick the first, applied on the current group membership view.) In application threads, the system calls *lock* and *unlock* (to acquire and release a mutex) are replaced with the functions *lsa_lock* and *lsa_unlock*.

The LSA algorithm uses a leader-follower scheme to enforce the same external behavior in all replicas so that replicas can participate in active replication schemes in which majority voting is used to mask Byzantine replica failures. (Note that we consider active replication to be a replication style in which all replicas concurrently serve requests and send replies so that a majority voting scheme can be employed. Active replication contrasts with passive replication, in which a single primary replica is operative, while a backup replica is on standby and becomes operational only when the primary fails.) Also, observe that our scheme is different from the leader-follower scheme of Delta-4 [23] proposed for semi-active replication, in which the leader is the only replica that replies to the clients and, consequently, must be assumed to be fail-silent. On the contrary, the LSA algorithm can support majority voting and can cope with a Byzantine leader who sends corrupt information to followers.

### 8.8.3 LSA Algorithm Overview

In a multithreaded application, threads' accesses to shared variables are serialized via mutexes. The manner in which threads are scheduled on common operating systems such as UNIX is nondeterministic. Assuming no a priori knowledge of the way replica threads request mutexes, determinism of replica state updates can be achieved by designating a selected replica, the leader, to decide the order in which mutexes are granted and to enforce an equivalent order in the other, follower, replicas. The followers enforce the leader's order of mutex acquisitions only with respect to the same mutex. This permits preservation of concurrency in the execution of follower threads that do not simultaneously acquire the same mutex, and it is possible as long as different mutexes protect different shared variables and the application threads are piecewise-deterministic.

Figure 8.14 depicts the execution of the LSA algorithm. All replicas begin executing simultaneously, and the leader threads freely execute while the order of mutex acquisitions is collected in a buffer, the *mutex table*, which is diffused to followers (both periodically and on becoming full) by means of a FIFO-ordered reliable multicast. On the left in Figure 8.14, the leader thread $t_1$ requests and acquires mutex $m_1$; then $t_2$ requests and acquires $m_2$. After $t_1$ releases $m_1$, $t_3$ requests and acquires that same mutex $(m_1)$. Consequently, the mutex table indicates the following sequence: $(m_1, t_1)$, $(m_2, t_2)$, $(m_1, t_3)$.

Followers unpack the mutex tables received from the leader in their projection queues. Each queue is associated with a mutex and contains the sequence of threads that can acquire the mutex, according to the leader's order. When a follower thread $t$ requests a mutex $m$, the thread is granted the mutex only if $t$ is at the top of the projection queue corresponding to $m$; otherwise, the thread is suspended.

In Figure 8.14, the follower's projection queues indicate that $m_1$ must be acquired first by $t_1$ and then by $t_3$. Note that the follower thread $t_2$ acquires $m_2$ before $t_1$ or $t_3$ acquires $m_1$, while, in the leader, $t_2$ acquires $m_2$ after $t_1$ acquires $m_1$. Also, in the follower, thread $t_3$ requests $m_1$ before $t_1$ does, but the mutex

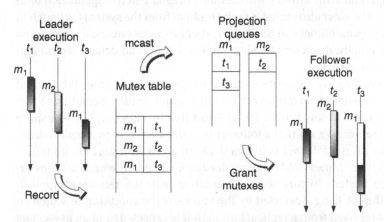

**Figure 8.14** LSA sample execution. *Source:* Basile et al. [39]/IEEE.

acquisition is delayed until $t_1$ releases $m_1$. This approach guarantees external correctness with respect to the leader.

### 8.8.3.1 Failure Behavior with Error-Free Leader-to-Followers Communication

The LSA algorithm introduces asymmetry in replicas (the leader and followers) and requires direct communication from the leader to the followers. This brings about failure modes not present in traditional replication schemes (e.g. [15]). This section analyzes the behavior of the LSA algorithm in the presence of a single, arbitrary replica failure. The group membership service and the FIFO-order reliable multicast used in the leader-to-followers communication are assumed not to fail (or, equivalently, are assumed to mask their Byzantine failures [14]). In this way, nonfaulty followers always have a consistent view of the replicas in the system and always receive the same sequence of messages from the leader.

Finally, we do not consider situations in which a failure propagates through the network by leading the recipient of a corrupted message to crash. We regard such cases as double-failure scenarios: a failure in the message sender, which sends a corrupted message, and a failure in the message recipient, which, by crashing, does not conform to its specification. (If a service specification does not cover all possible input combinations, then crashing because of an input set that was not considered at design time is not, strictly speaking, a violation of the service specification. Therefore, we extend the server specification with the additional requirement that a correct service implementation should not be affected by invalid inputs; for example, the implementation should detect and discard corrupted input data.) In principle, careful design and implementation can eliminate the occurrence of such failure types.

The architectural setup for the following discussion contains a single, independent voter in the system. The voter is in charge of detecting replica failures – crashes, hangs, and value errors – whether they originate in the application or in the LSA code. The voter also excludes faulty replicas from the system (although in general such responsibilities can be given to other processes outside the voter) and does not fail. Finally, the voter considers replica outputs and detects replica failures on a per-thread basis.

Before proceeding, we define two conditions: *deadlock* and *hang*. We say that a follower is in *deadlock on a mutex m* (i.e. in a *mutex deadlock* condition) if $m$ cannot be acquired by any thread, i.e. a thread that invokes *lsa_lock* to acquire $m$ will never return. We say that a follower is in *deadlock* (i.e. in a *replica deadlock* condition) if the follower is in deadlock on all its mutexes, i.e. no mutex can be acquired. Mutex and replica deadlocks happen when a follower-reconstructed leader's history is not compatible with the replicated application's algorithm. A *hang* – detected by the voter – is the condition in which an output is not received from a replica, although it is expected, and an associated timer expires in the voter.

*Failure modes.* In analyzing the possible failure modes, we distinguish between failures that originate in the leader replica and failures that originate in a follower replica.

- *Leader failures*: A faulty leader can crash (which would be signaled by the GCS as a view change) or produce incorrect output (or omit output) to the voter (which expects application output) and/or to the followers (which expect mutex tables). Errors from the leader can propagate to followers only via the transmission of mutex tables, which is the only leader-to-followers communication channel. As the application does not assume any particular mutex acquisition order, a faulty leader cannot cause a correct follower to perform invalid computation, only to diverge or deadlock. It is possible for those two conditions to manifest simultaneously. Some threads can diverge and produce inconsistent outputs w.r.t. the corresponding leader threads; note that if the outputs never differ despite the divergent behavior, then the error has no consequences for the system. Other threads can deadlock on a subset of mutexes, which would manifest as hangs to the voter; note that if the blocked threads are not supposed to produce output to the voter, then the error is immaterial to the system. That complex scenario can arise if the two groups of threads do not request common mutexes. If the properties of the GCS are preserved, then all nonfaulty followers receive the same sequence of messages from the leader, even if the leader sends corrupted messages. That guarantees that each pair of nonfaulty followers satisfies the correctness property. All nonfaulty followers consequently grant the same causally ordered set of mutexes. Thus, if the execution of a thread *t* at one nonfaulty follower diverges from the execution of the leader's thread *t*, then the same thing will occur at the other nonfaulty followers; similarly, if one nonfaulty follower deadlocks on a subset of mutexes, then all nonfaulty followers will deadlock on the same subset of mutexes.

- *Follower failures*: Corrupted mutex tables from a faulty leader cannot cause a follower to crash. (They can, however, result in either divergent behavior or deadlock of the follower, as discussed above.) When a follower crashes because faulty data from the leader have been mishandled, it is treated as a double-failure scenario: a failure in the leader and a failure in the follower caused by an implementation's failure. Thus, it can be assumed that a crash detected in a follower is contained within that follower and is isolated from the rest of the system. While a correct follower does not interact with other replicas, a misbehaving follower can impersonate the leader by sending messages (e.g. mutex tables) to other replicas. The leader unforgeably signs its messages so that the recipients can always discard messages from unexpected sources.

*Failure detection.* The voter considers replica outputs and detects replica failures on a per-thread basis. The following categories of replica behavior, as observed by the voter, can be distinguished: (i) *output*, i.e. a replica thread delivers an output to the voter; (ii) *no output*, i.e. a replica thread does not produce an output; and (iii) a *replica crash* detected by the GCS, which excludes the offending replica from the system (i.e. from the multicast group) and notifies the remaining replicas and the voter through a view change event.

Suppose that we observe replica threads' behavior at the voter for a sufficient amount of time. (In practice, the appropriate observation time is determined by the expiration of a dedicated time in the voter.) From the observational data, we can derive the possible combinations of leader and follower erroneous behavior (and corresponding voter decisions) induced by a single failure. The results can be seen in Table 8.1 for the faulty leader case, and in Table 8.2 for the faulty follower case.

The rule employed by the voter in detecting faulty replicas is as follows. (i) If all replicas send an output, the faulty replica is the one whose output differs from the majority output (as seen in cases L1 and F1). (ii) If the majority of replicas are hung, the leader is faulty (case L2).[6] (iii) If there is a single hung replica, that replica is faulty (cases L3 and F3). (iv) A replica that is sending a spurious output is faulty (cases L5 and F4).

**Table 8.1** Replica behavior under a faulty leader.

| Case | Expected behavior | Faulty leader's behavior | Followers' behavior | Diagnosis |
|------|-------------------|--------------------------|---------------------|-----------|
| L1 | Output | Output | Output | Compute majority value. If the leader is in the minority, it is faulty. |
| L2 | Output | Output | No output | Followers are in deadlock. Majority are hung, thus, the leader is faulty. |
| L3 | Output | No output | Output | The leader is the only hung replica, thus, it is faulty. |
| L4 | Output | No output | No output | Followers are in deadlock. All replicas are hung, thus, the leader is faulty. |
| L5 | No output | Output | No output | The leader sent a spurious output, thus, it is faulty. |
| L6 | No output | Output/No output | Output | Not possible. In nonfaulty replicas (even if contaminated), any mutex acquisition order results in the correct behavior. |
| L7 | No output | No output | No output | No faults has manifested. |

*Source:* Basile et al. [39]/IEEE.

---

6 In case L2, no output can be delivered to the client; however, after reconfiguration, surviving replicas restart execution (exiting from deadlock) and generate the expected output.

**Table 8.2** Replica behavior under a faulty follower.

| Case | Expected behavior | Faulty follower's behavior | Correct replicas' behavior | Diagnosis |
|------|-------------------|----------------------------|----------------------------|-----------|
| F1 | Output | Output | Output | Compute majority value. If the follower is in the minority, it is faulty. |
| F2 | Output | Output/No output | No output | Not possible since it violates the single failure assumption. |
| F3 | Output | No output | Output | The follower is the only hung replica, thus, it is faulty. |
| F4 | No output | No output | No output | The follower sent a spurious output, thus, it is faulty. |
| F5 | No output | Output/No output | Output | Not possible since it violates the single failure assumption. |
| F6 | No output | No output | No output | Not fault has manifested. |

*Source:* Basile et al. [39]/IEEE.

We name case L4 (in which all replicas are hung) a *leader impersonation failure* since the leader can be thought of as impersonating a follower by (i) stopping transmission of mutex tables, which causes the remaining replicas to deadlock; and (ii) waiting, as if it were a follower, to receive mutex tables in order to make progress. If we look only at replicas' behavior, a leader impersonation failure is indistinguishable from the correct scenario (cases L7 and F6) in which no output is expected and no replica sends any output. Two solutions are proposed to cope with leader impersonation failures:

1) *Application-specific information embedded in the voter:* After receiving a client request, the voter obtains knowledge on whether an output is expected to arrive from replicas. The knowledge can be derived from the client message contents. For example, for a replicated Apache server, the voter can inspect the HTTP header of the client message and determine whether it is a GET request (for which a response will follow) or a POST request (for which no response will follow).

2) *Follower-supported deadlock detection:* The LSA algorithm supports local mutex-deadlock detection during normal operation. When no responses to clients are generated despite open client connections, the voter periodically multicasts a message to followers, forcing them to initiate a self-check for a mutex deadlock condition. The followers communicate the outcome of the check to the voter, which determines the leader to be faulty if all followers indicate a mutex deadlock condition.

If the first solution is adopted, the timer for detecting replica hangs must be started when the voter receives a new client request for which replica output is expected. If the second solution is adopted, the timer can be started when the voter receives a new replica output for an open client connection. In both cases, voting occurs either upon receipt of an output from each replica for a client or upon timer expiration. The voting mechanism consists of taking both a majority vote on replica output values and a majority vote on replica hang conditions, on a per-thread basis. Using this information, the majority voter decides on the output to be delivered to the client and identifies any faulty replica and excludes it from the system. If the leader is excluded, the system must be reconfigured to elect a new leader. The exclusion of a follower does not require system reconfiguration. (That is, the system can continue operating if the number of remaining replicas is greater than one.)

*Reconfiguration.* Now we consider the reconfiguration of a system after a leader failure. The presented procedure does not require creation of new replicas, since the system is reconfigured around replicas that have not been excluded from the system. The reconfiguration procedure is initiated in each follower upon receipt of a view change event from the GCS corresponding to the leader's departure from the multicast group. The leader would have departed either by crashing or by being detected as faulty and terminated by the voter. A new leader can be selected after all surviving replicas have reached a replica deadlock condition, which represents a synchronization point. The reconfiguration procedure consists of the following steps:

1) The follower continues to execute until it detects a replica deadlock.
2) All projection queues are cleared to prepare the replica for resuming the execution. After deadlock has been reached, the remaining entries in the projection queues indicate a sequence of mutex acquisitions that is incompatible with the application's algorithm and must be removed.
3) The follower chooses the new leader from the group membership list. It is assumed that all replicas' group membership lists are identical so that a deterministic selection rule can be applied (e.g. pick the first). If the follower is not chosen to be the new leader, it waits in deadlock until it receives mutex tables from the new leader. The new leader awakens all its application threads so that they can execute *lsa_lock* as the leader replica.

If the leader-elect replica executes the reconfiguration procedure faster than the other replicas do, the other replicas may receive mutex tables from the new leader before they have reached a replica deadlock, i.e. before step (2). It is necessary, therefore, for the followers to buffer the mutex tables they received during the reconfiguration mode. The buffered mutex tables are unpacked into the projection queues after the new leader is chosen.

*Replica deadlock detection.* Replica deadlock defines a situation in which the LSA algorithm cannot grant more mutexes. That can happen, for example, if a projection queue is empty or has an invalid thread as its top entry. Assuming that the GCS is correct, all nonfaulty followers will grant the same causally ordered set of mutexes; therefore, they will reach a replica deadlock condition consistently, and the deadlock condition is thus a synchronization point for correct followers. Under the assumption that each application thread requests mutexes infinitely often, one can detect a replica deadlock during reconfiguration by checking whether all application threads have requested a mutex that cannot be granted (i.e. checking whether all threads are suspended).

However, it is possible to craft a pathological situation in which the above detection mechanism fails. A creation of an infinite number of threads (i.e. a situation in which a thread creates a child thread, which in turn creates another child thread, and so on) would infinitely delay replica deadlock detection. In [43], we proposed a more complex replica deadlock detection strategy, based on a dedicated mutex *mc*. That mechanism, in addition to handling infinite thread creation correctly, can also detect replica deadlock in advance, as it does not wait for all threads to be suspended.

### 8.8.3.2 Failure Behavior with Byzantine Errors in Leader-to-Followers Communication

This section analyzes the impact of failures in the leader-to-followers multicast communication under the single-failure scenario. We continue to assume that the group membership protocol does not fail. Violation of the properties of the FIFO-order reliable multicast because of a faulty leader can result in (i) failure to send a mutex table at all, (ii) sending of a mutex table only to some followers, or (iii) sending of a mutex table with different contents (or in different orders) to different followers. Those cases can cause followers to be inconsistent with each other. In this section, we suggest a solution that (i) does not require a multicast protocol that can tolerate Byzantine failures and (ii) takes action only after the voter has detected inconsistencies, without incurring extra overhead during normal operation.

*Failure detection.* The voter detects replica failures and decides upon system reconfiguration as described below:

1) Detection of a follower crash or spurious follower output indicates that the follower in question is the single faulty replica in the system. The system can continue without reconfiguration after the faulty follower has been excluded.
2) Detection of a follower hang or a follower value error indicates failure either of the follower or of the leader (if it has contaminated the follower). Both the follower and the leader must be excluded from the system since the two cases are indistinguishable.

3) Detection of a leader failure alone indicates that the leader is faulty and must be excluded from the system.

4) Detection of misbehavior of multiple replicas (e.g. crashes, hangs, or value errors) indicates that an error in the leader has contaminated the followers. Consequently, the leader is the single faulty replica and must be excluded. Note that in this scenario, because of the single-failure assumption, only the leader can crash.

*Reconfiguration*. We select a subset of the remaining correct followers (i.e. followers whose states are consistent with each other) from which the system can restart.[7] The reconfiguration procedure starts by having all followers send their states to the voter to determine the largest group of followers whose states agree; those in the largest group will survive the failure, and all other followers will be excluded from the system. For the state comparison to be meaningful, followers must capture their states when their corresponding threads are at the same logical point. Because of the absence of mutex table transmissions during reconfiguration, the followers will eventually deadlock and the replica state can be captured when that state is reached.

## 8.8.4 Specification of the PDS Algorithm

In the following, it is assumed that a total order relation "<" is imposed on the set of replica threads $T$ and that it can be used to sort the threads into an order that is the same for all replicas. Also, in the application threads, the system calls *lock* and *unlock* (to acquire and release a mutex) are replaced with the functions *pds_lock* and *pds_unlock*.

For ease of understanding, we first present an overview of the PDS-1 algorithm, in which each thread can acquire at most one mutex per round. We then provide specifications of the PDS-2 algorithm, which improves concurrency by allowing a thread to acquire up to two mutexes per round.[8]

### 8.8.4.1 PDS-1 Algorithm Overview

A replica's execution is broken into a sequence of rounds, and in each round, each thread can acquire at most one mutex. Upon requesting a mutex, a thread $t$ checks whether all other threads are suspended. If they are, $t$ triggers a new round;

---

7 Since potentially contaminated correct followers cannot perform an invalid computation, it would be sufficient to choose any follower as the single surviving replica and exclude all the other replicas.

8 Allowing a thread to acquire more than two mutexes per round leads to race conditions. Consequently, additional support must be provided.

otherwise, $t$ is suspended. When a new round is started, all threads' mutex requests are known, and therefore a DS of mutex acquisitions naturally occurs: threads that simultaneously request the same mutex acquire it according to increasing thread IDs. Because all threads must have requested a mutex in order for the next round to fire, it is important that no thread have an unbounded computation or blocking time between a mutex acquisition and the following mutex request, as required by the definition of a correct application (see Section 8.1). Figure 8.15 shows an execution in which only two threads are considered. At the beginning of round $n$, threads $t_1$ and $t_2$ have requested mutexes $m_1$ and $m_2$, respectively (indicated by small black circles in Figure 8.15a). Since the mutexes are different and no thread owns these mutexes, $t_1$ and $t_2$ can acquire them and run concurrently throughout round n (as indicated by the arrows pointing right in Figure 8.15b) until they both request the next mutex, namely $m_2$ for $t_1$ and $m_3$ for $t_2$ (see Figure 8.15c). At that point, round $n + 1$ fires, and thread $t_2$ can then acquire $m_3$, but $t_1$ cannot acquire $m_2$ because $m_2$ is held by $t_2$. Eventually, thread $t_2$ requests $m_4$ (see Figure 8.15d) and fires round $n + 2$. Thus, $t_2$ is granted $m_4$ and, by executing, has a chance to release $m_2$ and so let $t_1$ execute as well.

Figure 8.16 presents a more complex execution scenario for the PDS-1 algorithm. At the beginning of round $n$, threads $t_1$ and $t_2$ have requested $m_1$, while $t_3$ and $t_4$ have requested $m_2$. Threads $t_1$ and $t_3$ can execute concurrently because they have requested different mutexes and have the lowest IDs with respect to the mutexes they have requested. Threads $t_2$ and $t_3$ remain suspended (see Figure 8.16a).

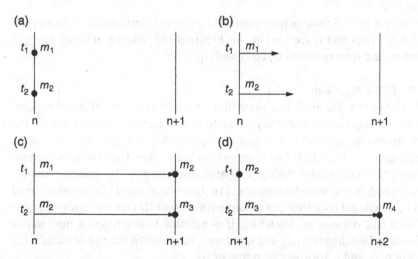

**Figure 8.15** Stages in PDS-1 first sample execution (a), (b), (c), and (d). *Source:* Basile et al. [39]/IEEE.

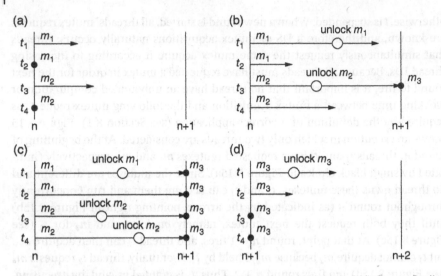

**Figure 8.16** Stages in PDS-1 second sample execution (a), (b), (c), and (d). *Source:* Basile et al. [39]/IEEE.

Later, $t_1$ releases $m_1$ and $t_3$ releases $m_2$ (as indicated by white circles in Figure 8.16b); in consequence, $t_2$ and $t_4$ can resume their execution. Thus, all threads can run concurrently. In Figure 8.16b, thread $t_3$ has been suspended upon requesting $m_3$. To ensure deterministic behavior, $t_3$ needs to wait for the other threads to declare their intentions in terms of which mutex they want to acquire next.

In Figure 8.16c, all threads have requested $m_3$ as the next mutex. At this point, round $n + 1$ fires and $t_1$ acquires $m_3$. In Figure 8.16d, when $t_1$ releases $m_3$, $t_2$ is granted $m_3$ and thus runs concurrently with $t_1$.

### 8.8.4.2 PDS-2 Algorithm

In this section, we discuss PDS-2 algorithm which improves the threads' concurrency by allowing each thread to acquire up to two mutexes per round. Figure 8.17a shows an instant in the PDS-1 execution represented in Figure 8.16, in which, during round $n$, threads $t_1$, $t_2$, and $t_3$ are suspended because the new round cannot fire unless $t_4$, which is still running, requests its next mutex. The waiting is unnecessary. Indeed, no matter which mutex $t_4$ requests next, say $m'$, in the next round $t_4$ will be scheduled only after any thread with a lower ID that has requested $m'$ is scheduled and releases $m'$. Therefore, it is possible to determine a new mutex acquisition scheduling for $t_1$, $t_2$, and $t_3$ before $t_4$ has reached the end of round n (as the ids of $t_1$, $t_2$, and $t_3$ are lower than that of $t_4$).

In the PDS-2 algorithm, each round is divided into two steps, and each thread can acquire at most two mutexes per round. Figure 8.17b shows the PDS-2

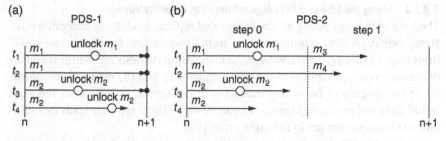

**Figure 8.17** Improving concurrency of PDS algorithm. (a) PDS-1 and (b) PDS-2. *Source:* Basile et al. [39]/IEEE.

execution corresponding to the PDS-1 execution of Figure 8.17a. $t_1$ and $t_2$ are each allowed to acquire their next mutex and proceed to step 1 before the higher-ID threads $t_3$ and $t_4$ have requested their first mutexes for that round, i.e. have completed step 0.

### 8.8.5 Application-Transparent Replication Framework

This section describes a software framework consisting of an implementation of the LSA and PDS algorithms, a virtual socket layer (VSL), and a voter/fanout process for supporting replication of multithreaded applications [39]. Figure 8.18 illustrates the configuration of a triplicated application employing the framework. (Ensemble [10] is used as the GCS).

Multiple instances of an application execute on different nodes, and the clients have the illusion of a service that is implemented by a single, nonfaulty server. Multiple clients interact with the voter as if it were the real server. The voter/ fanout forwards all data coming from clients to replicas by using a FIFO-order reliable multicast protocol. Socket operations invoked by a replica's code (e.g. to send a response back to the client) are converted into requests that are sent to the voter/fanout process. The voter collects the requests for socket operations from all the replicas and, after voting, performs the actual operation on the physical socket associated with the specific client.

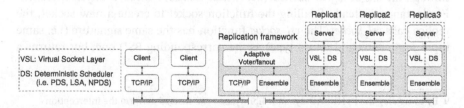

**Figure 8.18** Replication framework. *Source:* Basile et al. [39]/IEEE.

#### 8.8.5.1 Using the LSA and PDS Algorithms with Majority Voting

The issue of majority voting for single-threaded replicas is relatively straightforward. Here, majority voting requires replica *output consistency*, for which two conditions must be met: (i) *input consistency*, i.e. the input requests are identical and are delivered to correct replicas in the same order [44]; and (ii) *replica determinism*, i.e. in the absence of faults, any execution of the replica starting from the same initial state and processing the same ordered set of input requests leads to a set of output messages that are in the same order [15].

For multithreaded replicas, the condition of replica determinism is replaced with the condition of *piecewise thread determinism*. In addition, output consistency needs to hold only with respect to corresponding threads across replicas, while the voter must compare replica outputs on a per-thread basis.

Output comparison on a per-thread basis is necessary because the LSA and PDS algorithms synchronize replicas on shared state updates. In consequence, they do not guarantee any ordering on the outputs produced by different threads at different replicas. Threads can be scheduled in different orders and/or executed with different timings. To support output comparison on a per-thread basis, it is necessary for replicas (i) to use identical thread IDs for corresponding threads, and (ii) to tag their outputs with the logical ID of the thread that is generating the output.

#### 8.8.5.2 LSA and PDS Implementations

A prototype of the LSA and PDS algorithms has been implemented as a C/C++ DS library. The interception of lock/unlock operations on mutexes is performed transparently to the application through interception of the application calls to the POSIX thread (PTHREAD) library. A set of macros is employed to override the PTHREAD functions at compile time. The inclusion of the DS header file is the only change required to the application source code. Consequently, the application needs to be recompiled.[9] Selection between the LSA and PDS algorithms occurs at runtime by means of command-line arguments for the replica process.

#### 8.8.5.3 Virtual Socket Layer

The VSL is compatible with the BSD socket application programming interface and designed to hide the replication infrastructure from the replicated application through the use of logical sockets (i.e. *virtual sockets*) instead of physical sockets. For instance, instead of calling the function socket to create a new socket, the replica calls *vsl_socket*. The *vsl_socket* function has the same signature (i.e. same input arguments and return type) as the corresponding BSD one, but returns a

---

9 By overriding the PTHREAD dynamic library, one can instead perform the interception without requiring application recompilation.

logical socket descriptor instead of a physical socket descriptor. The substitution is automated with the help of preprocessor macros.

The VSL is responsible for (i) receiving/sending messages from the voter/fanout process and (ii) interacting with the replicated application. A dedicated network thread in each replica accepts messages from the voter/fanout process. (In our implementation, that thread is inside Ensemble.) The messages correspond to new data and new connection requests arriving from clients and are buffered in a data queue or a connection queue for the logical socket.

### 8.8.5.4 Voter/Fanout Process

The VSL separates the replicated application from the voter, and the voter separates the replication infrastructure from the client. The voting mechanism is specific to the replicated application. A bit-wise comparison is a simple yet popular voting mechanism. Other alternatives (e.g. a checksum verification, or voting only on chunks of the data) can be incorporated into our voter implementation as well.

While replicas use logical socket descriptors to interact with the VSL, the voter/fanout process uses real BSD sockets (physical sockets) and maps logical socket descriptors to physical socket descriptors.

In addition to voting on outgoing messages, the voter/fanout process forwards all client messages to the replicas by using a FIFO-order reliable multicast protocol. The voter also provides (i) adaptive timeout estimation, to minimize the probability of a false alarm while the voter is trying to detect hang errors; and (ii) *fast voting*, i.e. the voter can vote and send a response to the client as soon as the majority of replicas have provided corresponding outputs that agree.

### 8.8.6 Performance-Dependability Trade-Offs

The following sections discuss a conjunct experimental evaluation of the LSA and PDS algorithms from both the performance and dependability perspectives. Although a level of dependability assessment has been achieved formally, the process is not complete unless the algorithms are also evaluated experimentally, especially with regard to their responses under a wide range of failures. The goal of the dependability assessment is to evaluate the fault resilience of the algorithms. Whereas the goal of a DS algorithm is to support failure masking, it is critical that the algorithm itself does not constitute a major source of failures in the system.

We analyzed the LSA and PDS algorithms' performance/dependability characteristics through an experimental study of the performance-dependability trade-offs involved in selecting DS algorithms when one is replicating multithreaded applications. The considered algorithms include the LSA and PDS algorithms, and a nonpreemptive DS (NPDS) algorithm (which is based on the Transactional

Drago algorithm [28] proposed in the context of transactional applications) and also implemented in the VSL framework.

### 8.8.6.1 Performance Evaluation

We evaluated the performance by running a synthetic benchmark (described below) that emulated different levels of parallelism in a multithreaded replica execution in an active replication configuration with majority voting. Two performance measures were used: (i) the replicated server's throughput (i.e. the number of client requests served per second) and (ii) the replicated server's latency (i.e. the time interval between sending of a request and receipt of a response to the request), as seen by a client.

The experimental setup (see Figure 8.18) consisted of two Ethernet 100 Mbps LANs, one that connected the clients to a voter/fanout process and another that connected the voter/fanout process to three replicas. The replicas and voter executed on Pentium III 500 MHz-based machines running Linux 2.4, and Ensemble [10] were used for group communication.

*Synthetic benchmark.* A synthetic benchmark modeled a multithreaded, networked server in which 10 worker threads served requests coming concurrently from 15 clients. By setting the number of incoming client requests to be greater than the number of server threads, we could study the maximum server throughput. A client request was composed of a header, which specified the (random) type of the service requested (described later), and a payload message, which had random contents and size (where the size was uniformly distributed between 0 and 1000 bytes). Each client continuously generated random requests and waited for the response to arrive.

Serving of a client request involved two steps: (i) First, fast conversion of the payload was used solely to enable the voter to verify that corresponding server threads at different replicas were serving the same client requests. (We used lower-to-upper-case string conversion in the experiments; any inconsistency was detected as a value fault since the conversion result was included in the server response.) (ii) Secondly, we executed a sequence of (a) mutex acquisitions that modeled accesses to shared data, and (b) I/O activities (emulated by thread suspension) that modeled server accesses to persistent storage, e.g. a database. The two activities were interleaved to model variable workloads and allow different parallelisms in thread execution. The duration of I/O activity was a random variable uniformly distributed in $[0, D_{max}]$, where $D_{max}$ is a parameter that can be varied to emulate different levels of parallelism offered by the benchmark: the larger $D_{max}$ is, the more parallelism in thread execution.

*Triplicated server experiments.* Figure 8.19a shows the triplicated server's throughput, measured at the client side, as a function of $D_{max}$. All algorithms performed almost identically when $D_{max}$ was zero: since replicas ran on

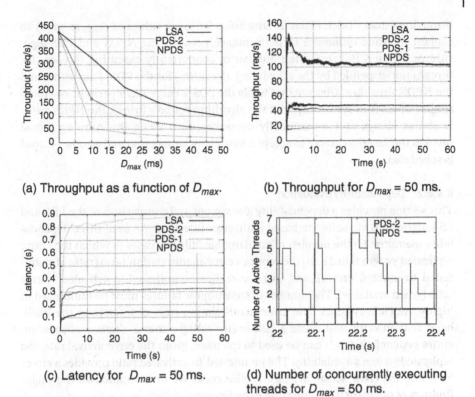

(a) Throughput as a function of $D_{max}$.

(b) Throughput for $D_{max} = 50$ ms.

(c) Latency for $D_{max} = 50$ ms.

(d) Number of concurrently executing threads for $D_{max} = 50$ ms.

**Figure 8.19** Evaluation results for triplicated server (a), (b), (c), and (d).

single-processor machines, threads were serialized. As $D_{max}$ increased, i.e. the potential concurrency in thread execution increased, the LSA algorithm performed the best, while the NPDS algorithm performed poorly. (LSA provides about five times more throughput than NPDS does.) The PDS algorithm stayed in the middle between LSA and NPDS, providing about two times the throughput of NPDS; therefore, PDS can be considered a compromise between aggressive concurrency at the expense of inter-replica communication (LSA), which gives better performance, and independent replica execution at expense of concurrency (NPDS), which provides better error resilience. The throughput of all algorithms decreased as $D_{max}$ grew because the service time increased while the number of server threads was fixed.

Figure 8.19b and c shows, respectively, the server throughput and latency as a function of experiment execution time for $D_{max}$ set to 50 ms. The two graphs, in addition to reinforcing our conclusions (from Figure 8.19a) on the relative performance of the tested algorithms, also show that PDS-2 provides about 12% more throughput than PDS-1. (That finding holds for lower values of $D_{max}$ as well.) To explain the wide difference in performance between the NPDS and PDS algorithms, Figure 8.19d shows the number of concurrently executing threads (i.e. threads not suspended by the scheduling algorithm) for the PDS-2 algorithm and the NPDS algorithm. Observe that while the PDS-2 curve has a periodic sawtooth shape (which is in synchrony with the algorithm round's firing), the NPDS curve is almost always at 1, occasionally decreasing to 0 when the running thread invokes the function *accept* to accept a new client connection and another thread is scheduled.

### 8.8.6.2 Dependability Evaluation

This section provides a dependability assessment and comparison of the PDS and LSA algorithms via software-based fault/error injection. We used three dependability measures: (i) the number of catastrophic failures (cases in which the entire replicated system failed), (ii) the replica's error-manifestation ratio (ratio of manifested to injected errors), and (iii) the replica's manifested-to-activated[10] error ratio (when available). The number of catastrophic failures must be minimized in highly available systems. The error manifestation ratio characterizes the likelihood that an error will cause a failure (including either a single replica or an entire system failure). It can be used to calculate, given the error arrival rate, the replicated system's availability. The manifested-to-activated ratio provides a closer look into the error sensitivity of a replica code. We now summarize the major findings of our error/fault-injection experiments:

1) About 36 000 single-bit errors were injected uniformly into text, data, and heap[11] segments of a replica process (which included Ensemble [10], which provides group communication primitives). The results indicate that PDS replicas have lower error sensitivity than LSA replicas do. The difference is due to the inter-replica communication required by LSA.
2) About 2800 single-bit errors were injected uniformly in the portion of a replica's text segment corresponding to a specific Ensemble function that was used by both a PDS replica and an LSA replica. We observed 81 catastrophic failures, which shows that Ensemble's fail-silence violations constitute an issue for highly available systems.
3) In (2), we did not observe a statistical difference, with respect to catastrophic failures, between LSA and PDS. Therefore, in an LSA leader, we injected errors into Ensemble functions used solely in LSA. (Note that all Ensemble functions used by PDS are also used by LSA replicas.) 31 catastrophic failures were

---

10 An error is activated if the injected data/instruction is used/executed.
11 More than one error may have been injected during a single heap experiment.

observed in 3600 injections, which confirms that LSA replicas are more sensitive to catastrophic failures.

4) Importantly, errors originating in the communication layer do propagate and lead to catastrophic failures of the entire replicated system. We report that not as an indictment of Ensemble (which is a well-engineered product), but to point out that those failures are due to fail-silence violations and propagation of errors in the communication layer, which are beyond the scope of the usual assumption of crash/omission failures. To limit or prevent propagation of errors across the network, the middleware on which fault-tolerant techniques are based (in our case, the reliable communication layer) must itself be fault-tolerant.

### 8.8.6.3 Injections into a Replica Process

We conducted a set of fault injection experiments to assess the impact of faults/errors in a replica's text, data, and heap memory segments. A replica here includes the application benchmark, the PDS/LSA algorithm, the VSL, and Ensemble. NFTAPE [31], a software framework for conducting automated fault injection experiments, was used to conduct the tests.

The error models considered are summarized in Table 8.3 and represent a combination of those used in past experimental studies (e.g. [45]). By injecting single bits into the targeted replica, we emulated errors in the main memory, the cache, the processor execution buffer, and the processor execution core, as well as errors that occur during transmission over a bus. Previous research on microprocessors [46–48] has shown that most (90–99%) device-level transients can be modeled as logic-level, single-bit errors. Data on operational errors also show that a majority of errors in the field are single-bit errors.

Manifested errors are divided into two major outcome categories: (i) *crash failures*, in which the injected replica stops executing and no incorrect state transition is performed before the failure, and (ii) *fail-silence violations*, in which the

**Table 8.3** Error models used in injection experiments.

| Error model | Description |
| --- | --- |
| TEXT | A single bit in the text segment of the target replica is flipped. |
| DATA | A single bit in the data segment of the target replica is flipped. |
| HEAP | A bit in allocated regions of the heap memory of the target replica is flipped periodically until the replica terminates or crashes. Note that more than one error may be injected during a single experiment. |

*Source:* Basile et al. [39]/IEEE.

**Table 8.4** Outcome categories.

| | |
|---|---|
| Crash failure | **SIGNAL:** the operating system terminates the target replica by sending a signal (e.g. SIGSEGV, SIGILL, SIGBUS, SIGFPE). |
| | **ASSERT:** the target replica shuts itself down owing to an internal check violation. |
| | **HANG:** the target replica does not terminate but no output is produced to the voter. |
| Fail silence violation | **VALUE ERROR:** the target replica produces a value different from other (nonfaulty) replicas. |
| | **TWO HUNG FOLLOWERS:** the target replica (LSA leader) sends output to the voter but stops sending mutex tables to followers[a]. |
| | **LEADER IMPERSONATION:** as the previous case except that no output is sent to the voter (the leader impersonates a follower)[b]. |
| | **CATASTROPHIC FAILURE:** the entire replicated system fails. |

[a] The LSA voter detects this case by noting that a majority of replicas are hung.
[b] The LSA voter detects this case by noting that no replica generated output before a dedicated timer expired, although output was expected.
*Source:* Basile et al. [39]/IEEE.

injected replica performs incorrect state transitions. The two categories and their corresponding subcategories are listed in Table 8.4.

Table 8.5 gives the results from error injection experiments for both the PDS and LSA algorithms (for LSA, we distinguish between leader and follower injections), and for each error model listed in Table 8.4. During each experiment, each of the 15 clients sent 10 requests and then terminated. This setup permitted us to observe the system for a sufficient amount of time after an error was injected (about 30 seconds). The experiment concluded when either all clients had terminated or a catastrophic failure occurred. The system was reset between experiments.

Except in five cases, the system was able to recover from the injected failure. In the case of PDS, the voter masked the failure. In the case of LSA, if the leader failed, the followers successfully elected a new leader after the failed leader had been excluded from the system; if a follower failed, the voter masked the failure. In discussing the fault injection results, we will distinguish between failures masked by the voter and catastrophic failures.

*Failures masked by the voter.* Text injections show a slightly larger error-manifestation ratio for LSA than for PDS: 10%, 8.3%, and 7.5% for an LSA leader, LSA follower, and PDS, respectively. The manifested-to-activated error ratios give a similar result: 73%, 65%, and 68% for an LSA leader, LSA follower, and PDS, respectively. The ratio variation could be explained by the different complexities of the two algorithms (as PDS is simpler than LSA). Because the difference in the algorithms' code sizes (14K for PDS and 25K for LSA) is small compared to the

**Table 8.5** Fault injection results.

| Error model | Total injected errors | Total activated errors | Total manifested errors[a] | Manifested errors[b] | | | | | | |
|---|---|---|---|---|---|---|---|---|---|---|
| | | | | Crash failures | | | Fail silence violations | | | |
| | | | | SIGNAL | ASSERT | HANG | VAL ERR | 2 H FOLL | LEAD IMP | CATAST FAIL |
| PDS TEXT | 5224 | 583 | 394 (7.5%) | 334 (85%) | 21 (5.3%) | 24 (6.1%) | 14 (3.6%) | N/A | N/A | 1 (0.25%) |
| DATA | 2152 | N/A | 6 (0.28%) | 5 | 1 | 0 | 0 | N/A | N/A | 0 |
| HEAP | 9158 | N/A | 869 (9.5%) | 782 (90%) | 0 | 32 (3.7%) | 55 (6.3%) | N/A | N/A | 0 |
| LSA-L TEXT | 5224 | 728 | 528 (10%) | 447 (85%) | 20 (3.8%) | 16 (3.0%) | 9 (1.7%) | 27 (5.1%) | 6 (1.1%) | 3 (0.57%) |
| DATA | 2139 | N/A | 5 (0.23%) | 4 | 1 | 0 | 0 | 0 | 0 | 0 |
| HEAP | 2036 | N/A | 523 (26%) | 501 (96%) | 0 | 3 (0.57%) | 8 (1.5%) | 11 (2.1%) | 0 | 0 |
| LSA-F TEXT | 5144 | 659 | 429 (8.3%) | 402 (94%) | 12 (2.8%) | 11 (2.6%) | 3 (0.70%) | N/A | N/A | 1 (0.23%) |
| DATA | 2153 | N/A | 5 (0.23%) | 5 | 0 | 0 | 0 | N/A | N/A | 0 |
| HEAP | 3010 | N/A | 961 (32%) | 927 (96%) | 0 | 9 (0.94%) | 25 (2.6%) | N/A | N/A | 0 |

[a] The error-manifestation ratio (i.e. the ratio of manifested to injected errors) is shown in parentheses.
[b] The percentage of the total number of manifested errors that are of the particular manifestation type is shown in parentheses.
Source: Basile et al. [39]/IEEE.

total replica code size (900K) and the errors are injected uniformly, we argue that the major cause of variations in the observed error manifestations is the *different types of usage of Ensemble* (whose code size is about 740K). While the PDS and LSA replicas both use Ensemble to communicate with the voter, an LSA replica also uses Ensemble for passing the order of mutex acquisitions from the leader to the followers. Profiling of the usage of Ensemble functions shows that a PDS replica and an LSA replica invoke, respectively, 343 and 391 Ensemble functions.

Data injections show a very low error-manifestation ratio. The reason is that a large part of the data segment (405K in total, 390K of which is part of Ensemble) is not used during normal execution. As a result, errors in the data segment do not contribute noticeably to the number of failures in the system.

Heap injections show an error-manifestation ratio for LSA that is about twice that for PDS. The reason can be found in the more extensive use of dynamic memory by (i) the LSA leader, which stores the mutex acquisition order on the heap memory; (ii) the LSA followers, which store the leader-decided order of mutex acquisitions in dynamic data structures (projection queues); and (iii) Ensemble (for both the leader and followers), which uses heap memory for internal message buffering and management in support of leader-to-followers communication. A larger error sensitivity can be observed for followers because each follower not only collects (in the projection queues) the leader-dictated order of mutex acquisitions but actively applies it in scheduling threads' executions. Therefore, corruption of the projection queues results in more crashes or divergent behavior of the follower, where divergent behavior manifests as a greater percentage of value errors.

To conclude, the experiments showed that an LSA-based replicated system is more sensitive than a PDS-based replicated system to voter-masked failures. Note that although such failures do not cause propagation of errors to clients, they do impact a replicated system's availability.

*Catastrophic failures.* Although the above discussion indicates that the PDS thread-scheduling strategy has higher error resilience than the LSA strategy does, the most important difference between the two algorithms appears when catastrophic failures are being analyzed. Because such failures cannot be masked by the voter, it is crucial that they be prevented in a replicated system. In our experiments, we observed five catastrophic failures, all of which were due to error propagation through the Ensemble communication layer. They are described below:

*PDS experiments.* An error injected into Ensemble's message-routing module (i.e. Unsigned) in the targeted replica caused the voter to crash in Ensemble's point-to-point communication module (i.e. Pt2pt), but the injected replica did not crash.

*LSA leader experiments.* Three catastrophic failures were caused by errors that originated in an Ensemble function used by the LSA leader. (i) An error injected in the intra-group failures-and-view module (i.e. intra) of the leader caused the voter to have an inconsistent group membership view with respect to other replicas,[12] and that violates the properties of reliable group communication. (ii) An error injected in the connection management module (i.e. Conn) of the leader caused the leader to hang and the two followers to crash in their reliable FIFO broadcast module (i.e. Mnak). (iii) Finally, an error injected in the unsigned module of the leader caused the two followers to crash in their Mnak module and the voter to crash in its Pt2pt module.

*LSA follower experiments.* An error injected in the Ensemble function *extern_rec()* of the targeted follower caused the voter and the other two replicas to raise an exception due to a corrupted control flow packet header. The *extern_rec()* function handles the interaction between the high-level part of Ensemble (e.g. reliable communication algorithms) written in ML and the low-level part (e.g. sockets) written in C.

### 8.8.6.4 Lessons Learned
Performance and failure analysis of the DS strategies of PDS, LSA, and NPDS revealed the following:

1) The LSA strategy provides the best performance (in terms of throughput and latency in response to client requests) at the expense of availability (measured in terms of resilience to errors). Because LSA relies on an inter-replica communication channel for efficient mutex acquisition scheduling, LSA is more sensitive to the underlying communication layer's fail silence violations than PDS. That leads to a larger number of catastrophic failures for LSA than for PDS. If it is crucial to minimize downtime (as it is for highly available systems), PDS is a more appropriate choice than LSA. If performance concerns have priority over minimized downtime, then LSA can be preferred to PDS.

2) The NPDS strategy provides correct execution through serialization, which eliminates the benefit of multithreading and results in poor performance compared to the PDS and LSA strategies. Although we did not explicitly evaluate NPDS's dependability characteristics, we argue that they are similar to those of PDS, especially with regard to catastrophic failures, because neither of the two algorithms uses inter-replica communication.

### 8.8.7 Conclusions

Replication schemes by their nature impose a significant performance overhead. For example, measurements reported for several existing approaches to replication indicate performance overheads ranging from three to ten times

---

12 The inconsistency caused the voter to receive a message from a replica that was not a member of the group seen by the voter. After that condition was detected, the voter terminated itself by raising an exception.

that of nonreplicated systems [27, 37, 38, 49]. Usually, only single-thread applications are replicated since multithreading does not easily conform to the state machine approach [15] widely used in software replication. However, if the replicas are multithreaded, then performance overhead due to replication can be reduced.

A simplistic approach is pursued by NPDSs (i.e. in Eternal [26] and in Transactional Drago [28]), which, although they provide correct execution, do not exploit concurrency in multithreaded replicas. In contrast, the *LSA* [43] captures the natural concurrency in a leader replica and projects it onto follower replicas through inter-replica communication. The *Preemptive Deterministic Scheduler (PDS)* algorithm removes the need for inter-replica communication yet preserves a large degree of replica concurrency. The absence of inter-replica communication gives PDS dependability advantages over LSA.

The architecture of a framework for transparent active replication of socket-based applications was also presented. The framework was used to replicate, with the LSA algorithm, the multithreaded version of the Apache web server. Performance measurements taken on a triplicated multithreaded Apache server showed a throughput degradation of approximately 23%.

We also discussed an experimental evaluation of the LSA and PDS algorithms from both the performance and dependability perspectives. The results show that PDS outperforms NPDSs. The PDS algorithm has lower throughput than LSA; however, it provides additional benefits in terms of system dependability and hence can be considered a trade-off between performance and dependability. We investigated those characteristics with fault injection. Fault-injection results show that the crash/omission failure semantics for the underlying communication layer (which was Ensemble in our experiments) is not sufficient for highly dependable systems. In a significant number of cases, errors that originated in the communication layer propagated and led to catastrophic failures of the entire replicated system. Therefore, we advocate the use of fault-tolerance middlewares that are themselves fault-tolerant [50].

## 8.9 Atomic Commit

An *atomic commit* is an operation in which a set of distinct changes is performed as a single operation. Upon success, the atomic commit applies all the changes. However, if a failure occurs before an atomic commit has been completed, it is *aborted*, and all the changes that have taken place up to the failure are revoked (*rolled back*). The purpose of atomic commit is to maintain the system in a consistent state even if there is a failure. The term *atomic commit* came from *atoms*, which were once thought to be the smallest indivisible particles of matter. In distributed systems, the atomic commit of the result of a set of operations, performed independently by multiple participants, is an important requirement. The two-phase commit protocol and the three-phase commit protocol, discussed in the following, are two of the algorithms that solve the problem of atomic commit.

Another common application of atomic commit is in revision control systems, to allow commitment of changes in multiple files with the guarantee that all changes to all files will be uploaded and merged to the source. The commitment is performed so transparently to the user that it is often taken almost for granted. Multiple files committed by a single user are assumed to be related to a single modification of the code base. Every user works on a stable version of the code that has either all or none of the modifications made by other users. The revision control systems also allow a user to roll back a modification (i.e. an entire commit operation).

### 8.9.1 The Two-Phase Commit Protocol

The two-phase commit protocol is a distributed algorithm that implements atomic commit for a transaction among multiple nodes in a distributed system. All nodes either commit the entire transaction or abort (i.e. remove any changes that were part of the partially executed transaction), in the event of a node failure or loss of messages. Skeen and Stonebraker [51] showed that the protocol cannot handle more than one random node failure at a time. One of the nodes is designated the *Coordinator*. The rest of the nodes are referred to as *Cohorts*. The two phases of the algorithm are (i) the Commit-Request phase, in which the Coordinator attempts to prepare all the Cohorts; and (ii) the Commit phase, in which the Coordinator completes the transactions at all Cohorts.

#### 8.9.1.1 Assumptions
The two-phase commit protocol assumes that:

i) One of the nodes (which we henceforward refer to as *node number 1*) is designated the Coordinator, and the other nodes act as Cohorts (which we refer to as *node numbers $i = 2, 3, \ldots, n$*).
ii) Stable storage exists at each node.
iii) Each node uses a write-ahead log (WAL).
iv) No node crashes forever.
v) Eventually, any two nodes can communicate with each other.

It can be argued that assumption (v) is reasonable since, even in the presence of a node or link failure, it may be possible to reroute and revive the network communication. However, assumption (iv) is a much stronger assumption.

### 8.9.1.2 Basic Algorithm

In the Commit-Request phase, the Coordinator broadcasts to all Cohorts a query to commit a "commit_request" message. It then waits for all the Cohorts to respond with an "agreed" message. If the transaction is successful, the Cohorts, using the WAL capability, write one entry to the undo log and another to the redo log. Then, they reply to the Coordinator with an "agreed" message. If the transaction fails at a Cohort, however, it sends an "abort" message to the Coordinator.

In the Commit phase, if the Coordinator receives an "agreed" message from all Cohorts, it adds a commit record to its log. It then broadcasts a "commit" message to all the Cohorts. If even one of the Cohorts does not send an agreement message or sends an "abort" message, the Coordinator sends an abort message. The Coordinator then waits for an ACK from the Cohorts. Note that, in this protocol, the Coordinator will block (i.e. wait) until all the ACKs from the Cohorts have come back. If a Cohort receives a "commit" message, it releases all the locks and resources held during the transaction and sends an ACK to the Coordinator. If the message is an "abort," then the Cohort undoes the transaction by using the undo log and releases the resources and locks held during the transaction. It then sends an ACK to the Coordinator. When ACKs are received from all Cohorts, the Coordinator writes a complete record to its log.

### 8.9.1.3 Disadvantages

The main drawback of the two-phase commit protocol is that it is a blocking protocol. A node blocks while waiting for a message. That means that other processes competing for resource locks held by the blocked processes will have to wait for the locks to be released. If the Coordinator fails permanently, some Cohorts will never resolve their transactions, and this can lead to a deadlock situation in which the resources are unavailable *forever*. The two-phase commit protocol also conservatively aborts transactions in favor of trying to reach a successful completion state.

### 8.9.1.4 The Detailed Two-Phase Commit Protocol

The following description is based on [3]:

*At the Coordinator:*

1) The Coordinator broadcasts the message to be committed (the "commit_request") to each Cohort and waits for responses from each of the Cohorts. (Now in preparing transaction or Commit-Request phase.)
2) a) If any Cohort responds with an "abort" message, then the Coordinator aborts the transaction (i.e. goes to step 7).
   b) If all Cohorts respond with an "agreed" message, then the Coordinator attempts to commit the transaction (i.e. goes to step 3).

c) If not all Cohorts have responded before a predetermined time expires, then the Coordinator either transmits "abort" messages to all Cohorts or retransmits "commit_request" messages selectively to only those Cohorts that have not responded. In either case, the protocol will eventually reach state 3 or state 7.

3) The Coordinator records a "Complete" entry in the log to indicate that the transaction is now complete.

4) The Coordinator sends a "commit" message to each of the Cohorts. It waits again until all the Cohorts have responded. All of them *must* respond with a "commit" ACK.

5) If, after some prespecified time period, some Cohorts have not sent the ACK, the Coordinator retransmits the "commit" message to those Cohorts. Once all Cohorts have replied with an ACK, the Coordinator erases all associated information from permanent memory (e.g. the Cohort list).

6) DONE.

7) The Coordinator sends the "abort" message to each Cohort.

*At Cohorts:*

1) a) If a "commit_request" message received from the Coordinator is for a transaction $t$ that is not known to the Cohort, the Cohort replies with an "abort" message. (A transaction could be unknown because it was never executed or because information about it was lost because of a crash, for example.)

a) If the transaction is identified, the Cohort writes the new state of the transaction to the undo and redo logs in permanent memory. The read locks of a transaction may be released at this time; however, the write locks will still be maintained. The Cohort sends an "agreed" message to the Coordinator.

2) If an "abort" message is received, then the Cohort kills the transaction: i.e. it uses the REDO and UNDO logs to delete the new state of the transaction and restore any state from before the occurrence of the transaction.

3) If a "commit" message is received, then the transaction is either prepared to be committed or has already been committed (because of the possible retransmissions from the Coordinator).

a) If the transaction is prepared, the Cohort updates the database and releases the remaining locks that the transaction possesses.

b) If the transaction has already been committed, the Cohort does not take any action, except that it responds with a commit ACK to the Coordinator.

The description in this chapter until now provides the theory of reliable distributed systems. This topic has been dealt with at great depth in prior research as illustrated in concepts and techniques thus far described. However, the future lies in extremely large-scale multi-cloud distributed systems. There are many vendors like Google, Microsoft, Amazon, etc., who are providing solutions for multi-cloud systems addressing public and commercial audiences in accordance with new standards and specifications such as CXL. CXL enables disaggregation of storage and memory. There are ongoing efforts for compute and accelerator resource disaggregation as well. All these offer an opportunity for users to execute large data projects while providing rapid response to failures, reducing performance bottlenecks, and enabling continuous adaptivity. The following section attempts to lead the reader into this upcoming combination of resource-disaggregation in the context of multi-cloud computing platforms.

## 8.10 Opportunities and Challenges in Resource-Disaggregated Cloud Data Centers

The distributed computing paradigm in data centers has continued to evolve to support increased performance, reliability, and efficiency. Resource disaggregation is the latest emerging paradigm. It builds upon previous work in remote direct memory access (RDMA) [52, 53], distributed shared memory (DSM) [54], and non-uniform memory access (NUMA) [55]. In disaggregated data centers, resources such as computing, storage, and memory are decoupled from their physical limits, allowing for dynamic allocation based on real-time demands and workloads. This approach enhances resource utilization, scalability, and flexibility, leading to reduced costs. While resource disaggregation has been a challenge historically, the emergence of the unified CXL [56] cache-coherent interconnect standard and improvement in network speeds (shown in Figure 8.20) relative to computing have enabled faster data movement and made disaggregation more feasible.

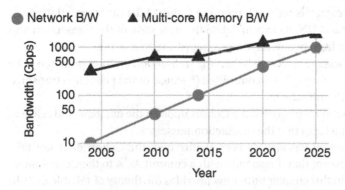

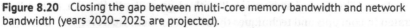

**Figure 8.20** Closing the gap between multi-core memory bandwidth and network bandwidth (years 2020–2025 are projected).

Disaggregation with CXL can resolve some of the limitations of previous approaches, as it is more scalable, has less network overhead, and is transparent to application developers. Specifically, while previous NUMA-based systems were limited to a single server [57], CXL can disaggregate multiple servers over the network; CXL cache coherence requires less overhead than previous DSM systems [58]; and applications can be ported to use disaggregation, as it relies on processor load/store semantics, unlike RDMA, which requires significant rewriting of code [59].

A large body of academic work [60–63] emulates memory disaggregation with a local memory cache backed by swapping from remote memory (similar to disk-based swapping). While these approaches demonstrate the practicality of disaggregation, they do not truly extend the address space like CXL-based systems.

Cloud providers have begun to adopt CXL-based resource disaggregation through initiatives like Pond [64] and ThymesisFlow [65]. Resource disaggregation is particularly beneficial for cloud providers because it reduces total cost of ownership (TCO) through the flexible resource allocation enabled by disaggregation, minimization of resource fragmentation and waste, and support for memory-intensive applications, such as LLM inference, that can benefit from memory expansion. Figure 8.21 depicts the architecture of CXL-based resource-disaggregated cloud datacenter system.

We here explore the key resilience and corresponding performance challenges of implementing resource disaggregation while keeping in mind the hardware constraints of current-generation devices. Specifically, we focus our discussion on three broad classes of resource control mechanisms: data movement, fault tolerance, and data consistency.

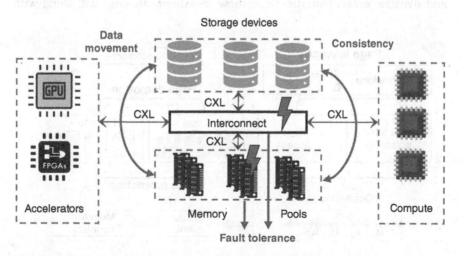

**Figure 8.21** Overview of a resource-disaggregated cloud data center.

### 8.10.1 Data Movement

To help meet increasing memory and storage demands, it is possible to use a range of memory expander modules in CXL, such as SSDs, NVMe, local DRAM, and CXL-attached memory. Each one makes a different trade-off among access type, access speed, and cost. Such hierarchical tiers of memory and storage introduce the challenges of memory allocation and page migration. The amount of memory from each tier allocated to an application should be determined based on the application's demand characteristics. More sensitive or critical applications must be allocated faster memory, while others can be allocated slower memory tiers to reduce cost. In addition, memory pages can be dynamically placed based on application access patterns to compensate for the slower access speeds of lower memory tiers.

*Case study of INDIGO.* We have studied the case of page migration among memory tiers with INDIGO. Previously proposed page migration mechanisms did not achieve the best performance in resource-disaggregated data centers because of their obliviousness to network transfer costs and reliance on inaccurate page access estimations. To address those limitations, we designed INDIGO, which uses novel page telemetry and a learning-based approach for network adaptation. We implemented INDIGO in the Linux kernel and evaluated it with common cloud and high-performance computing (HPC) applications on a real disaggregated memory system prototype, ThymesisFlow, which is based on the openCAPI interconnect (which is similar to CXL 1.0).

*INDIGO workflow.* The workflow of INDIGO is shown in Figure 8.22. INDIGO's page telemetry measures page access rates and coalesces similar measurements to estimate burst durations. The burst duration aids in differentiating between static and dynamic access patterns. Next, these measurements are used, along with

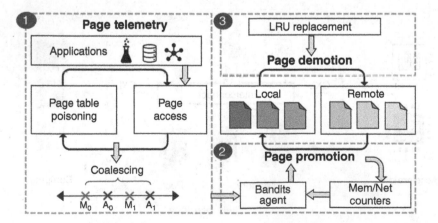

**Figure 8.22** Overview of INDIGO's workflow.

other system metrics, such as memory allocation and network telemetry (collected from memory and network counters, as shown in the figure), to determine the pages that should be migrated. The page migration decision is then taken by a contextual bandit agent driven by a neural network and trained in a feedback loop through use of application performance metrics. If the collection of training data is not feasible, INDIGO offers a network adaptive policy that adjusts promotion rates based on varying network conditions. Finally, infrequently accessed pages are demoted back to the remote memory pool via the regular Linux LRU replacement mechanism. Our evaluation of common cloud applications shows that INDIGO offers up to 50–70% improvement in application performance compared to other state-of-the-art page migration policies and reduces network traffic up to 3×.

### 8.10.2 Data Consistency

*Unified cache coherence.* Cache coherence protocols maintain a consistent state across multiple local processor/accelerator caches and memory. The cache coherency protocol in CXL (CXL.cache) is based on standard protocols like MESI [66]. However, such protocols may not scale to multiple devices because of the introduction of additional coherence traffic. To mitigate that issue, accelerators (such as programmable NICs and switches) may be used to implement strategies such as hierarchical coherence and directory-based coherence protocols.

Another beneficial feature is that accelerators, storage, and memory share a unified coherence model. While CXL supports byte addressability for accelerators and memory, it can also be extended for storage through use of a memory cache with background swapping [67].

### 8.10.3 Fault Tolerance

*Checkpointing and recovery.* The introduction of a network creates an additional source of failures compared to conventional data centers, introducing the need for additional recovery mechanisms, such as checkpointing. Typical fault-tolerance mechanisms that rely on replication of data followed by maintenance of a consistent checkpoint may not be viable, as they conflict with the efficiency targets of disaggregation. An alternative option is checkpointing, which has been widely used in other large memory systems, such as HPC [68] and applications like databases [69].

The exact consistency mechanism to be used depends on whether systemwide checkpointing [68], explicit application-level checkpointing [70], or a transaction-based model is used. In systemwide checkpointing, the entire program state, which includes variable values, stack state, and heap memory, is serialized and stored in the disk. However, this method is computationally expensive and impractical due to its high overhead [71], so we focus our discussion on the other two methods.

Application-level checkpointing exposes APIs to programmers so that they can create checkpoints from which the system can be recovered. If the application is distributed, a pause must be issued to all processes, and any messages in transit on the network must be delivered, before the checkpoint is taken. The pause ensures that all communication channels are empty before processes are allowed to checkpoint their states; the application state is then simply the concatenation of all the process states. The checkpoint annotation and integration can proceed in the background without requiring the application to pause. In transaction-based models, which are typically used by web microservices, the compute proceeds by interaction with a database via transactions. Therefore, the database is primarily responsible for ensuring the fault tolerance of the completed transaction.

*Challenges with checkpointing.* The unified coherence model simplifies the storing of checkpoints and the maintenance of consistency, but determination of the optimal storage location remains a challenge. It would be possible to leverage the memory-storage hierarchy by retaining the most recent checkpoints in local or remote memory, while selectively saving others to the disk. Furthermore, it is critical to establish a recovery chain for the application, and that involves several considerations: deciding whether the recovery process should be transparent to the storage tier (memory or disk), determining the procedure for restarting the system after a consistent checkpoint has been identified, and understanding what virtual structures (e.g. microservices) are appropriate for both creating and recovering from checkpoints.

*Networking and congestion control.* Conventional data center stacks have relied on TCP or kernel bypass using RDMA [52] for communication between microservices running on the compute components. CXL is intended to substantially reduce the software overhead associated with these communication stacks in favor of processor load/store semantics. However, such an approach makes it challenging to design a reliable networking stack that involves congestion control, retransmission mechanisms [72], and Quality of Service requirements, in several respects. Congestion control typically relies on measurements of buffer occupancy or round-trip times that may not be present in CXL systems, although CXL provides an opportunity to use other signals, such as ones indicating compute resource utilization. Retransmissions typically incur at an order of magnitude higher- timescale than network latency. This may in turn incur high overheads for sensitive traffic. To ensure Quality of Service, a mechanism for classifying the demand requirements of application traffic is required. It can be jointly implemented at both the switch and compute.

### 8.10.4  ML-based Orchestration and Validation

Machine learning can act as the linchpin for orchestrating disaggregated resources seamlessly. Machine learning can continuously analyze vast amounts of operational data to make real-time intelligent decisions, e.g. for resource allocation, and to perform offline analysis, e.g. for failure diagnosis. Previously, such decision-making tasks have been fine-tuned through painstaking manual human efforts, but the increase in system complexity that results from disaggregation makes manual effort untenable for future systems, highlighting the need for machine learning. Efficient orchestration is of particular importance to cloud providers, as they must meet strict performance and reliability guarantees for their customers.

FIRM [73] is an initial solution developed at the University of Illinois that explores the use of reinforcement learning (RL) to orchestrate multidimensional resources (e.g. horizontal scaling, CPU/memory allocation, and LLC partitioning) for distributed cloud services (e.g. microservices) such that performance guarantees are maintained. While FIRM provides significant performance improvements compared to static threshold-based resource management approaches, its applicability in production systems is limited by high training and retraining costs, an inability to handle multiple competing instances (in a multi-tenant platform), and a lack of fault tolerance against system failures.

Recent work in learning-based resource orchestration has addressed some of the limitations associated with a vanilla RL-based approach. AWARE [74] proposes the use of meta-learning to reduce the cost of training and retraining FIRM-like RL-based resource orchestrators on different applications and cloud environments. SIMPPO [75] has adopted a multi-agent formulation and models the competing agents as a "virtual agent" with mean field theory approximations to estimate the effect of the competing agents, thus reducing the cost of training a joint agent.

The need for retraining is amplified when the environment keeps updating because of failures or hardware updates. To further reduce the cost of such retraining, one can design hardware accelerators that reduce RL exploration costs by simultaneously running multiple copies of the environment in parallel, and through fast computation of model weight updates during gradient descent.

## References

1 Chandra, T.D. and Toueg, S. (1996). Unreliable failure detectors for reliable distributed systems. *Journal of the ACM* 43 (2): 225–267.

2 Mullender, S. (ed.) (1993). *Distributed Systems*, 2e. Reading, MA: Addison-Wesley.

3 Singhal, M. and Shivaratri, N. (1994). *Advanced Concepts in Operating Systems*. New York, NY: McGraw-Hill.

**4** Pease, M., Shostak, R., and Lamport, L. (1980). Reaching agreement in the presence of faults. *Journal of the ACM* 27 (2): 228–234.

**5** Fischer, M.J. and Lynch, N.A. (1982). A lower bound for the time to assure interactive consistency. *Information Processing Letters* 14 (4): 183–186.

**6** Lamport, L., Shostak, R., and Pease, M. (1982). The Byzantine generals problem. *ACM Transactions on Programming Languages and Systems* 4 (3): 382–401.

**7** Chockler, G., Keidar, I., and Vitenberg, R. (2001). Group communication specifications: a comprehensive study. *ACM Computing Surveys* 33 (4): 427–469.

**8** Birman, K.P. and Van Renesse, R. (1994). *Reliable Distributed Computing with the Isis Toolkit*. Los Alamitos, CA: IEEE Computer Society Press.

**9** Van Renesse, R., Birman, K., and Maffeis, S. (1996). Horus: a flexible group communication system. *Communications of the ACM* 39 (4): 76–83.

**10** Hayden, M. (1997). The Ensemble system. Ph.D. dissertation. Cornell University.

**11** Moser, L.E., Melliar-Smith, P.M., Agarwal, D.A. et al. (1996). Totem: a fault-tolerant multicast group communication system. *Communications of the ACM* 39 (4): 54–63.

**12** Amir, Y., Dolev, D., Kramer, S. et al. (1992). Transis: a communication subsystem for high availability. *Digest of Papers, the 22nd International Symposium on Fault-Tolerant Computing*, Boston, MA, USA (8–10 July 1992), 76–84. IEEE.

**13** Kihlstrom, K.P., Moser, L.E., and Melliar-Smith, P.M. (1998). The SecureRing protocols for securing group communication. *Proceedings of the 31st Annual Hawaii International Conference on System Sciences*, Kohala Coast, HI, USA (6–9 January 1998), vol. 3, 317–326. IEEE.

**14** Reiter, M.K. (1994). Secure agreement protocols: reliable and atomic group multicast in Rampart. *Proceedings of the 2nd ACM Conference on Computer and Communication Security*, Fairfax, VA, USA (2–4 November 1994), 68–80.

**15** Schneider, F.B. (1990). Implementing fault-tolerant services using the state machine approach: a tutorial. *ACM Computing Surveys* 22 (4): 299–319.

**16** Avižienis, A., Gilley, G.C., Mathur, F.P. et al. (1971). The STAR (Self-Testing And Repairing) computer: an investigation of the theory and practice of fault-tolerant computer design. *IEEE Transactions on Computers* C-20 (11): 1312–1321.

**17** Toy, W.N. (1978). Fault-tolerant design of local ESS processors. *Proceedings of the IEEE* 66 (10): 1126–1145.

**18** Jewett, D. (1991). Integrity S2: a fault-tolerant Unix platform. *Digest of Papers, the 21st International Symposium on Fault-Tolerant Computing*, Montreal, Canada (25–27 June 1991), 512–519. IEEE.

**19** Cristian, F., Aghili, H., Strong, R. et al. (1985). Atomic broadcast: from simple message diffusion to Byzantine agreement. *Digest of Papers, the 15th Annual International Symposium on Fault-Tolerant Computing*, Ann Arbor, MI, USA (19–21 June 1985), 200–206. IEEE Computer Society Press.

**20** Borg, A., Blau, W., Graetsch, W. et al. (1989). Fault tolerance under UNIX. *ACM Transactions on Computer Systems* 7 (1): 1–24.

**21** Bressoud, T.C. and Schneider, F.B. (1996). Hypervisor-based fault tolerance. *ACM Transactions on Computer Systems* 14 (1): 80–107.

**22** Wensley, J.H., Lamport, L., Goldberg, J. et al. (1978). SIFT: Design and analysis of a fault-tolerant computer for aircraft control. *Proceedings of the IEEE* 66 (10): 1240–1255.

**23** Chereque, M., Powell, D., Reynier, P. et al. (1992). Active replication in Delta-4. *Digest of Papers, the 22nd International Symposium on Fault-Tolerant Computing*, Boston, MA, USA (8–10 July 1992), 28–37. IEEE.

**24** Baysburd, A. and Birman, K. (1998). The Maestro approach to building reliable interoperable distributed applications. *Theory and Practice of Object Systems* 4 (2): 73–80.

**25** Felber, P., Guerraoui, R., and Schiper, A. (1998). The implementation of a CORBA object group service. *Theory and Practice of Object Systems* 4 (2): 93–105.

**26** Moser, L.E., Melliar-Smith, P.M., and Narasimhan, P. (1998). Consistent object replication in the Eternal system. *Theory and Practice of Object Systems* 4 (2): 81–92.

**27** Cukier, M., Ren, J., Sabnis, C. et al. (1998). AQuA: an adaptive architecture that provides dependable distributed objects. *Proceedings of the 17th IEEE Symposium on Reliable Distributed Systems*, West Lafayette, IN, USA (20–23 October 1998), 245–253. IEEE.

**28** Jiménez-Peris, R., Patiño-Martínez, M., and Arévalo, S. (2000). Deterministic scheduling for transactional multithreaded replicas. *Proceedings of the 19th IEEE Symposium on Reliable Distributed Systems*, Nürnberg, Germany (16–18 October 2000), 164–173. IEEE.

**29** Lamport, L. (2001). Paxos made simple. *ACM SIGACT News* 32 (4): 51–58. [In Rajsbaum, S. (2001). ACM SIGACT News distributed computing column 5. *ACM SIGACT News* 32 (4): 34–58.].

**30** Whittaker, M., Charapko, A., Hellerstein, J.M. et al. (2021). Read-write quorum systems made practical. *Proceedings of the 8th Workshop on Principles and Practice of Consistency for Distributed Data*, virtual (21 April 2021). New York, NY: Association for Computing Machinery. https://doi.org/10.1145/3447865.3457962.

**31** Hunt, P., Konar, M., Junqueira, F.P. et al. (2010). ZooKeeper: wait-free coordination for internet-scale systems. *Proceedings of the 2010 USENIX Annual Technical Conference*, Boston, MA, USA (23–25 June 2010). http://www.usenix.org/events/atc10/tech/full_papers/Hunt.pdf.

**32** Borthakur, D. (2007). The Hadoop distributed file system: architecture and design. https://svn.apache.org/repos/asf/hadoop/common/tags/release-0.16.3/docs/hdfs_design.pdf (accessed 19 October 2023).

**33** Kreps, J., Narkhede, N., and Rao, J. (2011). Kafka: a distributed messaging system for log processing. *Proceedings of the 6th International Workshop on Networking*

*Meets Databases*, Athens, Greece (12 June 2011). https://www.microsoft.com/en-us/research/wp-content/uploads/2017/09/Kafka.pdf.

**34** Weil, S.A., Brandt, S.A., Miller, E.L. et al. (2006). Ceph: a scalable, high-performance distributed file system. *Proceedings of the 7th Symposium on Operating Systems Design and Implementation*, Seattle, WA, USA (6–8 November 2006), 307–320. Berkeley, CA, USA: USENIX Association.

**35** Sivasubramanian, S. (2012). Amazon dynamoDB: a seamlessly scalable non-relational database service. *Proceedings of the 2012 ACM SIGMOD International Conference on Management of Data*, Scottsdale, AZ, USA (20–24 May 2012), 729–730. New York, NY: Association for Computing Machinery.

**36** Lakshman, A. and Malik, P. (2010). Cassandra: a decentralized structured storage system. *ACM SIGOPS Operating Systems Review* 44 (2): 35–40.

**37** Pleisch, S. and Schiper, A. (2001). FATOMAS: a fault-tolerant mobile agent system based on the agent-dependent approach. *Proceedings of the 2001 International Conference on Dependable Systems and Networks*, Gothenburg, Sweden (1–4 July 2001), 215–224. IEEE.

**38** Parrington, G.D., Shrivastava, S.K., Wheater, S.M. et al. (1995). The design and implementation of Arjuna. *Computing Systems* 8 (2): 255–308.

**39** Basile, C., Kalbarczyk, Z., and Iyer, R.K. (2006). Active replication of multithreaded applications. *IEEE Transactions on Parallel and Distributed Systems* 17 (5): 448–465.

**40** Goldberg, A.P. (1990). Transparent recovery of Mach applications. *Proceedings of the Usenix MACH Symposium*, Burlington, VT, USA (4–5 October 1990), 169–184.

**41** Lamport, L. (1978). Time, clocks and the ordering of events in distributed systems. *Communication of the ACM* 21 (7): 558–564.

**42** Elnozahy, E.N., Johnson, D.B., and Wang, Y.M. (1996). A survey of rollback-recovery protocols in message-passing systems. *School of Computer Science, Carnegie Mellon University Tech. Rep. CMU-CS-96-181*.

**43** Basile, C., Whisnant, K., Kalbarczyk, Z. et al. (2002). Loose synchronization of multithreaded replicas. *Proceedings of the 21st IEEE Symposium on Reliable Distributed Systems*, Suita, Japan (13–16 October 2002), 250–255. IEEE.

**44** Cristian, F., Aghili, H., Strong, R. et al. (1995). Atomic broadcast: from simple message diffusion to Byzantine agreement. *Information and Computation* 118 (1): 158–179.

**45** Madeira, H. and Silva, J.G. (1994). Experimental evaluation of the fail-silent behavior in computers without error masking. *Proceedings of the IEEE 24th International Symposium on Fault-Tolerant Computing*, Austin, TX, USA (15–17 June 1994), 350–359. IEEE.

**46** Rimen, M., Ohlsson, J., and Torin, J. (1994). On microprocessor error behavior modeling. *Proceedings of the IEEE 24th International Symposium on Fault-Tolerant Computing*, Austin, TX, USA (15–17 June 1994), 76–85. IEEE.

**47** Cha, H., Rudnick, E.M., Patel, J.H. et al. (1996). A gate-level simulation environment for alpha-particle-induced transient faults. *IEEE Transactions on Computers* 45 (11): 1248–1256.

**48** Choi, G.S., Iyer, R.K., and Saab, D.G. (1993). Fault behavior dictionary for simulation of device-level transients. *Proceedings of the 1993 IEEE International Conference on Computer-Aided Design*, Santa Clara, CA, USA (7–11 November 1993), 6–9. IEEE.

**49** Guerraoui, R., Felber, P., Garbinato, B. et al. (1998). System support for object groups. *Proceedings of the 13th ACM SIGPLAN Conference on Object-Oriented Programming Systems, Languages and Applications*, Vancouver, British Columbia, Canada (18–22 October 1998), 244–258. New York, NY: Association for Computing Machinery.

**50** Whisnant, K., Iyer, R.K., Jones, P. et al. (2002). An experimental evaluation of the REE SIFT environment for spaceborne applications. *Proceedings of the International Conference on Dependable Systems and Networks*, Washington, DC, USA (23–26 June 2002), 585–594. IEEE.

**51** Skeen, D. and Stonebraker, M. (1983). A formal model of crash recovery in a distributed system. *IEEE Transactions on Software Engineering* 9 (3): 219–228.

**52** Romanow, A. and Bailey, S. (2003). An overview of RDMA over IP. *1st International Workshop on Protocols for Fast Long-Distance Networks*, Geneva, Switzerland (3–4 February 2003).

**53** Shan, Y., Huang, Y., Chen, Y. et al. (2018). LegoOS: a disseminated, distributed OS for hardware resource disaggregation. *Proceedings of the 13th USENIX Symposium on Operating Systems Design and Implementation*, Carlsbad, CA, USA (8–10 October 2018), 69–87. USENIX.

**54** Protić, J., Tomašević, M., and Milutinović, V. (1996). Distributed shared memory: concepts and systems. *IEEE Parallel & Distributed Technology: Systems & Applications* 4 (2): 63–71.

**55** Lameter, C. (2013). NUMA (Non-Uniform Memory Access): an overview: NUMA becomes more common because memory controllers get close to execution units on microprocessors. *Queue* 11 (7): 40–51.

**56** Das Sharma, D, Blankenship, R, and Berger, D.S. (2023). An introduction to the Compute Express Link (CXL) interconnect. arXiv preprint arXiv:2306.11227.

**57** Gaud, F., Lepers, B., Funston, J. et al. (2015). Challenges of memory management on modern NUMA systems. *Communications of the ACM* 58 (12): 59–66.

**58** Gharachorloo, K. (1999). The plight of software distributed shared memory. *Invited talk at 1st Workshop on Software Distributed Shared Memory*, Rhodes, Greece (25 June 1999).

**59** Dragojević, A., Narayanan, D., Hodson, O. et al. (2014). FaRM: Fast Remote Memory. *Proceedings of the 11th USENIX Symposium on Networked Systems Design and Implementation*, Seattle, WA, USA (2–4 April 2014), 401–414. USENIX.

**60** Gu, J., Lee, Y., Zhang, Y. et al. (2017). Efficient memory disaggregation with Infiniswap. *Proceedings of the 14th USENIX Symposium on Networked Systems Design and Implementation*, Boston, MA, USA (27–29 March 2017), 649–667. USENIX.

**61** Al Maruf, H. and Chowdhury, M. (2020). Effectively prefetching remote memory with Leap. *Proceedings of the 2020 USENIX Annual Technical Conference* (15–17 July 2020), 843–857. USENIX.

**62** Amaro, E., Branner-Augmon, C., Luo, Z. et al. (2020). Can far memory improve job throughput? *Proceedings of the 15th European Conference on Computer Systems*, virtual (27–30 April 2020), article no. 14. https://doi.org/10.1145/3342195.3387522.

**63** Qiao, Y., Wang, C., Ruan, Z. et al. (2023). Hermit: Low-latency, high-throughput, and transparent remote memory via feedback-directed asynchrony. *Proceedings of the 20th USENIX Symposium on Networked Systems Design and Implementation*, Boston, MA, USA (17–19 April 2023), 181–198. USENIX.

**64** Li, H., Berger, D.S., Hsu, L. et al. (2023). Pond: CXL-based memory pooling systems for cloud platforms. *Proceedings of the 28th ACM International Conference on Architectural Support for Programming Languages and Operating Systems*, Vancouver, BC, Canada (25–29 March 2023), vol. 2, 574–587. New York, NY: Association for Computing Machinery.

**65** Pinto, C., Syrivelis, D., Gazzetti, M. et al. (2020). ThymesisFlow: a software-defined, HW/SW co-designed interconnect stack for rack-scale memory disaggregation. *Proceedings of the 2020 53rd Annual IEEE/ACM International Symposium on Microarchitecture*, Athens, Greece (17–21 October 2020), 868–880. IEEE.

**66** Papamarcos, M.S. and Patel, J.H. (1984). A low-overhead coherence solution for multiprocessors with private cache memories. *Proceedings of the 11th Annual International Symposium on Computer Architecture*, Ann Arbor, MI, USA (5–7 June 1984), 348–354. New York, NY: Association for Computing Machinery.

**67** Abulila, A., Mailthody, V.S., Qureshi, Z. et al. (2019). FlatFlash: Exploiting the byte-accessibility of SSDs within a unified memory-storage hierarchy. *Proceedings of the 24th International Conference on Architectural Support for Programming Languages and Operating Systems*, Providence, RI, USA (13–17 April 2019), 971–985. New York, NY: Association for Computing Machinery.

**68** Wang, L., Pattabiraman, K., Kalbarczyk, Z. et al. (2005, June). Modeling coordinated checkpointing for large-scale supercomputers. *Proceedings of the 2005 International Conference on Dependable Systems and Networks*, Yokohama, Japan (28 June–1 July 2005) 812–821. IEEE. https://doi.org/10.1109/DSN.2005.67

**69** Magalhaes, A., Monteiro, J.M., and Brayner, A. (2021). Main memory database recovery: A survey. *ACM Computing Surveys* 54 (2) article no. 46: 1–36. https://doi.org/10.1145/3442197.

**70** Bronevetsky, G., Marques, D., Pingali, K. et al. (2004). Application-level checkpointing for shared memory programs. *ACM SIGPLAN Notices* 39 (11): 235–247.

**71** Jones, W.M., Daly, J.T., and DeBardeleben, N. (2012). Application monitoring and checkpointing in HPC: Looking towards exascale systems. *Proceedings of the 50th ACM Southeast Regional Conference*, Tuscaloosa, AL, USA (29–31 March 2012), 262–267. New York, NY: Association for Computing Machinery.

**72** Cheng, Y., Cardwell, N., Dukkipati, N. et al. (2021). RFC 8985: The RACK-TLP Loss Detection Algorithm for TCP. https://www.rfc-editor.org/info/rfc8985 (accessed 19 October 2023).

**73** Qiu, H., Banerjee, S.S., Jha, S. et al. (2020). FIRM: an intelligent fine-grained resource management framework for SLO-oriented microservices. *Proceedings of the 14th USENIX Symposium on Operating Systems Design and Implementation*, virtual (4–6 November 2020), 805–825. USENIX.

**74** Qiu, H., Mao, W., Wang, C. et al. (2023). AWARE: Automate Workload Autoscaling with Reinforcement learning in production cloud systems. *Proceedings of the 2023 USENIX Annual Technical Conference*, Boston, MA, USA (10–12 July 2023), 387–402. USENIX.

**75** Qiu, H., Mao, W., Patke, A. et al. (2022, November). SIMPPO: a scalable and incremental online learning framework for serverless resource management. *Proceedings of the 13th Symposium on Cloud Computing*, San Francisco, CA, USA (7–11 November 2022), 306–322. New York, NY: Association for Computing Machinery.

# 9

# Checkpointing and Rollback Error Recovery

## 9.1 Introduction

Checkpointing is an important technique for recovery by means of rollback and re-execution of a process following error detection. There are two types of error recovery: *forward* error recovery and *backward* error recovery.

In forward error recovery, the currently executing process continues to execute from a point beyond the occurrence of the failure, with compensation for the corrupted and missed data. This type of error recovery makes the assumptions that (i) the precise error conditions that caused the detection and the resulting damage can be accurately assessed; (ii) the errors in the process's (system's) state can be removed; and (iii) the process (system) can move forward. An example of forward error recovery is exception handling and recovery.

In backward error recovery, the current process is rolled back to a certain error-free point, and the corrupted part of the process is re-executed so that the same requested service continues. The assumptions are that (i) the nature of faults cannot be foreseen, and errors in the process's (system's) states cannot be removed without re-execution; and (ii) the process's (system's) state can be restored to a previous error-free state. Checkpointing and rollback recovery is an example of this type of error recovery. These two approaches are summarized in Table 9.1.

The checkpoint and rollback mechanism is applicable when time redundancy is allowed. It applies to transient hardware faults and many software design faults, such as timing faults. It can be used with redundant and non-redundant architectures. It requires that it be feasible to determine checkpoints in an application. We define the *checkpoint data* as the state at the most recent checkpoint and the *active data* as the state accessed after the checkpoint.

*Dependable Computing: Design and Assessment*, First Edition. Ravishankar K. Iyer, Zbigniew T. Kalbarczyk, and Nithin M. Nakka.
© 2024 The IEEE Computer Society. Published 2024 by John Wiley & Sons, Inc.
Companion website: www.wiley.com/go/iyer/dependablecomputing1

**Table 9.1** Comparison of forward and backward error recovery.

|  | Advantages | Disadvantages |
|---|---|---|
| Forward error recovery | • Relatively low overhead | • Dependent on damage assessment and prediction<br>• Inappropriate for unanticipated damage<br>• Cannot provide a general recovery mechanism<br>• Design is specific to a particular system |
| Backward error recovery | • Applicable to all systems<br>• Independent of damage assessment (can recover from arbitrary damage)<br>• Can be application- or system-based | • Performance penalty (overhead of restoring state)<br>• Error may persist on re-execution<br>• Some component of the state may be unrecoverable |

Checkpointing preserves a precise system state or snapshot at regular intervals. The snapshot can be as small as one instruction. Typically, the checkpoint interval includes many instructions. Thus, it may not be ideal when the error detection latency is high. Rollback recovery is performed when an error is detected. It rolls back or restores processes to the saved state, i.e. the checkpoint, and then restarts the computation.

Implementation of checkpoint and rollback requires implementation of an appropriate error-detection mechanism. Appropriate mechanisms internal to the application include various self-checking mechanisms, such as data integrity, control-flow checking, and acceptance tests. External mechanisms include signals (e.g. abnormal termination), missing heartbeats, and watchdog timers. The data or process state to be checkpointed can be a volatile state: a program stack (consisting of local variables and return pointers of function calls), a program counter, a stack pointer, an open file descriptor, a signal handler, or static or dynamic data segments. Alternatively, the state to be checkpointed can be a persistent state, such as user files related to the current program execution. Whether to include the persistent state in the process state depends on the application; for example, the persistent state is often an important part of a long-running application. In any case, the checkpointed data must be stored in stable storage.

To implement checkpoint and rollback recovery, it is necessary to determine (i) the events to be logged and replayed, such as messages, events that triggered a message to be sent, or transactions, and (ii) the checkpoint times based on elapsed time, messages received or sent (as in parallel or distributed applications), amount of dirtied state (as in database applications), or critical function invocation/exit. Also required is a procedure to restart the computation and a means of handling a persistent error.

Checkpointing and rollback recovery can be implemented at the processor, memory management, operating system, compiler, or application level. Checkpointing and rollback recovery as a fault tolerance technique can be applied:

1) to single-threaded processes
2) to multithreaded processes running either on:
   a) a single processor
   b) in multiprocessors
   c) in a shared-memory multiprocessor architecture, or
   d) in a distributed system that is based on message passing.

## 9.2 Hardware-Implemented Cache-Based Schemes Checkpointing

### 9.2.1 Cache-Aided Rollback Error Recovery (CARER) for Uniprocessors

Cache-aided rollback error recovery (CARER) is a checkpointing and rollback recovery technique that involves the processor registers, the cache, and higher levels of memory [1]. When applied to a uniprocessor system, the processor registers and the cache contains the active data, and the checkpoint data are maintained in the main memory system. After a checkpoint, any modifications to the state are made only to the processor registers and cache. CARER assumes a writeback cache policy, wherein stores write the data to the cache only, and the updates are transferred to the main memory when a dirty cache line must be replaced because of a cache miss. It is necessary to take a checkpoint when a cache miss forces a dirty cache line to be written back to the main memory. Taking a checkpoint involves copying all registers and cache lines that have been modified to the main memory. When an error is detected, the corrupted state is discarded, and the system is rolled back to a previous consistent state by discarding all the processor registers and cache lines. That separation of the active state and checkpoint state is depicted in Figure 9.1.

In summary, the taking of a checkpoint involves two steps: (i) the processor registers are saved at a pre-allocated fixed region in memory, and (ii) the dirty cache lines are written back to the main memory. Rolling back to a checkpointed state requires (i) restoration of the processor registers from the fixed memory location where they were previously stored and (ii) discarding of all dirty cache lines.

To understand how the active state is created, let us begin with the machine in a stopped state, wherein valid checkpoint data are in the main memory, and the processor registers corresponding to the checkpoint data are saved in the main memory save area. There are no dirty lines in the cache or modified registers in the processor. To start machine execution from a previous valid checkpoint state,

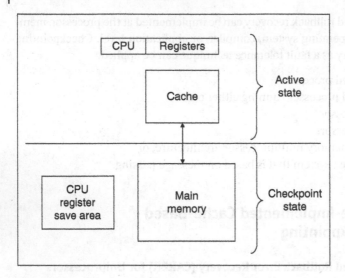

**Figure 9.1** Active and checkpoint states in processor-based checkpointing and rollback recovery.

the registers are restored from the main memory save area. During regular application execution, if a cache miss occurs, data from memory (considered valid from the previous checkpoint) are loaded into the cache. As discussed before, stores write only to the cache and are not written back to the memory. Only the cache and the processor registers contain any changes in the state since the last checkpoint, called the *active state*.

If a transient error is detected by one of the error detectors, the machine must be rolled back to the previous checkpoint. The processor registers and cache must be restored to that checkpoint, which is stored in the main memory. Only the dirty lines in the cache are part of the active state. The dirty lines can be invalidated selectively, or the entire cache can be invalidated to restore the cache to a clean state, the same state as that at the time of the checkpoint. Next, the processor registers are restored from their saved state in memory. The execution can now begin from the point of the previous checkpoint.

After the machine has executed past a previous checkpoint, to take a new checkpoint, the active state (i.e. the dirty cache lines and the processor registers) must be copied to the checkpoint state. To do so, all the dirty cache lines must be written back to memory, and the processor registers must be written into the main memory save area. A parameter in the hardware can trigger the taking of a checkpoint. However, because of a cache miss, if a dirty cache line is written back to memory, a checkpoint must be taken. The reason is that the dirty cache line is part of the active state, and the main memory is the checkpoint state. If the dirty cache line were written back before a checkpoint was taken, that would mix the checkpoint state with the active state.

One optimization to decrease checkpointing overhead is to use an internal set of backup registers. Another performance enhancement to decrease the time taken to write back all the dirty lines in the cache to the main memory is to mark all dirty cache lines to be *unchangeable* at the time of the checkpoint. Doing so allows a dirty line that is part of a checkpoint to remain in the cache without being written back to the main memory. With those optimizations in place, the checkpointed state consists of the backup internal registers, main memory, and all unchangeable lines in the cache. Before an unchangeable cache line is written, it must be written back to the memory.

The Sequoia multiprocessor [2] implements cache-based processor rollback recovery with the aforementioned optimizations and an additional mechanism for tolerating errors when the dirty cache lines are being written back to the checkpoint. Through the use of dual memory banks, an atomic checkpoint is provided that ensures the successful completion of a checkpoint or retaining of the previous checkpoint.

The six steps to flush a cache line to memory, as shown in Figure 9.2, are needed to provide an atomic checkpoint. A single failure at any point can be tolerated. The cache is written back sequentially to the two memory banks. A timestamp is written to the memory bank before ($T_{X1}$ or $T_{Y1}$) and after ($T_{X2}$ or $T_{Y2}$) the write back. Based on the relative values of those four timestamps, failures are detected according to the following scenarios, and appropriate recovery actions are taken:

1) $T_{X1} = T_{X2} = T_{Y1} = T_{Y2}$: No failure has occurred, and no action needs to be taken.
2) $T_{X1} > T_{X2} = T_{Y1} = T_{Y2}$: A failure has occurred during the write-back to bank X. The recovery action copies bank Y to bank X.

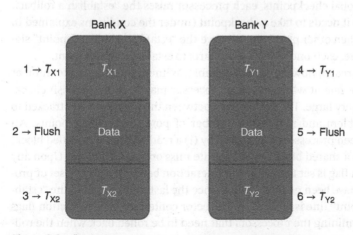

**Figure 9.2** Dual memory banks in the Sequoia multiprocessor.

3) We will consider two sub-cases:
   a) $T_{X1} = T_{X2} > T_{Y1} = T_{Y2}$: A failure has occurred after the write-back to bank X, but before the start of the write-back to bank Y.
   b) $T_{X1} = T_{X2} = T_{Y1} > T_{Y2}$: A failure has occurred during the flushing to bank Y. In either of the scenarios 3(a) and 3(b), the recovery involves copying bank X to bank Y to establish a correct checkpoint.

Both Career and Sequoia do not consistently support large-scale windows. SWICH [3] provides a prototype design implemented on an FPGA, which supports large windows continuously.

## 9.2.2  Multiprocessor Cache-Based Schemes

In a multiprocessor system, multiple processes running on different processors and any data dependencies that might exist among them pose a challenge to providing a consistent checkpointing and rollback mechanism. Data dependencies between processes force the rollback of one process on the rollback of another, and so on. That is commonly called *rollback propagation*. One possible way to avoid it is to maintain a global checkpoint, thereby removing the data dependencies.

The uniprocessor CARER scheme described in Section 9.2.1 can be extended to a multiprocessor architecture [4]. Each processor in the multiprocessor system has a private cache and shares a single bus-attached memory with the rest of the processors. To support the extensions to the multiprocessor architecture, the bus has three additional lines: (i) *shared*, wherein a block is being shared on the bus; (ii) *establish a rollback point*; and (iii) *rollback*, in which the system rolls back to a previous rollback point.

To maintain global checkpoints, each processor raises the "establish a rollback point" line when it needs to take a checkpoint (under the conditions explained in Section 9.2.1). When other processors observe the "establish a rollback point" signal on the bus line, each one of them also starts to establish a checkpoint.

That naïve approach, however, is not scalable. With an increase in the number of processors, the rate at which any one processor may need to establish checkpoints becomes very large. The interactions between the processors are tracked to alleviate the problem and reduce the number of potential rollback points. An interaction between processors is triggered by (i) a read miss on a modified block, (ii) a write hit on a shared block, or (iii) a write miss on a shared block. Upon any of those events, a flag is set to indicate an interaction between a pair or set of processors. If there have been no interactions since the last rollback point, the "establish a rollback point" line is ignored. A bit vector containing the interaction flags also aids in determining the processors that need to be rolled back when the rollback line is set.

Let us now consider a multiprocessor system in which the processors have private caches, and memory that is attached to the processors is shared through an interconnection network [5]. This approach does not have the advantage of a common bus to broadcast intentions. As in the uniprocessor scheme (as well as the prior multiprocessor scheme), a checkpoint is triggered whenever a dirty cache line needs to be written back to the main memory. However, that checkpoint does not require other processors to take checkpoints. To prevent rollback propagation, a checkpoint is triggered whenever a cache line on a processor that has been modified since the last checkpoint is read by another processor. By using checkpoint identifiers that associate a modified cache line with a specific checkpoint, we can reduce the number of dirty cache blocks that need to be checkpointed. The checkpoint identifier is a k-bit counter and is a generalization of the one-bit *unchangeable* flag in the uniprocessor CARER scheme. Every block has a checkpoint identifier associated with it, and the current checkpoint number is maintained in a global counter. To further reduce memory traffic, a recovery stack is used to temporarily store cache lines that need to be checkpointed. For all the unchangeable lines that need to be checkpointed, the data in the cache line, along with the cache line's checkpoint identifier, its cache coherence bits, and the address tag of the block, are pushed onto the recovery stack. When a checkpoint is taken, the recovery stack is cleared, and during rollback, the stack is written back to the cache.

Use of that scheme to take a checkpoint involves the following steps:

1) The global checkpoint number (GCPN) is incremented.
2) The GCPN is compared against the block number on all write hits.
   a) If the block number is less than the checkpoint number, the block is unwritable and must be pushed onto the recovery stack.
   b) The block counter is set equal to the global counter whenever a write is completed.

A pseudo-checkpoint is also allowed to exist for several cycles, but that requires two backup register sets and an extra pointer in the recovery stack.

### 9.2.3 ReVive: Cost-Effective Architectural Support for Rollback Recovery in Shared-Memory Multiprocessors

In the ReVive [6] approach to rollback recovery in shared memory multiprocessor systems, during error-free execution, it is necessary to interrupt all processors in order to take global checkpoints periodically. To establish a checkpoint, the caches must be flushed to memory, and a two-phase commit operation then takes place [7]. After a checkpoint has been taken, the main memory contains the checkpoint state. During normal operation after a checkpoint, the memory content will be modified by program execution. On the first write event to a line of checkpoint data in main memory, the previous content in memory is logged by the home directory controller to save the line's checkpoint state. All checkpoint data that have been overwritten can be found in the log when needed for recovery. During error-free operation, after the next checkpoint is taken, the logs can be freed and reused. In practice, depending on the worst-case error detection latency, multiple logs need to be saved to enable recovery across the required number of checkpoints.

When an error is detected, the logs are used to restore the state of the memory to the state at the time of the last checkpoint that immediately preceded the error. All the active data that have been in the caches since the checkpoint are eliminated through invalidation of the caches. The execution can then proceed. For errors that lead to loss of memory content, the ability to recover is provided via page-level parity. A parity page on a node is associated with a set of pages from different nodes. During error-free operation, upon each write event to the main memory, the home directory controller also updates the parity page located on another node. If a memory module on a node fails or is rendered unreachable, the parity information can be used to detect this error and recover the data in the memory module. The recovered memory content contains both the logs and the program state. First, the logs are recovered and used to perform the normal rollback procedure described before. After that step, the rest of the memory state is recovered in the background while the program execution is allowed to proceed.

When a new checkpoint is taken, the results of program execution since the previous checkpoint are committed. The steps involved in taking a checkpoint are (i) storing the execution context of the processor in a pre-allocated region of memory and (ii) writing back all the modified cache lines to memory. All the processors are interrupted to take a global checkpoint, and each processor waits until all its outstanding operations have been completed. The global checkpoint is then committed atomically on all processors through the use of a two-phase commit protocol [7] with the following sequence of actions: (i) synchronizing all processors, (ii) marking the state as tentatively committed, (iii) synchronizing the processors again, and (iv) fully committing the state. After the checkpoint has been taken, the space allocated to the log is freed. The number of most recent checkpoints that are maintained depends on the maximum detection latency. If an error occurs before a checkpoint has been established but is detected only after the checkpoint has been completely taken, the checkpoint would be corrupted. After rollback to the erroneous checkpoint, the error will surface again. In that situation, the system can attempt to roll back to an earlier checkpoint.

## 9.3   Memory-Based Schemes

This section discusses schemes that provide spatial redundancy through two (or more) physical memory locations for each piece of data.

### 9.3.1   Physical Memory-Based Schemes

The stable transaction memory (STM) [8] approach provides a mechanism for atomic updates to memory blocks using two memory banks. It is similar to the uniprocessor CARER technique implemented in the Sequoia processor. When the processor attempts to write to a memory location, all the redundant memory blocks associated with that memory location are also updated. The write to the multiple blocks is performed atomically using a transaction identifier. First, the transaction identifier is created via a create-transaction request. After the processor has written to all the blocks, it sends an "end-transaction" request to the STM. On receipt of the end-transaction request, the STM copies the data from the first bank to the second. If a failure occurs during the writing to the multiple memory blocks, it is detected by the STM through a time-out mechanism. Upon detecting the failure, the STM aborts that transaction by copying the original data from the second bank to the first bank, thus returning to a state before the write to memory began. A write-back cache policy is used to confine the changes locally within the cache. The modified cache lines are written back using the atomic commit mechanism described earlier. A process is marked to be dependent on another process (which may be running on another processor) if a modified block in the cache of the latter is read by the former. When the updates of a process are committed to memory, the updates of all its dependent processes are also committed in a group.

In a *sheaved* memory [9] architecture, a collection of physical page frames are bundled together (in a *sheaf*) with the "read one, write many" property. The number of frames bundled together within a sheaf can be set (that is, two, four, or eight frames per sheaf). All the frames bundled within a sheaf receive the data on a single write to memory. A checkpoint modifies the bundling of frames within the sheaf. By dropping a frame from a sheaf, the frame does not receive any subsequent writes to memory and thus holds the previous state of the sheaf.

### 9.3.2   Virtual Memory-Based Schemes

A *dual* scheme is one in which there is a mapping to two pieces of data (active and checkpoint) that are at the same level in the memory hierarchy. In this section, we examine schemes that achieve the *dual* nature through virtual mapping of the memory.

*Twin-Page Systems.* Twin Slot (also known as Twist) is a database recovery technique proposed by Reuter [10] in the category of twin-page systems. Twin-page systems are based on the basic property of moving-head disk drives, namely that a major component of the service time is seeking and latency time that depends on mechanical properties and that the actual transfer of data contributes only the remaining minor portion. Reuter has proposed that it would be possible to take advantage of that property and allocate enough space for each disk slot to contain two physical pages. For a page $P$, the twin page is referred to as $P'$. When $P$ is being accessed, accessing of $P'$ would not incur an additional delay due to mechanical properties.

The header for every disk page contains a timestamp. Each time the page is modified, the timestamp is updated. For the page $P$ and its twin, $P'$, we refer to the timestamps for the times when they were last modified as $T_P$ and $T_P'$, respectively. The global time of the last checkpoint will be referred to as $T_{chk}$. That value must be stored in a safe disk location (for example, a duplicate of the value could be stored on another disk).

When a page is fetched from the disk, its twin page and both pages' headers are also fetched into a buffer. Depending on the header information, specifically the timestamps, in the two pages, one of the pages is determined to be the active version and the other the checkpoint version. Only the active version of the page is delivered to the requestor. Two cases can arise in determining the active version of the page. Let $T_P$ be the timestamp of page $P$ (modified after page $P'$, that is, $T_P > T_P'$); the previous checkpoint was taken at $T_{chk}$, and the current fetch is done at time $t$ ($t > T_{chk}$).

Case I, shown in Figure 9.3, occurs when the page is fetched for the first time after the checkpoint has been taken. Here, $T_P' < T_P < T_{chk}$. Thus, $P$ is the checkpoint version of the page, and $P'$ is the version of the page from prior to the checkpoint and is not needed anymore. Therefore, the data in $P$ are used, and future write-backs to the page are written to $P'$. Thus, $P$ becomes the checkpoint version and $P'$ the active version. Note that on a write-back, only $P'$ is written, while $P$ is preserved in the slot.

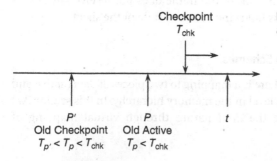

Checkpoint
$T_{chk}$

$P'$
Old Checkpoint
$T_{p'} < T_p < T_{chk}$

$P$
Old Active
$T_p < T_{chk}$

$t$

**Figure 9.3** Case I: First reference after the checkpoint.

**Figure 9.4** Case II: Page previously referenced.

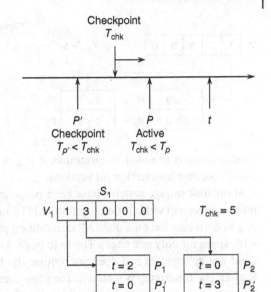

**Figure 9.5** Example of basic twist structure.

The second scenario, in which the page has been referred to and swapped out to the disk at least once from the point of the last checkpoint, is shown in Figure 9.4. Here, $T_P > T_{chk}$. In this case, $P$ is the active version of the page, and $P'$ is the checkpoint version. The data in page $P$ are used, and future swap-outs of the page are written to $P$.

Figure 9.5 shows the mapping of a segment. Each entry in the mapping vector contains a pointer to a disk slot referring to its twin pages. As discussed, both pages of the slot hold the timestamp of the time when the data were last written out to that page. In the example, since both pages were written before the last checkpoint ($T_{chk} = 5$), $P_1$ (changed at $t = 2$) and $P_2'$ (changed at $t = 3$) contain the checkpoint versions of the slots. $P_1'$ and $P_2$ are the versions of the data prior to the last checkpoint and are therefore not required. Now, let logical page 2 be fetched. The data are read from the slot $P_2'$ and passed to the requestor, and $P_2$ is made the destination for all future page swap-out operations. That preserves the checkpoint version while providing a working location for the active version.

Figure 9.6 shows the scenario in which a page has been modified and swapped out to disk. Here, $T_{P_2} > T_{chk}$. Therefore, slot $P_2$ contains the active page. If a system failure occurs at this point, the database needs to be scanned to detect all active pages that satisfy $T_{P_2} > T_{chk}$. If an active page is found on the disk during recovery, its timestamp is set to a value less than that of the checkpoint page. (For example, $T_{P_2} = 2$ would make $P_2'$ the checkpoint version.) The updated pages must be swapped out to disk to commit the changes. Once the pages have been written back, the current time is written as the checkpoint time so that all active pages can

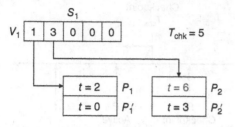

**Figure 9.6** Example of a modified page.

be atomically committed. For example, if $T_{chk} = 8$ is written to disk, then pages $P_1$ and $P_2$ become the checkpoint versions.

Many disk storage systems have been proposed based on the Twist storage system. A persistent virtual-memory system [11] has a single timestamp ($T_{chk}$) stored at a known location on a disk. All unmodified pages are stored in disk slots (each with space for only one page). The twin page, as in the generic twin-page system, need not be adjacent and does not require the header to contain the timestamp. Rather, the timestamp is stored in the page-translation table for external storage since the page tables are also checkpointed. For reads, the singleton page is used. However, upon a write, the singleton page is converted into a sibling page. If a page becomes inactive, its sibling page is converted to a singleton page. Following a crash, the system is rolled back to a prior checkpoint; in order to identify all active pages, either the entire disk space or the space where the timestamps are stored (i.e. the page translation table) is searched.

A recoverable distributed shared virtual-memory (RDSVM) system has also been developed based on the twin-page storage system [12]. It has a single virtual-address space that executes multiple processes. One goal of this scheme is to address the drawback faced by the generic twin-page system during system restart, namely the need to scan the entire database looking for active pages. A checkpoint sequence (CS) number and a rollback sequence (RS) number are assigned to each process. The CS is the counterpart of the $T_{chk}$ in the generic description. When a page is modified, the <CS, RS> pair, along with the time, is stored in the header field. Taking of a checkpoint involves forcing a swap out of all pages to disk and incrementing the CS value of the process. The CS value is then saved on disk.

## 9.4 Operating-System-Level Checkpointing

This section will address *libckpt*-based checkpointing under Unix. Building upon the *libckpt* primitive, we describe incremental checkpointing, forked checkpointing, fine-grained rollback and deterministic replay for software debugging, rollback of multithreaded processes, the transparent application checkpoint (TAC) module, and the RMK framework.

### 9.4.1 *libckpt*: Transparent Checkpointing Under Unix

*libckpt* performs near-transparent checkpointing [13] on uniprocessors that are executing Unix operating systems. It can take both incremental and copy-on-write checkpoints to optimize on checkpoint time. *libckpt* is implemented as a user-level library using only facilities commonly available under Unix.

Sequential checkpointing is the most naïve method for establishing a checkpoint under Unix. Application execution is suspended, and the entire contents of a process's memory and registers are written to a file. In this method, the disk transfers are not interleaved with the execution of the application, hence the name *sequential*.

Checkpointing with *libckpt* is not completely transparent. The *main()* procedure in C must be renamed ckpt_target() to give control of the program to *libckpt*. No other program modifications are needed. Once *libckpt* has control of a program, it generates a timer interrupt at regular intervals, and a sequential checkpoint is taken at each interrupt.

#### 9.4.1.1 Incremental Checkpointing

One optimization to sequential checkpointing is to save only that portion of the checkpoint that has been modified since the previous checkpoint. The unchanged portion is restored from previous checkpoints. This scheme is called *incremental checkpointing*. It uses page protection hardware to identify the unchanged pages in the checkpoint. This optimization reduces the size of each checkpoint and hence the checkpointing overhead.

In incremental checkpointing, old checkpoint files cannot be deleted because the program's data state is spread out over many checkpoint files. The cumulative size of incremental checkpoint files increases at a steady rate over time, perhaps because many updated values may be saved for the same page. One way to reduce the cumulative size of the incremental checkpoint files is to coalesce periodically (or upon a trigger event, such as the crossing of a space threshold) all old checkpoint files into one new file. The old files can then be discarded.

In *libckpt*, after initialization and after each checkpoint, the mprotect() system call is invoked to set the protection for all pages in the data space to *read-only*. When a write occurs to a memory location in a protected page, the SEGV (SEGmentation Violation) signal is raised. This signal is caught by a handler in *libckpt*. The access protection of the faulting page is set to *read-write*, and the page is marked as dirty. In the next checkpoint, *libckpt* includes only the dirty pages.

#### 9.4.1.2 Forked Checkpointing

Another alternative to sequential checkpointing is to make a copy of the program's data space and spawn an asynchronous thread to write the checkpoint file.

This is called *main-memory checkpointing*. However, it requires enough physical memory to hold the checkpoint, as the saving of the checkpoint to disk is overlapped with the execution of the application. *Copy-on-write* checkpointing is an enhancement to main-memory checkpointing. Here, the memory space of the process is copied using copy-on-write.

The *fork()* system call in Unix provides the mechanism needed to implement either main-memory checkpointing, or copy-on-write checkpointing. Using the fork() method in Unix for checkpointing is termed, most intuitively, as *forked checkpointing*. Depending on the operating system's implementation of fork(), forked checkpointing corresponds to either main-memory checkpointing or copy-on-write checkpointing.

To implement the main memory checkpointing through forked checkpointing, *libckpt* forks a child process, which creates and writes the checkpoint file in the background while the parent process returns to executing the application. The fork() system call provides a fixed snapshot of the parent's data space and a separate thread of control to the child process.

Most implementations of the fork() system call use a copy-on-write mechanism to optimize the copying of the parent's address space to that of the child. Initially, all virtual memory pages in the child's memory space refer to the same physical pages as the parent. Upon a write to a page, an exception is raised that is handled through the copying of the faulting page to the child's memory space, followed by a write to the newly allocated and copied page. In this case, forked checkpointing is implementing copy-on-write checkpointing.

## 9.4.2 Fine-Grained Rollback and Deterministic Replay for Software Debugging

*Flashback* [14] provides rollback and deterministic replay support to facilitate software debugging. It is implemented as a lightweight OS extension. It replicates a program's execution state using shadow processes. To enable subsequent deterministic re-execution, it also records interactions between the program and the rest of the system, such as system calls, signals, and memory-mapped regions.

A shadow process is created by "forking" a new process at the specified execution point (for example, at the time the checkpoint needs to be taken). The forked process maintains a copy of the original process's execution state in the main memory. After the shadow process is created, it is immediately suspended. If rollback is requested, the system kills the currently active process and creates a new active process from the shadow process that captured the execution state at the time of the checkpoint.

The shadow process is created through the allocation of a new shadow process structure in the kernel and copying the content of the original process's structures into it. That procedure is called *state capture*. The state information that is captured includes process memory (i.e. the stack and heap), registers, file descriptor tables, signal handlers, and other in-memory states associated with a process.

Flashback provides three primitives to support rollback and replay:

1) *stateHandle = Checkpoint( )*: This function causes the system to capture the execution state of the process at the current time. It returns a state handle for later use in rolling back to or discarding the stored (checkpointed) state.

2) *discard(stateHandle)*: This function deletes the copy of the process's execution state referred to by *stateHandle*. The program cannot then roll back to that state.

3) *replay(stateHandle)*: This function rolls the process back to the previous execution state specified by *stateHandle*. Then, the captured interactions between the process and the system are used to deterministically replay the execution until the point at which *replay( )* was called.

The effect of the above three primitives on the state of an executing process is shown in Figure 9.7. Upon calling the checkpoint( ) function, the process makes a clone of its execution state. The discard( ) function call removes the shadow state; if a rollback occurs through the replay( ) function call, the original execution state is deleted. The rollback and replay mechanism can be invoked either within a debugging environment, like *gdb*, or through explicit calls made within the program.

### 9.4.2.1 Rollback of Multithreaded Processes

Rollback of a multithreaded process requires special attention because, for a multithreaded process, several components of the process state are implicitly shared across all threads of the same process. For example, threads of a single process, implemented using the *pthread* package on Linux, share memory, file descriptors, and signal handlers with each other. User-space (and kernel) stacks are the only thread-private states. Such implicit sharing vastly complicates rollback because it is not possible for a thread to revert to its original version, as in the shadow state, without impacting the execution of other threads.

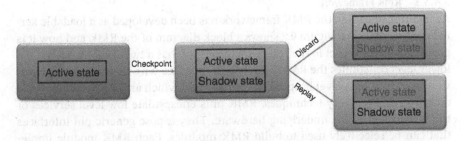

**Figure 9.7** Effect of Flashback primitives on process execution state.

There are two possible approaches for supporting the fine-grained rollback of multithreaded programs. The first is to capture the state for the entire process and, upon a failure, roll back all threads to that execution point. The second is to track thread dependencies. Threads that read from memory locations (or files) written to by another thread are marked as dependent on the latter thread. When a thread needs to be rolled back, it is sufficient to roll back other threads only if they depend on the erroneous thread.

Flashback uses the first approach for the rollback of multithreaded processes. At a checkpoint, the underlying operating system captures the execution state of all threads of a process. Similarly, upon a failure, Flashback reverts the execution state of all threads by rolling back to the original copy of the shared state. Thus, a consistent state is maintained among all threads. Implicitly, thread synchronization primitives, such as acquiring/releasing locks and semaphore operations, are also rolled back.

### 9.4.3 Transparent Application Checkpoint (TAC) Module

A TAC technique is implemented as a module in the Reliability MicroKernel (RMK) architecture [15]. RMK provides a framework for designing and deploying software-implemented modules that provide application-aware reliability services. The RMK architecture is deployed as a loadable Linux kernel module and can provide support for real-world applications, such as the Apache web server. Some examples of the application-aware reliability modules that have been developed to demonstrate the functionality of RMK include OS/application hang/crash detection and application-transparent checkpoint. RMK uses processor-level features that are available in the current generation of processors (such as debug registers and monitoring facilities) and interfaces exported by the operating system to define a set of basic services called *RMK pins*. RMK pins can be thought of as analogous to hardware pins in providing well-defined functionalities and inputs/outputs. The application-specific mechanisms called *RMK modules* make use of the RMK pins for runtime system monitoring and low-latency error detection.

#### 9.4.3.1 RMK Framework

As mentioned earlier, the RMK framework has been developed as a loadable kernel module in Linux. Figure 9.8 shows a block diagram of the RMK and how it is positioned with respect to the rest of the system. It has a two-level hierarchy: the lower level constitutes the RMK pins, which interface with the system and hardware, and the upper level hosts the RMK modules, which are application-specific detection and recovery techniques. RMK pins encapsulate low-level services of the system and of the underlying hardware. They expose generic pin interfaces that can be selectively used to build RMK modules. Each RMK module implements a specific error detection or recovery mechanism. Some example modules

**Figure 9.8** Reliability
MicroKernel architecture [15] /
with permission of IEEE.

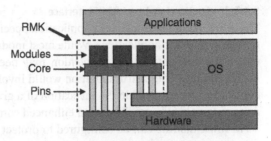

that have been designed and implemented are for the crash and hang detection of applications, hang detection of the operating system, and TAC and recovery. The installation and uninstallation of pins and modules are managed by the RMK core, which also invokes the pin functionalities on behalf of the RMK modules. The RMK core also provides a set of RMK APIs for the purpose of management. The following description of the RMK framework is based on [15].

#### 9.4.3.2 RMK Pins: System-Level RMK Interface

The RMK pins are the interface for the RMK with the operating system (or, more generally, with the runtime environment). A pin provides a specific service that is essential in providing reliability mechanisms. It uses a collection of OS functions to construct the service. Some examples of RMK pins that have been implemented in the RMK prototype are tabulated in Table 9.2.

**Table 9.2** RMK pins in the RMK prototype [15] / with permission of IEEE.

| RMK pin | Hardware/OS features | Pin functionalities |
|---------|---------------------|---------------------|
| P_PMC | Hardware counters available in modern processors for monitoring/measurement | Configures the counters; starts/stops counting; reads/writes counters; etc. |
| P_APIC | Advanced Programmable Interrupt Controller(APIC) provided in modern processors | Configures APIC for custom interrupt generation, e.g. generating an NMI interrupt when a performance counter reaches zero |
| P_DBR | Debug facilities available in hardware (e.g. debug registers) | Sets up a debug exception at a particular location; generates an event upon debug exception |
| P_INTR | Interrupt handling in operating system | Generates an event upon an interrupt through installed hooks |
| P_SCHL | Contexts are switched by the process scheduler in operating system | Intercepts context switches; generates an event upon a context switch |

### 9.4.3.3 Application-Level RMK Interface

The RMK modules implement application-specific detection and recovery techniques to monitor applications. While most modules are designed to be transparent to the application, the application may need to be instrumented for some RMK modules. The instrumentation would involve inserting a system call in the application code to enable the invocation of a given RMK module. That could be done automatically, possibly by an enhanced compiler.

An RMK module can be configured to protect a set of applications on the system. Users can associate a set of applications with RMK module(s). That information is kept in the dispatcher of the RMK core, which we will describe in Section 9.4.3.4. The RMK modules can be installed or removed as per the user requirements. The Configuration Manager, which is a specially designed RMK module, enables RMK reconfiguration.

### 9.4.3.4 RMK Core

The RMK core is provided as an interface between the RMK modules and the RMK pins. Its responsibilities include the following:

1) Maintaining mappings between events generated by pins and modules that subscribe to the events.
2) Delivering the events to modules.
3) Dispatching operation requests to pins.
4) Managing (e.g. installing) and configuring pins and modules.

### 9.4.3.5 An Example RMK Module: Transparent Application Checkpoint (TAC)

The TAC module takes an incremental checkpoint of an application. The approach is similar to that used by *libckpt* to checkpoint only the dirty memory pages. However, there are several differences. TAC (i) exploits knowledge of the application execution available at the OS level through the RMK pins, and (ii) decides when and how to checkpoint so as to avoid any inconsistency between the application image and the system state. The checkpoint is taken transparently to the application. A point to note is that step (ii) is made possible because of the knowledge that TAC obtains during step (i). In addition, the OS-level knowledge can be used to transparently synchronize threads in a multithreaded process and maintain consistency of process checkpoints in a distributed application. (For example, messages can be logged via invocations of the operations of the corresponding pins.)

Figure 9.9 shows the breakdown of the address space of a process executing under Linux. The kernel state of the process includes the process info, kernel stack, memory tables, signal/IPC (inter-process communication) status, wait queues, and tables for opened files. The process info includes process attributes

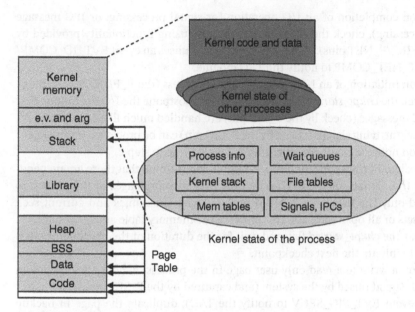

**Figure 9.9** User/kernel state of a process in Linux [15] / with permission of IEEE.

(e.g. process ID and schedule priority), process relations (e.g. parent and child), and user information (e.g. uid and gid). The wait queues deal with the pending asynchronous I/O operations and process/thread synchronization. The user state of the process consists of pages that constitute the memory segments for code, data, heap, stack, BSS (block starting symbol), and dynamically loaded libraries.

The checkpoint taken by the TAC module includes (i) the modified user memory pages and (ii) the processor state. The TAC module eliminates the need to checkpoint the kernel state of the process by taking a checkpoint only when the kernel state is in a *safe point*, i.e. there are no pending I/O, signals, or IPC messages in the context of the application process. Only the opened files table (containing the names and current seek offsets of all open files) and the memory table in the kernel state of the process are checkpointed. When the process is recovered upon a failure, the file table and memory table are restored in the process kernel state with no pending I/O, signals, or IPC messages and with an empty kernel stack. Consequently, after the checkpointed user memory pages have been restored, the recovered process is in a consistent state. The following steps outline the steps for application checkpointing in the TAC algorithm.

1) Periodically initiate a checkpoint by setting a *chkpt_started* flag to 1.
2) Check whether there is a pending I/O operation, signal, or IPC message in the target process. If TRUE go to sleep; otherwise, go to step 6.

3) Upon completion of an I/O operation (or signal processing, or IPC message processing), check the *chkpt_started* flag (by using functionality provided by P_FILE/P_NET pins). If the flag is set, the pin raises an event EVT_IO_COMP/EVT_NET_COMP to notify the TAC module.

4) Upon initiation of an I/O operation by the process (the P_FILE/P_NET pins), check the *chkpt_started* flag. If the flag is set, postpone the I/O operation. New IPC messages (check by the P_IPC pin) are handled much like I/O operations. Newly arriving signals (check by the P_SIG pin) can be processed immediately.

5) Upon notification of new event EVT_*_COMP, go to step 2.

6) Checkpoint the application process (after determining that there are no pending I/O, signals, or IPCs): (i) set all the user memory pages of the process to read-only (by using the P_MEM pin), (ii) save the names and current seek offsets of all open files, and (iii) preserve the memory table and CPU state.

7) Clear the *chkpt_started* flag and wait for the duration of the checkpoint interval to initiate the next checkpoint.

8) Upon a write to a read-only user page in the process, handle a segmentation fault signal raised by the system (and captured by the P_SIG pin, which raises an event EVT_SIG_SEGV to notify the TAC); duplicate the page in backup memory (which is hosted by a user-level dummy process) and enable writes to the page (by using the P_MEM pin).

## 9.5 Compiler-Assisted Checkpointing

This section describes compiler-assisted techniques for checkpointing (CATCH), defining potential checkpoints, sparse potential checkpoints, and adaptive checkpointing. Also included in this section is an analysis of compiler-assisted checkpointing using *libckpt*.

### 9.5.1 CATCH – Compiler-Assisted Techniques for Checkpointing

The goals of compiler-assisted techniques are to take the checkpoint in a manner that is transparent to the application and to minimize the size of the checkpoint without modifying the hardware or operating system. These techniques have been collectively referred to as *compiler-assisted techniques for checkpointing (CATCH)* [16].

The compiler inserts code in the program to trigger the taking of a checkpoint. Instead of randomly inserting checkpointing code into the application, the compiler uses sparse potential checkpoint code to maintain the desired interval between consecutive checkpoints while sacrificing performance as little as possible. For programs with large variations in memory usage, the checkpoint size is reduced through the use of a simple learning algorithm in *adaptive checkpointing*. The potential checkpoint time is reduced through the use of a *training* technique that identifies program locations where low-cost and high-coverage checkpoints can be performed.

The CATCH technique implements a library function named *_checkpoint(* ), which captures the state of the application. The compiler inserts calls to this routine at appropriate locations in the program so that at run-time, the application will periodically take checkpoints. Implementing the code for capturing a checkpoint of the application poses one level of difficulty in understanding the optimum amount of state that should be captured. If too much of the state is captured ("to err on the right side"), the checkpointing overhead will be prohibitively high. However, if the checkpoint includes too little of a state, then it would not be possible to recover from a failure in a robust manner.

Assuming that the application state can be identified, implementation of the checkpointing routine is not very difficult. A higher level of ingenuity, however, is needed to identify the appropriate locations in the application where the state should be captured. The checkpointing locations affect not only the frequency but also the size of the checkpoint that needs to be taken and are very crucial in determining space and time overheads for checkpointing.

### 9.5.1.1  Potential Checkpoints

Because of the dynamic nature of programs, depending on the size and nature of the input, it can be difficult to statically determine the precise locations in the application where the checkpointing code should be inserted. The following snippet of code, which contains a loop, illustrates the difficulty. Note that for loops, it is not always possible to statically determine the number of iterations, as the number may be input-dependent.

```
scanf ("%d", &k) ;
sum = 0;
for (i = 0; i < k; i++)
{
    sum += f (i);
}
printf ("%d\n", sum) ;
```

If the compiler decides to insert a call to *_checkpoint(* ) inside the loop, the checkpoint may need to be taken too frequently or many times, and the total time for checkpointing may be very high compared to the execution time of the application. If, however, the compiler inserts the call to *_checkpoint(* ) outside the loop, the application may execute for a long time within the loop and thus exceed the desired checkpoint interval before reaching the next checkpoint location.

Performance and reliability are competing goals in establishing the optimum checkpointing interval, and the dynamic nature of applications only exacerbates the problem of maintaining the length of the interval.

To address the issues discussed here, the CATCH technique identifies program locations where at run-time the clock is examined to decide whether or not to take a checkpoint. Those program locations are called *potential checkpoints*. Subroutine and loop entry points are candidate locations for inserting code for potential checkpoints.

There are two major objectives in the insertion of potential checkpoints: (i) keeping the checkpoint interval as close as possible to the optimal checkpoint interval (denoted by $T$), and (ii) minimizing the size of the checkpoint and time needed to establish one.

When the program reaches a potential checkpoint, it has the opportunity to take a checkpoint. The time at which the previous checkpoint was taken is noted. If the time that has elapsed since the last checkpoint is greater than $T$, then a checkpoint is taken at this location. Otherwise, the checkpointing code is bypassed. The optimum checkpoint interval is usually in the order of seconds or minutes. It should be ensured that the time that elapses between two subsequent potential checkpoint locations is small enough to keep the checkpoint interval as close as possible to $T$.

### 9.5.1.2 Sparse Potential Checkpoints

The time it takes to note the current system time and thereby determine how much time has elapsed since the previous checkpoint becomes increasingly significant as the number of locations with potential checkpoints increases, particularly for loops. Sparse potential checkpoints are used to reduce that performance overhead by imposing further criteria on the invocation of potential checkpoint code. The call to _potential( ) is replaced by the following conditional statement:

```
if(--counter <= 0)
        _potential();
```

where the counter is initialized to a reduction factor $l$. That reduces the number of calls to _potential( ) by almost a factor of $l$. There is a diminishing reduction in cost with an increase in $l$.

### 9.5.1.3 Adaptive Checkpointing

During their execution, some applications present large variations in the size of the state that needs to be saved to take a checkpoint. That motivates the need for a technique that can adapt itself to the dynamically changing requirements of the application. The variation of checkpoint size over time for the LUDCMP

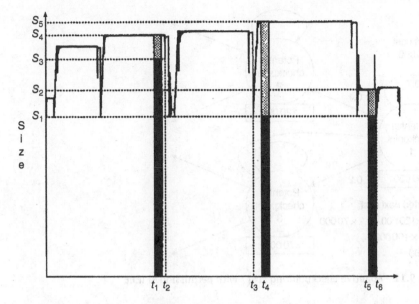

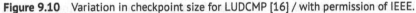

**Figure 9.10** Variation in checkpoint size for LUDCMP [16] / with permission of IEEE.

application is plotted in Figure 9.10. The plot shows that an application could benefit from such an adaptive checkpointing technique. LUDCMP decomposes 10 randomly generated matrices whose sizes are uniformly distributed from 1 to 50. For this application, the figure shows three scheduled checkpoints at $t_1$, $t_4$, and $t_5$ with checkpoint sizes of $s_4$, $s_5$, and $s_2$, respectively. However, as shown by the dotted vertical lines, if $t_1$ is shifted forward to $t_2$, $t_4$ backward to $t_3$, and $t_5$ forward to $t_6$, then the size of the checkpoint could be reduced to $s_3$, $s_1$, and $s_1$, respectively. Adaptive checkpointing uses a simple learning algorithm embedded in _potential() to enable a decision on whether or not to take a checkpoint at the current location based on the space and time requirements for the checkpoint.

The learning algorithm uses a transition graph, illustrated in Figure 9.11 to make that decision. The transition graph is built dynamically based on the application execution. When a potential checkpoint is encountered, a corresponding node is created in the transition graph (if it is not already present); otherwise, the previously created node is used. To enable estimation of the cost (in terms of space and time) of taking a checkpoint at each location, a cost is associated with each location. The node has outgoing edges to the next potential checkpoint locations. Each edge is labeled with the probability of reaching that location from the current location. The estimated cost and the transition probabilities are dynamically updated each time a potential checkpoint is reached.

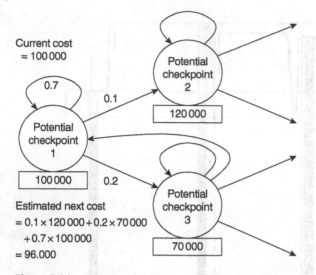

**Figure 9.11** Adaptive checkpointing [16] / with permission of IEEE.

The decision to establish a checkpoint is based on time (including $T$, which is the optimum checkpoint interval; $w$, the *checkpointing window size*; and the current time) and cost (the current cost and the estimated next cost). The checkpointing window size, $w$, presents a lower bound for the checkpointing interval. The estimated next cost is the sum of the costs of all immediate successors of the current node, weighted with the probability of reaching each such node, as specified by the label on the outgoing edge. The pseudocode for the rule is as follows:

```
if (the elapsed time since last checkpoint >= T)
    _checkpoint();
else if (((T - w) <= the elapsed time since last
            checkpoint) and (the estimated next cost >
            current cost))
    _checkpoint();
else
      defer the decision to next encountered
      potential checkpoint;
```

For example, in Figure 9.11, if the execution reaches node 1, then the current cost is 100 000. If the elapsed time since the last checkpoint is between $T - w$ and $T$, the decision on whether to take a checkpoint will be deferred to the next potential checkpoint location because the estimated next cost (96 000) is less than the current cost. However, if the elapsed time exceeds $T$, the program establishes a checkpoint immediately.

### 9.5.2 Compiler-Assisted Checkpointing Using *libckpt*

The following describes how compiler-assisted checkpointing [17] is used to help automate user-directed memory exclusion. Checkpointing optimizations based on memory exclusion improve the performance of checkpointing by omitting clean and dead portions of memory from each checkpoint. *Clean memory* is defined as memory that has not been modified since the previous checkpoint. The current value of a clean location does not need to be saved as part of a checkpoint because it may be recovered from an earlier checkpoint file. *Dead memory* is the memory that will be overwritten before it is next read. It does not need to be saved as part of a checkpoint because the values of such memory will never be needed. The following are checkpointing optimizations based on memory exclusion.

*Incremental Checkpointing.* With incremental checkpointing, page protection hardware is used to identify dirty pages that have been modified since the last checkpoint. Only the dirty pages are saved in each checkpoint file, i.e. all pages of clean memory are omitted. Upon recovery, the checkpointed state is rebuilt from all the checkpoint files. Incremental checkpointing can reduce overhead dramatically if the target program exhibits good locality. For programs with poor locality, incremental checkpointing can degenerate to the sequential case, saving the entire data memory. In that situation, the cost of catching page faults actually increases the checkpointing overhead. One extra cost of incremental checkpointing is increased use of disk space since old checkpoint files cannot be discarded.

*Word-Level Memory Exclusion.* Here, every read and write in the program is tracked so that both clean and dead memory can be excluded from checkpoint files. That leads to optimally (or near optimally) small checkpoint files. Word-level memory exclusion is useful for playback debugging, for which high runtime overheads are justified by the reduced storage requirements for checkpoint files.

With the help of safe programmer directives, sets of dead and *read-only* locations can be automatically derived by a compiler or preprocessor. The sets are expressed as the solution to a collection of data flow equations that can be solved efficiently using standard techniques. Compiler-assisted checkpointing uses automatically derived information to generate memory exclusion calls that are safe; the resulting checkpoints are guaranteed to be correct.

The *libckpt* runtime library implements three procedure calls to generate user-directed memory exclusion. To implement memory exclusion, *libckpt* maintains three lists of memory regions: I (include), E (exclude), and P (pending exclusion). Each word of memory has an entry in exactly one of these lists.

When *libckpt* takes a checkpoint, it writes all the memory in the I and P lists to the disk and then moves all elements of the P list to the E list. The user can manipulate these lists directly with two procedure calls, exclude_bytes(char *addr, int size, int usage) and include_bytes(char *addr, int size). *exclude_bytes( )* tells *libckpt* to exclude the specified region of memory from subsequent checkpoints. It is called when the user knows that those bytes are not necessary for the correct recovery of the program. *include_bytes( )* tells *libckpt* to move the specified bytes to the I list so that they will be included in the next and subsequent checkpoints.

In addition, *libckpt* provides a procedure *checkpoint_here( )* that allows the user to specify program locations at which to checkpoint. There is a runtime variable mintime that can be set so that checkpoints are not taken if *checkpoint_here( )* is called and mintime seconds have not passed since the previous checkpoint.

### 9.5.2.1 Compiler Directives

The goal of compiler-assisted checkpointing is for the programmer to place compiler directives into their code and have the compiler insert *exclude_bytes( )*, *include_bytes( )*, and *checkpoint_here( )* calls into the code based on static program analysis. Two such compiler directives have been introduced: EXCLUDE_HERE and CHECKPOINT_HERE.

- An EXCLUDE_HERE directive tells the compiler to compute memory exclusion information and insert memory exclusion calls at that program location.
- The CHECKPOINT_HERE directive indicates the program locations at which checkpoints can be taken. Program analysis assumes that checkpoints are taken only at these points, an assumption that can sharpen the analysis. If we remove this assumption, it is necessary to treat every statement as if it were followed by a CHECKPOINT_HERE directive.

The user should place these two directives in code locations that lead to the best use of memory exclusion. If the user chooses badly, the result is checkpointing that may be inefficient but is still correct. In contrast, incorrect memory exclusion calls inserted by a user can result in incorrect checkpointing.

## 9.6  Error Detection and Recovery in Distributed Systems

Processes in networked systems cooperate by exchanging information to accomplish a task. In distributed systems, they do so through message passing. In multiprocessor systems, they do so through shared memory. In both these classes of networked systems, the rollback of one process may require that other processes also roll back to an earlier state, also known as the domino effect. As a result, all cooperating processes need to establish recovery points. It is more difficult to roll back processes in concurrent systems than to roll back a single process because of the domino effect, lost messages, and livelocks. (A *livelock* is a situation in which the failure and consequent rollback of a single process can cause an infinite number of rollbacks, preventing the system from making progress.)

The domino effect is illustrated below in Figure 9.12. In the figure, X, Y, and Z are cooperating processes. A left bracket, [ , signifies a recovery point. Note that the rollback of X does not affect other processes, but a rollback of Z requires all three processes to roll back to their very first recovery points.

A strongly consistent set of checkpoints, or *recovery line*, corresponds to a strongly consistent global state. It needs to satisfy two properties during the interval spanned by checkpoints (between the earliest checkpoint in the set to the latest): (i) there must be one recovery point for each process in the set, and (ii) there must be no information flow between any two member processes in the set, or between any process in the set and any process outside the set.

A consistent set of checkpoints corresponds to a consistent global state. A strongly consistent recovery line $\{x_1, y_1, z_1\}$ and consistent recovery line $\{x_2, y_2, z_2\}$ (assuming all messages are logged) are illustrated in Figure 9.13.

In *synchronous checkpointing*, all processes synchronize their taking of checkpoints. The set of local checkpoints constitutes a consistent system state, i.e. the set of checkpoints forms a consistent memory line. The disadvantages of this approach are that additional messages must be exchanged to coordinate checkpointing and that synchronization delays are introduced during normal operations. In *asynchronous checkpointing*, checkpoints at each process are taken

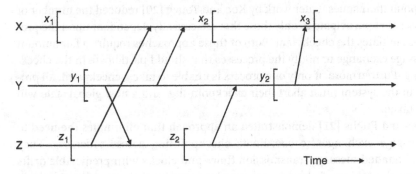

**Figure 9.12** Domino effect in recovering cooperating processes [18].

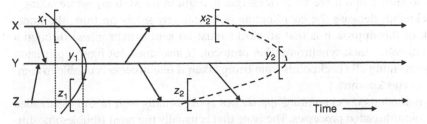

**Figure 9.13** Strongly consistent set (left) and consistent set (right) of checkpoints [18].

independently, without any synchronization among the processes. The disadvantages are that there is no guarantee that a set of local checkpoints will be a consistent set and that recovery algorithms must therefore search for the most recent consistent set before initiating recovery.

## 9.6.1 Synchronous Checkpointing

The goal of any rollback recovery is to restore the distributed system to a globally consistent state. A *globally consistent state* is one in which every message marked as having been received by a process is also marked as having been sent. If that condition does not hold, then the resulting state cannot be realizable through a valid execution of the distributed system.

In synchronous checkpointing, a single process initiates the taking of a checkpoint. Other processes also checkpoint their states at the same time if that is necessary to ensure a globally consistent state. Intuitively, it seems that if one could force all processes in a distributed system to checkpoint their states at exactly the same time, then the set of checkpoints would constitute a globally consistent state. The lack of a precise global clock, however, makes that infeasible.

Chandy and Lamport [19] performed early work in constructing globally consistent states. Their algorithm requires all processes in the distributed system to checkpoint their states. Later work by Koo and Toueg [20] reduced the number of processes that participate to only those that are causally dependent upon the process that initiates the checkpoint. Both of those approaches require a fair amount of message exchange to notify the processes that should participate in the checkpointing. Furthermore, if only one process is unable to take a checkpoint, all processes in the system must abort their checkpointing, and a new global state will not be taken.

Neves and Fuchs [21] demonstrated an approach that eliminates the need to use message exchanges to coordinate checkpointing across processes. They exploit bounded message transmission times and clocks with predictable drifts to trigger the taking of checkpoints based upon a local timer. After the timer expires, the processes wait for a calculated amount of time (i.e. the time necessary to ensure that there are no messages in flight in the system) before taking a checkpoint. Because the coordinating processes rely solely on time, the drawback of this approach is that all clocks must be kept synchronized through a system-wide clock synchronization protocol. It also does not have a provision for preventing all checkpoints from being taken if one process is unable to commit its checkpoint.

Synchronous checkpointing approaches apply equally well to single-threaded and multithreaded processes. The issue that is usually the most troublesome during multithreading and recovery stems from the nondeterministic nature of thread scheduling within a process. The same set of threads can cause different state changes in a process depending upon how they are scheduled. So, re-execution of threads during recovery is not guaranteed to produce the same effects that it would before a failure. However, with synchronous checkpointing, no process remains dependent upon threads that must be re-executed. If a process rolls back, all other processes that are dependent upon the recovered process are also rolled back to the same point in "time" (i.e. to the point in time when they were consistent with the recovered process).

### 9.6.2 Asynchronous Checkpointing: Message Logging

Asynchronous checkpointing allows each process in the distributed system to checkpoint itself independently of other processes. The advantage is that coordination with other processes is not needed in order to take checkpoints during normal execution. However, it comes at the cost of needing to ensure a consistent global state upon recovery.

Message logging is one way to make a recovered process consistent with the other processes in a system. We can make a failed process $P$ consistent with other processes by rolling back the state of $P$ to a checkpoint and then replaying all messages sent to $P$ after the checkpoint. The replayed messages are retrieved from message logs during recovery. The correctness of the reconstruction of the state of a process through replaying of logged messages holds only if the processes are piecewise deterministic (i.e. each incoming message begins a new state interval, and the state during the interval is dependent only upon the previous state and the incoming message).

Message logging has an advantage over synchronous checkpointing in that (potentially) fewer processes must roll back to recover from a failure. If process $P$ fails, then (ideally) only $P$ should need to roll back. If the recovered state of $P$ is consistent with the states of the other processes after messages have been replayed (i.e. no other process in the system depends upon a state of $P$ that was lost because of the failure), then no other processes are required to roll back.

To make sure that the state of $P$ is recoverable, pessimistic message logging mandates that an incoming message $M$ to $P$ be logged before $P$ begins processing $M$ (or, more correctly, before $P$ sends any outgoing messages after receiving $M$). Thus, the effects of $M$ on the process $P$ are recoverable. A simple approach is to log messages to stable storage before processing [22]. That adds a significant performance overhead because access to stable storage occurs in the critical path. It is a conceptually simple approach for two reasons: (i) the order in which messages are processed is naturally reflected by the order in which messages appear in the log, and (ii) all messages for a failed process are centrally located, which simplifies recovery.

Another approach is to log the messages at the sender. The order in which the messages were received by a process $P$ must still be maintained so that the messages to $P$ can be replayed in the correct order. When $P$ receives a message $M$, it assigns a receiver sequence number (RSN) to the message. It then sends the RSN back to the sender of $M$, and the sender appends it to the log entry for message $M$. The sender then sends an acknowledgment back to $P$ to confirm that $M$ has been fully logged. Process $P$ cannot send any outgoing message until it has received the acknowledgment that $M$ has been fully logged.

The advantages of sender-side logging over receiver-side logging are that the logging can be done to volatile memory (if only a single failure is to be tolerated) and that the logging can occur outside the critical path after the message has been sent. The primary disadvantage is that to recover a failed process $P$, all processes in the system may need to participate since all may have sent messages to $P$. Furthermore, the RSN for each replayed message must be examined to ensure that the messages are replayed in the correct order. The sender-based message-logging approach is described in greater detail in the following section.

## 9.6.3 Sender-Based Message Logging

Sender-based message logging [23] differs from other types of message-logging mechanisms in that the messages are logged in the local volatile memory on the machine from which each is sent. The sender assigns a unique sequence number, i.e. the *sender sequence number* (*SSN*), to each message that it sends. Keeping the message log in the sender's local memory makes it possible to recover from a single failure without the expense of synchronously logging each message to a special logging or backup process or to stable storage, and without having to roll back any processes other than the failed one to achieve a consistent state following recovery. The message log is then asynchronously written to stable storage as part of the sender's periodic checkpoint. That allows the stable storage logging to proceed independently of computation. This approach to fault-tolerant communication requires at most one extra message over non-fault-tolerant reliable message communication and incurs minimal additional delay due to synchronization. By distributing the overhead of logging across all the processes that are sending messages, it avoids the single point of failure that would otherwise be possible when a centralized logging facility is used. Since the logging is performed on the sender side, the logging overhead for a node is proportional to the number of messages that a process sends.

### 9.6.3.1 Design and Motivation

In sender-based message logging, the sender of a message stores the message in its own volatile memory. Apart from the logging of the messages, the entire process running at each node (machine) is checkpointed, and the state is written to stable storage. It is unlike synchronous checkpointing in that there is no coordination between the nodes when they take their individual checkpoints.

Upon receiving a message, the receiver assigns a sequence number, called the *receive sequence number (RSN)*, to the message and returns it to the sender. Since the receiver assigns the RSN to the message, it indicates the order in which the message was received relative to the other received messages. The sender adds the RSN to the message that is stored in its log. Upon the failure of a node, the process at the failed node is restarted from its previous checkpoint. Then, all the nodes that have sent messages to the failed node use the RSN (stored in their individual volatile logs) to resend messages in the order in which they were received and processed by the failed node (i.e. the receiver).

*Message-Logging Protocol.* Figure 9.14 depicts the sequence of events (and messages) involved in the sending of a message $M$ from process $X$ to process $Y$:

1) Process $X$ sends the message $M$ to process $Y$ and stores $M$ in its local volatile log.
2) Process $Y$ receives the message, assigns an RSN to it, and returns an acknowledgment to $X$ that includes the RSN value assigned to $M$.
   - If $X$ does not receive the RSN for the message in a fixed amount of time, it retransmits $M$. After a fixed number of retransmission attempts, $X$ declares that $Y$ has failed.
3) Process $X$ includes the RSN of a message along with its copy in the log and sends an acknowledgment of the RSN to $Y$.
   - If $Y$ does not receive an acknowledgment of the RSN in a fixed amount of time, it retransmits the acknowledgment along with the RSN. After a fixed number of retransmission attempts, $Y$ declares that $X$ has failed.

It should be noted that the sender logs a message completely in two independent steps: (i) it stores a copy of the message when it sends it to the intended recipient,

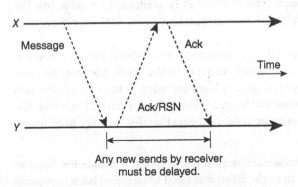

Any new sends by receiver
must be delayed.

**Figure 9.14** Operation of the message logging in the absence of transmission errors.

and (ii) it adds the RSN information sent by the receiver to the message log. It is possible that the receiver will fail before receiving the message or before sending out the acknowledgment of the message along with the RSN. If that happens, the sender would have a log of messages without their corresponding RSNs. Such messages are called *partially logged messages* and are dealt with in the failure recovery process.

*Failure Recovery.* When a node $N$ is determined to have failed, it is restarted on another processor from its previous checkpoint. After recovering from a checkpoint, the receiver broadcasts a request to all the nodes in the network for all the messages that were sent to it since the previous checkpoint. The retransmit request message contains the RSN of the last message that $N$ received before taking the checkpoint. Upon receiving the retransmission request from $N$, each node checks in its message log for any messages that it sent to $N$. All messages sent to $N$ that have the RSN information along with the message and whose RSNs are greater than the RSN sent in the retransmission request message are resent to $N$ in increasing RSN order. After all, such fully logged messages have been resent, the partially logged messages, as described earlier, are sent in no specific order.

The checkpoint state of a process contains the last SSN that the process used to send messages. After a failed process has been restored from its checkpoint, it begins execution and resends the messages that it had sent after it took the checkpoint but before it failed. Because it uses the SSN numbers following the SSN stored in the checkpoint, and because the processes are deterministic, the SSN for a message would be the same as that used for it before the process failed. The recipient of the message examines the SSN and rejects the message as a duplicate if the SSN is less than or equal to the highest SSN previously received from the sender. Depending on the time instant at which a checkpoint is taken, the receiver performs the following actions:

- If the receiver has not taken a checkpoint since it originally received this message, it returns an acknowledgment that includes the RSN that it assigned when it first received this message. The RSN value is available in a table (on the receiver) that stores the RSN value corresponding to an SSN from a particular sender.
- If the receiving process has taken a checkpoint since this message was originally received, the RSN value is not available in the table. Because the state change due to this message has already been included in the checkpoint, this message need not be retransmitted upon a failure of the receiver. Therefore, the receiver sends an indication to the sender process that this message need not be logged at the sender.

An important advantage of sender-based logging is that it avoids the domino effect, as no processes other than the failed one need to be rolled back to recover from a failure.

### 9.6.3.2 A Practical Implementation

The algorithm for sender-based message logging proposed by Johnson and Zwaenepoel [23] leaves a number of details to the choice of the implementer. In this section, we describe a functional implementation of sender-based message logging by Pandit and Alexander [24], along with some design decisions and assumptions used to design such a system.

We have implemented a distributed system of nodes that employ sender-based message logging for checkpointing and recovery. We also provided an API to allow application writers to specify the state that needs to be included in the checkpoint and the locations where the checkpoint is taken and to send messages to other nodes. Our implementation [25] was tested successfully on the trusted ILLIAC cluster at the University of Illinois at Urbana-Champaign.

A database server program (DB Server) manages the distributed system by handling requests to the database and providing a small amount of database-related functionality to the nodes. DB Server is responsible for the task of adding (or removing) nodes to (or from) the distributed system. When a node wants to join the network, it sends a message to the DB Server informing it of its presence and its IP and listening port. The DB Server then adds an entry for this node to the database and informs all other nodes of the new node's arrival.

When a node $A$ decides, because of repeated failed transmissions to another node $B$, that node $B$ has failed, $A$ asks the DB Server to remove node $B$ from the list. The DB Server then sends out a "remove node alert" to all the nodes, telling them to remove the crashed node from their peer list. The database maintained by DB Server contains three tables:

1) *Peers*: This table has a list of all the peers that join the network. Each peer has a name, an IP address, and a port on which it is listening for messages from the other nodes.
2) *Checkpoints*: This table holds all the checkpoints that the nodes take. A single entry in this table consists of fields for the *Checkpoint* object as defined by the application, the current values for SSN and RSN, and the other important data structures that the nodes maintain for implementing sender-based message logging.
3) *Logs*: This table is used for logging all the significant events that occur during the operation of the distributed system. The events are used for generating data that can be used to compare the implementation with other algorithms and implementations. The logs also help in identifying the successful completion of checkpointing and recovery. A snapshot of the logs table is shown in Figure 9.15. Messages are stored in the log in the following format:

*<timestamp>*     *<node that generated the message>: message*

| 01:00:52 | Server: Sending message to n1 2323. SSN = 2 |
| 01:00:52 | n1 2323: Received app msg from Server. SSN = 2, RSN = -1 |
| 01:00:52 | n1 2323: putting received message on receive queue. |
| 01:00:52 | Server: Received ack + rsn from n1 2323. SSN = 2, RSN = 3 |
| 01:00:52 | n1 2323: Received final ack from Server. SSN = 2, RSN = 3 |
| 01:00:52 | n2 2324: Adding message to send Queue (sendLock = 0) |
| 01:00:52 | n2 2324: Sending message to n2 2323. SSN = 1 |
| 01:00:52 | n2 2323: Received app msg from n2 2324. SSN = 1, RSN = -1 |
| 01:00:52 | n2 2323: putting received message on receive queue. |
| 01:00:52 | n2 2324: Received ack + rsn from n2 2323. SSN = 1, RSN = 3 |
| 01:00:52 | n2 2323: Received final ack from n2 2324. SSN = 1, RSN = 3 |
| 01:00:53 | n1 2323: Adding message to send Queue (sendLock = 0) |
| 01:00:53 | n1 2323: Sending message to n2 2323. SSN = 1 |
| 01:00:53 | n2 2323: Received app msg from n1 2323. SSN = 1, RSN = -1 |
| 01:00:53 | n2 2323: putting received message on receive queue. |
| 01:00:53 | n1 2323: Received ack + rsn from n2 2323. SSN = 1, RSN = 4 |
| 01:00:53 | n2 2323: Received final ack from n1 2323. SSN = 1, RSN = 4 |

**Figure 9.15** Snapshot of the logs table.

*Addition of a New Node to the Network.* Figure 9.16 shows the message sequence during the addition of new nodes to the network. The node being added to the network is n1 2324. The first set of highlighted messages shows the new node adding the remaining nodes, which are already in the database, as its peers. The second set of highlighted messages is logged by the remaining nodes in the system after they have identified the new node n1 2324.

*Checkpointing Message Trace.* One of the nodes in the network is labeled FailingNode. A failure, such as node crash, is simulated in this node. The message sequence shown in Figure 9.17 is generated when FailingNode initiates a checkpoint.

*Node Crash Message Sequence.* A crash failure is injected in the node named *FailingNode*. After FailingNode crashes, node n2 2323 attempts to deliver a message to it but fails. After a threshold number of failed delivery attempts, n2 2323 decides that the receiver node (in this case, FailingNode) has failed. The central

| msgID | timestamp | message |
|---|---|---|
| 1 | 2008-05-07 01:00:44 | n2 2323: There are no peers on the network currently. |
| 2 | 2008-05-07 01:00:44 | n2 2324: Added peer n2 2323. |
| 3 | 2008-05-07 01:00:44 | n1 2323: Added peer n2 2323. |
| 5 | 2008-05-07 01:00:44 | n1 2324: Added peer n2 2323. |
| 8 | 2008-05-07 01:00:44 | n2 2324: Added peer n1 2323. |
| 9 | 2008-05-07 01:00:44 | n1 2324: Added peer n1 2323. |
| 11 | 2008-05-07 01:00:44 | n1 2324: Added peer n2 2324. |
| 18 | 2008-05-07 01:00:44 | n1 2323: Received new node alert from DB. Adding peer n1 2324 to peers. |
| 19 | 2008-05-07 01:00:44 | n2 2323: Received new node alert from DB. Adding peer n1 2324 to peers. |
| 20 | 2008-05-07 01:00:44 | n1 2323: Received new node alert from DB. Adding peer n2 2324 to peers. |
| 21 | 2008-05-07 01:00:44 | n2 2323: Received new node alert from DB. Adding peer n2 2324 to peers. |
| 24 | 2008-05-07 01:00:44 | n2 2323: Received new node alert from DB. Adding peer n1 2323 to peers. |
| 25 | 2008-05-07 01:00:44 | n2 2324: Received new node alert from DB. Adding peer n1 2324 to peers. |

Node "n1 2324" adding peers that are already in DB

Peers get new node alert for node "n1 2324"

**Figure 9.16** Message sequence showing the addition of nodes to the network.

| msgID | timestamp | message |
|---|---|---|
| 7747 | 2008-05-07 01:04:48 | FailingNode: Checkpointing. |
| 7749 | 2008-05-07 01:04:48 | n2 2323: Adding message to send Queue (sendLock = 0) |
| 7750 | 2008-05-07 01:04:48 | n2 2323: Sending message to n1 2323. SSN = 157 |
| 7751 | 2008-05-07 01:04:48 | n1 2323: Received app msg from n2 2323. SSN = 157, RSN = -1 |
| 7752 | 2008-05-07 01:04:48 | n1 2323: putting received message on receive queue. |
| 7754 | 2008-05-07 01:04:48 | n2 2323: Received ack + rsn from n1 2323. SSN = 157, RSN = 162 |
| 7755 | 2008-05-07 01:04:48 | n1 2323: Received final ack from n2 2323. SSN = 157, RSN = 162 |
| 7757 | 2008-05-07 01:04:51 | Server: Adding message to send Queue (sendLock = 0) |
| 7758 | 2008-05-07 01:04:51 | FailingNode: Checkpointing succeeded. |

**Figure 9.17** Checkpointing message sequence.

DB Server broadcasts a message to all the remaining nodes in the network, telling them to remove FailingNode from their lists of peers. The sequence of messages is shown in Figure 9.18.

*Recovery*. After FailingNode recovers from a previous checkpoint, it sends a recovery alert to all the remaining nodes in the network. Each sending node has a separate log of all the messages that it sent to FailingNode before FailingNode crashed. Along with a recovery alert, FailingNode broadcasts requests for all the messages that the other nodes have sent to it since its last checkpoint. In Figure 9.19, those request messages are marked with dashed arrows. FailingNode receives an acknowledgment of its recovery alert from each of the nodes in the network. Those acknowledgment messages are marked with solid arrows.

| msgID | timestamp | message |
|---|---|---|
| 3527 | 2008-05-07 01:02:20 | n2 2323: Failed to send msg of type applicationMsg to FailingNode. SSN = 72, RSN = -1 |
| 3629 | 2008-05-07 01:02:23 | Server: Failed to send msg of type applicationMsg to FailingNode. SSN = 75, RSN = -1 |
| 3630 | 2008-05-07 01:02:23 | n2 2323: Failed to send msg of type applicationMsg to FailingNode. SSN = 72, RSN = -1 |
| 3659 | 2008-05-07 01:02:26 | Server: Failed to send msg of type applicationMsg to FailingNode. SSN = 75, RSN = -1 |
| 3660 | 2008-05-07 01:02:26 | n2 2323: Failed to send msg of type applicationMsg to FailingNode. SSN = 72, RSN = -1 |
| 3661 | 2008-05-07 01:02:29 | Server: Failed to send msg of type applicationMsg to FailingNode. SSN = 75, RSN = -1 |
| 3662 | 2008-05-07 01:02:29 | n2 2323: Failed to send msg of type applicationMsg to FailingNode. SSN = 72, RSN = -1 |
| 3663 | 2008-05-07 01:02:32 | Server: Failed to send msg of type applicationMsg to FailingNode. SSN = 75, RSN = -1 |
| 3664 | 2008-05-07 01:02:32 | n2 2323: Failed to send msg of type applicationMsg to FailingNode. SSN = 72, RSN = -1 |
| 3665 | 2008-05-07 01:02:32 | n2 2323: Final attempt failed. Remove peer FailingNode |
| 3666 | 2008-05-07 01:02:32 | n1 2324: Received remove node alert from DB. Removing FailingNode from peers. |
| 3667 | 2008-05-07 01:02:32 | n2 2324: Received remove node alert from DB. Removing FailingNode from peers. |
| 3668 | 2008-05-07 01:02:32 | n1 2323: Received remove node alert from DB. Removing FailingNode from peers. |
| 3669 | 2008-05-07 01:02:32 | n2 2323: Received remove node alert from DB. Removing FailingNode from peers. |

Peers receive remove node alert and remove "FailingNode" from peer list

**Figure 9.18** Messages in identifying and removing a crashed node.

| msgID | timestamp | message |
|---|---|---|
| 5005 | 2008-05-07 01:03:08 | FailingNode: Beginning Client Recovery Procedure |
| 5006 | 2008-05-07 01:03:08 | App: Restored Client node FailingNode |
| 5007 | 2008-05-07 01:03:08 | n2 2323: Received recovery alert from FailingNode. Requesting msgs with SSN > 44 ◄- - |
| 5008 | 2008-05-07 01:03:08 | n2 2324: Received recovery alert from FailingNode. Requesting msgs with SSN > 47 ◄- - |
| 5009 | 2008-05-07 01:03:08 | FailingNode: Received ack to recovery alert from n2 2323. ◄─── |
| 5010 | 2008-05-07 01:03:08 | Server: Received recovery alert from FailingNode. Requesting msgs with SSN > 45 ◄- - |
| 5011 | 2008-05-07 01:03:08 | n1 2324: Received recovery alert from FailingNode. Requesting msgs with SSN > 40 ◄- - |
| 5012 | 2008-05-07 01:03:08 | n1 2323: Received recovery alert from FailingNode. Requesting msgs with SSN > 47 ◄- - |
| 5013 | 2008-05-07 01:03:08 | FailingNode: Received ack to recovery alert from n2 2324. ◄─── |
| 5014 | 2008-05-07 01:03:08 | FailingNode: Received ack to recovery alert from Server. ◄─── |
| 5015 | 2008-05-07 01:03:08 | FailingNode: Received ack to recovery alert from n1 2324. ◄─── |
| 5016 | 2008-05-07 01:03:08 | FailingNode: Received ack to recovery alert from n1 2323. ◄─── |

◄- - Peers receiving recovery alert with request for messages higher than a certain SSN

◄─── "FailingNode" receiving acknowledgement for recovery alert

**Figure 9.19** FailingNode sending a recovery alert.

Figure 9.20 shows some of the messages retransmitted (in response to the recovery alert and message retransmission request) to FailingNode. Note that the messages that were received from the rest of the nodes and that are fully logged (i.e. the RSN is included in the message log) on the sender side are replayed to FailingNode in increasing RSN order. The messages begin with the next message after the current RSN is recorded in FailingNode's checkpoint. The figure also shows that the partially logged messages are sent (in no specific order) after all the fully logged messages have been sent.

After the recovery is complete, all nodes send a "Done Helping with Recovery" message, shown in Figure 9.21, to FailingNode.

| msgID | timestamp | message |
|-------|-----------|---------|
| 5110 | 2008-05-07 01:03:32 | FailingNode: Received app msg from n1 2324. SSN = 60, RSN = 60 |
| 5114 | 2008-05-07 01:03:35 | FailingNode: Received app msg from n2 2323. SSN = 59, RSN = 61 |
| 5118 | 2008-05-07 01:03:35 | FailingNode: Received app msg from Server. SSN = 65, RSN = 62 |
| 5122 | 2008-05-07 01:03:36 | FailingNode: Received app msg from n1 2323. SSN = 67, RSN = 63 |
| 5126 | 2008-05-07 01:03:38 | FailingNode: Received app msg from n2 2323. SSN = 63, RSN = 64 |
| 5128 | 2008-05-07 01:03:38 | FailingNode: Received app msg from n2 2324. SSN = 67, RSN = 65 |
| 5135 | 2008-05-07 01:03:39 | FailingNode: Received app msg from n1 2323. SSN = 68, RSN = 66 |
| 5140 | 2008-05-07 01:03:42 | FailingNode: Received app msg from n2 2324. SSN = 68, RSN = 67 |
| 5145 | 2008-05-07 01:03:44 | FailingNode: Received app msg from n1 2324. SSN = 67, RSN = 68 |
| 5149 | 2008-05-07 01:03:47 | FailingNode: Received app msg from Server. SSN = 70, RSN = 69 |
| 5154 | 2008-05-07 01:03:47 | FailingNode: Received app msg from n1 2324. SSN = 70, RSN = 70 |
| 5208 | 2008-05-07 01:03:50 | FailingNode: Received app msg from n2 2323. SSN = 72, RSN = -3 |
| 5218 | 2008-05-07 01:03:50 | FailingNode: Received app msg from Server. SSN = 75, RSN = -3 |

Partially logged messages

**Figure 9.20** Message retransmissions to FailingNode.

| msgID | timestamp | message |
|-------|-----------|---------|
| 5131 | 2008-05-07 01:03:38 | FailingNode: Received Done Helping with Recovery from n2 2323. |
| 5139 | 2008-05-07 01:03:39 | FailingNode: Received Done Helping with Recovery from n1 2323. |
| 5144 | 2008-05-07 01:03:42 | FailingNode: Received Done Helping with Recovery from n2 2324. |
| 5153 | 2008-05-07 01:03:47 | FailingNode: Received Done Helping with Recovery from Server. |
| 5158 | 2008-05-07 01:03:47 | FailingNode: Received Done Helping with Recovery from n1 2324. |

**Figure 9.21** Recovery completion.

Note that both the sender- and receiver-based message-logging approaches rely strongly on the piecewise-deterministic assumption about processes. The assumption holds true if the processes are single-threaded since the messages are processed serially. In this case, it is sufficient to record the order in which messages are received to record the order in which the piecewise-deterministic state changes are brought about in the process. If the process is multithreaded, however, it is no longer piecewise-deterministic. Several messages can be processed concurrently (each in its own thread), and the thread scheduler determines the ultimate order in which the threads update state in the process.

As an example of the nondeterminism and the effect it has on other processes, consider Figure 9.22, in which two clients send requests to a multithreaded server. Client A sends a request to purchase 10 items from the server's inventory, and Client B sends a request to calculate the current value of the server's inventory. The instructions from each request (i.e. thread) can be interleaved in a nondeterministic order, as shown in the close-up in Figure 9.22.

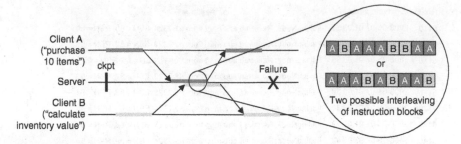

**Figure 9.22** A variety of state changes in the server that could occur because of the nondeterministic interleaving of instructions from multiple threads.

Suppose that the request (from Client A) to decrement the inventory by 10 items occurs before the request (from Client B) to query the present value of the inventory. The replies to the requests will be different if the order in which the requests are handled is reversed. Once the scheduler on the server has dictated an ordering of the state changes, the two clients become dependent upon this ordering (e.g. in the example, Client B learns the value of the inventory after the 10 items have been purchased by Client A).

If the server later fails and rolls back to the checkpoint indicated by the vertical bar in Figure 9.22 and message logging is used to recover the state of the server, the state changes in the server must be recreated in exactly the same order for the resulting server state to be consistent with what the two clients expect. Merely replaying messages in the original receive order would not work.

In addition to pessimistic message logging, optimistic and causal message-logging protocols have been developed. Optimistic message logging relaxes the requirement of pessimistic message logging that a message $M$ must be logged before $M$ can be processed [26, 27]. The result is that state changes from $M$ can be applied to $P$, and $P$ can send outgoing messages to other processes. As in Figure 9.22, other processes can become dependent upon this updated state (due to processing M) in $P$, and if $M$ is not fully logged when $P$ fails, then the state changes brought about by $M$ are not guaranteed to be recoverable. The lost state intervals are called the *orphan states* of $P$. Processes dependent upon orphan states must be rolled back as well, and to make that possible, each process must maintain a dependency vector [26] during normal execution. The dependency vector for $P$ specifies the state intervals in other processes on which $P$ is dependent.

Causal message logging attempts to combine the performance advantages of optimistic message logging during failure-free execution with the recovery simplicity of pessimistic message logging. No orphan states are created under causal message logging. Family-based message logging [28] utilizes sender-based logs to log the actual message data, much like the approach described in [23]. But family-based message logging makes use of the fact that a message needs to be fully logged (i.e. with the data plus RSN) only when another process becomes dependent upon it. The RSN for a received message $M$, therefore, is piggybacked on outgoing messages; the receiver of an outgoing message is responsible for recording the RSN for message $M$. Two processes must participate during recovery to replay message $M$ under that scheme: the sender of $M$ and the process that recorded the RSN for $M$.

Manetho [29] is another causal message-logging protocol. Manetho piggybacks onto outgoing messages an antecedent graph that specifies the history of state intervals upon which the current state of a process is dependent. The antecedent graphs are used during recovery to ensure that messages are replayed in the correct order. Logging is done just like family-based message logging: the sender logs the actual message data for $M$ sent to process $P$, and $P$ piggybacks its antecedent graph (which specifies that it is dependent on $M$) on outgoing messages.

Like pessimistic message logging, both optimistic and causal message logging assume that the processes are piecewise deterministic. In optimistic message logging, one can see that clearly by observing that state intervals are delineated only by the receipt of a message [26]. In causal message logging, the state changes between the receipt of a message and the transmission of an outgoing message are assumed to be deterministic. As a result, neither of those kinds of message-logging protocols has provisions for working with multithreaded processes. To account for multithreading, message logging must record the order of state changes to the processes rather than the order of message receipt.

## 9.7 Checkpointing Latency Modeling

Three metrics can be used to characterize a checkpointing scheme (see [30]):

- *Checkpoint overhead:* This is the additional execution time required by an application in order to take a checkpoint and is denoted by $C$.
- *Checkpoint latency:* This is the time that elapses between the taking of a checkpoint and the point at which the checkpoint is ready to be used for a future recovery. In essence, it is the time needed to save the checkpoint to stable storage. It is denoted by $L$.
- *Overhead ratio:* The overhead ratio is a measure of the increase in an application's execution time due to checkpointing relative to the time taken for the original, useful computation. (A formal definition and the analytical formulation of the overhead ratio, as presented in [30], will be discussed later in this section.)

Usually, when the checkpoint overhead, $C$, decreases, there is an increase in the checkpoint latency, $L$. As would be expected, the objective is to keep the overhead ratio as low as possible. A decrease in $C$ decreases the overhead ratio, whereas an increase in $L$ increases the overhead ratio. In [30], Vaidya shows that a relatively small decrease in checkpoint overhead $C$ can compensate for even a large increase in checkpoint latency $L$.

Time spent on *useful* computation is the time spent on the actual computations for the application, not including the time spent on checkpointing and rollback recovery. For equidistant checkpoints (with which the amount of useful work performed between two checkpoints is constant), the optimal checkpoint interval is typically independent of the checkpoint latency ($L$). Depending on whether or not the application is allowed to proceed while taking a checkpoint, there can be two kinds of checkpointing approaches:

1) *Sequential* checkpointing: The application is paused to take a checkpoint and is resumed only after the checkpoint has been completely saved to stable storage. The process continues to execute only *after* the state has been completely saved to the stable storage [13]. Figure 9.23 illustrates the sequential checkpointing scheme. The horizontal line represents processor execution, with time increasing from left to right. The shaded box represents the checkpointing operation, and $C$ = the width of the box = $L$. The latency for the sequential checkpointing approach is the *smallest* among all the available approaches, as the checkpoint is ready to be used for future recovery immediately after the checkpoint has been taken (i.e. as soon as the time taken for the checkpoint overhead has elapsed). However, since latency and overhead are usually conflicting requirements, the overhead for sequential latency is high relative to that for other approaches.

2) *Forked* checkpointing: In this approach, when a process needs to be checkpointed, a child process is forked from the main process. At the time of the fork, the state of the child process is identical to that of the main process. The main process continues executing, while the child process saves the

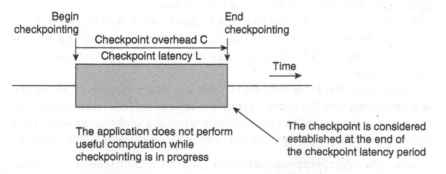

Figure 9.23 Sequential checkpointing [30] / with permission of IEEE.

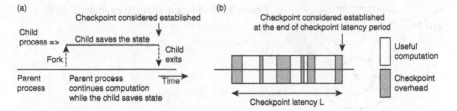

**Figure 9.24** Forked checkpointing (a) parent and child processes (b) interleaved execution [30] / with permission of IEEE.

checkpoint to stable storage in the background. Here we see that $C$ is much smaller than $L$. Figure 9.24a illustrates the overall approach with the parent and child processes. Figure 9.24b shows how the executions of the child and parent processes are interleaved on the same processor. As shown in the figure, the useful computation performed by the parent process is interleaved with the checkpointing operation performed by the child process.

When a checkpoint is ready to be used for a future recovery in the event of a failure, it is said to be *established*. From the definition of *checkpoint latency* ($L$) in the beginning of this section, it is clear that the checkpoint is established at the end of the checkpoint latency period. Figures 9.23 and 9.24 indicate the times at which a checkpoint is considered *established* in the sequential and forked checkpointing schemes, respectively. Processors are assumed to fail at intervals that follow an exponential distribution with rate $\lambda$. A processor can fail during normal operation, during checkpointing, or during rollback and recovery.

### Definitions

$T$: the amount of useful computation performed in each interval.

$G(t)$: the expected (average) execution time required to perform $t$ units of useful computation.

$\Gamma$: the expected execution time of a checkpoint interval.

Then, *overhead ratio* ($r$) is defined as:

$$r = \lim_{t \to \infty} \frac{G(t) - t}{t} = \lim_{t \to \infty} \frac{G(t)}{t} - 1$$

Considering a single checkpoint interval,

$$r = \frac{\Gamma}{T} - 1$$

To evaluate $\Gamma$, the system is described using a three-state discrete Markov chain, which is presented in Figure 9.25. State 0 is the initial state of the system at the start of a checkpoint interval. When the interval is completed without a failure, the

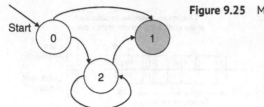

**Figure 9.25** Markov chain to evaluate $\Gamma$ [30].

system transitions from state 0 to state 1. If a failure occurs while the system is in state 0, then the system moves to state 2. After state 2 is entered, if no further failure occurs before the next checkpoint is established, then a transition to state 1 occurs. If, however, another failure occurs after state 2 has been entered and before the next checkpoint is established, then a transition is made from state 2 back to state 2.

Each transition $(X, Y)$ from state $X$ to state $Y$ in the Markov chain is associated with a transition probability $P_{XY}$ and a cost $K_{XY}$. The cost $K_{XY}$ of a transition $(X, Y)$ is the expected time spent in state $X$ before the transition to state $Y$. For the transitions shown in Figure 9.25, the transition probabilities and costs can be obtained as follows [30]:

$$P_{01} = e^{-\lambda(T+C)}$$

$$K_{01} = T + C$$

$$P_{02} = 1 - e^{-\lambda(T+C)}$$

$$K_{02} = \int_{0}^{T+C} (t)\frac{\lambda e^{-\lambda t}}{1-e^{-\lambda(T+C)}} dt = \lambda^{-1} - \frac{(T+C)e^{-\lambda(T+C)}}{1-e^{-\lambda(T+C)}}$$

$$P_{21} = e^{-\lambda(R+T+L)}$$

$$K_{21} = R + T + L$$

$$P_{22} = 1 - e^{-\lambda(R+T+L)}$$

$$K_{22} = \int_{0}^{R+T+L} (t)\frac{\lambda e^{-\lambda t}}{1-e^{-\lambda(R+T+L)}} dt = \lambda^{-1} - \frac{(R+T+L)e^{-\lambda(R+T+L)}}{1-e^{-\lambda(R+T+L)}}$$

Now, $\Gamma$, the expected cost of a path from state 0 to state 1, is given by:

$$\Gamma = P_{01}K_{01} + P_{02}\left( K_{02} + \frac{P_{22}}{1-P_{22}}K_{22} + K_{21} \right)$$

Substituting the expressions for various costs and transition probabilities into the above expression for $\Gamma$ and simplifying yield the following expression:

$$\Gamma = \lambda^{-1}\left(1-e^{-\lambda(T+C)}\right)e^{\lambda(R+T+L)} = \lambda^{-1}e^{\lambda(L-C+R)}\left(e^{\lambda(T+C)}-1\right)$$

Therefore, the overhead ratio $r$ is obtained as:

$$r = \frac{\Gamma}{T} - 1 = \frac{\lambda^{-1} e^{\lambda(L-C+R)} \left( e^{\lambda(T+C)} - 1 \right)}{T} - 1$$

The objective is to choose an appropriate value of $T$ to minimize the overhead ratio $r$. The optimal value of $T$ must satisfy the following equation:

$$\frac{\partial r}{\partial T} = \frac{\partial}{\partial T} \left[ \frac{\lambda^{-1} e^{\lambda(L-C+R)} \left( e^{\lambda(T+C)} - 1 \right)}{T} - 1 \right] = 0$$

$$\Rightarrow \frac{\partial}{\partial T} \left( \frac{e^{\lambda(T+C)} - 1}{T} \right) = 0 \tag{9.1}$$

Equation (9.1) yields $e^{\lambda(T+C)}(1 - \lambda T) = 1$. Thus, the positive values of $T$ for which $r$ is minimized or maximized must satisfy the above equation. It can be shown [31] that at the positive values of $T$ that satisfy Eq. (9.1),

$$\frac{\partial^2 r}{\partial T^2} > 0$$

(assuming $C > 0$). Therefore, function $r$ has only minimas (for $T > 0$). $r$ is not a constant function of $T$, and it is continuous for $T > 0$. Therefore, if it has no maxima (at $T > 0$), it cannot have more than one minimum at a positive $T$. Therefore, $r$ has only one minimum. It can be verified that if $C$ is smaller than $1/\lambda$, then

$$T_{opt} \approx \sqrt{\frac{2C}{\lambda}}$$

As (9.1) does not include $L$ or $R$, $T_{opt}$ is *not* dependent on $L$ and $R$, perhaps because checkpoint latency $L$ and overhead $R$ affect execution time only when a failure occurs.

## 9.8 Checkpointing in Main Memory Database Systems (MMDB)

Performance-critical applications may require the database with which they interface to access the data stored in the main memory directly. The performance requirements prohibit the use of inter-process communication for access to internal database structures; to meet its performance needs, the application should be able to access the database's internal structures directly. Software errors in the database management system (DBMS) adversely affect the availability of the database. However, the additional facilities provided to the application to enhance its performance, as described here, increase the risk of database unavailability. The reason is that errors in the application programs can also affect the database. "Addressing" errors have been shown to have a significant impact on DBMS availability [32] because of copy overruns and writes to incorrect locations through uninitialized pointers.

Even if memory protection primitives have been implemented in the operating system, their use is precluded by the high-performance needs of the application, as they have to be accessed through operating-system-level system calls. In addition, in a multithreaded application, where threads share the address space, one thread is allowed to access the pages of another thread without going through any protection mechanism implemented by the operating system. In light of those factors, there is a need for techniques that can directly protect data in a main-memory database (MMDB) management system.

This section summarizes various techniques proposed in the work by Bohannon et al. [33] to protect database states from software errors. Corruption of bytes due to an addressing error is referred to as *direct physical corruption*. An executing transaction that reads from the corrupted data may use the data for its own computation and write the results back to the database. The data derived and written from directly corrupted data are referred to as *indirectly corrupted*, and the transaction that wrote the indirectly corrupted data is said to have *carried* the corruption. An updated model that requires all updates to be in place and made through a predefined, fixed interface can be used to ensure protection from direct physical corruption. Those restrictions make it possible to distinguish correct updates from unintended or erroneous updates.

The database is divided into protection regions, and a codeword is associated with each to enable the protection of data from corruption. As per the updated model, data from a protection region can only be updated using the predefined prescribed interface. The interface ensures that an update of the data triggers a concomitant update of the codeword associated with that region (also called *codeword maintenance*). However, when a data value is updated because of an incorrect write or other addressing error, the update does not go through the prescribed interface; hence, with a high probability, the calculated codeword for the resultant data in the region will no longer match the codeword stored for that region.

Several codeword-based techniques have been presented for the prevention or detection of corruption. In Read Prechecking, the calculated and stored codewords for the data in a protection region are compared on each read operation. Transaction-carried corruption is thus prevented. One disadvantage of the Read Prechecking scheme is the high overhead introduced by the calculation and comparison of codewords on every read. To alleviate the overhead, the Data Codeword scheme asynchronously audits the codewords. The updates and audits of the codeword can still increase database contention. The Data Codewords with Deferred Maintenance scheme reduces the contention by using the database log to update the codewords. The Read Logging scheme has been introduced to detect indirect corruption. In Read Logging, a representative portion of information about each data item that is read by a transaction is added to the log.

*Multilevel Recovery.* A multilevel transaction-processing system consists of $n$ logical levels of abstraction, with operations at each level invoking operations at lower levels. Level 0 consists of physical updates that lead up to operations at level $n$ that are transactions themselves.

*Data Structures.* Figure 9.26 illustrates some of the data structures used in transaction management. The three main structures are the active transaction table (*ATT*), the system log, and checkpoint images. As shown in the figure, the undo and redo logs are stored on a per-transaction basis in the ATT. The ATT is essentially the local log. A portion of the local log is written out to stable storage and is indicated by the end_of_stable_log variable. The dirty page table, *dpt*, is a bitmap of the dirty pages and is used in checkpointing.

*Checkpointing.* In MMDBs, since the database is assumed to fit in the main memory, pages are not written back to the disk except during a checkpoint operation. During a checkpoint, the dpt is used to write dirty pages to disk. Two checkpoint images, Ckpt_A and Ckpt_B, are stored on disk along with a pointer to the most

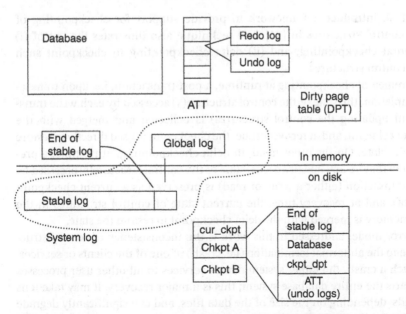

**Figure 9.26** Data structures in the Dali main-memory DBMS [33] / with permission of IEEE.

recent valid checkpoint, cur_ckpt. The purpose is to support what is commonly called *ping-pong checkpointing* [9]: at every checkpoint, the newly dirtied pages are written alternately to the two checkpoints. Only after all actions associated with the checkpoint have successfully completed is the cur_ckpt pointer switched to point to the new checkpoint.

To ensure that a checkpoint is free of corruption, every page in the database is audited after the checkpoint has been written out. If no page in the database has direct corruption, no indirect corruption could have occurred either. So, it is certain that the checkpoint itself was not corrupted.

*Recovery*. Upon detection of corruption, recovery starts from the last completed checkpoint image; all redo logs, starting with the *end_of_stable_log* specified by the checkpoint, are replayed. When the end of the log is reached, incomplete transactions are rolled back through the use of the logical undo information stored in either the ATT or the operation commit log records.

Until this point, we have discussed techniques that detect corruption on the database image. But the control structures of the database, such as lock information, are just as prone to corruption. The techniques summarized in this section do not address corruption in control structures. Next, we detail approaches for handling corruption in the control structures of MMDBs.

### 9.8.1 Checkpointing of MMDB Control Structures

Wang et al. introduce a framework to provide support for checkpointing of MMDB control structures in [34]. The technique also illustrates the use of (i) incremental checkpointing; and (ii) delta checkpointing to checkpoint such MMDB control structures.

In incremental checkpointing at runtime, a post-transaction, i.e. upon transaction completion, the state of the control structure(s) accessed by each write transaction (in updating the control structures) is collected and merged with the current checkpoint, and at recovery time, the checkpoint is used directly to restore the correct state. On the other hand, in delta checkpointing, at runtime, a pretransaction (before any updates occur) state of the control structure(s) accessed by a given transaction (either a write or read) is preserved as a current checkpoint (i.e. delta), and at recovery time, the current state of control structures in the shared memory is merged with the delta checkpoint to restore the state.

The error model addressed in this work is the inconsistency of control structures due to the abnormal termination (i.e. crash) of one of the clients or services. Upon such a crash, the target system denies services to all other user processes and restarts the entire database system; this is a major recovery. It may take tens of seconds, depending on the size of the data files, and can significantly degrade system availability, which is not acceptable for services provided to critical applications. A major reason for those problems is the way the database handles access to control structures stored in a separate database termed the *SysDB* (refer to Figure 9.27). The system employs multiple mutexes to guarantee the mutual exclusion semantic in accessing control structures by user processes. When a client or service crashes while still holding a mutex, the database may remain in an inconsistent state. Since there is no way for the system to tell which updates the crashed client has made, the cleanup process restarts the database to bring the system back into a consistent state.

Figure 9.27 depicts the example architecture of SysDB, which contains three tables: (i) the *process table*, which maintains process *ids* and *mutex lists* for each process as well as information on database mapping into the process address space; (ii) the *transaction table*, which maintains logs and locks for active transactions; and (iii) the *file table*, which keeps user database files. Each client/service process maps SysDB into its own address space before accessing the database.

### 9.8.1.1 Checkpointing Framework
The ARMOR infrastructure was used to provide the framework for implementing the checkpointing algorithms. The ARMOR architecture is designed to manage redundant resources across interconnected nodes, detect errors in both user applications and infrastructure components, and recover quickly from failures. ARMORs (Adaptive Reconfigurable Mobile Objects of Reliability) are multithreaded processes internally structured around objects called *elements* that contain their own private data and provide elementary functions or services. All

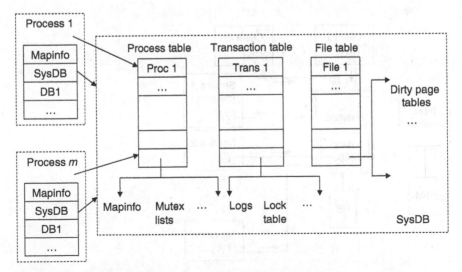

**Figure 9.27** Example control structures (SysDB) [34] / with permission of IEEE.

ARMORs contain a basic set of elements that provide core functionality, including the abilities to (i) implement reliable point-to-point message communication between ARMORs, (ii) respond to "are-you-alive?" messages from the local daemon, and (iii) capture ARMOR state. For more details on ARMOR architecture, the reader is referred to [35–38].

To expose ARMOR services, the database is instrumented in two ways. First, ARMOR stubs are embedded in the database processes, facilitating communication channel(s) between the database server and the ARMOR infrastructure. Second, functionalities for checkpointing SysDB data structures are embedded; the checkpointing functionality modifies selected library functions of the database but preserves function interfaces and hence is transparent to clients.

Figure 9.28 illustrates the basic architecture of the ARMOR infrastructure integrated with the target database. The FTM, FTM daemon, HB, and Daemon ARMORs constitute the skeleton of the ARMOR infrastructure. The solid lines are the ARMOR communication channels. An ARMOR element called the *image keeper* is embedded into the Daemon ARMOR to maintain the image (i.e. checkpoint) of the data structures in SysDB. When a client or service process opens the database, the database kernel library creates an *Embedded ARMOR (EA)* stub within the process and establishes a communication channel between the EA and the Daemon. From then on, the checkpoint data can be transmitted directly from the source process (with its EA stub) to the destination ARMOR, which maintains the image in memory. The image is then stored on a disk by ARMOR's checkpoint mechanism.

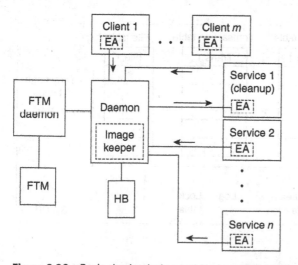

**Figure 9.28** Basic checkpointing architecture [34] / with permission of IEEE.

### 9.8.1.2 Incremental Checkpointing

In the incremental checkpointing scheme, only updates (incremental changes) to data are sent to the image keeper. The basic algorithm is as follows:

- After system initialization, the database server sends the image of all the control structures to the image keeper.
- In the following processing, a client/service acquires a mutex and then performs operations on the control structures. On each write operation, any changes to the data are stored in the local buffer.
- After all the updates have successfully finished, the mutex is released, and the client/service delivers the buffered increments to the image keeper to maintain an up-to-date checkpoint of the control structures.
- If a crash occurs while the mutex is being held, the cleanup service requests from the image keeper the latest checkpoint data and restores the corrupted control structures.

Handling mutex overlaps. In some cases, a single section of control structures is protected by multiple mutexes. To properly handle such a situation, the image keeper maintains, in addition to the checkpoint, a mapping between a mutex and the data section(s) protected by the mutex. To assist in the mapping, the checkpoint increments sent to the image keeper include the mutex id and the information necessary to identify the correct sections in the control structures.

Figure 9.29 depicts an example configuration of control structure images kept in the image keeper and illustrates the mapping of mutexes to control structures. With such mapping, overlapped data sections can be protected and their consistency with the corresponding copies in SysDB can be preserved, even when multiple mutexes are acquired at the same time.

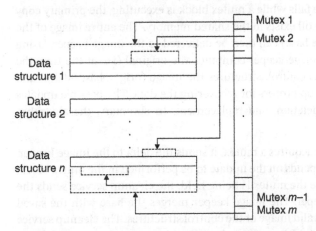

**Figure 9.29** Control structure images [34] / with permission of IEEE.

Handling data access without mutex protection. The proposed algorithm for incremental checkpointing works correctly so long as all updates to control structures are performed within the mutex blocks. There are, however, cases in which control structures are updated directly, without mutex protection, e.g. during database initialization (when it is assumed that no processes will try to access the database). While that example is a rather benign case, practice shows that application developers often make somewhat arbitrary decisions and allow accessing of control structures without mutex protection. To handle such scenarios, it is necessary (i) to locate, in the application code, all the places where updates might occur outside mutex blocks; and (ii) to augment the implementation to ensure that the checkpoint in the image keeper is up to date. This can be difficult given the size and complexity of real-world applications, such as our target database system. Delta checkpointing, discussed next, is an attempt to alleviate the problem.

### 9.8.1.3 Delta Checkpointing

The delta checkpointing algorithm is based on the following assumption: in a correctly implemented system, any access to control structures outside the mutex blocks, after system initialization, does not violate data consistency. Consequently, crashes outside the mutex blocks do not cause data inconsistency, and sections of control structures not updated by any currently executing mutex block are always consistent. As a result, the image keeper does not need to maintain a copy of all control structures (as in incremental checkpointing, discussed in the previous section). It is sufficient to preserve data sections modified during the execution of a given mutex block (plus information on the type and parameters of the update operation). In other words, the algorithm only needs to recognize, collect, and send to the image keeper the modified data section, i.e. the delta (which is a before-image). If a client/service fails while a mutex block is executing, the primary copy of the control structures still exists in the shared memory. The entire image of the related structures (i.e. the base) can then be delivered to the image keeper. Using the delta and base, the image keeper computes the original (i.e. at the time the mutex block was entered) control, structures the image (orig = base+delta) and sends it back to the cleanup process for recovering the data. The possible updates include data insertion, deletion, and replacement. In summary, the algorithm includes two basic steps:

1) When a client/service acquires a mutex, it sends the delta to the image keeper. The delta's content depends on the update to be performed in the mutex block.
2) If a crash occurs while the mutex is being held, the cleanup service sends the base to the image keeper. The image keeper merges the base with the saved delta and generates a valid image of the control structures. The cleanup service requests the regenerated image from the image keeper and restores the corrupted control structures.

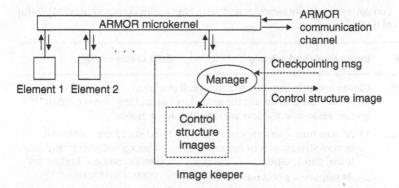

**Figure 9.30** Structure of the image keeper [34] / with permission of IEEE.

Observe that the image keeper merges the base with the latest delta it has received. To avoid the use of the wrong delta in a recovery, it is important to send out a delta at each mutex acquisition, even if the delta is empty, i.e. no changes to the control structures were performed during the current mutex block.

The *image keeper* is a separate element within the ARMOR process that collects and maintains checkpoint data representing the correct state of control structures. It is a passive component, which means that it is invoked only by the incoming messages (i.e. checkpoint updates) and that it performs proper actions according to the received messages. Figure 9.30 depicts the basic structure of the image keeper, which consists of (i) a set of memory blocks for preserving images of control data structures (i.e. *control structure images*), and (ii) management support (i.e. the *manager*) for updates of the checkpoint and recovery actions in response to client failures. The image keeper communicates with the database processes by means of the ARMOR communication channel.

The control structure images shown in Figure 9.29 represent a memory pool that stores the images of control structures in SysDB. Different mutexes map their corresponding data sections into the copy of control structures in the image keeper.

As a final note, Table 9.3 compares the incremental and delta checkpointing techniques.

## 9.9 Checkpointing in Distributed Database Systems

In a database that is serving transactions that might be critical, it is imperative to provide a mechanism for recovering safely from the effects of failures. The checkpointing mechanism should not introduce high costs in terms of space and time and thus affect the performance of the database system. Sequential checkpointing, as defined in Section 9.7, is not suitable for large databases, as it requires blocking of all transactions that are submitted to the system during a checkpoint.

**Table 9.3** Comparison of the incremental and delta checkpointing algorithms [34] / with permission of IEEE.

| Algorithm | Incremental checkpointing | Delta checkpointing |
|---|---|---|
| Similarities | Close checkpointing architecture; small overhead; no checkpoint taken for read-only access; the same way of handling mutex overlap and access to external devices while holding a mutex. | |
| Differences | 1) At start time – an image of all control structures is stored as an initial checkpoint;<br><br>2) At runtime – a post transaction (upon transaction completion) state of the control structure(s) accessed by each write transaction is collected and merged with the current checkpoint;<br><br>3) At recovery time – the checkpointed image of control structures is directly loaded to the shared memory from the image keeper;<br><br>4) Must checkpoint data updates due to operations within/outside mutex blocks. | 1) At start time – an initial checkpoint is an empty data set, i.e. no need to store any control structures;<br><br>2) At runtime – a prior transaction (before data updates occur) state of the control structure(s) accessed by a given transaction (write or read-only) is preserved as a current (delta) checkpoint;<br><br>3) At recovery time – the image of control structures from the shared memory is merged with the latest delta stored in the image keeper;<br><br>4) Must checkpoint only updates due to operations within mutex blocks. |

For large databases, the checkpointing mechanism should not interfere with the application processing, in this case, transactions.

In a distributed system, checkpointing should allow rollback recovery to a consistent state. That ability reduces the overhead of the recovery mechanism and avoids the need to synchronize all the participant nodes. For the checkpoint state to be globally consistent, the effects of a transaction on the database should be either completely included, or not included, in that state. Therefore, allowing transactions to be submitted while checkpoints are being taken conflicts with the goal of arriving at a globally consistent state. Here we describe the technique for checkpointing distributed database systems presented by Son and Agrawala in [39].

## 9.9.1 Definitions

This section defines a few terms that will be used in describing the checkpointing scheme. In particular, we define a *transaction* and the interactions that must take place between the nodes to commit a transaction.

A *transaction* is a basic unit of user activity in a database system. Transactions read and write data objects from the database. Data objects could be files, pages, records, fields, and so forth, in the database. To maintain a consistent state, a transaction is either *committed* (i.e. executed to completion) or *aborted* (i.e. not executed at all). The results of a transaction are reflected in the database only if it is committed. Each transaction is assigned a unique timestamp.

The nodes involved in a transaction are called *participants*, one of which is called the *coordinator*. The coordinator is responsible for initiating and terminating the transaction through message exchange with the rest of the participants.

To initiate a transaction, the coordinator creates and sends a transaction initiate message (TIM) to each of the participants. Upon receiving a TIM, each participant responds to the coordinator either with a TIM-ACK, if it can execute it, or with a TIM-NACK, if it is not in a position to execute it. If even one TIM-NACK is received, the coordinator aborts the transaction. If all the TIM-ACKs are received, then a start transaction message (STM) is sent to all participants. After receiving the STM, the participating node starts executing the transaction.

To enable atomic commit of transactions into the database state and also allow transactions during checkpoint establishment, transactions are divided into two groups depending on their time of occurrence relative to the start of the checkpoint: after-checkpoint transactions (ACPT) and before-checkpoint transactions (BCPT). The checkpointing scheme attempts to construct a state that will be reached when all the BCPTs are completed. The state changes due to the ACPTs are not included in the state. The scheme allows the conversion of an ACPT to a BCPT if it needs to be included in the state for consistency.

## 9.9.2  The Algorithm

As for a transaction, one of the participant nodes of the checkpointing operation is designated the *checkpoint coordinator* (CC), and the rest of the nodes are called *checkpoint subordinates* (CSs). The CC is responsible for initiating and terminating a checkpoint. Until a checkpoint is terminated, it is active. At any point in time, a CC cannot have more than one active checkpoint. The checkpointing algorithm consists of three phases.

The variables used in the algorithm are as follows:

1) *Local Clock (LC):* A clock, maintained at each site, that is manipulated by the clock rules of Lamport.
2) *Local Checkpoint Number (LCPN):* A number determined locally for the current checkpoint.
3) *Global Checkpoint Number (GCPN):* A globally unique number for the current checkpoint.
4) CONVERT: A Boolean variable showing the completion of the conversion of all the eligible transactions at the site.

In the first phase, each participant node provides its local checkpoint number (LCPN) to the CC. The CC determines the GCPN as the maximum of the LCPNs of all the participant nodes, and broadcasts it to all nodes. The second phase overlaps with the first phase and starts after a node has fixed its LCPN. All transactions at a site $k$ whose timestamps are less than or equal to $LCPN_k$ are marked as BCPT at that site. The remaining transactions are marked as ACPT and their results (i.e. data objects) are stored in buffers called *committed temporary versions* (*CTVs*). After a participant node has received the GCPN from the CC, it starts the third phase, in which any ACPT whose timestamp is less than or equal to the timestamp of the GCPN is converted to a BCPT. The updates of those converted transactions are also committed to the database from their corresponding CTVs. At a node, when the eligible ACPTs have been converted to BCPTs and all the BCPTs have completed execution, the site is ready to take a local checkpoint. After a checkpoint has been taken, the latest CTV for each data object (that has been modified by an ACPT) is committed to the database. The checkpointing algorithm works as follows:

1) The CC broadcasts a Checkpoint Request Message with a timestamp $LC_{cc}$. The LCPN of the coordinator is set to $LC_{cc}$. The coordinator sets the Boolean variable CONVERT to false ($CONVERT_{cc}$ = false) and marks all the transactions at the coordinator site whose timestamps are not greater than $LCPN_{cc}$ as BCPTs.

2) Upon receiving a Checkpoint Request Message, site $m$ updates its local clock, and $LCPN_m$ is determined by the CS as follows:

$$LC_m = \max\left(LC_{cc} + 1, LC_m\right)$$

$$LCPN_m = LC_m$$

The CS of site $m$ replies to the coordinator with $LCPN_m$, sets the Boolean variable CONVERT to false ($CONVERT_m$ = false), and marks all the transactions at site $m$ whose timestamps are not greater than $LCPN_m$ as BCPTs.

3) The coordinator broadcasts the GCPN, which is decided by:

$$GCPN = \max\left(LCPN_n\right) \quad n = 1,\ldots,N.$$

4) For all sites, after LCPN is fixed, all transactions with timestamps greater than LCPN are marked as temporary ACPT. If a temporary ACPT wants to update any data objects, those data objects are copied from the database to the buffer space of the transaction. When a temporary ACPT commits, updated data objects are not stored in the database as usual, but are maintained as *committed temporary versions* (*CTV*) of data objects. The data manager of each site maintains the permanent and temporary versions of data objects. When a read

request is made for a data object that has committed temporary versions, the value of the latest committed temporary version is returned. When a write request is made for a data object that has committed temporary versions, the previous committed temporary version is not overwritten; rather, another committed temporary version is created for it.

5) When the GCPN is known, each checkpointing process compares the timestamps of the temporary ACPTs to the GCPN. Transactions that satisfy the following condition become BCPTs; their updates are reflected in the database and included in the current checkpoint.

$$\text{LCPN} < \text{timestamp}(T) \leq \text{GCPN}.$$

The remaining temporary ACPTs are treated as actual ACPTs; their updates are not included in the current checkpoint but are included in the database after the current checkpointing has been completed. After the conversion of all the eligible ACPTs, the checkpointing process sets the Boolean variable CONVERT to true (CONVERT = true).

6) Local checkpointing is executed through the saving of the state of data objects when there is no active BCPT and the variable CONVERT is true.

7) After the execution of local checkpointing, the values of the latest committed temporary versions are used to replace the values of data objects in the database. Then, all committed temporary versions are deleted.

This checkpointing algorithm essentially consists of two phases. The function of the first phase (steps 1–3) is the assignment of a GCPN that is determined from the local clocks of the system. The second phase begins with the fixing of the LCPN at each site, which is necessary because each LCPN sent to the CC is a candidate to be the GCPN of the current checkpoint. In addition, the committed temporary versions must be created for the data objects updated by ACPTs. The notions of committed temporary versions and conversion from ACPT to BCPT are introduced to ensure that each checkpoint contains all the updates made by transactions with earlier timestamps than the GCPN of the checkpoint.

When a site receives a TIM, it sends a TIM-ACK, unless the following scenario occurs. Consider a TIM that is received while the node is participating in taking a checkpoint. If (i) the TIM is received after the node has indicated that it has converted all ACPTs whose timestamp(s) are less than the GCPN's timestamp to BCPTs, and (ii) the timestamp in the TIM is less than the GCPN's timestamp, then accepting the TIM would result in an additional BCPT, and that would be inconsistent with the view of the node from the other nodes. Therefore, in that specific case, a TIM-NACK would be sent by the node to the transaction coordinator.

### 9.9.2.1  Failure Recovery

The failure of a checkpointing subordinate can be tolerated by the algorithm presented earlier. Upon recovery, a node learns the GCPN of the latest checkpoint and executes all the transactions whose timestamps are not greater than that of the GCPN. Doing so brings the node's view of the database up to date. Other transactions are executed after the state of the data objects at the site has been saved by the checkpointing process.

However, the failure of a CC adversely affects the working of the algorithm. If the CC fails to broadcast the GCPN to the CSes, all transactions (including any newly arriving ones) become ACPTs. As a result, much more storage would be required for the committed temporary versions of the data objects modified by those transactions.

## 9.10  Multithreaded Checkpointing

There have been some approaches in academic research to investigate distributed checkpointing of multithreaded processes. Kasbekar and Das suggest an approach for forming coordinated checkpoints of multithreaded object-oriented processes to minimize the number of threads and objects that need to be rolled back [40]. A runtime component keeps track of thread-object dependencies, and the dependency information is scanned during recovery to select the set of threads and objects that must be rolled back. Because the scheme rolls back to a consistent set of checkpoints, it does not suffer from the problem of other processes' dependence upon the state of a rolled-back process. Its thread-object dependency graph, however, must be for the entire system, and modifying this centralized data structure upon every object invocation is certain to degrade performance.

Damani, Tarafdar, and Garg investigate issues in applying optimistic message logging to multithreaded distributed systems [41]. Their main contribution is the distinction between a failure unit and a recovery unit: failures are detected on the level of processes, but recovery is confined to individual threads. The scheme prevents what they call the "false causality problem." False causality arises when a process is rolled back as a whole even though only one thread in the process may have been dependent upon an orphan state in a failed process.

To account for the nondeterministic state changes brought about by multithreading, the authors of [41] created an abstract thread for each shared variable. Access to a shared variable is modeled as a message sent to the variable's artificial thread. Tracking of the order in which the artificial threads receive messages is equivalent to the tracking of the order in which state changes are applied to the shared variables, and the tracking can be done using traditional message-logging techniques. That approach, however, greatly increases the number of messages and threads in the system, especially for programs with a significant amount of data shared among threads. Consequently, algorithms whose time and space complexities depend upon the number of messages and threads (such as message log garbage collection or recovery) do not scale well.

### 9.10.1 Dealing with Nondeterminism

Slye and Elnozahy suggest that software interrupts can be used as the basis for tracking nondeterministic thread scheduling [42]. Their approach relies on a user-level threads library using software interrupts (such as Unix signals) to trigger the switch to another thread. They use instruction counters to record the number of instruction(s) between the interrupt events, and this log can be used to ensure that the interrupts occur in the same relative places within the instruction stream during recovery. The approach works only for uniprocessor computers, and it requires that two versions of the code exist: one instrumented for the normal operation that emulates the instruction counter in software and one instrumented for replay in which the execution can be interrupted so that logged interrupts can be applied. Because two versions of the code exist, the technique cannot tolerate more than one failure throughout the lifetime of the application (because the replay-instrumented version will be run after the first failure, and this version does not have the ability to log the interrupts).

Goldberg suggests adding support to the Mach operating system to track the order in which threads access synchronization objects such as mutual exclusion locks and semaphores [43]. Assuming that all accesses to shared data are protected through a mutual exclusion lock, the approach is equivalent to tracking the order in which threads access the data. The paper is not clear, however, on exactly how the logs are used to force a certain ordering during replay, or the overhead involved with such an approach. To track thread accesses to synchronization objects and enforce the same ordering during replay, Goldberg implicitly assumes that the replayed threads will be given the same identification numbers by the operating system. However, that cannot be guaranteed unless the threads are created in the same order, and Goldberg's only way to enforce an identical order during replay is through the access of synchronization objects. Since most applications do not view thread creation as an activity that must be synchronized, most applications do not acquire locks when creating new threads; thus, the ordering of thread creations during original execution is lost for replay purposes.

Dieter and Lumpp [44] present a user-level checkpointing library for multi-threaded programs that conform to the POSIX standard. The checkpointing library supports programs that access files sequentially and that use signals, but not those that randomly access files and communicate with other processes. A separate thread called the *checkpoint thread* is created with the explicit function of initiating a checkpoint. The checkpoint thread uses a signal to notify all the threads to synchronize and take a checkpoint. The library tracks all thread calls during program execution so that it will be possible to unlock and relock mutexes during a checkpoint to maintain program correctness. It also intercepts file open and close system calls to enable restoration of the state of an open file from the checkpoint.

This chapter has addressed some of the fundamental issues that relate to the design of checkpointing schemes. There are additional issues that impact the efficiency of checkpointing that we have not explicitly addressed. These refer to checkpointing frequency and its impact on availability as well as adaptive schemes. Methods to model the impact on checkpointing availability are also important and are addressed in the next chapter with an example of a large supercomputer system [45]. A newer important issue in present-day large systems is checkpointing in large data clusters and computing systems, particularly deep neural networks. These systems execute for extended periods of time during training and can experience failures due to software or hardware that call for the development of specialized checkpointing methods. Measurements on large-scale systems have shown that infrastructure failures are not uncommon (once every —six to seven days on NSF BlueWaters supercomputer and a comparable number on other large systems). ChecFreq [46] is a recent scheme that provides a balance between fine-grained checkpoint frequency and low overall performance overhead for DNN training. The system is integrated into PyTorch as a pluggable module.

# References

1 Hunt, D.B. and Marinos, P.N. (1987). A general-purpose cache-aided rollback error recovery technique. *Proceedings of the 17th Symposium on Fault-Tolerant Computing*, 170–175. Los Alamitos, CA: IEEE CS Press.

2 Bernstein, P.A. (1988). Sequoia: a fault-tolerant tightly coupled multiprocessor for transaction processing. *Computer* 21 (2): 37–45.

3 Teodorescu, R., Nakano, J., and Torrellas, J. (2006). SWICH: a prototype for efficient cache-level checkpointing and rollback. *IEEE Micro* 26 (5): 28–40. https://doi.org/10.1109/MM.2006.100.

4 Ahmed, R., Frazier, R., and Marinos, P. (1990). CARER: cache-aided rollback error recovery algorithm for shared-memory multiprocessors. *Proceedings of the 20th Annual International Symposium on Fault-Tolerant Computing*, Newcastle Upon Tyne, UK (26–28 June1990), 82–88.

5 Wu, K.-L., Fuchs, W., and Patel, J. (1990). Error recovery in shared memory multiprocessors using private caches. *IEEE Transactions on Parallel and Distributed Systems* 1 (2): 231–240.

**6** Prvulovic, M., Zhang, Z., and Torrellas, J. (2002). ReVive: cost-effective architectural support for rollback recovery in shared-memory multiprocessors. *Proceedings of the 29th Annual International Symposium on Computer Architecture* (25–29 May 2002), Anchorage, Alaska.

**7** Silberschatz, A., Korth, H.F., and Sudarshan, S. (1999). *Database System Concepts*, 3rde. McGraw-Hill.

**8** Banatre, M. and Joubert, P. (1990). Cache management in a tightly coupled fault-tolerant multiprocessor. *Proceedings 20th Symposium Fault-Tolerant Computing*, 89–96. Los Alamitos, CA: IEEE CS Press, Order No. 2051.

**9** Staknis, M.E. (1989). Sheaved memory: architectural support for state saving and restoration in paged systems. *Proceedings Third International Conference Architectural Support for Programming Languages and Operating Systems*, 96–102. New York: ACM.

**10** Reuter, A. (1980). A fast transaction-oriented logging scheme for undo recovery. *IEEE Transactions on Software Engineering* SE-6: 348–356.9.

**11** Thatte, S.M. (1986). Persistent memory: a storage architecture for object-oriented database systems. *Proceedings 1986 Int'l Workshop Object-Oriented Database Systems*, 148–159. Los Alamitos, CA: IEEE CS Press, Order No. 734 (microfiche only).

**12** Wu, K.L. and Fuchs, W.K. (1990). Recoverable distributed shared virtual memory. *IEEE Transactions on Computers* 39: 460–469.

**13** Plank, J., Beck, M., Kingsley, G., and Li, K. (1995). Libckpt: transparent checkpointing under unix. *Proceedings of USENIX*, New Orleans, LA, USA (16–20 January 1995).

**14** Srinivasan, S.M., Kandula, S., Andrews, C.R., and Zhou, Y. (2004). Flashback: a lightweight extension for rollback and deterministic replay for software debugging. *USENIX Annual Technical Conference, General Track*, Boston, MA, USA (27 June–2 July 2004), 29–44.

**15** Wang, L., Kalbarczyk, Z., Gu, W., and Iyer, R.K. (2007). Reliability MicroKernel: providing application-aware reliability in the OS. *IEEE Transactions on Reliability* 56 (4): 597–614.

**16** Li, C.-C.J. and Fuchs, W.K. (1995). CATCH - Compiler-Assisted Techniques for Checkpointing. *Twenty-Fifth International Symposium on Fault-Tolerant Computing, 1995, 'Highlights from Twenty-Five Years'* (27–30 June 1995), 213–220.

**17** Beck, M., Plank, J.S., and Kingsley, G. (1994). Compiler-assisted checkpointing. Technical Report UT-CS-94-269. Department of Computer Science, University of Tennessee.

**18** Singhal, M. and Shivaratri, N. (1994). *Advanced Concepts in Operating Systems*. New York: McGraw-Hill.

**19** Chandy, K.M. and Lamport, L. (1985). Distributed snapshots: determining global states of distributed systems. *ACM Transactions on Computer Systems* 3 (1): 63–75.

**20** Koo, R. and Toueg, S. (1987). Checkpointing and rollback-recovery for distributed systems. *IEEE Transactions on Software Engineering* 13 (1): 23–31.

**21** Neves, N. and Fuchs, W. (1998). Coordinated checkpointing without direct coordination. *Proceedings of IEEE International Computer Performance and Dependability Symposium*, Durham, NC, USA (7–9 September 1998), 23–31.

**22** Huang, Y. and Kintala, C. (1993). Software implemented fault tolerance: technologies and experience. *Proceedings of the 23rd Annual International Symposium on Fault-Tolerant Computing*, Toulouse, France (22–24 June 1993), 2–9.

**23** Johnson, D.B. and Zwaenepoel, W. (1987). Sender-based message logging. *Digest of Papers: 17th Annual International Symposium on Fault-Tolerant Computing*, Pittsburgh, PA, USA (6–8 July 1987), 14–19. IEEE Computer Society.

**24** Pandit, N. and Alexander, A. (2008). Implementation of sender based message logging. UIUC, ECE 542 Class Project Report.

**25** R. K. Iyer (2007). TRUSTED ILLIAC: a configurable hardware framework for a trusted computing base. *Proceedings of the 10th IEEE High Assurance Systems Engineering Symposium, 2007. HASE '07* (14–16 November 2007), 3-3.

**26** Strom, R. and Yemini, S. (1985). Optimistic recovery in distributed systems. *ACM Transactions on Computer Systems* 3 (3): 204–226.

**27** Damani, O. and Garg, V. (1996). How to recover efficiently and asynchronously when optimism fails. *Proceedings of the International Conference on Distributed Computing Systems*, Hong Kong (27–30 May 1996), 108–115.

**28** Alvisi, L., Hoppe, B., and Marzullo, K. (1993). Nonblocking and orphan-free message logging protocols. *Proceedings of the 23rd Annual Symposium on Fault-Tolerant Computing*, Toulouse, France (22–24 June 1993), 145–154.

**29** Elnozahy, E. and Zwaenepoel, W. (1992). Manetho: transparent rollback-recovery with low overhead, limited rollback, and fast output commit. *IEEE Transactions on Computers* 41 (5): 526–531.

**30** Vaidya, N. (1997). Impact of checkpoint latency on overhead ratio of a checkpointing scheme. *IEEE Transactions on Computers* 46 (8): 942–947.

**31** Vaidya, N.H. (1995). On checkpoint latency. Technical Report 95-015, Computer Science Department, Texas A&M University, College Station. *Presented in part at Pacific Rim Int'l Conf.* Fault-Tolerant Systems, Newport Beach, CA.

**32** Sullivan, M. (1993). System support for software fault tolerance in highly available database management systems. Technical Report ERL-93-5. Berkeley, CA: University of California.

**33** Bohannon, P., Rastogi, R., Seshadri, S. et al. (2003). Detection and recovery techniques for database corruption. *IEEE Transactions on Knowledge and Data Engineering* 15 (5): 1120–1136.

**34** Wang, L., Kalbarczyk, Z., and Iyer, R.K. (2004). Checkpointing of control structures in main memory database systems. *Proceedings Int'l Conf. Dependable*

*Systems and Networks (DSN 04)*, Florence, Italy (28 June–1 July 2004), 687–692. IEEE CS Press.

**35** Kalbarczyk, Z., Iyer, R., Bagchi, S., and Whisnant, K. (1999). Chameleon: a software infrastructure for adaptive fault tolerance. *IEEE Transactions on Parallel and Distributed Systems* 10 (6): 560–579.

**36** Whisnant, K., Iyer, R., Jones, P. et al. (2002). An experimental evaluation of the REE SIFT environment for spaceborne applications. *Proceedings International Conference on Dependable Systems and Networks (DSN)*, Bethesda, MA (23–26 June 2002), 585–594.

**37** Whisnant, K., Kalbarczyk, Z., and Iyer, R. (2003). A system model for dynamically reconfigurable software. *IBM Systems Journal* 42 (1): 45–59.

**38** Whisnant, K., Iyer, R., Kalbarczyk, Z. et al. (2004). The Effects of an ARMOR-based SIFT environment on the performance and dependability of user applications. *IEEE Transactions on Software Engineering* 30 (4): 257–277.

**39** Son, S.H. and Agrawala, A.K. (1989). Distributed checkpointing for globally consistent states of databases. *IEEE Transactions on Software Engineering* 15 (10): 1157–1167.

**40** Kasbekar, M., Narayanan, C., and Das, C. (1999). Selective checkpointing and rollbacks in multithreaded object-oriented environment. *IEEE Transactions on Reliability* 48 (4): 325–337.

**41** Damani, O., Tarafdar, A., and Garg, V. (1999). Optimistic recovery in multithreaded distributed systems. *Proceedings of the 18th Symposium on Reliable and Distributed Systems*, Lausanne, Switzerland (19–22 October 1999), 234–243.

**42** Slye, J. and Elnozahy, E. (1998). Support for software interrupts in log-based rollback-recovery. *IEEE Transactions on Computers* 47 (10): 1113–1123.

**43** Goldberg, A., Gopal, A., Li, K. et al. (1990). Transparent recovery of Mach applications. *Proceedings of the First USENIX Mach Workshop*, Burlington, VT, USA (4–5 October 1990), 169–183.

**44** Dieter, W. and Lumpp, Jr., J. (1999). A user-level checkpointing library for POSIX threads programs. *Proceedings of the 29th Annual International Symposium on Fault-Tolerant Computing*, Madison, WI, USA (15–18 June 1999), 224–227.

**45** Bauer, G.H., Bode, B., Enos, J. et al. (2018). Best practices and lessons from deploying and operating a sustained-petascale system: the blue waters experience. *SC18: International Conference for High Performance Computing, Networking, Storage and Analysis*, Dallas, TX, USA (11–16 November 2018), 673–684. doi: https://doi.org/10.1109/SC.2018.00056.

**46** Mohan, J., Phanishayee, A., and Chidambaram, V. (2021). CheckFreq: frequent, fine-grained DNN checkpointing. *Proceedings of the USENIX Conference on File and Storage Technologies (FAST 2021)* (23–25 February 2021). https://par.nsf.gov/biblio/10286595. Virtual Event.

# 10

# Checkpointing Large-Scale Systems

## 10.1  Introduction

This chapter focuses on checkpointing of high-performance scientific applications running on large-scale supercomputers, in which the number of processors is on the order of a hundred thousand. Although much work has been done in checkpointing for distributed applications, the high-performance parallel-computing community has not studied this problem in detail. While some tools for automated checkpointing were developed by CRAY for supercomputing applications based on synchronous checkpointing, such tools were of limited use due to their high custom design of the checkpointing/recovery support. Additionally, the diverse nature of the MPI support, network and storage support also makes it challenging to maintain and upgrade the checkpointing and recovery tools. Hence, the availability of transparent tools for challenging emerging applications is few and far between. However, that is changing with the advent of large-scale parallel machines. In these machines, it is not uncommon to have a processor fail every few hours, which is much shorter than the running time of many computational science applications. Here, application-level support for checkpointing with no modifications or OS-level hooks is much more the state of practice. The focus is on checkpointing generally multi-threaded applications and the goal is to ensure, to the extent possible, the checkpointing software is independent of the OS/MPI and other system facilities. The emergence of new hardware, which necessitates adapting the applications to new architectures will correspondingly require redesigning aspects of the checkpointing and recovery software and algorithms.

In the following subsection, we present an overview of various checkpointing techniques used in large-scale systems. Next, we discuss some of the existing

*Dependable Computing: Design and Assessment*, First Edition. Ravishankar K. Iyer, Zbigniew T. Kalbarczyk, and Nithin M. Nakka.
© 2024 The IEEE Computer Society. Published 2024 by John Wiley & Sons, Inc.
Companion website: www.wiley.com/go/iyer/dependablecomputing1

systems that employ these techniques and the lessons that can be learned from them. Finally, we present a testbed for studying the scalability and performance of the checkpointing schemes studied here for a large-scale system.

## 10.2 Checkpointing Techniques

Checkpointing techniques for large-scale systems are different from those used in regular clusters and supercomputers. Generally, there are three primary phases in the checkpointing of a parallel application running on a supercomputer. First, all the processes need to be coordinated so that they can take a consistent checkpoint. Next, the state of each process needs to be written to the I/O system, often over a shared network. Finally, the state needs to be restored from the last changed checkpoint if there is an error. Each of those phases incurs some overhead, which increases with the number of processors in the system. Hence, for a large-scale supercomputer, the overheads can be substantial, and specific techniques for reducing the overhead of each phase are essential. Such techniques are explored in the following sections.

### 10.2.1 Checkpoint Coordination Techniques

Checkpointing techniques can be broadly classified into *coordinated* (synchronous) and *uncoordinated* (asynchronous) checkpointing. In uncoordinated checkpointing, each processor takes a checkpoint at any time independent of the other processors. Although that approach has very little overhead, it may result in exponential rollback during restart. That problem can be solved by logging messages and playing them back to the failed process during restart. However, that is not a feasible solution for high-performance scientific applications because of the high overhead and the amount of storage required to store messages. Therefore, uncoordinated checkpointing is not a viable option in that setting.

Coordinated checkpointing techniques work by quiescing all processors and synchronizing them before a checkpoint is taken. They do so in two phases. A master processor first sends a *quiesce* signal to all processors. On receiving the signal, each processor stops its current computation, closes all open network connections, and suspends any I/O operations that are underway. It then sends a "ready" signal back to the master processor. When the master processor has received all the "ready" signals, it sends a "checkpoint now" signal that effectively causes all the processors to dump their states. That protocol has the effect of implementing a barrier across all the processors in the system.

The main problem with coordinated checkpointing is that the quiesce signal may not reach all processors simultaneously. Hence, different processors may be stopped at different points in their computation when they receive the quiesce signal. As a result, the process states across all the processors in the checkpoint may not be consistent. Consider, for example, the case in which processor $i$ sends a message to processor $j$ at the time of the checkpoint. Suppose the quiesce signal reaches processor $j$ before it reaches processor $i$. By the time processor $i$ sends the message, processor $j$ is already quiesced and cannot accept the message. But processor $i$ assumes that it has sent the message to processor $j$ and does not resend it when the system is restarted from the checkpoint. That leads to an inconsistency in the checkpoint.

One way to solve the problem is to modify the communication protocol to require acknowledgments for messages. If that is done, a message is considered sent only if the acknowledgment for the message has been received by the sending processor. In this example, processor $j$ did not send back the acknowledgment for the message received from processor $i$. Hence, processor $i$ considers the message unsent and will resend it when the application is started from the checkpoint, as illustrated in Figure 10.1. Many implementations of the Message Passing Interface (MPI) and other message-passing protocols already use acknowledgments for messages.

The coordinated checkpointing techniques discussed so far are *blocking*, meaning that all processors are brought to a standstill while the checkpoint is being taken. That incurs a high overhead and wastes computational resources. It is

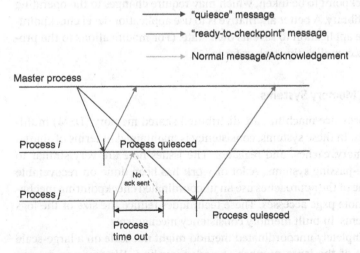

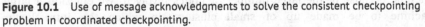

**Figure 10.1** Use of message acknowledgments to solve the consistent checkpointing problem in coordinated checkpointing.

possible to take a consistent checkpoint without stopping all the processors. The main problem in uncoordinated checkpointing is that messages can be *in-flight*, i.e. in transit, while a checkpoint is being taken. The problem occurs when the sending process dumps its state after sending the message, but the receiving process dumps its state before receiving the message. The result is that the message is lost at the receiving process when the system is restarted from the checkpoint. Another problem is early messages, in which a processor sends a message after dumping its state to a processor that has yet to dump its state. That would result in the message being counted at the receiving processor as part of the checkpoint, which is inconsistent with the global view of the system.

The Chandy–Lamport [1] protocol is the most widely deployed uncoordinated checkpointing protocol. It uses the notion of logical clocks at each processor, which corresponds to the processor's view of the highest-sequence-number message it has received so far. The assumptions are that messages are assigned local sequence numbers at each processor and that the message channels have FIFO delivery. The Chandy–Lamport protocol uses global tokens to solve the problems of early and in-flight messages. A single master process initiates the global checkpoint by saving its local state and sending markers on all its outgoing edges. The other processors, on receiving the token, first dump their state and send the token on all their outgoing edges. If the token has been seen by a processor already, it merely ignores it and does not forward it. That can be ensured by keeping track of the highest-sequence-number message sent so far by every other processor at this processor and discarding the message if it has been seen already.

The main disadvantage of the Chandy–Lamport protocol is that it requires a system-level checkpoint to be taken, which may require changes to the operating system and MPI library. A better alternative is to use application-level checkpointing and allow the application to save its own state. (For modifications to the protocol needed to accomplish this task, refer to [1].)

### 10.2.2 Shared Memory Systems

Many high-performance machines are distributed shared memory (DSM) multiprocessor systems. In these systems, consistency is maintained in terms of shared objects, like memory, caches, and registers. The issues here are very similar to those of message-passing systems. A lot of work has been done on recoverable DSMs [2–5]. Some of the approaches use an uncoordinated checkpointing mechanism and log remote page accesses. These techniques reduce the size of the logs by using the systems' in-built memory consistency mechanisms.

However, a completely uncoordinated method might not scale on a large-scale machine because of the large number of nodes involved. We envision a large machine to be made up of small clusters, in which the intra-cluster communication follows a shared memory model and the inter-cluster communication is through message passing. In such a system, intra-cluster checkpointing can be done in an uncoordinated fashion, in which each node takes periodic checkpoints independent of the other nodes in its clusters. However, the checkpointing periods of all the nodes in a cluster can be chosen to be very similar, so that the logging of dependencies is minimized. The inter-cluster checkpointing can follow a synchronized checkpoint approach.

### 10.2.3 I/O Techniques

The performance of any checkpoint/restart mechanism relies heavily on the I/O performance of the system. If there are many nodes, the demands on the I/O system can be much greater. I/O becomes an especially severe bottleneck in a synchronous checkpoint approach, wherein all the nodes decide to dump their memory image at the same time. In an asynchronous approach, the effect is not as pronounced because of the inherent staggering of checkpoints across the nodes. We can illustrate that phenomenon by evaluating a checkpoint scenario for the IBM Blue Gene supercomputer (BG/L). For a worst-case analysis, let us assume that all 64K nodes on the BG/L machine dump their complete memory images onto the disk at each checkpoint. The amount of storage required for a checkpoint is $64K \times 256$ MB, which is on the order of terabytes. Assuming that the connection to the external world is on the order of GB/s, it can take a few minutes to checkpoint the whole machine. Since the MTBF (mean time between failures) of the machine is on the order of hours, that constitutes a significant overhead for the checkpointing mechanism. Thus there is a need for a scalable I/O solution for checkpointing in terms of both the amount of data saved and the time taken to the checkpoint.

The I/O scalability can be partly addressed by having parallel file systems. Several parallel file systems are available for supercomputers and clusters, such as GPFS (the General Parallel File System), PVFS (the Parallel Virtual File System), and Lustre. They deal with the I/O bottleneck by allowing parallel applications to access files simultaneously. However, there are more processors writing to storage than disks in the storage system, which can lead to buffer overflows and throttle the I/O system, further degrading performance. One can avoid that problem by using a *staggering* approach, in which the compute nodes dump the checkpoint data onto some intermediate spare nodes, which act as proxies for performing the I/O. The proxies then write to the disk one at a time, thereby reducing the contention for the network and I/O resource. A possible configuration of such a system is illustrated in Figure 10.2. There is an *I/O Proxy* or *Checkpoint Server* for a set of $N$ compute nodes. Each node dumps its checkpoint image onto its assigned proxy. The proxies $P_1$ to $P_M$ then use a staggering approach to write out the data onto the

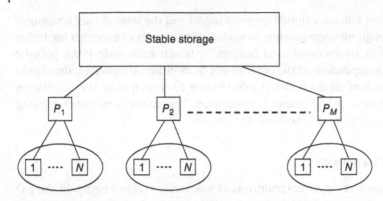

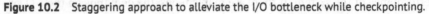

**Figure 10.2** Staggering approach to alleviate the I/O bottleneck while checkpointing.

stable storage. The size of each cluster (*N*) can be determined by a systematic study of the scalability of the I/O subsystem. Different staggering heuristics can be applied for optimal performance.

Another way of dealing with the I/O bottleneck is to reduce the amount of data written at each checkpoint. In a naive checkpointing approach, the complete memory state of each processor is dumped onto the disk. That leads to huge file sizes at each checkpoint and hence is not a scalable approach in a large-scale environment. Most scientific parallel applications have a very structured memory access pattern, and that property can be exploited to determine the necessary state to be dumped at each checkpoint. That approach has been adopted by incremental techniques, such that only the state changed from the previous checkpoint is dumped to the disk. It has been observed that a lot of savings in terms of file size can be obtained by using incremental techniques.

Incremental techniques can be broadly classified into *page-based techniques*, which track changes to memory at the granularity of pages, and *probabilistic techniques*, which track changes to memory at the granularity of variable-sized blocks. The main difference between a page-based approach and a probabilistic approach is that in a probabilistic approach, the memory changes are detected using hash functions rather than the hardware mechanisms used in the page-based approach. As a result, probabilistic approaches have the flexibility to use "variable-size" blocks and hence narrow down to the *near-exact* changed bytes. The effectiveness of the probabilistic approach depends to a great extent on the choice of the hash functions, as suitable hash functions (like MD5 and SHA-2) should be chosen to minimize the probability of aliasing. That has been explored in the context of IBM's Blue Gene supercomputer, and substantial savings in terms of the amount of state and the time taken to checkpoint have been obtained [6]. The checkpoint frequency is another important design parameter that must be considered. An optimum checkpoint interval can be obtained based on the system parameters and the behavior of the application. The performance gains obtained by incremental checkpoints also depend on how frequently the checkpoints are taken.

### 10.2.4 Recovery Techniques

Rollback recovery is triggered by the failure of components in a system. Depending upon whether system-wide checkpointing or application checkpointing is being used, either the entire system or the particular application affected by the failure is rolled back to the previous valid checkpoint state. Some of the issues related to rollback recovery are the following:

- The failed component must be removed from the routing table, and the routing table should be updated before rollback can begin. In short, the component availability map must be consistent throughout the system.
- All processors, memory units, and other routing hardware need to be reset before the rollback can take place. The service processor needs to selectively detect the components that need to be reset if application checkpointing is being used. Otherwise, all hardware can be reset.
- If the checkpoint is not present in stable storage, then it must be fetched from the disk, incurring the corresponding overhead.
- Threads must be migrated, and load balancing must be done to circumvent the failure. Sometimes it is better to remap an entire application and move it to another module rather than just remap a single failed thread to a different module.
- Once process states have been restored, all socket connections that were open at the time of checkpointing must be reestablished. File handles can be treated as socket connections. File pointers are restored after the file handle has been reestablished.
- If application checkpointing is done, it must be ensured that the locks and semaphores held by the threads of that application during checkpointing are restored to that application. Sometimes the thread handles and IDs cannot be restored to the initial state. Programmers must therefore make their code independent of the thread IDs.
- Assuming that all network transactions and window messages between successive checkpoints have been logged, the runtime environment (RTE) must ensure the replay of these logged messages at appropriate instances.
- If incremental checkpointing is used, the RTE must merge all the checkpoints to obtain a globally consistent state before the processes can be rolled back. Even before the need to roll back arises, it can do so by stealing cycles from the

I/O module for this purpose and coalescing the checkpoints during normal operation.

- All these mentioned issues should be aggressively fault-tolerant because the probability of a fault during rollback for a very large-scale system is not negligible.

Figure 10.3 shows the main steps in recovering from various types of failures. We consider four different failure modes of the system, namely (i) processor failure, (ii) I/O node failure, (iii) memory failure, and (iv) service processor failure. Keeping all these issues in mind, the overhead for rollback can be split into four parts:

1) *Initialization overhead:* This includes the time to update availability maps and routing tables, reset all associated hardware, fetch checkpoints from disk if necessary, and merge checkpoints (if incremental checkpointing is being done).
2) *Memory remap overhead:* This includes the time to remap memory and thread states so that the failed processes can be reinitialized elsewhere.
3) *I/O overhead:* This is the time to move the checkpoint from stable storage and set up the states in the memory and processors.
4) *Ramp-up overhead*: This is the time required to reestablish all socket network connections and file handles.

### 10.2.4.1 Use of Spares

One way to reduce the overhead of recovery is to designate some nodes in the supercomputer as standby nodes and move the computation to these nodes when a node fails. That would be a departure from the standard practice in high-performance computing of using all possible computational resources to increase performance, and it would involve designating some proportion of the resources specifically for rollback recovery. This technique is motivated by the following observations. First, there is a limit to the amount of speedup that can be obtained for an application by adding more nodes to the system. The reason is Amdahl's law, which states that the speedup of a parallel application is limited by its serial portion. Second, and more importantly, constant failures and consequent rollback to a previous checkpoint can severely degrade performance, as they do not constitute useful work for the application.

The question is what proportion of nodes in the system should be designated as spare nodes. Elnozahy et al. [7] have shown that the answer is dependent on a lot of factors, including the checkpoint interval and checkpoint latency, recovery time, the scalability of the application, and the mean time to failure (MTTF) and mean time to repair (MTTR) of the system. The assumption is that the system goes into a down phase when there are no spare nodes to take over the

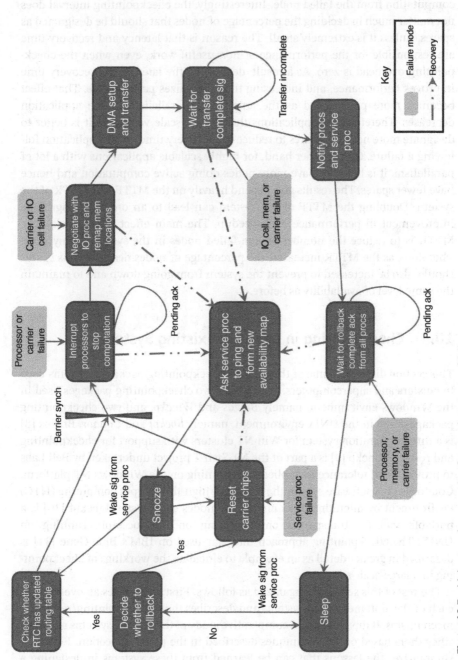

**Figure 10.3** Main steps in recovering from various types of failures.

computation from the failed node. Interestingly, the checkpointing interval does not matter much in deciding the percentage of nodes that should be designated as spares, unless it is extremely small. The reason is that latency and recovery time are responsible for the performance of non-useful work, even when the check-pointing overhead is zero. As a result, decreasing the latency and recovery time improves performance, and increasing them penalizes performance. That effect becomes more pronounced as the amount of parallelism in the application decreases. Therefore, for applications that do not scale very well, it is better to designate more nodes as spares to reduce the recovery time of the application following a failure. On the other hand, for highly scalable applications with a lot of parallelism, it is better to have more nodes doing active computation and hence have fewer spares. The results also depend heavily on the MTTF and MTTR of the system. Doubling the MTTF of the system can lead to an order of magnitude improvement in performance and speedup. The main effect of increasing the MTTR is to reduce the number of non-failed nodes in the system at any time. Therefore, as the MTTR increases, the percentage of nodes designated as spares should also be increased to prevent the system from going down and to maintain the same level of availability as before.

## 10.3 Checkpointing in Selected Existing Systems

This section discusses some of the existing checkpointing packages/systems used in clusters and supercomputers. We discuss two checkpointing packages used in the Windows environment, namely *Brazos* and *Winckp*, and two checkpointing packages used in the UNIX environment, namely *libckpt* and *Condor*. Brazos [8] is a thread-migration system for Win-NT clusters with support for checkpointing and restart. Winckp [9] is a part of the NT-SwiFT project undertaken by Bell Labs to provide fault tolerance to applications running on the Windows NT platform. Condor [2] is a software system that creates a high-throughput computing (HTC) environment by migrating tasks among the nodes of a cluster. Libckpt [10] is a portable tool for transparent checkpointing on uniprocessors running on UNIX. The checkpointing approach that was used on IBM's Blue Gene [11] is described in greater detail as an example to elucidate the workings of checkpointing in a large-scale system.

The rest of this section is organized as follows. First, it provides an overview of each of the aforementioned systems and describes their checkpointing/restarting mechanisms. It then presents a comparative study of the various systems and classifies them based on the techniques described in the previous section. Finally, it summarizes the lessons that can be learned from these systems in designing a checkpointing facility for a large-scale supercomputer.

## 10.3.1 Blue Gene

An incremental checkpoint algorithm was proposed for the Blue Gene/L machine [11]. It is a software-only approach that attempts to dynamically identify *near-exact*[1] changed blocks of memory so that only minimal data are stored on the disk. Initially, the application memory is split into blocks of equal sizes. Based on the past access patterns of the application, the memory partitioning is refined at every checkpoint. Through the partitioning scheme, the size of each changed block is reduced to be nearly equal to the actual amount changed, and the size of the unchanged blocks is increased. If that process is followed for several consecutive checkpoints, it is expected that the block sizes will then be as close as possible to the sizes of the changed portions of the page. That will reduce the size of the checkpoint (which is the size of the changed blocks) that needs to be stored on the disk.

Page-protection-based checkpointing mechanisms may not be feasible in large supercomputing systems such as the Blue Gene/L because of a lack of page-fault exception handlers. Because of the coarse granularity at the page level, the size of the checkpoint can be much larger than that of the modified sections. However, changing the page size either statically or dynamically is infeasible due to performance overheads and the need for kernel recompilation. That issue motivated the hash-based incremental checkpointing technique described in this section.

The hash-based incremental application-level checkpoint approach presented in [11] is user-initiated, while the restart is transparent. It is based on the hash-based checkpoint as proposed in Nam et al. [12]. Two questions need to be addressed to successfully implement even a hash-based checkpointing scheme:

1) What should be the appropriate block size?
2) Can there be a uniform block size for all applications?

As we noted from the experience of the coarse granularity of a page, one may conclude that the smaller the block size, the greater the reduction in the checkpoint size. However, one should bear in mind that decreasing the block size also increases the number of blocks and hence the overhead in storing into and looking up the hash table. It was seen in [11] that the memory access patterns changed dramatically within the execution of a single application. That calls for a dynamically adaptive technique that can use blocks of variable lengths depending on the memory access patterns of the application. The algorithm presented in [11] is depicted in Figure 10.4.

---

1 By "near-exact," we mean a block as close in size as possible to (although it is usually greater than) the exact number of changed bytes, limited by the adaptability of the algorithm on a particular dataset.

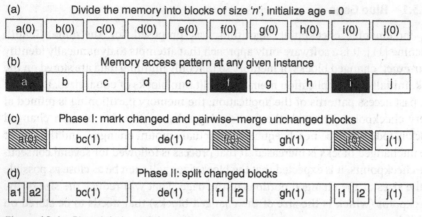

**Figure 10.4** Pictorial view of the split-merge algorithm (a) memory divided in blocks of size n (b) memory access pattern at a given instance (c) Phase I: Mark changed and Pairwise-Merge unchanged blocks (d) Phase II: Split changed blocks [11] / with permission of IEEE.

*Algorithm.* Each memory block is associated with a parameter called *age*, which defines the number of unchanged consecutive times. As shown in Figure 10.4a, the age of each block is initialized to zero. Through tracking of the age, blocks that have been unchanged the same number of times (or have the same age) can be identified and merged. If the principle of locality of reference is exploited, it is expected that such blocks will remain unchanged in the future or will change together.

The algorithm is based on the original hash-based algorithm in Nam et al. [12]. As in Nam et al.'s technique, the change in a block is identified through a comparison of the hash values at the previous and current checkpoints (see Figure 10.4b). If there is a difference, the block is changed (shaded black in the figure) and copied to the checkpoint file. Otherwise, the block is unchanged (no shading in the figure), and the age of the block is incremented.

Two consecutive blocks with the same age are merged to increase the size of unmodified blocks, as shown in Figure 10.4c. Each changed block is split into two blocks, in an attempt to decrease the size of the changed blocks that need to be copied to the incremental checkpoint file (as shown in Figure 10.4d). The reason is that it is expected that the half-block that was previously modified will also be modified in the future, thus enabling the exclusion of the other half-block from the checkpoint. For each block that is split, the age is reset to 0. The hope is that by such repeated splits and merges at every checkpoint, the block layout structure will stabilize to a state in which the size of the changed blocks is as small as possible, and the size of the unchanged blocks is as large as possible.

*Restarting the Application.* The incremental checkpoints are regularly merged, either manually or by a periodically triggered process, to generate a non-incremental checkpoint file representing a more recent state of the application. This checkpoint file is used for recovery if an error is detected. In the merge procedure, the final non-incremental checkpoint file is initialized to be empty. Then the incremental checkpoint files are scanned in reverse order of their creation times, and all blocks that have not been copied to the final merged file are copied to it. That guarantees that only the latest versions of all the blocks are written to the checkpoint file. After all the incremental checkpoint files and the initial non-incremental checkpoint have been merged, we obtain the checkpoint file for the application.

## 10.3.2 Brazos

The Brazos parallel programming environment is used on clusters of processors running Windows NT. In addition to providing programmers with the abstraction of running on a single shared-memory multiprocessor, Brazos supports message passing by implementing the MPI library. The work extends the use of thread migration to fault tolerance and cluster management. Migration is used to tolerate shutdowns due to scheduled maintenance or power loss by dynamically moving all computation threads and necessary data of the application to another available node without restarting the application. Problems in the context of stack pointers during thread migration are overcome by imposing the restriction that the desti-nation thread's stack must be located at the same virtual address as the source thread's stack. There are mechanisms for mapping the actual file handles before migration to the handles created at the new node. Those mechanisms require that all nodes have access to a common file system. File contents are not migrated; however, users have the option of flushing output file buffers prior to migration. Barrier synchronization is done before migration. During checkpointing, all states required for thread migration are saved, and upon rollback, these threads are migrated to a new node. Brazos synchronization objects such as locks and barriers do not need to be saved because checkpoints are created only at barriers. Thus, synchronization objects can be reinitialized during recovery.

## 10.3.3 Winckp

The goals of Winckp are to transparently checkpoint and recover applications on Windows NT. Winckp is a part of the NT-SwiFT project undertaken by Bell Labs to provide fault tolerance to applications running on the Windows NT platform. To take a snapshot, Winckp suspends all threads and stores state information into files. During a rollback operation, all threads are suspended, and the state information is restored from files along with the thread contexts. If the application process has died, Winckp starts a new process, suspends the main thread, restores all state infor-mation, and then resumes all the threads. To take a checkpoint, Winckp injects a checkpointing thread into the target application. That thread is in charge of saving system-call-related information in stable storage and replaying the system calls during rollback or recovery. Winckp also saves an application's memory, including the data, heap, and stack. To recover a window handle, Winckp first starts a new process and lets the new process create all related windows. Then, it creates a mapping between the old window handle value and the new window handle value. It also logs events coming from the mouse and keyboard and replays them to the process at appropriate instances during a rollback recovery. Some limitations of this scheme include its (i) lack of checkpoints during system calls, (ii) requirement that applications be independent of the thread handle and thread ID, (iii) inability to recover synchronization objects, and (iv) playback nondeterminism.

### 10.3.4 Condor

Condor is a software system that creates an HTC environment for UNIX clusters. Condor can manage a dedicated cluster of workstations. Its power comes from its ability to effectively harness non-dedicated, preexisting resources under distributed ownership. Condor provides checkpointing services to single-process jobs on a number of UNIX platforms. The application must be recompiled after it is linked with the Condor system call library, so it is not a transparent checkpointing scheme. When Condor sends a checkpoint signal to a process linked with this library, the provided signal handler writes the state of the process out to a file or a network socket. On the restart, the process reads that state from the file, and thus restores the stack, shared library and data segments, file state, signal handlers, and pending signals. If service is interrupted while a checkpoint is being performed (causing that checkpoint to fail), the process will restart from the previous checkpoint. Nodes within a Condor pool can be configured as checkpoint servers that act as repositories for checkpoints, hence saving valuable time for reading and writing of checkpoints. Some limitations of this scheme include its (i) lack of support for multi-process jobs, (ii) inability to perform checkpointing during network communication or IPC, (iii) lack of support for multiple kernel-level threads, (iv) inability to use memory-mapped files, and (v) loss of file locks between checkpoints.

### 10.3.5 Libckpt

Libckpt is a portable tool for transparent checkpointing on uniprocessors running on UNIX. It implements incremental and copy-on-write checkpointing. Libckpt has been ported to and tested on a wide variety of architectures and operating systems with no kernel modifications. While libckpt can be used in a mode that is almost totally transparent to the programmer, it also supports the incorporation of user directives into the creation of checkpoints. When a checkpoint is taken, only the portion of the checkpoint that has changed since the previous checkpoint needs to be saved. The unchanged portion can be restored from previous checkpoints. To place an upper bound on the cumulative size of incremental checkpoint files, libckpt coalesces all old checkpoint files into one new file and then discards the old files. It uses page protection to identify the pages that should be included in incremental checkpoints. Libckpt also supports forked checkpointing, i.e. it forks a child process, which creates and writes the checkpoint file while the parent process returns to executing the application. It also allows the programmer to manage memory exclusion explicitly through two procedure calls. For I/O operations, libckpt determines the state of the open file table at each checkpoint and saves it as part of each checkpoint. Upon recovery, the system is restored so that the states of open files are the same as they were at the time of the checkpoint. No other system state is either saved or restored by libckpt, and that is a limitation. Another limitation is that applications should be independent of the thread ID.

## 10.3.6 Classification of Checkpointing Approaches in Existing Systems

Table 10.1 classifies the systems presented in this section based on the following criteria:

1) Checkpointing level (application/system)
2) Coordination technique used (coordinated/uncoordinated, blocking/non-blocking)

**Table 10.1** Classification of checkpointing approaches in existing systems.

| System | Checkpointing level | Coordination technique | State-saving technique | Recovery techniques |
|---|---|---|---|---|
| Brazos | Application-level | Global coordination with blocking | Non-incremental | Thread migration |
| Winckp | System-level | Uncoordinated with message logging | Non-incremental | Message playback |
| Condor | System-level | None | Non-incremental | Unspecified |
| Libckpt | System level with application hints | None | Incremental | Unspecified |
| Blue Gene | Application level | Coordinated blocking | Incremental | Memory remapping and restoration |

3) State-saving technique used (incremental/non-incremental)
4) Recovery technique used

Of the systems presented, *Blue Gene* and *Brazos* explicitly support multiple processes or threads and hence support coordinated checkpointing. The others, namely *Winckp*, *Condor*, and *libckpt*, have no support for coordinated checkpointing, and the application must ensure coordination before taking the checkpoint. Likewise, *libckpt* and *Blue Gene* support incremental checkpointing and copy-on-write, whereas the others save the full state of the process onto disk. The recovery techniques used differ from system to system. *Brazos* allows restarting the application on a different configuration from the original system, while *Winckp* requires the systems to be identical. *Condor* and *libckpt* allow for some heterogeneity between the system on which the job is checkpointed and the system on which the job is restarted. The question of heterogeneity is not addressed in Blue Gene, as it was developed specifically for parallel supercomputers that have homogeneous nodes.

A number of lessons can be learned from the design of these systems to guide the building of a new checkpointing system/facility:

- Incremental checkpointing can yield substantial performance benefits compared to saving the full state of the process during a checkpoint.
- The system should be restartable on a configuration different from the configuration on which the checkpoint was taken.
- The checkpointing should be transparent to the application, although it can benefit from application-specified hints.

### 10.3.7 Example of Evaluation of Checkpointing Schemes for a Large-Scale System

This section briefly presents the characterization of checkpointing for the Blue Gene system. The Blue Gene supercomputer used a user-initiated checkpoint scheme to achieve fault tolerance. Table 10.2 depicts the performance of Blue Gene on a few NAS Parallel Benchmarks (programs for performance evaluation of supercomputers) while employing a non-incremental checkpoint mechanism [13]. The results show the numbers for a small machine of 8 nodes [12] and another with 512 nodes [7].

An interesting point about this table is that the checkpoint time of the system decreases as the number of nodes increases because of the decrease in the application footprint per node and consequent decrease in the amount of checkpoint data to be written to the disk. However, the I/O performance also degrades a little because of the increase in the number of nodes concurrently writing to the disk. Another thing to note is that increasing the number of nodes increases the

**Table 10.2** Checkpoint characterization on Blue Gene.

| Benchmarks | Number of checkpoints | Time taken per checkpoint (s) (8 nodes) | Time taken per checkpoint (s) (512 nodes) |
|---|---|---|---|
| LU (Lower-Upper Gauss-Seidel solver) | 5 | 91 | 14 |
| BT (block Tri-diagonal solver) | 10 | 256 | 40 |
| SP (scalar Penta-diagonal solver) | 5 | 85 | 23 |
| FT (discrete 3D fast Fourier Transform, all-to-all communication) | 6 | 175 | 107 |

coordination overhead. The combination of those factors results in nonlinear speedup. Thus, the optimal number of nodes for the application is dependent on the characteristics of the application, the checkpoint latency (including both I/O and coordination overhead), and the MTBF of the system.

### 10.3.8 Determining Optimal Checkpointing Interval

Many analytical models for computing the optimal checkpointing interval have been proposed in the literature. In 1974, Young [14] proposed $\tau_{opt} = \sqrt{2\delta M}$ as the optimum checkpoint interval, where $\delta$ is the time taken for checkpointing, and $M$ is the MTTF of the system. That interval was derived using a first-order approximation and assuming that the MTTF of the system is much larger than the time taken to restart from a checkpoint and that a failure cannot occur during restarts. That assumption is no longer valid for large-scale systems, as the MTTF may be on the same order as the time taken to the checkpoint. Another assumption made in the original model was that failures are equally distributed in any computation interval. That assumption, too, is invalid in a large-scale system, as failures are more apt to occur toward the beginning of a compute interval than toward the end because of the low MTTF of the system. Finally, the old model assumes that there is at most one failure during a compute interval, which is not true for a large-scale system.

Daly [15] presents a modification of Young's model to consider these factors. Daly's model can effectively track the simulation results even for low values of the MTTF. The model predicts that for low values of MTTF (less than three to four hours), it may be better to restrict the computation to fewer nodes to avoid frequent failures, as the cost of restart outweighs the performance gains from scaling the application. Using this model, it is possible to derive an optimum value of $n$, the number of nodes for the computation, although Daly's paper does not do so.

The model does not consider the increase in coordination overhead as the number of nodes increases or the scalability limits of the application due to Amdahl's law. Factoring those in would enable us to better understand the trade-offs in choosing the optimal number of nodes for the computation.

## 10.4 Modeling-Coordinated Checkpointing for Large-Scale Supercomputers

This section presents a model of a coordinated checkpointing protocol for large-scale supercomputers and studies its scalability by considering both the coordination overhead and the effect of failures. Unlike most of the prior checkpointing models, the model takes into account failures during checkpointing and recovery, as well as correlated failures. Stochastic activity networks (SANs) [16] are used to model the system, and the model is simulated to study the system's scalability, reliability, and performance. The description in this section is based on the work presented in [17].

It is assumed that each node of the supercomputing system is a tightly integrated unit consisting of multiple processors. For example, Blue Gene/L had two processors per node, and ASCI Q had four processors per node. Usually, large-scale supercomputing systems have dedicated nodes for job computation (*compute nodes*) and I/O operations (*I/O nodes*). The compute nodes in a set share the connections to an I/O node, and all the I/O nodes are connected to a parallel file system through a separate connection network. For example, IBM BG/L had 64K compute nodes and 1024 I/O nodes. The network bandwidth from 64 compute nodes to one I/O node was 350 MB/s, and the bandwidth from one I/O node to the file system was 1 GB/s.

Data writes from compute nodes to the file system are performed in two steps: from compute nodes to I/O nodes, and then from I/O nodes to the file system. The I/O nodes locally buffer the application data or checkpoint they receive from the compute nodes and then write it to the file system in the background while the compute nodes continue with the computation. The two steps are reversed for data reads, with the exception that reads cannot be done in the background, as the application may have to wait for the data to be read before proceeding, depending on the nature of the read.

In the protocol described in this section, a single coordinator node, or *master*, periodically initiates the checkpointing as follows:

1) The master broadcasts a "quiesce" request to all the compute nodes.
2) On receiving a "quiesce" request, each node quiesces its operations, i.e. stops all its activities at a consistent and interruptible state and replies "ready" to the master.

3) After receiving "ready" replies from all the compute nodes, the master broadcasts a "checkpoint" request to all the compute nodes.
4) On receiving a "checkpoint" request, each compute node dumps its state to an I/O node and then sends a "done" message to the master.
5) When the master has collected "done" messages from all the compute nodes, it broadcasts "proceed" to all the compute nodes, and the I/O nodes begin to write the checkpoint to the file system in the background.
6) On receiving the "proceed" message, each compute node continues its activity from the point at which it quiesced.

When a node is *quiesced*, it stops all the task-related activities in a consistent and interruptible state. Further, a timeout period is specified at the master to avoid an indefinite wait for the "ready" responses. An indefinite wait can occur as a result of an erroneous or failed node that does not respond to the quiesce request. If all the responses are not received within the timeout period, the master times out and broadcasts an "abort" message to all the compute nodes, causing them to abandon the checkpointing and proceed with their computations.

Note that the current checkpoint does not overwrite the previous checkpoint unless the checkpointing successfully completes and the checkpoint is verified to be correct. Therefore, whenever the checkpointing is abandoned, the previous checkpoint is still valid. Hence, the system can always recover to the last good checkpoint upon a compute node failure.

## 10.4.1 Failure and Recovery

On the failure of a compute node, the entire application rolls back to the last saved checkpoint and recovers. While permanent/persistent errors are not considered, checkpointing can still be used to recover from permanent hardware failures. However, that would require system reconfiguration and remapping of the checkpointed states into a new set of nodes (assuming that spare nodes are available).

Failures of compute nodes and I/O nodes are always detected without any latency. The mechanism for failure detection is not modeled. When an I/O node fails, all the I/O nodes need to be restarted. Most parallel scientific applications are written assuming the bulk-synchronous parallel (BSP) model [18]. This assumption is reasonable since, in the BSP model, the application needs the I/O operations on all the I/O nodes to be completed before continuing the computation.

When the master node fails when checkpointing is not in progress, it is assumed that the error is detected, and the master recovers independently of the other nodes. If the master fails during checkpointing, the checkpointing protocol is aborted, and the master goes back to the initial state. As nodes have multiple processors, the node failure rate is the product of the processor failure rate and the number of processors per node. (The system parameter *MTTF* refers to the per-node mean time to failure throughout this section unless specified otherwise. The *per-processor MTTF* is MTTF times the number of processors per node.) It is assumed that advanced design and error-handling techniques, e.g. the use of multiple cores on a chip, are applied to maintain low node failure rates.

## 10.4.2  SAN-Based Modeling

The modeled system is decomposed into several subsystems. Each subsystem is modeled as a separate SAN submodel; the overall model is obtained by integrating the submodels. All compute nodes are modeled as a single unit, and all the I/O nodes are modeled as another unit. As a result, the model can scale to a large number of nodes without incurring large simulation times. Figure 10.5 illustrates how the submodels (the ovals in Figure 10.5) are integrated into an overall model. The arrows in the figure illustrate the logical interactions between the submodels. These interactions are implemented by state sharing between the submodels. The dots in the submodels in Figure 10.5 indicate the initial positions of the tokens in the corresponding SAN. It should be emphasized that Figure 10.5 is not a state diagram in that the ovals do not represent the states of the system at any particular

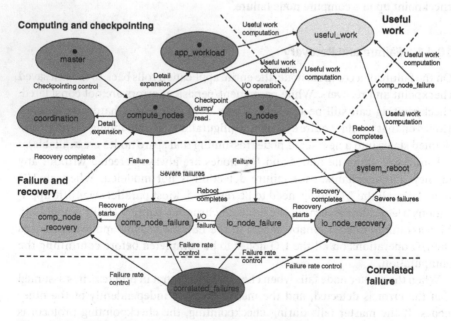

**Figure 10.5**  The overall composition of the model [17] / with permission of IEEE.

time. The submodels are organized into four modules: *computing and checkpointing, failure and recovery, correlated failure,* and *useful work.*

*Computing and Checkpointing Module.* The *compute_nodes* submodel depicts the computation, and checkpointing behavior of the compute nodes in the failure-free mode. While the compute nodes are executing, the application may be performing either computation or I/O operations, as represented in the *app_workload* submodel. The *master* submodel represents the master node in the coordinated checkpointing protocol. It triggers and coordinates the checkpointing, as modeled in the *compute_nodes* submodel.

The coordination among the compute nodes is modeled in the *coordination* submodel. The *io_nodes* submodel captures the I/O operations conducted by I/O nodes. It receives data from the *compute_nodes* submodel, writes/reads checkpoints to/from the file system, and writes data on behalf of the application in the *app_workload* submodel.

*Failure and Recovery Module.* A compute node or I/O node may fail in any of its states. The occurrence of failures in compute nodes is modeled in the *comp_node_failure* submodel. Recovery is initiated following the detection of the failure and is modeled in the *comp_node_recovery* submodel. As failures may also occur during recovery, compute nodes may experience multiple failures and subsequent recoveries in the *comp_node_recovery* submodel before the final successful recovery, after which the system resumes its normal execution and checkpointing cycle. Failures of compute nodes do not affect the I/O nodes if error propagation is not considered. The behavior of I/O nodes is similar, except that when an I/O node fails while writing application data to the file system, the application results are lost, and the system rolls back to the last checkpoint. That is represented in Figure 10.5 by an arrow from the *io_node_failure* submodel to the *comp_node_failure* submodel.

The recovery process occurs in two stages. First, the I/O nodes read the checkpoint from the file system and buffer it in their local memories. Then the compute nodes read the checkpoint from the I/O nodes and complete the recovery. The compute nodes then go back to the execution state, the master process gets reset, and the system exits the correlated failure window if there was one. The first stage is skipped if the checkpoint is already locally buffered in the I/O nodes when a compute node fails. If an I/O node fails while writing out a checkpoint, the checkpoint is aborted, and the I/O nodes get restarted, but the compute nodes are unaffected. If the number of unsuccessful recoveries in the *comp_node_recovery* and/ or *io_node_recovery* submodel exceeds a predefined threshold, the whole system, including the compute nodes and I/O nodes, is rebooted in *system_reboot* ("severe failures" transitions from *comp_node_recovery* and *io_node_recovery* to *system_reboot* in Figure 10.5). When the reboot completes, I/O processors are ready for execution but compute nodes still need to read the last checkpoint and recover.

Therefore, in Figure 10.5, the arrows of "reboot completes" from the *system_reboot* submodel point to the *io_nodes* and *comp_node_failure* submodels instead of the *compute_nodes* submodel.

*Correlated Failure Module.* The *correlated_failures* submodel depicts the semantics of correlated failures separately from the compute and I/O nodes' failure and recovery submodels. It controls the rates of all failures in the system. When a correlated failure occurs, the system enters a correlated failure window, in which it experiences failures at a rate that is higher than the independent failure rate. Note that independent failures can continue to occur when the system is within a correlated failure window.

*Useful Work Module.* The *useful_work* submodel calculates the useful work completed by the system. A positive reward is accumulated when the compute nodes perform job computation or I/O operations, and a negative reward, equal to the amount of the lost work, is applied when a compute node fails.

### 10.4.2.1 Modeling Compute and Checkpointing

In this section, the details of modeling the *computing and coordinated checkpointing* module are described. Figure 10.6 shows the SAN submodels for the *computing and coordinated checkpointing* module. States are shared among the submodels with the same names. Selected shared states are numbered in Figure 10.6 to help identify them.

When the application is started in the system, the compute nodes start out in the *execution* state, and the master is in the *master_sleep* state. We assume the application starts doing computation and that the *app_workload* is in the *compute* state. The I/O nodes are in the *ionode_idle* state. Initially, each of these states has a token; tokens are indicated by block arrows in Figure 10.6. In our model, the non-random events are modeled as deterministic activities, and exponential distribution is assumed for random events. To simplify the model, message transmissions are not explicitly modeled in the SAN, but the parameters of the corresponding events are appropriately set to include the message transmission latency. Also, the "done" and "proceed" message exchanges are not modeled in the interest of simplicity. The following steps detail the behavior of the model.

- First, assume that the checkpoint interval expires and the *checkpoint* activity is enabled. The master moves from the *master_sleep* state to the *master_checkpointing* state and starts a timer, as shown by the *start_timer* gate (Figure 10.6d).
- The compute nodes are initially in the state *execution*. When the master moves to *master_checkpointing*, the compute nodes move to the *quiescing* state after a latency of *recv_quiesce_bcast_time* (i.e. the broadcast overhead) (Figure 10.6a).
- Henceforth, the behavior depends on whether the application workload is performing computation or I/O. If the *app_workload* is in the *compute* state, the

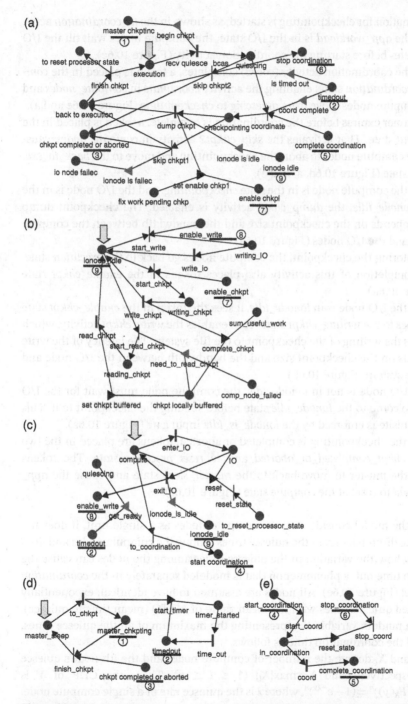

**Figure 10.6** Submodels for computing and checkpointing [17] / with permission of IEEE. (a) compute_nodes; (b) io_nodes; (c) app_workload; (d) master; and (e) coordination.

coordination for checkpointing is started, as shown in the *to_coordination* activity. If the *app_workload* is in the I/O state, the compute nodes wait till the I/O completes before starting the coordination activity (Figure 10.6c).

- After the coordination activity (*coord*) completes, a token is placed in the *complete_coordination* state, enabling the activity *coordinate* in *compute_nodes* and the compute nodes move from *quiescing* to *checkpointing* (Figure 10.6e and a).
- If the timer expires before the coordination is complete, a token is placed in the *timedout* state. That activates the *skip_chkpt2* activity in *compute_nodes*, causing the compute nodes to abort the checkpointing and move to the *back_to_execution* state (Figure 10.6d, a, and e).
- When the compute node is in the state *checkpointing*, and the I/O node is in the state *ionode_idle*, the *dump_chkpt* activity is enabled. The checkpoint dump time depends on the checkpoint size and the bandwidth between the compute nodes and the I/O nodes (Figure 10.6a).
- After storing the checkpoint, the compute nodes go back to the *execution* state. The completion of this activity also places tokens in the *enable_chkpt* state (Figure 10.6a).
- When the I/O node is in *ionode_idle*, it sees the token in the *enable_chkpt* state and goes to the *writing_chkpt* state. That enables the *write_chkpt* activity, which models the writing of the checkpoint to the file system. The latency of the write depends on the checkpoint size and the bandwidth between the I/O node and the file system (Figure 10.6b).
- If the I/O node is not in *ionode_idle*, the compute node must wait for the I/O node to come to the *ionode_idle* state before sending the checkpoint to it. This prerequisite is enforced by the *ionode_is_idle* input gate (Figure 10.6a).
- When the checkpointing is completed or aborted, tokens are placed in the two states *chkpt_completed_or_aborted* and *to_reset_processor_state*. The tokens cause the master to move back to the *master_sleep* state and cause the *app_workload* to reset at the *compute* state (Figure 10.6c).

Since the model considers all the compute nodes as a single unit, it does not reflect the discrepancies in the quiesce times among the compute nodes and does not show how the variation in the quiesce times among the nodes can cause the master to time out, a phenomenon that is modeled separately in the *coordination* submodel (Figure 10.6e). All nodes are assumed to have identical, exponentially distributed quiesce times with the mean value of MTTQ (mean time to quiesce). We use a random variable $Y$, representing the maximum of all the quiesce times, to model the coordination time as follows.

Let $n$ and $X_i$ denote the number of compute nodes and the $i$th node's quiesce time, respectively, and $Y = \max\{X_i\}$ $(1 \leq i \leq n)$. Then, the CDF of $Y$ is $F_Y(y) = (F_X(y))^n = (1 - e^{-\lambda y})^n$, where $\lambda$ is the quiesce rate of a single compute node.

$Y$ can be generated from a uniform random variable $U$ between 0 and 1 by $Y = -\frac{1}{\lambda} \times \log(1 - U^{1/n})$. The value of $Y$ is used as the latency in the *coord* activity in the *coordination* submodel that represents the coordination process.

### 10.4.2.2 Modeling Correlated Failures

Two categories of correlated failures are modeled: (i) correlated failures due to error propagation and (ii) generic correlated failures. Both are modeled by appropriately increasing the node/processor failure rates. This section describes how the increased rates are derived.

*Correlated Failures Due to Error Propagation.* When an independent failure occurs in the system, with some probability $p_e$ there is a conditional probability of a second failure due to the first. The result is an increased failure rate. We compute the failure rate increase for all nodes by multiplying the independent failure rate with a constant parameter called *frate_correlated_factor*.

Figure 10.7 shows the birth-death Markov process of correlated failures due to error propagation. $\lambda_i$ and $\lambda_c$ denote the rates of the system-wide independent failures and successive correlated failures, respectively. $\lambda$ is the independent failure rate of a single node. $\mu$ denotes the recovery rate of the system. $F_i$ is the system state in which $i$ failures have occurred before a successful recovery. (Three states, $F_0$, $F_1$, and $F_2$, are shown as examples in Figure 10.7.) As we assume that any successful recovery wipes off all latent errors, all the $F_i$ states transit directly to $F_0$ with the recovery rate. It is also assumed that the failure rates at all the $F_i$ states ($i > 0$) are the same. Thus, the conditional probability of another failure occurrence, provided that a failure has occurred, is

$$p = \frac{\lambda_c}{\lambda_c + \mu} \quad \Rightarrow \quad \lambda_c = \frac{p\mu}{1 - p}.$$

Let $n$ denote the number of nodes, and $r$ denote the multiple *frate_correlated_factor*. Then, according to the model,

$$\lambda_c = \lambda_i + nr\lambda = n\lambda(1 + r) \quad \Rightarrow \quad r = \frac{p\mu}{(1 - p)n\lambda} - 1$$

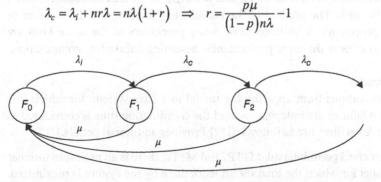

**Figure 10.7** Birth-death Markov process of correlated failures [17] / with permission of IEEE.

**Table 10.3** Parameters for modeling generic correlated failures [17] / with permission of IEEE.

| | |
|---|---|
| $\lambda_s$ | Failure rate of the entire system |
| $\lambda_{si}$ | Rate of independent failures in the system |
| $\lambda_{sc}$ | Rate of correlated failures in the system |
| $\lambda$ | Independent failures per node |
| $r$ | Increased failure rate due to correlated failures |
| $\rho$ | Correlated failure coefficient |
| $n$ | Number of nodes |

As long as $\lambda_c > \lambda_i$, $r$ can be chosen independently to study a range of correlated failure effects. For example, when $n = 1024$, $p = 0.3$, MTTR $= 10$ minutes, and MTTF $= 25$ years, $r$ is about 600.

*Generic Correlated Failures.* The system may suffer from generic correlated failures at any instant of the system's life. A correlated failure coefficient $\lambda$ is assumed to model generic correlated failures; it is the unconditional probability that a correlated failure will occur at any time.

Table 10.3 lists the parameters used for modeling generic correlated failures. The failure rate of generic correlated failures is given by

$$\lambda_s = \lambda_{si} + \rho\lambda_{sc} = n\lambda + \rho rn\lambda = n\lambda(1 + \rho r).$$

Note that $\lambda_{si}$, $\lambda_{sc}$, and $\rho$ are not the same as the $\lambda_i$, $\lambda_c$, and $p_e$ in the discussion of correlated failures due to error propagation, because they model different probabilities. The symbols $n$, $\lambda$, and $r$ have the same meanings in both models.

The following two metrics are used to evaluate system performance:

- *Useful work fraction:* Fraction of time the system makes forward progress toward the completion of a job. It does not include work that is repeated because of failures.
- *Total useful work:* The product of the useful work fraction and the number of compute processors. It indicates how many processors of the same kind are required to achieve the same performance, assuming failure-free computation.

### 10.4.2.3 Results
The key observations from applying the model to a base system, for which it is assumed that failures are independent and the coordination time is considered to be a fixed quiesce time, are as follows. ([17] Provides additional details.)

- For a given checkpoint interval, MTTR, and MTTF, there is an optimum number of processors for which the total useful work done by the system is maximized. Adding more processors beyond that optimum number will hurt system performance because of failure effects. The rationale is as follows. On the one hand, more processors provide higher computing power for the job; on the other hand, more processors incur more frequent failures, and hence more computation is wasted because of failures. For small numbers of processors, the former factor dominates, while for sufficiently large numbers of processors, the latter outweighs the former. Consider how the optimum number of processors varies with the MTTF, MTTR, and checkpoint interval: it decreases with smaller MTTFs, increases with smaller MTTRs, and decreases with larger checkpoint intervals. The reasons are that smaller MTTFs increase the failure rate, larger MTTRs increase the penalty of a failure, and larger checkpoint intervals cause more work to be lost upon a failure. All three aggravate the effects of failures and thus lower the equilibrium point between the computing power and the failure effect.

- For the system to be scalable, checkpoints should be taken on the granularity of minutes rather than hours, as is the current practice. While in theory, there is an optimal checkpoint interval, for any practical range, there is no optimal checkpoint interval for which the useful work is maximized, contrary to what other studies have shown (e.g. see [14, 15]). The reason is that the overhead of checkpointing is relatively low when the checkpoint writing is done in the background, and the effect of failures dominates the effect of taking checkpoints frequently.

- The useful work fraction steadily decreases as the number of processors increases because the greater number of processors does not contribute to the useful work fraction, and the failure effect degrades the useful work fraction. Thus, even when the maximum total useful work is achieved at the optimum number of processors, the useful work fraction is still small. For example, for an MTTF of one year per node, the peak of total useful work is obtained with 128K processors, for which the useful work fraction is only about $56\,000/131\,072 = 42.7\%$, i.e. over 50% of system time is spent in handling failures. Thus, the overall failure rate of the system must substantially decrease for the useful work fraction to improve.

- Failures during checkpointing/recovery do not exert as significant an effect on the useful work fraction as failures during computation. The reason is that the duration of checkpointing/recovery is much smaller than that of computation and hence incurs less loss of useful work.

**10.4.2.3.1 *Effect of Correlated Failures*** We consider two categories of correlated failures.

*Correlated Failures Due to Error Propagation Only.* Correlated failures due to error propagation are modeled with three parameters: *probability of correlated failure* $(p_e)$, *frate_correlated_factor* $(r)$, and *correlated failure window*. The results show that the useful work fraction is not susceptible to correlated failures due to error propagation. The reason is that we assume these failures occur only during recovery, and we observed that failures during recovery do not significantly affect the useful work fraction.

*Generic Correlated Failures.* Generic correlated failures are modeled with two parameters: *correlated failure factor* ($r$) and *correlated failure coefficient* ($\rho$). Therefore, the entire system failure rate gets doubled because of generic correlated failures. The results show that when generic correlated failures, unlike correlated failures due to error propagation, are present, there is a large amount of performance degradation, and the performance degradation prevents the system from scaling well.

## 10.5 Checkpointing in Large-Scale Systems: A Simulation Study

In this section, findings from a simulation study on the scalability of coordinated checkpointing in large-scale computing systems [7] are described; coordinated checkpointing is assumed. With the delivered performance fixed at 1 PF/s, the number of nodes in the system were varied to obtain different configurations. If other parameters, like checkpointing interval, MTTF, and MTTR, were varied, their effect on the checkpointing and recovery capabilities of the system could also be evaluated. The findings of this study suggest that it is not ideal to use a large number of small COTS components to build a supercomputing cluster, even though doing so is the current trend. An intuitive explanation for that result is that when many such unreliable components operate together, their failure rates add up to make the cumulative failure rate very significant.

Although use of coordinated checkpointing as the rollback recovery technique was assumed in the study, it has been projected that in future large-scale system implementations, local checkpoints will be taken on each node, and those local checkpoints will then be committed to a stable storage system in the background. It is expected that that approach will prevent the stable storage from becoming the performance bottleneck when all nodes are trying to commit their checkpoints to it at the same time [19].

As mentioned earlier, the delivered performance of the system was constant at 1 PF/s (petaflops per second) while the number of nodes were varied during the evaluation. Each processor was assumed to contribute a performance of 1 GF/s. The specifications of the different configurations are summarized in Table 10.4. For example, consider a single node with 25 processors. That node would contribute a performance of 250 GF/s ($25 \times 10$ GF/s). To attain a total system performance of 1 PF/s, we need 4000 such nodes; this configuration is shown in the second row (i.e. Large SMP) of Table 10.4.

**Table 10.4** Different configurations for a notional PF/s system [7] / with permission of IEEE.

| Node type | Processors in node | Node performance | Number of nodes $N$ |
|---|---|---|---|
| Large-Scale NUMA (Non-Uniform Memory Access) | 1000 | 10 TF/s | 100 |
| Large SMP (Symmetric Multiprocessors) | 25 | 250 GF/s | 4000 |
| Small SMP | 4 | 40 GF/s | 24000 |
| System-on-a-chip | 1 | 10 GF/s | 100000 |

A node may be in either of two states: (i) functional, meaning it is available for use; or (ii) failed, meaning it is unavailable for use. Failed nodes can be repaired and thus transitioned to the functional state. Let $N$ be the total number of nodes in the system, and among them, let $N_f$ be the number of nodes that are functional. At any time, let $a$ nodes be executing the applications on the system. The rest of the $(N - a)$ nodes can be used as spares in the event of a failure of one of the $a$ active nodes. The following is a list of definitions in terms of the nomenclature used in [20].

- The system is said to be *functional* when there are at least $a$ active nodes ($N_f \geq a$).
- When nodes fail, they are replaced with nodes from the spare pool.
- The time that a failed node takes to recover from its previous checkpoint is $R$.
- A coordinated checkpoint is taken every $I$ seconds after computation begins until an active node fails.
- The checkpoint latency, $L$, is the time that it takes for the checkpoint to be available for recovery.
- The overhead of checkpoint, $C$, is the computation time needed to take the checkpoint.

The system can be in one of three states: *Up*, *Recovery*, or *Down*. In the *Up* state, the system performs computation and checkpoints its state at intervals of $I$ seconds. When an active node fails, one of two situations arises: if ($N_f \geq a$), then the system enters the *Recovery* state; otherwise, it transitions to the *Down* phase. The *Recovery* phase starts with the failure of an active node. The node recovers and the system takes a checkpoint. When the checkpoint is available for recovery (after the checkpoint latency, $L$), the system enters the *Up* state. When the system is in the *Down* state, the recovery of an active node again leads to two possible state transitions: node ($N_f \geq a$) either recovers and thus reaches the *Recovery* state, or remains in the *Down* state. The possible transitions are depicted in Figure 10.8.

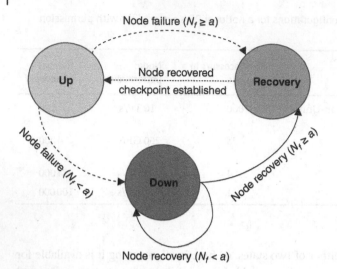

**Figure 10.8**   State transition diagram for the supercomputing system.

Useful work (*W*) is defined as the amount of system computation time that will be lost in the event of a failure. It is given by:

$$W = \begin{cases} I \text{ if state} = \text{Recovery} \\ I - C \text{ if state} = Up \text{ per completed checkpoint} \\ 0 \text{ if state} = \text{Down} \end{cases}$$

Let *T* be the total running time of the application. The useful work factor/fraction (*U*) is defined as the ratio of the useful work to the total time:

$$U = W \big/ T$$

To begin our experiment, we varied the number of active nodes (*a*) and the checkpointing interval (*I*) to determine the set of parameters that yields the best useful work factor/fraction. Table 10.5 illustrates the conflicting positive and

**Table 10.5**   Effect of parameter variation on useful work factor/fraction (*U*).

| Parameter variation | Positive effect (*U*↑) | Negative effect (*U*↓) |
|---|---|---|
| (*a* = # nodes executing applications)↑ | (total computation time)↓ → *U*↑ | (#*spares* (*N* − *a*))↓ → (time spent in *Down* state)↑ → *U*↓ |
| (*I* = checkpointing interval)↑ | (checkpointing overhead)↓ → *U*↑ | (upon a failure, work lost since the last checkpoint)↑ → *U*↓ |

negative effects of those parameters on $U$. An informed choice of the parameters is needed for each system.

For different values of $N$, the fraction of active nodes, $\left(\frac{a}{N}\right)$, were varied from $\frac{1}{4}$ to 1, and the best value for $U$ was determined. Specifically, for each choice of $\left(\frac{a}{N}\right)$, we used a binary search algorithm to search the checkpoint interval range to choose the best value of $U$. The experiment showed that as $N$ increases, $U$ decreases. The reason is that the number of nodes that can fail increases as $N$ increases, leading to a lower value of $U$. Note that the failure of a node takes the system to the *Recovery* state, in which the useful work is lower than in the *Up* state. A similar trend was observed when $a$ increased (while $N$ was kept constant). In particular, when $a$ approached $N$, $U$ decreased sharply. The reason is that the number of spare nodes available, $(N - a)$, decreased, and the system spent more time in the *Down* state, in which $W$ (useful work) is 0.

Consider an application with a serial portion $S$ and a parallelizable portion $P$. With $a$ active nodes, the time taken would be $S + P/a$. Normalizing the speedup to that on a single-node system so that $S + P = 1$ or, alternatively, $P = (1 - S)$, the speedup is given by:

$$\text{Speedup}(S, a) = \frac{1}{\left(S + \frac{(1-S)}{a}\right)} = \frac{a}{\left((a-1)S + 1\right)}.$$

To take checkpointing, failures, and consequent recovery into account, the amount of useful work performed with checkpointing must be considered. Therefore, with checkpointing the speedup is given by speedup$(S, a, U) = U$speedup$(S, a)$.

Using speedup$(S, a, U)$ as a metric the effect of varying the various parameters [7] was evaluated. The parameters studied were the number of nodes $N$, the degree of parallelization $S$ (or, more precisely, the extent of serialization in the program), the checkpoint overhead $C$, the checkpoint latency $L$, the recovery time $R$, the MTTF, and the MTTR. The conclusions are summarized next.

1) When $N$ increased, the obtained speedup reached a saturation point, perhaps because the application could not scale beyond some point, and the failure rate became too high, requiring a higher frequency of checkpointing.
2) When the overheads due to checkpointing and recovery were made negligible (to simulate an ideal system that detects failures and repairs the nodes almost instantaneously), we found that the system could attain near-optimal performance. The reason is that the system spent very little time, if any, in the *Down* state.
3) As expected, when the checkpointing overhead was reduced, the performance improved, and vice versa.

4) The checkpointing overhead had a greater impact on programs with less parallelism. The reason is that even with a larger number of active nodes, multiple checkpoints could be taken between a recovery and a failure, particularly in the serial portion of the code.

5) With programs that had a higher degree of parallelization ($P$), increases of $a$ decreased the time between a recovery and a failure, even to the point that not even one checkpoint could be completed before the next failure occurred. In such a case, $L$ and $R$ dominated over $C$ in their impact on performance.

6) Increases in the MTTF increased the performance, and that was expected because the amount of useful work before a failure occurred was increased. A corresponding trend was noted when the MTTF decreased.

7) As for the effect of MTTR on performance, it was expected that when $a$ was very close to $N$, the impact of the MTTR would be higher because the system would stay in the *Down* state for a longer amount of time. As the optimal $\left( a/N \right)$ decreased, the impact of MTTR would decrease as well. That hypothesis was confirmed in our study.

In summary, our study concluded that if most failures are transient, then clusters built from larger symmetric multiprocessors (SMP) will provide higher performance. However, if failures are not transient, smaller nodes will perform better in building the cluster. To bring those two conclusions together: medium-sized nodes would perform the best in a scenario in which there is a mixture of transient and permanent failures.

## 10.6 Cooperative Checkpointing

The amount of state in an application is not constant throughout its execution. Taking a checkpoint periodically without knowing the current state of the application is not as effective as deciding to take a checkpoint based on the state of the application and the system. The latter would have less impact on performance in terms of both the time and space utilized.

At application design and implementation time, the designer does not understand the runtime execution environment in which the application will be deployed. Furthermore, at runtime, the system cannot perfectly determine the most desirable points at which checkpoints could be taken. However, those two independent pieces of information are key to determining what and when to checkpoint. *Cooperative checkpointing* attempts to make the "best use of both worlds" to improve the performance of checkpointing [21].

From the application side, the user can initiate a "potential" checkpoint at selected points in the code. They could be points where the state of the application is minimal so that low overhead is incurred by checkpointing. At runtime, the calls to these "potential" checkpoints generate *requests* to the system for a checkpoint. The system either *grants* or *denies* permission to take the checkpoint based on its runtime state. Within the system, the entity responsible for deciding whether to take a checkpoint is called *the gatekeeper*.

### 10.6.1 Other Terms and Definitions

The cooperative checkpointing approach presented in [21] uses the following terminology:

- A *failure* is defined as any event in hardware or software that results in the immediate failure of a running application. Any unsaved computation is lost at the time of the failure, and execution must be restarted from the most recently completed checkpoint.
- *I* is the checkpointing interval, i.e. the time that elapses between two consecutive checkpoints.
- *C* is the *checkpoint overhead*, i.e. the amount of time the application is paused so that a checkpoint can be taken.
- *L* is the checkpoint latency, i.e. the time after initiation of the checkpoint at which the checkpoint is available for use in recovery.
- A *node-second* is a unit of work and is the amount of work performed by an application if a node is occupied for one second by the application.
- *Wasted work* is time spent on a node by the application in doing work other than making progress on the application's own work. It includes time spent sitting idle, recomputing lost work because of a failure, or taking a checkpoint.
- *Saved work* is the inverse of *wasted work* and is obtained by subtracting the amount of *wasted work* from the total node execution time of the application.

### 10.6.2 Cooperative Checkpointing vs. Periodic Checkpointing

The obvious question about the cooperative checkpointing approach is, how does the gatekeeper decide which checkpoints to skip?

The analysis presented in [21] uses competitive analyses to compare *cooperative checkpointing* and the *periodic checkpointing* approaches. An online checkpointing algorithm *A* has an expected competitive ratio $\omega$ (i.e. *A* is $\omega$-competitive) if the expected amount of work saved by the optimal offline algorithm (OPT) is at most $\omega$ times the expected amount of work saved by *A*.

The *optimal offline cooperative checkpointing algorithm* performs the latest checkpoint in each failure-free interval such that the checkpoint completes before the end of the interval (if one exists) and skips every other checkpoint.

The details of the analytical comparison are presented in [21]. For a better understanding of the technique, we present here a numerical example (from [21]) that illustrates the benefits of cooperative checkpointing over periodic checkpointing. The Blue Gene/L system was taken as a reference, as the various parameters were derived from earlier analyses of this supercomputing cluster [22].

In the example, the checkpoint overhead ($C$) was set to 6 minutes (i.e. 360 seconds), which is half of the estimated upper bound for checkpointing on BG/L (i.e. 12 minutes, or 720 seconds). A BG/L supercomputer with 65 536 nodes was considered.

For a 4096-node BG/L prototype, Liang et al. [22] estimated the mean time between failures to be 3.7 failures/day (MTBF = 6.5 hours). Assuming that the failure rate scales linearly with the number of nodes, the 65 536-node machine will have an MTBF of slightly over 24 minutes (i.e. more precisely, 1459 seconds). The MTBF roughly corresponds to a three-year component lifetime.

From [20], it can be estimated that on this BG/L machine, the optimal periodic checkpointing algorithm would checkpoint every 17 minutes $\left(\left(\sqrt{2C/\lambda}\right) = \sqrt{2CE[F]} = \sqrt{2 \times 360 \times 1459} = 1025 \text{ seconds}\right)$. With a checkpoint overhead ($C$) of six minutes, it would spend 26% of the machine's time performing checkpoints.

Consider a non-exponential failure distribution, such as $\chi(t) = a\delta(t - t_1) + (1 - a)\delta(t - t_2)$, that may better describe the failure behavior of the BG/L. In [22], the maximum uptime of the BG/L system was estimated to be about 504 000 seconds. Pick $t_1$ to be small, $t_2$ to be very large, and $a$ to be nearly 1. Assume that cooperative checkpointing grants every other request for a checkpoint from the application, beginning with the second. Then, $I = 512$ seconds. The MTBF is 1459 seconds. $t_2$ is chosen to be 504 000 seconds, and $t_1$ is set to $I + C = 872$ seconds. We get:

$$1459 = at_1 + (1 - a)t_2 = 872a + (1 - a)504000$$

which fixes $a$ at 0.9988. In other words, 99.88% of the time, the application fails at time $I + C$, a situation in which the periodic checkpointing algorithm saves no work, but OPT saves $I$. Oliner et al. show in [21] that in an infinite execution under those system parameters and that failure distribution, cooperative checkpointing can accomplish four times as much useful work in a given amount of machine time compared to even the optimal periodic checkpointing algorithm.

# References

1 Chandy, K.M. and Lamport, L. (1985). Distributed snapshots: determining global states of distributed systems. *ACM Transactions on Computer Systems* 3 (1): 63–75.

**2** Litzkow, M., Tannenbaum, T., Basney, J. et al. (1997). Checkpoint and migration of UNIX processes in the condor distributed processing system. Technical Report #1346. Computer Sciences Department, University of Wisconsin–Madison. https://minds.wisconsin.edu/bitstream/handle/1793/60116/TR1346. pdf?sequence=1&isAllowed=y (accessed 22 July 2023).

**3** Janakiraman, G. and Tamir, Y. (1994). Coordinated checkpointing-rollback error recovery for distributed shared memory multicomputers. *Proceedings of the IEEE 13th Symposium on Reliable Distributed Systems*, 42–51, Dana Point, CA (25–27 October 1994). IEEE.

**4** Neves, N., Castro, M., and Guedes, P. (1994). A checkpoint protocol for an entry consistent shared memory system. *Proceedings of the 13th Annual ACM Symposium on Principles of Distributed Computing*, 121–129, Los Angeles, CA (August 1994). New York: Association for Computing Machinery.

**5** Janssens, B. and Fuchs, W.K. (1995). Ensuring correct rollback recovery in distributed shared memory systems. *Journal of Parallel and Distributed Computing* 29 (2): 211–218.

**6** Agarwal S., Garg, R., Gupta, M.S. et al. (2004). Adaptive incremental checkpointing for massively parallel systems. *Proceedings of the 18th International Conference on Supercomputing*, 277–286, Malo, France (26 June–1 July 2004). New York: Association for Computing Machinery.

**7** Elnozahy, E.N., Plank, J.S., and Fuchs, W.K. (2004). Checkpointing for peta-scale systems. *IEEE Transactions on Dependable and Secure Computing* 1 (2): 97–108.

**8** Speight, E. and Bennett, J.K. (1997). Brazos: a third-generation DSM system. *Proceedings of the USENIX Windows NT Workshop*, 95–106, Seattle, WA (11–13 August 1997).

**9** Chung, P.E., Lee, W.-J., Huang, Y. et al. (1999). Winckp: a transparent checkpointing and rollback recovery tool for Windows NT applications. *Digest of Papers, the 29th Annual International Symposium on Fault-Tolerant Computing*, 220–223, Madison, WI (15–18 June 1999). IEEE.

**10** Plank, J.S., Beck, M., Kingsley, G. et al. (1995). Libckpt: transparent checkpointing under Unix. *Proceedings of the Usenix Winter 1995 Technical Conference*, 213–223, New Orleans, LA (January 1995).

**11** Nam, H., Kim, J., Hong, S.J. et al. (2002). Probabilistic checkpointing. *IEICE Transactions on Information and Systems* E85-D (7): 1093–1104.

**12** NASA Advanced Supercomputing (NAS) Division. (2021). NAS parallel benchmarks. https://www.nas.nasa.gov/publications/npb.html (accessed August 2021).

**13** Schulz, M., Bronevetsky, G., Fernandes, R. et al. (2004). Implementation and evaluation of a scalable application-level checkpoint-recovery scheme for MPI programs. *Proceedings of the 2004 ACM/IEEE Conference on Supercomputing*, Pittsburgh, PA (6–12 November 2004). IEEE.

**14** Young, J.W. (1974). A first order approximation to the optimum checkpoint interval. *Communications of the ACM* 17 (9): 530–531.

**15** Daly, J. (2003). A model for predicting the optimum checkpoint interval for restart dumps. *Proceedings of the International Conference on Computational Science*, 3–12, Part IV, Melbourne, Australia and St. Petersburg, Russia (2–4 June 2003), (ed. P.M.A. Sloot, D. Abramson, A.V. Bogdanov et al.). *Lecture Notes in Computer Science*, vol. 2660. Berlin, Heidelberg: Springer.

**16** Sanders, W. and Meyer, J. (2001). Stochastic activity networks: formal definitions and concepts. In: *Lectures on Formal Methods and PerformanceAnalysis*, EEF School 2000. Lecture Notes in Computer Science, vol 2090 (ed. E. Brinksma, H. Hermanns, and J.P. Katoen), 315–343. Berlin, Heidelberg: Springer.

**17** Wang, L., Pattabiraman, K., Kalbarczyk, Z. et al. (2005). Modeling coordinated checkpointing for large-scale supercomputers. *Proceedings of the 2005 International Conference on Dependable Systems and Networks*, 812–821, Yokohama, Japan (28 June–1 July 2005). IEEE.

**18** Valiant, L.G. (1990). A bridging model for parallel computation. *Communications of the ACM* 33 (8): 103–111.

**19** Vaidya, N.H. (1996). On staggered checkpointing. *Proceedings of the 8th IEEE Symposium on Parallel and Distributed Processing*, 572–580, New Orleans, LA (23–26 October 1996). IEEE.

**20** Vaidya, N.H. (1997). Impact of checkpoint latency on overhead ratio of a checkpointing scheme. *IEEE Transactions on Computers* 46 (8): 942–947.

**21** Oliner, A., Rudolph, L., and Sahoo, R. (2006). Cooperative checkpointing theory. *Proceedings of the 20th IEEE International Parallel & Distributed Processing Symposium*, Rhodes Island, Greece (25–29 April 2006). IEEE. https://doi.org/10.1109/IPDPS.2006.1639368

**22** Liang, Y., Zhang, Y., Sivasubramaniam, A. et al. (2005). Filtering failure logs for a BlueGene/L prototype. *Proceedings of the International Conference on Dependable Systems and Networks*, 476–485, Yokohama, Japan (28 June–1 July 2005). IEEE.

# 11

# Internals of Fault Injection Techniques

## 11.1 Introduction

The computer industry appears to be experiencing a fairly strong shift away from the performance-focused paradigm to a service-based paradigm that promises high dependability, such that users can justifiably trust a delivered service.

One of the trends shaping system dependability research has been the changes in failure rates and the dominant sources of failures, both hardware and software [1]. Hardware failure rates are going down, while the relative contribution of software is showing an upward trend. The concern for soft errors, however, is increasing as device sizes shrink and complexity increases. At the same time, the number of end users has grown by an order of magnitude, further reducing systems' tolerance of failures.

To achieve high dependability, systems are designed with fault-tolerance features to detect errors and then mask or recover from the effects of those errors. Thus, the testing of those fault-tolerance features is extremely important to understand how dependable a system with incorporated fault-tolerance mechanisms is, and to gain insight into the success and behavior of error detection and recovery. Fault/error injection can be applied to conduct detailed studies of the complex interactions between faults/errors and the fault-tolerance features designed to handle them. For more than three decades, fault injection has been recognized as a means of effectively testing and stressing fault-tolerance mechanisms so that a system's behavior can be studied prior to its deployment. Typically, fault injection is employed either at an early design stage (via simulation-based tools) or at the prototype/development stage (via hardware- and software-based fault injection).

The objective of fault injection is to mimic faults and errors and consequently force the exercise of the fault-tolerance components of the target system. To maximize the efficacy of each injection, the locations, timing, and conditions for faults

*Dependable Computing: Design and Assessment*, First Edition. Ravishankar K. Iyer, Zbigniew T. Kalbarczyk, and Nithin M. Nakka.
© 2024 The IEEE Computer Society. Published 2024 by John Wiley & Sons, Inc.
Companion website: www.wiley.com/go/iyer/dependablecomputing1

being injected must be carefully chosen. In fault injection, the condition upon which a fault is to be injected into a target datum or instruction is called a *trigger*. Note that the parameters in the trigger condition could be independent of the target data or instructions.

One important step in the evolution of fault injection was the formalization of the key components of a fault injection experiment: the fault set, the set of activations, the set of readouts, and the derived measurements. Before delving into the details of the different approaches to fault injection, we provide a few important definitions:

- A *fault* is a low-level anomaly that causes a deviation in the system state. The deviation in the system state is called an *error* [2]. Specifically, *fault injection* is the emulation of faults. However, because the emulation of errors often has the same effect as the emulation of faults and is often easier to implement, the term *fault injection* is conventionally used to refer to both types of emulation collectively.
- *Fault activation* refers to the activation of, or access to, injected faults. For example, a fault injected into a register is activated when that register is read before the register is overwritten. Faults that are not accessed will not have any effect on the system and therefore are similar to faults that are not activated. We used this view of fault activation because the determination that a fault has been accessed is relatively easy to make.
- *Fault activation level* refers to the ratio of the number of activated faults ($F_a$) to the total number of injected faults ($F_i$). Therefore,

$$Fault\ activation\ level = \frac{F_a}{F_i}$$

The concepts of the fault set, activation, and measurements were further extended by formalizing failure acceleration (i.e. injecting faults at a high rate to increase the number of failures observed).

Accelerated fault injection was first applied to an IBM 370 mainframe [3]. The early implementations of fault injectors used pin-level injection [4]. The leading advance in fault injection in the late 1980s was the idea of using software instead of hardware to inject faults because hardware fault injectors often damaged the target system and were expensive to build. The idea is called *software-implemented fault injection* (*SWIFI*). Another important method of injecting faults was the use of radiation sources to induce single-event upsets (SEUs) on exposed integrated circuits [5]. Power supply fault injections attempt to mimic the effects of transients on the power bus of a circuit or system [6]. Laser fault injection (LFI) has emerged as a preferred contactless method of inducing SEUs in semiconductor circuits. In LFI, a laser beam mimics the effects of heavy-ion radiation [7]. Hardware-injected faults most closely resemble the faults one would expect in a hostile environment. The hardware approaches are nonintrusive; that is, the system operates exactly as it otherwise would while faults are being injected (until the fault manifests). However, most hardware approaches are very costly and, further, may cause permanent damage to systems.

Only a few studies have claimed to use more than one type of analysis (physical, SWIFI, or simulation). Young et al. developed a "HYBRID" [8] approach that combined hardware triggering with SWIFI. Guthoff and Sieh [9] combined SWIFI with simulation by taking a checkpoint of a target program running on a real system, simulating the effect of a low-level transient, and injecting the symptom back into the real system. FlexFi [10] used a separate background debug mode microcontroller (a COTS processor common on microprocessor boards) to inject faults into a Motorola 68K processor in real time. Kanawati et al. [11] offered the first example of combining hardware and software fault injection and triggering. Specifically, they used FERRARI [11] to trigger a hardware monitor (via the serial port), which in turn activated a pin-level hardware injector to inject faults into the system bus after the system had returned from the SWIFI fault injector to the user mode.

This chapter focuses on the underlying techniques for *SWIFI*. Section 11.2 describes the history of software fault injection and the categorization of its techniques. Section 11.3 presents fault model attributes. Sections 11.4, 11.5, and 11.6 describe how fault injection is applied in real-world systems. The attributes of the injections that can be used to benchmark systems are defined in Section 11.7. Section 11.8 presents a case study of a sample system, NFTAPE (Networked Fault Tolerance and Performance Evaluator) [12], to illustrate how to use the tools to conduct a set of operating system evaluation activities. Section 11.9 introduces a new generate of fault-injection techniques that are Bayesian based and demonstratively more comprehensive, and is deployed to assess autonomous vehicles' (AVs') safety. Concluding remarks are offered in Section 11.10.

## 11.2 Historical View of Software Fault Injection

The fault/error model assumed in software fault injection is not contingent upon the error origin, i.e. an error could have occurred anywhere (source code, disk, network, memory, or CPU) and anytime (and could be either transient or permanent).

In a well-designed system, multiple mechanisms for protecting against errors may be available (e.g. parity, ECC, or memory scrubbing); however, errors can still exist. Errors could be, for example, timing issues due to hardware/software problems, a noise source such as undershoot or overshoot, or noise on the address bus that results in writing or reading of the wrong data to/from the memory. In the last case, the data may not have been altered by the address bus noise, but the wrong location will be accessed. Software fault/error injection experiments employ source code errors, memory errors, and CPU register errors that emulate the diverse origins and impact of actual errors.

Siewiorek and his colleagues from Carnegie Mellon University introduced one of the first SWIFI tools, FIAT [13], a tool that added functions to test trigger conditions and inject faults at compile time. FIAT could thus trigger a fault on a condition such as the arrival of a message from a particular node.

Soon after FIAT was introduced, Kanawati et al. [11] from the University of Texas at Austin created a method that used the UNIX *ptrace* system call to set breakpoints in a process and to access its memory and registers. The *ptrace* call is generally used by debuggers to control a traced process. Kanawati et al.'s tool, FERRARI, allowed the user to inject memory and register faults without recompiling a target application running in the SunOS.

Dawson et al. [14] from the University of Michigan developed ORCHESTRA to inject protocol (communication) faults into distributed systems. ORCHESTRA tested network protocols by inserting code into the network protocol stack on Mach and Solaris systems to inject faults upon the arrival of certain messages. Han et al. [15] presented another tool from the University of Michigan, DOCTOR, which injected communication messages and bit flips into memory and registers in the HARTS real-time OS.

EFA [16], a project from the University of Dortmund, Germany, proposed an environment for general fault injection, but it made several assumptions about the target system (e.g. the target must be a distributed application, and the fault injector must be triggered by message arrivals). The approach also required the programmer to include fault injection functions in the target program and to enumerate all possible faults that can be injected.

Researchers at the University of Illinois at Urbana-Champaign created a set of general-purpose fault injection tools. FINE [17] used traps to allow fault injection into the OS to assess the propagation of faults in UNIX systems. Kao and Iyer [18] followed it with DEFINE, an extension to FINE that added distributed support and injected software faults by replacing functions in memory with corrupted machine code compiled from the same source files. DEFINE then grew into another tool, FTAPE, in which Tsai et al. [19] injected faults and I/O errors into a fault-tolerant computer, the Tandem Integrity S2. Through the use of FTAPE, it was found that stress-based triggering led to a higher fault activation rate than either path- or time-based triggering. NFTAPE [12] is a tool for conducting automated fault-injection-based dependability campaigns in distributed computer systems, where a *campaign* is defined as a set of fault injection experiments that are identical or closely related with respect to a defined category. NFTAPE [20–22] supports a wide variety of functionalities, including injecting into the operating system kernel's code section (including drivers), data structures, stack, or CPU register; into the user application's code, data (including network-communication-related faults), stack, or registers; or into a configurable field-programmable gate array (FPGA) or software simulator.

FPGAs have become increasingly popular, e.g. in space applications and many other critical systems. The ability to reconfigure is central in systems that dynamically determine the best architectures in which faulty blocks can be isolated through remapping of the original design or through scrubbing of the device. Alderighi et al. [23] proposed a software fault injection tool for static random-access memory (SRAM)-based FPGAs that addressed faults in the configuration bitstreams.

Carreira et al. [24] from the University of Coimbra in Portugal presented Xception, a SWIFI tool that uses the debugging registers of modern CPUs to trigger faults. Another tool from the University of Illinois, Loki [25], can trigger faults by constructing a software *probe* in the user's application source code when the distributed system is in particular states, without explicit synchronization. MAFALDA [26] injected faults into a ChorusOS-based system by adding functions to the microkernel; the associated research revealed the importance of having low-level error detection to measure the propagation of faults.

Analysis of monitored data drives the development (or extension) of fault injection tools. For example, with FTAPE [19], stress-based fault injection was employed to evaluate one of the first UNIX-based fault-tolerant systems developed by Tandem (now a division of HP). The stress-based approach ensures that faults/errors are injected into system components when they are being heavily used (i.e. are highly stressed). It allows meaningful comparison of systems and was an important step toward system benchmarking.

While fault/error injection methods and techniques have been extensively studied in academia, the industry also employs fault injection. Merenda and Merenda [27] report on fault injection-based testing of recovery and serviceability in the IBM ES/9000 systems. Fault injection and software testing were used by Ansaldo-CRIS in Italy to assess the dependability of a new generation of railway control systems [28]. In [29], physical fault injection at the pin level was employed to validate error-handling mechanisms of the Teraflops supercomputer developed by Intel.

Simulation-based tools can be used to test fault-tolerant designs by emulating the effects of fault injection. In 1990, Goswami and Iyer [30] introduced DEPEND, a simulation-based environment for modeling systems and faults at the system level. DEPEND was used to demonstrate a hierarchical method in which the behavior at one level can be used at a higher level (e.g. the transistor-level analysis can be used at the processor level). Jenn et al. [31] introduced MEFISTO to test faulty circuit behavior by inserting faults into VHDL (Very High-Speed Integrated Circuit Hardware Description Language) models. Choi and Iyer [32] used FOCUS to measure the sensitivity of circuits to transient upsets at the device level. Clark and Pradhan [33] used REACT to evaluate multiprocessor architectures. Ghosh and Johnson [34] used the ADEPT simulator to model complex real-time distributed systems. Saggese et al. [20] studied the impact of soft errors in a microprocessor that was a gate-level implementation (i.e. a fully synthesized design) of a relatively simple processor.

In conclusion, software fault injection has been used to inject faults/errors into targets whose operations can be reached by software, so that the outcomes can be monitored and documented. The rest of this chapter discusses the internals of three types of *SWIFI* techniques, namely (i) compile-time injection, (ii) runtime injection, and (iii) simulation-based injection. Figure 11.1 shows a categorization of the software fault injection techniques that we will address in the following sections.

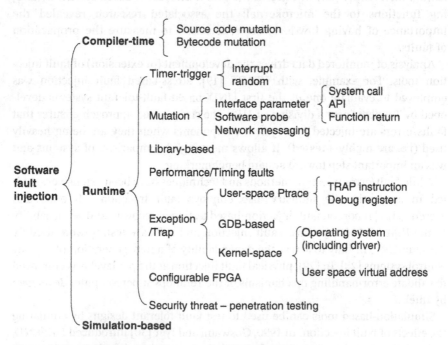

**Figure 11.1** Categories of software fault injection techniques.

## 11.3 Fault Model Attributes

The following four attributes can be used to characterize a fault/error injection; different fault injection experiments may have different focuses.

- *Trigger (When?)*. A fault/error injection can be triggered when (i) a target datum is read/written for stack/data injection, (ii) a target instruction in a given function is reached, (iii) a register is used, (iv) an event happens, or (v) a software/hardware timer expires at a predetermined time, or (vi) at any random time.
- *Location (Where?)*. (i) Randomly selected locations such as code section, stack, static/dynamic data, or CPU register; or (ii) targets of special interest, such as most frequently used functions, major data structures, or an assignment statement of the source code. Modification of memory contents has been chosen as one of the basic techniques used in software fault injections because faults are likely to contaminate certain parts of memory.
- *Type (What?)*. (i) Bit faults that are suitable for emulating hardware/environment faults, (ii) delays (performance penalties), or (iii) source code mutations that are designed to focus on emulating software bugs.
- *Duration (How Long?)*. Either transient or permanent.

A *campaign* is a set of identical or closely related fault injection experiments in terms of a defined category. One example of a fault injection campaign would be the random injection of 1000 faults (with three-bit flips per word) to the memory where the operating system *schedule()* function is located, followed by the running of a user-level TPC-C online transaction processing benchmark as a workload.

In general, while one is conducting a fault injection campaign, it is advisable to create a representative mixture of classes of faults/errors that fit the needs of the system and to include possible external features (such as the environment or operational conditions) in the fault model.

Sections 11.4 through 11.6, below, introduce the key characteristics of software fault injectors when implemented to be used at the *compile time*, at *runtime*, and in *simulation*, respectively. Table 11.1 summarizes the key features of the software fault injection techniques discussed in those three sections.

## 11.4 Compile-Time Fault Injection

Compile-time injection (i.e. software mutation or code insertion) is an injection technique whereby source code (i.e. assembler code or bytecode) is modified and emulated faults are injected before the code is loaded for the execution.

**Table 11.1**  Characteristics of software fault injection techniques.

| Software fault injection hierarchy | | | Main property | Fault type | Advantages | Disadvantages |
|---|---|---|---|---|---|---|
| Compile time | Software mutation | Source code mutation | A modified version of high-level source code is loaded to emulate common practical fault patterns. | Mutation | Better emulation of real software mistakes/bugs; suitable for emulating permanent faults. | Case-specific; requires manual intervention; it is hard to emulate transient faults; it is necessary to recompile. |
| | | Bytecode mutation | Applied at the bytecode level (for JAVA and C#). | Bit flips, mutation | No source code needs to be modified. | Additional tools are needed to transform the bytecode. |
| Runtime | | Time-trigger | Software/hardware interrupt; random. | Bit flips, mutation | Random; can be combined with other types of injections. | Hard to recreate the faulted scenario (low reproducibility). |
| | Mutation | Interface (parameter) | APIs; system calls; function parameters. | Mutation | Good portability; can be implemented to run automatically. | Limited operating system space is tested. |
| | | Code; bytecode | Emulation, including performance faults. | Mutation | Match faults in reality; injects into virtual machine's object attribute values and methods parameters | Case-specific; hard to run automatically. |
| | User-space Ptrace) | TRAP instruction | Code; register; crash; crash latency. | Bit flips | Multiple breakpoints; automatic experiments; emulates transient/permanent faults. | Cannot monitor data access; target process must agree to be traced. |
| | | Debug register | Code; register; crash; crash latency. | Bit flips | Injects to code/data/stack parts; automatic experiments; emulates transient/permanent faults. | Not all kernels support debug register access in *ptrace*. |

| Simulation | | Fault target | Fault model | Advantages | Disadvantages |
|---|---|---|---|---|---|
| Kernel-space | Kernel | Code; register; crash; crash latency. | Bit flips | Uses debugging and performance features; automation; emulates transient/permanent faults. | Need knowledge of the kernel. |
| Kernel-space | User virtual address | Virtual address injection; code; register; crash; crash latency. | Bit flips | No need to use *ptrace*; minimum interference with applications; automatic experiments; emulates transient/permanent faults. | Need to use additional code to differentiate overlapped virtual address space for different processes. |
| FPGA | Configuration bit file | Reconfigurable FPGA | Bit flips | Runtime injects directly to FPGA; evaluates hardware prototypes. | Hard to monitor behavior after injections; must have knowledge of FPGA; must recompute checksum. |
| FPGA | Code mutations | Reconfigurable FPGA | Mutation, bit flips | Fast and cheap; effective. | Impact testing; inefficient. |
| Security threat | | Penetration testing | | | |
| Simulation-related | | Processor-level; combinational logic, flip-flops. | Bit flips | Easy to monitor system behavior in the presence of faults. | Results are based on the design of the simulator. |

## 11.4.1 Source Code Mutation

It has been claimed that faults created in source code are very similar to those produced by programming faults, errors, and defects. A source code mutant that is supposed to be semantically different from the original code (in terms of instructions or static data structures) can be created to emulate a fault inside the source. The injected mutants generate a scenario that can be used to test the system's ability to handle certain types of faults. The code mutation to the original program syntax makes use of the source code and is therefore a "white-box" technique. The benefit of using source code is that it gives instant access to logical code layouts and data structures, but it also suffers from the same level of intractability as exhaustive testing. Source code mutation is extremely useful in examining a fault-tolerant system's attributes or behavior in the presence of predesign faults. Examples of tools that use this approach include Pisces Safety Net [35], an extension of Xception [36], and FIRE [37]. Permanent faults [15] as well as transient faults can be emulated by embedding faults/errors into the executable object files at compile time, during which no perturbation to the target process is introduced during process execution.

One of the main drawbacks of source code mutation is that because it requires modification of the source code, the source code must be available (which it won't be for certain systems). Also, since the code is modified, there is a chance that unintended faults will be introduced. Further, this technique cannot be used as part of a certification process because the system under test will be different from what is shipped.

Compile-time code/data mutations introduce a large amount of injection complexity and demand a considerable effort. It is reasonable to investigate what faults (or mistakes or bugs) occur more often than others in real programs for performing targeted injections to reduce the total injection time without losing fault coverage.

Faults can be emulated in a high-level language such as C/C++ and Java, and it is also possible to mutate low-level code through a set of mutation operators (i.e. key programming structures at the machine-code level whereby high-level software faults can be emulated) [35]. Using this method, faults can be injected into targets for which source code is not available. One implementation of the approach would be to disassemble the target executable code to assembly language, apply the library of common programmer mistakes, and then assemble the code back to low-level mutated executable code. The technique can be applied to binary files prior to execution or to in-memory running processes. FIRE [37] is designed to validate object-oriented applications; it requires the instrumentation of the target source code to add reflection-related information.

### 11.4.2 Bytecode Mutation

A bytecode injection or mutation modifies bytecode, the intermediate representation of high-level programs such as Java and C#. The representation behaves as the machine language of a virtual machine. It is a variant of fault injection through the mutation of user code/data. Since it directly handles an off-the-shelf program or library supplied in bytecode without source code, the bytecode mutation has advantages over a source-level injection (SLI), and it can be performed on-demand at load time when a virtual machine loads a class file. *Jaca* [38] uses this approach to fault injection. Jaca injects high-level software faults by using a Java Reflection-based programming tool named *Javassist* to affect the attributes and methods of an object's public interface. Reflection is achieved by subdividing a system's architecture into two levels: the functional (or base) level, in which the application's functionality is implemented, and the nonfunctional (or meta) level which performs monitoring and manipulation of the base-level structure or behavior.

## 11.5 Runtime Fault Injection

This section presents an extensive analysis of runtime techniques for fault injection in the user space and the kernel space. Runtime approaches can be classified based on either the type of triggers used or the component of the software subsystem that is the target of the injection.

### 11.5.1 Time Trigger Faults

An injection can be triggered at a predefined time when the temporal trigger is implemented through the internal timer available in most modern processors. This temporal-trigger-based methodology requires no modifications to the application or workload program. Since it injects faults based on time rather than specific events or system states, it produces unpredictable fault effects and program behavior. As a result, the injected faults are hard to reproduce because of uncertainty in program executions. The approach is, however, suitable for emulating transient faults and intermittent hardware faults.

### 11.5.2 Runtime Mutation

Mutations can happen during runtime with or without compile-time processing. The most commonly used approach is the runtime modification of the parameters of system calls and the bytecode of the Java virtual machine.

### 11.5.2.1 Mutation of APIs and System Call Parameters

Operating systems do not always check all the input parameters and their combinations of system calls and application programming interfaces (APIs). That gives software designers the ability to trade off speed and robustness. Runtime API and system call parameter mutations enable users to probe the effectiveness of the exception-handling scheme of the operating system, library functions, or third-party software packages. It is mainly a "black-box" technique. MAFALDA [26] and Ballista [39] are examples of this caller-based fault injection method, which can make operating systems crash/hang and can also cause abnormal terminations of the library or software packages, instead of graceful returns.

The methodology of parameter mutations of system calls and APIs is likely to find problems that are caused by exceptional conditions or improper handling of exceptions that aren't tested or encountered during operating system development. Exceptional condition tests can be automatically generated. Since faults are introduced to operating systems through system calls, this approach offers a way to evaluate the dependability of operating systems over different platforms. The method is especially suitable if the source code for a module that is to be hardened is unavailable and/or cannot be modified. The results are aimed in part at quantitatively comparing the robustness of multiple implementations of the same system call and/or API [39].

### 11.5.2.2 Software Probe

Fault injections can be performed based on a view of the global state of a system. Although in practice it is infeasible to obtain complete knowledge of the global state without significant intrusion into the system, it is possible to catch a partial view of the global state of systems for an injection. Those partial states (which depend on the particular system being studied) and the faults being injected form software probes. The Loki [25] fault injector is a good example. It is capable of performing such state-based injections. The benefit of this type of injection is that it may facilitate fault removal by identifying the particular global state/fault combinations that lead to system failures, and it may help with dependability assessment by permitting faults to be correctly injected in representative system states.

### 11.5.2.3 Network Messaging Faults

The emphasis of network messaging injections is on identifying specific problems, such as timing errors in a communication protocol or its implementation, instead of on evaluating system dependability. The fault injection is done at the message level through interception and manipulation of incoming and outgoing messages of a target protocol, or through the probing of the state of the protocol to inject spontaneous messages into the system. There is no need to instrument any of the source codes of the protocol. Example network-messaging fault injection tools include ORCHESTRA [14] and NFTAPE [40].

This fault injection approach can test the fault-tolerance capabilities of protocol implementations under various failure models commonly found in the distributed systems literature, including process crash failures, link crash failures, send omission failures, receive omission failures, timing/performance failures, and arbitrary Byzantine failures [14].

In ORCHESTRA, a protocol fault-injection layer is inserted in the protocol stack to test the target protocol, which sits above the fault-injection layer. Experiments may reveal major design or implementation errors as well as subtle violations of protocol specifications. Basile et al. [40] discuss the impact of errors in the messages exchanged by Ensemble processes; if a single-bit error is injected in a randomly selected message sent by a target process, the corrupted message then propagates to other processes and may cause a failure at the receiving end.

### 11.5.3  Library-Based Faults

FIMD-MPI [41], ORCHESTRA [14], and the method of Tsai et al. [42] introduce faults in the system call or API, which is at the boundary of the application and the operating system, to conduct a shared library-based injection. Instead of randomly modifying the parameters of the system call or API, one must instead instrument the shared library itself based on the fault models of interest, which depend on the application's needs. In principle, no source code, either in applications or in the operating system, must be modified. The library-based injection is especially suitable for evaluating application and operating system behavior under exceptional situations, such as resource exhaustion. A good example of library-based injection would be to change the *free()* function in the libleak.so library to create a memory leak scenario that can support evaluation of the memory leak detection algorithm.

### 11.5.4  Performance/Timing Faults

Instead of injecting bit faults, the injector can emulate a set of performance faults, such as finite-size queues, bandwidth limitations, a limited timing loop, or communication and computation delays, that degrade the system's performance. Performance faults are triggered either by events or by random timers within the operating system's kernel space and/or application user space. The faults themselves are introduced by one of the following methods: (i) execution of a loop routine to consume CPU cycles, (ii) modification of the queue size, (iii) squeezing of the sender/receiver buffer, or (iv) holding of a lock/mutex for some time.

### 11.5.5 User-Space *Ptrace*-Based Faults

*Ptrace()* system calls allow the injector process in the user space to inject faults into the target process that is running in the system. To accurately obtain the dependability attributes of applications, a monitoring scheme must be created in the injection environment so that the data of interest can be sampled and documented for analysis. One such crucial dependability attribute (or metric) is the fault/error activation rate. The use of a breakpoint has been commonly recognized as a way to monitor the runtime fault activation; it has a significant advantage over compile-time code/data mutations. In the user space, the breakpoint could be created by a TRAP instruction or by using the GNU Debugger (GDB) tool (discussed in Section 11.5.6).

#### 11.5.5.1 Fault Injection Using Trap Instruction

The trap instruction scheme achieves its versatility by using traps and *ptrace()* system calls to enable software to emulate the effects of both permanent and transient errors. Those mechanisms allow the injection of complex and subtle error behavior into the target system, and provide more control over the type, location, and time of injection of the faults and errors. FERRARI [11] leverages the *ptrace*-based TRAP instructions to set a breakpoint for triggering the injection of a fault.

#### 11.5.5.2 Fault Injection Using Debug Register

The debug register approach uses the advanced debugging and performance monitoring features that exist in most modern processors to inject faults and then monitor the faults' activation and impact on the target system. Faults are injected such that there is a minimum of interference with the target application; no application source code is modified, and no software traps are inserted. Since the target process must be set into the trace mode through a *ptrace()* system call, the application's performance is degraded, but only in a minimal way. This approach for setting breakpoints is used in tools such as Xception [24, 36]. Its most important advantage is that by using instruction and data breakpoint registers, respectively, we can not only inject into and monitor the target process's instruction flow but potentially supervise the application's data flow as well.

### 11.5.6 Fault Injection Using GDB

The general debugger tool GDB is different from the *ptrace*-based injector. It provides richer functionality to support injection into and monitoring of the target user process. GDB is a general-purpose debugging utility that includes interactive user operations and works for almost all UNIX-based environments. Users can make use of both its fault injection and system-debugging capabilities at the same time. The major disadvantage of the GDB-based injector is that it adds too much overhead (such as the interactive dialogue) to the application and may affect the application's performance. Distributed systems evaluation is one area in which the GDB-based approach is nevertheless suitable.

The use of GDB to set a breakpoint for fault injection can be found in SFIDA [43] and NFTAPE [40]. SFIDA [43] has been integrated with GDB for both program debugging and fault injection, and it is capable of injecting software design or implementation faults into a distributed application, in addition to injecting hardware faults in single nodes. NFTAPE [40] uses *expect* (a programmed dialogue with interactive programs) to incorporate GDB and injects faults into Ensemble, a popular group communication system.

### 11.5.7 Kernel Space

Understanding an operating system's sensitivity to errors and identifying error propagation patterns are important in system dependability benchmarking, in selecting a computing platform, and in assessing trade-offs of cost, reliability, and performance. To gain insight into those issues, it would be necessary to perform fault/error injection experiments to determine (i) how an operating system kernel responds to errors that impact the kernel code, kernel data, kernel stack, and processor system registers; and (ii) how the processor hardware architecture (i.e. the instruction set architecture and register set) impacts the kernel behavior in the presence of errors.

The operating system kernel provides rich information on processes and threads running in the system, including the kernel threads themselves. The injectors and their monitoring environment instrumented inside the kernel take advantage of kernel information and gather system behavior attributes as much as possible.

Although any fault models can be implemented, such as code/data mutations with or without kernel/application source code, the most commonly used fault model in the runtime kernel-space injection is that of random bit flips that target all system memory areas plus processors and I/O devices. It is largely a "black box" technique, and no source code is needed. In consequence, injection campaigns can be conducted automatically. That gives users the privilege of being able to automate most, if not all, faulty situations, including both transient and permanent faults. Kernel-space injectors target not only the operating system kernel, but also user-space applications, and are minimally intrusive to the application. Soft errors in the system are becoming an increasingly important consideration, and systems must be designed to be immune to SEUs or soft errors. One area in which the kernel-space injector could be applied is in uniform injection of the whole memory space of systems, including the kernel and user space, to emulate the effect of soft errors on the system.

### 11.5.7.1 Kernel Fault Injection

The kernel scheme, which has been implemented in NFTAPE [22], FINE [17], Xception [24], and MAFALDA [26], targets the operating system kernel through instrumented kernel space injectors that have the ability to reach all the kernel instructions and data. Compared to the kernel approach, mutation of system call parameters is easy to implement and has good portability, but suffers from the limitation of mainly targeting part of the exception handling of system calls. On the other hand, the kernel space injector is more flexible in that it can locate any kernel objects based on triggers of interest or at a random time. However, the kernel space injector has the disadvantage that the kernel image must be modified to hold the injector and its monitoring.

### 11.5.7.2 Driver

The driver subsystem contributes a large portion of the operating system kernel in terms of code size [22] for Linux. Drivers of varying complexity are commonly developed and customized by third-party vendors and then integrated into the kernel. A significant proportion of operating system failures can be traced back to faulty drivers [44]. A kernel space injector can be used to inject bit-flip errors into the driver subsystem. Faults are injected into drivers to evaluate the design of a specific device or fault detection/recovery scheme. The fault model could be bit flips, parameter mutations, or code/data mutations. The injectors of NFTAPE [21, 22], Albinet et al. [45], and Durães and Madeira [46] can perform kernel space injection into driver code.

### 11.5.7.3 User Virtual Address

If errors are injected from the kernel space into an application running in the user space, the application can execute normally; there is no need to set it to TRACE mode. Thus, there is no impact on performance. This method also provides a comprehensive set of fault triggers, including spatial/temporal triggers and triggers related to the manipulation of data in memory. Injected faults can impact any process running on the target system, and no application source code is needed. This capability is available in NFTAPE [21, 22].

The methodology is similar to that used in the design of kernel injectors, but the following questions need to be addressed: How does a kernel module access a target process's virtual address in user space? How do we break the target process with minimum interference? How do we monitor and record the behavior of target applications under faults?

The CPU's debug registers can be used to set breakpoints in the application's virtual address space. When a debugged instruction is executed or the data are accessed with the virtual address in the debug registers, then the same breakpoint handler that is used by the kernel injector is called. Faults can be injected only into the target application process's space, and if another process triggers the breakpoint, then the breakpoint handler records this event, resets the breakpoint, and causes the injector to wait for the target process to trigger the breakpoint.

### 11.5.8 Configurable FPGAs

Configurable FPGAs not only accelerate the system development process and assist with reprogramming in the field to regulate design but also provide the flexibility to evaluate system activities under faulty hardware and software. Partially reconfigurable FPGAs make it possible to emulate soft errors in the hardware. Two fault models are often used for fault injection into FPGA-based systems: (i) HDL source code mutations, and (ii) bit errors in the configuration bitstreams. The tools used in Alderighi et al. [23], NFTAPE [20], and Civera et al. [47] have the ability to inject into FPGAs. Faults in the configuration bit may cause permanent errors in the mapped design. FPGAs are more susceptible than ASICs to SEUs, and their behavior under errors in configuration bitstreams needs to be evaluated.

Alderighi et al. [23] proposed a fault injection tool for SRAM-based FPGAs that is based on fault emulation. Faults are injected by modifying the configuration bitstreams while they are being loaded into the device, without using standard synthesis tools or available commercial software, such as JBits (Java-based APIs for handling bitstreams). That makes the tool independent of the system used for design/development and allows quick fault injection. Also, any device configuration cell can be accessed, allowing one to study the effects of possible contentions or shorts.

Source code (such as VHDL) mutations can also be applied to the FPGA design. Figure 11.2 presents an architecture that adds a set of flip-flops (FFs), including a Mask Chain, to combinational circuits for storing the information on which states should be affected (through bit flips) and the logic for performing fault injections. The signal *inject* triggers the injections, and module *M* is responsible for complementing the output of the combinational circuitry that is loaded into the FF module.

### 11.5.9 Security Threats

Parameter mutations in penetration testing [48] inject illegal data for inputs either through the standard entrance or through the environment. That is much like what attackers do when they test programs for vulnerabilities. Property-based testing examines conformance to specific security properties, which can be used to generate test cases that exercise the source code to determine whether the code

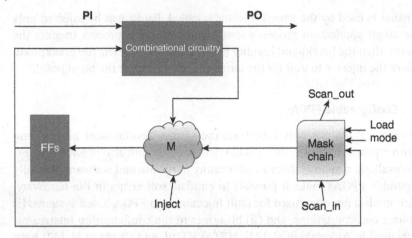

**Figure 11.2** Injecting faults into combinational circuits by adding injection logic. *Source:* Adapted from Civera et al. [47].

fails to satisfy the properties. Transient errors may also create security holes, and it is necessary to investigate the security outcomes of soft errors [49, 50].

Injection of environmental faults is more realistic and reflective of attacks because hackers try to exploit such faults. Meanwhile, observations [48] show that some security flaws are caused by a program's inappropriate interactions with the environment and are triggered by a user's malicious perturbation of the environment (i.e. an environment fault). Environment faults can be injected into a system, and failure to tolerate those faults is an indicator of a potential security flaw in the system.

An exciting research avenue in which fault/error injection has been applied is the possibility of security violations due to errors. In [49], it is shown that naturally occurring hardware errors can cause security vulnerabilities in network applications such as FTP (the File Transfer Protocol) and SSH (Secure Shell). As a result, relatively passive but malicious users can exploit these vulnerabilities. While such events are unlikely, the large number of systems operating in the field means that such vulnerabilities must not be neglected. In another study, fault/error injection was employed to experimentally evaluate and model the security vulnerabilities caused by errors, and the resulting security violations, in two Linux kernel-based firewall facilities (IPChains and Netfilter) [50]. Based on data on field failures, data from the error injection experiments, and system performance parameters such as processor cache miss and replacement rates, a SAN (stochastic activity network) model was developed and simulated to predict the mean time to security vulnerability and the duration of the window of vulnerability under realistic conditions.

The results indicated that error-caused vulnerabilities can be a nonnegligible source of security violations.

## 11.6 Simulation-Based Fault Injection

In simulation-based fault injection, the whole system's behavior is modeled, and faults are injected into the simulated model of the system. This technique is often applied in the design phases to test and validate error-handling techniques before a physical prototype is available, allowing design faults to be detected at an early stage so that the cost of correcting them may be reduced. Several tools have been developed to perform simulation-based fault injection. A few examples are DEPEND [51], ASPHALT [52], MEFISTO [31], FOCUS [32], REACT [33], ADEPT [34], and NFTAPE [20]. Simulation has the advantage of being able to inject any fault models, and it is useful for quick and approximate measurements of a system. However, simulations do not always capture the behavior of a system correctly, and they usually do not account for implementation errors in the real system.

Simulation-based fault injection has high controllability and observability and can be done at the electrical (transistor) level, logic (gate) level, or functional (algorithm) level, depending on the abstraction level employed when the system was simulated. The efficiency is generally greater for higher abstraction levels, while the reachability is lower. Faults may be injected using additional components, either via alteration of the simulation model (mutations) or through built-in simulator commands. The intrusiveness is obviously much higher in the former case than the latter.

In [52], simulated fault injection is compared with other types of software fault injections. The researchers used a low-level injector on a simulated Myrinet network and a software fault injector on the real system. The comparison showed that the simulation did a poor job of covering how the system behaved in invalid or unspecified states. The reason was either that the specifications were ambiguous or that the behavior was undefined (e.g. if the simulation says that the network card should read data from an incorrect address in the host system's memory, then the data are undefined in the simulation). The simulation was accurate when the system operated in valid states.

An example of a simulation-based fault injection experiment in NFTAPE is presented in [20]. A framework was developed to facilitate experiments on a publicly available mixed behavioral/RTL (register-transfer level) VHDL model description of a superscalar processor. The VHDL design of the processor was modified to make it synthesizable. The design hierarchy was extracted from the original description to selectively inject faults in various portions of the processor and to trace the effect of the faults across the functional units.

## 11.7 Dependability Benchmark Attributes

A well-accepted dependability benchmark for evaluating operating systems and applications is not yet available. Nevertheless, a set of dependability attributes that can be evaluated using fault injection can be used for quantitative dependability evaluation and comparison of systems/applications. These attributes are as follows:

- *Crash*: The operating system/application stops working, e.g. there is a bad trap, system panic, or bus error. Crash handlers embedded in the operating system can be enhanced to enable the dumping of failure data (processor and memory state), which can be used to trace the root cause of the crash.
- *Crash latency*: The number of CPU cycles or instructions executed between an activated fault and the actual crash.
- *Propagation*: During injections, errors injected and activated in one module/subsystem may propagate to others, causing the system/application to crash. Analysis of dynamic error propagation patterns can minimize the problem and support detection and control schemes.
- *Hang*: System/application resources are exhausted, resulting in a nonoperational system/application, e.g. deadlock.
- *Crash severity*: For operating systems, the severity of the crash failures resulting from the injected errors can be categorized into three levels, according to the system downtime due to the failure:
  1) *Most severe*, such that recovering from an error injection requires a complete reformatting of the file system on the disk, and the process of bringing up the system may take up to an hour.
  2) *Severe*, such that the rebooting of the system requires the user to interactively run a facility/tool (e.g. *fsck* in Linux) to recover the partially corrupted file system. Although reinstallation is not needed, the process can still take more than five minutes and requires user interference.
  3) *Normal*. At this least severe level, the system may automatically reboot under the instrumentation of a crash-recovery scheme, and the rebooting usually takes less than four minutes, depending on the types of machines and configurations.
- *Robustness of system calls*: The operating system's ability to handle invalid arguments in the invocation of system calls or library functions.
- *Recovery*: The length of time it takes a system/application to return to working condition after fault injections.
- *Sensitivity to errors*: An overall property based on error activation rate, manifestation rate, crash latency, crash/hang rate, and propagation.

The question of how to extract the above attributes from the various operating systems while ensuring a fair comparison between the operating systems still needs to be addressed. We present some possible approaches to tackling this challenge. While operating systems from different vendors have different designs and implementations, there are specific fundamental functionalities that operating systems need to provide to the system. Some of them could be provided (or not) by the user during the installation of his or her specific system. If we focus on the common functionalities, such as process scheduling, file system management, inter-process communication and shared memory allocation and use, and the device driver interface, we can understand the portions of the operating system that are responsible for implementing those subsystems. It is possible to do so through dynamic kernel profiling of applications that target each specific subsystem. When those portions are individually tested through fault injection, we can arrive at a comparison metric for the entire operating system for that particular subsystem. The different subsystems interface with each other, so some overlap of the operating system "slices" that implement the subsystems is to be expected. However, the slicing mechanism reveals the modularity, i.e. the independence, of the subsystems that was designed into the operating system.

## 11.8 Architecture of a Fault Injection Environment: NFTAPE Fault/Error Injection Framework Configured to Evaluate Linux OS

This section presents a sample fault/error injection framework, NFTAPE [12], to illustrate how to architect the key components of a fault injection environment to enable automated benchmarking of operating systems. NFTAPE's architecture and methodology are discussed in the context of two Linux systems: an Intel Pentium 4 running RedHat Linux 9, and a Motorola PowerPC G4 running YellowDog Linux 3.0. Note that the results from the fault injection-based assessment of the two systems are discussed in Chapter 7.

### 11.8.1 Fault Injection Environment

The error injection environment, shown in Figure 11.3, consists of (i) kernel-embedded components (the injection controller, breakpoint handler, crash handler, and crash dumper); (ii) a user-level control host that prepares the target addresses/registers (to be injected), starts the workload, and logs injection data for analysis; (iii) a hardware monitor that detects system hangs/crashes to provide auto reboot if needed; and (iv) a remote crash data collector that resides on the control host or a server to receive crash data via UDP (User Datagram Protocol) connections.

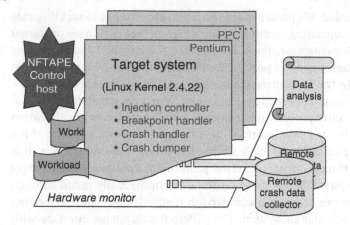

**Figure 11.3** Error injection environment.

### 11.8.2 Approach Overview

An automated error injection process, illustrated in Figure 11.4, includes the following major steps:

- *Step 1: Generate injection targets.* The target generator provides error injection targets, including addresses/registers for the following types of injections: (i) code injection (into randomly chosen instruction breakpoint locations from selected kernel functions, kernel subsystems, and kernel code address ranges); (ii) stack injection (the bit patterns to inject randomly into chosen locations in the kernel process stack); (iii) system register injection (system registers to inject); and (iv) data injection (random locations in both the initialized and uninitialized portions of the kernel data section). The error injection targets are generated and stored before the control host calls the injector manager to conduct injections.

- *Step 2: Inject errors.* The control host employs pregenerated information on the injection target and performs the error injections by calling the injector manager. This process includes starting the workload, enabling performance registers to measure crash latency, and injecting errors.

- *Step 3: Collect data.* Depending on the outcome of the error injection, one of the following actions is taken:
  - *Error not activated.* Go to Step 1 and proceed to the next injection without rebooting the target machine.
  - *Error activated.* Two sets of possible outcomes are classified based on the action to be performed: (i) *not manifested, fail silence violation,* or *system hang,* whereby the results are logged, the target system is rebooted, and the system proceeds to the next injection; or (ii) *crash,* wherein the dumped data are collected following a crash, the target system is rebooted, and the system

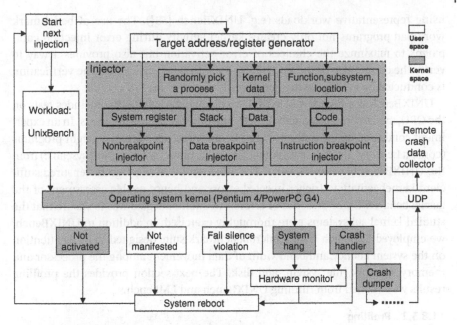

**Figure 11.4** Automated process of injecting errors.

proceeds to the next injection. Crash causes, crash latency (cycles-to-crash), and kernel function return addresses are collected using crash handlers embedded in the kernel. That information is then packaged as a UDP-like packet and sent to a remote crash data collector (i.e. reliable storage) through a UDP connection. Since the file system may not behave properly after the kernel crashes, the crash handler bypasses the kernel's underlying file system and sends the packets directly to the network card's packet-sending function.

## 11.8.3 Kernel Profiling

The Kernel-profiling technique allows the user to meaningfully target kernel code sections that are failure sensitive, and hence, responsive to fault injection methods. Hardware monitoring enables the detection of the operating system's status if there are kernel hangs and kernel crashes. The control host, working in the user space, manages components such as the target generator, workload, watchdog, and injector manager.

### 11.8.3.1 Workload

Because of the size of the kernel, it is impractical to target the entire kernel code for error injection. Depending on the workload, different kernel functions are activated with varied frequencies. To determine the relative importance of different subsystems and the most frequently used functions, the kernel can be profiled using representative workloads (e.g. UNIXBench [53]). The use of benchmark workload programs not only creates kernel activity during error injection campaigns to maximize the chances of error activation but also provides a way to verify the correctness of the underlying operating system kernel. The verification is conducted by modifying the benchmark source code.

UNIXBench is a high-level UNIX/Linux benchmark suite that includes tests on the CPU, memory management, file I/O, and other kernel components. In an experiment conducted by the authors of this book, we selected for study eight programs (context1.c, dhry_2.c, fstime.c, hanoi.c, looper.c, pipe.c, spawn.c, and syscall.c) from the UNIXBench benchmark suite. The selection of those programs ensured sufficient kernel activity to trigger injected errors and hence enable assessment of the kernel behavior in the presence of errors. An additional goal was to ensure that the studied kernel subsystems were thoroughly exercised. In addition to UNIXBench, we employed LMbench [54], a microbenchmark suite designed to focus attention on the system latency and bandwidth of data movement among the processor and memory, network, file system, and disk. The next section provides the profiling results we obtained from running UNIXBench and LMbench.

### 11.8.3.2 Profiling

To determine targets (i.e. the most active kernel functions) for error injection campaigns, a Linux kernel profiler (e.g. [55]) can be used to profile kernel functions while the benchmark workloads are being executed. The profiling procedure consists of three steps: (i) activating the profiling module within the kernel, (ii) launching the benchmark programs, and (iii) deactivating the profiling module and reporting a list of all activated kernel functions. Each function on the list is associated with a *profiling value* that indicates the number of times the sampled program counter falls into a given function. After we ran all eight programs sequentially, a total of 403 kernel functions had been profiled. Figure 11.5 shows the distribution of the profiling values of the profiled kernel functions. The x-axis

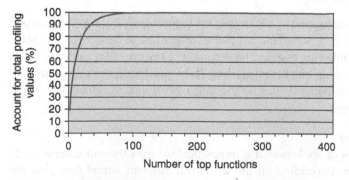

**Figure 11.5** Distribution of profiled functions.

in Figure 11.5 gives the number of top functions, which are sorted according to the profiling value. The *y*-axis shows the percentage of the profiling values of the top functions against the sum of all profiling values. The figure indicates that the top 32 functions account for 95% of all profiling values. These functions were selected as the targets for the error injection experiments. Table 11.2 provides a list of the functions that were the top 32 when UNIXBench was run on the IA-32 architecture, together with a brief description of their functionalities.

Table 11.3 gives the distribution of profiled functions among the kernel modules running the UNIXBench benchmarks. Clearly, the *arch*, *fs*, *kernel*, *mm*, and *drivers* subsystems contribute most of the functions used.

When we ran the LMbench benchmark (a total of 23 programs) while employing the same profiling scheme, 846 kernel functions were observed to execute. Of the 37 most frequently used kernel functions for LMbench, 60% were also among the top 50 functions executed when UNIXBench was run.

### 11.8.4 Hardware Monitoring

To enable automated system reboot following kernel crashes or hangs, a watchdog card can be installed on the system in the form of, for example, a PCI (peripheral component interconnect) card. A counter inside the card is continuously incremented, and, upon reaching a configurable terminal count, it resets the processor. The watchdog driver (i.e. a kernel daemon) controlled by the control host part of NFTAPE can be used to interface with the PCI card, and to reset the counter frequently enough so that during normal operation, the watchdog does not reset the system. However, if the kernel hangs, then the daemon cannot clear the watchdog card's counter, and the system is rebooted. In our experimental environment, the control host reset the watchdog counter by regularly sending the resetting-counter message to the watchdog daemon.

### 11.8.5 Control Host Overview

The control host is the injection campaign controller that supervises the whole procedure by calling components such as the target generator, workload, watchdog, and injector manager. Figure 11.6 depicts the control host hierarchy and the system architecture.

The function of the control host is to generate targets for the kernel injector, start the workload, verify the correctness of the operating system, keep the watchdog monitor working, and, finally, call the injector manager to launch injections based on the targets provided by the target generator. The control host may execute on the same node as the target kernel or on a different node. For simplicity, we assume that the control host and target kernel are on the same node.

**Table 11.2** Most frequently used kernel functions when UNIXBench is run.

| # | Function name | Subsystem | Description |
|---|---|---|---|
| 1 | default_idle | arch | Default loop waiting for rescheduling |
| 2 | system_call | arch | Assembler routine to handle system calls |
| 3 | fget | fs | Map file descriptor to a file structure |
| 4 | fput | fs | Decrement the number of descriptor references, close file if possible |
| 5 | schedule | kernel | Decide which process should be executed |
| 6 | pipe_read | fs | Copy data contained in the buffer intended for the user |
| 7 | generic_file_write | mm | Write to a file through the page cache |
| 8 | pipe_write | fs | Write to the pipe data passed as parameters from the buffer within the limit |
| 9 | file_read_actor | mm | Copy data to user space |
| 10 | sys_write | fs | Write bytes to the descriptor |
| 17 | free_pages | mm | Decrement the page's reference count, hand blocks back to the zone allocator |
| 18 | zap_page_range | mm | Remove user pages in a given range |
| 19 | wake_up | kernel | Wake up all the processes in the wait queue |
| 20 | do_generic_file_read | mm | After a page is read from the disk, copy the data from the Page Cache into the user buffer |
| 21 | block_prepare_write | fs | Write page function for block devices, prepare address space |
| 22 | exit_notify | kernel | Send signals to all closest relatives to let them know this object is dead |
| 23 | copy_page_range | mm | Copy one vm_area from one task to the other |
| 24 | unlock_page | mm | Unlock the page and wake up sleepers |
| 25 | find_lock_page_helper | mm | Scan the hash list to find page, return with write lock held |
| 26 | locate_fd | fs | Find a free file descriptor |

| # | Function | Category | Description |
|---|---|---|---|
| 11 | do_page_fault | arch | Page fault handler |
| 12 | generic_copy_to_user | arch | User address space access function |
| 13 | do_wp_page | mm | Shared page handler |
| 14 | generic_copy_from_user | arch | User address space access functions |
| 15 | sys_read | fs | Read bytes from file |
| 16 | block_commit_write | fs | Prepare to write to the disk and mark buffer dirty |
| 27 | pipe_wait | fs | Drop the inode semaphore and wait for a pipe event |
| 28 | flush_tlb_page | arch | Flush one page |
| 29 | fd_install | fs | Install a file pointer in the fd array |
| 30 | dupfd | fs | Generate a copy of the file descriptor |
| 31 | find_lock_page | mm | Lock the page, scan hash list, return with write lock held |
| 32 | copy_mm | kernel | Create a new process address space |

**Table 11.3** Function distribution among kernel modules.

| Subsystem name | Total number of functions within a subsystem | Contribution to the core 32 functions |
|---|---|---|
| arch | 40 | 5 |
| fs | 154 | 12 |
| kernel | 62 | 5 |
| mm | 71 | 10 |
| drivers | 64 | 0 |
| ipc | 1 | 0 |
| lib | 6 | 0 |
| net | 5 | 0 |
| Total | 403 | 32 |

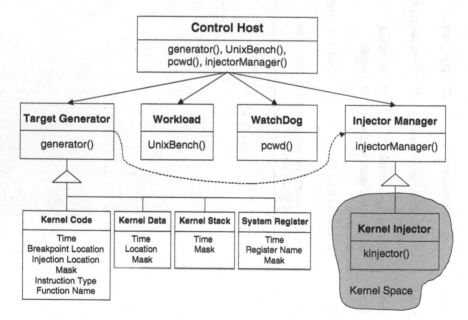

**Figure 11.6** Control host hierarchy.

### 11.8.5.1 Target Generator

The target generator provides the following inputs to the injector manager.

1) **Kernel code section injection.**
   - *Random time*: Time from when the control host calls the injector manager until the kernel injector starts. For example, "Random Time 3000" means

that 3000 ms after the injector manager starts executing, the kernel injector
sets a breakpoint.

- *Breakpoint location*: The kernel injector uses the CPU's instruction breakpoint
  mechanism to check the fault activation and perform injection. By running the
  workload and profiling the corresponding kernel usage, one can identify the
  most frequently used kernel functions. Provided we have the kernel object file,
  i.e. *vmlinux*, and the kernel function name, then the command *objdump* can be
  run to display the linear address of a kernel function. That address is the breakpoint location, which the kernel injector uses to set an instruction breakpoint.
- *Injection location*: In our injection campaigns, the injection location was
  assigned the same value as the breakpoint location. In principle, it could be
  any location in which we are interested.
- *Mask*: A pattern of 32-bit binary values that are used to invert certain bits in
  a data word during error injections. For example, 0x00000010 means that bit
  4 will be flipped in the injection. The expression 0xffff0000 means that bit 31
  to bit 16 is to be flipped.
- *Instruction type*: The instruction mnemonic or opcode, e.g. add, b (branch),
  blt (branch if less than), or stw (store word). This is used to simplify the data
  analysis.
- *Function name*: The kernel function name passed to the kernel injector and
  used to help in the data analysis.

2) **Kernel data section injection.**
- *Random time, mask*: The definitions are the same as given for code section
  injection.
- *Location*: The location corresponds to the linear address at which the kernel
  injector sets the data breakpoint for triggering injections. The addresses are
  randomly selected in the kernel-initialized data section and kernel-
  uninitialized data sections.

3) **Process stack injection.**
- It is impractical to define the kernel stack in advance; therefore, we leave the
  functionality of generating the kernel stack address to the kernel injector.
- *Random time, mask*: The definitions are the same as given for code section
  injection.

4) **System register injection.**
- *Random time, mask*: The definitions are the same as given for code section
  injection.
- *Register name*: The generator randomly picks a system register for injection.

### 11.8.5.2 Injector Manager

The injector manager executes in the user space and constitutes an interface
between the control host and the underlying kernel. The injector manager also

receives outputs from the target generator, communicates with the kernel injector through the *syscall* (*ioctl*) interface, and then passes the injection status from the kernel to the user space.

The injector manager is initialized after the control host has obtained the targets from the target generator and installed the kernel module called the *injection controller* (see next section). Three events take place inside the injector manager: (i) it delays the setting of the breakpoint for a random amount of time; (ii) it starts the kernel injection by passing the target data produced in the target generator to the kernel module; and (iii) it checks the injection status, including error activation and corrupted data in the target location.

## 11.8.6 Kernel-Level Support

This section concentrates on the essential injection work that occurs inside the kernel as specified by four kernel components: the injection controller, breakpoint handler, crash handler, and crash dumper. Among them, the injection controller is a kernel module installed by the control host before the injector manager is called, and the other three parts are compiled together with the kernel.

System register injection is conducted in the injection controller because it does not need breakpoint support. However, code/data/stack errors are injected in the breakpoint handler. If the kernel does not crash/hang, the control host gets the error activation message by calling the injection controller. Otherwise, either the watchdog monitor can detect the kernel hang, or the crash handler catches the kernel crash. In the latter case, the crash handler directly calls the crash dumper to save relevant data to a remote crash data collector. This scenario is illustrated in Figure 11.7. A dashed arrow indicates a possible consequence of a component's execution; the arrow points to the next component that can be activated. A solid arrow indicates that one component is directly calling another.

### 11.8.6.1 Injection Controller

The injection controller is a kernel module or a device driver; it controls the kernel part of the injection campaign. Its main tasks include keeping a kernel injection's status, setting an instruction breakpoint for the code section injection, randomly selecting a kernel stack to set a data breakpoint for stack injections, setting a data breakpoint for the data section injection, and injecting an error into a system register.

*Injection Status Buffer.* A set of global variables, collectively called the *injection status buffer*, is used to maintain the injection status in the kernel. The variables include the breakpoint address, injection location, mask, system register name, the original value at the injection target, the new value after injection, instruction opcode, injection type (code, data, stack, or system register), random number,

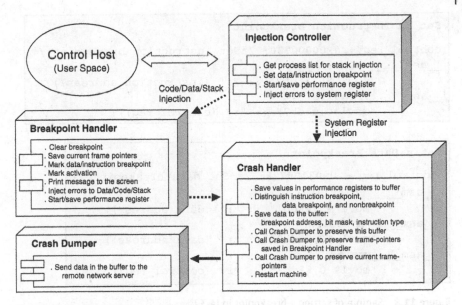

**Figure 11.7** Kernel injector components.

current node IP address, remote crash data collector IP address, activation status, and error message. Different injectors may use different variables, e.g. stack injection does not need instruction opcode.

*Debugging Support.* The kernel injector uses the CPU's debugging facilities (i.e. the breakpoint exception supported by the CPU) to monitor the activation of error injections. The debug events can interrupt normal program flow to inject errors while the program continues to run. The debug registers are used to support instruction breakpoints (for code section injection) and data breakpoints (for data section and stack injection), e.g. DB0 (debug address register 0) through DB7 in Intel IA-32, and IABR/DABR in the PowerPC architecture.

Figure 11.8 gives the sample source code for setting a breakpoint in IA-32. *Instruction_address* and *data_address* are the linear addresses in the kernel space where the breakpoint is to occur.

When an instruction breakpoint is set in DB2, the CPU breaks on instruction execution at that location, no matter which kernel process is running. For data breakpoints, to differentiate between data read and data write, two data breakpoints (DB1 and DB2) are set by assigning DB2 to break on data reads or writes but not on instruction fetches, and DB1 to break on data writes only.

*Performance Monitoring.* The performance monitor is employed to measure cycles-to-crash or instructions-to-crash while errors are being injected. Figure 11.9 shows the source code (in the PowerPC architecture) for monitoring counter registers PMC1 (SPR 953) and PMC2 (SPR 954), which are 32-bit counters used to

```
Set an Instruction Breakpoint

control_reg = 0x00000730; /*Set instruction breakpoint*/
__asm__ __volatile__(
        "movl %0,%%db2" :: "r" (instruction_address));
__asm__ __volatile__(
        "movl%0,%%db7" :: "r" (control_reg));
```

```
Set a Data Breakpoint

control_reg = 0x03100728; /* Set data breakpoint */
__asm__ __volatile__(
        "movl %0,%%db1" :: "r" (data_address));
__asm__ __volatile__(
        "movl %0,%%db2" :: "r" (data_address));
__asm__ __volatile__(
        "movl% 0,%%db7" :: "r" (control_reg));
```

**Figure 11.8** Sample of setting a breakpoint in IA-32.

```
i=0;
__asm__ __volatile__("mtspr 952, %0" :: "r" (i));
__asm__ __volatile__("mtspr 953, %0" :: "r" (i));
__asm__ __volatile__("mtspr 954, %0" :: "r" (i));
i = 0x00000042;
__asm__ __volatile__("mtspr 952, %0" :: "r" (i));
```

**Figure 11.9** Starting performance registers to count cycles-to-crash.

collect those measures. The monitor mode control register MMCR0 (SPR 952) selects PMC1 for counting processor cycles and PMC2 for counting instructions completed.

To keep the *mtspr* (move to special-purpose register) instruction from being performed out of order, we need a serializing instruction that forces the preceding instructions in the program stream to be completed before the program can continue. Examples of such instructions include the *isync/sync* in the PPC (PowerPC microprocessor) and the *35upid* (32-bit user-posted interrupt descriptor) in the IA-32 architecture. Performance registers are started in the injection controller for system register injection only, and they are activated in the breakpoint handler for other injections.

*Process Kernel Stack Injection.* We conducted the kernel stack injection by locating the area where a process kernel stack was located. Inside the kernel, a circular, doubly linked list linked all existing process descriptors and their process kernel

```
p = current;
while ((p=p->next_task) != current) {
   if ( pick this process stack ){
      break;
   }
}
```

```
stack_top = p + sizeof(union task_union);

This process kernel stack is in the range of
{p->thread.ksp, stack_top }
```

**Figure 11.10**   Locating the target process stack.

stacks together. Figure 11.10 shows how to traverse the kernel process list to pick a process and then locate the linear address range of the corresponding process kernel stack for injection.

*System Register Injection.* System registers in the PowerPC architecture can be classified as configuration registers, memory management registers, exception-handling registers, performance-monitoring registers, or miscellaneous registers. In Intel IA-32, registers can be classified as system flags, control registers, debug registers, memory-management registers, or miscellaneous registers. All system register injections occur inside the injection controller, and breakpoints do not need to be set.

### 11.8.7   Breakpoint Handler

A kernel exception handler is called when the processor reports an instruction breakpoint while it is attempting to execute an instruction at a given address or when it reports a data breakpoint as it is attempting to access a memory location. The handler named *do_debug()* is located in the file arch/i386/kernel/traps.c (for the IA-32 architecture) to handle the debug exception with interrupt vector 1 for both the instruction breakpoint and the data breakpoint. A PowerPC processor supports the instruction address breakpoint exception with exception vector offset 0x01300 to handle the instruction breakpoint and supports the DSI (data storage interrupt) exception with the exception vector offset 0x00300 to handle the data breakpoint. Thus, there are two exception handlers in the PPC kernel: one named *InstructionBreakpoint()* that is located in the file arch/ppc/kernel/traps.c, and another named *do_page_fault()* that is located in the file arch/ppc/mm/fault.c.

Figure 11.7 shows the breakpoint handler's main functionality and relationship with other kernel components. Concisely, the breakpoint handler performs the following functions: (i) clears all breakpoints when multiple breakpoints have been reached; (ii) saves current function return addresses in the process kernel stack to enable an analysis of error propagations within kernel functions and kernel subsystems; (iii) reserves the current injection status for the injection status buffer that contains error activation data, injection targets, original value, and breakpoint type; (iv) carries on the error injection by flipping the bits specified in the *mask*, which were saved in the injection status buffer, at this breakpoint location; and (v) starts the performance registers to count the events such as CPU cycles and instructions completed. In an IA-32 processor, performance registers are read and saved to the injection status buffer. In a PPC, performance registers can be reset to zero.

### 11.8.8 Crash Handler

In instrumenting the kernel, we first tracked the locations in the source code responsible for handling kernel errors that could cause kernel crashes, e.g. *printk (KERN_ALERT "Unable to handle kernel NULL pointer dereference")*. Then we replaced that code with the crash handler *nftape_crash_handler()*. Table 11.4 lists

**Table 11.4** Instrumented kernel crashes in IA-32.

| No | Crash causes | Files | No | Crash causes | Files |
|----|--------------|-------|----|--------------|-------|
| 1 | Unable to handle kernel NULL pointer dereference | fault.c | 14 | NMI error | traps.c |
| 2 | Unable to handle kernel paging request | fault.c | 15 | Overflow | traps.c |
| 3 | Kernel panic | panic.c | 16 | Bound error | traps.c |
| 4 | Bed trap | traps.c | 17 | Invalid opcode | traps.c |
| 5 | General protection fault | traps.c | 18 | Device not available | traps.c |
| 6 | Memory parity error | traps.c | 19 | Double fault | traps.c |
| 7 | I/O check error | traps.c | 20 | Coprocessor segment overrun | traps.c |
| 8 | Unknown NMI error | traps.c | 21 | Invalid TSS | traps.c |
| 9 | Do coprocessor error | traps.c | 22 | Segment not present | traps.c |
| 10 | Simd math error | traps.c | 23 | Stack segment error | traps.c |
| 11 | Simd error, cache flush denied | traps.c | 24 | Alignment check | traps.c |
| 12 | Spurious interrupt bug | traps.c | 25 | Machine check | traps.c |
| 13 | Divide error | traps.c | | | |

the crash locations instrumented with embedded crash handlers in the IA-32 architecture. The locations for the PowerPC kernel are similar.

The crash handler itself, as shown in Figure 11.7, is responsible for the following:

1) Saving current performance register values to the dumper buffer (i.e. the buffer used by the crash dumper to send data to the remote crash collector). The difference between the current values and the values previously saved/reset is a measure of the cycles-to-crash and instructions-to-crash.
2) Copying the current injection status to the dumper buffer. The status includes the crash cause, injection type, injection location, crash location, and mask.
3) Calling *crash_dumper()* to dump the data inside the dumper buffer, to dump the function return address to which the frame pointers (that were saved in the injection status buffer in the breakpoint handler before injection happened) point, and to dump the current function return address to which the frame pointers point.
4) Restarting the system for the next injection.

### 11.8.9   Crash Dumper

Linux-embedded kernel-logging schemes cannot guarantee that logging messages will be saved when the kernel crashes. The rationale for using a crash dumper routine is that we cannot assume that the file system layer will be available if the kernel crashes. There are two ways to guarantee a kernel dump. One is to save the system memory image to the disk, e.g. by performing a swap partition before a crash has taken place, and then retrieving the kernel dump after the system reboots. The other is to save the memory image to a centralized server by sending the image over the network. The classical UNIX and Linux Kernel Crash Dump (LKCD) use the former approach, and *netdump* [44] uses the latter.

Our crash dumper adapts the *netdump* to assemble a UDP-like data packet automatically and to directly call the network card driver that sends the packet to the remote crash data collector.

### 11.8.10   Component Interactions

This section presents the component interactions in terms of sequence diagrams. The control host controls all the injection campaigns. We illustrate only the cases in which breakpoints are used to inject errors, i.e. code/data/stack injections. The system register injections are similar. Figure 11.11 shows that the kernel is crashed after error injections and that the crash handler/crash dumper saves the crash data. Figure 11.12 shows that injected errors are activated but not manifested. The control host decided on that approach by checking the results from the workload and the kernel injection status (i.e. errors are activated).

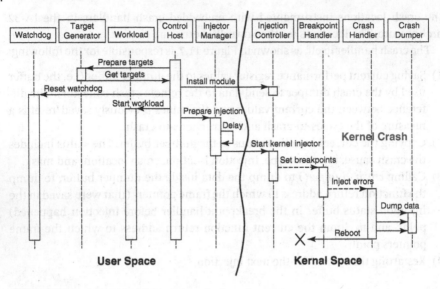

**Figure 11.11** Component interactions for kernel crash.

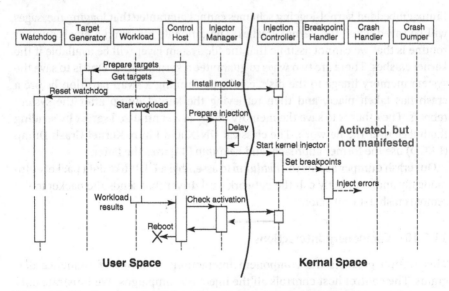

**Figure 11.12** Component collaborations for unmanifested injection.

Figure 11.13 shows that errors have not been activated because the breakpoint has not been reached, and, hence, errors have not been injected. Thus, the control host documents this situation and starts the next injection, using the next target.

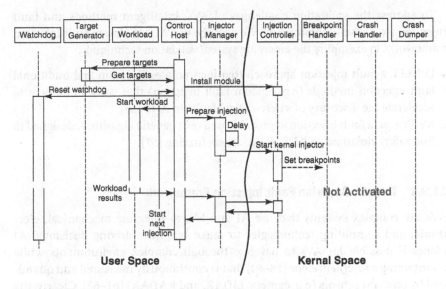

**Figure 11.13** Component interactions for an inactivated injection.

## 11.9 ML-Based Fault Injection: Evaluating Modern Autonomous Vehicles

In recent years, AI/ML (artificial intelligence/machine learning) methods have become a driving force in meeting the growing sophistication and complexity of emerging applications (e.g. AVs or robotic systems). While those applications hold significant potential to increase productivity and improve quality of life, they also bring new vulnerabilities that may cause serious failures, leading to property damage and/or loss of human lives. Consequently, it is critical to validate the robustness of ML algorithms in the presence of disturbances (including accidental faults and/or malicious attacks) under representative execution scenarios. The complexity of such systems makes the test space extremely large. Hence, novel validation methods are required to guarantee the performance of a high-quality validation in an acceptable/reasonable time frame. In this context, traditional fault-injection methods (e.g. random fault injection) may be inadequate to achieve comprehensive coverage and, most importantly, identify vulnerabilities (or design flaws) that could lead to catastrophic system/application failures. In the following, we use autonomous driving systems (ADS) as an example of complex AI/ML-driven applications as we discuss challenges and present novel fault-injection approaches for empirically assessing the fault propagation, resilience, and safety characteristics of an ADS.

To address the validation challenges of AVs, intelligent methods and fault injection tools have been proposed. We describe two AI/ML-driven fault-injection frameworks to exemplify the emerging system validation techniques.

- DriveFI, a fault injection approach that incorporates Bayesian and traditional fault injection methods (e.g. random fault injection) that work in tandem to accelerate the discovery of safety-critical faults in ADS [56].
- AV-Fuzzer, a fault injection approach based on a genetic algorithm, designed to find safety violations in ADS via AI-driven fuzzing [57].

## 11.9.1 DriveFI: Bayesian Fault Injection Framework

AVs are complex systems that use AI and ML to integrate mechanical, electronic, and computing technologies to make real-time driving decisions. AI makes it possible for AVs to navigate through complex environments while maintaining a *safety envelope* [58–60] that is continuously measured and quantified by onboard sensors (e.g. camera, LiDAR, and RADAR) [61–63]. Clearly, the safety and resilience of AVs are of significant concern, as exemplified by several headline-making AV crashes [64, 65], as well as prior work characterizing AV resilience during road tests [66]. Hence there is a compelling need for a comprehensive assessment of AV technology. AV development today involves verification [67–70], validation [71], and testing [72, 73] as well as other forms of assessment throughout the lifecycle. However, assessment of these systems in realistic execution environments, especially given the occurrence of random faults, has been challenging. Fault injection (FI) is a well-established method for testing the resilience and error-handling capabilities of computing and cyber-physical systems [74] under faults. FI-based assessment of AVs presents a unique challenge, not only because of AVs' complexity but also because of the centrality of AI in a free-flowing operational environment [75]. Also, AVs represent a complex integration of software [76] and hardware technologies [77] that have been shown to be vulnerable to hardware and software errors (e.g. SEUs [78, 79], *Heisenbugs* [80]). Future trends of increasing code complexity and shrinking feature sizes will only exacerbate the problem.

This section presents *DriveFI*, an intelligent FI framework for AVs that addresses the above challenge by identifying hazardous situations that can lead to collisions and accidents. DriveFI includes (i) an FI engine that can modify the software and hardware states of an ADS to simulate the occurrence of faults, and (ii) an ML-based fault selection engine, which we call *Bayesian fault injection*, that can find the situations and faults that are most likely to lead to violations of safety conditions. In contrast, traditional FI techniques [74] often do not focus on safety violations, and in practice have low manifestation rates and require enormous amounts of time under test [81, 82]. Note that given a fault model, DriveFI can also perform random FI to obtain a baseline.

*Contributions.* DriveFI's Bayesian FI framework is able to find safety-critical situations and faults through causal and counterfactual reasoning about the behavior of the ADS under a fault. It does so by (1) *integrating domain knowledge* in the form of vehicle kinematics and AV architecture, (2) *modeling safety* based on lateral and longitudinal stopping distance, and (3) using *realistic fault models* to mimic soft errors and software errors. Items (1), (2), and (3) are integrated into a *Bayesian network* (BN). BNs provide a favorable formalism in which to model the propagation of faults across AV system components with an interpretable model. The model, together with fault injection results, can be used to design and assess the safety of AVs. Further, BNs enable rapid probabilistic inference, which allows DriveFI to quickly find safety-critical faults. The Bayesian FI framework can be extended to other safety-critical systems (e.g. surgical robots). The framework requires specification of the safety constraints and the system software architecture to model causal relationships between system subcomponents. We have demonstrated the capabilities and generality of this approach on two industry-grade, level-4 ADSes [83]: DriveAV [61] (a proprietary ADS from NVIDIA) and Apollo 3.0 [62] (an open-source ADS from Baidu).

*Results.* We use three fault models: (1) random and uniform faults in non-ECC-protected processor structures, (2) random and uniform faults in ADS software module outputs (corrupted with min or max values), and (3) faults in which ADS module outputs are corrupted with Bayesian FI. The major results of our injection campaigns include the following:

- Using fault model (2) we compiled a list of 98 400 faults. An exhaustive evaluation of all 98 400 faults in our simulated driving scenarios would have taken 615 days. In comparison, our Bayesian FI was able to find 561 faults that maximally impact AV safety in less than four hours. Thus, Bayesian FI achieves 3690× acceleration. Two cases found by Bayesian FI are described in Section 11.9.1.4; one, in particular, mimics the Tesla vehicle crash [64].
- Bayesian FI is able to find critical faults and scenes that led to safety hazards. Out of the 561 identified faults, 460 manifested as safety hazards. These 460 faults were found to be associated with 68 safety-critical scenes[1] (out of 7200 scenes).
- In comparison, several weeks of 5000 random FI experiments did not result in discovery of a single safety hazard. Only 1.93% of the single-bit injections led to silent-data corruption (SDC) that caused actuation errors. The ADS recovered from all of these errors without any safety violations. In 7.35% of the FIs, kernel

---

1 A scene is represented by one camera frame.

panics and hangs occurred. It is expected that recovery from such faults can be done with the backup/redundant systems that are present in AVs today. We believe that the mining of critical situations by Bayesian FI will have wider applicability beyond our fault injections here. Combining results from a range of fault injection experiments to create a library of situations will help manufacturers develop rules and conditions for AV testing and safe driving.

*Putting DriveFI in Perspective.* Early work studied the safety of AVs using system-theoretic approaches [84, 85]. More recent studies have focused on the resilience of constituent modules of an ADS (described in Section 11.9.3), e.g. [82, 86–88]. Another line of work [89, 90] has used FI to study sensor-related resilience in AVs. In contrast to DriveFI, none of the prior approaches has considered the resilience of modern end-to-end AI-driven systems that use industry-grade ADSes to mine faults that lead to safety hazards.

### 11.9.1.1 Autonomous Driving System Overview

This section provides an overview of the AI-driven Bayesian FI approach advocated here. We now introduce the formalism that is used in the remainder of this section. Figure 11.14 illustrates the basic control architecture of an AV (henceforth also referred to as *Ego Vehicle* or *EV*). It consists of mechanical components and actuators that are controlled by an ADS, which represents the computational

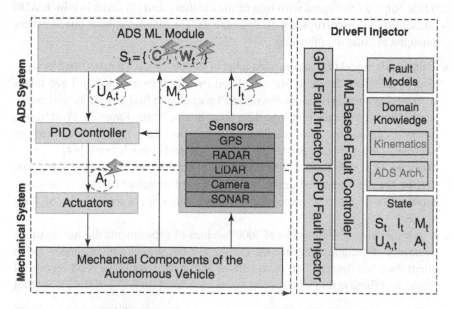

**Figure 11.14** A high-level overview of an AV's autonomous and mechanical systems, and its interaction with DriveFI.

(hardware and software) component of the AV. At every instant in time, $t$, the ADS system takes input from sensors $\mathbf{I_t}$ (e.g. cameras, LiDAR, and GPS), takes inertial measurements $\mathbf{M_t}$ from the mechanical components (e.g. velocity $v_t$ and acceleration $a_t$), and infers actuation commands $\mathbf{A_t}$ (e.g. throttle $\zeta$, brake $b$, and steering angle $\varphi$). For clarity, we further subdivide the ADS into two components: (i) an ML module (responsible for perception and planning) that takes inputs $\mathbf{I_t}$ and $\mathbf{M_t}$ and produces raw-actuation commands $\mathbf{U_{A,t}}$, and (ii) a PID controller [91] that is responsible for smoothing the output $\mathbf{U_{A,t}}$ to produce $\mathbf{A_t}$. The PID controller ensures that the AV does not make any sudden changes in $\mathbf{A_t}$. The ADS ML module has an instantaneous state $\mathbf{S_t}$ that consists of configuration parameters C (e.g. neural network weights to perceive input camera data) and a *world model* $\mathrm{W}_t$, which maintains and tracks the trajectories of all static objects (e.g. lane markings) and dynamic objects (e.g. other vehicles) perceived by the ADS.

### 11.9.1.2 Defining Safety

We define the instantaneous safety criteria of an AV in terms of the longitudinal (i.e. direction of motion of the vehicle) and lateral (i.e. perpendicular to the direction of the vehicle motion) Cartesian distance travelled by the AV (see Figure 11.15). Those criteria form a "primal" definition of safety based on collision avoidance, which can be extended with other notions of safety, e.g. using traffic rules. The extended notions of safety are not considered here, as they can vary based on the laws of the jurisdictions in which they are applied.

---

**Definition 1**

The *stopping distance* $d_{\text{stop}}$ is defined as the maximum distance the vehicle will travel before coming to a complete stop while the maximum comfortable deceleration $a_{\text{max}}$ is being applied.

---

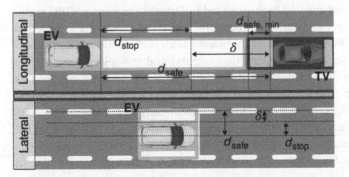

**Figure 11.15** Definition of $d_{\text{stop}}$, $d_{\text{safe}}$, and $\delta$ for lateral and longitudinal movement of the car. Non-AV vehicles are labeled as target vehicles ("TV").

---

**Definition 2**

The *safety envelope* $d_{safe}$ [58, 60] of an AV is defined as the maximum distance an AV can travel without colliding with any static or dynamic object.

---

A safety envelope is used to ensure (through constraints on $\mathbf{U}_{A,t}$) that the vehicle trajectory is collision-free. Production ADSes use techniques such as those in [92, 93] to estimate vehicle and object trajectories, thereby computing $d_{safe}$ whenever an actuation command is sent to the mechanical components of the vehicle. These ADSes generally set a minimum value of $d_{safe}$ (i.e. $d_{safe,min}$) to ensure that a human passenger is never uncomfortable about approaching obstacles.

---

**Definition 3**

The *safety potential* $\delta$ is defined as $\delta = d_{safe} - d_{stop}$. An AV is defined to be in a *safe state* when $\delta > 0$ in both lateral and longitudinal directions.[2]

---

### 11.9.1.3 Fault Injection

The goal of DriveFI is to test ADSes in the presence of faults to identify hazardous situations that can lead to accidents (e.g. loss of property or life). To accomplish that goal, DriveFI includes (i) an FI engine that can modify the software and hardware states of the ADS to simulate the occurrence of faults, and (ii) an ML-based fault selection engine that can find faults and scenes that are most likely to lead to violations of safety conditions and, hence, can be used to guide the fault injection. Taken together, these components of DriveFI can identify hazardous situations that lead to accidents similar to the Tesla crash described later in this section.

*Fault Model.* We assume that faults injected in DriveFI can corrupt GPU architectural state. Memory and caches (of both the CPUs and GPUs) are assumed to be protected with SECDED codes. Each injected fault is characterized by its location (in this case, its dynamic instruction counts) and the injected value. The faults injected into the architectural states of these processors can manifest as *errors* in the inputs, outputs, and internal state of the ADS modules described above (i.e. $\mathbf{I}_t$, $\mathbf{M}_t$, $\mathbf{S}_t$, $\mathbf{U}_{A,t}$, and $\mathbf{A}_t$). DriveFI can directly inject errors into ADS outputs by corrupting the variables that store ADS outputs. ADS software input/output variables are ultimately stored in different levels of storage hierarchies, e.g. registers or caches. Single- or multiple-bit faults cause corruption of variables

---

2 We use the shorthand $\delta > 0$ to mean both lateral and longitudinal $\delta$s.

when not masked in hardware [94]. Hence, faults are being injected into these memory units, but the variables are corrupted to emulate the faults. Therefore, our fault injectors target each element in the internal ADS software state ($S_t$), sensor inputs ($I_t$), vehicle inertial measurements ($M_t$), and actuation commands ($U_t, A_t$), as shown in Figure 11.23. We define any error that causes safety issues for the AV as *hazardous*. For simplicity and clarity, in the remainder of this chapter, we refer to both injected faults and errors as *faults*.

To build a baseline for the ML-based targeted injections, we used DriveFI to perform random injections into the GPU architectural state and ADS module outputs for two production ADS systems from NVIDIA and Baidu. In contrast to prior work [82, 88], which reported significant SDC rates (as high as 20%) for the ADS system's constituent deep-learning models (ConvNets that deal with perception, namely object recognition and tracking), we observed that random injections rarely cause hazardous errors. These faults are masked because of the natural resilience of the ADS stack. Specifically, (i) for production ADS systems that make real-time inferences at 60–100 Hz, transient faults have little chance to propagate to actuators before a new system state is recalculated; (ii) the ADS system architecture is inherently resilient, as it uses algorithms like extended Kalman filtering [95] (for sensor fusion) and PID control (for output smoothing); and (iii) not all driving scenes/frames are hazardous even under faults. Environmental conditions, such as the presence of other objects on the streets, are fundamental in defining the safety envelope.

*Bayesian Fault Injection.* Consider a fault $f$ that changes the value of one of the aforementioned variables. The goal of the ML-based fault injector is to find a *critical situation* that is inherently safe (i.e. $\delta > 0$) and becomes unsafe after injection of fault $f$ (i.e. $\delta_{\text{do}(f)} \leq 0$). The set of all faults $\mathbf{F}_{\text{crit}}$ in which that condition holds is defined as

$$\mathbf{F}_{\text{crit}} = \left\{ f : \delta > 0 \wedge \hat{\delta}_{\ do(f)} \leq 0 \right\}. \tag{11.1}$$

The solution to that problem requires causal and counterfactual reasoning about the behavior of the ADS under a fault. DriveFI performs that reasoning by modeling the ADS system using a Bayesian network (BN, shown in Figure 11.16), which can capture causal relationships [96]. The BN describes statistical relationships between the variables $w_t$, $\mathbf{M_t}$, $\mathbf{U_{A,t}}$, and $\mathbf{A_t}$ at a time $t$, as well as relationships between the variables over time. The topology of the BN is derived from the architecture of the ADS system, i.e. Figure 11.16 has the same graphical structure as Figure 11.14. DriveFI uses the BN to calculate the maximum likelihood

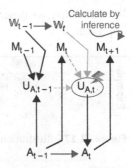

**Figure 11.16** Bayesian FI.

estimate (MLE)[3] of the value $\hat{M}_{t+1}$ and then uses the MLE value to calculate $\hat{\delta}_{do(f)}$ based on the kinematic model of the AV described later in Section 11.9.2. We use probabilistic inference over the posterior distribution of the BN to calculate

$$\hat{M}_{t+1} = argmax_m \Pr[M_{t+1} = m|do(f)]$$ (11.2)

The do(·) notation is based on the *do-calculus* defined in [96]. It marks an FI action as an intervention in the BN model. It replaces certain probabilities with constants and removes statistical conditional dependencies that are a target of the intervention (i.e. dashed lines in Figure 11.16), but preserves all other statistical dependencies. We call this notion of counterfactual reasoning about the importance of a fault in performing targeted injections *Bayesian fault injection*.

#### 11.9.1.4 Case Studies

To explain the need for a high-efficiency FI mechanism (such as our ML-based fault injector), we discuss a real-world example of a car accident due to faults.

*Example: Real-World Crash.* Figure 11.17 shows a real-world example of a fatal accident that was shown to have been caused by a problem in Tesla Autopilot [64]. In Scene 2.A, the EV (shown in beige) followed the lead vehicle (TV#1). A few seconds later, TV#1 changed lanes (shown in Scene 2.A, 2.B); Autopilot then decided to accelerate to match the allowed highway speed. However, TV#1 had been behind another vehicle (TV#2), and the EV had no knowledge of TV#2; it was too late for the EV to recognize TV#2 and slow down to avoid an accident. While this crash was attributed to a design problem (i.e. delayed recognition) in the perception subsystem of the ADS, one can imagine that a runtime fault (that delays the perception of an object) could lead to the same fatal outcome. As we show later, our Bayesian-based fault injector is able to recreate such scenarios.

### 11.9.2 Bayesian Fault Injection

In this section, we describe in detail the formulation of the *Bayesian fault injection* approach.

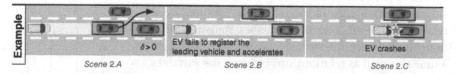

**Figure 11.17** Illustration of Tesla Autopilot problem similar to a Bayesian fault injection.

---

3 The estimated value of $x$ is denoted by $\hat{x}$.

### 11.9.2.1 Kinematics-Based Model of Safety

Consider an EV moving in two-dimensional space as shown in Figure 11.18. The vehicle at time $t$ has an instantaneous position $(x_t, y_t)$, speed $v_t$, heading $\theta_t$, and steering angle $\varphi_t$. The equations of motion for the vehicle are

$$\frac{dx_t}{dt} = v_t \cos\theta_t; \frac{dy_t}{dt} = vt \sin\theta_t; \frac{d\theta_t}{dt} = \frac{v_t \tan\varphi_t}{L}, \tag{11.3}$$

where $L$ is the distance between the wheels of the EV [97]. Here $v_t$ and $\varphi_t$ are determined by the control model for the EV. In our case, $v_t$ is defined based on the output of the ADS $\mathbf{A_t}$, i.e. $v_t = f(\zeta_t, b_t, \varphi_t)$.

Note that a more complete model of the EV motion might include other dynamics, e.g. *sliding* and *skidding* of the EV's wheels. We have not added these complications to our model, as that would require us to make additional assumptions that are beyond the scope of this chapter, e.g. about the EV's tires, road conditions, road banking, and weather. Similarly, we do not consider the 3-D motion of the EV, as doing so would require further assumptions about the topology of the maps (e.g. elevation) in the FI campaign. Our approach can be extended to consider those additional factors.

We can compute the maximum stopping distance $d_{\text{stop}}$ from (11.3) by first computing the time $t_{\text{stop}}$ taken to bring the vehicle to a complete halt, i.e.

$$\left.\frac{d\theta_t}{dt}\right|_{t=t_{\text{stop}}} = 0 \text{ and } \left.\frac{dy_t}{dt}\right|_{t=t_{\text{stop}}} = 0. \tag{11.4}$$

$d_{\text{stop}}$ is then calculated as $[x_{t_{\text{stop}}} - x_0, y_{t_{\text{stop}}} - y_0]^T$, where $(x_0, y_0)$ is the position of the EV at the beginning of the maneuver. Closed-form solutions to the system of differential equations (11.3) and (11.4) are intractable for arbitrary control procedures (i.e. $v_t$ and $\varphi_t$) and have to be solved by iterative numerical solution methods like the Runge-Kutta methods [98].

**Figure 11.18** Orientation of the EV when in motion.

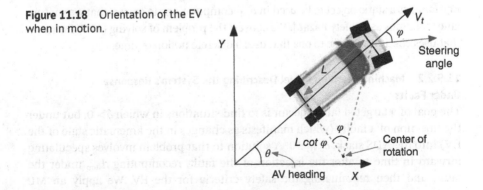

*The Emergency Stop Maneuver.* To simplify our analysis, we assume that the EV executes a special maneuver we call an *emergency stop* to bring the vehicle to a halt. This procedure is characterized by

$$\frac{dv_t}{dt} = -a_{max} \quad \text{and} \quad \frac{d\varphi_t}{dt} = 0. \tag{11.5}$$

That corresponds to the deceleration of the EV with the maximum deceleration to come to a halt. Equation (11.5) reduces (11.3) to

$$\frac{d^2 x_t}{dt^2} = -a_{max} \sin\theta_t \left( \frac{d\theta_t}{dt} \right) \tag{11.6a}$$

$$\frac{d^2 y_t}{dt^2} = -a_{max} \cos\theta_t \left( \frac{d\theta_t}{dt} \right) \tag{11.6b}$$

$$\frac{d\theta_t}{dt} = \frac{\left( \sqrt{ \left( \frac{dx_t}{dt} \right)^2 + \left( \frac{dy_t}{dt} \right)^2 } \right)}{L} \tan\varphi_0, \tag{11.6c}$$

where $\varphi_0$ is the steering angle of the car at the beginning of the maneuver. DriveFI uses the system of equations defined in (11.4) and (11.6) to find $d_{stop}$. We use the shorthand $P$ to denote the procedure (iterative numerical integration) used to compute

$$d_{stop} = P\left( a_{max}, v_0, \theta_0, \varphi_0, x_0, y_0 \right) \tag{11.7}$$

from the above equations and the initial kinematic state of the EV (i.e. $v_0$, $\theta_0$, $\varphi_0$, $x_0$, and $y_0$) at the start of the maneuver. Recall from Section 11.9.1.1 that $\delta = d_{safe} - d_{stop}$ and that $\delta > 0$ defines the safety of the EV. The $d_{safe}$ value is assumed to be computed directly from the sensors of the EV. It is the distance to the closest object (static or dynamic) in the longitudinal or lateral path of the EV. As a result, $d_{safe}$ changes with time, and is updated at the sensor's (e.g. LiDAR's or camera's) refresh rate. We include the boundaries of the lane in which the EV is traveling (henceforth referred to as the *Ego lane*) as a static object to be used in $d_{safe}$ computations to ensure that we capture lane violations as a safety hazard. We convert the problem of solving (11.7) from one that uses continuous time to one that uses a discrete notion of time.

### 11.9.2.2 Machine Learning Model Describing the System's Response Under Faults

The goal of a targeted fault injector is to find situations in which $\delta > 0$, but under the injection of a fault $f$ (which manifests as changes in the kinematic state of the EV) into the ADS stack, $\delta_{do(f)} \leq 0$. A solution to that problem involves speculating forward in time to after the injection of the fault, recomputing $d_{stop}$ under the fault, and then reevaluating the safety criteria for the EV. We apply an ML algorithm, which has been trained as a predictor of the EV's kinematic state, as the mechanism for speculation. We now describe the design of the model and its training and inference.

*The Model.* Consider a situation in which a fault is injected into the EV's ADS at time point $k$. We want to estimate the value of $d_{\text{stop}}$ at time $k + 1$ when the (corrupted) actuation commands of the previous time step have been acted upon. As we showed in the previous section, we can do so using (11.7). However, that would require knowing the values $x_{k+1}$, $y_{k+1}$, $v_{k+1}$, $\theta_{k+1}$, and $\varphi_{k+1}$ as the initial conditions to start the emergency stop maneuver. DriveFI estimates those values based on a maximum likelihood estimation over the posterior distribution of a probabilistic model that captures the components of the ADS.

DriveFI uses a Dynamic Bayesian Network (DBN) [99], specifically a 3-Temporal Bayesian Network (TBN), i.e. a DBN unfolded thrice, to model $x_{k+1}$, $y_{k+1}$, $v_{k+1}$, $\theta_{k+1}$, and $\varphi_{k+1}$. The model is illustrated in Figure 11.19. The core idea of DBNs is to model each point in time with a static BN and to add temporal links from one time slice to the next (as shown by red arrows in Figure 11.19). Usually all the time points have identical BN topologies and hyper-parameter settings. BNs are directed acyclic graphs in which nodes represent random variables and arcs represent the causal connections among the variables [100]. Each random variable in the BN is henceforth referred to as a *node* to avoid confusion with the ADS variables. Each node $x$ is associated with a probability table that provides conditional probability distributions (CPDs, i.e. $\Pr(x \mid \pi(x))$) of a node's possible value given the value of its parent nodes $\pi(x)$.

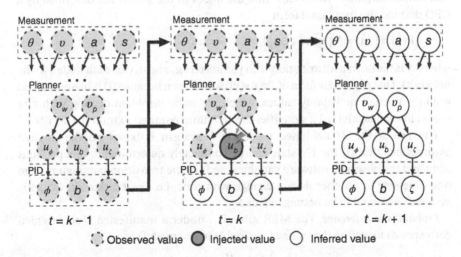

**Figure 11.19** 3-Temporal Bayesian network modeling the ADS.

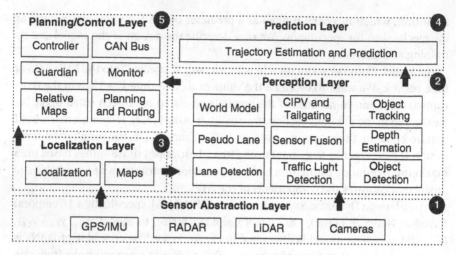

**Figure 11.20** ADS architecture.

The 3-TBN model (see Figure 11.19) is constructed based on the topological structure shown in Figure 11.14. A detailed version of this figure for the Apollo and DriveFI ADSes is described in Section 11.9.3 and shown in Figure 11.20. The variables in each of the ADS modules are connected in a parent-child fashion that reflects the data flow shown in this figure. For example, the edges between $u\zeta$ and $\zeta$ (in Figure 11.19) represent the CPD $\Pr(\zeta|u\zeta)$. This approximates the PID control for $\zeta$. Similarly, other components of the ADS are modeled based on their input and output variables. We assume that the nodes in the 3-TBN are described by a CPD that has the functional form

$$\Pr\left(x|\pi\left(x\right)\right) = N\left(\mu_X^T\pi\left(x\right), \sigma_x\right),$$

where $N$ is the normal distribution with parameters $\mu_\mathbf{x}$ and $\sigma_x$ (for each node $x$ in the network). That particular form of $\Pr(x|\pi(x))$ was chosen because (i) it has numerical stability at small probability values, which are common when dealing with rare events like faults, and (ii) it simplifies the algorithm required to train the 3-TBN.

The use of the 3-TBN-based modeling formalism is based on the implicit assumptions that (i) the EV state can be completely determined by its previous state and the observed software variables, and (ii) the transition parameters from one time step to another do not change with time, i.e. the Markovian dynamic system is assumed to be homogeneous.

*Probabilistic Inference.* The MLE value $\hat{v}_{k+1}$ under a manifested fault $f$ (which corresponds to setting the value of a variable in the model) is

$$\hat{v}_{k+1} = argmax_v \Pr(v_{k+1} = v \,|do\left(f\right), \mathbf{O}_\mathbf{k}^{(f)}). \tag{11.8}$$

Given that we can execute a simulation of the EV under non-fault conditions, all variables that are not children of the injected variable can be observed to have values from the correct run. These "golden" observations are labeled $O_k^{(f)}$. Equation (11.8) is solved by first estimating the posterior distribution of $v_{k+1}$ by using *Markov chain Monte Carlo* methods [99] and then estimating the most likely value of $v_{k+1}$. A similar procedure can be used to compute $\hat{\theta}_{k+1}$ and $\hat{\varphi}_{k+1}$. The values of $\hat{x}_{k+1}$ and $\hat{y}_{k+1}$ can then be computed using time-discretized versions of (11.3).

Finally, from (11.7), we get

$$\hat{d}_{stop} = P\left(a_{max}, \hat{x}_{k+1}, \hat{y}_{k+1}, \hat{v}_{k+1}, \hat{\theta}_{k+1}, \hat{\varphi}_{k+1}\right). \tag{11.9}$$

*Training.* The 3-TBN described above defines a probability distribution $\Pr(X_{k-1}, X_k, X_{k+1})$, where $X_k = M_k \cup S_k \cup U_{A,k} \cup A_k$. Via the BN formalism, $\Pr(X_{k-1}, X_k, X_{k+1})$ is defined as

$$\Pr\left(X_{k-1}, X_k, X_{k+1}\right) = \frac{1}{Z} \prod_{x \in X_{k-1} \cup X_k \cup X_{k+1}} \Pr\left(x | \pi\left(x\right)\right),$$

where $Z$ is the partition function that normalizes $P$ to be a probability distribution. We use the *Expectation-Maximization algorithm* [101] to compute

$$\hat{\mu}, \hat{\sigma} = argmax \, E_{X|D,\mu,\sigma}\left[logP\left(X|\mu,\sigma\right)\right], \tag{11.10}$$

where $D$ refers to a training dataset that contains values of $X_{k-1}$, $X_k$, and $X_{k+1}$ under normal operation as well as during FIs. Here, the computation of $Z$ is intractable because of the combinatorially large size of $X_{k-1} \times X_k \times X_{k+1}$. However, (11.8) does not require the computation of $Z$, as it is a common multiplicand to all values of the objective function.

*Training Data.* The variables in $X_k$ are measured by executing the ADS in several driving scenarios in a simulator. We describe the setup of this simulator in Section 11.9.3. Simply capturing the data under normal operation is not sufficient to capture abnormalities created in the ADS state because of faults. Therefore, in addition to running driving scenarios without faults, we run the driving scenarios while injecting random faults (i.e. the baseline described in Section 11.9.1.1) one at a time. The FI campaign that corresponds to the training data is described in Section 11.9.4. We recreate the process of injecting a fault into a uniformly randomly selected scene 20–50 times for each fault. The reason for varying the number of faults is that some variables (such as $\zeta$, $b$, and $\varphi$) exhibit all possible values during simulated runs with no injections, while others, such as stateful variables, simply do not vary naturally. The computation of $F_{crit}$ (from (11.1)) is done offline for every frame in every driving scene. The FI procedure executes as follows (see Figure 11.21). For each driving scenario, a non-fault-injected "golden" execution of the simulation is performed. At each

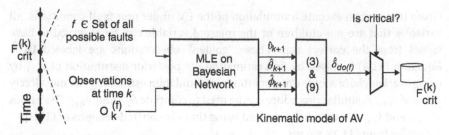

**Figure 11.21** BN MLE inference is executed offline for every simulated time point to find the set of critical faults.

instant $k$, the variables in $X_k$ are measured and stored. These "golden" values of $X_k$ are stepped through with (11.9) to build $\mathbf{F}_{crit}^{(k)}$ for every scene/frame, based on (11.1). An FI campaign is carried out on the simulated EV to execute $(k)$ faults in $\cup_k \mathbf{F}_{crit}^{(k)}$ one frame and one fault at a time.

### 11.9.3 The ADS Architecture and Simulation

#### 11.9.3.1 Overview of ADS

An AV uses ADS technology to control the vehicle's steering, acceleration, and monitoring of the surrounding environment (e.g. other vehicles/pedestrians) [102]. The ADS's key components are as follows. The *Sensor Abstraction Layer* (❶ in Figure 11.20) is responsible for preprocessing of input data, noise filtering, gains control [103], tone-mapping [104], demosaicking [105], and extraction of regions of interest, depending on the sensor type. The *Perception Layer* (❷ in Figure 11.20) takes the input from the *Sensor Abstraction Layer* and uses computer vision techniques (including deep learning [106]) to detect and track [107] static objects (e.g. lanes, traffic signs, and barriers) and dynamic objects (e.g. passenger vehicles, trucks, cyclists, and pedestrians). The perception layer calculates various useful metrics such as "closest in path obstacle" (CIPO) and "tailgating distance" for each object. Such association of an object with measured or inferred metrics (e.g. CIPO and tailgating distance) is defined as the *world model* of the AV. The *Localization Layer* (❸ in Figure 11.20) is responsible for aggregating data from various sources to locate the AV in the world model. The *Prediction Layer* (❹ in Figure 11.20) is responsible for generating trajectories for detected objects by using information from the world model (e.g. positions, headings, velocities, and accelerations). It can probabilistically identify obstacles in an AV's path [108]. The *Planning & Control Layer* (❺ in Figure 11.20) is responsible for generating navigation plans based on the origin and destination and for sending control signals (actuation, brake, and steer) to the AV while maintaining safety. The surveillance system monitors all the modules in the vehicle, including hardware. The "Monitor module" receives data from various modules and passes them on to a human-machine interface for the human driver to view to ensure that all the modules are operating normally. In the event of a module or hardware failure, the monitor triggers an alert in the "Guardian module," which then chooses an action to be taken to prevent an accident.

### 11.9.3.2 Simulation Platform

This study uses *Unreal Engine (UE)* based simulation platforms (CARLA [109] and DriveSim [110]) that are capable of simulating complex urban and freeway driving scenarios by using a library of urban layouts, buildings, pedestrians, vehicles, and weather conditions (e.g. sunny, rainy, and foggy). The simulation platforms are capable of generating sensor data at regular intervals (from cameras and LiDARs) that can be fed to the ADS platform.

Figure 11.22 represents the most common driving scenarios encountered by humans on a daily basis.

### 11.9.4 DriveFI Architecture

The software architecture of DriveFI (shown in Figure 11.23) simulates driving scenarios and controls the AV in simulation by using an AI agent. The scenario manager coordinates the simulator and AI agent and monitors the state of the software and the safety of the AV. In addition, the campaign manager selects a fault model, software or hardware module sites for FI, the number of faults, and a driving scenario. The campaign manager uses the specified

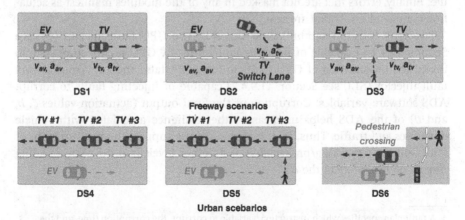

**Figure 11.22** Driving scenarios supported by simulation engine.

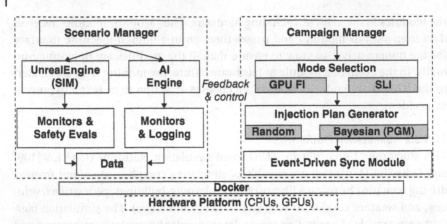

**Figure 11.23** DriveFI architecture.

configuration to profile the ADS workload, generate a fault plan,[4] and inject a specified number of faults into the ADS. The "Event-driven synchronization" module helps coordinate among all the toolkits (the UE-based driving scenario simulator, monitoring agents, campaign manager, fault injectors, and AI agent).

DriveFI output is used to characterize error propagation and masking (i) in computational elements, (ii) in the ADS, and (iii) in vehicle dynamics and traffic. Low-level circuit, microarchitectural, and RTL faults manifest as architectural-state faults in computational elements. The architectural-state faults that do not get masked manifest as errors in the internal state of the ADS modules, and the errors that do not get masked in the module propagate to the output of the module. Finally, errors that are not masked in any of the modules manifest as actuation command errors that are sent to the AV.

Two fault injectors are built into DriveFI: (i) a GPU fault injector (GI, see Section 11.9.4.1) capable of injecting faults into the GPU architecture state to reveal the propagation of GPU faults to the ADS state, and (ii) a source-level fault injector (SLI, see Section 11.9.4.2) capable of injecting faults to corrupt ADS software variables. Corruption of the final output (actuation values $\zeta$, $b$, and $\theta$) of the ADS helps us measure the resilience associated with vehicle dynamics and traffic. Thus, fault injection results support the measurement of fault and error masking/propagation at different levels and the corresponding impact on the safety of the AV.

---

4 A fault plan specifies which instruction/variable to corrupt, the corruption time, and the corruption value.

### 11.9.4.1 Injecting into Computational Elements: GPU Fault Models

We consider transient faults in the functional units (e.g. arithmetic and logic units, and load-store units), latches, and unprotected SRAM structures of the GPU processor. Such transient faults are modeled by injecting bit-flips (single and double) in the outputs of executing instructions. If the destination register is a general-purpose register or a condition code, one or two bits are randomly selected to be flipped. For store instructions, we flip a randomly selected bit (or bits) in the stored value. Since we inject faults directly into the live state (destination registers), our fault model does not account for various masking factors in the lower layers of the hardware stack, such as circuit-, gate-, and microarchitecture-level masking, as well as masking due to faults in architecturally untouched values. The GI employs an approach similar to that of SASSIFI [81] and includes a profiling pass and fault-injection plan generation. We do not consider faults in cache, memory, and register files, as they are protected by ECC.

### 11.9.4.2 Injecting Faults into ADS Module Output Variables

The goal of SLI is to corrupt the internal state of the ADS by modifying the ADS module output variables (hence the input variables of another module) of the ADS components. SLI is implemented as a library that is statically linked to the ADS software. Users must identify software variables that store the outputs of ADS modules that play a critical role in inferring the actuation commands of the AV. Source-code modification is required in order to mark the output variable and invoke the corresponding module injector to get a corrupted value (using the fault model provided in the XML config file). Table 11.5 shows some of the variables from each of the ADS modules (see Figure 11.20) that were targeted using SLI.

The SLI-supported fault models are described below.

*1-Fixed.* A single fault is injected at the *k*th scene of a given ADS software module output. Across experiments, a constant value is used to corrupt the given ADS software module output. There are a total of 41 "1-Fixed" fault types, each defined by (i) the ADS module output and (ii) the corruption value. The bounded continuous outputs are corrupted to the maximum or minimum possible value for those outputs. For example, to inject into brake actuation output, SLI uses a maximum brake value of 1.0 or a minimum brake value of 0.0. Unbounded continuous output values (e.g. $v$, $a$, and *pos*) are corrupted to double or half of the current output value.[5] For categorical output variables, the output value is corrupted to one of the categorical values; e.g. the object/obstacle class can be corrupted to "do not care/disappear," "pedestrian," "vehicle," and "cyclist."

---

5 We limit ourselves to corruption of the outputs to double or half, as otherwise the ADS may detect the injected faults as errors.

**Table 11.5** Examples of SLI-supported ADS module outputs.

| FI Target (Output Variables) |
|---|
| **Path Perception Module** |
| `lane_type, lane_width` |
| **Object Perception Module** |
| `camera_object_distance, camera_object_class,`<br>`lidar_object_distance, lidar_object_class,`<br>`sensor_fused_obstacle_distance, sensor_fused_obstacle_class` |
| **Planning & Control Module** |
| `vehicle_state_measurements` (*pos*, *v*, *a*)`, obstacle_state_measurements`<br>`(pos, v, a), actuator_values` ($\zeta$, *b*, $\varphi$)`, pid_measured_value,`<br>`pid_output` |

*M-Fixed.* $m$ faults are injected into a given set of ADS software module output starting at scene $k$, and faults continue to be injected into the ADS software module output until scene $K + m$. $m$ is chosen uniformly and randomly between 10 and 100. The range selected for $m$ is large enough to support the study of a threshold value for a number of consecutive frames/scenes that must be injected to cause a hazardous situation. Again, there are 41 "M-Fixed" fault types.

*1-Random.* A single fault is injected at the $k$th scene in a uniformly and randomly chosen set of ADS module outputs. The injected fault value is also chosen uniformly and randomly from the range of values of the selected ADS module output.

*M-Random.* $m$ faults are injected in a set of randomly chosen ADS software module output starting at scene $k$, and faults continue to be injected in the ADS software module output until scene $K + M$. $m$ is chosen uniformly and randomly between 10 and 100. In this case, both the ADS module and the corruption value are selected uniformly and randomly.

## 11.9.5 Results

In this section, we characterize the impact of fault and error injection on the safety of the EV. We used a UE-based simulator to study three freeway driving scenarios (DS1–DS3) and three urban driving scenarios (DS4–DS6). DS1–DS3 were controlled by DriveAV, whereas DS4–DS6 were controlled by Apollo. We verified the safety of the EV at any given scene by calculating the CIPO (the closest in-path obstacle) and LK distance (lateral distance from the center of the lane). A safety hazard occurs when $d_{min} < 1.0$ m in the longitudinal direction, which corresponds to less than 1.0 m of minimum distance from CIPO, or when the EV crosses the Ego lane, which corresponds to a 0.80-m displacement from the center of the lane. Hence, the minimum CIPO distance (min-CIPO) and maximum LK distance (max-LK) across all scenes characterize the safety hazard for the entire simulation.

Because of space restrictions, without any loss of generality, we limit our discussion to DS1, in which the EV was controlled by DriveAV, and DS6, in which the EV was controlled by Apollo. Figure 11.11a–d shows the boxplots of min-CIPO and max-LK for Apollo (DS6) and DriveAV (DS1), respectively, across all fault injection experiments and golden runs (defined below). The experiments are summarized in Table 11.6. A boxplot shows the distribution of quantitative data in a way that facilitates comparisons between variables or across levels of a categorical variable. The boxplot shows the quartiles of the dataset, while the whiskers extend to show the rest of the distribution (maximum and minimum samples), except for points that are determined to be outliers [111]. To understand the

**Table 11.6** Fault injection experiments.

| Campaign | Target module | #Faults/Experiment |
| --- | --- | --- |
| 1-GPU-all | All GPU kernels | 1 |
| 1-RANDOM | All software module outputs | 1 |
| 1-Fixed_throttle_max | Actuator – throttle | 1 |
| 1-Fixed_brake_max | Actuator – brake | 1 |
| 1-Fixed_Steer_max | Actuator – steer | 1 |
| 1-Fixed_obstacle_rem | Perception – obstacle disappear | 1 |
| 1-Fixed_obstacle_dist | Perception – obstacle distance | 1 |
| 1-Fixed_lane_rem | Perception – lane disappear | 1 |
| M-Random | All software module outputs | 10–100 |
| M-Fixed_throttle_max | Actuator – throttle | 10–100 |
| M-Fixed_brake_max | Actuator – brake | 10–100 |
| M-Fixed_Steer_max | Actuator – steer | 10–100 |
| M-Fixed_obstacle_rem | Perception – obstacle disappear | 10–100 |
| M-Fixed_obstacle_dist | Perception – obstacle distance | 10–100 |
| M-Fixed_lane_rem | Perception – lane disappear | 10–100 |
| 1-PGM | All software modules | 1 |

simulation and safety characteristics of the driving scenarios, we ran 50 end-to-end simulations for each scenario without any injection. We call those runs *golden runs*. The golden runs serve as a reference against which we compare injected simulation runs in the rest of this chapter. The median min-CIPO and max-LK distances are 16 m (see "golden" in Figure 11.24c) and 0.019 m (see "golden" in Figure 11.24d) for DriveAV, and 11.19 m (see "golden" in Figure 11.24a) and 0.31 m (see "golden" in Figure 11.24b) for Apollo. None of the golden runs resulted in safety hazards.

### 11.9.5.1 GPU-Level Fault Injection

We conducted 800 GPU-level FI experiments for each driving scenario (DS1, DS2, and DS3) in DriveAV. The min-CIPO and max-LK of DS1 simulated in DriveAV are labelled as "1GPU" in Figure 11.24c and d, respectively. We conducted only

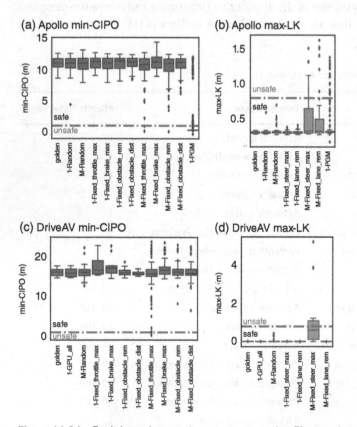

**Figure 11.24** Fault/error impact characterization using FI campaigns. (a) and (b) use DS6; (c) and (d) use DS1.

800 GPU-level FI experiments per scenario because we did not observe any safety violations during the runs, and running more experiments would have been prohibitively expensive (2.7 days per driving scenario, 800*5 min/FI). In FI experiments labelled "1-GPU_all," faults were chosen uniformly randomly from across all dynamic instructions in the ADS. We did not conduct any GPU FI experiments on Apollo because of a CUDA driver version mismatch between GI and Apollo. Resolving the issue would have required vendor support and fixes. In Figure 11.24c and d, we can observe that the EV is always safe, even after FI, and that the distribution is similar to the one in the golden case.

*Fault Propagation and Masking in GPUs.* Across all GPUFI experiments on the DS1–DS3 driving scenarios, representing a total of 2400 FI experiments, 1.9% of injected faults led to SDC (i.e. caused corruption of the actuation outputs that were the final outputs of the ADS module), and 0.02% led to object misclassification errors.[6] None of the object misclassification errors resulted in actuation output corruption. Our results indicate that the perception module (which is responsible for object detection and classification) is more resilient than other ADS modules. The reason is that the perception software takes advantage of sensor fusion (i.e. redundancy in sensing devices can compensate for a fault of a single sensor). Across all driving scenarios, the SDCs did not result in any EV safety breach.

7.35% of faults resulted in detectable uncorrectable errors (DUEs) that led to ADS software crashes (61%) or hangs (39%). The ADS is equipped to handle detectable errors and take corresponding corrective or safety measures. Although DUEs are more common than SDCs, it is expected that systems can recover from such faults via backup/redundant systems. However, errors may persist for multiple frames. In 2% of the misclassification error cases (recall that 0.02% of GPU-level FIs led to misclassification errors), ADS perception module outputs were incorrectly classified for more than one frame, i.e. the impact of the injected fault persisted for more than one frame.

In our data, we observed misclassification of objects for up to eight continuous frames. In those cases, errors did get masked eventually because of the temporal nature of the ADS platform. For example, ADS is fed with new sensor data at regular intervals, e.g. 7.5 times per second in our study. This observation suggests the need for a more thorough study of fault masking and propagation in ADSes at the software level to handle cases in which faults persist for more than one frame.

### 11.9.5.2 Source-Level Fault Injections
We observed in the previous section that the ADS was able to compensate for injected transient faults. To further understand the ADS platform's susceptibility

---

6 *Object misclassification* refers to incorrect classification of an object, e.g. a pedestrian may be interpreted as a vehicle.

to faults and its robustness in the case of persistent errors, we conducted targeted FI with SLI to inject one or more faults directly into the ADS module outputs. We conducted 84 SLI-based FI campaigns for each driving scenario (scenarios 1–3 in DriveAV and 4–6 in Apollo). Of the 43 campaigns, 1 corresponded to "1-Random," 1 corresponded to "M-Random," 41 corresponded to 41 fault types under "M-Fixed," and 41 corresponded to 41 fault types under "M-Random." Labels are shown across the *x*-axis in Figure 11.24.

*Robustness of the ADS to Single and Multiple Faults.* The ADS platform was found to be robust to the injection of a single fault ("1-Random" campaign). To understand the robustness to the persistence of fault-generating multiple random errors, we conducted FI campaigns on driving scenarios by using "1-Random" and "M-Random" fault models. The distributions of min-CIPO and max-LK for "M-Random" were found to be statistically different from those in the golden runs for Apollo (see "M-Random" in Figure 11.24a and b) and DriveAV (see "M-Random" in Figure 11.24c and d). For both the "1-Random" and "M-Random" campaigns, none of the injected faults led to a hazardous driving situation; however, the ADS safety was found to be more vulnerable[7] to the "M-Random" fault model (especially for lane keep functionality). For example, the minimum min-CIPO observed across all injections decreased from 8.7 to 8.0 m, and max-LK increased from 0.34 to 0.7 m for Apollo. Similarly, in DriveAV, min-CIPO increased from 15.2 to 12.6 m, and max-LK decreased from 0.024 to 0.43 m.

*Robustness of the ADS Modules to Single and Multiple Faults.* A persistent fault within a component of the ADS module continuously generates errors for the corresponding module. We tested the robustness of the ADS to a faulty module by subjecting one of the chosen module outputs to multiple faults. In these campaigns, we used "1-Fixed" and "M-Fixed" fault models. There are a total of 41 fault types for the "M-Fixed" and "1-Fixed" fault types (e.g. "throttle max," "obstacle removal," and "lane removal"). Here, we discuss the results of only select campaigns. The selected campaigns (shown in Figure 11.24) include (i) actuation module output corruption (in which the brake, throttle, and steering were all changed to the "max" allowed value); (ii) sensor fusion output corruption (in which the obstacle class was changed to "disappear" and the distance that could be considered in trajectory planning was changed to "max"); and (iii) lane output corruption (in which the lane type was changed to "disappear"). The FI experiments that led to safety breaches appear as data points below the red line for min-CIPO and above the red line for max-LK. Clearly, none of the FI campaigns conducted under the "1-Fixed" fault model led to safety hazards, but a few were observed for "M-random" FI campaigns. We rank ADS modules by their module

---

7 The AV came closer to the other vehicle/pedestrian than it did when no fault was injected.

vulnerability factor (MVF), which we calculated by finding the percent of simulations that resulted in either (i) a min-CIPO distance less than the minimum min-CIPO distance across the golden runs, or (ii) a max-LK distance more than the maximum max-LK distance across the golden simulation runs. Using that method, we found that "steer angle" (MVF = 46%), "lane classification" (MVF = 43%), "obstacle classification" (MVF = 10%), and "throttle" (MVF = 7%) are the most vulnerable for Apollo; for DriveAV, we found the same components to be vulnerable, except for "lane classification" and "obstacle removal."

The higher resilience of "lane classification" and "obstacle removal" in DriveAV can be attributed to DriveAV's free-space detection module (not present in Apollo) and the scene attributes. The free-space detection module helps the DriveAV EV detect drivable space (using a dedicated DNN network tasked with finding drivable space) even if the object is misclassified or its attributes (such as distance and velocity) are corrupted. The free-space detection module ensures safety without requiring complete replication of the obstacle detection and classification modules. The masking of faults in both modules can also be attributed to obstacle registration and tracking in the world model that helps track the obstacle over time.

*Compensation in ADS.* An ADS automatically compensates for any change in EV state (i.e. $\theta$, $v$, $a$, and $s$) that leads to an unsafe state caused by one or more faults/errors. It does so by issuing actuation commands that bring the EV to a safe state. For example, the EV may compensate for an increased $v$ by braking ($b$), a decreased $v$ by throttling ($\zeta$), or a change in heading angle by steering ($\varphi$). Figure 11.25 shows throttle ($\zeta$) values for golden and injected runs (Figure 11.25a) and compensation achieved by braking (Figure 11.25b) for an FI experiment in which $\zeta$ was corrupted in 30 consecutive frames/scenes. Compensation at time step $K$ is calculated as the difference between the cumulative sums of "brake"

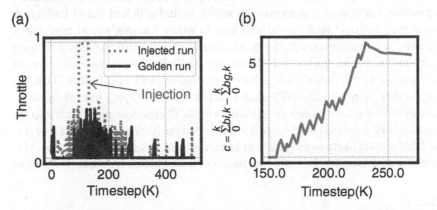

**Figure 11.25** Impact of 30 continuous faults on $\zeta$ in DriveAV. (a) $\zeta$ for a golden simulation (in black) and an injected simulation (in red); (b) compensation $c$.

values observed at time step $K$ in the injected run and in the golden runs. The injection leads to an increase in the velocity of the vehicle, which is compensated for by braking. In Figure 11.25b, we show that the compensation increases until time step $K = 232$ to undo the effects of multiple faults, and then flattens out as the brake values in the golden run and faulty run (i.e. the run with the fault injection) become equal. We observed similar compensation behavior for the faults injected into the brake and steer values.

The ability of an ADS to compensate for injected faults depends on the number of faults and the time of injection. The outlier data point below the red line in Figure 11.24a for "M-Fixed_throttle_max" corresponds to 30 consecutive frames/ scenes injected with faults into $\zeta$ values. In this FI experiment (not shown in Figure 11.25), the vehicle was unable to compensate for the injected faults, as the faults were injected at $K = 400$ and there was not sufficient time for the vehicle to stop, i.e. the EV reached an unsafe state at the end of the injections. In Apollo, only 20 injected faults into $\zeta$ values led to unsafe states. *Persistent errors have a significant impact on the EV's state, and the ADS's ability to compensate for the impact of errors depends on the time and location of FIs.*

### 11.9.5.3 Results of Bayesian FI-Based Injections

So far, in the FI campaigns, hazardous driving conditions (accidents and lane violations) were created only when multiple faults had been injected into the ADS (i.e. multiple consecutive frames/scenes had been injected). However, in the real world, it is more likely that a single fault will occur, and therefore it is important to find conditions under which a single fault can lead to hazardous driving conditions. One way to approach the problem of finding all such single faults (i.e. critical faults) is to inject every single fault while running a driving scenario in a simulator. That approach, however, would be prohibitively costly and is infeasible in practice. For example, an exhaustive search to find which of the 41 fault types under the "1-Fixed" fault model will lead to safety hazards would have taken 272 days[8] in our simulation platform. Another way to find critical faults is to inject faults uniformly and randomly. However, the results from GPU hardware-level FI (see Section 11.9.5.1) and ADS software module-level FI (see Section 11.9.5.2) suggest that we need a smart FI method capable of identifying hazardous situations in driving scenarios and using them to guide FI experiments. A fault injector based on such a method would inject a fault when the ADS is most vulnerable (i.e. the fault is most likely to propagate to actuators) and in such a way that the ADS cannot compensate for the fault. The Bayesian fault injector is able to find *critical*

---

8 615 days/DS = 9 min/DS*41 fault types *2400 scenes. Note that traditional FI is sampling-based, so 615 days represents the worst case of enumeration of all faults.

*situations* that are inherently safe (i.e. $\delta > 0$) but become unsafe after injection of fault $f$ (i.e. $\delta_{do(f)} \leq 0$). We have shown the effectiveness of Bayesian FI by injecting faults into driving scenarios DS4–DS6 controlled by Apollo.

*Effectiveness of Bayesian FI.* When we used Bayesian FI, 82% of injected faults resulted in hazards. (95% of the hazards were accidents involving a pedestrian, and 5% were lane violations.) Bayesian FI selects one of the 41 fault types of the "1-Fixed" fault model, and uses SLI to inject a single fault into an ADS module output variable. Recall that in the "1-Fixed" fault model, the fault location (i.e. the ADS module output variable) and corruption value are defined by the fault type. In comparison, none of the random single FIs led to safety hazards. The Bayesian FI results are marked as "1-PGM" in Figure 11.24a and b. All data points below the red line in Figure 11.24a correspond to collisions, and all data points above the red line in Figure 11.24b correspond to lane violations. The median min-CIPO distance was 0.32 m, which is significantly less than the 11.19-m median value for golden runs. Although the median max-LK value did not change for the "1-PGM" campaign compared to golden runs, 5% of the hazards were due to lane violations.

*Mining Critical Faults and Critical Scenes.* As discussed before, injection of all fault types under the "1-Fixed" fault model of SLI would be prohibitively expensive. Bayesian FI helped us find all critical faults $|F_{crit}|$ for every scene and mine driving scenes that are more susceptible to faults. The critical faults mined by Bayesian FI can help designers understand the weaknesses of the system and corner cases under which a fault may lead to hazards, whereas the critical scenes can be used by designers to inject random faults (using GI or SLI) only in those scenes to help them understand the architecture vulnerability factor (AVF). We believe that the mining of critical scenes by Bayesian FI will have wider applicability beyond our FIs here. The combination of results from a range of FI experiments to create a library of scenes will help manufacturers develop rules and conditions for AV testing and safe driving. Table 11.7 gives summary statistics of mined critical faults and scenes in the driving scenarios DS4–DS6. A total of 561 faults were found to be critical across DS4–DS6. Upon inspecting the mined critical faults, we

**Table 11.7** Summary of PGM-based fault injection.

| Driving scenario | Crit. scenes % | Crit. faults % | Hazard rate |
|---|---|---|---|
| DS4 (2400 scenes) | 0 | 0.0 | 0.0 |
| DS5 (2400 scenes) | 0.88 | 0.20 | 0.36 |
| DS6 (2400 scenes) | 1.96 | 0.36 | 0.20 |

Total faults (TF) in the "FIXED" fault model = #scenes/DS * #error types = 98400/DS.
Critical scenes % = #scenes in which critical faults were found by #scenes/DS.
Critical faults % = (Critical faults mined by Bayesian FI/TF).

found that the top 3 most susceptible ADS module outputs for vehicle collision are the throttle value (24% of 561 critical faults), the PID controller input (18%), and the sensor-fusion obstacle class value (15% of 561 critical faults). ADS module outputs targeted by Bayesian FI for creating lane violations are the (i) lane type value (2% of 561), (ii) throttle (1.4%), and (iii) steer (1.4%). 56% of the fault types were never used by Bayesian FI; for example, Bayesian FI never injected into the output of the camera-sensor object classification module.

For DS4, we did not find any critical scene or error. That was expected, as there was no trailing or leading vehicle around the EV in our driving scenarios. All the vehicles were in the other lane following a completely different trajectory, and one fault in this case would not be sufficient to make the EV cross into the adjacent lane. For DS5, 0.88% of the scenes and 0.20% of the faults were found to be critical. The critical scenes in this case correspond to a scene in which (1) the object (i.e. pedestrian) is first registered into the world model and (2) the EV then starts braking. In the case of (1), the Bayesian FI chooses to remove the obstacle (e.g. by removing the obstacle, or misclassifying the object), and in the case of (2), the Bayesian FI chooses to accelerate the vehicle (e.g. by corrupting PID outputs or planner outputs). For DS6, we observed that 1.96% of the scenes and 0.36% of the faults were critical. We made a similar observation for DS5. However, in addition, we found the EV to be susceptible to faults around turns. Bayesian FI in those cases chooses faults that correspond to a disappearing lane or steering value corruptions. The EV tends to follow the lead vehicle when the lane markings are missing. However, in turns for which there is no lead vehicle to follow, such errors become critical. It is worthwhile to note that Bayesian FI was able to mine critical faults and scenes in 4 hours and took approximately 54 hours to simulate all the extracted faults in the simulator.

## 11.9.6 AV-Fuzzer: Fault Injection Framework Based on AI-Driven Fuzzing

AV-Fuzzer is an efficient AV testing framework for generating test cases that determine an AV's safety violations in an evolving traffic environment. We perturb the driving maneuvers of traffic participants (e.g. other vehicles in the environment) to create situations in which an AV runs into safety violations. The AV-Fuzzer approach is based on the following insights and observations. (i) One can formulate the search for the perturbations to be introduced as an optimization problem that can be solved using a genetic algorithm and domain knowledge of the vehicle dynamics. We minimize the safety potential of an AV over its projected trajectory, and the values of the perturbation determined via this process provide participants' parameters that define their trajectories. (ii) The efficiency of finding safety violations can be improved by designing a local fuzzer that dynamically increases the exploitation of local optima in the areas where highly likely safety-hazardous situations (i.e. near-miss accidents) are observed. (iii) One can develop a restart mechanism that repeats the optimization with significantly different starting points in the unexplored search space to determine diverse safety-hazardous situations in which the AV runs into safety violations.

AV-Fuzzer was demonstrated on Baidu's Apollo, an industrial-grade, level-4 AV software stack widely used to control AVs on public roads [58]. AV-Fuzzer found several safety-critical deficiencies in Apollo that had not been discovered or reported before, and it was able to find these safety violations in a relatively short period of search time. Specifically, 13 critical scenarios were identified in which Apollo ran into hazardous situations that led to crashes. In contrast, other techniques, such as random fuzzing and adaptive stress testing [4], have found only 1 and 5 safety violations, respectively, in the same amount of search time. The overarching causes of the safety violations AV-Fuzzer reports in Apollo can be classified into five distinct types that map to various categories of software deficiencies in that system. While AV-Fuzzer found all five types within 20 hours of search, existing techniques [112] have found at most two distinct types, even given 10× the search time (200 hours). Because AV-Fuzzer is both efficient and effective, it can be integrated into the AV development cycle.

## 11.9.7 Related Work

AV research has traditionally focused on the improvement of ML/AI techniques. However, when models are deployed at a large scale on computing platforms, the focus changes to the assessment of the resilience and safety features of the compute stack that drives the AV. Assessment of the safety and resilience of AVs requires robust testing techniques that are scalable and directly applicable in real-world driving scenarios. It is not scalable or practical to base a safety argument solely on statistical measures such as a billion miles on roads, or on simulations done on platforms such as CARLA [109] or openpilot [63, 113, 114]. Testing the robustness of an ADS has proven to be challenging and mostly ad hoc or experience-based [75]. In particular, to test the functionality and design of the hardware and software components of an ADS, current methods rely on the injection of invalid or perturbed inputs [86, 89, 90] or faults and errors [82, 89, 115] into an ADS in simulation or ADS components, and accrual of millions of miles on roads [116, 117].

However, those methods are not scalable because (i) they lack simulated or real datasets that would represent all kinds of driving scenarios [113]; (ii) it would take billions of miles of driving to add functionality or do a bug fix, in order to drive statistical measures [118]; (iii) they are restricted to DNNs [82, 114, 119–121] and sensors [89, 90], even when DNNs form only a small part of the whole ecosystem; and (iv) once the easy bugs have been fixed, finding rare hazardous events would be exponentially more expensive, as faults might manifest only under specific conditions (e.g. a certain software state).

## 11.10  Insights and Concluding Remarks

In this chapter, we discussed fault injection as an effective means of testing and stressing fault-tolerance mechanisms before they are deployed in the field on an actual system. Fault injection can be done through hardware or software, and the focus of this chapter was on the techniques and tools used in SWIFI. First, we presented a historical view of fault injection in which we studied various software-based fault injection tools. Software-based fault injection tools have been broadly classified as compile-time, runtime, and simulation-based techniques, and each of those categories can be further broken down based on the specific component in the system that is corrupted. We explained the different types by featuring example fault injection tools that implement the various techniques. Based on a broad study of current and earlier fault injection techniques and our experience in developing fault injectors at various levels, we arrived at a set of fault-injection-based dependability attributes for benchmarking systems in general and operating systems in particular. Finally, we talked about architecting a fault injection environment, using the NFTAPE fault/error injection framework as a representative example. We concluded with a brief discussion of a new direction in fault injection, the use of AI/ML methods, by presenting two AI/ML-driven fault injection frameworks (DriveFI, which is a Bayesian fault injector, and AV-Fuzzer, which performs AI-driven fuzzing) for safety assessment of ADS, to exemplify these emerging system validation techniques.

## References

1 Siewiorek, D.P., Chillarege, R., and Kalbarczyk, Z.T. (2004). Reflections on industry trends and experimental research in dependability. *IEEE Transactions on Dependable and Secure Computing* 1 (2): 109–127.

2 Laprie, J.-C. (1985). Dependable computing and fault tolerance: concepts and terminology. *Proceedings of the 15th International Symposium on Fault-Tolerant Computing*, Ann Arbor, MI (19–21 June 1985), 2–11.

3 Chillarege, R. and Bowen, N.S. (1989). Understanding large system failures: a fault injection experiment. *Digest of Papers, the 19th International Symposium on Fault-Tolerant Computing*, Chicago, IL (21–23 June 1989), 356–363. IEEE.

4 Arlat, J., Crouzet, Y., and Laprie, J.-C. (1989). Fault injection for dependability validation of fault-tolerant computer systems. *Digest of Papers, the 19th International Symposium on Fault-Tolerant Computing*, Chicago, IL (21–23 June 1989), 348–355. IEEE.

5 Gunneflo, U., Karlsson, J., and Torin, J. (1989). Evaluation of error detection schemes using fault injection by heavy-ion radiation. *Digest of Papers, the*

*19th International Symposium on Fault-Tolerant Computing*, Chicago, IL (21–23 June 1989), 340–347. IEEE.

6 Wagner, K.D. and McCluskey, E.J. (1985). Effect of supply voltage on circuit propagation delay and test application. *Proceedings of the 1985 International Conference on Computer-Aided Design*, Santa Clara, CA (11–14 November 1985), 42–44.

7 Samson, J.R., Moreno, W., and Falquez, F. (1998). A technique for automated validation of fault tolerant designs using laser fault injection (LFI). *Digest of Papers, the 28th Annual International Symposium on Fault-Tolerant Computing*, Munich, Germany (23–25 June 1998), 162–167. IEEE.

8 Young, L.T., Alonso, C., Iyer, R.K. et al. (1993). A hybrid monitor assisted fault injection environment. In: *Proceedings of the 3rd IFIP International Working Conference on Dependable Computing for Critical Applications, Mondello, Sicily, Italy (14–16 September 1992), Dependable Computing and Fault-Tolerant Systems*, vol. 8 (ed. C.E. Landwehr, B. Randell, and L. Simoncini), 281–302. Vienna, Austria: Springer-Verlag.

9 Guthoff, J. and Sieh, V. (1995). Combining software-implemented and simulation-based fault injection into a single fault injection method. *Digest of Papers, the 25th International Symposium on Fault-Tolerant Computing*, Pasadena, CA (27–30 June 1995), 196–206. IEEE.

10 Benso, A., Rebaudengo, M., and Sonza Reorda, M. (1999). FlexFi: A flexible fault injection environment for microprocessor-based systems. In: *Proceedings of the 18th International Conference on Computer Safety, Reliability and Security (SAFECOMP'99), Toulouse, France (27–29 September 1999), Lecture Notes in Computer Science*, vol. 1698 (ed. M. Felici and K. Kanoun), 323–335. Berlin, Heidelberg, Germany: Springer.

11 Kanawati, N.A., Kanawati, G.A., and Abraham, J.A. (1995). Dependability evaluation using hybrid fault/error injection. *Proceedings of the 1995 IEEE International Computer Performance and Dependability Symposium*, Erlangen, Germany (24–26 April 1995), 224–233. IEEE.

12 Stott, D.T., Floering, B., Burke, D. et al. (2000). NFTAPE: a framework for assessing dependability in distributed systems with lightweight fault injectors. *Proceedings of the IEEE International Computer Performance and Dependability Symposium*, Chicago, IL (27–29 March 2000), 91–100. IEEE.

13 Segall, Z., Vrsalovic, D., Siewiorek, D. et al. (1988). FIAT: fault injection based automated testing environment. *Digest of Papers, the 18th International Symposium on Fault-Tolerant Computing*, Tokyo, Japan (27–30 June 1988), 102–107. IEEE.

14 Dawson, S., Jahanian, F., Mitton, T. et al. (1996). Testing of fault-tolerant and real-time distributed systems via protocol fault injection. *Proceedings of the 26th International Symposium on Fault-Tolerant Computing*, Sendai, Japan (25–27 June 1996), 404–414. IEEE.

**15** Han, S., Shin, K.G., and Rosenberg, H.A. (1995). DOCTOR: an integrated software fault injection environment for distributed real-time systems. *Proceedings of the 1995 IEEE International Computer Performance and Dependability Symposium*, Erlangen, Germany (24–26 April 1995), 204–213. IEEE.

**16** Echtle, K. and Leu, M. (1992). The EFA fault injector for fault-tolerant distributed system testing. *Proceedings of the IEEE Workshop on Fault-Tolerant Parallel and Distributed Systems*, Amherst, MA (6–7 July 1992), 28–35.

**17** Kao, W., Iyer, R.K., and Tang, D. (1993). FINE: a fault injection and monitoring environment for tracing the UNIX system behavior under faults. *IEEE Transactions on Software Engineering* 19 (11): 1105–1118.

**18** Kao, W.-L. and Iyer, R.K. (1994). DEFINE: a distributed fault injection and monitoring environment. *Proceedings of the IEEE Workshop on Fault-Tolerant Parallel and Distributed Systems*, College Station, TX (12–14 June 1994), 252–259. IEEE.

**19** Tsai, T.K., Hsueh, M.-C., Zhao, H. et al. (1999). Stress-based and path-based fault injection. *IEEE Transactions on Computers* 48 (11): 1183–1201.

**20** Saggese, G.P., Vetteth, A., Kalbarczyk, Z. et al. (2005). Microprocessor sensitivity to failures: control vs. execution and combinational vs. sequential logic. *Proceedings of the 2005 International Conference on Dependable Systems and Networks*, Yokohama, Japan (28 June–1 July 2005), 760–769. IEEE.

**21** Gu, W., Kalbarczyk, Z., and Iyer, R.K. (2004). Error sensitivity of the Linux kernel executing on PowerPC G4 and Pentium 4 processors. *Proceedings of the 2004 International Conference on Dependable Systems and Networks*, Florence, Italy (28 June–1 July 2004), 887–896. IEEE.

**22** Gu, W., Kalbarczyk, Z., Iyer, R.K. et al. (2003). Characterization of Linux kernel behavior under errors. *Proceedings of the 2003 International Conference on Dependable Systems and Networks*, San Francisco, CA (22–25 June 2003), 459–468. IEEE.

**23** Alderighi, A., Candelori, A., Casini, F. et al. (2005). SEU sensitivity of Virtex configuration logic. *IEEE Transactions on Nuclear Science* 52 (6): 2462–2467.

**24** Carreira, J., Madeira, H., and Silva, J.G. (1998). Xception: a technique for the evaluation of dependability in modern computers. *IEEE Transactions on Software Engineering* 24 (2): 125–136.

**25** Cukier, M., Chandra, R., Henke, D. et al. (1999). Fault injection based on a partial view of the global state of a distributed system. *Proceedings of the 18th IEEE Symposium on Reliable Distributed Systems*, Lausanne, Switzerland (19–22 October 1999), 168–177. IEEE.

**26** Rodríguez, M., Salles, F., Fabre, J.-C. et al. (1999). MAFALDA: Microkernel assessment by fault injection and design aid. In: *Proceedings of the European Dependable Computing Conference (EDCC-3), Prague, Czech Republic*

*(15–17 September 1999)*, *Lecture Notes in Computer Science*, vol. 1667 (ed. J. Hlavička, E. Maehle, and A. Pataricza), 143–160. Berlin, Heidelberg: Springer.

27 Merenda, A.C. and Merenda, E. (1992). Recovery/serviceability system test improvements for the IBM ES/9000 520 based models. *Digest of Papers, the 22nd International Symposium on Fault-Tolerant Computing*, Boston, MA (8–10 July 1992), 463–467. IEEE.

28 Amendola, A.M., Impagliazzo, L., Marmo, P. et al. (1997). Experimental evaluation of computer-based railway control systems. *Proceedings of the IEEE 27th International Symposium on Fault-Tolerant Computing*, Seattle, WA (24–27 June 1997), 380–384. IEEE.

29 Constantinescu, C. (1998). Validation of the fault/error handling mechanisms of the Teraflops supercomputer. *Digest of Papers, the 28th Annual International Symposium on Fault-Tolerant Computing*, Munich, Germany (23–25 June 1998), 382–389. IEEE.

30 Goswami, K.K. and Iyer, R.K. (1990). DEPEND: A design environment for prediction and evaluation of system dependability. *Proceedings of the 9th IEEE/ AIAA/NASA Conference on Digital Avionics Systems*, Virginia Beach, VA (16–18 October 1990), 87–92. IEEE.

31 Jenn, E., Arlat, J., Rimén, M. et al. (1994). Fault injection into VHDL models: the MEFISTO tool. *Proceedings of the IEEE 24th International Symposium on Fault-Tolerant Computing*, Austin, TX (15–17 June 1994), 66–75. IEEE.

32 Choi, G.S. and Iyer, R.K. (1992). FOCUS: an experimental environment for fault sensitivity analysis. *IEEE Transactions on Computers* 41 (12): 1515–1526.

33 Clark, J.A. and Pradhan, D.K. (1993). REACT: a synthesis and evaluation tool for fault-tolerant multiprocessor architectures. *Proceedings of the Annual Reliability and Maintainability Symposium*, Atlanta, GA (26–28 January 1993), 428–435. IEEE.

34 Ghosh, A.K. and Johnson, B.W. (1995). System-level modeling in the ADEPT environment of a distributed computer system for real-time applications. *Proceedings of the 1995 IEEE International Computer Performance and Dependability Symposium*, Erlangen, Germany (24–26 April 1995), 194–203. IEEE.

35 Voas, J., Charron, F., McGraw, G. et al. (1997). Predicting how badly "good" software can behave. *IEEE Software* 14 (4): 73–83.

36 Madeira, H., Costa, D., and Vieira, M. (2000). On the emulation of software faults by software fault injection. *Proceedings of the International Conference on Dependable Systems and Networks*, New York, NY (25–28 June 2000), 417–426. IEEE.

37 Martins, E. and Rosa, A.C.A. (2000). A fault injection approach based on reflective programming. *Proceedings of the International Conference on Dependable Systems and Networks*, New York, NY (25–28 June 2000), 407–416. IEEE.

**38** de Oliveira Moraes, R.L. and Martins, E. (2003). Jaca: A software fault injection tool. *Proceedings of the 2003 International Conference on Dependable Systems and Networks*, San Francisco, CA (22–25 June 2003), 667. IEEE.

**39** Koopman, P. and DeVale, J. (2000). The exception handling effectiveness of POSIX operating systems. *IEEE Transactions on Software Engineering* 26 (9): 837–848.

**40** Basile, C., Wang, L., Kalbarczyk, Z. et al. (2003). Group communication protocols under errors. *Proceedings of the 22nd International Symposium on Reliable Distributed Systems*, Florence, Italy (6–8 October 2003), 35–44. IEEE.

**41** Blough, D.M. and Liu, P. (2000). FIMD-MPI: A tool for injecting faults into MPI applications. *Proceedings of the 14th International Parallel and Distributed Processing Symposium*, Cancun, Mexico (1–5 May 2000), 241–247. IEEE.

**42** Tsai, T., Vaidyanathan, K., and Gross, K. (2006). Low-overhead run-time memory leak detection and recovery. *Proceedings of the 2006 12th Pacific Rim International Symposium on Dependable Computing*, Riverside, CA (18–20 December 2006), 329–340. IEEE.

**43** Lee, H., Song, Y., and Shin, H. (2000). SFIDA: A software implemented fault injection tool for distributed dependable applications. *Proceedings of the 4th International Conference/Exhibition on High Performance Computing in the Asia-Pacific Region*, Beijing, China (14–17 May 2000), vol. 1, 410–415. IEEE.

**44** Chou, A., Yang, J., Chelf, B. et al. (2001). An empirical study of operating systems errors. *Proceedings of the 18th ACM Symposium on Operating Systems Principles*, Banff, Alberta, Canada (21–24 October 2001), 73–88. New York: Association for Computing Machinery.

**45** Albinet, A., Arlat, J., and Fabre, J.-C. (2004). Characterization of the impact of faulty drivers on the robustness of the Linux kernel. *Proceedings of the International Conference on Dependable Systems and Networks*, Florence, Italy (28 June–1 July 2004), 867–876. IEEE.

**46** Durães, J. and Madeira, H. (2002). Characterization of operating systems behavior in the presence of faulty drivers through software fault emulation. *Proceedings of the 2002 Pacific Rim International Symposium on Dependable Computing*, Tsukuba City, Ibaraki, Japan (16–18 December 2002), 201–209. IEEE.

**47** Civera, P., Macchiarulo, L., Rebaudengo, M. et al. (2001). Exploiting FPGA for accelerating fault injection experiments. *Proceedings of the 7th International On-Line Testing Workshop*, Taormina, Italy (9–11 July 2001), 9–13. IEEE.

**48** Du, W. and Mathur, A.P. (2000). Testing for software vulnerability using environment perturbation. *Proceedings of the International Conference on Dependable Systems and Networks*, New York, NY (25–28 June 2000), 603–612. IEEE.

**49** Xu, J., Chen, S., Kalbarczyk, Z. et al. (2001). An experimental study of security vulnerabilities caused by errors. *Proceedings of the 2001 International Conference on Dependable Systems and Networks*, Göteborg, Sweden (1–4 July 2001), 421–430. IEEE.

**50** Chen, S., Xu, J., Kalbarczyk, Z. et al. (2004). Modeling and evaluating the security threats of transient errors in firewall software. *Performance Evaluation* 56 (1–4): 53–72.

**51** Goswami, K., Iyer, R., and Young, L. (1997). DEPEND: A simulation-based environment for system level dependability analysis. *IEEE Transactions on Computers* 46 (1): 60–74.

**52** Yount, C. and Siewiorek, D. (1996). A methodology for the rapid injection of transient hardware errors. *IEEE Transactions on Computers* 45 (8): 881–891.

**53** Carvalho, G. (2016). How to benchmark a linux server using UnixBench. https://www.copahost.com/blog/benchmark-linux-unixbench/ (accessed 28 July 2021).

**54** McVoy, L. and Staelin, C. (2012). LMbench: Tools for performance analysis. http://www.bitmover.com/lmbench/ (accessed 28 July 2021).

**55** Kern, R., Korobov, M., Forbes, M.M. et al. (2020). Line_profiler and kernprof. https://github.com/rkern/line_profiler (accessed 28 July 2021).

**56** Jha, S., Banerjee, S., Tsai, T. et al. (2019). ML-based fault injection for autonomous vehicles: a case for Bayesian fault injection. *Proceedings of the 2019 49th Annual IEEE/IFIP International Conference on Dependable Systems and Networks*, Portland, OR (24–27 June 2019), 112–124. IEEE.

**57** Li, G., Li, Y., Jha, S. et al. (2020). AV-FUZZER: Finding safety violations in autonomous driving systems. *Proceedings of the 2020 IEEE 31st International Symposium on Software Reliability Engineering*, Coimbra, Portugal (12–15 October 2020), 25–36. IEEE.

**58** Erlien, S.M. (2015). Shared vehicle control using safe driving envelopes for obstacle avoidance and stability. PhD dissertation. Stanford University.

**59** Erlien, S.M., Fujita, S., and Gerdes, J.C. (2016). Shared steering control using safe envelopes for obstacle avoidance and vehicle stability. *IEEE Transactions on Intelligent Transportation Systems* 17 (2): 441–451.

**60** Suh, J., Kim, B., and Yi, K. (2016). Design and evaluation of a driving mode decision algorithm for automated driving vehicle on a motorway. *IFACPapersOnLine* 49 (11): 115–120.

**61** NVIDIA (2022). Nvidia DRIVE SDK v6.0.5. https://developer.nvidia.com/drive/drive-sdk (accessed 1 December 2022).

**62** Baidu (2022). Apollo Open Platform v8.0.0. apollo.auto. https://developer.apollo.auto/ (accessed 1 December 2022).

**63** Comma.ai (2023). Openpilot. https://github.com/commaai/openpilot (accessed 12 September 2018).

**64** Alvarez, S. (2018). Research group demos why Tesla Autopilot could crash into a stationary vehicle. https://www.teslarati.com/tesla-research-group-autopilot-crash-demo/ (accessed 1 December 2022).

**65** TS (2018). Why Uber's self-driving car killed a pedestrian. *The Economist,* 29 May. https://www.economist.com/the-economist-explains/2018/05/29/why-ubers-self-driving-car-killed-a-pedestrian (accessed 29 May 2018).

**66** Banerjee, S.S., Jha, S., Cyriac, J. et al. (2018). Hands off the wheel in autonomous vehicles? A systems perspective on over a million miles of field data. *Proceedings of the 2018 48th Annual IEEE/IFIP International Conference on Dependable Systems and Networks*, Luxembourg, Luxembourg (25–28 June 2018), 586–597. IEEE.

**67** Fan, C., Qi, B., Mitra, S. et al. (2017). DryVR: Data-driven verification and compositional reasoning for automotive systems. In: *Proceedings of the 29th International Conference on Computer Aided Verification, Heidelberg, Germany (24–28 July 2017), Lecture Notes in Computer Science*, vol. 10426 (ed. R. Majumdar and V. Kunčak), Part I, 441–461. Cham: Springer.

**68** Clarke, E.M. and Grumberg, O. (1987). The model checking problem for concurrent systems with many similar processes. In: *[Proceedings of the Colloquium on] Temporal Logic in Specification, Altrincham, UK (8–10 April 1987), Lecture Notes in Computer Science*, vol. 398 (ed. B. Banieqbal, H. Barringer, and A. Pnueli), 188–201. Berlin, Heidelberg: Springer.

**69** Clarke, E.M., Emerson, E.A., and Sistla, A.P. (1983). Automatic verification of finite state concurrent systems using temporal logic specifications: a practical approach. *Proceedings of the 10th ACM SIGACT-SIGPLAN Symposium on Principles of Programming Languages*, Austin, TX (24–26 January 1983), 117–126. New York, NY: Association for Computing Machinery.

**70** Bitner, J., Jain, J., Abadir, M., et al. (1994). Efficient algorithmic circuit verification using indexed BDDs. *Proceedings of the IEEE 24th International Symposium on Fault-Tolerant Computing*, Austin, TX (15–17 June 1994), 266–275. IEEE.

**71** Shen, J. and Abraham, J.A. (1998). Native mode functional test generation for processors with applications to self test and design validation. *Proceedings of the International Test Conference*, Washington, DC (18–23 October 1998), 990–999. IEEE.

**72** Roy, R.K., Niermann, T.M., Patel, J.H. et al. (1988). Compaction of ATPG-generated test sequences for sequential circuits. *Digest of Technical Papers, 1988 IEEE International Conference on Computer-Aided Design*, Santa Clara, CA (7–10 November 1988), 382–385. IEEE.

**73** Hamzaoglu, I. and Patel, J.H. (2000). Deterministic test pattern generation techniques for sequential circuits. *Proceedings of the 2000 IEEE/ACM International Conference on Computer-Aided Design*, San Jose, CA (5–9 November 2000), 538–543. IEEE.

**74** Hsueh, M.-C., Tsai, T.K., and Iyer, R.K. (1997). Fault injection techniques and tools. *Computer* 30 (4): 75–82.

**75** Fraade-Blanar, L., Blumenthal, M.S., Anderson J.M. et al. (2018). Measuring Automated Vehicle Safety: Forging a Framework. *RAND Corporation Research Report RR-2662*. https://www.rand.org/pubs/research_reports/RR2662.html (accessed 1 December 2022).

**76** Zax, D. (2012). Many cars have a hundred million lines of code. *MIT Technology Review* (3 December). https://www.technologyreview.com/2012/12/03/181350/many-cars-have-a-hundred-million-lines-of-code/ (accessed 22 June 2023).

**77** Hawkins, A.J. (2017). NVIDIA says its new supercomputer will enable the highest level of automated driving. *The Verge* (10 October). https://www.theverge.com/2017/10/10/16449416/nvidia-pegasusself-driving-car-ai-robotaxi (accessed 22 June 2023).

**78** Esmaeilzadeh, H., Blem, E., St. Amant, R. et al. (2011). Dark silicon and the end of multicore scaling. *Proceedings of the 2011 38th Annual International Symposium on Computer Architecture*, San Jose, CA (4–8 June 2011), 365–376. IEEE.

**79** Karnik, T. and Hazucha, P. (2004). Characterization of soft errors caused by single event upsets in CMOS processes. *IEEE Transactions on Dependable and Secure Computing* 1 (2): 128–143.

**80** Musuvathi, M., Qadeer, S., Ball, T. et al. (2008). Finding and reproducing Heisenbugs in concurrent programs. *Proceedings of the 8th USENIX Conference on Operating Systems Design and Implementation*, San Diego, CA (8–10 December 2008), 267–280. Berkeley, CA: USENIX Association.

**81** Hari, S.K.S., Tsai, T., Stephenson, M. et al. (2017). SASSIFI: An architecture-level fault injection tool for GPU application resilience evaluation. *Proceedings of the 2017 IEEE International Symposium on Performance Analysis of Systems and Software*, Santa Rosa, CA (24–25 April 2017), 249–258. IEEE.

**82** Li, G., Hari, S.K.S., Sullivan, M. et al. (2017). Understanding error propagation in deep learning neural network (DNN) accelerators and applications. *Proceedings of the International Conference for High Performance Computing, Networking, Storage and Analysis*, Denver, CO (12–17 November 2017), 8:1–8:12. https://doi.org/10.1145/3126908.3126964.

**83** NHTSA (2017). Automated driving systems: a vision for safety. https://www.nhtsa.gov/sites/nhtsa.gov/files/documents/13069a-ads2.0_090617_v9a_tag.pdf (accessed 15 April 2023).

**84** Abdulkhaleq, A., Lammering, D., Wagner, S. et al. (2017). A systematic approach based on STPA for developing a dependable architecture for fully automated driving vehicles. *Procedia Engineering* 179: 41–51.

**85** Leveson, N. (2004). A new accident model for engineering safer systems. *Safety Science* 42 (4): 237–270.

**86** Pei, K., Cao, Y., Yang, J. et al. (2017). DeepXplore: automated whitebox testing of deep learning systems. *Proceedings of the 26th Symposium on Operating Systems*

*Principles*, Shanghai, China (28 October 2017), 1–18. New York: Association for Computing Machinery.

87 Salami, B., Unsal, O., and Kestelman, A. C. (2018). On the resilience of RTL NN accelerators: fault characterization and mitigation. *2018 30th International Symposium on Computer Architecture and High Performance Computing (SBAC-PAD)*, Lyon, France (24–27 September 2018), 322–329.

88 Reagen, B., Gupta, U., Pentecost, L. et al. (2018). Ares: A framework for quantifying the resilience of deep neural networks. *Proceedings of the 55th Annual Design Automation Conference*, San Francisco, CA, USA (24–29 June 2018), article no. 17. New York: Association for Computing Machinery. https://doi.org/10.1145/3195970.3195997.

89 Jha, S., Banerjee, S.S., Cyriac, J. et al. (2018). AVFI: Fault injection for autonomous vehicles. *Proceedings of the 2018 48th Annual IEEE/IFIP International Conference on Dependable Systems and Networks Workshops*, Luxembourg, Luxembourg (25–28 June 2018), 55–56. IEEE.

90 Rubaiyat, A.H.M., Qin, Y., and Alemzadeh, H. (2018). Experimental resilience assessment of an open-source driving agent. *2018 IEEE 23rd Pacific Rim International Symposium on Dependable Computing (PRDC)*, Taipei, Taiwan (4–7 December 2018), 54–63.

91 Åström, K.J. and Hägglund, T. (1995). *PID Controllers: Theory, Design, and Tuning*, 2e. Research Triangle Park, NC: Instrument Society of America.

92 Erlien, S.M., Fujita, S., and Gerdes, J.C. (2013). Safe driving envelopes for shared control of ground vehicles. *IFAC Proceedings Volumes* 46 (21): 831–836.

93 Anderson, S.J., Karumanchi, S.B., and Iagnemma, K. (2012). Constraint-based planning and control for safe, semi-autonomous operation of vehicles. *Proceedings of the 2012 IEEE Intelligent Vehicles Symposium*, Madrid, Spain (3–7 June 2012), 383–388. IEEE.

94 Avižienis, A., Laprie, J.-C., Randell, B. et al. (2004). Basic concepts and taxonomy of dependable and secure computing. *IEEE Transactions on Dependable and Secure Computing* 1 (1): 11–33.

95 Julier, S.J. and Uhlmann, J.K. (1997). New extension of the Kalman filter to nonlinear systems. *Proceedings SPIE 3068, Signal Processing, Sensor Fusion, and Target Recognition VI*, Orlando, FL (28 July 1997), 182–194. https://doi.org/10.1117/12.280797.

96 Pearl, J. (2018). Theoretical impediments to machine learning with seven sparks from the causal revolution. *Proceedings of the 11th ACM International Conference on Web Search and Data Mining*, Marina Del Rey, CA (5–9 February 2018). New York: Association for Computing Machinery. https://doi.org/10.1145/3159652.3176182.

97 LaValle, S.M. (2006). *Planning Algorithms*. Cambridge, UK: Cambridge University Press.

**98** DeVries, P.L. (1994). *A First Course in Computational Physics*. New York: Wiley.

**99** Koller, D., Weber, J., Huang, T, et al. (1994). Towards robust automatic traffic scene analysis in real-time. *Proceedings of the 12th International Conference on Pattern Recognition*, Jerusalem, Israel (9–13 October 1994), 126–131. IEEE.

**100** Pearl, J. (1988). *Probabilistic Reasoning in Intelligent Systems: Networks of Plausible Inference*. San Francisco, CA: Morgan Kaufmann.

**101** Dempster, A.P., Laird, N.M., and Rubin, D.B. (1977). Maximum likelihood from incomplete data via the EM algorithm. *Journal of the Royal Statistical Society. Series B (Methodological)* 39 (1): 1–38.

**102** SAE International (2021). Taxonomy and definitions for terms related to driving automation systems for on-road motor vehicles. https://www.sae.org/standards/content/j3016_202104/ (accessed 22 June 2023).

**103** Watson, A.B. and Solomon, J.A. (1997). Model of visual contrast gain control and pattern masking. *Journal of the Optical Society of America A* 14 (9): 2379–2391.

**104** Ashikhmin, M. (2002). A tone mapping algorithm for high contrast images. *Proceedings of the 13th Eurographics Workshop on Rendering*, Pisa, Italy (26–28 June 2002), 145–156. Goslar, Germany: Eurographics Association.

**105** Menon, D. and Calvagno, G. (2011). Color image demosaicking: an overview. *Signal Processing: Image Communication* 26 (8–9): 518–533.

**106** Redmon, J., Divvala, S., Girshick, R. et al. (2016). You only look once: unified, real-time object detection. *Proceedings of the IEEE Conference on Computer Vision and Pattern Recognition*, Las Vegas, NV (27–30 June 2016), 779–788. IEEE.

**107** Reid, D.B. (1979). An algorithm for tracking multiple targets. *IEEE Transactions on Automatic Control* AC-24 (6): 843–854.

**108** Houenou, A., Bonnifait, P., Cherfaoui, V. et al. (2013). Vehicle trajectory prediction based on motion model and maneuver recognition. *Proceedings of the 2013 IEEE/RSJ International Conference on Intelligent Robots and Systems*, Tokyo, Japan (3–7 November 2013), 4363–4369.

**109** Dosovitskiy, A., Ros, G., Codevilla, F. et al. (2017). CARLA: An open urban driving simulator. *Proceedings of the 1st Annual Conference on Robot Learning*, Mountain View, CA (13–15 November 2017) [*Proceedings of Machine Learning Research* 78: 1–16].

**110** NVIDIA (2022). NVIDIA DRIVE Sim, 1 December 2022. https://developer.nvidia.com/drive/simulation (accessed 15 April 2023).

**111** Waskom, M. (2022). seaborn.boxplot. https://seaborn.pydata.org/generated/seaborn.boxplot.html (accessed 22 June 2023).

**112** Lee, R., Mengshoel, O.J., Saksena, A. et al. (2020). Adaptive stress testing: finding likely failure events with reinforcement learning. *Journal of Artificial Intelligence Research* 69: 1165–1201.

**113** Anderson, J.M., Kalra, N., Stanley, K.D. et al. (2016). Autonomous Vehicle Technology: A Guide for Policymakers. *RAND Corporation research report RR-443-2-RC*.

**114** Kalra, N. and Paddock, S.M. (2016). Driving to safety: how many miles of driving would it take to demonstrate autonomous vehicle reliability? *Transportation Research Part A: Policy and Practice* 94: 182–193.

**115** Jha, S., Tsai, T., Hari, S.K.S. et al. (2018). Kayotee: a fault injection-based system to assess the safety and reliability of autonomous vehicles to faults and errors. *3rd IEEE International Workshop on Automotive Reliability & Test*, Phoenix, AZ (1–2 November 2018).

**116** Molly From Gasgoo (2018). Baidu Apollo given another 20 licenses by Beijing for autonomous car road tests. *Gasgoo* (26 December). http://autonews.gasgoo.com/china_news/70015513.html (accessed 1 December 2022).

**117** Waymo LLC (2021). *Waymo Safety Report*. https://ltad.com/resources/waymo-safety-report-2021.html (accessed 21 April 2023).

**118** Koopman, P. and Wagner, M. (2018). Toward a Framework for Highly Automated Vehicle Safety Validation. *SAE International Technical Paper 2018-01-1071*.

**119** Lu, J., Sibai, H., Fabry, E., and Forsyth, D. (2017). No need to worry about adversarial examples in object detection in autonomous vehicles. https://doi.org/10.48550/arXiv.1707.03501.

**120** Pei, K., Zhu, L., Cao, Y., and Jana, S. (2017). Towards practical verification of machine learning: the case of computer vision systems. arXiv preprint arXiv:1712.01785.

**121** Lakkaraju, H., Kamar, E., Caruana, R. et al. (2017). Identifying unknown unknowns in the open world: representations and policies for guided exploration. *Proceedings of the 31st AAAI Conference on Artificial Intelligence*, San Francisco, CA (4–9 February 2017), 2124–2132. AAAI Press.

# 12
# Measurement-Based Analysis of Large-Scale Clusters: Methodology

## 12.1 Introduction

The dependability of a system can be experimentally evaluated at different phases of its lifecycle. In the design phase, computer-aided design (CAD) environments are used to evaluate the design via simulation, including simulated fault injection. Such fault injection tests the effectiveness of fault-tolerance mechanisms and evaluates system dependability, providing timely feedback to system designers. Simulation, however, requires accurate input parameters and validation of output results. Although the parameter estimates can be obtained from past measurements, this is often complicated by design and technology changes. In the prototype phase, the system runs under controlled workload conditions; controlled physical fault injection is used to evaluate the system behavior under faults, including the detection coverage and the recovery capability of various fault-tolerance mechanisms. Fault injection on a real system can provide information about the failure process from fault occurrence to system recovery, including error latency, propagation, detection, and recovery (which may involve reconfiguration). However, that type of fault injection can only study artificial faults; it cannot provide certain important dependability measures, such as mean time between failures (MTBFs) and availability. In the operational phase, a direct measurement-based approach can be used to measure systems in the field under real workloads. The collected data contain a large amount of information about naturally occurring errors/failures. Analysis of these data can provide an understanding of actual error/failure characteristics and insight into analytical models. Although measurement-based analysis is useful for evaluating real systems, it is limited to detecting errors. Further, conditions in the field may vary widely, casting doubt on the statistical validity of the results. Thus, all three approaches – simulated fault

*Dependable Computing: Design and Assessment*, First Edition. Ravishankar K. Iyer, Zbigniew T. Kalbarczyk, and Nithin M. Nakka.
© 2024 The IEEE Computer Society. Published 2024 by John Wiley & Sons, Inc.
Companion website: www.wiley.com/go/iyer/dependablecomputing1

injection, physical fault injection, and measurement-based analysis – are valuable in dependability analysis.

In the design phase, simulated fault injection can be conducted at various levels: the electrical level, the logic level, and the function level. The objective of simulated fault injection is to identify dependability bottlenecks, coverage of error detection/recovery mechanisms, the effectiveness of reconfiguration schemes, performance loss, and other dependability measures. The feedback from simulation can be extremely useful in the cost-effective redesign of a system. A thorough discussion of various techniques for simulated fault injection can be found in [1].

In the prototype phase, while the objectives of physical fault injection are similar to those of simulated fault injection, the methods differ radically, as real fault injection and monitoring facilities are involved. Physical faults can be injected at the hardware level (as logic or electrical faults) or at the software level (as code or data corruption). Heavy-ion radiation techniques can also be used to inject faults and stress the system. A detailed treatment of the instrumentation involved in fault injection experiments, with real examples and including several fault injection environments, is given in [1].

In the operational phase, a measurement-based analysis must address issues such as how to monitor computer errors and failures and how to analyze measured data to quantify system dependability characteristics. Although methods for the design and evaluation of fault-tolerant systems have been extensively researched, little is known about how well these strategies work in the field. Studies of production systems are valuable not only for accurate evaluation but also to identify reliability bottlenecks in a system's design. The measurement-based analysis in [1] is based on over 200 machine-years of data gathered from IBM, Digital Equipment Corporation (DEC), and Tandem systems that were not networked.

In this chapter, we focus on the operational phase. The results from this phase can inform both the design and prototype phases as well as new or revised designs.

System dependability in the operational phase is affected by workload effects, hardware problems, and environmental factors. Thus, the system in the operational phase cannot be characterized through the simple application of analytical models proposed for the design or development phase. In addition, the operational phase of software is very different from the development phase. The operational phase involves frequent changes and updates installed either by system managers or vendors. Often, a vendor will install a change (i.e. patch) to fix a fault found at some other installation. In a sense, the system being measured represents an aggregate of all such systems being maintained by the vendor.

This chapter discusses past and current research and methodologies for measurement-based dependability analysis of a range of systems. Examples of actual operational systems are provided to illustrate different approaches, introduce measurement and analysis methods for failure characterization of systems, and assess error-handling mechanisms. The selected examples range from earlier work on IBM-MVS and Tandem (now HP) machines to high-performance computing (HPC) systems, smartphones, Software-as-a-Service clouds, and medical devices.

## 12.2 Related Research

Measurement-based dependability analysis of operational systems has evolved significantly over the past decades. Past studies have addressed one or more of the following issues: basic error characteristics, dependency analysis, modeling and evaluation, software dependability, and fault diagnosis. Table 12.1 provides an overview of the issues addressed in the literature over the last 40 years.

In the 1970s, studies were done on the Chi/OS for the Univac [124], and the collected data were used to calculate the MTBF of the considered systems. Over the following years, the scope of research broadened to address a wide set of systems and pursue several objectives. The 1980s and the 1990s were characterized by field failure data analysis (FFDA) studies on mainframe and multicomputer systems, such as the IBM 370 with the MVS OS [3, 50, 65, 74, 82, 89], the DEC VAX [21, 27–29, 51, 60, 75], and Tandem systems [2, 4, 32].

Early studies in measurement-based analysis investigated transient errors in DEC computer systems and found that more than 95% of all detected errors were intermittent or transient [27, 28]. The studies also showed that the interarrival times of transient errors followed a Weibull distribution with a decreasing error rate. The distribution was also shown to fit the software failure data collected from an IBM operating system [54]. Several studies have investigated the relationship between system activity and failures. In the 1980s, analysis of measurements from IBM [49, 52] and DEC [53] machines revealed that the average system failure rate was strongly correlated with the average workload on the system. The effect of workload-imposed stress on software was investigated in [50, 53, 54]. A study of failure data from three different operating systems showed that time to error (TTE) can be represented by a multistage gamma distribution for a single-machine operating system and by a hyperexponential distribution for the distributed operating systems measured by the authors [84]. Other analyses of DEC VAX [60] and Tandem [4] multicomputer systems showed that correlated failures across processors are not negligible, and their impacts on availability and reliability are significant [57, 60, 61]. In [65], analytical modeling and measurements were combined to develop measurement-based reliability/performability models based on data collected from an IBM mainframe. The results showed that a semi-Markov process is better than a Markov process for modeling system behavior. Markov reward

**Table 12.1** Classification of related research.

| Category | Research milestones | References | Representative environment |
|---|---|---|---|
| Data coalescing | Data coalescence heuristics | [2–10] | IBM 370/168, Blue Gene/P, Dell cluster, VAX/VMS, telephony switch, Blue Waters petascale supercomputer |
| | Data filtering | [11–19] | |
| | Assessment of data coalescence heuristics | [20–22] | |
| | Data mining of event logs | [23–26] | |
| Basic error characteristics | Transient faults/errors | [27–29] | SMP/Numa clusters, VAX/VMS, Bluetooth PAN, cellphones, medical devices, Windows 2000, storage, Blue Waters petascale supercomputer |
| | Failure characteristics | [29–42] | |
| | TTE, TTF, error and fault latency, failure rate distributions | [9, 10, 43–48] | |
| Dependency | Failure/workload dependency | [49–59] | IBM z/OS and IBM Z systems, Blue Waters petascale supercomputer |
| | Two-way and multiway failure correlation | [60–64] | |
| Modeling and evaluation | Performability models | [29, 56, 57, 65–73] | IBM z/OS and IBM Z systems, Blue Waters petascale supercomputer |
| | Reward model for distributed system | [29] | |
| Software dependability | Error recovery | [74] | IBM z/OS and IBM Z systems, Blue Waters petascale supercomputer |
| | Hardware-related and correlated software errors | [75–77] | |
| | Software fault tolerance | [75, 78–80] | |
| | Software defect classification | [81–88] | |
| Fault diagnosis | Heuristic trend analysis | [5, 22] | Blue Waters highspeed network and storage system. |
| | Statistical analysis of symptoms | [89–93] | |
| | Network fault signature | [90, 94, 95] | |
| | Failure prediction | [96–100] | |
| Network availability | Network failures, congestions, and performance impact | [37, 94, 95, 101–110] | A mixture of systems and networks: Blue Waters highspeed network and storage system. |
| | Internet and datacenter failures | [111–117] | |
| Autonomous vehicles and surgical robots' failures | Data analysis | [118–123] | Autonomous vehicles and surgical robots |

modeling techniques were applied to distributed systems [29] and fault-tolerant systems [83] to quantify performance loss due to errors/failures for both hardware and software.

A 1990 census of Tandem system availability, which indicated that software faults were the major source of system outages in the measured fault-tolerant systems [32], increased interest in software fault tolerance and reliability. Analyses of field data from various software systems investigated several dependability issues, including the effectiveness of error recovery [74], hardware-related software errors [76], correlated software errors in distributed systems [75], software fault tolerance [81, 83], and software defect classification [82, 88]. Measurement-based fault diagnosis and failure prediction issues were investigated in [5, 22, 89, 90, 94]. Measurements also enabled the development of the Orthogonal Defect Classification (ODC) approach [87]. It assumes the existence of measurable cause-and-effect relationships in a software development process and consists of a technique that provides an in-process measurement paradigm for extracting key information from defects and enabling the metering of cause-and-effect relationships.

Subsequent research addressed the study of LAN computers with commodity operating systems, such as the various flavors of Microsoft Windows [37, 100, 103] as well as UNIX-based [44, 94, 116, 117] operating systems. In the late 1990s and beyond, as the Internet increased in popularity, several studies focused on the dependability of a network of networks [93, 94, 106] and Internet hosts [55, 112, 116]. For example, in [104], a methodology for collecting and analyzing failures in a network of UNIX-based workstations is presented. The majority of observed failures (68%) were network-related. Machine reboots collected in a network of Windows NT-based servers are analyzed in [103]. The failure behavior of a typical machine and of the network as a whole was modeled in terms of a finite state machine, providing insights into the typical problems encountered and their dynamics.

The reliability of Internet hosts from the users' perspective is studied in [116]. In [112], the mean time to failure (MTTF), mean time to repair (MTTR), availability, and reliability of Internet hosts are evaluated. In [115], the vagaries of end-to-end Internet routing are analyzed, and major routing pathologies and properties are identified. In [19], faults that occurred in three large open-source applications (an Apache web server, a GNOME desktop environment, and a MySQL database) are studied using information contained in bug reports and source code. Faults are classified based on how they depend on the operating environment, and the results show (i) that 72–87% of the faults were independent of the operating environment and were hence deterministic (non-transient), and (ii) that half of the remaining faults depended on a condition in the operating environment that was likely to persist on retry. Only 5–14% of the faults were triggered by transient conditions, such as timing and synchronization, that are naturally repaired during recovery.

More recent work has addressed an even broader spectrum of topics, adding contributions to cloud computing [125], web-based applications [41], and tele-communication systems [46, 95]. The focus of such work has been on categorizing the nature of failures [41, 126], identifying bottlenecks [42, 127, 128] and bugs [99, 129, 130], and measuring the reliability of the system being analyzed [131, 132]. Several failure studies [126, 133] show that most of the failures experienced in enterprise software systems are caused by recurrent faults in a small proportion of the total code base. The authors of [126] demonstrate with empirical data that the 80–20 Pareto rule for operational failures (i.e. 20% of the modules are responsible for 80% of the failures) holds in operational software. In [133], the two most common problems are found to account for about 40% of crashes, and fewer than half of the total problems are responsible for 80% of the crashes. In [41], the failures of SCOPE, a general-purpose framework used at Microsoft Bing that has been adopted by thousands of developers around the world to create data-parallel programs (e.g. data mining over large datasets), are studied in detail. The work shows that for a variety of analyzed data-manipulation jobs, the majority of failures (84.5%) are due to unexpected values in the processed data.

Several studies have attempted to evaluate large-scale parallel systems [8, 11, 12, 20, 36, 43, 45, 69, 96]. Analysis of event logs from about 400 parallel server machines with the AIX operating system [36] demonstrated that despite improvements in system robustness, the failure rates of large-scale machines were still significant and highly variable. Schroeder and Gibson [43] analyzed failure data made publicly available by one of the largest HPC sites. The data, collected over nine years at Los Alamos National Laboratory (LANL), included 23 000 failures recorded on more than 20 different systems, mostly large clusters of SMP and NUMA nodes. The study classifies failure occurrences and models failure times (with Weibull and gamma distributions) and recovery times (with the lognormal distribution). The authors show that failure and recovery rates vary widely across systems. Moreover, their analysis shows that the curve of the failure rate over the lifetime of an HPC system is often very different from the traditional bathtub curve.

More recent studies focus on the interplay of high-speed networks, storage systems, and application services in [107–110]. [9] focuses on multiple levels of failures in Blue Waters over several years of its operation. In [10], the authors focus on HPC application resilience. [108] addresses on-line/real-time analysis to differentiative between performance-related failures and "reliability failure." This can be an important question because each requires a different approach to mitigation.

## 12.2.1 Failure Data Analysis in Specific Application Domains

In addition to the general-purpose and HPC systems discussed above, measurement-based analysis has been applied to several other old and new domains.

Representative examples are discussed in the remainder of this section, with an emphasis on the current growing interest in safety-critical medical devices.

*Nuclear Reactors.* An analysis of data on 11 years of operation of safety-critical software for nuclear reactors is presented in [80]. The study was conducted by Technicatome, a French company specializing in the design of nuclear reactors deployed in submarines and aircraft carriers of the French Navy. Several conclusions can be drawn from the study. The paper claims that the analysis of data is an efficient means for improving development processes. Further, it notes that emergent formal methods would have been of little help in preventing the errors encountered in operation since the observed failures were concerned with HW/SW interactions and real-time issues that are extremely difficult to model. In fact, since it is very difficult to reproduce real load and asynchronous situations in a laboratory environment, some very specific situations can be encountered only in a life-size trial.

*Mobile Phones.* The authors of [31] developed one of the first examples of a logging platform for the dependability analysis of mobile phones, specifically targeting the Symbian OS. The work used failure logs from 25 volunteer smartphone users, who recorded failure events and panics (or kernel-generated warnings in Symbian OS). The paper characterizes kernel panics (e.g. bursts) and the relation between panics and user-visible failures. The work found that (i) the majority of kernel exceptions (56%) are due to memory access violation errors and heap management problems; (ii) system panics often occur in bursts of two or more panic events in quick succession; and (iii) users experience a failure (the phone freezes or shuts itself down) every 11 days, on average. The paper also characterizes the recovery actions performed by users following observed failures. The study was beneficial in revealing the failure characteristics of the observed mobile operating systems and in relating the failures to user-initiated recovery actions. For instance, the work showed that there are specific software problems that lead to severe failures that require forcible manual shutdown of the cellphone via detaching of the battery.

*Java Virtual Machines.* In [39], the dependability of the Java Virtual Machine (JVM) is characterized by bug databases. The study found that JVM's built-in error detection mechanisms were incapable of detecting a considerable percentage of failures (45.03%) and that the JVM could not be expected to achieve the same level of dependability on different platforms.

*Mobile Robots.* The work in [48] analyzed the dependability of mobile robots based on failure reports gathered on 673 hours of actual usage of 13 robots from three manufacturers. The study shows that mobile robots have an MTBF of about eight hours and availability lower than 50%. The platform itself was the source of most failures for field robots, whereas the biggest source of failure in indoor robots was the wireless communication link.

*Wireless Sensor Networks.* Wireless sensor network (WSN) failures were presented with respect to an experimental testbed for the first time in [134]. The authors performed an in-depth study of the application of a WSN to real-world habitat monitoring on Great Duck Island in the state of Maine in the USA. The paper provides important insights on the cumulative probability of node failure through experimental evaluation and analysis. The work demonstrated that in a harsh environment, 50% of the nodes became unavailable within just four days of the start of a three-month deployment. Similar results were later found [135] for a WSN used for monitoring habitat in a redwood forest.

*Autonomous Vehicles.* Autonomous vehicles (AV) are sophisticated driving machines, as they are equipped with mini "supercomputers" on board and a dense network of sensing devices. Most recently, the safety and services of Tesla have been criticized by both NHTSA and others against the company's Autopilot claims and careless deployments. These unintended accelerations, brake failures, and collapsing wheels caused NHTSA to launch a probe into 765 000 vehicles after Tesla crashes into fire truck in February 2023 [136]. Failures on AV are critically important as they affect driver's lives as well as others. Banerjee et al. [123] found that AVs are 15–4000 times worse than human drivers for accidents per cumulative mile driven, based on over a million miles of field data from California DMV (2014–2017). Unlike accidents, which is an actual collision with other vehicles, pedestrians, or property; a disengagement is a failure that causes the control of the vehicle to switch from the software to the human driver. It was estimated that the majority cause of disengagement failures was because of machine-learning-based systems: 44% of perception, 20% control and decision, and 33.6% computing systems. The paper categorized ten different fault tags related to disengagements such as: sensor, planner, network, AV controllers. Most importantly, failures were analyzed from different perspectives such as: AV manufacturers, maturity of AV technologies, and alertness of human driver. *In summary, the present state of the practice is that AVs drivers are not completely free from driving; they need to be as alert as drivers of non-AVs.*

*Safety-Critical Medical Devices.* Analysis of safety-critical failures in robots and on the impact of targeted attacks on teleoperated surgical robots are discussed in [121, 122]. In the biomedical and clinical engineering community, there have been several efforts to address the failure analysis of medical devices based on the causes of adverse events and recalls. Most of that work has been limited to the analysis of software-related recalls [118] based on data collected by the U.S. Food and Drug Administration (FDA) up to the year 2005 [119] or for the one-year period of 2009 [120]. Other than [118], almost none of the related work in the area of medical device safety did extensive analysis of the root causes of failures and their symptoms. There have also been a few efforts to analyze MDR (Medical Device Recalls) or MAUDE (explained below) databases, but they have been limited to certain types of devices, such as implantable cardiac defibrillators (ICDs) [137–140].

In [30], to identify the major causes of failures that impact patient safety, the authors focus on computer-related recalls related to failures of computer-based medical devices. They used two public FDA databases: the Medical and Radiation Emitting Device Recalls database (referred to as the "Recalls" database), and the Manufacturer and User Facility Device Experience ("MAUDE" or "Adverse Event Reports") database. Analysis of adverse event reports allowed the authors to measure the impact of device failures in terms of actual adverse consequences (for example, serious injuries or deaths) reported to the FDA.

*Supercomputers.* Failures are a significant concern in HPC. For example, the Frontier Exascale supercomputer at the ORNL has "Mean time between failure on a system this size is hours, it's not days." – Justin Whitt, Program Director [141]. A more detailed analysis of Blue Waters, the world's first sustained petaflops machine, shows that sustaining failure-free operation is a challenge [9].

## 12.2.2 Analysis of Data on Security Incidents

Several studies have attempted to characterize and model system vulnerabilities and attacks starting from field data on security incidents. A honeypot can be regarded as an information system resource whose value lies in unauthorized or illicit use of that resource [142]. The CAUDIT system operates a non-interactive Secure Shell (SSH) honeypot and attracted the largest number of attack attempts (~405 million) to date [143]. The study in [144] aimed at using data collected by honeypots to validate fault assumptions made during the design of intrusion-tolerant systems. Analysis of honeypot data demonstrated that, in most cases, attackers know in advance which ports are open on each machine, without having to perform any port scan. Moreover, there were no substantial differences between the attacks made on different operating systems.

Some studies [145, 146] have analyzed attack data to build formal models that involve both single and multiple nodes. Several authors have proposed models that correlate alerts to incidents. Other sources that collect attack data include honeypot experiments [147]. Red teams have often been used to collect network vulnerability data; these data are generally not published. Several studies focus on classification of security flaws, vulnerabilities, and attacks; examples include [145, 148, 149]. The work in [150] exploits data from the Bugtraq database and proposes a classification of vulnerabilities. The measured vulnerabilities are dominated by five categories: input validation errors (23%), boundary condition errors (21%), design errors (18%), failures to handle exceptional conditions (11%), and access validation errors (10%). The primary reason for the dominance of these categories is that they include the most prevalent vulnerabilities, such as buffer overflow and format string vulnerabilities. Starting from those data and helped by code inspections, the authors propose finite-state machine models of vulnerabilities that elucidate the vulnerabilities' behavior and/or uncover new ones. In [151], the authors describe an in-depth study of forensic data on security incidents that occurred over a period of five years at the National Center for Supercomputing Applications (NCSA) at the University of Illinois. Their proposed methodology combines automated analysis of data from security monitors and system logs with human expertise to extract and process relevant data to (i) determine the progression of an attack, (ii) establish incident categories and characterize their severity, (iii) associate alerts with incidents, and (iv) identify incidents missed by monitoring tools and examine why they were overlooked. In [152], the authors investigated the root causes of 447 K authentication failures in a distributed identity federation called CILogon. A fault-tree with probabilities of each failure type was presented. In summary, the measurement and analysis of security vulnerabilities, incidents, and compromises are acknowledged to be an important area of study.

## 12.3 Steps in Field Failure Data Analysis

There is no better way to understand the dependability characteristics of computer systems (including networked systems) than by direct measurements and analysis. However, the question of what and how to measure is a difficult one. Measuring a real system means monitoring and recording naturally occurring errors and failures in the system while it is running under user workloads. Analysis of such measurements can provide valuable information on actual error/ failure behavior, identify system bottlenecks, quantify dependability measures, and verify assumptions made in analytical models.

From a statistical point of view, sound evaluations require a considerable amount of data. In modern computer systems, failures are infrequent, so to obtain meaningful data, measurements must be taken over a long period of time. Also, the measured system must be exposed to a wide range of usage conditions for the results to be representative. Clearly, in a real system, only detected errors can be measured. There are many possible sources of errors, including untested manufacturing faults and software defects; errors due to transient errors induced by radiation, power surges, or other physical processes; operator errors; and environmental factors. The occurrence of errors is also highly dependent on the workload running on the system. A distribution of operational outages from various error sources for several major commercial systems is reported in [153].

Figure 12.1 outlines a conceptual framework for data-driven studies where ellipses represent input and output files. Given field error data collected from a

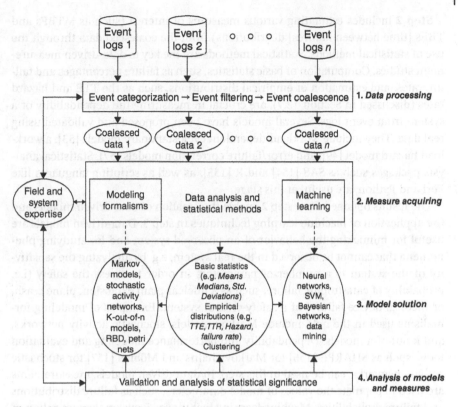

**Figure 12.1** Conceptual framework and steps for field failure data analysis (FFDA).

real system, a measurement-based study consists of four major steps: (i) data processing, (ii) model identification and parameter estimation, (iii) model solution if necessary, and (iv) analysis of models and measures.

**Step 1** consists of processing the event data to extract the necessary information. Event data are categorized, and all the unneeded data, such as informational data or data on debug events, are filtered out from the dataset. The remaining events are then grouped together (coalesced) in accordance with their presumed source. More specifically, in computer systems, a single problem commonly results in the occurrence of many repeated error events in rapid succession. To ensure that the analysis is not biased by such repeated observations of the same problem, all error entries that have the same error type and occur within a short time interval (e.g. five minutes) of each other coalesce into a single record. The output of this step is a form of coalesced data in which errors and failures are identified. This step is highly dependent on the measured system. Coalescing algorithms have been proposed in [2, 5, 6, 89].

**Step 2** includes estimating various measures of interest (such as MTBFs and TBFs [time between failures] distributions) from the coalesced data through the use of statistical methods. Statistical methods are the key to data-driven measurement studies. Computation of basic statistics, such as failure percentages and failure rates, and estimation of empirical distributions, such as the TTE and hazard rates (discussed in Section 12.7), are crucial in measuring the dependability of a system from event logs. Several models have been proposed and validated using real data. They include workload-dependent cyclostationary models [53], a workload hazard model [49], and error/failure correlation models [57]. Statistical analysis packages such as SAS [154] and R [155], as well as scripting languages like Perl and Python, are useful at this stage.

The results obtained from step 2 enable the creation of data-driven models and the application of machine learning techniques in step 3. Data-driven models are useful for mimicking the behavior of an observed system and for studying phenomena that cannot be observed in the real system, e.g. by analyzing the sensitivity of the system to a number of parameters in order to assess the safety (i.e. probability of catastrophic failure, such as a nuclear plant explosion, plane crash, or medical device failure) of a safety-critical system. Examples of modeling formalisms used in the field include Markov models, stochastic activity networks, and k-out-of-n models. Dependability and performance modeling and evaluation tools, such as SHARPE [156] for Markov chains and Möbius [157] for stochastic activity networks, can be used in this step. In data-driven models, measurements are used to populate the values of model parameters, such as failure distributions and failure probabilities. Machine learning techniques focus on the realization of models that can learn from the data. Statistical methods such as data clustering, analysis of variance, and principal component analysis are at the core of many machine learning methods. Data and estimated measurements, including failure rates, are used to train specific models to both predict and detect errors and potential failures. Bayesian networks, neural networks, and support vector machines (SVMs) are a few examples of commonly used ways to create data-driven failure detectors and predictors.

**Step 4**, the most creative part of a measurement-based study, involves careful interpretation of the models and measures obtained from the data, e.g. to identify reliability bottlenecks or determine a design enhancement's impact on availability. The analysis methods can vary significantly from one study to another, depending on project goals. This step includes the use of statistical tests and other validation techniques to validate the results of the analysis and hypothesize on failure causes and relationships.

During each of the foregoing steps, the analysis normally requires a strong interaction with field and system experts, such as system administrators for large-scale machines and physicians for the analysis of medical device failures.

The interaction with system and field experts is beneficial for the analysis and must be considered a key point to address.

In the following sections, we analyze the described steps in detail, providing several examples from past and current systems.

## 12.4 Failure Event Monitoring and Logging

All major systems provide a way to collect operational data in the form of event logs. Event logs represent a valuable source of data that can be used in conducting a failure analysis. The logs are machine-generated, often human-readable files that report sequences of entries (the log events) generated by the hardware, operating system and daemons, middleware, network devices, and applications in relation to regular and anomalous activities that occur during the system's operational phase. This section provides an overview of the most common techniques used for collecting the operational data of computers in the form of event logs.

There are two principal ways to collect field data from operational systems: manual logging and online automated logging. Since failures are relatively rare events, it is necessary to meticulously collect and analyze error data for many months before the results of the data analysis can be considered representative and statistically valid. The main advantage of online automatic logging is its ability to record a large amount of information about transient errors and to provide details of automatic error recovery processes. Its disadvantages are that an online log does not usually include information about the cause and propagation of the error or about the offline diagnosis. Importantly, only detected events can be logged. In other words, not all the possible erroneous conditions are logged. Thus, with this technique, it might be hard to pinpoint the root causes of each failure event. Also, under some crash scenarios, the system may fail too quickly for any error messages to be recorded.

### 12.4.1 Automated Error Logging

Automated error logging software is provided by many large computer systems' operating systems, such as those of IBM, Cray machines, and HP NonStop systems [153]. Similarly, commercial operating systems, such as UNIX and Microsoft OSes, as well as smartphone platforms, such as Android and Apple iOS, offer capabilities for error logging. Typically, the event-logging software records information on errors that occur in the various subsystems, such as the memory, storage, and network subsystems, as well as other system events, such as reboots and shutdowns. The reports usually include information on the location, time, and type of the error, and the system state at the time of the error; they sometimes include error recovery (e.g. retry) information. The reports are stored chronologically in a permanent system file. The following sections provide examples of well-established techniques for automated event logging in commercial systems as well as examples of manual failure reports.

### 12.4.1.1 Syslog

The Syslog protocol is defined by RFC 5424, which was published by the Internet Engineering Task Force [158]. It provides a message format that allows vendor-specific extensions to be provided in a structured way. It runs as a background process and records events generated by different local sources: the kernel, system components (disk, network interfaces, and memory), daemons, and application processes that are configured to communicate with the Syslog daemon, which stores the events in plain-text files. The definition of the Syslog standard allows for customization of the information logged and how such data are collected, for instance, on a specific file server node or database. Basic information logged by the Syslog protocol includes (i) the timestamp of the event; (ii) the facility, indicating the type of software that generated the message; (iii) the severity level (from those shown in Table 12.2), indicating the severity of the logged message; (iv) identification of the node that generated the message; (v) the process, including its PID (process identifier), that logged the event; and, finally, (vi) a description of the event.

### 12.4.1.2 Blue Waters Logs

Table 12.3 shows examples of Syslog messages collected from the Cray XE-6/XK-7 Blue Waters, which was installed at the National Center for Supercomputing Applications (NCSA) in 2013. The format of the messages extends the basic Syslog format, and logs are collected through dedicated software called Cray Lightweight Log Management (LLM). An instance of how LLM extends the Syslog format is as follows: the node field indicates the cabinet (c-X-X), the chassis in the cabinet (cX), the slot in the chassis (sX), and the node number (nX), and the logs show how much time had passed since the last reboot. In addition to Syslog, Blue Waters collected information from the Sonexion parallel file system, from the cabinet controllers (including environmental and power information), and from the integrated Hardware Supervisory System (HSS), an independent system with its own control processors and supervisory network that monitored and managed all major hardware and software components in Blue Waters. Because of the huge volume of logs[1] produced, Cray developed a set of tools to filter and query data provided by the error logs.

---

1 In a typical week of operation, Blue Waters could collect up to 800 GB of event logs.

**Table 12.2** Levels of severity for Syslog.

| Code | Severity | Keyword | Description | General description |
|------|----------|---------|-------------|---------------------|
| 0 | Emergency | emerg (panic) | System is unusable. | A "panic" condition, usually affecting multiple apps/servers/sites. For messages logged at this level, the system would usually notify all tech staff on call. |
| 1 | Alert | alert | Action must be taken immediately. | Should be corrected immediately; therefore, notify staff who can fix the problem. |
| 2 | Critical | crit | Critical conditions. | Should be corrected immediately, but indicates a failure in a secondary system. |
| 3 | Error | err (error) | Error conditions. | Non-urgent failures; these should be relayed to developers or admins, and each item must be resolved within a given amount of time. |
| 4 | Warning | warning (warn) | Warning conditions. | Warning messages; they do not indicate that an error has occurred, but that an error will occur if action is not taken. |
| 5 | Notice | notice | Normal but significant condition. | Events that are unusual but not error conditions; might be summarized in an email to developers or admins so they can spot potential problems; no immediate action required. |
| 6 | Informational | info | Informational messages. | Normal operational messages; no action required. |
| 7 | Debug | debug | Debug-level messages. | Info useful to developers for debugging the application; not useful during operations. |

In addition to automated logs, Blue Waters also have significant human-written logs, referred to as failure reports. System failure reports are human-written documents that record each event in the system that required the attention of the system managers, such as failures, maintenance, system upgrades, and bugs signaled to the manufacturer. Each entry contains several distinct fields, including (i) start time of the event, (ii) repair time and date, (iii) category of the event, (iv) affected facility, (v) textual description of the event, (vi) number of nodes offline because of the event, (vii) System-Wide Outage (SWO) flag, and (viii) Field

**Table 12.3** Snippets of logs collected from Cray XE-6/XK-7 Blue Waters at NCSA.

| Date | Facility | Severity | Node | Process [PID] | Reboot time | Message |
|---|---|---|---|---|---|---|
| 10/6/12 19:28:17.481499 | local 3 | 6 | c16-0c1s4n1 | erd[32539] | 10/2/12 19:18:16 | [hss_erd@34] ecconsole log\|src:::c16- 0c1s4n1\|pri:0x0\|seqn um:0x0\|svc:::c16-0c1s4n1\|.c:1116: kg- nilnd tx done()) $$ error -113 on tx xffff88081d1b5248-><?> id 0/0 state GNILND_TX_ALLOCD age 65s msg |
| 10/6/12 19:28:17.482756 | local 3 | 6 | c7-11c2s0n1 | xtconsole[13063] | 10/2/12 19:18:16 | [console@34] LNet: 12283:0:(gnilnd_cb.c:1116: kg-nilnd_ tx_done()) $$ error -113 on tx 0xffff881011fa7db0-><?> id 0/0 state GNILND_TX_ALLOCD age 65s msg@0xffff881011fa7e30 m/v/ty/ck/pck/pl b00fbabe/8/2/0/ffff/0 x0: GNILND_MSG_IMMEDIATE |
| 10/6/12 19:28:17.483199 | local 3 | 6 | c9-8c1s0n2 | erd[32539] | 10/2/12 19:18:16 | hss_erd@34] ec_console_log\|src:::c9-8c1s0n2\|pri:0x0\| seqnum:0x0\|svc:::c9-8c1s0n2\|: kgnilnd_tx_done()) $$ error -113 on tx 0xffff880e65d56000-><?> id 0/0 state GNILND_ TX_ALLOCD age 65s msg@0xffff880e65d |

Replaced Unit (FRU). Over 1978 distinct entries (including scheduled mainte-nance, system expansions, and failure events) were being reported during the measurement interval of 261 days.

### 12.4.1.3 IBM Z/OS Logs

The IBM Z/OS operating system collects detailed diagnostic data in several machine-generated logs. The main sources of diagnostic data are the messages provided by the system in the logs shown in Table 12.4. The z/OS error log con-tains data related to hardware and software errors. Application program abnormal ends are always accompanied by messages in the system log (Syslog) and the job log, which indicates the abend code and, usually, a reason code. Many abnormal ends also generate a symptom dump in the Syslog and job log. Table 12.5 shows an example of IBM Syslog logs.

**Table 12.4**  Log types provided by IBM Z/OS.

| | |
|---|---|
| **Console log** | Messages sent to a console with master authority are intended for the operators. The system writes in the hard copy log all messages sent to a console, regardless of whether the message is displayed. |
| **Hard-copy log** | The hard-copy log is a record of all system message traffic, including messages to and from all consoles, commands entered by the operator, and the output response of the commands. In a dump, these messages appear in the master trace. With JES3, the hard-copy log is always written to the Syslog. With JES2, the hard-copy log is usually written to the Syslog, but can be written to a console printer, if the installation chooses. |
| **Syslog** | An installation typically prints the Syslog periodically to check for problems. The Syslog consists of (i) all messages issued through macros, (ii) all messages entered by LOG operator commands, (iii) usually, the hard-copy log, and (iv) any messages routed to the Syslog from any system component or program. |
| **Job log** | Messages sent to a job log are intended for the programmer who submitted the job. |
| **OPERLOG** | OPERLOG is an MVS system logger application that records and merges messages about programs and system functions (the hardcopy message set) from each system. OPERLOG, rather than the system log, is used as a permanent log of operating conditions and maintenance for all systems. |
| **Logrec** | The Logrec log stream is an MVS System Logger application that records hardware failures, selected software errors, and selected system conditions across the sysplex. The use of a Logrec log stream rather than a Logrec data set for each system can streamline Logrec error recording. |

**Table 12.5**  Example of IBM Syslog Logs.

| | | | |
|---|---|---|---|
| STC18213 | 00000090 | $HASP100 | BPXAS ON STCINRDR |
| STC18213 | 00000090 | $HASP373 | BPXAS STARTED |
| STC18213 | 80000010 | IEF403I | BPXAS - STARTED - TIME=13.36.36 - ASID=001F - SC53 STC16316 00000291 IST663I IPS SRQ REQUEST FROM ISTAPNCP FAILED, SENSE=08570002 |
| 111 | 00000291 | IST664I | REAL OLU=USIBMSC.S52TOS48 REAL DLU=USIBMSC.S48TO 111 00000291 IST889I SID = ED0385CAAEEAAF28 |
| 111 | 00000291 | IST264I | REQUIRED RESOURCE S48TOS52 NOT ACTIVE |
| 111 | 00000291 | IST314I | END |
| STC16352 | 00000291 | IST663I | IPS SRQ REQUEST FROM ISTAPNCP FAILED, SENSE=087D0001 883 00000291 IST664I REAL OLU=USIBMSC.S52TOS48 ALIAS DLU=USIBMSC.S48TO 883 00000291 IST889I SID = ED0385CAAEEAAF28 |
| 883 | 00000291 | IST314I | END |
| STC28215 | 00000291 | IST663I | IPS SRQ REQUEST TO ISTAPNCP FAILED, SENSE=08570002 86 864 00000291 IST664I REAL OLU=USIBMSC.S52TOS48 ALIAS DLU=USIBMSC.S48TO 864 00000291 IST889I SID = ED0385CAAEEAAF28 |

A symptom dump is another useful source of information that may provide enough basic diagnostic information to enable diagnosis of an abend or other problem. Table 12.6 shows the last error record contained in the system dump messages extracted from a collected crash dump.

Logged codes consist of specific system codes and include system completion codes (or abend codes) identified by three hexadecimal digits, and user completion codes identified by four decimal digits; they are usually the result of the abnormal ending of a system or an application program. The completion code indicates the reason for the abnormal end wait states, e.g. a hang of the program. The symptom dump in Table 12.6 shows that (i) the active load module ABENDER is located at address X'00006FD8'; (ii) the failing instruction was at offset X'12' in load module ABENDER; and (iii) the address space identifier (ASID) for the failing task was X'000C'.

#### 12.4.1.4  IBM Blue Gene RAS Events

The RAS (reliability, availability, and serviceability) log contains error, trace, and informational records called *RAS messages*. Figure 12.2 shows a snippet of a log in the event log in row format [159], collected from the IBM supercomputer Blue Gene/P.

**Table 12.6** Example IBM system dump message.

IEA995I SYMPTOM DUMP OUTPUT
SYSTEM COMPLETION CODE=0C4 REASON CODE=00000004
TIME=16.44.42 SEQ=00057 CPU=0000 **ASID=000C**
PSW AT TIME OF ERROR 078D0000 00006FEA ILC 4 INTC 04
ACTIVE LOAD MODULE=ABENDER **ADDRESS=00006FD8 OFFSET=00000012**
DATA AT PSW 00006FE4 - 00105020 30381FFF 58E0D00C
GPR 0-3 FD000008 00005FF8 00000014 00FD6A40
GPR 4-7 00AEC980 00AFF030 00AC4FF8 FD000000
GPR 8-11 00AFF1B0 80AD2050 00000000 00AFF030
GPR 12-15 40006FDE 00005FB0 80FD6A90 00006FD8
END OF SYMPTOM DUMP

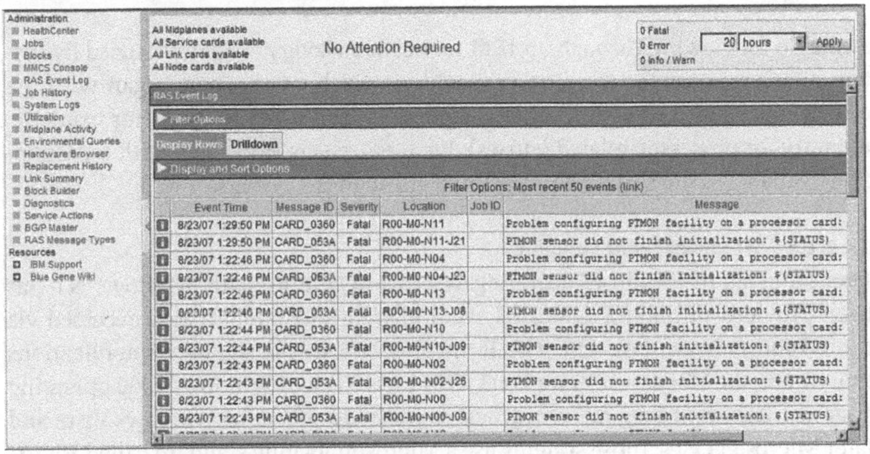

**Figure 12.2** Example Blue Gene/P RAS log [159].

Figure 12.3 shows an example of the details associated with the RAS messages shown in Figure 12.2. Every RAS event has the following relevant attributes: (i) EVENT TIME, which is the time stamp associated with that event; (ii) Message ID, identifying the subsystem that generated the event; (iii) SEVERITY of the event, as identified by one of the levels INFO, WARNING, SEVERE, ERROR, FATAL, or FAILURE, in order of increasing severity; (iv) LOCATION of the event, identifying the rack (R), midplane (M), and node (N); (v) JOB ID, which denotes the job that detected this event; and (vi) ENTRY DATA, which provides a short description of the event. A finite number of RAS messages were used on Blue Gene/P, and each one had an identification (ID) number and a detailed message. The list of RAS events that have occurred or that might occur on a system is

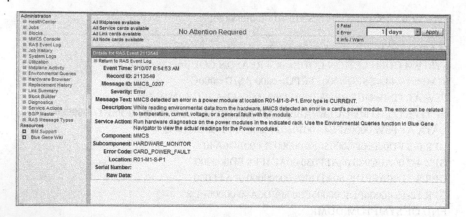

**Figure 12.3** Example of details of the RAS message in Figure 12.2 [159].

available for viewing through an IBM tool called Navigator that was used by system administrators for monitoring machines. Each error report began with the error's label and had a suffix that categorized each error by type (for example, memory- or processor-related entries). Each entry was associated with a description available to the system administrator through the Navigator tool.

### 12.4.1.5 Windows Event Logging

Event logging in Windows operating systems beginning with Windows NT has been provided through a dedicated event-logging subsystem that is accessed via the Windows Event Log API. The Event Log API was designed for applications that ran on the Windows Server 2003, Windows XP, and Windows 2000 operating systems. The event-logging infrastructure was redesigned for Windows Vista and later Microsoft OSes; those systems use a Microsoft logging standard called EVTX.

EVTX includes many additional features and enhancements that offer various properties, including the use of channels to publish events, an extensible markup-language-based log format (XML), and a dedicated event viewer. Information about each event conforms to an XML schema, and the XML representing a given event can be accessed through a specific API. In addition, EVTX files are organized in an internal database that can be queried with a SQL-like command utility (i.e. the event log parser) to ease the analysis of logs. The fields in the EVTX Windows event log are shown in Table 12.7.

Later Microsoft Windows products, such as Windows 8 and Windows Server 2008, included two categories of event logs: operating system logs called Windows Logs, and Applications and Services Logs. The Windows Logs include logs of all the events generated by application and security policies and the operating system. In addition to the Application, System, and Security logs supported in the

**Table 12.7**  Fields in EVTX Windows Event Logs.

| Property name | Description |
|---|---|
| Source | The software that logged the event, as indicated by either a program name, such as "SQL Server," or a component of the system or of a large program, such as a driver name. For example, "Elnkii" indicates an EtherLink II driver. |
| Event ID | A number identifying the particular event type. The first line of the description usually contains the name of the event type. For example, "6005" is the ID of the event that occurs when the Event Log service is started. The first line of the description of such an event is "The Event log service was started." The Event ID and the Source can be used by product support representatives to troubleshoot system problems. |
| Level | A classification of the event severity. Events with the following severity levels can appear in the system and application logs: <br><br> • **Information**. Indicates that a change in an application or component has occurred, e.g. an operation has been successfully completed, a resource has been created. <br><br> • **Warning**. Indicates that an issue has occurred that can impact service or result in a more serious problem if action is not taken. <br><br> • **Error**. Indicates that a problem has occurred that might impact functionality that is external to the application or component that triggered the event. <br><br> • **Critical**. Indicates that a failure has occurred from which the application or component that triggered the event notification cannot automatically recover. <br><br> The following event severity levels can occur in the security log: <br><br> • **Success Audit**. Indicates that the exercise of a user right has succeeded. <br><br> • **Failure Audit**. Indicates that the exercise of a user right has failed. <br><br> In the Event Viewer normal list view, the levels are represented by symbols. |
| User | The name of the user on whose behalf the event occurred. It is the client ID if the event was actually caused by a server process, or the primary ID if impersonation is not taking place. A security log entry may contain both the primary and impersonation IDs. Impersonation occurs when the server allows one process to take on the security attributes of another. |
| Operational Code | Contains a numeric value that identifies the activity or a point within an activity that the application was performing when it raised the event notification, for example, initialization or closing. |
| Log | The name of the log in which the event was recorded. |
| Task Category | Used to represent a subcomponent or activity of the event publisher. |
| Keywords | A set of categories or tags that can be used to filter or search for events. Examples include "Network," "Security," or "Resource not found." |
| Computer | The name of the computer on which the event occurred. It is typically the name of the local computer, but it might be the name of a computer that forwarded the event, or it might be the name of the local computer before its name was changed. |
| Date and Time | The date and time when the event was logged. |

previous versions of Windows, they also include two other logs, the Setup Log and the Forwarded Events Log. In the *Application (program) Log*, events are classified as errors, warnings, or information, depending on the severity of the event. The *System Log* contains events logged by Windows system components. For example, the failure of a driver or other system component to load during startup is recorded in the System Log. The event types logged by system components are predetermined by Windows. The *Security Log* contains events such as valid and invalid logon attempts, as well as events related to resource use, such as the creation, opening, or deletion of files or other objects. Administrators can specify what events are recorded in the Security Log. For example, attempts to log on to the system are recorded in the Security Log. Computers that are configured as domain controllers will have additional logs displayed in the *Setup Log*. The *Forwarded Events Log* is used to store events collected from remote computers. The *Applications and Services Log* contains events logged by applications or background services. For example, a database program might record a file error in the Applications and Services Log. Program developers decide which events to log. All the abovementioned logs can be viewed via the Microsoft Event Viewer application, shown in Figure 12.4.

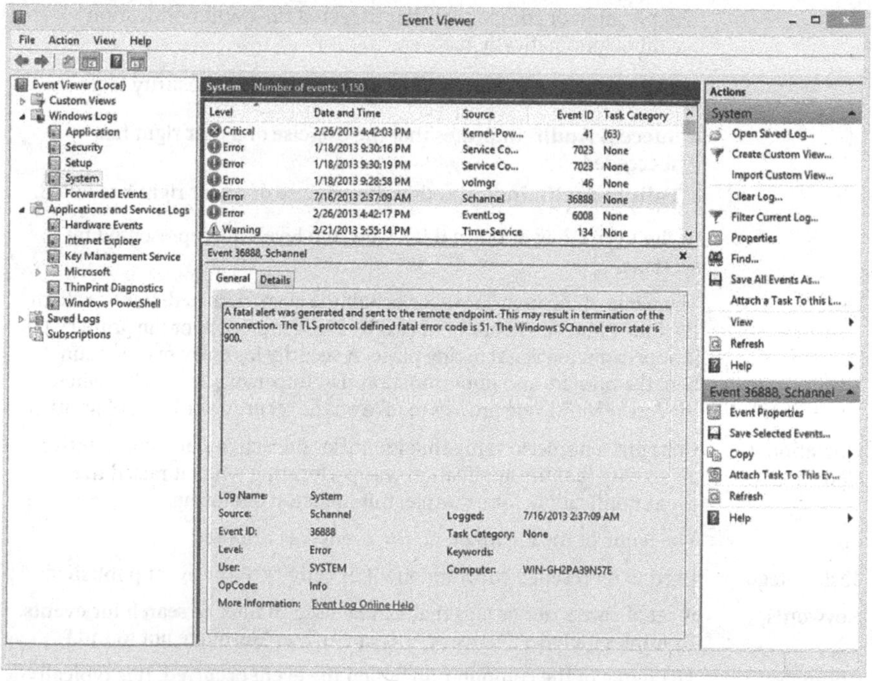

**Figure 12.4** Snapshot of the Microsoft EVTX Event Viewer from a Windows 8 machine.

## 12.4.2 Human-Generated Failure Reports

Human-generated failure reports are extensively used to keep track of failures in large-scale and enterprise systems. Human-generated software failure reports contain detailed information about the underlying faults, failure symptoms, and fixes. As a result, such reports can be used to address many software dependability issues. Typically, in large-scale data centers, system administrators produce human-generated failure reports documenting the actions taken by automated detection mechanisms that are initiated by automatic monitoring and failure reporting tools.

While they are a rich and useful source of information on failures, human-generated failure reports have disadvantages. Specifically, there are two major challenges in evaluating manual reports. First, underreporting can be significant. Ideally, cross-referencing between automated event logs generated by the operating system and manual reports should be possible. Second, since the reports contain textual descriptions provided by analysts, they cannot be readily analyzed by automatic tools. The raw data must usually be reorganized into a structured database after accurate parsing, which often uses data mining techniques, including natural language data processing procedures. That reorganization involves standardization of the language used in the report, including data categorization, i.e. generation of categories and counting of instances for each category starting from the description in natural language, the quality of which will depend on the operators' skills. That challenge can be serious, as the bulk of the evaluation efforts might be spent on that data reorganization. The problem can be mitigated by enforcing strict policies on the creation of failure reports, including the generation of well-defined categories a priori so that analysts can simply choose and mark the most appropriate category when they close a case.

### 12.4.2.1 Bug Databases and Public User Forums

Bug databases and public user forums are an extreme kind of manual failure report. They consist of unstructured reports, typically written by untrained people, that contain user-oriented descriptions of problems experienced with a specific device or piece of software and how the user fixed the problem. They are a readily available source of information on user-perceived failures and can be useful in building a first-level failure characterization.

Several products offer open-source bug- and problem-tracking systems. A non-comprehensive list includes Bugzilla [160], Mantis [161], and Trac [162], as well as other, product-specific tools, such as the Oracle/Sun [163] and MySQL [164] bug databases.

The authors of [31] describe an example public user forum in which mobile phone users post information on their experiences with handheld devices. The posts were used by the authors to provide a high-level characterization of

Symbian-based phone failures between January 2003 and March 2006. A total of 533 reports were studied. Phone models from all major vendors were considered: Motorola, Nokia, Samsung, Sony-Ericsson, LG, Kyocera, Audiovox, HP, BlackBerry, Handspring, and Danger. The posted data had a free format and a relatively small number of posts reported on device errors/failures.

In the following, we provide a few examples of manual failure reports for the Tandem Guardian90 and HPC clusters at LANL.

*Tandem Guardian90 OS.* An example of human-generated software failure reports is described in [81], which considered the Tandem Product Report (TPR) database, a component of the Tandem Product Reporting System (PRS). TPRs were used to report all problems, questions, and requests for enhancements by customers or Tandem employees concerning any Tandem products. A TPR consists of a header and a body. The header provides fixed fields for information such as the date, problem type, urgency, customer and system identifications, and a brief problem description. The body of a TPR is a textual description of all actions taken by Tandem analysts in diagnosing the problem. If a TPR reports a software failure, the body also includes the log of memory dump analyses performed by Tandem analysts.

*Los Alamos National Laboratory Computer Failure Reports.* An example of an effective policy for the creation of manual failure reports is the one enforced at LANL. At LANL, failures are detected by an automated monitoring system that alerts operations staff (via a page) whenever a node is down [43], reducing the possibility of underreporting. The operations staff then create a failure record in the database that specifies the start time of the failure and the system and node affected. The next action is to send the report to a system administrator, who consequently starts the repair action. Following the repair, the system administrator notifies the operations staff of it; they then put the node back into the list of available nodes and add the end time to the failure record. The output is a well-structured failure report, as shown in Table 12.8. Each failure report contains several pieces of information, including the time when the failure started, the time when it was resolved, the system and node affected, the type of workload running on the node, and the root cause, which could be any of the following: (i) human error; (ii) the environment, including power outages or A/C failures; (iii) a network failure; (iv) a software failure; and (v) a hardware failure. Such information is provided by the system administrator, who includes detailed information on the root cause, such as the particular hardware component affected by a hardware failure.

## 12.5 Data Processing

Usually, logs contain a large amount of redundant and irrelevant information in various formats. Thus, data filtering, manipulation, and processing must be performed to classify the information and put it into a flat format to facilitate

**Table 12.8** Example failure report from LANL [43].

| System | 2 |
|---|---|
| Machine Type | cluster |
| Nodes | 49 |
| procstot | 6152 |
| procsinnode | 80 |
| nodenum | 0 |
| nodenumz | 0 |
| node install | 5-Apr |
| node prod | 5-Jun |
| cputype | |
| Purpose | graphics.fe |
| Prob Started (mm/dd/yy hh:mm) | 6/21/05 10:54 |
| Prob Fixed (mm/dd/yy hh:mm) | 6/21/05 11:00 |
| Down-time | 6 |
| Facilities | — |
| Hardware | Graphics Accel Hdwr |
| Human Error | — |
| Network | — |
| Undetermined | — |
| Software | — |

subsequent analyses. The design of the flat format depends on the needs of the subsequent analyses.

Section 12.3 provided an overview of the steps involved in the analysis of operational data. In the following sections, we explore each of the major steps that were outlined in Figure 12.1. Figure 12.5 illustrates the steps in the processing of failure data. The figure also indicates, for each step, the order of magnitude of the datasets typically obtained when one is analyzing data from HPC systems.

The first step in data processing is event categorization. Logs, indeed, contain much information that is not related to failure events. The event categorization step aims to reduce the initial dataset and to concentrate attention only on a significant set of data. For instance, an event of interest may consist of error and failure events generated by specific devices or with a specific level of severity.

There is no uniform or best approach to event categorization, as different systems have different hardware and software architectures. Therefore, the event categorization step requires a deep understanding of the underlying architecture of the systems, how the data are logged, and the benefit of interplay with system

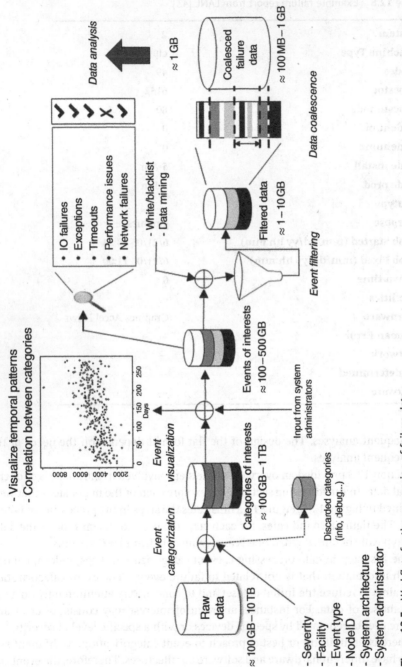

**Figure 12.5** Workflow for the processing of failure data.

administrators. This step often requires the creation of an ad hoc data parser to parse the data into a specific format that can ease the next steps of the analysis. An example is to parse Syslog events (stored in tab-separated text files) into specific SQL databases to make it possible to query the data. That process typically requires several data manipulation tasks (e.g. standardization of the date-time format or string manipulation). Data are typically transformed into an internal format before being used in the later steps of the analysis. The design of the flat format depends on the needs of the subsequent analyses. With manual failure reports, the difficulty of this step is exacerbated by the presence of natural language free-form text.

Typically, the event categorization step is time-consuming, because it requires frequent interactions with the system administrator and manual inspection of the log content to provide a meaningful categorization. Once data have been categorized, the questions that analysts ask are as follows: What message content and occurrence rate are normal? Does each message type have an associated "normal" occurrence rate (e.g. hourly, weekly, or bursty when users start work in the morning)? What message categories occur at the same time or in close time proximity to one another, and over what time span? A good way of answering those questions is to plot the error/failure times in terms of the identified categories to visualize the dataset. Often, a cross-correlation analysis and a visual plot of the failure times of one failure category against another will also be useful in identifying potential correlations between failure categories and suggest that some entries can be discarded to further reduce the dataset.

## 12.5.1 Data Filtering

After error classification, the following data processing steps can be broadly divided into two phases: (i) data filtering to remove events that are not of interest, and (ii) data coalescing of redundant or equivalent events. The goal is to select only useful entries such as error, failure, and reboot reports (and to discard unneeded entries, such as disk volume change reports) from the log file and transform the data set into a flat format.

Two basic filtering strategies are typically adopted: blacklist and whitelist strategies. The *blacklist* strategy can be thought of as using a list of all the terms that identify events that are not of interest to analysts. The blacklist filtering discards all events whose descriptive messages contain one or more of the black-listed terms. On the contrary, the *whitelist* strategy uses a list of all terms judged to pertain to events of interest; events that contain these terms are not rejected. In some cases, hybrid filtering can be employed (whitelisting plus blacklisting). The creation of effective filters can be a time-consuming task that often relies on the expertise of the analyst. Often, the knowledge of system administrators is crucial to the success of this task, which often takes more time than the rest of the analysis. Effective ways of building filters are based on the automated creation of regular expressions from the data in order to summarize the content of a potentially vast data set in a few hundreds or thousands of templates. Several tools for easing that process are available, such as Loghound [165] and SEC [166]. Such filtering techniques have been employed for a variety of systems, ranging from supercomputers to enterprise telephone systems. For instance, in [12], the authors demonstrate how their filtering strategy can remove over 99.96% of the entries of an event log gathered from an IBM Blue Gene/L prototype. Importantly, such aggressive filtering still preserves the information contained in the dataset.

### 12.5.1.1 Example: Processing of Public Computer-Related Recalls Databases for Safety-Critical Medical Devices

An example of data processing that, in addition to traditional statistical methods, involves natural language processing, is presented in [30] in the context of safety-critical computer failures in medical devices. Figure 12.6 shows the workflow used in [30] to extract failure data on computer-based medical devices from two public computer-related recalls databases: the Medical and Radiation Emitting Device Recalls database (referred to as the "Recalls" database) and the Manufacturer and User Facility Device Experience ("MAUDE" or "Adverse Event Reports") database [167]. The process involved the analysis of 13413 records reported to the FDA between 1 January 2006 and 31 December 2011 (see Figure 12.6, step 1).

Each FDA recall database record consists of several fields, including human-written, unstructured text explaining the main reason for the recall and the recovery actions the manufacturer took to address the recall. Many of the recall records have the same reasons because the same component or part is used in different devices or models manufactured by the same company. After eliminating the duplicate values in the "Reason for Recalls" list (using Microsoft Excel to remove duplicate entries), the authors came up with 5294 unique recall events (or what we call *recalls*) in the FDA database.

In step 2, the approach identified the computer-related recalls by analyzing the "Reason for Recall" and "Action" fields in the FDA Recalls database records (see Figure 12.6, step 2). For that purpose, the Natural Language Toolkit (NLTK, a suite of Python libraries for natural language processing) was used to identify a dictionary of keywords that could be used to classify the database entries and to extract the most frequently used nouns and adjectives in the human-written "Reason for Recall" fields (see Figure 12.6, step 3). After that step, the content of the created dictionary was manually reviewed, and, finally, a ranked dictionary of 461 common computer-related keywords that might represent failures of computer-based devices was obtained. The terms in the dictionary were further

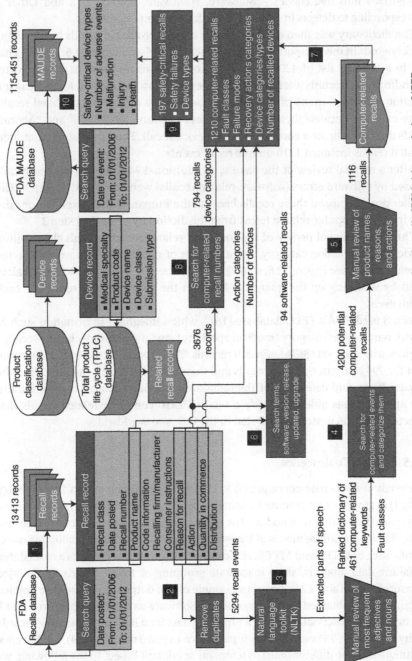

**Figure 12.6** Data processing workflow for analyzing safety-critical computer-related recalls [30]/with permission of IEEE.

categorized into five classes – Software, Hardware, Battery, I/O, and Other – corresponding to defects in the device's different components.

The dictionary was then used to identify computer-related recalls by searching for keywords in the "Reason for Recall" descriptions (see Figure 12.6, step 4). That led to a reduced list of 4200 potentially computer-related recalls, whose corresponding recall records were manually reviewed for validation and further categorization. In step 5, many of the records from the list of computer-related recalls were excluded because their "Product Name," "Reason for Recall," and "Action" fields did not indicate a computer-based device recall. The final list of computer-related recalls included 1116 unique recall events.

After a manual review of the results, an additional 94 computer-related recalls caused by software errors (software-related recalls) were identified in step 6. The earlier process missed those recalls because the human-written explanations did not include computer-related terms from the dictionary created in step 3.

Through a manual review of the computer-related recalls, a fault class, failure mode, recovery action category, and a number of recalled devices were extracted for each recall (see Figure 12.6, step 7). The number of recalled devices was calculated by summing up the quantities listed in the recall records related to each recall event.

Step 8 used FDA's TPLC database [167], which integrates information such as device name, type, category (medical specialty), and a regulatory class of recalled devices with a subset (3676) of recall records. The process extracted that information for 794 computer-related recalls and then used it as a training set to find the names, types, and categories of the remaining computer-related recalls. Finally, the approach was able to identify a total of 1210 computer-related recalls that affected 12 24 836 devices distributed in the U.S. and worldwide.

## 12.5.2 Data Coalescence

The goals of data coalescence are (i) to eliminate redundant events from the log, and (ii) to group events potentially initiated by the same cause with respect to time and space (i.e. on different nodes). The output is then used to characterize the failures, classify the failure modes of the system, and evaluate dependability measurements, such as MTBF and MTTR. Hence, data coalescence represents a crucial step in failure data analysis, since inaccurate grouping of failures leads to distorted measurements. Table 12.9 shows an example of the output of coalescence applied to failure data obtained from a production Software-as-a-Service platform [168]. An interesting observation is that a tuple may last for a long time and may include many entries (e.g. 245 events in the tuple shown in row 3 of Table 12.9). Coalescence techniques can be differentiated as temporal or content-based. In the following, we discuss examples of heuristics used in the analysis of failure data.

**Table 12.9** Example output of coalescence analysis [168].

| Time stamp | Tuple length [s] | # Entries in the tuple | Content in the tuple | Example of entries (from the logs) | Failure type |
|---|---|---|---|---|---|
| 1 325 479 405 | 289 | 2 | PLATFORM(2) | IT4_TRNF{SQL Connection Exception} | Query failed |
| 1 346 964 193 | 2996 | 73 | APPLOG(65) PLATFORM(1) OS(2) EXCEPTION(5) | **PlatformError**{System Error(Package Validation/ Execution Failed.)} <br> **OSError**{-RestartManager->[. . .]} <br> **OSError**{Transaction (Process ID 103) was deadlocked on lock \| communication buffer resources with another process and has been chosen as the deadlock victim. Rerun the transaction.} | IT4_L2 <br> Package Validation + Deadlock |
| 1 348 581 699 | 535 | 245 | APPLOG(123) OS(2) EXCEPTION(120) | **OSError**{event{Error Reporting->\|0\|APPCRASH\|Not available\|0\|CcmExec.exe\|4.0.6487.2000\|4ab33e4d\|ntdll. dll}; <br> **OSError**{The application-specific permission settings do not grant Local Activation permission for the COM Server application with CLSID {} | Security Permission + app crash |

#### 12.5.2.1 Time-Based Coalescence

Time-based coalescence, or *tupling* [2], exploits the heuristic of the tuple, i.e. a collection of events that occur close in time. Observations of event logs indicate that events tend to occur during relatively short periods of high activity. This suggests that it would be appropriate to apply a time-based coalescence heuristic. One common heuristic consists of considering all events that occur within a fixed time of each other as having been caused by the same source. The heuristic is based on the observation that in many systems, multiple events are caused by a single fault, and the effects may be observed first by hardware and subsequently by software drivers and the operating system, and then by other portions of the system. Moreover, the same fault may persist or repeat often over time.

Figure 12.7 shows an example of how a single fault can produce multiple reports of events. At the left is a set of random fault processes. Effects of faults will propagate through the system, possibly generating one or more errors. Hardware and software mechanisms will detect errors as the fault effects propagate through various layers of the system and report them to the error logger. Many situations can prevent the accurate reporting of errors: errors can pass undetected, errors can be detected by multiple sensors, and a system crash may result in failure to detect errors. Errors reported in the event log can be a function of the system state as well as the original fault. Multiple error effects can appear to combine and be detected as a single error, or the order in which errors are detected can be affected by the system state [2]. Figure 12.8 gives other examples of commonly used temporal coalescence heuristics.

Algorithm 1 in Figure 12.8 consists of the standard tupling defined in [2]. It groups together all the events that happen within a time window of $W$ from one another. Figure 12.9 shows the variation of the tuple count with clustering time. It is worth noting that with Algorithm 1, the time window slides after each coalesced entry, creating a tuple with a variable length. The assumption is that we should expect to see relatively small interarrival times between related errors, and relatively large interarrival times between tuples. For that reason, we would expect a high sensitivity to $W$ for values of $W$ close to the typical interarrival time

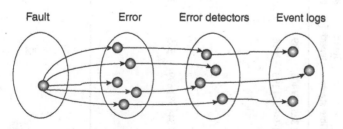

**Figure 12.7** Multiple event reporting phenomenon. *Source:* Adapted from [2].

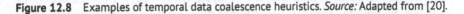

| ALGORITHM 1. Tupling with sliding windows | ALGORITHM 2. Tupling with Tsao's Rule | ALGORITHM 3. Spherical Covariance (SC07) |
|---|---|---|
| 1. W = find_knee_time_window(); | 1. foreach event in the log { | 1. ttr = current est. of MTTR; |
| 2. /* W is the time window size */ | 2. If (T(next)-T(curr) < 2.8 min.) | 2. theta = current est. of inter-failure time; |
| 3. do temporal_coalescence(){ | 3. add next to the current tuple; | 3. C = threshold parameter; |
| 4. foreach event in the log { | 4. else | 4. foreach event in the log { |
| 5. If (T(next)-T(curr) < W) | If (T(next)-T(curr) < 22.5 min. | 5. D = T(next) − T(curr); |
| 5. add next to the current tuple { | and Type(next) already in the tuple) | 6. if (D < ttr and Type(next) = Type(curr)) |
| 6. else | 5. add next to the current tuple; | 7. add next to the current tuple; |
| 7. create a new tuple; | 6. else | 8. elseif (D < theta) |
| 8. } | 7. create a new tuple; } | 9. c = 1 − αD/theta + β(D/theta)³; |
| 9. } | | 10. if (c > C) |
| | | 11. add next to the current tuple; |
| | | 12. else create a new tuple; |
| | | 13. else create a new tuple; |
| | | 14. } |

**Figure 12.8** Examples of temporal data coalescence heuristics. *Source:* Adapted from [20].

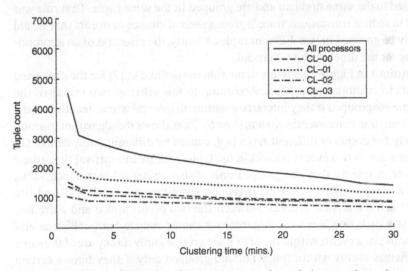

**Figure 12.9** Effect of the value of the coalescence time windows on the tuple count for five Tandem TNS II machines [2]/with permission of IEEE.

between related events, and a small sensitivity for values of $W$ larger than the interarrival time between related events. That would explain the L-shaped curve in the experimental data and suggests a method for choosing a clustering time. The vertex of the "L" represents the internal clustering time of the system. The size $W$ of the time window should be chosen to be greater than the point on the "knee" of the curve. In [2], a heuristic for the selection of a single coalescence time window for the Tandem TNS II system is presented. The authors found that the number of tuples of a given log is a monotonically decreasing function of the time window and has a characteristic L-shaped curve, as shown in Figure 12.9. According to their findings, the knee of the curve represents the internal clustering time of the system, i.e. after a time greater than the value on the knee, all the events that happen with a small interarrival time are coalesced together. Therefore, the time window should be chosen right after the knee.

An alternative to that technique consists of adopting a fixed coalescence window, such that an event is added to the current tuple if its timestamp is at most $W$ seconds from the first event in the tuple. In that case, the time windows do not shift, and the time is always counted from the first entry.

Algorithm 2 in Figure 12.8 adds the so-called *Tsao's rule* [5] to the grouping scheme. With it, two windows are used; the first is fixed at 2.8 minutes, and the second at 22.5 minutes. Just as in the classical sliding scheme, if two events fall within the first window, then they are grouped. Otherwise, if they are distant in time (e.g. within the second window) but of the same type, then presumably they are related to the same problem and are grouped in the same tuple. That rule was defined to reduce truncations since it gives a second chance to events that would normally be grouped in two different tuples. Clearly, the selection of an appropriate value for the time window is crucial.

Algorithm 3 in Figure 12.8 refers to the scheme defined in [7] for the clustering of events in coalitions of clusters. According to this scheme, two events of the same type are grouped if they interarrive within an interval whose length is equal to the mean time to recover the system (line 6). That allows the algorithm to group separately the events of different types (e.g. caused by different subsystems). On the other hand, if two events fall within the typical failure interarrival time (the $\theta$ parameter in line 8), they are grouped only if their spherical covariance value, defined as $c = 1 - \alpha(D/\theta) + \beta(D/\theta)^3$, is above a given threshold $C$ (lines 9 and 10), where $D$ is the temporal distance between the two events and $\alpha$ and $\beta$ are two parameters such that $\alpha = 1 + \beta$. Algorithm 3 should reduce both collisions and truncations since events within the MTTR are grouped only if they are of the same type, whereas events within the MTBF are grouped only if they have a certain degree of correlation. The problem is that the algorithm requires initial estimations of the mean time to recover and the failure interarrival based on administrative logs, which might be unavailable or inaccurate.

An additional step of the time-based coalescence is a coalescence of events that occur close in time but on different nodes of the system under study. It is typically applied to analyze large-scale distributed systems, such as supercomputers, and consists of applying time coalescence techniques on log files obtained by merging the logs of individual nodes [11, 57, 96, 100].

#### 12.5.2.2 Problems with Time-Based Coalescence
It is known that data coalescence can distort the results of an analysis because of imperfect groupings caused by *truncations* and *collisions* [2, 21]. Figure 12.10 provides an example of truncations and collisions with reference to time and spatial coalescence. *Truncation* occurs when the time between two or more events caused

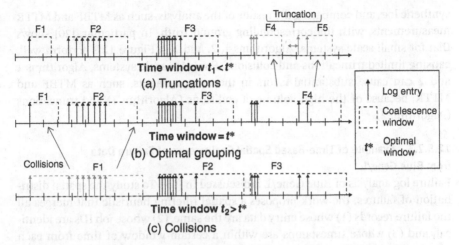

**Figure 12.10** Example of wrong grouping: truncations (a) and collisions (c) with respect to optimal grouping (b) [20]/with permission of IEEE.

by a single failure is greater than the clustering time so that the events are split into multiple tuples (Figure 12.10a). A *collision* occurs when two independent failures occur close enough in time such that their events overlap and are erroneously combined into a single tuple (Figure 12.10c). Consequently, the quality of the results of a coalescence process is strictly dependent on the selected time window [2].

Interpretation of failure data often requires interaction with the people who run the systems and collect the data [43] to validate the result of the coalescence. Therefore, a substantial effort in the analysis process should be devoted to validating the results of the coalescence.

One approach often used in the field to validate the quality of a coalescence process is to analyze manual failure reports filed by system administrators [16], if available, since they contain exact information on the diagnosed failures and on the remedies applied to the system, i.e. the ground truth on the failures that happened. That analysis is valuable in providing solid understanding of the failure data and can often suggest better strategies for coalescing the failure entries, for instance, by coalescing together only those failures that belong to specific types (e.g. disk and parallel file system errors).

An additional approach that can be used to improve a time-based coalescence heuristic is found in [20]. The work proposes an approach for generating synthetic logs that mimic the syslog format, along with the ground truth on the underlying failure process. The log can be generated using several parameters so that the sensitivity of the coalescence techniques to system parameters (e.g. failure rate and workload) can be assessed. The assessment is conducted by coalescing the synthetic logs and comparing the results of the analysis, such as MTBF and MTTR measurements, with the corresponding ground truth. In particular, [20] shows that for small-scale systems, Algorithms 1, 2, and 3 in Figure 12.8 perform well, causing limited truncations and collisions. For large-scale systems, Algorithms 1 and 2 can cause substantial errors in the measurements, such as MTBF and MTTR, because of the high volume of collisions (Algorithm 1) and truncations (Algorithm 2).

### 12.5.2.3 Example of Time-Based Spatial Coalescence of Failure Data from Blue Gene/L

Failure log analysis of Blue Gene/L is discussed in [96]. To study the spatial distribution of failures, the work proposes a spatial filtering heuristic that merges all the failure records (1) whose entry data are the same, (2) whose job IDs are identical, and (3) whose timestamps are within a certain window of time from each other, such that they are coalesced into one single failure record only within the boundary of a midplane. Those failure records, which satisfy conditions 1–3 (but from different midplanes), then stay uncompressed, i.e. if the same failure has impacts on several midplanes, and then the heuristic considers those impacts to reflect multiple different failures.

Figure 12.11 shows that failures from different components demonstrate different spatial behaviors. Comparable to the case in temporal distribution, memory failures are fairly evenly distributed across all the midplanes; 104 out of 128 midplanes have reported failures, and the maximum number of memory failures per midplane is 7. That observation indicates that all midplanes have similar probabilities of failing in their memory subsystems and that there is not a real spatial pattern between the machines. Similarly, the authors also observed that all midplanes have comparable numbers of application I/O failures. (Refer to Figure 12.11d). The reason, however, is not that all midplanes have uniform probabilities of failing in the I/O subsystem, but that an application I/O failure can be detected/reported by many midplanes simultaneously because of the nature of the deployed parallel I/O subsystem.

Network failures show more pronounced skewness in the spatial distribution. Among the 128 midplanes, 61 have network failures, and midplane 103 alone experienced 35 failures (26% of the total network failures). In addition, 6% of the midplanes encountered 61% of the failures.

### 12.5.2.4 Content-Based Event Coalescence

Time and spatial coalescence are limited to the evaluation of the time distances between events; hence, they cannot avoid accidental overlaps of independent events. For that reason, content-based coalescence techniques emerged [8, 14, 16,

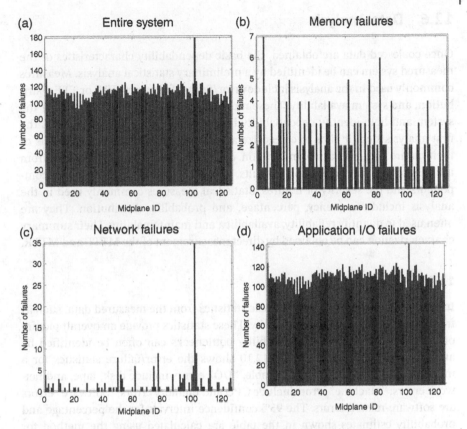

**Figure 12.11** Number of failures for each midplane after the spatial coalescence. Failures in (a) the entire system; (b) memory; (c) network; (d) application I/O.
*Source:* Adapted from [96].

26, 165] that based the grouping of events on the specific content of log messages. For instance, in [26], the authors describe how to combine data mining and statistical analysis techniques to transform chaotic log files into a standard form for visualization. In [15], signal analysis concepts are used to characterize the content of logs. The work in [8] and [14] applies the *lift* [169] data mining operator to find frequent event patterns starting from log content and hence isolating accidental patterns. In [16], the content of logs is mined to encode the position of words and to classify events by the nodes that produced them. Despite promising results for content-based coalescence, time (and spatial) coalescence techniques are the most used in the literature, such as in [2, 6, 7, 12, 35–37, 96, 100, 103, 117], because of the simplicity of the underlying algorithms.

## 12.6 Data Analysis

Once coalesced data are obtained, the basic dependability characteristics of the measured system can be identified by a preliminary statistical analysis. Measures commonly used in the analysis include error/failure frequency, TTE or TTF distribution, and system availability. These measures provide an overall picture of the system and help identify dependability bottlenecks. Failure classification is the first analysis step; it aims to categorize all the observed failures on the basis of their nature and/or location. In addition, descriptive statistics can be derived from the data to analyze the location of faults, errors, and failures among system components and the severity of failures. Statistical measures commonly used in the analysis include frequency, percentage, and probability distribution. They are often used to quantify reliability, availability, and maintainability. Their summary characterization can be obtained by direct measurement of the MTTF and MTTR.

### 12.6.1 Basic Statistics

It is important but easy to obtain basic statistics from the measured data, such as frequency, percentage, and probability. These statistics provide an overall picture of the measured system. Dependability bottlenecks can often be identified by analysis of these statistics. Table 12.10 shows the error/failure statistics for a measured VAXcluster [29]. In the table, "I/O" errors include disk, tape, and network errors; "Machine" errors include CPU and memory errors; "Software" errors are software-related errors. The 95% confidence intervals for the percentage and probability estimates shown in the table are calculated using the method for proportions.

Two bottlenecks can be identified from the table. First, the major error category is I/O errors (93%), i.e. errors from shared resources. I/O errors have a very high

**Table 12.10** Error/failure statistics for a VAXcluster [29].

| Category | Error | | Failure | | |
| | Frequency | Percentage | Frequency | Percentage | Recovery probability |
| --- | --- | --- | --- | --- | --- |
| I/O | 25 807 | $92.876 \pm 0.30$ | 105 | $42.86 \pm 6.20$ | $0.9966 \pm 0.001$ |
| Machine | 1721 | $6.196 \pm 0.28$ | 5 | $2.04 \pm 1.77$ | $0.9706 \pm 0.002$ |
| Software | 69 | $0.256 \pm 0.06$ | 62 | $25.31 \pm 5.44$ | $0.1016 \pm 0.071$ |
| Unknown | 191 | $0.696 \pm 0.10$ | 73 | $29.80 \pm 5.73$ | $0.6186 \pm 0.069$ |
| All | 27 788 | 100 | 245 | 100 | $0.991 \pm 0.001$ |

recovery probability (0.996) but cause nearly 43% of all failures. Therefore, although the system is generally robust with respect to I/O errors, the shared resources still constitute a major reliability bottleneck due to the sheer number of errors. To improve such a system, it may be necessary to use an ultra-reliable network and a disk system to reduce the raw error rate, not just provide high recoverability.

Second, although software errors constitute only a small part of all errors (0.3%), they result in a significant number of failures (25%). The reason is that software errors have a very low recovery probability (0.1). This software failure estimation is conservative because there are significant unknown failures (30%). Some of the unknown failures could be attributed to software problems. Thus, software-related problems are severe in the measured system.

Table 12.11 lists Mean Time Between Errors (MTBE), Mean Time to Error Recovery (MTTER), Mean Time Between Failures (MTBF), and Mean Time to Failure Recovery (MTTFR) for each type of error (averaged over all machine hours). On average, every 1.5 hours, there is an error event on each machine, and it is most likely the result of a disk problem (disk MTBE = 2.1). The table shows that software and disk problems are major reliability bottlenecks in the system (i.e. they have the lowest MTBF). However, the mean recovery time for disk failures (110 minutes) is longer than that for software failures (24 minutes), and also longer than those of other types of failures. That is, it takes a relatively long time to repair a faulty disk or drive. Table 12.12 shows MTBF for the individual machines in the VAXcluster. It can be seen that the longest MTBF (13.89 days for

**Table 12.11** MTBE, MTTER, MTBF, and MTTFR by type for VAXcluster [29].

| Measure | MTBE (h) | MTTER (min) | MTBF (h) | MTTFR (min) |
|---------|----------|-------------|----------|-------------|
| CPU | 252 | 0.86 | 84000 | 24.8 |
| Memory | 27 | 1.39 | NA | NA |
| Disk | 2.13 | 0.91 | 656 | 110 |
| Network | 12 | 1.05 | 1400 | 54.4 |
| Software | 609 | 21.9 | 677 | 24.4 |
| **All** | **1.51** | **1.3** | **171** | **50.6** |

**Table 12.12** MTBF (days) for individual machines [29].

| Earth | Europa | Jupiter | Leo | Mars | Mercury | Saturn |
|-------|--------|---------|-----|------|---------|--------|
| 5.56 | 3.33 | 8.93 | 13.89 | 12.5 | 8.33 | 8.62 |

Leonardo) is more than four times longer than the shortest MTBF (3.33 days for Europa). Thus, although these machines are operating in similar environments, their individual characteristics vary significantly. The average MTBF for the seven machines is approximately 7.1 days. Confidence intervals for these figures can easily be calculated from the distributions given in Section 12.6.2.

## 12.6.2 Repair Rates

A good approach for modeling the rate of occurrence of failures (ROCIOF) consists in the estimation of the repair rates (not to be confused with the length of time for a repair). Times are measured in terms of system power-on hours from initial turn-on at time zero, to the end of system life or occurrence of a failure. Failures occur as a system ages and is repaired to a state that may be the same as new, or better, or worse. The frequency of repairs may increase, decrease, or stay at a roughly constant rate.

Let $N(t)$ be a counting function that keeps track of the cumulative number of failures a given system has had from time zero to time $t$. $N(t)$ is a step function that increases by 1 every time a failure occurs and stays at the new level until the next failure. The ROCOF, or repair rate, is defined as the rate at which failures occur during system operation time (and are then repaired).

Every system will have its own observed $N(t)$ function over time. If we observed the $N(t)$ curves for a large number of similar systems (e.g. the nodes of a supercomputer or the virtual machines in a cloud datacenter) and "averaged" these curves, we would have an estimate of $M(t) =$ the expected number (i.e. average number) of cumulative failures by time $t$ for these systems.

The derivative of $M(t)$, denoted by $m(t)$, is defined to be the repair rate, or the ROCOF, at time $t$.

One possible model for $M(t)$ is $M(t) = \lambda t$, and the repair rate (or ROCOF) is the constant $m(t) = \lambda$. That model comes about when the interarrival times between failures are independent and identically distributed according to the exponential distribution, with parameter $\lambda$. It is also known as a *homogeneous Poisson process (HPP)*.

In the remainder of this section, we discuss examples of basic analysis that provide a first level of failure characterization, e.g. failure rate, recovery procedures, failure types, and root cause analysis.

### 12.6.2.1 Example: Root Cause Analysis from 20 HPC Systems at LANL

Table 12.13 gives an overview of 22 high-performance computing (HPC) systems at LANL analyzed in [43]. The systems were in production use between 1996 and November 2005. Most of them were large clusters of either NUMA (non-uniform memory access) nodes, or 2-way and 4-way SMP (symmetric multiprocessing)

**Table 12.13** Overview of systems. Systems 1–18 were SMP-based, and systems 19–22 were NUMA-based [43].

| | (I) High-level system information | | | (II) Information per node category | | | |
| --- | --- | --- | --- | --- | --- | --- | --- |
| HW | ID | Nodes | Procs | Procs/node | Production Time | Mem (GB) | NICs |
| A | 1 | 1 | 8 | 8 | N/A – 12/99 | 16 | 0 |
| B | 2 | 1 | 32 | 32 | N/A – 12/03 | 8 | 1 |
| C | 3 | 1 | 4 | 4 | N/A – 04/03 | 1 | 0 |
| D | 4 | 164 | 328 | 2 | 04/01 – now | 1 | 1 |
| | | | | 2 | 12/02 – now | 1 | 1 |
| E | 5 | 256 | 1024 | 4 | 12/01 – now | 16 | 2 |
| | 6 | 128 | 512 | 4 | 09/01 – 01/02 | 16 | 2 |
| | 7 | 1004 | 4096 | 4 | 05/02 – now | 8 | 2 |
| | | | | 4 | 05/02 – now | 16 | 2 |
| | | | | 4 | 05/02 – now | 32 | 2 |
| | | | | 4 | 05/02 – now | 352 | 2 |
| | 8 | 1024 | 4096 | 4 | 10/02 – now | 8 | 2 |
| | | | | 4 | 10/02 – now | 16 | 2 |
| | | | | 4 | 10/02 – now | 32 | 2 |
| | 9 | 128 | 512 | 4 | 09/03 – now | 4 | 1 |
| | 10 | 128 | 512 | 4 | 09/03 – now | 4 | 1 |
| | 11 | 128 | 512 | 4 | 09/03 – now | 4 | 1 |
| | 12 | 32 | 128 | 4 | 09/03 – now | 4 | 1 |
| | | | | 4 | 09/03 – now | 16 | 1 |
| F | 13 | 128 | 256 | 2 | 09/03 – now | 4 | 1 |
| | 14 | 256 | 512 | 2 | 09/03 – now | 4 | 1 |
| | 15 | 256 | 512 | 2 | 09/03 – now | 4 | 1 |
| | 16 | 256 | 512 | 2 | 09/03 – now | 4 | 1 |
| | 17 | 256 | 512 | 2 | 09/03 – now | 4 | 1 |
| | 18 | 512 | 1024 | 2 | 09/03 – now | 4 | 1 |
| | | | | 2 | 03/05 – 06/05 | 4 | 1 |
| G | 19 | 16 | 2048 | 128 | 12/96 – 09/02 | 32 | 4 |
| | | | | 128 | 12/96 – 09/02 | 64 | 4 |
| | 20 | 49 | 6152 | 128 | 01/97 – now | 128 | 12 |
| | | | | 128 | 01/97 – 11/05 | 32 | 12 |
| | | | | 80 | 06/05 – now | 80 | 0 |
| | 21 | 5 | 544 | 128 | 10/98 – 12/04 | 128 | 4 |
| | | | | 32 | 01/98 – 12/04 | 16 | 4 |
| | | | | 128 | 11/02 – now | 64 | 4 |
| | | | | 128 | 11/05 – 12/04 | 32 | 4 |
| H | 22 | 1 | 256 | 256 | 11/04 – now | 1024 | 0 |

**Table 12.14** Detailed root-cause breakdown of LANL data [43].

| Hardware root causes (%) | | Hardware root causes (%) excluding type E systems | | Software root causes (%) | | Environmental root causes (%) | |
|---|---|---|---|---|---|---|---|
| CPU | 42.8 | Memory DIMM | 30.1 | Other Software | 30.0 | Power Outage | 48.4 |
| Memory DIMM | 21.4 | Node Board | 16.4 | OS | 26.0 | UPS | 21.2 |
| Node Board | 6.8 | Other | 11.8 | Parallel File System | 11.8 | Power Spike | 15.1 |
| Other | 5.1 | Power Supply | 9.7 | Kernel Software | 6.0 | Chillers | 9.8 |
| Power Supply | 4.4 | Interconnect Interface | 6.6 | Scheduler Software | 4.9 | Environment | 5.3 |
| Interconnect Interface | 3.1 | Interconnect Soft Error | 3.1 | Cluster File System | 3.6 | | |
| Disk Drive | 2.0 | CPU | 2.4 | Resource Mgmt System | 3.2 | | |
| Interconnect Soft Error | 1.3 | Fan Assembly | 1.8 | Network | 2.7 | | |
| System Board | 0.9 | Router Board | 1.5 | User Code | 2.4 | | |
| PCI Backplane | 0.8 | Fibre Raid Controller | 1.4 | NFS | 1.6 | | |

nodes. Here the time instant *now* indicates the system is still in production as of the time of publication of [43].

Table 12.14 shows the 10 most common root causes gathered from the manual failure reports produced at LANL within the high-level hardware, software, and environmental categories, and their percentages. As the first column in the table indicates, a large fraction (more than 40%) of all hardware-related outages at LANL were attributed to CPUs. The second most commonly blamed hardware component was memory DIMMs. However, a closer look at the data reveals that for most systems, memory was a far more common root cause than CPUs were. The only exception was for systems of type E. System E experienced a very high percentage (more than 50%) of CPU-related failures because of a design flaw in the type E CPU.

The second column in Table 12.14 presents a breakdown of hardware failures into low-level root causes across all LANL systems, except for type E systems; it shows that nearly a third of all hardware-related node failures among non-type-E systems were due to memory. In fact, we find that systems' memory-related failures made up a significant portion of all failures, not just hardware failures.

Memory was the single most common "low-level" root cause for all system failures (across all failures, not only hardware failures), except for system E. For each system covered by the data (including type E systems), more than 10% of all failures (not only hardware failures) were due to memory.

The third column in Table 12.14 provides a breakdown of software-related failures into low-level root-cause categories.

Unfortunately, a significant fraction of software failures were not specified but were assigned to the "Other Software" category. When looking at individual systems, we found that the detailed breakdowns for software-related failures varied quite a bit across systems. For system F, the most common software failure was related to the parallel file system; for system H, to the scheduler software; and for system E, to the operating system. For systems D and G, a large portion of the software failures was not specified further (i.e. were "Other Software").

The fourth column in Table 12.14 provides a breakdown of failures with environmental root causes. Nearly half of them were due to power outages. The second most common root cause was problems with an uninterruptible power supply (UPS) device, followed by power spikes. For network failures and human errors, the data do not contain more detailed breakdowns, so there are no corresponding columns in Table 12.14.

### 12.6.2.2 Example: Analysis of Smartphone Users' Failure Reports

Our analysis of smartphone failure reports revealed that the most frequent types of failures are output failures (36.3%), followed by freezes (25.3%), unstable behavior (18.5%), self-shutdowns (16.9%), and input failures (3%). Despite their high occurrence, output failures are often of low severity, since repeating the action is often sufficient to restore correct device operation (5.79%; see Table 12.15). On the

**Table 12.15** Failure frequency distribution with respect to failure types and recovery actions; the numbers are percentages of the total number of failures [31].

| | Recovery action | | | | | |
|---|---|---|---|---|---|---|
| Failure type | Service phone | Reboot | Battery removal | Wait | Repeat | Unrepairable | Percentage of failures |
| Freeze | 3.65 | 2.36 | 9.01 | 4.29 | 0 | 6.01 | 25.32 |
| Input failure | 0.64 | 0.64 | 0.21 | 0 | 0.64 | 0.86 | 2.99 |
| Output failure | 6.87 | 8.80 | 0.43 | 0.64 | 5.79 | 13.73 | 36.26 |
| Self-shutdown | 6.65 | 0 | 2.15 | 0.43 | 0 | 7.73 | 16.96 |
| Unstable behavior | 6.87 | 1.72 | 0.21 | 0.21 | 0.64 | 8.80 | 18.45 |

other hand, self-shutdown and unstable behavior can be considered high-severity failures because one can effectively recover from them only by servicing the phone or removing the battery. Phone freezes are usually of medium severity since reboot and battery removal usually recover and reestablish proper operation in 2.4% and 9.0% of freeze failures respectively (see Table 12.15). In only about 3.7% of cases (see Table 12.15) must the user seek assistance.

To elucidate the relationship between failure types and recovery actions, Table 12.15 reports a failure distribution with respect to failure types and corresponding recovery actions. From the recovery action perspective, it should be noted that reboots are an effective way to recover from output failures: reboots are used to recover from 8.8% of all output failures. The implication is that output failures are often due to temporary corruptions of the software state, which are cleaned up by reboots. That hypothesis is confirmed by the fact that repeating an action is often sufficient to restore correct device operation. Users usually recover phones from freezes by pulling out the battery (9.01%), although a significant number of them (4.29%) recover simply by waiting some amount of time for the phone to respond. This suggests that some battery removals and reboots in response to freezes happen only because users are impatient. That suggestion led us to reflect that freezes are more annoying than output failures, for which the user rarely needs to pull out the battery.

The analyzed data also allowed us to correlate failure occurrences with user activity at the time of the failure. In particular, 13% of failures occurred during voice calls; 5.4% during creation, sending, or receiving of text messages; 3.6% during Bluetooth use; and 2.4% while the user was manipulating images. Finally, several reports (which, we conjecture, came from relatively sophisticated users) provide insight into the failure causes, e.g. there were indications of memory leaks, incorrect use of device resources, bad handling (by the software) of indexes/pointers to objects, and incorrect management of buffer sizes.

### 12.6.2.3 Example: Analysis of Failures from LANs of Windows NT Machines

In the following discussion, failure data collected from a LAN of Windows NT-based servers are used to illustrate analysis methods for obtaining detailed failure characterizations of a system's behavior [102]. The data for the study were obtained from event logs (i.e. logs of machine events that are maintained and modified by the Windows NT operating system) collected over a six-month period from the mail routing network of a commercial organization.

In the networked systems on which we focus here, the origin of faults is a basic yet useful way to classify faults. A networked computing environment has two major types of faults, based on their source:

- *Machine-related.* A computation node (workstation) encounters failure conditions because of problems that are local to that workstation.

- *Network-related.* A computation node encounters a failure because of a problem in a network component. For example, a failure condition encountered on a client because of a failed server would be classified as a network-related failure.

The fields in the event or error log are:

- Date and time of the event
- Severity of the event (1 indicates an Error, 2 indicates a Warning, 4 indicates an Information message)
- Event ID
- The source that logged the event
- The machine on which the event was logged
- Event-specific information

Table 12.16 summarizes the classification of errors collected for a LAN of Windows NT machines [102]. It shows that most of the problems in the Windows NT-based network were machine-related. The reason is that for the Windows NT-based system, we analyzed only machine reboots, most of which could be attributed to machine-related problems. The above classification is very generic and does not provide enough insight into the real nature of failures observed in the networked system. A more detailed analysis is needed to identify the weak points in the system.

Our initial breakdown of the data on system reboots was based on the events that preceded the current reboot by no more than an hour and occurred after the previous reboot. For each instance of a reboot, the most severe and frequently occurring events (hereinafter referred to as *prominent events*) were identified. The corresponding reboot was then categorized based on the sources and IDs of these prominent events. In some cases, the prominent events were specific enough to identify the problem that caused the reboot. In other cases, only a high-level description of the problem could be obtained based on knowledge of the prominent events. Table 12.17 shows a breakdown of the reboots by category. (These data pertain to reboots in the domain over a period of six months.)

**Table 12.16** Network-related and machine-related problems in a LAN of Windows NT machines [102].

| Type of environment | Commercial environment |
|---|---|
| Type and number of machines | 68 mail servers based on Windows NT 4.0 |
| Period of data collection | 6 months |
| Failure context | Machine reboots logged in a server system log |
| Machine-related failures | 69% |
| Network-related failures | 31% |

**Table 12.17** Breakdown of reboots based on prominent events [102].

| Category | Frequency | Percentage |
|---|---|---|
| *Total reboots* | *1100* | *100* |
| Hardware or firmware problems | 105 | 9 |
| Connectivity problems | 241 | 22 |
| Crucial application failures | 152 | 14 |
| Problems with a software component | 42 | 4 |
| Normal shutdowns | 63 | 6 |
| Normal reboots/power-off (no indication of any problems) | 178 | 16 |
| Unknown | 319 | 29 |

The categories in Table 12.17 should be interpreted as follows:

- *Hardware- or firmware-related problems:* This category includes events that indicated a problem with hardware components (e.g. network adapter or disk), their associated drivers (typically, failures of drivers to load because of problems with devices), or some firmware (e.g. some events indicated that the power on self-test had failed).
- *Connectivity problems:* This category comprises events that indicated that either a system component (e.g. a redirector or server) or a critical application (e.g. an MS Exchange system attendant) could not retrieve information from a remote machine. In these scenarios, it is not possible to pinpoint the cause of the connectivity problem. Some of the connectivity failures resulted from network adapter problems and hence are categorized as hardware-related.
- *Crucial application failure:* This category encompasses reboots that were preceded by severe problems with, and possibly shutdown of, critical application software (such as the Message Transfer Agent). In such cases, it wasn't clear why the application reported problems. If an application shutdown occurred as a result of a connectivity problem, then the corresponding reboot is categorized as connectivity-related.
- *Problems with a software component:* Typically, these reboots were characterized by startup problems (such as a failure to load a critical system component, or a failure to find a driver entry point). Another significant problem in this category is situations in which the machine ran out of virtual memory, possibly because of a memory leak in a software component. In many of these cases, the component that caused the problem is not identifiable.
- *Normal shutdowns:* This category covers reboots that were not preceded by warnings or error messages, as well as events that indicated the shutting down

of critical application software and some system components (e.g. the browser). These represent shutdowns for maintenance or for correcting problems not captured in the event logs.

- *Normal reboots/power-off:* This category covers reboots that were typically not preceded by shutdown events, but do not appear to have been caused by any problems, either. No warnings or error messages appear in the event log before the reboot.

Based on the data in Table 12.17, we can make the following observations about the failures:

1) 28% of the reboots cannot be categorized. Such reboots were preceded by events of severity 2 or lower, but there is not enough information available to determine (a) whether the events were severe enough to force a reboot of the machine, or (b) the nature of the problem that the events reflected.
2) A significant percentage (22%) of the reboots have reported connectivity problems, which is unsurprising considering that the workload on the machines was network I/O-intensive.
3) Only a small percentage (10%) of the reboots can be traced to a system hardware component. Most of the identifiable problems were software-related.
4) Nearly 50% of the reboots were abnormal (i.e. were due to a problem with the machine rather than a normal shutdown).
5) In nearly 15% of cases, severe problems with a crucial mail server application forced a reboot of the machine.
6) Some of the reboots due to connectivity problems may have resulted from failures that propagated in the domain. Furthermore, it is possible that the machines functioning as the master browser and the primary domain controller (PDC) were potential reliability bottlenecks for the domain.

*Analysis of the Failure Behavior of Individual Machines.* After our preliminary investigation of the causes of failures, we probed failures from the perspective of an individual machine as well as the whole network. First, we focused on the failure behavior of individual machines in the domain to obtain (i) estimates of machine up-times and down-times, (ii) an estimate of the availability of each machine, and (iii) a finite state model to describe the failure behavior of a typical machine in the domain. The following discussion is based on the results of the analysis of failure data collected from a LAN of Windows NT-based servers. Machine up-times and down-times were estimated as follows.

- For every reboot event encountered, the timestamp of the reboot was recorded.
- The timestamp of the event immediately preceding the reboot was also recorded. (It would have been the last event logged by the machine before it went down.)

- A smoothing factor of one hour was applied to the reboots (i.e. for multiple reboots that occurred within a period of one hour, all except the last reboot were disregarded). (Since intermediate reboots indicate incomplete recovery from a failure, the machine would have to be considered as having been down until the last such reboot occurred.)
- Each up-time estimate was generated by calculating the time difference between a reboot timestamp and the timestamp of the event that preceded the next reboot.
- Each down-time estimate was obtained by calculating the time difference between a reboot timestamp and the timestamp of the event that preceded it.

Machine up-times are presented in Table 12.18, which reflects an analysis of five months of data. As the standard deviation suggests, there was a great degree of variation in the machine up-times. The longest up-time was nearly three months. The average is skewed because of some of the longer up-times. The median is more representative of the typical up-time. Machine down-times are provided in Table 12.19, which, again, reflects analysis of five months of data. As the table

**Table 12.18**  Machine up-time statistics [102].

| Item | Value |
| --- | --- |
| Number of entries | 616 |
| Maximum | 85.2 days |
| Minimum | 1 hour |
| Average | 11.82 days |
| Median | 5.54 days |
| Standard deviation | 15.656 days |

**Table 12.19**  Machine down-time statistics [102].

| Item | Value |
| --- | --- |
| Item | Frequency |
| Number of entries | 682 |
| Maximum | 15.76 days |
| Minimum | 1 second |
| Average | 1.97 hours |
| Median | 11.43 minutes |
| Standard deviation | 15.86 hours |

clearly shows, 50% of the down-times lasted about 12 minutes, which is so little time that we presume that hardware components could not have been replaced, and the machine reconfigured, during those down-times.

The implication is that the majority of problems were software-related (e.g. memory leaks, misloaded drivers, or application errors). The maximum value is unrealistic and might have been due to the machine's being temporarily taken offline and recommissioned after a fortnight.

*Discussion of Up-times and Down-times.* Since the machines under consideration were dedicated mail servers, bringing down one or more of them would potentially have disrupted the storage, forwarding, reception, and delivery of mail. Such disruptions could have been prevented if explicit rerouting had been performed to avoid the machines that were down. But it is not clear whether such rerouting was done or could have been done. In that context, the following observations are causes for concern: (i) the average measured down-time was nearly two hours, and (ii) 50% of the measured up-time samples were about five days or less.

Having estimated the machine's up-time and down-time, we can estimate the availability of each machine. That availability is evaluated as the ratio

$$\left[ \langle \text{average up-time} \rangle \Big/ \big( \langle \text{average up-time} \rangle + \langle \text{average down-time} \rangle \big) \right] * 100.$$

Table 12.20 summarizes the availability measurements. It shows that the majority of the machines had an availability of 99.7% or higher. Also, there is not a great deal of variation among the individual values. That is surprising, considering the rather large degree of variation in the average up-times. It follows that machines with smaller average up-times also had correspondingly smaller average down-times, so that the ratios are not very different. Hence, broadly speaking, the domain had two types of machines: those that rebooted often but recovered quickly, and those that stayed up longer but took longer to recover from a failure.

**Table 12.20**  Machine availability [102].

| Item | Value |
| --- | --- |
| Number of machines | 66 |
| Maximum | 99.99% |
| Minimum | 89.39% |
| Median | 99.76% |
| Average | 99.35% |
| Standard deviation | 1.52 |

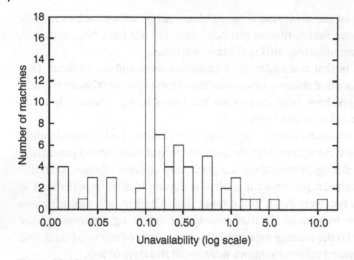

**Figure 12.12** Unavailability distribution [102]/with permission of Springer Nature.

Figure 12.12 shows the unavailability distribution across the machines. (Unavailability was evaluated as 100 – Availability.) Less than 20% of the machines had an availability of 99.9% or higher. However, nearly 90% of the machines had an availability of 99% or higher. It should be noted that these numbers indicate the fraction of time the machine was alive. They do not necessarily indicate the ability of the machine to provide useful service, because the machine could have been alive but unable to provide the service expected of it. To elaborate, each of the machines in the domain acted as a mail server for a set of user machines. Hence, if one of the mail servers had problems that prevented it from receiving, storing, forwarding, or delivering mail, then that server would effectively have been unavailable to the user machines, even though it was up and running.

Hence, to obtain a better estimate of machine availability, it would be necessary to examine how long a machine was able to provide service to user machines.

## 12.7 Estimation of Empirical Distributions

TTE/TTF probability distributions and error/failure hazard rates are commonly used to investigate how errors and failures occur across time. It is relatively easy to obtain empirical TTE/TTF distributions from data with the aid of statistical analysis packages like R [155] or SAS [154]. To that end, the real data can be fitted with theoretical continuous-time distributions. In practice, the family of the distribution and its associated parameters have to be estimated from the collected data. Usually, a family of the distribution is chosen, and the fitting is conducted via a parameter estimation, e.g. a maximum likelihood estimation.

Goodness-of-fit tests can be conducted to determine whether the data can reasonably be declared to belong to the chosen family.

Often, a realistic, analytical form of TTE/TTF distributions is essential in modeling and evaluating computer system dependability. For simplicity, or because of a lack of information, the TTF is assumed to be exponentially distributed. The exponential distribution was first adopted to model the TTF and time to repair electronic components. Early measurement-based studies found that the Weibull distribution with a decreasing failure rate was representative of the time between failures (TBFs) in a measured DEC computer system [28] and for a measured IBM-VM/SP operating system [54]. A comparative study of the dependability of the Tandem Guardian, DEC VAX VMS, and IBM MVS operating systems showed that the software TTE in a single machine can be represented by a multistage gamma distribution and that the software TTE in multicomputers can be represented by a hyperexponential distribution [84]. The reason is the simplistic memoryless property of the exponential distribution. If a process consists of alternate phases – that is, during any single experiment, the process experiences one and only one of many alternate phases, and these phases have exponential distributions – then the overall distribution is hyperexponential.

The lognormal distribution has been recognized as a proper distribution for software failure rates [170]. Many successful analytical models of software behavior share assumptions suggesting that the distribution of software event rates will asymptotically approach lognormal. The lognormal distribution has its origin in the complexity of software systems (estimated by the depth of conditionals), and in the understanding that an essentially multiplicative process can be used to determine event rates. The central limit theorem links these properties to the lognormal: just as the normal distribution arises when one is summing many random terms, the lognormal distribution arises when the value of a variable is determined by the multiplication of many random factors.

The Weibull distribution has been used to describe fatigue failures and electronic component failures. It is perhaps the most widely used parametric family of failure distributions because one can obtain an increasing, decreasing, or constant failure rate distribution by choosing an appropriate *shape parameter* for it. Therefore, it can be used for all phases of the bathtub mortality curve [1].

### 12.7.1 Hazard Rate Estimation

The hazard rate gives the probability that a failure will occur within the coming unit of time, given that no failure has occurred since the last failure occurrence. The mathematical definition of the hazard rate is the following:

$$h(t) = \frac{Pr\{errorin(t, t + \Delta t)\}}{Pr\{noerrorsin(0, t)\}dt} = \frac{f(t)}{(1 - F(t))} \tag{12.1}$$

where $F(T)$ is the CDF (and $1 - F(T)$ is the survival function), and $f(t)$ is the probability density function (PDF) of the variable. The hazard rate expresses the propensity to fail in the next small interval of time $\Delta t$, given the survival time of $t$. It can be interpreted as the failure rate in the following sense. If a large number of items (say $n(t)$) are in operation at time $t$, then $n(t) \times h(t)$ is approximately equal to the number of failures per unit time per unit at risk. The unit of $h(t)$ is the fraction of failed units per unit time.

The empirical hazard functions are constructed based on the empirical TBF estimation, using the same time scale used for the TBF estimation. However, when one is estimating the hazard rate from empirical data, certain issues concerning the application of hazard rate estimators must be addressed in order to obtain meaningful results. It has been noted that bias problems occur when one is estimating near the endpoints of the data. It is often noted that numerical differentiation increases the noise. That is why the empirical hazard rate peaks at the end: because of the increased noise amplified by the $f(t)$ at the numerator of the hazard rate formula. These peaks in the empirical hazard rate are usually referred to as *boundary effects*. Below we provide examples of hazard analysis in real systems.

Figure 12.13 depicts the PDF for disk errors in the CMU Andrew file system [153]. Analysis shows that the instantaneous error rate (hazard function) for the data is a decreasing function of time.

The data are seen to best fit a Weibull distribution, i.e. the PDF, $f(t)$, is given by

$$f(t) = \alpha\lambda t^{\alpha-1}e^{-\lambda t^{\alpha}} \tag{12.2}$$

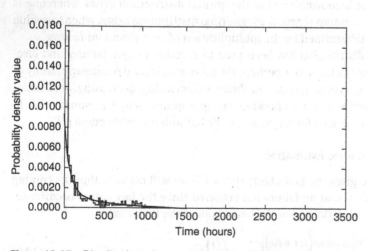

**Figure 12.13** Distribution of Andrew file system disk errors. Data taken from [153].

and the hazard (error rate) function is given by

$$h(t) = \alpha \lambda t^{\alpha-1} \tag{12.3}$$

where $\alpha$ is the shape parameter and $\lambda$ is the scale or rate parameter. Note that if $\alpha == 1$, then the hazard function reduces to a constant (i.e. $f(t)$ reduces to the exponential). The Weibull function has been found to describe a wide variety of hardware and software errors; it is superimposed upon the actual data presented in Figure 12.13. Note that $\alpha$ is usually much less than 1, which means the hazard function is decreasing.

We present TTE distributions for the three operating systems studied in [84], but first, we explain how a TTE distribution is obtained from a multicomputer system. In a multicomputer system, typically, all the constituent machines work in a similar environment and run the same version of the operating system. The whole system can be treated as a single entity in which multiple instances of an operating system are running concurrently. Every software error in the system is sequentially ordered, and a distribution is constructed. The constructed TTE distribution reflects the software error characteristics for the whole system. We will call this distribution the *multicomputer software TTE distribution*.

Figure 12.14 gives the analytical TTE or TTH distributions that were extracted, using SAS, from data on the three systems. All three empirical distributions failed

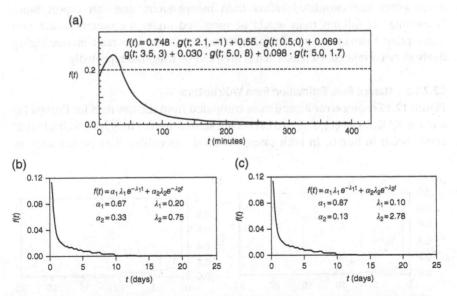

**Figure 12.14** Analytic software TTE (or TTH) distributions. (a) IBM MVS software TTE distribution, (b) VAXcluster software TTE distribution, and (c) Tandem software TTH distribution [84]/with permission of IEEE.

to fit simple exponential functions. The fitting was tested using the Kolmogorov-Smirnov or Chi-square test at a 0.05 significance level. The two-phase hyperexponential distribution provided satisfactory fits for the VAXcluster and Tandem multicomputer software TTE distributions. An attempt to fit the MVS TTE distribution to a phase-type exponential distribution led to a large number of stages. As a result, a multistage gamma distribution was used [84].

It was found that a 5-stage gamma distribution provided a satisfactory fit, which means that the software TTE distribution on the MVS had a complicated mode. Figure 12.14b, c shows that the multicomputer software TTE distribution can be modeled as a probabilistic combination of two exponential random variables, indicating that there are two dominant error modes. The higher error rate, $\lambda_2$, which has an occurrence probability of $\alpha_2$, captures both the error bursts (i.e. multiple errors that occur on the same operating system within a short period of time) and the concurrent errors (i.e. multiple errors on different instances of an operating system within a short period of time) on these systems. The lower error rate, $\lambda_1$, with an occurrence probability of $\alpha_1$, captures regular errors and provides an inter-burst error rate.

Error bursts can be explained as repeated occurrences of the same software problem or as multiple effects of an intermittent hardware fault on the software. Software error bursts have also been observed in laboratory experiments reported in [171]. The study showed that if the input sequences of the software under investigation are correlated rather than independent, one can expect more "bunching" of failures than would be predicted under a constant failure rate assumption. In an operating system, input sequences (i.e. user requests) are highly likely to be correlated. Hence, a defect area can be triggered repeatedly.

### 12.7.1.1 Hazard Rate Estimation from VAXclusters

Figure 12.15 shows error hazard rates computed from the raw data for Europa (a) and the VAXcluster (b). The two curves are similar in that they both indicate that errors occur in bursts. In both cases, the most susceptible time period after an

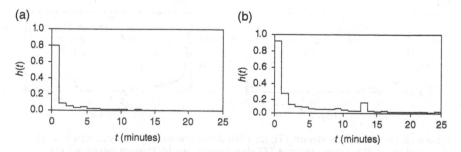

**Figure 12.15** Error hazard for (a) Europa, (b) VAXcluster [29]/with permission of IEEE.

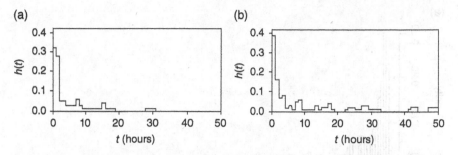

**Figure 12.16** Failure hazard for (a) Europa, (b) VAXcluster [29]/with permission of IEEE.

error occurrence is the following minute. That is, if no new error is observed within the first minute after an error, the error occurrence probability decreases considerably. However, the time window (i.e. the time interval between two successive error observations) in which the second error is likely to occur is longer than just a minute. For Europa, the susceptible time window is around five minutes, which is consistent with the time interval used in the coalescing algorithm employed (which assumes that, within the interval, two error observations of the same type are likely to have been caused by the same problem). For the VAXcluster, the susceptible time window is about 15 minutes. That is, when a burst of errors involves multiple machines, it can last 15 minutes.

Figure 12.16 shows the failure hazard rates computed from the failure event data for Europa (a) and the VAXcluster (b). The curves show that, like errors, failures occur in bursts for both the single machine and the VAXcluster. The failure hazard rate for the VAXcluster is generally higher than that for Europa. In both cases, the time windows in which the system is susceptible to failures are around five to ten hours.

In summary, despite a high probability of recovery from errors in shared resources, the sheer numbers of such errors mean that they cause a significant portion of all failures, making shared resources a reliability bottleneck for the VAXcluster. The error and failure distributions and hazard rates revealed that not only errors but also failures, occurred in bursts for both the single machine and the entire VAXcluster.

### 12.7.1.2 Hazard Rate Estimation from a Software-as-a-Service Platform

Figure 12.17 shows the PDF (a) and failure hazard rate (b) of a production Software-as-a-Service platform. The shape of the hazard function (decreasing to an almost constant value) is due to the heavy-tailed distribution of the TBFs shown in Figure 12.17a.

Random variables that follow heavy-tailed distributions are characterized as exhibiting many *small values* (i.e. short intervals between two subsequent events)

(a)

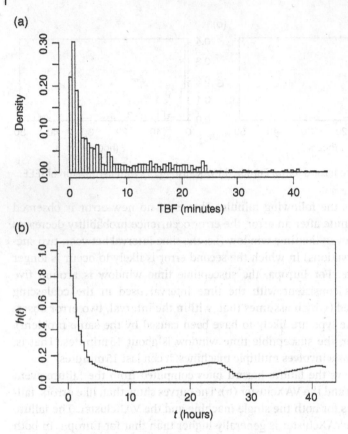

(b)

**Figure 12.17** Example of the TBFs and the hazard rate for a Software-as-a-Service platform: (a) PDF for the TBFs and (b) hazard rate.

mixed with a few *large values* (i.e. long intervals between two subsequent events). In our case, a lot of failures happen in close proximity with each other, and in a relatively few cases, two subsequent failures happen far apart in time. As a result, in observations (or dataset) corresponding to a random variable with heavy-tailed distribution, most of the observations (i.e. values the variable takes) are *small values*, but most of the contributions to the variable mean (or variance) come from the rare *large values*. In particular, for data samples "in the tail," $E[X|X > k]$ is approximately equal to $k$. This is referred to as the *expectation paradox*. For failure distributions, the expectation paradox implies that (i) most failures happen in bursts since the majority of the observations of the TTF are small values; and (ii) if we are observing heavy-tailed failure interarrivals, then, after a given point (when we are about to enter the tail), the probability that a failure will happen in the next time unit decreases as time passes.

Error bursts can be explained as repeated occurrences of the same software problem or as multiple effects of an intermittent hardware fault on the software. In an operating system, input sequences (i.e. user requests) are highly likely to be correlated. That phenomenon is well-modeled by Weibull and lognormal distribution. The lognormal distribution can be interpreted as the result of overlapping and mutually influencing dynamics, proving that there is a component of autocorrelation in the failure times. For instance, for the data in Figure 12.17b, after the first five to six hours, the chances of having another failure in the next minute decrease, and then are constant for a while. In other words, Figure 12.17b shows that the platform can be subjected to a burst of failures within a vulnerable time window of five to six hours (the knee on the curve). After that, the hazard rate sets to a low value in the range of 0.06–0.16. Interestingly, that phenomenon is similar to the one shown in Figure 12.17a. A difference is that for the SaaS platform, the hazard rate shows a slight increase toward the 24th hour, and then an additional step toward lower values after that. That effect is due to clients' resubmissions of failed jobs the day after the jobs failed. In many cases, failures are caused by unexpected values in user data. The hazard plots confirm that if we do not observe any failures for 24 hours, there is very likely to be an increase in the hazard rate due to the resubmission of jobs that failed 24 hours ago and will eventually fail again, and then contribute to the increase around hour 24. After that interval, the hazard rate decreases sharply, showing that if the system does not have any failures for more than 24 hours, then it is very unlikely that new failures will happen within the following hours. Finally, the increase in the hazard slope toward 40 hours is due to the boundary effects mentioned earlier in this section.

## 12.8 Dependency Analysis

Many underlying dependencies exist among measured parameters and components. Examples are the dependency between workload and failure rate, and the dependency or correlation among failures on different components. Understanding and quantifying such dependencies is important for developing realistic models and hence better designs. The workload/failure dependency issue was studied in the early 1980s, and the correlated failure issue has been investigated subsequent years.

Dependency between workloads and failures has been addressed via two approaches: statistical quantification of the dependence between workload and failure rate [52, 76], and stochastic modeling of failures as functions of workload [53]. Both approaches have demonstrated a strong correlation between workload and failure rate. The results have indicated that dependability models cannot be considered representative unless the system workload is taken into account. Based on that result, several workload-dependent analytical models have been proposed [172–174].

Early measurements on VAXclusters [51, 56] and Tandem machines [4] found correlated failures in those systems. Other studies showed that even a small correlation can have a major impact on system dependability [60, 61, 75]. Neither traditional models that assume failure independence, nor those that are believed to take correlation into account are representative of the actual occurrence process of correlated failures observed in measured systems.

In the following subsections, dependency analysis is illustrated through discussion of two issues: (i) dependency between workload and failure, and (ii) dependency among errors/failures on different components in a computer system.

## 12.8.1 Workload/Failure Dependency

An early study [52] introduced a workload-dependent cyclostationary model to characterize system failure processes. The basic assumption in the model was that the instantaneous failure rate of a system resource can be approximated by a function of the usage of the resource considered. Specifically, the failure rate of a particular resource, $\lambda(t)$, was assumed to be

$$\lambda(t) = au(t) + b \tag{12.4}$$

where $u(t)$ is a usage function of the resource, which in turn consists of a deterministic, periodic function of time, $m(t)$, and a modified, stationary Gaussian process, $z(t)$:

$$u(t) = m(t) + z(t) \tag{12.5}$$

The failure arrivals were assumed to follow a Poisson process. Thus, the failure process involved two stochastic processes: a Poisson process and a Gaussian process. Such a failure process is defined as a doubly stochastic process. The model was applied to a PDP-10 machine running a modified version of the standard TOPS-10 operating system. It was shown that the TTF distribution predicted by the model and the one observed from the real system had a very good fit at the significance level 0.36 in a $\chi^2$ test.

The work in [52] introduced a workload-dependent software probabilistic model to predict the differences in manifestations of software errors and transient hardware errors as a function of system workload. The model was applied to a modified version of the TOPS-10 operating system running on a PDP-10 machine. The central argument behind this study was that the observed software failure rate depends on the instantaneous complexity of the data to be processed, while the system failure rate due to hardware transients is insensitive to the data complexity. If a system doubles its average fraction of time spent in the kernel mode, its failure rate due to hardware transients increases linearly. Thus, deviations from the expected linearity can be attributed to software errors.

In [49], a load hazard model was introduced to measure the risk of failure as system activity increases. Given a workload variable $X$, the load hazard is defined as

$$z(x) = \frac{Pr\left[\text{failure in load interval}(x, x + \Delta x)\right]}{Pr\left[\text{no failure in load interval}(0, x)\right]\Delta x} = \frac{g(x)}{1 - G(x)} \tag{12.6}$$

where $g(x)$ is the PDF of the variable "a failure occurs at a given workload value $x$" and $G(x)$ is the corresponding CDF That is,

$$g(x) = Pr\left[\text{failure occurs}\,|\,X = x\right] = \frac{f(x)}{l(x)} \tag{12.7}$$

where $l(x)$ is the PDF of the workload under consideration:

$$l(x) = Pr\left[X = x\right] \tag{12.8}$$

and $f(x)$ is the joint PDF of the system state (failure state or nonfailure state) and the workload. One can think of $g(x)$ as the probability of a failure at a given load when all loads are equally represented; it is the conditional failure probability.

An analogy to illustrate the above distinction between $f(x)$ and $g(x)$ is that automobiles traveling at 150 mph have a higher accident probability than those traveling at 55 mph; however, far more accidents occur at 55 mph. To obtain an accurate representation of the risks involved in traveling at high speeds, we must divide the number of accidents that occur at each speed by the number of autos traveling at that speed.

A constant hazard rate implies that failures occur randomly with respect to the workload. An increasing hazard rate on the increase of $X$ implies that there is an increasing failure rate with an increasing workload.

The load hazard model was applied to the software failure and workload data collected from an IBM 370 system running the VM operating system. Based on the collected data, $l(x)$, $f(x)$, $g(x)$, and $z(x)$ were computed for each workload variable.

In each hazard plot, $z(x)$ has been calculated and plotted as a function of a chosen workload variable, $x$. In developing hazard plots for load failure data, an important factor to consider is that in the real world, failures can occur for several reasons. Some examples are temperature, humidity, random noise, mechanical failures, and design errors. Factors not related to load can be expected to appear as noise in a load failure analysis. If the non-load factors are predominant, we can expect to find no discernible pattern. An easily discernible pattern, on the other hand, would indicate that the load-failure dependence dominates relative to other factors. The strength of such a relationship can be measured through regression.

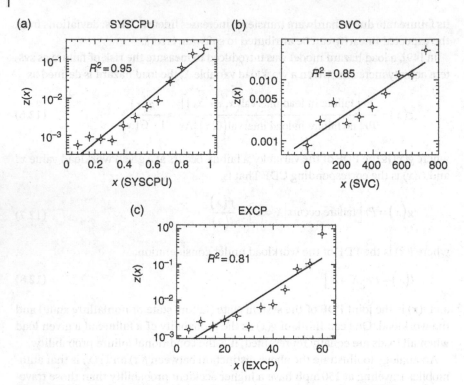

**Figure 12.18** Hazard plots for three selected load parameters in the IBM 370 system: (a) SYSCPU – CPU utilization for system (a fraction between 0 and 1); (b) SVC – Supervisor calls (rate per second) used for operating system services, e.g., memory allocation; (c) EXCP – the I/O initiation rate by batch jobs (I/O per second). The vertical scale on the plots of $z(x)$ is logarithmic [52]/with permission of IEEE.

Figure 12.18a–c depicts the hazard plots for the three selected load parameters. The regression coefficient $R^2$, which is an effective measure of the goodness of fit, is provided for each plot. Quite simply, it measures the amount of variability in the data that can be accounted for by the regression model. $R^2$ values of greater than 0.6 (corresponding to an $R > 0.75$) are generally interpreted as strong relationships.

The hazard plots show that the workload parameters appear to be acting as stress factors and suggest that they can be used as predictors of the load-related reliability measures, i.e. the failure rate increases as the workload increases. The effect is particularly strong in the case of the CPU-intensive workload. The correlation coefficients of 0.95 show that the failure closely fits an increasing load hazard model. In such a case, as shown in Figure 12.18, the measured percentage of CPU utilization (SYS-CPU) is "reliability-sensitive," i.e. when the system CPU increases from 0.3 to 0.9, there is an almost hundredfold increase in the load hazard ($10^{-3}$ to $10^{-1}$). Note that the vertical scale on the plots is logarithmic, indicating that the relationship between the load hazard $z(x)$ and the workload variable is exponential, i.e. the risk of a software failure increases exponentially with increasing workload.

The risk of failure also increases with an increasing rate of supervisor calls, although at a somewhat lower correlation (0.85). A change in SVC (supervisor calls) from 20 to 550/seconds results in only a tenfold increase in $z(x)$.

The above experimental results have been incorporated into analytical dependability models. The authors of [172] proposed a general, analytical approach to the study of workload effects on computer system dependability. In their study, a Markov renewal process model was established to represent the interaction between workload and fault accumulation in a system. Two types of interaction were considered: the workload may help detect/correct a correctable fault, or it may cause the system to fail by activating an uncorrectable fault. The faults considered in the model in [172] were transient and were modeled as dormant, soft internal faults in the system. Such faults can accumulate in the system and be activated by workload.

The modeled workload discussed in [172] consisted of various types of task arrivals that had different processing requirements. The relationship between workload and system states was defined as follows: for each type of task $i$, there is a corresponding threshold value $m_i$. If the total number of dormant faults in the system does not exceed $m_i$, arrival of a type $i$ task activates and corrects any existing faults via fault-tolerance mechanisms provided by the system and brings the system back to the fault-free state. Otherwise, if the total dormant faults in the system exceed $m_i$, a service request of a type $i$ task cannot be met, and the system fails. The threshold value $m_i$ is called fault margin associated with the type $i$ task. The fault margin characterizes the fault tolerance of the system.

The study in [172] examined some specific examples (of input tasks as workload, and internal activity or self-exercising as workload) and showed how the probability nature of "time to failure" can be formulated directly in terms of workload, fault arrival, and fault margins. It also examined the role of self-exercising in fault-tolerant systems and showed how self-exercising and fault tolerance interact in their influence on TTF. The results provided new insights into how workload affects the dependability of fault-tolerant systems.

Later, another methodology was proposed in [173] for evaluating systems with nonhomogeneous workloads and fault arrivals. The proposed methodology employed analytic techniques based on Markov processes and stochastic activity networks. The modeled environment was assumed to vary between different utilization phases (e.g. a passive use period and an active use period) of random duration that have different workload effects on fault occurrence and recovery. External faults due to physical or human causes as well as internal design and operational faults were considered in the model. The study addressed questions about the system at random times, e.g. system availability at a phase transition or MTTF relative to the beginning of some phase. Since the methodology accounts for a nonhomogeneous environment, it can be used to evaluate the use of different fault recovery techniques during different phases.

In [174], a workload-dependent memory fault model was developed. The overall model consists of two submodels: (i) a memory fault occurrence model that depends on several workload parameters, such as the page references and the execution time of tasks, and (ii) a performance model that accounts for the influence of memory faults on system performance. Additional workload produced by fault handling was also taken into account. The study used queuing network analysis methods to evaluate the average performance loss caused by memory faults. The transient task reliability, which quantifies the risk that a single task will suffer a memory fault, was also evaluated. The results demonstrated that the performance decrease caused by memory errors depends on system workload and operating system characteristics.

## 12.8.2  Failure Dependency Among Components

The correlation coefficient can be used to quantify the linear dependence between two variables.

The correlation coefficient, $Corr(X_1, X_2)$, between the random variables $X_1$ and $X_2$ is defined as:

$$Corr\left(X_1, X_2\right) = \frac{E\left[\left(X_1 - \mu_1\right)\left(X_2 - \mu_2\right)\right]}{\sigma_1 \sigma_2} \qquad (12.9)$$

where $\mu_1$ and $\mu_2$ are the means of $X_1$ and $X_2$, and $\sigma_1$ and $\sigma_2$ are the standard deviations of $X_1$ and $X_2$, respectively. If we use $\rho$ to denote the correlation coefficient, then $\rho$ satisfies $-1 \leq \rho \geq 1$. The correlation coefficient is a measure of the linear relationship between two variables. When $|\rho| = 1$, we have $X_1 = aX_2 + b$, where $b > 0$ if $\rho = 1$, or $b < 0$ if $\rho = -1$. In this boundary case, there is an exact linear relationship between $X_1$ and $X_2$. When $|\rho| \neq 1$, there is no exact linear relationship between $X_1$ and $X_2$. In that case, $\rho$ measures the goodness of the linear relationship $X_1 = aX_2 + b$ between $X_1$ and $X_2$. Usually, a $\rho$ value of 0.5 or above is considered reasonably high. Correlation analysis can be used to quantify error or workload dependency between two components in a system.

Given random variables $X_1$, $X_2$, and $X_3$ and correlation coefficients between each pair $\rho_{12}$ (for $X_1$, $X_2$), $\rho_{23}$ (for $X_2$, $X_3$), and $\rho_{13}$ (for $X_1$, $X_3$), we know these variables are related to each other by $\rho_{12}, \rho_{23},$ and $\rho_{13}$. Since $X_1$ is related to $X_2$, and $X_2$ is related to $X_3$, a partial dependence between $X_1$ and $X_3$ may be due to $X_2$.

The partial correlation coefficient defined below quantifies the partial dependence:

$$\rho_{13.2} = \frac{\rho_{13} - \rho_{13}\rho_{23}}{\left(1 - \rho_{12}^2\right)\left(1 - \rho_{23}^2\right)} \tag{12.10}$$

The partial correlation coefficient can be considered a measure of the common relationship among the three variables. If a random variable, $X$, is defined on time series, the correlation coefficient can be used to quantify the time serial dependence in the sample data of $X$. Given a time window $\Delta t > 0$, the autocorrelation coefficient of $X$ on the time series $t$ is defined as

$$Autocor\left(X, \Delta t\right) = Corr\left(X\left(t\right), X\left(t + \Delta t\right)\right) \tag{12.11}$$

where $t$ is defined on the discrete values ($\Delta t$, $2\Delta t$, $3\Delta t$, ...). We treat $X(t)$ and $X(t + \Delta t)$ as two different random variables, and the autocorrelation coefficient is actually the correlation coefficient between the two variables. That is, $Autocor(X,\Delta t)$ measures the time serial correlation of $X$ with a window $\Delta t$ (lag). When errors/failures on two components are related, the correlation coefficient between the two components is a good measure of such dependence. The question is how to obtain it from measured data.

### 12.8.2.1 Steps in Correlation Analysis

The first step in correlation analysis is to build a data matrix based on the measured data. Assume that there are $n$ components in the measured system and that the measured period is divided into $m$ equal intervals of $\Delta t$ (e.g. five minutes). An $m \times n$ data matrix can then be constructed in the following way. The $n$ columns of the matrix represent the $n$ components in the measured system. The $m$ rows of the matrix represent the $m$ time intervals. Element ($i, j$) of the matrix is set to the number of errors (or set to 1 in the failure case) occurring within interval $i$ on component $j$. Column $j$ can be regarded as a sample of the random variable, $X_j$, which represents the state of component $j$ in the system.

The second step is to calculate correlation coefficients using Eq. (12.11) based on the data matrix. Each time, we pick up two columns ($X_i$ and $X_j$) to calculate $Corr(X_i, X_j)$. This step can be automated by using a statistical package such as SAS. Table 12.21 lists the average correlation coefficients of the 21 pairs of machines in a VAXcluster for different types of errors and failures [60]. Generally, the error correlation is high (0.62) and the failure correlation is low (0.06). Disk and network errors are strongly correlated, because the processors in the system heavily use and share the disks and the network concurrently.

We have seen that the failure correlation coefficient in Table 12.21 is low (0.06). An important question is: Does such a low correlation have an impact on

**Table 12.21** Average correlation coefficients for VAXcluster errors [60].

| | | Error | | | | Failure |
| --- | --- | --- | --- | --- | --- | --- |
| All | CPU | Memory | Disk | Network | Software | All |
| 0.62 | 0.03 | 0.01 | 0.78 | 0.7 | 0.02 | 0.06 |

dependability? Through different approaches, two independent studies, [61] and [4], showed that even a small correlation can have a significant impact on system unavailability. Here, we discuss the approach used in [61].

In [61], another type of correlation coefficient, different from that discussed above, was introduced to quantify the correlation between the $i$th and $(i+1)$th failure. Let $A$ and $B$ be random variables representing failures of the first and second components, respectively. $A$ takes a value of 1 if the first component is in the failure state, and 0 if it is not; $B$ takes a value of 1 if the second component is in the failure state, and 0 if it is not. (Thus, $A$ and $B$ are similar to $X_i$ in the matrix discussed above.) The steady-state linear correlation coefficient between $A$ and $B$ was defined as follows:

$$\rho_{AB} = \frac{E\left[(A-m_A)(B-m_B)\right]}{E\left[(A-m_A)^2\right]E\left[(B-m_B)^2\right]} \tag{12.12}$$

where $m_A$ and $m_B$ are the time average (mean) of $A$ and $B$, respectively. Given the failure rate of the first component, $\lambda_1$, $\rho_{AB}$ can be used to determine the failure rate of the second component by

$$\lambda_2 = \frac{\mu\left(\lambda_1 + \lambda_1\rho_{AB} + \mu\rho_{AB}\right)}{\mu - \lambda_1\rho_{AB} - \mu\rho_{AB}} \tag{12.13}$$

where $\mu$ is the recovery rate of components 1 and 2.

The study in [61] applied the methodology to solve Markov models of two-, three-, and four-component systems subject to permanent, intermittent, and transient correlated failures under a range of assumed correlation coefficients. Table 12.22 lists the evaluated unavailability for systems with 2, 3, and 4 components under several different correlation coefficients, given a set of component failure and recovery rates. The results show that a correlation coefficient as small as 0.0001–0.01 can increase the unavailability of a system by several orders of magnitude.

If errors/failures on more than two components are related, the correlation coefficient is not enough to quantify the dependence among these components (i.e. the multiway correlation). In such a case, the factor analysis method can be used to uncover the multiway correlation. In the following, the application of

**Table 12.22** Sensitivity study of the unavailability computed for systems with 2, 3, and 4 components, for different correlation coefficients [61].

|  | 0 | 0.0001 | 0.001 | 0.01 |
|---|---|---|---|---|
| 2-Component System | $4.84 \times 10^{-8}$ | $7 \times 10^{-8}$ | $4.28 \times 10^{-7}$ | $2.27 \times 10^{-6}$ |
| 3-Component System | $1.06 \times 10^{-11}$ | $3.63 \times 10^{-10}$ | $6.71 \times 10^{-9}$ | $1.97 \times 10^{-7}$ |
| 4-Component System | $2.34 \times 10^{-15}$ | $2.93 \times 10^{-11}$ | $1.40 \times 10^{-9}$ | $8.64 \times 10^{-8}$ |

factor analysis is illustrated using the processor failure data collected from a Tandem fault-tolerant system [4].

Much as in the correlation analysis discussed above, the first step is to build an $m \times n$ data matrix based on measurements, where $n$ is the number of components in the system and $m$ is the number of measured time intervals. The element $(i, j)$ of this matrix has a value of 1 if processor $j$ halts during the $i$th time interval; otherwise, it has a value of 0. The $j$th column of the matrix represents the sample halt history of processor $j$, while the $i$th row of the matrix represents the state of the eight processors in the $i$th time interval. The matrix is called a *processor halt matrix*.

In [4], the factor analysis approach was applied to data collected from an 8-processor Tandem fault-tolerant system (i.e. $n = 8$). The time interval ($\Delta t$) used was 30 minutes. Results obtained by applying the SAS procedure FACTOR to the processor halt matrix are shown in Table 12.23. The numbers in the middle of the table are factor loadings, and the last column shows commonality. The bottom

**Table 12.23** Effect of correlation on unavailability for systems with two to four components [4].

| Processor | Factor 1 | Factor 2 | Factor 3 | Factor 4 | Commonality |
|---|---|---|---|---|---|
| 1 | 0.997 | −0.004 | −0.069 | 0.023 | 1 |
| 2 | 0 | 0 | 0 | 0 | 0 |
| 3 | 0.061 | 0.012 | 0.853 | −0.133 | 0.75 |
| 4 | 0.001 | 0.999 | −0.011 | 0.021 | 1 |
| 5 | 0.982 | 0 | 0.188 | −0.018 | 1 |
| 6 | −0.001 | 0.447 | −0.005 | 0.009 | 0.2 |
| 7 | 0.047 | −0.002 | 0.862 | 0.506 | 1 |
| 8 | −0.007 | 0.762 | 0.09 | 0.641 | 1 |
| Var. | 1.965 | 1.781 | 1.519 | 0.685 | |
| Var. % | 24.6 | 22.3 | 19 | 8.6 | |

two rows show the amount of variance attributed to the common factors and the percentages of the total variance that they represent.

According to [175], factor loadings greater than 0.5 are considered significant. However, in reliability analysis, factor loadings lower than 0.5 can be significant. The results show that there are four common factors. Factor 1 captures the dependence between processor 1 and processor 5 and accounts for 24.6% of the total variance. Factor 2 captures the multiway dependence among processors 4, 6, and 8, although the contribution of processor 6 is small (0.4472). Factor 2 explains 22.3% of the total variance. Factor 3 captures the dependence between processor 3 and processor 7 and contributes 19% of the total variance. Factor 4 captures the dependence, although it is lower (with factor loadings of 0.506 and 0.641), between processor 7 and processor 8 and accounts for 8.6% of the total variance.

### 12.8.3 Error Interaction Analysis

When software is running in a complex system, interactions between hardware and software, and interactions among multiple processors, can cause software error scenarios that cannot be seen during testing. Investigation of such error scenarios is helpful for understanding the characteristics of software errors in operational systems. In the following, hardware-related software errors that result from interactions between hardware and software are discussed.

#### 12.8.3.1 Hardware-Related Software Errors

In [76], software errors related to hardware errors were described as hardware-related software errors. More precisely, if a software error (or failure) occurs in close time proximity (within a minute) of a hardware error, it is called a *hardware-related software (HW/SW) error* (or *failure*). There are several causes of hardware-related software errors. For instance, a hardware error, such as a flipped memory bit, may change the software conditions, resulting in a software error. Therefore, even though the error is reported as a software error, it is caused by faulty hardware. Another possibility is that the software may fail to handle an unexpected hardware problem, such as an abnormal condition in the network communication. This can be attributed to a software design flaw. Sometimes, both the hardware error and the software error are symptoms of another, unidentified problem.

Table 12.24 shows the frequency and percentage of hardware-related software errors/failures (among all software errors/failures) measured from an IBM 3081 system running MVS [54] and two VAXclusters [75].

In the IBM system, approximately 33% of all observed software failures were hardware related. HW/SW errors were found to have large error-handling times (i.e. high recovery overhead). The system failure probability for HW/SW errors is close to three times that for software errors in general. The VAXcluster data show

**Table 12.24** Hardware-related software errors/failures [76].

| Category | HW/SW Errors | | HW/SW Failures | |
|----------|--------------|-----------|----------------|-----------|
| *Measures* | Frequency | Percent | Frequency | Percent |
| *IBM/MVS* | 177 | 11.4 | 94 | 32.8 |
| *VAX/VMS* | 32 | 18.9 | 28 | 21.4 |

that most hardware errors involved in HW/SW errors are network errors (75%), which indicates that the major sources of hardware-related software problems in the measured VAXclusters are network-related hardware or software components. A high percentage of failures related to the network (be it in hardware or in software) is a unique feature in a multicomputer system, in which processes rely heavily on intercommunications through the network. The next chapter builds upon the methods described in this chapter by providing detailed case studies of failure analysis of real-world systems.

# References

1 Iyer, R.K. and Tang, D. (1996). Experimental analysis of computer system dependability. In: *Fault-Tolerant Computer System Design* (ed. D.K. Pradhan), 282–392. Upper Saddle River, NJ: Prentice Hall.

2 Hansen, J.P., and Siewiorek, D.P. (1992). Models for time coalescence in event logs. *Digest of Papers, the 22nd International Symposium on Fault Tolerant Computing*, Boston, MA (8–10 July 1992), 221–227. IEEE.

3 Iyer, R.K., Rossetti, D.J., and Hsueh, M.C. (1986). Measurement and modeling of computer reliability as affected by system activity. *ACM Transactions on Computer Systems* 4 (3): 214–237.

4 Lee, I., Iyer, R.K., and Tang, D. (1991). Error/failure analysis using event logs from fault tolerant systems. *Digest of Papers, the 21st International Symposium on Fault-Tolerant Computing*, Montreal, Quebec, Canada (25–27 June 1991), 10–17. IEEE.

5 Tsao, M.M. and Siewiorek, D.P. (1983). Trend analysis on system error files. *Digest of Papers, the 13th International Symposium on Fault-Tolerant Computing*, Milan, Italy (28–30 June 1983), 116–119. IEEE Computer Society Press.

6 Di Martino, C. (2013). One size does not fit all: clustering supercomputer failures using a multiple time window approach. In: *Proceedings of the International Supercomputing Conference, Lecture Notes in Computer Science*, vol. 7905, 302–316. Berlin, Heidelberg: Springer.

**7** Fu, S. and Xu, C.-Z. (2007). Exploring event correlation for failure prediction in coalitions of clusters. *Proceedings of the 2007 ACM/IEEE Conference on Supercomputing*, Reno, NV (10–16 November 2007). New York, NY: Association for Computing Machinery.

**8** Pecchia, A., Cotroneo, D., Kalbarczyk, Z. et al. (2011). Improving log-based field failure data analysis of multi-node computing systems. *Proceedings of the 2011 IEEE/IFIP 41st International Conference on Dependable Systems & Networks*, Hong Kong, China (27–30 June 2011), 97–108. IEEE.

**9** Di Martino C., Kalbarczyk Z., Iyer R.K. et al. (2014). Lessons learned from the analysis of system failures at petascale: the case of Blue Waters. *Proceedings of the 2014 44th Annual IEEE/IFIP International Conference on Dependable Systems and Networks*, Atlanta, GA (23–26 June 2014), 610–621. IEEE.

**10** Di Martino, C., Kramer, W., Kalbarczyk, Z. et al. (2015). Measuring and understanding extreme-scale application resilience: a field study of 5,000,000 HPC application runs. *Proceedings of the 2015 45th Annual IEEE/IFIP International Conference on Dependable Systems and Networks*, Rio de Janeiro, Brazil (22–25 June 2015), 25–36. IEEE.

**11** Oliner, A. and Stearley, J. (2007). What supercomputers say: a study of five system logs. *Proceedings of the 37th Annual IEEE/IFIP International Conference on Dependable Systems and Networks*, Edinburgh, Scotland (25–28 June 2007), 575–584. IEEE.

**12** Liang, Y., Zhang, Y., Sivasubramaniam, A. et al. (2005). Filtering failure logs for a BlueGene/L prototype. *Proceedings of the 2005 International Conference on Dependable Systems and Networks*, Yokohama, Japan (28 June–1 July 2005), 476–485. IEEE.

**13** Jain, S., Singh, I., Chandra, A. et al. (2009). Extracting the textual and temporal structure of supercomputing logs. *Proceedings of the 2009 International Conference on High Performance Computing*, Kochi, India (16–19 December 2009), 254–263. IEEE.

**14** Zheng, Z., Lan, Z., Park, B. H. et al. (2009). System log pre-processing to improve failure prediction. *Proceedings of the 2009 IEEE/IFIP International Conference on Dependable Systems & Networks*, Lisbon, Portugal (29 June–2 July 2009), 572–577. IEEE.

**15** Gainaru, A., Cappello, F., and Kramer, W. (2012). Taming of the shrew: Modeling the normal and faulty behaviour of large-scale HPC systems. *Proceedings of the 2012 IEEE 26th International Parallel Distributed Processing Symposium*, Shanghai, China (21–25 May 2012), 1168–1179. IEEE.

**16** Stearley, J. and Oliner, A.J. (2008). Bad words: finding faults in Spirit's syslogs. *Proceedings of the 2008 8th IEEE International Symposium on Cluster Computing and the Grid*, Lyon, France (19–22 May 2008), 765–770. IEEE.

17  Fu, X. Ren, R., Zhan, J. et al. (2012). LogMaster: mining event correlations in logs of large-scale cluster systems. *Proceedings of the 2012 IEEE 31st Symposium on Reliable Distributed Systems*, Irvine, CA (8–11 October 2012), 71–80. IEEE.

18  Gainaru, A., Cappello, F., Snir, M. et al. (2012). Fault prediction under the microscope: a closer look into HPC systems. *Proceedings of the International Conference on High Performance Computing, Networking, Storage and Analysis*, Salt Lake City, UT (10–16 November 2012). IEEE.

19  Chandra, S. and Chen, P.M. (2000). Whither generic recovery from application faults? A fault study using open-source software. *Proceedings of the International Conference on Dependable Systems and Networks*, New York, NY (25–28 June 2000), 97–106. IEEE.

20  Di Martino, C., Cinque, M., and Cotroneo, D. (2012). Assessing time coalescence techniques for the analysis of supercomputer logs. *Proceedings of the IEEE/IFIP International Conference on Dependable Systems and Networks*, Boston, MA (25–28 June 2012). IEEE.

21  Buckley M.F. and Siewiorek, D.P. (1996). A comparative analysis of event tupling schemes. *Proceedings of the Annual Symposium on Fault-Tolerant Computing*, Sendai, Japan (25–27 June 1996), 294–303. IEEE.

22  Lin, T.-T.Y. and Siewiorek, D.P. (1990). Error log analysis: statistical modeling and heuristic trend analysis. *IEEE Transactions on Reliability* 39 (4): 419–432.

23  Oliner, A.J., Aiken, A., and Stearley, J. (2008). Alert detection in system logs. *Proceedings of the 2008 8th IEEE International Conference on Data Mining*, Pisa, Italy (15–19 December 2008), 959–964. IEEE.

24  Cinque, M., Cotroneo, D., and Pecchia, A. (2013). Event logs for the analysis of software failures: a rule-based approach. *IEEE Transactions on Software Engineering* 39 (6): 806–821.

25  Krizak, P. (2010). Log analysis and event correlation using Variable Temporal Event Correlator (VTEC). *Proceedings of the 24th Large Installation System Administration Conference*, San Jose, CA (7–12 November 2010), 147–162. The USENIX Association.

26  Lim, C., Singh, N., and Yajnik, S. (2008). A log mining approach to failure analysis of enterprise telephony systems. *Proceedings of the 2008 IEEE International Conference on Dependable Systems and Networks with FTCS and DCC*, Anchorage, AK (24–27 June 2008), 398–403. IEEE.

27  Siewiorek, D.P., Kini, V., Mashburn, H. et al. (1978). A case study of C.mmp, Cm*, and C.vmp: part I—experiences with fault tolerance in multiprocessor systems. *Proceedings of the IEEE* 66 (10): 1178–1199.

28  McConnel, S.R., Siewiorek, D.P. and Tsao, M.M. (1979). The measurement and analysis of transient errors in digital computer systems. *Proceedings of the 9th*

*Annual International Symposium on Fault-Tolerant Computing*, Madison, WI (20–22 June 1979), 67–70. IEEE Computer Society.

29 Tang, D. and Iyer, R.K. (1993). Dependability measurement and modeling of a multicomputer system. *IEEE Transactions on Computers* 42 (1): 62–75.

30 Alemzadeh, H., Iyer, R.K., Kalbarczyk, Z. et al. (2013). Analysis of safety-critical computer failures in medical devices. *IEEE Security & Privacy* 11 (4): 14–26.

31 Cinque, M., Cotroneo, D., Kalbarczyk, Z. et al. (2007). How do mobile phones fail? A failure data analysis of Symbian OS smart phones. *Proceedings of the 37th Annual IEEE/IFIP International Conference on Dependable Systems and Networks*, Edinburgh, Scotland (25–28 June 2007), 585–594. IEEE.

32 Gray, J. (1990). A census of Tandem system availability between 1985 and 1990. *IEEE Transactions on Reliability* 39 (4): 409–418.

33 Schroeder, B., Pinheiro, E., and Weber, W.-D. (2009). DRAM errors in the wild: a large-scale field study. *ACM SIGMETRICS Performance Evaluation Review* 37 (1): 193–204.

34 Cinque, M., Cotroneo, D., and Russo, S. (2006). Collecting and analyzing failure data of Bluetooth personal area networks. *Proceedings of the International Conference on Dependable Systems and Networks*, Philadelphia, PA (25–28 June 2006), 313–322. IEEE.

35 Ganapathi, A. and Patterson, D. (2005). Crash data collection: a Windows case study. *Proceedings of the 2005 International Conference on Dependable Systems and Networks*, Yokohama, Japan (28 June–1 July 2005), 280–285. IEEE.

36 Sahoo, R.K., Sivasubramaniam, A., Squillante, M.S. et al. (2004). Failure data analysis of a large-scale heterogeneous server environment. *Proceedings of the International Conference on Dependable Systems and Networks*, Florence, Italy (28 June –1 July 2004), 772–781. IEEE.

37 Simache, C., Kaâniche, M., and Saidane, A. (2002). Event log based dependability analysis of Windows NT and 2K systems. *Proceedings of the 2002 Pacific Rim International Symposium on Dependable Computing*, Tsukuba City, Ibaraki, Japan (16–18 December 2002), 311–315. IEEE.

38 Jiang, W., Hu, C., Zhou, Y. et al. (2008). Are disks the dominant contributor for storage failures? A comprehensive study of storage subsystem failure characteristics. *ACM Transactions on Storage* 4 (3): 7:1–7:25. https://doi.org/10.1145/1416944.1416946.

39 Cotroneo, D., Orlando, S., and Russo, S. (2006). Failure classification and analysis of the Java Virtual Machine. *Proceedings of the 26th IEEE International Conference on Distributed Computing Systems*, Lisboa, Portugal (4–7 July 2006), article no. 17. IEEE.

40 Buckley, M.F. and Siewiorek, D.P. (1995). VAX/VMS event monitoring and analysis. *Digest of Papers, 25th International Symposium on Fault-Tolerant Computing*, Pasadena, CA (27–30 June 1995), 414–423. IEEE.

**41** Li, S., Zhou, H., Lin, H. et al. (2013). A characteristic study on failures of production distributed data-parallel programs. *Proceedings of the 2013 35th International Conference on Software Engineering*, San Francisco, CA (18–26 May 2013), 963–972. IEEE.

**42** Yin, Z., Ma, X., Zheng, J. et al. (2011). An empirical study on configuration errors in commercial and open source systems. *Proceedings of the 23rd ACM Symposium on Operating Systems Principles*, Cascais, Portugal (23–26 October 2011), 159–172. New York: Association for Computing Machinery.

**43** Schroeder, B. and Gibson, G.A. (2010). A large-scale study of failures in high-performance computing systems. *IEEE Transactions on Dependable and Secure Computing* 7 (4): 337–350.

**44** Chillarege, R., Biyani, S., and Rosenthal, J. (1995). Measurement of failure rate in widely distributed software. *Digest of Papers, the 25th International Symposium on Fault-Tolerant Computing*, Pasadena, CA (27–30 June 1995), 424–433. IEEE.

**45** Schroeder, B. and Gibson, G.A. (2007). Disk failures in the real world: What does an MTTF of 1,000,000 hours mean to you? *Proceedings of the 5th USENIX Conference on File and Storage Technologies,* San Jose, CA (13–16 February 2007), 1–16. USENIX.

**46** Matz, S.M., Votta, L.G., and Malkawi, M. (2002). Analysis of failure and recovery rates in a wireless telecommunications system. *Proceedings of the International Conference on Dependable Systems and Networks,* Washington, DC (23–26 June 2002), 687–693. IEEE.

**47** Chillarege, R. and Iyer, R.K. (1987). Measurement-based analysis of error latency. *IEEE Transactions on Computers* C-36 (5): 529–537.

**48** Carlson, J. and Murphy, R.R. (2003). Reliability analysis of mobile robots. *Proceedings of the 2003 IEEE International Conference on Robotics and Automation*, Taipei, Taiwan (14–19 September 2003), vol. 1, 274–281. IEEE.

**49** Iyer, R.K. and Rossetti, D.J. (1982). A statistical load dependency model for CPU errors at SLAC. *Digest of Papers, the 12th International Symposium on Fault-Tolerant Computing*, Santa Monica, CA (21–24 June 1982), 363–372. IEEE.

**50** Iyer, R.K., Butner, S.E., and McCluskey, E.J. (1982). A statistical failure/load relationship: results of a multicomputer study. *IEEE Transactions on Computers* C-31 (7): 697–706.

**51** Wein, A.S. and Sathaye, A. (1990). Validating complex computer system availability models. *IEEE Transactions on Reliability* 39 (4): 468–479.

**52** Butner, S.E. and Iyer, R.K. (1980). Statistical study of reliability and system load at SLAC. *Digest of Papers, 10th International Symposium on Fault-Tolerant Computing*, Kyoto, Japan (1–3 October 1980), 207–209. IEEE Computer Society.

**53** Castillo, X. and Siewiorek, D.P. (1982). Workload dependent software reliability prediction model. *Digest of Papers, the 12th Annual International Symposium on Fault-Tolerant Computing*, Santa Monica, CA (22–24 June 1982), 279–286. IEEE Computer Society Press.

**54** Iyer, R.K. and Rossetti, D.J. (1985). Effect of system workload on operating system reliability: a study on IBM 3081. *IEEE Transactions on Software Engineering* SE-11 (12): 1438–1448.

**55** Ganesan, R., Sarkar, S., Goel, G. et al. (2012). Measurements-based analysis of workload-error relationship in a production SaaS cloud. *Proceedings of the 2012 IEEE 23rd International Symposium on Software Reliability Engineering Workshops*, Dallas, TX (27–30 November 2012), 96–105. IEEE.

**56** Tang, D., Iyer, R.K., and Subramani, S.S. (1990). Failure analysis and modeling of a VAXcluster system. *Digest of Papers, 20th International Symposium on Fault-Tolerant Computing*, Newcastle upon Tyne, UK (26–28 June 1990), 244–251. IEEE.

**57** Tang, D. and Iyer, R.K. (1992). Analysis and modeling of correlated failures in multicomputer systems. *IEEE Transactions on Computers* 41 (5): 567–577.

**58** Tian, J., Rudraraju, S., and Li, Z. (2004). Evaluating web software reliability based on workload and failure data extracted from server logs. *IEEE Transactions on Software Engineering* 30 (11): 754–769.

**59** Beaudry, M.D. (1978). Performance-related reliability measures for computing systems. *IEEE Transactions on Computers* C-27 (6): 540–547.

**60** Tang, D. and Iyer, R.K. (1992). Impact of correlated failures on dependability in a VAXcluster system. In: *Dependable Computing for Critical Applications 2, Dependable Computing and Fault-Tolerant Systems*, vol. 6 (ed. J.F. Meyer and R.D. Schlichting), 175–194. Vienna, Austria: Springer.

**61** Dugan, J.B. (1992). Correlated hardware failures in redundant systems. In: *Dependable Computing for Critical Applications 2, Dependable Computing and Fault-Tolerant Systems*, vol. 6 (ed. J.F. Meyer and R.D. Schlichting), 157–174. Vienna: Springer.

**62** Zimmermann, T., Nagappan, N., Herzig, K. et al. (2011). An empirical study on the relation between dependency neighborhoods and failures. *Proceedings of the 2011 4th IEEE International Conference on Software Testing, Verification and Validation*, Berlin, Germany (21–25 March 2011), 347–356. IEEE.

**63** El-Sayed, N. and Schroeder, B. (2013). Reading between the lines of failure logs: understanding how HPC systems fail. *Proceedings of the 2013 43rd Annual IEEE/IFIP International Conference on Dependable Systems and Networks*, Budapest, Hungary (24–27 June 2013). IEEE.

**64** Schroeder, B. and Gibson, G.A. (2007). Understanding failures in petascale computers. *Journal of Physics: Conference Series* 78: 012022. [*Proceedings of 3rd Annual Scientific Discovery Through Advanced Computing Conference*, Boston, MA (24–28 June 2007). Bristol: IOP Publishing.].

**65** Hsueh, M.C., Iyer, R.K., and Trivedi, K.S. (1988). Performability modeling based on real data: a case study. *IEEE Transactions on Computers* 37 (4): 478–484.

**66** Hac, A. (1985). A system reliability model with classes of failures. *IEEE Transactions on Reliability* R-34 (1): 29–33.

**67** Hacker, T.J., Romero, F., and Carothers, C.D. (2009). An analysis of clustered failures on large supercomputing systems. *Journal of Parallel and Distributed Computing* 69 (7): 652–665.

**68** Yigitbasi, N., Gallet, M., Kondo, D. et al. (2010). Analysis and modeling of time-correlated failures in large-scale distributed systems. *Proceedings of the 2010 11th IEEE/ACM International Conference on Grid Computing*, Brussels, Belgium (25–28 October 2010), 65–72. IEEE.

**69** Heien, E., Kondo, D., Gainaru, A. et al. (2011). Modeling and tolerating heterogeneous failures in large parallel systems. *Proceedings of the 2011 International Conference for High Performance Computing, Networking, Storage and Analysis,* Seattle, WA (12–18 November 2011), article no. 45. New York: Association for Computing Machinery.

**70** Kulkarni, V.G., Nicola, V.F., and Trivedi, K.S. (1986). On modelling the performance and reliability of multimode computer systems. *Journal of Systems and Software* 6 (1–2): 175–182.

**71** Trivedi, K.S., Vaidyanathan, K., and Goseva-Popstojanova, K. (2000). Modeling and analysis of software aging and rejuvenation. *Proceedings of the 33rd Annual Simulation Symposium*, Washington, DC (16–20 April 2000), 270–279. IEEE.

**72** Di Martino, C., Cinque, M., and Cotroneo, D. (2012). Automated generation of performance and dependability models for the assessment of wireless sensor networks. *IEEE Transactions on Computers* 61 (6): 870–884.

**73** Yang, X., Wang, Z., Xue, J. et al. (2012). The reliability wall for exascale supercomputing. *IEEE Transactions on Computers* 61 (6): 767–779.

**74** Velaardi, P. and Iyer, R.K. (1984). A study of software failures and recovery in the MVS operating system. *IEEE Transactions on Computers* C-33 (6): 564–568.

**75** Tang, D. and Iyer, R.K. (1992). Analysis of the VAX/VMS error logs in multicomputer environments: a case study of software dependability. *Proceedings of the 3rd International Symposium on Software Reliability Engineering*, Research Triangle Park, NC (7–10 October 1992), 216–226. IEEE.

**76** Iyer, R.K. and Velardi, P. (1985). Hardware-related software errors: measurement and analysis. *IEEE Transactions on Software Engineering* 11 (2): 223–231.

**77** Li, X., Shen, K., Huang, M.C. et al. (2007). A memory soft error measurement on production systems. *Proceedings of the USENIX Annual Technical Conference,* Santa Clara, CA (17–22 June 2007), 275–280. USENIX Association.

**78** Tsai, T., Theera-Ampornpunt, N., and Bagchi, S. (2012). A study of soft error consequences in hard disk drives. *Proceedings of the 2012 IEEE/IFIP International Conference on Dependable Systems and Networks*, Boston, MA (25–28 June 2012). IEEE.

**79** Cinque, M., Cotroneo, D., Natella, R. et al. (2010). Assessing and improving the effectiveness of logs for the analysis of software faults. *Proceedings of the*

*2010 IEEE/IFIP International Conference on Dependable Systems and Networks,* Chicago, IL (28 June–1 July 2010), 457–466. IEEE.

80  Laplace, J.-C. and Brun, M. (1998). Critical software for nuclear reactors: 11 years of field experience analysis. *Proceedings of the 9th International Symposium on Software Reliability Engineering*, Paderborn, Germany (4–7 November 1998), 364–368. IEEE.

81  Lee, I. and Iyer, R.K. (1993). Faults, symptoms, and software fault tolerance in the Tandem GUARDIAN90 operating system. *Digest of Papers, the 23rd International Symposium on Fault-Tolerant Computing*, Toulouse, France (22–24 June 1993), 20–29. IEEE.

82  Sullivan, M. and Chillarege, R. (1991). Software defects and their impact on system availability: a study of field failures in operating systems. *Digest of Papers, the 21st International Symposium on Fault-Tolerant Computing*, Montreal, Quebec, Canada (25–27 June 1991), 2–9. IEEE.

83  Lee, I. and Iyer, R.K. (1992). Analysis of software halts in the Tandem GUARDIAN operating system. *Proceedings of the 3rd International Symposium on Software Reliability Engineering*, Research Triangle Park, NC (7–10 October 1992), 227–236. IEEE.

84  Lee, I., Tang, D., Iyer, R.K. et al. (1993). Measurement-based evaluation of operating system fault tolerance. *IEEE Transactions on Reliability* 42 (2): 238–249.

85  Chou, A., Yang, J., Chelf, B. et al. (2001). An empirical study of operating systems errors. *Proceedings of the 18th ACM Symposium on Operating Systems Principles*, Banff, Alberta, Canada (21–24 October 2001), 73–88. New York: Association for Computing Machinery.

86  Chillarege, R., Bhandari, I.S., Chaar, J.K. et al. (1992). Orthogonal defect classification: a concept for in-process measurements. *IEEE Transactions on Software Engineering* 18 (11): 943–956.

87  Sullivan, M. and Chillarege, R. (1992). A comparison of software defects in database management systems and operating systems. *Digest of Papers, the 22nd International Symposium on Fault-Tolerant Computing*, Boston, MA (8–10 July 1992), 475–484. IEEE.

88  Maxion, R.A. (1990). Anomaly detection for diagnosis. *Digest of Papers, the 20th International Symposium on Fault-Tolerant Computing*, Newcastle upon Tyne, UK (26–28 June 1990), 20–27. IEEE.

89  Iyer, R.K., Young, L.T., and Iyer, P.V.K. (1990). Automatic recognition of intermittent failures: an experimental study of field data. *IEEE Transactions on Computers* 39 (4): 525–537.

90  Xu, W., Huang, L., Fox, A. et al. (2009). Online system problem detection by mining patterns of console logs. *Proceedings of the 2009 9th IEEE International Conference on Data Mining*, Miami, FL (6–9 December 2009), 588–597. IEEE.

**91** Kıcıman, E. and Subramanian, L. (2005). A root cause localization model for large scale systems. *Proceedings of the 1st Workshop on Hot Topics in System Dependability*, Yokohama, Japan (30 June 2005).

**92** Kim, S., Zimmermann, T., and Nagappan, N. (2011). Crash graphs: an aggregated view of multiple crashes to improve crash triage. *Proceedings of the 2011 IEEE/IFIP 41st International Conference on Dependable Systems & Networks*, Hong Kong, China (27–30 June 2011), 486–493. IEEE.

**93** Maxion, R.A. and Feather, F.E. (1990). A case study of Ethernet anomalies in a distributed computing environment. *IEEE Transactions on Reliability* 39 (4): 433–443.

**94** Maxion, R.A. and Olszewski, R.T. (1993). Detection and discrimination of injected network faults. *Digest of Papers, the 23rd International Symposium on Fault-Tolerant Computing*, Toulouse, France (22–24 June 1993), 198–207. IEEE.

**95** Salfner, F., Schieschke, M., and Malek, M. (2006). Predicting failures of computer systems: a case study for a telecommunication system. *Proceedings of the 20th IEEE International Parallel & Distributed Processing Symposium*, Rhodes Island, Greece (25–29 April 2006). IEEE.

**96** Liang, Y., Zhang, Y., Jette, M. et al. (2006). BlueGene/L failure analysis and prediction models. *Proceedings of the International Conference on Dependable Systems and Networks*, Philadelphia, PA (25–28 June 2006), 425–434. IEEE.

**97** Michalak, S.E., Harris, K.W., Hengartner, N.W. et al. (2005). Predicting the number of fatal soft errors in Los Alamos National Laboratory's ASC Q supercomputer. *IEEE Transactions on Device and Materials Reliability* 5 (3): 329–335.

**98** Fu, S. and Xu, C.-Z. (2007). Quantifying temporal and spatial correlation of failure events for proactive management. *Proceedings of the 2007 26th IEEE International Symposium on Reliable Distributed Systems*, Beijing, China (10–12 October 2007), 175–184. IEEE.

**99** Guo, P.J., Zimmermann, T., Nagappan, N. et al. (2010). Characterizing and predicting which bugs get fixed: an empirical study of Microsoft Windows. *Proceedings of the 32nd ACM/IEEE International Conference on Software Engineering*, Cape Town, South Africa (1–8 May 2010), 495–504, vol. 1. New York: Association for Computing Machinery.

**100** Xu, J., Kalbarczyk, Z., and Iyer, R.K. (1999). Networked Windows NT system field failure data analysis. *Proceedings of the 1999 Pacific Rim International Symposium on Dependable Computing*, Hong Kong, China (16–17 December 1999), 178–185. Los Alamitos, CA: IEEE Computer Society.

**101** Thakur, A. and Iyer, R.K. (1996). Analyze-NOW: an environment for collection & analysis of failures in a network of workstations. *IEEE Transactions on Reliability* 45 (4): 561–570.

**102** Iyer, R.K., Kalbarczyk, Z., and Kalyanakrishnan, M. (2000). Measurement-based analysis of networked system availability. In: *Performance Evaluation: Origins and Directions, Lecture Notes in Computer Science*, vol. 1769 (ed. G. Haring, C. Lindemann, and M. Reiser), 161–199. Berlin, Heidelberg: Springer.

**103** Kalyanakrishnam, M., Kalbarczyk, Z. and Iyer, R. (1999). Failure data analysis of a LAN of Windows NT based computers. *Proceedings of the 18th IEEE Symposium on Reliable Distributed Systems*, Lausanne, Switzerland (19–22 October 1999), 178–187. Los Alamitos, CA: IEEE Computer Society.

**104** Simache, C. and Kaâniche, M. (2001). Measurement-based availability analysis of Unix systems in a distributed environment. *Proceedings of the 12th International Symposium on Software Reliability Engineering*, Hong Kong, China (27–30 November 2001), 346–355. IEEE.

**105** Simache, C. and Kaâniche, M. (2005). Availability assessment of SunOS/Solaris Unix systems based on Syslogd and wtmpx log files: A case study. *Proceedings of the 11th Pacific Rim International Symposium on Dependable Computing*, Hunan, China (12–14 December 2005). IEEE.

**106** Oppenheimer, D. and Patterson, D.A. (2002). Studying and using failure data from large-scale internet services. *Proceedings of the 10th ACM SIGOPS European Workshop*, Saint-Emilion, France (1 July 2002), 255–258. New York: Association for Computing Machinery.

**107** Patke, A., Qiu, H., Jha, S. et al. (2022). Evaluating hardware memory disaggregation under delay and contention. *Proceedings of the 2022 IEEE International Parallel and Distributed Processing Symposium Workshops*, Lyon, France (30 May–3 June 2022), 1221–1227. IEEE.

**108** Jha, S., Cui, S., Banerjee, S.S. et al. (2020). Live forensics for HPC systems: a case study on distributed storage systems. *Proceedings of the International Conference for High Performance Computing, Networking, Storage and Analysis*, Atlanta, GA [virtual] (9–19 November 2020). IEEE.

**109** Patke, A., Jha, S., Qiu, H. et al. (2021). Delay sensitivity-driven congestion mitigation for HPC systems. *Proceedings of the ACM International Conference on Supercomputing*, Virtual (14–17 June 2021), 342–353. New York: Association for Computing Machinery.

**110** Jha, S., Patke, A., Brandt, J. et al. (2020). Measuring congestion in high-performance datacenter interconnects. *Proceedings of the 17th USENIX Conference on Networked Systems Design and Implementation*, Santa Clara, CA (25–27 February 2020), 37–58. USENIX Association, USA.

**111** Gill, P., Jain, N., and Nagappan, N. (2011). Understanding network failures in data centers: measurement, analysis, and implications. *Proceedings of the ACM SIGCOMM 2011 Conference*, Toronto, Ontario, Canada (15–19 August 2011), 350–361. New York: Association for Computing Machinery.

**112** Long, D., Muir, A., and Golding, R. (1995). A longitudinal survey of Internet host reliability. *Proceedings of the 14th Symposium on Reliable Distributed Systems*, Bad Neuenahr, Germany (13–15 September 1995), 2–9. IEEE.

**113** Arlitt, M.F. and Williamson, C.L. (1996). Web server workload characterization: the search for invariants. *Proceedings of the 1996 ACM SIGMETRICS International Conference on Measurement and Modeling of Computer Systems*, Philadelphia, PA, USA (23–26 May 1996), 126–137, New York: Association for Computing Machinery.

**114** Benson, T., Akella, A., and Maltz, D.A. (2010). Network traffic characteristics of data centers in the wild. *Proceedings of the 10th ACM SIGCOMM Conference on Internet Measurement*, Melbourne, Australia (1–3 November 2010), 267–280. New York: Association for Computing Machinery.

**115** Paxson, V. (2006). End-to-end routing behavior in the Internet. *ACM SIGCOMM Computer Communication Review* 26 (4): 25–38.

**116** Kalyanakrishnan, M., Iyer, R.K., and Patel, J. (1997). Reliability of Internet hosts: a case study from the end user's perspective. *Proceedings of the 6th International Conference on Computer Communications and Networks*, Las Vegas, NV (22–25 September 1997), 418–423. IEEE.

**117** Lal, R. and Choi, G. (1998). Error and failure analysis of a UNIX server. *Proceedings of the 3rd IEEE International High-Assurance Systems Engineering Symposium*, Washington, DC (13–14 November 1998), 232–239. IEEE.

**118** Wallace, D.R. and Kuhn, D.R. (2001). Failure modes in medical device software: an analysis of 15 years of recall data. *International Journal of Reliability, Quality and Safety Engineering* 8 (4): 351–371.

**119** Bliznakov, Z., Mitalas, G., and Pallikarakis, N. (2007). Analysis and classification of medical device recalls. In: *World Congress on Medical Physics and Biomedical Engineering 2006*, IFMBE Proceedings, vol. 14 (ed. R. Magjarevic and J.H. Nagel), 3782–3785. Berlin, Heidelberg: Springer.

**120** Yang, H. and Hyman, W.A. (2010). An analysis of software-related recalls of medical devices. *Journal of Clinical Engineering* 35 (3): 153–156.

**121** Alemzadeh, H., Chen, D., Li, X. et al. (2016). Targeted attacks on teleoperated surgical robots: dynamic model-based detection and mitigation. *Proceedings of the 2016 46th Annual IEEE/IFIP International Conference on Dependable Systems and Networks*, Toulouse, France (28 June–1 July 2016), 395–406. IEEE.

**122** Alemzadeh, H., Raman, J., Leveson, N. et al. (2016). Adverse events in robotic surgery: a retrospective study of 14 years of FDA data. *PLoS ONE* 11 (4): e0151470. https://doi.org/10.1371/journal.pone.0151470.

**123** Banerjee, S.S., Jha, S., Cyriac, J. et al. (2018). Hands off the wheel in autonomous vehicles? A systems perspective on over a million miles of field data. *Proceedings of the 2018 48th Annual IEEE/IFIP International Conference* *on Dependable Systems and Networks*, Luxembourg, Luxembourg (25–28 June 2018), 586–597. IEEE.

**124** Lynch, W.C., Langner, J.W., and Schwartz, M.S. (1975). Reliability experience with Chi/OS. *IEEE Transactions on Software Engineering* SE-1 (2): 253–257.

**125** Vishwanath, K.V. and Nagappan, N. (2010). Characterizing cloud computing hardware reliability. *Proceedings of the 1st ACM Symposium on Cloud Computing [Proceedings of the ACM SIGMOD-SIGOPS Workshop on Cloud Computing in Conjunction with SIGMOD 2010]*, Indianapolis, IN (10–11 June 2010), 193–204. New York: Association for Computing Machinery.

**126** Fenton, N.E. and Ohlsson, N. (2000). Quantitative analysis of faults and failures in a complex software system. *IEEE Transactions on Software Engineering* 26 (8): 797–814.

**127** Han, S., Dang, Y., Ge, S. et al. (2012). Performance debugging in the large via mining millions of stack traces. *Proceedings of the 2012 34th International Conference on Software Engineering*, Zurich, Switzerland (2–9 June 2012), 145–155. IEEE.

**128** Jin, G., Song, L., Shi, X. et al. (2012). Understanding and detecting real-world performance bugs. *Proceedings of the 33rd ACM SIGPLAN Conference on Programming Language Design and Implementation*, Beijing, China (11–16 June 2012), 77–88. New York: Association for Computing Machinery.

**129** Glerum, K., Kinshumann, K., Greenberg, S. et al. (2009). Debugging in the (very) large: ten years of implementation and experience. *Proceedings of the ACM SIGOPS 22nd Symposium on Operating Systems Principles*, Big Sky, MT (11–14 October 2009), 103–116. New York: Association for Computing Machinery.

**130** Murtaza, S.S., Madhavji, N., Gittens, M. et al. (2011). Diagnosing new faults using mutants and prior faults (NIER track). *Proceedings of the 2011 33rd International Conference on Software Engineering*, Honolulu, HI (21–28 May 2011), 960–963. IEEE.

**131** Banerjee, S., Srikanth, H., and Cukic, B. (2010). Log-based reliability analysis of software as a service (SaaS). *Proceedings of the 2010 IEEE 21st International Symposium on Software Reliability Engineering*, San Jose, CA (1–4 November 2010), 239–248. IEEE.

**132** Li, P.L., Kivett, R., Zhan, Z. et al. (2011). Characterizing the differences between pre- and post-release versions of software. *Proceedings of the 2011 33rd International Conference on Software Engineering*, Honolulu, HI (21–28 May 2011), 716–725. IEEE.

**133** Brodie, M., Ma, S., Rachevsky, L. et al. (2005). Automated problem determination using call-stack matching. *Journal of Network and Systems Management* 13 (2): 219–237.

**134** Szewczyk, R., Mainwaring, A., Polastre, J. et al. (2004). An analysis of a large-scale habitat monitoring application. *Proceedings of the 2nd International*

*Conference on Embedded Networked Sensor Systems*, Baltimore, MD (3–5 November 2004), 214–226. New York: Association for Computing Machinery.

**135** Tolle, G., Polastre, J., Szewczyk, R. et al. (2005). A macroscope in the redwoods. *Proceedings of the 3rd International Conference on Embedded Networked Sensor Systems*, San Diego, CA (2–4 November 2005), 51–63. New York: Association for Computing Machinery.

**136** Bellan, R. (2023). NHTSA requests info after Tesla crashes into fire truck. *Tech Crunch* (20 February). https://techcrunch.com/2023/02/20/nhtsa-requests-info-after-tesla-crashes-into-fire-truck/ (accessed 12 March 2023).

**137** Castro, F.P., Chimento, G., Munn, B.G. et al. (1997). An analysis of Food and Drug Administration medical device reports relating to total joint components. *The Journal of Arthroplasty* 12 (7): 765–771.

**138** Brown, S.L., Morrison, A.E., Parmentier, C.M. et al. (1997). Infusion pump adverse events: experience from medical device reports. *Journal of Intravenous Nursing* 20 (1): 41–49.

**139** Brixey, J., Johnson, T.R., and Zhang, J. (2002). Evaluating a medical error taxonomy. *Proceedings of the Annual Symposium of the American Medical Informatics Association (AMIA)*, San Antonio, TX (9–13 November 2002), 71–75. Philadelphia, PA: Hanley & Belfus, Inc.

**140** Hauser, R.G. and Maron, B.J. (2005). Lessons from the failure and recall of an implantable cardioverter-defibrillator. *Circulation* 112 (13): 2040–2042.

**141** Swinhoe, D. (2022). Frontier supercomputer suffering 'daily hardware failures' during testing. https://www.datacenterdynamics.com/en/news/frontier-supercomputer-suffering-daily-hardware-failures-during-testing/ (accessed 12 March 2023).

**142** The Honeynet Project (2022). The Honeynet Project website. www.honeynet.org (accessed 21 December 2022).

**143** Cao, P.M., Wu, Y., Banerjee, S.S. et al. (2019). CAUDIT: Continuous auditing of SSH servers to mitigate brute-force attacks. *Proceedings of the 16th USENIX Symposium on Networked Systems Design and Implementation*, Boston, MA (26–28 February 2019), 667–682.

**144** Dacier, M., Pouget, F. and Debar, H. (2004). Honeypots: practical means to validate malicious fault assumptions. *Proceedings of the 10th IEEE Pacific Rim International Symposium on Dependable Computing*, Papeete, Tahiti, French Polynesia (3–5 March 2004), 383–388. IEEE.

**145** Landwehr, C.E., Bull, A.R., McDermott, J.P. et al. (1994). A taxonomy of computer program security flaws. *ACM Computing Surveys* 26 (3): 211–254.

**146** Treinen, J.J. and Thurimella, R. (2006). A framework for the application of association rule mining in large intrusion detection infrastructures. *Proceedings of the 9th International Symposium on Recent Advances in Intrusion Detection,*

Hamburg, Germany (20–22 September 2006), 1–18. *Lecture Notes in Computer Science*, vol. 4219. Berlin, Heidelberg: Springer.

**147** Cukier, M., Berthier, R., Panjwani, S. et al. (2006). A statistical analysis of attack data to separate attacks. *Proceedings of the International Conference on Dependable Systems and Networks*, Philadelphia, PA (25–28 June 2006), 383–392. IEEE.

**148** Cheswick, W.R., Bellovin, S.M., and Rubin, A.D. (2003). *Firewalls and Internet Security: Repelling the Wily Hacker*, 2e. Boston, MA: Addison-Wesley Longman.

**149** Cohen, F.B. (1995). *Protection and Security on the Information Superhighway*. New York: Wiley.

**150** Chen, S., Kalbarczyk, Z., Xu, J. et al. (2003). A data-driven finite state machine model for analyzing security vulnerabilities. *Proceedings of the 2003 International Conference on Dependable Systems and Networks*, San Francisco, CA (22–25 June 2003), 605–614. IEEE.

**151** Sharma, A., Kalbarczyk, Z., Barlow, J. et al. (2011). Analysis of security data from a large computing organization. *Proceedings of the 2011 IEEE/IFIP 41st International Conference on Dependable Systems & Networks*, Hong Kong, China (27–30 June 2011), 506–517. IEEE.

**152** Basney, J., Cao, P., and Fleury, T. (2020). Investigating root causes of authentication failures using a SAML and OIDC observatory. *Proceedings of the 2020 IEEE 6th International Conference on Dependability in Sensor, Cloud and Big Data Systems and Application[s]*, Nadi, Fiji (14–16 December 2020), 119–126. IEEE.

**153** Siewiorek, D.P. and Swarz, R.S. (1998). *Reliable Computer Systems: Design and Evaluation*, 3e. Natick, MA: A K Peters.

**154** SAS (2022). SAS website. sas.com (accessed 23 March 2023).

**155** The R Foundation (2023). The R project for statistical computing. www.r-project.org (accessed 21 December 2022).

**156** Hirel, C., Sahner, R., Zang, X. et al. (2000). Reliability and performability modeling using SHARPE 2000. *Proceedings of the 11th International Conference on Computer Performance Evaluation: Modelling Techniques and Tools*, Schaumburg, IL (27–31 March 2000), 345–349. *Lecture Notes in Computer Science*, vol. 1786. Berlin, Heidelberg: Springer.

**157** Deavours, D.D., Clark, G., Courtney, T. et al. (2002). The Möbius framework and its implementation. *IEEE Transactions on Software Engineering* 28 (10): 956–969.

**158** Gerhards, R. (2009). The Syslog protocol. Internet Engineering Task Force (IETF) Request for Comments (RFC) 5424, March 2009. http://www.ietf.org/rfc/rfc5424.txt (accessed 21 December 2022).

**159** Lakner, G. (2009). *IBM System Blue Gene Solution: Blue Gene/P System Administration*. IBM. http://www.redbooks.ibm.com/redbooks/pdfs/sg247417.pdf (accessed 14 June 2023).

**160** Mozilla Corporation (2022). Bugzilla website. bugzilla.mozilla.org (accessed 21 December 2022).

**161** Mantis Bug Tracker (2022). Mantis Bug Tracker website. mantisbt.org (accessed 21 December 2022).

**162** Edge Wall Software (2020). Welcome to the Trac open source project. 21 April 2020. trac.edgewall.org (accessed 21 December 2022).

**163** Oracle (2021). How to track/check a bug in My Oracle Support (Doc ID 1304801.1). 24 September 2021. https://support.oracle.com/knowledge/Support%20Tools/1304801_1.html (accessed 21 December 2022).

**164** MySQL (2022). Bugs home. bugs.mysql.com (accessed 21 December 2022).

**165** Vaarandi, R. (2008). Mining event logs with SLCT and LogHound. *Proceedings of the 2008 IEEE Network Operations and Management Symposium*, Salvador, Bahia, Brazil (7–11 April 2008), 1071–1074. IEEE.

**166** Ristov (2022). Simple event correlator. http://simple-evcorr.sourceforge.net/ (accessed 14 June 2023).

**167** U.S. Food and Drug Administration (2022). Medical device databases. https://www.fda.gov/medical-devices/device-advice-comprehensive-regulatory-assistance/medical-device-databases (accessed 21 December 2022).

**168** Martino, C., Sarkar, S., Ganesan, R. et al. (2017). Analysis and diagnosis of SLA violations in a production SaaS cloud. *IEEE Transactions on Reliability* 66 (1): 54–75.

**169** Brin, S., Motwani, R., Ullman, J.D. et al. (1997). Dynamic itemset counting and implication rules for market basket data. *ACM SIGMOD Record* 26 (2): 255–264.

**170** Mullen, R.E. (1998). The lognormal distribution of software failure rates: origin and evidence. *Proceedings of the 9th International Symposium on Software Reliability Engineering*, Paderborn, Germany (4–7 November 1998), 124–133. Los Alamitos, CA: IEEE Computer Society.

**171** Bishop, P.G. and Pullen, F.D. (1988). PODS revisited: a study of software failure behaviour. *Digest of Papers, the 18th International Symposium on Fault-Tolerant Computing*, Tokyo, Japan (27–30 June 1988), 2–8. IEEE.

**172** Meyer, J.F. and Wei, L. (1988). Analysis of workload influence on dependability. *Digest of Papers, the 18th International Symposium on Fault-Tolerant Computing*, Tokyo, Japan (27–30 June 1988), 84–89. IEEE.

**173** Aupperle, B.E., Meyer, J.F., and Wei, L. (1989). Evaluation of fault-tolerant systems with nonhomogeneous workloads. *Digest of Papers, the 19th International Symposium on Fault-Tolerant Computing*, Chicago, IL (21–23 June 1989), 159–166. IEEE.

**174** Dunkel, J. (1990). On the modeling of workload dependent memory faults. *Digest of Papers, the 20th International Symposium on Fault-Tolerant Computing*, Newcastle upon Tyne, UK (26–28 June 1990), 348–355. IEEE.

**175** Dillon, W.R. and Goldstein, M. (1984). *Multivariate Analysis*. Chichester, UK: Wiley.

# 13
# Measurement-Based Analysis of Large Systems: Case Studies

## 13.1 Introduction

The previous chapter presented the techniques employed in the measurement-based analysis of large-scale clusters and substantiated them with relevant examples. This chapter provides detailed case studies to illustrate the use of concepts and techniques described in the preceding chapter. Specifically, we focus on the failure characterization of three different computing platforms: (i) a cloud-based Software-as-a-Service (SaaS) platform that supports business data processing [1], (ii) a high-performance supercomputing platform that supports a high volume of computationally intensive scientific and engineering applications [2], and (iii) autonomous vehicle (AV) technology [3].

## 13.2 Case Study I: Failure Characterization of a Production Software-as-a-Service Cloud Platform

The SaaS platform analyzed in this case study uses virtualization technology and is deployed over several processing nodes (i.e. application servers) and database servers. The application server is responsible for the communication between the thin client used by the users (e.g. web browsers) and the platform core services. It collects user business data and dispatches the data to the specific components downstream in charge of the needed processing (e.g. inventory or sales accounting). The database server is responsible for storing raw and processed data, as well as tracking the status of the computation of the platform components and customer transactions. The application server is organized to provide multi-stage data processing across seven key computing stages. (The relevant computing stages are discussed

*Dependable Computing: Design and Assessment*, First Edition. Ravishankar K. Iyer, Zbigniew T. Kalbarczyk, and Nithin M. Nakka.
© 2024 The IEEE Computer Society. Published 2024 by John Wiley & Sons, Inc.
Companion website: www.wiley.com/go/iyer/dependablecomputing1

below.) Because of the confidentiality of the information, in the following, the names of the components have been replaced with fictitious names.

- *Data validation (P1):* Data are periodically received from the clients. This stage checks the structure and validity of the data format (e.g. number and type of fields).
- *Data notification (P2):* This component sends notifications to various stakeholders when errors are encountered, for instance, concerning the data format.
- *Data verification (P3):* Received data are scanned for potential viruses and verified at the semantic level for correctness and consistency according to prespecified formats.
- *Data transformation (P4):* Business transformations are applied to harmonize the data.
- *Data commit (P5):* Data are sorted and moved to their respective final repositories, where they are committed.
- *Data archiving (P6):* All data are archived for audit purposes.
- *Data distribution (O4):* The processed and harmonized data are sent to downstream systems for inventory management and business intelligence.

Each stage of the platform is implemented as a set of .NET applications. All services are independent of one another and perform their functions by periodically polling for relevant files, status code changes, and database entries. The system integrates several commercial off-the-shelf (COTS) components for common functionalities, such as data manipulation and transformation.

### 13.2.1 Data Source

The considered data were collected in several log files, summarized in Table 13.1. They cover a period of 283 days in which the system received 275 790 files from 42 customers in 11 different countries and include (i) platform logs produced by the

**Table 13.1** Summary of the considered logs [1] / with permission from Association for Computing Machinery.

| Log files | | # of entries | | |
| --- | --- | --- | --- | --- |
| | | Info | Warnings, errors, failures | Total |
| App server OS | Application logs | N/A | 17 487 | 17 487 |
| | Exception logs | 363 106 | 27 112 | 400 593 |
| | OS logs | 34 447 | 1723 | 36 180 |
| DB server OS | DB logs | 61 092 | 19 488 | 101 223 |
| **Platform logs** | | **2 015 618** | **1475** | **2 017 093** |

applications under study; (ii) OS logs collected by the guest machines hosting the core services; (iii) DB logs produced by the staging backend database; (iv) application logs, collected by the OS, that encompass all the errors encountered by the platform modules and captured by the OS; and (v) exception logs that include the stack trace of the generated exceptions.

*Platform logs* consist of several files, stored as plain text, that are generated by specific logging procedures implemented as part of the platform code. Entries are collected as client data traverse through the processing stages and include detailed information, such as the size of the file, the number of records in the file, client information, time, and, in the case of a failure, the computing stages involved in the failure and logged exit code. *OS, application*, and *exception logs* are obtained from the event-logging service in the Windows Server 2008 operating system. The event-logger software records information on errors that occur in the various subsystems, such as memory, disk, and network subsystems, as well as information on other system events, such as reboots and shutdowns. The reports usually include information on the error location, time, type, system state at the time of the error, and, sometimes, error recovery (e.g. retry) actions.

The impact of an error can range from a minor problem to a platform hang/crash or database corruption. Two types of data failures are considered. The first, referred to as *validation failures*, are due to errors caused by user mistakes (e.g. a wrong/corrupted client file) and are detected during the first stage (P1) of the computation (i.e. the data validation stage). Files that fail the validation stage are not processed by the platform. Instead, they are sent back to the client with a detailed report on the causes of the rejection. The second type of failure, referred to as *platform failures*, can manifest in any stage of the computation and are caused by system-related issues, including residual bugs, operating system errors, and hardware/network problems. In this study, we focus on the analysis of platform failures because of their higher impact.

## 13.2.2 Failure Analysis Workflow

The workflow for analyzing the logs consists of three main steps:

*Step 1: Data collection, filtering, and event extraction:* Initially, the data are collected from the platform and the operating systems (the application server and database server) in the form of logs. Collected data are filtered to leave only events of interest, i.e. warning, error, or failure events. Data are transformed into an internal format by specific preprocessing modules before being used in the later steps of the analysis. The transformed logs are hosted in a staging database to ease the analysis.

*Step 2: Data coalescence:* Failure events that happen at around the same time may be different manifestations of the same fault/error in the system, e.g. multiple error detectors might be triggered (resulting in multiple logged events), or the same cause might generate different failures in close proximity. Time coalescence is based on the assumption that logged events that have the same cause will be close to each other in time. All logs (platform OS, application, exception, and DB) are merged together and ordered by their timestamps. Then, all entries that have the same error type and are within the same time window are grouped in a single tuple: i.e. a collection of a number of events (failure entries) that happened near each other in time are considered to be related to the same cause. The duration of the tuple indicates the amount of time that passed between the first and last failure entries that are grouped together. We estimated a suitable coalescence time window of 820 seconds by using a heuristic similar to one proposed in [4].

*Step 3: Failure analysis:* Coalesced data are used to classify the failure modes of the platform under study and to acquire a set of measures, such as mean time between failures (MTBF) and failure rate. Finally, statistical inference tests are applied to the dataset to identify specific models and potential trends in the data.

## 13.2.3 Failure Characterization

In the considered period of 283 days, the system received 275 290 files. The vast majority (86.13%) of the files were processed successfully. In 37 822 cases (13.25%), the files generated a validation failure during the initial validation stages and hence were not processed. In 1475 other cases (0.62%), the processing of the customer files failed because of platform failures, the subject of this case study. In particular, the results of the coalescence process show that:

- Customer data are responsible for 34.1% of platform failures. Most of those failures are caused by unexpected values in customer data that escape the initial validation stages of the platform; such problems are difficult to foresee during the coding phase. Results show that one can eliminate 10.6% of these errors by performing intensive robustness testing or fault-injection-based studies.
- 32% of the platform failures are due to timeout errors, which tend to accumulate over time. For the analyzed platform, elimination of timeout errors would increase the MTBF by a factor of 1.94, e.g. from 7 hours, 2 minutes to 13 hours, 41 minutes.
- The coalescence shows that 73.1% of all failures are of just three failure types. In total, the logs contain 42 different failure types.

### 13.2.3.1 Output of the Coalescence Process

Figure 13.1a shows the outcome of the coalescence of all the data logs. Recall that the coalescence process aims to group together failure events that happen near each other in time (within the chosen time window of 820 seconds). Therefore, the number of tuples obtained after the coalescence is lower than the number of entries contained in the raw data (i.e. before the coalescence). The coalesced data, summarized in Table 13.2, consist of 1639 tuples. 1475 platform failures are coalesced in 918 tuples and constitute 56.1% of the total tuples. The remaining 721 (43.9%) of the tuples contain entries from the OS, DB,

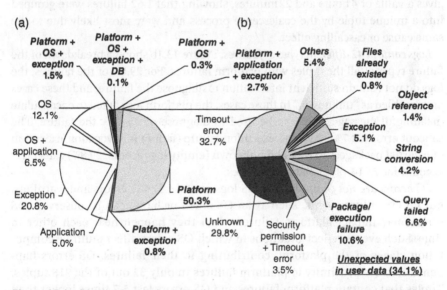

**Figure 13.1** Distribution of the (a) tuple type after the coalescence process, (b) failure types (explosion of platform failures in (a)) [1] / with permission from Association for Computing Machinery.

**Table 13.2** Summary of the coalescence process [1] / with permission from Association for Computing Machinery.

| Entries (raw data) | | Tuples (after the coalescence) | |
|---|---|---|---|
| 67 285 | | 1639 | |
| Platform failures | OS, DB, application, exception failures (no platform failures) | With platform failures | No platform failures |
| | | 918 (56.1%) | 721 (43.9%) |
| 1475 | 65810 | 1 entry | > 1 entry |
| | | 679 (74%) | 239 (26%) |

application, and exception logs that do not represent events that happened in close time proximity to any platform failure. 239 (26%) of the 918 tuples with platform failures have more than one event/entry; in 82% of the 239 cases, the multiple events are failure events generated in the same execution stage. In the remaining 74% of the 918 tuples, each tuple contains only a single platform failure.

*The MTBF* of 7 hours and 2 minutes is estimated as the mean time between tuples in the set of 918 into which the 1475 platform failures were grouped. Computation of the MTBF as the MTBF in the set of 1475 platform failure entries gives a value of 4 hours and 22 minutes, showing that 1.62 failures were grouped into a unique tuple by the coalescence process and were most likely due to the same cause or cascading effect.

*Logs contain 42 different types of failures.* Figure 13.1b shows a breakdown of the failure types of all the tuples with platform failures. For 29.8% of the failures, the logs do not contain sufficient information to diagnose the failure, and these cases are classified as "unknown." In those cases, the platform logs failed to encapsulate meaningful messages that can be used to diagnose or classify the failure. The timeout error (32.7%), package/execution failure (failure in invocation/execution of external packages; 10.6%), and unknown (empty log records; 29.8%) categories account for 73.1% of all platform failures.

*OS errors are not common.* The OS logs contain 37 481 errors and warnings, but no OS failure events, such as an OS crash or hang, can be observed. OS errors may impact platform failures when they happen near each other in time. Such events reflect situations in which OS errors affect multiple computation stages of the platform, contributing to their failures. OS errors happened in close proximity to platform failures in only 32 out of the 918 tuples. Tuples that contain platform failures and OS errors last 5.7 times longer than tuples with only platform failures, with an average duration of 697 seconds, compared with 113 seconds for tuples with only platform failures. Platform failures were due to timeout errors in 94% of the tuples which include platform failures and OS errors.

*Timeout errors* are a known problem in the world of Microsoft SQL and .NET applications (e.g. [5]). In SQL Server, those errors appear to be due to performance, concurrency, and network problems. Business-oriented systems like the platform under analysis are characterized by small numbers of big transactions. The transactions are frequently INSERT and JOIN operations. Timeout errors can be caused by a query that is taking a long time (e.g. for data insertion into a large indexed table), forcing other queries on the same table to wait and potentially violate the timeout. Another factor that may cause timeout errors is the level of concurrency in the system. Typically, a .NET application creates a query by instantiating a specific SQL Client thread from a pool of available threads. If the thread runs out of SqlInternalConnection objects, it is placed on a waiting list. If the load and/or the level of concurrent queries is high, then the wait time can be bigger than the programmed timeout, causing timeout errors.

Finally, *network problems* also play an important role in timeout errors. The platform uses UDP packets to connect to the SQL Server to obtain the connection endpoint (i.e. the TCP port number or named pipe), and packets can be dropped and never retransmitted. That is likely to happen in a virtualized environment subjected to high processor or I/O load, which may cause transient failures of the virtual network interfaces.

An example of failures due to timeout errors in the coalesced data is shown in Table 13.3. The snippet of the logs shows that five OS errors and four platform failures are grouped in the same tuple. The OS errors are due to (i) temporary restrictions on the permission to access one or more Distributed Component Object Model (DCOM) components, and (ii) services' failure to (re)start, including some side services, like Remote Desktop Protocol (RDP), and some critical services, like the *LanmanServer* (the core service for the management of LAN services). From the example in Table 13.3, it is clear that timeout failures in a single component may cascade and cause the failures of several other components downstream.

**Table 13.3** Example of a complex failure as reported after the coalescence.

| Tuple details | Messages from the logs |
| --- | --- |
| **Time Stamp:** 2012/05/23 12:16:06 **Duration (s):** 1594 **Entries:** 9 **Type (num):** OS (5) PLATFORM (4) **Failure Type:** Service/Driver failure + Package/Execution + Timeout Error | `ERR{SCM->A timeout was reached while waiting for a transaction response from the LanmanServer service.} ERR{DCOM->The application-specific permission settings do not grant Local Activation permission for the COM Server application [...]} ERR{SCMr->A timeout was reached [...] (30000|Netman)} ERR{SCM->A timeout was reached [...] (30000|UmRdpService)}` **`P4_STG{FILE_ID>Platform(Timeout expired. The timeout period elapsed prior to completion of the operation or the server is not responding.)}`** `WARN{RDPDR->An Io Request to the device did not complete or canceled within the specific timeout [...] }` **`P4_STG{FILE_ID->Platform(Timeout expired. The timeout period elapsed [...])}`** **`P4_STG{FILE_ID->Platform(Timeout expired. The timeout period elapsed [...])}`** |

Entries from platform failures are in bold font [1] / with permission from Association for Computing Machinery.

### 13.2.3.2 Key Factors Impacting Platform Failures

*Unexpected values in customer data cause 34.1% of platform failures.* Based on the content uploaded by the user (e.g. inventory data or sales data), the platform selects the required processing. The platform extracts data for processing from the received files and feeds the data to downstream stages that handle data manipulation and transformation. For that reason, the platform enforces a strict validation of customer data once the data are uploaded. Because of the huge volume of data and the high volume of customers, unexpected values might be present and elude the initial validation checks. A simple example is a field containing an unexpected null or empty value that is then uploaded to an SQL table that does not accept the null value. Another example is an overflow or division by zero caused by an unexpected numerical value in the data. Our analysis indicates that such failures lead to 34.1% of the total platform failures. In particular, data-induced errors cause (i) string conversion failures (4.2%), (ii) problems in extracting table/column (6.6%) and file (0.8%) names in the parsed data, (iii) references to null objects (1.4%), (iv) data out of range and arithmetic exceptions (5.1%), (v) failure in the invocation/execution of external packages due to wrong parameters/value ranges (10.6%), and (vi) other data-related exceptions (5.4%).

*Software exceptions are present in 5.1% of platform failures.* Exception handlers embedded in the platform code are effective in capturing runtime exceptions 94.9% of the time. A total of 922 different software exceptions are present in the data. As illustrated in Figure 13.1a, they are coalesced in 25.9% of the 1639 total tuples (where 25.9% is the sum of the percentages of the tuple types that include exceptions). On average, 2.2 different exceptions are present in each tuple, with a peak of 29 in one case, showing that they tend to occur in rapid succession, namely within the assumed coalescence time window. The high effectiveness of exception-handling mechanisms is in part due to the strong support provided by the programming language (.NET) used to implement the platform that enforces the use of try-catch blocks when invoking string/array functions and accessing communication channels. That finding indicates that exception-handling code can be improved based on understanding of the data errors that lead to platform failures. Such code improvement would in turn substantially reduce the impact of errors such as string conversion problems, references to null objects, and arithmetic exceptions. In addition, understanding of unexpected data could also be used to design thorough robustness-testing campaigns to fix failures due to invocation of library functions with incorrect parameters or value ranges (10.6%).

*Five platform stages are responsible for 95% of platform failures.* Recall that the platform executes in fixed processing stages, and all the components are subjected to the same load since all the stages are executed in sequence. Table 13.4 shows a breakdown of the platform failures per processing stage, relating the number of component failures to the size of the component expressed in lines of code (LOC).

**Table 13.4** Size (% of total LOC count) and failure density (number of failures/LOC) of the modules that exhibit platform failures [1] / with permission from Association for Computing Machinery.

| Stage | % LOC | # failures | failure density |
|---|---|---|---|
| P3_P | 14.39% | 35 | 0.013 |
| P3_PP (6 threads) | 0.72% | 120 | 0.89 (0.148/thread) |
| P4_PREP | 2.54% | 69 | 0.15 |
| P4_STG | 2.56% | 179 | 0.37 |
| P4_TRNF | 2.74% | 215 | 0.41 |
| P5 | 3.75% | 178 | 0.26 |
| P6 | 0.35% | 9 | 0.14 |
| O4 | 11.11% | 692 | 0.32 |

For each component, we show the *failure density* expressed as the total number of failures divided by the size of the component in LOC. Interestingly, P3_PP shows an overall higher failure density than the other components. The main reason is that P3_PP is the only multithreaded component and it executes six concurrent threads. In detail, the failure density of P3_PP, normalized with respect to the number of threads, is comparable with that of the other data preparation stages (e.g. P4_PREP and P6), which indicates the presence of a failure cause that is persistent across different threads. P3_P shows the lowest failure density despite being the largest software component in the platform.

Finally, all components in charge of data manipulation, transformation, and archiving (P4_STG, P4_TRNF, P5, and O4) show higher failure density than the others. In particular, P4_TRNF and P4_STG include a unique COTS library for data manipulation, written in .NET, that is seven times the size of the biggest component in the platform.[1] The library contributes to a substantial number of platform failures classified as either package/execution failures (10.6% of the total failures) or string conversions (4.2%); see Figure 13.1b. Such failures are mainly caused by bad/corrupted values passed as parameters of the library functions, which are not robust to unexpected data values.

Another component showing high failure density is O4 (data distribution). Failures exhibited by O4 include timeout errors (47%), unknown failures (23%), and simultaneous occurrences of failures due to wrong security permissions (for instance, to move/create files in specific folders), among others. While we

---

1 For reasons of confidentiality, we are not disclosing the absolute LOC count for the platform components.

cannot diagnose the failures classified as "unknown," we can note that the platform tends to fail because of timeout errors mainly in the components that deal with querying of the database, such as O4. In summary, (i) P3_P, P4_L2, P4_STG, P4_TRNF, P5, and O4 account for 95% of the total failures; (ii) data manipulation and transformation components are more sensitive to unexpected/corrupted values in the customer data; (iii) many failures are due to external components used for standard data manipulation and transformation tasks, such as dart parsing and harmonization; and (iv) components in charge of querying the database to dump and archive the data are more susceptible to failures due to wrong security permissions and/or timeout errors (addressed in Section 13.2.3.3). Therefore, we can conclude that in the considered platform, testing of the robustness of data manipulation and transformation components could help reduce the impact of unexpected customer data values on platform failures.

### 13.2.3.3 Impact of Timeout Errors

Figure 13.2a illustrates the distribution of TBF for the coalesced data. The distribution shows that about 30% of failures happen within one hour after prior failures. After the first hour, the probability of a second failure in rapid succession drops sharply. Interestingly, the data can be successfully fitted to a fatigue life distribution [6]. The Kolmogorov–Smirnov test shows a p-value of 0.04, indicating, with a confidence of 96%, that the null hypothesis that the data follow a fatigue life distribution cannot be rejected. Other distributions, like Weibull, lognormal, and exponential, do not obtain a sufficiently good fit to allow rejection of the null hypothesis. For instance, the p-value obtained for fitting the data to an exponential distribution is 0.21.

Fatigue life distributions have been extensively used in mechanical reliability to model the fatigue damage process in metals subject to cyclic load above a critical threshold. Cracks (comparable to errors) accumulate and eventually generate a failure of the metal structure. Hence, in our case, the distribution of the observed TBF data is similar to one dominated by an underlying process of error accumulation triggered by stressful workload cycles.

To investigate potential error accumulation, we identified the failure types that dominated the observed distribution. The analysis consisted of eliminating one failure type at a time and recomputing the distribution fitting and TBF. The objective was to observe what type of failure dominates the TBF.

It was possible to fit the resulting dataset with a fatigue life distribution (p-value of 0.14), only in the case where the tuples corresponding to timeout errors are eliminated. Interestingly, the same dataset with timeout errors eliminated can be successfully fitted (with a p-value of 0.07) to an exponential distribution with a rate of $1/13.69[h]$ (see Figure 13.2b), i.e. in the case of no failures

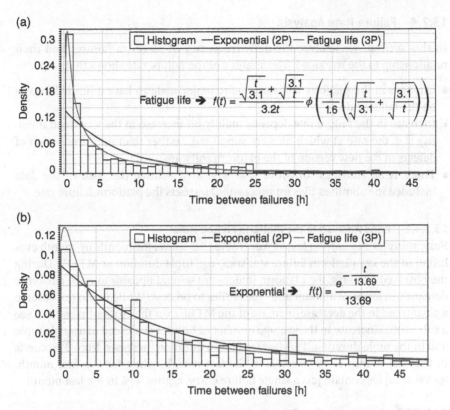

**Figure 13.2** TBF density function distribution for (a) all failure types, (b) all failure types except timeout failures [1] / with permission from Association for Computing Machinery.

due to timeout errors, the TBF goes from 7 hours, 2 minutes to 13 hours, 41 minutes. In particular, for the whole dataset, the reliability drops to 90% in 48 minutes, while for the same system without timeout errors, that reliability level is reached after 91 minutes.

The reason for the exponential interarrival of failures is that the elimination of timeout failures means that a significant number of the remaining failures (34.1%) happen because of an unexpected value in the customer data. Since customers submit files independently, we are likely to observe independent failure interarrivals, as illustrated in Figure 13.2b. Elimination of the timeout failures (which happen with 94% of the OS errors and have a longer duration than other failures) would substantially reduce the risk that failures will occur in rapid succession because of error accumulation and would increase the reliability by a factor of 1.94.

## 13.2.4 Failure Rate Analysis

In this section, we analyze the daily frequency of platform failures and their relationship to the workload. The analysis of the failure rate shows that:

- Changes in the platform software due to major updates have a limited impact on the failure rate.
- Increase in the failure rate depends mainly on increase in the workload intensity (i.e. the rate at which files are submitted), rather than on introduction of defects in the new version of the platform software.
- There is no statistical evidence that workload volume (i.e. size of the data included in submitted files for processing) impacts the platform failure rate.

### 13.2.4.1 Trend Analysis of the Platform Failure Rate

*Basic statistics on platform failure rate.* Table 13.5 shows the month-by-month evolution of the key platform failure statistics (e.g. tuple duration or MTBF). During the observed 283 days, the platform underwent several updates to meet customer demands in terms of amount and type of files to process. While we do not observe a clear trend in the decrease/increase of the MTBF over the 10 months, we can see a substantial increase in the average number of failures coalesced in a single tuple and in the tuple duration. The average failure duration increased from 37 seconds in the first month to 484 seconds in the last month, while for the first month, 90.6% of tuples contain just a single failure entry, against 44% in the last month.

**Table 13.5** Breakdown of synthetic statistics per month [1] / with permission from Association for Computing Machinery.

| Month | Num failures | Tuples with a single failure entry | Average duration tuples (s) | MTBF (h) | Median TBF (h) | Avg. entries per tuple |
|---|---|---|---|---|---|---|
| 1 | 106 | 96 (90.6%) | 37 | 6.80 | 3.81 | 1.1 |
| 2 | 67 | 53 (79.1%) | 103 | 10.20 | 4.9 | 1.3 |
| 3 | 85 | 73 (85.9%) | 123 | 8.74 | 4.68 | 1.8 |
| 4 | 92 | 71 (77.2%) | 135 | 7.83 | 2.73 | 1.9 |
| 5 | 143 | 115 (80.4%) | 125 | 5.26 | 2 | 1.4 |
| 6 | 132 | 105 (79.5%) | 108 | 5.42 | 1.78 | 1.4 |
| 7 | 104 | 71 (68.3%) | 105 | 7.06 | 2.69 | 1.5 |
| 8 | 96 | 63 (65.6%) | 253 | 7.77 | 1.94 | 2.0 |
| 9 | 109 | 44 (40.4%) | 376 | 6.76 | 2.68 | 2.2 |
| 10 | 25 | 5 (20.0%) | 484 | 8.00 | 4.23 | 2.5 |

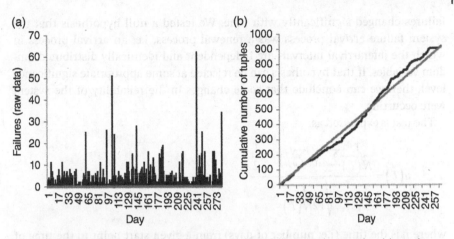

**Figure 13.3** Distribution of the number of platform failure entries per day: (a) number of failures per day; (b) cumulative number of failures per day (line between the first and last values added to show an ideal constant pattern) [1] / with permission from Association for Computing Machinery.

Figure 13.3 shows the temporal distribution of the number of platform failure entries per day. Only 25 days out of 283 passed without platform failures. Specifically, it can be observed that:

- *Days 1–96*: The platform exhibited 324 failures in three months (21% of the total failures, with a failure rate of 3.4 failures/day).
- *Day 97*: The LATAM (LATin-AMerican) version of the software was deployed with new features for data processing. The update introduced two new software components and modified a subset of core modules (e.g. the data verification and data manipulation components of the platform) to handle the new workload.
- *Days 98–187*: The platform exhibited 630 failures (43% of total failure entries) in three months (a failure rate of seven failures/day, twice that of the first three months).
- *Days 188 to 241*: The platform exhibited 200 failures (13% of total failure entries) in two months (a failure rate of 3.7 failures/day, comparable with that of the first three months).

Figure 13.3b shows the cumulative number of platform failures per day. A constant daily failure rate would have resulted in a linear increase in the cumulative number of failures, as illustrated by the straight line in Figure 13.3.

*Trend analysis.* In our analysis, we employed the Laplace trend test [7], which is useful in analyzing trends in the platform failure rate and in validating the presence of a constant failure rate (i.e. an exponential distribution of failure times). The objective of the Laplace trend test was to determine whether the arrival of failures changed significantly with time. We tested a null hypothesis that the system failure arrival process was a renewal process, i.e. an arrival process in which the interarrival intervals are independent and identically distributed random variables. If that hypothesis can be rejected at some appropriate significance level, then we can conclude that some changes in the reliability of the system were occurring.

The test is expressed as:

$$u(T) = \frac{\frac{1}{N(T)}\sum_{i=1}^{N(T)}\sum_{j=i}^{i} t_j - \frac{T}{2}}{T\sqrt{\frac{1}{12N(T)}}}$$

where $t_j$ is the time (i.e. number of days) from a given start point to the time of each event (failure), $N(T)$ is the number of events (i.e. failures), and $T$ is the time from the start point to the end of the observation period.

A test score greater than zero means that there is an upward or increasing trend, and a score less than zero means there is a downward or decreasing trend. When the score is greater than +1.96 or less than −1.96, we are at least 95% confident that there is a significant trend upward or downward, respectively. The implication is that successive interarrival failure times tend to become larger for an improving system, and smaller for a deteriorating system. A score of zero means that the trend is a horizontal line. Figure 13.4 shows the result of the Laplace test. In particular:

- There was no substantial change in the reliability of the platform until the deployment of the LATAM version of the software on Day 97.

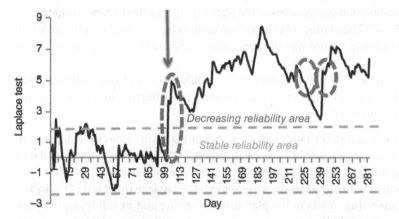

**Figure 13.4** Laplace trend test [1] / with permission from Association for Computing Machinery.

- The deterioration of the platform reliability (i.e. the increase in the platform failure rate), indicated by the sharp increase (beyond the 1.96 mark) in the Laplace test results, happened just after the platform update.
- The temporary reversion to the older version of the software on Day 213 changed the trend until Day 241 when the LATAM version of the platform software was restored again.

A decrease in reliability may not, and usually does not, mean that software has more bugs. A higher failure rate may be due to changes in the operational profile, e.g. software upgrades and/or an increase in the workload processed by the system (e.g. due to new clients). The impact of those two factors on platform failures is discussed in the following sections.

### 13.2.4.2 Impact of Platform Software Upgrades

The platform software upgrade on Day 97 made it possible to process new files from the Latin American market, thus increasing the number of clients using the platform. Recall that the workload consists of files submitted to the platform for processing. Figure 13.5 shows the workload in terms of *intensity* (files submitted to the platform per day, regardless of the file size) and *volume* (amount of data submitted per day, regardless of the number of files submitted for processing). Note that (i) the higher the number of files, the higher the level of concurrency in the platform; and (ii) the larger the files, the longer the processing time for each component of the platform. Figure 13.5 shows that the number of submitted files per day increased by a factor of 2.5 toward the end of the period because of an increasing number of customers using the platform.

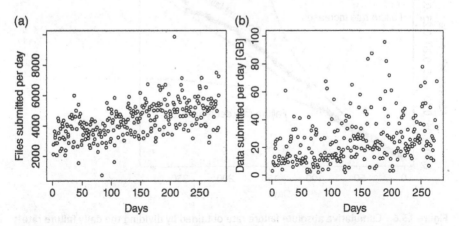

**Figure 13.5** Workload: (a) intensity (number of files per day); (b) volume (amount of data submitted per day) [1] / with permission from Association for Computing Machinery.

To obtain a distribution of the failure rate in which all the failures are equally represented regardless of the potential interaction with the workload, we normalized the daily failure rate and workload distribution by dividing the daily failure rate by the daily workload rate in terms of intensity (i.e. number of files submitted per day) and volume (GB of data submitted per day). We refer to those obtained failure rate figures as the *absolute failure rate*, i.e. the failure rate per processed file or processed GB of data. Figure 13.6 shows the cumulative absolute failure rate computed with respect to the workload intensity. Interestingly, the distribution shows linear behavior for the observed period, except for a jump around the day of the platform software upgrade (Day 97). The introduction of software defects with the software upgrade would eventually cause the curve to have an increasing slope (see Figure 13.6), and the elimination of defects with an upgrade would eventually cause the curve to have a decreasing slope. The plot of the empirical data shows that the software upgrade did not introduce additional defects or reduce the slope of the graph. The jump around Day 97 corresponds to a number of transient failures that manifested during the replacement of the core services of the platform with the LATAM components. We obtained similar results (not shown here) for the absolute failure rate computed with respect to the workload volume. We can conclude that, with the exception of a few days (e.g. Day 97 and Day 241; see Figure 13.3), the platform failure rate was substantially immune to the changes introduced by the platform software upgrade.

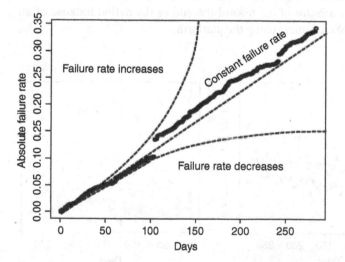

**Figure 13.6** Cumulative absolute failure rate obtained by dividing the daily failure rate by the workload intensity (number of files processed per day) [1] / with permission from Association for Computing Machinery.

**Table 13.6** Breakdown of the workload and failures by day of the week [1] / with permission from Association for Computing Machinery.

|  | Mon | Tue | Wed | Thu | Fri | Sat | Sun |
|---|---|---|---|---|---|---|---|
| # failures | 239 | 248 | 213 | 310 | 233 | 131 | 101 |
| % failures per day | 16.2% | 16.8% | 14.4% | 21% | 15.8% | 8.9% | 6.9% |
| % received files | 16.1% | 15.2% | 14.4% | 16.6% | 14.6% | 11% | 11.9% |
| data (GB) | 970 | 800 | 780 | 930 | 1390 | 1200 | 790 |
| average file size (MB) | 24 | 20 | 21 | 22 | 37 | 42 | 78 |
| **failures per GB of data** | 2.44 | 3.02 | 2.73 | 3.36 | 1.68 | 1.08 | 1.29 |
| **failures per # files per day** | 0.58% | 0.64% | 0.58% | 0.73% | 0.62% | 0.46% | 0.33% |

### 13.2.4.3 Impact of the Workload Volume on the Platform Failure Rate

Let us consider the typical workload week (Monday to Sunday) and relate the failure rate to it. Table 13.6 provides a breakdown of the workload and failure data per day of the week. As one might expect, the number of files submitted over the weekend is substantially lower (48–66% lower than for the other days). However, by the end of the week, customers submit larger files to compute (mostly reports on the week's sales), which can reach 2–3 times the average size of the files submitted earlier in the week. As shown in Table 13.6, the ratio of failures to GB of data varies slightly for the first four days of the week and drops by a factor of 1.5 to 3 for the remaining three days.[2] In fact, during the weekend, the platform processes fewer files, but the files are larger than those processed on the other days of the week; we can conclude that the platform can tolerate a high volume of data without being affected.

### 13.2.4.4 Impact of the Workload Intensity on the Platform Failure Rate

During the workweek, customers submit daily or hourly reports on their inventory or sales; those reports are smaller, but more frequent, than the weekly reports sent over the weekend. Recall that the platform is organized in computation stages that work in a pipeline. Therefore, a higher-intensity workload forces a higher level of concurrency in the system, as more threads are active in parallel to handle the larger amount of files to be processed. On days with higher concurrency (Mondays and Thursdays), the percentage of failed files is

---

2 An analysis of variance, not included here, confirmed the hypothesis.

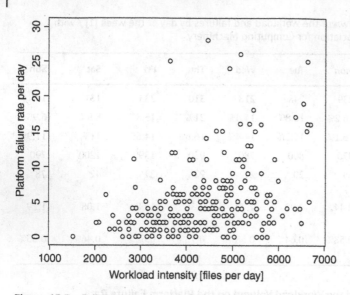

**Figure 13.7** Failure rate vs. workload per day [1] / with permission from Association for Computing Machinery.

higher than on the other days, while, for instance, on Sundays, the percentage drops to about 50% of that of the other days.

To confirm that a change in the workload causes a change in the failure rate, we consider the Mann-Kendall statistical trend test. It evaluates whether $y$ values tend to increase or decrease over $x$ values through what is essentially a nonparametric form of monotonic trend regression analysis. If we plot the workload intensity over the failure rate, this test evaluates the null hypothesis that the failure rate data have no trend over the workload data, as illustrated in Figure 13.7. The result of the test shows a $\tau$ value of 0.485 (correlation) and p-value $= 2.22E-9$, which suggests that the null hypothesis can be rejected, i.e. that there is a trend in the data. Therefore, we can conclude that (i) the increment in the platform failure rate is due to the increment in the intensity of the workload (see Figure 13.5a), and (ii) the level of concurrency enforced in the platform by intensive workloads leads to an increase in the failure rate. In other words, the reliability of the platform software remains constant over time (with respect to the absolute failure rate), while the usage of the platform grows in intensity. Therefore, the number of failures grows too.

## 13.2.5 Conclusions

While this case study focuses on the failure characterization of a specific SaaS platform, the lessons learned are valid in a broad context of large computing clusters and applications. An in-depth analysis of failure data reveals factors that impact platform failure type and frequency. Those analytical results can be used to improve the effectiveness of a testing effort by focusing on error-prone components.

In particular, our analysis showed that 37% of the total LOC of the platform software is responsible for 95% of the platform failures. The majority of failures belong to just a few failure types (3 out of 42 in our case), and 34.1% of all failures are due to unexpected values in customer data. That knowledge can be used to guide design, testing, and configuration of the system to improve resiliency and performance. Understanding unexpected values in customer data can guide the design of effective exception handling and the creation of robustness-testing campaigns. For instance, queries, as a general practice, are typically generated by automated tools to reduce the incidence of human mistakes and to handle complex table structures. In addition, most of the problems due to unexpected data values can be fixed without any major change to the platform code. For instance, a number of platform failures (i.e. 6.6% of failures) happen because of query failures, e.g. because of the impossibility of inserting null values into one or more tables. A subset of failures could be addressed by leveraging the semantics of the data and allowing null values where possible. Hence, data on logged failures could also be fed to an automated tool to support the implementation of effective exception handlers and to validate DB schemes and queries.

The analysis also shows (i) that the level of concurrency due to intensive workloads acts as a stress factor for the platform, increasing its susceptibility to failures, and (ii) that the platform is insensitive to the workload volume (i.e. the size of the data included in submitted files for processing). The relationship between the workload intensity and system/application susceptibility to failures can be attributed to (i) load-induced software failures, namely failures triggered under high-concurrency conditions; and (ii) the increased likelihood of receiving data with unexpected values when more intense workloads (e.g. larger numbers of different files submitted per day) are being dealt with. In our case, such load-induced failures happen because of timeout errors, which account for 32.7% of all the failures. The analysis also demonstrated that keeping even a low constant amount of residual bugs over successive updates may not imply constant reliability of the data-processing software and may eventually lead to major failures. The intensity and semantics of the large amount of data that future systems will be called to process should be taken into account during development to mitigate data-induced failures.

Our analyses indicate that failures due to unexpected values in user data occur independently in 93% of the cases. Other errors, such as those due to timeouts, can propagate and cause extended failures of several components, indicating a lack of failure-containment mechanisms, despite the modular design of the platform. In particular, our data show that shared resources such as the DB can become the real bottleneck in data-processing systems when they are subjected to high levels of concurrency. Although increasing the value of the timeout could have a negative impact on a number of aspects of the system (e.g. the size of allocated buffers), tuning of the platform based on a judicious analysis of the failure data could be the cornerstone of a "low-hanging fruit" kind of reliability improvement. Timeout errors could also be mitigated by keeping the system updated with the latest patches, which might solve newly discovered performance bugs [8].

## 13.3 Case Study II: Analysis of Blue Waters System Failures

This case study focuses on the analysis of system failures of Blue Waters, a petascale high-performance computing (HPC) system at the National Center for Supercomputing Applications (NCSA) at the University of Illinois Urbana-Champaign. Until 2022, Blue Waters was a sustained petaflop system capable of delivering approximately 13.1 petaflops (at peak) for a range of real-world scientific and engineering applications. The system was equipped with:

- 276 Cray liquid-cooled cabinets hosting 26 496 nodes and 1.49 PB of RAM across 197 032 RAM DIMMs. Each cabinet consisted of an L1 cabinet controller, several fan trays, power conversion electronics, breakers, a blower and chiller, and related piping. Each cabinet was organized into three chassis, and each chassis hosted eight blades.
- 22 640 compute nodes (based on AMD Opteron processors) with a total of 724 480 cores.
- 3072 GPU hybrid nodes equipped with Nvidia K20X GPU accelerators and AMD Opteron processors.
- 784 service nodes with a total of 5824 available cores.
- The high-speed Cray Gemini network, to provide node connectivity.
- The online storage system, consisting of 198 Cray Sonexion 1600 storage units equipped with 20 196 hard-disk drives (HDDs), and 396 solid-state drives (SSDs) (used to store file system metadata) that provided access to 26 petabytes (36 raw) of usable storage over a Lustre distributed file system.
- 300 petabytes (380 raw) of usable near-line tape storage.

*Compute node hardware.* Compute nodes were hosted in 5660 Cray XE6 blades, with four nodes per blade. A compute node consisted of two 16-core AMD Opteron 6276 processors at 2.6 GHz. Each Opteron processor included eight dual-core AMD Bulldozer modules, each with an $8 \times 64$ kB L1 instruction cache, $16 \times 16$ kB L1 data cache, $8 \times 2$ MB L2 cache (shared between the cores of each Bulldozer module), and $2 \times 8$ MB L3 cache (shared by all the cores). Each node was equipped with 64 GB of DDR3 RAM in 8 GB DIMMs. System memory was protected with $\times 8$

Chipkill [9, 10] code that used eighteen 8-bit symbols to make a 144-bit ECC word made up of 128 data bits and 16 check bits for each memory word. The ×8 code was single-symbol-correcting code, i.e. it detected and corrected errors of up to eight bits. Caches were protected with parity and ECC. In particular, L3, L2, and L1 data caches were protected with ECC, while all others (tag caches, TLBs, and L2 and L1 instruction caches) were protected with parity.

*GPU node hardware.* GPU nodes were hosted in 768 Cray XK7 blades, with four nodes per blade. A GPU node consisted of a 16-core Opteron 6272 processor equipped with 32 GB of DDR3 RAM in 4 GB DIMMs and an Nvidia K20X accelerator. The accelerators were equipped with 2880 single-precision Cuda cores, 64 kB of L1 cache, 1536 kB of dedicated L2 cache, and 6 GB of ECC-protected DDR5 RAM memory.

*Service node hardware.* Service nodes were hosted on 166 Cray XIO blades and 30 XE6 blades, with four nodes per blade. Each XIO service node consisted of a six-core AMD Opteron 2435 working at 2.3 GHz and equipped with 16 GB of DDR2 memory in 4 GB DIMMs protected by ×4 Chipkill (single-symbol error correction and dual-symbol error detection). Service nodes hosted special PCI-Express cards such as Infiniband and fiber-channel cards. A service node could be configured as (i) a boot node to orchestrate systemwide reboots; (ii) a system database node to collect event logs; (iii) a MOM node for scheduling jobs; (iv) a network node to bridge external networks through Infiniband QDR IB cards; or (v) an Lnet (Lustre file system network) node to handle metadata (via Lustre metadata servers, or MDSes, to keep track of the location of the files in the storage servers) and file I/O data (via Lustre Object Storage Servers, or OSSes, to store the data stripes across the storage modules) for file system servers and clients. All the blades were powered through four dual-redundant voltage regulator modules fed by a power distribution unit (PDU) installed in the cabinet and attached to the blade through a dedicated connector.

*Network.* The Blue Waters high-speed network consisted of the Cray Gemini System Interconnect. Each blade included a network mezzanine card that housed two network chips, each one shared by two nodes via the HyperTransport AMD bus and powered by two dual-redundant voltage regulator modules. The topology was a three-dimensional (3D) 23 × 24 × 24 reentrant torus, and each node had six possible links to other nodes, i.e. right, left, up, down, in, and out. The ends of the mesh looped back to eliminate the problem of programming for a mesh with edges.

*Hardware Supervisor System (HSS) and system resiliency features.* Figure 13.8 shows a simplified schema of the Cray HSS architecture and how it interacted with the components of Blue Waters. Every node in the system was checked and managed by the HSS. The core components of the HSS system included (i) the HSS network; (ii) blade (L0) and cabinet (L1) controllers in charge of monitoring the nodes, replying to heartbeat signal requests, and collecting data on temperature,

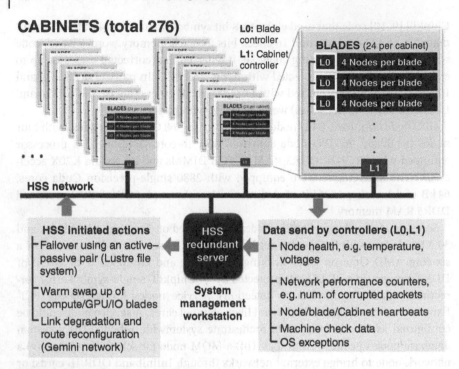

**Figure 13.8** The Hardware Supervisor System: Resiliency features.

voltage, power, network performance counters, and runtime software exceptions; and (iii) the HSS manager in charge of collecting node health data and executing the management software. The HSS manager, upon detection of a failure, e.g. a missing heartbeat, triggered failure mitigation mechanisms. They included (i) warm swap of a compute/GPU blade to allow the system operator to remove and repair system blades without disrupting the workload; (ii) service node and Lustre node failover mechanisms, e.g. replacement of I/O nodes with warm-standby replicas; and (iii) link degradation and route reconfiguration to enable routing around failed nodes in the topology. The procedure in the communication path route consisted of (i) waiting 10 seconds to aggregate failures; (ii) determining which blade(s) were alive; (iii) quiescing the Gemini network traffic; (iv) asserting a new route in the Gemini chips; and (v) cleaning up and resuming Gemini. The total time to execute that procedure was around 30–60 seconds. In the case of Gemini link failures, applications running on the affected blades were either killed or, in the case of a warm swap-out, allowed to complete.

*System software.* Compute and GPU nodes executed the lightweight kernel Compute Node Linux (CNL) developed by Cray. The operating system was reduced to a bare minimum to minimize the overhead on the nodes and included only essential components, such as a process loader, a Virtual Memory Manager, and a set of Cray ALPS agents for loading and controlling jobs. Service nodes executed a full-featured version of Linux, the Cray Linux Environment (CLE), which is based on the Suse Linux Enterprise Server 11 kernel 3.0.42.

Jobs were scheduled through a suite of cooperating software that included (i) Cray ALPS (the Application Level Placement Scheduler) [11] for the placement, launch, and monitoring of all the applications composing a single job; and (ii) Moab and TORQUE [12] for resource management and scheduling decisions. Jobs were assigned at the granularity of the node.

*File system features.* All blades were diskless and used the shared parallel file system for I/O operations. The Blue Waters Lustre installation consisted of a parallel file system used to manage data stored in Cray Sonexion 1600 storage modules. Each Sonexion module had 2 SSD of 2 TB in a RAID 1 configuration for journaling and logging, 22 disks of 2 TB for metadata storage, and 80 disks of 2 TB for data storage, organized in units of 8 disks in RAID 6. All disks were connected to two redundant RAID controllers. In each unit, two additional disks served as hot spares, which automatically provided failover for a failed drive. Data were accessed transparently from the nodes via the Lustre service nodes (Lnet), which interfaced with the Sonexion storage modules. Blue Waters included three file systems, i.e. project, scratch, and home, and provided up to 26 PB of usable storage over 36 PB of raw disk space. Each pair of a Lustre service node and Sonexion module was configured as an active-passive pair connected to a shared storage device. In that configuration, when a failure of a Lustre node was detected by HSS, the passive replica node became active and took over from the failed node; the shared storage device was then mounted in a read-only mode to avoid data inconsistency until the failed node had been replaced with the standby replica. After failure recovery, clients reconnected and replayed their requests serially to reconstruct the state on the replaced node. Until a client received a confirmation that a given transaction had been written to stable storage, the client held on to the transaction (waiting on a timeout), in case it needed to be replayed. If the timeout was reached, all the jobs waiting to reconnect failed. The recovery process (i.e. the boot-up of the warm standby and the reconstruction of the state lost in the failure) might have taken 5–30 minutes (60 for MDS), depending on the number of clients using the file system at the moment of the failure.

*Workload.* The workload processed by Blue Waters consisted of large-scale scientific simulations, including ones addressing molecular dynamics, hurricanes and tornadoes, supernovae, galaxy formation, earthquakes, and fluid dynamics. Blue Waters was capable of delivering above 1 PF/s of sustained performance, and jobs could use compute nodes, GPU nodes, or both. The average load (utilization) in terms of used nodes, computed over 24 hours for the measured period, was 71%.

## 13.3.1 Data and Methodology

The results discussed in this case study are based on analysis of manual reports generated by Blue Waters system maintenance engineers over a period of 261 days from January 3 to November 17, 2013. In addition, we use automatically collected event data logs to provide an in-depth understanding of specific failures, such as uncorrectable machine checks, e.g. hardware exceptions caused by parity or ECC errors.

*Manual reports.* System reports are human-written documents that record each event in the system that required the attention of the system managers, such as failures, maintenance, system upgrades, and bugs signaled to the manufacturer. Each entry contains several distinct fields, including (i) start time of the event, (ii) repair time and date, (iii) category of the event, (iv) affected facility, (v) textual description of the event, (vi) number of nodes offline because of the event, (vii) systemwide outage (SWO) flag, and (viii) field replaced unit (FRU). Over 1978 distinct entries (including scheduled maintenance, system expansions, and failure events) were reported during the 261-day measurement interval. Table 13.7 shows a snippet of the reports.

**Table 13.7** Example Blue Waters incident report.

| Start time | End time | Category | Facility | Subject | Failed nodes | SWO | FRU |
|---|---|---|---|---|---|---|---|
| 3/6/13 7:38 | 3/7/13 17:00 | Single/ multiple node | | c2-8c1s3n3 (RQ12110251) memory error | 1 | 0 | DIMM |
| 3/11/13 21:11 | 3/12/13 0:21 | Interrupt | Sonexion | SCSI and SAS errors on snx1003n181 crashed and automatic failure failed | 26563 | 1 | |
| 3/28/13 2:52 | 3/29/13 14:52 | Failure (no interrupt) | Sonexion | snx11003n354 Slot 47 disk failure | 0 | 0 | Disk |
| 4/22/13 7:28 | 4/22/13 18:08 | Interrupt | | c5-8c0s6 (rq11520016) node failure made the HSN non-routable | 26534 | 1 | Comp. blade |
| 4/29/13 16:28 | 4/29/13 16:49 | Failure (no impact) | Sonexion | snx11003n warning fan at speed 0 RPM | 0 | 0 | Fan tray |
| 5/30/13 4:50 | 5/30/13 9:48 | Interrupt | Gemini | Blade failed. Replaced, warm-swapped, then there was a throttle and routes hung | 26573 | 1 | |

Entries include only a subset of the fields used in this study [2] / with permission from IEEE.

*Failure categories.* Entries in the failure reports were produced upon arrival of alerts from automated detection mechanisms and failure-reporting tools. The Blue Waters maintenance specialists used the following categories to classify each entry added to the failure report.

1) *Failure (No Interrupt):* Failures that were naturally tolerated by the architecture, i.e. did not cause node/system downtime or trigger failover actions (e.g. cooling hardware or performance problems).
2) *Interrupt (Failover):* A critical problem that was successfully handled by the automatic failover mechanisms.
3) *Link and Node Failure (Job Failed):* A failure of one or more nodes and one or more links that caused the failure of one or more user jobs.
4) *Link Failure (No Job Failed):* Failures of a single or multiple node(s) that caused a link failure that was successfully handled by the automatic network failover mechanisms.
5) *Link Failure (Job Failed):* Link failures that caused job loss.
6) *Single/Multiple Node Failure:* Failures of single/multiple compute, GPU, or service node(s) that required repair, but did not impact core system functionalities.
7) *Interruption (Systemwide Outage):* The whole system was unavailable, e.g. because of a systemwide repair or restart. An SWO occurred if specific requirements could not be met, including (i) the ability to access all data blocks of all files in the file system; (ii) the ability of users to log in; (iii) full interconnection between nodes; (iv) access to an external storage server (esDM, or external data mover); (v) the ability to support user application submission, scheduling, launch, and/or completion; (vi) the ability to recover from file system or network failures through automated failover operations; and (vii) performance (e.g. network bandwidth or file system throughput) above acceptable levels.

Human-generated reports present several challenges. They contain textual descriptions in natural language and cannot be readily analyzed by automatic tools. Failure reports must be filtered from nonfailure events to avoid biasing the analysis. Therefore, an early step of our analysis consisted of purging the nonfailure entries and reorganizing the content into a structured database. In close partnership with NCSA and Cray engineers, we manually reviewed each data record in the failure reports and combined redundant or overlapping records. Finally, manual failure reports may suffer from misdetection and underreporting of noncritical failures. We extensively investigated the potential for underreporting, and concluded that the incidents of failure underreporting were negligible. The reasons are that each manual report was based on an automatic failure/alert trigger provided by the HSS's extensive system-logging mechanisms, and the technical staff of Blue Waters was meticulous about recordkeeping. After fixing the problem, the staff updated the error report with the identified cause of the event, the fixes applied, and, where applicable, the FRU.

*Machine check data.* Machine checks were errors detected by the machine check architecture in the northbridge of the processor. Machine check errors may be related to several causes, such as hard or soft memory errors (e.g. bit flips) as well as processor or memory voltage ripple or motherboard problems. Machine check data include a timestamp, the ID of the node that experienced the machine check, and information on the type (e.g. correctable/uncorrectable or detected by the hardware scrubber), physical address, error syndrome, and involved operation (e.g. reading from the memory or loading of the L2 data cache), all encoded into a 64-bit word in the logged data obtained after the content of the machine-check status register had been fetched [9]. In the case of an uncorrectable error, the operating system was configured to panic. Consequently, the event would be detected by a system console, which switched the status of the node from up to down.

*Failure root causes* identified in the reports are classified into the following exclusive categories: hardware, software, missing heartbeat,[3] network, environment, and unknown (i.e. failures for which the cause could not be determined). Our assignment of an outage to the hardware or software category was guided by the type of corrective action taken (e.g. replacement with a spare part or installation of software patches) and based on our interactions with system administrators. After that step, we reduced the number of reports from 1978 to 1490 entries that include only recorded failures.

### 13.3.1.1 Characterization Methodology

In characterizing failures from the manual failure reports, we (i) associated failures with the corresponding root-cause categories, i.e. hardware, software, network, environment, missing heartbeat/node down, and unknown, and measured the failure rate and repair times across them; (ii) determined how the hardware and software failures evolved in the considered measurement window; (iii) evaluated the hardware error resiliency; and (iv) evaluated systemwide failure and repair time distributions and their statistical properties. Computed metrics included the relative failure frequency, mean, and standard deviation. In addition, we evaluated the density distributions of the TBF and relative frequency of root causes. We also measured the error resiliency of the memory and processors by using the machine check data. Specifically, we computed (i) the failure rate in FITs (Failures in Time) (i.e. failures in $10^9$ hours of operation) per GB of memory

---

3 We consider this a separate category of failure. Missing heartbeats were detected by the system but automatically recovered from before they were diagnosed.

for RAM and GPU accelerator onboard memory; (ii) MTBF and annualized failure rate (AFR) for the processor, memory, GPU accelerator, disks, and SSDs; and (iii) probability of uncorrectable errors per GB of memory, for both GPU accelerator and memory errors.

The analysis of the data required us to develop several techniques and tools (i) to handle large amounts of textual data (i.e. 3.7 TB of system logs for the considered period), (ii) to extract and decode specific types of system events (e.g. the 64-bit machine-check status register for all the logged machine checks), and (iii) to harmonize and mine the manual failure reports. Details of the developed toolset are not included here because of our focus on measurements.

## 13.3.2 Blue Waters Failure Causes

In this section, we analyze the data and information in the failure reports to address how often Blue Waters failed and how much time was needed to fix the causes of a failure. We discuss (i) the distribution of failures' root causes across all the failure categories defined, and (ii) the root causes of the failures, as identified by the Cray and Blue Waters maintenance specialists.

### 13.3.2.1 Breakdown of Failures

Table 13.8 provides a breakdown of the failure reports, MTBF, and MTTR (mean time to recovery/repair) across the defined failure categories. In the measured period of 261 days, the system experienced 1490 failures, of which 1451 (97.4%) were tolerated and 39 (2.6%) resulted in SWOs. Key observations are:

- On average, there was a failure (across all categories) every 4.2 hours, while the system suffered SWOs approximately every 160 hours.
- 58.3% of failures resulted in single/multiple node failures (category 6 in Table 13.8) that caused node unavailability. Such failures were the most common, occurring every 4.2 hours; they were allowed to accumulate to optimize the cost of field intervention, and they were repaired, on average, in 32 hours.
- About one-fourth (25.7%) of failures were potentially severe events from which the system recovered by means of system-level failovers without job failures (categories 2 and 4 in Table 13.8). Only 2.6% caused job failures (categories 3 and 5 in Table 13.8) without resulting in an SWO.
- 11% of failures (category 1 in Table 13.8) consisted of noncritical events that were tolerated by the redundant design of Blue Waters without requiring any automatic failover operation. Such events included, for instance, failures of (redundant) power supplies in the compute or service blades, failures of cooling hardware (fan trays or water cooling valves), job-scheduling performance problems, and resource manager crashes. Such failures caused no machine

**Table 13.8** Failure statistics.

| Failure category | Count | Percent | MTBF (h) | MTTR (h) | $\sigma_{TBF}$ (h) | $\sigma_{TTR}$ (h) |
|---|---|---|---|---|---|---|
| 1) Failure (no interrupt) | 164 | 11% | 35.17 | 13.5 | 70.8 | 35.3 |
| 2) Interrupt (failover) | 99 | 6.6% | 58 | 14.7 | 92 | 42.2 |
| 3) Link & node failure (job failed) | 19 | 1.3% | 297.7 | 6.1 | 427.3 | 5.4 |
| 4) Link failure (no job failed) | 285 | 19.1% | 19.9 | 32.7 | 51.9 | 91.2 |
| 5) Link failure (job failed) | 19 | 1.3% | 291.6 | 16 | 444 | 26.7 |
| 6) Single/ multiple-node failure | 868 | 58.2% | 4.2 | 32.7 | 6.3 | 72 |
| 7) **Interruption (systemwide outage)** | **39** | **2.62%** | **159.2** | **5.16** | **174.2** | **8.1** |
| ALL | **1490** | 100% | 4.2 | 34.5 | 13.3 | 50.5 |

The last row refers to the statistics calculated across all the failure categories [2] / with permission from IEEE.

downtime and little or no unavailability of software services (e.g. of the job scheduler). They occurred on average every 35.12 hours, and their interarrival times showed high variance due to the heterogeneity of the root cause (e.g. cooling hardware and job scheduling software).

*Software failures contributed to 53% of node downtime hours.* Figure 13.9a shows how hardware, software, network, heartbeat, and environment root causes were distributed across the failure categories given in Table 13.8. As seen in other systems (e.g. [13]), failures with hardware root causes were the predominant cause of single/multiple node failures. They occurred 442 times (51%) over 868 single/multiple node failures documented in the failure reports, and constituted 42% of the total number of failures across all the categories (see rightmost bar in Figure 13.9a). Conversely, failures with software root causes represented 20% of the total number of failures and only 7.9% of the single/multiple node failures. However, an interesting conclusion can be drawn from the relative impacts that hardware and software causes had on the total number of node repair hours (i.e. total number of node hours required to repair failures due to the same root cause) shown in Figure 13.9b. The key observation is that failures with software root causes were

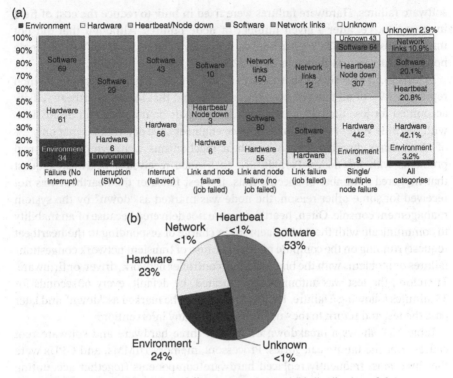

**Figure 13.9** (a) Breakdown of the failure categories, and (b) distribution of the cumulative node repair hours across hardware, software, network, unknown, heartbeat, and environment root causes [2] / with permission from IEEE.

responsible for 53% of the total node repair hours, although they constituted only 20% of the total number of failures. Hardware root causes, however, despite causing 42% of all failures, resulted in only 23% of the total repair time. As we shall see, hardware problems were well managed by the system.

To identify a reason for those differences, we analyzed the distribution of the number of nodes involved in failures with hardware or software root causes. We found that failures with hardware root causes that did not cause SWOs propagated outside the boundary of a single blade in only 0.7% of the cases. Examples of failures due to hardware root causes that impacted a full blade include failures in the voltage converter module (VRM) of the mezzanine and/or problems with the cabinet controller. The data show that 96.7% of failures with hardware root causes were limited to a single node, and 99.3% were limited to a single blade (i.e. four nodes). Conversely, software failures, if they didn't cause systemwide failures, propagated to another node 14% of the time, i.e. 20 times more often than hardware failures did. In addition, hardware failures were easier to diagnose than software failures. Hardware failures were fixed in bulk to reduce the cost of field intervention, i.e. after a given number of node failures. Although that did not impact the system MTTR (5.16 hours), it did result in a larger MTTR for single nodes (32.7 hours), as shown in Table 13.8.

Figure 13.9b also shows that failures whose root causes are unknown (which represent 2.9% of all failures; see Figure 13.9a) and that lacked heartbeat activity accounted for less than 2% of the total node repair hours. Based on discussions with the Blue Waters system maintenance engineers, we determined that only 2% of the failures detected by the heartbeat mechanisms were symptoms of real problems with the nodes. Periodically, each node received a heartbeat request that triggered a number of specific tests. If a test failed or the heartbeat was not received for some other reason, the node was marked as "down" by the system management console. Often, heartbeats were not delivered because of an inability to communicate with the ALPS daemon (in charge of responding to the heartbeat request) running on the compute node or because of transient network congestion/ failures or problems with the blade/cabinet controller network, driver, or firmware. Therefore, the test was automatically repeated, by default, every 60 seconds for 35 minutes following a failure. Hence, a node could be marked as "down" and later pass the test and return to the "up" state without any intervention.

Table 13.9 shows a breakdown of the top three hardware and software root causes over the failure categories. Processors, memory DIMMs, and GPUs were the three most frequently replaced hardware components (together accounting for 72% of the replaced components), out of an extensive list of 69 replaced units. As discussed in the next section, processors were replaced when the maintenance specialists observed specific hardware exceptions (e.g. L1 cache parity errors) in the system console logs. In many cases, the replaced processors were tested and found to be free of problems, and the failure was attributed to a problem with the socket or the voltage regulator. Problems in the node or mezzanine voltage regulator accounted for about 14% of single/multiple node failures in our gathered data. In one case, the mezzanine voltage regulator failed because of a bug in the L0 node controller firmware, causing a SWO and showing that software can have an impact on low-level hardware failures. Lustre, the CLE OS, and Sonexion/storage software were the top three software root causes among the failure categories. In particular, the Lustre file system and related software caused 44% of the single/ multiple node failures attributed to software root causes, while the CLE OS and Sonexion/storage caused as much as 28% and 9% of the total single and multiple node failures, respectively.

Lustre includes a rich software stack of more than 250K LOC. It played a crucial role in Blue Waters, since all the compute nodes were diskless and relied on Lustre for file system access. Lustre problems were the most widespread cause of failures and were present in six of the seven failure categories shown in Table 13.9. Blue

Table 13.9 Breakdown of the counts of the top three hardware and software failure root causes [2] / with permission from IEEE.

| | Failure (No interrupt) | Interrupt (SWO) | Interrupt (Failover) | Link failure (User job failed) | Link & node failure (User job failed) | Single/Multiple node failure |
|---|---|---|---|---|---|---|
| HW | PSU 20 | EPO 1 | Disks 45 | Optic 12 | GPU 2 | Processor 160 |
| | IPMI 15 | Compute blade 2 | IPMI 5 | RAM 9 | Gemini ASIC 1 | RAM 158 |
| | Fan tray assy 14 | Storage module 2 | Storage module 2 | Gemini voltage regulator 8 | Compute blade 2 | GPU 38 |
| SW | Moab TORQUE 33 | Lustre 18 | Lustre 29 | Lustre Net (Lnet) 2 | CLE kernel 1 | Lustre 30 |
| | CLE kernel 17 | Moab TORQUE 6 | Sonexion storage 8 | Sonexion storage 6 | | CLE kernel 16 |
| | Warm swap 5 | Gemini 5 | CLE kernel 4 | CLE kernel 3 | | Sonexion storage 5 |

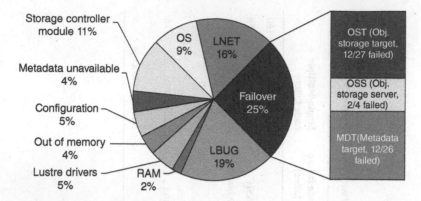

**Figure 13.10** Breakdown of the Lustre failures [2] / with permission from IEEE.

Waters experienced a total of 104 different failures attributed to Lustre, and 18 of the 104 escalated to SWOs.

Figure 13.10 shows the breakdown of the root causes of Lustre failures. The failure of any Lustre component triggered failover operations, which were successful 75% of the time, as shown in the figure. If the automated failover procedure failed to recover the normal state of the system, the automated procedures were overridden by the technical staff, and the system was manually recovered. A common cause of Lustre issues was detection of the so-called LBUG (19%), i.e. a panic-style assertion in the storage node kernel. The unavailability of the Object Storage Target (OST) or of the metadata (i.e. MDS, MDT, and MGS in Lustre) that provide low-level support for the storage system is another important Lustre failure category. Configuration problems contributed to 5% of the Lustre failures, but they were not critical and often manifested as performance issues, i.e. Lustre became slow. About 13% of Lustre failures were due to hardware problems (2% were due to problems with RAM, and 11% were due to problems with the Controller Module), and the failover mechanism recovered from all of them.

### 13.3.2.2 Effectiveness of Failover

On average, each day, the system recovered from 1 or 2 critical failures that triggered automatic failover procedures. About 28% of all failures triggered some type of failover mechanism. That included 39 SWOs, 99 interrupt-failovers, 285 link failures in which no user job failed, 19 link failures in which a user job failed, and 19 node failures in which a user job failed, out of a total of 1490 failures. The data contain information on 138 triggered failover operations due to failures attributed to hardware or software causes. Out of 138 recorded failover operations, SWOs occurred 24.6% of the time (in 39 out of the 138 cases); the system successfully recovered from the remaining 99 failures (see Figure 13.9a.)

*Lustre failover.* The failure recovery of Lustre is a complex procedure that typically requires movement of a large volume of data over the network, and synchronization of the nodes participating in data movement. Twenty-six out of 104 failover attempts failed; specifically, (i) the failover of the metadata target (MDT) failed 12 times out of 26, (ii) the failover of the Object Storage Server (OSS) failed 2 times out of 4, and (iii) the failover of the Object Storage Target (OST) failed 12 times out of 27. As one might expect, the most critical failover procedures were those involving the storage and metadata server nodes. Under heavy job loads, those procedures were time-consuming (taking between 15 and 30 minutes). Recovery from a client failure in Lustre was based on revocation and lock of resources, so the surviving clients could continue their work uninterrupted. Because of the way the Lustre Distributed Lock Manager handles parallel operations, threads could block on a single resource. Moreover, threads had to hold a resource until clients acknowledged completion of an operation. Even though the system was configured to support 512 service threads, they could all quickly become consumed because of the blocking. In particular, the data show that for about 20% of the Lustre failover failures that caused a SWO, the reason for the outage was that lock timeouts fired because of the high volume of clients that needed to recover during the failover (e.g. the large number of OSSes). Those results indicate that the mechanisms behind Lustre failover procedures (e.g. timeouts) operated at their limit at the Blue Waters scale when they had to deal with high workload conditions and a large number of clients were involved in the recovery.

*Gemini failover.* Out of 323 documented link failures (categories "Link & node failure (job failed)," "Link failure (no job failed)," and "Link failure (job failed)" in Table 13.8), 38 caused the loss of one or more user jobs, while the Gemini-supported failover mechanism succeeded in 285 cases.

In the Gemini network, when a lane (a part of a Gemini network link) fails, the network is automatically able to run in degraded mode (i.e. diverting the traffic to the remaining links at the price of reduced speed). Lane failures have three main causes: (i) bad cable interconnections, (ii) failure of a routing node or a Gemini mezzanine card, and (iii) network congestion. Evidence shows that the network is agile and fault-tolerant. We speculate that more attention has been paid to Gemini software stack testing, while Lustre is naturally more vulnerable to failures due to (i) its richer software stack, (ii) the community-driven nature of the product, and (iii) the inability to test how critical modules such as the failover would behave over large-scale deployments like Blue Waters. In addition, because of the long recovery time and the dual-redundant configuration of Lustre servers, the chances that failures will occur during the time needed to recover, as we have seen, are not insignificant. Hence, we claim that more effort is required to create better failover and testing techniques for software at the petascale and above.

### 13.3.3 Hardware Error Resiliency

The Blue Waters maintenance specialists diagnosed processor- and memory-related problems by looking at the machine-check exceptions contained in the system logs. In looking at the system logs produced by Blue Waters nodes, we counted 1 544 398 machine-check events in the measurement period, of which only 28 consisted of uncorrectable errors, i.e. errors that could not be corrected by either ECC or Chipkill and might cause loss of data, corruption of processor state, or both. That indicates an unusual degree of containment of hardware problems that we further investigate in this section. Table 13.10 shows a breakdown of the machine-check errors over the different node types.

In total, 12 721 nodes (46% of the total Blue Waters nodes) experienced at least a memory error; 82.3% of the nodes that manifested machine checks were compute nodes, 19.4% were GPU nodes, and 7.34% were service nodes. 6.6% of all the memory DIMMs that generated at least a correctable error occurred during the observation window. In our data, 55% of the nodes generated only one machine check, while 92% of the machine checks were generated by only 19% of the nodes.

*Memory errors breakdown.* Table 13.11 shows a breakdown of the memory errors observed in Blue Waters. The table shows that about 70.01% of the memory errors involved a single bit, and 29.98% involved two to eight consecutive bits (i.e. less than or equal to two symbols, where a symbol is four bits), confirming prior results for a smaller-scale Cray supercomputer [14]. Chipkill could correct errors involving up to two symbols (×8 Chipkill on compute and GPU nodes); without Chipkill, 30% of the analyzed memory errors would be uncorrectable, e.g. if one used only ECC. Hence, a key finding is that ECC/Chipkill techniques were

**Table 13.10** Breakdown of the machine-check errors [2] / with permission from IEEE.

|  | Compute | | GPU | | Service | | ALL | |
|---|---|---|---|---|---|---|---|---|
|  | Count | Error/MB | Count | Error/MB | Count | Error/MB | Total | Error/MB |
| L1 | 27 522 | 1.62 | 594 | 0.26 | 632 | 3.48 | 28 748 | 1.48 |
| L2 | 18 590 | 0.05 | 1098 | 0.02 | 1566 | 0.17 | 21 254 | 0.05 |
| L3 | 292 920 | 0.81 | 2282 | 0.01 | 23 030 | 1.98 | 318 232 | 0.75 |
| Memory | 840 322 | 5.66E-4 | 97 974 | 9.73E-4 | 93 590 | 3.93E-3 | 1 031 886 | 6.42E-4 |
| Other | 101 388 | — | 1102 | — | 41 788 | — | 144 278 | |
| % CPU | 34.39% | | 4.93% | | 41.73% | | 33.19% | |
| % RAM | 65.61% | | 95.07% | | 58.27% | | 54.41% | |
| Total | 1 280 742 | | 103 050 | | 160 606 | | 1 544 398 | |

**Table 13.11** Breakdown of the count of memory errors [2] / with permission from IEEE.

| Type | Count | % |
| --- | --- | --- |
| Total memory errors | 1 031 886 | 66.81% |
| ECC/Chipkill single bit | 722 526 | 70.01% |
| Chipkill (more than 2 bits) | 309 359 | 29.98% |
| Uncorrectable ECC/Chipkill | 28 | 2.71E-05% |

effective in correcting 99.997% of the memory errors that occurred, i.e. we observed only 28 cases of uncorrectable errors out of 1 544 398 errors.

The data also show that about 8.2% of the DIMMs manifest correctable errors, matching the data in earlier large-scale studies [15]. However, in our study, we found that fewer than 0.1% of the machines and 0.0014% of the total DIMMs generated uncorrectable errors, i.e. one order of magnitude lower than the incidences of 1.3%–4% for the machines and 0.05%–0.08% for DDR2 DIMMs with uncorrectable errors described in [15]. In particular, the number of uncorrectable errors we found over the total number of handled errors was more than 3 orders of magnitude lower than that for DDR2 memory systems reported in an independent large-scale study [15], even though Blue Waters generated two orders of magnitude more machine checks than previous generations of HPC systems [13, 15]. That shows that the error resiliency of DDR3 to multiple-bit errors has improved substantially over that of DDR2. A key implication is that the joint use of ECC and ×8 Chipkill techniques in Blue Waters was able to fix 99.998% of the errors generated in 1.476 PB of DDR3 RAM and in a total size of 1.5 TB of L1, L2, and L3 caches across all Blue Waters processors. Only 0.002% of errors were uncorrectable, as compared to the 1.29% reported for the previous generation of HPC systems [15] when they employed only ECC and/or ×4 Chipkill (i.e. single-symbol correction and dual-symbol detection). The expectation among hardware designers has been that the numbers of both transient and permanent hardware failures may rise uncontrollably as device sizes shrink, especially in large-scale machines like Blue Waters. However, our results indicate that we are far from that situation. Because of the high numbers of nodes and errors, we claim that the results provided in this section have strong statistical significance for the characterization of processor and memory error resiliency features.

### 13.3.3.1 Rate of Uncorrectable Errors Across Different Node Types

Table 13.10 shows that the rates of correctable and uncorrectable errors per node varied across compute, GPU, and service nodes. If we look to the rates of errors detected by the memory scrubber for compute, GPU, and service nodes (not shown in Table 13.10), we notice that the nodes had similar levels of physical susceptibility to memory or cache errors, i.e. 29 errors per compute node, 28.5 errors per GPU node, and 30 errors per service node. Therefore, we ruled out the possibility that uncorrectable error rates might have been related to the different hardware characteristics (e.g. total installed RAM or different AMD Opterons).

A first observation is that nodes adopted different Chipkill techniques, i.e. ×4 for service nodes, but ×8 for compute and GPU nodes. In particular, service nodes were able to correct errors on four consecutive bits and detect errors on up to eight consecutive bits, while compute and GPU nodes could detect and correct errors affecting up to eight bits. That impacted the capacity of service nodes to tolerate multiple-bit errors (of more than four bits). In particular, our measurements show that about 1% of the memory errors of compute and GPU nodes, but only 0.2% of the memory errors on service nodes, involved four to eight bits. The reason for the difference is that those errors were not critical for compute and GPU nodes, but they caused uncorrectable errors on service nodes.

The difference in the Chipkill technique used explains only some of the measurements. In particular, as shown in Table 13.12, the rate of memory errors per node was 48.1 for service nodes, but only 37.1 for compute nodes (i.e. 23% fewer errors per node) and 31.1 for GPU nodes (i.e. 56% fewer errors per node). We observed that compute and GPU nodes executed a lightweight OS rather than the full OS run by service nodes.

The level of multitasking was different for the different OSes, with one application per core for compute and GPU nodes, against several background services for service nodes.

In addition, service nodes showed a higher percentage of used memory because of their lower amount of installed memory, i.e. 16 GB vs. 64 GB for compute nodes. The high number of active services on service nodes translated into a sparser memory access pattern than found on compute or GPU nodes, which usually worked on big chunks of data. (For example, the matrices used by compute and GPU nodes were stored in consecutive memory locations, e.g. in the same

**Table 13.12** Breakdown of the uncorrectable memory errors (UE) [2] / with permission from IEEE.

| | RAM (GB) | Errors/Node | UE | UE/GB | MTBF (UE) |
|---|---|---|---|---|---|
| Compute | 1 448 960 | 37.1 | 14 | 1.08E-05 | 1617 h |
| GPU | 127 104 | 31.1 | 4 | 3.88E-05 | 768 h |
| Service | 23 232 | 48.1 | 10 | 6.22E-05 | 193 h |
| GPU Card | 18 432 | 9.76E-3 | 38 | 2.06E-03 | 80 h |

memory chip or DIMM, for the purpose of compiler optimization.) Hence, we speculate that service nodes were more susceptible than compute/GPU nodes to uncorrectable memory errors because of the service nodes' higher levels of multi-tasking, disparities in memory access patterns, and higher memory loads.

### 13.3.3.2 Hardware Failure Rates

The procedure enforced at NCSA for Blue Waters hardware replacement was to replace (i) the processor when uncorrectable or parity errors were observed, and (ii) memory when the rate of corrected ECC errors over a single address was above a programmed threshold. A similar replacement policy was enforced for storage devices and GPU accelerators, which were replaced when uncorrectable errors were detected, e.g. when a RAID controller detected uncorrectable disk errors or when a GPU accelerator manifested a double-bit error. In fact, GPU accelerator memory was protected only by ECC and therefore was vulnerable to multiple-bit errors.

Table 13.13 shows the AFR (which is the percentage of failed units in a population, scaled to a per-year estimation), MTBF, and FIT rate for processor, memory DIMM, GPU, and storage devices (including disks and SSDs). Table 13.13 also shows the estimated failure rate expressed in FITs/devices. The MTBF for a single component is computed as the total number of working hours divided by the AFR.

Interestingly, the DDR3 DIMMs show the highest MTBF, at 7 821 488 hours. The processors and disks show an MTBF about half the size of the DDR3 DIMM MTBF, specifically 3 771 492 hours for the processors and 2 807 692 for the disks. The GPU accelerators show an MTBF of 506 394 hours, i.e. 15 times smaller than the DDR3 DIMM MTBF (about 200 times smaller than the FIT/GB).

In fact, disks were found to provide a high level of reliability. During the 261-day period of observation, only 45 disks from the pool of 20 196 devices were replaced. The computed AFR for disks was lower than the observed values of 2–6% given in other studies of disk failures [16], although the population of disks in Blue Waters was smaller than that considered in other studies. Our numbers,

**Table 13.13** AFR, MTBF, and FIT for the top five hardware root causes [2] / with permission from IEEE.

|                | Total   | AFR     | MTBF      | FIT/Device | FIT/GB |
|----------------|---------|---------|-----------|------------|--------|
| Processor      | 49 258  | 0.23%   | 3 771 492 | 265.15     | N/A    |
| DIMMs          | 197 032 | 0.112%  | 7 821 488 | 127.84     | 15.98  |
| GPU card (6 GB)| 3072    | 1.732%  | 506 394   | 1974.11    | 329.02 |
| Disks (2 TB)   | 20 196  | 0.312%  | 2 807 692 | 356.16     | 0.174  |
| SSD (2 TB)     | 392     | 0.717%  | 1 230 795 | 812.48     | 0.397  |

however, confirm the MTBF values provided by the manufacturer and show no tangible evidence of defective disk units, and we measured an SSD MTBF lower than the manufacturer's declared value of 2 000 000. An uncorrectable error of an SSD or a disk often implies a permanent error on the device. (Note that no permanent error was observed for processors or GPU accelerators.)

*Rate of uncorrectable errors for GPU cards.* Table 13.11 reports the rates of uncorrected memory errors in Blue Waters nodes and GPU accelerators. We note (i) that for uncorrectable memory errors, the DDR5 memory on the GPU accelerator shows an MTBF one order of magnitude smaller than that for the DDR3 constituting the GPU node RAM, and 2 orders of magnitude smaller than that of compute nodes (a similar comparison holds for the FIT/GB shown in Table 13.13); and (ii) that the disparity is even higher if we look at the number of uncorrectable errors per GB shown in Table 13.12. In particular, we note that the rate of uncorrectable errors per GB on GPU node DDR3 memory is 2 orders of magnitude smaller than that on the GPU accelerator DDR5 onboard memory and that the FIT rate per GB of memory of GPU accelerators is 10 times higher than that for the DDR3 RAM of the nodes. An implication is that enforcement of Chipkill coding for compute, service, and GPU node DDR3 RAM can decrease the rate of uncorrectable errors per GB by a factor of 100, compared to the rate for the ECC-protected memories (e.g. the DDR5 memory on the GPU card).

### 13.3.3.3 Hardware Failure Trends

Our data cover the early months of production of Blue Waters. Therefore, it is important to assess how the failure rates evolved during the measured period. To do so, we first plotted the arithmetic mean of the TBF for failures due to hardware and software root causes, and we looked for any trend. Second, we used the Laplace test [7] to determine whether the arrival of failures changed significantly over time.

*The failure rate distribution trended to a constant failure rate toward the end of the measured period.* Figure 13.11 shows that the TBF for failures due to hardware root causes increased by a factor of 2 toward the end of the measured period. The ripples on the first months of the plot were caused by (i) failures of defective units, and (ii) preproduction tests run between March 1 and March 27, 2013 (the start of the production time). It is interesting that after users started to use Blue Waters, there was a constant rate of discovery and fix of hardware problems. More specifically, Figure 13.11a shows that the TBFs started to improve in April and continued to improve constantly until they stabilized toward the end of the period under study (i.e. the slopes of the charts decrease). By the end of the observation period, the hardware MTBF had grown to 10.9 hours. Figure 13.11c shows the Laplace score computed over the examined period. In particular, Figure 13.11c confirms that in the first months of production, the hardware reliability was not stable

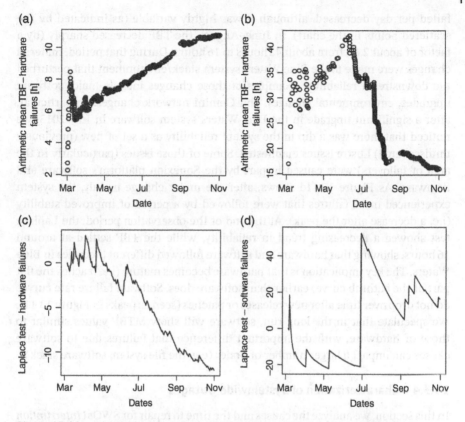

**Figure 13.11** Arithmetic mean of the TBF for failures due to (a) hardware, (b) software root causes. Laplace test for the number of nodes that fail per day because of (c) hardware, (d) software root causes [2] / with permission from IEEE.

(i.e. the score oscillates around zero). From July on, the reliability of the system improved (shown by a Laplace score lower than −1.96) because permanent and non-independent failures had been fixed, so most of the remaining failures were those that occurred with independent inter-failure times. The implication is that over those few months, Blue Waters' hardware configuration matured, going toward the flat part of the bathtub curve. It is interesting to note that Figure 13.11c shows a peak around July. During that peak time, the system was suspended for replacement of several blades; the new hardware added to the system caused a transient upward trend in the Laplace score, showing that new defects were fixed soon after the installation of the new hardware.

*The reliability of the software deteriorated over the measured months.* Figure 13.11b shows that in the first months, the TBF of failures due to software improved until June, while Figure 13.11d shows that the number of nodes that failed per day decreased, although it was highly variable (as indicated by the scattered points in the chart). In June–August, the TBF decreased sharply (by a factor of about 2.6), from about 42 hours to 16 hours. During that period, material changes were made to the Blue Waters system stack/environment that perturbed the downstream reliability. Examples of those changes include major software upgrades, environmental changes, and Gemini network changes. In particular, after a significant upgrade in the Blue Waters system software in July 2013, we noticed that there was a dip in the system reliability as a set of new (previously undiscovered) Lustre issues manifested. Some of those issues (particularly in the area of failovers) were caused in part by the Sonexion platform's software and firmware. As Figure 13.11d shows, after the major change in July, the system experienced more failures that were followed by a period of improved stability (i.e. a decrease after the peak). At the end of the observation period, the Laplace test showed a decreasing trend in reliability, while the TBF settled at around 16 hours, showing that hardware and software followed different lifecycles in Blue Waters. The key implication is that hardware becomes mature (i.e. reaches the flat part of the bathtub curve) earlier than software does. Software failure rate curves do not drop over time after new releases or patches (seen as peaks in Figure 13.11). We speculate that in the long run, software will show MTBF values similar to those of hardware, with the important difference that failures due to software causes can impact a larger number of nodes (e.g. the file system software stack).

### 13.3.4 Characterization of Systemwide Outages

In this section, we analyze the causes and the time to repair for SWOs (*Interruption* failure category in Table 13.8) in Blue Waters.

*Basic statistics.* Table 13.14 shows the statistics for 39 SWOs presented in the failure reports. On average, the system experienced a SWO every 159.22 hours.

**Table 13.14** Systemwide outage statistics [2] / with permission from IEEE.

| | |
|---|---|
| Availability | 0.9688 |
| Total Time | 261 d |
| Unscheduled Downtime | 8.375 d |
| MTBF (SWO) | 6.625 d |
| MIN TBF | 3.35 h |
| MAX TBF | 37 d |
| MTTR | 5.12 h |
| Min TTR | 0.58 h |
| Max TTR | 12 h |

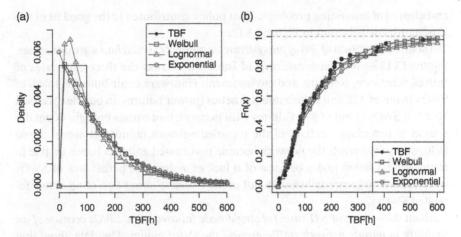

**Figure 13.12** Distribution fitting for systemwide outages' TBF: (a) PDF, (b) CDF [2] / with permission from IEEE.

In 90% of those cases, the system was brought back to full capacity within 3.28 hours from the start of the outage, with an MTTR of 5.12 hours. The quick repair of SWOs contributed to a system availability of 0.9688.

Figure 13.12 shows the probability density function (PDF) and cumulative distribution function (CDF) of the distribution of the times between SWOs. The exponential, Weibull, and lognormal distributions have an acceptable goodness of fit (i.e. a p-value of less than 0.1), as shown in Table 13.15. Note that the good fit for the lognormal distribution indicates a hazard rate that first increases and then decreases ($\sigma > 1$), modeling the case in which an SWO might depend on the preceding one. Interestingly, the reports document only one case in which an SWO was attributed to the same cause as the preceding SWO, which had occurred 3 hours and 51 minutes earlier,[4] while all the other cases were clearly unrelated. In addition, after each systemwide repair, the system was rebooted

**Table 13.15** Parameters for the estimated systemwide outage TBF distributions [2] / with permission from IEEE.

| Distribution | G.O.F. (Kolmogorov) | Parameters |
| --- | --- | --- |
| Lognormal | 0.072 | $\mu = 4.58$, $\sigma = 1.08$ |
| Weibull | 0.073 | $\alpha = 1.07$, $\beta = 152$ |
| Exponential | 0.08 | $\lambda = 0.006$ |

4 Both outages were associated with Lustre.

and cleared of remaining problems. That policy contributed to the good fit of the exponential distribution in Figure 13.12.

*About 74.4% (29 out of 39) of the systemwide outages (SWOs) had software causes.* Figure 13.13 shows the breakdown of the SWOs across the three categories of causes: hardware, software, and environment. Hardware contributed to 15.4% of SWOs (6 out of 39), and environmental issues (power failures, in our case) caused 10.2% of SWOs (4 out of 39). Failures with network root causes brought down the system in two cases, i.e. 0.6% of the recorded network failures. However, those failures resulted when the network became partitioned and was hence unable to route around failed nodes because of a lack of redundant paths. 46% of SWOs were caused by Lustre failures (18 out of 39, which is about 62% of all software-related SWOs).

*About 0.7% (6 out of 831 cases) of single-node failures led to SWOs because of an inability to reroute network traffic around the failed blades.* The data show that node failures due to hardware problems became critical when they affected the Gemini routing or access to the Lustre file system. The full 3D torus topology was effective in providing a number of redundant paths, and the link degradation mechanisms and distributed routing tables ensured protection against transient errors, e.g. corruption of the routing table. The Gemini network uses dimension-ordered routing. In an error-free network, a packet first travels along the X dimension until it reaches the destination node's X coordinate. The packet then travels in the Y dimension to the destination node's Y coordinate. Finally, the packet moves in the Z dimension until it reaches the final destination. If the standard X–Y–Z ordering does not work, Gemini tries an alternative route until it finds a routable path.

Certain failure patterns, such as multiple errors in the same loop along the Z dimension, can leave Gemini unable to find a valid route. While such failures are rare, for Blue Waters, they required the longest recovery time, with an MTTR of 8.1 hours. The failure reports contain three cases of SWOs due to routing problems: (i) a mishap of the failover procedure during the warm swap of a failed service, causing a system partition; (ii) a partial failure of the Gemini network that did not trigger the link recovery procedure, causing all the jobs to abort because of lack of communication; and (iii) a crash of the Gemini routing algorithm that caused the routes to hang. In the last case, while the Gemini crash's cause is unknown, system logs revealed a high rate of misrouted packets and routing data corruption within a one-hour time window before the incident.

## 13.3.5 Conclusions

Our Blue Waters case study offers an in-depth failure analysis of a sustained peta-flop system. The overall failure characterization indicates that failures due to software were a major contributor to Blue Waters' total repair time (53%), although

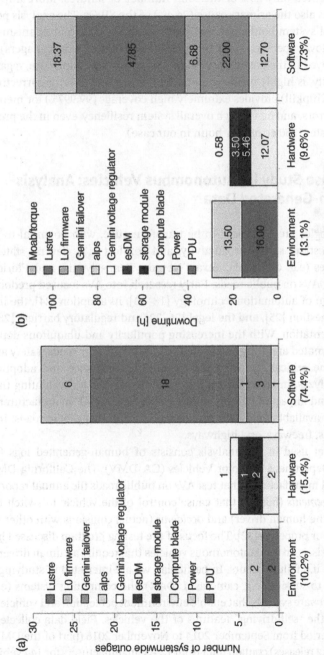

**Figure 13.13** Breakdown of (a) SWO root causes and (b) repair times [2] / with permission from IEEE.

they represented only 20% of the total number of failures. More importantly, software was also the primary cause (74.4%) of the SWOs. The analysis points out that the real system bottleneck was the inadequacy of the mechanisms behind complex failover operations (e.g. timeout and distributed lock managers), such as those employed in the Lustre file system. To our surprise, hardware, regardless of its complexity, is highly resilient. In particular, the use of error-correcting codes (including Chipkill) provides extremely high coverage (99.997%) for memory and processor errors, and hence high overall system resiliency, even in the presence of high error rates (250 errors per hour, in our case).

## 13.4 Case Study III: Autonomous Vehicles: Analysis of Human-Generated Data

AV technologies are advertised to be transformative, with potential to improve traffic congestion, safety, productivity, and comfort [17]. Several states in the United States (e.g. California, Texas, Nevada, Pennsylvania, and Florida) have been testing AVs on public roads. Early research into AVs focused predominantly on the design of automation technology [18–23], its adoption [24], the impact of AVs on congestion [25], and the legal [26, 27] and regulatory barriers [28–31] for AV implementation. With the increasing popularity and ubiquitous deployment of semiautomated and fully automated vehicles on public roads, safety and reliability became critical requirements for public acceptance and adoption. This chapter analyzes, in broad terms, the reliability of AVs by evaluating the cause, dynamics, and impact of failures across a wide range of AV manufacturers, utilizing publicly available field data from tests on California public roads, including urban streets, freeways, and highways.

The dataset used in the analysis consists of human-generated logs from the California Department of Motor Vehicles (CA DMV). The California DMV mandates that all manufacturers that test AVs on public roads file annual reports detailing *disengagements* (failures that cause control of the vehicle to switch from the software to the human driver) and *accidents* (actual collisions with other vehicles, pedestrians, or property) [32]. The focus of the testing program discussed here, and of our analysis, is on semiautonomous vehicles that require a human driver to serve as a fallback if a failure occurs. In particular, we are interested in studying failures that pertain to sensing (e.g. cameras, LIDAR) and computing systems (e.g. hardware and software systems that enable environment perception and vehicle control) that enable the "self-driving" features of the vehicles. Field data collected over a 26-month period from September 2014 to November 2016 (part of the DMV's 2016 and 2017 data releases) contain data from 12 AV manufacturers for 144 vehicles that drove a cumulative 1 116 605 autonomous miles. Across all manufacturers, we observed a total of 5328 disengagements, 42 of which led to accidents.

This study presents (i) an end-to-end workflow for analyzing AV failure data, and (ii) several insights about failure modes in AVs (across a single manufacturer's fleet, across different manufacturers, and over time) gained by executing the proposed workflow on the available data. The analysis of the 2014–2016 data shows that:

- Drivers of AVs need to be as alert as drivers of non-AV vehicles. Further, the small size of the overall action window (detection time + reaction time) would make reaction-time-based accidents a frequent failure mode with the widespread deployment of AVs.
- For the same number of miles driven, for the manufacturers that reported accidents, human-driven non-AVs were 15 to 4000× less likely than AVs to have an accident.
- 64% of disengagements were the result of problems in, or untimely decisions made by, the machine learning system.
- In terms of reliability per mission, AVs were 4.22× worse than airplanes, and 2.5× better than surgical robots. These findings demonstrate that at the time period covered by the dataset, while individual components of AV technology (e.g. vision systems, control systems) might have matured, entire AV systems were still in a "burn-in" phase.

The analysis also shows a distinct improvement in the performance of AVs over time. However, it demonstrates the need for continued improvement in the dependability of this technology. It is conceivable (indeed, expected) that AV manufacturers are performing similar analyses of data from their testing fleet. The results of these analyses are usually proprietary to the manufacturers. The California DMV data and analysis characterize failures of AVs in that fleet and can be used to inform the design of future AVs.

Figure 13.14 shows the end-to-end pipeline for processing failure data from AVs. The next subsections describe Figure 13.14 in greater detail. Section 13.4.1 discusses two real examples of AV disengagement and failure in real traffic on California roads; Section 13.4.2 discusses our data collection methodology (Stage I of the pipeline); Section 13.4.3 describes the preprocessing, filtering, and natural language processing (NLP) steps required to convert the data to a format suitable for analysis (Stages II and III of the pipeline); and Section 13.4.4 describes the statistical analysis of the failure data and summarizes the insights derived from the analysis (Stage IV of the pipeline).

### 13.4.1 Examples of AV-Related Accidents

This section details two representative incidents based on real events that occurred on the streets of Mountain View, CA. They illustrate how problems in the perception, learning, and control systems of an AV can manifest as an accident.

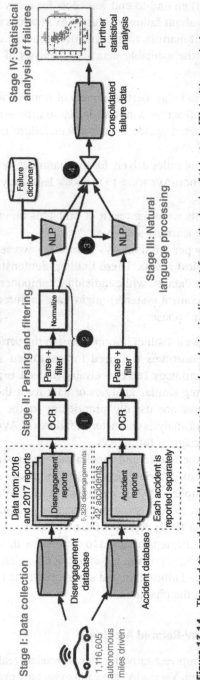

**Figure 13.14** The end-to-end data collection, processing, and analysis pipeline that forms the basis of this study [3] / with permission from IEEE.

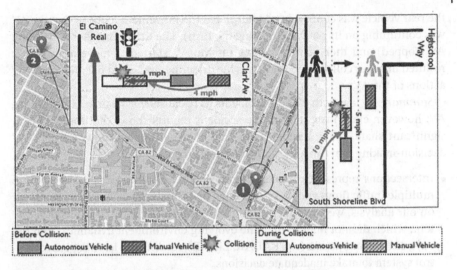

**Figure 13.15** Accident scenarios [3] / with permission from IEEE.

*Incident I: Real-time decisions.* Example (1) in Figure 13.15 shows a case in which the human driver of the AV proactively took over control of the vehicle from the autonomous agent (to prevent an accident) but was unable to rectify decisions made by the autonomous agent in time to prevent an accident. The disengagement report (i.e. error logs from the AV combined with post-mortem analysis performed by the manufacturer) logs the error as either "disengage for a recklessly behaving road user" or "incorrect behavior prediction." For example, a Waymo prototype vehicle was in autonomous mode at an intersection when a pedestrian started to cross the street. According to the accident report, the AV decided to yield to the pedestrian but did not stop. The test driver proactively took control of the car as a precaution. At the same time, there was a car in front of the AV that was also yielding to the pedestrian, and another vehicle to the rear in the adjacent lane that was making a lane change. In this complex scenario, the driver did not have many options other than to brake, and the rear vehicle collided with the back of the AV.

*Incident II: Anticipating AV behavior.* Example (2) in Figure 13.15 shows a case in which a Waymo prototype vehicle was running in autonomous mode and was hit by a manually controlled vehicle from the rear at an intersection. The disengagement report logs the cause as "disengage for a recklessly behaving road user." In this case, the AV had signaled a right turn and had started to decelerate for the turn. To gauge the traffic coming from the other side in order to make a safe turn, it came to a complete stop before it started moving again toward the intersection. The movement toward the intersection was required to allow the recognition system to analyze the scene and produce a movement plan for the car. The driver of the rear vehicle was confused and interpreted the movement to mean that the AV was continuing on its path (i.e. making the turn). The driver first stopped (as the AV stopped) and then started moving (as the AV started to move again). This resulted in a rear collision on the AV, as the driver behind could not anticipate the actions of the AV.

*Summary.* By law, both of those accidents were caused by the drivers in the non-AV; however, close inspection of the accident reports shows that the AV had a significant share of the responsibility. The above examples showcase poor AV decision-making that can eventually lead to accidents.

- Intersections represent complex scenarios in which the AV needs to analyze multiple traffic flows and make decisions in a constrained environment. Based on our analysis, we attribute the failures to the learning-based perception system, which did not infer in time the evolving environment dynamics from the onboard sensor systems (e.g. RADAR, LiDAR), leading the learning-based control system to make inadequate decisions.
- In both cases, drivers either voluntarily took or were forced to take control of the autonomous system in complex and dynamic traffic scenarios that gave them very little time to react and undo the AV's actions. Perception and reaction times are crucial in accident avoidance.
- Drivers of nearby non-AVs often cannot anticipate decisions made by AVs, which frequently also leads to accidents.

Using the limited publicly available information about the designs of AV systems (e.g. [33–36]), we have drawn our conclusions by analyzing human-entered textual logs that contain information about accidents and disengagements. Our method localizes failures to the learning, perception, and decision-and-control subsystems of an AV to reveal the causes of disengagements and accidents.

### 13.4.2  AV System Description and Data Collection

An AV is any vehicle that uses an autonomous driving system (ADS) technology capable of supporting and assisting a human driver in the tasks of (i) controlling[5] the main functions of steering and acceleration, and (ii) monitoring the surrounding environment (e.g. other vehicles, pedestrians, traffic signals, and road markings) [37]. The Society of Automotive Engineers (SAE) defines six levels of autonomy that are based on the extent to which the technology can support and assist in driving tasks [37]. The levels of autonomy go from 0 (no automation) to 5 (full, unrestricted automation). Levels 0–2 (e.g. anti-lock braking, cruise control)

---

5 Here, "control" incorporates both decision and control.

require a human driver to be responsible for monitoring the environment of the vehicle, with different levels of automation available to support vehicle control tasks. Levels 3–5 are thought of as truly automated driving systems in which the AV both monitors the environment and controls the vehicle. The subject of this study is Level 3 vehicles.

*AV disengagements.* Level 3 requires the presence (and attention) of a human driver to serve as a fallback when the autonomous system fails. A transfer of control from the autonomous system to the human driver following a failure is called *disengagement*. Disengagements can be initiated either manually by the driver or autonomously by the car. Manual disengagements initiated by the driver are cautionary (e.g. if one feels uncomfortable, or wants to adopt a proactive approach to prevent a potential accident). Automated disengagements are indicative of a design limitation of the AV.

*AV accidents.* An *accident* is an actual collision with other vehicles, pedestrians, or other objects. Note that not all disengagements lead to collisions. As we show later in this chapter, according to the data analyzed, most disengagements are handled safely by human operators, with only a small fraction leading to accidents. For example, in some reported collisions, the test driver initiated a manual disengagement before the collision (though it could be argued that what we are seeing here is an artifact of the AV safety-pilots training program [32]).

### 13.4.2.1 AV Hierarchical Control Structure

Manufacturers have not disclosed the architectures of their AVs. However, to identify multidimensional causes of AV disengagements/accidents, we built a hierarchical control structure for AVs by using the systems-theoretic hazard modeling and analysis abstraction Systems-Theoretic Process Analysis (STPA) [38]. Figure 13.16 shows an AV hierarchical control structure derived based on technical documentation [39], [40–43]. We assert that these information sources are representative and provide a conceptual view of AV systems that is sufficiently detailed to enable creation of an STPA model. We refer to this system as the "Autonomous Driving System" (ADS). The major components of the ADS are (i) "sensors" (e.g. GPS, RADAR, LiDAR, and cameras) that are responsible for collecting environment-related data, (ii) a "recognition/perception system" that uses sensor data to identify the objects and changes in the environment around the AV, (iii) a "planner and controller" system that is responsible for planning the next motion of the car based on the current parameters of the AV and the environment (e.g. speed, location, and other vehicles), and (iv) a "follower" system that signals the "actuators" to drive the vehicle along the path chosen by the "planner and controller."

STPA employs concepts from systems and control theories to model hierarchical control structures in which the components at each level of the hierarchy

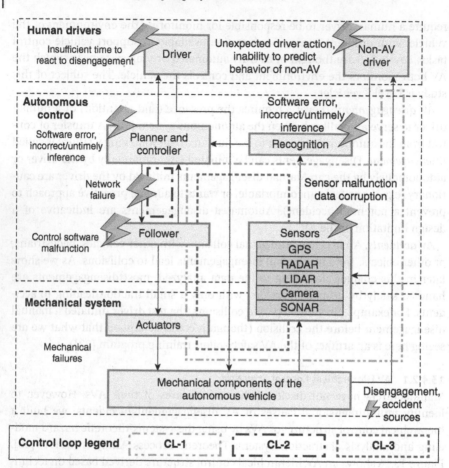

**Figure 13.16** Autonomous vehicle hierarchical control structure drawn based on [21]. Examples of control loops are highlighted as CL-1, CL-2, and CL-3 [3] / with permission from IEEE.

impose safety constraints on the activity of the levels below and communicate their conditions and behavior to the levels above them. Accidents and disengagements are complex, dynamic processes resulting from inadequate perception control and decision-making at different layers of the system control structure. Accidents and disengagements seen in the data were overlaid on this structure. In every control loop, the planner and controller system uses an algorithm to generate the control actions based on a model of the current state of the process that it is controlling. The control actions (e.g. "decelerate") taken by the planner and controller system (i.e. the ADS) change the state of the controlled process (e.g. mechanical components of the AV). The feedback message (e.g. the state of the traffic lights) sent back from the controlled process (e.g. the AV control software) updates the process model used (e.g. the mental model the driver has of the AV status) by the controller. Analysis of dependencies along those control loops allows for the identification of inadequate controls and the potential causes of unsafe control actions through examination of the operation of components and their interactions in each loop of the control structure. Any flaws or inadequacies in the algorithm, the process model, or the feedback used by a controller are considered potential causal factors leading to unsafe control actions and resultant disengagements/accidents.

Figure 13.16 highlights three control loops (CL-1, CL-2, and CL-3, indicated with different types of dashed lines) to illustrate details of the interactions among the driver (both AV and Non-AV), AV control, and AV hardware/software components. Our analysis couples that STPA approach with manufacturers' reports. The most complex control loop, CL-1, involves interaction among the *autonomous control* (including sensors, recognition system, planner, and controller), *mechanical system* (actuators and mechanical components of the vehicle), and *human drivers* (drivers of non-AVs). The Non-AV Driver module represents the AV system's ability to (i) collect the data on Non-AV driver behavior through the sensors, and (ii) provide information (e.g. on brake signals, turn indicators, or horn) to Non-AV drivers. Examples of failures in this control loop were discussed in the two case studies presented earlier.

### 13.4.2.2 Data Sources

California driving conditions are representative of urban situations, and the state DMV has a strong mandate to collect data on driving conditions and to make the data publicly available. California law requires manufacturers that operate and test AVs to file reports on disengagements (reported annually) and accidents (reported within ten business days of the incident) [32, 44]; these reports are eventually made public. The reports are available in two databases, as follows:

- *AV disengagement reports.* These reports contain aggregated information about fleet size, monthly autonomous miles traveled, and the number of disengagements observed. Each manufacturer provides its own data format, resulting in a fragmented set of data. Some manufacturers provide additional information, including timestamps, road type (e.g. urban streets, highway, freeway), weather conditions (e.g. sunny, raining, overcast), driver reaction times (time taken for the driver to disengage from autonomous mode), and other factors contributing to the disengagements. We use the additional data whenever they are available.
- *AV accident reports.* These reports contain timestamped information about the AV involved, the location of the accident, descriptions of other vehicles involved (e.g. class of vehicle, speed), and a human-written textual description of the incident and its severity.

Both datasets consisted of scanned documents containing both tabulated data and natural-language text. Unlike previous analyses [45, 46], which were based solely on the data provided, we focus on building an analysis workflow that processes substantive amounts of human-generated disengagement and accident reports by using NLP.

*Summary of datasets.* The CA DMV datasets analyzed cover a period of 26 months from 2014 to 2016 for 12 AV manufacturers (Bosch, Delphi Automotive, Google, Nissan, Mercedes-Benz, Tesla Motors, BMW, GMCruise, Ford, Honda, Uber, and Volkswagen). The datasets include data on 144 AVs that drove a cumulative 1 116 605 autonomous miles across distinct road types (31.7% on city streets, 29.26% on highways, 14.63% on interstates, 9.75% on freeways, and the remaining 14.6% on parking lots, on suburban roads, and on rural roads). Uber, BMW, Ford, and Honda reported too few disengagements for us to draw statistically significant conclusions, so are left out of the analysis here. At the time of the study, across all manufacturers, we observe a total of 5328 disengagements[6] and 42 accidents. Aggregating per car and per manufacturer, we observe an average of 262 autonomous miles driven per disengagement, and one accident event for every 127 disengagements. Also, we observe a significant skew in the number of autonomous miles driven (see Table 13.16). For example, the study shows that Waymo tested their AV prototypes more extensively than the other manufacturers (for over 1 000 000 miles, compared to 15 000 miles for the next highest testing manufacturer). This suggests that Waymo's AVs might perform better than those of its competitors because of the extensive testing of the ADS platform. Note that not all manufacturers provided all the data needed to compute the summary statistics; those omissions are indicated by dashes in Table 13.16.

### 13.4.3 Data-Analysis Workflow: Parsing, Filtering, Normalization, and NLP

Figure 13.14 illustrates the methodology (workflow) for converting raw disengagement and accident reports into a consolidated form that lends itself to further analysis. Below, we describe the key steps involved in Stages II and III of the workflow.

*Data normalization.* The CA DMV did not enforce any data format specification for the reports, leading to disparities (across manufacturers and across time) in the data schema and granularity of the information available through the reports. Hence, we needed to filter, parse, and normalize (labeled as (1) and (2) in Figure 13.14) the data into machine-encoded text to produce structured datasets

---

6 Two of the manufacturers (Bosch and GMCruise) reported all their disengagement data as planned tests. Our understanding, based on all the DMV reports, is that the tests were planned, but the disengagements occurred naturally. Together, the two manufacturers had 14 accidents during "tests."

**Table 13.16** Summary of fleet size, autonomous miles driven, and failure incidents across all manufacturers in CA DMV datasets.

| Manufacturer | 2015–2016 Report | | | | 2016–2017 Report | | | |
|---|---|---|---|---|---|---|---|---|
| | Cars | Miles | Disengagements | Accidents | Cars | Miles | Disengagements | Accidents |
| Mercedes-Benz | 2 | 1739.08 | 1024 | — | | 673.41 | 336 | — |
| Bosch | 2 | 935.1 | 625 | — | 3 | 983 | 1442 | — |
| Delphi | 2 | 16661 | 405 | 1 | 2 | 3090 | 167 | — |
| GM Cruise | — | 285.4 | 135 | — | — | 9729.8 | 149 | 14 |
| Nissan | 4 | 1485.4 | 106 | — | 3 | 4099 | 29 | 1 |
| Tesla | — | — | — | — | 5 | 550 | 182 | — |
| Volkswagen | 2 | 14946.11 | 260 | — | — | — | — | — |
| Waymo (Google) | 49 | 424332 | 341 | 9 | 70 | 635868 | 123 | 16 |
| Uber ATC | — | — | — | — | — | — | — | 1 |
| Honda | — | — | — | — | 0 | 0 | 0 | — |
| Ford | — | — | — | — | 2 | 590 | 3 | — |
| BMW | — | — | — | — | — | 638 | 1 | — |
| Total | 61 | 460384.1 | 2896 | 10 | 83 | 656221 | 2432 | 32 |

Dashes indicate the absence of data in the manufacturer's report [3] / with permission from IEEE.

that have uniform schema across manufacturers and time (i.e. across reports made by the same manufacturer at different times).

*Labeling and tagging of the reported disengagement and accident causes.* The pipeline uses an NLP-based technique (labeled as (3) in Figure 13.14) to map a given disengagement event to a corresponding fault tag and a failure category. First, several passes are made over the datasets to construct a "Failure Dictionary" that is used in a voting scheme (based on the maximum number of shared keywords) to assign a disengagement cause to a fault tag. In the event that this procedure is unsuccessful, the disengagement cause is marked with the "Unknown-T" tag. Next, an ontology (based on Figure 13.16) of failure categories on top of the tags (derived from [47]) is constructed. Specifically, we apply our understanding of the ADS system to select keywords and phrases that differentiate fault tags from each other. The tags are chosen to localize faults in the computing system (e.g. software and hardware systems) and in the machine learning algorithms/design (e.g. perception and control algorithms), thereby identifying potential targets for improving the safety and reliability of the AV. Table 13.17 provides examples of the raw log to tag and category mapping; Table 13.18 lists the fault tags used in this study. The following failure categories were considered: (i) faults in the design of the machine learning system responsible for "perception" tasks (dealing with data from sensors) and "planning and control" tasks (dealing with control of steering and acceleration); (ii) faults in the computing system (dealing with hardware and software problems); and (iii) an "Unknown-C" category consisting of tags we cannot classify into any of the above categories.

**Table 13.17** Sample of disengagement reports from the CA DMV datasets [3] / with permission from IEEE.

| Manufacturer | Raw disengagement report (Log) | Category | Tags |
| --- | --- | --- | --- |
| Nissan | **1/4/16 – 1:25 PM – Software module froze.** As a result driver safely disengaged and resumed manual control. – City and highway – Sunny/Dry | System | Software |
| Nissan | **5/25/16 – 11:20** AM – Leaf #1 (Alfa) – The AV **didn't see** the lead vehicle, driver safely disengaged and resumed manual control | ML/ Design | Recognition System |
| Waymo Volkswagen | May-**16** – Highway – Safe Operation – Disengage for a **recklessly behaving** road user **11/12/14 – 18:24:03** – Takeover-Request – **watchdog error** | ML/ Design System | Environment Computer System |

We use the "–" to denote field separators.
Note that log formats vary across manufacturers and time.
Bold-face text represents phrases analyzed by the NLP engine to categorize log lines.

**Table 13.18** Definition of fault tags and categories that are assigned to disengagements [3] / with permission from IEEE.

| Tag | Category | Definition |
|---|---|---|
| Environment | ML/Design | Sudden change in external factors (e.g. construction zones, emergency vehicles, accidents) |
| Computer System | System | Computer-system-related problem (e.g. processor overload) |
| Recognition System | ML/Design | Failure to recognize outside environment correctly |
| Planner | ML/Design | Planner failed to anticipate the other driver's behavior |
| Sensor | System | Sensor failed to localize in time |
| Network | System | Data rate too high to be handled by the network |
| Design Bug | ML/Design | AV was not designed to handle an unforeseen situation |
| Software | System | Software-related problems such as hang or crash |
| AV Controller | System <br> ML / Design | "System" when AV controller does not respond to commands <br><br> "ML/Design" when AV controller makes wrong decisions/predictions |
| Hang/Crash | System | Watchdog timer error |

*Digitization of the accident and disengagement reports.* The logs were available in the form of scanned images of digital documents (for disengagement reports) and handwritten reports (for accident reports). The first task was to preprocess and convert these scanned reports into a machine-encoded format. Examples of such machine-encoded disengagement reports are shown in Table 13.17. The analysis proceeded with optical character recognition (OCR; labeled as (1) in Figure 13.14), using Google Tesseract [48] on the scanned documents. In certain cases, where the Tesseract OCR failed (because of low-resolution scans or inability to recognize some table formats), we manually converted the documents to machine-encoded text.

## 13.4.4 Statistical Analysis of Failures in AVs

Traditional approaches to evaluating the resilience of a system [49] require the computation of *availability*, *reliability*, and *safety*. These metrics require information about operational periods of the AV (e.g. the active time of the vehicle). As this information is not available in the CA DMV datasets, we used the 5324 disengagements (across eight manufacturers) and 42 accidents as the basis for deriving statistics on fault classes, failure modes of AVs, and their evolution over time. These statistics allow us to draw conclusions and answer the following questions:

- *Question 1:* How do we assess the stability/maturity of the AV technology?
- *Question 2:* What is the primary cause of disengagements (and potentially accidents) observed in AVs?
- *Question 3:* Are manufacturers indeed building better and more reliable AVs over time?
- *Question 4:* What level of alertness[7] of the human driver of an AV guarantees safety?
- *Question 5:* How well do AVs compare with human drivers?

### 13.4.4.1 Analysis of AV Disengagement Reports

*Question 1: Assessment of AV technology.* Based on the available data, we computed the following metrics from the disengagement reports to assess AVs: (i) number of disengagements observed per autonomous mile driven (DPM, shown in Figure 13.17), and (ii) total number of disengagements observed (shown in Figure 13.18).

*Comparing DPMs across manufacturers.* Most manufacturers had a median DPM $\in [0.1, 0.01]$ $m^{-1}$ per car, with the 99th percentile DPM around 1 $m^{-1}$ (see Figure 13.17). There was a significant disparity (nearly 100×) between median DPMs across all manufacturers. This substantiates our initial hypothesis that the cumulative miles driven by a manufacturer (see Table 13.16) are indicative of

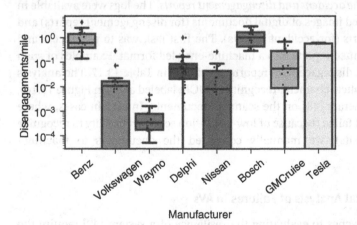

**Figure 13.17** Comparison of the distributions of DPM per car across manufacturers [3] / with permission from IEEE.

---

7 Measured here as reaction times of human drivers to disengagements.

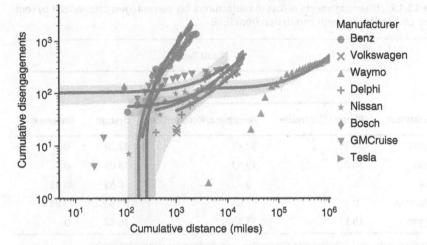

**Figure 13.18** Disengagements reported per cumulative miles driven across manufacturers represented in a log-log plot. Lines represent linear regression fits [3] / with permission from IEEE.

better performance. For example, Waymo (Google) did ~100× better than its competitors in terms of both the median and 99th percentile DPMs; at the same time, it was responsible for more than 90% of the total miles driven in the datasets.

*Maturity of AV technology.* Figure 13.18 demonstrates a strong linear correlation (based on the linear regression fits) between the number of disengagements observed and the number of cumulative autonomous miles driven. We expect that in an ideal case, mature AV technology will show a decrease in DPM (i.e. the slopes of the lines in Figure 13.18) that asymptotically reaches toward a horizontal line (or close to it, i.e. zero DPM or a very low DPM). The reason is that the data collected from the planned testing of AVs validate the computing system (e.g. by identifying software bugs) and train the machine learning algorithms that monitor the environment and control the steering and acceleration of the AV. Eventually, that enables the AVs to handle more fault scenarios, thus contributing to a decreasing DPM. Within the 2014–2016 data we examined, we found that to be true for most manufacturers to varying degrees, except for Volkswagen, Bosch, and GM Cruise. An important conclusion is that despite its million miles driven, Waymo was still not quite approaching the target asymptote. This indicates that Waymo and other manufacturers were still in the "burn-in" phase during the period covered by our study.

*Question 2: Causes of AV disengagements.* We present a categorization of the sources of faults that cause disengagements from two different perspectives: (i) cause of occurrence, and (ii) modality of occurrence.

*Machine-learning-related faults.* First, we consider disengagements by *cause of occurrence*, i.e. categorization of the cause of a disengagement. In the following,

**Table 13.19** Disengagements across manufacturers (as percentages) categorized by root failure categories [3] / with permission from IEEE.

| | Fault Type | | | |
|---|---|---|---|---|
| | **ML/Design** | | | |
| **Manufacturer** | **Planner/Controller** | **Perception/Recognition** | **System** | **Unknown-C** |
| Delphi | 37.59 | 50.17 | 12.24 | 0 |
| Nissan | 36.3 | 49.63 | 14.07 | 0 |
| Tesla | 0 | 0 | 1.65 | 98.35 |
| Volkswagen | 0 | 3.08 | 83.08 | 13.85 |
| Waymo | 10.13 | 53.45 | 36.42 | 0 |

ML/Design is divided into Planner/Controller- and Perception-related problems.

we ignore the numbers for Tesla, as most of their categorical labels are marked "Unknown-C." Machine-learning-related faults, mainly ones pertaining to the perception system (e.g. improper detection of traffic lights, lane markings, holes, and bumps), were the dominant cause of disengagements across most manufacturers. They account for ~44% of all reported disengagements (see Table 13.19).[8] The second major contributor to reported disengagements was the machine learning related to the control and decision framework (e.g. improper motion planning), which accounted for ~20% of the total disengagements. The computing system, i.e. hardware issues (e.g. problems with the sensor and processor) and software issues (e.g. hangs, crashes, bugs), accounted for ~33.6% of the total disengagements reported. Further, we observe that the perception-based machine learning faults were responsible for DPM measurements in the upper three quartiles. Therefore, we conclude that the faults in the perception system were directly responsible for higher DPMs across manufacturers.

*Comparing Waymo to others using fault categorization.* As stated earlier, we observed that AV prototypes from Waymo performed significantly better than those of its competitors. Our fault categorization allows us to speculate on reasons for this behavior. We observed (see Figure 13.19) that Waymo reported significantly higher percentages of disengagements related to system faults (i.e. software or hardware issues) than to machine learning/design issues, unlike other manufacturers.

---

8 We consider external fault sources such as undetected construction zones, cyclists, pedestrians, emergency vehicles, and weather phenomena (e.g. rain or sun glare) as perception-related, machine-learning-related disengagements, as they deal with interpretation of the environment from sensor data.

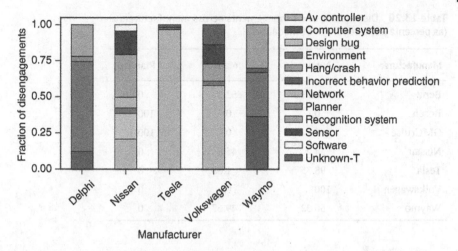

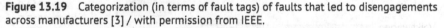

**Figure 13.19** Categorization (in terms of fault tags) of faults that led to disengagements across manufacturers [3] / with permission from IEEE.

Extensive on-road testing (over 1 060 200 cumulative autonomous miles, which was ~70× more than any other manufacturer at the time period covered by this study) allowed Waymo to eliminate many fault scenarios relating to perception and control. Even though Waymo had resolved key control and decision-making issues in the machine learning system, perception and system issues still dominated as of the end of the 2014–2016 period covered by the data. We observe that most accidents were the result of poor decisions made by the machine learning system in complex traffic scenarios, as shown in the two real examples of AV-related accidents discussed earlier. Faults in the perception systems often propagated to the decision system, leading to complex failure scenarios.

Last, we consider disengagements by *modality of occurrence*, i.e. whether the disengagement was initiated automatically by the AV, or manually by the driver, or as part of a planned fault injection campaign. Table 13.20 lists the distribution of these modalities across multiple manufacturers. We observe that an average of 48% of all disengagements were initiated automatically by the system. Note that this measurement is biased by manufacturers like Mercedes-Benz and Waymo that reported a larger number of disengagements.

*Question 3: Dynamics of AV disengagements.* As suggested by Figure 13.18, we expect that AV technology (including perception, decision, and control) gets tuned over time, resulting in decreasing DPMs. This hypothesis is true to varying degrees across manufacturers. In this section, we further assess its validity. We look at (i) the temporal dynamics of DPMs (i.e. does DPM decrease with time?), and (ii) the dynamics of DPM with the cumulative number of miles driven (i.e. does DPM decrease with more extensive testing?).

**Table 13.20** Distribution of disengagements across manufacturers
(as percentages) categorized by modality [3].

| Manufacturer | Automatic | Manual | Planned |
|---|---|---|---|
| Benz | 47.11 | 52.89 | 0 |
| Bosch | 0 | 0 | 100 |
| GMCruise | 0 | 0 | 100 |
| Nissan | 54.2 | 45.8 | 0 |
| Tesla | 98.35 | 1.65 | 0 |
| Volkswagen | 100 | 0 | 0 |
| Waymo | 50.32 | 49.67 | 0 |

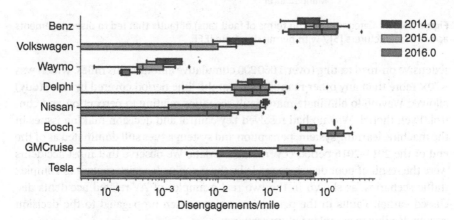

**Figure 13.20** Evolution of DPMs per car with cumulative miles driven
(all manufacturers) [3] / with permission from IEEE.

*Temporal trends.* Figure 13.20 illustrates the temporal dynamics of the distribution of DPM per car across manufacturers aggregated per year. First, we
observe that there was a distinct decreasing trend for the median DPM across
most manufacturers. Some manufacturers, like Bosch, that showed an increase
in median DPM per year claimed that their disengagements resulted from
planned fault injection experiments (see Table 13.20). In fact, some manufacturers showed a decrease of as much as 10× in median DPM across the three-year
analysis window. Second, we see a significant increase in the variance of
the DPM across cars over the period of interest. This increase suggests that the
median performance improved over time. However, the worst-case performance
did not, since the variance relative to the median was large. In fact, for some

manufacturers, like Delphi, the 75th percentile DPM across years changed by less than 50%. Waymo was an exception to this trend, demonstrating a nearly 8× decrease in median DPM with a significant decrease in variance across the three years of measurement. Recall from Question 1 that Waymo nevertheless did not approach the asymptote.

*Trend with cumulative miles driven.* While the temporal trends are important, an alternative approach is to look at disengagements per mile (DPMs) as a function of miles driven. Since manufacturers did not all drive the same number of autonomous miles each month, this measure enables a more equitable analysis of AVs across manufacturers. Aggregating across all manufacturers, we observe that there was a strong negative correlation between DPM and cumulative miles driven (as shown in Figure 13.21). We observe that the log(DPM) and log (cumulative autonomous miles) are correlated with a Pearson coefficient of −0.87 (at a p-value of $7 \times 10^{-56}$). Figure 13.22 shows this relationship across different manufacturers, with linear regression fit lines describing the trends mentioned above. It suggests that the manufacturers were continuously improving their ADSes, with some manufacturers making more headway than others (as represented by the slope of the fitted lines). Further, we observe that manufacturers with larger DPMs seemed to make more significant improvements over the same number of miles driven; this suggests that some of the faults/problems fixed as a result of the testing represented the "low-hanging fruit."

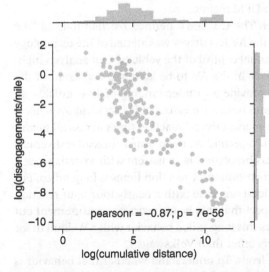

**Figure 13.21** Linear statistical relationship between DPM per car and the cumulative number of autonomous miles [3] / with permission from IEEE.

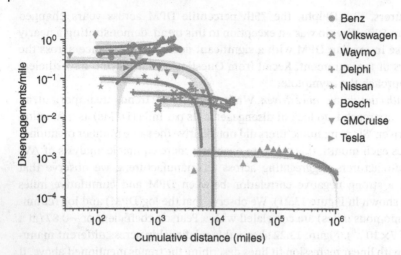

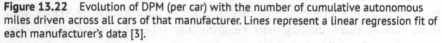

**Figure 13.22** Evolution of DPM (per car) with the number of cumulative autonomous miles driven across all cars of that manufacturer. Lines represent a linear regression fit of each manufacturer's data [3].

While the temporal trends may be more indicative of how actual users would drive these cars (i.e. the AVs will be used with a mix of idle and driving times), the trends with cumulative miles provide a more robust alternative for comparisons, wherein the miles driven are the only basis for comparison. Both show a decreasing trend. The first shows an increasing variance; neither shows that any of the cars approached a very low or zero DPM regime.

*Question 4: Driver alertness level.* The CA DMV defined *reaction time* as "the period of time elapsed from when the AV test driver was alerted of the technology failure, and the driver assumed manual control of the vehicle." Our analysis highlights the need for the human driver in the AV to be alert and cognizant of the environment. The reaction times provide an understanding of how quickly an individual would react to a fault, and hence are essential for accident avoidance. Figure 13.23 gives the distribution of test drivers' reaction times across all manufacturers. We observe an average 0.85-second reaction time across all test vehicle drivers and all manufacturers. This observation is consistent with a similar observation made in [50]. Further, the distribution of reaction times is long-tailed. For example, Volkswagen reported at least one case with a nearly four-hour reaction time for a disengagement; we suspect that this is an incorrect measurement but cannot confirm. Figure 13.24 shows this long-tailed behavior with a Weibull fit for the reported data for manufacturers other than Volkswagen.

*Comparison to human alertness levels.* To understand whether that behavior is indeed representative of human alertness levels when driving, we compared those results with those presented in [51] for non-AVs, which found the reaction time

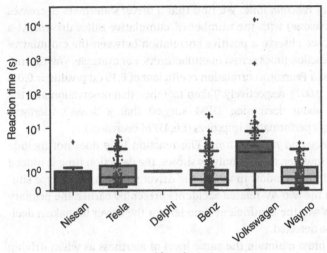

**Figure 13.23** Distribution of reaction times for drivers following disengagement across all manufacturers [3] / with permission from IEEE.

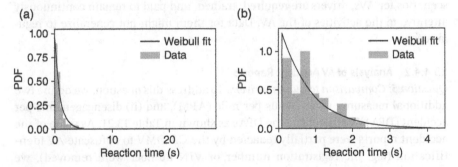

**Figure 13.24** Distribution of reaction times for: (a) Mercedes-Benz and (b) Waymo fleets [3] / with permission from IEEE.

for braking in test vehicles to be 0.82 seconds. This observation is consistent with our study. Further, [51] reports that a driver's ownership of a vehicle (i.e. it is his or her own property) increased reaction time by approximately 0.27 seconds. Hence, we assume 1.09 seconds to be the average time for a human driver in a non-AV to respond to any situation on the road. The observation implies that semi-AVs (which are the most commonly deployed AVs on public streets) would require continuous human supervision and alertness much as human-controlled non-AVs do. Echoing the results of Question 3, that in turn suggests that the technology may not be mature enough to allow human drivers to be engaged in other activities, contrary to what has been advertised.

*Temporal behavior of reaction time.* We find that a driver's alertness decreases (i.e. reaction time increases) with the number of cumulative miles driven. At a 99% confidence level, we observe a positive correlation between the cumulative miles driven and the reaction times across manufacturers. For example, Waymo and Mercedes-Benz showed a Pearson's correlation coefficient of 0.19 (at p-value = 0.01) and 0.11 (at p-value = 0.007), respectively. Taken together, that observation and the previous observation about decreasing DPM suggest that a driver's alertness decreases as the system's performance improves (i.e. DPM decreases).

*Fault detection latency and reaction time.* The reaction time does not include fault detection time. However, as our analysis shows, the detection time is indeed part of the end-to-end time window in which the driver reacts to an adverse situation. For example, in the two AV-related accidents presented earlier, the primary cause of the accidents was the insufficient time left for the driver to make a decision after the fault was detected.

The drivers of AVs must maintain the same level of alertness as when driving non-AVs. This suggests that the small size of the overall action window (detection time + reaction time) can make reaction-time-based accidents a frequent failure mode with the widespread deployment of AVs. We also note that in planned test scenarios for AVs, drivers are required, trained, and paid to remain continuously attentive to the activities of the AV. Data for them might not generalize to regular users.

### 13.4.4.2 Analysis of AV Accident Reports

*Question 5: Comparison to human drivers.* To address this question, we define two additional measures: (i) accidents per mile (APM), and (ii) disengagements per accident (DPA). We calculated the DPAs as shown in Table 13.21. As some of the accident reports were partially redacted by the CA DMV to obfuscate AV identification (e.g. the registration number or VIN number were removed), we

**Table 13.21** Summary of accidents reported by manufacturers [3] / with permission from IEEE.

| Manufacturer | Accidents | Fraction of Total | DPA |
| --- | --- | --- | --- |
| Waymo | 25 | 59.52 | 18 |
| Delphi | 1 | 2.38 | 572 |
| Nissan | 1 | 2.38 | 135 |
| GMCruise | 14 | 33.33 | 20 |
| Uber ATC | 1 | 2.38 | – |

DPA = Disengagements per accident.

**Table 13.22** Reliability of AVs compared to human drivers [3] / with permission from IEEE.

| Manufacturer | Median DPM (mile$^{-1}$) | Median APM (mile$^{-1}$) | Rel. to HAPM |
|---|---|---|---|
| Mercedes-Benz | 0.565 | — | — |
| Volkswagen | 0.0181 | — | — |
| Waymo | 0.000745 | $4.140 \times 10^{-5}$ | 20.7× |
| Delphi | 0.0263 | $4.599 \times 10^{-5}$ | 22.99× |
| Nissan | 0.0413 | $3.057 \times 10^{-4}$ | 15.285× |
| Bosch | 0.811 | — | — |
| GMCruise | 0.177 | $8.843 \times 10^{-3}$ | 4421.5× |
| Tesla | 0.250 | — | — |

HAPM – Human APM.
Human APM = $2 \times 10^{-6}$ mile$^{-1}$ [37, 38].
Column 4 = AV APM/Human APM.

cannot compute the APM per vehicle directly. We instead compute APM using the equation APM = DPM/DPA. Even though the number of accidents is small compared to the number of disengagements, we use the approach in [52] to test the statistical significance of our results. Our calculations for two of the four manufacturers (i.e. Waymo and GMCruise) were made at > 90% significance.

*Comparison of APMs across manufacturers.* We observed that there is great variability (~100×) in APMs across manufacturers (see Table 13.22). For example, Waymo was responsible for 59.52% of accidents reported (see Table 13.21) but had the lowest DPM ($7.45 \times 10^{-4}$), the lowest DPA (18), and the lowest APM ($4.14 \times 10^{-5}$). In contrast, GM Cruise had a similar DPA (20) but performed 238× worse in terms of DPM, and 214× worse in terms of APM, compared to Waymo (see Table 13.22). This indicates that there was significant variability across manufacturers in classifying the severity of disengagements, which again indicates the immaturity of the AV technology at the time addressed by the study. Also, the observed APM metric variability can be partially attributed to test drivers' proactive disengagement of the ADS (i.e. manual disengagement) to prevent accidents. We compared the accident rate of AVs with that of manual vehicles using data from [53, 54], which report that one accident is expected every 500 000 miles (i.e. APM = $2 \times 10^{-6}$). We found that compared to human drivers, AVs performed 15–22× worse (see Table 13.22) in terms of APM.[9]

---

9 Note that [53, 54] report only crashes on highways and freeways. However, AV manufacturers are required to report any crash on all types of roads.

When they are calculated using first principles (i.e. not using DPA as done before), for vehicles that can be identified in the accident reports, we observe a strong positive correlation between the number of accidents observed per mile and the number of autonomous miles driven (with a Pearson correlation coefficient of 0.98 at p-value < 0.01). Comparing that number to the trends in the DPM seen in Figure 13.21, we see that there is a much stronger correlation of the APM with cumulative miles. This behavior might be indicative of the manufacturers' priority on fixing problems in their ADSes (i.e. they identified problems related to accidents and fixed them quickly).

The foregoing analysis shows that for the same number of miles driven, for manufacturers that reported accidents, human-driven cars (non-AVs) were 15–4000× less likely than AVs to have an accident.

*Collision speeds and locations.* All the accidents reported in the datasets occurred at low speeds and in the vicinity of intersections on urban streets. Figure 13.25 shows that more than 80% of the accidents occurred when the relative speed of the colliding vehicles was less than 10 mph. In most of the cases in which the non-AV vehicle was determined to be at fault, the underlying cause can be attributed to the failure of the vehicle's driver to anticipate AV behavior. This observation points to the need for better understanding of the driving interactions and behaviors that

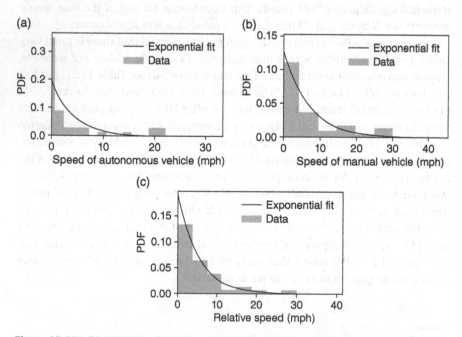

**Figure 13.25** Distribution of vehicular speeds for all reported accidents: (a) speed of AV, (b) speed of MV, and (c) relative speed.

drivers expect from other on-road vehicles. Most of the accidents were minor (either rear-end or side-swipe collisions), and no serious injuries were reported.

Our data show that good situational awareness needs to be provided by ADSes (in particular, the machine learning algorithms) to preemptively avoid accidents in a timely fashion.

### 13.4.5 Discussion

*Comparison with other safety-critical autonomous systems.* Airplanes [55] and surgical robots [56] are safety-critical semiautonomous systems that have seen ubiquitous deployment, as well as a significant body of work characterizing and improving their resilience. We will now compare AVs to both of those systems in terms of the accidents per mission (APMi), to gauge the maturity of the AVs at the time period covered by the study vis-à-vis these systems. We define a *mission* as the continuous operation of the system of interest from the time of activity commencement to the end of the activity. For airplanes and cars, a mission is equivalent to one departure (i.e. trip), and for the surgical robot, a mission is equivalent to a surgical procedure.

We use data presented in [57] (9.8 accidents per 100 000 departures for airplanes) and [58] (1043 accidents per 100 000 procedures for surgical robots) as the baseline for comparison. We estimated the APMi of an AV by using data pertaining to the average length of a vehicle ride on U.S. public roads as presented in [59], a median of 10 miles per trip.

Using the APMi metrics in Table 13.23, our analysis shows that AVs did surprisingly well per mission. Compared to airplanes (which utilize sophisticated resilience models and techniques), AVs were merely 4.22× worse, and AVs were 2.5× better than surgical robots (see Table 13.23). However, if all cars are replaced by AVs in the future, AVs will make ~96 billion trips per year [60], compared to the 9.6 million trips of airlines. This means that AVs will make 10 000× more trips

**Table 13.23** Reliability of AVs compared to other safety-critical autonomous systems [3] / with permission from IEEE.

| Manufacturer | APMi | Aviation Industry APMi/Airline APM [41] | Surgical Robotics APM/SR APM [42] |
| --- | --- | --- | --- |
| Waymo | $4.140 \times 10^{-4}$ | 4.22 | 0.0398 |
| Delphi | $4.599 \times 10^{-4}$ | 4.69 | 0.0442 |
| Nissan | $3.057 \times 10^{-3}$ | 31.19 | 0.293 |
| GMCruise | $8.843 \times 10^{-2}$ | 902.34 | 8.502 |

APMi = Accidents per mission for an AV.
Airline APM = $9.8 \times 10^{-5}$.
Surgical Robot (SR) APM = $1.04 \times 10^{-2}$.

than airlines, leading to a higher number of accidents per year than for airplanes. Further, the average length of a mission in terms of time and miles covered is significantly different for airplanes and AVs. Hence a holistic comparison across these systems would need to consider operational time per mission and also account for competing failures across concurrent deployments of these systems.

*Traditional reliability metrics.* While we have made an approximate comparison above, the more traditional and accurate method for comparing the resilience of AVs with that of airplanes (which are also highly automated systems) is via operational hours to failure. That metric, however, is unavailable for cars, since we do not have information about the idle time for these vehicles or their distribution. We propose an alternative metric based on the number of miles driven to disengagement/accident. This metric will be available across transportation systems.

To make it possible to obtain this measure directly, there needs to be a small change in the data collection by the DMV: manufacturers and the DMV should collect data on miles between disengagements per vehicle to enable the computation of the metrics.

## 13.4.6 Limitations of this Study

This empirical study is subject to vagaries arising from heterogeneous data collection systems (e.g. the inclusion or exclusion of data points, or the disparate information content across data formats), hampering our ability to draw generalized conclusions. Dealing with such issues is not uncommon in analyzing system reliability/resilience from multiple data sources. It is important that new studies across other datasets be continually conducted so that robust conclusions can become available. Some of the limitations of our study are outlined below.

"Internal validity" implies that there are no systematic errors and biases. We studied the datasets available from 12 different manufacturers and reported only generalized trends in order to eliminate any biases and micro-observations (observations with low statistical significance) that might be artifacts of bad logging or biases from the manufacturers in reporting the disengagements and accidents. For example:

- *Data underreporting*: To obtain an AV testing permit, companies are legally required to catalogue and submit to the DMV reports of all disengagements and accidents that (i) pertained to technology failures and safe operation of the AVs, and (ii) required the AV test driver to disengage the autonomous mode and take immediate manual control of the vehicle. The interpretation of "safe" operation and technology "failure" can vary across manufacturers, leading to underreporting. Further, regulatory oversight and enforcement of regulations are difficult and may result in underreporting. Given the available data, we cannot accurately estimate the scale of underreporting.
- *Not all miles are equivalent*: One manufacturer may hold the tests of its AVs in more challenging environments than others do, e.g. at night or during bad

weather. Not all manufacturers report environmental conditions during tests. Where available, we report the testing conditions and disengagements caused by environmental factors (see "Environment" in Figure 13.19).

- *Validity of fault tags and failure categories*: There is no consistent data format for the provided disengagement/accident reports across manufacturers. Our NLP framework for tagging and categorization may lead to systematic errors; therefore, the dictionaries were verified manually by the study team to ensure their correctness. We explicitly labeled data points as "Unknown-T/C" when there was uncertainty in the tags and categories given by the NLP framework.

"External validity" concerns the extent to which a study can be generalized to other systems or datasets. To the best of our knowledge, the CA DMV datasets may be the only publicly available datasets pertaining to AV failures. Until we work with manufacturers on proprietary data (which might not be disclosed publicly) or with other datasets, we cannot comment on the general external validity of the techniques presented here.

### 13.4.7 Related Work

The majority of the earlier research into AV systems focused on the functionality of vehicle guidance systems. Numerous demonstrations of end-to-end computing systems for AVs have been done (e.g. [18–23, 61, 62]). The accepted practice for vehicular safety, based on the ISO 26262 safety standard [63], is to consider human drivers to have ultimate responsibility for safety. That is the basis for most AV testing programs on public roads, which require a human driver to be in the vehicle to monitor the vehicle. This driver is expected to intervene if a system failure occurs; indeed, several such incidents are recorded in the CA DMV datasets. In such a scenario, safety considerations for the AV are driven by (i) the AV's ability to alert the driver about a failure, (ii) the driver's ability to recognize the abilities of the AV and the limits of the system, (iii) the AV's ability to anticipate the behavior of other road users who might not always conform to the rules, and (iv) the other road users' ability to anticipate the behavior of the AV [64, 65]. How this will be handled in AVs remains an open question [66]. Safety is also emphasized in several publications, including [67, 68]. Waymo has published a report on the safety precautions considered for their AVs [41].[10]

A model for estimating the number of miles AVs must be driven to demonstrate their reliability with statistical confidence is presented in [52]. In [46, 50], the authors provide summary statistics (e.g. driver reaction times and AV speed in accident scenarios) from tabulated data in the DMV datasets. Our approach uses

---

10 For their trained drivers, Waymo seems to suggest there was one accident for 2.3 million miles; we cannot substantiate that.

an STPA-based ontology and NLP techniques to parse a significant amount of unstructured data presented as natural text.

Other related work has focused on the safety and reliability of AVs as they apply to legal (e.g. [26, 27]) and regulatory barriers (e.g. [28–31]) for AV deployment and implementation. Security and privacy measures to encompass system-level attacks and failures of AVs have also been studied [69, 70].

## 13.4.8 Insights and Conclusions

While the methodology of data analytics is based on sound statistical analysis, the process of getting data from a large system and converting those data into a meaningful summary of a system's reliability and availability and an error characterization remains more of an art than a science. Chapter 12 outlined useful techniques in as generic a way as possible, so they can be applied to other systems at scale. The examples and detailed case studies in this chapter involve a step-by-step approach that serves to illustrate the underlying techniques and to convey a sound understanding of the systems analyzed. The extraction of system reliability parameters and failure characteristics for the Blue Waters supercomputer also provides a deeper understanding of the resilience of supercomputers. In this context, the early-stage reliability problems of the Frontier exascale supercomputer [71] demonstrate that reliability will remain a core issue in future large-scale systems. Application to other systems, however, will continue to require some adaptation and customization of the methodology described here.

AV technologies have seen significant improvement since the time period covered by our study. For example, Waymo surpassed a total of 10 million miles in 2020 [72], with Cruise not far behind. The DPMs of the leaders have improved significantly. For example, Waymo claims a median DPM of 0.00003 in 2020, a 30× improvement compared to the median DPM in our study. There has also been an increase in autonomous driving participants from companies around the globe, with manufacturers from East Asian countries like China gaining significant momentum [73]. However, despite the stellar improvements over the past few years, fatal incidents involving AVs [74] are still making headlines. According to the latest statistics from the U.S. National Highway Traffic Safety Administration (NHTSA), in 2021, automakers reported 500 crashes involving advanced driver assistance systems; Tesla, which is generally viewed as being at the forefront of self-driving technologies, topped the chart with 273 accidents in that period. Leading manufacturers continue to "reclassify" [75] their self-driving technologies to conform more realistically with the actual performance and safety of the technologies. For example, instead of being classified as fully autonomous (Level 4), most AVs have been reclassified as Level 2.5, or Level 3 at best [76]. While leading companies like Cruise and Waymo have reached key milestones by launching their AVs to the general public as ride-sharing services [77, 78], they operate in relatively confined geographic locations at times when traffic is limited [79]. Building a fully AV that can operate in a wide range of locations and conditions remains a significant reliability and safety challenge. In particular, the challenges related to fully AVs (Levels 4 and 5, currently under development) and today's semi-AVs are often underestimated. We believe the following concerns require the attention of reliability and safety researchers and practitioners. While the term "autonomous vehicle" makes the reader imagine cars driving independent of human input, this is not yet the reality with safety being a significant concern. For example, Tesla states that their current "Autopilot, Enhanced Autopilot and Full Self-Driving Capability" require active human supervision and "do not make the vehicle autonomous" [80].

- There is ongoing research on the verification and validation of the safety properties of individual system components (e.g. the control, communication, and mechanical system components) using the STAMP framework [67]. However, this study shows the importance of using rigorous theoretical models (like STPA models) for evaluating AV technologies.
- The machine learning systems responsible for perception and control need further research and assessment under fault conditions via stochastic modeling and fault injection to augment data collection.
- Going forward, there is a strong possibility that both AVs and semi-AVs will coexist with non-AVs (with human drivers completely in charge) within several years. Hence, the urgency of more independent studies driven by data and models of the kind reported here needs to be emphasized.

# References

1 Di Martino, C., Kalbarczyk, Z., Iyer, R.K. et al. (2014). Characterization of operational failures from a business data processing SaaS platform. In: *Companion Proceedings of the 36th International Conference on Software Engineering*, Hyderabad, India (31 May–7 June 2014), 195–204. New York, NY, USA: Association for Computing Machinery.

2 Di Martino, C., Kalbarczyk, Z., Iyer, R.K. et al. (2014). Lessons learned from the analysis of system failures at petascale: the case of Blue Waters. In: *Proceedings of the 2014 44th Annual IEEE/IFIP International Conference on Dependable Systems and Networks*, Atlanta, GA, USA (23–26 June 2014), 610–621. IEEE.

3 Banerjee, S.S., Jha, S., Cyriac, J. et al. (2018). Hands off the wheel in autonomous vehicles?: a systems perspective on over a million miles of field data. In: *Proceedings of the 2018 48th Annual IEEE/IFIP International Conference on Dependable Systems and Networks*, Luxembourg, Luxembourg (25–28 June 2018), 586–597. IEEE.

**4** Di Martino, C. (2013). One size does not fit all: clustering supercomputer failures using a multiple time window approach. In: *Proceedings of the 28th International Supercomputing Conference*, Leipzig, Germany (16–20 June 2013), *Lecture Notes in Computer Science*, vol. 7905 (ed. J.M. Kunkel, T. Ludwig, and H.W. Meuer), 302–316. Berlin and Heidelberg, Germany: Springer.

**5** Payne, R. (2022). SQL best practices. *Database Journal* (20 December). https://www.databasejournal.com/features/sql-best-practices/.

**6** Lee, Y.-L., Barkey, M.E., and Kang, H.-T. (2012). *Metal Fatigue Analysis Handbook: Practical Problem-Solving Techniques for Computer-Aided Engineering*. Amsterdam, The Netherlands: Elsevier (Butterworth-Heinemann).

**7** Lyu, M.R. (ed.) (1996). *Handbook of Software Reliability Engineering*. Hightstown, NJ, USA: McGraw-Hill.

**8** Jin, G., Song, L., Shi, X. et al. (2012). Understanding and detecting real-world performance bugs. In: *Proceedings of the 33rd ACM SIGPLAN Conference on Programming Language Design and Implementation*, Beijing, China (11–16 June 2012), 77–88. New York, NY, USA: Association for Computing Machinery.

**9** Advanced Micro Devices, Inc. (2016). *BIOS and Kernel Developer's Guide (BKDG) for AMD Family 16h Models 30h-3Fh Processors*. 52740 Rev. 3.06 (18 March). https://www.amd.com/system/files/TechDocs/52740_16h_Models_30h-3Fh_BKDG.pdf (accessed 1 June 2022).

**10** Dell, T.J. (1997). *A White Paper on the Benefits of Chipkill-Correct ECC for PC Server Main Memory*. IBM Microelectronics Division.

**11** Karo, M., Lagerstrom, R., Kohnke, M. et al. (2006). The application level placement scheduler. In: *CUG 2006 Final Program and Proceedings*, Lugano, Switzerland (8–11 May 2006). Cray User Group, Inc. https://cug.org/5-publications/proceedings_attendee_lists/2006CD/S06_Proceedings/pages/Authors/Karo-4C/Karo_alps_paper.pdf (accessed 1 June 2022).

**12** Adaptive Computing, Inc (2022). Moab HPC Suite. https://adaptivecomputing.com/moab-hpc-suite/ (accessed 11 September 2022).

**13** Schroeder, B. and Gibson, G.A. (2010). A large-scale study of failures in high-performance computing systems. *IEEE Transactions on Dependable and Secure Computing* 7 (4): 337–350.

**14** Sridharan, V., Stearley, J., DeBardeleben, N. et al. (2013). Feng shui of supercomputer memory: positional effects in DRAM and SRAM faults. In: *Proceedings of the International Conference on High Performance Computing, Networking, Storage and Analysis*, Denver, CO, USA (17–22 November 2013), 22:1–22:11. New York, NY, USA: Association for Computing Machinery https://doi.org/10.1145/2503210.2503257.

**15** Schroeder, B., Pinheiro, E., and Weber, W.-D. (2009). DRAM errors in the wild: a large-scale field study. *ACM SIGMETRICS Performance Evaluation Review* 37 (1): 193–204.

**16** Schroeder, B. and Gibson, G.A. (2007). Disk failures in the real world: What does an MTTF of 1,000,000 hours mean to you? In: *Proceedings of the 5th USENIX Conference on File and Storage Technologies*, San Jose, CA, USA (13–16 February 2007). USENIX https://www.usenix.org/legacy/events/fast07/tech/.

**17** Gerla, M., Lee, E.-K., Pau, G. et al. (2014). Internet of vehicles: From intelligent grid to autonomous cars and vehicular clouds. In: *Proceedings of the 2014 IEEE World Forum on Internet of Things*, Seoul, Korea (6–8 March 2014), 241–246. IEEE.

**18** Ozguner, U., Stiller, C., and Redmill, K. (2007). Systems for safety and autonomous behavior in cars: the DARPA grand challenge experience. *Proceedings of the IEEE* 95 (2): 397–412.

**19** Buehler, M., Iagnemma, K., and Singh, S. (2008). Special Issue on the 2007 DARPA Urban Challenge, Part I. *Journal of Field Robotics* 25 (8): 423–566.

**20** Urmson, C., Anhalt, J., Bagnell, D. et al. (2008). Autonomous driving in urban environments: boss and the urban challenge. *Journal of Field Robotics* 25 (8): 425–466.

**21** Chatham, A. (2013). Google's self-driving cars: the technology, capabilities & challenges. In: *Proceedings of the 2013 Embedded Linux Conference*, San Francisco, CA, USA (20–24 February 2013), 20–24. The Linux Foundation.

**22** Urmson, C. (2015). Progress in self-driving vehicles. In: *Frontiers of Engineering: Reports on Leading-Edge Engineering from the 2014 Symposium*, 5–9. Washington, DC, USA: The National Academies Press.

**23** Paden, B., Čáp, M., Yong, S.Z. et al. (2016). A survey of motion planning and control techniques for self-driving urban vehicles. *IEEE Transactions on Intelligent Vehicles* 1 (1): 33–55.

**24** Payre, W., Cestac, J., and Delhomme, P. (2014). Intention to use a fully automated car: attitudes and *a priori* acceptability. *Transportation Research Part F: Traffic Psychology and Behaviour* 27 (Part B): 252–263.

**25** Shladover, S.E., Su, D., and Lu, X.-Y. (2012). Impacts of cooperative adaptive cruise control on freeway traffic flow. *Transportation Research Record: Journal of the Transportation Research Board* 2324 (1): 63–70.

**26** Marchant, G.E. and Lindor, R.A. (2012). The coming collision between autonomous vehicles and the liability system. *Santa Clara Law Review* 52 (4): 1321–1340.

**27** Parent, M., Tona, P., Csepinszky, A., et al. (2013). Legal issues and certification of the fully automated vehicles: best practices and lessons learned. *CityMobil2 Report*. D26.1.

**28** Anderson, J.M., Kalra, N., Stanley, K.D. et al. (2016). Autonomous vehicle technology: a guide for policymakers. *RAND Corporation research report RR-443-2-RC*.

**29** Fagnant, D.J. and Kockelman, K. (2015). Preparing a nation for autonomous vehicles: opportunities, barriers and policy recommendations. *Transportation Research Part A: Policy and Practice* 77: 167–181.

**30** Fraade-Blanar, L. and Kalra, N. (2017). Autonomous vehicles and federal safety standards: an exemption to the rule? *RAND Corporation perspective PE-258-RC*.

**31** Kalra, N. and Groves, D.G. (2017). The enemy of good: estimating the cost of waiting for nearly perfect automated vehicles. *RAND Corporation research report RR-2150-RC*.

**32** State of California, Department of Motor Vehicles (2022). California Autonomous Vehicle Regulations. https://www.dmv.ca.gov/portal/vehicle-industry-services/autonomous-vehicles/california-autonomous-vehicle-regulations/ (accessed 21 April 2023).

**33** Chen, C., Seff, A., Kornhauser, A. et al. (2015). DeepDriving: learning affordance for direct perception in autonomous driving. In: *Proceedings of the IEEE International Conference on Computer Vision*, Santiago, Chile (7–13 December 2015), 2722–2730. IEEE.

**34** Petti, S. and Fraichard, T. (2005). Safe motion planning in dynamic environments. In: *Proceedings of the 2005 IEEE/RSJ International Conference on Intelligent Robots and Systems*, Edmonton, AB, Canada (2–5 August 2005), 2210–2215. IEEE.

**35** Li, G., Hari, S.K.S., Sullivan, M. et al. (2017). Understanding error propagation in deep learning neural network (DNN) accelerators and applications. In: *Proceedings of the International Conference for High Performance Computing, Networking, Storage and Analysis*, Denver, CO, USA (12–17 November 2017), 8:1–8:12. New York, NY, USA: Association for Computing Machinery https://doi.org/10.1145/3126908.3126964.

**36** NVIDIA (2023). NVIDIA Drive, Scalable AI Platform for Autonomous Driving. https://www.nvidia.com/en-us/self-driving-cars/drive-platform (accessed 14 April 2023).

**37** SAE International (2021). Taxonomy and definitions for terms related to driving automation systems for on-road motor vehicles. https://www.sae.org/standards/content/j3016_202104/.

**38** Leveson, N. (2011). *Engineering a Safer World: Systems Thinking Applied to Safety*. Cambridge, MA, USA: MIT Press.

**39** Mujica, F. (2014). *Scalable Electronics Driving Autonomous Vehicle Technologies*. Texas Instruments White Paper.

**40** Abdulkhaleq, A., Lammering, D., Wagner, S. et al. (2017). A systematic approach based on STPA for developing a dependable architecture for fully automated driving vehicles. *Procedia Engineering* 179: 41–51.

**41** Waymo LLC (2021). *Waymo Safety Report*. https://ltad.com/resources/waymo-safety-report-2021.html (accessed 21 April 2023).

**42** Amer, N.H., Zamzuri, H., Hudha, K. et al. (2017). Modelling and control strategies in path tracking control for autonomous ground vehicles: a review of state of the art and challenges. *Journal of Intelligent & Robotic Systems* 86 (2): 225–254.

**43** Geiger, A., Lenz, P., and Urtasun, R. (2012). Are we ready for autonomous driving? The KITTI Vision Benchmark Suite. In: *Proceedings of the 2012 IEEE*

*Conference on Computer Vision and Pattern Recognition*, Providence, RI, USA (16–21 June 2012), 3354–3361. IEEE.

44  State of California, Department of Motor Vehicles (2021). Autonomous Vehicles. https://www.dmv.ca.gov/portal/vehicle-industry-services/autonomous-vehicles/ (accessed 14 April 2023).

45  Favarò, F.M., Nader, N., Eurich, S.O. et al. (2017). Examining accident reports involving autonomous vehicles in California. *PLoS One* 12 (9): e0184952. https://doi.org/10.1371/journal.pone.0184952.

46  Favarò, F., Eurich, S., and Nader, N. (2018). Autonomous vehicles' disengagements: trends, triggers, and regulatory limitations. *Accident Analysis & Prevention* 110: 136–148.

47  Alemzadeh, H. (2016). Data-driven resiliency assessment of medical cyberphysical systems. PhD dissertation. University of Illinois at Urbana-Champaign.

48  Smith, R. (2007). An overview of the Tesseract OCR Engine. In: *Proceedings of the 9th International Conference on Document Analysis and Recognition*, Curitiba, Brazil (23–26 September 2007), vol. 2, 629–633. IEEE.

49  Avižienis, A., Laprie, J.-C., Randell, B. et al. (2004). Basic concepts and taxonomy of dependable and secure computing. *IEEE Transactions on Dependable and Secure Computing* 1 (1): 11–33.

50  Dixit, V.V., Chand, S., and Nair, D.J. (2016). Autonomous vehicles: disengagements, accidents and reaction times. *PLoS One* 11 (12): e0168054. https://doi.org/10.1371/journal.pone.0168054.

51  Fambro, D.B., Fitzpatrick, K., and Koppa, R.J. (1997). Determination of stopping sight distances. *National Cooperative Highway Research Program, Report 400*. Transportation Research Board, National Research Council. Washington, DC, USA: National Academy Press.

52  Kalra, N. and Paddock, S.M. (2016). Driving to safety: how many miles of driving would it take to demonstrate autonomous vehicle reliability? *Transportation Research Part A: Policy and Practice* 94: 182–193.

53  National Highway Traffic Safety Administration (NHTSA) (2016). 2015 motor vehicle crashes: overview. *Traffic Safety Facts: Research Note, DOT HS 812 318*. U.S. Department of Transportation.

54  Federal Highway Administration (FHWA) (2023). Traffic volume trends. https://www.fhwa.dot.gov/policyinformation/travel_monitoring/tvt.cfm (accessed 14 April 2023).

55  Federal Aviation Administration (1988). System design and analysis. *Advisory Circular AC* 25: 1309–1A.

56  Alemzadeh, H., Raman, J., Leveson, N. et al. (2016). Adverse events in robotic surgery: a retrospective study of 14 years of FDA data. *PLoS One* 11 (4): e0151470. https://doi.org/10.1371/journal.pone.0151470.

**57** National Transportation Safety Board (2023). General aviation accident dashboard: 2012–2021. https://www.ntsb.gov/safety/data/Pages/GeneralAviationDashboard.aspx (accessed 14 March 2023).

**58** Alemzadeh, H., Iyer, R.K., Kalbarczyk, Z. et al. (2013). Analysis of safety-critical computer failures in medical devices. *IEEE Security & Privacy* 11 (4): 14–26.

**59** Office of Highway Policy Information (2008). Our Nation's Highways: 2008. *Federal Highway Administration publication FHWA-PL-08-021*, U.S. Department of Transportation. https://www.fhwa.dot.gov/policyinformation/pubs/pl08021.

**60** Plötz, P., Jakobsson, N., and Sprei, F. (2017). On the distribution of individual daily driving distances. *Transportation Research Part B: Methodological* 101: 213–227.

**61** Stanek, G., Langer, D., Müller-Bessler, B. et al. (2010). Junior 3: a test platform for advanced driver assistance systems. In: *Proceedings of the 2010 IEEE Intelligent Vehicles Symposium*, La Jolla, CA, USA (21–24 June 2010), 143–149. IEEE.

**62** Levinson, J., Askeland, J., Becker, J. et al. (2011). Towards fully autonomous driving: systems and algorithms. In: *Proceedings of the 2011 IEEE Intelligent Vehicles Symposium*, Baden-Baden, Germany (5–9 June 2011), 163–168. IEEE.

**63** International Organization for Standardization (December 2018). Road Vehicles—Functional Safety. International Organization for Standardization, Geneva, CH, Standard, p. 33. https://www.iso.org/standard/68383.html.

**64** Casner, S.M., Hutchins, E.L., and Norman, D. (2016). The challenges of partially automated driving. *Communications of the ACM* 59 (5): 70–77.

**65** Reschka, A. (2016). Safety concept for autonomous vehicles. In: *Autonomous Driving: Technical, Legal and Social Aspects* (ed. M. Maurer, J.C. Gerdes, B. Lenz, et al.), 473–496. Berlin, Heidelberg, Germany: Springer.

**66** Koopman, P. and Wagner, M. (2017). Autonomous vehicle safety: an interdisciplinary challenge. *IEEE Intelligent Transportation Systems Magazine* 9 (1): 90–96.

**67** Leveson, N. (2004). A new accident model for engineering safer systems. *Safety Science* 42 (4): 237–270.

**68** Fan, C., Qi, B., Mitra, S. et al. (2017). DRYVR: data-driven verification and compositional reasoning for automotive systems. In: *Proceedings of the 29th International Conference on Computer Aided Verification*, Heidelberg, Germany (24–28 July 2017), Part I, *Lecture Notes in Computer Science*, vol. 10426, 441–461. Cham, Switzerland: Springer.

**69** Society of Automotive Engineers (SAE) (2021). *Cybersecurity Guidebook for Cyber-Physical Vehicle Systems*. SAE International.

**70** Joy, J. and Gerla, M. (2017). Privacy risks in vehicle grids and autonomous cars. In: *Proceedings of the 2nd ACM International Workshop on Smart, Autonomous, and Connected Vehicular Systems and Services*, Snowbird, UT, USA (16 October 2017), 19–23. New York, NY, USA: Association for Computing Machinery.

**71** Swinhoe, D. (2022). Frontier supercomputer suffering 'daily hardware failures' during testing. *Data Center Dynamics* (10 October). https://www. datacenterdynamics.com/en/news/frontier-supercomputer-suffering-daily-hardware-failures-during-testing/.

**72** Crowe, S. (2021). Cruise, Waymo lead way in Calif. autonomous vehicle testing. *The Robot Report* (10 February). https://www.therobotreport.com/cruise-waymo-lead-way-calif-autonomous-vehicle-tests/.

**73** Fannin, R. (2022). Where the billions spent on autonomous vehicles by U.S. and Chinese giants is heading. *CNBC* (21 May). https://www.cnbc.com/2022/05/21/why-the-first-autonomous-vehicles-winners-wont-be-in-your-driveway.html.

**74** Wakabayashi, D. (2018). Self-driving uber car kills pedestrian in Arizona, where Robots Roam *The New York Times*. https://www.nytimes.com/2018/03/19/technology/uber-driverless-fatality.html (accessed 29 September 2023)

**75** Proactive (2022). Tesla out front in autonomous driving crash tally, US watchdog says. *Proactive* (16 June). https://www.proactiveinvestors.com/companies/news/985046/tesla-out-front-in-autonomous-driving-crash-tally-us-watchdog-says-985046.html.

**76** Witzenburg, G. (2021). Ford Blue Cruise: call it level 2.5. *WardsAuto* (11 August). https://www.wardsauto.com/vehicles/ford-blue-cruise-call-it-level-25.

**77** Moon, M. (2023). Cruise's robotaxis have driven 1 million miles with nobody behind the wheel. *Engadget* (22 February). https://www.engadget.com/cruise-robotaxi-1-million-driverless-miles-170051724.html.

**78** Bassett, A. (2022). Waymo's new robotaxi is an all-electric people mover with no steering wheel. *The Verge* (21 November). https://www.theverge.com/2022/11/21/23471183/waymo-zeekr-geely-autonomous-vehicle-av-robotaxi.

**79** McFarland, M. (2022). GM's robotaxis are only coming out after dark. *CNN* (8 February). https://www.cnn.com/2022/02/08/tech/cruise-robotaxis-night/index.html.

**80** Tesla (2023). Autopilot and full self-driving capability. https://www.tesla.com/en_eu/support/autopilot (accessed 11 September 2023).

# 14

# The Future: Dependable and Trustworthy AI Systems

## 14.1   Introduction

The emergence of artificial intelligence (AI) systems and their ubiquitous adoption in automating tasks that involve humans in critical application domains (e.g. autonomous vehicles (AVs), medical assistants/devices, manufacturing, agriculture, and smart buildings) means that it is of paramount importance that we are able to place trust in these technologies.

In a broad sense, a trustworthy AI system must be both dependable (i.e. ensure the safety, resilience, robustness, and security of both itself and its operational environment) and explainable (i.e. provide the reasoning behind the decisions/actions produced). The absence of such features remains a major impediment to the public acceptance of these technologies and their deployment in human- and mission-critical applications, despite successful demonstrations. Also, there are ongoing concerns, from both algorithmic and experimental perspectives, regarding the reliability, safety, and security of machine learning (ML) technologies and systems that incorporate ML technologies, and whether such systems may be vulnerable to security hacks and crashes that can ultimately impact human safety. As Schneier states in [57], traditionally, computers have outperformed humans only with respect to speed, scale, and scope, whereas humans have excelled at thinking, reasoning, adapting, and understanding. However, AI is changing the landscape, such that computers can now infer relationships, discover patterns, and react and adapt to changes while keeping their strength in speed, scale, and scope. In the new era of smart systems, AI has successfully demonstrated the possibility of accelerating and automating processes that were previously the jobs of human actors (e.g. driving, medical diagnosis, or navigation). The successful demonstrations and fascinating possibilities of AI have changed the paradigm for system design.

*Dependable Computing: Design and Assessment*, First Edition. Ravishankar K. Iyer, Zbigniew T. Kalbarczyk, and Nithin M. Nakka.
© 2024 The IEEE Computer Society. Published 2024 by John Wiley & Sons, Inc.
Companion website: www.wiley.com/go/iyer/dependablecomputing1

In conventional systems, humans in the decision loop monitor, reason about, and validate decisions (if not made by the humans themselves) and the feedback that follows. In contrast, in production AI systems, decisions are inferred by AI models, and actuators execute actions without human validation. That change in paradigm, such that a human is no longer integral to the decision loop, presents the need to assure the dependability of AI systems and their actions. Further, systems' proximity to and direct interaction with humans and their surroundings, and the probabilistic nature of the underlying algorithms, raise the stakes with respect to the trust that must be placed in the actions of such systems.

For instance, AVs use ML methods to derive real-time driving decisions that could easily have life-or-death consequences. Despite their benefits in enabling autonomous control and management and in rapid response to anomalous system or application events, AI/ML technologies bring new challenges in terms of their robustness, resilience, and safety. ML algorithms, particularly the ones used in AVs, are known to be brittle to rare driving scenarios and accidental or malicious perturbations. Further, uncertainties in their environments and the decision process, software/hardware runtime errors, design bugs, and malicious attacks can contribute to erratic behavior of AVs. Uncertain decisions may lead to safety hazards, such as accidents, which can result in loss of human life or property damage. In March 2018, for example, an automated test vehicle fatally injured a pedestrian who was pushing a bicycle across a road at a point where there was no crosswalk. The automated driving system (ADS) failed to classify the victim as a pedestrian or to predict her path. The ADS recognized the likely collision only after the situation had exceeded the response specifications of the braking system. The vehicle operator was responsible for monitoring the ADS and for responding to emergency situations (i.e. for taking control of the ADS when needed), but the vehicle operator was glancing away from the road and redirected her gaze ahead only about a second before impact [51]. AI failures are not limited to the transportation industry; they have been reported for many AI applications, including some that are already in service [18, 58, 65, 73]. These failures are challenging our trust in AI and AI applications.

The resilience and safety challenges cannot be solved simply by redeploying the usual redundancy methods used in life- and mission-critical systems. The uncertainty introduced in emerging computing systems with AI/ML support or in full-fledged AI systems will require new techniques and methods to address the consequent resilience challenges in these systems, which include AVs, hybrid and multicloud systems, smart power grids, the new generation of AI-enabled healthcare systems, emerging secure computing systems and techniques, and high-performance computing, among others.

**System** *trustworthiness* is a relatively well-studied concept in computing systems. Avižienis et al. [93] describe a trustworthy system in the context of availability, reliability, safety, confidentiality, integrity, and maintainability. While the context is much broader when applied to AI/ML systems and includes several additional aspects like ethics, explainability, interpretability, and fairness, we will largely confine ourselves to their description and bring in other issues as relevant [93]. A significant body of literature addresses the design, measurement, and modeling of trustworthy mission- and life-critical systems (e.g. space programs, high-speed trains, and large-scale computing infrastructure) and ways to detect, prevent, and tolerate incidents that corrupt the operation of such systems [91, 92]. However, the emergence of AI systems and those that incorporate AI in management and control, and their trustworthy/dependability requirements, raise new challenges in assuring trust in system design, validation, and verification. Joint probability distributions are the basis of quantifying the multifaceted characteristics of system trustworthiness and dependability. When we introduce into that mix, the additional uncertainties characteristic of high-dimensionality, heterogeneous data, and the complexities intrinsic to AI systems, the problem becomes challenging. Overall, we can generally classify those uncertainties in three ways, as follows.

1) *Uncertainty in the inputs:* The challenge is to identify and handle the uncertainty in the input caused by (i) measurement errors, and (ii) adversarial perturbations. For example, recent research indicated that an AV may fail to recognize a stop sign or estimate target object trajectories because of corrupted inputs from sensors due to a fault or an adversarial attack [80, 83, 84]. Further, ML systems in general have been shown to be vulnerable to noisy inputs. For instance, an AI-driven eye-screening system that demonstrated a promising eye-disorder detection rate during its development struggled with significant rejection rates when deployed in practice. Post-deployment investigation showed that numerous factors, such as the expertise of the staff, procedures followed, or environmental characteristics (e.g. poor lighting), affected the quality of the input [88].

2) *Uncertainty in AI/ML models and data (epistemic and aleatoric uncertainties):* The challenge here is to identify and handle the model and data uncertainties in a system that are likely to impact AI/ML inference and decision making. For example, in an ADS, such uncertainties are often related to (i) variability in the data collection process, lack of comprehensive training data, and inability of the ML model to handle rare inputs; (ii) underfitting/overfitting of ML model parameters (e.g. neural network weights and Kalman filter parameters); and (iii) implementation and integration of an ensemble of ML models (e.g. uncertainty that propagates and snowballs from object detectors to vehicle actuation commands). Such uncertainty in the model outputs cannot be solved simply through conventional methods.

3) *Uncertainty in system operation:* The challenge here is in handling uncertainty in the behavior of the underlying system components that execute the ML models and vehicle kinematics. The uncertainty may be caused by a wide

range of failure modes across the components. Examples include faults in mechanical components such as the engine and brakes, performance anomalies, and bugs and faults in software and hardware components. Although many such challenges can be handled using traditional resiliency techniques, the inadequacy of the training combined with the uncertainties endemic in AI modeling can significantly impact the inferences made by AI/ML models, hence the compelling need to design ML models that can inherently handle those failure modes and produce outputs to ensure the safe operation of the AVs under real-time dynamical conditions.

This chapter discusses challenges in assuring trustworthiness in AI systems and presents a model that can start to enumerate and represent the trustworthiness of a system and its components. The challenges are discussed in the context of three representative application domains for which potential advances from adopting AI technology have been demonstrated: transportation, enterprise computing systems, and healthcare. Further, we provide a survey of state-of-the-art technologies that address such challenges, which span various layers of the AI system architecture, and we consider their limitations to help us envision a research path toward trustworthy AI/ML systems. We summarize in Table 14.1 samples of recent catastrophic incidents involving trustworthy AI systems discussed in this section.

## 14.2 Building Trustworthy AI Systems

System trustworthiness in the context of an AI system, and/or systems that are controlled or managed by AI/ML techniques (wherein AI algorithms are the principal decision-makers and inference drivers), raises new problems. In this section, we describe the key components of an AI system and discuss how its trustworthiness differs from the conventional understanding of trustworthiness.

### 14.2.1 An AI System and Its Key Components

As depicted in Figure 14.1, an AI system consists of three core components: the knowledge base (*data*) from which the intelligence is inferred, the learning algorithm (*AI*) that derives/infers a representative model from the data, and an actuation module (*actor*) that executes the action and interacts with the surrounding environment and the human users.

Data are the knowledge base from which the AI system learns, infers, and derives intelligence. The data are collected through various methods (e.g. sensors, monitors, questionnaires, or surveys) to represent the users and/or the environment under study. As AI models are driven by data, the representativeness and fairness of the data are critical in assuring the performance of the decision model.

**Table 14.1** Sample incidents involving trustworthy AI systems.

| Application | Description | Year |
|---|---|---|
| Autonomous vehicle | Uber self-driving AI failed to detect pedestrians. | 2018 |
| Autonomous vehicle | Tesla vehicle failed to detect lane divider. | 2018 |
| Autonomous vehicle | Nearly 400 crashes by cars with ADS or L2-ADS in the United States. | 2022 |
| Autonomous vehicle | Waymo's driverless cars were involved in two crashes and 18 'minor contact events' over 1 million miles. | 2023 |
| Autonomous vehicle | Tesla's full self-driving system could cause crashes. At least 17 people have died in the 35 crashes. | 2023 |
| Autonomous vehicle | Tesla Autopilot's vision system did not consistently detect and track the truck as an object or threat as it crossed the path of the car. | 2023 |
| Autonomous vehicle | Cruise stops all driverless taxi operations in the United States. | 2023 |
| High-performance computing | Supercomputer running COVID-19 research taken offline because of security breaches. | 2020 |
| High-performance computing | Frontier supercomputer at Oak Ridge Leadership Computing Facility experiences outages (MTBF: few hours) | 2023 |
| Cloud computing | Google's data center shutdown during UK heatwave due to cooling failure and extreme temperatures. (Duration: few hours) | 2022 |
| Cloud computing | Multiple Google Cloud services faced outages due to a recent rollout of the management plane (Duration: 7+ h) | 2023 |
| Cloud computing | Google Compute Engine Control Plane health checks failed for any changes made to newly added health checks (Duration: 13 h) | 2023 |
| Cloud computing | Microsoft Wide-area networking (WAN) routing change: Azure; Outlook email, calendar & Teams (Duration: 5 h) | 2023 |
| Cloud computing | Microsoft Teams outage due to expired authentication certificate (Duration: 3 h) | 2020 |
| Cloud computing | Zoom outage during the pandemic (Duration: 4 h) | 2020 |
| Cloud computing | AWS DNS Resolution affecting customers including Facebook, Disney, Ring (Duration: 11 h) | 2021 |
| Cloud computing | Cloudflare network backbone misconfigurations led to 50% traffic drop across the network (Duration: 27 min) | 2020 |

*(Continued)*

**Table 14.1** (Continued)

| Application | Description | Year |
|---|---|---|
| Cloud computing | Facebook, WhatsApp, and Instagram inaccessible due to DNS error (Duration: 6 h) | 2021 |
| Cloud computing | Google Cloud entire data center failed due to fire and flood (Duration: 10 h) | 2023 |
| Cloud computing | IBM Cloud worldwide outage due to a 3rd-party network provider (Duration: several hours) | 2020 |
| Government | NOIRLab Astronomical observations at the International Gemini Observatory suspended | 2023 |
| Healthcare | Clinically relevant vulnerabilities of deep machine learning systems for skin cancer diagnosis | 2020 |
| Healthcare | Racial bias in an algorithm used to predict comorbidity risk score for follow-up patient care | 2019 |
| Healthcare | IBM Watson fails to detect cancer | 2018 |
| Healthcare | Model for prescribing antipsychotic medication for schizophrenia fails to generalize | 2024 |
| Healthcare | AI models rely on spurious correlations to diagnose COVID-19 from chest X-ray | 2021 |
| Healthcare | DNN predict genetic mutations by relying on cancer subtype | 2022 |
| Healthcare | Biased chest X-ray models lead to misdiagnosis by clinicians | 2023 |
| Healthcare | Google ML-driven eye-scanning system suffers in clinical practice | 2020 |
| Healthcare | ChatGPT misdiagnoses 80% of pediatric cases | 2024 |
| Healthcare | Recalled more than 1000 Medtronic's MiniMed insulin pumps due to a potential cyber security risk | 2018 |

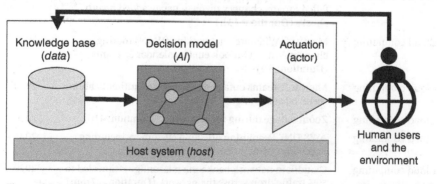

**Figure 14.1** Generic representation of an AI system/application.

A *decision model* is the abstraction of the intelligence learned/derived from the data by an AI algorithm. Given a set of data (and prior knowledge regarding the problem under study), a set of AI algorithms locate information, infer patterns, or detect anomalies to answer the problem under study. An ideal decision model would effectively (i.e. accurately and in a timely manner) mimic a human operator, making decisions for the given problem.

An *actor* is the system component that executes the decision as derived by the decision model. The actor interacts with the human users and the surrounding environment. An incorrect action by the actor can have hazardous impacts (e.g. a safety violation). Often, the specification of the actor defines performance constraints in the decision model to assure the trustworthiness of the system.

Users and the environment are the entities that interact with the AI system. The users and the environment experience the results of the decisions made by the decision model and the actions taken by the actor. Different AI systems may interact with humans and/or the environment in different ways. For instance, in the case of AVs, humans are fully immersed in the driving environment, while in the case of medical devices, humans can be both the subject and the administrator of the device. Design, assessment, and validation of trustworthy AI systems require full understanding and modeling of the interaction between the AI system and its environment.

### 14.2.2 A System Perspective on Trust in AI Systems

This section focuses on the system perspective wherein AI has a critical role as a principal decision-maker. We find that among the general attributes that define trust, *reliability*, *security*, and *safety* are the key attributes that can be assessed, addressed, and validated. We describe how these key attributes apply to a generic AI system in the context of its architecture (introduced in Section 14.2.1).

*Reliability* means that continuity of correct service is assured as required for the AI system. To keep the AI system reliable, data should properly represent the knowledge base that the system needs to learn or infer. Data correctness is a common measure for assuring that the data are reliable. In addition, the decision model should be correct (given proper data) and robust against faults in the data from which it learns. Finally, an actor should not fail in executing the actions chosen by the decision model, and the actions should properly cover all edge cases and possible combinations that affect the state of the environment and the decision made by the model (as derived from the data).

*Security* is a system's vulnerability to malicious activities. Security is often described in the context of confidentiality, integrity, and availability. To keep an AI system secure, data should be confidential so that no unauthorized entity can access the system (a concept related to privacy). Also, the data integrity should be preserved so that the original data are not corrupted by malicious actions; the decision model (or the underlying system that hosts the decision model) should detect inconsistencies and corruptions in the data and be able to tolerate any poisoning of the data. Further, no unauthorized entity should be able to access the learned decision model or its critical parameters, and the actor should properly execute the decision without corruption(s) from an external entity.

*Safety* is an assurance that there will not be catastrophic consequences for the entities that interact with the system (i.e. the users and the environment). The safety of the system cannot be studied at the level of the data or the decision model, but only after considering the action to be taken by the actor and its impact. An actor of an AI system should accurately execute a decision as derived by the decision model. Further, safety barriers and policies should be designed to prevent hazardous consequences for the entities with which the system interacts. In assessing, addressing, and validating the reliability, security, and safety of AI systems, the following attributes should also be considered.

*Performance* measures the timeliness of the decision and the action. The safety window, as defined by the system specifications of the actor and its interaction with the user or the environment, introduces constraints on the performance of the system. For instance, the same AI model can result in different consequences, depending on the sensitivity of the action to the performance (e.g. accuracy or timeliness) of the decision model. In that context, measuring and modeling the performance of the subcomponents of an AI system is critical in studying and designing trustworthy AI systems.

*Interpretability* of models is critical. Models inferred by ML algorithms (e.g. deep neural networks) are often treated as black boxes. Without fully understanding the internals, researchers, and engineers often evaluate a model through the output that the model provides. However, that approach can result in a failure to recognize possible faults in the decision logic or other vulnerabilities that can benefit malicious entities. Interpretability and explainability are complicated research topics, but understanding this aspect of AI systems is critical in assuring that a system is trustworthy.

Two broad categories of methods can be employed to build resilient AI systems in the presence of uncertainties in the inputs, the ML model, and the system. They are the offline identification of resilience deficiencies during the development phase and the online detection and mitigation of resilience deficiencies after deployment of the system. Offline methods encompass techniques like formal verification, fault injection, and falsification that try to uncover bugs and resilience issues with the system design and implementation before deployment. While these techniques are not new and indeed existed before the advent of AI systems, the additional uncertainty introduced by the ML algorithms makes resilience evaluation using these methods more challenging. In addition, research in adversarial learning continues to uncover a new class of resilience issues that are specific to neural networks and associated algorithms. They must be addressed at design time to ensure the trustworthiness of the ML system. In most cases, it is impossible to identify and fix all the resilience issues during development, as many ML systems are complex and operate in complex environments. For that reason, it is important to use online detection and mitigation algorithms that can capture resilience issues at runtime and take appropriate actions to mitigate any negative impact on the performance or safety of the system. In Sections 14.3 and 14.4, we discuss some offline and online techniques that have been proposed to ensure the resilience of AI systems and the challenges that hinder the assurance of resilience in AI systems.

## 14.3 Offline Identification of Deficiencies

This section describes offline methods that identify, at an early phase of system development, design, and implementation deficiencies that may lead to uncertainties. The analyses are performed offline and aim to reveal and address deficiencies before system deployment.

### 14.3.1 Assessment and Validation of a System and Its Design

#### 14.3.1.1 Formal Verification
Formal verification techniques use rigorous mathematical reasoning to prove whether the design of a system is correct with respect to the intended system specification and requirements [4]. Formal methods take a system model and a requirement (e.g. safety) as input and provide supporting proof if the model satisfies the requirement, or a counterexample if it does not. The advantage of formal methods over empirical methods for safety verification is that they can provide safety guarantees over a range of inputs for a model, eliminating the need to test each scenario manually; a well-developed model can thus provide increased confidence in system resilience. However, it is not possible to apply traditional formal verification techniques to real-world systems, as verification problems are known to be theoretically undecidable for typical real-world systems [31]. Furthermore, purely model-based verification techniques have difficulty with nonlinear, hybrid [64], or other systems at scale, especially systems that do not have complete and precise model specifications [23]. Hence, many newer verification methods have resorted to approximations and incorporation of uncertainties [19, 24, 25].

In [50], Mitra et al. verify the safety of a model helicopter controller using the hybrid input/output automaton (HIOA). HIOA is used to verify the desired properties (in this case safety) of an automaton by induction. HIOA, which is an alternative to algorithmic verification, can model a larger class of hybrid systems; proofs using HIOA are tractable. In [50], the design and verification of a supervisory controller for the model helicopter are described. The supervisory controller periodically observes the pitch angle and pitch angular velocity and overrides the user control when it decides that the helicopter is heading to an unsafe state. However, certain key assumptions in the safety proof could limit the extension of the approach to general self-driving tasks. The sensors used by the supervisory systems are parameterized by the sampling period $\Delta$ and sensor errors for pitch angle $\epsilon_0$ and velocity $\epsilon_1$. It is unclear whether the safety proof applies to configurations beyond $\Delta, \epsilon_0, \epsilon_1$. For example, in the event of a fault that affects the sensors, the initial parameters of the sensors can no longer be guaranteed. Hence, an extension of the proof to cover this condition may be required. Making any of the parameters too large (to cover more drastic scenarios) will impact the helicopter's operation, as the supervisory agent might interfere too often. Also, the designed supervisory model assumes that the dynamics of the helicopter depend only on the input from the user or the environment. That is a valid assumption if the helicopter is operated in a closed and controlled environment. However, no safety guarantees can be made if other environmental forces (e.g. wind shear, thunderstorms, or external actors) are applied to the helicopter during operation.

A data-driven verification method is used in [23] to address some of the challenges of formal verification for real-world autonomous systems; by using numerical simulations together with static analysis of the models, the method allows verification of nonlinear models that do not have closed-form analytical solutions as well as models without precise specifications. Data-driven verification is done by performing sensitivity analysis and then integrating simulations of the model with model-based reachability analysis. Fan et al. developed the C2E2 [25] tool to perform sensitivity analysis on nonlinear and hybrid systems with known models. The outcome of a sensitivity analysis of a system can be used to determine the worst-case bounds or probabilistic bounds of output changes due to small changes in the input. Sensitivity analysis can also be used to generalize the results of data-driven verification from an individual execution to a general set of reachable states.

DRYVR [24] is a data-driven framework for verifying the safety of hybrid control systems (found in many self-driving applications). In this context, a *hybrid control system* can be defined as one that contains both continuous-time and discrete-event components [64]. For example, a lane-keeping controller in a self-driving car is a discrete-event system, while the dynamics of the car are modeled as a continuous-time system. Fan et al. [24] claim that it is nearly impossible to formulate a concise mathematical formula for complex continuous-time systems like the dynamics of a vehicle. Instead, they describe a hybrid control system as a combination of white-box and black-box components. In the example of an automatic emergency braking (AEB) system, the white-box component will describe the high-level logic of a discrete-event controller, while the black-box component will model the dynamics of the vehicle, which may have hundreds of parameters. Since the control logic of the AEB system is discrete and clearly defined, one can construct a transition graph (which is a directed acyclic graph) depicting the different states of the control system and their transitions. The black box is modeled using the trajectories of the dynamics of the car over time in a simulated environment. After the model is constructed, the safety property of a system can be verified using simulation-driven reachability analysis. DRYVR [24] has been applied to verify several advanced driver-assistance systems (ADAS), e.g. autonomous emergency braking (ΛEB), auto-passing, and auto-lane changing. While DryVR has demonstrated promising results, limitations exist. It requires each scenario to be specified, together with the initial state, transition graphs, and unsafe states of the AV for a driving scenario. Scenarios can include a small number of vehicles and usually no other environmental factors. DRYVR's ability to scale to a larger number of scenarios is unclear. It works well for a highly specialized ADAS (e.g. a lane-change system) with a restricted set of input scenarios, but may not scale well for general self-driving tasks that must navigate many driving scenarios. Further, DRYVR assumes a well-defined control logic represented by a transition graph. Emerging self-driving systems use deep neural networks in their control and decision loops and it may be difficult to obtain accurate transition graphs without uncertainty.

In [19], the authors propose a formal verification framework for verifying robotic behaviors in the presence of bounded uncertainties. This work is based on the observation that the mathematical models described via the differential equations used in the formal verification of robots are insufficiently accurate due to model simplifications or inaccuracies in model parameter specifications. Their framework uses interval analysis to verify robotic behaviors with bounded uncertainties in the mathematical models. The authors combine an interval constraint programming approach with validated numerical integration methods to deal with differential equations. They illustrate their framework with an example application to robust path planning.

Dutta et al. present a method for quantifying trust in an autonomous system in the presence of adversarial attacks on sensor measurements [22]. An estimation method based on set membership is used to identify safe states of the system. Furthermore, they use statistical/probabilistic model-checking to give probabilistic guarantees on whether various subsystems of the vehicle will satisfy safety specifications within a time interval. In [22], a case study of an adaptive cruise control unit of a vehicle is described. The study used the confidence analysis results generated during the proposed verification process to quantify trust.

A common shortcoming of all the formal verification techniques discussed so far is that they do not account for possible failures in the systems they are trying to prove safe. The techniques discussed perform formal verification of the design and the corresponding algorithm of the system under test, assuming the system works exactly as implemented. Although these proofs are valuable in verifying the safety of AVs deployed on public roads, it is necessary to account for potential failures and their effects. Zhang et al. [77] provide a framework for theoretically modeling these failures using probabilistic hybrid systems, and for automatically checking safety properties. In this probabilistic setting for safety verification, a system can be deemed safe if the probability that a system trajectory will reach an unsafe state from the initial state can be bounded by an acceptable probability threshold. Zhang et al. model the jumps or state transitions in the hybrid automata model as probability distributions, which makes it possible to model component failures, message losses, and other faults. In [77], they describe how they demonstrated their technique on a thermostat control system with discrete probabilities (i.e. probability mass functions). However, it is not clear how their technique could scale to larger cyber-physical systems (CPSes) and more complex failure modes that are represented using probability density functions. That may be one reason why there has been limited work on using Zhang et al.'s probabilistic hybrid automaton for safety verification in more complex CPSes, such as AVs.

Another approach to formally proving the safety of a CPS is to use model-based design (MBD) and metric temporal logic (MTL) [40] specifications. Since the verification problem for hybrid automata is generally undecidable even for simple safety requirements [31], research on hybrid automata safety verification has focused on finding classes of hybrid automata for which the safety verification is decidable [5]. However, for more complex safety requirements, MTL is preferred, as safety properties can be expressed concretely in mathematical notation. Abbas et al. [1] present a Monte Carlo optimization technique for finding system behaviors that falsify an MTL property. They show that by minimizing a robustness metric when performing a random walk over the input space, their technique can automatically falsify properties with more consistency than other methods, like random uniform sampling of the input space. In this context, *falsification* is the process of finding counterexamples that prove that the MTL property is not satisfied. A robustness metric for a signal in MTL is the amount of perturbation it can tolerate before it inverts its Boolean truth value. The larger the robustness metric, the greater the perturbation it can withstand. The sign of the robustness metric indicates whether the MTL property is satisfied (positive +) or falsified (negative −). As stated in [5], this method finds counterexamples that violate safety properties, it cannot assess the probability of a failure or safety violation, but can only detect such failures or violations. While useful, such methods are unable to prove that a CPS system is safe under all operational conditions. MBD can be used to develop models at different levels of abstraction. For example, there might be a nominal model (referred to as a *derived model*) that specifies the behavior and architecture of the system that is then implemented. Certain safety properties could have been rigorously proven for one of the models, but other safety properties might not be formally checkable. S-TaLiRo [6] is a tool that can check the conformance (i.e. similarity) between the nominal model and the derived model by computing a quantitative estimate of the closeness between the behaviors of the two models. The level of conformance can then be used to understand how the verification results from one model transfer to the other [32]. This conformance testing between two models for CPS can be done using falsification [2]. In [2], the conformance between two models is defined by a distance metric called $(T, J, (\tau, \epsilon))$-closeness, where $T$ is the test duration, and $J$ is the maximum number of mode switches in the hybrid automaton. Two models are said to be $(T, J, (\tau, \epsilon))$-*close* or *conformant with degree* $(T, J, (\tau, \epsilon))$ if within any time window $2\tau$, there is a time when the output trajectories of both models are within $\epsilon$ of each other, given the same set of inputs and initial conditions. The method in [2] finds how close two models are by using falsifying trajectory pairs for a $(T, J, (\tau, \epsilon))$ distance. Since Abbas et al. [1, 2] show that $(T, J, (\tau, \epsilon))$ is monotonic, if a particular $(T, J, (\tau, \epsilon))$ is nonconformant, then all smaller values of $(\tau, \epsilon)$ are also nonconformant. Hence, they are able to find an optimal $(\tau, \epsilon)$ conformance of two models to transfer the verification results from one model to another. Essentially, they address the question that if a verified model $(T, J, (\tau, \epsilon))$ is conformant with its implementation, then at what values of $(\tau, \epsilon)$ is it possible to claim that the implementation is also safe?

Certification of neural networks is another research thrust in the verification of AI algorithms. CNN-Cert [11] is a proposed framework for finding the lower bound on the maximum distortion in the input a neural network can accommodate without changing the output label it produces. This lower bound of the distortion in the input is used as a metric to certify a neural network. (That is, if a neural network is certified with a lower bound $\rho cert$, then no attack on input that has a norm of distortions less than $\rho cert$ will cause the output classification to change.) In [11], this is achieved by applying a pair of linear upper/lower bounds on the neuron outputs at each layer. Furthermore, the method achieves higher lower bounds and generates the bounds much faster than prior methods. Unlike previous certification methods, the framework can be applied to a more general class of convolutional neural network (CNN) models. However, the certification depends on determining the range of the inputs to each layer's activation, which depends on the inputs used at certification time. It is unclear what guarantees the certification can provide for unexplored or untested inputs.

There are inherent challenges in applying traditional formal verification methods to AI algorithms. Wing [74] discusses the differences and questions that must be considered to move from traditional formal methods to formal methods for AI; high-level differences identified include the probabilistic nature of ML systems and the stochastic nature of inputs to the system. Hence, the properties that need to be verified must also be defined probabilistically. To do so, we must develop new scalable verification techniques that can work with probabilities and nonlinear functions. Wing [74] also emphasizes that the use of data to train ML systems makes verification of those systems significantly more difficult than that of traditional systems. Various issues, such as specification of unseen data and checking of the data for desired properties, must be addressed to enable the verification of AI algorithms.

### 14.3.1.2 Traditional End-to-End Random Fault Injection

Another conventional method for enhancing the reliability of a system is through aggressive testing of the system's operation under adverse events. In this approach, one randomly injects adverse values into select parameters of the system and studies the impact. The approach often reveals vulnerabilities or faults in the system design/implementation that were not activated in earlier phases.

To assess the safety of AVs, Jha et al. [36] provide a framework called AVFI that allows users to inject random faults into the inputs, outputs, and decision logic of an AV and measure the end-to-end resiliency of the AV in simulation. Some of the input injections include random occlusions and noise in the images that are fed into the decision-making logic in the AV; such occlusions and noise can occur during the operational lifespan of an AV. Output injections include perturbations in the actuation values sent out from the decision logic to see whether the AV can correct itself and prevent dangerous situations. As fault injections were performed while the AV was driving in a virtual world, the authors were able to consider the performance of the entire AV stack (including the dynamics of the car) in evaluating the fault tolerance of the AV system.

### 14.3.1.3 Model-driven Fuzzing, Falsification, and Fault Injection

A random fault injection technique can enable holistic testing of AV systems by finding components in the AV that are relatively sensitive to faults. Li et al. [42] characterize the propagation of soft errors (e.g. a single-bit flip due to radiation) from hardware to DNN application software. Their paper proposes cost-effective silent data corruption (SDC) mitigation mechanisms in both hardware and software and evaluates them on common image-recognition neural networks such as CaffeNet, NiN, and ConvNet. However, their technique evaluates the neural network in isolation and does not focus on safety violations; in practice, it has low manifestation rates and requires enormous amounts of time under test. Relying only on random fault injection campaigns to find safety-critical faults is ineffective due to the large fault space. Guided or targeted fault injection [75] can accelerate the discovery of safety-critical faults by narrowing down the fault injection space through the application of domain knowledge about the AV system and the environment to identify relatively vulnerable states of the system.

Rubaiyat et al. [56] propose an end-to-end fault injection framework in which they can use domain knowledge obtained using the STPA (System Theoretic

Process Analysis) technique to narrow down the fault injection space for finding safety-critical faults. Their approach starts by using STPA to identify potentially hazardous situations in AVs. The algorithm performs fault injection in the AV during a simulation of the hazardous situations at the specific time and fault location obtained from the STPA analysis. The results show that Rubaiyat et al.'s STPA-embedded fault injection framework obtains a better fault manifestation rate (5.9% improvement) and better hazard coverage (6.8% improvement) than random injections can. However, the STPA approach requires that the tester be responsible for manually analyzing and defining hazardous scenarios. Since the number of possible driving scenarios in the world is extremely huge, it would be impractical to define all dangerous scenarios manually, and it would be easy to miss edge cases.

Jha et al. [35] address that issue by taking some of the responsibility for manually identifying all hazardous situations away from the tester. They use a kinematics model (i.e. a set of differential equations modeling the kinematics of the car) to define safe and unsafe longitudinal and lateral distances from the AV to other actors. They then use domain knowledge about the structure of the AV architecture to create a temporal Bayesian network (TBN) that can be used to predict the next architectural state of the AV based on the current and previous architectural states of the AV. A data-driven approach is employed to train the TBN model to learn the relationships between the different state variables across time. The training data are collected from AV runs in the simulator with and without random fault injection. Since the TBN is a well-defined interpretable model, it is possible to target architectural states that might cause safety violations under faults and perturb those states according to a fault model. Then, probabilistic inference can be done on the perturbed TBN to check whether the AV reaches an unsafe situation. If it does, the fault will be added to a collection of safety-critical faults, and simulation will be used to verify whether the predicted faults lead to unsafe situations. This method of fault injection, in which domain knowledge and data are used via probabilistic models to consider both the temporal nature of AVs and the dynamics of the car, has been shown to accelerate the identification of safety-critical faults by three orders of magnitude.

Guided or targeted fault injections have enabled a higher error manifestation rate and hazard coverage in AV systems. Although such guided injection techniques have accelerated the discovery of safety-critical faults, it is challenging to measure how much of the fault space the experiments cover. The main reason is that just because a fault does not cause a safety violation in one driving scenario does not necessarily imply that it will not cause a safety violation in another scenario. Furthermore, the techniques discussed here rely on already having potentially dangerous driving scenarios. Generation of potentially unsafe driving scenarios that provide good coverage of real-world scenarios is another current research challenge.

### 14.3.2 Post-Mortem Analysis to Track the Causes of Incidents Systematically

AV safety assessment can also be performed by analyzing failure data from field testing of AVs [7, 27, 71]. Such analysis will help in assessing the level of safety of an AV in the real world, which may be hard to quantify with high certainty using predeployment safety assessment techniques. The California Department of Motor Vehicles (CA DMV) requires all manufacturers that test AVs on public roads to report disengagements (i.e. failures that cause the control of the vehicle to switch from the software to the human driver) and accidents (i.e. collisions with other vehicles, pedestrians, or property).

Banerjee et al. [7] investigated the causes, dynamics, and impacts of such AV failures by analyzing disengagement and accident reports obtained from public DMV databases [13] such as California's. To identify the multidimensional causes of AV disengagements/accidents, they used STPA to build a hierarchical control structure for AVs. Doing so was necessary because many manufacturers do not disclose the architectures of their AVs. Through a combination of failure data analysis and STPA techniques [7] traces back from reported failures to the system components that were responsible for the faults. The resulting characterization of failures and their causes allowed the authors to reveal that 64% of the reported disengagements were due to issues with the machine-learning-based perception and decision-and-control systems. Furthermore, although the data showed that manufacturers improved over time, the authors of [7] (published in 2018) found that the then-current AVs were at least 15 times more likely to have an accident than a human driver over the same number of miles driven. Hence (at the time of their study), they concluded that AVs were not yet ready to be deployed on public roads and that more research and development must be done to improve AV safety.

There are some challenges in assessing AV safety through post-mortem data analysis. First, statistically showing that an AV is safe based on the number of miles driven safely is not a viable approach [38]. Kalra and Paddock [38] claim that statistically showing that an AV is as safe as a human (i.e. 1.09 fatalities per 100 million miles) with 95% confidence would require 250 million failure-free miles of autonomous driving. Assessing safety over 250 million miles whenever there is a change in the design or implementation of an AV system would make the development cycle unreasonably long. Second, the effectiveness of post-mortem failure analysis depends on the granularity and accuracy with which failure scenarios are recorded. Highly detailed logging of failure events within an AV system may result in a better understanding of a failure's causes and effects during analysis. However, the end-to-end latency constraints on the AV system restrict how much data can be logged in every perception-decision-actuation cycle in the AV.

**14.3.2.1 Adversarial Learning: A Red Team Approach**

Uncertainty in AI systems and their components can offer tempting vulnerabilities for adversaries who wish to corrupt a system. However, by thinking ahead from the adversaries' perspective, we can pre-emptively identify vulnerabilities and flaws before an attacker has exploited the system. We can use observations of the system's responses to adversarial actions (e.g. corrupted data points, injected faults, or carefully crafted malicious input) as a knowledge base for improving the trustworthiness of AI systems. Next, we discuss state-of-the-art approaches that use AI methods to identify trust-related issues in critical systems.

**14.3.2.2 Adversarial Learning: A Systematic Approach to Mislead AI Systems**

*Adversarial learning* can be defined as the process of crafting malicious inputs that can mislead trained ML models into misclassification or misdetection, while usually remaining imperceptible to humans. The vulnerability of neural networks to adversarial attacks was first put forward by Szegedy et al. [66]. Although the underlying reason for the vulnerability is not fully understood (because of the poor interpretability of deep neural networks), the authors show that the assumption that the deep stack of nonlinearities can encode a smooth nonlocal generalization prior over the input space is false. Small, imperceptible perturbations to the input can therefore cause a neural network classifier to misclassify the input with high confidence. Szegedy et al. also show that the crafted adversarial examples can transfer to other neural networks working on similar input-output spaces. Akhtar and Mian [3] and Chakraborty et al. [14] provide good surveys of adversarial attacks on deep learning networks [3], and focus on vulnerabilities of computer vision models. Table 14.2 summarizes and analyzes some interesting work related to adversarial learning on deep neural networks.

Tramèr et al. [67] analyze claims about the effectiveness of fast single-step adversarial training methods. They show that adversarial training using those methods produces only weak perturbations, and that the models remain vulnerable to strong black-box attacks because the algorithm converges to a degenerate minimum. Hence, previous claims that the robustness of a single-step adversarial trained model transfers to other models are wrong. Furthermore, the authors also introduce and explain the notion of Ensemble Adversarial Training, with which they decouple the generation of adversarial examples from the models being trained. The training data are augmented with adversarial examples from other pretrained models to avoid the degenerate minimum problem and increase the model robustness to black-box attacks transferred from other models.

Liu et al. [44] present a novel targeted attack for neural networks that involves a concept called the *Trojan attack*. The attack works as a three-step process on a pretrained, publicly available model and does not require access to most of the original

**Table 14.2** Summary and analysis of work related to adversarial learning in deep neural networks.

| Paper | Summary | Comments |
| --- | --- | --- |
| Adversarial examples that fool detectors [46] | Constructs adversarial stop sign examples that fool 2 standard object detectors, Faster RCNN and YOLO. | Pros: Were able to create both digital and physical perturbations for stop signs that cause object detectors to misclassify a stop sign. Cons: The attacks are susceptible to lighting conditions and viewing angles. Only stop signs with large perturbations can fool detectors in the physical world. |
| Ensemble adversarial training: attacks and defenses [67] | The proposed method decouples the generation of adversarial examples from the training step. Adversarial examples from other pretrained models are used to train the target network to improve the robustness to black-box attacks and avoid the degenerate minimum problem. | Pros: The identification of a degenerate solution to the optimization problem, and its parallel to reward hacking, is insightful. Ensemble training is an easy-to-implement technique, as pretrained models can be used. Cons: There is a notable loss in accuracy of the adversarially trained network, and it is not robust to white-box attacks. Adversarial examples increase the required data set size, making models more data-hungry and limiting scalability. |
| Neural cleanse: identifying and mitigating backdoor attacks in neural networks [70] | Provides a framework for detecting and mitigating backdoor attacks in neural networks. It can reverse-engineer the input perturbations and identify the malicious target labels and Trojaned neurons. Mitigation is done through the filtering of inputs or patching of the network model. | Pros: The approach is generalizable and not tailored to a specific attack model. The detection scheme is low-cost and scalable. Cons: There is no evaluation of the increase in latency due to the detection and mitigation steps. Also, the approach assumes that the majority of the labels are uninfected, which may not always be true. |
| Trojan attacks on neural networks [44] | Proposes a method for injecting malicious behavior into neural networks by retraining a small part of the network to misclassify images when a specially crafted trigger patch is inserted in the input image. Even with the Trojan injected, the neural network performs almost as well as the original model on benign inputs. | Pros: The attack does not require access to the original data and requires little retraining time to inject the Trojan. The authors comprehensively evaluate their attack on multiple types of neural networks and scenarios. Cons: The Trojan stamps on the input images are easily detectable by a human observer, so the authors' claim that the stamps are stealthy may not always hold. The attack works only if the attacker can modify the target neural network. Many safety-critical applications don't expose their network models. |

training data. (i) A small patch in the input is crafted as a Trojan trigger that activates specified internal neurons. (ii) New training data are generated that can maximize the likelihood of classifying an image with the trigger as an incorrect class, and without the trigger as the original, correct class. (iii) The model is retrained on these newly generated data. The paper shows that the attack has minimal impact on the performance of the neural network on the original benign data set, but can misclassify stamped images with high probability. However, the attack increases robustness only against black-box attacks and not white-box attacks. Furthermore, Ensemble Adversarial Training reduces the accuracy of the original model, and that may be significant, depending on the application domain. Although the attack has a high degree of success on neural networks that are performing different classification tasks, the authors' claim that the Trojan stamp is stealthy may not be valid in general. A human observer can easily perceive the stamp if shown a malicious image. Furthermore, to insert the Trojan effectively, the attacker must have access to the model, retrain it, and get others to use it. Therefore, safety-critical system manufacturers should train their models in-house and not make them public.

Wang et al. [70] propose techniques both to detect and mitigate some neural network backdoor attacks. Their backdoor detection method checks whether certain labels are easier to misclassify through small changes in the input space. A byproduct of this step is that it allows sample triggers to be reverse-engineered. The paper also presents two mitigation techniques: neuron pruning (in which neurons that are activated by the backdoor trigger when inference is being performed are discarded) and unlearning (in which the network is retrained with triggers or adversarial examples so that they are not misclassified). Wang et al.'s detection and mitigation techniques are generic enough that they can be applied to many classification models covering varied attack models so long as the target label can be distinguished via their outlier method. However, they did not present or evaluate their techniques' impact on latency when applied to the models. Certain applications (like AVs) have low latency requirements that may be violated if the techniques are not fast enough. In addition, Wang et al.'s attack does not work well if there are multiple target labels for the Trojan attack, as it will be more difficult to find the outlier labels.

### 14.3.2.3  Generative Adversarial Networks

A *generative adversarial network* (GAN) is a method for training a generative model such that it learns the distribution of a particular data set and generates random samples from the learned distribution. The generated samples need not be identical to any of the samples in the original data set. Wang et al. [72] give a comprehensive overview of GANs and their applications. GANs have been applied to data augmentation [54] and image synthesis techniques like super-resolution (upscaling image resolution) [41], completion/repair [43], matting [47], and image-to-image translation [33]. They have also been used for video generation [68] as well as in adversarial attacks against ML systems, which will be discussed in detail later.

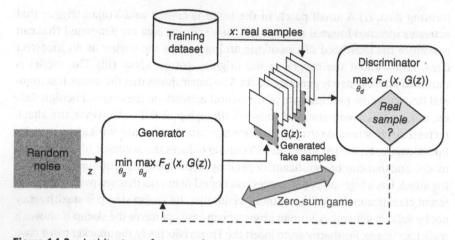

**Figure 14.2** Architecture of a generative adversarial network (GAN).

A GAN, as depicted in Figure 14.2, takes a game-theoretic approach wherein the overall objective function can be represented as a minimax function involving a generator $G$ and a discriminator $D$. Goodfellow et al. [28] formalize the optimization of the objective function as follows:

$$ss \min_G \max_D V(D,G) = E_{x \sim P_{\text{data}}}\Big[\log D(x)\Big] + E_{z \sim p_z(z)}\Big[\log\big(1 - D\big(G(z)\big)\big)\Big] \tag{14.1}$$

where $P_{\text{data}}$ is the true data distribution, and $p_z(z)$ is the prior distribution on the input noise variables used to learn the generator distribution $p_g$. $D(x)$ denotes the probability that $x$ is from the true data distribution $p_{\text{data}}$ instead of the generator distribution $p_g$.

Both $G$ and $D$ are modeled as multilayer perceptrons. The generator is responsible for learning the real data distribution so that it can generate synthetic samples $G(z)$ that resemble the real data. The role of the discriminator $D$ is to distinguish between real data samples $x$ and the generated samples $G(z)$. In this setting, the generator *minimizes* the objective function (i.c. $V$ ($D$, $G$) in Equation (14.1)) that the discriminator tries to *maximize* by identifying fake samples from the pool of inputs. Iterating over the training data sets enables the generator and discriminator to tune their parameters ($\theta_G$ and $\theta_D$). Goodfellow et al. [28] theoretically prove that if both $G$ and $D$ have enough capacity, then the minimax algorithm on the objective function $V(D, G)$ will converge such that the distribution of samples generated by $G$ will be equal to the real data distribution. However, in practice, neither $G$ nor $D$ has infinite capacity; hence, the generated distribution is never guaranteed to converge to the real data distribution. However, the good performance of the multilayer perceptrons in GANs in practice makes them a reasonable generative model even without theoretical guarantees.

Since the inception of the original GAN by Goodfellow et al., various other types of GAN architectures have been developed. The architectures generally differ by the type of neural networks used for the generator and discriminator. Creswell et al. [17] broadly classify GANs into (i) fully connected GANs, (ii) convolutional GANs, (iii) conditional GANs, and (iv) GANs with inference models. Fully connected GANs have their generator and discriminator modeled as a fully connected neural network and were used in simple image data sets like MNIST and CIFAR-10. Convolutional GANs use CNNs, an approach that is more suitable for working with images than for fully connected networks. Conditional GANs [49] extend the original GAN by conditioning the generator and discriminator on some extra information $y$, such as the label or class of the data. The advantage of conditional GANs is that they offer some level of control over the modes of the generated data by helping direct the data generation process. The class and the prior input noise $p_z(z)$ are combined into a joint hidden representation. The objective function in Equation (14.1) now becomes

$$\min_{G} \max_{D} V\left(D,G\right) = E_{x \sim P_{\text{data}}} \left[ \log D\left(x|y\right) \right] + E_{z \sim p_z(z)} \left[ \log\left(1 - D\left(G\left(z|y\right)\right)\right) \right]. \quad (14.2)$$

GANs with inference models provide a way to map the data $x$ to the latent space $z$. For example, in bidirectional GANs [20], the generator consists of the traditional GAN generator $G$ that maps from $z$ space to $x$ space as well as an encoder $E$ that is responsible for learning the inverse mapping. Both $G$ and $E$ are jointly optimized using the discriminator.

*Examples.* As discussed in [26], deep neural networks are vulnerable to well-designed input samples, known as *adversarial examples*, that can mislead DNNs into classifying objects incorrectly, although a human may not be able to tell the difference between the benign and adversarial inputs. This problem has been most widely demonstrated in computer vision, for which imperceptible changes in an image cause the DNN to give incorrect output. This poses a cybersecurity risk with respect to password cracking, malware detection, and facial recognition. For example, in [63], the authors consider a threat in which an attacker can deploy a black-box API attack against online ML services (e.g. intrusion detection systems). In such an attack, an adversary can, without any prior knowledge of the ML algorithm and the training data, infer and/or replicate the ML model likely used in the online service. However, during such an attack, security barriers, such as rate limitations, restrict the collection of observation data, resulting in a lack of training data. In [63], the authors demonstrate that in a GAN, adversaries can generate synthetic training data, despite the limited number of data samples, either to poison the training process of an intrusion detection system or to mislead the classifier into making incorrect decisions. It is shown in [63] that when the synthetic training data generated by the GAN are used to train the inferred classifier, the difference between the labels returned by the target and by the inferred classifier drops from about 45% to 28%. In [62], the authors demonstrate that an adversary can generate and transmit wireless signals that cannot be distinguished from intended GAN signals. The generator is located in the adversarial transmitter, while the discriminator is placed in the adversarial receiver. The attackers might be able to use the trained generator of the GAN to fool a defense mechanism, such as radio frequency (RF) fingerprinting, of a vulnerable receiver. Otherwise, the discriminator of the trained GAN can be used to enhance vulnerable detectors to identify spoofing signals. In [62], the authors evaluate GAN performance by showing that a GAN-based spoofing attack significantly increases the probability of success from 36.2% (for a replay attack) to 76.2% (for GAN-based spoofing), even when a deep learning classifier is used as the defense at the receiver. In [12], the authors demonstrate that by using a deep GAN, attackers can synthesize spoofing attacks on speaker recognition systems, which are deployed for security-critical applications such as banking and home automation. In particular, the authors were able to fool a CNN-based speaker verifier regardless of whether they conducted a targeted attack (in which an adversary wants to be identified as a particular target person) or an untargeted attack (in which an adversary wants to be verified as any benign speaker). The authors used an improved Wasserstein GAN to generate spectrogram images that fooled the voice recognition system.

*Insights.* The adversarial use cases of GANs described above show that GANs can model the true data distribution to a certain extent and thus can increase the success rate of attacks on deep learning systems through generated data samples. However, GANs are not a one-stop solution for exploiting any ML system, as not all the samples generated by GANs fool AI systems, and the efficacy of attacks varies across use cases. Furthermore, the same adversarial examples generated by GANs to exploit an ML system can be used to make the ML system more robust to attacks.

*Other non-GAN-based adversarial examples.* Sharif et al. present an attack on a facial biometric system that is widely used in surveillance and access control; they used a systematic method to generate a pattern that allowed the attacker to evade recognition or impersonate another individual [61]. Similarly, the authors of [55] present an attack on an intelligent personal assistant in which they played an inaudible voice command that utilized the frequency range that can be captured by microphones but not heard by human ears. In [10], the authors demonstrate that an adversary can cause an infraction or collision of an AV by adding double lanes on the road that cause the AV to take a left turn where a right turn is needed.

*GAN for trustworthy AI.* Use of GANs to attack and compromise ML algorithms used in perception, recognition, and control has been demonstrated many times, but there has also been work in which GANs make ML models more robust. GANs may threaten the trustworthiness of AI applications, either by poisoning the model in the training phase or by feeding fake data to systems deployed in practice. However, one can also compensate for a limited input data set by exemplifying the training data set with GANs, or by training the GAN against likely adversarial samples (with the right labels) to prepare the GAN to defend against potential attacks empowered by adversarial learning. For instance, a social GAN [30], given a partially observed history of some pedestrians, uses GANs and sequence prediction to predict multiple socially acceptable trajectories for those pedestrians, assuming they want to avoid getting too close to each other. Furthermore, the authors in [30] propose a novel mechanism for increasing the accuracy of the predicted trajectories by learning the social norms whereby humans walk past each other. This work can aid in training algorithms used in AVs and social robots that need to operate in crowded environments. DeepRoad [78], on the other hand, uses a GAN to synthetically produce driving scenes in various weather conditions without using traditional image transformation techniques. Images produced by GANs tend to have greater diversity than those produced by image transformation methods, increasing the test coverage of scenarios. DeepRoad also validates generated images before using them in testing to reduce the mismatch between the training and application domains; if that were not done, the accuracy of the ML system would be dramatically degraded. DeepRoad was able to detect thousands of inconsistent behaviors for well-known DNN-based autonomous driving systems in the Udacity self-driving car challenge.

*Insights.* Although GANs can be used to find examples and edge cases empirically to make AI more robust, there are no theoretical guarantees of completeness. The improvement in safety is hard to quantify because the universal set of inputs is too large to enumerate. Furthermore, it is possible for errors to occur within the GAN itself, and that may cause critical examples to be missed.

*Mitigation.* A number of researchers have proposed ways to improve the robustness of learning models [29, 45, 48]. Furthermore, in certain applications, the physical constraints of a problem allow a system to overcome adversarial examples, preventing temporal misclassification from cascading into critical decisions made by the application software. The creators of TequilaGAN [87] take an alternative approach, in which they aim to detect GAN-generated fake examples by identifying the characteristics of fake samples. They conducted a study over four data sets from image processing and audio analysis: the MNIST handwritten digits database, the CIFAR-10 tiny images data set, a Bach chorales data set, and the NIST 2004 specch database. The authors found that fake, GAN-generated samples are distinguishable from training data sets because of their significant divergence from the training data sets, the smooth approximation in their distribution (if they were produced by a generator that had been trained using a stochastic gradient descent and an asymptotically converging activation function), or their violation of the specifications of real data (e.g. specifications that define the style of music).

Further, although digital attacks on perception systems are of significant concern, prototype attacks often assume that the attacker can gain access to an AI system's decision module. However, connecting to a remote system and, further, gaining sufficient privilege are nontrivial tasks, especially if the system is not connected to a public network (e.g. AVs). Second, if the attacker has full access to the AV's computer, there are many other components (e.g. decision and control systems) that the attacker can more easily manipulate to cause a safety hazard. Hence, attacks on the perception system through environment modifications (e.g. a physical adversarial stop sign) may be a more plausible attack mode that needs to be addressed. An extensive survey of adversarial attacks and their defenses can be found in [89].

### 14.3.3 Smart Malware with Self-Learning Capabilities

While adversarial learning approaches investigate how attackers can come up with adversarial input (or methods for generating fake input) to mislead AI modules, one can also consider the potential for launching attacks that embed AI modules into malware to automate exploits, to customize attack payloads, and to execute attacks with minimal intervention from the human attacker. A number of researchers have recently asserted their concerns about the possibility of smart malware that can be embedded with learning capabilities.

Chung et al. demonstrated that with the help of statistical and learning methods, malware (after being installed in the system with privileges) can analyze local data that describe the operational patterns of a water distribution system in a smart building [15]. The malware infers anomalies that are likely to be capable of triggering systemwide outages in the compute infrastructure (CI), which relies heavily on water distribution. The malware then injects such an anomaly into the system to trigger an outage-causing scenario. The prototype malware, presented in [15] and tested in a simulated environment, was able to infer successful attack strategies that would be hard to distinguish from accidental failures. In [16], the authors discuss prototype malware that uses a density-based spatial clustering algorithm, called DBSCAN, to identify times at which a surgical robot is likely to be performing sensitive surgical operations, to determine the opportune time to trigger the attack payload. The various pieces of prototype malware were able to infer when and how to attack the target system, despite minimal prior knowledge regarding the victim system. In [39], the authors demonstrate that an attacker can encode the specifics of the target in a DNN (i.e. can train a DNN with a data set that specifies the attack target) so that a certain piece of ransomware will activate only in the target's system. As discussed in [39], in addition to minimizing unnecessary activations of an attack (which would reveal the existence of the malware), the use of DNNs impedes the reverse-engineering process by taking advantage of the difficulty of interpreting an AI model.

AI technology is not always beneficial to the general public and can be used by adversaries. (An extensive survey of this topic can be found in [37].) While certain mitigation methods (e.g. encryption or two-factor authentication) can impede malware's incursion into a system, no existing prevention technology has been proven to be perfect. Further, in an endless cat-and-mouse game, attackers have always been able to find vulnerabilities in advancing security barriers. A study to define trustworthy AI can provide a starting point for protecting our systems against smart malware. The vulnerabilities identified by such a study can be the baseline for determining how to neutralize AI-driven threats.

## 14.4 Online Detection and Mitigation

While offline analysis can provide insight that could improve the design of a system to enhance trust, the development of a comprehensive method for detecting all deficiencies, in advance, is a challenging problem. For instance, certain edge cases are activated in rare circumstances that offline methods might not easily capture. Next, we discuss online methods that detect unforeseen circumstances or behaviors and that mitigate the uncertainties in operation.

### 14.4.1 Formalization

Here we describe the design and development of current monitoring and mitigation methods for trustworthy AI systems. An AI system continuously performs an array of tasks that affect internal and external systems in response to user input. These tasks must be executed such that the system maintains its trust properties, such as robustness, integrity, reliability, performance, safety, and security. For example, a user of a self-driving car provides a navigation goal by specifying a destination on a map. In response to that input, the vehicle must perform two key types of tasks: (i) *external tasks*, such as driving in the environment, and (ii) *internal tasks*, such as scheduling of computational tasks. These tasks are executed using computational algorithms and models (henceforth referred to as *agents*).

### 14.4.2 Monitoring

Most of the AI algorithms in AVs include a data-driven approach for training and testing their predictions given a set of inputs, and measuring or ensuring the safety of such systems may also require an empirical approach. Use of a statistical approach to prove that an AV is as safe as a human driver is not viable because the measurement collection requires so much time and money [38]. Hence, researchers have moved to defining formal models of AV safety that do not rely on empirical methods.

Formal models of safety allow the deterministic evaluation of the safety of an AV, given an accurate representation or measurement of the world. Examples of research in this direction can be found in [53, 60].

The safety force field [53], introduced by NVIDIA, uses the concept of safety potentials to define safe or unsafe states between two actors on a road. If an AV is in an unsafe state with respect to another actor or object (such that their safety potentials are high and their trajectories intersect), the AV applies a safety procedure that reduces the safety potential between them. The model considers vehicle kinematics and actor trajectories when calculating safety potentials. Shalev-Shwartz et al. propose a similar approach, although their proposed formal model was based on a responsibility-sensitive safety (RSS) model for multiagent safety [60]. RSS is a mathematical formalization of "duty of care" law, which states that individuals must be reasonably careful when performing tasks that may injure others. Both [53, 60] proved that no collision can occur if all actors behave as they are required to by the formal model, given an accurate perception of the world.

The key drawback of the above formal models is in assuming that (i) the models have access to accurate representations of the world and the car, and (ii) the implementation of the formal model will be fault-free. Neither of these assumptions holds in real life. First, the perception systems used in AVs are not perfect and are the cause of many safety issues [7]. Second, the implementations of the formal models in AVs are bound to have faults that arise from a variety of sources, like AI algorithms, software and hardware implementation bugs, and adversarial attacks. Hence, these formalisms are meant not to replace existing self-driving technologies, but to complement them to improve the safety of AVs.

### 14.4.3 Mitigation

In controlling a self-driving vehicle, it is critical to ensure the safety not only of the vehicle and its passengers, but also of the surrounding environment. However, in the context of the vehicle's decision-making, the intents of entities in the environment remain unknown, meaning there is uncertainty in the inputs. The authors of [21] combine the pedestrian intent model, using LSTM (long short-term memory) and lane detection modules, to detect safety hazards online and plan a path for the vehicle to avoid a collision. The approach assumes that all map information and possible pedestrian intentions define a set of possible goals (e.g. a pedestrian might cross the road at a crosswalk, or might take a path that ignores the crosswalk). Hence, if a pedestrian takes an unexpected action (e.g. following a ball or animal into the road), the module's ability to make good decisions may be questionable.

On the other hand, inputs are noisy and uncertain, and learning algorithms typically incorporate domain knowledge into decision models to mitigate this uncertainty. In this approach, the domain knowledge, represented as a graphical model (e.g. a Markov decision process [MDP] or a partially observable Markov decision process [POMDP]), is a skeleton that bounds the decision/model surface with details (e.g. transition probability, decision policy, or strategy) to be fleshed out by the observed data. In particular, we find that certain learning models are commonly deployed to mitigate the uncertainty in different layers of the AI system architecture.

A decision process is often represented as a Markov decision process with a set of states and actions. However, we often lack a complete understanding of the environment because the underlying state is not observable. To account for this restriction, POMDP models introduce the concept of a *set of observations*, an indirect measure that provides information to predict the likely state. (An MDP does not need the observation state, as the agent knows the current state with certainty.) For instance, Abbas et al. [1], in the context of autonomous driving, acknowledge that temporal evolution of situations cannot be predicted without uncertainty because of the stochastic behavior of other users who share the environment (i.e. the road). Furthermore, users can perceive only a limited part of their current situation, as sensors are noisy and the majority of the environment is occluded. To address this problem, the authors present a continuous POMDP solver that can merge into traffic under nontrivial occlusions (e.g. with dead angles or with important objects hidden behind obstacles).

Reinforcement learning (RL) is an approach commonly deployed to approximately solve an MDP by replacing the sum of rewards over all states with a Monte Carlo approximation. (In other words, the value and reward functions are updated only for states that are actually visited.) To accommodate the incompleteness of the underlying decision model, an RL algorithm combines exploitation (i.e. making the best decision given the current information) with exploration (i.e. gathering more information that might lead to better decisions in the future).

Akhtar and Mian [3] adopted RL to automatically navigate a mobile robot in an unknown environment while avoiding collisions. For a robot to learn collision avoidance, it should experience collisions, which, however, could cause physical damage. Instead, the authors let their robot experience collisions only at low speed until the robot gained confidence. The approach was driven by an uncertainty-aware cost function, whereby the agent chooses to proceed cautiously in an unfamiliar environment and makes confident movements (e.g. with increased velocity) only in settings for which it has high confidence. Similarly, Banerjee et al. [82] adopted a Bayesian network to estimate computing infrastructure resource utilization. The domain knowledge regarding the processor is represented by the underlying model, while the noisy measurements (e.g. performance counters from the processors) drive the analysis. To account for uncertainty in measurements [82], systematically modeled the variance of the measurements and applied the model to a Bayesian network. The experimental results show that their approach drastically reduces job completion times (determined by optimizing the resource utilization) despite the relatively limited model training time and data (compared to conventional methods). Similar approaches for quantifying the uncertainty in medical images and decision models are discussed in [6–9].

Abbas et al. [2] combine the advantages of approximate POMPDs and deep RL in collision-free navigation of self-driving vehicles in an environment that is not fully observable by the car. In particular, HyLEAP lets the approximated POMDP exploit the DRL network, as a critic, to plan the path of the vehicle. The experimental results demonstrate that the hybrid method outperforms DRL or POMDP methods used in isolation, especially against unusual pedestrian movement patterns; in other words, the method results in fewer collisions and lower impact speeds.

Beede et al. [8] apply RL in active breast lesion detection from DCE-MRI (dynamic contrast-enhanced magnetic resonance imaging). Conventional detection methods rely on handcrafted features and exhaustive search mechanisms (which are computationally complex and potentially suboptimal) in handling the variability in lesion appearance, shape, location, and size. State-of-the-art learning methods have been adopted to address this problem. However, the need for large annotated training sets, and the approach's sensitivity to variability in the input data set, call into question the practicality of the approach. Instead, the authors present a deep Q-network (DQN)-driven learning method that reduces the runtime without loss of detection accuracy. Their experimental results show detection accuracy comparable to that of state-of-the-art methods (e.g. CNN) while reducing the detection time by 55%.

In summary, state-of-the-art research is demonstrating that it is possible to mitigate uncertainty that can challenge the trustworthiness of AI applications. It can be achieved either by reducing the uncertainty in the different layers of the system by modeling the noise and uncertainty and inferring the underlying truth, or by augmenting the data-driven methods with domain and expert knowledge that provides a bound for the truth to be inferred.

## 14.5 Trust Model Formulation

The precise definition of *trust*, or the determination of which property (e.g. reliability, security, safety, and performance, among others) matters most, is specific to the application domain or system under study. Hence, studying and assessing system trustworthiness are not trivial tasks. The interdependency across properties further complicates the problem. Each property that contributes to trust has been well-studied in the literature. For instance, the authors of [79] present a framework that models the security of a CPS from the physical to supervisory levels, and they demonstrate a game-theoretic approach for deriving a strategic solution to secure the system.

### 14.5.1 An Illustrative Trust Model

In the following, we describe a generic model that spans four trust properties (i.e. reliability, security, safety, and performance). Unlike existing methods that are

**Table 14.3** Parameters.

| Parameter | Description |
|---|---|
| $C_{reward}$ | Reward per unit of time for providing the system functionality |
| $f_f$ | Failure density function of the system |
| $m(t)$ | Renewal density function of the system |
| $g(t)$ | Repair density function of the system |
| $W(t)$ | Reward rate of the system |
| $C_{down}$ | Downtime cost per unit time |
| $C_{repair}$ | Repair cost per unit time |

specific to a single property, our model captures the relationship across multiple properties and represents the overall trustworthiness of a system.

In this formulation, described by the parameters listed in Table 14.3, the system collects reward $C_{reward}$ if it is alive and functional. Upon failure, the system incurs the following penalties: (i) downtime or service-level agreement (SLA) violation cost ($C_{down}$), and (ii) repair cost ($C_{repair}$). On repair, the system is renewed, and the failure density function remains $f_f(t)$.

In our formulation, we consider two states: up and down. The system starts in an up state and transitions to a down state upon failure. After failing, the system is repaired. Following completion of the repair, the system transitions back to an up state. Considering the downtime and repair cost, the reward rate ($W(t)$) for the system is given by Equation (14.7). Here the system is given a reward $C_{reward}$ for useful work and incurs the penalties of $C_{down}$ and $C_{repair}$ upon failure. Thus, we must calculate the probability that the system is in an up state or a down state to calculate $W(t)$.

$$W(t) = C_{reward} \cdot A(t) - \{1 - A(t)\}\{C_{down} + C_{repair}\} \tag{14.3}$$

where $A(t)$, which is the reward for useful work, is given by Equation (14.4), and $R(t)$ is given by Equation (14.5).

$$A(t) = R(t) + \int_0^t R(t-u)m(u)\,du \tag{14.4}$$

$$R(t) = 1 - \int_0^t f_f(t)\,dt \tag{14.5}$$

Most of the time, a violation in a trust property will have a cascading impact on other properties that are related. For instance, a security breach can lead to a safety violation, or a reliability problem can introduce new security vulnerabilities.

To capture such effects, we extend the model as follows with the addition of an expected cost (where $\mathbb{C}_i$ is the expected cost of cascading):

$$W(t) = \mathbb{C}_{\text{reward}} \cdot A(t) - \{1 - A(t)\}\left\{\mathbb{C}_{\text{down}} + \mathbb{C}_{\text{repair}} + \sum_{i \in \mathbb{P}} J_i(\vec{\theta}, \vec{\eta})\mathbb{C}_i\right\} \quad (14.6)$$

The parameters in Equation (14.4) are described in Table 14.4, and additional parameters are described in Table 14.5.

*Example: AV model.* In this model, in addition to incurring the cost of SLA violations and repairs, we also incur the cost of safety violations, $\mathbb{C}_{\text{safety}}$. The probability that the system will experience a safety violation is $p_{s|f}$. We omit the calculation of $p_{s|f}$, as it would require a deep dive into the AV system.

$$W(t) = \mathbb{C}_{\text{reward}} \cdot A(t) - \{1 - A(t)\}\left\{p_{s|f}(t)d \cdot \mathbb{C}_{\text{safety}}(w_m(t)) + \mathbb{C}_{\text{down}} + \mathbb{C}_{\text{repair}}\right\} \quad (14.7)$$

This section has described a system perspective of trust and a way to develop analytical models in terms of system-level trust metrics including reliability, security, safety, and performance. It described the major components that provide a framework for quantifying the trustworthiness of an AI system in terms of domain-specific reward models (e.g. reliability, security, safety, and performance). In the next section, we will discuss three representative application domains in which AI systems play a critical role. We will identify challenges that

**Table 14.4** Parameters for extended formulation.

| Parameter | Description |
| --- | --- |
| $J_i$ | Joint distribution where a property violation results in the violation of another property $i$ |
| $P$ | Set of system properties that are critical in ensuring trust |
| $\eta^{\circledast}$ | Generic system parameters that represent system state |
| $\circledast$ | Global system parameters that are shared across properties |
| $\theta$ | Parameter of the joint distribution |

**Table 14.5** Additional notation.

| Parameter | Description |
| --- | --- |
| $w_m(t)$ | State of the world (environment) at time $t$ |
| $\mathbb{C}_{\text{safety}}(w_m(t))$ | Safety cost per unit time |
| $p_{s|f}$ | Probability of the occurrence of a safety violation (s), given a failure (f) |

are specific to each application area and describe how we apply our model framework to problems that are specific to each domain.

## 14.6 Modeling the Trustworthiness of Critical Applications

As AI technology matures, AI components have been deployed in various application domains. For instance, auto manufacturers are developing self-driving vehicles that automatically maneuver themselves in response to dynamically changing environments. In healthcare, researchers are looking into the use of ML technology for the detection of anomalies in health records (e.g. medical images, sensor readings, or test results) to help physicians detect potential diseases early. Nevertheless, several unfortunate incidents have raised flags about reckless adoption of new technology, and point to the need for careful investigation of the trustworthiness of such systems. For example, prototype AV systems from companies leading the self-driving vehicle industry have reported several fatal incidents in which the decision module failed to detect objects (e.g. a pedestrian or lane divider) in a timely manner, resulting in a collision [81, 83]. Sensors are noisy by nature, which has driven current design practices in which decisions are derived from an ensemble of sensor measurements. However, recent incidents hint at the limitations of such methods and suggest the need for a systematic approach to assessing the trustworthiness of the technology and the system. The failure of IBM Watson, the machine that beat human champions on the TV show Jeopardy!, in healthcare (specifically for clinical decision support) and the struggle that Google's ML-driven eye-scanning system faced when deployed in practice illustrated the limitations of the current assessment and evaluation methods and settings in representing the real environment with which the system must interact and in which it operates.

AI technology has been adopted, and demonstrated success, in many societally important application domains (e.g. manufacturing, supply chain management, the justice system, and human resources). In this section, we limit our scope to three representative domains in which a lack of trustworthiness in operation can have critical impacts on humans and their environment. Here, we adopt the abstraction of AI systems and the definitions of trustworthy AI described in Section 14.2, and apply them to the following three trust-sensitive applications: transportation (AVs), enterprise computing systems' infrastructure management, and healthcare.

### 14.6.1 Autonomous Vehicles and Transportation

AV technologies are understood to be transformative, with the potential to improve traffic congestion, safety, productivity, and comfort. AVs are complex systems that use AI and ML to integrate mechanical, electronic, and computing technologies to make real-time driving decisions. AI enables AVs to navigate through complex environments while maintaining a safety envelope (e.g. the maximum distance an AV can travel without colliding with any static or dynamic object) that is continuously measured and quantified by onboard sensors (e.g. camera, LiDAR, and RADAR).

The trustworthiness of traditional vehicles has been well-studied and has been improving since the mid-1930s. Today, the mechanical [9] and electrical [76] components of traditional cars conform to strict reliability standards. Furthermore, vehicle safety ratings [69] ensure that cars are structurally and mechanically safe for the driver and the passengers in the event of a collision [52]. Intelligent vehicle safety systems, such as collision avoidance systems, further enhance safety [34] and greatly reduce fatalities. Hence, traditional vehicles are generally seen as trustworthy systems.

When studying and assessing trustworthiness in traditional cars, we do not consider the erroneous decisions of the driver as a safety hazard; we rely on the driver as the last resort to respond to any faults or failures of the vehicle. However, with the advent of AVs, the vehicle is responsible for making driving decisions that directly impact the safety of its passengers as well as other users who share the road. Figure 14.3 shows an advanced AV, or a driver assist system (ADAS)-based vehicle, with an array of error/failure detection recovery methods (discussed in earlier chapters) to control and manage failures. It also shows the role of AI/ML in managing the system and keeping it safe. Hence, the trustworthiness of AVs depends not only on the trustworthiness of vehicles as traditionally defined but also on the trustworthiness of the AI system that makes the driving decisions.

| Components | Functionality | Fault tolerance techniques |
|---|---|---|
| Planning, Localization, Prediction, Perception, Sensor abstraction | Location orientation, Object speed detection, Worldview build up, Visual information detection | Hazard analysis, Scenario-based verification, Simulated deployments |

ML-based control

| Components | Fault tolerance techniques |
|---|---|
| Camera, LiDAR, RADAR, Ultrasonic, GPS, IMU | Full redundancy (up to 20), Overlapping field of view |

Sensors

| Hardware components | Fault tolerance techniques |
|---|---|
| Memory, Processor, Accelerators (GPU), Ethernet and InfiniBand networks, CAN bus | Error correction and detection codes, Dedicated safety islands, Flow control, Traffic prioritization, Frame checks, Differential signaling |

Compute (Fully duplicated)

**Figure 14.3** Autonomous vehicle, with an array of error detection recovery methods to manage failures. *Source:* Adapted from https://waymo.com/media-resources/

Clearly, the safety and resilience of AVs are of significant concern; several headline-making AV crashes [80, 81], as well as prior work characterizing AV resilience during road tests [7], show that AVs do not outperform human drivers with respect to safety. An outstanding issue for AVs is the need for rigorous demonstration and validation of their safety and trustworthiness. The self-adaptive, context-sensitive behavior of AVs can cause unexpected emergent behavior or interactions with external actors not foreseen at the architectural stage of design. The causes of "unexpected" or unsafe behaviors may include unforeseen interactions between an autonomous action and the vehicle's kinematics, various failure and hazard scenarios, faults (both design and physical), and security threats. It is therefore necessary to develop performance-sensitive and at-scale resilient implementations of the autonomous functions and architectures to ensure safe and correct system operation under challenging conditions.

### 14.6.1.1 Addressing Uncertainty

A generic representation of an AV stack and its operating environment, indicating points at which challenges to safe operations arise, is shown in Figure 14.4. As indicated in the figure, pedestrians and a bicyclist are crossing the road. The question is whether the AV's perception systems (RADAR, LiDAR, and the camera sensor and its controller) can handle the situation correctly in the presence of uncertainty in each measurement.

Uncertainty in the inputs of AVs arises from measurement errors or noisy inputs from the various sensors (e.g. camera, LiDAR, and RADAR). AV sensors are noisy by nature, and misdetections or bad decisions stemming from such noisy input can have fatal results [80]. For instance, in 2016, the sensors on a Tesla Model S failed to detect a white 18-wheeler truck [81] against a bright sky background and drove into it, killing the driver. In addition to naturally occurring noise, AVs are at risk from adversaries who can intentionally perturb input data to corrupt the operation and safety of the AV [84, 85].

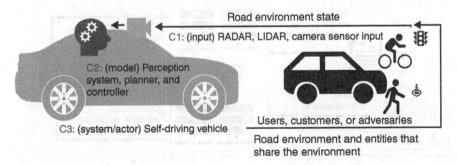
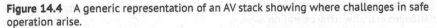

**Figure 14.4** A generic representation of an AV stack showing where challenges in safe operation arise.

Uncertainties in ML models of AVs manifest themselves in the perception and decision-and-control modules and are propagated through the pipeline to the actuators (e.g. gas, brake, and steering). In Silicon Valley in February 2016, a Google Lexus SUV crashed into the side of a bus when merging into traffic after it stopped to avoid an obstacle. The AV misjudged the trajectory of the bus, and wrongly assumed that the bus would yield to it. (No one was injured, but the vehicles were damaged.)

Uncertainty in system operation can be caused by the failure of any mechanical, hardware, or software component in the AV such that the failure bypasses fault tolerance mechanisms and manifests itself as an erroneous actuation. It is imperative to ensure that the ML models behave safely in the presence of such failures.

## 14.6.2 Large-Scale Computing Infrastructure

As depicted in Figure 14.5, large-scale computing infrastructure (e.g. high-performance computers or cloud systems) provides aggregated computing power to solve large problems at speed. To optimize the utilization of compute and data-related resources and minimize the runtime of the programs/applications processed on these resources, data centers have been adding CI in the form of instrumentation, computing, communications and control for system management, and real-time/back-end analysis (C1, C2, and C3 in Figure 14.5) to collect and analyze detailed information about all aspects of operation. However, such additional CI increases the volume (by tens of terabytes per day per system) and dimensionality (by thousands of different instrumentation points) of data available to human administrators, who have limited capacity to analyze the data to identify root causes of problems. In addition, any delay between a problem's occurrence and its diagnosis limits the utilization of current CI systems with respect to automated feedback and optimization of runtime resources and configuration.

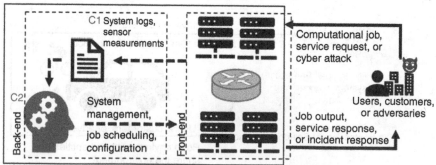

**Figure 14.5** Generic representation of a compute infrastructure showing where challenges in trustworthy operation arise.

The convergence of AI with cloud, mid-tier, and top-tier high-performance computing (HPC) centers has rapidly emerged as an alternative way to handle the disruptive effects of the big-data revolution. The design and training of AI algorithms require novel cyber-tools, such as distributed training schemes in HPC platforms, but once these algorithms have been fully trained, they enable real-time inference studies that use minimal resources, e.g. on-demand, in the cloud, GPU-accelerated solutions or field-programmable gate arrays (FPGAs), to further boost computing acceleration. For instance, AI can reduce the complexity of designing and operating CI. By definition, CI is highly interconnected, and systems are co-dependent; hence, it is difficult to design, build, and operate such systems to provide the desired level of security. AI can reduce the "time to discovery of an attack" and correspondingly, the "time to respond" to discovered attacks. Given the growing data sizes and complexities of systems, the human ability to discover and respond to anomalies, inefficiencies, bottlenecks, faults, and security vulnerabilities in a timely manner is limited. To address that limitation, AI methodologies can be applied to effectively locate and extract insights from large, complex data and support automated responses. When AI takes care of the most trivial (yet common) problems, the system administrators can focus on the rare, more significant problems that cannot be handled by AI-driven automation.

### 14.6.2.1 Model Formulation

Large computing infrastructure is commonly a target for attackers, who typically try to corrupt the availability of the system or its services. A traditional threat (e.g. denial of service attacks) would target the CI. In contrast, in [15], the authors demonstrate an indirect attack that deploys learning malware in a chilled water system (i.e. a CPS that supports a CI) to corrupt the operation of the computing infrastructure. An attacker intrudes into the control server of the supporting CPS that regulates the chilled water, which is critical for managing the operational environment of the CI. (Failure to meet the SLA, for instance by delivering chilled water that is hotter than a specified maximum temperature, can damage circuits in the CI.) The learning malware analyzes CPS measurements to infer anomalies that are likely to be related to computing infrastructure outages. By injecting the anomalies into the CPS, the malware can trigger a failure incident and disguise its malicious action as an accidental failure. The formulation of this problem is as follows:

$$W(t) = \mathbb{C}_{\text{reward}} \cdot A(t) - \{1 - A(t)\}\{\mathbb{C}_{\text{down}} + \mathbb{C}_{\text{repair}} + p_{\text{sec}|f} \cdot \mathbb{C}_{\text{down}}(x(t))\} \quad (14.8)$$

- $A(t) = R(t) + \int_0^t R(t-u)m(u)\mathrm{d}u$, where $A(t)$ is the reward for useful work and $R(t)$ is a function of $\eta$, the temperature deviation of the chilled water. $\mathbb{C}_{\text{down}}$ is the SLA violation cost, and $\mathbb{C}_{\text{repair}}$ is the repair cost. $\mathbb{C}_{\text{down}}(x(t))$ is the (expected) safety cost.

- $p_{sec|f}$ (i.e. probability that given a system failure, the cause was a security incident) can be represented as a function of malware accuracy, detection accuracy, and CI workload. Higher malware accuracy and higher CI workload increase $p_{sec|f}$, while a higher incident detection accuracy decreases $p_{sec|f}$.
- The security attack mimics a reliability failure. Hence, the impact will be identical: $(\mathbb{C}_{down})$, i.e. $\mathbb{C}_{security} = \mathbb{C}_{down} \cdot p_{sec|f}$.

### 14.6.2.2 Addressing Uncertainty

The deployment of AI technology is advancing the automation of computer infrastructure management [94]. We must carefully investigate how the adoption of AI technology impacts the trustworthiness of the computing infrastructure. In particular, for large-scale computing systems, it is important to keep the system available and secure. However, as for other trust-sensitive systems, we face challenges in assuring the trustworthiness of AI in CI management. Those challenges stem from three layers of the system, as follows:

1) *Uncertainty in the input:* Given the complexity of CIs, devising the input space of the associated AI system is nearly impossible. Incident reports disclose how unexpected sequences or combinations of events have caused management/control software to make decisions that congest the limited resources of the computing infrastructure. Such congestion often results in worse throughput or availability than can be achieved by conventional management methods. Also, input data sources commonly used in CIs (e.g. performance counters in hardware architectures, or security monitors that audit user and system activities) are noisy by nature. To secure the improvement that AI-driven systems promise in CI operation, it is critical for systems to actively account for the uncertainty in the input.

2) *Uncertainty in the model:* The probabilistic nature of AI technology, particularly ML methods, can easily result in an outage of the system or a security vulnerability that malicious entities can exploit. Cybersecurity incident detection is a problem that researchers and engineers must consider during deployment of ML technology. Whereas humans serve as the end-actuators for healthcare systems and AVs (at least during the current phase of development, in which the driver is responsible for the final impact), cybersecurity instead relies heavily on automated systems (including monitors and detection systems), while the attention of human system administrators focuses more narrowly on incident response and aftermath. As a result, a failure of a detection system can easily lead to failure of system components and outage of the system. Furthermore, recent research has demonstrated that attackers can exploit the probabilistic nature of a model by learning data sets that can mislead or neutralize the AI classifiers.

3) *Uncertainty in the system:* Computing infrastructures are also challenged with respect to managing uncertainty, especially in executing life- and

mission-critical applications. Assuring the reliability of large-scale systems (whose computing power may be at the scale of petaflops or even exaflops) is a unique research question by itself, and CIs are constantly subject to errors, failures, and malicious attacks. To the best of our knowledge, the risk and impact of executing an AI application on a system platform that is itself at risk are only now being investigated. Interesting research questions, such as how to notify the AI application of the status of the underlying system, or how to respond to adverse events in the host system to minimize their impact (e.g. safe or soft failures), are challenges to be addressed.

### 14.6.3 Healthcare AI/ML

Healthcare is an important trust-sensitive domain in which AI is making significant progress, e.g. in robotics and AI-driven prognosis and treatment. Researchers are investigating deep learning methods, among many other ML methods, for deployment in translational bioinformatics, medical imaging, pervasive sensing, medical informatics, and public health. For instance, deep learning in medical image analysis can help physicians determine a tumor's grade, and ML methods can analyze EEG signals that capture neural oscillations (i.e. brain waves) to help physicians localize seizure onset zones [95].

Figure 14.6 shows how AI is integrated into healthcare. In a traditional setup, healthcare providers take input from a patient in varying forms (marked C1 in Figure 14.6; e.g. medical images, measurement data, and questionnaire entries), and the physician will consider such input in diagnosing and treating the patient (C3 in Figure 14.6). Various automated monitoring systems (e.g. vital sign monitors) reduce the need for human observation of patients. In performing AI-driven causal inference (C2 in Figure 14.6), the system and the healthcare providers

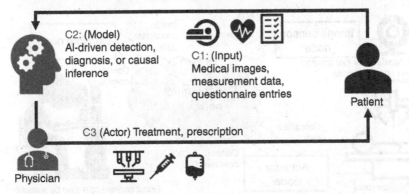

**Figure 14.6** Generic representation of a healthcare system, showing where challenges to trustworthy operation arise.

must propose an individualized diagnosis for the patient. Instead of aiming for AI technology to replace physicians in the same sense that AVs may remove drivers from behind the wheel, healthcare providers seek assistance from AI technology in performing preliminary analysis so that the physician can diagnose diseases and their causes faster and more accurately [97]. While the oversight of physicians will limit the consequences of AI failure, poor decisions by AI can still corrupt healthcare operations. For instance, in [8], the authors describe the deployment of a deep-learning-driven system for assessing diabetic retinopathy in 11 clinics in Thailand. Having shown promising results during the development process (i.e. >90% sensitivity and specificity), the system was expected to reduce the length of the eye-screening process (i.e. from the taking of photos to patients' receipt of results) from up to 10 weeks to 10 minutes. However, when the system was deployed in practice, 21% of the 1838 images put through the system were rejected by it for not satisfying system requirements, as defined by the developers according to a grading scheme designed to guarantee decision accuracy; the patients were referred to ophthalmologists to have the images read manually. As the rejected images were readable by the nurses who had taken the photos and deemed them appropriate, the high rejection rate created frustration for the providers and the patients, eventually resulting in opposition to using the system.

### 14.6.3.1 Model Formulation

Consider a surgical robotic system consisting of an image sensor that monitors an operating room, a console from which the surgeon operates the robot, and the robot itself, which executes the operation as controlled by the surgeon (see Figure 14.7). Each system component is connected to a computing node that communicates over the control network via a publish–subscribe pattern.

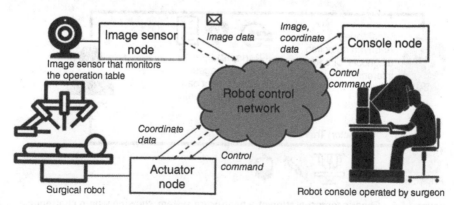

**Figure 14.7** Operation of an experimental surgical robot [96].

Consider the threat model in [16], whereby an attacker gains access to the control network and installs learning malware that can eavesdrop on the data packets (i.e. coordinate data) to infer the small time interval during which the robot arm is likely to be closest to the patient. Using a deep RL method, Deep Q-Learning [90], the malware triggers an attack payload (i.e. corruption of sensor data sent to the surgeon) that can put the patient at risk. As the self-learning malware triggers the payload, the image sensor node is unregistered from the robotic control network,[1] and the other nodes subscribe to the malicious node that is crafting the image data. With the corrupted image data as input, the virtual visual and haptic representation derived by the console node is no longer valid. The formulation of this problem is as follows:

The core idea is to extract the resource usage patterns and to ensure that the monitoring performed by the self-learning malware allows the computation and data exfiltration within the noise margin of the victim system. This automation of the process of determining the pattern of network traffic frees the attacker from those restrictions, and the attack encoded with learning methods can move laterally across the system to resources that a human attacker could not have reached [86].

$$W(t) = \mathbb{C}_{\text{reward}} \cdot A(t) - \left\{1 - A(t)\right\} \left\{\mathbb{C}_{\text{down}} + \mathbb{C}_{\text{repair}} + p_{\text{sec}|\text{s}} \cdot \mathbb{C}_{\text{down}}(x(t))\right\} \quad (14.9)$$

- $A(t) = R(t) + \int_0^t R(t-u)m(u)\mathrm{d}u$, where
  - $A(t)$ is the reward for useful work,
  - $R(t)$ is the probability that the system remains operational without an intrusion up to time $t$, and
  - $m(u)$ is the probability that the system mitigates (i.e. detects and responds to) the attack within $u$ time units.
- $\mathbb{C}_{\text{down}}$ is the SLA violation cost.
- $\mathbb{C}_{\text{repair}}$ is the repair cost.
- $\mathbb{C}_{\text{down}}(x(t))$ is the (expected) safety cost.
- $p_{\text{sec}|\text{s}}$ (i.e. probability that given a safety hazard, the cause was a security incident) is a function of the surgeon's input traces, the distance between the robot and the patient, the robot's maximum movement per time unit, and the latency of the safety engine. A larger variation in surgeon input and a longer distance to the patient reduce $p_{\text{sec}|\text{s}}$, while a larger maximum movement and a longer latency (i.e. time taken by the safety engine to respond to the incident) increase $p_{\text{sec}|\text{s}}$.

---

1 As discussed in [16], ROS1 (Robot Operating System) has a vulnerability such that an attacker with access to the control network can register itself as a genuine node, which can conflict with other registrants and can result in unregistering of a node with the same name.

Now, assume that an attacker has intruded into the console[2], a Linux machine that hosts the *omni-client* node on top of ROS (the Robot Operating System), and has installed self-learning malware (see Figure 14.8). The malware, with its access to the coordinates of the robot end-effector, monitors the movements of the robot. When micro-movements occur that are represented by the spatial density of the robot arm traces, the learning algorithm labels a cluster in which the robot arm is in close proximity to the patient and is performing sensitive operations; the malware defines this as a sensitive region. After collecting the data on the sensitive regions, the malware triggers the attack payload (i.e. inverts the actuation command) to make the robot move in the opposite direction from what the surgeon had intended. When the malware detects a responsive movement of the surgeon, trying to undo the malicious movement (i.e. movement of the haptic device in the opposite direction), the malware disengages its control and passes the genuine actuation command to the robot. Thus it tries to disguise the attack as a temporal fault. If the surgeon proceeds with the operation, either with or without restarting the system, the malware will detect another instance in which the robot has again reached the sensitive region and will again trigger the attack payload.

Unlike a failure incident, a security violation does not imply an immediate transition to the down state. Nevertheless, system operation after such an attack is detected cannot be trusted. Hence, in this analysis, the system is considered to be down once an attack has been triggered. System downtime is the sum of the time to detection and time to repair. As in our generic framework, $C_{down}$ is directly proportional to the downtime, and $C_{repair}$ is inversely proportional to the repair time. (For example, consider two repair service models in which, respectively,

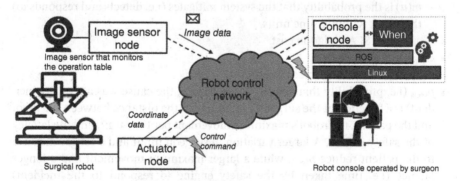

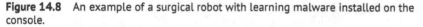

**Figure 14.8** An example of a surgical robot with learning malware installed on the console.

---

2 Viable intrusion channels include phishing attacks (if the system is connected to a public network) or media devices, as was the case in the Stuxnet attack.

the vendor immediately responds to an incident, or the vendor only makes routine visits.) While a security violation does not directly imply a safety violation, there is a probability that a security problem will impact the safety of the system, as captured by $p_{sec|s}$.

$$W(t) = \mathbb{C}_{reward} \cdot A(t) - \{1 - A(t)\}$$

$$\left\{ \int_0^\infty \mathbb{C}_{down} \cdot t \cdot p_{detect}(t) dt + \mathbb{C}_{repair} + p_{sec|s} \cdot \mathbb{C}_{safety}(x(t)) \right\}, \qquad (14.10)$$

where $A(t)$ is the reward for useful work, $p_{detect}(t)dt$ is the probability of detection, $\mathbb{C}_{repair}$ is the repair cost, and $\mathbb{C}_{safety}(x(t))$ is the (expected) safety cost.

### 14.6.3.2 Addressing Uncertainty

Healthcare systems, like any trust-sensitive AI systems, face challenges in addressing uncertainties that stem from three layers of the system, as follows:

1) *Uncertainty in the input:* The challenge is to identify and handle the uncertainty in the input. In healthcare, physicians (and AI applications that support health providers) process information in various formats. For instance, medical images (e.g. MRI, X-ray, and ultrasound) play a critical role in locating problems (e.g. inflammation or a tumor). However, such images are noisy by nature, and each patient or case may contain unique patterns that can easily confuse the diagnosis process. On the other hand, questionnaires and score systems are heavily used to assess patients and quantify patients' symptoms. However, such measures (and their interpretation) are subjective, such that the result itself does not represent the ground truth. Further, as demonstrated in [8], AI systems in practice are vulnerable in less-controlled environments (i.e. several socio-environmental factors impact model performance, nursing workflows, and hence the patient experience). Also, the accuracy of detection methods (i.e. that compare the output of the model with the ground truth) is a common measure for assessing the reliability of medical systems. However, that method is highly sensitive to the input to the model (i.e. data), and choosing a representative data set is a hard research problem by itself.

2) *Uncertainty in the model:* ML methods are often treated as black boxes of which only the output is available, while the internal computations are not easily explainable and cannot be interpreted. In healthcare, however, for which trustworthiness matters, explainable AI methods are of paramount importance. For example, a physician must be able to explain to a patient why an AI algorithm gave a certain patient-specific response. In addition, the reliability and safety of the data and the algorithm should be investigated. For

example, an AI system for early detection of diabetic retinopathy, which is a leading cause of blindness in diabetic people, was held back by the FDA for seven years. The challenge was in evaluating the system and assuring its accuracy and safety given that the AI algorithm (in particular, the model derived by the AI and its inputs) is hard to interpret or explain [59]. Also, IBM Watson, which was supposed to learn by ingesting medical literature on cancer and health records of real cancer patients, demonstrated the limitations of AI's statistical thinking and proved that it could not read and learn the way a doctor would. Further, Watson failed to adopt new treatment methods, for a lack of sufficient data points [65].

3) *Uncertainty in the system:* Because its service model keeps humans in the decision loop, AI in healthcare depends greatly on the environmental setup and the humans who take part in the system. Further, the AI faces variation and uncertainty in the operational environment that are unlike what it encounters in the development phase, and failure to mitigate such uncertainty can affect the performance of the system. For instance, the AI system described in [88] demonstrated success in its development phase on historical data, but its efficacy in practice remains to be seen. Moreover, the performance of the system varied depending on the clinic that was running the system, e.g. because of the darkness of the room where images were taken or the expertise of the nurses. That is the reality that we must deal with, and the system should, at a minimum, detect and acknowledge the uncertainty, if not tolerate it.

## 14.7   Conclusion: How Can We Make AI Systems Trustworthy?

The use of AI in accelerating and automating processes that were previously the jobs of human actors (e.g. in AVs, medical assistants/devices, manufacturing, agriculture, and smart buildings) has been successfully demonstrated. These successful demonstrations and the fascinating possibilities of AI are rapidly changing the foundational paradigms of system design, and it is of paramount importance that we be able to place trust in these technologies. However, the question of errors and consequent failures of AI and AI-enabled systems, while well-publicized, is just beginning to be addressed. This book has attempted to bring together the important classical methods of dependability and fault tolerance, from fundamental hardware techniques to techniques for software and systems. This chapter has emphasized the impact of the emergent AI and ML techniques that serve to fully manage and automate systems; we noted that the resilience and safety challenges cannot be solved simply by redeploying the usual redundancy methods, even those currently used in mission-critical systems. The uncertainty introduced in emerging computing systems with AI/ML support or in full-fledged AI systems will require new techniques and methods to address the consequent resilience challenges in these systems, which include AVs, hybrid and multicloud systems, smart power grids, the new generation of AI-enabled healthcare systems, emerging secure computing systems and techniques, and high-performance computing systems, among others.

Figures 14.9 and 14.10 show how the classical resiliency techniques interface with machine intelligence. Unlike traditional systems, ML/AI systems introduce a range of errors in perception, inference, and decision-making that are inherent in probabilistic decision-making. Addressing these challenges will be an important direction for resilience research and development, and will be necessary to provide the safe, resilient, and dependable AI systems of the future.

As this book goes to press, the emergence of GPT models with massive data and many erroneous inferences (lying, cheating, and hallucinations) stands to exacerbate the problems. We believe the real approach will be to introduce methods and technologies that are human brain-inspired, which are highly resilient, and can compute successfully in the face of massive uncertainty and, above all, will be self-repairing while maintaining their performance. The major challenge is how to continually check and validate such systems and, more importantly, how to check the checker.

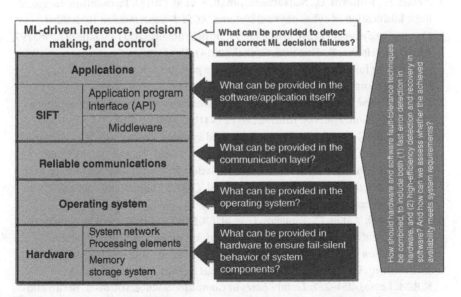

**Figure 14.9** System view of dependable computing, incorporating AI/ML challenges.

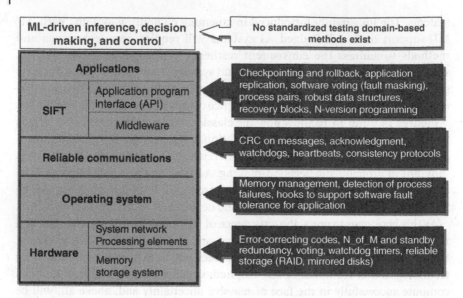

**Figure 14.10** How to achieve the objectives: interfacing classical solution techniques with emerging machine intelligence.

# References

**1** Abbas, H., Fainekos, G., Sankaranarayanan, S. et al. (2013). Probabilistic temporal logic falsification of cyber-physical systems. *ACM Transactions on Embedded Computing Systems* 12 (2s): article no. 95. https://doi.org/10.1145/2465787.2465797.

**2** Abbas, H., Hoxha, B., Fainekos, G. et al. (2014). Conformance testing as falsification for cyber-physical systems. *arXiv preprint* arXiv:1401.5200 https://arxiv.org/abs/1401.5200.

**3** Akhtar, N. and Mian, A. (2018). Threat of adversarial attacks on deep learning in computer vision: a survey. *IEEE Access* 6: 14410–14430.

**4** Alur, R. (2011). Formal verification of hybrid systems. *Proceedings of the 9th ACM International Conference on Embedded Software*, Taipei, Taiwan (9–14 October 2011), 273–278. New York, NY, USA: Association for Computing Machinery.

**5** Alur, R., Henzinger, T.A., Lafferriere, G. et al. (2000). Discrete abstractions of hybrid systems. *Proceedings of the IEEE* 88 (7): 971–984.

**6** Annpureddy, Y., Liu, C., Fainekos, G. et al. (2011). S-TaLiRo: a tool for temporal logic falsification for hybrid systems. *Proceedings of the 17th International Conference on Tools and Algorithms for the Construction and Analysis of Systems*, Saarbrücken, Germany (26 March–3 April 2011), (eds. P.A. Abdulla and K.R.M. Leino), 254–257. *Lecture Notes in Computer Science*, vol. 6605. Berlin and Heidelberg, Germany: Springer.

**7** Banerjee, S.S., Jha, S., Cyriac, J. et al. (2018). Hands off the wheel in autonomous vehicles?: a systems perspective on over a million miles of field data. *Proceedings of the 2018 48th Annual IEEE/IFIP International Conference on Dependable Systems and Networks (DSN)*, Luxembourg (25–28 June 2018), 586–597. IEEE.

**8** Beede, E., Baylor, E., Hersch, F. et al. (2020). A human-centered evaluation of a deep learning system deployed in clinics for the detection of diabetic retinopathy. *Proceedings of the 2020 CHI Conference on Human Factors in Computing Systems*, Honolulu, HI, USA (25–30 April 2020). New York, NY, USA: Association for Computing Machinery. https://doi.org/10.1145/3313831.3376718.

**9** Bertsche, B. (2008). *Reliability in Automotive and Mechanical Engineering: Determination of Component and System Reliability*. Berlin and Heidelberg, Germany: Springer.

**10** Boloor, A., He, X., Gill, C. et al. (2019). Simple physical adversarial examples against end-to-end autonomous driving models. *Proceedings of the 2019 IEEE International Conference on Embedded Software and Systems*, Las Vegas, NV, USA (2–3 June 2019). https://doi.org/10.1109/icess.2019.8782514.

**11** Boopathy, A., Weng, T.-W., Chen, P.-Y. et al. (2019). CNN-Cert: an efficient framework for certifying robustness of convolutional neural networks. *Proceedings of the AAAI Conference on Artificial Intelligence* 33 (1): 3240–3247.

**12** Cai, W., Doshi, A., and Valle, R. (2018). Attacking speaker recognition with deep generative models. *arXiv preprint* arXiv:1801.02384 https://arxiv.org/abs/1801.02384.

**13** California Department of Motor Vehicles (2017). Testing of autonomous vehicles. https://www.dmv.ca.gov/portal/dmv/detail/vr/autonomous/testing (accessed 05 March 2020).

**14** Chakraborty, A., Alam, M., Dey, V. et al. (2018). Adversarial attacks and defences: a survey. *arXiv preprint*. arXiv:1810.00069. https://arxiv.org/abs/1810.00069.

**15** Chung, K., Kalbarczyk, Z.T., and Iyer, R.K. (2019). Availability attacks on computing systems through alteration of environmental control: smart malware approach. *Proceedings of the 10th ACM/IEEE International Conference on Cyber-Physical Systems*, Montreal, Quebec, Canada (16–18 April 2019). New York, NY, USA: Association for Computing Machinery. https://doi.org/10.1145/3302509.3311041.

**16** Chung, K., Li, X., Tang, P. et al. (2019). Smart malware that uses leaked control data of robotic applications: the case of Raven-II surgical robots. *Proceedings of the 22nd International Symposium on Research in Attacks, Intrusions and Defenses*, Beijing, China (23–25 September 2019), 337–351. USENIX Association.

**17** Creswell, A., White, T., Dumoulin, V. et al. (2018). Generative adversarial networks: an overview. *IEEE Signal Processing Magazine* 35 (1): 53–65.

**18** Dastin, J. (2018). Amazon scraps secret AI recruiting tool that showed bias against women. Reuters (10 October). https://www.ml.cmu.edu/news/news-archive/ 2016-2020/2018/october/amazon-scraps-secret-artificial-intelligence-recruiting-engine-that-showed-biases-against-women.html (accessed 2 March 2024).

**19** Dit Sandretto, J.A., Chapoutot, A., and Mullier, O. (2017). Formal verification of robotic behaviors in presence of bounded uncertainties. *Proceedings of the 2017 1st IEEE International Conference on Robotic Computing*, Taichung, Taiwan (10–12 April 2017), 81–88. IEEE.

**20** Donahue, J., Krähenbühl, P., and Darrell, T. (2016). Adversarial feature learning. *arXiv preprint*. arXiv:1605.09782 https://arxiv.org/abs/1605.09782.

**21** Du, P., Huang, Z., Liu, T. et al. (2019). Online monitoring for safe pedestrian-vehicle interactions. *arXiv preprint* arXiv:1910.05599. https://arxiv.org/abs/ 1910.05599.

**22** Dutta, R.G., Guo, X., and Jin, Y. (2016). Quantifying trust in autonomous system under uncertainties. *Proceedings of the 2016 29th IEEE International System-on-Chip Conference*, Seattle, WA, USA (6–9 September 2016), 362–367. IEEE.

**23** Fan, C. (2019). Formal methods for safe autonomy: data-driven verification, synthesis, and applications. PhD dissertation, University of Illinois at Urbana-Champaign.

**24** Fan, C., Qi, B., Mitra, S. et al. (2017). DryVR: data-driven verification and compositional reasoning for automotive systems. *Proceedings of the 29th International Conference on Computer Aided Verification*, Heidelberg, Germany (24–28 July 2017), (eds. R. Majumdar and V. Kunčak), Part I, 441–461. *Lecture Notes in Computer Science*, vol. 10426. Cham, Switzerland: Springer.

**25** Fan, C., Qi, B., Mitra, S. et al. (2016). Automatic reachability analysis for nonlinear hybrid models with C2E2. *Proceedings of the 28th International Conference on Computer Aided Verification*, Toronto, ON, Canada (17–23 July 2016), (eds. S. Chaudhuri and A. Farzan), Part I, 531–538. *Lecture Notes in Computer Science*, vol. 9779. Cham, Switzerland: Springer.

**26** Fournaris, A.P., Lalos, A.S., and Serpanos, D. (2019). Generative adversarial networks in AI-enabled safety-critical systems: friend or foe? *Computer* 52 (9): 78–81.

**27** Favarò, F.M., Nader, N., Eurich, S.O. et al. (2017). Examining accident reports involving autonomous vehicles in California. *PLoS One* 12 (9): e0184952. https://doi.org/10.1371/journal.pone.0184952.

**28** Goodfellow, I., Pouget-Abadie, J., Mirza, M. et al. (2014). Generative adversarial nets. *Advances in Neural Information Processing Systems* 27 (NeurIPS Proceedings), (eds. Z. Ghahramani, M. Welling, C. Cortes et al.), 2672–2680. https://papers.nips.cc/paper/2014.

**29** Gu, S. and Rigazio, L. (2014). Towards deep neural network architectures robust to adversarial examples. *arXiv preprint* arXiv:1412.5063. https://arxiv.org/abs/ 1412.5068.

**30** Gupta, A., Johnson, J., Li, F.-F. et al. (2018). Social GAN: socially acceptable trajectories with generative adversarial networks. *Proceedings of the 2018 IEEE/ CVF Conference on Computer Vision and Pattern Recognition*, Salt Lake City, UT, USA (18–23 June 2018), 2255–2264. IEEE.

**31** Henzinger, T.A., Kopke, P.W., Puri, A. et al. (1998). What's decidable about hybrid automata? *Journal of Computer and System Sciences* 57 (1): 94–124.

**32** Hoxha, B., Bach, H., Abbas, H. et al. (2014). Towards formal specification visualization for testing and monitoring of cyber-physical systems. *International Workshop on Design and Implementation of Formal Tools and Systems*, Lausanne, Switzerland (20 October 2014). http://fmgroup.polito.it/cabodi/difts2014/papers/difts2014_submission_9.pdf (accessed 27 November 2023).

**33** Isola, P., Zhu, J.-Y., Zhou, T. et al. (2017). Image-to-image translation with conditional adversarial networks. *Proceedings of the 2017 IEEE Conference on Computer Vision and Pattern Recognition*, Honolulu, HI, USA (21–26 July 2017), 5967–5976. IEEE.

**34** Jarašuniene, A. and Jakubauskas, G. (2007). Improvement of road safety using passive and active intelligent vehicle safety systems. *Transport* 22 (4): 284–289.

**35** Jha, S., Banerjee, S., Tsai, T. et al. (2019). ML-based fault injection for autonomous vehicles: a case for Bayesian fault injection. *Proceedings of the 2019 49th Annual IEEE/IFIP International Conference on Dependable Systems and Networks*, Portland, OR, USA (24–27 June 2019), 112–124. IEEE.

**36** Jha, S., Banerjee, S.S., Cyriac, J. et al. (2018). AVFI: Fault injection for autonomous vehicles. *Proceedings of the 2018 48th Annual IEEE/IFIP International Conference on Dependable Systems and Networks Workshops*, Luxembourg (25–28 June 2018), 55–56. IEEE.

**37** Kaloudi, N. and Li, J. (2021). The AI-based cyber threat landscape: a survey. *ACM Computing Surveys* 53 (1): article no. 20. https://doi.org/10.1145/3372823.

**38** Kalra, N. and Paddock, S.M. (2016). Driving to safety: how many miles of driving would it take to demonstrate autonomous vehicle reliability? *Transportation Research Part A: Policy and Practice* 94: 182–193.

**39** Kirat, D., Jang, J., and Stoecklin, M.P. (2018). DeepLocker: concealing targeted attacks with AI locksmithing. *Proceedings of Blackhat USA*. https://i.blackhat.com/us-18/Thu-August-9/us-18-Kirat-DeepLocker-Concealing-Targeted-Attacks-with-AI-Locksmithing.pdf (accessed 2 March 2024).

**40** Koymans, R. (1990). Specifying real-time properties with metric temporal logic. *Real-Time Systems* 2 (4): 255–299.

**41** Ledig, C., Theis, L., Huszár, F. et al. (2017). Photo-realistic single image super-resolution using a generative adversarial network. *Proceedings of the 2017 IEEE Conference on Computer Vision and Pattern Recognition*, Honolulu, HI, USA (21–26 July 2017), 105–114. IEEE.

**42** Li, G., Hari, S.K.S., Sullivan, M. et al. (2017). Understanding error propagation in deep learning neural network (DNN) accelerators and applications.

*Proceedings of the International Conference for High Performance Computing, Networking, Storage and Analysis*, Denver, CO, USA (12–17 November 2017), article no. 8. New York, NY, USA: Association for Computing Machinery. https://doi.org/10.1145/3126908.3126964.

**43** Li, Y., Liu, S., Yang, J. et al. (2017). Generative face completion. *Proceedings of the 2017 IEEE Conference on Computer Vision and Pattern Recognition*, Honolulu, HI, USA (21–26 July 2017), 5892–5900. IEEE.

**44** Liu, Y., Ma, S., Aafer, Y. et al. (2018) Trojaning attack on neural networks. *In 25th Annual Network and Distributed System Security Symposium* (NDSS 2018), 18–21 February 2018. San Diego, CA, USA.

**45** Lu, J., Issaranon, T., and Forsyth, D. (2017). SafetyNet: detecting and rejecting adversarial examples robustly. *Proceedings of the 2017 IEEE International Conference on Computer Vision*, Venice, Italy (22–29 October 2017), 446–454. IEEE.

**46** Lu, J., Sibai, H., and Fabry, E. (2017). Adversarial examples that fool detectors. *arXiv preprint* arXiv:1712.02494. https://arxiv.org/abs/1712.02494.

**47** Lutz, S., Amplianitis, K., and Smolic, A. (2018). AlphaGAN: generative adversarial networks for natural image matting. *arXiv preprint*. arXiv:1807.10088. https://arxiv.org/abs/1807.10088.

**48** Metzen, J.H., Genewein, T., Fischer, V. et al. (2017). On detecting adversarial perturbations. *5th International Conference on Learning Representations*, Toulon, France (24–26 April 2017). Unpublished poster presentation. https://openreview. net/pdf?id=SJzCSf9xg (accessed 2 March 2024).

**49** Mirza, M. and Osindero, S. (2014). Conditional generative adversarial nets. *arXiv preprint*. arXiv:1411.1784. https://arxiv.org/abs/1411.1784.

**50** Mitra, S., Wang, Y., Lynch, N. et al. (2003). Safety verification of model helicopter controller using hybrid input/output automata. *Proceedings of the 6th International Workshop on Hybrid Systems: Computation and Control*, Prague, Czech Republic (3–5 April 2003), (eds. O. Maler and A. Pnueli), 343–358. *Lecture Notes in Computer Science*, vol. 2623. Berlin and Heidelberg, Germany: Springer.

**51** National Transportation Safety Board (2019). Collision Between Vehicle Controlled by Developmental Automated Driving System and Pedestrian, Tempe, Arizona, March 18, 2018. *Tech. Rep. (Accident Rep.) NTSB/HAR-19/03, PB2019-101402*. https://www.ntsb.gov/investigations/AccidentReports/Reports/HAR1903.pdf.

**52** Newstead, S., Watson, L., and Cameron, M. (2009). Vehicle Safety Ratings Estimated from Police Reported Crash Data: 2009 Update: Australian and New Zealand Crashes During 1987–2007. *Tech Rep. 287*. Victoria, Australia: Monash University Accident Research Centre.

**53** Nistér, D., Lee, H.-L., Ng, J. et al. (2019). The Safety Force Field. *Tech Rep.* Nvidia. https://developer.nvidia.com/drive/secure/docs/the-safety-force-field.pdf.

**54** Odena, A. (2016). Semi-supervised learning with generative adversarial networks. *arXiv preprint.* arXiv:1606.01583. https://arxiv.org/abs/1606.01583.

**55** Roy, N., Shen, S., Hassanieh, H. et al. (2018). Inaudible voice commands: the Long-Range attack and defense. *Proceedings of the 15th USENIX Symposium on Networked Systems Design and Implementation,* Renton, WA, USA (9–11 April 2018). USENIX Association. https://www.usenix.org/conference/nsdi18/presentation/roy.

**56** Rubaiyat, A.H.M., Qin, Y., and Alemzadeh, H. (2018). Experimental resilience assessment of an open-source driving agent. *Proceedings of the 2018 IEEE 23rd Pacific Rim International Symposium on Dependable Computing,* Taipei, Taiwan (4–7 December 2018), 54–63. IEEE.

**57** Schneier, B. (2018). Artificial intelligence and the attack/defense balance. *IEEE Security and Privacy* 16 (2): 96. https://doi.org/10.1109/MSP.2018.1870857.

**58** Schwartz, O. (2019). In 2016, Microsoft's racist chatbot revealed the dangers of online conversation. *IEEE Spectrum* 11: 2019. https://spectrum.ieee.org/in-2016-microsofts-racist-chatbot-revealed-the-dangers-of-online-conversation.

**59** Scudellari, M. (2018). AI diagnostics move into the clinic. *IEEE Spectrum* 55 (2) https://spectrum.ieee.org/ai-diagnostics-move-into-the-clinic.

**60** Shalev-Shwartz, S., Shammah, S., and Shashua, A. (2017). On a formal model of safe and scalable self-driving cars. *arXiv preprint.* arXiv:1708.06374. https://arxiv.org/abs/1708.06374.

**61** Sharif, M., Bhagavatula, S., Bauer, L. et al. (2016). Accessorize to a crime: Real and stealthy attacks on state-of-the-art face recognition. *Proceedings of the 2016 ACM SIGSAC Conference on Computer and Communications Security,* Vienna, Austria (24–28 October 2016), 1528–1540. New York, NY, USA: Association for Computing Machinery.

**62** Shi, Y., Davaslioglu, K., and Sagduyu, Y.E. (2019). Generative adversarial network for wireless signal spoofing. *Proceedings of the ACM Workshop on Wireless Security and Machine Learning,* Miami, FL, USA (15–17 May 2019), 55–60. New York, NY, USA: Association for Computing Machinery.

**63** Shi, Y., Sagduyu, Y.E., Davaslioglu, K. et al. (2018). Generative adversarial networks for black-box API attacks with limited training data. *Proceedings of the 2018 IEEE International Symposium on Signal Processing and Information Technology,* Louisville, KY, USA (6–8 December 2018), 453–458. IEEE.

**64** Stiver, J.A. and Antsaklis, P.J. (1992). Modeling and analysis of hybrid control systems. *Proceedings of the 31st IEEE Conference on Decision and Control,* Tucson, AZ, USA (16–18 December 1992), 3748–3751. IEEE.

**65** Strickland, E. (2019). IBM Watson, heal thyself: how IBM overpromised and underdelivered on AI health care. *IEEE Spectrum* 56 (4): 24–31.

**66** Szegedy, C., Zaremba, W., Sutskever, I. et al. (2013). Intriguing properties of neural networks. *arXiv preprint.* arXiv:1312.6199. https://arxiv.org/abs/1312.6199.

**67** Tramèr, F., Kurakin, A., Papernot, N. et al. (2017). Ensemble adversarial training: attacks and defenses. *arXiv preprint*. arXiv:1705.07204. https://arxiv.org/abs/1705.07204.

**68** Tulyakov, S., Liu, M.-Y., Yang, X. et al. (2018). MoCoGAN: Decomposing motion and content for video generation. *Proceedings of the 2018 IEEE/CVF Conference on Computer Vision and Pattern Recognition*, Salt Lake City, UT, USA (18–23 June 2018), 1526–1535. IEEE.

**69** van Ratingen, M.R. (2016). Saving lives with safer cars: The past, present and future of consumer safety ratings. *International Research Council on the Biomechanics of Injury Conference Proceedings*, Malaga, Spain (14–16 September 2016). http://www.ircobi.org/wordpress/downloads/irc16/default.htm.

**70** Wang, B., Yao, Y., Shan, S. et al. (2019). Neural cleanse: identifying and mitigating backdoor attacks in neural networks. *Proceedings of the 2019 IEEE Symposium on Security and Privacy*, San Francisco, CA, USA (19–23 May 2019), 707–723. IEEE.

**71** Wang, S. and Li, Z. (2019). Exploring causes and effects of automated vehicle disengagement using statistical modeling and classification tree based on field test data. *Accident Analysis & Prevention* 129: 44–54. https://doi.org/10.1016/j.aap.2019.04.015.

**72** Wang, Z., She, Q., and Ward, T.E. (2019). Generative adversarial networks in computer vision: a survey and taxonomy. *arXiv preprint*. arXiv:1906.01529 https://arxiv.org/abs/1906.01529.

**73** Winder, D. (2019). Apple's iPhone FaceID hacked in less than 120 seconds. *Forbes* (10 August). https://www.forbes.com/sites/daveywinder/2019/08/10/apples-iphone-faceid-hacked-in-less-than-120-seconds/#53f89d7921bc (accessed 1 March 2024).

**74** Wing, J.M. (2020). Trustworthy AI. *arXiv preprint*. arXiv:2002.06276 https://arxiv.org/abs/2002.06276.

**75** Xu, X. and Li, M.-L. (2012). Understanding soft error propagation using efficient vulnerability-driven fault injection. *Proceedings of the IEEE/IFIP International Conference on Dependable Systems and Networks*, Boston, MA, US (25–28 June 2012). IEEE. https://doi.org/10.1109/DSN.2012.6263923

**76** Zanoni, E. and Pavan, P. (1993). Improving the reliability and safety of automotive electronics. *IEEE Micro* 13 (1): 30–48.

**77** Zhang, L., She, Z., Ratschan, S. et al. (2010). Safety verification for probabilistic hybrid systems. *Proceedings of the 22nd International Conference on Computer Aided Verification*, Edinburgh, UK (15–19 July 2010), (eds. T. Touili, B. Cook, and P. Jackson), 196–211. *Lecture Notes in Computer Science*, vol. 6174. Berlin and Heidelberg, Germany: Springer.

**78** Zhang, M., Zhang, Y., Zhang, L. et al. (2018). DeepRoad: GAN-based metamorphic testing and input validation framework for autonomous driving systems. *Proceedings of the 2018 33rd IEEE/ACM International Conference on*

*Automated Software Engineering*, Montpellier, France (3–7 September 2020), 132–142. IEEE.

**79** Jha, S., Cui, S., Banerjee, S. et al. (2020). ML-driven malware that targets AV safety. *Proceedings of the 2020 50th Annual IEEE/IFIP International Conference on Dependable Systems and Networks*, Valencia, Spain (29 June–2 July 2020), 113–124. IEEE.

**80** Alvarez, S. (2018). Research group demos why Tesla Autopilot could crash into a stationary vehicle. *Teslarati* (14 June 2018). https://www.teslarati.com/tesla-research-group-autopilot-crash-demo/#google_vignette (accessed 18 January 2024).

**81** Castro, J. (2016). Tesla self-driving car fails to detect truck in fatal crash. *ABC 7 News* (1 July). https://abc7news.com/tesla-s-autopilot-self-driving-car-officials-investigating-teslas-autopilot-feature-after-fatal-crash/1410042/ (accessed 1 March 2024).

**82** Banerjee, S., Jha, S., Kalbarczyk, Z., and Iyer, R. (2020). Inductive-bias-driven reinforcement learning for efficient schedules in heterogeneous clusters. *Proceedings of the 37th International Conference on Machine Learning*, Virtual (13–18 July 2020), vol. 119, 629–641. Proceedings of Machine Learning Research. Vienna, Austria.

**83** Lu, Y. (2023). Cruise stops all driverless taxi operations in the United States. *The New York Times* (26 October 2023). https://www.nytimes.com/2023/10/26/technology/cruise-driverless-taxi-united-states.html (accessed 1 March 2024).

**84** Jia, Y., Lu, Y., Shen, J. et al. (2020). Fooling detection alone is not enough: adversarial attack against multiple object tracking. *Proceedings of the 8th International Conference on Learning Representations*, Virtual (30 April 2020). https://openreview.net/forum?id=rJl31TNYPr.

**85** Cao, Y., Xiao, C., Yang, D. et al. (2019). Adversarial objects against LiDAR-based autonomous driving systems. *arXiv preprint* arXiv:1907.05418. http://arxiv.org/abs/1907.05418.

**86** Chung, K., Cao, P., Kalbarczyk, Z.T., and Iyer, R.K. (2023). StealthML: data-driven malware for stealthy data exfiltration. *Proceedings of the 2023 IEEE International Conference on Cyber Security and Resilience*, Venice, Italy (31 July–2 August 2023), 16–21. IEEE.

**87** Valle, R., Cai, W., and Doshi, A. (2018). TequilaGAN: how to easily identify GAN samples. *arXiv preprint*. arXiv:1807.04919. https://arxiv.org/abs/1807.04919.

**88** Abràmoff, M.D., Lavin, P.T., Birch, M. et al. (2018). Pivotal trial of an autonomous AI-based diagnostic system for detection of diabetic retinopathy in primary care offices. *NPJ Digital Medicine* 1: article no. 39. https://doi.org/10.1038/s41746-018-0040-6.

**89** Akhtar, N., Mian, A., Kardan, N. et al. (2021). Advances in adversarial attacks and defenses in computer vision: a survey. *IEEE Access* 9: 155161–155196. https://doi.org/10.1109/ACCESS.2021.3127960.

**90** Mnih, V., Kavukcuoglu, K., Silver, D. et al. (2015). Human-level control through deep reinforcement learning. *Nature* 518 (7540): 529–533. https://doi.org/10.1038/nature14236.

**91** Trivedi, K.S. (2016). *Probability and Statistics with Reliability, Queuing and Computer Science Applications*. Wiley.

**92** Siewiorek, D.P., Chillarege, R., and Kalbarczyk, Z.T. (2004). Reflections on industry trends and experimental research in dependability. *IEEE Transactions on Dependable and Secure Computing* 1 (2): 109–127.

**93** Avizienis, A., Laprie, J.-C., Randell, B., and Landwehr, C. (2004). Basic concepts and taxonomy of dependable and secure computing. *IEEE Transactions on Dependable and Secure Computing* 1 (1): 11–33.

**94** Qiu, H., Banerjee, S.S., Jha, S. et al. (2020). FIRM: an intelligent fine-grained resource management framework for SLO-oriented microservices. *Proceedings of the 14th USENIX Conference on Operating Systems Design and Implementation*, virtual (4–6 November 2020), 805–825. Berkeley, CA, USA: USENIX Association.

**95** Varatharajah, Y., Chong, M.J., Saboo, K., Berry, B. et al. (2017). EEG-GRAPH: a factor-graph-based model for capturing spatial, temporal, and observational relationships in electroencephalograms. *Advances in Neural Information Processing Systems* 30 (NIPS 2017), (eds. I. Guyon, U. Von Luxburg, S. Bengio et al.). https://proceedings.neurips.cc/paper/2017/hash/fb3f76858cb38e5b7fd113e0bc1c0721-Abstract.html.

**96** Alemzadeh, H., Chen, D., Li, X. et al. (2016). Targeted attacks on teleoperated surgical robots: Dynamic model-based detection and mitigation. *Proceedings of the 2016 46th Annual IEEE/IFIP International Conference on Dependable Systems and Networks*, Toulouse, France (28 June–1 July 2016), 395–406. IEEE.

**97** Ng, A.Y., Oberije, C.J.G., Ambrózay, É. et al. (2023). Prospective implementation of AI-assisted screen reading to improve early detection of breast cancer. *Nature Medicine* 29, pp. 3044–3049.

# Index

Note: Page number with "n" denotes footnote numbers.

*Dependable Computing: Design and Assessment*, First Edition. Ravishankar K. Iyer,
Zbigniew T. Kalbarczyk, and Nithin M. Nakka.
© 2024 The IEEE Computer Society. Published 2024 by John Wiley & Sons, Inc.
Companion website: www.wiley.com/go/iyer/dependablecomputing1